CALIFORNIA CAMPING

FOGHORN OUTDOORS®

CALIFORNIA CAMPING

The Complete Guide to More Than 1,500 Tent and RV Campgrounds

THIRTEENTH EDITION

Tom Stienstra

AVALON
TRAVEL

FOGHORN OUTDOORS
CALIFORNIA CAMPING
The Complete Guide to More Than
1,500 Tent and RV Campgrounds

Thirteenth Edition

Tom Stienstra

Text © 2003 by Tom Stienstra
All rights reserved.
Illustrations and maps © 2003 by
Avalon Travel Publishing.
All rights reserved.
Avalon Travel Publishing is a division
of Avalon Publishing Group, Inc.

Some photos and illustrations are used by permission
and are the property of the original copyright owners.

ISBN: 1-56691-486-8
ISSN: 1531-8109

Editor: Rebecca K. Browning
Series Manager: Marisa Solís
Copy Editor: Karen Gaynor Bleske
Proofreader: Erika Howsare
Senior Research Editor: Stephani Cruickshank
Research Editor: Pamela S. Padula
Graphics Coordinator: Melissa Sherowski
Illustrator: Bob Race
Production Coordinator: Darren Alessi
Cover Designer: Jacob Goolkasian
Interior Designer: Darren Alessi
Map Editor: Olivia Solís
Cartographers: Kat Kalamaras, Mike Morgenfeld, Suzanne Service, CHK America
Indexers: Rebecca K. Browning, Beth Polzin

Front cover photo: © Larry Prosor

Printed in the United States of America by Delta Printing Solutions

Please send all feedback about this book to:

ⒻOGHORN OUTDOORS®
California Camping
Avalon Travel Publishing
1400 65th Street, Suite 250
Emeryville, CA 94608, USA
email: atpfeedback@avalonpub.com
website: www.foghorn.com

Printing History
1st edition—1987
13th edition—March 2003
5 4 3

About the Author

© KURT ROGERS

Tom Stienstra has made it his life's work to explore the West, traveling 150 days a year—camping, hiking, fishing, biking, boating, and flying—searching for the best of the outdoors and then writing about it.

Tom is the nation's top-selling author of outdoor guidebooks. He has been named California Outdoor Writer of the Year four times and has twice been awarded National Outdoor Writer of the Year, newspaper division, by the Outdoor Writers Association of America. As the outdoors columnist for the *San Francisco Chronicle,* Tom and his articles have also appeared on www.SFGate.com and in newspapers around the country.

His wife, Stephani Stienstra, has co-authored two books with him. They live with their sons in Northern California.

You can contact Tom directly via the website www.TomStienstra.com. His other books are also available on his website, including:

Foghorn Outdoors California Fishing
Foghorn Outdoors California Hiking (with Ann Marie Brown)
Foghorn Outdoors California Recreational Lakes & Rivers
Foghorn Outdoors California Wildlife (with illustrator Paul Johnson)
Foghorn Outdoors Northern California Cabins & Cottages (with Stephani Stienstra)
Foghorn Outdoors Oregon Camping
Foghorn Outdoors Pacific Northwest Camping
Foghorn Outdoors Washington Camping (with Stephani Stienstra)

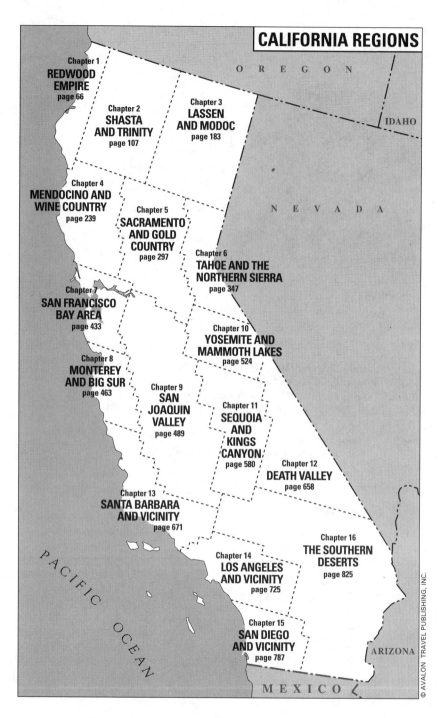

CALIFORNIA REGIONS

Chapter 1
REDWOOD EMPIRE
page 66

Chapter 2
SHASTA AND TRINITY
page 107

Chapter 3
LASSEN AND MODOC
page 183

Chapter 4
MENDOCINO AND WINE COUNTRY
page 239

Chapter 5
SACRAMENTO AND GOLD COUNTRY
page 297

Chapter 6
TAHOE AND THE NORTHERN SIERRA
page 347

Chapter 7
SAN FRANCISCO BAY AREA
page 433

Chapter 10
YOSEMITE AND MAMMOTH LAKES
page 524

Chapter 8
MONTEREY AND BIG SUR
page 463

Chapter 9
SAN JOAQUIN VALLEY
page 489

Chapter 11
SEQUOIA AND KINGS CANYON
page 580

Chapter 12
DEATH VALLEY
page 658

Chapter 13
SANTA BARBARA AND VICINITY
page 671

Chapter 16
THE SOUTHERN DESERTS
page 825

Chapter 14
LOS ANGELES AND VICINITY
page 725

Chapter 15
SAN DIEGO AND VICINITY
page 787

OREGON

IDAHO

NEVADA

ARIZONA

PACIFIC OCEAN

MEXICO

© AVALON TRAVEL PUBLISHING, INC.

Contents

Chapter 4—Mendocino and Wine Country

Including: Bodega Bay • Boonville • Cache Creek • Calistoga • Clear Lake • Cobb Mountain • Covelo • East Van Arsdale Reservoir • Fort Bragg • Fort Ross • Gualala • Healdsburg • Hopland • Howard Lake • Indian Valley Reservoir • Kelseyville • Lake Berryessa • Lake Mendocino • Lake Pillsbury • Lake Sonoma • Letts Lake • Little Stony Creek • Lower Blue Lake • Manchester State Beach • Mendocino • Mendocino National Forest • Middletown • Napa • Navarro River • Navarro River Redwoods State Park • Noyo River • Petaluma • Plaskett Lakes • Point Arena • Rumsey • Russian River • Santa Rosa • Scotts Creek • Snow Mountain Wilderness • Sonoma Coast State Beach • Sonoma County Regional Park • Spring Lake • Stony Creek • Ukiah • Upper Blue Lake • Willits

Chapter 5—Sacramento and Gold Country

Including: Arnold • Auburn • Bear River • Big Reservoir • Black Butte Lake. • Bucks Lake • Bullards Bar Reservoir • Calaveras Big Trees State Park • Camanche Reservoir • Colfax • Collins Lake • Columbia • Colusa • Cosumnes River • Dunnigan • Eldorado National Forest • Feather River • Folsom Lake State Recreation Area • Georgetown • Grass Valley • Jackson • Jenkinson Lake • Lake Oroville • Little Grass Valley Reservoir • Loomis • Marysville • Mokelumne River • Nevada City • New Hogan Reservoir • North Yuba River • Orland • Oroville • Paradise • Pardee Reservoir • Placerville • Plumas National Forest • Plymouth • Rock Creek • Rollins Lake • Sacramento • Sacramento River • Sly Creek Reservoir • Stanislaus National Forest • Stanislaus River • Stockton • Sugar Pine Reservoir • Tahoe National Forest • Twain Harte • Vacaville • Williams • Yuba River

Chapter 6—Tahoe and the Northern Sierra

Including: American River • Arnold • Bear River Reservoir • Bear Valley Creek • Big Silver Creek • Blairsden • Blue Lakes • Boca Reservoir • Bowman Lake • Carson Pass • Carson River • Clark Fork • Consumes River • Donner Lake • Eldorado National Forest • Emigrant Gap • Faucherie Lake • French Meadows Reservoir • Frenchman Lake • Gerle Creek Reservoir • Graeagle • Haypress Creek • Hell Hole Reservoir • Humboldt-Toiyabe National Forest • Ice House Reservoir • Indian Creek Reservoir • Jackson Meadow Reservoir • Lake Alpine • Lake Davis • Lake Tahoe Basin • Lake Valley Reservoir • Little Last Chance Creek • Little Truckee River • Long Canyon Creek • Loon Lake • Markleeville • Markleeville Creek • Mill Creek • Mokelumne River • Molybdenite Creek • Mosquito Lake • Niagara Creek • Pacific Creek • Packer Creek • Packer Lake • Pine Creek • Plumas National Forest • Prosser Creek Reservoir • Rattlesnake Creek • Rubicon River • Silver Fork • Silver Lake • Spicer Reservoir • Stampede Lake • Stanislaus National Forest • Stanislaus River • Stumpy Meadows • Tahoe National Forest • Topaz Lake • Truckee River • Truckee • Union Valley Reservoir • Walker River • Woodfords • Yuba River

Our Commitment

We are committed to making *Foghorn Outdoors California Camping* the most accurate, thorough, and enjoyable camping guide to the state. With this thirteenth edition, you can rest assured that every camping spot in this book has been carefully reviewed and accompanied by the most up-to-date information available. It is possible in few cases, primarily at a small number of private RV parks, that some campground fees will be raised after we have gone to press. If you have a specific need or concern, it's a good idea to call the campground ahead of time.

If you would like to comment on the book, whether it's to suggest a tent or RV spot we overlooked, or to let us know about any noteworthy experience—good or bad—that occurred while using *Foghorn Outdoors California Camping* as your guide, we would appreciate hearing from you. Please address correspondence to:

Foghorn Outdoors California Camping, Thirteenth Edition
Avalon Travel Publishing
1400 65th Street, Suite 250
Emeryville, CA 94608, U.S.A.

email: atpfeedback@avalonpub.com
If you send us an email, please put "California Camping" in the subject line.

How to Use This Book

Foghorn Outdoors California Camping is divided into 16 chapters based on major geographic regions in the state. Each chapter begins with a map of the region, which is further broken down into detail maps. These detail maps show the location of all the campgrounds in that chapter.

This guide can be navigated easily in two ways:

1. If you know the name of the specific campground you want to use, or the name of the surrounding geographical area or nearby feature (town, national or state park, forest, mountain, lake, river, etc.), look it up in the index and turn to the corresponding page.

2. If you know the general area you want to visit, turn to the map at the beginning of the chapter that covers the area. Each chapter map is broken down into detail maps, which show by number all the campgrounds in that chapter. You can then determine which campgrounds are in or near your destination by their corresponding numbers. Campgrounds are listed sequentially in each chapter so you can turn to the page with the corresponding map number for the site you're interested in.

© TOM STIENSTRA

ABOUT THE CAMPGROUND PROFILES

Each campground in this book is listed in a consistent, easy-to-read format to help you choose the ideal camping spot. From a general overview of the setting to detailed driving directions, the profile will provide all the information you need. Here is an example:

Map number and campground name →

General location of the campground named by its proximity to the nearest major town or landmark →

Icons noting activities and facilities at or nearby the campground

Scenic rating, on a scale of 1–10

Map the campground can be found on and page number the map can be found on

1 SOMEWHERE USA CAMPGROUND

Rating: 10

South of Somewhere USA Lake.

Map 1.2, page 4

Each campground in this book begins with a brief overview of its setting. The description typically covers ambience, information about the attractions, and activities popular at the campground.

Campsites, facilities: This section provides the number of campsites for both tents and RVs and notes whether hookups are available. Facilities such as restrooms, picnic areas, recreation areas, laundry, and dump stations will be addressed, as well as the availability of piped water, showers, playground, stores, and others amenities. The campground's pet policy is also mentioned here.

Reservations, fees: This section notes whether reservations are accepted, and the rates for tent sites and RV sites. If there are additional fees for parking or pets, or discounted weekly or seasonal rates, those will also be noted here.

Directions: This section provides mile-by-mile driving directions to the campground from the nearest major town.

Contact: This section provides an address, a phone number, and an Internet address, if available, for each campground.

ABOUT THE ICONS

The icons in this book are designed to provide at-a-glance information on activities, facilities, and services provided that are available on-site or within walking distance of each campground. The icons are not meant to represent every activity or service, but rather those that are most significant.

— Hiking trails are available.

— Biking trails or routes are available. This usually refers to mountain biking, although it may represent road cycling as well. Refer to the text for that campground for details.

— Swimming opportunities are available.

— Fishing opportunities are available.

— Boating opportunities are available. Various types of vessels apply under this umbrella activity, including motorboats and personal watercrafts (Jet Skis). Refer to the text for that campground for more details, including mph restrictions and boat ramp availability.

— Winter sports are available. This general category may include activities such as downhill skiing, cross-country skiing, snowshoeing, snowmobiling, snowboarding, and ice skating. Refer to the text for that campground for more details on which sports are available.

— Hot or cold springs are located nearby. Refer to the text for that campground for more information.

— Pets are permitted. Campgrounds that allow pets may require an additional fee or that pets be leashed. Campgrounds may also restrict pet size or behavior. Refer to the text for that campground for specific instructions or call in advance.

— A playground is available. A campground with a playground can be desirable for campers traveling with children.

— Wheelchair access is provided, as advertised by campground managers. However, concerned persons are advised to call the contact number of a campground to be certain that their specific needs will be met.

— The campground is in a remote location or may be difficult to reach. The icon represents the 5% of American vacationers who actively seek to escape the crowds and to discover California's hidden gems.

— RV sites are provided.

— Tent sites are provided.

ABOUT THE MAPS

This book is divided into several chapters based on established regions; an overview map of these regions follows the table of contents. At the start of each chapter, you'll find a map of the entire region, enhanced by a grid that divides the region into smaller sections. These sections are then enlarged into individual detail maps. Campgrounds are noted by their map numbers on the detail maps.

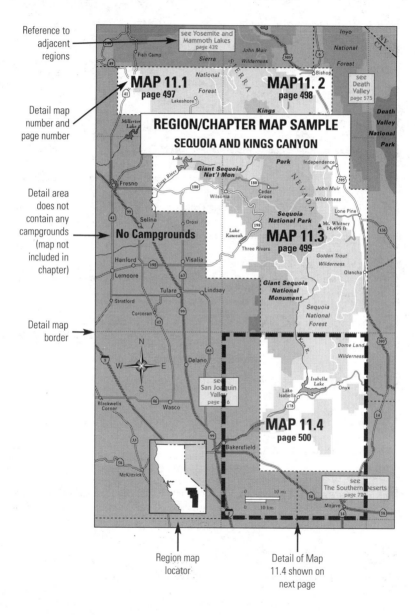

Reference to adjacent regions

Detail map number and page number

Detail area does not contain any campgrounds (map not included in chapter)

Detail map border

Region map locator

Detail of Map 11.4 shown on next page

see Yosemite and Mammoth Lakes page 432

see Death Valley page 575

REGION/CHAPTER MAP SAMPLE

SEQUOIA AND KINGS CANYON

MAP 11.1 page 497

MAP11. 2 page 498

No Campgrounds

MAP 11.3 page 499

MAP 11.4 page 500

see San Joaquin Valley page 6

see The Southern Deserts page 790

Map number → **Map 11.4**

Campgrounds shown on detail map and the page range where those campgrounds are listed →
**Campgrounds 108–117
Pages 564–570**

Indicates adjacent detail maps within region

Detail map locator

11.3

1 2
3
4

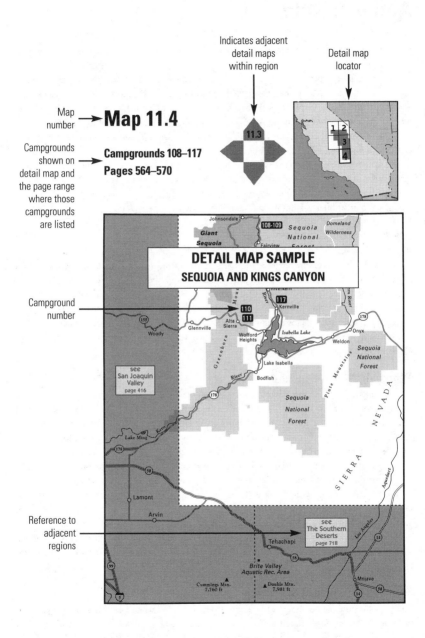

Johnsondale
Giant Sequoia
108-109
Sequoia National Forest
Domeland Wilderness
Fairview

DETAIL MAP SAMPLE

SEQUOIA AND KINGS CANYON

Campground number →
110 111
117 Kernville
Alta Sierra
178
Glennville
Woody
Isabella Lake
Onyx
Wofford Heights
Weldon
155
see San Joaquin Valley page 416
Lake Isabella
Bodfish
178
Sequoia National Forest
Piute Mountains
Sequoia National Forest
N E V A D A
Lake Ming
178
Kern River
S I E R R A
Aqueduct
58
Lamont
Arvin
Reference to adjacent regions →
see The Southern Deserts page 718
Tehachapi
Los Angeles
14
99
Brite Valley Aquatic Rec. Area
58
Cummings Mtn. 7,760 ft
Double Mtn. 7,981 ft
Mojave
58
5
14

Author's Note

We have made it a personal mission to win your trust and put the best possible guidebook in your hands.

I've written every word. Every page has been reviewed for accuracy by multiple people: a ranger, recreation officer, or park owner; then again by me; two research editors, Stephani Cruickshank and Pam Padula; and two editors, Rebecca Browning and Karen Bleske. We challenged each other to produce the most accurate, up-to-date, easy-to-use, and complete outdoor guide out there.

We have gone to these lengths to make *Foghorn Outdoors California Camping* your book of choice, the book you will trust, the book you keep in your car during your upcoming getaways.

The primary value of the book is simple: You will never again get stuck without a spot for the night. Never. Instead, as you roam about and learn the state as I have, you will discover the hundreds of little-known lakes, streams, trailheads, and coastal parks that can help transform your life into one of wonder, adventure, and happiness.

All-new Format for Easy Use

If this book looks different from anything you've seen, that's because it is.

We started this edition by breaking the state into 16 distinct geographic regions. Each of these regions represents a chapter, almost as if it were a miniature book on its own. Then, within that chapter, we split the regions into detailed maps with a new, easy-to-follow numbering system so you can find any location in California in a matter of seconds. We've accomplished this by numbering the chapters and maps serially, somewhat like a textbook. Of course, this book will lead you to fun, not a grade. With this new format, I believe you'll find *Foghorn Outdoors California Camping* much easier to navigate.

What You'll Find Inside

My first intent was to capture what I've seen and learned in 25 years of roaming around as a full-time outdoors writer, covering nearly one million miles in California alone. I've explored all 58 counties; 20,000 hiking miles; 1,000 lakes; the entire coast; 20 national forests; 50 wilderness areas; and 250 state, national, regional, and county parks. I'm always looking for another place to explore and capture the outdoor experience, and there always seems to be another place to discover and explore.

I also want the book to steer you in the right direction. Imprecise directions have always bugged me. So for this edition, I rewrote directions with a new style for all 1,500 campgrounds in California: Every direction in the book is written as if the passenger is reading it to the driver. In many cases, the accuracy is now to the one-tenth of a mile. I admit, it's a huge improvement over anything I've previously published, especially for the central Sierra and Southern California.

Note that the prices listed for each camp were provided to us for the 2003 season. Over seasons and years, prices go up. Count on it. If price is a bottom-line concern, call the contact number listed before planning your visit.

"No Place Left to Go?"

The way this book came about is filled with irony. It started when I kept hearing people complaining, "There is nowhere left to go in California." I used to think that myself. In the 1980s, I even started planning to move to Alaska or the Northwest Territories to be a bush plane pilot and guide. In the process of being certified as a pilot, I looked down on the vast California landscape and started seeing another world out there, a world outside the tunnel of freeway traffic, where all things great and wonderful seemed possible. My mission suddenly changed. I wanted to explore all of these beautiful places that were being unveiled to me from the air.

This book largely details that lifelong adventure, including:

- Coverage of 384 lakes you can drive to, including 190 without boat ramps, where with a canoe, kayak, or inflatable you can create your own personal paradise, often for free or at a very low cost.
- Details on 800 national forest campgrounds, including 600 not listed on any reservation service, which are often remote and beautiful spots at lakes, rivers, or trailheads.
- Every national park, state park, county park, regional park, and city park with campgrounds, including little-known sites that have space available even on three-day weekends.
- Information about 20 million acres of national forest, 17.5 million acres of land managed by the Bureau of Land Management, 1,100 miles of coast, a dozen islands, 55 prominent wilderness areas, and every landscape form that exists, including coast, bays, rivers, lakes, and estuaries mountains, valleys, wetlands, desert, and forest.
- Listings including 600 boat ramps, 280 lakes where swimming is allowed, 130 lakes with power boating, and 45 rivers where rafting or canoeing is allowed.
- Detailed information about each camp's setting, facilities, fees, reservation policies, and nearby recreation.
- Helpful notes about how to put the fun into every trip, including tips on catching fish, dealing with bears, and finding the best camp tents, bags, food, water purifiers, and more.
- Icons that quickly identify activities and services at each camp.
- Telephone numbers for each campground.
- Over 100 easy-to-use, detailed maps.
- The most accurate driving directions of any outdoor book in the state.
- Suggestions and recommendations from readers. We get tons of email and read each one carefully. We've often used this feedback for updates or bookwide upgrades. Your comments are always welcome and appreciated.

The Best Time to Go Is Now

As you may have realized, this is not a hobby for me, as it is for some part-time writers who publish books. With my work as outdoors columnist for the *San Francisco Chronicle* and writing guidebooks, this is my full-time job—and has been for 25 years. I spend up to 200 days a year in the field, traveling an average of 30,000 to 40,000 miles per year; it works because I often fly to cut time, and I don't commute to a job or watch TV. This has given me years' worth of extra time in the outdoors. In the process, I see first-hand how seriously people take their fun, what they need to know to make their trip work, and how their underlying fears of getting stuck without a spot for the night can take the life out of what should be a rejuvenating experience. Sound familiar?

Solve these problems by taking my advice. Never go anywhere without this book on your front seat!

Outdoor adventure is good for the soul, especially when shared with the people you care for most. If you don't think you have enough time to be outdoors enjoying what nature has to offer, do what I do and schedule time for outdoor activities. It's a great way to beat the time trap. If you schedule it, you'll do it, and there's no better time than right now to enjoy the outdoors. See you out there!

Tom Stienstra, March 2003
website: www.TomStienstra.com

Author's Picks

Can't decide where to camp this weekend? Here are my picks for the best campgrounds to visit in California. I've organized my selections by activity. These campgrounds have been chosen for their proximity to the activity and are listed in alphabetical order.

CAMPGROUNDS IN THE BEST SCENIC DESTINATIONS

Bridalveil Creek, Yosemite National Park, page 552.
Del Norte Coast Redwoods State Park, Redwood National Park, pages 77–78.
Diablo, Sardine Lakes, page 359.
Emerald Bay State Park and Boat-In, Lake Tahoe, page 399.
Lake Siskiyou Camp-Resort, Mt. Shasta, page 132.
Mill Flat, Kings River in Sequoia National Forest, pages 613–614.
Pfeiffer Big Sur State Park, Big Sur, pages 481–482.
Steep Ravine Environmental Campsites, Mt. Tamalpais State Park, page 445.
Sunset, Sequoia National Park, page 617.
Whitney Portal and Whitney Portal Group, Mt. Whitney, page 627.

CAMPGROUNDS IN THE BEST FAMILY DESTINATIONS

Alpine Campground, Lake Alpine, page 420.
Camp Shelley, South Lake Tahoe, page 400.
Convict Lake, Inyo National Forest, pages 569–570.
Lake Siskiyou Camp-Resort, Mt. Shasta, page 132.
Mono Hot Springs, Sierra National Forest, page 592.
Refugio State Beach/El Capitan Canyon (Goleta Beach), near Santa Barbara, pages 692–693.
Serrano, Big Bear Lake in San Bernadino National Forest, pages 755–756.
Trinity River, Shasta-Trinity National Forest, pages 139–140.
Upper Pines, Yosemite Valley in Yosemite National Park, page 553.
Yosemite Lakes (Rainbow Pool), Tuolumne River, page 544.

BEST BOAT-IN CAMPGROUNDS

Azalea Cove Hike-In/Boat-In, Union Valley Reservoir, page 395.
Brannan Island State Recreation Area, Sacramento River, page 443.
Emerald Bay State Park and Boat-In, Lake Tahoe, page 399.
Greens Creek Boat-In, Shasta Lake, page 167.
Lake Sonoma Recreation Area, Lake Sonoma, page 276.
Madrone Cove Boat-In, Bullards Bar Reservoir, page 316.
Ridgeville Boat-In Camp, Trinity Lake, page 155.
Santa Rosa Island Boat-In, Channel Islands National Park, page 720.
Stone Lagoon Boat-In, Humboldt Lagoons State Park, page 83.
Tree of Heaven, Klamath National Forest, page 126.

BEST CAMPGROUNDS FOR FISHING

Chula Vista Marina and RV Park, Chula Vista, page 809.
El Capitan Canyon, Santa Barbara, pages 692–693.

Hermit Gulch, Catalina Island, pages 766–767.
Hirz Bay, Shasta Lake, page 162.
Lake Cachuma Recreation Area, Lake Cachuma, page 701.
Lower Twin Lake, Humbolt-Toiyabe National Forest, pages 534–535.
Moccasin Point, Don Pedro Reservoir, page 506.
Woodson Bridge State Recreation Area, Sacramento River, page 303.

BEST CAMPGROUNDS FOR WHITE-WATER RAFTING
Auburn State Recreation Area, Middle Fork of the American River, pages 330–331.
Dillon Creek, Klamath River, page 117.
Elk Creek Campground, Klamath River, pages 113–114.
Hobo, Kern River, page 652.
Kirch Flat, Kings River, page 612.
Limestone, Kern River, pages 638–639.
Lumsden, Main Stem Tuolumne River, page 537.
Mathews Creek, Salmon River, page 122.
Sand Flat, South Fork of the American River, page 403.

BEST CAMPGROUNDS FOR WATER-SKIING
Lake Elsinore Recreation Area, Lake Elsinore, page 774.
Lake Nacimiento Resort, Lake Nacimiento, pages 680–681.
Lake Perris State Recreation Area, Lake Perris, page 770.
Lake Piru Recreation Area, Lake Piru, pages 718–719.
Lakeshore Villa RV Park, Shasta Lake, page 159.
Los Alamos, Pyramid Lake, page 716.
Moabi Regional Park (Lake Havasu), Colorado River, pages 847–848.
Rainbo Beach Resort and Marina, Colorado River, page 846.
Santee Lakes Regional Park, near Santee, page 808.

BEST CAMPGROUNDS WITH ACCESS TO TRAILHEADS
Crystal Springs, Kings Canyon National Park, page 618.
Horseshoe Meadow, Inyo National Forest, page 628.
Onion Valley, Inyo National Forest, pages 621–622.
Tuolumne Meadows, Yosemite National Park, page 547.
Wild Plum, Tahoe National Forest, page 361.

BEST CAMPGROUNDS NEAR WATERFALLS
Big Basin Redwoods State Park, near Santa Cruz, pages 454–455.
Bridalveil Creek, Yosemite National Park, page 552.
Camp 4, Yosemite National Park, page 551.
French Meadows (Grouse Falls), Tahoe National Forest, page 382.
Lower Pines, Yosemite National Park, page 552.
McArthur-Burney Falls Memorial State Park, near Burney, pages 193–194.
Milsap Bar, Plumas National Forest, page 311.

BEST CAMPGROUNDS FOR COASTAL HIKES/WALKS

Chula Vista Marina and RV Park, Chula Vista, page 809.
Coast Camp Hike-In, Point Reyes National Seashore, page 439.
Henry Cowell Redwoods State Park, near Santa Cruz, pages 468–469.
Montaña de Oro State Park, near Morro Bay, page 683.
Nadelos and Wailaki, King Range, page 101.
Patrick's Point State Park, near Trinidad, pages 84–85.
Saddle Mountain Recreation Park, Carmel River, pages 477–478.
San Elijo State Beach, Cardiff by the Sea, pages 796–797.
Sinkyone Wilderness, Sinkyone Wilderness State Park, pages 101–102.

BEST ISLAND CAMPGROUNDS

Angel Island State Park Walk-In, Angel Island, page 450.
Little Harbor Hike-In, Catalina Island, pages 765–766.
Parson's Landing Hike-In, Catalina Island, pages 764–765.
San Miguel Island Boat-In and Hike-In, Channel Islands National Park, pages 693–694.
Santa Cruz Island Boat-In, Channel Islands, page 713.
Santa Rosa Island Boat-In, Channel Islands National Park, page 720.
Two Harbors, Catalina Island, page 765.

BEST CAMPGROUNDS FOR ENJOYING FALL COLORS

Convict Lake, Inyo National Forest, pages 569–570.
Diamond "O" (Carlon Falls), Stanislaus National Forest, page 544.
Fallen Leaf Campground, Lake Tahoe Basin, pages 400–401.
Lundy Canyon Campground, Lundy Lake, page 536.
McGee Creek, Inyo National Forest, pages 570–571.
North Lake, Bishop Creek, pages 604–605.
Palomar Mountain State Park, near the Palomar Observatory, pages 797–798.
Paso Picacho, Cuyamaca Rancho State Park, page 811.
William Heise County Park, near Julian, page 805.

State Park Fee Changes

As this book went to press, some fee changes at California parks were ordered as part of the governor's emergency budget package. The campsite fee at state parks was raised one dollar to a standard $13 per night, and several add-on fees will return. For instance, an extra $6 will be charged for RV hookups. Other add-on fees will be charged for extra vehicles at a campsite, premium sites, and boat launching.

© TOM STIENSTRA

Introduction

Camping Tips

FOOD AND COOKING GEAR

It was a warm, crystal clear day, the kind of day when if you had ever wanted to go skydiving, you would go skydiving. That was exactly the case for my old pal Foonsky, who had never before tried the sport. But a funny thing happened after he jumped out of the plane and pulled on the rip cord: his parachute didn't open.

In total free fall, Foonsky watched the earth below getting closer and closer. Not one to panic, he calmly pulled the rip cord on the emergency parachute. Again nothing happened. No parachute, no nothing.

The ground was getting ever closer, and as he tried to search for a soft place to land, Foonsky detected a small object shooting up toward him, growing larger as it approached. It looked like a camper.

Figuring this was his last chance, Foonsky shouted as they passed in midair, "Hey, do you know anything about parachutes?"

The other fellow just yelled back as he headed off into space, "Do you know anything about lighting camping stoves?"

Well, Foonsky got lucky and his parachute opened. As for the other guy, well, he's probably in orbit like a NASA weather satellite. If you've ever had a mishap while lighting a camping stove, you know exactly what I'm talking about.

When it comes to camping, all gear is not created equal. Nothing is more important than lighting your stove easily and having it reach full heat without feeling as if you're playing with a short fuse to a miniature bomb. If your stove does not work right, your trip can turn into a disaster, regardless of how well you have planned the other elements. In addition, a bad stove will add an underlying sense of foreboding to your day. You will constantly have the inner suspicion that your darn stove is going to foul up again.

Camping Stoves

If you are buying a camping stove, remember this one critical rule: do not leave the store with a new stove unless you have been shown exactly how to use it.

Know what you are getting. Many stores that specialize in outdoor recreation equipment now provide experienced campers/employees who will demonstrate the use of every stove they sell and while they're at it, describe their respective strengths and weaknesses.

An innovation by Peak 1 is a two-burner backpacking stove that allows you to boil water and heat a pot of food simultaneously. While that has long been standard for car campers using Coleman's legendary camp stove, it was previously unheard of for wilderness campers in high-elevation areas.

A stove that has developed a cultlike following is the little Sierra, which burns small twigs and pinecones, then uses a tiny battery-driven fan to develop increased heat and cooking ability. It's an excellent alternative for long-distance backpacking trips, as it solves the problem of carrying a fuel bottle, especially on expeditions for which large quantities of fuel would otherwise be needed. Some tinkering with the flame (a very hot one) is required, and they are legal and functional only in the alpine zone where dry wood is available. Also note that in years with high fire danger, the U.S. Forest Service will enact rules prohibiting open flames, and fires are also often prohibited above an elevation of 10,000 feet.

For expeditions, I prefer a small, lightweight stove that uses white gas so I can closely gauge fuel consumption. My pal Foonsky uses one with a butane bottle because it lights so easily. We have contests to see who can boil a pot of water faster, and the difference is usually negligible. Thus, other factors are important when choosing a stove.

Of these, ease of cleaning the burner is the most important. If you camp often, especially with a smaller stove, the burner holes will eventually become clogged. Some stoves have a built-in cleaning needle; a quick twist of the knob and you're in business. Others require disassembly and a protracted session using special cleaning tools. If a stove is difficult to clean, you will tend to put off doing it, and your stove will sputter and pant while you feel humiliated watching the cold pot of water sitting there.

Before making a purchase, have the salesperson show you how to clean the burner head. Except in the case of large, multiburner family camping stoves, which rarely require cleaning, this test can do more to determine the long-term value of a stove than any other factor.

Fuels for Camping Stoves

White gas and butane have long been the most popular camp fuels, but a newly developed fuel could dramatically change that.

LPG (liquid petroleum gas) comes in cartridges for easy attachment to a stove or lantern. At room temperature, LPG is delivered in a combustible gaseous form. When you shake the cartridge, the contents sound liquid; that is because the gas liquefies under pressure, which is why it is so easy to use. Large amounts of fuel are compressed into small canisters.

While convenience has always been the calling card for LPG, recent innovations have allowed it to become a suitable choice for winter and high-altitude mountaineering expeditions,

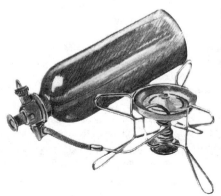

Stoves are available in many styles and burn a variety of fuels. These are three typical examples. Top: **White gas stoves** are the most popular because they are inexpensive and easy to find; they do require priming and can be explosive. Middle: **Gas canister stoves** burn propane, butane, isobutane, and mixtures of the three. These are the easiest to use but have two disadvantages: 1) Because the fuel is bottled, determining how much fuel is left can be difficult. 2) The fuel is limited to above-freezing conditions. Bottom: **Liquid fuel stoves** burn Coleman fuel, denatured alcohol, kerosene, and even gasoline; these fuels are economical and have a high heat output, but most must be primed.

coming close to matching white gas performance specs. For several years now, MSR, Epi (Coleman), Coleman, Primus, Camping Gaz, Markill, and other makers have been mixing propane, butane, and isobutane to improve performance capabilities.

Two important hurdles that stood in the way of LPG's popularity have been leaped. Coleman, working in cooperation with the U.S. Postal Service, has developed a program in which three-packs of 170-gram Coleman Max fuel cartridges can be shipped by mail to any address or post office in the 50 states and Puerto Rico. Also, each Coleman Max fuel cartridge is now made of aluminum and comes with a special device that allows the consumer to puncture the cartridge safely once the fuel is gone and then toss it into any aluminum recycling container.

The following details the benefits and drawbacks of other available fuels:

White gas: White gas is the most popular camp fuel because it is sold at most outdoor recreation stores and many supermarkets and is inexpensive and effective. It burns hot, has virtually no smell, and evaporates quickly when spilled. If you are caught in wet, miserable weather and can't get a fire going, you can use white gas as an emergency fire starter; however, if you do so, use it sparingly and never on an open flame.

During times of high fire danger the U.S. Forest Service will enact rules prohibiting open flames. Fires are also often prohibited above an elevation of 10,000 feet.

White gas is a popular fuel both for car campers, who use the large, two-burner stoves equipped with a fuel tank and a pump, and for hikers who carry a lightweight backpacking stove. On the latter, lighting can require priming with a gel called priming paste, which some people dislike. Another problem with white gas is that it can be extremely explosive.

As an example, I once almost burned my beard completely off in a mini-explosion while lighting one of the larger stoves designed for car camping. I was in the middle of cooking dinner when the flame suddenly shut down. Sure enough, the fuel tank was empty, and after refilling it, I pumped the tank 50 or 60 times to regain pressure. When I lit a match, the sucker ignited from three feet away. The resulting explosion was like a stick of dynamite going off, and immediately the smell of burning beard was in the air. In a flash, my once thick, dark beard had been reduced to a mass of little yellow burned curlicues.

My error? After filling the tank, I forgot to shut the fuel cock off while pumping up the pressure in the tank. As a result, the stove burners were slowly producing the gas/air mixture as I pumped the tank, filling the air above the stove. Then strike a match from even a few feet away and ka-boom!

Butane: The explosive problem can be solved by using stoves that burn bottled butane fuel. Butane requires no pouring, pumping, or priming, and butane stoves are the easiest to light. Just turn a knob and light—that's it. On the minus side, because it comes in bottles, you never know precisely how much fuel you have left. And when a bottle is empty, you have a potential piece of litter. (Never litter. Ever.)

The other problem with butane is that it just plain does not work well in cold weather or when there is little fuel left in the cartridge. Since you cannot predict mountain weather in spring or fall, you can wind up using more fuel than originally projected. That can be frustrating, particularly if your stove starts wheezing when there are still several days left to go. In addition, with most butane cartridges, if there is any chance of the temperature's falling below freezing, you often have to sleep with the cartridge to keep it warm or forget about using it come morning.

Coleman Max Performance Fuel: This new fuel offers a unique approach to solving the consistent burn challenge facing all pressurized gas cartridges: operating at temperatures at or below 0°F. Using a standard propane/butane blend for high-octane performance, Coleman gets around the drop-off in performance other cartridges experience by using a version of fuel injection. A hose inside the cartridge pulls liquid fuel into the stove, where it vaporizes—a switch from the standard approach of pulling only a gaseous form of the fuel into a stove. By drawing liquid out of the cartridge, Coleman gets around the tendency of propane to burn off first and allows each cartridge to deliver a consistent mix of propane and butane to the stove's burners throughout the cartridge's life.

Butane/Propane: This blend offers higher octane performance than butane alone, solving the cold temperature doldrums somewhat. However, propane burns off before butane, so there will be a performance drop as the fuel level in the cartridge lowers.

Propane: Now available for single-burner stoves using larger, heavier cartridges to accommodate higher pressures, propane offers the very best performance of any of the pressurized gas canister fuels.

Primus Tri-Blend: This blend is made up of 20 percent propane, 70 percent butane, and 10 percent isobutane and is designed to burn with more consistent heat and efficiency than standard propane/butane mixes.

Denatured alcohol: Though this fuel burns cleanly and quietly and is virtually explosion-proof, it generates much less heat than pressurized or liquid gas fuels.

Kerosene: Never buy a stove that uses kerosene for fuel. Kerosene is smelly and messy, generates low heat, needs priming, and is virtually obsolete as a camp fuel in the United States. As a test I once tried using a kerosene stove. I could scarcely boil a pot of water. In addition, some kerosene leaked out when the stove was packed, ruining everything it touched. The smell of kerosene never did go away. Kerosene remains popular in Europe only because most campers there haven't yet heard much about white gas. When they do, they will demand it.

Building Fires

One summer expedition took me to the Canadian wilderness in British Columbia for a 75-mile canoe trip on the Bowron Lake Circuit, a chain of 13 lakes, six rivers, and seven portages. It is one of the truly great canoe trips in the world, a loop that ends just a few hundred feet from its starting point. But at the first camp at Kibbee Lake, my stove developed a fuel leak at the base of the burner, and the nuclear-like blast that followed just about turned Canada into a giant crater.

As a result, the final 70 miles of the trip had to be completed without a stove, cooking done on open fires each night. The problem was compounded by the weather. It rained eight of the 10 days. Rain? In Canada, raindrops the size of silver dollars fall so hard they actually bounce on the lake surface. We had to stop paddling a few times to empty the rainwater out of the canoe. At the end of the day we'd make camp and then face the test: either make a fire or go to bed cold and hungry.

With an ax, at least we had a chance for success. As soaked as all the downed wood was, I was able to make my own fire-starting tinder from the chips of split logs; no matter how hard it rains, the inside of a log is always dry.

In miserable weather, matches don't stay lit long enough to get the tinder started. Instead we used either a candle or the little waxlike fire-starter cubes that remain lit for several minutes. From those we could get the tinder going. Then we added small, slender strips of wood that had been axed from the interior of the logs. When the flame reached a foot high, we added the logs, their dry interior facing in. By the time the inside of the logs had caught fire, the outside would be drying from the heat. It wasn't long before a royal blaze was brightening the rainy night.

Keep It Wild Tip 1: Campfires

1. Fire use can scar the backcountry. If a fire ring is not available, use a light-weight stove for cooking.
2. Where fires are permitted, use existing fire rings away from large rocks or overhangs.
3. Don't char rocks by building new rings.
4. Gather sticks from the ground that are no larger than the diameter of your wrist.
5. Don't snap branches of live, dead, or downed trees, which can cause personal injury and also scar the natural setting.
6. Put the fire "dead out" and make sure it's cold before departing. Remove all trash from the fire ring and sprinkle dirt over the site.
7. Remember that some forest fires can be started by a campfire that appears to be out. Hot embers burning deep in the pit can cause tree roots to catch fire and burn underground. If you ever see smoke rising from the ground, seemingly from nowhere, dig down and put the fire out.

That's a worst-case scenario, and I hope you will never face anything like it. Nevertheless, being able to build a good fire and cook on it can be one of the more satisfying elements of a camping trip. At times just looking into the flames can provide a special satisfaction at the end of a good day.

However, never expect to build a fire for every meal or in some cases even to build one at all. Many state and federal campgrounds have been picked clean of downed wood, or forest fire danger forces rangers to prohibit fires altogether during the fire season. In either case you must use your camp stove or go hungry.

But when you can build a fire and the resources for doing so are available, it will enhance the quality of your camping experience. Of the campgrounds listed in this book, those where you are permitted to build fires will usually have fire rings. In primitive areas where you can make your own fire, you should dig a ring eight inches deep, line the edges with rock, and clear all the needles and twigs in a five-foot radius. The next day, when the fire is dead, you can discard the rocks, fill over the black charcoal with dirt, and then scatter pine needles and twigs over it. Nobody will even know you camped there. That's the best way I know to keep a secret spot a real secret.

When you start to build a campfire, the first thing you will notice is that no matter how good your intentions, your fellow campers will not be able to resist moving the wood around. Watch. You'll be getting ready to add a key piece of wood at just the right spot, and your companion will stick his mitts in, confidently believing he has a better idea. He'll shift the fire around and undermine your best-thought-out plans.

So I enforce a rule on camping trips: one person makes the fire while everybody else stands clear or is involved with other camp tasks such as gathering wood, getting water, putting up tents, or planning dinner. Once the fire is going strong, then it's fair game; anyone adds logs at his or her discretion. But in the early, delicate stages of the campfire, it's best to leave the work to one person.

Before a match is ever struck, you should gather a complete pile of firewood. Then start small, with the tiniest twigs you can find, and slowly add larger twigs as you go, crisscrossing them like a miniature tepee. Eventually you will get to the big chunks that will produce high heat. The key is to get one piece of wood burning into another, which then burns into another, setting off what I call the chain of flame. Conversely, single pieces of wood set apart from each other will not burn.

On a dry summer evening at a campsite where plenty of wood is available, about the only way you can blow the deal is to get impatient and try to add the big pieces too quickly. Do that and you'll get smoke, not flames, and it won't be long before every one of your fellow campers is poking at your fire. It will drive you crazy, but they just won't be able to help it.

Cooking Gear

I like traveling light, and I've found that all I need for cooking is a pot, small frying pan, metal pot grabber, fork, knife, cup, and matches. If you want to keep the price of food low and also cook customized dinners each night, a small pressure cooker can be just the ticket. (See Keeping the Price Down on page 8.) I store all my gear in one small bag that fits into my pack. If I'm camping out of my four-wheel-drive rig, the little bag of cooking gear is easy to keep track of. Going simple, not complicated, is the key to keeping a camping trip on the right track.

You can get more elaborate by buying complete kits with plates, a coffeepot, large pots, and other cookware, but what really counts is having a single pot that makes you happy. It needs to be just the right size, not too big or small, and stable enough so it won't tip over, even if it is at a slight angle on a fire, full of water at a full boil. Mine is just 6 inches wide and 4.5 inches deep. It holds better than a quart of water and has served me well for several hundred camp dinners.

The rest of your cook kit is easy to complete. The frying pan should be small, light-gauge aluminum, and Teflon-coated, with a fold-in handle so it's no hassle to store. A pot grabber is a great addition. It's a little aluminum gadget that clamps to the edge of pots and allows you to lift them and pour water with total control without burning your fingers. For cleanup take a plastic scrubber and a small bottle filled with dish cleaner, and you're in business.

A sierra cup, a wide aluminum cup with a wire handle, is an ideal item to carry because you can eat out of it as well as use it for drinking. This means no plates to scrub after dinner, so cleanup is quick and easy. In addition, if you go for a hike, you can clip it to your belt with its handle.

If you want a more formal setup complete with plates, glasses, silverware, and the like, you can end up spending more time preparing and cleaning up from meals than you do enjoying the country you are exploring. In addition, the more equipment you bring, the more loose ends you will have to deal with, and loose ends can cause plenty of frustration. If you have a choice, go simple.

And remember what Thoreau said: "A man is rich in proportion to what he can do without."

Food and Cooking Tricks

On a trip to the Bob Marshall Wilderness in western Montana, I woke up one morning, yawned, and said, "What've we got for breakfast?"

The silence was ominous. "Well," finally came the response, "we don't have any food left."

"What!?"

"Well, I figured we'd catch trout for meals every other night."

On the return trip, we ended up eating wild berries, buds, and, yes, even roots (not too tasty). When we finally landed the next day at a suburban pizza parlor, we nearly ate the wooden tables.

Running out of food on a camping trip can do more to turn reasonable people into violent grumps than any other event. There's no excuse for it, not when a system for figuring meals can be outlined with precision and little effort. You should not go out and buy a bunch of food, throw it in your rig, and head off for yonder. That leaves too much to chance. And if you've ever been in the woods and real hungry, you'll know it's worth taking a little effort to make sure a day or two of starvation will not occur. Here's a three-step solution:

1. Draw up a general meal-by-meal plan and make sure your companions like what's on it.
2. Tell your companions to buy any specialty items (such as a special brand of coffee) on their own and not to expect you to take care of everything.
3. Put all the food on your living room floor and literally plan out every day of your trip, meal by meal, putting the food in plastic bags as you go. That way you will know exact food quotas and will not go hungry.

Fish for your dinner? There's one guarantee as far as that goes: if you expect to catch fish for meals, you will most certainly get skunked. If you don't expect to catch fish for meals, you will probably catch so many they'll be coming out of your ears. I've seen it a hundred times.

Keeping the Price Down

"There must be some mistake," I said with a laugh. "Whoever paid $750 for camp food?"

But the amount was as clear as the digital numbers on the cash register: $753.27.

"How is this possible?" I asked the clerk.

"Just add it up," she responded, irritated.

Then I started figuring. The freeze-dried backpack dinners cost $6 apiece. A small pack of beef jerky went for $2, the beef sticks for $.75, granola bars for $.50. Multiply it all by four hungry men, including Foonsky, for 21 days. This food was to sustain us on a major expedition—four guys hiking 250 miles over three weeks from Mt. Whitney to Yosemite Valley.

The dinners alone cost close to $500. Add in the usual goodies—jerky, granola bars, soup, dried fruit, oatmeal, Tang, candy, and coffee—and I felt as if an earthquake had struck when I saw the tab.

How to Make Beef Jerky in Your Own Kitchen

Start with a couple pieces of meat: lean top round, sirloin, or tri-tip. Cut it into 3/16-inch strips across the grain, trimming out the membrane, gristle, and fat. Marinate the strips for 24 hours in a glass dish. The fun begins in picking a marinade. Try two-thirds teriyaki sauce, one-third Worcestershire sauce. You can customize the recipe by adding pepper, ground mustard, bay leaf, red wine vinegar, garlic, and, for the brave, Tabasco sauce.

After a day or so, squeeze out each strip of meat with a rolling pin, lay them in rows on a cooling rack over a cookie sheet, and dry them in the oven at 125 degrees for 12 hours. Thicker pieces can take as long as 18 to 24 hours.

That's it. The hardest part is cleaning the cookie sheet when you're done. The easiest part is eating your own homemade jerky while sitting at a lookout on a mountain ridge. The do-it-yourself method for jerky may take a day or so, but it is cheaper and can taste better than any store-bought jerky.

A lot of campers have received similar shocks. In preparation for their trips, campers shop with enthusiasm. Then they pay the bill in horror.

Well, there are solutions, lots of them. You can eat gourmet style in the outback without having your wallet cleaned out. But it requires do-it-yourself cooking, more planning, and careful shopping. It also means transcending the push-button I-want-it-now attitude that so many people can't leave behind when they go to the mountains.

The secret is to bring along a small pressure cooker. A reader in San Francisco, Mike Bettinger, passed this tip on to me. Little pressure cookers weigh about two pounds, which may sound like a lot to backpackers and backcountry campers. But when three or four people are on a trip, it actually saves weight.

The key is that it allows campers to bring items that are difficult to cook at high altitudes, such as brown and white rice; red, black, pinto, and lima beans; and lentils. You pick one or more for a basic staple and then add a variety of freeze-dried ingredients to make a complete dish. Available are packets of meat, vegetables, onions, shallots, and garlic. Sun-dried tomatoes, for instance, reconstitute wonderfully in a pressure cooker. Add herbs, spices, and maybe a few rainbow trout and you will be eating better out of a backpack than most people do at home.

"In the morning, I have used the pressure cooker to turn dried apricots into apricot sauce to put on the pancakes we made with sourdough starter," Bettinger said. "The pressure cooker is also big enough for washing out cups and utensils. The days when backpacking meant eating terrible freeze-dried food are over. It doesn't take a gourmet cook to prepare these meals, only some thought beforehand."

Now when Foonsky, Mr. Furnai, Rambob, and I sit down to eat such a meal, we don't call it "eating." We call it "hodgepacking" or "time to pack your hodge." After a particularly long day on the trail, you can do some serious hodgepacking.

If your trip is a shorter one, say for a weekend, you can bring more fresh food to add some sizzle to the hodge. You can design a hot soup/stew mix that is good enough to eat at home.

Start by bringing a pot of water to a full boil, then adding pasta, ramen noodles, or macaroni. While it simmers, cut in a potato, carrot, onion, and garlic clove, and cook for about 10 minutes. When the vegetables have softened, add in a soup mix or two, maybe some cheese, and you are just about in business. But you can still ruin it and turn your hodge into slodge. Make sure you read the directions on the soup mix to determine cooking time. It can vary widely. In addition, make sure you stir the whole thing up; otherwise you will get these hidden dry clumps of soup mix that taste like garlic sawdust.

How do I know? Well, it was up near Kearsage Pass in the Sierra Nevada, where, feeling half-starved, I dug into our nightly hodge. I will never forget that first bite—I damn near gagged to death. Foonsky laughed at me, until he took his first bite (a nice big one) and then turned green.

Another way to trim food costs is to make your own beef jerky, the trademark staple of campers for more than 200 years. A tiny packet of beef jerky costs $2, and for that 250-mile expedition, I spent $150 on jerky alone. Never again. Now we make our own and get big strips of jerky that taste better than anything you can buy.

If all this still doesn't sound like your idea of a gourmet but low-cost camping meal, well, you are forgetting the main course: rainbow trout. Remember: if you don't plan on catching them for dinner, you'll probably snag more than you can finish in one night's hodgepacking.

Some campers go to great difficulties to cook their trout, bringing along frying pans, butter, grills, tinfoil, and more, but all you need is some seasoned salt and a campfire.

Rinse the gutted trout, and while it's still wet, sprinkle on a good dose of seasoned salt, both inside and out. Clear any burning logs to the side of the campfire, then lay the trout right on the coals, turning it once so both sides are cooked. Sound ridiculous? Sound like you are throwing the fish away? Sound like the fish will burn up? Sound like you will have to eat the campfire ash? Wrong on all counts. The fish cooks perfectly, the ash doesn't stick, and after cooking trout this way, you may never fry trout again.

But if you can't convince your buddies, who may insist the trout should be fried, then make sure you have butter to fry them in, not oil. Also make sure you cook them all the way through, so the meat strips off the backbone in two nice, clean fillets. The fish should end up looking like one that Sylvester the Cat just drew out of his mouth—only the head, tail, and a perfect skeleton.

You can supplement your eats with sweets, nuts, freeze-dried fruits, and drink mixes. In any case, make sure you keep the dinner menu varied. If you and your buddies look into your dinner cups and groan, "Ugh, not this again," you will soon start dreaming of cheeseburgers and french fries instead of hiking, fishing, and finding beautiful campsites.

If you are car camping and have a big ice chest, you can bring virtually anything to eat and drink. If you are on the trail and don't mind paying the price, the newest freeze-dried dinners provide another option.

Some of the biggest advances in the outdoors industry have come in the freeze-dried dinners now available to campers. Some of them are almost good enough to serve in restaurants. Sweet-and-sour pork over rice, tostadas, Burgundy chicken—it sure beats the poopy goop we used to eat, like the old soupy chili-mac dinners that tasted bad and looked so unlike food that consumption was near impossible, even for my dog, Rebel. Foonsky usually managed to get it down, but just barely.

To provide an idea of how to plan a menu, consider what my companions and I ate while hiking 250 miles on California's John Muir Trail:

- Breakfast: instant soup, oatmeal (never get plain), one beef or jerky stick, coffee or hot chocolate.
- Lunch: one beef stick, two jerky sticks, one granola bar, dried fruit, half cup of pistachio nuts, Tang, one small bag of M&Ms.
- Dinner: instant soup, one freeze-dried dinner, one milk bar, rainbow trout.

What was that last item? Rainbow trout? Right! Unless you plan on it, you can catch them every night.

CLOTHING AND WEATHER PROTECTION

What started as an innocent pursuit of a perfect campground evolved into one heck of a predicament for Foonsky and me.

We had parked at the end of a logging road and then bushwhacked our way down a canyon to a pristine trout stream. On my first cast—a little flip into the plunge pool of a waterfall—I caught a 16-inch rainbow trout, a real beauty that jumped three times. Magic stuff.

Then just across the stream, we saw it: The Perfect Camping Spot. On a sandbar on the edge of the forest, there lay a flat spot, high and dry above the river. Nearby was plenty of downed wood collected by past winter storms that we could use for firewood. And, of course, this beautiful trout stream was bubbling along just 40 yards from the site.

But nothing is perfect, right? To reach it, we had to wade across the river, although it didn't appear to be too difficult. The cold water tingled a bit, and the river came up surprisingly high, just above the belt. But it would be worth it to camp at The Perfect Spot.

Once across the river, we put on some dry clothes, set up camp, explored the woods, and fished the stream, catching several nice trout for dinner. But late that afternoon, it started raining. What?

Rain in the summertime? Nature makes its own rules. By the next morning, it was still raining, pouring like a Yosemite waterfall from a solid gray sky.

That's when we noticed The Perfect Spot wasn't so perfect. The rain had raised the river level too high for us to wade back across. We were marooned, wet, and hungry.

"Now we're in a heck of a predicament," said Foonsky, the water streaming off him.

Getting cold and wet on a camping trip with no way to warm up is not only unnecessary and uncomfortable, it can be a fast ticket to hypothermia, the number one killer of campers in the woods. By definition, hypothermia is a condition in which body temperature is lowered to the point that it causes illness. It is particularly dangerous because the afflicted are usually unaware it is setting in. The first sign is a sense of apathy, then a state of confusion, which can lead eventually to collapse (or what appears to be sleep), then death.

You must always have a way to get warm and dry in short order, regardless of any conditions you may face. If you have no way of getting dry, then you must take emergency steps to prevent hypothermia. (Those steps are detailed in First Aid and Insect Protection section on page 28.)

But you should never reach that point. For starters, always have spare sets of clothing tucked away so no matter how cold and wet you might get, you have something dry to put on. On hiking trips I always carry a second set of clothes, sealed to stay dry, in a plastic garbage bag. I keep a third set waiting back at the truck.

If you are car camping, your vehicle can cause an illusory sense of security. But with an extra set of dry clothes stashed safely away, there is no illusion. The security is real. And remember, no matter how hot the weather is when you start your trip, always be prepared for the worst. Foonsky and I learned the hard way.

So both of us were soaking wet on that sandbar, and with no other choice we tried holing up in the tent for the night. A sleeping bag with Quallofil or another polyester fiberfill can retain warmth even when wet, because the fill is hollow and retains its loft. So as miserable as it was, we made it through the night.

The rain stopped the next day and the river dropped a bit, but it was still rolling big and angry. Using a stick as a wading staff, Foonsky crossed about 80 percent of the stream before he was dumped, but he made a jump for it and managed to scramble to the riverbank. He waved for me to follow. "No problem," I thought.

It took me 20 minutes to reach nearly the same spot where Foonsky had been dumped. The heavy river current was above my belt and pushing hard. Then in the flash of an instant, my wading staff slipped on a rock. I teetered in the river current and was knocked over like a bowling pin. I became completely submerged. I went tumbling down the river, heading right toward the waterfall. While underwater I looked up at the surface, and I can remember how close it seemed yet how out of control I was. Right then this giant hand appeared, and I grabbed it. It was Foonsky. If it weren't for that hand, I would have sailed right over the waterfall.

My momentum drew Foonsky right into the river, and we scrambled in the current, but I suddenly sensed the river bottom under my knees. On all fours, the two of us clambered ashore. We were safe.

"Thanks, ol' buddy," I said.

"Man, we're wet," he responded. "Let's get to the rig and get some dry clothes on."

The Art of Layering

The most important element in enjoying the outdoor experience in any condition is to stay dry and warm. There is no substitute. You must stay dry and you must stay warm.

Thus comes the theory behind layering, which suggests that as your body temperature fluctuates or the weather shifts, you simply peel off or add available layers as needed—and have a waterproof shell available in case of rain.

The introduction of a new era of outdoor clothing has made it possible for campers to turn choosing clothes into an art form. Like art, it comes much more expensive than throwing on a pair of blue jeans, a T-shirt, and some flannel, but for many it is worth the price.

In putting together your ideal layering system, there are some general considerations. What you need to do is create a system that effectively combines elements of breathability, wicking, rapid drying, insulation, durability, wind resistance, and water repellence while still being lightweight and offering the necessary freedom of movement, all with just a few garments.

The basic intent of a base layer is to manage moisture. Your base layer will be the first article of clothing you put on and the last to come off. Since your own skin will be churning out the perspiration, the goal of this second skin is to manage the moisture and move it away from you. That is why the best base layer available is from bicomponent knits, that is, blends of polyester and cotton, which work to provide wicking and insulating properties in one layer.

The way it works is that the side facing your skin is water hating, while the side away from your skin is water loving; thus it pulls or "wicks" moisture through. You'll stay dry and happy, even with only one layer on, something not possible with old single-function weaves. The best include Thermax, Capilene, Driclime, Lifa, and Polartec 100. The only time that cotton should become a part of your base layer is if you wish to keep cool, not warm, such as in a hot desert climate where evaporative cooling becomes your friend, not your enemy.

Stretch fleece and microdenier pile also provide a good base layer, though they can be used as a second layer as well. Microdenier pile can be worn alone or layered under or over other pieces, and it has excellent wicking capability as well as more windproof potential.

The next layer should be a light cotton shirt or a long-sleeved cotton/wool shirt, or both, depending on the coolness of the day. For pants, many just wear blue jeans when camping, but blue jeans can be hot and tight, and once wet, they tend to stay that way. Putting on wet blue jeans on a cold morning is a torturous way to start the day. (I tell you this from experience, since I have suffered that fate a number of times.) A better choice is pants made from a cotton/canvas mix, which are available at outdoors stores. They are light, have a lot of give, and dry quickly. If the weather is quite warm, shorts that have some room to them can be the best choice.

Finally, you'll top the entire ensemble off with a thin windproof, water-resistant layer. You want this layer to breathe like crazy, yet not be so porous that rain runs through it like floodwaters through a leaking dike. Patagonia's Velocity shell is one of the best. Its outer fabric is DWR (durable water-repellent) treated, and the coating is by Gore. Patagonia calls it Pneumatic (Gore now calls it Activent, while Marmot, Moonstone, and North Face all offer their own versions). Though condensation will still build up inside, it manages to get rid of enough moisture.

It is critical to know the difference between "water-resistant" and "waterproof." (This is covered later in the chapter under the Rain Gear section.)

But hey, why does anybody need all this fancy stuff just to go camping? Fair question. Like the introduction of Gore-Tex years ago, all this fabric and fiber mumbo jumbo has its skeptics, including me. You don't have to opt for this aerobic-function fashion statement; it is unnecessary on many camping trips. But the fact is you must be ready for anything when you venture into the outdoors. And the truth is that the new era of outdoor clothing works, and it works better than anything that has come before.

Regardless of what you choose, weather should never be a nuisance or cause discomfort, regardless of what you experience. Instead it should provide a welcome change of pace.

About Hats

One final word of advice: always pack along a warm hat for those times when you need to seal in warmth. You lose a large percentage of heat through your head. I almost always wear a wide-brimmed hat, something like the legendary outlaws wore 150 years ago. There's actually logic behind it: my hat is made of kangaroo skin (waterproof), is rigged with a lariat (it can be cinched down when it's windy), and has a wide brim that keeps the tops of my ears from being sunburned (years ago they once were burned to a red crisp on a trip where I was wearing a baseball hat). But to be honest, I like how it looks, kind of like my pal Waylon Jennings.

Vests and Parkas

In cold weather you should take the layer system one step further with a warm vest and a parka jacket. Vests are especially useful because they provide warmth without the bulkiness of a parka. The warmest vests and parkas are either filled with down or Quallofil, or they are made with a cotton/wool mix. Each has its respective merits and problems. Down fill provides the most warmth for the amount of weight, but becomes useless when wet, closely resembling a wet dishrag. Quallofil keeps much of its heat-retaining quality even when wet, but it is expensive. Vests made of cotton/wool mixes are the most attractive and also are quite warm, but they can be as heavy as a ship's anchor when wet.

Sometimes the answer is combining the two. One of my best camping companions wears a good-looking cotton/wool vest and a parka filled with Quallofil. The vest never gets wet, so weight is not a factor.

Rain Gear

One of the most miserable nights I ever spent in my life was on a camping trip where I didn't bring my rain gear or a tent. Hey, it was early August, the temperature had been in the 90s for weeks, and if anybody had said it was going to rain, I would have told him to consult a brain doctor. But rain it did. And as I got wetter and wetter, I kept saying to myself, "Hey, it's summer, it's not supposed to rain." Then I remembered one of the 10 commandments of camping: forget your rain gear and you can guarantee it will rain.

To stay dry, you need some form of water-repellent shell. It can be as simple as a $5 poncho made out of plastic or as elaborate as a Gore-Tex rain jacket-and-pants set that costs $300. What counts is not how much you spend, but how dry you stay.

The most important thing to realize is that waterproof and water-resistant are completely different things. In addition, there is no such thing as rain gear that is both waterproof and breathable. The more waterproof a jacket is, the less it breathes. Conversely, the more breathable a jacket is, the less waterproof it becomes.

Waterproof: impervious to water. Though rain won't penetrate waterproof material, if you're at all mobile you'll soon find yourself wet from perspiration that can't evaporate. **Water-resistant: resistant but not impervious to water.** You'll stay dry using water-resistant material only if it isn't pouring.

If you wear water-resistant rain gear in a downpour, you'll get soaked. Water-resistant rain gear is appealing because it breathes and will keep you dry in the light stuff, such as mist, fog, even a little splash from a canoe paddle. But in rain? Forget it.

So what is the solution?

I've decided that the best approach is a set of fairly light but 100 percent-waterproof rain gear. I recently bought a hooded jacket and pants from Coleman, and my assessment is that it is the most cost-efficient rain gear I've ever had. All I can say is, hey, it works: I stay dry, it doesn't weigh much, and it didn't cost a fortune.

You can also stay dry with any of the waterproof plastics and even heavy-duty rubber-coated outfits made for commercial fishermen. But these are uncomfortable during anything but a heavy rain. Because they are heavy and don't breathe, you'll likely get soaked anyway (that is, from your own sweat), even if it isn't raining hard.

On backpacking trips, I still stash a super lightweight water-repellent slicker for day hikes, and a poncho, which I throw over my pack at night to keep it dry. But otherwise I never go any-where—*anywhere*—without my rain gear.

Some do just fine with a cheap poncho, and note that ponchos can serve other uses in addition to a raincoat. Ponchos can be used as a ground tarp, as a rain cover for supplies or a backpack, or can be roped up to trees in a pinch to provide a quick storm ceiling if you don't have a tent. The problem with ponchos is that in a hard rain, you just don't stay dry. First your legs get wet, then they get soaked. Then your arms follow the same pattern. If you're wearing cotton, you'll find that once part of the garment gets wet, the water will spread until, alas, you are dripping wet, poncho and all. Before long you start to feel like a walking refrigerator.

One high-cost option is buying a Gore-Tex rain jacket and pants. Gore-Tex is actually not a fabric as is commonly believed, but a laminated film that coats a breathable fabric. The result is lightweight, water-repellent, breathable jackets and pants. They are perfect for campers, but they cost a fortune.

Some hiking buddies of mine have complained that the older Gore-Tex rain gear loses its water-repellent quality over time. However, manufacturers insist that this is the result of water seeping through seams, not leaks in the jacket. At each seam, tiny needles have pierced the fabric, and as tiny as the holes are, water will find a way through. An application of Seam Lock, especially at major seams around the shoulders of a jacket, can usually fix the problem.

If you don't want to spend the big bucks for Gore-Tex rain gear but want more rain protection than a poncho affords, a coated nylon jacket is the compromise that many choose. They are inexpensive, have the highest water-repellency of any rain gear, and are warm, providing a good outer shell for your layers of clothing. But they are not without fault. These jackets don't breathe at all, and if you zip them up tight, you can sweat a river.

My brother Rambob gave me a nylon jacket before a mountain climbing expedition. I wore that $20 special all the way to the top with no complaints; it's warm and 100 percent waterproof. The one problem with nylon is when temperatures drop below freezing. It gets so stiff that it feels as if you are wearing a straitjacket. But at $20, it seems like a treasure, especially compared to a $180 Gore-Tex jacket.

There's one more jacket-construction term to know: DWR, or durable water-repellent finish. All of the top-quality jackets these days are DWR-treated. The DWR causes water to bead up on the shell. When the DWR wears off, even a once-waterproof jacket will feel like a wet dishrag.

Also note that ventilation is the key to coolness. The only ventilation on most shells is often the zipper. But waterproof jackets need additional openings. Look for mesh-backed pockets and underarm zippers, as well as cuffs, waists, and hems that can be adjusted to open wide. Storm flaps (the baffle over the zipper) that close with hook-and-loop material or snaps let you leave the zipper open for airflow into the jacket.

Other Gear—and a Few Tips

What are the three items most commonly forgotten on a camping trip? A hat, sunglasses, and lip balm.

A hat is crucial, especially when you are visiting high elevations. Without one you are constantly exposed to everything nature can give you. The sun will dehydrate you, sap your energy, sunburn your head, and in worst cases, cause sunstroke. Start with a comfortable hat. Then finish with sunglasses, lip balm, and sunscreen for additional protection. They will help protect you from extreme heat.

To guard against extreme cold, it's a good idea to keep a pair of thin ski gloves stashed away with your emergency clothes, along with a wool ski cap. The gloves should be thick enough to keep your fingers from stiffening up, but pliable enough to allow full movement so you don't have to take them off to complete simple tasks, like lighting a stove. An alternative to gloves is glovelets, which look like gloves with no fingers. In any case, just because the weather turns cold doesn't mean that your hands have to.

And if you fall into a river as Foonsky and I did—well, I hope you have a set of dry clothes waiting back at your rig. Oh, and a hand reaching out to you.

HIKING AND FOOT CARE

We had set up a nice little camp in the woods, and my buddy, Foonsky, was strapping on his hiking boots, sitting against a big Douglas fir.

"New boots," he said with a grin. "But they seem pretty stiff."

We decided to hoof it down the trail for a few hours, exploring the mountain wildlands that are said to hide Bigfoot and other strange creatures. After just a short while on the trail, a sense of peace and calm seemed to settle in. The forest provides the chance to be purified with clean air and the smell of trees, freeing you from all troubles.

But it wasn't long before a look of trouble was on Foonsky's face. And no, it wasn't from seeing Bigfoot.

"Got a hot spot on a toe," he said.

Immediately we stopped. He pulled off his right boot, then his socks, and inspected the left side of his big toe. Sure enough, a blister had bubbled up, filled with fluid, but hadn't popped. From his medical kit, Foonsky cut a small piece of moleskin to fit over the blister and taped it to hold it in place. In a few minutes we were back on the trail.

A half hour later, there was still no sign of Bigfoot. But Foonsky stopped again and pulled off his other boot. "Another hot spot." On the little toe of his left foot was another small blister, over which he taped a Band-Aid to keep it from further chafing against the inside of his new boot.

In just a few days, ol' Foonsky, a strong, 6-foot-5, 200-plus-pound guy, was walking around like a sore-hoofed horse that had been loaded with a month's worth of supplies and ridden over sharp rocks. Well, it wasn't the distance that had done Foonsky in; it was those blisters. He had them on eight of his 10 toes and was going through Band-Aids, moleskin, and tape like a walking emergency ward. If he used any more tape, he would've looked like a mummy from an Egyptian tomb.

If you've ever been in a similar predicament, you know the frustration of wanting to have a good time, wanting to hike and explore the area where you have set up a secluded camp, only to be held up by several blisters. No one is immune—all are created equal before the blister god. You can be forced to bow to it unless you get your act together.

That means wearing the right-style boots for what you have in mind and then protecting your feet with carefully selected socks. If you are still so unfortunate as to get a blister or two, it means knowing how to treat them fast so they don't turn your walk into a sore-footed endurance test.

What causes blisters? In almost all cases, it is the simple rubbing of a foot against the rugged interior of a boot. That can be worsened by several factors:

1. A very stiff boot or one in which your foot moves inside as you walk, instead of the boot flexing as if it were another layer of skin.
2. Thin, ragged, or dirty socks. This is the fastest route to blisters. Thin socks will allow your feet to move inside of your boots, ragged socks will allow your skin to chafe directly against the boot's interior, and dirty socks will wrinkle and fold, also rubbing against your feet instead of cushioning them.
3. Soft feet. By themselves, soft feet will not cause blisters, but in combination with a stiff boot or thin socks, they can cause terrible problems. The best way to toughen up your feet is to go barefoot. In fact, some of the biggest, toughest-looking guys you'll ever see, from Hell's Angels to pro football players, have feet that are as soft as a baby's butt. Why? Because they never go barefoot and don't hike much.

The Perfect Boot

Every hiker eventually conducts a search for the perfect boot in the mission for ideal foot comfort and to stay free of blisters. While there are many entries in this search, in fact, so many that it can be confusing, there is a way to find that perfect boot for you.

To stay blister-free, the most important factors are socks and the flexibility of a boot. If there is any foot slippage from a thin sock or a stiff boot, you can rub up a blister in minutes. For instance, I never wear stiff boots and I always wear two fresh sets of SmartWools ($13 a pop).

This search for the perfect boot included discussions with the nation's preeminent long-distance hikers, Brian Robinson of Mountain View (7,200 miles in 2001) and Ray Jardine of Oregon (2,700 miles of Pacific Crest Trail in three months). Both believe that the weight of a boot (or athletic shoe, as they often use) is the defining factor when selecting hiking footware. They both go as light as possible, believing that heavy boots will eventually wear you out by forcing you to pick up several pounds on your feet over and over again. A compatriot at the *San Francisco Chronicle,* outdoors writer Paul McHugh, offers the reminder that arch support may be even more vital, especially for people who hike less frequently and thus have not developed great foot strength as have Robinson and Jardine.

It is absolutely critical to stay away from very stiff boots and thin socks. Always wear the right-style boots for what you have in mind and then protect your feet with carefully selected socks. If you are still so unfortunate as to get a blister or two, it means knowing how to treat them fast so they don't turn your walk into a sore-footed endurance test.

What Causes Blisters

What causes blisters? In almost all cases, it is the simple rubbing of a foot against the rugged interior of a boot. That can be worsened by several factors:

1. A very stiff boot or one in which your foot moves inside as you walk, instead of the boot flexing as if it were another layer of skin.
2. Thin, ragged, or dirty socks. This is the fastest route to blisters. Thin socks will allow your feet to move inside your boots, ragged socks will allow your skin to chafe directly against the

boot's interior, and dirty socks will wrinkle and fold, also rubbing against your feet instead of cushioning them.

3. Soft feet. By themselves, soft feet will not cause blisters, but in combination with a stiff boot or thin socks, they can cause terrible problems. The best way to toughen up your feet is to go barefoot. In fact, some of the biggest, toughest-looking guys you'll ever see, from Hells Angels to pro football players, have feet that are as soft as a baby's butt. Why? Because they never go barefoot and don't hike much.

Selecting the Right Boots

When I hiked the John Muir Trail, I hiked 400 miles in three months, that is, 250 miles in three weeks from Mt. Whitney to Yosemite Valley, then another 150 miles in an earlier general training program. In that span I got just one blister, suffered on the fourth day of the 250-miler. I treated it immediately and suffered no more. One key is wearing the right boot, and for me, that means a boot that acts as a thick layer of skin that is flexible and pliable to my foot. I want my feet to fit snugly in them, with no interior movement.

There are four kinds of hiking footwear, most commonly known as: 1. Hiking boots; 2. Hunting boots; 3. Mountaineering boots; 4. Athletic shoes. Select the right one for you or pay the consequences.

One great trick when on a hiking vacation is to bring all four, and then for each hike, wear different footwear. This has many benefits. By changing boots, you change the points of stress for your feet and legs, greatly reducing soreness and the chance of creating a hot spot on a foot. It also allows you to go light on flat trails, and heavy on steep trails, where additional boot weight can help traction in downhill stretches.

Hiking Boots

Hiking boots can resemble low-cut leather/Gore-Tex hunting boots or Gore-Tex walking shoes, almost as if they were heavy athletic shoes. They are designed for day walks or short backpacking trips. Some of the newer models are like rugged athletic shoes, designed with a Gore-Tex top for lightness and a Vibram sole for traction. These are perfect for people who like to walk but rarely carry a heavy backpack. Because they are flexible, they are easy to break in, and with fresh socks they rarely cause blister problems. Because they are light, general hiking fatigue is greatly reduced.

On the negative side, because hiking boots are light, traction can be far from good on steep, slippery surfaces. In addition, they provide less than ideal ankle support, which can be a problem in rocky areas, such as along a stream where you might want to go trout fishing. Turn your ankle and your trip can be ruined.

For day-hiking, they are the footwear of choice for most.

Hunting Boots

Hunting boots are also called backpacking boots, super boots, or wilderness boots. They feature high ankle support, deep Vibram lug sole, built-in orthotics and arch support, and waterproof exterior.

Many larger backpackers prefer them because of the additional support they provide when carrying a heavy pack. They also can stand up to hundreds of miles of wilderness use, constantly being banged against rocks and walked through streams while supporting 200 pounds. On the negative side, they can be quite hot, weigh a ton, and if they get wet, take days to dry. Because they are heavy, they can wear you out. Often the extra weight can add days to long-distance expeditions, cutting into the number of miles a hiker is capable of on a daily basis.

Mountaineering Boots
Mountaineering boots are identified by midrange tops, laces that extend almost as far as the toe area, and ankle areas that are as stiff as a board. The lack of "give" is what endears them to mountaineers. Their stiffness is preferred when rock-climbing, walking off-trail on craggy surfaces, or hiking along the edge of streambeds where walking across small rocks can cause you to turn your ankle. Because these boots don't give on rugged, craggy terrain, they reduce ankle injuries and provide better traction.

The drawback to stiff boots is that if you don't have the proper socks and your foot starts slipping around in the boot, you will get a set of blisters that can have you using so much tape and moleskin that you can end up looking like a mummy. If you just want to go for a walk or a good tromp with a backpack, then hiking shoes or hunting boots will serve you better.

Athletic Shoes
Athletic shoes are built so well these days that they often can make good hiking footwear. They are often featherlight, so the long-term wear on your legs is minimal. For many short walks, they are ideal. For those with very strong feet and arches, they are popular even on multiday trips, where you carry a small pack.

But there can be many problems with such a shoe. On steep sections, you can lose your footing, slip, and fall. If you stub your toe, you have little protection, and it hurts like heck. If you try to carry a backpack and don't have a strong arch, your arch can collapse, or at the minimum, overstress your ankles and feet. In addition, heavy socks usually are not a good fit in these lightweight shoes; if you go with a thin cotton sock and if folds over, you can rub up a blister in minutes.

At the Store
There are a many styles, brands, and price ranges to choose from. If you wander about comparing all their many features, you will get as confused as a kid in a toy store.

Instead, go into the store with your mind clear about what you want, find it, and buy it. If you want the best, expect to spend $85–150 for hiking boots, $100–175 for hunting boots, $140–200 for mountaineering boots, and $50–90 for athletic shoes. If you go much cheaper, well, then you are getting cheap.

Yet you don't always get what you pay for. Once I spent $250 for hiking boots custom-made in Germany that I have worn for close to 2,000 miles, yet which weighed four pounds each! Another time, trying to go light, I spent $185 on some low-cut hiking boots; they turned out to be miserable blister makers. Even after a year of trying to get my money's worth, they never worked right on the trail and now occupy a dark place deep in my closet.

This is one area where you don't want to scrimp, so try not to yelp about the high cost.

Instead, walk out of the store believing you deserve the best, and that's exactly what you just paid for. Another trick I have learned is to stash several pairs of different-style hiking boots in my vehicle. Then, when out on adventures, I can pick the perfect boot for the type of terrain. I have seven sets of boots and constantly rotate them. Use heavy boots for steep trails with loose footing, lightweight models for flat routes with a hard surface. This works wonders to avoid blisters and muscle soreness because you are constantly changing the point of attack.

Keep It Wild Tip 2: Travel Lightly

1. Visit the backcountry in small groups.
2. Below tree line, always stay on designated trails.
3. Don't cut across switchbacks.
4. When traveling cross-country where no trails are available, follow animal trails or spread out with your group so no new routes are created.
5. Read your map and orient yourself with landmarks, a compass, and an altimeter. Avoid marking trails with rock cairns, tree scars, or ribbons.

If you plan to use the advice of a shoe salesperson, first look at what kind of boots he or she is wearing. If he or she isn't even wearing boots, then any advice the salesperson might tender may not be worth much. Most people I know who own quality boots, including salespeople, will wear them almost daily if their jobs allow, since boots are the best footwear available. However, even these well-meaning folks can offer sketchy advice. Every hiker I've ever met will tell you he wears the world's greatest boot! Instead of asking how great the boot is, ask, "How many blisters did you get when you hiked 12 miles a day for a week?"

Enter the store with a precise use and style in mind. Rather than fish for suggestions, tell the salesperson exactly what you want, try two or three brands of the same style, and always try on both boots in a pair simultaneously so you know exactly how they'll feel. If possible, walk up and down stairs with them. Are they too stiff? Are your feet snug yet comfortable, or do they slip? Do they have that "right" kind of feel when you walk?

If you get the right answers to those questions, then you're on your way to blister-free, pleasure-filled days of walking.

Socks

People can spend so much energy selecting the right kind of boot that they virtually overlook wearing the right kind of socks. One goes with the other.

Your socks should be thick enough to cushion your feet as well as fit snugly. Without good socks you might try to get the bootlaces too tight—and that's like putting a tourniquet on your feet. You should have plenty of clean socks on hand, or plan on washing what you have on your trip. As socks are worn, they become compressed, dirty, and damp. If they fold over, you'll rub up a blister in minutes.

My companions believe I go overboard when it comes to socks, that I bring too many and wear too many. But it works, so that's where the complaints stop. So how many do I wear? Well, it varies. On day hikes, I have found a sock called a SmartWool that makes my size 13s feel as if I'm walking on pillows. I always wear two of them, that is, two on each foot.

Do not wear cotton socks. Your foot can get damp and mix with dirt, which can cause a hot spot to start on your foot. Eventually you get blisters, lots of them.

SmartWool socks and other similar socks are a synthetic composite. They can partially wick moisture away from the skin.

The exterior sock can be wool or its equivalent. This will cushion your foot, provide that just-right snug fit in your boot, and give you some additional warmth and insulation in cold weather. It is critical to keep the sock clean. If you wear a dirty wool sock over and over again, it will compact and lose its cushion and start wrinkling while you hike, and then your feet will catch on fire from the blisters that start popping up. Of course, when wearing multiple socks, especially a wool composite, you will likely need to go up a boot size so they fit comfortably.

A Few More Tips

If you are like most folks—that is, the bottoms of your feet are rarely exposed and quite soft—you can take additional steps in their care. The best tip is keeping a fresh foot pad made of sponge rubber in your boot. But note that brand-new foot pads are often slippery for a few days, and that can cause blisters. They need to be broken in before an expedition, just as with new boots.

Another cure for soft feet is to get out and walk or jog on a regular basis before your camping trip. On one trip, I ran into the long-distance master Jardine, and he swore that going barefoot regularly is the best way to build up foot strength, arch support, and to toughen up the bottom of your feet.

If you plan to use a foot pad and wear two heavy socks, you will need to use these items when sizing boots. It is an unforgiving error to wear thin cotton socks when buying boots and later try to squeeze all this stuff, plus your feet, into them. There just won't be enough room.

Treating Blisters

The key to treating blisters is fast work at the first sign of a hot spot. If you feel a hot spot, never keep walking, figuring that the problem will go away or that you will work through it. Wrong! Stop immediately and go to work.

Before you remove your socks, check to see if the sock has a wrinkle in it, a likely cause of the problem. If so, either change socks or pull them tight, removing the tiny folds, after taking care of the blister.

To take care of the blister, cut a piece of moleskin to cover the offending toe, securing the moleskin with white medical tape. If moleskin is not available, small Band-Aids can do the job, but these have to be replaced daily, and sometimes with even more frequency. At night, clean your feet and sleep without socks. That will allow your feet to dry and heal.

Tips in the Field

Two other items that can help your walking are an Ace bandage and a pair of gaiters.

For sprained ankles and twisted knees, an Ace bandage can be like an insurance policy to get you back on the trail and out of trouble. In many cases a hiker with a twisted ankle or sprained knee has relied on a good wrap with a four-inch bandage for the added support to get home. Always buy the Ace bandages that come with the clips permanently attached, so you don't have to worry about losing them.

Gaiters are leggings made of Gore-Tex that fit from just below your knees, over your calves, and attach under your boots. They are of particular help when walking in damp areas or in places where rain is common. As your legs brush against ferns or low-lying plants, gaiters will deflect the moisture. Without them, your pants will be soaking wet in short order.

Should your boots become wet, a good tip is never to try to force-dry them. Some well-meaning folks will try to dry them quickly at the edge of a campfire or actually put the boots in an oven. While this may dry the boots, it can also loosen the glue that holds them together, ultimately weakening them until one day they fall apart in a heap.

A better bet is to treat the leather so the boots become water-repellent. Silicone-based liquids are the easiest to use and least greasy of the treatments available.

A final tip is to have another pair of lightweight shoes or moccasins that you can wear around camp and in the process give your feet the rest they deserve.

SLEEPING GEAR

One mountain night in the pines on an eve long ago, my dad, brother, and I had rolled out our sleeping bags and were bedded down for the night. After the pretrip excitement, a long drive, an evening of trout fishing, and a barbecue, we were like three tired doggies who had played too much.

But as I looked up at the stars, I was suddenly wide awake. This kid was still wired. A half hour later? No change—wide awake.

And as little kids can do, I had to wake up ol' dad to tell him about it. "Hey, Dad, I can't sleep."

"This is what you do," he said. "Watch the sky for a shooting star and tell yourself that you cannot go to sleep until you see at least one. As you wait and watch, you will start getting tired, and it will be difficult to keep your eyes open. But tell yourself you must keep watching. Then you'll start to really feel tired. When you finally see a shooting star, you'll go to sleep so fast you won't know what hit you."

Well, I tried it that night and I don't even remember seeing a shooting star, I went to sleep so fast.

It's a good trick, and along with having a good sleeping bag, ground insulation, maybe a tent, or a few tricks for bedding down in a pickup truck or motor home, you can get a good night's sleep on every camping trip.

More than 20 years after that camping episode with my dad and brother, we made a trip to the planetarium at the Academy of Sciences in San Francisco to see a show on Halley's Comet. The lights dimmed, and the ceiling turned into a night sky, filled with stars and a setting moon. A scientist began explaining phenomena of the heavens.

After a few minutes, I began to feel drowsy. Just then, a shooting star zipped across the planetarium ceiling. I went into a deep sleep so fast it was like I was in a coma. I didn't wake up until the show was over, the lights were turned back on, and the people were leaving.

Feeling drowsy, I turned to see if ol' Dad had liked the show. Oh yeah? Not only had he gone to sleep too, but he apparently had no intention of waking up, no matter what. Just like a camping trip.

Sleeping Bags

Question: What could be worse than trying to sleep in a cold, wet sleeping bag on a rainy night without a tent in the mountains?

Answer: Trying to sleep in a cold, wet sleeping bag on a rainy night without a tent in the mountains when your sleeping bag is filled with down.

Water will turn a down-filled sleeping bag into a mushy heap. Many campers do not like a high-tech approach, but the state-of-the-art polyfiber sleeping bags can keep you warm even when wet. That factor, along with temperature rating and weight, is key when selecting a sleeping bag.

A sleeping bag is a shell filled with heat-retaining insulation. By itself it is not warm. Your body provides the heat, and the sleeping bag's ability to retain that heat is what makes it warm or cold.

The old-style canvas bags are heavy, bulky, cold, and when wet, useless. With other options available, their use is limited. Anybody who sleeps outdoors or backpacks should choose otherwise.

Buy and use a sleeping bag filled with down or one of the quality poly-fills. Down is light, warm, and aesthetically pleasing to those who don't think camping and technology mix. If you choose a down bag, be sure to keep it double wrapped in plastic garbage bags on your trip to keep it dry. Once it's wet, you'll spend your nights howling at the moon.

The polyfiber-filled bags are not necessarily better than those filled with down, but they can be. Their one key advantage is that even when wet, some poly-fills can retain up to 85 percent of your body heat. This allows you to sleep and get valuable rest even in miserable conditions. And my camping experience is that no matter how lucky you may be, there comes a time when you will get caught in an unexpected, violent storm and everything you've got will get wet, including your sleeping bag. That's when a poly-fill bag becomes priceless. You either have one and can sleep, or you don't have one and suffer. It is that simple. Of the synthetic fills, Quallofil made by DuPont is the industry leader.

But just because a sleeping bag uses a high-tech poly-fill doesn't necessarily make it a better bag. There are other factors.

The most important are a bag's temperature rating and weight. The temperature rating of a sleeping bag refers to how cold it can get before you start actually feeling cold. Many campers make the mistake of thinking, "I only camp in the summer, so a bag rated at 30 or 40°F should be fine." Later they find out it isn't so fine, and all it takes is one cold night to convince them of that. When selecting the right temperature rating, visualize the coldest weather you might ever confront, and then get a bag rated for even colder weather.

For instance, if you are a summer camper, you may rarely experience a night in the low 30s or high 20s. A sleeping bag rated at 20°F would be appropriate, keeping you snug, warm, and asleep. For most campers, I advise bags rated at 0 or 10°F.

If you buy a poly-filled sleeping bag, never leave it squished in your stuff sack between camping trips. Instead, keep it on a hanger in a closet or use it as a blanket. One thing that can reduce a poly-filled bag's heat-retaining qualities is if you lose the loft out of the tiny hollow fibers that make up the fill. You can avoid this with proper storage.

The weight of a sleeping bag can also be a key factor, especially for backpackers. When you have to carry your gear on your back, every ounce becomes important. Sleeping bags that weigh just three pounds are available, although they are expensive. But if you hike much, it's worth the price to keep your weight to a minimum. For an overnighter, you can get away with a four- or 4.5-pound bag without much stress. However, bags weighing five pounds and up should be left back at the car.

I have two sleeping bags: a seven-pounder that feels like a giant sponge, and a little three-pounder. The heavy-duty model is for pickup truck camping in cold weather and doubles as a blanket at home. The lightweight bag is for hikes. Between the two, I'm set.

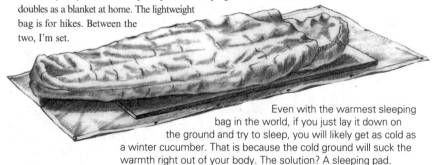

Even with the warmest sleeping bag in the world, if you just lay it down on the ground and try to sleep, you will likely get as cold as a winter cucumber. That is because the cold ground will suck the warmth right out of your body. The solution? A sleeping pad.

Insulation Pads

Even with the warmest sleeping bag in the world, if you just lay it down on the ground and try to sleep, you will likely get as cold as a winter cucumber. That is because the cold ground will suck the warmth right out of your body. The solution is to have a layer of insulation between you and the ground. For this you can use a thin Insulite pad, a lightweight Therm-a-Rest inflatable pad, a foam pad or mattress, air bed, or a cot. Here is a capsule summary of all three:

- **Insulite pads:** They are light, inexpensive, roll up quick for transport, and can double as a seat pad at your camp. The negative side is that in one night, they will compress, making you feel that you are sleeping on granite.
- **Therm-a-Rest pads:** These are a real luxury because they do everything an Insulite pad does, but also provide a cushion. The negative side is that they are expensive by comparison, and if they get a hole in them, they become worthless without a patch kit.
- **Air beds, foam mattresses, and cots:** These are excellent for car campers. The new line of air beds available are outstanding, especially the thicker ones, and inflate quickly with an electric motor inflator that plugs into a power plug or cigarette lighter in your vehicle. Foam mattresses are also excellent, in fact, the most comfortable of all, but their size precludes many from considering them. I've found that cots work great, too. I finally wore out an old wood one just before this book went to press; replaced it immediately with one of the new high-tech and light metal ones. For camping in the back of a pickup truck with a camper shell, the cots with three-inch legs are best, of course.

A Few Tricks

When surveying a camp area, the most important consideration should be to select a good spot to sleep. Everything else is secondary. Ideally, you want a flat spot that is wind-sheltered and on ground soft enough to drive stakes into. Yeah, and I want to win the lottery, too.

Sometimes that ground will have a slight slope to it. In that case, always sleep with your head on the uphill side. If you sleep parallel to the slope, every time you roll over, you'll find yourself rolling down the hill. If you sleep with your head on the downhill side, you'll get a headache that feels as if an ax is embedded in your brain.

When you've found a good spot, clear it of all branches, twigs, and rocks, of course. A good tip is to dig a slight indentation in the ground where your hip will fit. Since your body is not flat, but has curves and edges, it will not feel comfortable on flat ground. Some people even get severely bruised on the sides of their hips when sleeping on flat, hard ground. For that reason alone they learn to hate camping. What a shame, especially when the problem is solved easily with a Therm-a-Rest pad, foam insulation, air bed, or a cot.

After the ground is prepared, throw a ground cloth over the spot, which will keep much of the morning dew off you. In some areas, particularly where fog is a problem, morning dew can be heavy and get the outside of your sleeping bag quite wet. In that case, you need overhead protection, such as a tent or some kind of roof, like a poncho or tarp with its ends tied to trees.

Tents and Weather Protection

All it takes is to get caught in the rain once without a tent and you will never go anywhere without one again. A tent provides protection from rain, wind, and mosquito attacks. In exchange, you can lose a starry night's view, though some tents now even provide moon roofs.

A tent can be as complex as a four-season, tubular-jointed dome with a rain fly or as simple as two ponchos snapped together and roped up to a tree. They can be as cheap as a $10 tube tent, which is nothing more than a hollow piece of plastic, or as expensive as a $500 five-person deluxe expedition dome model. They vary greatly in size, price, and put-up time. If you plan on getting a good one, plan on doing plenty of shopping and asking lots of questions. With a little bit of homework, you can get the right answers to these questions:

Will It Keep Me Dry?

On many one-person and two-person tents, the rain fly does not extend far enough to keep water off the bottom sidewalls of the tent. In a driving rain, water can also drip from the rain fly and to the bottom sidewalls of the tent. Eventually the water can leak through to the inside, particularly through the seams where the tent has been sewn together.

You must be able to stake out your rain fly so it completely covers all of the tent. If you are tent shopping and this does not appear possible, then don't buy the tent. To prevent potential leaks, use a seam waterproofer such as Seam Lock, a gluelike substance, to close potential leak areas on tent seams. For large umbrella tents, keep a patch kit handy. Starting in 2003, note that Coleman tents are now guaranteed to keep campers dry.

Another way to keep water out of your tent is to store all wet garments outside the tent, under a poncho. Moisture from wet clothes stashed in the tent will condense on the interior tent walls. If you bring enough wet clothes into the tent, by the next morning you can feel as if you're camping in a duck blind.

How Hard Is It to Put Up?

If a tent is difficult to erect in full sunlight, you can just about forget it at night, especially the first night out. Some tents can go up in just a few minutes, without requiring help from another camper. This might be the kind of tent you want.

The way to compare put-up time of tents when shopping is to count the number of connecting points from the tent poles to the tent and the number of stakes required. The fewer the better. Think simple. My two-person-plus-a-dog tent has seven connecting points and, minus the rain fly, requires no stakes. It goes up in a few minutes. If you need a lot of stakes, it is a sure tip-off to a long put-up time. Try it at night or in the rain, and you'll be ready to cash your chips and go for broke. My bigger family tent, which has three rooms with walls, so we can keep our two kids, Jeremy and Kris, isolated on each side, takes about a half hour to put up. That's without anybody's help. With their help, add about 15 minutes, heh, heh.

Another factor is the tent poles themselves. Some small tents have poles that are broken into small sections that are connected by bungee cords. It takes only an instant to convert them to a complete pole.

Some outdoor shops have tents on display on their showroom floors. Before buying the tent, have the salesperson take the tent down and put it back up. If it takes him more than five minutes, or he says he doesn't have time, then keep looking.

Is It Roomy Enough?

Don't judge the size of a tent on floor space alone. Some tents small on floor space can give the illusion of roominess with a high ceiling. You can be quite comfortable in them and snug.

But remember that a one-person or two-person tent is just that. A two-person tent has room for two people plus gear. That's it. Don't buy a tent expecting it to hold more than it is intended to.

How Much Does It Weigh?

If you're a hiker, this becomes the preeminent question. If it's much more than six or seven pounds, forget it. A 12-pound tent is bad enough, but get it wet and it's like carrying a piano on your back. On the other hand, weight is scarcely a factor if you camp only where you can take your car. My dad, for instance, used to have this giant canvas umbrella tent that folded down to a neat little pack that weighed about 500 pounds.

Family Tents

It is always worth spending the time and money to buy a tent you and your family will be happy with.

Many excellent family tents are available for $125–175, particularly from Coleman, Cabela's, and Remington. Guide-approved expedition tents for groups cost higher, generally $350–600. Here is a synopsis of some of best tents available:

Coleman Weathermaster

800/835-3278
website: www.coleman.com
$150–200

The Weathermaster series features tents with multiple rooms, walls, and ample headroom, and they are guaranteed to keep rain out. The 17- by 9-foot model sleeps six to eight, has a 76-inch ceiling, and has zippered dividers. This is the tent I bought for my family. Since the dividers are removable, you can configure the tent in many designs. The frame is designed with poles that are not moved around yet are adjustable to three different heights to accommodate uneven ground.

Coleman Modified Dome

800/835-3278
website: www.coleman.com
$70–230

Coleman Modified Dome tents are available in six different single- and multi-room designs. The

A-frame style **tents** have gone the way of the dinosaur. With the world going high-tech, tents of today vary greatly in complexity, size, price, and put-up time. And they wouldn't be fit for this new millennium without offering options such as moon roofs, rain flies, and tent wings. Be sure to buy the one that's right for your needs.

pole structure is unique, with all four upright poles and one ridgepole shock-corded together for a integrated system that makes setup extremely fast and easy. Yet the tent has passed tests in high winds because of the engineering of the ridgepole. Mesh panels in the ceiling are a tremendous plus for ventilation.

Coleman Sundome
800/835-3278
website: www.coleman.com
$60–160

This tent is the traditional square and rectangular dome tents that are widely known for their simple setup with two-pole construction and roomy design. A standard feature is the tub floor, which wraps partially up the outer wall for increased water resistance. Mesh roof vents, D-shaped doors, shock-corded poles, and three-quarter-length rainflies are standard.

Cabela's Three-Room Cabin
800/237-4444
website: www.cabelas.com
$270

A beautiful three-room tent colored forest green and featuring a 10- by 20-foot floor available in different configurations with removable interior walls. Three doors mean everybody doesn't tromp through the center room for access to the side rooms. It will stand up to wind, rain, and frequent use.

Cabela's Alaskan Vestibule
800/237-4444
website: www.cabelas.com
$129–250

The new Alaskan Vestibule series for 2003 is based around a dome tent that can be connected by a tube to another dome tent. In use, it looks like a giant caterpillar, with dome tents that sleep four, or six to eight, on each end of a connector tube. It allows privacy without having to buy separate tents. A favorite for both family use and professionals.

Kelty Nirvana
800/423-2320
website: www.kelty.com
$325

The Nirvana is a top-of-the-line tent based on a sleek dome profile. This is a great package, with mesh sides, tops, and doors, along with a full awning fly and coverage for weather protection. Clip sleeves and rubber-tipped poles for easy slide during set-up are a nice bonus.

Bivouac Bags
If you like going solo and choose not to own a tent at all, a bivy bag, short for bivouac bag and pronounced "bivvy" as in dizzy, and not "bivy" as in ivy, can provide the extremely lightweight weather protection you require. A bivy bag is a water-repellent shell in which your sleeping bag fits. It is light and tough, and for some is the perfect alternative to a heavy tent. My own bivy weighs 31 ounces and cost me $240; it's made by OR (Outdoor Research), and I just plain love

Keep It Wild Tip 3: Camp with Care

1. Choose an existing, legal site. Restrict activities to areas where vegetation is compacted or absent.
2. Camp at least 75 steps (200 feet) from lakes, streams, and trails.
3. Always choose sites that won't be damaged by your stay.
4. Preserve the feeling of solitude by selecting camps that are out of view when possible.
5. Don't dig trenches or build structures or furniture.

the thing on expeditions. On the downside, however, it can be a bit difficult getting settled just right in it, and some say they feel claustrophobic at the close quarters. Once you get used to a bivy, then spend a night in a tent, the tent feels like a room at the Mirage.

My biggest fear was the idea of riding out a storm. You can hear the rain hitting you, and sometimes even feel the pounding of the drops through the bivy bag. For some, it can be unsettling to try to sleep under such circumstances. On the other hand, I've always looked forward to it. In cold weather, a bivy also helps keep you warm. I've had just one miserable night in mine. That was when my sleeping bag was a bit wet when I started the night. By the middle of the night, the water was condensing from the sleeping bag on the interior walls of the bivy, and then soaking the bag, like a storm cycle. The night hit only about 45°F but I just about froze to death anyway. Otherwise, I've used it on multiweek expeditions with great results, with warm, dry nights and deep, restful sleeps by night, and a pack lightened without carrying a tent by day.

Pickup Truck Campers

If you own a pickup truck with a camper shell, you can turn it into a self-contained campground with a little work. This can be an ideal way to go: it's fast, portable, and you are guaranteed a dry environment.

But that does not necessarily mean it is a warm environment. In fact, without insulation from the metal truck bed, it can be like trying to sleep on an iceberg. That is because the metal truck bed will get as cold as the air temperature, which is often much colder than the ground temperature. Without insulation, it can be much colder in your camper shell than it would be on the open ground.

When I camp in my rig, I use a large piece of foam for a mattress and insulation. The foam measures four inches thick, 48 inches wide, and 76 inches long. It makes for a bed as comfortable as anything one might ask for. In fact, during the winter, if I don't go camping for a few weeks because of writing obligations, I sometimes will throw the foam on the floor, lay down the old sleeping bag, light a fire, and camp right in my living room. It's in my blood, I tell you. Air beds and cots are also extremely comfortable and I've used both many times. Whatever you choose, just make sure you have a comfortable sleeping unit. Good sleep makes for great camping trips.

RVs

The problems RVers encounter come from two primary sources: lack of privacy and light intrusion.

The lack of privacy stems from the natural restrictions of where a land yacht can go. Without careful use of the guide section of this book, motor-home owners can find themselves in parking lot settings, jammed in with plenty of neighbors. Because RVs often have large picture windows, you lose your privacy, causing some late nights; then, come daybreak, light intrusion forces an early wake up. The result is you get shorted on your sleep.

The answer is to carry inserts to fit over the inside of your windows. This closes off the outside and retains your privacy. And if you don't want to wake up with the sun at daybreak, you don't have to. It will still be dark.

FIRST AID AND INSECT PROTECTION

The mountain night could not have been more perfect, I thought as I lay in my sleeping bag.

The sky looked like a mass of jewels and the air tasted sweet and smelled of pines. A shooting star fireballed across the sky, and I remember thinking, "It just doesn't get any better."

Just then, as I was drifting into sleep, a mysterious buzz appeared from nowhere and deposited itself inside my left ear. Suddenly awake, I whacked my ear with the palm of my hand, hard enough to cause a minor concussion. The buzz disappeared. I pulled out my flashlight and shined it on my palm, and there, lit in the blackness of night, lay the squished intruder: a mosquito, dead amid a stain of blood.

Satisfied, I turned off the light, closed my eyes, and thought of the fishing trip planned for the next day. Then I heard them. It was a squadron of mosquitoes flying landing patterns around my head. I tried to grab them with an open hand, but they dodged the assault and flew off. Just 30 seconds later another landed in my left ear. I promptly dispatched the invader with a rip of the palm.

Now I was completely awake, so I got out of my sleeping bag to retrieve some mosquito repellent. But en route, several of the buggers swarmed and nailed me in the back and arms. After I applied the repellent and settled snugly again in my sleeping bag, the mosquitoes would buzz a few inches from my ear. After getting a whiff of the poison, they would fly off. It was like sleeping in a sawmill.

The next day, drowsy from little sleep, I set out to fish. I'd walked but 15 minutes when I brushed against a bush and felt this stinging sensation on the inside of my arm, just above the wrist. I looked down: a tick had his clamps in me. I ripped it out before he could embed his head into my skin.

After catching a few fish, I sat down against a tree to eat lunch and just watch the water go by. My dog, Rebel, sat down next to me and stared at the beef jerky I was munching as if it were a T-bone steak. I finished eating, gave him a small piece, patted him on the head, and said, "Good dog." Right then, I noticed an itch on my arm where a mosquito had drilled me. I unconsciously scratched it. Two days later, in that exact spot, some nasty red splotches started popping up. Poison oak. By petting my dog and then scratching my arm, I had transferred the oil residue of the poison oak leaves from Rebel's fur to my arm.

When I returned home, Foonsky asked me about the trip.

"Great," I said. "Mosquitoes, ticks, poison oak. Can hardly wait to go back."

"Sorry I missed out," he answered.

Mosquitoes, No-See-Ums, Gnats, and Horseflies

On a trip to Canada, Foonsky and I were fishing a small lake from the shore when suddenly a black horde of mosquitoes could be seen moving across the lake toward us. It was like when the French army looked across the Rhine and saw the Wehrmacht coming. There was a buzz in the air. We fought them off for a few minutes, then made a fast retreat to the truck and jumped in, content the buggers had been fooled. But in some way still unknown to us, the mosquitoes gained entry to the truck. In 10 minutes, we squished 15 of them as they attempted to plant their oil drills into our skins. Just outside the truck, the black horde waited for us to make a tactical error such as rolling down a window. It finally took a miraculous hailstorm to foil the attack.

When it comes to mosquitoes, no-see-ums, gnats, and horseflies, there are times when there is nothing you can do. However, in most situations you can muster a defense to repel the attack.

The first key with mosquitoes is to wear clothing too heavy for them to drill through. Expose a minimum of skin, wear a hat, and tie a bandanna around your neck, preferably one that has been sprayed with repellent. If you try to get by with just a cotton T-shirt, you will be declared a federal mosquito sanctuary.

So first your skin must be well covered, exposing only your hands and face. Second, you should have your companion spray your clothes with repellent. Third, you should dab liquid repellent directly on your skin.

At night, the easiest way to get a good sleep without mosquitoes buzzing in your ear is to sleep in a bug-proof tent. If

Mosquito Repellent: Taking vitamin B1 and eating garlic are reputed to act as natural insect repellents, but I've met a lot of mosquitoes that are not convinced. A better bet is to examine the label of the repellent in question for N, N-diethyl-metatoluamide, commonly known as DEET. That is the poison, and the percentage of it in the container must be listed and will indicate that brand's effectiveness. Inert ingredients are mainly fluids used to fill the bottles.

the nights are warm and you want to see the stars, new tent models are available that have a skylight covered with mosquito netting. If you don't like tents on summer evenings, mosquito netting rigged with an air space at your head can solve the problem. Otherwise prepare to get bitten, even with the use of mosquito repellent.

If your problems are with no-see-ums or biting horseflies, then you need a slightly different approach.

No-see-ums are tiny black insects that look like nothing more than a sliver of dirt on your skin. Then you notice something stinging, and when you rub the area, you scratch up a little no-see-um. The results are similar to mosquito bites, making your skin itch, splotch, and when you get them bad, swell. In addition to using the techniques described to repel mosquitoes, you should go one step further.

The problem is that no-see-ums are tricky little devils. Somehow they can actually get under your socks and around your ankles where they will bite to their hearts' content all night long while you sleep, itch, sleep, and itch some more. The best solution is to apply a liquid repellent to your ankles, then wear clean socks.

Horseflies are another story. They are rarely a problem, but when they get their dander up, they can cause trouble you'll never forget.

One such episode occurred when Foonsky and I were paddling a canoe along the shoreline of a large lake. This giant horsefly, about the size of a fingertip, started dive-bombing the canoe. After 20 minutes, it landed on Foonsky's thigh. He immediately slammed it with an open hand, then let out a blood-curdling "Yeeeee-ow!" that practically sent ripples across the lake. When Foonsky whacked it, the horsefly had somehow turned around and bit him on the hand, leaving a huge red welt.

In the next 10 minutes, that big fly strafed the canoe on more dive-bomb runs. I finally got my canoe paddle, swung it as if it were a baseball bat, and nailed that horsefly as if I'd hit a home run. It landed about 15 feet from the boat, still alive and buzzing in the water. While I was trying to figure what it would take to kill this bugger, a large rainbow trout surfaced and snatched it out of the water, finally avenging the assault.

If you have horsefly or yellow jacket problems, you'd best just leave the area. One, two, or a few can be dealt with. More than that and your fun camping trip will be about as fun as being roped to a tree and stung by an electric shock rod.

On most trips, you will spend time doing everything possible to keep from getting bitten by mosquitoes or no-see-ums. When that fails, you must know what to do next, and fast, if you are among those ill-fated campers who get big red lumps from a bite inflicted from even a microscopic mosquito.

A fluid called After Bite or a dab of ammonia should be applied immediately to the bite. To start the healing process, apply a first-aid gel (not a liquid), such as the one made by Campho-Phenique.

DEET Versus "Natural" Repellents

What is DEET? You're not likely to find the word DEET on any repellent label. That's because DEET stands for N,N diethyl-m-toluamide. If the label contains this scientific name, the repellent contains DEET. Despite fears of DEET-associated health risks and the increased attention given natural alternatives, DEET-based repellents are still acknowledged as by far the best option when serious insect protection is required.

What are the health risks associated with using DEET? A number of deaths and a number of medical problems have been attributed in the press to DEET in recent years—events that those in the DEET community vehemently deny as being specifically DEET-related, pointing to reams of scientific documentation as evidence. It does seem logical to assume that if DEET can peel paint, melt nylon, destroy plastic, wreck wood finishes, and damage fishing line, then it must be hell on the skin—perhaps worse.

On one trip, I had a small bottle of mosquito repellent in the same pocket as a Swiss army knife. Guess what happened? The mosquito repellent leaked a bit and literally melted the insignia right off the knife. DEET will also melt synthetic clothes. That is why in bad mosquito country, I'll expose a minimum of skin, just hands and face (with full beard), and apply the repellent only to my cheeks and the back of my hands, perhaps wear a bandanna sprinkled with a few drops as well. That does the trick, with a minimum of exposure to the repellent.

Although nothing definitive has been published, there is a belief among a growing number in the scientific community that repeated applications of products containing low percentages of DEET can be potentially dangerous. It is theorized that this actually puts consumers at a greater risk for absorbing high levels of DEET into the body than if they had just used one application of a 30–50 percent DEET product with an efficacy of four to six hours. Also being studied is the possibility that low levels of DEET, which might not otherwise be of toxicological concern, may become hazardous if they are formulated with solvents or dilutents (considered inert ingredients) that may enhance the absorption rate.

Are natural alternatives a safer choice? To imply that essential oils are completely safe because they are a natural product is not altogether accurate. Essential oils, while derived from plants that grow naturally, are chemicals too. Some are potentially hazardous if ingested, and most are downright painful if they find their way into the eyes or onto mucus membranes. For example, pennyroyal is perhaps the most toxic of the essential oils used to repel insects and can be deadly if taken internally. Other oils used include citronella (perhaps the most common, it's extracted from an aromatic grass indigenous to Southern Asia), eucalyptus, cedarwood, and peppermint.

Three citronella-based products, Buzz Away (manufactured by Quantum), Avon's Skin-So-Soft, and Natrapel (manufactured by Tender), have received EPA registration and approval for sale as repellents for use in controlling mosquitoes, flies, gnats, and midges.

How effective are natural repellents? While there are numerous studies cited by those on the DEET and citronella sides of the fence, the average effective repelling time of a citronella product appears to range from 1.5 to two hours. Tests conducted at Cambridge University, England, comparing Natrapel to DEET-based Skintastic (a low-percentage DEET product) found citronella to be just as effective in repelling mosquitoes. The key here is effectiveness and the amount of time until reapplication.

Citronella products work for up to two hours and then require reapplication (the same holds true for other natural formulations). Products using a low-percentage level of DEET also require reapplication every two hours to remain effective. So if you're going outside for only a short period in an environment where insect bites are more an irritant than a hazard, you would do just as well to go natural.

What other chemical alternatives are there? Another line of defense against insects is the chemical permethrin, used on clothing, not on skin. Permethrin-based products are designed to repel and kill arthropods or crawling insects, making them a preferred repellent for ticks. The currently available products will remain effective, repelling and killing mosquitoes, ticks, and chiggers, for two weeks and through two launderings.

Ticks

Ticks are nasty little vermin that will wait in ambush, jump on unsuspecting prey, and then crawl to a prime location before filling their bodies with their victim's blood.

Keep It Wild Tip 4: Sanitation

If no refuse facility is available:
1. Deposit human waste in "cat holes" dug six to eight inches deep. Cover and disguise the cat hole when finished.
2. Deposit human waste at least 75 paces (200 feet) from any water source or camp.
3. Use toilet paper sparingly. When finished, carefully burn it in the cat hole, then bury it.
4. If no appropriate burial locations are available, such as in popular wilderness camps above tree line in granite settings, then all human refuse should be double-bagged and packed out.
5. At boat-in campsites, chemical toilets are required. Chemical toilets can also solve the problem of larger groups camping for long stays at one location where no facilities are available.
6. To wash dishes or your body, carry water away from the source and use small amounts of biodegradable soap. Scatter dishwater after all food particles have been removed.
7. Scour your campsites for even the tiniest piece of trash and any other evidence of your stay. Pack out all the trash you can, even if it's not yours. Finding cigarette butts, for instance, provides special irritation for most campers. Pick them up and discard them properly.
8. Never litter. Never. Or you become the enemy of all others.

I call them Dracula bugs, but by any name they can be a terrible camp pest. Ticks rest on grass and low plants and attach themselves to those who brush against the vegetation (dogs are particularly vulnerable). Typically they are no more than 18 inches above ground, and if you stay on the trails, you can usually avoid them.

There are two common species of ticks. The common coastal tick is larger, brownish in color, and prefers to crawl around before putting its clamps on you. The latter habit can be creepy, but when you feel it crawling, you can just pick it off and dispatch it. The coastal tick's preferred destination is usually the back of your neck, just where the hairline starts. The other species, the wood tick, is small and black, and when he puts his clamps in, it's immediately painful. When a wood tick gets into a dog for a few days, it can cause a large red welt. In either case, ticks should be removed as soon as possible.

If you have hiked in areas infested with ticks, it is advisable to shower as soon as possible, washing your clothes immediately. If you just leave your clothes in a heap, a tick can crawl out and invade your home. They like warmth, and one way or another, they can end up in your bed. Waking up in the middle of the night with a tick crawling across your chest can really give you the creeps.

Once a tick has its clampers in you, you must decide how long it has been there. If it has been a short time, the most painless and effective method for removal is to take a pair of sharp tweezers and grasp the little devil, making certain to isolate the mouth area, then pull him out. Reader Johvin Perry sent in the suggestion to coat the tick with Vaseline, which will cut off its oxygen supply, after which it may voluntarily give up the hunt.

If the tick has been in longer, you may wish to have a doctor extract it. Some people will burn a tick with a cigarette, or poison it with lighter fluid, but this is not advisable. No matter how you do it, you must take care to remove all of it, especially its clawlike mouth.

The wound, however small, should then be cleansed and dressed. This is done by applying liquid peroxide, which cleans and sterilizes, and then applying a dressing coated with a first-aid gel such as First-Aid Cream, Campho-Phenique, or Neosporin.

Lyme disease, which can be transmitted by the bite of the deer tick, is rare but common enough to warrant some attention. To prevent tick bites, some people tuck their pant legs into their hiking socks and spray tick repellent, called Permamone, on their pants.

The first symptom of Lyme disease is that the bite area will develop a bright red, splotchy rash. Other possible early symptoms include headache, nausea, fever, and/or a stiff neck. If this happens, or if you have any doubts, you should see your doctor immediately. If you do get Lyme disease, don't panic. Doctors say it is easily treated in the early stages with simple antibiotics. If you are nervous about getting Lyme disease, carry a small plastic bag with you when you hike. If a tick manages to get his clampers into you, put it in the plastic bag after you pull it out. Then give it to your doctor for analysis to see if the tick is a carrier of the disease.

During the course of my hiking and camping career, I have removed ticks from my skin hundreds of times without any problems. However, if you are worried about ticks, you can buy a tick removal kit from any outdoors store. These kits allow you to remove ticks in such a way that their toxins are guaranteed not to enter your bloodstream.

If you are particularly wary of ticks or perhaps even have nightmares of them, wear long pants that are tucked into the socks, as well as a long-sleeved shirt tucked securely into the pants and held with a belt. Clothing should be light in color, making it easier to see ticks, and tightly woven so ticks have trouble hanging on. On one hike with my mom, Eleanor, I brushed more than 100 ticks off my blue jeans in less than an hour, while she did not pick up a single one on her polyester pants.

Perform tick checks regularly, especially on the back of the neck. The combination of DEET insect repellents applied to the skin and permethrin repellents applied directly to clothing is considered to be the most effective line of defense against ticks.

Poison Oak

After a nice afternoon hike, about a five-miler, I was concerned about possible exposure to poison oak, so I immediately showered and put on clean clothes. Then I settled into a chair with my favorite foamy elixir to watch the end of a baseball game. The game went 18 innings; meanwhile, my dog, tired from the hike, went to sleep on my bare ankles.

A few days later I had a case of poison oak. My feet looked as though they had been on fire and put out with an ice pick. The lesson? Don't always trust your dog, give him a bath as well, and beware of extra-inning ball games.

You can get poison oak only from direct contact with the oil residue from the leaves. It can be passed in a variety of ways, as direct as skin-to-leaf contact or as indirect as leaf to dog, dog to sofa, sofa to skin. Once you have it, there is little you can do but itch yourself to death. Applying Caladryl lotion or its equivalent can help because it contains antihistamines, which attack and dry the itch.

A tip that may sound crazy but seems to work is advised by my pal Furniss. You should expose the afflicted area to the hottest water you can stand, then suddenly immerse it in cold water. The hot water opens the skin pores and gets the "itch" out, and the cold water then quickly seals the pores.

In any case, you're a lot better off if you don't get poison oak to begin with. Remember that poison oak can disguise itself. In the spring, it is green; then it gradually turns reddish in the summer. By fall, it becomes a bloody, ugly-looking red. In the winter, it loses its leaves altogether and appears to be nothing more than barren, brown sticks of a small plant. However, at any time and in any form, its contact with skin can quickly lead to infection.

Avoiding Poison Oak: Remember the old Boy Scout saying: "Leaves of three, let them be."

Some people are more easily afflicted than others, but if you are one of the lucky few who aren't, don't cheer too loudly. While some people can be exposed to the oil residue of poison oak with little or no effect, the body's resistance can gradually be worn down with repeated exposure. At one time I could practically play in the stuff and the only symptom would be a few little bumps on the inside of my wrist. Now, more than 15 years later, my resistance has broken down. If I merely rub against poison oak now, in a few days the exposed area can look as if it were used for a track meet.

So regardless of whether you consider yourself vulnerable or not, you should take heed to reduce your exposure. That can be done by staying on trails when you hike and making sure your dog does the same. Remember, the worst stands of poison oak are usually brush-infested areas just off the trail. Protect yourself also by dressing so your skin is completely covered, wearing long-sleeved shirts, long pants, and boots. If you suspect you've been exposed, immediately wash your clothes and then wash yourself with aloe vera, rinsing with a cool shower.

And don't forget to give your dog a bath as well.

Sunburn

The most common injury suffered on camping trips is sunburn, yet some people wear it as a badge of honor, believing that it somehow enhances their virility. Well, it doesn't. Neither do suntans. And too much sun can lead to serious burns or sunstroke.

It is easy enough to avoid. Use a high-level sunscreen on your skin, apply lip balm with sunscreen, and wear sunglasses and a hat. If any area gets burned, apply first-aid cream, which will soothe and provide moisture for your parched, burned skin.

The best advice is not to get even a suntan. Those who do are involved in a practice that can be eventually ruinous to their skin and possibly lead to cancer.

A Word about Giardia and Cryptosporidium

You have just hiked in to your backwoods spot, you're thirsty and a bit tired, but you smile as you consider the prospects. Everything seems perfect—there's not a stranger in sight, and you have nothing to do but relax with your pals.

You toss down your gear, grab your cup, dip it into the stream, and take a long drink of that ice-cold mountain water. It seems crystal pure and sweeter than anything you've ever tasted. It's not till later that you find out it can be just like drinking a cup of poison.

Whether you camp in the wilderness or not, if you hike, you're going to get thirsty. And if your canteen runs dry, you'll start eyeing any water source. Stop! Do not pass Go. Do not drink.

By drinking what appears to be pure mountain water without first treating it, you can ingest a microscopic protozoan called *Giardia lamblia*. The pain of the ensuing abdominal cramps can make you feel that your stomach and intestinal tract are in a knot, ready to explode. With that comes long-term diarrhea that is worse than even a bear could imagine.

Treating Your Water Means Avoiding Diarrhea: The only sure way to beat giardia and other water-borne diseases is to filter or boil your water before drinking, eating, or brushing your teeth. And the best way to prevent the spread of giardia is to bury your waste products at least eight inches deep and 200 feet away from natural waters.

Doctors call the disease giardiasis, or giardia for short, but it is difficult to diagnose. One friend of mine who contracted giardia was told he might have stomach cancer before the proper diagnosis was made.

Drinking directly from a stream or lake does not mean you will get giardia, but you are taking a giant chance. There is no reason to assume such a risk, potentially ruining your trip and enduring weeks of misery.

A lot of people are taking that risk. I made a personal survey of campers in the Yosemite National Park wilderness, and found that roughly only one in 20 was equipped with some kind of water-purification system. The result, according to the Public Health Service, is that an average of 4 percent of all backpackers and campers suffer giardiasis. According to the Parasitic Diseases Division of the Center for Infectious Diseases, the rates range from 1 percent to 20 percent across the country.

But if you get giardia, you are not going to care about the statistics. "When I got giardia, I just about wanted to die," said Henry McCarthy, a California camper. "For about 10 days, it was the most terrible thing I have ever experienced. And through the whole thing, I kept thinking, 'I shouldn't have drunk that water, but it seemed all right at the time.'"

That is the mistake most campers make. The stream might be running free, gurgling over boulders in the high country, tumbling into deep, oxygenated pools. It looks pure. Then in a few days, the problems suddenly start. Drinking untreated water from mountain streams is a lot like playing Russian roulette. Sooner or later the gun goes off.

Filters

There's really no excuse for going without a water filter: handheld filters are getting more compact, lighter, easier to use, and often less expensive. Having to boil water or endure chemicals that leave a bad taste in the mouth has been all but eliminated.

With a filter, you just pump and drink. Filtering strains out microscopic contaminants, rendering the water clear and somewhat pure. How pure? That depends on the size of the filter's pores—what manufacturers call pore-size efficiency. A filter with a pore-size efficiency of one micron or smaller will remove protozoa such as *Giardia lamblia* and cryptosporidium, as well as parasitic eggs and larva, but it takes a pore-size efficiency of less than 0.4 microns to remove bacteria. All but one of the filters recommended here do that.

A good backcountry water filter weighs less than 20 ounces, is easy to grasp, simple to use, and a snap to clean and maintain. At the very least, buy one that will remove protozoa and bacteria. (A number of cheap, pocket-sized filters remove only *Giardia lamblia* and cryptosporidium. That, in my book, is risking your health to save money.) Consider the flow rate, too: a liter per minute is good.

All filters will eventually clog—it's a sign that they've been doing their job. If you force water through a filter that's becoming difficult to pump, you risk injecting a load of microbial nasties into your bottle. Some models can be backwashed, brushed, or, as with ceramic elements, scrubbed to extend their useful lives. And if the filter has a prefilter to screen out the big stuff, use it: it will give your filter a boost in mileage, which can then top out at about 100 gallons per disposable element. Any of the filters reviewed here will serve well on an outing into the wilds, providing you always play by the manufacturer's rules. They cost about $35–75, up to more than $200, depending on the volume of water they are constructed to filter.

- **First Need Deluxe:** The 15-ounce First Need Deluxe from General Ecology does something no other handheld filter will do: it removes protozoa, bacteria, and viruses without using chemicals. Such effectiveness is the result of a fancy three-stage matrix system. Unfortunately, if you drop the filter and unknowingly

Water filters are a wise investment since all wilderness water should be considered contaminated. Make sure the filter can be easily cleaned or has a replaceable cartridge. The filter pores must be 0.4 microns or less to remove bacteria.

crack the cartridge, all the little nasties can get through. General Ecology's solution is to include a bottle of blue dye that indicates breaks. The issue hasn't scared off too many folks, though: the First Need has been around since 1982. Additional cartridges cost $30. A final note: the filter pumps smoothly and puts out more than a liter per minute. A favorite of mine.

- **PentaPure Oasis:** The PentaPure Oasis Water Purification System from WTC/Ecomaster offers drinkable water with a twist: you squeeze and sip instead of pumping. Weighing 6.5 ounces, the system packages a three-stage filter inside a 21-ounce-capacity sport bottle with an angled and sealing drinking nozzle, ideal for mountain bikers. The filter removes and/or kills protozoa, bacteria, and viruses, so it's also suitable for world travel. It's certainly convenient: just fill the bottle with untreated water, screw on the cap, give it a firm squeeze (don't expect the easy flow of a normal sport bottle; there's more work being done), and sip. The Oasis only runs into trouble if the water source is shallow; you'll need a cup for scooping.

- **Basic Designs Ceramic:** The Basic Designs Ceramic Filter Pump weighs eight ounces and is as stripped-down a filter as you'll find. The pump is simple, easy to use, and quite reliable. The ceramic filter effectively removes protozoa and bacteria, making it ideal and cost effective for backpacking—but it won't protect against viruses. Also, the filter element is too bulbous to work directly from a shallow water source; like the PentaPure, you'll have to decontaminate a pot, cup, or bottle to transfer your unfiltered water. It's a great buy, though, for anyone worried only about *Giardia lamblia* and cryptosporidium.

- **SweetWater WalkAbout:** The WalkAbout is perfect for the day hiker or backpacker who obsesses on lightening the load. The filter weighs just 8.5 ounces, is easily cleaned in the field, and removes both protozoa and bacteria: a genuine bargain. There are some trade-offs, however, for its diminutiveness. Water delivery is a tad slow at just under a liter per minute, but redesigned filter cartridges ($12.50) are now good for up to 100 gallons.

- **MSR MiniWorks:** Like the WalkAbout, the bargain-priced MiniWorks has a bigger and more expensive water-filtering brother. But in this case the differences are harder to discern: the new 14.3-ounce MiniWorks looks similar to the $140 WaterWorks II, and like the WaterWorks is fully field-maintainable, while guarding against protozoa, bacteria, and chemicals. But the Mini is the best-executed, easiest-to-use ceramic filter on the market, and it attaches directly to a standard one-quart Nalgene water bottle. Too bad it takes 90 seconds to filter that quart.

- **PUR Explorer:** The Explorer offers protection from all the bad guys—viruses as well as protozoa and bacteria—by incorporating an iodine matrix into the filtration process. An optional carbon cartridge ($20) neutralizes the iodine's noxious taste. The Explorer is also considered a trusty veteran among water filters because of its smooth pumping action and nifty backwashing feature: with a quick twist, the device switches from filtering mode to self-cleaning mode. It may be on the heavy side (20 ounces) and somewhat pricey, but the Explorer works very well on iffy water anywhere.

- **Katadyn U.S.A. Mini Filter:** The Mini Filter is a much more compact version of Katadyn's venerable Pocket Filter. This one weighs just eight ounces, ideal for the minimalist backcountry traveler, and it effectively removes protozoa and bacteria. A palm-of-the-hand-size filter, however, makes it challenging to put any kind of power behind the pump's tiny handle, and the filtered water comes through at a paltry half-liter per minute. It also requires more cleaning than most filters—though the good news is that the element is made of long-lasting ceramic. Ironically, one option lets you buy the Mini Filter with a carbon element instead of the ceramic. The pumping is easier, the flow rate is better, and the price is way down ($99), but I'd only go that route if you'll be pumping from clear mountain streams.

- **MSR WaterWorks II Ceramic:** At 17.4 ounces the WaterWorks II isn't light, but for the same price as the Katadyn you get a better flow rate (90 seconds per liter), an easy pumping action, and—like the original Mini Filter—a long-lasting ceramic cartridge. This filter is a good match for the person who encounters a lot of dirty water—its three-stage filter weeds out protozoa, bacteria, and chemicals—and is mechanically inclined. The MSR can be completely disassembled afield for troubleshooting and cleaning. (If you're not so endowed, take the filter apart at home only, as the potential for confusion is somewhat high.) By the way, the company has corrected the clogging problem that plagued a previous version of the WaterWorks. The big drawback with filters is that if you pump water from a mucky lake, the filter can clog in a few days. Therein lies the weakness. Once plugged up, it is useless, and you have to replace it or take your chances.

One trick to extend the filter life is to fill your cook pot with water, let the sediment settle, then pump from there. As an insurance policy, always have a spare filter canister on hand.

Boiling Water

Except for water filtration, this is the only treatment that you can use with complete confidence. According to the federal Parasitic Diseases Division, it takes a few minutes at a rolling boil to be certain you've killed *Giardia lamblia.* At high elevations, boil for three to five minutes. A side benefit is that you'll also kill other dangerous bacteria that live undetected in natural waters.

But to be honest, boiling water is a thorn for most people on backcountry trips. For one thing, if you boil water on an open fire, what should taste like crystal-pure mountain water tastes instead like a mouthful of warm ashes. If you don't have a campfire, it wastes stove fuel. And if you are thirsty *now,* forget it. The water takes hours to cool.

The only time boiling always makes sense, however, is when you are preparing dinner. The ash taste will disappear in whatever freeze-dried dinner, soup, or hot drink you make.

Water-Purification Pills

Pills are the preference for most backcountry campers, and this can get them in trouble. At just $3–8 per bottle, which can figure up to just a few cents per canteen, they do come cheap. In addition, they kill most of the bacteria, regardless of whether you use iodine crystals or potable aqua iodine tablets.

The problem is they just don't always kill *Giardia lamblia,* and that is the one critter worth worrying about on your trip. That makes water-treatment pills unreliable and dangerous.

Another key element is the time factor. Depending on the water's temperature, organic content, and pH level, these pills can take a long time to do the job. A minimum wait of 20 minutes is advised. Most people don't like waiting that long, especially when they're hot and thirsty after a hike and thinking, "What the heck, the water looks fine."

And then there is the taste. On one trip, my water filter clogged and we had to use the iodine pills instead. It doesn't take long to get tired of the iodine-tinged taste of the water. Mountain water should be one of the greatest tasting beverages of the world, but the iodine kills that.

No Treatment

This is your last resort and, using extreme care, can be executed with success. One of my best hiking buddies, Michael Furniss, is a nationally renowned hydrologist, and on wilderness trips he has showed me the difference between safe and dangerous water sources.

Long ago, people believed that just finding water running over a rock was a guarantee of its purity. Imagine that. What we've learned is that the safe water sources are almost always small springs in high, craggy mountain areas. The key is making sure no one has been upstream from where you drink. We drink untreated water only when we can see the source, such as a spring.

Furniss mentioned that another potential problem in bypassing water treatment is that even in settings free of *Giardia lamblia,* you can still ingest other bacteria that cause stomach problems.

Hypothermia

No matter how well planned your trip might be, a sudden change in weather can turn it into a puzzle for which there are few answers. Bad weather or an accident can set in motion a dangerous chain of events.

Such a chain of episodes occurred for my brother Rambob and me on a fishing trip one fall day just below the snow line. The weather had suddenly turned very cold, and ice was forming along the shore of the lake. Suddenly, the canoe became terribly imbalanced, and just that quick it flipped. The little life vest seat cushions were useless, and using the canoe as a paddleboard, we tried to kick our way back to shore where my dad was going crazy at the thought of his two sons drowning before his eyes.

It took 17 minutes in that 38-degree water, but we finally made it to shore. When they pulled me out of the water, my legs were dead, not strong enough even to hold up my weight. In fact, I didn't feel so much cold as tired, and I just wanted to lie down and go to sleep.

I closed my eyes, and my brother-in-law, Lloyd Angal, slapped me in the face several times, then got me on my feet and pushed and pulled me about.

In the celebration over our making it to shore, only Lloyd had realized that hypothermia was setting in. Hypothermia is the condition in which the temperature of the body is lowered to the point that it causes poor reasoning, apathy, and collapse. It can look like the afflicted person is just tired and needs to sleep, but that sleep can be the first step toward a coma.

Ultimately my brother and I shared what little dry clothing remained. Then we began hiking around to get muscle movement, creating internal warmth. We ate whatever munchies were available because the body produces heat by digestion. But most important, we got our heads as dry as possible. More body heat is lost through wet hair than any other single factor.

A few hours later, we were in a pizza parlor replaying the incident, talking about how only a life vest can do the job of a life vest. We decided never again to rely on those little flotation seat cushions that disappear when the boat flips.

Almost by instinct we had done everything right to prevent hypothermia: don't go to sleep, start a physical activity, induce shivering, put dry clothes on, dry your head, and eat something. That's how you fight hypothermia. In a dangerous situation, whether you fall in a lake or a stream or get caught unprepared in a storm, that's how you can stay alive.

After being in that ice-bordered lake for almost 20 minutes and then finally pulling ourselves to the shoreline, we discovered a strange thing. My canoe was flipped right-side up and almost all of its contents were lost: tackle box, flotation cushions, and cooler. But remaining were one paddle and one fishing rod, the trout rod my grandfather had given me for my 12th birthday.

Lloyd gave me a smile. "This means that you are meant to paddle and fish again," he said with a laugh.

Getting Unlost

You could not have been more lost. But there I was, a guy who is supposed to know about these things, transfixed by confusion, snow, and hoofprints from a big deer.

I discovered it is actually quite easy to get lost. If you don't get your bearings, getting found is

the difficult part. This occurred on a wilderness trip where I'd hiked in to a remote lake and then set up a base camp for a deer hunt.

"There are some giant bucks up on that rim," confided Mr. Furnai, who lives near the area. "But it takes a mountain man to even get close to them."

That was a challenge I answered. After four-wheeling it to the trailhead, I tromped off with pack and rifle, gut-thumped it up 100 switchbacks over the rim, then followed a creek drainage up to a small but beautiful lake. The area was stark and nearly treeless, with bald granite broken only by large boulders. To keep from getting lost, I marked my route with piles of small rocks to act as directional signs for the return trip.

To keep from getting lost (above tree line or in sparse vegetation), mark your route with **trail ducks,** small piles of rock which act as directional signs for the return trip.

But at daybreak the next day, I stuck my head out of my tent and found eight inches of snow on the ground. I looked up into a gray sky filled by huge, cascading snowflakes. Visibility was about 50 yards, with fog on the mountain rim. "I better get out of here and get back to my truck," I said to myself. "If my truck gets buried at the trailhead, I'll never get out."

After packing quickly, I started down the mountain. But after 20 minutes, I began to get disoriented. You see, all the little piles of rocks I'd stacked to mark the way were now buried in snow, and I had only a smooth white blanket of snow to guide me. Everything looked the same, and it was snowing even harder now.

Five minutes later I started chewing on some jerky to keep warm, then suddenly stopped. Where was I? Where was the creek drainage? Isn't this where I was supposed to cross over a creek and start the switchbacks down the mountain?

Right then I looked down and saw the tracks of a huge deer, the kind Mr. Furnai had talked about. What a predicament: I was lost and snowed in and seeing big hoofprints in the snow. Part of me wanted to abandon all safety and go after that deer, but a little voice in the back of my head won out. "Treat this as an emergency," it said.

The first step in any predicament is to secure your present situation, that is, to make sure it does not get any worse. I unloaded my rifle (too easy to slip, fall, and have a misfire), took stock of my food (three days' worth), camp fuel (plenty), and clothes (rain gear keeping me dry). Then I wondered, "Where the hell am I?"

I took out my map, compass, and altimeter, then opened the map and laid it on the snow. It immediately began collecting snowflakes. I set the compass atop the map and oriented it to north. Because of the fog, there was no way to spot landmarks, such as prominent mountaintops, to verify my position. Then I checked the altimeter, which read 4,900 feet. Well, the elevation at my lake was 5,320 feet. That was critical information.

I scanned the elevation lines on the map and was able to trace the approximate area of my position, somewhere downstream from the lake, yet close to a 4,900-foot elevation. "Right here," I said, pointing to a spot on the map with a finger. "I should pick up the switchback trail down the mountain somewhere off to the left, maybe just 40 or 50 yards away."

Slowly and deliberately, I pushed through the light, powdered snow. In five minutes, I suddenly stopped. To the left, across a 10-foot depression in the snow, appeared a flat spot that veered off to the right. "That's it! That's the crossing."

In minutes, I was working down the switchbacks, on my way, no longer lost. I thought of the hoofprints I had seen, and now that I knew my position, I wanted to head back and spend the day hunting. Then I looked up at the sky, saw it filled with falling snowflakes, and envisioned my truck buried deep in snow. Alas, this time logic won out over dreams.

In a few hours, now trudging through more than a foot of snow, I was at my truck at a spot called Doe Flat, and next to it was a giant, all-terrain U.S. Forest Service vehicle and two rangers.

"Need any help?" I asked them.

They just laughed. "We're here to help you," one answered. "It's a good thing you filed a trip plan with our district office in Gasquet. We wouldn't have known you were out here."

"Winter has arrived," said the other. "If we don't get your truck out now, it will be stuck here until next spring. If we hadn't found you, you might have been here until the end of time."

They connected a chain from the rear axle of their giant rig to the front axle of my truck and started towing me out, back to civilization. On the way to pavement, I figured I had gotten some of the more important lessons of my life. Always file a trip plan and have plenty of food, fuel, and a camp stove you can rely on. Make sure your clothes, weather gear, sleeping bag, and tent will keep you dry and warm. Always carry a compass, altimeter, and map with elevation lines, and know how to use them, practicing in good weather to get the feel of it.

And if you get lost and see the hoofprints of a giant deer, well, there are times when it is best to pass them by.

CATCHING FISH, AVOIDING BEARS, AND HAVING FUN

Feet tired and hot, stomachs hungry, we stopped our hike for lunch beside a beautiful little river pool that was catching the flows from a long but gentle waterfall. My brother Rambob passed me a piece of jerky. I took my boots off, then slowly dunked my feet into the cool, foaming water.

I was gazing at a towering peak across a canyon when suddenly, Wham! There was a quick jolt at the heel of my right foot. I pulled my foot out of the water to find that, incredibly, a trout had bitten it.

My brother looked at me as if I had antlers growing out of my head. "Wow!" he exclaimed. "That trout almost caught himself an outdoors writer!"

It's true that in remote areas trout sometimes bite on almost anything, even feet. On one high-country trip I caught limits of trout using nothing but a bare hook. The only problem is that the fish will often hit the splitshot sinker instead of the hook. Of course, fishing isn't usually that easy. But it gives you an idea of what is possible.

America's wildlands are home to a remarkable abundance of fish and wildlife. Deer browse with little fear of man, bears keep an eye out for your food, and little critters such as squirrels and chipmunks are daily companions. Add in the fishing, and you've got yourself a camping trip.

Your camping adventures will evolve into premium outdoor experiences if you can work in a few good fishing trips, avoid bear problems, and occasionally add a little offbeat fun with some camp games.

Trout and Bass

He creeps up on the stream as quiet as an Indian scout, keeping his shadow off the water. With his little spinning rod he'll zip his lure within an inch or two of its desired mark, probing along rocks, the edges of riffles, pocket water, or wherever he can find a change in river habitat. Rambob is trout fishing, and he's a master at it.

In most cases he'll catch a trout on his first or second cast. After that it's time to move up the river, giving no spot much more than five minutes' due. Stick and move, stick and move, stalking the stream like a bobcat zeroing in on an unsuspecting rabbit. He might keep a few trout for dinner, but mostly he releases what he catches. Rambob doesn't necessarily fish for food. It's the feeling that comes with it.

Why We Fish: Fishing can give you a sense of exhilaration, like taking a hot shower after being coated with dust. On your walk back to camp, the steps come easy. You suddenly understand what John Muir meant when he talked of developing a oneness with nature, because you have it. That's what fishing can provide.

You don't need a million dollars' worth of fancy gear to catch fish. What you need is the right outlook, and that can be learned. That goes regardless of whether you are fishing for trout or bass, the two most popular fisheries in the United States. Your fishing tackle selection should be as simple and clutter free as possible.

At home I've got every piece of fishing tackle you might imagine, more than 30 rods and many tackle boxes, racks and cabinets filled with all kinds of stuff. I've got one lure that looks like a chipmunk and another that resembles a miniature can of beer with hooks. If I hear of something new, I want to try it and usually do. It's a result of my lifelong fascination with the sport.

But if you just want to catch fish, there's an easier way to go. And when I go fishing, I take that path. I don't try to bring everything. It would be impossible. Instead I bring a relatively small amount of gear. At home I will scan my tackle boxes for equipment and lures, make my selections, and bring just the essentials. Rod, reel, and tackle will fit into a side pocket of my backpack or a small carrying bag.

So what kind of rod should be used on an outdoor trip? For most camper/anglers, I suggest the use of a light, multipiece spinning rod that will break down to a small size. The lowest-priced, quality six-piece rod on the market is the Daiwa 6.5-foot pack rod, number 6752, which is made of a graphite/glass composite that gives it the quality of a much more expensive model. And it comes in a hard plastic carrying tube for protection. Other major rod manufacturers, such as Fenwick, offer similar premium rods. It's tough to miss with any of them.

The use of graphite/glass composites in fishing rods has made them lighter and more sensitive, yet stronger. The only downside to graphite as a rod material is that it can be brittle. If you rap your rod against something, it can crack or cause a weak spot. That weak spot can eventually snap under even light pressure, like setting a hook or casting. Of course, a bit of care will prevent that from ever occurring.

If you haven't bought a fishing reel in some time, you will be surprised at the quality and price of micro spinning reels on the market. The reels come tiny and strong, with rear-control drag systems. Sigma, Shimano, Cardinal, Abu, and others all make premium reels. They're worth it. With your purchase, you've just bought a reel that will last for years and years.

The one downside to spinning reels is that after long-term use, the bail spring will weaken. The result is that after casting and beginning to reel, the bail will sometimes not flip over and allow the reel to retrieve the line. Then you have to do it by hand. This can be incredibly frustrating, particularly when stream fishing, where instant line pickup is essential. The solution is to have a new bail spring installed every few years. This is a cheap, quick operation for a tackle expert.

You might own a giant tackle box filled with lures, but on your fishing trip you are better off to fit just the essentials into a small container. One of the best ways to do that is to use the Plano Micro-Magnum 3414, a tiny two-sided tackle box for trout anglers that fits into a shirt pocket. In mine, I can fit 20 lures in one side of the box and 20 flies, splitshot, and snap swivels in the other. For bass lures, which are bigger, you need a slightly larger box, but the same principle applies.

There are more fishing lures on the market than you can imagine, but a few special ones can do the job. I make sure these are in my box on every trip. For trout, I carry a small black Panther Martin spinner with yellow spots, a small gold Kastmaster, a yellow Roostertail, a gold Z-Ray with red spots, a Super Duper, and a Mepps Lightning spinner.

You can take it a step further using insider's wisdom. My old pal Ed "the Dunk" showed me his trick of taking a tiny Dardevle spoon, spray painting it flat black, and dabbing five tiny red dots on it. It's a real killer, particularly in tiny streams where the trout are spooky.

The best trout catcher I've ever used on rivers is a small metal lure called a Met-L Fly. On days when nothing else works, it can be like going to a shooting gallery. The problem is that the lure is nearly impossible to find. Rambob and I consider the few we have remaining so valuable that if the lure is snagged on a rock, a cold swim is deemed mandatory for its retrieval. These lures are as hard to find in tackle shops as trout can be to catch without one.

For bass, you can also fit all you need into a small plastic tackle box. I have fished with many bass pros, and all of them actually use just a few lures: a white spinner bait, a small jig called a Gits-It, a surface plug called a Zara Spook, and plastic worms. At times, as when the bass move into shoreline areas during the spring, shad minnow imitations like those made by Rebel or Rapala can be dynamite. My favorite is the one-inch, blue-silver Rapala. Every spring as the lakes begin to warm and the fish snap out of their winter doldrums, I like to float and paddle around in my small raft. I'll cast that little Rapala along the shoreline and catch and release hundreds of bass, bluegill, and sunfish. The fish are usually sitting close to the shoreline, awaiting my offering.

Fishing Tips

There's an old angler's joke about how you need to think like a fish. But if you're the one getting zilched, you may not think it's so funny.

The irony is that it is your mental approach, what you see and what you miss, that often determines your fishing luck. Some people will spend a lot of money on tackle, lures, and fishing clothes, and that done, just saunter up to a stream or lake, cast out, and wonder why they are not catching fish. The answer is their mental outlook. They are not attuning themselves to their surroundings.

You must live on nature's level, not your own. Try this and you will become aware of things you never believed even existed. Soon you will see things that will allow you to catch fish. You can get a head start by reading about fishing, but to get your degree in fishing, you must attend the University of Nature.

On every fishing trip, regardless what you fish for, try to follow three hard-and-fast rules:

1. Always approach the fishing spot so you will be undetected.
2. Present your lure, fly, or bait in a manner so it appears completely natural, as if no line was attached.
3. Stick and move, hitting one spot, working it the best you can, then move to the next.

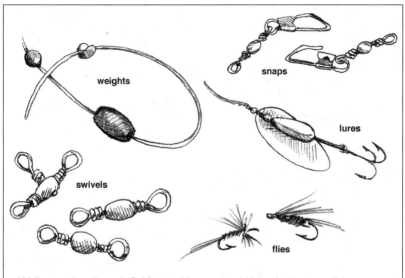

While camping, the only **fishing tackle** you should bring is the essentials: several varying weights, about 20 lures, and about 20 flies, splitshot, and snap swivels. These should all fit into a container just bigger than a deck of cards.

Approach

No one can just walk up to a stream or lake, cast out, and start catching fish as if someone had waved a magic wand. Instead, give the fish credit for being smart. After all, they live there.

Your approach must be completely undetected by the fish. Fish can sense your presence through sight and sound, though this is misinterpreted by most people. By sight, this rarely means the fish actually see you; more likely they will see your shadow on the water or the movement of your arm or rod while casting. By sound, it doesn't mean they hear you talking, but that they will detect the vibrations of your footsteps along the shore, kicking a rock, or the unnatural plunking sound of a heavy cast hitting the water. Any of these elements can spook them off the bite. In order to fish undetected, you must walk softly, keep your shadow off the water, and keep your casting motion low. All of these keys become easier at sunrise or sunset, when shadows are on the water. At midday a high sun causes a high level of light penetration in the water, which can make the fish skittish to any foreign presence.

Like hunting, you must stalk the spots. When my brother Rambob sneaks up on a fishing spot, he is like a burglar sneaking through an unlocked window.

Presentation

Your lure, fly, or bait must appear in the water as if no line were attached, so it looks as natural as possible. My pal Mo Furniss has skin-dived in rivers to watch what the fish see when somebody is fishing.

"You wouldn't believe it," he said. "When the lure hits the water, every trout within 40 feet,

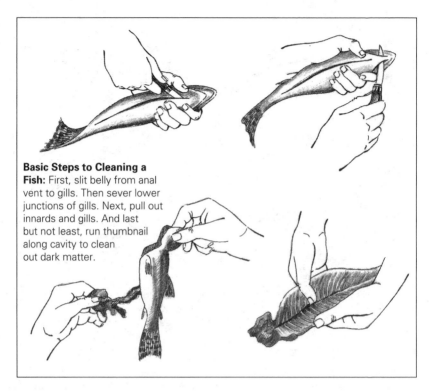

Basic Steps to Cleaning a Fish: First, slit belly from anal vent to gills. Then sever lower junctions of gills. Next, pull out innards and gills. And last but not least, run thumbnail along cavity to clean out dark matter.

like 15, 20 trout, will do a little zigzag. They all see the lure and are aware something is going on. Meanwhile, onshore the guy casting doesn't get a bite and thinks there aren't any fish in the river."

If your offering is aimed at fooling a fish into striking, it must appear as part of its natural habitat, like an insect just hatched or a small fish looking for a spot to hide. That's where you come in.

After you have sneaked up on a fishing spot, you should zip your cast upstream and start your retrieval as soon as it hits the water. If you let the lure sink to the bottom and then start the retrieval, you have no chance. A minnow, for instance, does not sink to the bottom, then start swimming. On rivers, the retrieval should be more of a drift, as if the "minnow" is in trouble and the current is sweeping it downstream.

When fishing on trout streams, always hike and cast upriver and retrieve as the offering drifts downstream in the current. This is effective because trout will sit almost motionless, pointed upstream, finning against the current. This way they can see anything coming their direction, and if a potential food morsel arrives, all they need to do is move over a few inches, open their mouths, and they've got an easy lunch. Thus you must cast upstream.

Conversely, if you cast downstream, your retrieval will bring the lure from behind the fish, where he cannot see it approaching. And I've never seen a trout that had eyes in its tail. In addition, when retrieving a downstream lure, the river current will tend to sweep your lure inshore to the rocks.

The rule of the wild is that wildlife will congregate wherever there is a distinct change in habitat. To find where fish are hiding, look where a riffle pours into a small pond, where a rapid plunges into a deep hole and flattens, and around submerged trees, rock piles, and boulders in the middle of a long riffle.

Finding Spots

A lot of anglers don't catch fish, and a lot of hikers never see any wildlife. The key is where they are looking.

The rule of the wild is that fish and wildlife will congregate wherever there is a distinct change in the habitat. This is where you should begin your search. To find deer, for instance, forget probing a thick forest, but look for where it breaks into a meadow or a clear-cut has splayed a stand of trees. That's where the deer will be.

In a river, it can be where a riffle pours into a small pool, a rapid that plunges into a deep hole and flattens, a big boulder in the middle of a long riffle, a shoreline point, a rock pile, a submerged tree. Look for the changes. Conversely, long, straight stretches of shoreline will not hold fish—the habitat is lousy.

On rivers, the most productive areas are often where short riffles tumble into small oxygenated pools. After sneaking up from the downstream side and staying low, you should zip your cast so the lure plops gently into the white water just above the pool. Start your retrieval instantly; the lure will drift downstream and plunk into the pool. Bang! That's where the trout will hit. Take a few more casts and then head upstream to the next spot.

With a careful approach and lure presentation and by fishing in the right spots, you have the ticket to many exciting days on the water.

Of Bears and Food

The first time you come nose-to-nose with a bear can make your skin quiver.

Even the sight of mild-mannered black bears, the most common bear in America, can send shock waves through your body. They weigh 250–400 pounds and have large claws and teeth that are made to scare campers. When they bound, the muscles on their shoulders roll like ocean breakers.

Bears in camping areas are accustomed to sharing the mountains with hikers and campers. They have become specialists in the food-raiding business. As a result, you must be able to make a bear-proof food hang or be able to scare the fellow off. Many campgrounds provide bear- and raccoon-proof food lockers. You can also stash your food in your vehicle, but that limits the range of your trip.

If you are staying at one of the easy backpack sites listed in this book, there will be no food lockers available. Your car will not be there, either. The solution is to make a bear-proof food hang, suspending all of your food wrapped in a plastic garbage bag from a rope in midair, 10 feet from the trunk of a tree and 20 feet off the ground. (Counterbalancing two bags with a rope thrown over a tree limb is very effective, but finding an appropriate limb can be difficult.)

This is accomplished by tying a rock to a rope, then throwing it over a high but sturdy tree limb. Next, tie your food bag to the rope and hoist it in the air. When you are satisfied with the position of the food bag, tie off the end of the rope to another tree. In an area frequented by bears, a good food bag is a necessity—nothing else will do.

I've been there. On one trip my pal Foonsky and my brother Rambob left to fish, and I was stoking up an evening campfire when I felt the eyes of an intruder on my back. I turned around and saw a big bear heading straight for our camp. In the next half hour I scared the bear off twice, but then he got a whiff of something sweet in my brother's pack.

The bear rolled into camp like a truck, grabbed the pack, ripped it open, and plucked out the Tang and the Swiss Miss. The 350-pounder then sat astride a nearby log and lapped at the goodies like a thirsty dog drinking water.

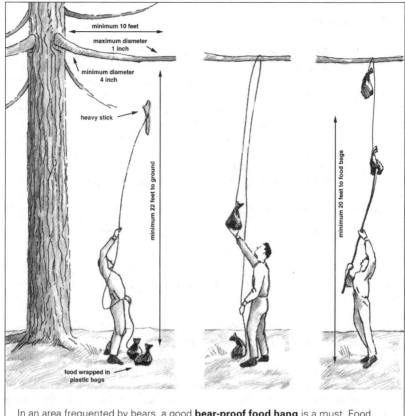

In an area frequented by bears, a good **bear-proof food hang** is a must. Food should be stored in a plastic bag 10 feet from the trunk of the tree and at least 20 feet from the ground.

Once a bear gets his mitts on your gear, he considers it his. I took two steps toward the pack, and that bear jumped off the log and galloped across the camp right at me. Scientists say a man can't outrun a bear, but they've never seen how fast I can go up a granite block with a bear on my tail.

Shortly thereafter, Foonsky returned to find me perched on top of the rock and demanded to know how I could let a bear get our Tang. It took all three of us, Foonsky, Rambob, and me, charging at once and shouting like madmen, to clear the bear out of camp and send him off over the ridge. We learned never to let food sit unattended.

The Grizzly

When it comes to grizzlies, well, my friends, you need what we call an attitude adjustment. Or that big ol' bear may just decide to adjust your attitude for you, making your stay at the park a short one.

Bear Territory

If you are hiking in a wilderness area that may have grizzlies, it becomes a necessity to wear bells on your pack. That way the bear will hear you coming and likely get out of your way. Keep talking, singing, or maybe even debating the country's foreign policy, but do not fall into a silent hiking vigil. And if a breeze is blowing in your face, you must make even more noise (a good excuse to rant and rave about the government's domestic affairs). Noise is important, because your smell will not be carried in the direction you are hiking. As a result the bear will not smell you coming.

If a bear can hear you and smell you, it will tend to get out of the way and let you pass without your knowing it was even close by. The exceptions are if you are carrying fish or lots of sweets in your pack or if you are wearing heavy, sweet deodorants or makeup. All of these are bear attractants.

Grizzlies are nothing like black bears. They are bigger, stronger, have little fear, and take what they want. Some people believe there are many different species of this critter, such as Alaskan brown, silvertip, cinnamon, and Kodiak, but the truth is they are all grizzlies. Any difference in appearance has to do with diet, habitat, and life habits, not speciation. By any name, they all come big.

The first thing you must do is determine if there are grizzlies in the area where you are camping (if you're in California, is no need to worry—grizzlies do not live in the state). That can usually be done by asking local rangers. If you are heading into Yellowstone or Glacier National Park, or the Bob Marshall Wilderness of Montana, well, you don't have to ask. They're out there, and they're the biggest and potentially most dangerous critters you could run into.

One general way to figure the size of a bear is from his footprint. Take the width of the footprint in inches, add one to it, and you'll have an estimated length of the bear in feet. For instance, a nine-inch footprint equals a 10-foot bear. Any bear that big is a grizzly, my friends. In fact, most grizzly footprints average about nine to 10 inches across, and black bears (though they may be brown in color) tend to have footprints only 4.5 to six inches across.

Most encounters with grizzlies occur when hikers fall into a silent march in the wilderness with the wind in their faces, and they walk around a corner and right into a big, unsuspecting grizzly. If you do this and see a big hump just behind its neck, well, don't think twice. It's a grizzly.

And then what should you do? Get up a tree, that's what. Grizzlies are so big that their claws cannot support their immense weight, and thus they cannot climb trees. And although their young can climb, they rarely want to get their mitts on you.

If you do get grabbed, every instinct in your body will tell you to fight back. Don't believe it. Play dead. Go limp. Let the bear throw you around a little, because after awhile you become unexciting play material and the bear will get bored. My grandmother was grabbed by a grizzly in Glacier National Park and after a few tosses and hugs, was finally left alone to escape.

Some say it's a good idea to tuck your head under his chin, since that way the bear will be unable to bite your head. I'll take a pass on that one. If you are taking action, any action, it's a signal that you are a force to be reckoned with, and he'll likely respond with more aggression. And bears don't lose many wrestling matches.

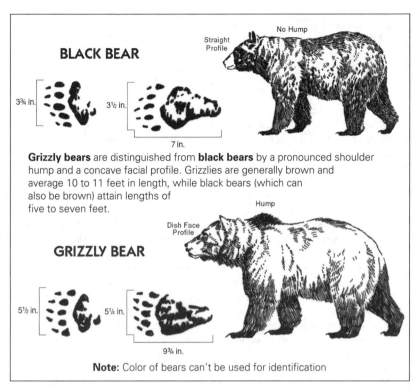

BLACK BEAR

3¾ in. 3½ in.

7 in.

Grizzly bears are distinguished from **black bears** by a pronounced shoulder hump and a concave facial profile. Grizzlies are generally brown and average 10 to 11 feet in length, while black bears (which can also be brown) attain lengths of five to seven feet.

Straight Profile

No Hump

Dish Face Profile

Hump

GRIZZLY BEAR

5½ in. 5¼ in.

9¾ in.

Note: Color of bears can't be used for identification

What grizzlies really like to do, believe it or not, is to pile a lot of sticks and leaves on you. Just let them, and keep perfectly still. Don't fight them; don't run. And when you have a 100 percent chance (not 98 or 99) to dash up a nearby tree, that's when you let fly. Once safely in a tree, you can hurl down insults and let your aggression out.

In a wilderness camp there are special precautions you should take. Always hang your food at least 100 yards downwind of camp and get it high; 30 feet is reasonable. In addition, circle your camp with rope and hang the bells from your pack on it. Thus, if a bear walks into your camp, he'll run into the rope, the bells will ring, and everybody will have a chance to get up a tree before ol' griz figures out what's going on. Often the unexpected ringing of bells is enough to send him off in search of a quieter environment.

You see, more often than not, grizzlies tend to clear the way for campers and hikers. So be smart, don't act like bear bait, and always have a plan if you are confronted by one.

My pal Foonsky had such a plan during a wilderness expedition in Montana's northern Rockies. On our second day of hiking, we started seeing scratch marks on the trees 13 to 14 feet off the ground.

"Mr. Griz made those," Foonsky said. "With spring here, the grizzlies are coming out of hibernation and using the trees like a cat uses a scratch board to stretch the muscles."

The next day, I noticed Foonsky had a pair of track shoes tied to the back of his pack. I just laughed.

"You're not going to outrun a griz," I said. "In fact, there's hardly any animal out here in the wilderness that man can outrun."

Foonsky just smiled.

"I don't have to outrun a griz," he said. "I just have to outrun you!"

Fun and Games

"Now what are we supposed to do?" the young boy asked his dad.

"Yeah, Dad, think of something," said another son.

Well, Dad thought hard. This was one of the first camping trips he'd taken with his sons and one of the first lessons he received was that kids don't appreciate the philosophic release of mountain quiet. They want action and lots of it. With a glint in his eye, Dad searched around the camp and picked up 15 twigs, breaking them so each was four inches long. He laid them in three separate rows, three twigs in one row, five twigs in another, and seven in the other.

"OK, this game is called 3-5-7," said Dad. "You each take turns picking up sticks. You are allowed to remove all or as few as one twig from a row, but here's the catch: you can pick only from one row per turn. Whoever picks up the last stick left is the loser."

I remember this episode well because those two little boys were my brother Bobby, as in Rambobby, and me. And to this day, we still play 3-5-7 on campouts, with the winner getting to watch the loser clean the dishes. What I have learned in the span of time since that original episode is that it does not matter what your age is: campers need options for camp fun.

Some evenings, after a long hike or ride, you are likely to feel too worn out to take on a serious romp downstream to fish, or a climb up to a ridge for a view. That is especially true if you have been in the outback for a week or more. At that point a lot of campers will spend their time resting and gazing at a map of the area, dreaming of the next day's adventure, or just take a seat against a rock, watching the colors of the sky and mountain panorama change minute by minute. But kids in the push-button video era, and a lot of adults too, want more. After all, "I'm on vacation; I want some fun."

There are several options, such as the 3-5-7 twig game, and they should be just as much a part of your trip planning as arranging your gear.

For kids, plan on games, the more physically challenging the competition, the better. One of the best games is to throw a chunk of wood into a lake and challenge the kids to hit it by throwing rocks. It wreaks havoc on the fishing, but it can keep kids totally absorbed for some time. Target practice with a wrist-rocket slingshot is also all consuming for kids, firing rocks away at small targets like pinecones set on a log.

You can also set kids off on little missions near camp, such as looking for the footprints of wildlife, searching out good places to have a "snipe hunt," picking up twigs to get the evening fire started, or having them take the water purifier to a stream to pump some drinking water into a canteen. The latter is an easy, fun, yet important task that will allow kids to feel a sense of equality they often don't get at home.

For adults, the appeal should be more to the intellect. A good example is star and planet identification, and while you are staring into space, you're bound to spot a few asteroids or shooting stars. A star chart can make it easy to find and identify many distinctive stars and constellations, such as Pleiades (the Seven Sisters), Orion, and others from the zodiac, depending on the time of year. With a little research, this can add a unique perspective to your trip. You could point to Polaris, one of the most easily identified of all stars, and note that navigators in the 1400s used it to find their way. Polaris, of course, is the North Star and is at the end of the handle of the Little Dipper. Pinpointing Polaris is quite easy. First find the Big Dipper and then find the outside stars of the ladle of the Big Dipper. They are called the "pointer stars" because they point right at Polaris.

A tree identification book can teach you a few things about your surroundings. It is also a good idea for one member of the party to research the history of the area you have chosen and another to research the geology. With shared knowledge, you end up with a deeper love of wild places.

Another way to add some recreation into your trip is to bring a board game, a number of which have been miniaturized for campers. The most popular are chess, checkers, and cribbage. The latter comes with an equally miniature set of playing cards. And if you bring those little cards, that opens a vast set of other possibilities. With kids along, for instance, just take three queens out of the deck and you can play Old Maid.

But there are more serious card games, and they come with high stakes. Such occurred on one high-country trip where Foonsky, Rambob, and I sat down for a late-afternoon game of poker. In a game of seven-card stud, I caught a straight on the sixth card and felt like a dog licking on a T-bone. Already I had bet several Skittles and peanut M&Ms on this promising hand.

Then I examined the cards Foonsky had face up. He was showing three sevens, and acting as happy as a grizzly with a pork chop—or a full house. He matched my bet of two peanut M&Ms, then raised me three SweetTarts, one Starburst, and one sour apple Jolly Rancher. Rambob folded, but I matched Foonsky's bet and hoped for the best as the seventh and final card was dealt.

Just after Foonsky glanced at that last card, I saw him sneak a look at my grape stick and beef jerky stash.

"I raise you a grape stick," he said.

Rambob and I both gasped. It was the highest bet ever made, equivalent to a million dollars laid down in Las Vegas. Cannons were going off in my chest. I looked hard at my cards. They looked good, but were they good enough?

Even with a great hand like I had, a grape stick was too much to gamble, my last one with 10 days of trail ahead of us. I shook my head and folded my cards. Foonsky smiled at his victory.

But I still had my grape stick.

Old Tricks Don't Always Work

Most people are born honest, but after a few camping trips, they usually get over it.

I remember some advice I got from Rambob, normally an honest soul, on one camping trip. A giant mosquito had landed on my arm and he alerted me to some expert advice.

Keep It Wild Tip 5: Keep the Wilderness Wild

1. Let nature's sound prevail. Avoid loud voices and noises.
2. Leave radios and tape players at home. At drive-in camping sites, never open car doors with music playing.
3. Careful guidance is necessary when choosing any games to bring for children. Most toys, especially any kind of gun toys with which children simulate shooting at each other, shouldn't be allowed on a camping trip.
4. Control pets at all times or leave them with a sitter at home.
5. Treat natural heritage with respect. Leave plants, rocks, and historical artifacts where you find them.

"Flex your arm muscles," he commanded, watching the mosquito fill with my blood. "He'll get stuck in your arm, then he'll explode."

For some reason, I believed him. We both proceeded to watch the mosquito drill countless holes in my arm.

Alas, the unknowing face sabotage from their most trusted companions on camping trips. It can arise at any time, usually in the form of advice from a friendly, honest-looking face, as if to say, "What? How can you doubt me?" After that mosquito episode, I was a little more skeptical of my dear old brother. Then the next day, when another mosquito was nailing me in the back of the neck, out came this gem:

"Hold your breath," he commanded. I instinctively obeyed. "That will freeze the mosquito," he said, "then you can squish him."

But in the time I wasted holding my breath, the little bugger was able to fly off without my having the satisfaction of squishing him. When he got home, he probably told his family, "What a dummy I got to drill today!"

Over the years, I have been duped numerous times with dubious advice:

On a grizzly bear attack: "If he grabs you, tuck your head under the grizzly's chin; then he won't be able to bite you in the head." This made sense to me until the first time I came face-to-face with a nine-foot grizzly 40 yards away. In seconds, I was at the top of a tree, which suddenly seemed to make the most sense.

On coping with animal bites: "If a bear bites you in the arm, don't try to jerk it away. That will just rip up your arm. Instead force your arm deeper into his mouth. He'll lose his grip and will have to open it to get a firmer hold, and right then you can get away." I was told this in the Boy Scouts, and when I was 14, I had a chance to try it out when a friend's dog bit me as I tried to pet it. What happened? When I shoved my arm deeper into his mouth, he bit me three more times.

On cooking breakfast: "The bacon will curl up every time in a camp frying pan. So make sure you have a bacon stretcher to keep it flat." As a 12-year-old Tenderfoot, I spent two hours looking for the bacon stretcher until I figured out the camp leader had forgotten it. It wasn't for several years that I learned that there is no such thing.

On preventing sore muscles: "If you haven't hiked for a long time and you are facing a rough climb, you can keep from getting sore muscles in your legs, back, and shoulders by practicing the 'Dead Man's Walk.' Simply let your entire body go slack, and then take slow, wobbling steps. This will clear your muscles of lactic acid, which causes them to be so sore after a rough hike." Foonsky pulled this one on me. Rambob and I both bought it and tried it while we were hiking up Mt. Whitney, which requires a 6,000-foot elevation gain in six miles. In one 45-minute period, about 30 other hikers passed us and looked at us as if we were suffering from some rare form of mental aberration.

Fish won't bite? No problem: "If the fish are not feeding or will not bite, persistent anglers can still catch dinner with little problem. Keep casting across the current, and eventually, as they hover in the stream, the line will feed across their open mouths. Keep reeling and you will hook the fish right in the side of the mouth. This technique is called 'lining.' Never worry if the fish will not bite, because you can always line 'em." Of course, heh, heh, heh, that explains why so many fish get hooked in the side of the mouth.

How to keep bears away: "To keep bears away, urinate around the borders of your campground. If there are a lot of bears in the area, it is advisable to go right on your sleeping bag." Yeah, surrrrrre.

What to do with trash: "Don't worry about packing out trash. Just bury it. It will regenerate into the earth and add valuable minerals." Bears, raccoons, skunks, and other critters will dig up your trash as soon as you depart, leaving one huge mess for the next camper. Always pack out everything.

Often the advice comes without warning. That was the case after a fishing trip with a female companion, when she outcaught me two to one, the third such trip in a row. I explained this to a shopkeeper, and he nodded, then explained why.

"The male fish are able to detect the female scent on the lure, and thus become aroused into striking."

Of course! That explains everything!

Getting Revenge

I was just a lad when Foonsky pulled the old snipe-hunt trick on me. It took nearly 30 years to get revenge.

You probably know about snipe hunting. The victim is led out at night in the woods by a group, and then is left holding a bag.

"Stay perfectly still and quiet," Foonsky explained. "You don't want to scare the snipe. The rest of us will go back to camp and let the woods settle down. Then when the snipe are least expecting it, we'll form a line and charge through the forest with sticks, beating bushes and trees, and we'll flush the snipe out right to you. Be ready with the bag. When we flush the snipe out, bag it. But until we start our charge, make sure you don't move or make a sound or you will spook the snipe and ruin everything."

I sat out there in the woods with my bag for hours, waiting for the charge. I waited, waited, and waited. Nothing happened. No charge, no snipe. It wasn't until well past midnight that I figured something was wrong. When I finally returned to camp, everybody was sleeping.

Well, I tell ya, don't get mad at your pals for the tricks they pull on you. Get revenge. About 25 years later, on the last day of a camping trip, the time finally came.

"Let's break camp early," Foonsky suggested to Mr. Furnai and me. "Get up before dawn, eat breakfast, pack up, and be on the ridge to watch the sun come up. It will be a fantastic way to end the trip."

"Sounds great to me," I replied. But when Foonsky wasn't looking, I turned his alarm clock ahead three hours. So when the alarm sounded at the appointed 4:30 A.M. wake-up time, Mr. Furnai and I knew it was actually only 1:30 A.M.

Foonsky clambered out of his sleeping bag and whistled with a grin. "Time to break camp."

"You go ahead," I answered. "I'll skip breakfast so I can get a little more sleep. At the first sign of dawn, wake me up, and I'll break camp."

"Me, too," said Mr. Furnai.

Foonsky then proceeded to make some coffee, cook a breakfast, and eat it, sitting on a log in the black darkness of the forest, waiting for the sun to come up. An hour later, with still no sign of dawn, he checked his clock. It now read 5:30 A.M. "Any minute now we should start seeing some light," he said.

He made another cup of coffee, packed his gear, and sat there in the middle of the night, looking up at the stars, waiting for dawn. "Anytime now," he said. He ended up sitting there all night long.

Revenge is sweet. Before a fishing trip at a lake, I took Foonsky aside and explained that the third member of the party, Jimbobo, was hard of hearing and very sensitive about it. "Don't mention it to him," I advised. "Just talk real loud."

Meanwhile, I had already told Jimbobo the same thing. "Foonsky just can't hear very good." We had fished less than 20 minutes when Foonsky got a nibble.

"GET A BITE?" shouted Jimbobo.

"YEAH!" yelled back Foonsky, smiling. "BUT I DIDN'T HOOK HIM!"

"MAYBE NEXT TIME!" shouted Jimbobo with a friendly grin.

Well, they spent the entire day yelling at each other from the distance of a few feet. They never did figure it out. Heh, heh, heh.

That is, I thought so, until we made a trip salmon fishing. I got a strike that almost knocked my fishing rod out of the boat. When I grabbed the rod, it felt as if Moby Dick were on the other end. "At least a 25-pounder," I said. "Maybe bigger."

The fish dove, ripped off line, and then bulldogged. "It's acting like a 40-pounder," I announced, "Huge, just huge. It's going deep. That's how the big ones fight."

Some 15 minutes later, I finally got the "salmon" to the surface. It turned out to be a coffee can that Foonsky had clipped on the line with a snap swivel. By maneuvering the boat, he made the coffee can fight like a big fish.

This all started with a little old snipe hunt years ago. You never know what your pals will try next. Don't get mad. Get revenge.

CAMPING OPTIONS
Boat-in Seclusion

Most campers would never think of trading in their cars, pickup trucks, or RVs for a boat, but people who go by boat on a camping trip enjoy virtually guaranteed seclusion and top-quality outdoor experiences.

Camping with a boat is a do-it-yourself venture in living under primitive circumstances. Yet at the same time you can bring along any luxury item you wish, from giant coolers, stoves, and lanterns to portable gasoline generators. Weight is almost never an issue.

Many outstanding boat-in campgrounds in beautiful surroundings are available in California. The best are on the shores of lakes accessible by canoe or skiff, and at offshore islands reached by saltwater cruisers. Several boat-in camps are detailed in this book.

If you want to take the adventure a step further and create your own boat-in camp, perhaps near a special fishing spot, this is a go-for-it deal that provides the best way possible to establish your own secret campsite. But most people who set out freelance style forget three critical items for boat-in camping: a shovel, a sunshade, and an ax. Here is why these items can make a key difference in your trip:

Shovel: Many lakes and virtually all reservoirs have steep, sloping banks. At reservoirs subject to drawdowns, what was lake bottom in the spring can be a campsite in late summer. If you want a flat area for a tent site, the only answer is to dig one out yourself. A shovel gives you that option.

Sunshade: The flattest spots to camp along lakes often have a tendency to support only sparse tree growth. As a result, a natural shield from sun and rain is rarely available. What? Rain in the summer? Oh yeah, don't get me started. A light tarp, set up with poles and staked ropes, solves the problem.

Ax: Unless you bring your own firewood, which is necessary at some sparsely wooded reservoirs, there is no substitute for a good, sharp ax. With an ax, you can almost always find dry firewood, since the interior of an otherwise wet log will be dry. When the weather turns bad is precisely when you will most want a fire. You may need an ax to get one going.

In the search to create your own personal boat-in campsite, you will find that the flattest areas are usually the tips of peninsulas and points, while the protected back ends of coves are often steeply sloped. At reservoirs, the flattest areas are usually near the mouths of the feeder streams and the points are quite steep. On rivers, there are usually sandbars on the inside of tight bends that make for ideal campsites.

Almost all boat-in campsites developed by government agencies are free of charge, but you are on your own. Only in extremely rare cases is piped water available.

Any way you go, by canoe, skiff, or power cruiser, you end up with a one-in-a-million campsite you can call your own.

Desert Outings

It was a cold, snowy day in Missouri when 10-year-old Rusty Ballinger started dreaming about the vast deserts of the West.

"My dad was reading aloud from a Zane Grey book called *Riders of the Purple Sage*," Ballinger said. "He would get animated when he got to the passages about the desert. It wasn't long before I started to have the same feelings."

That was in 1947. Ballinger, now in his 60s, has spent a good part of his life exploring the West, camping along the way. "The deserts are the best part. There's something about the uniqueness of each little area you see," Ballinger said. "You're constantly surprised. Just the time of day and the way the sun casts a different color. It's like the lady you care about. One time she smiles, the next time she's pensive. The desert is like that. If you love nature, you can love the desert. After awhile, you can't help but love it."

A desert adventure is not just an antidote for a case of cabin fever in the winter. Whether you go by RV, pickup truck, car, or on foot, it provides its own special qualities.

If you go camping in the desert, your approach has to be as unique as the setting. For starters,

---

Keep It Wild Tip 6: Respect Other Users

1. Horseback riders have priority over hikers. Step to the downhill side of the trail and talk softly when encountering horseback riders.
2. Hikers and horseback riders have priority over mountain bikers. When mountain bikers encounter other users even on wide trails, they should pass at an extremely slow speed. On very narrow trails they should dismount and get off to the side so hikers or horseback riders can pass without having their trip disrupted.
3. Mountain bikes aren't permitted on most single-track trails and are expressly prohibited in designated wilderness areas and all sections of the Pacific Crest Trail. Mountain bikers breaking these rules should be confronted and told to dismount and walk their bikes until they reach a legal area.
4. It's illegal for horseback riders to break off branches that may be in the path of wilderness trails.
5. Horseback riders on overnight trips are prohibited from camping in many areas and are usually required to keep stock animals in specific areas where they can do no damage to the landscape.

don't plan on any campfires, but bring a camp stove instead. And unlike in the mountains, do not camp near a water hole. That's because an animal such as a badger, coyote, or desert bighorn might be desperate for water, and if you set up camp in the animal's way, you may be forcing a confrontation.

In some areas, there is a danger of flash floods. An intense rain can fall in one area, collect in a pool, then suddenly burst through a narrow canyon. If you are in its path, you could be injured or drowned. The lesson? Never camp in a gully.

"Some people might wonder, 'What good is this place?'" Ballinger said. "The answer is that it is good for looking at. It is one of the world's unique places."

CAMP ETHICS AND POLITICS

The perfect place to set up a base camp turned out to be not so perfect. In fact, according to Doug Williams of California, it did not even exist.

Williams and his son, James, had driven deep into Angeles National Forest, prepared to set up camp and then explore the surrounding area on foot. But when they reached their destination, no campground existed.

"I wanted a primitive camp in a national forest where I could teach my son some basics," said the senior Williams. "But when we got there, there wasn't much left of the camp, and it had been closed. It was obvious that the area had been vandalized."

It turned out not to be an isolated incident. A lack of outdoor ethics practiced by a few people using the unsupervised campgrounds available on national forestland has caused the U.S. Forest Service to close a few of them and make extensive repairs to others.

"There have been sites closed, especially in Angeles and San Bernardino National Forests in Southern California," said David Flohr, regional campground coordinator for the U.S. Forest Service. "It's an urban type of thing, affecting forests near urban areas, and not just Los Angeles. They get a lot of urban users and they bring with them a lot of the same ethics they have in the city. They get drinking and they're not afraid to do things. They vandalize and run. Of course, it is a public facility, so they think nobody is getting hurt."

But somebody is getting hurt, starting with the next person who wants to use the campground. And if the ranger district budget doesn't have enough money to pay for repairs, the campground is then closed for the next arrivals. Just ask Doug and James Williams.

In an era of considerable fiscal restraint for the U.S. Forest Service, vandalized campgrounds could face closure instead of repair in the next few years. Williams had just a taste of it, but Flohr, as camping coordinator, gets a steady diet.

"It starts with behavior," Flohr said. "General rowdiness, drinking, partying, and then vandalism. It goes all the way from the felt-tip pen things (graffiti) to total destruction, blowing up toilet buildings with dynamite. I have seen toilets destroyed totally with shotguns. They burn up tables, burn barriers. They'll burn up signs for firewood, even the shingles right off the roofs of the bathrooms. They'll shoot anything, garbage cans, signs. It can get a little hairy. A favorite is to remove the stool out of a toilet building. We've had people fall in the open hole."

The National Park Service had a similar problem some years back, especially with rampant littering. Park Director Bill Mott responded by creating an interpretive program that attempts to teach visitors the wise use of natural areas, and to have all park workers set examples by picking up litter and reminding others to do the same.

The U.S. Forest Service has responded with a similar program, making brochures available that detail the wise use of national forests. The four most popular brochures are titled: "Rules for Visitors to the National Forest," "Recreation in the National Forests," "Is the Water Safe?" and "Backcountry Safety Tips." These include details on campfires, drinking water from lakes or streams, hypothermia, safety, and outdoor ethics. They are available free by writing to Public Affairs, U.S. Forest Service, 630 Sansome St., San Francisco, CA 94111.

Flohr said even experienced campers sometimes cross over the ethics line unintentionally. The most common example, he said, is when campers toss garbage into the outhouse toilet, rather than packing it out in a plastic garbage bag.

"They throw it in the vault toilet bowls, which just fills them up," Flohr said. "That creates an extremely high cost to pump it. You know why? Because some poor guy has to pick that stuff out piece by piece. It can't be pumped."

At most backcountry sites, the U.S. Forest Service has implemented a program called "Pack it in, pack it out," even posting signs that remind all visitors to do so. But a lot of people don't do it, and others may even uproot the sign and burn it for firewood.

On a trip to a secluded lake near Carson Pass in the Sierra Nevada, I arrived at a small, little-known camp where the picnic table had been spray painted and garbage had been strewn about. A pristine place, the true temple of God, had been defiled.

Getting Along with Fellow Campers

The most important thing about a camping, fishing, or hunting trip is not where you go, how many fish you catch, or how many shots you fire. It often has little to do with how beautiful the view is, how easily the campfire lights, or how sunny the days are.

Oh yeah? Then what is the most important factor? The answer: the people you are with. It is that simple.

Who would you rather camp with? Your enemy at work or your dream mate in a good mood? Heh, heh. You get the idea. A camping trip is a fairly close-knit experience, and you can make lifetime friends or lifelong enemies in the process. That is why your choice of companions is so important. Your own behavior is equally consequential.

Yet most people spend more time putting together their camping gear than considering why they enjoy or hate the company of their chosen companions. Here are 10 rules of behavior for good camping mates:

Two Dogs: "There are two dogs inside of you," my dad once said, "a good one, and a bad one. The one you feed is the one that will grow. Always try to feed the good dog."

1. **No whining:** Nothing is more irritating than being around a whiner. It goes right to the heart of adventure, since often the only difference between a hardship and an escapade is simply whether or not an individual has the spirit for it. The people who do can turn a rugged day in the outdoors into a cherished memory. Those who don't can ruin it with their incessant sniveling.

2. **Activities must be agreed upon:** Always have a meeting of the minds with your companions over the general game plan. Then everybody will possess an equal stake in the outcome of the trip. This is absolutely critical. Otherwise they will feel like merely an addendum to your trip, not an equal participant, and a whiner will be born (see number one).

3. **Nobody's in charge:** It is impossible to be genuine friends if one person is always telling another what to do, especially if the orders involve simple camp tasks. You need to share the space on the same emotional plane, and the only way to do that is to have a semblance of equality, regardless of differences in experience. Just try ordering your mate around at home for a few days. You'll quickly see the results, and they aren't pretty.

4. **Equal chances at the fun stuff:** It's fun to build the fire, fun to get the first cast at the best fishing spot, and fun to hoist the bagged food for a bear-proof food hang. It is not fun to clean the dishes, collect firewood, or cook every night. So obviously there must be an equal distribution of the fun stuff and the not-fun stuff, and everybody on the trip must get a shot at the good and the bad.

5. **No heroes:** No awards are bestowed for achievement in the outdoors, yet some guys treat mountain peaks, big fish, and big game as if they are prizes in a trophy competition. Actually, nobody cares how wonderful you are, which is always a surprise to trophy chasers. What people care about is the heart of the adventure, the gut-level stuff.

6. **Agree on a wake-up time:** It is a good idea to agree on a general wake-up time before closing your eyes for the night, and that goes regardless of whether you want to sleep in late or get up at dawn. Then you can proceed on course regardless of what time you crawl out of your sleeping bag in the morning, without the risk of whining (see number one).

7. **Think of the other guy:** Be self-aware instead of self-absorbed. A good test is to count the number of times you say, "What do you think?" A lot of potential problems can be solved quickly by actually listening to the answer.

8. **Solo responsibilities:** There are a number of essential camp duties on all trips, and while they should be shared equally, most should be completed solo. That means that when it is time for you to cook, you don't have to worry about me changing the recipe on you. It means that when it is my turn to make the fire, you keep your mitts out of it.

9. **Don't let money get in the way:** Of course everybody should share equally in trip expenses, such as the cost of food, and it should be split up before you head out yonder. Don't let somebody pay extra, because that person will likely try to control the trip. Conversely, don't let somebody weasel out of paying a fair share.

10. **Accordance on the food plan:** Always have complete agreement on what you plan to eat each day. Don't figure that just because you like Steamboat's Sludge, everybody else will, too, especially youngsters. Always, always, always check for food allergies such as nuts, onions, or cheese, and make sure each person brings his or her own personal coffee brand. Some people drink only decaffeinated; others might gag on anything but Burma monkey beans.

Obviously, it is difficult to find companions who will agree on all of these elements. This is why many campers say that the best camping buddies they'll ever have are their mates, who know all about them and like them anyway.

OUTDOORS WITH KIDS

How do you get a boy or girl excited about the outdoors? How do you compete with the television and remote control? How do you prove to a kid that success comes from persistence, spirit, and logic, which the outdoors teaches, and not from pushing buttons?

The answer is in the **Ten Camping Commandments for Kids.** These are lessons that will get youngsters excited about the outdoors, and that will make sure adults help the process along, not kill it. I've put this list together with the help of my own kids, Jeremy and Kris, and their mother, Stephani. Some of the commandments are obvious, some are not, but all are important:

1. Take children to places where there is a guarantee of action. A good example is camping in a park where large numbers of wildlife can be viewed, such as squirrels, chipmunks, deer, and even bears. Other good choices are fishing at a small pond loaded with bluegill, or hunting in a spot where a kid can shoot a .22 at pinecones all day. Boys and girls want action, not solitude.

2. Enthusiasm is contagious. If you aren't excited about an adventure, you can't expect a child to be. Show a genuine zest for life in the outdoors, and point out everything as if it is the first time you have ever seen it.

3. Always, always, always be seated when talking to someone small. This allows the adult and child to be on the same level. That is why fishing in a small boat is perfect for adults and kids. Nothing is worse for youngsters than having a big person look down at them and give them orders. What fun is that?

4. Always *show* how to do something, whether it is gathering sticks for a campfire, cleaning a trout, or tying a knot. Never tell—always show. A button usually clicks to "off" when a kid is lectured. But kids can learn behavior patterns and outdoor skills by watching adults, even when the adults are not aware they are being watched.

5. Let kids be kids. Let the adventure happen, rather than trying to force it within some preconceived plan. If they get sidetracked watching pollywogs, chasing butterflies, or sneaking up on chipmunks, let them be. A youngster can have more fun turning over rocks and looking at different kinds of bugs than sitting in one spot, waiting for a fish to bite.

6. Expect short attention spans. Instead of getting frustrated about it, use it to your advantage. How? By bringing along a bag of candy and snacks. Where there is a lull in the camp activity, out comes the bag. Don't let them know what goodies await, so each one becomes a surprise.

7. Make absolutely certain the child's sleeping bag is clean, dry, and warm. Nothing is worse than discomfort when trying to sleep, but a refreshing sleep makes for a positive attitude the next day. In addition, kids can become quite scared of animals at night. A parent should not wait for any signs of this, but always play the part of the outdoor guardian, the one who will take care of everything.

8. Kids quickly relate to outdoor ethics. They will enjoy eating everything they kill, building a safe campfire, and picking up all their litter, and they will develop a sense of pride that goes with it. A good idea is to bring extra plastic garbage bags to pick up any trash you come across. Kids long remember when they do something right that somebody else has done wrong.

9. If you want youngsters hooked on the outdoors for life, take a close-up photograph of them holding up fish they have caught, blowing on the campfire, or completing other camp tasks. Young children can forget how much fun they had, but they never forget if they have a picture of it.

10. The least important word you can ever say to a kid is "I." Keep track of how often you are saying "Thank you" and "What do you think?" If you don't say them very often, you'll lose out. Finally, the most important words of all are: "I am proud of you."

PREDICTING WEATHER

Foonsky climbed out of his sleeping bag, glanced at the nearby meadow, and scowled hard.

"It doesn't look good," he said. "Doesn't look good at all."

I looked at my adventure companion of 20 years, noting his discontent. Then I looked at the meadow and immediately understood why: *"When the grass is dry at morning light, look for rain before the night."*

"How bad you figure?" I asked him.

"We'll know soon enough, I reckon," Foonsky answered. "Short notice, soon to pass. Long notice, long it will last."

Keep It Wild Tip 7: Plan Ahead and Prepare

1. Learn about the regulations and issues that apply to the area you're visiting.
2. Avoid heavy-use areas.
3. Obtain all maps and permits.
4. Bring extra garbage bags to pack out any refuse you come across.

When you are out in the wild, spending your days fishing and your nights camping, you learn to rely on yourself to predict the weather. It can make or break you. If a storm hits the unprepared, it can quash the trip and possibly endanger the participants. But if you are ready, a potential hardship can be an adventure.

You can't rely on TV weather forecasters, people who don't even know that when all the cows on a hill are facing north, it will rain that night for sure. God forbid if the cows are all sitting. But what do you expect from TV's talking heads?

Foonsky made a campfire, started boiling some water for coffee and soup, and we started to plan the day. In the process, I noticed the smoke of the campfire: it was sluggish, drifting and hovering.

"You notice the smoke?" I asked, chewing on a piece of homemade jerky.

"Not good," Foonsky said. "Not good." He knew that sluggish, hovering smoke indicates rain.

"You'd think we'd have been smart enough to know last night that this was coming," Foonsky said. "Did you take a look at the moon or the clouds?"

"I didn't look at either," I answered. "Too busy eating the trout we caught." You see, if the moon is clear and white, the weather will be good the next day. But if there is a ring around the moon, the number of stars you can count inside the ring equals the number of days until the next rain. As for clouds, the high, thin clouds called cirrus indicate a change in the weather.

We were quiet for a while, planning our strategy, but as we did so, some terrible things happened: a chipmunk scampered past with his tail high, a small flock of geese flew by very low, and a little sparrow perched on a tree limb quite close to the trunk.

"We're in for trouble," I told Foonsky.

"I know, I know," he answered. "I saw 'em, too. And come to think of it, no crickets were chirping last night either."

"Damn, that's right!"

These are all signs of an approaching storm. Foonsky pointed at the smoke of the campfire and shook his head as if he had just been condemned. Sure enough, now the smoke was blowing toward the north, a sign of a south wind. *"When the wind is from the south, the rain is in its mouth."*

"We'd best stay hunkered down until it passes," Foonsky said.

I nodded. "Let's gather as much firewood now as we can, get our gear covered up, then plan our meals."

"Then we'll get a poker game going."

As we accomplished these camp tasks, the sky clouded up, then darkened. Within an hour we had gathered enough firewood to make a large pile, enough wood to keep a fire going no matter how hard it rained. The day's meals had been separated out of the food bag so it wouldn't have to be retrieved during the storm. We buttoned two ponchos together, staked two of the corners with ropes to the ground, and tied the other two with ropes to different tree limbs to create a slanted roof/shelter.

As the first raindrop fell with that magic sound on our poncho roof, Foonsky was just starting to shuffle the cards.

"Cut for deal," he said.

Just as I did so, it started to rain a bit harder. I pulled out another piece of beef jerky and started chewing on it. It was just another day in paradise.

Weather lore can be valuable. Small signs provided by nature and wildlife can be translated to provide a variety of weather information. Here is the list I have compiled over the years:

When the grass is dry at morning light,
Look for rain before the night.

Short notice, soon to pass.
Long notice, long it will last.

When the wind is from the east,
'Tis fit for neither man nor beast.

When the wind is from the south,
The rain is in its mouth.

When the wind is from the west,
Then it is the very best.

Red sky at night, sailors' delight.
Red sky in the morning, sailors take warning.

When all the cows are pointed north,
Within a day rain will come forth.

Onion skins very thin, mild winter coming in.
Onion skins very tough, winter's going to be very rough.

When your boots make the squeak of snow,
Then very cold temperatures will surely show.

If a goose flies high, fair weather ahead.
If a goose flies low, foul weather will come instead.

A thick coat on a woolly caterpillar means a big, early snow is coming.

Chipmunks will run with their tails up before a rain.

Bees always stay near their hives before a rainstorm.

When the birds are perched on large limbs near tree trunks, an intense but short storm will arrive.

On the coast, if groups of seabirds are flying a mile inland, look for major winds.

If crickets are chirping very loud during the evening, the next day will be clear and warm.

If the smoke of a campfire at night rises in a thin spiral, good weather is assured for the next day.

If the smoke of a campfire at night is sluggish, drifting, and hovering, it will rain the next day.

If there is a ring around the moon, count the number of stars inside the ring, and that is how many days until the next rain.

If the moon is clear and white, the weather will be good the next day.

High, thin clouds, or cirrus, indicate a change in the weather.

Oval-shaped lenticular clouds indicate high winds.

Two levels of clouds moving in different directions indicate changing weather soon.

Huge, dark, billowing clouds, called cumulonimbus, suddenly forming on warm afternoons in the mountains mean that a short but intense thunderstorm with lightning can be expected.

When squirrels are busy gathering food for extended periods, it means good weather is ahead in the short term, but a hard winter is ahead in the long term.

And God forbid if all the cows are sitting down. . . .

© TOM STIENSTRA

Chapter 1
Redwood Empire

Chapter 1—Redwood Empire

Visitors come from around the world to the Redwood Empire for one reason: to see the groves of giant redwoods, the tallest trees in the world. On a perfect day in the redwoods here, refracted sunlight beams through the forest canopy, creating a solemn, cathedral-like effect. It feels as if you are standing in the center of the earth's pure magic.

But the redwood forests are only one of the attractions to this area. The Smith River canyon, Del Norte and Humboldt Coasts, and the remote edge of the Siskiyou Wilderness in Six Rivers National Forest all make this region like none other in the world.

On sunny days in late summer, some visitors are incredulous that so few people live in the Redwood Empire. The reason why is the same one that explains why the trees grow so tall: rain in the winter—often for weeks at a time—and fog in the summer. If the sun does manage to appear, it's an event almost worthy of calling the police to say you've spotted a large, yellow Unidentified Flying Object. So most folks are content to just visit.

Three stellar areas should be on your must-see list for outstanding days of adventure here: the redwood parks from Trinidad to Klamath River, the Smith River Recreation Area, and the Lost Coast.

I've hiked every trailhead from Trinidad to Crescent City and believe that the hikes here feature some of the best adventuring day trips in Northern California. A good place to start is Prairie Creek Redwoods State Park, where you can see fantastic herds of Roosevelt elk. Then head over to the beach by hiking Fern Canyon, where you walk for 20 minutes at the bottom of a canyon adjacent to vertical walls covered with ferns, and then continue north on the Coastal Trail, where you'll pass through pristine woodlands and fantastic expanses of untouched beaches. All the trails through the redwoods north of the Klamath River are winners; it's just a matter of matching your level of ambition to the right hike.

The Smith River Recreation Area is equally gorgeous. The Smith is one of the last major free-flowing rivers in America. Wild, pristine, and beautiful, it's set in a series of gorges and bordered by national forest. The centerpiece is Jedediah Smith State Park and its grove of monster-sized redwoods. South Fork Road provides an extended tour into Six Rivers National Forest along the South Fork Smith River, with the option of visiting many of the largest trees in Jedediah Smith State Park. The turnoff is on U.S. 199 just northeast of the town of Hiouchi. Turn right, cross two bridges, and you will arrive at a fork in the road. Turning left at the fork will take you along the South Fork Smith River and deep into Six Rivers National Forest. Turning right at the fork will take you to a series of trailheads for hikes into redwoods. Of these, the best is the Boy Scout Tree Trail.

The Lost Coast is often overlooked by visitors because of the difficulty in reaching it; your only access is via a slow, curvy road through the Mattole River Valley, past Petrolia, and out to a piece of coast. The experience is like being in suspended animation—your surroundings peaceful and pristine, with a striking lack of people. One of the best ways to capture the sensation is to drive out near the mouth of the Mattole, then hike south on the Coast Trail long enough to get a feel for the area.

Compared to other regions in California, this corner of the state is somewhat one-dimensional. The emphasis here is primarily on exploring the redwoods and the coast, and to some extent, the Smith River. Most of the campgrounds here are designed with that in mind.

Many private campgrounds are set on U.S. 101 as well as near the mouths of the Smith and Klamath Rivers. These make fine base camps for fishing trips when the salmon are running. The state and national park campgrounds in the redwoods are in high demand, and reservations are often necessary in the peak vacation season. On the opposite end of the spectrum are primitive and remote settings, in Six Rivers National Forest, the Lost Coast, and even a few surprise nuggets in Redwood National Park.

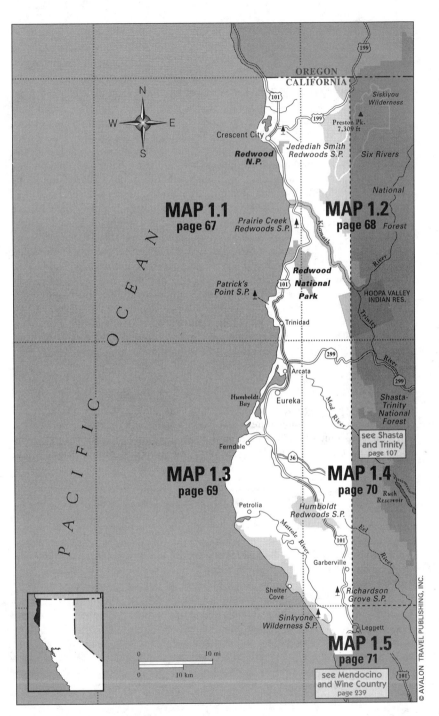

Map 1.1

Campgrounds 1–34
Pages 72–87

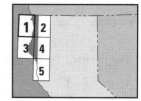

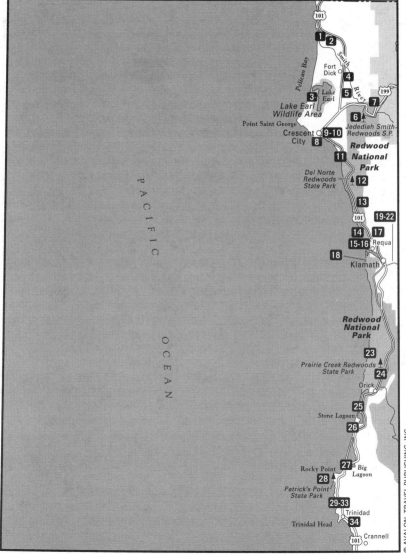

© AVALON TRAVEL PUBLISHING, INC.

Map 1.2

Campgrounds 35–38
Pages 88–89

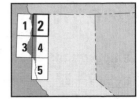

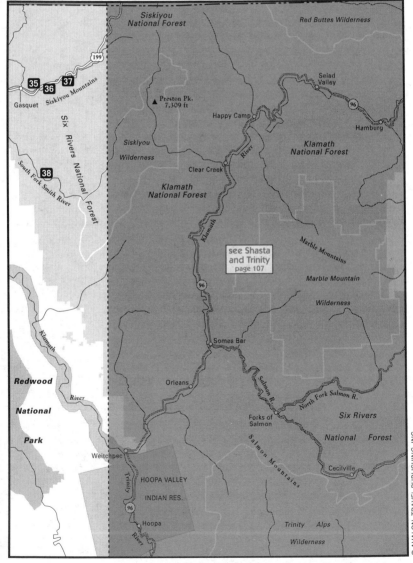

© AVALON TRAVEL PUBLISHING, INC.

Map 1.3

Campgrounds 39–51
Pages 90–95

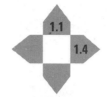

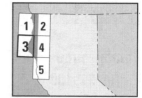

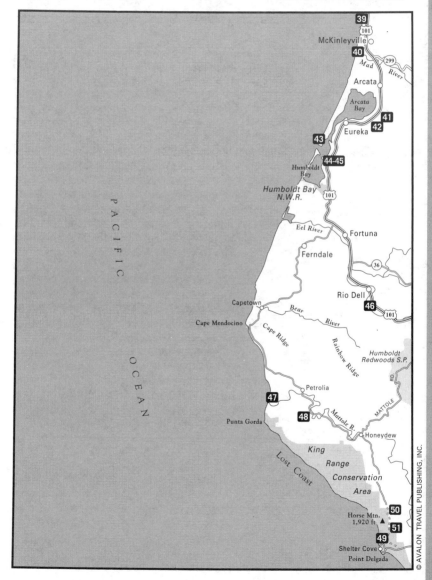

Map 1.4

Campgrounds 52–63
Pages 95–100

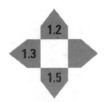

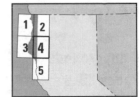

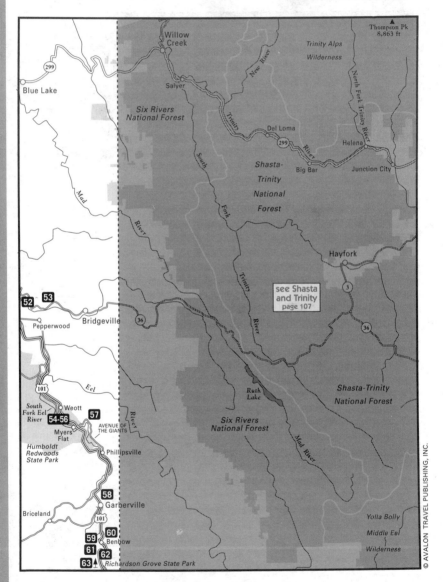

Map 1.5

Campgrounds 64–69
Pages 101–103

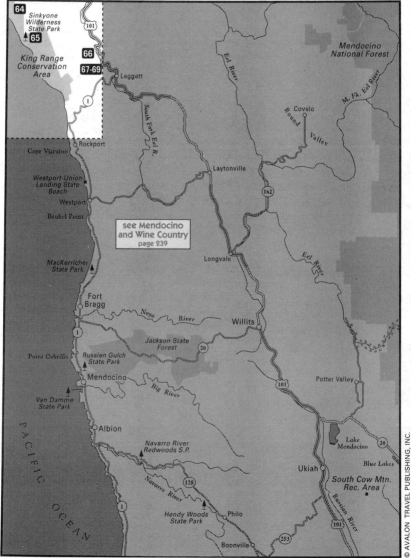

© AVALON TRAVEL PUBLISHING, INC.

1 SALMON HARBOR RESORT

Rating: 6

On the Smith River.

Map 1.1, page 67

If location is everything, this privately operated campground rates high for salmon fishermen in the fall. It is set near the mouth of the Smith River, where salmon enter and school in the deep river holes in October. The fish are big, often in the 20-pound range, occasionally surpassing even 40 pounds. Year-round this is a good layover for RV cruisers looking for a spot near the Oregon border. It is actually an RV parking area with hookups, set within a mobile home park. Salmon Harbor Resort overlooks the ocean, with good beachcombing and driftwood and agate hunting nearby.

Campsites, facilities: There are 93 sites for tents or RVs, 88 with full hookups and cable TV for RVs up to 40 feet long. Picnic tables and fire grills are provided. Drinking water, flush toilets, showers, telephones, coin laundry, storage sheds, modem hookups, and a recreation room are available. A grocery store, ice, gas, a restaurant, and a bar are available within three miles. Leashed pets are permitted.

Reservations, fees: Reservations are accepted at 800/332-6139. The fee is $25 per night, $1.50 per person for more than two people. Senior discount available. Open year-round.

Directions: From Crescent City, drive north on U.S. 101 for 13 miles to the town of Smith River. Continue three miles north on U.S. 101 to the Salmon Harbor Road exit. Turn left on Salmon Harbor Road, drive a short distance, and look for Salmon Harbor Resort at the end of the road.

Contact: Salmon Harbor Resort, 707/487-3341.

2 BEST WESTERN & SHIP ASHORE RESORT RV PARK

Rating: 7

On the Smith River.

Map 1.1, page 67

This is a famous spot for Smith River fishermen in late fall and all through winter, when the tales get taller as the evening gets late. In the summer, the resort has become quite popular with people cruising the coast on U.S. 101. The park is set on five acres of land adjacent to the lower Smith River. The salmon and steelhead seem to come in one size here—big—but they can be as elusive as Bigfoot. If you want to hear how big these fish can be, just check into the Captain's Galley restaurant any fall or winter evening. Salmon average 15–25 pounds, occasionally bigger, with 50-pounders caught each year, and steelhead average 10–14 pounds, with bigger fish occasionally hooked as well.

Campsites, facilities: There are 200 RV sites, including 80 permanent sites for mobile homes, some pull-through sites, most with full hookups, and a separate area for 10–15 tents. Motel rooms are also available. Picnic tables are provided. Flush toilets, showers, boat dock, boat ramp, and some patios are available. A coin laundry, LP gas, and a restaurant are also available. A grocery store is two miles away. Leashed pets are permitted.

Reservations, fees: Reservations are accepted. The fee is $10 for two people for the first night, $15 per night thereafter. Major credit cards accepted. Open year-round.

Directions: From Crescent City, drive north on U.S. 101 for 16 miles, three miles past the town of Smith River, to the Ship Ashore sign at Chinook Street. At Chinook Street, turn left and drive a short distance (less than half a block) to the motel lobby to register.

Contact: Best Western & Ship Ashore Resort RV Park, 707/487-3141, fax 707/487-7070.

❸ TOLOWA DUNES STATE PARK

🚶 🚲 ⛵ 🏊 🐕 ⛰️

Rating: 9

Near Crescent City.

Map 1.1, page 67

This campground is one of the great discoveries available to people who love the outdoors. The walk-in sites are extremely secluded, quiet, and sheltered, set off little spur trails from the main access trail/road. With forested rolling hills, a benign climate, and a combination of marshes, sandy soil, and proximity to the ocean, the Smith River and Lake Earl are not only pretty and pleasant, but they attract a wide variety of bird life. This is a 5,000-acre park that takes in some of the best wetlands habitat along California's northern coast. It encompasses ocean beach, river, and open and vegetated sand dunes, wood ridges, wetlands, and a large but shallow lake. The access trail to and from camp provides an outstanding bike trip along the adjacent wildlife area. The campgrounds are not set near Lake Earl, but the lake is accessible with a short drive. Lakes Earl and Tolowa are connected by a curving piece of water, with Tolowa to the west and Earl to the east. Tolowa borders coastal sand dunes and, after heavy rainfall, sometimes runs into the ocean. That is how sea-run cutthroat trout and flounder enter the brackish waters, caught rarely at the narrows between the lakes. Lakes Earl and Tolowa offer 7.5 miles of ocean frontage, 15 miles of horseback riding trails, numerous hiking trails, opportunities for canoeing and kayaking, and the bonus of having the Smith River nearby to the north. This park is named after the Tolowa people, the most recent Native Americans to occupy the area. The wetlands are an important stopover for thousands of migrating ducks, geese, swans, and other waterfowl on the Pacific Flyway, along with hundreds of species of other birds. Another bonus: there are great wildflower displays in spring and early summer.

Campsites, facilities: There are six primitive sites and a ride-in horse camp with 16 individual corrals and food lockers. There is no drinking water, but picnic tables are provided. Pit toilets are available. Fire rings are provided for the walk-in sites and fire pits for the horse camp. Leashed pets are permitted.

Reservations, fees: Reservations are not accepted. The fee is $7 per night for walk-in sites. In the horse camp, there is a $3 fee per night per horse and rider, and a group rate of $45 per night for 15 or more riders. Registration is required at Del Norte Coast Redwoods State Park, Jedediah Smith Redwoods State Park, or Crescent City Information Center. Senior discount available.

Directions: In Crescent City, drive on U.S. 101 to the lighted intersection at Northcrest Drive. Turn left (northwest) and drive about five miles (Northcrest becomes Lake Earl Drive) to Lower Lake Road. Turn left and drive 2.5 miles. Turn left on Kellogg Road and drive one-half mile. A small metal gate, for which the combination is given at registration, and parking area large enough for a few cars is the access point on the right side of the road.

For the horse camp: In Crescent City, turn northwest on Northcrest Drive and drive five miles to Lower Lake Road. At Lower Lake Road, turn left and drive about seven miles to Pala Road. At Pala Road, turn left and drive to the parking area. The horse camp is about a mile southwest of the Pala Road parking lot.

For trail and walk-in beach access: In Crescent City, turn northwest on Northcrest Drive and continue 1.5 miles to Old Mill Road. Turn west (left) on Old Mill Road and drive three miles to Sand Hill Road. For the state park trailhead, turn left at Sand Hill Road and drive one-quarter mile to the trail entrance. For Fish and Game trail and walk-in beach access, continue on Old Mill Road to the locked gate at the road's end (about 100 yards past the Sand Hill Road turnoff). The trail begins at the parking lot.

For the Lake Earl boat launch: In Crescent City, turn northwest on Northcrest Drive and drive about 3.5 miles to Lake View Road. At Lake View Road, turn left and drive a mile to the road's end at Lake Earl.

For the drive-in beach access: From Crescent City, turn northwest on Northcrest Drive and drive north for about five miles to Lower Lake Road. At Lower Lake Road, turn left and drive 2.5 miles to Kellogg Road. At Kellogg Road, turn left and drive 1.5 miles to the beach parking lot at the end of the road.

For picnicking and bird-watching: In Crescent City, turn northwest on Northcrest Drive and drive north for about five miles to Lower Lake Road. At Lower Lake Road, turn left and drive about seven miles to Pala Road on the left. Note: refer to trail notes and walk-in beach access.

Contact: Tolowa Dunes State Park, 707/464-6101, ext. 5151.

4 RAMBLIN' ROSE RESORT

Rating: 8

Near the Smith River.

Map 1.1, page 67

Ramblin' Rose is an RV park set amid redwood trees, some of them giant, with Tyrone Creek running just behind the campground. The big trees are the highlight of the area, of course, with Redwood National Park and Jedediah Smith Redwoods State Park just to the east on U.S. 199. Nearby attractions include the beach to the immediate west and the Smith River to the north.

Campsites, facilities: There are 93 RV sites with full hookups, including some drive-through sites, and seven tent sites. Picnic tables are provided. There is also a separate mobile park with full-time residents. Restrooms, drinking water, showers, and a recreation hall, volleyball, horseshoes, croquet, and badminton are available. A miniconvenience store, ice, and a coin laundry are also available. Leashed pets are permitted.

Reservations, fees: Reservations are accepted.

The fee is $20 per night for RV sites and $15 per night for tent sites, $2 per person for more than two people. For reservations, 877/387-4831. Open year-round.

Directions: From Crescent City, take U.S. 101 north for four miles to the junction of U.S. 199. Continue north on U.S. 101 for another four miles to the campground, 6701 U.S. 101 N in Crescent City.

Contact: Ramblin' Rose Resort, 707/487-4831, website: www.ramblinroserv.com.

5 CRESCENT CITY REDWOODS KOA

Rating: 6

Five miles north of Crescent City.

Map 1.1, page 67

This KOA camp is on the edge of a recreation wonderland, a perfect jump-off spot for a vacation. The camp itself includes those little KOA Kamping Kabins, which are cute log cabins with electricity and heat, as well as the larger Kamping Kottages; just make sure you bring your sleeping bag and pillows. The park covers 20 acres, featuring both open and wooded areas. In addition, there are two nine-hole golf courses nearby. The camp is only a 10-minute drive to Redwood National Park, Jedediah Smith Redwoods State Park, and the Smith River National Recreation Area. It is also only a 10-minute drive to the beach and Tolowa Dunes Wildlife Area to the east and to Crescent City Harbor to the south.

Campsites, facilities: There are 44 tent sites and 44 sites with full hookups for RVs up to 40 feet long; 17 cabins and one cottage are also available. Picnic tables and fire grills are provided. An RV dump station, flush toilets, showers, a coin laundry, and a playground are available. LP gas, groceries, ice, and wood are also available. A recreation room, pool table, ping pong, horseshoes, go-carts, basketball, and volleyball are on the property. Leashed pets are permitted.

Reservations, fees: Reservations are accepted

at 800/562-5754. The fee is $21 per night ($39–45 for two-room cabins), $3.50 per person for more than two people, 12 and under are free. Senior discount available. Major credit cards accepted. Open year-round.

Directions: From Crescent City, take U.S. 101 north for five miles to the junction of U.S. 101 and U.S. 199. Continue north on U.S. 101 for one mile and look for the campground entrance on the right (east) side of the road.

Contact: Crescent City Redwoods KOA, 707/464-5744, website: www.koa.com.

6 JEDEDIAH SMITH REDWOODS STATE PARK

Rating:10

On the Smith River.

Map 1.1, page 67

This is a beautiful park set along the Smith River, where the campsites are sprinkled amid a grove of old-growth redwoods. Reservations are usually a necessity during the summer. This park covers 10,000 acres on both sides of the Smith River, a jewel, the last major free-flowing river in California. There are 20 miles of hiking and nature trails, river access, a visitor center with exhibits, and a nature store. The park has hiking trails that lead right out of the campground; one is routed along the beautiful Smith River, and another heads through forest, across U.S. 199, and hooks up with the Simpson-Reed Interpretive Trail. In the summer, interpretive programs are available. There is also a good put-in spot at the park for river access in a drift boat, canoe, or raft. The fishing is best for steelhead from mid-January through March. The best hikes are on the south side of the Smith River, accessible via Howland Hill Road, including the Boy Scout Tree Trail and Stout Grove (for access, see the entry for Hiouchi Hamlet RV Resort). Note that in winter, 100 inches of cumulative rainfall is common.

Campsites, facilities: There are 107 sites for tents or RVs up to 36 feet long and trailers up to 31 feet long, and five hike-in/bike-in sites. Picnic tables, fire grills, and food lockers are provided. Drinking water, flush toilets, coin-operated showers, and an RV dump station are available. Propane gas, groceries, and a coin laundry are available within one mile. Leashed pets are permitted only in the campground and on roads. Some facilities are wheelchair-accessible.

Reservations, fees: Reservations are accepted with a $7.50 reservation fee at 800/444-PARK (800/444-7275) and website www.Reserve America.com. The fee is $12 per night, and $1 per person per night for hike-in, bike-in sites. Senior discount available. Open year-round.

Directions: From Crescent City, drive north on U.S. 101 for four miles to the junction with U.S. 199. Turn east at U.S. 199 and drive five miles. Turn right at the well-signed entrance station.

Contact: Redwood National and State Parks, 1111 2nd St., Crescent City, CA 95531, 707/464-6101, fax 707/464-1812.

7 HIOUCHI HAMLET RV RESORT

Rating: 7

Near the Smith River.

Map 1.1, page 67

This park is out of the wind and fog you get on the coast and set instead in the heart of the forest country. It makes a good base camp for a steelhead trip in winter. Insiders know that right next door, the fried chicken at the Hamlet's market is always good for a quick hit. An excellent side trip is to drive just east of Hiouchi on U.S. 199, turn right, and cross over two bridges, where you will reach a fork in the road. Turn left for a great scenic drive along the South Fork Smith River or turn right to get backdoor access to Jedediah Smith Redwoods State Park and three great trailheads for hiking in the redwoods. My favorite of the latter is the Boy Scout Tree Trail.

Campsites, facilities: There are 125 sites for

RVs of any length, most with full hookups and cable TV, and six tent sites. The RV sites include some drive-through sites and 40 full-time residents. Park-model RVs and furnished apartments with kitchenettes are also available. Flush toilets, showers, an RV dump station, coin laundry, modem hookups, horseshoe pits, groceries, LP gas, deli, and groceries are available. A motel and café are nearby. A golf course is available within three miles. Some facilities are wheelchair-accessible. Leashed pets are permitted.

Reservations, fees: Reservations are accepted. The fee is $15–24.50 per night. Senior discount available. Major credit cards accepted. Open year-round.

Directions: From Crescent City, drive five miles north on U.S. 101 to U.S. 199. Turn east (right) on U.S. 199 and drive about five miles (just past the entrance to Jedediah Smith State Park) to the town of Hiouchi. In Hiouchi, turn left at the well-signed campground entrance.

Contact: Hiouchi Hamlet RV Resort, 800/722-9468 or 707/458-3321, fax 707/458-4223.

8 BAYSIDE RV PARK

Rating: 6

In Crescent City.

Map 1.1, page 67

If you are towing a boat, you just found your personal heaven: this RV park is directly adjacent to the boat docking area in Crescent City Harbor. There are several walks in the immediate area, including exploring the harbor and ocean frontage. For a quick change of scenery, it is only a 15-minute drive to Redwood National Park and Jedediah Smith Redwoods State Park along U.S. 199 to the north.

Campsites, facilities: There are 110 sites, including 35 permanent residents, for RVs up to 34 feet, including some drive-through sites, with full hookups, including cable TV. Picnic tables are provided. Flush toilets, showers, and a coin laundry are available. A modem hookup is available at the park office. Leashed pets are permitted.

Reservations, fees: Reservations are accepted at 800/446-9482. The fee is $15 per night, $2 per person for more than two people. Open year-round.

Directions: From U.S. 101 at the southern end of Crescent City, turn west at Citizen Dock Road and drive a very short distance to the campground.

Contact: Bayside RV Park, 707/464-9482.

9 VILLAGE CAMPER INN RV PARK

Rating: 7

In Crescent City.

Map 1.1, page 67

Woods and water, that's what attracts visitors to California's north coast. Village Camper Inn provides nearby access to big woods and big water. This RV park is on 20 acres of wooded land, with the giant redwoods along U.S. 199 about a 10-minute drive away. In addition, you find some premium beachcombing for driftwood and agates a mile away on the spectacular rocky beaches just west of town.

Campsites, facilities: There are 135 RV sites, including some drive-through sites, most with full hookups, and a separate area for tents. Picnic tables are provided. Drinking water, an RV dump station, flush toilets, and showers are provided; a coin laundry and cable TV hookups are available. Leashed pets are permitted.

Reservations, fees: Reservations are accepted. The fee is $16–20 per night, $2 per person for more than two people, $1 for children. Major credit cards accepted. Open year-round.

Directions: On U.S. 101, driving north in Crescent City: Drive north on U.S. 101 to the Parkway Drive exit. Take that exit and drive one-half mile to the campground on the right.

On U.S. 101, driving south in Crescent City:

Drive south on U.S. 101 to the Washington Boulevard exit. Turn left on Washington Boulevard and drive one block to Parkway Drive. Turn left on Parkway and drive one block to the campground on the right.

Contact: Village Camper Inn RV Park, 707/464-3544.

10 SUNSET HARBOR RV PARK

Rating: 4

In Crescent City.

Map 1.1, page 67

People camp here with their RVs to be close to the action in Crescent City and to the nearby harbor and beach frontage. For starters, drive a few minutes to the northwest side of town, where the sea is sprinkled with gigantic rocks and boulders, for dramatic ocean views and spectacular sunsets. For finishers, go down to the west side of town for great walks along the ocean parkway or south to the harbor and adjacent beach, which is long and expansive.

Campsites, facilities: There are 69 sites with full hookups, including cable TV, for RVs up to 40 feet long. Picnic tables are provided. Flush toilets, showers, and coin laundry are available. A modem hookup is available in the park office. A grocery store and a recreation room are available nearby. Restrooms and showers are wheelchair-accessible. Leashed pets are permitted.

Reservations, fees: Reservations are accepted. The fee is $22 per night, $2 per person for more than two people, monthly rates are available. Major credit cards accepted. Open year-round.

Directions: In Crescent City on U.S. 101, drive to King Street. At King Street, turn east and drive one block to the park entrance at the end of the road.

Contact: Sunset Harbor RV Park, 707/464-3423.

11 NICKEL CREEK WALK-IN

Rating: 8

In Redwood National Park.

Map 1.1, page 67

This camp is set 100 yards from the beach on a bluff, right near the mouth of Nickel Creek. One of the least-known national park campgrounds in the whole state, Nickel Creek Walk-In provides a backpacking-type experience, yet it requires only a short walk. In return for the effort, you get seclusion and beach frontage, with seashore walks and tide pool exploration available.

Campsites, facilities: There are five hike-in tent sites. There is no drinking water. Picnic tables and fire grills are provided. Composting toilets are available. You must pack out garbage. No pets are allowed.

Reservations, fees: Reservations are not accepted. There is no fee for camping. Open year-round.

Directions: From Crescent City, drive south on U.S. 101 for two miles to Enderts Beach Road, turn right on Enderts Beach Road, and drive about a mile to the trailhead at the end of the road. From the trailhead, hike in a half mile to the campground.

Contact: Redwood National and State Parks, 1111 2nd St., Crescent City, CA 95531, 707/464-6101, fax 707/464-1812.

12 DEL NORTE COAST REDWOODS STATE PARK

Rating: 8

Near Crescent City.

Map 1.1, page 67

The campsites are set in a series of loops in the forest, so while there are a lot of camps, you still feel a sense of privacy here. In addition to redwoods, there are also good stands of alders, along with a rambling stream fed by several creeks. It makes for a very pretty setting, with a good loop hike available right out of the camp. This park covers 6,400 acres, featuring 50 percent old-growth coastal redwoods and eight miles of wild coastline. Topography is fairly steep, with elevations ranging from sea level to 1,277 feet. This range is oriented in a north-to-south direction, with steep cliffs adjacent to the ocean. That makes most of the rocky seacoast generally inaccessible except by the Damnation Trail and Footsteps Rock Trail. The best coastal access is at Wilson Beach or False Klamath Cove, where there is a half mile of sandy beach bordered by excellent tide pools. The forest interior is dense, with both redwoods and tanoaks, madrones, red alder, big leaf maple, and California bay. One reason for the lush growth is what rangers call the "nurturing" coastal climate. Nurturing, in this case, means rain like you wouldn't believe in the winter, often more than 100 inches in a season, and lots of fog in the summer. Interpretive programs are conducted here. Insider's note: hike-in and bike-in campers beware. There is a 900-foot elevation change over the course of two miles between the U.S. 101 access road and the campground.

Campsites, facilities: There are 38 tent sites and 107 sites for tents or RVs up to 31 feet long and trailers up to 27 feet long. Hike-in/bike-in sites are also available. Picnic tables, fire grills, and food lockers are provided. Drinking water, RV dump station, flush toilets, and coin-operated showers are available. Some facilities are wheelchair-accessible. Leashed pets are permitted only in the campground.

Reservations, fees: Reservations are accepted with a $7.50 reservation fee at 800/444-PARK (800/444-7275) and website www.Reserve America.com. The fee is $12 per night, $1 per person per night for hike-in/bike-in sites. Open May through September.

Directions: From Crescent City, drive seven miles south on U.S. 101 to a signed access road for Del Norte Coast Redwoods State Park. Turn left at the park entrance.

Contact: Redwood National and State Parks, 1111 2nd St., Crescent City, CA 95531, 707/464-6101, fax 707/464-1812.

13 DE MARTIN

Rating: 8

In Redwood National Park.

Map 1.1, page 67

For hikers on the Pacific Coastal Trail, this camp is ideal for an overnight spot. It is set in a grassy prairie area on a bluff overlooking the ocean along the De Martin section of the trail, aside Wilson Creek. Sound good? You can chase the waves, hike the Coastal Trail, or just hunker down and let the joy of a peaceful spot renew your spirit.

Campsites, facilities: There are 10 tent sites. Caches for food storage are provided. Composting toilets are available. There is no drinking water and you must pack out your garbage. No pets are allowed.

Reservations, fees: Reservations are not accepted. There is no fee for camping. Open year-round.

Directions: From Crescent City, drive south for approximately 18 miles on U.S. 101 to Wilson Creek Road. At Wilson Creek Road, turn left and drive one-quarter mile to the trailhead at the end of the road. From the trailhead, hike in about 2.5 miles to the campground.

Contact: Redwood National and State Parks, 1111 2nd St., Crescent City, CA 95531, 707/464-6101, fax 707/464-1812.

14 MYSTIC FOREST RV PARK

Rating: 6

Near the Klamath River.

Map 1.1, page 67

Yes, Paul Bunyan exists. After all, how do you think the Mojave got turned into a desert? Babe, the giant blue ox, is still around too, as you will discover at the Trees of Mystery north of Klamath, where a dinosaur-sized Paul Bunyan guards the parking lot. Less than a mile away is the Mystic Forest RV Park. Though Mystic Forest and the Trees of Mystery are not associated commercially, the link is obvious as soon as you arrive. The park features gravel roads, redwood trees, and grassy sites amid a 50-acre park designed primarily for RVs with a separate area for tents.

Campsites, facilities: There are 30 RV sites, including 15 drive-through, with full hookups, and a separate area for tents with 14 sites. Picnic tables and fire rings are provided. Drinking water, flush toilets, showers, playground, a coin laundry, small store and gift shop, and wood are available. A clubhouse with kitchen is available for groups. Some facilities are wheelchair-accessible. Leashed pets are permitted.

Reservations, fees: Reservations are accepted. The fee is $14–20 per night, $2 per person for more than two people. Major credit cards accepted. Open year-round.

Directions: From Eureka, drive north on U.S. 101 to Klamath and continue north for four miles. Look for the entrance sign on the left side of the road. If you reach the Trees of Mystery, you have gone a mile too far north.

Contact: Mystic Forest RV Park, 707/482-4901, fax 707/482-0704, website: www./mystic forestrv.com.

15 RIVERSIDE RV PARK

Rating: 7

On the Klamath River.
Map 1.1, page 67

This RV park features lots of trees and grassy areas along the Klamath River. This is one in a series of RV parks near the town of Klamath along the lower Klamath River. It provides an option for RV cruisers looking for a layover spot on a U.S. 101 tour or a base of operations for a Klamath River fishing trip. There's good salmon fishing starting in late summer, peak-ing at Labor Day, and continuing into fall on the Klamath River.

Campsites, facilities: There are 93 sites, including 30 drive-through, with full hookups for RVs and tents. Flush toilets, showers, and cable TV are available. Boat rentals and a dock are also available. A restaurant is available within one mile. Leashed pets are permitted.

Reservations, fees: Reservations are accepted. The fee is $9–20 per night. Monthly rates available. Open year-round.

Directions: From Eureka, drive north on U.S. 101 to Klamath. Continue north for two miles to the campground on the west (on the left if driving north).

Contact: Riverside RV Park, 707/482-2523.

16 CHINOOK RV RESORT

Rating: 7

On the Klamath River.
Map 1.1, page 67

The camping area at this park consists of grassy RV sites that overlook the Klamath River. Chinook RV Resort is another of the more well-known parks on the lower Klamath. A boat ramp, fishing supplies, and all the advice you can ask for are available.

Campsites, facilities: There are 70 RV sites with full hookups, including some drive-through sites, with a tent area available in a grassy area. Picnic tables and fire grills are provided. Flush toilets, showers, cable television and modem hookups, a playground, coin laundry and recreation room, LP gas, groceries, RV supplies, boat ramp, boat rentals, and a tackle shop are available. Leashed pets are permitted.

Reservations, fees: Reservations are accepted. The fee is $22 per night, plus $2 per person per night for more than two people, $2 per extra vehicle. Major credit cards accepted. Senior discount available. Open year-round.

Directions: From Eureka, drive north on U.S. 101 to Klamath. After crossing the bridge at the Klamath River, continue north on U.S. 101 for a mile to the campground on the left. **Contact:** Chinook RV Resort, 707/482-3511, fax 707/482-3030.

17 CAMP MARIGOLD

Rating: 7

Near the Klamath River.
Map 1.1, page 67

Camp Marigold is surrounded by wonder: Redwood National Park, towering redwoods, Pacific Ocean beaches, driftwood, agates, fossilized rocks, blackberries, Fern Canyon, Lagoon Creek Park, and the Trees of Mystery. Fishing is available nearby, in season, for several species, including king salmon, steelhead, red tail perch, and candlefish. The camp has 3.5 acres of landscaped gardens with hiking trails. . . get the idea? Well, there's more: it is only two miles to the Klamath River, in case you can't find enough to do already.

Campsites, facilities: There are 40 sites with full hookups for tents or RVs up to 35 feet. Park-model RVs are also available. Picnic tables and barbecues are provided. Restrooms, hot showers, cable TV, and a coin laundry are available. Cabins (with fully equipped kitchenettes and bedding, for two to six people) and a group lodge (with kitchen, for up to 15 people) are also available. Small leashed pets are permitted.

Reservations, fees: Reservations are recommended. The fee is $10–15 per night, $5 for each additional person (maximum 15). Monthly rates available. Major credit cards are accepted. Open year-round.

Directions: From Eureka, drive 60 miles north on U.S. 101 to the campground at 16101 U.S. 101, four miles north of the Klamath River Bridge, on the right side of the road. The camp is a mile south of the Trees of Mystery.

Contact: Camp Marigold, 800/621-8513 or 707/482-3585, website: www.northcoast .com/~campmar.

18 FLINT RIDGE WALK-IN

Rating: 7

In Redwood National Park.
Map 1.1, page 67

This little-known camp is on a grassy bluff overlooking the ocean along the Flint Ridge section of the Pacific Coastal Trail. From the parking area at the trailhead, it's only a five-minute walk to reach a meadow surrounded by a thicket of wild blackberries, alders, and redwoods, with the ocean looming huge to the west. The parking area, by the way, is an excellent perch to watch for the "puff-of-smoke" spouts from passing whales. A hike out of camp is routed into the forest; it's a two-mile climb to reach a hill filled solid with redwoods. The only problem is that there is no real destination—just in and then back.

Campsites, facilities: There are 10 hike-in tent sites. Composting toilets are available. There is no drinking water. You must pack out garbage. No pets are allowed.

Reservations, fees: Reservations are not accepted. There is no fee for camping. Open year-round.

Directions: From Eureka, drive north on U.S. 101 to the Klamath River. Just before reaching the bridge at the Klamath River, take the Coastal Drive exit and head west up the hill for four miles to a dirt parking area on the right side of the road. Park here. The campground trailhead is adjacent to the parking area on the east side of the road. Hike five minutes to the camp.

Contact: Redwood National and State Parks, 1111 2nd St., Crescent City, CA 95531, 707/464-6101, fax 707/464-1812.

19 CAMPER CORRAL

Rating: 6

On the Klamath River.
Map 1.1, page 67

This resort offers 3,000 feet of Klamath River

frontage, grassy tent sites, berry picking, access to the ocean, and hiking trails nearby. And, of course, in the fall it has salmon, the main attraction on the lower Klamath. Organized recreation is available in summer.

Campsites, facilities: There are 140 sites, including 100 drive-through sites, many with full hookups, for RVs or tents. Picnic tables and fire grills are provided. Drinking water, flush toilets, showers, a heated swimming pool, recreation hall, playground, RV dump station, coin laundry, cable TV, ice, and a bait and tackle shop are available. Basketball, volleyball, badminton, shuffleboard, horseshoes, and tetherball are also available. Leashed pets are permitted.

Reservations, fees: Reservations are accepted. The fee is $14–20 per night, $2 per night for each additional vehicle, $2 per person per night for more than two people. Monthly rates are available. Major credit cards accepted. Open April through October.

Directions: From Eureka, drive north on U.S. 101 to Klamath. Just after crossing the Klamath River Bridge, take the Terwer Valley Road exit. At the stop sign, turn left and drive a short distance west to the campground.

Contact: Camper Corral, 707/482-5741, fax 707/482-6625, website: www. campercorral.net.

20 CRIVELLI'S RESTAURANT, BAR, AND TRAILER PARK

Rating: 5

Near the Klamath River.
Map 1.1, page 67

Crivelli's Trailer Park is adjacent to a motel, surrounded by trees, and only one-quarter mile away from the Klamath River. It's a good base camp for a salmon fishing trip during the fall run, so when the salmon arrive en masse, it can be difficult to get a reservation. Some regulars show up every year, same time, same place, staying for a week or more and fishing daily for salmon in the lower river. A restaurant and lounge are available. Once the fishing season is over in November, the restaurant is closed until late May.

Campsites, facilities: There are 31 RV sites with full hookups, including some pull-through sites; about half are permanent residents. Some facilities are wheelchair-accessible. Flush toilets, showers, a coin laundry, restaurant, and a lounge are available. Leashed pets are permitted.

Reservations, fees: Reservations are recommended. The fee is $10–15 per night. Major credit cards accepted. Open year-round.

Directions: From Eureka, drive north on U.S. 101 to Klamath and the junction with Highway 169. Turn east (right) on Highway 169 and drive 2.5 miles to the trailer park entrance on the left.

Contact: Crivelli's Trailer Park, 707/482-3713.

21 STEELHEAD LODGE

Rating: 6

On the Klamath River.
Map 1.1, page 67

Many anglers use this park as headquarters when the salmon and steelhead get going in August. The park has grassy sites near the Klamath River.

Campsites, facilities: There are 36 sites, including 10 drive-through, with full hookups for RVs or tents. Picnic tables are provided. Drinking water, flush toilets, showers, and ice are available. A bar, restaurant, and motel are also available. Bar and restaurant are wheelchair-accessible. Leashed pets are permitted.

Reservations, fees: Reservations are accepted. The fee is $15 per night. Major credit cards accepted. Open year-round.

Directions: From Eureka, drive north on U.S. 101 to Klamath and the junction with Highway 169. Turn east on Highway 169 and drive 3.2 miles to Terwer Riffle Road. Turn right (south) on Terwer Riffle Road and drive one block to Steelhead Lodge on the right.

Contact: Steelhead Lodge, 707/482-8145. For a fishing report, 707/482-7775.

22 TERWER PARK

Rating: 7

On the Klamath River.
Map 1.1, page 67

This RV park is situated near the Terwer Riffle, one of the better shore-fishing spots for steelhead and salmon on the lower Klamath River. You get grassy sites, river access, and some fair trails along the Klamath. When the salmon arrive in late August and September, Terwer Riffle can be loaded with fish, as well as boaters and shore anglers—a wild scene. Note that at this park, tent campers are separated from the RV park, with tent camping at a grassy area near the river.

Campsites, facilities: There are 87 RV sites, including 12 drive-through sites, with full hookups and with a few long-term residents. A separate tent area is available. Picnic tables are provided. Flush toilets, hot showers, and a coin laundry are available. A pulley boat launch is available nearby. Leashed pets are permitted.

Reservations, fees: Reservations are accepted. The fee is $10–13.50 per night, $5 for a second vehicle. Monthly rates available. Open year-round.

Directions: From Eureka, drive north on U.S. 101 to Klamath and the junction with Highway 169. Turn east on Highway 169 and drive 3.5 miles to Terwer Riffle Road. Turn right on Terwer Riffle Road and drive seven blocks (about a half mile) to the park at the end of the road (641 Terwer Riffle Rd).

Contact: Terwer Park, 707/482-3855, website: www.terwerpark.com.

23 GOLD BLUFF BEACH

Rating: 8

In Prairie Creek Redwoods State Park.
Map 1.1, page 67

The campsites here are set in a sandy, exposed area with man-made windbreaks with a huge, expansive beach on one side and a backdrop of 100- to 200-foot cliffs on the other side. You can walk for miles at this beach, often without seeing another soul, and there is a great trail routed north through forest, with many hidden little waterfalls. In addition, the Fern Canyon Trail, one of the best 30-minute hikes in California, is at the end of Davison Road. Hikers walk along a stream in a narrow canyon, its vertical walls covered with magnificent ferns. There are some herds of elk in the area, often right along the access road. These camps are rarely used in the winter because of the region's heavy rain and winds. The expanse of beach here is awesome, covering 10 miles of huge, pristine ocean frontage. Campfire programs are offered in summer. See previous listing for more information about Prairie Creek Redwoods.

Campsites, facilities: There are 25 sites for tents or RVs up to 24 feet long (no trailers or vehicles wider than eight feet). Fire grills, food lockers, and tables are provided. Drinking water, flush toilets, and solar showers are available. Leashed pets are permitted.

Reservations, fees: Reservations are not accepted. The fee is $12 per night. Senior discount available. Open year-round, weather permitting.

Directions: From Eureka, drive north on U.S. 101 for 45 miles to Orick. At Orick, continue north on U.S. 101 for three miles to Davison Road. Turn left (west) on Davison Road and drive six miles to the campground on the left. Note: no vehicles more than 24 feet long or more than eight feet wide are permitted on Davison Road, which is narrow and very bumpy.

Contact: Prairie Creek Redwoods State Park, 707/464-6101, ext. 5301 or 5300 (Visitor Center).

24 ELK PRAIRIE

Rating: 9

In Prairie Creek Redwoods State Park.
Map 1.1, page 67

Herds of Roosevelt elk wander free in this

remarkable 14,000-acre park. Great opportunities for photographs abound, with the elk often found right along the highway and access roads. Where there are meadows, there are elk; it's about that simple. An elky here, an elky there, making this one of the best places to see wildlife in California. Remember that these are wild animals, they are huge, and they can be unpredictable; in other words, enjoy them, but don't harass them or get too close. This park consists of old-growth coastal redwoods, prairie lands, and 10 miles of scenic, open beach (Gold Bluff Beach). The interior of the park can be reached by 75 miles of hiking, biking, and nature trails, including a trailhead for a great bike ride at the campground. There are many additional trailheads and a beautiful tour of giant redwoods along the Drury Scenic Parkway. A visitor center and summer interpretive programs with guided walks and junior ranger programs are available. Because of the prevalent coastal fog, the understory of the forest is very dense. Western azalea and rhododendron bloom in May and June, and the Rhododendron Trail is a favorite for seeing this display. From November through May, always bring your rain gear. Summer temperatures range 40–75°F; winter temperatures range 35–55°F.

Campsites, facilities: There are 75 sites for tents, RVs up to 27 feet long, or trailers up to 24 feet long. Picnic tables, fire grills, and bear-proof food lockers are provided. Drinking water, flush toilets, and coin-operated showers are available. Some facilities are wheelchair-accessible. Leashed pets are permitted.

Reservations, fees: Reservations are accepted with a $7.50 reservation fee at 800/444-PARK (800/444-7275) and website www.Reserve America.com. The fee is $12 per night. Senior discount available. Open year-round.

Directions: From Eureka, drive 45 miles north on U.S. 101 to Orick. At Orick, continue north on U.S. 101 for five miles to the Newton B. Drury Scenic Parkway. Take the exit for the Newton B. Drury Scenic Parkway and drive

north for a mile to the park. Turn left at the park entrance.

Contact: Prairie Creek Redwoods State Park, 707/464-6101, ext. 5301 or 5300 (Visitor Center).

25 STONE LAGOON BOAT-IN

Rating:10

In Humboldt Lagoons State Park.

Map 1.1, page 67

Virtually nobody knows about this ideal spot for canoeists. While Stone Lagoon is directly adjacent to U.S. 101, the camp is set in a cove that is out of sight of the highway. That makes it a secret spot for many. It is a great place to explore by canoe or kayak, especially paddling upstream to the lagoon's inlet creek. After setting up camp, it is possible to hike to a secluded sand spit and stretch of beachfront. You may see elk in this area on the rare occasion. The water is usually calm in the morning but often gets choppy from afternoon winds. Translation: get your paddling done early on Stone Lagoon. There is also good fishing for cutthroat trout here. In the early 1900s, several dairy ranches were established along the shore of Stone Lagoon. Today the marshland habitat has returned to support a rich variety of marsh plants, birds, and other animals.

Campsites, facilities: There are six primitive tent sites accessible by boat only. There is no drinking water. Picnic tables, food lockers, and fire rings are provided. Pit toilets are available. Garbage must be packed out. No pets are allowed.

Reservations, fees: Reservations are not accepted. The fee is $7 per night. Senior discount available. Open year-round.

Directions: From Eureka, drive 41 miles north on U.S. 101 (15 miles north of Trinidad) to Stone Lagoon. At Stone Lagoon, turn left at the visitor information center. The boat-in campground is in a cove directly across the lagoon from the visitor center. The campsites are dispersed in an area covering about 300 yards in the landing area.

Contact: Humboldt Lagoons State Park, Visitor Center, 707/488-2041; Humboldt County Parks, 707/445-7652.

26 DRY LAGOON WALK-IN

Rating: 8

In Humboldt Lagoons State Park.
Map 1.1, page 67

This is a walk-in camp; that is, you need to walk about 200 yards from the parking area to reach the campsites. This makes it a dream for members of the 5 Percent Club, because many tourists are unwilling to walk at all. It is beautiful here, set in the woods, with ocean views and beach access. In the early 1900s, Dry Lagoon was drained by farmers and several types of crops were attempted. The farming projects were colossal failures and the lagoon was allowed to refill. This spot receives 60 inches of rain, on the average, in winter, with spring and fall pleasant. In summer, it can be foggy, cool, and damp, so bring warm, layered clothing. The park has a visitor center and bookstore. A highlight here is a three-mile segment of the Coastal Trail.

Campsites, facilities: There are six primitive tent sites. Picnic tables, fire rings, and food lockers are provided. Pits toilets are available. There is no drinking water. Garbage must be packed out. No pets are allowed.

Reservations, fees: Reservations are not accepted. The fee is $7 per night. All campers must register at the Patrick's Point State Park entrance station to obtain the combination to the gate lock. Senior discount available. Open year-round.

Directions: From Eureka, drive north on U.S. 101 for 22 miles to Trinidad. At Trinidad, continue north on U.S. 101 for 13 miles to Dry Lagoon Road. Turn left and drive approximately one mile to the gate at the end of the road. Open gate combination (see previous note) and drive one-quarter mile to the trailhead. Park and walk 200 yards to the camp.

Contact: Humboldt Lagoons State Park, Vis-

27 BIG LAGOON COUNTY PARK

Rating: 7

Overlooking the Pacific Ocean.
Map 1.1, page 67

This is a remarkable, huge lagoon that borders the Pacific Ocean. It provides good boating, excellent exploring, fair fishing, and good duck hunting in the winter. It's a good spot to paddle a canoe around on a calm day. A lot of out-of-towners cruise by, note the lagoon's proximity to the ocean, and figure it must be salt water. Wrong! Not only is it freshwater, but it provides a long shot for anglers trying for rainbow trout. One reason not many RV drivers stop here is that most of them are drawn farther north (another eight miles) to Freshwater Lagoon.

Campsites, facilities: There are 26 sites for tents or RVs. Picnic tables and fire grills are provided. Drinking water and flush toilets are available. Some facilities are wheelchair-accessible. A boat ramp is also available. Leashed pets are permitted.

Reservations, fees: Reservations are not accepted. The fee is $12 per night per vehicle, $1 per pet per night. Open year-round.

Directions: From Eureka, drive 22 miles north on U.S. 101 to Trinidad. At Trinidad, continue north on U.S. 101 for eight miles to Big Lagoon Park Road. Turn left (west) at Big Lagoon Park Road and drive two miles to the park.

Contact: Humboldt County Parks, 707/445-7652; Humboldt Lagoons State Park, Visitor Center, 707/488-2041.

28 PATRICK'S POINT STATE PARK

Rating: 9

Near Trinidad.
Map 1.1, page 67

This pretty park covers 640 acres of coastal

headlands and it is filled with Sitka spruce, dramatic ocean lookouts, and several beautiful beaches, including one with agates, one with tidepools, and another with an expansive stretch of beachfront leading to a lagoon. You can best see it on the Rim Trail, which has many little cut-off routes to the lookouts and down to the beaches. The campground is sheltered in the forest, and while it is often foggy and damp in the summer, it is always beautiful. A Native American village, constructed by the Yurok tribe, is also here. At the north end of the park, a short hike to see the bizarre "Octopus Trees" is a good side trip, with trees that are growing atop downed logs, their root systems exposed like octopus tentacles; the trail here loops through a grove of old-growth Sitka spruce. In addition, there are several miles of pristine beach to the north that extends to the lagoons. Interpretive programs are available. The forest here is dense, with spruce, hemlock, pine, fir, and red alder covering an ocean headland. Night and morning fog are common almost year-round, and there are periods where it doesn't lift for days. This area gets 60 inches of rain per year on the average. For camping, plan on making reservations.

Campsites, facilities: There are 124 sites for tents or RVs, including 39 sites for RVs only up to 31 feet long. Fire grills, food lockers, and picnic tables are provided. Drinking water, flush toilets, and coin-operated showers are available. Some facilities are wheelchair-accessible. Leashed pets are permitted at campsites, but not on trails or beaches.

Reservations, fees: Reservations are accepted with a $7.50 reservation fee at 800/444-PARK (800/444-7275) and website www.Reserve America.com. The fee is $12 per night. Senior discount available. Open year-round.

Directions: From Eureka, drive north on U.S. 101 for 22 miles to Trinidad. At Trinidad, continue north on U.S. 101 for 5.5 miles to Patrick's Point Drive. Take that exit and at the stop sign, turn left and drive one-half mile to the park entrance.

Contact: Patrick's Point State Park, 707/677-3570 or 707/488-5555.

29 SOUNDS OF THE SEA RV PARK

Rating: 6

In Trinidad.

Map 1.1, page 67

The Trinidad area, about 20 miles north of Eureka, is one of the great places on this planet. Nearby Patrick's Point State Park is one of the highlights, with a Sitka spruce forest, beautiful coastal lookouts, a great easy hike on the Rim Trail, and access to several secluded beaches. To the nearby south at Trinidad Head is a small harbor and dock, with deep-sea and salmon fishing trips available. A breezy beach is to the immediate north of the Seascape Restaurant. A bonus at this privately operated RV park is good berry picking.

Campsites, facilities: There are 52 RV sites, including some drive-through, with full hookups. Picnic tables and fire rings are provided. Restrooms, showers, an RV dump station, a coin laundry, grocery store, gift shop, cable TV, and ice are available. Leashed pets are permitted.

Reservations, fees: Reservations are accepted. The fee is $21 per night. Major credit cards accepted. Open year-round.

Directions: From Eureka, drive north on U.S. 101 for 28 miles to Trinidad. In Trinidad, continue north on U.S. 101 for five miles to the Patrick's Point exit. Take the Patrick's Point exit, turn left, and drive a half mile to the campground.

Contact: Sounds of the Sea RV Park, 707/677-3271, website: www.northcoast.com/~gupie.

30 SYLVAN HARBOR RV PARK AND CABINS

Rating: 8

In Trinidad.

Map 1.1, page 67

This park is designed as an RV park and fish

camp, with cleaning tables and canning facilities available on site. It is a short distance from the boat hoist at Trinidad Pier. Beauty surrounds Sylvan Harbor on all sides for miles. Visitors come to enjoy the various beaches, go agate hunting, or look for driftwood on the beach. Nearby Patrick's Point State Park is an excellent getaway side trip. This is one of several privately operated parks in the Trinidad area, offering a choice of shaded or open sites near the ocean. (For more information about recreation options nearby, see the entry for Sounds of the Sea.)

Campsites, facilities: There are 70 sites with full hookups, including cable TV, for RVs up to 35 feet long. Three cabins are available. Restrooms, showers, an RV dump station, a coin laundry, and LP gas are available. Leashed pets are permitted.

Reservations, fees: Reservations are accepted for cabins only. The fee is $18 per night for RV sites, $2 per person for more than two people; call for cabin fees. Open year-round.

Directions: From Eureka, drive north on U.S. 101 for 28 miles to Trinidad. Take the Trinidad exit to the stop sign at Seawood Drive. Turn left and drive a short distance under the freeway to Patrick's Point Drive. Turn right and drive one mile to the campground on the right.

Contact: Sylvan Harbor RV Park and Cabins, tel./fax 707/677-9988, website: www.sylvan harbor.com.

31 VIEW CREST LODGE & CAMPGROUND

Rating: 8

In Trinidad.

Map 1.1, page 67

View Crest Campground is one of the premium spots in Trinidad, with pretty cottages available as well as campsites for RVs and tents. A bonus here is the remarkable flights of swallows, many of which have nests at the cottages. Recreation options include deep-sea and sal-

mon fishing at Trinidad Harbor to the nearby south, and outstanding easy hiking at Patrick's Point State Park to the nearby north.

Campsites, facilities: There are 25 RV sites with full hookups, including nine drive-through sites, and a separate area for tents; 12 cottages are available. Picnic tables and fire rings are provided. Restrooms, showers, playground, an RV dump station, cable TV hookups, RV storage, a coin laundry, and wood are available. Leashed pets are permitted only in the campground.

Reservations, fees: Reservations are accepted. The fee is $16–20 per night, $1 per person per night for more than two people. Major credit cards accepted. Open year-round.

Directions: From Eureka, drive north on U.S. 101 for 28 miles to Trinidad. Take the Trinidad exit to the stop sign at Seawood Drive. Turn left and drive a short distance under the freeway to Patrick's Point Drive. Turn right and drive two miles to the campground on the right.

Contact: View Crest Lodge Campground, 707/677-3393, fax 707/677-9363, website: www.viewcrestlodge.com.

32 MIDWAY RV PARK

Rating: 6

In Trinidad.

Map 1.1, page 67

This is one of several privately developed campgrounds in Trinidad. In the summer, salmon fishing can be excellent just off Trinidad Head. In the fall, rock fishing is the way to go, and in winter, crabbing is tops. Patrick's Point State Park provides a nearby side-trip option to the north.

Campsites, facilities: There are 65 RV sites with full hookups and four sites for tents. Picnic tables are provided. Restrooms, showers, cable TV, club room, a playground, propane, coin laundry, fish-cleaning station, and RV storage are available. Some facilities are wheelchair-accessible. Leashed pets are permitted.

Reservations, fees: Reservations are recommended in the summer. The fee is $16–23 per night, $3 per person per night for more than two people. Senior discount available. Major credit cards accepted. Open year-round.

Directions: From Eureka, drive north on U.S. 101 for 28 miles to Trinidad. Take the Trinidad exit to the stop sign at Seawood Drive. Turn left and drive a short distance under the freeway to Patrick's Point Drive. Turn right on Patrick's Point Drive and drive a half mile to the campground on the right.

Contact: Midway RV Park, tel./fax 707/677-3934.

33 EMERALD FOREST

Rating: 5

In Trinidad.

Map 1.1, page 67

This campground is set on 12 acres of redwoods, often dark and wet, with the ocean at Trinidad Head only about a five-minute drive away. Nice spot with nice folks.

Campsites, facilities: There are 55 sites for RVs, including 14 drive-through sites, with full or partial hookups, and 30 tent sites. There are also 15 cabins with kitchens. Picnic tables, fire rings, and barbecues are provided. Restrooms, showers, free cable TV in RV and tent sites, and a playground are available. A minimart, ice, wood, coin laundry, meeting hall with kitchen and fireplace (seats about 40), and LP gas are also available. Modem hookups, volleyball, horseshoes, badminton, and video arcade are on-site. Leashed pets are permitted, except in the tent sites.

Reservations, fees: Reservations are recommended in the summer. The fee is $19–25 per night, $2 per person per night for more than two people. Call for cabin prices for pets. Major credit cards accepted. Open year-round.

Directions: From Eureka, drive north on U.S. 101 for 28 miles to Trinidad. Take the Trinidad exit to the stop sign at Seawood Drive. Turn left and drive a short distance under the freeway to

Patrick's Point Drive. Turn right on Patrick's Point Drive and drive about .7 mile north to the campground on the right side of the road.

Contact: Emerald Forest, 707/677-3554, fax 707/677-0963, website: www.cabinsinthered woods.com.

34 HIDDEN CREEK

Rating: 5

In Trinidad.

Map 1.1, page 67

To tell you the truth, there really isn't much hidden about this RV park, but you might be hard-pressed to find year-round Parker Creek. Regardless, it is still in a pretty location in Trinidad, with the Trinidad pier, adjacent harbor, restaurants, and beach all within a drive of just a minute or two. Some of California's best deep-sea fishing for salmon, lingcod, and rockfish is available on boats out of Trinidad Harbor, and there are annual derbies for salmon, lingcod, and halibut. Crab and albacore tuna are also caught here, and there's beachcombing for agates and driftwood on the beach to the immediate north.

Campsites, facilities: There are 56 RV sites with full or partial hookups, including cable TV, six drive-through sites, and some with permanent residents, four sites for tents, and one mobile home. Several group sites are also available. Picnic tables are provided. Patios, restrooms, showers, LP gas, fishing cleaning station, ice, and an RV dump station are available. Leashed pets are permitted.

Reservations, fees: Reservations are recommended in the summer. The fee is $14–21 per night, $2 per person per night for more than two people. Long-term rates available. Senior discount available. Open year-round.

Directions: From Eureka, drive north on U.S. 101 for 28 miles to Trinidad. Take the Trinidad exit to the stop sign. Turn right at Westhaven Drive and drive a short distance to the RV park on the left at 199 N. Westhaven.

Contact: Hidden Creek RV Park, 707/677-3775, fax 707/677-3886.

35 PANTHER FLAT

Rating: 8

On the Smith River in Six Rivers National Forest.

Map 1.2, page 68

This is an ideal alternative to the often-crowded Jedediah Smith Redwoods State Park. The park provides easy road access since it is set right along U.S. 199, the two-laner that runs beside the Smith River. This is the largest and one of the feature campgrounds in the Smith River National Recreation Area, with excellent prospects for salmon and steelhead fishing in the fall and winter respectively, and outstanding hiking and backpacking in the summer. A great nearby hike is the Stony Creek Trail, an easy walk along the North Fork Smith River; the trailhead is in nearby Gasquet on Stoney Creek Road. Redwood National Park is a short drive to the west. The Siskiyou Wilderness is a short drive to the southeast via forest roads detailed on Forest Service maps. The wild and scenic Smith River system provides swimming, sunbathing, kayaking for experts, and beautiful scenery.

Campsites, facilities: There are 39 sites for tents, trailers up to 40 feet long, and RVs up to 35 feet long. Picnic tables and fire grills are provided. Drinking water, flush toilets, and hot showers are available. A camp host is on site. Propane gas, groceries, and coin laundry are available nearby. Several campsites are wheelchair-accessible. Leashed pets are permitted.

Reservations, fees: Reservations are recommended and may be made with a $9 reservation fee at 877/444-6777 or website www.ReserveUsa.com. The fee is $15 per night, $5 fee for extra vehicles. Senior discount available. Open year-round.

Directions: From Crescent City, drive north on U.S. 101 for four miles to the junction with U.S. 199. At U.S. 199, turn east and drive 15 miles to Gasquet. From Gasquet, continue for 2.3 miles east on U.S. 199 and look for the entrance to the campground on the left side of the highway.

Contact: Smith River National Recreation Area, Six Rivers National Forest, P.O. Box 228, Gasquet, CA 95543, 707/457-3131, fax 707 457-3794.

36 GRASSY FLAT

Rating: 4

On the Smith River in Six Rivers National Forest.

Map 1.2, page 68

This is one in a series of three easy-to-reach Forest Service camps set near U.S. 199 along the beautiful Smith River. It's a classic wild river, popular in the summer with kayakers, and the steelhead come huge in the winter for the crafty few. The camp itself is set directly across from a CalTrans waste area, and if you hit it when the crews are working, it can be noisy here. Most of the time, however, it is peaceful and quiet. In the winter when the camp is closed, fishermen will often park at the piped gate, and then walk past the camp to a good steelhead spot.

Campsites, facilities: There are four walk-in tent sites and 15 sites for tents or RVs up to 30 feet long. Picnic tables and fire grills are provided. Drinking water and vault toilets are available. Propane gas and groceries are available nearby. Some facilities are wheelchair-accessible. Leashed pets are permitted.

Reservations, fees: Reservations are accepted with a $9 reservation fee at 877/444-6777 and website www.ReserveUsa.com. The fee is $10 per night, $5 for each extra vehicle. Senior discount available. Open late May through mid-September.

Directions: From Crescent City, drive north on U.S. 101 for four miles to the junction with U.S. 199, turn east on U.S. 199, and drive 15 miles to Gasquet. From Gasquet, continue east on U.S. 199 for 4.4 miles and look for the campground entrance on the right side of the road.

Contact: Smith River National Recreation Area, Six Rivers National Forest, P.O. Box 228, Gasquet, CA 95543, 707/457-3131, fax 707/457-3794.

37 PATRICK CREEK

Rating: 8

In Six Rivers National Forest.

Map 1.2, page 68

This is one of the prettiest spots along U.S. 199, where Patrick Creek enters the upper Smith River. This section of the Smith looks something like a large trout stream, rolling green past a boulder-lined shore, complete with forest canopy. There are no trout of course, but rather salmon and steelhead in the fall and winter, and only their little smolts pooling up in the summer. A big plus for this camp is its nearby access to excellent hiking in the Siskiyou Wilderness, especially the great day hike to Buck Lake. It is essential to have a map of Six Rivers National Forest, both for driving directions to the trailhead and for the hiking route. You can buy maps at the information center for the Smith River National Recreation Area on the north side of U.S. 199 in Gasquet. An option at this camp is Patrick Creek Lodge, on the opposite side of the highway from the campground, which has a fine restaurant and bar. A paved trail connects the campground to Patrick Creek Lodge.

Campsites, facilities: There are 13 sites for tents and RVs up to 35 feet long. Picnic tables and fire grills are provided. Drinking water, flush toilets, and restrooms are available. Some facilities are wheelchair-accessible. Leashed pets are permitted.

Reservations, fees: Reservations are accepted with a $9 reservation fee at 877/444-6777 and website www.ReserveUsa.com. The fee is $13 per night, $5 for each extra vehicle. Senior discount available. Open late May through mid-September.

Directions: From Crescent City, drive north on U.S. 101 for three miles to the junction with U.S. 199, turn east on U.S. 199, and drive 15 miles to Gasquet. From Gasquet, continue east on U.S. 199 for 7.5 miles and look for the campground entrance on the right side of the road.

Contact: Smith River National Recreation Area, Six Rivers National Forest, P.O. Box 228, Gasquet, CA 95543, 707/457-3131, fax 707/457-3794.

38 BIG FLAT

Rating: 7

On Hurdygurdy Creek in Six Rivers National Forest.

Map 1.2, page 68

This camp provides an ideal setting for those who know of it, which is why it gets quite a bit of use for a relatively remote camp. Set along Hurdygurdy Creek, near where the creek enters the South Fork of the Smith River, it provides nearby access to the South Kelsey Trail, an outstanding hiking route whether you are walking for a few hours or backpacking for days. In the summer, it is a good layover for rafters or kayakers paddling the South Fork of the Smith River.

Campsites, facilities: There are 28 sites for tents or RVs up to 22 feet long. Picnic tables and fire grills are provided. Vault toilets are available. There is no drinking water and you must pack out your garbage. Leashed pets are permitted.

Reservations, fees: Reservations are not accepted. The fee is $8 per night, $5 per night for each extra vehicle. Senior discount available. Open May through mid-September.

Directions: From Crescent City, drive north on U.S. 101 for four miles to the junction with U.S. 199, turn east on U.S. 199, and drive five miles to Hiouchi. Continue just past Hiouchi, turn right at South Fork Road, and cross two bridges. At the Y, turn left on South Fork Road and drive about 14 miles to Big Flat Road/County Road 405. At Big Flat Road, turn left and drive one-quarter mile to the campground entrance road (Forest Road 15N59) on the left. Turn left and drive a short distance to the camp on the left.

Contact: Smith River National Recreation Area, Six Rivers National Forest, P.O. Box 228, Gasquet, CA 95543, 707/457-3131, fax 707/457-3794.

39 CLAM BEACH COUNTY PARK

Rating: 7

Near McKinleyville.

Map 1.3, page 69

Here awaits a beach that seems to stretch on forever, one of the great places to bring a lover, dog, children, or, hey, all three. While the campsites are a bit exposed, making winds out of the north a problem in the spring, the direct beach access largely makes up for it. The park gets its name from the good clamming that is available, but you must come equipped with a clam gun or special clam shovel, and then be out when minus low tides arrive at daybreak. Most people just enjoy playing tag with the waves, taking long romantic walks, or throwing sticks for the dog.

Campsites, facilities: There are 12 sites for tents and RV parking is allowed on the paved lot. No hookups. Picnic tables and fire rings are provided. Drinking water and vault toilets are available. Propane gas, grocery store, and a coin laundry are available in McKinleyville. Leashed pets are permitted.

Reservations, fees: Reservations are not accepted. The fee is $8 per night per vehicle, $1 per pet per night. Open year-round.

Directions: From Eureka, drive north on U.S. 101 to McKinleyville. Just past McKinleyville, turn west at the sign for Clam Beach and drive two blocks to the campground, which is adjacent to Little River State Beach.

Contact: Humboldt County Parks, 707/445-7652.

40 MAD RIVER RAPIDS RV PARK

Rating: 7

In Arcata.

Map 1.3, page 69

This camp is near the farmlands on the outskirts of town, in a pastoral, quiet setting. There is a great bike ride nearby on a trail routed along the Mad River, and it is also excellent for taking a dog for a walk. Nearby Arcata is a unique town, a bit of the old and a bit of the new, and the Arcata Marsh at the north end of Humboldt Bay provides a scenic and easy bicycle trip, as well as an excellent destination for hiking, sight-seeing, and bird-watching.

Campsites, facilities: There are 92 RV sites with full hookups, including 50 long-term rentals and 40 drive-through sites. Picnic tables are provided. Fire grills are provided at two sites. Patios, restrooms, showers, an RV dump station, recreation room, tennis courts, fitness room, playground, basketball courts, horseshoe pits, swimming pool, spa, cable TV, VCR rentals, restaurant, grocery store, and coin laundry are available. Some facilities are wheelchair-accessible. Leashed pets are permitted.

Reservations, fees: Reservations are accepted. The fee is $26–33 per night. Major credit cards accepted. Senior discount available. Open year-round.

Directions: From the junction of U.S. 101 and Highway 299 in Arcata, drive a quarter mile north on U.S. 101 to the Guintoli Lane exit. At the exit, turn left (west) on Janes Road and drive two blocks west to the park on the left.

Contact: Mad River Rapids RV Park, 800/822-7776 or 707/822-7275, fax 707/822-7286, website: www.madriverrv.com.

41 WIDOW WHITE CREEK RV PARK

Rating: 5

In McKinleyville.

Map 1.3, page 69

This privately operated park provides extremely

easy access from the highway. Nearby recreation options include the Mad River, where there is a nice picnic site near the hatchery, productive steelhead fishing in the winter, and good perch fishing in the surf where the Mad River enters the ocean. Ocean fishing for salmon is nearby in the summer. Get this—nearby are the "world's largest totem poles." They'll tell you all about it.

Campsites, facilities: There are 40 RV sites, including 30 long-term rentals and some drive-through sites, with full hookups and a separate area for tents. Picnic tables are provided. Restrooms, showers, playground, an RV dump station, and a coin laundry are available. Some facilities are wheelchair-accessible. Leashed pets are permitted.

Reservations, fees: Reservations are accepted. The fee is $18–22 per night. Monthly rates available. Open year-round.

Directions: From Eureka, drive north on U.S. 101 and continue for 4.5 miles past the junction with Highway 299 to the Murray Road exit. Take the exit, turn right (east) on Murray Road, and drive one-half block to the park on the left.

Contact: Widow White Creek RV Park, 707/839-1137.

42 EUREKA KOA

Rating: 2

In Eureka.

Map 1.3, page 69

This is a year-round KOA camp for U.S. 101 cruisers looking for a layover spot in Eureka. A bonus here is a few of those little KOA Kamping Kabins, the log-style jobs that win on cuteness alone. The closest significant recreation option is the Arcata Marsh on Humboldt Bay, a richly diverse spot with good trails for biking and hiking or just parking and looking at the water. Another option is excellent salmon fishing in June, July, and August.

Campsites, facilities: There are eight bike-in/

hike-in sites, 26 tent sites, and 140 RV sites (42 drive-through with full hookups and some partial hookups). Group sites, 10 camping cabins, and two cottages are available. Picnic tables and fire pits are provided. Drinking water, flush toilets, showers, playground, recreation room, heated swimming pool, two hot tubs, grocery store, coin laundry, RV dump station, LP gas, ice, wood, fax machine, and computer kiosks are available. Some facilities are wheelchair-accessible. Leashed pets are permitted.

Reservations, fees: Reservations are accepted at 800/562-3136. The fee is $20–28 per night, $3 per person for more than two people. Cabins are $40 per night for four people, cottages are $120 per night for four people. Major credit cards accepted. Open year-round.

Directions: From Eureka, drive north on U.S. 101 for four miles to KOA Drive (well signed on east side of highway). Turn right on KOA Drive and drive to 4050 N. U.S. 101.

Contact: Eureka KOA, 707/822-4243, fax 707/822-0126, website: www.koa.com.

43 SAMOA BOAT LAUNCH COUNTY PARK

Rating: 7

On Humboldt Bay.

Map 1.3, page 69

The nearby vicinity of the boat ramp, with access to Humboldt Bay and the Pacific Ocean, makes this a star attraction for campers towing their fishing boats. At the park you get good beachcombing and clamming at low tides and a chance to see a huge variety of seabirds, highlighted by egrets and herons. There's a reason: directly across the bay is the Humboldt Bay National Wildlife Refuge. This park is set near the famed all-you-can-eat, logger-style Samoa Cookhouse.

Campsites, facilities: There are 26 sites for RVs or tents. Picnic tables and fire grills are provided. Drinking water and flush toilets are available. A boat ramp, grocery store, LP gas, and a coin laundry are available in Eureka (about five miles away). Leashed pets are permitted.

Reservations, fees: Reservations are not accepted. The fee is $12 per night per vehicle, $1 per pet per night. Open year-round.

Directions: From U.S. 101 in Eureka, turn west on Highway 255 and drive two miles until it dead-ends at New Navy Base Road. At New Navy Base Road, turn left and drive five miles to the end of the Samoa Peninsula and the campground entrance.

Contact: Humboldt County Parks, 707/445-7652.

44 E-Z LANDING RV PARK AND MARINA

Rating: 7

On Humboldt Bay.
Map 1.3, page 69

This is a good base camp for salmon trips in July and August when big schools of king salmon often teem just west of the entrance of Humboldt Bay. A nearby boat ramp with access to Humboldt Bay has been in disrepair and was scheduled for repair and a return to operation by 2003; call first if you plan on launching a boat here. It's not the prettiest camp in the world, with quite a bit of asphalt, but most people use this camp as a simple parking spot for sleeping and getting down to the business of the day: fishing. This spot is ideal for ocean fishing, clamming, beachcombing, and boating.

Campsites, facilities: There are 45 RV sites with full hookups, including about half long-term and 20 drive-through sites. Patios, flush toilets, showers, modem hookups, marine gas, ice, coin laundry, party boat for fishing, bait, and tackle are available. Some facilities are wheelchair-accessible. Leashed pets are permitted.

Reservations, fees: Reservations are accepted. The fee is $19 per night. Major credit cards accepted. Open year-round.

Directions: From Eureka, drive 3.5 miles south on U.S. 101 to King Salmon Avenue. Turn

west (right) on King Salmon Avenue (it becomes Buhne Drive) and drive for a half mile to where the road turns. Turn left (south) on Buhne Drive and go a half mile to the park on the left (1875 Buhne Drive).

Contact: E-Z Landing RV Park and Marina, 707/442-1118, fax 707/442-1999.

45 JOHNNY'S MARINA AND RV PARK

Rating: 5

On Humboldt Bay.
Map 1.3, page 69

This is a good base camp for salmon fishing during the peak season—always call, since the season changes each year as set by the Department of Fish and Game. Mooring for private boats is available, a nice plus for campers trailering boats. Other recreation activities include beachcombing, clamming, and perch fishing from shore. The owners have run this place for more than 50 years.

Campsites, facilities: There are 53 RV sites with full hookups, including several long-term rentals and four drive-through sites. Patios, restrooms, showers, and an RV dump station are provided. A coin laundry and boat dock are available. Leashed pets are permitted.

Reservations, fees: Reservations are accepted. The fee is $20 per night. Open year-round.

Directions: From Eureka, drive 3.5 miles south on U.S. 101 to King Salmon Avenue. Turn west (right) on King Salmon Avenue (it becomes Buhne Drive). Continue about a half mile to the park on the left (1821 Buhne Drive).

Contact: Johnny's Marina and RV Park, 707/442-2284, fax 707/443-4608.

46 STAFFORD RV PARK

Rating: 6

Near Scotia.
Map 1.3, page 69

This is a privately operated park for RVs that

provides several side-trip options: a tour of the giant sawmill in Scotia, a tour of giant redwoods on the Avenue of the Giants, access to the nearby Eel River, and best of all, the nearby Redwood National Park. One of the better park information centers in California is here, with maps and information about hikes, bike rides, and driving tours.

Campsites, facilities: There are 50 RV sites, including many drive-through sites, with full or partial hookups, 30 tent sites, group sites, and four sleeping cabins. Picnic tables and fire grills are provided. Drinking water, flush toilets, showers, and a coin laundry are available. Some facilities are wheelchair-accessible. Leashed pets are permitted.

Reservations, fees: Reservations are accepted. The fee is $10–20 per night. Major credit cards accepted in summer only. Monthly rates available. Open year-round, with a reduced number of sites in the winter.

Directions: From Eureka, drive south on U.S. 101 to Scotia. At Scotia, continue south for three miles to Stafford Road. Turn right (west) on Stafford Road and at the first stop sign, turn left under the overpass, and drive a short distance to North Road. At North Road, turn right and drive a quarter mile to the park on the right (385 North Road).

Contact: Stafford RV Park, 707/764-3416.

47 MATTOLE

Rating: 8

On the Pacific Ocean.

Map 1.3, page 69

This is a little-known camp set at the mouth of the Mattole River, right where it pours into the Pacific Ocean. It is beautiful and isolated. An outstanding hike leads to the Punta Gorda Lighthouse. Hike from the campground to the ocean and head south. It's a level walk, and at low tide, there's a chance to observe tidepool life. Perch fishing is good where the Mattole flows into the ocean, best during low tides. In

the winter, the Mattole often provides excellent steelhead fishing. Check the Department of Fish and Game regulations for closed areas. Be sure to have a full tank on the way out— the nearest gas station is quite distant.

Campsites, facilities: There are 14 sites for tents or RVs up to 15 feet long. Picnic tables and fire rings are provided. Pit toilets are available. No drinking water is available. Leashed pets are permitted.

Reservations, fees: Reservations are not accepted. The fee is $5 per night suggested donation. Open year-round.

Directions: From U.S. 101 north of Garberville, take the South Fork-Honeydew exit and drive west to Honeydew. At Honeydew, turn right on Mattole Road and drive toward Petrolia. At the second bridge over the Mattole River, one mile before Petrolia, turn west on Lighthouse Road and drive five miles to the campground at the end of the road.

Contact: Bureau of Land Management, Arcata Field Office, 707/825-2300, fax 707/825-2301.

48 A. W. WAY COUNTY PARK

Rating: 8

On the Mattole River.

Map 1.3, page 69

This secluded camp provides a home for visitors to the "Lost Coast," the beautiful coastal stretch of California far from any semblance of urban life. The highlight here is the Mattole River, a great steelhead stream when flows are suitable between January and mid-March. Nearby is excellent hiking in the King Range National Conservation Area. For the great hike out to the abandoned Punta Gorda Lighthouse, drive to the trailhead on the left side of Lighthouse Road (see the Mattole listing). This area is typically bombarded with monsoon-level rains in winter.

Campsites, facilities: There are 30 sites for tents or RVs. Picnic tables and fire grills are provided. Drinking water, flush toilets, and showers are available. A grocery store, coin laundry, and propane gas are available nearby. Leashed pets are permitted.

Reservations, fees: Reservations are not accepted. The fee is $12 per night per vehicle, $1 per pet. Open year-round.

Directions: From Garberville, drive north on U.S. 101 to the South Fork-Honeydew exit. Turn west on South Fork-Honeydew Road and drive 31 miles (the road alternates between pavement, gravel, dirt, then pavement again, steep and curvy) to the park entrance on the left side of the road. The park is 7.5 miles south of the town of Petrolia.

Contact: Humboldt County Parks, 707/445-7652.

49 SHELTER COVE CAMPGROUND & DELI

Rating: 9

Overlooking the Pacific Ocean.

Map 1.3, page 69

This is a prime oceanside spot to set up a base camp for deep-sea fishing, whale-watching, tidepool gazing, beachcombing, and hiking. A six-lane boat ramp makes it perfect for campers who have trailered boats and don't mind the long drive. Reservations are strongly advised here. The park's backdrop is the King Range National Conservation Area, offering spectacular views. The deli is well known for its fish-and-chips. The salmon and halibut fishing is quite good here in the summer season; always call first for current regulations and seasons, which change every year. Crabbing is good in December, clamming best during winter's low tides, and hiking in the King Mountain Range during the summer. There is heavy rain in winter. On occasional Saturday nights from Memorial Day through Labor Day, there are barbecues with live entertainment, weather permitting. Note that two miles north is one of the only black sand beaches in the continental United States.

Campsites, facilities: There are 103 sites, many with full hookups, for tents or RVs, including 15 drive-through sites. These include some long-term renters. Picnic tables and fire rings are provided. Restrooms, showers, an RV dump station, a coin laundry, grocery store, deli, LP gas, ice, and RV supplies are available. A boat ramp and marina is across the street. Leashed pets are permitted.

Reservations, fees: Reservations are recommended. The fee is $16–27 per night, $3 per person per night for more than two people. Major credit cards accepted. Open year-round.

Directions: From Eureka, drive 60 miles south on U.S. 101 to the Redway/Shelter Cove exit. Take that exit and drive 2.5 miles north on Redwood Road to Briceland-Shelter Cove Road. Turn right (west) and drive 24 miles (following the truck/RV route signs) to Upper Pacific Drive. Turn left (south) on Upper Pacific Drive and proceed (it becomes Machi Road) a half mile to the park on the right.

Contact: Shelter Cove Campground & Deli, 707/986-7474, fax 707/986-7101.

50 HORSE MOUNTAIN

Rating: 6

In the King Range.

Map 1.3, page 69

Few people know of this spot. The campground is set along the northwest flank of Horse Mountain. A primitive road (Saddle Mountain Road) leads west from the camp and then goes left at the Y, up to Horse Mountain (1,929 feet), which offers spectacular ocean and coastal views on clear days. If you turn right at the Y, the road leads to the trailhead for the King Crest Trail near Saddle Mountain (3,290 feet). This hike is an ambitious climb to King Peak (4,087 feet), rewarding hikers with a fantastic panorama, including Mt. Lassen poking above the Yolla Bolly Wilderness to the east.

Campsites, facilities: There are nine sites for tents or RVs up to 20 feet long. Picnic tables and fire rings are provided. Pit toilets are available. No drinking water is available. Leashed pets are permitted.

Reservations, fees: Reservations are not accepted. The fee is $5 per night. Senior discount available. Open year-round.

Directions: From Eureka, drive 60 miles south on U.S. 101. Take the Redway/Shelter Cove exit onto Redwood Drive in the town of Redway. Look on the right for the King Range Conservation Area sign. Turn right on Briceland-Thorne Road (which will become Shelter Cove Road) and drive 17 miles to King Peak Road (Horse Mountain). Turn right and continue six miles to the campground on the right.

Contact: Bureau of Land Management, Arcata Field Office, 707/825-2300, fax 707/825-2301.

51 TOLKAN

Rating: 6

In the King Range.
Map 1.3, page 69

This remote camp is set at 1,840 feet, a short drive south of Horse Mountain. (For nearby side-trip options, see the entry for Horse Mountain.)

Campsites, facilities: There are nine sites for tents or RVs up to 20 feet long. Picnic tables and fire rings are provided. Vault toilets are available. No drinking water is available. Some facilities are wheelchair-accessible. Leashed pets are permitted.

Reservations, fees: Reservations are not accepted. The fee is $8 per night. Senior discount available. Open year-round.

Directions: From Eureka, drive 60 miles south on U.S. 101 to the Redway exit. Take the Redway/Shelter Cove exit onto Redwood Drive into the town of Redway. Look on the right for the King Range Conservation Area sign, turn right on Briceland-Thorne Road (which will become Shelter Cove Road), and drive 17 miles to Kings Peak (Horse Mountain) Road. Turn right on Kings Peak Road and continue 3.5 miles to the campground on the right.

Contact: Bureau of Land Management, Arcata Field Office, 707/825-2300, fax 707/825-2301.

52 VAN DUZEN COUNTY PARK

Rating: 6

On the Van Duzen River.
Map 1.4, page 70

This campground is set at the headwaters of the Van Duzen River, one of the Eel River's major tributaries. The river is subject to tremendous fluctuations in flows and height, so low in the fall that it is often temporarily closed to fishing by the Department of Fish and Game, so high in the winter that only fools would stick their toes in. For a short period in late spring, it provides a benign run for rafting and canoeing, putting in at Grizzly Creek and taking out at Van Duzen. In October, you'll find an excellent salmon fishing spot where the Van Duzen enters the Eel.

Campsites, facilities: There are 30 sites for tents or RVs. Picnic tables and fire grills are provided. Drinking water, flush toilets, and showers are available. A grocery store and coin laundry are available nearby. Some facilities are wheelchair-accessible. Leashed pets are permitted.

Reservations, fees: Reservations are not accepted. The fee is $12 per night per vehicle, $1 per pet per night. Open year-round.

Directions: From Eureka, drive south on U.S. 101 to the junction of Highway 36 at Alton. Turn east on Highway 36 and drive 12 miles to the campground.

Contact: Humboldt County Parks, 707/445-7652.

53 GRIZZLY CREEK REDWOODS STATE PARK

Rating: 7

Near Bridgeville.
Map 1.4, page 70

Most summer vacationers hit the campgrounds

on the Redwood Highway, that is, U.S. 101. However, this camp is just far enough off the beaten path to provide some semblance of seclusion. It is set in redwoods, quite beautiful, with fair hiking and good access to the adjacent Van Duzen River. The park encompasses only a few acres, yet it is very quiet and private. There are 4.5 miles of hiking trails, a visitor center with exhibits, and a bookstore. The Cheatham Grove in this park is an exceptional stand of coast redwoods. In the winter one of the better holes for steelhead fishing is accessible here. Nearby attractions include the Victorian village of Ferndale and Fort Humboldt to the north, Humboldt Redwoods State Park to the south, and Ruth Lake to the more distant east.

Campsites, facilities: There are 18 tent sites and 12 sites for RVs up to 30 feet long or trailers up to 18 feet. Picnic tables and fire grills are provided. Drinking water, flush toilets, and showers are available. A grocery store is available within 3.5 miles. Some facilities are wheelchair-accessible. Leashed pets are permitted in campground, but not on trails or day-use beach area.

Reservations, fees: Reservations are accepted with a $7.50 reservation fee at 800/444-PARK (800/444-7275) and website www.Reserve America.com. The fee is $12 per night. Senior discount available. Open year-round.

Directions: From Eureka, drive south on U.S. 101 to the junction of Highway 36 at Alton. Turn east on Highway 36 and drive about 17 miles to the campground on the right.

Contact: Grizzly Creek Redwoods State Park, 707/777-3683, fax 707/777-3159.

54 ALBEE CREEK

Rating: 8

In Humboldt Redwoods State Park.

Map 1.4, page 70

Humboldt Redwoods State Park is a massive sprawl of forest that is known for some unusual giant trees in the Federation Grove and Big Tree Area. The park covers 52,000 acres, including more than 7,000 acres of old-growth coast redwoods. It has 100 miles of hiking trails, many excellent, both short and long. The camp is set in a redwood grove, and the smell of these trees has a special magic. Nearby Albee Creek, a benign trickle most of the year, can flood in the winter after heavy rains. A visitor center with exhibits, season interpretive programs, campfire talks, nature walks, and junior ranger programs are available.

Campsites, facilities: There are 39 sites for tents and 33 sites for RVs up to 31 feet long and trailers up to 21 feet long. Picnic tables, fire grills, and food lockers are provided. Drinking water, flush toilets, and showers are available. Leashed pets are permitted.

Reservations, fees: Reservations are accepted with a $7.50 reservation fee at 800/444-PARK (800/444-7275) and website www.Reserve America.com. The fee is $12 per night. Senior discount available. Open May through September.

Directions: From Eureka, drive south on U.S. 101 about 11 miles to the Honeydew exit (if you reach Weott, you have gone two miles too far). At Mattole Road, turn west and drive five miles to the campground on the right.

Contact: Humboldt Redwoods State Park, 707/946-2409, fax 707/946-2326.

55 BURLINGTON

Rating: 7

In Humboldt Redwoods State Park.

Map 1.4, page 70

This camp is one of the centerpieces of Humboldt Redwoods State Park. This park is California's largest redwood state park. It includes the Rockefeller Forest, the largest remaining contiguous old-growth coast redwood forest in the world. The trees here are thousands of years old and have never been logged; they are as pristine now as 200 years ago. This camp is often at capacity during the tourist months. You get shady campsites with big redwood stumps that kids can play on. There's good hiking on trails routed through the redwoods, and in winter, steelhead fishing is often good on the nearby Eel River. The park has 100 miles of trails, but it is the little half-mile Founders Grove Nature Trail that has the quickest payoff and requires the least effort. The average rainfall here is 65 inches per year, with most occurring between October and May. Morning and evening fog in the summer keeps the temperature cool in the river basin.

Campsites, facilities: There are 57 sites for tents or RVs up to 33 feet long or trailers up to 24 feet. Picnic tables, fire grills, and food lockers are provided. Drinking water, flush toilets, and showers are available. Some facilities are wheelchair-accessible. Leashed pets are permitted.

Reservations, fees: Reservations are accepted with a $7.50 reservation fee at 800/444-PARK (800/444-7275) and website www.Reserve America.com. The fee is $12 per night. Senior discount available. Open year-round.

Directions: From Eureka, drive south on U.S. 101 for 45 miles to the Weott/Newton Road exit. Turn right on Newton Road and continue to the T junction where Newton Road meets the Avenue of the Giants. Turn left on the Avenue of the Giants and drive two miles to the campground entrance on the left.

Contact: Humboldt Redwoods State Park, 707/946-2409, fax 707/946-2326.

56 HIDDEN SPRINGS

Rating: 7

In Humboldt Redwoods State Park.

Map 1.4, page 70

This camp gets heavy use from May through September, but the campsites have been situated in a way that offers relative seclusion. Side trips include good hiking on trails routed through redwoods and a touring drive on Avenue of the Giants. The park has more than 100 miles of hiking trails, many of them amid spectacular giant redwoods, including the Bull Creek Flats Trail and Founders Grove Nature Trail. Bears are occasionally spotted by mountain bikers on rides out to the park's outskirts. In winter, nearby High Rock on the Eel River is one of the better shoreline fishing spots for steelhead. (For more information on Humboldt Redwoods, see notes for Albee Creek and Burlington campgrounds.)

Campsites, facilities: There are 154 sites for tents or RVs up to 33 feet long or trailers up to 24 feet. Picnic tables, fire grills, and food lockers are provided. Drinking water, flush toilets, and showers are available. A grocery store and coin laundry are available within one mile in Myers Flat. Leashed pets are permitted.

Reservations, fees: Reservations are accepted with a $7.50 reservation fee at 800/444-PARK (800/444-7275) and website www.Reserve America.com. The fee is $12 per night. Senior discount available. Open May through September.

Directions: From Eureka, drive south 50 miles on U.S. 101 to the Myers Flat/Avenue of the Giants exit. Continue south and drive less than a mile to the campground entrance on the left.

Contact: Humboldt Redwoods State Park, 707/946-2409, fax 707/946-2326.

57 GIANT REDWOODS RV AND CAMP

Rating: 8

On the Eel River.

Map 1.4, page 70

This privately operated park is set in a grove of redwoods and covers 23 acres, much of it fronting the Eel River. Trip options include the scenic drive on Avenue of the Giants.

Campsites, facilities: There are 26 tent sites and 57 RV sites (34 drive-through), many with full or partial hookups. Picnic tables and fire rings are provided. Restrooms, showers, modem hookups, a store, ice, coin laundry, playground, and a recreation room are available. Limited facilities in winter. Pets are welcome with a dog "freedom area" available at the river bar.

Reservations, fees: Reservations are recommended in the summer. The fee is $20–30 per night, $2.50 per person per night for more than two people, $2 per pet per night. Seventh night free. Major credit cards accepted. Senior discount available. Open year-round.

Directions: From Eureka, drive south 50 miles on U.S. 101 to the Myers Flat/Avenue of the Giants exit. Turn right on Avenue of the Giants and make a quick left onto Myers Avenue. Drive a quarter mile on Myers Avenue to the campground entrance.

Contact: Giant Redwoods RV and Camp, 707/943-3198, fax 707/943-3359, website: www .giantredwoodsrvcamp.com.

58 DEAN CREEK RESORT

Rating: 7

On the South Fork of the Eel River.
Map 1.4, page 70

This year-round RV park is set on the South Fork of the Eel River. This is a very family-oriented resort. In the summer, it makes a good base camp for a redwood park adventure, with Humboldt Redwoods State Park (well north of here) providing 100 miles of hiking trails, many routed through awesome stands of giant trees. In the winter heavy rains feed the South Fork Eel, inspiring steelhead upstream on their annual winter journey. Fishing is good in this area, best by shore at nearby High Rock. Bank access is good at several other spots, particularly upstream near Benbow and in Cooks Valley. An excellent side trip is to drive three miles south to the Avenue of the Giants, a tour through giant redwood trees. The campground also offers volleyball, shuffleboard, badminton, and horseshoes. You get the idea.

Campsites, facilities: There are 64 sites with full or partial hookups for RVs or tents, 12 drive-through sites, and an 11-unit motel. Pic-

nic tables and fire grills are provided. Restrooms, showers, a recreation room, a coin laundry, store, RV supplies, wood, ice, giant spa, sauna, pool (heated only in summer), RV dump station, and a playground are available. Minigolf is available on site. Some facilities are wheelchair-accessible. Leashed pets are permitted.

Reservations, fees: Reservations are recommended in the summer and may be made at 877/923-2555. The fee is $25–33 per night, $3.50 per person per night for more than two people, $1.50 per pet, $1.50 per extra vehicle per night for more than one vehicle. Major credit cards accepted. Open year-round.

Directions: From Eureka, drive 60 miles south on U.S. 101 to the Redwood Drive exit. Exit onto Redwood Drive and continue about one-half block to the campground entrance on the right.

Contact: Dean Creek Resort, 707/923-2555, fax 707/923-2547, website: www. deancreek resort.com.

59 BENBOW LAKE STATE RECREATION AREA

Rating: 7

On the Eel River.
Map 1.4, page 70

This camp is set along the South Fork of the Eel River, with easy access from U.S. 101. It gets heavy use in the summer. In theory, Benbow Lake is created each summer when the river is dammed on a temporary basis, creating a 1,000-acre lake for swimming and light boating. This seasonal dam is projected to be installed in mid-June and kept in place until mid-September. However, there is no guarantee this will occur. There was no lake in 2000 or 2002 because of dam repairs and ensuring downstream passage of steelhead smolts. If you're making a vacation planned around lake recreation, always call first. In the winter, this stretch of river can be quite good for steelhead fishing.

Campsites, facilities: There are 77 sites for tents or RVs up to 30 feet long; two sites have full hookups. Picnic tables, food lockers, and fire grills are provided. Drinking water, flush toilets, and coin-operated showers are available. A boat ramp (no motors) and boat rentals are available nearby. There is an RV dump station at the park entrance. Supplies and a coin laundry are available in Garberville. Leashed pets are permitted at campsites only.

Reservations, fees: Reservations are accepted with a $7.50 reservation fee at 800/444-PARK (800/444-7275) and website www.Reserve America.com. The fee is $12–17 per night. Senior discount available. Open April through October, weather permitting.

Directions: From the junction of U.S. 101 and Highway 1 in Leggett, drive north on U.S. 101 past Richardson Grove State Park to the Benbow exit (two miles south of Garberville). Take that exit and drive 2.7 miles to the park entrance.

Contact: Benbow Lake State Recreation Area, 707/923-3238.

60 BENBOW VALLEY RV RESORT & GOLF COURSE

Rating: 7

On the Eel River.

Map 1.4, page 70

This is an RV park set along U.S. 101 and the South Fork Eel River, with both a pretty nine-hole regulation golf course and little Benbow Lake providing nearby recreation. It takes on a dramatically different character in the winter, when the highway is largely abandoned, the river comes up, and steelhead migrate upstream to the stretch of water here. Cooks Valley and Benbow provide good shore fishing access. Note that fishing restrictions for steelhead are extremely severe and subject to constant change; always check with DFG before fishing for steelhead. (See the note on Benbow Lake State Recreation Area on the status of Benbow Lake.)

Campsites, facilities: There are 112 RV sites (60 drive-through) with full hookups, including three "VIP" sites, plus cottage and RV cabin rentals. Picnic tables are provided. Cable TV, restrooms, showers, coin laundry, grocery store, snack bar, playground, recreation room, heated swimming pool, whirlpool, RV supplies, and a nine-hole golf course are available. A boat dock and boat rentals (in summer) are available within 100 feet at Benbow Lake. Leashed pets are permitted. A doggy playground and pet wash are available.

Reservations, fees: Reservations are accepted. The fee is $29–45 per night, $2.50 per person per night for more than two people, $2 per pet per night. Major credit cards accepted. Open February to December.

Directions: From the junction of U.S. 101 and Highway 1 in Leggett, drive north on U.S. 101 past Richardson Grove State Park to the Benbow exit (two miles south of Garberville). Take that exit and turn north on Benbow Drive and drive a short distance to the campground.

Contact: Benbow Valley RV Resort & Golf Course, 707/923-2777, fax 707/923-2821, website: www.benbowrv.com.

61 MADRONE AND HUCKLEBERRY

Rating: 8

In Richardson Grove State Park.

Map 1.4, page 70

The highway cuts a swath right through Richardson Grove State Park, and everyone slows to gawk at the tallest trees in the world, one of the most impressive groves of redwoods you can drive through in California. To explore further, there are several campgrounds available at the park, as well as a network of outstanding hiking trails. The best of these are the short Redwood Exhibit Trail, Settlers Loop, and Toumey Trail. The park is one of the prettiest and most popular state parks, making reservations a necessity from Memorial Day through Labor Day weekend. When arriving from points south on U.S. 101, this is the first park in the Redwood Empire where you will encounter significant old-growth redwood. There are nine miles of hiking trails, fishing in the winter for steelhead, and several trees of significant note. These include the ninth-tallest coast redwood, results of a tree ring study conducted on fallen trees in 1933, and a walk-through tree.

Campsites, facilities: At Madrone Camp, there are 40 sites for tents or RVs up to 30 feet long. At Huckleberry, there are 36 sites for tents or RVs up to 30 feet long. Picnic tables, food lockers, and fire grills are provided. Drinking water, flush toilets, and coin-operated showers are available. A minimart and RV dump station (three miles away) are available nearby. Some facilities are wheelchair-accessible. Leashed pets are permitted at campsites only.

Reservations, fees: Reservations are accepted with a $7.50 reservation fee at 800/444-PARK (800/444-7275) and website www.Reserve America.com. The fee is $12 per night. Senior discount available. Open year-round, but subject to occasional winter closures.

Directions: From the junction of U.S. 101 and Highway 1 in Leggett, drive north on U.S. 101 for 20 miles (past Piercy) to the park entrance along the west side of the road (note: Garberville is nine miles north on U.S. 101).

Contact: Richardson Grove State Park, 707/247-3318.

62 OAK FLAT

Rating: 8

In Richardson Grove State Park.
Map 1.4, page 70
Oak Flat is on the eastern side of the Eel River in the shade of forest and provides easy access to the river. The campground is open only in the summer. (For side-trip information, see the entries for Madrone and Huckleberry.)

Campsites, facilities: There are 100 sites for tents or RVs up to 24 feet long and trailers up to 21 feet long. Picnic tables, food lockers, and

fire grills are provided. Drinking water, flush toilets, and coin-operated showers are available. A grocery store and propane gas are available nearby. Leashed pets are permitted.

Reservations, fees: Reservations are accepted with a $7.50 reservation fee at 800/444-PARK (800/444-7275) and website www.Reserve America.com. The fee is $12 per night. Senior discount available. Open mid-June to mid-September.

Directions: From the junction of U.S. 101 and Highway 1 in Leggett, drive north on U.S. 101 for 20 miles (past Piercy) to the park entrance on the west side of the road (nine miles south of Garberville).

Contact: Richardson Grove State Park, 707/247-3318.

63 RICHARDSON GROVE CAMPGROUND & RV PARK

Rating: 7

On the Eel River.
Map 1.4, page 70
This private camp provides a nearby alternative to Richardson Grove State Park, complete with cabin rentals. The state park, with its grove of giant redwoods and excellent hiking, is the primary attraction. The park is family-oriented, with volleyball and basketball courts and horseshoe pits. The adjacent South Fork Eel River may look like a trickle in the summer, but there are some good swimming holes. It also provides good steelhead fishing in January and February, with especially good shore fishing access here as well as to the south in Cooks Valley (check DFG regulations before fishing). This campground is owned and operated by the Northern California/Nevada District Assemblies of God. Because of their nonprofit status, several cabins and a dorm are no longer available for rent.

Campsites, facilities: There are 91 sites for tents or RVs (28 drive-through), many with full or partial hookups, and two log cabins.

Picnic tables and fire rings are provided. Restrooms, showers, RV dump station, playground, coin laundry, grocery store, LP gas, and ice are available. Leashed pets are permitted.

Reservations, fees: Reservations are recommended. The fee is $15–20 per night for individual sites. Group rates available. Major credit cards accepted. Open year-round.

Directions: From the junction of U.S. 101 and Highway 1 in Leggett, drive north on U.S. 101 (one mile before reaching Richardson Grove State Park) to the camp entrance on the west side (left) of the road.

Contact: Richardson Grove Campground, 707/247-3380, fax 707/247-9806, website: www.redwoodfamilycamp.com.

64 NADELOS AND WAILAKI

Rating: 7

In the King Range.

Map 1.5, page 71

Nadelos and Wailaki campgrounds are set a short distance apart at 1,840 feet near the South Fork Bear Creek at the southern end of the King Range National Conservation Area. This provides access to a rare geographic dynamic, where mountains and coast adjoin. Nearby Chemise Mountain, elevation 2,598 feet, is one of the highest points in California within two miles of the sea, and it provides a dramatic lookout on clear days.

Campsites, facilities: There are eight single tent sites at Nadelos. There are 13 sites for tents and RVs at Wailaki. Picnic tables and fire grills are provided. Drinking water and vault toilets are available. Some facilities are wheelchair-accessible. Leashed pets are permitted.

Reservations, fees: Reservations are not accepted. The fee is $8 per night. Senior discount available. Open year-round.

Directions: From U.S. 101 north of Garberville, take the Redway exit, turn west on Shelter Cove Road, and drive 17 miles to Chemise Mountain Road. Turn left on Chemise Moun-

tain Road and drive one mile to Nadelos Campground on the right. To reach Wailaki Campground from Nadelos, continue .4 miles to the camp on the right.

Contact: Bureau of Land Management, Arcata Field Office, 707/825-2300, fax 707/825-2301, website: www.ca.blm.gov/arcata.

65 SINKYONE WILDERNESS

Rating:10

In Sinkyone Wilderness State Park.

Map 1.5, page 71

This is a great jump-off point for a backpacking trip in the Sinkyone Wilderness on the Lost Coast, one of the few wilderness areas where a trip can be made any month of the year. The terrain is primitive, steep, and often wet, but it provides a rare coastal wilderness experience. Starting at the northern trailhead at Orchard Camp, or the southern trailhead at the Usal Beach campground, it's an ambitious weekend tromp of 17 miles. This is a unique 7,367-acre park that is named after the Sinkyone Indians, who once lived in this area. It is called the Lost Coast because there are no highways that provide direct access. Regardless, it has become surprisingly popular for backpackers on the Coast Trail. Annual rainfall is up to 80 inches per year, mostly between November and May. Summer temperatures range 45–75°F, with morning and evening fog common.

Campsites, facilities: At Usal Beach, there are 35 tent sites. Picnic tables and fire rings are provided. Pit toilets are provided. No drinking water is available. Between Bear Harbor and Jones Beach there are 23 primitive tent sites with picnic tables, fire rings, and pit toilets. Drinking water is available at the Needle Rock Visitor Center (see directions below). Garbage service is provided at Usal Beach only; otherwise garbage must be packed out. Leashed pets are permitted at campsites only.

Reservations, fees: Reservations are not accepted.

The fee is $7 per night. Senior discount available. Open year-round, weather permitting.

Directions: To reach the northern boundary of the Sinkyone Wilderness from U.S. 101 north of Garberville, take the Redway exit, turn west on Briceland Road, and drive 17 miles to Whitethorn. From Whitethorn continue six more miles to the four-corners fork. Drive straight ahead to the middle left fork and continue 3.5 miles on a dirt road to the Needle Rock Ranger Station.

To reach the southern boundary of the Sinkyone Wilderness from Leggett on U.S. 101, turn southwest on Highway 1 (toward Fort Bragg) and drive 14.66 miles to Mile Marker 90.88 at County Road 431. Turn right on County Road 431 (a dirt road, often unsigned) and drive six miles to the Usal Beach Campground. Note: the roads can be quite rough. Trailers and RVs are not recommended.

Contact: Sinkyone Wilderness State Park, 707/986-7711 or 707/247-3318, fax 707/247-3300.

66 REDWOODS RIVER RESORT

Rating: 8

On the Eel River.

Map 1.5, page 71

This resort is situated in a 21-acre grove of redwoods on U.S. 101 and features 3,000 feet of river frontage. Many of the campsites are shaded. A hiking trail leads from the resort to the Eel River, a walk of just over a quarter mile. This is one in a series of both public and private campgrounds along the highway between Leggett and Garberville. Steelhead and salmon fishing are popular here in the winter, and the resort provides nearby access to state parks. The elevation is 700 feet.

Campsites, facilities: There are 14 tent sites and 27 RV sites with full hookups, including nine drive-through sites, eight cabins, and eight lodge rooms. Cabins and lodge rooms have fully furnished kitchenettes and private bath-

rooms. Lodge rooms have decks with barbecues and picnic tables. Cabins have wood-burning stoves. At campsites, picnic tables and fire rings are provided. Restrooms, hot showers, heated pool (summer only), playground, recreation room, minimart, coin laundry, group kitchen, RV dump station, and an evening campfire (in summer) are available. Some facilities are wheelchair-accessible. Leashed pets are permitted.

Reservations, fees: Reservations are recommended in the summer. The fee is $14–30 per night, $2.50 per person for more than two people, $1 for pets. Major credit cards accepted. Open year-round.

Directions: From the junction of U.S. 101 and Highway 1 in Leggett, drive north on U.S. 101 for seven miles to the campground entrance on the left.

Contact: Redwoods River Resort, 707/925-6249, fax 707/925-6413, website: www.redwoodriverresort.com.

67 REDWOOD CAMPGROUND

Rating: 8

On the Eel River in Standish-Hickey State Recreation Area.

Map 1.5, page 71

This is one of three camps in Standish-Hickey State Recreation Area, and it is by far the most unusual. To reach Redwood Campground requires driving over a temporary "summer bridge," which provides access to a pretty spot along the South Fork Eel River. In early September, out comes the bridge and up comes the river. The elevation is 800 feet. Standish-Hickey is the gateway to the tall trees country. It covers 1,012 acres set in an inland river canyon. The South Fork Eel provides two miles of river frontage. One of the few virgin stands of redwoods in this area can be seen on the Grove Trail. Note that two other campgrounds are available at this park, and that this camp is open only in summer.

Campsites, facilities: There are 63 sites for tents or RVs up to 18 feet long. No trailers, including pop-up tent trailers, are permitted. Picnic tables and fire rings are provided. Drinking water, coin-operated showers, and flush toilets are available. Some facilities are wheelchair-accessible. Leashed pets are permitted.

Reservations, fees: Reservations are accepted with a $7.50 reservation fee at 800/444-PARK (800/444-7275) and website www.Reserve America.com. The fee is $12 per night. Open July through Labor Day weekend.

Directions: From the junction of U.S. 101 and Highway 1 in Leggett, drive north on U.S. 101 for one mile to the park entrance.

Contact: Standish-Hickey State Recreation Area, 707/925-6482, fax 707/925-6402.

68 ROCK CREEK

Rating: 8

On the Eel River in Standish-Hickey State Recreation Area.

Map 1.5, page 71

This is one of two main campgrounds set in a redwood grove at Standish-Hickey State Recreation Area (the other is Hickey). It is the classic state park camp, with numbered sites, flat tent spaces, picnic tables, and food lockers. Hiking is only fair in this park, but most people enjoy the short tromp down to the nearby South Fork Eel River. In the winter, steelhead migrate through the area. (See listing for Redwood Campground for more details on this park.)

Campsites, facilities: There are 35 sites for tents or RVs up to 27 feet long and trailers to 24 feet long. There is one hike-in/bike-in site that accommodates up to eight people. Picnic tables and fire rings are provided. Drinking water, coin-operated showers, and flush toilets are available. Some facilities are wheelchair-accessible. Leashed pets are permitted.

Reservations, fees: Reservations are accepted

with a $7.50 reservation fee at 800/444-PARK (800/444-7275) and website www.Reserve America.com. The fee is $12 per night. Senior discount available. The hike-in, bike-in site is $1 per person per night.

Directions: From the junction of U.S. 101 and Highway 1 in Leggett, drive north on U.S. 101 for one mile to the park entrance on the west side of the road.

Contact: Standish-Hickey State Recreation Area, 707/925-6482, fax 707/925-6402.

69 HICKEY

Rating: 8

On the Eel River in Standish-Hickey State Recreation Area.

Map 1.5, page 71

This is an ideal layover for U.S. 101 cruisers yearning to spend a night in the redwoods. The park is best known for its campsites set amid redwoods and for the nearby South Fork Eel River with its steelhead fishing in the winter. The elevation is 800 feet. (See details about Standish-Hickey State Recreation Area in the note for Redwood Campground.)

Campsites, facilities: There are 65 sites for tents or RVs up to 27 feet long and trailers to 24 feet long. Picnic tables and fire rings are provided. Drinking water, coin-operated showers, and flush toilets are available. A grocery store is available nearby. Some facilities are wheelchair-accessible. Leashed pets are permitted.

Reservations, fees: Reservations are accepted with a $7.50 reservation fee at 800/444-PARK (800/444-7275) and website www.Reserve America.com. The fee is $12 per night. Senior discount available. Open year-round.

Directions: From the junction of U.S. 101 and Highway 1 in Leggett, drive north on U.S. 101 for one mile to the park entrance on the left.

Contact: Standish-Hickey State Recreation Area, 707/925-6482, fax 707/925-6402.

© TOM STIENSTRA

Chapter 2
Shasta and Trinity

Chapter 2—Shasta and Trinity

At 14,162 feet, Mt. Shasta rises like a diamond in a field of coal. Its sphere of influence spans a radius of 125 miles, and its shadow is felt everywhere in the region. This area has much to offer with giant Shasta Lake, the Sacramento River above and below the lake, the McCloud River, and the wonderful Trinity Divide country with its dozens of pretty backcountry lakes and several wilderness areas. This is one of the best regions anywhere for an outdoor adventure—especially hiking, fishing, power boating, rafting, and exploring.

In this area, you can find campgrounds that are truly remote, set near quiet wilderness, and that offer the potential for unlimited adventures. Of all the regions in this book, this is the easiest one in which to find a campground in a secluded setting near great recreation opportunities. That is the main reason people visit.

There are hundreds of destinations, but the most popular are Shasta Lake, the Trinity Alps and its surrounding lakes and streams, and the Klamath Mountains, known as "Bigfoot Country" by the locals.

Shasta Lake is one of America's top recreation lakes. It is the one destination that is big enough to handle all who love it. The massive reservoir boasts 370 miles of shoreline, 1,200 campsites, 21 boat launches, 11 marinas, 35 resorts, and numerous houseboat and cabin rentals. A remarkable 22 species of fish live in the lake. Many of the campgrounds feature lake views. In addition, getting here is easy—a straight shot off I-5.

At the charmed center of this beautiful region is the Trinity Alps, where lakes are sprinkled everywhere. It's also home to the headwaters for feeder streams to the Trinity River, Klamath River, New River, Wooley Creek, and others. Trinity Lake provides outstanding boating and fishing, and just downstream, smaller Lewiston Lake offers a quiet alternative. One advantage to Lewiston Lake is that it is always full of water, even all summer long, making for a very pretty scene. Downstream of Lewiston, the Trinity River provides low-cost rafting and outstanding shoreline access along Highway 299 for fishing for salmon and steelhead.

The neighboring Klamath Mountains are well known as Bigfoot Country. If you drive up the Forest Service road at Bluff Creek, just off Highway 96 upstream of Weitchpec, you can even find the spot where the famous Bigfoot movie was shot in the 1960s. Well, we haven't seen Bigfoot, but we have discovered tons of outdoor recreation. This remote region features miles of the Klamath and Salmon Rivers, as well as the Marble Mountain Wilderness. Options include canoeing, rafting, and fishing for steelhead on the Klamath River, or hiking into your choice of more than 100 wilderness lakes.

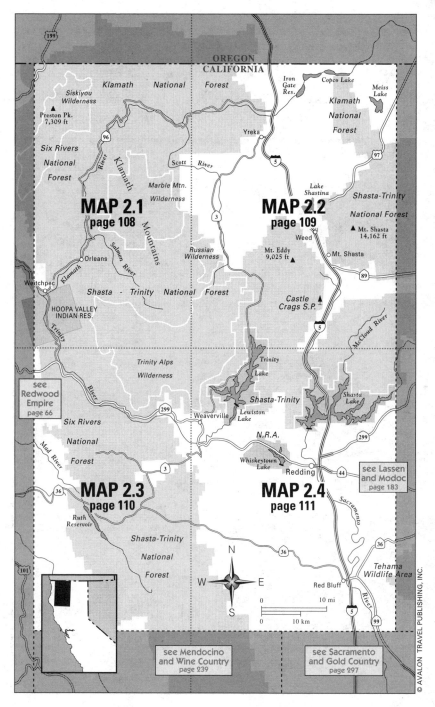

Map 2.1

Campgrounds 1–27
Pages 113–124

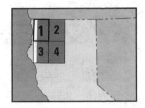

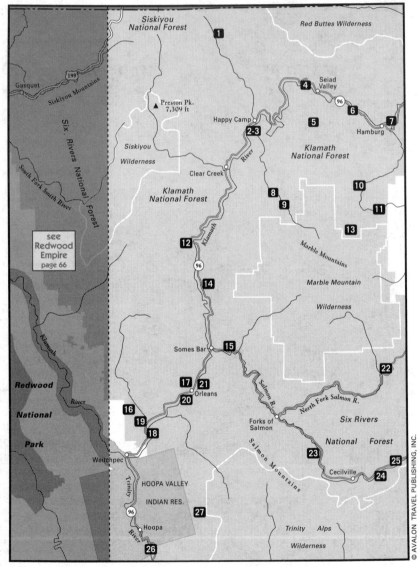

see
Redwood
Empire
page 66

© AVALON TRAVEL PUBLISHING, INC.

Map 2.2

Campgrounds 28–63
Pages 125–141

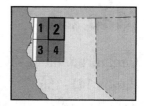

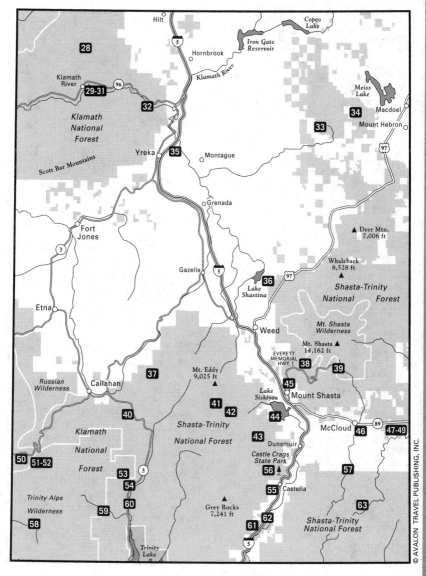

Map 2.3

Campgrounds 64–84
Pages 141–150

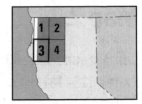

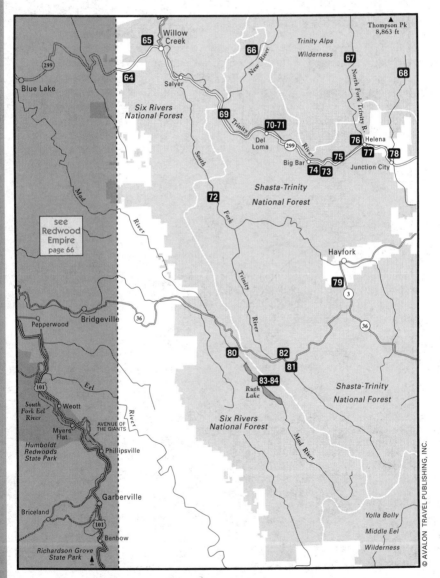

© AVALON TRAVEL PUBLISHING, INC.

Map 2.4

Campgrounds 132–155
Pages 171–180

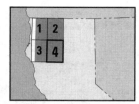

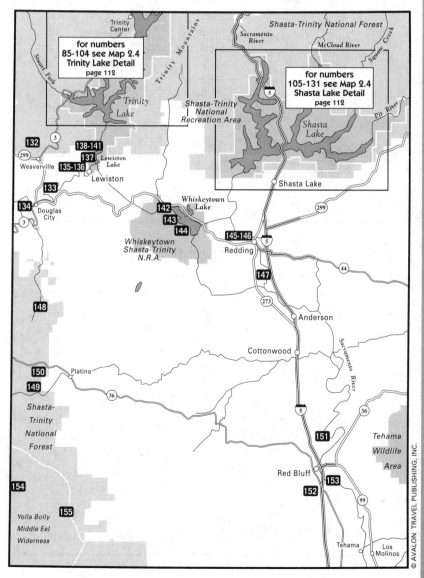

Map 2.4
Trinity Lake Detail

Campgrounds 85–104
Pages 150–158

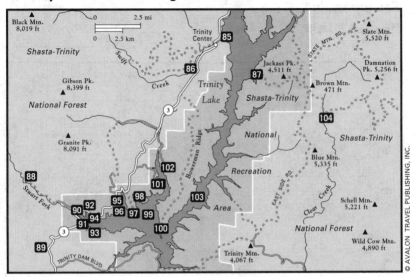

Map 2.4
Shasta Lake Detail

Campgrounds 105–131
Pages 159–170

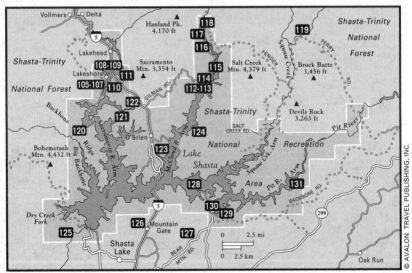

1 WEST BRANCH

Rating: 6

In Klamath National Forest.

Map 2.1, page 108

This is a virtually unknown, low-charge camp, set in a canyon near Indian Creek. This is deep in Klamath National Forest at 2,200 feet in elevation. The best side trip here is the winding four-mile drive on a bumpy dirt road to Kelly Lake, little known and little used. A remote Forest Service station is on the opposite side of Indian Creek Road from the campground. It is a 20-minute drive from the town of Happy Camp.

Campsites, facilities: There are 15 sites for tents or RVs up to 32 feet long. Picnic tables and fire grills are provided. Drinking water and vault toilets are available. There are RV dump stations in Happy Camp at the Elk Creek Campground and the Happy Camp Open Dump. Pack out your garbage. Leashed pets are permitted.

Reservations, fees: Reservations are not accepted. The fee is $6 per night. Two vehicles maximum per site. Senior discount available. Open May through October.

Directions: From Happy Camp on Highway 96, turn north on Indian Creek Road (a paved road) and drive 14.5 miles to the camp on the right side of the road.

Contact: Klamath National Forest, Happy Camp Ranger District, 530/493-2243, fax 530/493-1796.

2 CURLY JACK

Rating: 7

On the Klamath River in Klamath National Forest.

Map 2.1, page 108

This campground is set at 1,075 feet in elevation on the Klamath River, providing opportunities for fishing, light rafting, and kayaking.

What's special about Curly Jack, though, is that the water is generally warm enough through the summer for swimming.

Campsites, facilities: There are 17 sites for tents or RVs up to 22 feet, with some specially designed sites for RVs up to 60 feet, and two group sites. Fire grills are provided. Drinking water and vault toilets are available. Some facilities are wheelchair-accessible. Leashed pets are permitted. A camp host is on-site in summer.

Reservations, fees: Reservations are required for group camps only. The fee is $10 per night, $30 per night for a group campsite (reservation required). Senior discount available. A maximum of two vehicles is allowed per site. Open year-round, but services available only from May through September.

Directions: From the town of Happy Camp on Highway 96, turn south on Elk Creek Road and drive about one mile. Turn right on Curly Jack Road and drive one block to the campground entrance.

Contact: Klamath National Forest, Happy Camp Ranger District, 530/493-2243, fax 530/493-1796.

3 ELK CREEK CAMPGROUND

Rating: 8

On the Klamath River.

Map 2.1, page 108

Elk Creek Campground is a year-round RV park set where Elk Creek pours into the Klamath River. It is a beautiful campground, with sites right on the water in a pretty, wooded setting. The section of the Klamath River nearby is perfect for inflatable kayaking and rafting. Guided trips are available for families or experts, with a wide scope of white water available, rated all the way from the easy Class I stuff all the way to the Class V to hell-and-back rapids. In addition, the water is quite warm in the summer and flows are maintained throughout the year, making it ideal for water sports. The park also has 25 miniature show horses boarded on the property with surreys and buckboards. In addition, horseshoe tournaments are occasionally held.

Campsites, facilities: There are 45 sites, including some drive-through sites and 10 long-term rentals, for RVs up to 60 feet, many with full or partial hookups, and a separate area for tents. Three rental trailers are also available. Picnic tables and fire grills are provided. Restrooms, hot showers, recreation room, beach, coin laundry, RV dump station, ice, propane, and wood are available. Leashed pets are permitted. Private horse boarding is available.

Reservations, fees: Reservations are accepted. The fee is $7 per person for tent campers, $3 per person for more than two people, $18–20 for RVs. Major credit cards accepted. Open year-round.

Directions: From Highway 96 in the town of Happy Camp, turn south on Elk Creek Road and drive one mile to the campground on the right.

Contact: Elk Creek Campground, 530/493-2208, fax 530/493-2029, website: www.elkcreek campground.com.

4 FORT GOFF

Rating: 7

In Klamath National Forest.
Map 2.1, page 108

This small, primitive campground is set right along the Klamath River, an ideal location for both fishing and rafting. Many of the most productive shoreline fishing spots on the Klamath River are in this area, with fair trout fishing in summer, good steelhead fishing in the fall and early winter, and a wild card for salmon in late September. There are pullouts along Highway 96 for parking, with short trails/scrambles down to the river. This is also a good spot for rafting, especially in inflatable kayaks, and commercial rafting operations have trips available on this stretch of river. On the opposite side of Highway 96 (within walking distance

to the west) is a trailhead for a hike that is routed along Little Fort Goff Creek, an uphill tromp for five miles to Big Camp and the Boundary National Recreation Trail. The creek also runs near the camp.

Campsites, facilities: There are five tent sites. Picnic tables and fire grills are provided. Vault toilets are available. There is no drinking water and you must pack out your garbage. Supplies are available in Seiad Valley. Leashed pets are permitted.

Reservations, fees: Reservations are not accepted. There is no fee for camping. Open May through October.

Directions: From Yreka, drive north on I-5 to the junction with Highway 96. At Highway 96, turn west and drive to Seiad Valley. At Seiad Valley, continue west on Highway 96 for five miles to the campground on the left side of the road.

Contact: Klamath National Forest, Happy Camp Ranger District, 530/493-2243, fax 530/493-1796.

5 GRIDER CREEK

Rating: 6

In Klamath National Forest.
Map 2.1, page 108

This obscure little camp is used primarily by hikers, since a trailhead for the Pacific Crest Trail is available, and by deer hunters in the fall. The camp is set at 1,700 feet along Grider Creek. Access to the PCT is provided from a bridge across the creek built in 2002. From here, the Pacific Crest Trail is routed uphill along Grider Creek into the Marble Mountain Wilderness, about an 11-mile ripper to Huckleberry Mountain at 6,303 feet. There are no lakes along the route, only small streams and feeder creeks.

Campsites, facilities: There are 10 sites for tents or RVs up to 16 feet long. Picnic tables and fire grills are provided. Vault toilets are available. No drinking water is provided.

Garbage must be packed out. Leashed pets are permitted.

Reservations, fees: Reservations are not accepted. There is no fee for camping. Two vehicles maximum per site. Open May through October.

Directions: From Yreka, drive north on I-5 to the junction with Highway 96. At Highway 96, turn west and drive to Walker Creek Road/Forest Road 46N64, one mile before Seiad Valley. Turn left to enter Walker Creek Road and stay to the right as it runs adjacent to the Klamath River to Grider Creek Road. At Grider Creek Road, turn left and drive south for three miles to the camp entrance.

Contact: Klamath National Forest, Happy Camp Ranger District, 530/493-2243, fax 530/493-1796.

⑥ O'NEIL CREEK

Rating: 7

In Klamath National Forest.
Map 2.1, page 108

This camp is set near O'Neil Creek, and though it's not far from the Klamath River, access to the river is not easy. To fish or raft, most people will use this as a base camp, then drive out for recreation during the day. That creates a predicament for RV owners, who lose their campsites every time they drive off. During the fall hunting season, this is a good base camp for hunters branching out into the surrounding national forest. There are also historic mining sites nearby.

Campsites, facilities: There are 18 sites for tents or RVs up to 22 feet. Picnic tables and fire grills are provided. Drinking water and vault toilets are available. Garbage must be packed out. Supplies can be obtained in Seiad Valley. Leashed pets are permitted.

Reservations, fees: Reservations are not accepted. The fee is $6 per night. A maximum of two vehicles is allowed per site. Senior discount available. Open May through October.

Directions: From Yreka drive north on I-5 to the junction with Highway 96. Turn west on Highway 96 and drive past Hamburg, continuing west for three miles to the campground.

Contact: Klamath National Forest, Happy Camp Ranger District, 530/493-2243, fax 530/493-1796.

⑦ SARAH TOTTEN

Rating: 7

On the Klamath River in Klamath National Forest.
Map 2.1, page 108

This is one of the more popular Forest Service camps on the Klamath River, and it's no mystery why. In the summer, its placement is perfect for rafters, who camp here and use it as a put-in spot. In fall and winter, fishermen arrive for the steelhead run. It's in the "banana belt," or good weather area of the Klamath, in a pretty grove of oak trees. Fishing is often good here for salmon in early October and for steelhead from November through spring, providing there are fishable water flows.

Campsites, facilities: There are 12 tent sites, five sites for tents and RVs up to 22 feet long, and a group site. Picnic tables and fire grills are provided. Drinking water and vault toilets are available. There's a small grocery store nearby. Leashed pets are permitted.

Reservations, fees: Reservations are accepted only for the group site at 877/444-6777. The fee is $10 for family sites, two vehicles maximum per site, $30 per night for group sites. Senior discount available. Open May through October.

Directions: From Yreka, drive north on I-5 to the junction with Highway 96. At Highway 96, turn west and drive to Horse Creek, continuing west for five miles to the campground on the right side of the road. If you reach the town of Hamburg, you have gone a half mile too far.

Contact: Klamath National Forest, Happy Camp Ranger District, 530/493-2243, fax 530/493-1796.

8 SULPHUR SPRINGS

Rating: 8

On Elk Creek in Klamath National Forest.

Map 2.1, page 108

This hidden spot is set along Elk Creek on the border of the Marble Mountain Wilderness. The camp is at a trailhead that provides access to miles and miles of trails that follow streams into the backcountry of the wilderness area. It is a 12-mile backpack trip one way and largely uphill to Spirit Lake, one of the prettiest lakes in the entire wilderness. Sulphur Springs Camp is set at 3,100 feet. The nearby hot springs (which are actually lukewarm) provide a side attraction. There are also some swimming holes nearby in Elk Creek, but these aren't hot springs, so expect the water to be cold.

Campsites, facilities: There are several walk-in tent sites. Picnic tables and fire grills are provided. Vault toilets are available. No drinking water is available. Pack out your garbage. Leashed pets are permitted.

Reservations, fees: Reservations are not accepted. There is no fee for camping. Two vehicles maximum per site. Open late May through early October.

Directions: From Yreka, drive north on I-5 to the junction with Highway 96. At Highway 96, turn west and drive to Happy Camp. In Happy Camp, turn south on Elk Creek Road and drive 14 miles to the campground.

Contact: Klamath National Forest, Happy Camp Ranger District, 530/493-2243, fax 530/493-1796.

9 NORCROSS

Rating: 7

Near Happy Camp in Klamath National Forest.

Map 2.1, page 108

Set at 2,400 feet in elevation, this camp serves as a staging area for various trails that provide access into the Marble Mountain Wilderness. There is also access to the popular Kelsey Trail and to swimming and fishing activities.

Campsites, facilities: There are eight sites for tents or RVs. Picnic tables and fire pits are provided. Vault toilets are available. No drinking water is available. Pack out all garbage. Leashed pets are permitted.

Reservations, fees: Reservations are not accepted. There is no fee for camping. Two vehicles maximum per site. Open year-round.

Directions: From Yreka on I-5, drive west on Highway 96 to the town of Happy Camp. In Happy Camp, turn south onto Elk Creek Road and drive 16 miles to the campground.

Contact: Klamath National Forest, Happy Camp Ranger District, 530/493-2243, fax 530/493-1796.

10 BRIDGE FLAT

Rating: 7

In Klamath National Forest.

Map 2.1, page 108

This camp is set at 2,000 feet along the Scott River. Though commercial rafting trips are only rarely available here, the river is accessible during the early spring for skilled rafters and kayakers, with a good put-in and take-out spot four miles downriver. For backpackers a trailhead for the Kelsey Trail is nearby, leading into the Marble Mountain Wilderness.

Campsites, facilities: There are four sites for tents or RVs up to 22 feet long. Picnic tables and fire grills are provided. Vault toilets are available and wheelchair-accessible. There is no drinking water. Garbage must be packed out. Leashed pets are permitted.

Reservations, fees: Reservations are not accepted. There is no fee for camping. Open year-round.

Directions: From Redding, drive north on I-5 to Yreka. In Yreka, turn southwest on Highway 3 and drive 16.5 miles to Fort Jones. In Fort Jones, turn right on Scott River Road and drive 21 miles to the campground on the right side of the road.

Contact: Klamath National Forest, Scott River Ranger District, 530/468-5351, fax 530/468-1290.

11 INDIAN SCOTTY

Rating: 7

On the Scott River in Klamath National Forest.

Map 2.1, page 108

This popular camp provides direct access to the adjacent Scott River. Because it is easy to reach (no gravel roads) and shaded, it gets a lot of use. The camp is set at 2,400 feet. The levels, forces, and temperatures on the Scott River fluctuate greatly from spring to fall. In the spring, it can be a raging cauldron, cold from snowmelt. Come summer it quiets, with some deep pools providing swimming holes. By fall, it can be reduced to a trickle. Keep your expectations flexible according to the season.

Campsites, facilities: There are 28 sites and a group site for tents or RVs up to 38 feet long. Picnic tables and fire grills are provided. Drinking water and vault toilets are available. There is a playground in the group-use area. Leashed pets are permitted.

Reservations, fees: Reservations are accepted on for group sites. The fee is $10 per night during summer, free during winter. Groups sites are $30 per night. Senior discount available. Open year-round.

Directions: From Redding, drive north on I-5 to Yreka. In Yreka, turn southwest on Highway 3 and travel 16.5 miles to Fort Jones. In Fort Jones, turn right on Scott River Road and drive 14 miles to a concrete bridge and the adjacent signed campground entrance.

Contact: Klamath National Forest, Scott River Ranger District, 530/468-5351, fax 530/468-1290.

12 DILLON CREEK

Rating: 7

On the Klamath River in Klamath National Forest.

Map 2.1, page 108

This is a prime base camp for rafting or a steelhead fishing trip. A put-in spot for rafting is adjacent to the camp, with an excellent river run available from here on down past Presido Bar to the takeout at Ti-Bar. If you choose to go on, make absolutely certain to pull out at Green Riffle river access and takeout, or risk death at Ishi Pishi Falls. The water is warm here in the summer, and there are also many excellent swimming holes in the area. In addition, this is a good stretch of water for steelhead fishing in September to February, best in early winter from Dillon Beach to Ti-Bar. The elevation is 800 feet.

Campsites, facilities: There are 10 tent sites and 11 RV sites. Picnic tables and fire grills are provided. Drinking water and vault toilets are available. There is a RV dump station in Happy Camp 25 miles north of the campground and at Aikens Creek nine miles west of the town of Orleans. Leashed pets are permitted.

Reservations, fees: Reservations are not accepted. The fee is $9 fee per night. Open year-round.

Directions: From Yreka on I-5, turn west on Highway 96 and drive to the town of Happy Camp. Continue west from Happy Camp for 35 miles and look for the campground on the right side of the road. Coming from the west, from Somes Bar, drive 15 miles north on Highway 96.

Contact: Six Rivers National Forest, Orleans Ranger District, 530/627-3291, fax 530/627-3401.

13 LOVERS CAMP

Rating: 5

In Klamath National Forest.

Map 2.1, page 108

Lovers Camp isn't set up for lovers at all, but for horses and backpackers. This is a trailhead camp set at 4,300 feet at the edge of the Marble Mountain Wilderness, one of the best in the entire wilderness for packers with horses. The trail here is routed up along Canyon Creek to the beautiful Marble Valley at the foot of Black Marble Mountain. The most common destination is Sky High Lakes, a good one-day huff-and-puff away. Now there's a place for lovers.

Campsites, facilities: There are five walk-in sites. Picnic tables and fire grills are provided. Vault toilets are available and wheelchair-accessible. There are also facilities for stock unloading and a corral. There is no drinking water, but water is available for stock. Garbage must be packed out. Leashed pets are permitted.

Reservations, fees: Reservations are not accepted. There is no fee for camping. Open June through October.

Directions: From Redding, drive north on I-5 to Yreka. In Yreka, turn southwest on Highway 3 and drive to Fort Jones. In Fort Jones, turn right and drive 18 miles on Scott River Road to Forest Road 43N45. Turn south on Forest Road 43N45 and drive nine miles to the campground at the end of the road.

Contact: Klamath National Forest, Scott River Ranger District, 530/468-5351, fax 530/468-1290.

14 MARBLE MOUNTAIN RANCH

Rating: 6

Near the Klamath River.

Map 2.1, page 108

The lodge is set just across the road from the Klamath River, an ideal location as headquarters for a rafting trip in the summer or a steelhead fishing trip in the fall. This ranch is considered a vacation destination, with most people staying for a week. Commercial rafting trips are available here, with guided trips offered by the ranch. This piece of river is beautiful and fresh with lots of wildlife and birds, yet not dangerous. However, be absolutely certain to take out at Green Riffle boat access before reaching Ishi Pishi Falls, which cannot be run. If you like privacy and comfort, the cabin rentals available here are a nice bonus. There's also a full pack station at the ranch for guided trail rides lasting from one hour to overnight. Guided mountain bike trips are also available. In addition, there is a sporting clays target range.

Campsites, facilities: There are 30 tent sites, 11 cabins, two houses, and 10 RV sites with full hookups. Picnic tables and fire grills are provided. Restrooms, drinking water, hot showers, coin laundry, ice, wood, recreation room, horseshoe pits, and volleyball and basketball courts are available. Leashed pets are permitted.

Reservations, fees: Reservations are required. The fee is $5 per person for tent sites, $15 for RV sites, $2 per person for more than two people. Major credit cards are accepted. Open year-round.

Directions: From the junction of U.S. 101 and Highway 299 near Arcata, turn east on Highway 299 and drive to Willow Creek. In Willow Creek, turn north (left) on Highway 96 east and drive to Somes Bar. At Somes Bar, continue for 7.5 miles to Mile Marker 7.5 and Marble Mountain Ranch on the right.

Contact: Marble Mountain Ranch, 530/469-3322 or 800/KLAMATH (800/552-6284), fax 530/469-3357, website: www.marblemountain ranch.com.

15 OAK BOTTOM ON THE SALMON RIVER

Rating: 7

In Klamath National Forest.

Map 2.1, page 108

This camp is just far enough off Highway 96

that it gets missed by zillions of out-of-towners every year. It is set across the road from the lower Salmon River, a pretty, clean, and cold stream that pours out of the surrounding wilderness high country. Swimming is very good in river holes, though the water is cold, especially when nearby Wooley Creek is full of snowmelt pouring out of the Marble Mountains to the north. In the fall, there is good shoreline fishing for steelhead, though the canyon bottom is shaded almost all day and gets very cold.

Campsites, facilities: There are 26 sites for tents and small RVs. Picnic tables and fire grills are provided. Drinking water and vault toilets are available. There is an RV dump station at the Elk Creek Campground in Happy Camp and at Aikens Creek, 13 miles southwest of the town of Orleans. Supplies are available in Somes Bar. Leashed pets are permitted.

Reservations, fees: Reservations are not accepted. The fee is $10 per night. Open April through November, weather permitting.

Directions: From the junction of U.S. 101 and Highway 299 near Arcata, turn east on Highway 299 and drive to Willow Creek and Highway 96. Turn north on Highway 96 and drive to Somes Bar-Etna Road (one-quarter mile before Somes Bar). Turn right on Somes Bar-Etna Road and drive two miles to the campground on the left side of the road.

Contact: Klamath National Forest, Ukonom Ranger District, 530/627-3291, fax 530/627-3401.

16 FISH LAKE

Rating: 8

In Six Rivers National Forest.

Map 2.1, page 108

This is a pretty little lake that provides good fishing for stocked rainbow trout from the season opener on Memorial Day weekend through July. The camp gets little pressure in other months. It's in the heart of Bigfoot country,

with numerous Bigfoot sightings reported near Bluff Creek. No powerboats are permitted on the lake, but it's too small for that anyway, being better suited for a canoe, float tube, raft, or pram. The elevation is 1,800 feet. The presence here of Port Orford cedar root disease, spread by spores in the mud, forces closure from October through April.

Campsites, facilities: There are 10 sites for tents and 14 sites for tents or RVs up to 35 feet long. Picnic tables and fire grills are provided. Drinking water and vault toilets are available; a camp host is on-site. Leashed pets are permitted.

Reservations, fees: Reservations are not accepted. The fee is $9 per night. Senior discount available. Open May through September, weather permitting.

Directions: From I-5 in Redding, turn west on Highway 299 and drive to Willow Creek. At Willow Creek, turn north on Highway 96 and drive to Weitchpec, continuing seven miles north on Highway 96 to Fish Lake Road. Turn left on Fish Lake Road and drive five miles (stay to the right at the Y) to Fish Lake.

Contact: Six Rivers National Forest, Orleans Ranger District, 530/627-3291, fax 530/627-3401.

17 THE PINES TRAILER PARK

Rating: 6

On the Klamath River.

Map 2.1, page 108

This is an option for RV cruisers touring Highway 96 and looking for a stopover in Orleans. The steelhead fishing is good in this area in the fall. The campground is in a wooded setting, across the highway from the Klamath River.

Campsites, facilities: There are 25 sites with full hookups, including some long-term rentals, for RVs up to 40 feet long, and a separate area for tents. Picnic tables are provided. Restrooms, showers, cable TV hookups, RV dump station, and a coin laundry are available. Leashed pets are permitted.

Reservations, fees: Reservations are accepted. The fee is $13 per night, $1 per person for more than two people. Monthly rates available. Open year-round.

Directions: From the junction of U.S. 101 and Highway 299 near Arcata, drive east on Highway 299 to Willow Creek. At Willow Creek, turn north (left) on Highway 96, drive past Weitchpec, and continue to Orleans. In Orleans, look for the park entrance on the left side of the road.

Contact: The Pines Trailer Park, 530/627-3425.

18 AIKENS CREEK WEST

Rating: 7

On the Klamath River in Six Rivers National Forest.

Map 2.1, page 108

The Klamath River is warm and green here in summer, and this camp provides an ideal put-in spot for a day of easy rafting, especially for newcomers in inflatable kayaks. The camp is set at 340 feet in elevation along the Klamath. From here to Weitchpec is an easy paddle, with the takeout on the right side of the river just beyond Muddy Creek. The river is set in a beautiful canyon with lots of birds and enters the Yurok Indian Reservation. The steelhead fishing can be good in this area from August through mid-November, and it's best downstream at Johnson's Bar from a boat, boondogging Glo Bugs. Highway 96 is a scenic but slow cruise. Note: the camp may be closed periodically because of flooding. In winter and spring, check its status before planning your trip.

Campsites, facilities: There are dispersed sites for tents or RVs. Picnic tables and fire grills are provided. Vault toilets are available. No drinking water is available. A camp host is on-site in summer. There are reduced services in winter, and all garbage must be packed out. Leashed pets are permitted.

Reservations, fees: Reservations are not accepted.

The fee is $7 per night. Senior discount available. Open year-round.

Directions: From the junction of U.S. 101 and Highway 299 near Arcata, turn east on Highway 299 and drive to Willow Creek. In Willow Creek, turn north on Highway 96 and drive to Weitchpec, continuing on Highway 96 for five miles to the campground on the right side of the road.

Contact: Six Rivers National Forest, Orleans Ranger District, 530/627-3291, fax 530/627-3401.

19 E-NE-NUCK

Rating: 7

In Six Rivers National Forest.

Map 2.1, page 108

The campground gets its name from a Karuk Indian chief who lived in the area in the late 1800s. It's a popular spot for anglers; Bluff Creek and the Klamath are within walking distance and Fish Lake is eight miles to the west. Bluff Creek is the legendary site where the Bigfoot film of the 1960s was shot. Whether the film is genuine or a phony, it still has put Bluff Creek on the map.

Campsites, facilities: There are 11 campsites for tents or RVs up to 22 feet long. Picnic tables and cast-iron firebox stoves are provided. Drinking water, vault toilets are available; a camp host is on-site. Leashed pets are permitted.

Reservations, fees: Reservations are not accepted. The fee is $9 per night, $5 per additional vehicle. Senior discount available. Open late spring through early November.

Directions: From the junction of U.S. 101 and Highway 299 near Arcata, turn east on Highway 299 and drive to Willow Creek. In Willow Creek, turn north on Highway 96 and drive to Weitchpec, continuing on Highway 96 for about five miles to the campground. E-Ne-Nuck is just beyond Aikens Creek West Campground.

Contact: Six Rivers National Forest, Orleans Ranger District, 530/627-3291, fax 530/627-3401.

20 KLAMATH RIVERSIDE RV PARK AND CAMPGROUND

Rating: 8

On the Klamath River.

Map 2.1, page 108

Klamath Riverside RV Park and Campground is an option for RV cruisers touring Highway 96—designated the Bigfoot Scenic Byway—and looking for a place in Orleans. The camp has large grassy sites set amid pine trees, right on the river. There are spectacular views of Mt. Orleans and the surrounding hills. A 12-foot Bigfoot statue is on the property. Over the years, we've seen many changes at this park. It has been transformed from a dusty fishing spot to a park more resembling a rural resort. One big plus is that the park offers guided trips during the season for fishing and rafting.

Campsites, facilities: There are 45 RV sites, some drive-through, with full hookups and a separate area for tents. Two cabins, duplex, and five rental trailers are also available. Picnic tables and fire rings are provided. Restrooms, showers, a hot tub, group pavilion, a small store, and a coin laundry are available. A swimming pool is available in summer. River rafting services and guided drift boat fishing in season are available. Horseback riding is available within 12 miles. Leashed pets are permitted.

Reservations, fees: Reservations are accepted. The fee is $15–22 per night, $5 per person for more than two people for tent camping, $2 per person for more than two people for RV camping. Group rates available. Monthly rates available. Open year-round.

Directions: From the junction of U.S. 101 and Highway 299 near Arcata, drive east on Highway 299 to Willow Creek, turn north (left) on Highway 96, and drive past Weitchpec to Or-

leans. This campground is at the west end of the town of Orleans on Highway 96 on the right.

Contact: Klamath Riverside RV Park and Campground, 800/627-9779 or 530/627-3239, fax 530/627-3755, website: www.klamathriversidervpark.com.

21 PEARCH CREEK

Rating: 7

On the Klamath River in Six Rivers National Forest.

Map 2.1, page 108

This is one of the premium Forest Service camps on the Klamath River because of its easy access from the highway and easy access to the river. The camp is set on Pearch Creek, about a quarter mile from the Klamath at a deep bend in the river. It is open year-round. Indeed, the fishing is often excellent for one- to five-pound steelhead from August through November. The elevation is 400 feet.

Campsites, facilities: There are nine sites for tents and two sites for tents or RVs up to 22 feet long. Picnic tables and fire grills are provided. Drinking water and vault toilets are available; a camp host is on-site in summer. A grocery store, coin laundry, and propane gas are available within one mile. Leashed pets are permitted.

Reservations, fees: Reservations are not accepted. The fee is $9 per night, $5 for each additional vehicle. Senior discount available. Open May to late October.

Directions: From I-5 in Redding, turn west on Highway 299 and drive to Willow Creek. In Willow Creek, turn north on Highway 96, drive past Weitchpec, and continue to Orleans. In Orleans, continue for one mile and look for the campground entrance on the right side of the road.

Contact: Six Rivers National Forest, Orleans Ranger District, 530/627-3291, fax 530/627-3401.

22 IDLEWILD

Rating: 8

On the North Fork of the Salmon River in Klamath National Forest.

Map 2.1, page 108

This is one of the prettiest drive-to camps in the region, set near the confluence of the Salmon River and its south fork, a beautiful, cold, clear stream and a major tributary to the Klamath River. Most campers are using the camp for its nearby trailhead (two miles north on a dirt Forest Service road out of camp). The hike here is routed to the north, climbing alongside the Salmon River for miles into the Marble Mountain Wilderness (wilderness permits are required). It's a rugged 10-mile, all-day climb to Lake of the Island with several other lakes (highlighted by Hancock Lake) to the nearby west, accessible on week-long trips.

Campsites, facilities: There are 23 sites, including two group sites, for tents or RVs up to 22 feet long. Picnic tables and fire grills are provided. Drinking water and vault toilets are available. Leashed pets are permitted.

Reservations, fees: Reservations are not accepted. The fee is $6 per night. Senior discount available. Open June through October.

Directions: From Redding, drive north on I-5 to Yreka. In Yreka, turn southwest on Highway 3 and drive to Etna. In Etna, turn west on Etna-Somes Bar Road (Main Street in town) and drive about 16 miles to the campground on the right side of the road. Note: a shorter, more scenic, and more complex route is available from Gazelle (North of Weed on Old Highway 99). Take Gazelle-Callahan Road west over the summit and continue north to Etna.

Contact: Klamath National Forest, Salmon River Ranger District, 530/468-5351, fax 530/468-1290.

23 MATTHEWS CREEK

Rating: 8

On the Salmon River in Klamath National Forest.

Map 2.1, page 108

This camp is set in a dramatic river canyon, with the beautiful South Fork of the Salmon River nearby. Rafters call it the "Cal Salmon," and good put-in and take-out spots are found every few miles all the way to the confluence with the Klamath. In early summer the water is quite cold from snowmelt, but by mid-summer it warms up significantly. The best fishing for steelhead on the Salmon is in December in the stretch of river downstream from Forks of Salmon (check regulations for closed areas). In winter the mountain rims shield the canyon floor from sunlight and it gets so cold you'll feel like a human glacier. The elevation is 1,700 feet.

Campsites, facilities: There are seven sites for tents or RVs up to 16 feet long and seven sites for tents only. Picnic tables and fire grills are provided. Drinking water and vault toilets are available during the summer. The toilets are wheelchair-accessible. Leashed or controlled pets are permitted.

Reservations, fees: Reservations are not accepted. The fee is $8 per night, free during the off-season. Senior discount available. Open year-round, weather permitting.

Directions: From the junction of U.S. 101 and Highway 299 near Arcata, head east on Highway 299 and drive to Willow Creek. In Willow Creek, turn north on Highway 96 and drive past Orleans to Somes Bar. At Somes Bar, turn east on Salmon River Road/Forest Road 2B01 and drive to the town of Forks of Salmon. Turn right on Cecilville Road/Forest Road 1002 and drive about nine miles to the campground. Cecilville Road is very narrow.

Contact: Klamath National Forest, Salmon River Ranger District, 530/468-5351, fax 530/468-1290.

24 EAST FORK

Rating: 6

On the Salmon River in Klamath National Forest.

Map 2.1, page 108

This is one of the more spectacular areas in the fall when the leaves turn different shades of gold. It's set at 2,400 feet along the Salmon River, just outside the town of Cecilville. Directly adjacent to the camp is Forest Road 37N02, which leads to a Forest Service station four miles away, and to a trailhead for the Trinity Alps Wilderness three miles beyond that. Note to steelhead anglers: check the Department of Fish and Game regulations for closed areas on the Salmon River.

Campsites, facilities: There are six tent sites and three sites for RVs up to 16 feet long. Picnic tables and fire grills are provided. Vault toilets are available. No drinking water is available. Leashed pets are permitted.

Reservations, fees: Reservations are not accepted. There is no fee for camping. Open year-round, weather permitting.

Directions: From Redding, drive north on I-5 past Weed to the Edgewood exit. Take the Edgewood exit, turn left at the stop sign, and drive a short distance to another stop sign at Old Stage Road. Turn right at Old Stage Road, drive to Gazelle, turn left on Gazelle-Callahan Road, and drive to Callahan. In Callahan, turn southwest on Cecilville Road and drive about 30 miles to the campground on the right side of the road. If you reach the town of Cecilville, you have gone two miles too far.

Contact: Klamath National Forest, Salmon River Ranger District, 530/468-5351, fax 530/468-1290.

25 SHADOW CREEK

Rating: 7

In Klamath National Forest.

Map 2.1, page 108

This tiny spot, secluded and quiet, is along little Shadow Creek where it enters the East Fork Salmon River, adjacent to a deep bend in the road. An unusual side trip is to take the Forest Service road out of camp (turn north off Cecilville Road) and follow it as it winds back and forth, finally arriving at Grouse Point, 5,409 feet in elevation, for a view of the western slopes of the nearby Russian and Trinity Alps Wilderness Areas. There are three trailheads six miles to the east of the camp: Fish Creek, Long Gulch, and Trail Gulch. Note: the river adjacent to the campground is a spawning area and is closed to salmon and steelhead fishing, but you can take trout.

Campsites, facilities: There are five tent sites and five sites for RVs up to 16 feet long. Picnic tables and fire grills are provided. Vault toilets are available. No drinking water is available. All garbage must be packed out. Leashed pets are permitted.

Reservations, fees: Reservations are not accepted. There is no fee for camping. Open year-round.

Directions: From Redding, drive north on I-5 past Weed to the Edgewood exit. Take the Edgewood exit, turn left at the stop sign, and drive a short distance to another stop sign at Old Stage Road. Turn right at Old Stage Road, drive to Gazelle, turn left on Gazelle-Callahan Road, and drive to Callahan. In Callahan, turn southwest on Cecilville Road and drive about 25 miles to the campground on the left side of the road.

Contact: Klamath National Forest, Salmon River Ranger District, 530/468-5351, fax 530/468-1290.

26 TISH TANG

≋ 🚣 🐕 🚐 ⛺

Rating: 8

In Six Rivers National Forest.
Map 2.1, page 108
This campground is adjacent to one of the best swimming holes in all of Northern California. By late July the adjacent Trinity River is warm and slow, perfect for tubing, falling in "by accident," and paddling a canoe. There is a large gravel beach, and some people will bring along their shorty lawn chairs and just take a seat on the edge of the river in a few inches of water. Though Tish Tang is a good put-in spot for rafting in the late spring and early summer, the flows are too slow and quiet for most rafters to even ruffle a feather during the summer. The elevation is 400 feet.

Campsites, facilities: There are 21 sites for tents and 19 sites for tents or RVs up to 30 feet long and trailers up to 22 feet long. Picnic tables and fire grills are provided. Drinking water and vault toilets are available, and there is a camp host. Leashed pets are permitted.

Reservations, fees: Reservations are not accepted. The fee is $10 per night, $5 for each additional vehicle, $15 per night for multiple-family sites. Open late May to late October.

Directions: From the junction of U.S. 101 and Highway 299 near Arcata, turn east on Highway 299 and drive to Willow Creek. In Willow Creek, turn north on Highway 96 and drive eight miles north to the campground entrance on the right side of the road.

Contact: Hoopa Valley Tribal Council, Forestry Department, 530/625-4284, fax 530/625-4230.

27 MILL CREEK LAKE HIKE-IN

🏃 ≋ 🚣 🐕 ⛺

Rating: 4

On the border of the Trinity Alps Wilderness.
Map 2.1, page 108
In 1999, a forest fire severely affected this area and caution should be used when hiking. Occasional falls of dead trees are inevitable. Because of the fire, few people are expected to visit the lake. In time, this will again become something of a secret camp. It now is surrounded largely by tree skeletons. Mill Creek Lake is a secret three-acre lake set at 5,000 feet on the edge of the Trinity Alps Wilderness. Reaching it requires a two-mile hike from the wilderness boundary, with the little lake set just north of North Trinity Mountain (6,362 feet). This is a rare chance to reach a wilderness lake with such a short walk, backpacking without having to pay the penalty of days of demanding hiking. The lake features excellent swimming, with warmer water than in higher and more remote wilderness lakes, and decent fishing for rainbow trout. It is stocked with fingerlings yearly by airplane.

Campsites, facilities: There are three primitive tent sites at locations around the lake. Fire rings are provided. No drinking water is available. Pack out all garbage. Leashed pets are permitted.

Reservations, fees: Reservations are not accepted. There is no fee for camping. A free wilderness permit is required from the U.S. Forest Service. Open when weather permits access.

Directions: From the junction of U.S. 101 and Highway 299 near Arcata, turn east on Highway 299 and drive to Willow Creek. In Willow Creek turn north on Highway 96, drive into the Hoopa Valley, turn east on Big Hill Road, and drive 12 miles to the national forest boundary. Turn right on Forest Road 10N02 and drive about 3.5 miles, where you will reach another junction. Turn left at the signed junction to the Mill Creek Lake Trailhead and drive a short distance to the parking area. A one-hour walk is then required to reach the lake.

Contact: Six Rivers National Forest, Lower Trinity Ranger District, 530/629-2118, fax 530/629-2102. For a map, send $6 to U.S. Forest Service, Attn: Map Sales, P.O. Box 9035, Prescott, AZ 86313, 928/443-8285 with credit card, website: www.fs.fed.us/maps/. Ask for the Six Rivers National Forest.

28 BEAVER CREEK

Rating: 8

In Klamath National Forest.
Map 2.2, page 109

This camp is set along Beaver Creek, a feeder stream to the nearby Klamath River, with two small creeks entering Beaver Creek on the far side of the river near the campground. It is quiet and pretty. There are several historic mining sites in the area; you'll need a map of Klamath National Forest (available for $6 at the district office) to find them. In the fall, this campground is usually taken by deer hunters.

Campsites, facilities: There are eight sites for tents or small RVs. Picnic tables and fire grills are provided. Drinking water and vault toilets are available. Garbage must be packed out. Leashed pets are permitted.

Reservations, fees: Reservations are not accepted. There is no fee for camping. Open year-round.

Directions: From Redding, drive north on I-5 to Highway 96. Turn west on Highway 96 and drive approximately 15 miles (if you reach the town of Klamath River, you have gone a half mile too far) to Beaver Creek Road. Turn right on Beaver Creek Road/Forest Road 11 and drive four miles to the campground.

Contact: Klamath National Forest, Scott River Ranger District, 530/468-5351, fax 530/468-1290.

29 THE OAKS RV PARK

Rating: 7

On the Klamath River.
Map 2.2, page 109

Fishing? Rafting? Canoeing? Hiking? This camp provides a good headquarters for all of these adventures. This stretch of the Klamath

is ideal for boating, with summer flows warm and often at perfect levels for rafting and canoeing, with a small beach area available. Fishing is best in the fall, when salmon, and later steelhead, migrate through the area.

Campsites, facilities: There are 10 sites with full hookups for tents and 12 sites for RVs. Picnic tables are provided. Drinking water, restrooms, hot showers, ice, and coin laundry are available. A restaurant and lounge are available within walking distance next door. Groceries can be obtained within three miles in the town of Klamath River. A golf course is nearby. Leashed pets are permitted.

Reservations, fees: Reservations are accepted. The fee is $10–12 per night. Open year-round.

Directions: From Redding, drive north on I-5 to Highway 96. Turn west on Highway 96 and drive approximately 20 miles to the town of Klamath River. Look for the park entrance on the left, across from the town post office.

Contact: The Oaks RV Park, 530/465-2323, fax 530/465-2312.

30 QUIGLEY'S GENERAL STORE AND TRAILER PARK

Rating: 7

On the Klamath River.
Map 2.2, page 109

This year-round, privately operated park is set along the Klamath River, highlighted by 13 riverfront sites. Many of the parking sites have clear views of the river, as well as good mountain views. Quigley's General Store is well stocked for such a remote little shop, and you can usually get reliable fishing information here, too.

Campsites, facilities: There are 20 sites with full hookups for RVs up to 40 feet long, including seven sites with long-term rentals. Picnic tables are provided. Restrooms, hot showers, a store, deli, and coin laundry are available. Some facilities are wheelchair-accessible. Leashed pets are permitted.

Reservations, fees: Reservations are accepted. The fee is $15 per night, $1 per person for more than two people. Monthly rates available. Major credit cards accepted. Open year-round.

Directions: From Redding, drive north on I-5 to Highway 96. Turn west on Highway 96 and drive approximately 15 miles to the town of Klamath River. Look for the campground entrance on the left.

Contact: Quigley's General Store and Trailer Park, 530/465-2224, fax 530/465-2422.

31 FISHER'S KLAMATH RIVER TRAILER PARK

Rating: 8

On the Klamath River.
Map 2.2, page 109

This privately operated RV park is in one of the prettiest areas of the Klamath River. There's a good piece of river here for summer rafting or fall steelhead fishing. For rafting, the river is sprinkled with Class II and III rapids, ideal for inflatable kayaks, and several commercial rafting companies operate in this area. Every site has a view of the river and the beautiful Siskiyou Mountains.

Campsites, facilities: There are 17 RV sites with full hookups. Picnic tables, restrooms, hot showers, and a coin laundry are available. Leashed pets are permitted.

Reservations, fees: Reservations are accepted. The fee is $12 per night. For more than two people, $1 extra per person per night. Monthly rates available. Open year-round.

Directions: From Redding, drive north on I-5 to Highway 96. Turn west on Highway 96 and drive approximately 15 miles to the campground entrance on the left (if you reach the town of Klamath River, you have gone a mile too far).

Contact: Fisher's Klamath River Trailer Park, 530/465-2297.

32 TREE OF HEAVEN

Rating: 7

In Klamath National Forest.
Map 2.2, page 109

This outstanding riverside campground provides excellent access to the Klamath River for fishing, rafting, and hiking. The best deal is to put in your raft, canoe, or drift boat upstream at the ramp below Iron Gate Reservoir, then make the all-day run down to the takeout at Tree of Heaven. This section of river is an easy paddle and also provides excellent steelhead fishing in the winter. There is also a trail out of the camp that is routed along the river and probes through vegetation, ending at a fair fishing spot (a better spot is nearby at the mouth of the Shasta River). On the drive in from the highway, you can watch the landscape turn from high chaparral to forest.

Campsites, facilities: There are 20 sites for tents and moderate-sized RVs. Picnic tables and fire grills are provided. Drinking water and vault toilets are available. A river access spot for put-in and takeout for rafts and drift boats is available (some facilities are wheelchair-accessible here). Leashed pets are permitted.

Reservations, fees: Reservations are accepted. The fee is $10 per night. Senior discount available. Open year-round.

Directions: From Redding, drive north on I-5 to Highway 96. Turn west on Highway 96 and drive seven miles to the campground entrance on the left side of the road.

Contact: Klamath National Forest, Scott River Ranger District, 530/468-5351, fax 530/468-1290.

33 MARTINS DAIRY

Rating: 8

On the Little Shasta River in Klamath National Forest.
Map 2.2, page 109

This camp is set at 6,000 feet, where the deer

get big and the country seems wide open. A large meadow is nearby, directly across the road from this remote camp, with fantastic wildflower displays in late spring. This is one of the prettiest camps around in the fall, with dramatic color from aspens and other hardwoods. It also makes a good base camp for hunters in the fall. Before heading into the surrounding backcountry, obtain a map of Klamath National Forest, available for $6 at the Goosenest Ranger Station on Highway 97, on your way in to camp.

Campsites, facilities: There are eight sites for tents or small RVs and a horse camp site. Picnic tables and fire grills are provided. Drinking water and wheelchair-accessible vault toilets are available. Leashed pets are permitted.

Reservations, fees: Reservations are not accepted. The fee is $8 per night. Senior discount available. Open Memorial Day weekend through mid-October, weather permitting.

Directions: From Redding, drive north on I-5 to Weed. In Weed, turn north on U.S. 97 and drive to Grass Lake. Continue about seven miles to Forest Road 70/46N10 (if you reach Hebron Summit, you have driven about a mile too far). Turn left, drive about 10 miles to a Y, take the left fork, and drive three miles (including a very sharp right turn) to the campground on the right side of the road. A map of Klamath National Forest is advised.

Contact: Klamath National Forest, Goosenest Ranger District, 530/398-4391, fax 530/398-5749.

34 JUANITA LAKE

Rating: 7

In Klamath National Forest.
Map 2.2, page 109
Small and relatively unknown, this camp is set along the shore of Juanita Lake at 5,100 feet. It is stocked with rainbow trout, brown trout, bass, and catfish, but a problem with golden shiners has cut into the lake's fishing produc-

tivity. It's a small lake and forested, set near the Butte Valley Wildlife Area in the plateau country just five miles to the northeast. The latter provides an opportunity to see waterfowl and, in the winter, bald eagles. Campers will discover a network of Forest Service roads in the area, providing an opportunity for mountain biking. There is also a paved trail around the lake that is wheelchair-accessible and spans approximately 1.25 miles.

Campsites, facilities: There are 12 tent sites, 11 sites for RVs up to 32 feet, and a group site that can accommodate 50 people. Picnic tables and fire grills are provided. Drinking water and vault toilets are available. Boating is allowed, but no motorboats are permitted on the lake. Many facilities are wheelchair-accessible. Leashed pets are permitted.

Reservations, fees: Reservations are accepted only for group sites. The fee is $10 per night, group sites are $30 per night. Senior discount available. Open May through October.

Directions: From Redding, drive north on I-5 to Weed. In Weed, turn north on U.S. 97 and drive approximately 37 miles. Turn left on Ball Mountain Road and drive 2.5 miles, veer right at the fork, and continue to the campground entrance at the lake.

Contact: Klamath National Forest, Goosenest Ranger District, 530/398-4391, fax 530/398-5749.

35 WAIIAKA TRAILER HAVEN

Rating: 4

Near Yreka.
Map 2.2, page 109
If it's late, you're tired, and you're hunting for a spot to hunker down for the night, this is your only bet in the immediate Yreka vicinity. A string of fast-food restaurants is available nearby on the west side of the highway. A small hill blocks the view of Mt. Shasta to the south.

Campsites, facilities: There are 60 drive-through sites with full hookups for RVs of any length, including 30 long-term rentals, and a separate grassy area for tents. Restrooms, showers, playground, horseshoes, and a recreation room are provided. A coin laundry and propane gas are available. Leashed pets are permitted. No campfires are permitted.

Reservations, fees: Reservations are accepted. The fee is $10–22 per night, $1.50 per person for more than two people. Major credit cards accepted. Open year-round.

Directions: From Redding, drive north on I-5 to Yreka, take the Fort Jones exit, and drive one block east to Fairlane Road. At Fairlane Road, turn left (north) and drive to Sharps Road. At Sharps Road, bear left (east) and drive one block to the RV park entrance (just past the fairgrounds parking lot) on the left.

Contact: Waiiaka Trailer Heaven, 530/842-4500.

36 LAKE SHASTINA

Rating: 7

Near Klamath National Forest and Weed.
Map 2.2, page 109

Lake Shastina is set at the northern foot of Mt. Shasta. It offers spectacular views, good swimming on hot summer days, and fishing for catfish and bass in the spring and summer, an occasional opportunity for crappie, and good fishing for trout when the wind is down in late winter and spring. One reason the views of Mt. Shasta are so good is that this is largely high sagebrush country with few trees. As such, it can get very dusty, windy, and in the winter, nasty cold. When the lake is full, the wind is down, and the weather is good, there are few complaints. But that is only rarely the case. The lake level is often low, with the water drained for hay farmers to the north, and they'd turn this lake into a 10-foot puddle if they could get away with it. This is one of the few lakes in Northern California that has property with lakeside housing, consisting of several small developments. Alas, the water slide, once of-

fering great fun for kids, is now off-limits to the public.

Campsites, facilities: There is a small primitive area designated for camping in tents or self-contained RVs only. There is no drinking water. A chemical toilet is available and a boat launch is available nearby; the boat ramp is nonfunctional when the lake level drops below the concrete ramp. Garbage service available May to September only. Supplies can be obtained five miles away in Weed. Leashed pets are permitted.

Reservations, fees: Reservations are not accepted. There is no fee for camping. Open May through September.

Directions: From Redding, drive north on I-5 to Weed. In Weed, turn north on U.S. 97 and drive about five miles to Big Springs Road. Turn left (west) on Big Springs Road and drive about one mile to Jackson Ranch Road. Turn left (west) on Jackson Ranch Road and drive a half mile to Emerald Isle Road (watch for the signed turnoff). Turn right and drive two miles to the campground.

Contact: Siskiyou County Public Works, 530/842-8250.

37 KANGAROO LAKE/WALK-IN

Rating: 10

In Klamath National Forest.
Map 2.2, page 109

A remote paved road leads right to Kangaroo Lake, set at 6,050 feet, providing a genuine rarity: a beautiful and pristine mountain lake with a walk-in campground, good fishing for brook and rainbow trout, and an excellent trailhead for hikers. The walk to the campsites is very short, one to three minutes, with many sites very close. Reaching the lake requires another five minutes, but a paved wheelchair-accessible trail is available. In addition, a switchbacked ramp for wheelchairs makes it one of the best wheelchair-accessible fishing areas in California. For hiking, a trail rises up steeply out of the campground and connects to the Pacific Crest Trail, from which you turn left to gain a dramatic lookout of Northern California peaks as well as the lake below.

Campsites, facilities: There are 13 drive-in sites for RVs or trailers up to 25 feet and five walk-in sites for tents. Picnic tables and fire grills are provided. Drinking water and vault toilets are available. Some facilities are wheelchair-accessible, including a nearby fishing pier. Leashed pets are permitted.

Reservations, fees: Reservations are not accepted. The fee is $10 per night. Senior discount available. Open June through October, weather permitting.

Directions: From Redding, drive north on I-5 just past Weed and take the Edgewood turnoff. At the stop sign, turn left and drive a short distance to the stop sign at Old Stage Road. Turn right on Old Stage Road and drive six miles to Gazelle. In Gazelle, turn left at Gazelle-Callahan Road and drive over the summit. From the summit, continue about five miles to Rail Creek Road. Turn left at Rail Creek Road and drive approximately five miles to where the road dead-ends at Kangaroo Lake Walk-In.

Contact: Klamath National Forest, Scott River Ranger Station, 530/468-5351, fax 530/468-1290.

38 MCBRIDE SPRINGS

Rating: 8

In Shasta-Trinity National Forest.
Map 2.2, page 109

This camp is set at 5,000 feet on the slopes of the awesome Mt. Shasta (14,162 feet), California's most majestic mountain. Stargazing is fantastic here, and during full moons, an eerie glow is cast on the adjoining high mountain slopes. A good side trip is to drive to the end of Everitt Memorial Highway, which tops out above 7,000 feet. You get great lookouts to the west and a jump-off point for a Shasta expedition or day hike to Panther Meadows.

Campsites, facilities: There are 10 sites for tents or small RVs. Picnic tables and fire grills are provided. Drinking water (from a single well with a hand pump at the north end of the campground) and vault toilets are available. Supplies and a coin laundry are available in the town of Mt. Shasta. Leashed pets are permitted.

Reservations, fees: Reservations are not accepted. The fee is $10 per night. Senior discount available. Open Memorial Day weekend through October, weather permitting.

Directions: From Redding drive north on I-5 to the town of Mt. Shasta and take the Central Mt. Shasta exit. Turn right and continue on Lake Street through town; once out of town, it turns to the left and becomes Everitt Memorial Highway. Continue on Everitt Memorial Highway for four miles to the campground entrance on the left side of the road.

Contact: Shasta-Trinity National Forest, Mt. Shasta Ranger District, 530/926-4511, fax 530/926-5120.

39 PANTHER MEADOWS WALK-IN

Rating: 9

In Shasta-Trinity National Forest.
Map 2.2, page 109

This quiet site, on the slopes of Mt. Shasta at 7,400 feet, features access to the pristine Panther Meadows, a high mountain meadow set just below tree line. It's a sacred place, regardless of your religious orientation. The hiking is excellent here, with a short hike out to Gray Butte (8,108 feet) for a perfect look to the south of Castle Crags, Mt. Lassen, and the Sacramento River Canyon. A three-night maximum stay is enforced to minimize long-term impacts.

Campsites, facilities: There are 10 walk-in tent sites (trailers not recommended). Picnic tables and fire grills are provided. Vault toilets are available. No drinking water is available. Garbage must be packed out. Supplies are available in the town of Mt. Shasta. Leashed pets are permitted.

Reservations, fees: Reservations are not accepted. There is no fee for camping. Open mid-June to mid-October, weather permitting.

Directions: From Redding, drive north on I-5 to the town of Mt. Shasta and take the Central Mt. Shasta exit. Turn right and continue on Lake Street through town; once out of town, Lake Street turns to the left and becomes Everitt Memorial Highway. Continue on Everitt Memorial Highway for about 10 miles to the Bunny Flat parking area (where the road is gated). Park, walk past the gate, and continue for one mile to the campground entrance on the right side of the road. Note: when the gate is open, the walk takes only a few minutes.

Contact: Shasta-Trinity National Forest, Mt. Shasta Ranger District, 530/926-4511, fax 530/926-5120.

40 SCOTT MOUNTAIN

Rating: 7

In Shasta-Trinity National Forest.
Map 2.2, page 109

This camp is a jump-off point for hikers, with the Pacific Crest Trail passing right by here. If you hike southwest, it leads into the Scott Mountains and skirts the northern edge of the Trinity Alps Wilderness. Another option here is driving on Forest Road 40N08, which begins directly across from camp and Highway 3. On this road, it's only two miles to Big Carmen Lake, a small, largely unknown and pretty little spot. Campground elevation is 5,400 feet.

Campsites, facilities: There are seven tent sites. Picnic tables and fire grills are provided. Vault toilets are available. No drinking water is available. All garbage must be packed out. Leashed pets are permitted.

Reservations, fees: Reservations are not accepted. There is no fee for camping. Open year-round.

Directions: From Redding, drive north on I-5 just past Weed and take the Edgewood turnoff. At the stop sign, turn left and drive a short distance to the stop sign at Old Stage Road. Turn right on Old Stage Road and drive six miles to Gazelle. In Gazelle, turn left at Gazelle-Callahan Road and drive to Callahan. In Callahan, turn south on Highway 3 and drive to Scott Mountain Summit and look for the campground on the right side of the road.

Contact: Shasta-Trinity National Forest, Weaverville Ranger Station, 530/623-2121, fax 530/623-6010.

41 TOAD LAKE WALK-IN

Rating: 9

In Shasta-Trinity National Forest.
Map 2.2, page 109

If you want the remote beauty and splendor of an alpine lake on the Pacific Crest Trail, yet you don't want to walk far to get there, this is the place. Little Toad Lake is no easy trick to get to, with a bone-jarring ride for the last half hour, followed by a 15-minute walk, but it's worth the effort. It's a beautiful little lake set at 6,900 feet in the Mt. Eddy Range, with lakeside sites, excellent swimming, fair fishing for small trout, and great hiking. The best of the latter is a 45-minute hike out of the Toad Lake Basin (follow the trail counterclockwise around the lake and up to the ridge) to Porcupine Lake, a pristine mountain lake.

Campsites, facilities: There are six walk-in tent sites. A vault toilet is provided, but it not always functioning. No drinking water is available. All garbage must be packed out. Leashed pets are permitted.

Reservations, fees: Reservations are not accepted. There is no fee for camping. Access roads may be closed because of flooding; call ahead for status. Open May through October, weather permitting.

Directions: From the town of Mt. Shasta on I-5, take the Central Mt. Shasta exit and drive to the stop sign. Turn west and drive a short distance to Old Stage Road. Turn left and drive a quarter mile to a Y at W. A. Barr Road. Bear right and drive past Box Canyon Dam and the entrance to Lake Siskiyou, and continue up the mountain (the road becomes Forest Road 26). Just past a concrete bridge, turn right at the sign for Toad Lake, drive .2 mile, then turn left on a dirt Forest Service road and continue for 11 miles to the parking area. The road is extremely bumpy and twisty, and the final half mile to the trailhead is rocky and rough. High-clearance, four-wheel-drive vehicles are recommended. Walk in about one-half mile to the lake and campsites.

Contact: Shasta-Trinity National Forest, Mt. Shasta Ranger District, 530/926-4511, fax 530/926-5120.

42 GUMBOOT LAKE

Rating: 9

In Shasta-Trinity National Forest.

Map 2.2, page 109

This pretty spot provides a few small camps set beside a small yet beautiful high mountain lake, the kind of place many think you can reach only with long hikes. Not so with Gumboot. In addition, the fishing is good here, with rainbow trout in the 12-inch class. The lake is small, almost too small for even a canoe, and better suited to a pram, raft, or float tube. No motors of any kind are permitted, including electric motors. When the fishing gets good, it can get crowded, with both out-of-towners and locals making casts from the shoreline. An option is hiking 10 minutes through forest to Upper Gumboot Lake, which is more of a pond with small trout. Another excellent hike is available here, tromping off-trail beyond Upper Gumboot Lake and up the back slope of the lake to the Pacific Crest Trail, then turning left and scrambling to a great lookout of Mt. Shasta in the distance and Gumboot in the foreground.

Campsites, facilities: There are four sites for tents or RVs up to 10 feet long, and across the creek there are four tent sites. Picnic tables are provided. Vault toilets are available. No drinking water is available. Garbage must be packed out. Leashed pets are permitted.

Reservations, fees: Reservations are not accepted. There is no fee for camping. Open May through October, weather permitting.

Directions: From the town of Mt. Shasta on I-5, take the Central Mt. Shasta exit and drive to the stop sign. Turn west and continue a short distance to Old Stage Road. Turn left and drive a quarter mile to a Y at W. A. Barr Road. Bear right on W. A. Barr Road and drive past Box Canyon Dam and the Lake Siskiyou Campground entrance. Continue 10 miles to a fork, signed for Gumboot Lake. Bear left and drive one-half mile to the lake and campsites.

Contact: Shasta-Trinity National Forest, Mt. Shasta Ranger District, 530/926-4511, fax 530/926-5120.

43 CASTLE LAKE

Rating:10

In Shasta-Trinity National Forest.

Map 2.2, page 109

Castle Lake is a beautiful spot, a deep blue lake set in a granite bowl with a spectacular wall on the far side. The views of Mt. Shasta are great, fishing is good (especially ice fishing in winter), canoeing or floating around on a raft is a lot of fun, and there is a terrific hike that loops around the left side of the lake, rising to the ridge overlooking the lake for dramatic views. The campground is not right beside the lake, to ensure the pristine clear waters remain untouched, but is rather just a short distance downstream along Castle Lake Creek. The elevation is 5,450 feet.

Campsites, facilities: There are six sites for tents or RVs up to 16 feet long. Picnic tables and fire grills are provided. Vault toilets are available.

No drinking water is available. Leashed pets are permitted.

Reservations, fees: Reservations are not accepted. There is no fee for camping. Open May through October, weather permitting.

Directions: From the town of Mt. Shasta on I-5, take the Central Mt. Shasta exit and drive to the stop sign. Turn west and drive a short distance to Old Stage Road. Turn left and drive a quarter mile to a Y at W. A. Barr Road. Bear right on W. A. Barr Road and drive past Box Canyon Dam. Turn left at Castle Lake Road and drive seven miles to the campground access road on the left. Turn left and drive a short distance to the campground. Note: Castle Lake is another quarter mile up the road; there are no legal campsites along the lake's shoreline.

Contact: Shasta-Trinity National Forest, Mt. Shasta Ranger District, 530/926-4511, fax 530/926-5120.

44 LAKE SISKIYOU CAMP-RESORT

Rating: 9

Near Mt. Shasta.

Map 2.2, page 109

This is a true gem of a lake, a jewel set at the foot of Mt. Shasta. The lake level is almost always full and offers a variety of quality recreation options, with great swimming, low-speed boating, and fishing. The campground complexes are huge, yet they are tucked into the forest so visitors don't get their style cramped. The water is clean and fresh, and the swimming can be a euphoric sensation on a hot summer afternoon. There is an excellent beach and swimming area, the latter protected by a buoy line. In spring, the fishing is good for trout, and then as the water warms, for smallmouth bass. A good boat ramp and boat rentals are available, and a 10-mph speed limit is strictly enforced, keeping the lake pristine and quiet.

Campsites, facilities: There are 150 sites for RVs, 25 with partial hookups and 125 with full hookups, including some drive-through sites, and 225 additional sites for tents, six of which are group areas. There are also 20 cabins and park-model cabins, and six RV rentals. Picnic tables and fire grills are provided. Drinking water, flush toilets, showers, playground, propane, grocery store, gift shop, deli, coin laundry, and an RV dump station are available. There are also a marina, boat rentals (canoes, kayaks, motorized boats), free boat launching, fishing dock, fish-cleaning station, swimming beach, and a banquet room. A free movie plays every night in the summer. Some facilities are wheelchair-accessible. Leashed pets are permitted.

Reservations, fees: Reservations are accepted. The fee is $18–25 per night, $1–2.50 per person for more than two people, $4 per night for each additional vehicle, $1 per pet per night. Major credit cards are accepted. Open April through October, weather permitting.

Directions: From the town of Mt. Shasta on I-5, take the Central Mt. Shasta exit and drive to the stop sign. Turn west and drive a short distance to Old Stage Road. Turn left and drive one-quarter mile to a Y at W. A. Barr Road. Bear right on W. A. Barr Road and drive past Box Canyon Dam. Two miles farther, turn right at the entrance road for Lake Siskiyou Campground and Marina and drive a short distance to the entrance station.

Contact: Lake Siskiyou Camp-Resort, 530/926-2618 or 888/926-2618, website: www.lakesis.com.

45 KOA MT. SHASTA

Rating: 7

In Mt. Shasta city.

Map 2.2, page 109

Despite this KOA camp's relative proximity to the town of Mt. Shasta, the extended driveway, wooded grounds, and view of Mt. Shasta offer some feeling of seclusion. A bonus here is that those cute little KOA log cabins are available, providing additional privacy. There are many excellent side trips. The best is driving up Everitt Memorial Highway, which rises up the slopes of Mt. Shasta to the tree line at Bunny Flat, where you can take outstanding, short day hikes with great views to the south of the Sacramento River Canyon and Castle Crags. In the winter, you can play in the snow, including heading up to Bunny Flat for snowplay or to the Mt. Shasta Board & Ski Park for developed downhill and cross-country skiing. One of the biggest events of the year in Mt. Shasta is the Fourth of July Run For Fun and associated parade and fireworks display at nearby Lake Siskiyou.

Campsites, facilities: There are 41 sites with full hookups for RVs, including many drive-through sites, 89 additional sites for tents or RVs (partial hookups), and four camping cabins. Picnic tables and fire grills are provided. Restrooms, showers, a playground, propane gas, a grocery store, horseshoe pit, shuffleboard, a swimming pool, and coin laundry are available. Some facilities are wheelchair-accessible. Leashed pets are permitted.

Reservations, fees: Reservations are accepted at 800/562-3617. The fee is $15–27 per night, $2–3 per person for more than two people. Major credit cards accepted. Open year-round.

Directions: From Redding, drive north on I-5 to the town of Mt. Shasta. Continue past the first Mt. Shasta exit and take the Central Mt. Shasta exit. Turn right at the stop sign and drive to Mt. Shasta Boulevard. Turn left and drive a half mile to East Hinckley Boulevard. Turn right (signed KOA) on East Hinckley, drive a very short distance, then turn left at the entrance to the extended driveway for KOA Mt. Shasta.

Contact: KOA Mt. Shasta, 530/926-4029, website: www.koa.com.

46 MCCLOUD DANCE COUNTRY RV PARK

Rating: 6

In McCloud.

Map 2.2, page 109

Dance Country RV Park is very popular with square dancers in the summer. The town of McCloud is the home of McCloud Dance Country Hall, a large dance hall dedicated to square and round dancing. The park is sprinkled with old-growth pine trees and bordered by Squaw Valley Creek, a pretty stream. The RV sites are grassy and manicured, many shaded. McCloud River's three waterfalls are accessible from the McCloud River Loop, five miles south of the park on Highway 89. Mt. Shasta Board & Ski Park also offers summer activities such as biking, mountain climbing, and chairlift rides to great views of the surrounding forests. The ski park access road is six miles west of McCloud off Highway 89 at Snowman's Hill Summit. The McCloud River Railroad runs an excursion and a dinner train on summer weekends out of McCloud; reservations are available in town. If you're lucky you might see "Old Engine No. 25," one of the few remaining steam engines in service. (For more information, see Fowler's Camp.)

Campsites, facilities: There are 137 sites, most with full hookups and the rest with water and electricity, for RVs of any length, a grassy area for dispersed tent camping, and seven park-model cabins. There are a few long-term rentals. Picnic tables are provided. Drinking water, restrooms with hot showers, a central barbecue and campfire area, cable TV, modem access, coin laundry, RV dump station, propane, horseshoes, fish-cleaning station, and two pet walks are available. Some facilities are wheelchair-accessible. Large groups are welcome. Leashed pets are permitted.

Reservations, fees: Reservations are recommended. The fee is $15–24 per night for two people, $1.50 for each additional child 6–12 years old, and $3 for each additional camper 13 years of age or older. Major credit cards accepted. Open year-round.

Directions: From Redding, drive north on I-5 and continue just past Dunsmuir to the junction with Highway 89. Turn east on Highway 89 and drive nine miles to McCloud and Squaw Valley Road. Turn right on Squaw Valley Road and then turn immediately left into the park entrance.

Contact: McCloud Dance Country RV Park, 530/964-2252, website: www.mccloudrvpark.com.

47 FOWLER'S CAMP

Rating:10

On the McCloud River in Shasta-Trinity National Forest.

Map 2.2, page 109

This campground is set beside the beautiful McCloud River, providing the chance for an easy hike to two waterfalls, including one of the most dramatic in Northern California. From the camp, the trail is routed upstream through forest, a near-level walk for only 15 minutes, then arrives at awesome Middle Falls, a wide-sweeping and powerful cascade best viewed in April. By summer, the flows subside and warm to the point that some people will swim in the pool at the base of the falls. Another trail is routed from camp downstream to Lower Falls, an outstanding swimming hole in midsummer. Fishing the McCloud River here is fair, with trout stocks made from Lakim Dam on downstream to the camp. If this camp is full, Cattle Camp and Algoma offer overflow areas.

Campsites, facilities: There are 39 sites for tents or RVs up to 30 feet long. Picnic tables and fire grills are provided. Drinking water and vault toilets are available. Some facilities are wheelchair-accessible. Leashed pets are permitted.

Reservations, fees: Reservations are not accepted. The fee is $12 per night. Senior discount available. Open May through October.

Directions: From Redding, drive north on I-5 and continue just past Dunsmuir to the junction with Highway 89. Turn east on Highway 89 and drive 12 miles to McCloud. From McCloud, drive five miles southeast on Highway 89 to the campground entrance road on the right. Turn right and drive a short distance to a Y, then turn left at the Y to the campground.

Contact: Shasta-Trinity National Forest, McCloud Ranger District, 530/964-2184, fax 530/964-2938.

48 ALGOMA

Rating: 7

On the McCloud River in Shasta-Trinity National Forest.

Map 2.2, page 109

This little-known, undeveloped spot along the McCloud River is quite dusty in August. It is an alternative to Fowler's Camp and Cattle Camp. (See those entries for side trip options.) A dirt road out of Algoma Camp (turn right at the junction) follows along the headwaters of the McCloud River, past Cattle Camp to Upper Falls. There is a parking area for a short walk to view Middle Falls and on to Fowler's Camp and Lower Falls.

Campsites, facilities: There are eight sites for tents or RVs. Picnic tables and fire grills are provided. A vault toilet is available intermittently; if this is of concern, call first. No drinking water is available. Leashed pets are permitted.

Reservations, fees: Reservations are not accepted. There is no fee for camping. Open late April to October, weather permitting.

Directions: From Redding, drive north on I-5 and continue just past Dunsmuir to the junction with Highway 89. Turn east on Highway 89 and drive to McCloud. From McCloud, drive 14 miles east on Highway 89 to the campground entrance road on the right (signed). Turn right and drive one mile to the campground on the right side of the road.

Contact: Shasta-Trinity National Forest, McCloud Ranger District, 530/964-2184, fax 530/964-2938.

49 CATTLE CAMP

Rating: 5

On the McCloud River in Shasta-Trinity National Forest.

Map 2.2, page 109

This campground is ideal for RV campers who want a rustic setting, or as an overflow area if the more attractive Fowler's Camp is filled. One of the best swimming holes in the Mc-Cloud River is near the camp, although the water is typically cold. There are several good side trips in the area, including fishing on the nearby McCloud River, visiting the three waterfalls near Fowler's Camp, and exploring the north slopes of Mt. Shasta (a map of Shasta-Trinity National Forest details the back roads).

Campsites, facilities: There are 27 sites for tents or RVs. Picnic tables and fire grills are provided. Drinking water and vault toilets are available. Some facilities are wheelchair-accessible, including toilets. Leashed pets are permitted.

Reservations, fees: Reservations are not accepted. The fee is $12 per night. Senior discount available. Open late April to October, weather permitting.

Directions: From Redding, drive north on I-5 and continue just past Dunsmuir to the junction with Highway 89. Turn east on Highway 89 and drive to McCloud. From McCloud, drive 11 miles east on Highway 89 to the campground entrance road on the right. Turn right and drive a half mile to the campground on the left side of the road.

Contact: Shasta-Trinity National Forest, McCloud Ranger District, 530/964-2184, fax 530/964-2938.

50 TRAIL CREEK

Rating: 7

In Klamath National Forest.
Map 2.2, page 109

This simple and quiet camp is set beside Trail Creek, a small tributary to the upper Salmon River, at an elevation of 4,700 feet. A trailhead is about a mile to the south, accessible via a Forest Service road, providing access to a two-mile trail routed along Fish Creek and leading to little Fish Lake. From Fish Lake the trail climbs steeply, switchbacking at times, for another two miles to larger Trail Gull Lake,

a very pretty spot set below Deadman Peak (7,741 feet).

Campsites, facilities: There are seven sites for tents or RVs up to 22 feet long and eight sites for tents only. Picnic tables and fire grills are provided. Drinking water and vault toilets are available. Leashed pets are permitted.

Reservations, fees: Reservations are not accepted. The fee is $6 per night. Senior discount available. Open May through October.

Directions: From Redding, drive north on I-5 past Weed to the Edgewood exit. Take the Edgewood exit, turn left at the stop sign, and drive a short distance to another stop sign at Old Stage Road. Turn right at Old Stage Road and drive to Gazelle. In Gazelle, turn left on Gazelle-Callahan Road and continue to Callahan. In Callahan, turn southwest on Cecilville Road and drive 17 miles to the campground.

Contact: Klamath National Forest, Scott River Ranger District, 530/468-5351, fax 530/468-1290.

51 HIDDEN HORSE

Rating: 7

In Klamath National Forest.
Map 2.2, page 109

Hidden Horse Camp provides an alternate horse camp to nearby Carter Meadows. The horse camps are in close proximity to the Pacific Crest National Scenic Trail, which passes through the area and serves as access to the Russian Wilderness to the north and the Trinity Alps Wilderness to the south. Trail Creek and East Fork are nearby.

Campsites, facilities: There are six sites for tents or RVs. Picnic tables and fire grills are provided. Drinking water and vault toilets are available. A horse-mounting ramp and corral hitching posts are also available. There is no designated water for stock available. Some facilities are wheelchair-accessible.

Reservations, fees: Reservations are not accepted. The fee is $10 per night. Senior discount available. Open late May to mid-October, weather permitting.

Directions: From Redding, drive north on I-5 past Weed. Take the Edgewood exit, turn left at the stop sign, and drive a short distance. Turn right on Old Stage Road, drive to Gazelle, turn left on Gazelle-Callahan Road, and continue to Callahan. In Callahan turn southwest on Cecilville Road and drive 11 miles to Carter Meadows Horse Camp. Continue one-quarter mile to the campground on the left.

Contact: Klamath National Forest, Scott River Ranger District, 530/468-5351, fax 530/468-1290.

52 CARTER MEADOWS HORSE CAMP

Rating: 7

In Klamath National Forest.
Map 2.2, page 109

Carter Meadows offers an extensive trail network for riding and hiking. The Pacific Crest National Scenic Trail passes through the area and serves as access to the Russian Wilderness to the north and the Trinity Alps Wilderness to the south. Stream fishing is another option here. Trail Creek and East Fork are nearby.

Campsites, facilities: There is one group equestrian site for tents or RVs, with three large horse corrals. Group barbecues and picnic tables are provided. Drinking water and vault toilets are available. One toilet is wheelchair-accessible. Stock water troughs are also available.

Reservations, fees: Reservations are required with a $9 reservation fee at 800/444-6777 or website www.ReserveUsa.com. The rate is $30 per night. Open mid-June to mid-October, weather permitting.

Directions: From Redding, drive north on I-5 past Weed. Take the Edgewood exit, turn left at the stop sign, and drive a short distance. Turn right on Old Stage Road, drive to Gazelle, turn left on Gazelle-Callahan Road, and continue to Callahan. In Callahan turn southwest

on Cecilville Road and drive 11 miles to the campground.

Contact: Klamath National Forest, Scott River Ranger District, 530/468-5351, fax 530/468-1290.

53 HORSE FLAT

Rating: 6

On Eagle Creek in Shasta-Trinity National Forest.
Map 2.2, page 109

This camp is used by commercial pack operations as well as horse owners preparing for trips into the Trinity Alps. The camp even has a corral, though it was unused on our visit. A trail starts right out of camp and is routed deep into the Trinity Alps Wilderness. It starts at 3,200 feet in elevation, then climbs all the way along Eagle Creek to Eagle Peak, where it intersects with the Pacific Crest Trail, then drops over the ridge to little Telephone Lake, a nine-mile hike. Note: horse owners should call for the condition of the corral before making the trip.

Campsites, facilities: There are five tent sites and 11 sites for tents or RVs up to 16 feet long. Picnic tables and fire grills are provided. Vault toilets are available. No drinking water is available. Horse corrals are available. Garbage must be packed out. Leashed pets are permitted.

Reservations, fees: Reservations are not accepted. There is no fee for camping. Open mid-May through October.

Directions: From Redding, drive west on Highway 299 to Weaverville and Highway 3. Turn north on Highway 3 and drive to Trinity Center at the north end of Trinity Lake. From Trinity Center, continue north on Highway 3 for 16.5 miles to Eagle Creek Campground (on the right) and Forest Road 38N27 on the left. Turn left on Forest Road 38N27 and drive two miles to the campground.

Contact: Shasta-Trinity National Forest, Weaverville Ranger Station, 530/623-2121, fax 530/623-6010.

54 EAGLE CREEK

Rating: 7

In Shasta-Trinity National Forest.
Map 2.2, page 109

This campground is set where little Eagle Creek enters the north Trinity River. Some campers use it as a base camp for a fishing trip, with the rainbow trout often abundant but predictably small in this stretch of water. The campground is open year-round, but there is no drinking water in the winter. The elevation is 2,800 feet.

Campsites, facilities: There are five tent sites and 12 sites for tents or RVs up to 27 feet long. Picnic tables and fire grills are provided. Drinking water (spring, summer, and fall only) and vault toilets are available, and there is a camp host. Leashed pets are permitted.

Reservations, fees: Reservations are not accepted. The fee is $9 per night. Senior discount available. Open year-round.

Directions: From Redding, drive west on Highway 299 to Weaverville and Highway 3. Turn north on Highway 3 and drive to Trinity Center at the north end of Trinity Lake. From Trinity Center, continue north on Highway 3 for 16.5 miles to the campground on the right side of the road.

Contact: Shasta-Trinity National Forest, Weaverville Ranger Station, 530/623-2121, fax 530/623-6010.

55 RAILROAD PARK RV & CAMPGROUND

Rating: 7

South of Dunsmuir.
Map 2.2, page 109

This camp was designed in the spirit of the railroad, when steam trains ruled the rails. The property features old stage cars (available for overnight lodging) and a steam locomotive. Many good side trips are available in the area, including excellent hiking and sightseeing at Castle Crags State Park (where there is a series of awesome granite spires) and outstanding trout fishing on the upper Sacramento River. At night, the sound of occasional passing trains soothes some, wakes others.

Campsites, facilities: There are 24 sites with full hookups for RVs, including some drive-through sites, four sites for RVs with no hookups, and a separate area with 17 sites for tents only. Restrooms, hot showers, satellite TV hookups, ice, coin laundry, recreation room, playground, and horseshoes are available. A restaurant and lounge are within walking distance. Some facilities are wheelchair-accessible. Leashed pets are permitted.

Reservations, fees: Reservations are accepted with a deposit. The fee is $18–25 fee per night, $2 per person per night for more than two people. Major credit cards accepted. Open April through October.

Directions: From Redding, drive north on I-5 for 45 miles to the exit for Cragview Drive/Railroad Park Road. Take that exit and drive a half mile (the road becomes Railroad Park Road). Turn left under the freeway and continue to the campground on the left.

Contact: Railroad Park RV & Campground, 530/235-0420, website: www.rrpark.com

56 CASTLE CRAGS STATE PARK

Rating: 9

On the Sacramento River.
Map 2.2, page 109

This park is named for the awesome granite spires that tower 6,000 feet above the park. Beyond to the north is giant Mt. Shasta (14,162 feet), making for a spectacular natural setting. The campsites are set in forest, shaded, very pretty, and sprinkled along a paved access road. But not a year goes by when people don't write in complaining of the highway noise from I-5 echoing in the Sacramento River Canyon, as well as of the occasional passing freight trains in the night. Pristine quiet, this campground is not. At the end of the access road is a parking area for the two-minute walk to the Crags Lookout, a beautiful view. Nearby is the trailhead (at 2,500 feet elevation) for hikes up the Crags, featuring a 6.2-mile round-trip that rises to Castle Dome at 4,966 feet, the leading spire on the crag's ridge. Again, road noise echoing up the canyon provides a background once you clear the tree line. Trout fishing is good in the nearby Sacramento River but requires driving, walking, and exploring to find the best spots. There are also some good swimming holes, but the water is cold. This is a popular state park, with reservations often required in summer, but with your choice of any campsite even in late spring.

Campsites, facilities: There are 64 sites for tents or RVs up to 27 feet, an overflow area with 12 sites and limited facilities, and six primitive walk-in sites (100-yard walk required). Picnic tables, food lockers, and fire grills are provided. Drinking water, wood, hot showers, and flush toilets are available. Leashed pets are permitted at campsites only.

Reservations, fees: Reservations are accepted with a $7.50 reservation fee at 800/444-PARK (800/444-7275) and website www.Reserve America.com. The fee is $12 per night. Senior discount available. Open year-round.

Directions: From Redding, drive north on I-5 for 45 miles to the Castle Crags State Park exit. Turn west and drive to the well-signed park entrance on the right side of the road.

Contact: Castle Crags State Park, 530/235-2684, fax 530/235-1965.

57 FRIDAY'S RV RETREAT & MCCLOUD FLY FISHING RANCH

🏃 🏊 🐕 ♿ 🚐 ⛺

Rating: 7

Near McCloud.

Map 2.2, page 109

Friday's offers great recreation opportunities for every member of the family. The property features a private fishing pond, a casting pond, 1.5 miles of Squaw Valley Creek frontage, and five miles of hiking trails. In addition, the McCloud River's wild trout section is a half-hour drive to the south, the beautiful McCloud Golf Course (nine holes) is within a five-minute drive, and a trailhead for the Pacific Crest Trail is also only five minutes away. The park covers 400 wooded and grassy acres. Owner Bob Friday is quite a character, and he figured out that if he planted giant rainbow trout in the ponds for catch-and-release fishing, fly fishers would stop to catch a monster and take a photograph, and then tell people they caught the fish on the McCloud River, where they are smaller and elusive. Also available is the dinner and excursion train that runs out of McCloud on summer weekends. See Ah-Di-Na and McCloud Dance Country RV Park for other information and side trip options.

Campsites, facilities: There are 30 sites with full hookups, including mostly drive-through sites, for RVs of any length, a large, grassy area for dispersed tent camping, and two cabins. Picnic tables and fire pits are provided. Drinking water, restrooms with hot showers and flush toilets, cable TV, laundry room, pay phone, propane gas, and a recreation room are available. A flyfishing school is available by arrangement. Some facilities are wheelchair-accessible. Leashed pets are permitted.

Reservations, fees: Reservations are recommended. The fee is $15–22 per night for two people, $3 per person for more than two people. Monthly rates available. Open mid-May to mid-September, weather permitting.

Directions: From Redding, drive north on I-5 and continue just past Dunsmuir to the junction with Highway 89. Bear right on Highway 89 and drive nine miles to McCloud and Squaw Valley Road. Turn right at Squaw Valley Road and drive six miles to the park entrance on the right.

Contact: Friday's, 530/964-2878, website: www.fridaysflyshop.com.

58 BIG FLAT

Rating: 8

On Coffee Creek in Klamath National Forest.

Map 2.2, page 109

This is a great jump-off spot for a wilderness backpacking trip into the adjacent Trinity Alps. An 11-mile hike will take you into the beautiful Caribou Lakes Basin for lakeside campsites, excellent swimming, dramatic sunsets, and fair trout fishing. The trail is routed out of camp, crosses the stream, then climbs a series of switchbacks to the ridge. From here it gets easier, rounding a mountain and depositing you in the basin. Bypass Little Caribou, Lower Caribou, and Snowslide Lakes, and instead head all the way to Caribou, the biggest and best of the lot. Big Flat is set at 5,000 feet in elevation along Coffee Creek, and on the drive in, you'll see big piles of boulders along the stream, evidence of past gold mining activity.

Campsites, facilities: There are nine sites for tents or RVs up to 16 feet long. Picnic tables and fire grills are provided. Vault toilets are available. No drinking water is available. Garbage must be packed out. Leashed pets are permitted.

Reservations, fees: Reservations are not accepted. There is no fee for camping. Open year-round, weather permitting.

Directions: From Redding, turn east on Highway 299 and drive to Weaverville. In Weaverville, turn north on Highway 3 and drive just past the north end of Trinity Lake to Coffee Creek Road/Forest Road 104, adjacent to a Forest Service ranger station. Turn left on Coffee Creek Road and drive 21 miles to the campground at the end of the road.

Contact: Klamath National Forest, Salmon River Ranger District, 530/468-5351, fax 530/468-1290.

59 GOLDFIELD

Rating: 6

In Shasta-Trinity National Forest.

Map 2.2, page 109

For hikers, this camp makes a perfect first stop after a long drive. You wake up, get your gear organized, then take the trailhead to the south. It is routed along Boulder Creek, and with a left turn at the junction (about four miles in) will take you to Boulder Lake (another two miles), set inside the edge of the Trinity Alps Wilderness. Former 49er coach George Seifert first told me about the beauty of this place and how perfectly this campground is situated for the hike. Campground elevation is 3,000 feet.

Campsites, facilities: There are six tent sites. Picnic tables and fire grills are provided. Vault toilets and hitching posts for horses are available. No drinking water is available. Pack out all garbage. Leashed pets are permitted.

Reservations, fees: Reservations are not accepted. There is no fee for camping. Open year-round.

Directions: From Redding, head east on Highway 299 and drive to Weaverville. Turn north on Highway 3 and drive just past the north end of Trinity Lake to Coffee Creek Road/Forest Road 104, adjacent to a Forest Service ranger station. Turn left on Coffee Creek Road/Forest Road 104 and drive 6.5 miles to the campground on the left side of the road.

Contact: Shasta-Trinity National Forest, Weaverville Ranger Station, 530/623-2121, fax 530/623-6010.

60 TRINITY RIVER

Rating: 7

In Shasta-Trinity National Forest.

Map 2.2, page 109

This camp offers easy access off Highway 3, yet it is fairly secluded and provides streamside access to the upper Trinity River. It's a good base camp for a fishing trip when the upper Trinity is loaded with small trout. The elevation is 2,500 feet.

Campsites, facilities: There are seven sites for tents or RVs up to 32 feet long. Picnic tables and fire grills are provided. Drinking water (spring, summer, and fall only) and vault toilets are available, and there is a camp host. Leashed pets are permitted.

Reservations, fees: Reservations are not accepted. The fee is $9 per night. Senior discount available. Open year-round, but there's no drinking water in the winter.

Directions: From Redding, drive west on Highway 299 to Weaverville and Highway 3. Turn north on Highway 3 and drive to Trinity Center at the north end of Trinity Lake. From Trinity Center, continue north on Highway 3 for 9.5 miles to the campground on the left side of the road.

Contact: Shasta-Trinity National Forest, Weaverville Ranger Station, 530/623-2121, fax 530/623-6010.

61 BEST IN THE WEST RESORT
Rating: 3

Near Dunsmuir.

Map 2.2, page 109

This is a good layover spot for RV cruisers looking to take a break. The proximity to Castle Crags State Park, the Sacramento River, and Mt. Shasta make the location a winner. Trains make regular runs every night in the Sacramento River Canyon and the noise is a problem for some visitors.

Campsites, facilities: There are 16 sites, most with full hookups, for RVs, and a separate grassy area for dispersed tent camping, five cabins, and a lodge. Picnic tables are provided. Restrooms, hot showers, cable TV, coin laundry, and playground are available. Leashed pets are permitted.

Reservations, fees: Reservations are accepted.

The fee is $15 per night. Monthly rates available. Open year-round.

Directions: From Redding, drive north on I-5 for about 40 miles to the Sims Road exit. Take the Sims Road exit and drive one block west on Sims Road to the campground on the left.

Contact: Best in the West Resort, 530/235-2603, website:eggerbestwest.com.

62 SIMS FLAT
Rating: 7

On the Sacramento River.

Map 2.2, page 109

The upper Sacramento River is again becoming one of the best trout streams in the West that provides easy and direct access off an interstate highway. This camp is a good example. Sitting beside the upper Sacramento River at an elevation of 1,600 feet, it provides access to some of the better spots for trout fishing, particularly from mid-May through July. The trout population has recovered since the devastating spill from a train derailment that occurred in 1991, and there's good trout fishing in this area. There is a wheelchair-accessible interpretive trail. If you want to literally get away from it all, there is a trailhead about three miles east on Sims Flat Road that climbs along South Fork, including a terrible, steep, one-mile section near the top, eventually popping out at Tombstone Mountain. The noise from passing trains can be a shock for newcomers.

Campsites, facilities: There are 19 sites for tents or RVs up to 16 feet. Picnic tables and fire grills are provided. Drinking water and flush and vault toilets are available. A grocery store is nearby. Some facilities are wheelchair-accessible. Leashed pets are permitted.

Reservations, fees: Reservations are not accepted. The fee is $12 per night. Senior discount available. Open April through October.

Directions: From Redding, drive north on I-5 for about 40 miles to the Sims Road exit. Take the Sims Road exit (on the east side of the highway) and drive south for a mile to the campground.

Contact: Shasta-Trinity National Forest, Mt. Shasta Ranger District, 530/926-4511, fax 530/926-5120.

63 AH-DI-NA

Rating: 9

On the McCloud River in Shasta-Trinity National Forest.

Map 2.2, page 109

This is the perfect base camp for trout fishing on the lower McCloud River, with campsites just a cast away from one of the prettiest streams in California. Downstream of the camp is a special two-mile stretch of river governed by the Nature Conservancy, where all fish must be released, no bait is permitted, single, barbless hooks are mandated, and only 10 rods are allowed on the river at any one time. Wildlife is abundant in the area, the Pacific Crest Trail passes adjacent to the camp, and an excellent nature trail is also available along the river in the McCloud Nature Conservancy.

Campsites, facilities: There are 17 tent sites. Picnic tables and fire grills are provided. Drinking water and flush toilets are available. Leashed pets are permitted.

Reservations, fees: Reservations are not accepted. The fee is $8 per night. Senior discount available. Open late April to mid-November, weather permitting.

Directions: From Redding, drive north on I-5 past Dunsmuir to the junction with Highway 89. Turn right and drive nine miles to McCloud and Squaw Valley Road. Turn right on Squaw Valley Road and drive to Lake McCloud. Turn right at Lake McCloud and continue along the lake to a signed turnoff on the right side of the road (at a deep cove in the lake). Turn right (the road turns to dirt) and drive four miles to the campground entrance on the left side of

the road. Turn left and drive a short distance to the campground.

Contact: Shasta-Trinity National Forest, McCloud Ranger District, 530/964-2184, fax 530/964-2938.

64 EAST FORK WILLOW CREEK

Rating: 9

On Willow Creek.

Map 2.3, page 110

This is a beautiful spot along Willow Creek. Set at a 2,000-foot elevation, it's one of the prettiest campgrounds in the area. In August and September the river is often quite warm, ideal for swimming or tubing. In the winter it is one of the better camps for shoreline steelhead fishing. Way back in the 1950s and early 1960s this was one of the better-known campgrounds in the area, but the flood of 1964 wiped it out. Only recently have rehabilitation efforts restored it to life.

Campsites, facilities: There are 13 sites for tents and RVs up to 35 feet long. Picnic tables and fire rings are provided. Vault toilets with wheelchair access are available. No drinking water is available. Leashed pets are permitted.

Reservations, fees: Reservations are not accepted. The fee is $8 per night, $5 per night for additional vehicles, two vehicles maximum per site. Senior discount available. Open May through October.

Directions: From the junction of U.S. 101 and Highway 299 near Arcata, turn east on Highway 299 and drive 32 miles (six miles west of Willow Creek) and look for the camp's entrance road (well signed) on the right (south) side of the road.

Contact: Six Rivers National Forest, Lower Trinity Ranger District, 530/629-2118, fax 530/629-2102. For a map, send $6 to U.S. Forest Service, Attn: Map Sales, P.O. Box 9035, Prescott, AZ 86313, 928/443-8285 with credit card, website: www.fs.fed.us/maps/; ask for the Six Rivers National Forest.

65 BOISE CREEK

Rating: 7

In Six Rivers National Forest.

Map 2.3, page 110

This camp features a quarter-mile-long trail down to Boise Creek and nearby access to the Trinity River. If you have ever wanted to see Bigfoot, you can do it while camping here because there's a giant wooden Bigfoot on display in nearby Willow Creek. After your Bigfoot experience, your best bet during summer is to head north on nearby Highway 96 (turn north in Willow Creek) to the campground at Tish Tang, where there is excellent river access, swimming, and rafting in the late summer's warm flows. The Trinity River also provides good salmon and steelhead fishing during fall and winter, respectively, with the best nearby access upriver along Highway 299 at Burnt Ranch. Note that fishing is prohibited in nearby Willow Creek. Also note that in the past, drinking water was available at this campground and that the required repairs to the water system were not scheduled as of the publication date in 2003.

Campsites, facilities: There are several sites for bicyclists and hikers and 17 sites for tents or RVs up to 35 feet long. Picnic tables and fire grills are provided. No drinking water. Vault toilets are available, and a camp host is on-site. A grocery store, gas station, restaurant, and propane gas are available nearby. Leashed pets are permitted.

Reservations, fees: Reservations are not accepted. The fee is $10 per night, $4 for an extra vehicle. Senior discount available. Open year-round, with limited services in winter.

Directions: From the intersection of U.S. 101 and Highway 299 near Arcata, drive 38 miles east on Highway 299 and look for the campground entrance on the left side of the road. If you reach the town of Willow Creek, you have gone 1.5 miles too far.

Contact: Six Rivers National Forest, Lower Trinity Ranger District, 530/629-2118, fax 530/629-2102.

66 DENNY

Rating: 8

On the New River in Shasta-Trinity National Forest.

Map 2.3, page 110

This is a secluded and quiet campground along the New River, a tributary to the Trinity River and a designated Wild and Scenic River. The stream here is OK for swimming but too cold to even dip a toe in until late summer. If you drive north from the camp on Denny Road, you will find several trailheads for trips into the Trinity Alps Wilderness. The best of them is at the end of the road, where there is a good parking area, with a trail that is routed along the East Fork New River up toward Limestone Ridge. Note that the stretch of river near the camp is closed to fishing year-round. The campground is set at 1,400 feet.

Campsites, facilities: There are 16 tent sites and six sites for tents or RVs up to 25 feet long. Picnic tables and fire grills are provided. Vault toilets are available. No drinking water is available. All garbage must be packed out. Leashed pets are permitted. Supplies are available about one hour away in Salyers Bar.

Reservations, fees: Reservations are not accepted. There is no fee for camping. Open year-round.

Directions: From the junction of U.S. 101 and Highway 299 near Arcata, turn east on Highway 299 and drive to Willow Creek. In Willow Creek, continue east on Highway 299 and, after reaching Salyer, continue for four miles to Denny Road/County Road 402. Turn north on Denny Road and drive about 14 miles on a paved but very windy road to the campground.

Contact: Shasta-Trinity National Forest, Big Bar Ranger Station, 530/623-6106 or 530/623-6123.

67 HOBO GULCH

Rating: 7

On the North Fork of the Trinity River in Shasta-Trinity National Forest.

Map 2.3, page 110

Only the ambitious need apply. This is a trailhead camp set on the edge of the Trinity Alps Wilderness, and the reason only the ambitious show up is that it is a 20-mile uphill haul all the way to Grizzly Lake, set at the foot of the awesome Thompson Peak (8,663 feet), with no other lakes available en route. The camp is set at 2,900 feet along the North Fork of the Trinity River. The adjacent slopes of the wilderness are known for little creeks, woods, and a few pristine meadows, and are largely devoid of lakes.

Campsites, facilities: There are 10 sites for tents or RVs. Picnic tables and fire grills are provided. Vault toilets are available. No drinking water is available. Garbage must be packed out. Supplies can be obtained in Junction City, about one hour away. Leashed pets are permitted.

Reservations, fees: Reservations are not accepted. There is no fee for camping. Open year-round, weather permitting.

Directions: From Redding, turn west on Highway 299, drive past Weaverville, and continue 13 miles to Helena. In Helena, turn right and drive four miles on County East Fork Road to Hobo Gulch Road. At Hobo Gulch Road, turn north and drive 16 miles to the end of the road at the campground.

Contact: Shasta-Trinity National Forest, Big Bar Ranger Station, 530/623-6106, fax 530/623-6123.

68 RIPSTEIN

Rating: 8

On Canyon Creek in Shasta-Trinity National Forest.

Map 2.3, page 110

This is one of the great trailhead camps for the neighboring Trinity Alps. It is set at 2,600 feet on the southern edge of the wilderness and is a popular spot for a late-night arrival followed by a backpacking trip the next morning. Waiting are the Canyon Creek Lakes via a six-mile uphill hike along Canyon Creek. The destination is extremely beautiful—two alpine lakes set in high granite mountains. The route passes Canyon Creek Falls, a set of two different waterfalls, about 3.5 miles out. This is one of the most popular backpacking destinations in Northern California.

Campsites, facilities: There are 10 tent sites. Picnic tables and fire grills are provided. Vault toilets are available. No drinking water is available. Garbage must be packed out. Supplies can be obtained 45 minutes away in Junction City. Leashed pets are permitted.

Reservations, fees: Reservations are not accepted. There is no fee for camping. Open year-round.

Directions: From Redding, head west on Highway 299 and drive to Junction City. At Junction City, turn right on Canyon Creek Road and drive 15 miles to the campground on the left side of the road.

Contact: Shasta-Trinity National Forest, Big Bar Ranger Station, 530/623-6106, fax 530/623-6123.

69 BURNT RANCH

Rating: 7

On the Trinity River in Shasta-Trinity National Forest.

Map 2.3, page 110

This campground is set on a bluff above the Trinity River and is one of its most compelling spots. Burnt Ranch Falls isn't much of a waterfall, but it provides a fantastic spot to watch salmon and steelhead leap like hurdlers to make it past the falls and into a calm pool above. The peak migration periods are in mid-September for salmon and in early winter and early spring for steelhead. On their migratory route, the fish will hold below the falls, gaining strength for their upriver surge, making it a natural fishing spot. This section of river is very pretty, with deep, dramatic canyons nearby. The elevation is 1,000 feet.

Campsites, facilities: There are 16 sites for tents or RVs up to 25 feet long, and a group site for up to eight people. There is a maximum of two vehicles per unit, except at the group site. Picnic tables and fire grills are provided. Drinking water and vault toilets are available. Garbage must be packed out. Supplies can be obtained in Hawkins Bar about one hour away. Leashed pets are permitted.

Reservations, fees: Reservations are not accepted. The fee is $8 per night in season. Senior discount available. Open year-round, weather permitting.

Directions: From Redding, take Highway 299 west and drive past Weaverville to Burnt Ranch. In Burnt Ranch, continue a half mile and look for the campground entrance on the right side of the road.

Contact: Shasta-Trinity National Forest, Big Bar Ranger Station, 530/623-6106, fax 530/623-6123.

70 DEL LOMA RV PARK AND CAMPGROUND

Rating: 7

On the Trinity River.

Map 2.3, page 110

RV cruisers looking for a layover spot near the Trinity River will find just that at Del Loma. Shady sites and sandy beaches are available here along the Trinity. Rafting and tubing trips are popular in this area during the summer. Salmon fishing is best in the fall, steelhead fishing in the winter. This camp is popular for family reunions and groups. Salmon fishing can be sensational on the Trinity in the fall and some anglers will book a year in advance to make certain they get a spot. The park was largely remodeled in 2001 and 2002.

Campsites, facilities: There are 41 sites, including two drive-through, with full or partial hookups for RVs and tents, two park-model cabins, and 29 apartments. Picnic tables, fire grills, flush toilets, hot showers, and an RV dump station are provided. A grocery store, RV supplies, firewood, coin laundry, recreation room, volleyball, 18-hole minigolf, and horseshoe pits are available. Leashed pets are permitted.

Reservations, fees: Reservations are accepted at 800/839-0194. The fee is $18.75 per night, $2 per person for more than two people. Group and monthly rates available. Major credit cards accepted. Open year-round.

Directions: From the junction of U.S. 101 and Highway 299 in Arcata, turn east on Highway 299 and drive to Burnt Ranch. From Burnt Ranch, continue 10 miles east on Highway 299 to the town of Del Loma and look for the campground entrance on the right.

Contact: Del Loma RV Park and Campground, 800/839-0194 or 530/623-2834, website: www.del lomarv.com.

71 HAYDEN FLAT/GROUP

Rating: 7

On the Trinity River in Shasta-Trinity National Forest.

Map 2.3, page 110

This campground is split into two pieces, with most of the sites grouped in a large, shaded area across the road from the river and a few on the river side. A beach is available along the river; it is a good spot for swimming as well as a popular put-in and takeout for rafters. The elevation is 1,200 feet.

Campsites, facilities: There are 35 sites for tents or RVs up to 25 feet long and five sites for RVs up to 35 feet in length. Picnic tables and fire grills are provided. Drinking water and vault toilets are available. Some facilities are wheelchair-accessible. Leashed pets are permitted.

Reservations, fees: Reservations are accepted for group sites 10–23 with an advance payment of $30 for three sites up to 24 people. Reservations are not accepted for individual sites. The fee is $10 per night, $6 in off-season. Senior discount available. Open year-round.

Directions: From the junction of U.S. 101 and Highway 299 in Arcata, head east on Highway 299 and drive to Burnt Ranch. From Burnt Ranch, continue 10 miles east on Highway 299 and look for the campground entrance along the left side of the road. If you reach the town of Del Loma, you have gone a half mile too far.

Contact: Shasta-Trinity National Forest, Big Bar Ranger Station, 530/623-6106, fax 530/623-6123.

72 BIG SLIDE

Rating: 7

On the South Fork of the Trinity River in Shasta-Trinity National Forest.

Map 2.3, page 110

This camp is literally out in the middle of nowhere. Free? Of course it's free. Otherwise, someone would actually have to show up now and then to collect. It's a tiny, secluded, little-visited spot set along the South Fork of the Trinity River. The elevation is 1,250 feet.

Campsites, facilities: There are seven sites for tents or small RVs, and one site for tents only. No trailers. Picnic tables and fire grills are provided. Vault toilets are available. No drinking water is available. Leashed pets are permitted.

Reservations, fees: Reservations are not accepted. There is no fee for camping. Open May through October.

Directions: From Redding, head west on Highway 299 and drive over the Buckhorn Summit to the junction with Highway 3 near Douglas City. Turn south on Highway 3 and drive to Hayfork. From Hayfork, turn right on County Road 301 and drive about 20 miles to the town of Hyampom. In Hyampom, turn right on Lower South Fork Road/County Road 311 and drive five miles on County Road 311 to the campground on the right.

Contact: Shasta-Trinity National Forest, Hayfork Ranger Station, 530/628-5227, fax 530/628-5212.

73 SKUNK POINT GROUP CAMP

Rating: 7

On the Trinity River in Shasta-Trinity National Forest.

Map 2.3, page 110

This is an ideal site for groups on rafting trips, and starting in 2003, commercial rafting groups will be urged to use this site over all others on the Trinity River. To facilitate that, no group reservation fee is charged. You get easy access to the nearby Trinity River with a streamside setting and privacy for the group. A beach on the river is nearby. In the spring, this section of river offers primarily Class II rapids (only more difficult during high water), but most of it is rated Class I. By late summer, the water is warm and benign, ideal for families. Guided rafting trips and inflatables are available for hire and rent in nearby Big Flat. The camp elevation is 1,200 feet.

Campsites, facilities: There are two group sites that hold up to 30 people each. Picnic tables and fire grills are provided. Vault toilets are available. No drinking water is available. Some facilities are wheelchair-accessible. Leashed pets are permitted.

Reservations, fees: Reservations are required. The fee is $20 per night for 10 or fewer campers, $2 each additional camper to a maximum of 30 people. Open year-round.

Directions: From Redding, head west on Highway 299, driving past Weaverville, Junction City, and Helena, and continue for about seven miles. Look for the campground entrance on the left side of the road. If you reach the town of Big Bar, you have gone two miles too far.

Contact: Shasta-Trinity National Forest, Big Bar Ranger Station, 530/623-6106, fax 530/623-6123.

74 BIG BAR

Rating: 6

Near the Trinity River in Shasta-Trinity National Forest.

Map 2.3, page 110

You name it, you got it—a quiet, small campground with easy access, and good fishing nearby (in the fall). In addition, there is a good put-in spot for inflatable kayaks and rafts. It is an ideal piece of water for newcomers, with Trinity River Rafting offering inflatable rentals for as low as $25, including shuttle service. The elevation is 1,200 feet. If the shoe fits. . . .

Campsites, facilities: There are three tent sites. Picnic tables and fire grills are provided. Vault toilets are available. No drinking water is available. Supplies are available one mile away. Leashed pets are permitted.

Reservations, fees: Reservations are not accepted. There is no fee for camping. Open year-round.

Directions: From Redding, turn west on Highway 299, drive past Weaverville, continue for 25 miles to the ranger station one mile east of Big Bar, and look for Corral Bottom Roads (across from the ranger station). Turn left and drive a quarter mile to the campground on the left.

Contact: Shasta-Trinity National Forest, Big Bar Ranger Station, 530/623-6106, fax 530/623-6123.

75 BIG FLAT

Rating: 6

On the Trinity River in Shasta-Trinity National Forest.

Map 2.3, page 110

This level campground is set off Highway 299, just across the road from the Trinity River. The sites are close together, and it can be hot and dusty in midsummer. No problem. That is when you will be on the Trinity River, taking the lowest-priced rafting trip available anywhere in the West—as low as $25 to rent an inflatable kayak from Trinity River Rafting in nearby Big Bar, which includes shuttle service. It's fun, exciting, easy (newcomers are welcome), and cheap.

Campsites, facilities: There are 10 sites for tents or RVs up to 25 feet long. Picnic tables and fire grills are provided. Drinking water and vault toilets are available. Leashed pets are permitted.

Reservations, fees: Reservations are not accepted. The fee is $8 per night in season, $6 in winter. Senior discount available. Open year-round, weather permitting.

Directions: From Redding, turn west on Highway 299, drive past Weaverville, Junction City, and Helena, and continue for about seven miles. Look for the campground entrance on the right side of the road. If you reach the town of Big Bar, you have gone three miles too far.

Contact: Shasta-Trinity National Forest, Big Bar Ranger Station, 530/623-6106, fax 530/623-6123.

76 PIGEON POINT

Rating: 7

On the Trinity River in Shasta-Trinity National Forest.

Map 2.3, page 110

In the good old days, huge flocks of bandtail pigeons flew the Trinity River Canyon, swooping and diving in dramatic shows. Nowadays you don't see too many pigeons, but this camp still keeps its namesake. It is better known for its access to the Trinity River, with a large beach for swimming. The elevation is 1,100 feet.

Campsites, facilities: There are 10 sites for tents or RVs up to 25 feet long. Picnic tables and fire grills are provided. Vault toilets are available. No drinking water is available. Supplies can be obtained within 10 miles in Big Bar or Junction City. Some facilities are wheelchair-accessible. Leashed pets are permitted.

Reservations, fees: Reservations are not accepted. The fee is $6 per night. Senior discount available. Open year-round.

Directions: From Redding, head west on Highway 299 and drive to Weaverville. Continue west on Highway 299 to Helena and continue a half mile to the campground on the left (south) side of the road.

Contact: Shasta-Trinity National Forest, Big Bar Ranger Station, 530/623-6106, fax 530/623-6123.

77 BIGFOOT CAMPGROUND AND RV PARK

Rating: 8

On the Trinity River.
Map 2.3, page 110

This private RV park is set along the Trinity River and has become one of the most popular spots on the Trinity River. The low-cost raft trips are a feature, along with cabin rentals. It is also a popular layover for Highway 299 cruisers but provides the option for longer stays with rafting, gold panning, and in the fall and winter, fishing for salmon and steelhead, respectively. RV sites are exceptionally large, and a bonus is that a storage area is available. A three-acre site for tent camping is set along the river.

Campsites, facilities: There are 46 sites with full or partial hookups for RVs, a separate area for tent camping, and four cabins. From December 1 to May 1 there are no tents allowed or RV hook-ups provided, only self-contained vehicles are permitted. Picnic tables and barbecues are provided. Flush toilets, coin showers, coin laundry, grocery store, RV dump station, television, propane gas, solar-heated swimming pool (summer only), and horseshoe pits are available. Modem hookups, fishing licenses, and a tackle shop are also available. Some facilities are wheelchair-accessible. Leashed pets are permitted.

Reservations, fees: Reservations are recom-

mended from June through October. The fee is $17–21 per night, $2 per night per person for more than two people. Major credit cards accepted. Open year-round.

Directions: From Redding, turn west on Highway 299 and drive to Junction City. Continue west on Highway 299 for three miles to the camp on the left.

Contact: Bigfoot Campground and RV Park, 800/422-5219 or 530/623-6088, fax 530/623-3573, website: www.bigfootRVcabins.com.

78 JUNCTION CITY

Rating: 7

On the Trinity River in Shasta-Trinity National Forest.
Map 2.3, page 110

Some of the Trinity River's best fall salmon fishing is in this area in September and early October, with steelhead following from mid-October into the winter. That makes it an ideal base camp for a fishing or camping trip.

Campsites, facilities: There are 22 sites for tents and RVs up to 28 feet long. Picnic tables, fire grills, and bearproof food lockers are provided. Drinking water and vault toilets are available, and camp hosts are on-site; note that from November through April, drinking water is available only from the pump house. Groceries and propane gas are available within two miles in Junction City. Leashed pets are permitted.

Reservations, fees: Reservations are not accepted. The fee is $8 per night from May through October. Senior discount available. Open year-round.

Directions: From Redding, turn west on Highway 299 and drive to Junction City. At Junction City, continue west on Highway 299 for 1.5 miles to the camp on the right.

Contact: Bureau of Land Management, Redding Field Office, 530/224-2100, fax 530/224-2172.

79 PHILPOT

🏃 🎣 🐕 5% 🚐 ⛺

Rating: 7

On the North Fork of Salt Creek in Shasta-Trinity National Forest.

Map 2.3, page 110

It's time to join the 5 Percent Club; that is, the 5 percent of the people who know the little-used, beautiful spots in California. This is one of those places, set on the North Fork of Salt Creek on national forest land. The elevation is 2,600 feet. Remember: 95 percent of the people use just 5 percent of the available open space. Why would anyone come here? To join the 5 Percent Club, that's why. Note: the road is too rough for many vehicles, and the sites are too small for most RVs. Trailers and RVs are not recommended.

Campsites, facilities: There are six sites for tents or small RVs. Picnic tables and fire grills are provided. Vault toilets are available. No drinking water is available. Leashed pets are permitted.

Reservations, fees: Reservations are not accepted. There is no fee for camping. Open late May through October.

Directions: From Redding, turn west on Highway 299, drive over the Buckhorn Summit, and continue to the junction with Highway 3 near Douglas City. Turn south on Highway 3 and drive to Hayfork. From Hayfork, continue southwest on Highway 3 for eight miles to County Road 353 (Rattlesnake Creek Road). Turn right and drive one mile to Forest Road 30N31. Turn right and drive a half mile to the campground on the left. Trailers and RVs are not recommended.

Contact: Shasta-Trinity National Forest, Hayfork Ranger Station, 530/628-5227, fax 530/628-5212.

80 MAD RIVER

🎣 🚗 🐕 🚐 ⛺

Rating: 7

In Six Rivers National Forest.

Map 2.3, page 110

This Forest Service campground is set along an alluvial flood terrace, a unique landscape for this region, featuring a forest of manzanita and Douglas fir. It is often hot, always remote, in a relatively unknown section of Six Rivers National Forest at an elevation of 2,600 feet. The headwaters of the Mad River pour right past the campground, about two miles downstream from the Ruth Lake Dam. People making weekend trips to Ruth Lake sometimes end up at this little-used camp. Ruth Lake is a designated Watchable Wildlife Site and is the only major recreation lake within decent driving range of Eureka, offering a small marina with boat rentals and a good boat ramp for access to trout fishing, bass fishing, and water-skiing.

Campsites, facilities: There are 40 sites, a few of which are for RVs up to 22 feet long or trailers up to 30 feet long. Picnic tables and fire grills are provided. Drinking water is available from approximately mid-May to mid-October. Vault toilets are available. Leashed pets are permitted.

Reservations, fees: Reservations are not accepted. The fee is $12 per night, $5 per extra vehicle. Senior discount available. Open year-round.

Directions: From Eureka, drive south on U.S. 101 to Alton. Turn east on Highway 36 and drive about 50 miles to the town of Mad River. Turn southeast on Lower Mad River Road and drive four miles to the camp on the right side of the road.

Contact: Six Rivers National Forest, Mad River Ranger District, 707/574-6233, fax 707/574-6273.

81 HELL GATE

Rating: 7

On the South Fork of the Trinity River in Shasta-Trinity National Forest.

Map 2.3, page 110

This is a pretty spot bordering the South Fork of the Trinity River. The prime feature is for hikers. The South Fork National Recreation Trail begins at the campground and follows the river for many miles. Additional trails branch off and up into the South Fork Mountains. This area is extremely hot in summer. The elevation is 2,300 feet. It gets moderate use and may even fill on three-day weekends. Insider's note: if Hell Gate is full, there are seven primitive campsites at Scott's Flat Campground, a half mile beyond Hell Gate, that can accommodate RVs and trailers of all sizes.

Campsites, facilities: There are 12 tent sites and three sites for tents or RVs up to 16 feet long. Picnic tables and fire grills are provided. Drinking water and vault toilets are available. Some facilities are wheelchair-accessible. Leashed pets are permitted. If Hell Gate is full, there are seven additional campsites that will take tents and RVs up to 20 feet long, just a half mile beyond this campground at Scott's Flat Campground.

Reservations, fees: Reservations are not accepted. The fee is $6 per night. Senior discount available. Open May through October.

Directions: From Red Bluff, turn west on Highway 36 (very twisty) and drive past Platina to the junction with Highway 3. Continue west on Highway 36 for 10 miles to the campground entrance on the left side of the road. If you reach Forest Glen, you have gone a mile too far.

Contact: Shasta-Trinity National Forest, Hayfork Ranger Station, 530/628-5227, fax 530/628-5212.

82 FOREST GLEN

Rating: 7

On the South Fork of the Trinity River in Shasta-Trinity National Forest.

Map 2.3, page 110

If you get stuck for a spot in this region, this camp almost always has sites open, even during three-day weekends. It is on the edge of a forest near the South Fork of the Trinity River. If you hit it wrong, during a surprise storm, a primitive shelter is available at the nearby Forest Glen Guard Station—a historic cabin that sleeps eight and rents out from the Forest Service for $35 a night.

Campsites, facilities: There are 15 sites for tents or RVs up to 15 feet long. Picnic tables and fire grills are provided. Vault toilets are available. No drinking water is available. Some facilities are wheelchair-accessible. Leashed pets are permitted.

Reservations, fees: Reservations are not accepted. The fee is $6 per night. Senior discount available. Open May through October.

Directions: From Red Bluff, turn west on Highway 36 (very twisty) and drive past Platina to the junction with Highway 3. Continue west on Highway 36 for 11 miles to Forest Glen. The campground is at the west end of town on the right side of the road.

Contact: Shasta-Trinity National Forest, Hayfork Ranger Station, 530/628-5227, fax 530/628-5212.

83 FIR COVE

Rating: 7

On Ruth Lake in Six Rivers National Forest.

Map 2.3, page 110

This spot is situated along Ruth Lake adjacent to Bailey Cove. Groups can reserve a section of the campground Monday through Thursday. The elevation is 2,600 feet.

Campsites, facilities: There are 19 single or

three group sites for tents and RVs. Several sites can accommodate RVs up to 22 feet long. Picnic tables and fire grills are provided. Drinking water and vault toilets are available. Leashed pets are permitted.

Reservations, fees: Reservations are accepted only for group sites through the Mad River Ranger District station. Reservations are not accepted for single sites. The fee is $12 per night, $5 per night for additional vehicles, $40–50 per night for group sites. Open on summer weekends only, from Friday after 2 P.M. to Monday at 2 P.M. Open May through October.

Directions: From Eureka, drive south on U.S. 101 to Alton and the junction with Highway 36. Turn east on Highway 36 and drive about 50 miles to the town of Mad River. Turn right at the sign for Ruth Lake/Lower Mad River Road and drive 12 miles to the campground on the right side of the road.

Contact: Six Rivers National Forest, Mad River Ranger District, 707/574-6233, fax 707/574-6273.

84 BAILEY CANYON

Rating: 7

On Ruth Lake in Six Rivers National Forest.
Map 2.3, page 110

Ruth Lake is the only major lake within a reasonable driving distance of U.S. 101, although some people might argue with you over how reasonable this twisty drive is. Regardless, you end up at a camp along the east shore of Ruth Lake, where fishing for trout or bass and water-skiing are popular. What really wins out is that it is hot and sunny all summer, the exact opposite of the fogged-in Humboldt coast. The elevation is 2,600 feet.

Campsites, facilities: There are 25 sites, a few of which are for RVs up to 22 feet long. Picnic tables and fire grills are provided. Drinking water and vault toilets are available. A boat ramp and small marina are available nearby. Leashed pets are permitted.

Reservations, fees: Reservations are not accepted. The fee is $12 per night, $5 for an extra vehicle. Senior discount available. Open May through October.

Directions: From Eureka, drive south on U.S. 101 to Alton and the junction with Highway 36. Turn east on Highway 36 and drive about 50 miles to the town of Mad River. Turn right at the sign for Ruth Lake/Lower Mad River Road and drive 13 miles to the campground on the right side of the road.

Contact: Six Rivers National Forest, Mad River Ranger District, 707/574-6233, fax 707/574-6273.

85 WYNTOON RESORT

Rating: 8

On Trinity Lake.
Map 2.4 Trinity Lake Detail, page 112

This huge resort is an ideal family vacation destination. Set in a wooded area covering 70 acres on the north shore of Trinity Lake, it provides opportunities for fishing, boating, swimming, and water-skiing, with access within walking distance. The lake sits at the base of the dramatic Trinity Alps, one of the most beautiful regions in the state.

Campsites, facilities: There are 78 tent sites and 136 sites, including many drive-through, with full hookups for trailers or RVs, 19 cottages, and five trailers. Picnic tables and fire rings are provided. Drinking water, restrooms, showers, a coin laundry, a playground, heated pool (Memorial Day through Labor Day), RV dump station, gasoline, grocery store, ice, snack bar, fish-cleaning area, boat rentals, slips, and a boat launch are available. Some facilities are wheelchair-accessible. Leashed pets are permitted.

Reservations, fees: Reservations are accepted. The fee is $22–25 per night, $3 per person for more than two people, $1 per pet per night. Monthly rates available. Major credit cards accepted. Open year-round.

Directions: From Redding, turn west on Highway 299 and drive to Weaverville at Highway 3. Turn north on Highway 3 and drive to Trinity Lake. At Trinity Center, continue a half mile north on Highway 3 to the resort on the right.

Contact: Wyntoon Resort, 800/715-3337 or 530/266-3337, fax 530/266-3820, website: wyntoonresort.com.

86 PREACHER MEADOW

Rating: 7

In Shasta-Trinity National Forest.
Map 2.4 Trinity Lake Detail, page 112

The winter of 2000 was one of the strangest on record here, where a localized wind storm knocked down 66 trees and put this campground temporarily out of commission. It reopened in summer of 2000. The anomaly of a tree blowdown makes a constant subject of discussion for campers here. But it isn't long and your attention will shift to the view of the Trinity Alps, excellent from the right vantage point. Otherwise, compared to all the other camps in the area so close to Trinity Lake, it has trouble matching up in the quality department. If the lakeside camps are full, this camp provides an overflow option.

Campsites, facilities: There are 45 sites for tents or RVs up to 32 feet long. Picnic tables and fire grills are provided. Drinking water and vault toilets are available, and there is a camp host. Supplies, a coin laundry, and a small airport are available nearby. Leashed pets are permitted.

Reservations, fees: Reservations are not accepted. The fee is $8 per night. Senior discount available. Open mid-May through October.

Directions: From Redding, turn west on Highway 299 and drive to Weaverville at Highway 3. Head north on Highway 3 and drive to Trinity Lake. Continue toward Trinity Center and look for the campground entrance on the left side of the road (if you

reach Trinity Center you have gone two miles too far).

Contact: Shasta-Trinity National Forest, Weaverville Ranger Station, 530/623-2121, fax 530/623-6010.

87 JACKASS SPRINGS

Rating: 6

On Trinity Lake in Shasta-Trinity National Forest.
Map 2.4 Trinity Lake Detail, page 112

If you're poking around for a more secluded campsite on this end of the lake, halt your search and pick the best spot you can find at this campground, since it's the only one in this area of Trinity Lake. The campground is one mile from Trinity Lake, but you can't see the lake from the camp. It is most popular in the fall as a base camp for deer hunters. The elevation is 2,500 feet.

Campsites, facilities: There are 21 sites for tents or RVs up to 32 feet long. Picnic tables and fire grills are provided. Vault toilets are available. No drinking water is available. Garbage must be packed out. Leashed pets are permitted.

Reservations, fees: Reservations are not accepted. There is no fee for camping. Open year-round, weather permitting.

Directions: From Redding head west on Highway 299 and drive to Weaverville and the junction with Highway 3. Turn north on Highway 3 and drive 29 miles to Trinity Center. Continue five miles past Trinity Center to County Road 106. Turn right on County Road 106 and drive 12 miles to the Jackass Springs/County Road 119 turnoff. Turn right on County Road 119 and drive five miles to the campground at the end of the road.

Contact: Shasta-Trinity National Forest, Weaverville Ranger Station, 530/623-2121, fax 530/623-6010.

88 BRIDGE CAMP

Rating: 8

On Stuarts Fork in Shasta-Trinity National Forest.

Map 2.4 Trinity Lake Detail, page 112

This remote spot is an ideal jump-off point for backpackers. It's at the head of Stuarts Fork Trail, about two miles from the western shore of Trinity Lake. The trail leads into the Trinity Alps Wilderness, along Stuarts Fork, past Oak Flat and Morris Meadows, and up to Emerald Lake and the Sawtooth Ridge. It is a long and grueling climb, but fishing is excellent at Emerald Lake as well as at neighboring Sapphire Lake. There's a great view of the Alps from this camp. It is set at 2,700 feet and remains open year-round, but there's no piped water in the winter and it gets mighty cold up here.

Campsites, facilities: There are 10 sites for tents or trailers up to 12 feet long. Picnic tables and fire grills are provided. Drinking water, vault toilets, and horse corrals are available; there is a camp host. Leashed pets are permitted.

Reservations, fees: Reservations are not accepted. The fee is $10 per night, free in winter. Senior discount available. Open year-round, weather permitting.

Directions: From Redding, head west on Highway 299 and drive to Weaverville. In Weaverville, turn north on Highway 3 and drive 17 miles to Trinity Alps Road (at Stuarts Fork of Trinity Lake). At Trinity Alps Road, turn left and drive about 2.5 miles to the campground on the right side of the road.

Contact: Shasta-Trinity National Forest, Weaverville Ranger Station, 530/623-2121, fax 530/623-6010.

89 RUSH CREEK

Rating: 4

In Shasta-Trinity National Forest, north of Weaverville.

Map 2.4 Trinity Lake Detail, page 112

This small, primitive camp provides overflow space during busy holiday weekends when the camps at Lewiston and Trinity Lakes are near capacity. It may not be much, but hey, at least if you know about Rush Creek you'll never get stuck for a spot. The camp borders Rush Creek and is secluded, but again, it's nearly five miles to the nearest access point to Trinity Lake.

Campsites, facilities: There are 10 sites for tents only. Picnic tables and fire pits are provided. Vault toilets are available. No drinking water is available.

Reservations, fees: Reservations are not accepted. The fee is $6 per night. Senior discount available. Open May to mid-September.

Directions: From Redding, go west on Highway 299 and drive to Weaverville. In Weaverville, turn north on Highway 3 and drive about eight miles to the signed turnoff on the left side of the road. Turn left and drive a quarter mile on the short spur road to the campground on the left side of the road. If you get to Forest Road 113, you've gone too far.

Contact: Shasta-Trinity National Forest, Weaverville Ranger Station, 530/623-2121, fax 530/623-6010.

90 STONEY POINT

Rating: 7

On Trinity Lake in Shasta-Trinity National Forest.

Map 2.4 Trinity Lake Detail, page 112

This is a popular spot at Trinity Lake, easily discovered and easily reached. Set near the inlet of Stuarts Fork, it often fills up, but two other campgrounds close by provide overflow options. The elevation is 2,400 feet.

Campsites, facilities: There are 22 sites for tents only. Picnic tables and fire grills are provided. Drinking water and flush toilets are available. Leashed pets are permitted.

Reservations, fees: Reservations are not accepted. The fee is $11 per night in season, free in winter. Senior discount available. Open year-round, weather permitting.

Directions: From Redding, head west on Highway 299 and drive to Weaverville. In Weaverville, turn north on Highway 3 and drive 14 miles (about a quarter mile past the Stuarts Fork Bridge) to the campground.

Contact: Shasta-Trinity National Forest, Weaverville Ranger Station, 530/623-2121, fax 530/623-6010.

91 PINEWOOD COVE RESORT

Rating: 7

On Trinity Lake.

Map 2.4 Trinity Lake Detail, page 112

This is a privately operated camp with full boating facilities at Trinity Lake. If you don't have a boat but want to get on Trinity Lake, this can be a good starting point. A reservation is advised during the peak summer season. The elevation is 2,300 feet.

Campsites, facilities: There are 50 sites with full or partial hookups for RVs up to 40 feet long, and 28 tent sites, including 10 RV sites rented for the entire season and wait-listed. There are also eight park-model cabins, six trailer rentals, and one A-frame cabin. Picnic tables and fire grills are provided. Restrooms, showers, a coin laundry, RV dump station, RV supplies, free movies three nights a week, recreation room, pinball and video machines, grocery store, ice, fishing tackle, library, boat dock with 32 slips, beach, and boat rentals are available. Some facilities are wheelchair-accessible. Leashed pets are permitted.

Reservations, fees: Reservations are recommended in the summer. The fee is $20–27.50 per night, $3 per person for more than two

people, $2 per pet per night. Major credit cards accepted. Senior discount available. Open mid-April through October.

Directions: From Redding, turn west on Highway 299 and drive to Weaverville. In Weaverville, turn north (right) on Highway 3 and drive 14 miles to the campground entrance on the right.

Contact: Pinewood Cove Resort, 800/988-5253 (reservations only) or 530/286-2201, fax 530/286-2202, website: www.pinewoodcove.com.

92 STONEY CREEK GROUP CAMP

Rating: 7

On Trinity Lake in Shasta-Trinity National Forest.

Map 2.4 Trinity Lake Detail, page 112

A series of camps sits on the northern shore of the Stuarts Fork arm of Trinity Lake. This is one of two designed for groups (the other is Bushy Tail), and it is clearly the better. It is set along the Stoney Creek arm, a cove with a feeder creek, with the camp large but relatively private. A swimming beach nearby is a bonus. The elevation is 2,400 feet.

Campsites, facilities: This group campground can hold up to 50 people. Sites are for tents only. Drinking water (spring, summer, and fall only; no drinking water in the winter), flush toilets, picnic tables, and fire grills are available. Leashed pets are permitted.

Reservations, fees: Reservations are required with a $9 reservation fee at 877/444-6777 or website www.ReserveUsa.com. The fee is $65 per night during season. Open year-round.

Directions: From Redding, turn west on Highway 299 and drive to Weaverville. In Weaverville, turn north on Highway 3 and drive 14.5 miles (about a half mile past the Stuarts Fork Bridge) to the campground.

Contact: Shasta-Trinity National Forest, Weaverville Ranger Station, 530/623-2121, fax 530/623-6010.

93 TANNERY GULCH
🚶 ♨ 🛶 🚤 🏕 🚙 ⛺

Rating: 8

On Trinity Lake in Shasta-Trinity National Forest.

Map 2.4 Trinity Lake Detail, page 112

This is one of the more popular Forest Service camps on the southwest shore of huge Trinity Lake. There's a nice beach near the campground, provided the infamous Bureau of Reclamation hasn't drawn the lake level down too far. It can be quite low in the fall. The elevation is 2,400 feet.

Campsites, facilities: There are 83 sites for tents or RVs up to 40 feet long and four multifamily sites. Picnic tables and fire grills are provided. Drinking water, flush and vault toilets, and a boat ramp area available, and there is a camp host. A grocery store is available nearby. Leashed pets are permitted.

Reservations, fees: Reservations are accepted with a $9 reservation fee at 877/444-6777 and website www.ReserveUsa.com. The fee is $15–20 per night, $5 for an extra vehicle. Senior discount available. Open May through September.

Directions: From Redding, head west on Highway 299 and drive to Weaverville. In Weaverville, turn north on Highway 3 and drive 13.5 miles north to County Road 172. Turn right on County Road 172 and drive 1.5 miles to the campground on the left side of the road.

Contact: Shasta-Trinity National Forest, Weaverville Ranger Station, 530/623-2121, fax 530/623-6010.

94 FAWN GROUP CAMP
♨ 🛶 🚤 🏕 🚙 ⛺

Rating: 7

On Trinity Lake in Shasta-Trinity National Forest.

Map 2.4 Trinity Lake Detail, page 112

If you want Trinity Lake all to yourself, one way to do it is to get a group together and then reserve this camp near the shore of Trinity Lake. The elevation is 2,500 feet.

Campsites, facilities: This group campground can hold up to 300 people. Sites are for tents or RVs up to 37 feet long. Picnic tables and fire grills are provided. Drinking water and flush toilets are available. Leashed pets are permitted.

Reservations, fees: Reservations are required with a $9 reservation fee at 877/444-6777 or website www.ReserveUsa.com. The fee is $80 group fee per night. Open May through September.

Directions: From Redding, head west on Highway 299 and drive to Weaverville. In Weaverville, turn north on Highway 3 and drive 15 miles to the campground.

Contact: Shasta-Trinity National Forest, Weaverville Ranger Station, 530/623-2121, fax 530/623-6010.

95 BUSHY TAIL GROUP CAMP
🚶 ♨ 🛶 🚤 🏕 🚙 ⛺

Rating: 7

On Trinity Lake in Shasta-Trinity National Forest.

Map 2.4 Trinity Lake Detail, page 112

This is a huge group camp at Trinity Lake, the kind of place where you might want to have a political convention. Then you could tell some politician to go jump in a lake. (Haven't you always wanted to do that?) What the heck, it's pretty enough to want to jump in yourself, and with a boat launch nearby, you get a bonus. The elevation is 2,500 feet.

Campsites, facilities: This group campground can hold up to 200 people in 30 sites. Sites are for tents or RVs up to 20 feet long. Picnic tables and fire grills are provided. Drinking water and flush toilets are available. Supplies and a boat ramp are available nearby. Leashed pets are permitted.

Reservations, fees: Reservations are required with a $9 reservation fee at 877/444-6777 or website www.ReserveUsa.com. The fee is $60 group fee per night. Open May through September.

Directions: From Redding, head west on Highway 299 and drive to Weaverville. In Weaverville, turn north on Highway 3 and drive about 16 miles (approximately 3.5 miles past the Stuarts Fork Bridge) to the campground entrance road on the right. Turn right and drive a short distance to the camp on the left side of the road.

Contact: Shasta-Trinity National Forest, Weaverville Ranger Station, 530/623-2121, fax 530/623-6010.

96 MINERSVILLE

Rating: 7

On Trinity Lake in Shasta-Trinity National Forest.

Map 2.4 Trinity Lake Detail, page 112

The setting is near lakeside, quite beautiful when Trinity Lake is fullest in the spring and early summer. This is a good camp for boaters, with a boat ramp in the cove a short distance to the north. But note that the boat ramp is not always functional. When the lake level is 65 feet below full, the ramp is not usable. The elevation is 2,500 feet.

Campsites, facilities: There are 21 sites for tents or RVs up to 18 feet long. Picnic tables and fire grills are provided. Drinking water (spring, summer, and fall only), flush toilets, and a low-water boat ramp are provided. There is a camp host. Leashed pets are permitted.

Reservations, fees: Reservations are not accepted. The fee is $12–20 per night, free in winter. Senior discount available. Open year-round, but note that there is no drinking water in the winter.

Directions: From Redding, head west on Highway 299 to Weaverville. Turn north on Highway 3 and drive about 18 miles (if you reach the Mule Creek Ranger Station, you have gone a half mile too far). Turn right at the signed campground access road and drive a half mile to the camp.

Contact: Shasta-Trinity National Forest, Weaver-

ville Ranger Station, 530/623-2121, fax 530/623-6010.

97 RIDGEVILLE BOAT-IN CAMP

Rating: 9

On Trinity Lake in Shasta-Trinity National Forest.

Map 2.4 Trinity Lake Detail, page 112

This is one of the ways to get a camping spot to call your own—go by boat. The camp is exposed on a peninsula, providing beautiful views. Prospects for water-skiing and trout or bass fishing are often outstanding. The early part of the season is the prime time here for boaters, before the furnace heat of full summer, with both trout and bass on the bite. A great view of the Trinity Alps is a bonus. The only downer is the typical lake drawdown at the end of summer and beginning of fall, when this boat-in camp is left a long traipse from water's edge.

Campsites, facilities: There are 21 tent sites. Picnic tables and fire grills are provided. Vault toilets are available. No drinking water is available. Garbage must be packed out. A camp host is on-site in summer. Boat ramps can be found near Clark Springs, Alpine View, or farther north at Trinity Center. Leashed pets are permitted.

Reservations, fees: Reservations are not accepted. There is no fee for camping. Open year-round.

Directions: From Redding, head west on Highway 299 and drive to Weaverville. In Weaverville, turn north on Highway 3 and drive seven miles to the Stuarts Fork arm of Trinity Lake. You'll find boat launches at Stuarts Fork. After launching, drive your boat to the mouth of Stuarts Fork. The campground is set on the western shore at the end of a peninsula at the entrance to that part of the lake.

Contact: Shasta-Trinity National Forest, Weaverville Ranger Station, 530/623-2121, fax 530/623-6010.

98 CLARK SPRINGS

Rating: 7

On Trinity Lake in Shasta-Trinity National Forest.

Map 2.4 Trinity Lake Detail, page 112

This used to be a day-use-only picnic area, but because of popular demand, the Forest Service has opened it for camping. That makes sense because people were bound to declare it a campground anyway, since it has a nearby boat ramp and a beach. The elevation is 2,400 feet.

Campsites, facilities: There are 21 tent sites. Picnic tables and fire grills are provided. Drinking water (spring, summer, and fall only) and flush toilets are available. A grocery store and boat ramp are available nearby. Leashed pets are permitted.

Reservations, fees: Reservations are not accepted. The fee is $8 per night, free in winter. Senior discount available. Open year-round, but no drinking water is available in the winter.

Directions: From Redding, head west on Highway 299 and drive to Weaverville. In Weaverville, turn north on Highway 3 and drive 16.5 miles (about four miles past the Stuarts Fork Bridge) to the campground entrance road on the right.

Contact: Shasta-Trinity National Forest, Weaverville Ranger Station, 530/623-2121, fax 530/623-6010.

99 RIDGEVILLE ISLAND BOAT-IN CAMP

Rating: 9

On Trinity Lake in Shasta-Trinity National Forest.

Map 2.4 Trinity Lake Detail, page 112

How would you like to be on a deserted island? You'll learn the answer from this tiny, little-known island with a great view of the Trinity Alps. It is one of several boat-in camps

in the Trinity Lake region. The elevation is 2,500 feet. Note that the lake level at Trinity Lake is typically dropped significantly from September through October.

Campsites, facilities: There are three tent sites. Picnic tables and fire grills are provided. Vault toilets are available. No drinking water is available. Garbage must be packed out. Boat ramps can be found at Clark Springs campground, Bowerman Boat Ramp at Alpine View, or farther north at Trinity Center. Leashed pets are permitted.

Reservations, fees: Reservations are not accepted. There is no fee for camping. Open year-round.

Directions: From Redding, head west on Highway 299 and drive to Weaverville. In Weaverville, turn north on Highway 3 and drive seven miles to the Stuarts Fork arm of Trinity Lake. You'll find boat launches at Stuarts Fork. After launching, drive your boat to the mouth of Stuarts Fork; the campground is set on a small island here.

Contact: Shasta-Trinity National Forest, Weaverville Ranger Station, 530/623-2121, fax 530/623-6010.

100 MARINERS ROOST BOAT-IN CAMP

Rating: 8

On Trinity Lake in Shasta-Trinity National Forest.

Map 2.4 Trinity Lake Detail, page 112

A perfect boat camp? This comes close at Trinity since it's positioned perfectly for boaters, with spectacular views of the Trinity Alps to the west, and it is an ideal spot for water-skiers. That is because it is on the western side of the lake's major peninsula, topped by Bowerman Ridge. Secluded and wooded, this area is set at 2,400 feet elevation.

Campsites, facilities: There are seven tent sites. Picnic tables and fire grills are provided. Vault toilets are available. No drinking water is available. Boat ramps are available at Clark Springs campground, near Alpine View campground, or farther north at Trinity Center. Leashed pets are permitted.

Reservations, fees: Reservations are not accepted. There is no fee for camping. Open year-round.

Directions: From Redding, head west on Highway 299 and drive to Weaverville. In Weaverville, turn north on Highway 3 and drive seven miles to the Stuarts Fork arm of Trinity Lake. You'll find boat launches at Stuarts Fork. After launching, drive your boat to the mouth of Stuarts Fork and look for the camp on the peninsula, just east and on the opposite shore of Ridgeville Island Boat-In Camp.

Contact: Shasta-Trinity National Forest, Weaverville Ranger Station, 530/623-2121, fax 530/623-6010.

101 HAYWARD FLAT

Rating: 7

On Trinity Lake in Shasta-Trinity National Forest.

Map 2.4 Trinity Lake Detail, page 112

When giant Trinity Lake is full of water, Hayward Flat is one of the prettiest places you could ask for. The camp has become one of the most popular Forest Service campgrounds on Trinity Lake because it sits right along the shore and offers a "private" beach for Hayward Flat campers only. The elevation is 2,400 feet.

Campsites, facilities: There are 98 sites for tents or RVs up to 40 feet long and four multifamily sites. Picnic tables and fire grills are provided. Drinking water and flush toilets, and there is a camp host. Supplies and a boat ramp are available nearby. Leashed pets are permitted.

Reservations, fees: Reservations are accepted with a $9 reservation fee at 877/444-6777 and website www.ReserveUsa.com. The fee is $15–20 per night, $5 for each additional vehicle. Se-

nior discount available. Open mid-May through mid-September.

Directions: From Redding, head west on Highway 299 and drive to Weaverville. In Weaverville, turn north on Highway 3 and drive about 20 miles, approximately three miles past the Mule Creek Ranger Station. Turn right at the signed access road for Hayward Flat and drive about three miles to the campground at the end of the road.

Contact: Shasta-Trinity National Forest, Weaverville Ranger Station, 530/623-2121, fax 530/623-6010.

102 ALPINE VIEW

Rating: 9

On Trinity Lake in Shasta-Trinity National Forest.

Map 2.4 Trinity Lake Detail, page 112

This is an attractive area, set on the shore of Trinity Lake at a creek inlet. The boat ramp nearby provides a bonus. It's a very pretty spot, with views to the west across the lake arm and to the Trinity Alps, featuring Granite Peak. The Forest Service also runs tours from the campground to historic Bowerman Barn, which was built in 1894. The elevation is 2,400 feet.

Campsites, facilities: There are 66 sites for tents or RVs up to 32 feet long. Picnic tables and fire grills are provided. Drinking water and flush toilets are available, and there is a camp host. Some facilities are wheelchair-accessible. The Bowerman Boat Ramp is next to the camp. Leashed pets are permitted.

Reservations, fees: Reservations are not accepted. The fee is $12–18 per night, $5 for an extra vehicle. Senior discount available. Open mid-May through mid-September (rarely, it is closed temporarily when lake levels are extremely low).

Directions: From Redding, turn west on Highway 299 and drive to Weaverville. In Weaverville, turn north on Highway 3 and drive to Covington Mill (six miles south of Trinity

Center). Turn right (south) on Guy Covington Road and drive three miles to the camp (one mile past Bowerman Boat Ramp) on the right side of the road.

Contact: Shasta-Trinity National Forest, Weaverville Ranger Station, 530/623-2121, fax 530/623-6010.

103 CAPTAIN'S POINT BOAT-IN CAMP

🏞️ 🛶 � 🏕️ 5% 🏕️

Rating: 7

On Trinity Lake in Shasta-Trinity National Forest.

Map 2.4 Trinity Lake Detail, page 112

The Trinity River arm of Trinity Lake is a massive piece of water, stretching north from the giant Trinity Dam for nearly 20 miles. This camp is the only boat-in camp along this entire stretch of shore, and it is situated at a prominent spot, where a peninsula juts well into the main lake body. This is a perfect boat-in site for water-skiers or fishermen. The fishing is often excellent for smallmouth bass in the cove adjacent to Captain's Point, using grubs. The elevation is 2,400 feet.

Campsites, facilities: There are three tent sites. Picnic tables and fire grills are provided. Vault toilets are available. No drinking water is available. Garbage must be packed out. Boat ramps can be found near Clark Springs and Alpine View, or farther north at Trinity Center. Leashed pets are permitted.

Reservations, fees: Reservations are not accepted. There is no fee for camping. Open year-round.

Directions: From Redding, head west on Highway 299 and drive to Weaverville. In Weaverville, turn north on Highway 3 and drive about seven miles to the signed turnoff on the right side of the road for the Trinity Alps Marina. Turn right and drive approximately 10 miles to the marina and boat ramp. Launch your boat and cruise north about four miles up the main Trinity River arm of the lake.

Look for Captain's Point on the left side of the lake.

Contact: Shasta-Trinity National Forest, Weaverville Ranger Station, 530/623-2121, fax 530/623-6010.

104 CLEAR CREEK

🚶 🐴 5% 🚐 🏕️

Rating: 6

In Shasta-Trinity National Forest.

Map 2.4 Trinity Lake Detail, page 112

This is a primitive, little-known camp that gets little use. It is set near Clear Creek at 3,500 feet elevation. In fall hunters will occasionally turn it into a deer camp, with the adjacent slopes of Blue Mountain and Damnation Peak in the Trinity Divide country providing fair numbers of large bucks, three points or better. Trinity Lake is only seven miles to the west, but it seems as if it's in a different world.

Campsites, facilities: There are two tent sites and six sites for tents or RVs up to 22 feet long. Picnic tables and fire grills are provided. Vault toilets are available. No drinking water is available. Garbage must be packed out. Leashed pets are permitted.

Reservations, fees: Reservations are not accepted. There is no fee for camping. Open year-round.

Directions: From Redding, turn west on Highway 299 and drive 17 miles to Trinity Lake Road (just west of Whiskeytown Lake). Turn north on Trinity Lake Road and continue past the town of French Gulch for about 12 miles to the Trinity Mountain Ranger Station. Turn right on County Road 106/East Side Road (gravel) and drive north for about 11 miles to the campground access road (dirt) on right. Turn right on the access road and drive two miles to the campground.

Contact: Shasta-Trinity National Forest, Weaverville Ranger District, 530/623-2121, fax 530/623-6010.

105 LAKESHORE VILLA RV PARK

Rating: 7

On Shasta Lake.

Map 2.4 Shasta Lake Detail, page 112

This is a large campground with level, shaded sites for RVs, set near the northern Sacramento River arm of giant Shasta Lake. Most of the campers visiting here are boaters coming for the water sports, water-skiing, wakeboarding, or tubing. The sites are level and graveled.

Campsites, facilities: There are 92 sites, including some drive-through sites and 75 with full hookups, for RVs and tents, and two RV rentals. Restrooms, hot showers, ice, RV dump station, cable TV, coin laundry, playground, recreation room, and a boat dock are available. Leashed pets are permitted.

Reservations, fees: Reservations are accepted with a deposit. The fee is $22–25 per night. A few long-term rentals available. Major credit cards are accepted. Open year-round.

Directions: From Redding, drive north on I-5 for 24 miles to the Lakeshore-Antlers Road exit in Lakehead. Take that exit, turn left at the stop sign, and drive under the freeway to Lakeshore Drive. Turn left on Lakeshore Drive and drive a half mile to the campground on the right.

Contact: Lakeshore Villa RV Park, 530/238-8688, website: www.american-rvresorts.com.

106 LAKESHORE INN & RV

Rating: 7

On Shasta Lake.

Map 2.4 Shasta Lake Detail, page 112

Shasta Lake is a boater's paradise and an ideal spot for campers with boats, with a nearby boat ramp and private marina available. It is on the Sacramento River arm of Shasta Lake.

Campsites, facilities: There are 35 sites, including some drive-through sites, with partial and full hookups for RVs and tents, and 10

cabins. Picnic tables are provided. Restrooms, hot showers, swimming pool (summer only), playground, video arcade, coin laundry, bar and restaurant (summer only), and a small grocery store (summer) are available. Family barbecues are held on Sunday in season, 5 P.M.–9 P.M. Live music is scheduled most Friday and Saturday nights. A marina and boat rentals are available nearby. Some facilities are wheelchair-accessible. Leashed pets are permitted.

Reservations, fees: Reservations are recommended. The fee is $22–28 per night, $2 per person for more than two people, $1 per pet per night. Major credit cards accepted. Open year-round, with limited winter facilities.

Directions: From Redding, drive north on I-5 for 24 miles to the Lakeshore-Antlers Road exit in Lakehead. Take that exit, turn left at the stop sign, and drive under the freeway to Lakeshore Drive. Turn left on Lakeshore Drive and drive one mile to the campground.

Contact: Lakeshore, 530/238-2003, fax 530/238-2832, website: www.shastacamping.com

107 SHASTA LAKE RV RESORT AND CAMPGROUND

Rating: 7

On Shasta Lake.

Map 2.4 Shasta Lake Detail, page 112

Shasta Lake RV Resort and Campground is one of a series on the upper end of Shasta Lake with easy access off I-5 by car, then easy access by boat to premium trout or bass fishing as well as water-skiing.

Campsites, facilities: There are 53 sites, including some drive-through, with full hookups for RVs, 21 tent sites, and four trailers. Picnic tables, barbecues, and fire rings are provided. Restrooms, hot showers, seasonal convenience store, wood, coin laundry, playground, and a swimming pool (summer) are available. There is also a private dock with 36 boat slips. Leashed pets are permitted.

Reservations, fees: Reservations are accepted

with a deposit. The fee is $17–25 per night, $1 per pet per night. Major credit cards accepted. Open year-round.

Directions: From Redding, drive north on I-5 for 24 miles to the Lakeshore-Antlers Road exit in Lakehead. Take that exit, turn left at the stop sign, and drive under the freeway to Lakeshore Drive. Turn left on Lakeshore Drive and drive 1.5 miles to the campground on the right.

Contact: Shasta Lake RV Resort and Campground, 800/374-2782 or 530/238-2370, website: www.shastalakerv.com.

108 ANTLERS RV PARK AND CAMPGROUND

Rating: 7

On Shasta Lake.

Map 2.4 Shasta Lake Detail, page 112

Antlers Park is set along the Sacramento River arm of Shasta Lake at 1,215 feet. Note that no long-term rentals are allowed, which can be a desirable factor for many visitors. This is a full-service spot for campers, boaters, and anglers, with access to the beautiful Sacramento River arm. The camp often fills in summer, including on weekdays.

Campsites, facilities: There are 70 sites for RVs, including three drive-through and many with full hookups, and 36 sites for tents. Restrooms, hot showers, seasonal grocery store and snack bar, ice, coin laundry, recreation room, playground, volleyball court, and swimming pool (summer). Boat rentals, houseboats, moorage, and a complete marina are available adjacent to the park. Some facilities are wheelchair-accessible. Leashed pets are permitted.

Reservations, fees: Reservations are accepted with a deposit. The fee is $14–28.50 per night, $3 per person for more than two people, $3 per pet per night. Major credit cards accepted. Open year-round.

Directions: From Redding, drive north on I-5 for 24 miles to the Lakeshore-Antlers Road exit

in Lakehead. Take that exit, turn right at the stop sign, and drive a short distance to Antlers Road. At Antlers Road, turn right and drive 2.5 miles south to the campground on the left.

Contact: Antlers RV Park and Campground, 800/642-6849 or 530/238-2322, website: www.antlersrv.com.

109 ANTLERS

Rating: 7

On Shasta Lake in Shasta-Trinity National Forest.

Map 2.4 Shasta Lake Detail, page 112

This spot is set on the primary Sacramento River inlet of giant Shasta Lake. Antlers is a well-known spot that attracts returning campers and boaters year after year. It is the farthest upstream marina/camp on the lake. Because of that, lake levels can fluctuate greatly from spring through fall, and the operators will move their docks to compensate. Easy access off I-5 is a big plus for boaters.

Campsites, facilities: There are 41 single sites and 18 double sites for tents or RVs up to 30 feet long. Picnic tables and fire grills are provided. Drinking water and flush and vault toilets are available, and there is a camp host in summer. A boat ramp, grocery store, and coin laundry are available nearby. Leashed pets are permitted.

Reservations, fees: Reservations are accepted with a $9 reservation fee at 877/444-6777 and website www.ReserveUsa.com. The fee is $16 per night for a single site, $26 for a double site, $5 for an extra vehicle. Senior discount available. Open year-round.

Directions: From Redding, drive north on I-5 for 24 miles to the Lakeshore-Antlers Road exit in Lakehead. Take that exit, turn right at the stop sign, and drive a short distance to Antlers Road. At Antlers Road, turn right and drive one mile south to the campground.

Contact: Shasta-Trinity National Forest, Shasta Lake Ranger District, 530/275-1587, fax 530/275-1512; Shasta Lake Visitor Center, 530/275-1589.

110 LAKESHORE EAST

Rating: 7

On Shasta Lake in Shasta-Trinity National Forest.

Map 2.4 Shasta Lake Detail, page 112

Lakeshore East is near the full-service community of Lakehead and is on the Sacramento arm of Shasta Lake. It's a nice spot, with a good boat ramp and marina nearby at Antlers or Sugarloaf.

Campsites, facilities: There are 26 sites for tents or RVs up to 30 feet long. Picnic tables and fire grills are provided. Drinking water and flush toilets are available, and thre is a camp host. A boat ramp, grocery store, and coin laundry are available nearby. Some facilities are wheelchair-accessible. Leashed pets are permitted.

Reservations, fees: Reservations are accepted with a $9 reservation fee at 877/444-6777 and website www.ReserveUsa.com. The fee is $16 per night for single sites, $26 for double sites. Senior discount available. Open May through September.

Directions: From Redding, drive north on I-5 for 24 miles to the Antlers exit at Lakehead. Take the Antlers exit, turn left at the stop sign, and drive under the freeway to Lakeshore Drive. Turn left on Lakeshore Drive and drive three miles. Look for the campground entrance on the left side of the road.

Contact: Shasta-Trinity National Forest, Shasta Lake Ranger District, 530/275-1587, fax 530/275-1512; Shasta Lake Visitor Center, 530/275-1589.

111 GREGORY CREEK

Rating: 7

On Shasta Lake in Shasta-Trinity National Forest.

Map 2.4 Shasta Lake Detail, page 112

This is one of the more secluded Forest Service campgrounds on Shasta Lake, and it has become extremely popular with the younger crowd. It is set just above lakeside, on the eastern shore of the northern Sacramento River arm of the lake. When the lake is fullest in the spring and early summer, this is a great spot.

Campsites, facilities: There are five tent sites and 13 sites for tents or RVs up to 16 feet long. Picnic tables and fire grills are provided. Drinking water and flush toilets are available. Leashed pets are permitted.

Reservations, fees: Reservations are not accepted. The fee is $13 per night, $5 for each additional vehicle. Senior discount available. Open May through September.

Directions: From Redding, drive north on I-5 for 21 miles to the Salt Creek/Gilman Road exit. Take that exit and drive over the freeway to Gregory Creek Road. Turn right and drive 10 miles to the campground at the end of the road.

Contact: Shasta-Trinity National Forest, Shasta Lake Ranger District, 530/275-1587, fax 530/275-1512; Shasta Lake Visitor Center, 530/275-1589.

112 HIRZ BAY GROUP CAMP

Rating: 7

On Shasta Lake in Shasta-Trinity National Forest.

Map 2.4 Shasta Lake Detail, page 112

This is the spot for your own private party—providing you get a reservation—set on a point at the entrance of Hirz Bay on the McCloud River arm of Shasta Lake. A boat ramp is only a half mile away on the camp access road, giving access to the McCloud River arm. This is an excellent spot to make a base camp for a fishing trip, with great trolling for trout in this stretch of the lake.

Campsites, facilities: There are two group sites for tents and RVs up to 30 feet long. Picnic tables and fire grills are provided. Drinking water, vault toilets, and a group picnic area are available. Leashed pets are permitted.

Reservations, fees: Reservations are accepted with a $9 reservation fee at 877/444-6777 or website www.ReserveUsa.com. Camp One accommodates up to 120 people and is $90 per night; Camp Two accommodates up to 80 people and is $65 per night. Open year-round.

Directions: From Redding, drive north on I-5 for about 20 miles to the Salt Creek/Gilman exit. Turn right on Gilman Road/County Road 7H009 and drive northeast for 10 miles to the campground/boat launch access road. Turn right and drive a half mile to the camp on the left side of the road. The group camp is past the family campground.

Contact: Shasta-Trinity National Forest, Shasta Lake Ranger District, 530/275-1587, fax 530/275-1512; Shasta Lake Visitor Center, 530/275-1589.

113 HIRZ BAY

Rating: 7

On Shasta Lake in Shasta-Trinity National Forest.

Map 2.4 Shasta Lake Detail, page 112

This is one of two camps in the immediate area (the other is Hirz Bay Group Camp) that provides nearby access to a boat ramp (a half mile down the road) and the McCloud River arm of Shasta Lake. The camp is set on a point at the entrance of Hirz Bay. This is an excellent spot to make a base camp for a fishing trip, with great trolling for trout in this stretch of the lake.

Campsites, facilities: There are 37 single sites and 10 double sites for tents or RVs up to 30 feet long. Picnic tables and fire grills are provided. Drinking water and flush and vault toilets are available. A boat ramp is nearby. Some facilities are wheelchair-accessible. Leashed pets are permitted.

Reservations, fees: Reservations are accepted with a $9 reservation fee at 877/444-6777 or website www.ReserveUsa.com. The fee is $16 per night for a single, $25 for a double, $5 for an extra vehicle. Senior discount available. Open year-round.

Directions: From Redding, drive north on I-5 for about 20 miles to the Salt Creek/Gilman exit. Turn right on Gilman Road/County Road 7H009 and drive northeast for 10 miles to the campground/boat launch access road. Turn right and drive a half mile to the camp on the left side of the road.

Contact: Shasta-Trinity National Forest, Shasta Lake Ranger District, 530/275-1587, fax 530/275-1512; Shasta Lake Visitor Center, 530/275-1589.

114 DEKKAS ROCK GROUP CAMP

Rating: 8

On Shasta Lake in Shasta-Trinity National Forest.

Map 2.4 Shasta Lake Detail, page 112

The few people who know about this camp love this little spot. It is an ideal group camp, set on a flat above the McCloud arm of Shasta Lake, shaded primarily by bays and oaks, with a boat ramp two miles to the south at Hirz Bay. The views are pretty here, looking across the lake at the limestone ridge that borders the McCloud arm. In late summer and fall when the lake level drops, it can be a hike from the camp down to water's edge.

Campsites, facilities: There is one group site for tents, and four parking spaces for RVs up to 16 feet long. A central meeting area with preparation tables, picnic tables, and large barbecue is provided. Drinking water and vault toilets are available. Leashed pets are permitted.

Reservations, fees: Reservations are accepted with a $9 reservation fee at 877/444-6777 and website www.ReserveUsa.com. The fee is $90 per night for the group site for up to 60 campers.

Directions: From Redding, drive north on I-5 for about 20 miles to the Salt Creek/Gilman exit. Turn right on Gilman Road/County Road 7H009 and drive northeast for 11 miles to the campground on the right side of the road.

Contact: Shasta-Trinity National Forest, Shasta Lake Ranger District, 530/275-1587, fax 530/275-1512; Shasta Lake Visitor Center, 530/275-1589.

115 MOORE CREEK

Rating: 7

On Shasta Lake in Shasta-Trinity National Forest.

Map 2.4 Shasta Lake Detail, page 112

The McCloud arm of Shasta Lake is the most beautiful of the five arms at Shasta, with its emerald green waters and limestone canyon towering overhead to the east. That beautiful setting is taken advantage of at this camp, with a good view of the lake and limestone, along with good trout fishing on the adjacent section of water.

Campsites, facilities: There are 12 sites for tents or RVs up to 16 feet long. Picnic tables and fire grills are provided. Drinking water and vault toilets are available. Leashed pets are permitted.

Reservations, fees: Reservations are accepted with a $9 reservation fee only for the group site at 877/444-6777 or website www.Reserve Usa.com. The fee is $13 per night for single sites, $5 for each additional vehicle, $90 for group site. Senior discount available. Open May through September.

Directions: From Redding, drive north on I-5 for about 20 miles to the Salt Creek/Gilman exit. Take that exit and turn right on Gilman Road/County Road 7H009 and drive northeast for 14 miles to the campground on the right side of the road.

Contact: Shasta-Trinity National Forest, Shasta Lake Ranger District, 530/275-1587, fax 530/275-1512; Shasta Lake Visitor Center, 530/275-1589.

116 ELLERY CREEK

Rating: 7

On Shasta Lake in Shasta-Trinity National Forest.

Map 2.4 Shasta Lake Detail, page 112

This camp is set at a pretty spot where Ellery Creek empties into the upper McCloud arm of Shasta Lake. Several sites are set on the pavement with an unobstructed view of the beautiful McCloud arm. This stretch of water is excellent for trout fishing in the summer, with bank-fishing access available two miles upstream at the McCloud Bridge. In the spring, there are tons of small spotted bass along the shore from the camp on upstream to the inlet of the McCloud River. Boat launching facilities are available five miles south at Hirz Bay.

Campsites, facilities: There are 19 sites for tents or RVs up to 30 feet long. Picnic tables and fire grills are provided. Drinking water and vault toilets are available, and there is a camp host. Toilets are wheelchair-accessible. Leashed pets are permitted.

Reservations, fees: Reservations are accepted with a $9 reservation fee at 877/444-6777 and website www.ReserveUsa.com. The fee is $13 per night, $5 for each additional vehicle. Senior discount available. Open April through September.

Directions: From Redding, drive north on I-5 for about 20 miles to the Salt Creek/Gilman exit. Turn right on Gilman Road/County Road 7H009 and drive northeast for 15 miles to the campground on the right side of the road.

Contact: Shasta-Trinity National Forest, Shasta Lake Ranger District, 530/275-1587, fax 530/275-1512; Shasta Lake Visitor Center, 530/275-1589.

117 PINE POINT

Rating: 7

On Shasta Lake in Shasta-Trinity National Forest.

Map 2.4 Shasta Lake Detail, page 112

Pine Point is a pretty little camp, set on a ridge above the McCloud arm of Shasta Lake amid oak trees and scattered ponderosa pines. The view is best in spring, when lake levels are generally highest. Boat launching facilities are available at Hirz Bay; boaters park their boats on shore below the camp while the rest of their party arrives at the camp by car. That provides a chance not only for camping, but also for boating, swimming, waterskiing, and fishing. Note: from July through September, this campground can be reserved as a group site only.

Campsites, facilities: There are 14 sites for tents or RVs up to 24 feet. Picnic tables and fire rings are provided. Drinking water and vault toilets are available. Leashed pets are permitted.

Reservations, fees: Reservations are accepted with a $9 reservation fee only for group sites at 877/444-6777 or website www.Reserve Usa.com. The fee is $13 per night, $5 for each additional vehicle, $90 per night for group sites. Senior discount available. Open May through September.

Directions: From Redding, drive north on I-5 for about 20 miles to the Salt Creek/Gilman exit. Turn right on Gilman Road/County Road 7H009 and drive northeast for 17 miles to the campground entrance road on the right.

Contact: Shasta-Trinity National Forest, Shasta Lake Ranger District, 530/275-1587, fax 530/275-1512; Shasta Lake Visitor Center, 530/275-1589.

118 MCCLOUD BRIDGE

Rating: 7

On Shasta Lake in Shasta-Trinity National Forest.

Map 2.4 Shasta Lake Detail, page 112

Even though reaching this camp requires a long drive, it remains popular. That is because the best shore-fishing access at the lake is available at nearby McCloud Bridge. It is common to see 15 or 20 people shore fishing here for trout on summer weekends. In the fall, big brown trout migrate through this section of lake en route to their upstream spawning grounds.

Campsites, facilities: There are 14 sites for tents or RVs up to 16 feet long. Picnic tables and fire grills are provided. Drinking water, vault toilets, and a group picnic area are available. Some facilities are wheelchair-accessible, including the picnic area. Leashed pets are permitted.

Reservations, fees: Reservations are not accepted. The fee is $16 per night for single sites, $26 for double sites, $5 for each additional vehicle. Senior discount available. Open May through September.

Directions: From Redding, drive north on I-5 for about 20 miles to the Salt Creek/Gilman exit. Turn right on Gilman Road/County Road 7H009 and drive northeast for 18.5 miles. Cross the McCloud Bridge and drive one mile to the campground entrance on the right.

Contact: Shasta-Trinity National Forest, Shasta Lake Ranger District, 530/275-1587, fax 530/275-1512; Shasta Lake Visitor Center, 530/275-1589.

119 MADRONE CAMP

Rating: 7

On Squaw Creek in Shasta-Trinity National Forest.

Map 2.4 Shasta Lake Detail, page 112

Tired of people? Then you've come to the right place. This remote camp is set along Squaw

Creek, a feeder stream of Shasta Lake, which lies to the southwest. It's way out there, far away from anybody. Even though Shasta Lake is relatively close, about 10 miles away, it's literally in another world. A network of four-wheel-drive roads provides a recreation option, detailed on a map of Shasta-Trinity National Forest.

Campsites, facilities: There are 13 sites for tents or RVs up to 16 feet long. Picnic tables and fire grills are provided. Vault toilets are available, and there is a camp host in summer. No drinking water is available. Leashed pets are permitted.

Reservations, fees: Reservations are not accepted. There is no fee for camping. Open year-round, with limited winter facilities.

Directions: From Redding, drive 29 miles east on Highway 299 to the town of Montgomery Creek. Turn left on Fenders Ferry Road/Forest Road 27 and drive 22 miles to the camp (the road starts as gravel and then becomes dirt).

Contact: Shasta-Trinity National Forest, Shasta Lake Ranger District, 530/275-1587, fax 530/275-1512; Shasta Lake Visitor Center, 530/275-1589.

120 GOOSENECK COVE BOAT-IN

Rating: 4

On Shasta Lake in Shasta-Trinity National Forest.

Map 2.4 Shasta Lake Detail, page 112

You want a camp all to yourself? There's a good chance of that here at Gooseneck Cove. One reason is because it is well hidden, set well back in a cove on the west side of the Sacramento River arm of giant Shasta Lake. The other reason is there was some fire damage here in 1999, and some burned oaks and manzanita will take years to grow out. So there is a blackened hill in view. That will likely keep the few who know of this place away. So there you have it, a chance any day of the year to

have a campground all to yourself. The fishing on the Sacramento River arm of Shasta Lake is very good, both trolling for trout all summer, especially at the headwaters in midsummer, and for bass in the spring on plastic worms. Water-skiing is also excellent here, with water temperatures in the high 70s for most of summer.

Campsites, facilities: There are eight boat-in sites for tents. Picnic tables and fire grills are provided. Vault toilets are available. No drinking water is available. Garbage must be packed out. Small stores with supplies are available at Antlers. Leashed pets are permitted.

Reservations, fees: Reservations are not accepted. There is no fee for camping. A $6 fee is charged for boat launching. Open year-round.

Directions: From Redding, drive north on I-5 for 24 miles to the Lakeshore-Antlers Road exit in Lakehead. Take that exit, turn left at the stop sign, and drive a short distance to Antlers Road. At Antlers Road, turn right and drive one mile south to the campground and nearby boat launch. Launch your boat and cruise seven miles south to the boat-in campground.

Contact: Shasta-Trinity National Forest, Shasta Lake Ranger District, 530/275-1587, fax 530/275-1512; Shasta Lake Visitor Center, 530/275-1589.

121 TRAIL IN RV CAMPGROUND

Rating: 7

Near Shasta Lake.

Map 2.4 Shasta Lake Detail, page 112

This is a privately operated campground near the Salt Creek arm of giant Shasta Lake. Open, level sites are available. The lake is about a quarter mile away and offers fishing, boating, and swimming. Its proximity to I-5 makes this a popular spot, fast and easy to reach, which is extremely attractive for drivers of RVs and trailers who want to avoid the many twisty roads surrounding Shasta Lake.

Campsites, facilities: There are 39 sites,

including 10 pull-through, with full hookups for RVs, and two sites for tents. Picnic tables and fire grills are provided. Restrooms, hot showers, TV hookups, RV dump station, swimming pool, convenience store, ice, wood, and coin laundry are available. Leashed pets are permitted.

Reservations, fees: Reservations are accepted with a deposit. The fee is $22.25 per night for RV camping ($14 for tent camping) plus $2 per person per night for more than two people, monthly rates available, $1 per pet per night. Major credit cards accepted. Open year-round.

Directions: From Redding, drive 22 miles north on I-5 to the Gilman Road/Salt Creek Road exit. Take that exit and turn left on Salt Creek Road and drive a short distance to Gregory Creek Road. Turn right and drive one-quarter mile to the campground on the right.

Contact: Trail In RV Campground, 530/238-8533.

122 NELSON POINT

Rating: 7

On Shasta Lake in Shasta-Trinity National Forest.

Map 2.4 Shasta Lake Detail, page 112

This is an easy-to-reach campground, only a few minutes from I-5. It's set beside the Salt Creek inlet of Shasta Lake, deep in a cove. In low-water years, or when the lake level is low in the fall and early winter, this camp can seem quite distant from water's edge.

Campsites, facilities: There are eight sites for tents or RVs up to 16 feet long. Vault toilets, picnic tables, and fire grills are provided. No drinking water is available. A grocery store and coin laundry are nearby in Lakehead. Leashed pets are permitted.

Reservations, fees: Reservations are accepted with a $9 reservation fee only for group sites, July through September, at 877/444-6777 or website www.ReserveUsa.com. The fee is $8

for single-site use, $5 for each additional vehicle, and $65 per night for group sites. Senior discount available. Open May through September.

Directions: From Redding, drive north on I-5 for about 20 miles to the Salt Creek Road/Gilman Road exit. Take that exit, turn left and drive a quarter mile to Gregory Creek Road. Turn right and drive one mile to Conflict Point Road. Turn left and drive one mile to the campground on the left.

Contact: Shasta-Trinity National Forest, Shasta Lake Ranger District, 530/275-1587, fax 530/275-1512; Shasta Lake Visitor center, 530/275-1589.

123 HOLIDAY HARBOR

Rating: 7

On Shasta Lake.

Map 2.4 Shasta Lake Detail, page 112

This camp is one of the more popular family-oriented, all-service resorts on Shasta Lake. It is set on the lower McCloud arm of the lake, which is extremely beautiful with a limestone mountain ridge off to the east. It is an ideal jump-off for all water sports, especially houseboating, boating, all water sports, and fishing. A good boat ramp, boat rentals, and store with all the goodies are bonuses. Another plus is the nearby side trip to Shasta Caverns, a privately guided adventure (fee charged) into limestone caves. This camp often fills in summer, even on weekdays. We've worked with the management here for years, and whoever you talk to has always been friendly, helpful, and smart.

Campsites, facilities: There are 27 sites with full hookups for RVs up to 40 feet long, with tents allowed in several sites. Picnic tables and barbecues are provided. Restrooms, hot showers, grocery store, coin laundry, boat moorage, playground, propane gas, and boat rentals are available. Some facilities are wheelchair-accessible. Leashed pets are permitted.

Reservations, fees: Reservations are recommended. The fee is $19.50–25.50, $3–5.25 per person for more than two people, $4.50 per night for each additional vehicle, and $6.50–8.50 per night for boat moorage. Major credit cards accepted. Open April through October.

Directions: From Redding, drive 18 miles north on I-5 to the Shasta Caverns Road exit. Turn right at Shasta Caverns Road and drive about one mile to the campground entrance on the right.

Contact: Holiday Harbor, 800/776-2628 or 530/238-2383, website: www.shastalake.com.

124 GREENS CREEK BOAT-IN

Rating:10

On Shasta Lake in Shasta-Trinity National Forest.

Map 2.4 Shasta Lake Detail, page 112

This is one of my favorite spots on the planet on a warm spring day, maybe mid-April, but it is always special. This boat-in campsite provides an exceptional base camp and boat-in headquarters for a recreation paradise. The camp is set at the foot of dramatic limestone formations on the McCloud arm of Shasta Lake. On land, there is a steep but fantastic hike that leads to a dramatic lookout of the lake. By boat, this is one of the best fishing spots, trolling for 16- to 18-inch trout with Z-Rays, Kastmasters, and Cripplures; proper depth is critical, and experts using downriggers have a huge advantage. The campsites are in a region well wooded, little traveled, with good opportunities in the evening to see wildlife.

Campsites, facilities: There are nine boat-in sites for tents. Picnic tables and fire grills are provided. Vault toilets are available. No drinking water is available. Garbage must be packed out. Small stores with supplies are available at Holiday Harbor. Leashed pets are permitted.

Reservations, fees: Reservations are not accepted. There is no fee for camping. A $6 fee is charged for boat launching. Open year-round.

Directions: From Redding, drive north on I-5 over the Pit River Bridge at Shasta Lake to the O'Brien Road/Shasta Caverns Road exit. Turn east (right) on Shasta Caverns Road and drive one-quarter mile to a signed turnoff for Bailey Cove. Turn right and drive one mile to Bailey Cove Boat Ramp. Launch your boat and cruise four miles northeast up the McCloud Arm. Land your boat and pick your campsite.

Contact: Shasta-Trinity National Forest, Shasta Lake Ranger District, 530/275-1587, fax 530/275-1512; Shasta Lake Visitor Center, 530/275-1589.

125 SHASTA

Rating: 6

On the Sacramento River in Shasta-Trinity National Forest.

Map 2.4 Shasta Lake Detail, page 112

Because campers must drive across Shasta Dam to reach this campground, access was closed in 2002 for national security reasons. Call before planning a visit. We believe it will reopen to the public since the route also provides access to an adjacent OHV area, one of the few in the north state. When open, this place is thus for quads and dirt bikes, loud and wild, and hey, it's a perfect spot for them. It's barren because of past mining in the area, but the view of the river and Shasta Dam are incredible. Nearby dam tours are unique and memorable.

Campsites, facilities: There are 22 sites for tents or RVs up to 24 feet long. Picnic tables and fire rings are provided. Drinking water and vault toilets are available. A boat ramp is nearby. Groceries and bait are available in Shasta Lake City. Leashed pets are permitted.

Reservations, fees: Reservations are not accepted. The fee is $10 per night, $5 for each additional vehicle. Open year-round.

Directions: From I-5 in Redding, drive north for three miles to the exit for the town of Shasta Lake City and Shasta Dam Boulevard. Take that exit and bear west on Shasta Dam

Boulevard and drive three miles to Lake Boulevard. Turn right on Lake Boulevard and drive two miles. Cross Shasta Dam and continue four miles to the signed campground.

Contact: Bureau of Reclamation Visitor Center, 530/275-4463; Shasta-Trinity National Forest, Shasta Lake Ranger District, 530/275-1587, fax 530/275-1512; Shasta Lake Visitor Center, 530/275-1589.

126 WONDERLAND MOBILE HOME & RV PARK

Rating: 5

Near Shasta Lake.
Map 2.4 Shasta Lake Detail, page 112

This RV park is within a mobile home park south of Shasta Lake. The tour of Shasta Caverns is a recreation option, via a short drive to Holiday Harbor. Other options include the city of Redding's extensive visitor center, the Turtle Bay Museum and Exploration Park, the Carter House Natural History Museum in Caldwell Park, public golf courses, and the Sacramento River trails, which are paved, making them accessible for wheelchairs and bikes.

Campsites, facilities: There are 30 sites for RVs, many with full hookups and some drive-through, and a grassy area for dispersed tent camping. Picnic tables, restrooms, showers, coin laundry, cable TV, seasonally heated swimming pool, and horseshoes are available. Some facilities are wheelchair-accessible. Leashed pets are permitted.

Reservations, fees: Reservations are accepted. The fee is $11–15 per night, $2.50 per person per night for more than two people. Senior discount available. Major credit cards accepted. Open year-round.

Directions: From Redding, drive north on I-5 for 11 miles to the Fawndale exit. Take that exit west onto Wonderland Boulevard and drive a quarter mile to the park on the left (15203 Wonderland Boulevard).

Contact: Wonderland Mobile Home & RV Park, 530/275-1281.

127 BEAR MOUNTAIN RV RESORT & CAMPGROUND

Rating: 5

Near Shasta Lake.
Map 2.4 Shasta Lake Detail, page 112

This is a privately operated park set up primarily for RVs in the remote Jones Valley area along Shasta Lake. It is set on 52 acres. A hiking trail leaves from the campground, rises up a hill, and provides a great view of Redding.

Campsites, facilities: There are 97 sites with full or partial hookups for RVs, including some drive-through sites, 24 tent sites, and four park-model cabins. Picnic tables and fire rings are provided. Drinking water, flush toilets, coin showers, coin laundry, modem access, convenience store, RV dump station, a seasonal pool, recreation hall, arcade, and two playgrounds, volleyball, and horseshoe pit are available. Some facilities are wheelchair-accessible. A boat ramp is within three miles. Leashed pets are permitted.

Reservations, fees: Reservations are accepted. The fee is $14–20 per night. Monthly rates available. Major credit cards accepted. Senior discount available. Open year-round.

Directions: From Redding, drive north on I-5 for three miles to the Oasis Road exit. Take that exit and turn right on Oasis Road/Old Oregon Trail and drive 3.5 miles to Bear Mountain Road. Turn right on Bear Mountain Road and drive 3.5 miles to the campground on the left.

Contact: Bear Mountain RV Resort, 530/275-4728 or 800/952-0551, fax 530/275-8459, website: www.campshasta.com.

128 SKI ISLAND BOAT-IN

Rating: 8

On Shasta Lake in Shasta-Trinity National Forest.
Map 2.4 Shasta Lake Detail, page 112

Could there be any secrets left about Shasta

Lake? You bet, with boat-in campsites providing the best of all worlds for people willing to rough it just a little. Ski Island is an outstanding place to set up camp, then boat, fish, ski, or explore this giant lake. It is on the Pit River Arm of the lake about three miles upstream from the Pit River (I-5) bridge. The closest boat ramp to Ski Island is at Silverthorn Resort, which is in a cove on the Pit River arm of the lake. Here you will find this three-acre island with a boat-in campground and several little trails. It is well out of sight, and out of mind for most campers as well. One note: in wet weather, the reddish, iron-based soil on the island will turn the bottom of your boat rust-colored with even a minimum of tracking in.

Campsites, facilities: There are 23 boat-in sites for tents. Picnic tables and fire grills are provided. Vault toilets are available. No drinking water is available. Garbage must be packed out. Small stores with supplies are available at Silverthorn Resort and Jones Valley Resort. Leashed pets are permitted.

Reservations, fees: Reservations are not accepted. There is no fee for camping. A $6 fee is charged for boat launching. Open year-round.

Directions: From Redding, drive north on I-5 to the Oasis exit and drive east to Bear Mountain Road. Turn right and drive to Dry Creek Road. Turn left on Dry Creek Road and drive seven miles to a fork in the road. Bear right at the fork and drive to Jones Valley Boat Ramp (a left at the fork takes you to Silverthorn Resort). Launch your boat and head west (to the left) for four miles to Ski Island. Land and pick your campsite.

Contact: Shasta-Trinity National Forest, Shasta Lake Ranger District, 530/275-1587, fax 530/275-1512; Shasta Lake Visitor Center, 530/275-1589.

129 UPPER AND LOWER JONES VALLEY CAMPS

Rating: 7

On Shasta Lake in Shasta-Trinity National Forest.

Map 2.4 Shasta Lake Detail, page 112

Lower Jones is a small, pretty camp sheltered by oaks and bays along a deep cove in the remote Pit River arm of Shasta Lake. There is a trailhead at the camp that provides access to the Clickapudi Trail, a great hiking and biking trail that traces the lake's shore, routed through pretty woodlands. Two nearby resorts, Jones Valley and Silverthorn, provide boat rentals and supplies.

Campsites, facilities: There are 21 sites for tents or RVs up to 16 feet long in two adjacent campgrounds. Picnic tables and fire grills are provided. Drinking water and vault toilets are available. Some facilities are wheelchair-accessible. A boat ramp at Jones Valley is two miles from camp. Leashed pets are permitted.

Reservations, fees: Reservations are not accepted. Upper Jones sites are $13 per night, Lower Jones sites are $16 for a single site and $26 for a double. Senior discount available. Lower Jones is open year-round. Upper Jones is open May through September.

Directions: From Redding, turn east on Highway 299 and drive 7.5 miles just past the town of Bella Vista. At Dry Creek Road, turn left and drive nine miles to a Y in the road. Bear right at the Y (left will take you to Silverthorn Resort) and drive a short distance to the campground entrances, on the left side for Lower Jones and on the right side for Upper Jones.

Contact: Shasta-Trinity National Forest, Shasta Lake Ranger District, 530/275-1587, fax 530/275-1512; Shasta Lake Visitor Center, 530/275-1589.

130 JONES VALLEY INLET

Rating: 7

On Shasta Lake in Shasta-Trinity National Forest.

Map 2.4 Shasta Lake Detail, page 112

This is one of the few primitive camp areas on Shasta Lake, set on the distant Pit River arm of the lake. It is an ideal camp for hiking and biking, with the nearby Clickapudi Trail routed for miles along the lake's shore, in and out of coves, and then entering the surrounding foothills and oak/bay woodlands. The camp is pretty, if a bit exposed, with two nearby resorts, Jones Valley and Silverthorn, providing boat rentals and supplies.

Campsites, facilities: There is an area for dispersed, primitive camping for tents or RVs up to 30 feet long. Vault toilets are available. No drinking water is available. A boat ramp at Jones Valley is two miles from camp. Groceries are available nearby. Leashed pets are permitted.

Reservations, fees: Reservations are not accepted. The fee is $6 per vehicle per night. Senior discount available. Open March through mid-October.

Directions: From Redding, turn east on Highway 299 and drive 7.5 miles just past the town of Bella Vista. At Dry Creek Road turn left and drive nine miles to a Y in the road. Bear right at the Y (left will take you to Silverthorn Resort) and drive a short distance to the campground entrance on the left side of the road.

Contact: Shasta-Trinity National Forest, Shasta Lake Ranger District, 530/275-1587, fax 530/275-1512; Shasta Lake Visitor Center, 530/275-1589.

131 ARBUCKLE FLAT BOAT-IN

Rating: 8

On Shasta Lake in Shasta-Trinity National Forest.

Map 2.4 Shasta Lake Detail, page 112

How could anything be secluded on Northern California's most popular recreation lake? Well, here is your answer. Arbuckle Flat is a truly secluded boat-in campground well up the Pit River arm of the lake, set far back in a deep cove. You will feel a million miles away from all the fast traffic back at the main lake body. Specifically, it is five miles east of the Jones Valley Boat Ramp, set on the right (south) side of a deep cove. You pay a small price for this seclusion. After landing your boat, you must then carry your gear up a hill to the campsites. When the lake is low, this is like a march up Cardiac Hill. The landscape surrounding the campsites is peppered with oak. The fishing in the area is often good for bass, and where you find submerged trees, for crappie as well.

Campsites, facilities: There are 11 boat-in sites for tents. Picnic tables and fire grills are provided. Vault toilets are available. No drinking water is available. Garbage must be packed out. Small stores with supplies are available at Silverthorn Resort and Jones Valley Resort. Leashed pets are permitted.

Reservations, fees: Reservations are not accepted. There is no fee for camping. A $6 fee is charged for boat launching. Open year-round.

Directions: From Redding, drive north on I-5 to the Oasis exit and drive east to Bear Mountain Road. Turn right and drive to Dry Creek Road. Turn left on Dry Creek Road and drive seven miles to a fork in the road. Bear right at the fork and drive to Jones Valley Boat Ramp (a left at the fork takes you to Silverthorn Resort). Launch your boat and head east (to the right) for five miles. The last major arm off to your right hides the campground at the back of the cove, in the oaks above the shore. Land and pick your campsite.

Contact: Shasta-Trinity National Forest, Shasta Lake Ranger District, 530/275-1587, fax 530/275-1512; Shasta Lake Visitor Center, 530/275-1589.

132 EAST WEAVER

Rating: 6

On the east branch of Weaver Creek in Shasta-Trinity National Forest.

Map 2.4, page 111

This camp is set along East Weaver Creek. Another mile to the west on East Weaver Road, the road dead-ends at a trailhead, a good side trip. From here, the hiking trail is routed four miles, a significant climb, to tiny East Weaver Lake, set to the southwest of Monument Peak (7,771 feet elevation). The elevation at East Weaver is 2,700 feet.

Campsites, facilities: There are eight tent sites and seven sites for tents or RVs up to 16 feet long. Picnic tables and fire grills are provided. Drinking water (spring, summer, and fall only) and vault toilets are available. Supplies and a coin laundry are available in Weaverville. Leashed pets are permitted.

Reservations, fees: Reservations are not accepted. The fee is $9 per night. Senior discount available. Open year-round.

Directions: From Redding, go west on Highway 299 and drive to Weaverville. In Weaverville, turn north on Highway 3 and drive about two miles to East Weaver Road. Turn left on East Weaver Road and drive 3.5 miles to the campground.

Contact: Shasta-Trinity National Forest, Weaverville Ranger Station, 530/623-2121, fax 530/623-6010.

133 STEELBRIDGE

Rating: 7

On the Trinity River.

Map 2.4, page 111

Very few campers know of this spot, yet it was renovated in 2000 and it can be a prime spot for anglers and campers. It's one of the better stretches of water in the area for steelhead, with good shore fishing access. The prime time is from October through December. In the summer, the shade of conifers will keep you cool. Don't forget to bring your own water. The elevation is 1,700 feet.

Campsites, facilities: There are nine sites for tents or RVs up to 20 feet long. Picnic tables and fire grills are provided. Pit toilets are available; there is a camp host in summer. No drinking water is available. Supplies are available within three miles in Douglas City. Leashed pets are permitted.

Reservations, fees: Reservations are not accepted. The fee is $5 per night. Senior discount available. Open year-round.

Directions: From Redding, head west on Highway 299, drive over Buckhorn Summit, and continue toward Douglas City to Steel Bridge Road (if you reach Douglas City, you have gone 2.3 miles too far). At Steel Bridge Road, turn right and drive about four miles to the campground at the end of the road.

Contact: Bureau of Land Management, Redding Field Office, 530/224-2100, fax 530/224-2172.

134 DOUGLAS CITY AND STEINER FLAT

Rating: 7

On the Trinity River.

Map 2.4, page 111

If you want to camp along this stretch of the main Trinity River, these camps are your best bet (they're along the river about two miles from each other). They are set off the main road, near the river, with good bank fishing access (the prime season is from mid-August through winter for salmon and steelhead). There's paved parking and two beaches at Douglas City Campground. Steiner Flat, a more primitive camp, provides better access for fishing. This can be a good base camp for an off-season fishing trip on the Trinity River or a lounging spot during the summer. The elevation is 1,700 feet.

Campsites, facilities: There are 18 sites for tents or RVs up to 30 feet long at Douglas City with dispersed camping at Steiner Flat. At Douglas City, picnic tables and fire grills are provided. Restrooms, flush toilets, and sinks are available. Drinking water is available in summer only. At Steiner Flat, a pit toilet is available. No drinking water is available. Supplies are available within one mile in Douglas City. Leashed pets are permitted.

Reservations, fees: Reservations are not accepted. The fee is $10 per night. Senior discount available. Open year-round.

Directions: From Redding, go west on Highway 299 and continue over the bridge at the Trinity River near Douglas City to Steiner Flat Road. Turn left on Steiner Flat Road and drive a half mile to Douglas City campground on the left. To reach Steiner Flat, continue two more miles and look for the campground on the left.

Contact: Bureau of Land Management, Redding Field Office, 530/224-2100, fax 530/224-2172.

135 OLD LEWISTON BRIDGE RV RESORT

Rating: 7

On the Trinity River.
Map 2.4, page 111

This is a popular spot for calm-water kayaking, rafting, and fishing. Though much of the water from Trinity and Lewiston Lakes is diverted via tunnel to Whiskeytown Lake (en route to the valley and points south), enough escapes downstream to provide a viable stream here near the town of Lewiston. This upstream section below Lewiston Lake is prime in the early summer for trout, particularly the chance for a huge brown trout (special regulations in effect). The campground is in a hilly area but has level sites, with nearby Lewiston Lake also a major attraction. Damage from a major fire in the general area in summer of 1999, set as a "controlled burn," is still evident.

Campsites, facilities: There are 52 sites with full hookups for RVs, including some long-term rentals, a separate area for tents, and five rental trailers. Picnic tables are provided. Restrooms, hot showers, coin laundry, a grocery store, ice, and propane gas refills are available. A group picnic area is available by reservation. Supplies can be obtained within walking distance in Lewiston. Leashed pets are permitted.

Reservations, fees: Reservations are accepted. The fee is $24 per night for RVs, $14 per night per vehicle for tent campers, $2 per person for more than two people. Monthly rates available. Major credit cards accepted. Open year-round.

Directions: From Redding, head west on Highway 299, drive over Buckhorn Summit, and continue for five miles to Trinity Dam Boulevard. Turn right on Trinity Dam Boulevard and drive four miles to Lewiston, and continue north to Rush Creek Road. Turn left (west) on Rush Creek Road and drive three-quarters of a mile to the resort on the left.

Contact: Old Lewiston Bridge RV Resort, 800/922-1924 or tel./fax 530/778-3894, website: www.lewistonbridgerv.com.

136 TRINITY RIVER LODGE RV RESORT

Rating: 7

On the Trinity River.
Map 2.4, page 111

For many, this privately operated park has an ideal location. You get level, grassy sites with shade trees along the Trinity River, yet it is just a short drive north to Lewiston Lake or a bit farther to giant Trinity Lake. Lake or river, take your pick. The resort covers nearly 14 acres, pretty enough that about half the sites are rented for the entire summer.

Campsites, facilities: There are 60 sites with full hookups for RVs up to 40 feet long, including about 30 summer rentals, five tent sites, and one cottage. Restrooms, hot showers, a coin laundry, cable TV, recreation room, lending library, clubhouse, recreation field, propane gas, camp store, ice, wood, furnished trailer rentals, boat and trailer storage, horseshoes, and picnic area are available. Some facilities are wheelchair-accessible. Leashed pets are permitted.

Reservations, fees: Reservations are recommended. The fee is $14–24 per night. Major credit cards accepted. Open year-round.

Directions: From Redding, go west on Highway 299, drive over Buckhorn Summit, and continue for five miles to Trinity Dam Boulevard. Turn right on Trinity Dam Boulevard and drive four miles to Lewiston. Continue on Trinity Dam Boulevard to Rush Creek Road. Turn left on Rush Creek Road and drive 2.3 miles to the campground on the left.

Contact: Trinity River Lodge RV Resort, 800/761-2769 or 530/778-3791, website: www.rvdestinations.com/trinityriver.

137 MARY SMITH

Rating:10

On Lewiston Lake in Shasta-Trinity National Forest.

Map 2.4, page 111

This is one of the prettiest spots you'll ever see, set along the southwestern shore of Lewiston Lake. When you wake up and peek out of your sleeping bag, the natural beauty of this serene lake can take your breath away. Hand-launched boats, such as canoes, are ideal here. Birdwatching is good in this area. The best fishing is from Lakeview Terrace and the tules on upstream to just below Trinity Dam. The elevation is 2,000 feet.

Campsites, facilities: There are 18 sites for tents only, some requiring a very short walk. Picnic tables and fire grills are provided. Drinking water and flush and vault toilets are available,

and there is a camp host. Supplies and a coin laundry are available in Lewiston. Leashed pets are permitted.

Reservations, fees: Reservations are not accepted. The fee is $9 per night. Open May through October.

Directions: From Redding, head west on Highway 299, drive over Buckhorn Summit, and continue for five miles to Trinity Dam Boulevard. Turn right on Trinity Dam Boulevard and drive four miles to Lewiston, and then continue on Trinity Dam Boulevard for 2.5 miles to the campground.

Contact: Shasta-Trinity National Forest, Weaverville Ranger Station, 530/623-2121, fax 530/623-6010.

138 COOPER GULCH

Rating: 8

On Lewiston Lake in Shasta-Trinity National Forest.

Map 2.4, page 111

Here is a nice spot along a beautiful lake, featuring a short trail to Baker Gulch, where a pretty creek enters Lewiston Lake. The trout fishing is good on the upper end of the lake (where the current starts) and upstream. The lake was recently designated a wildlife viewing area, with large numbers of waterfowl and other birds often spotted near the tules off the shore of Lakeview Terrace. Bring all of your own supplies and plan on hunkering down here for a while.

Campsites, facilities: There are five sites for tents or RVs up to 16 feet long. Picnic tables and fire grills are provided. Vault toilets are available. No drinking water is available. Some facilities are wheelchair-accessible. Supplies and a coin laundry are available in Lewiston. Leashed pets are permitted.

Reservations, fees: Reservations are not accepted. The fee is $12 per night. Senior discount available. Open April through November.

Directions: From Redding, head west on Highway 299, drive over Buckhorn Summit, and continue for five miles to Trinity Dam Boulevard. Turn right on Trinity Dam Boulevard, drive four miles to Lewiston, and then continue on Trinity Dam Boulevard another four miles north to the campground.

Contact: Shasta-Trinity National Forest, Weaverville Ranger Station, 530/623-2121, fax 530/623-6010.

139 LAKEVIEW TERRACE RESORT

Rating: 8

On Lewiston Lake.
Map 2.4, page 111

This might be your Golden Pond. It's a terraced RV park—with cabin rentals also available—that overlooks Lewiston Lake, one of the prettiest drive-to lakes in the region. Fishing for trout is excellent from Lakeview Terrace on upstream toward the dam. Lewiston Lake is perfect for fishing, with a 10 mph speed limit in effect (all the hot boats go to nearby Trinity Lake), along with excellent prospects for rainbow and brown trout. The topper is that Lewiston Lake is always full to the brim, just the opposite of the up-and-down nightmare of its neighboring big brother, Trinity.

Campsites, facilities: There are 40 sites, including some drive-through, with full hookups for RVs up to 40 feet, and cabins with one to five bedrooms. Picnic tables and barbecues are provided. Restrooms, hot showers, coin laundry, heated pool (summer only), propane gas, ice, horseshoes, playground, bait, and boat rentals are available. Supplies are available within five miles. Leashed pets are permitted.

Reservations, fees: Reservations are recommended. The fee is $18–21 per night, $2 per person for more than two people. Major credit cards accepted. Open year-round.

Directions: From Redding, drive west on Highway 299, drive over Buckhorn Summit, and continue for five miles to Trinity Dam Boulevard. Turn right on Trinity Dam Boulevard and drive 10 miles (five miles past Lewiston) to the resort on the left side of the road.

Contact: Lakeview Terrace Resort, 530/778-3803, fax 530/778-3960, website: www.camp grounds.com/lakeview.

140 TUNNEL ROCK

Rating: 7

On Lewiston Lake in Shasta-Trinity National Forest.
Map 2.4, page 111

This is a very small, primitive alternative to Ackerman, which is more developed and another mile up the road to the north. The proximity to the Pine Cove boat ramp and fish-cleaning station, less than two miles to the south, is a primary attraction. The elevation is 1,700 feet.

Campsites, facilities: There are six tent sites. Picnic tables and fire grills are provided. Vault toilets are available. No drinking water is available. Leashed pets are permitted.

Reservations, fees: Reservations are not accepted. The fee is $6 per night. Senior discount available. Open year-round.

Directions: From Redding, go west on Highway 299, drive over Buckhorn Summit, and continue for five miles to County Road 105/Trinity Dam Road. Turn right on Trinity Dam Road and drive four miles to Lewiston, and then continue another seven miles north on Trinity Dam Boulevard to the campground.

Contact: Shasta-Trinity National Forest, Weaverville Ranger Station, 530/623-2121, fax 530/623-6010.

141 ACKERMAN

Rating: 7

On Lewiston Lake in Shasta-Trinity National Forest.
Map 2.4, page 111

Of the camps and parks at Lewiston Lake,

Ackerman is closest to the lake's headwaters. This stretch of water below Trinity Dam is the best area for trout fishing on Lewiston Lake. Nearby Pine Cove boat ramp, two miles south of the camp, offers the only boat launch on Lewiston Lake with docks and a fish-cleaning station—a popular spot for anglers. When the Trinity powerhouse is running, trout fishing is excellent in this area. The elevation is 2,000 feet.

Campsites, facilities: There are 66 sites for tents or RVs up to 40 feet long. Picnic tables and fire grills are provided. Drinking water (spring, summer, and fall only; no drinking water in the winter), flush toilets, and RV dump station are available, and there is a camp host. Leashed pets are permitted.

Reservations, fees: Reservations are not accepted. The fee is $6–11 per night. Senior discount available. Open year-round.

Directions: From Redding, head west on Highway 299, drive over Buckhorn Summit, and continue for five miles to Trinity Dam Boulevard. Turn right on Trinity Dam Boulevard and drive four miles to Lewiston. Continue north on Trinity Dam Boulevard for eight miles to the campground.

Contact: Shasta-Trinity National Forest, Weaverville Ranger Station, 530/623-2121, fax 530/623-6010.

142 OAK BOTTOM

Rating: 7

On Whiskeytown Lake.
Map 2.4, page 111

The prettiest hiking trails at Whiskeytown Lake are at the far western end of the reservoir, and this camp provides excellent access to them. One hiking and biking trail skirts the north shoreline of the lake and is routed to the lake's inlet at the Judge Carr Powerhouse. The other, with the trailhead just a short drive to the west, is routed along Mill Creek, a pristine, clear-running stream with the trail jumping over the

water many times. The campground sites seem a little close, but the camp is next to a beach area. There are junior ranger programs for youngsters 7–12 years old, and evening ranger programs at the Oak Bottom Amphitheater are available three nights per week from mid-June through Labor Day. A self-guided nature trail is five miles away at the visitor center.

Campsites, facilities: There are 102 walk-in tent sites with picnic tables and fire grills. There are 22 sites for self-contained RVs or trailers in the large parking area near the launch ramp. Drinking water, restrooms, flush toilets, coin-operated showers, groceries, ice, wood, RV dump station, boat ramp, and boat rentals are available. Some facilities are wheelchair-accessible. Leashed pets are permitted.

Reservations, fees: Reservations are accepted in summer at 800/365-CAMP (800/365-2267) or website reservations.nps.gov; reservations are not accepted in the off-season. The fee is $7–18 per night, plus a park use permit of $5 per day, $10 per week, or $20 per year. Senior discount available. Open year-round.

Directions: From Redding, drive west on Highway 299 for 15 miles (past the visitor center) to the campground entrance road on the left. Turn left and drive a short distance to the campground.

Contact: Whiskeytown National Recreation Area, 530/242-3400, fax 530/246-5154.

143 DRY CREEK GROUP CAMP

Rating: 7

On Whiskeytown Lake.
Map 2.4, page 111

If you're in a group and take the time to reserve this spot, you'll be rewarded with some room and the quiet that goes along with it. This is the most remote drive-to camp at Whiskeytown Lake. A boat ramp is about two miles away (to the east) at Brandy Creek. You'll pass it on the way in. Note: reservations are an absolute must, available five months in advance.

Campsites, facilities: There are two tents-only group sites that can accommodate 50 people each. Picnic tables and fire grills are provided. Drinking water and pit toilets are available. Leashed pets are permitted.

Reservations, fees: Reservations are accepted at 800/365-CAMP (800/365-2267) or website reservations.nps.gov. The fee is $75 per night, plus a park use permit of $5 per day, $10 per week, or $20 per year. Open year-round, weather permitting.

Directions: From Redding, drive west on Highway 299 for 10 miles to the visitor center. Turn left at the visitor center (Kennedy Memorial Drive) and drive six miles to the campground on the right side of the road.

Contact: Whiskeytown National Recreation Area, 530/242-3400, ext. 221, fax 530/246-5154.

144 BRANDY CREEK

Rating: 7

On Whiskeytown Lake.
Map 2.4, page 111

For campers with boats, this is the best place to stay at Whiskeytown Lake, with a boat ramp less than a quarter mile away. Whiskeytown is popular for sailing and windsurfing, as it gets a lot more wind than other lakes in the region. Fishing for kokanee salmon is good in the early morning before the wind comes up.

Campsites, facilities: There are 37 sites for self-contained RVs and trailers up to 35 feet long. Drinking water and a RV dump station are available. Leashed pets are permitted.

Reservations, fees: Reservations are not accepted. The fee is $14 per night during the summer, $7 per night during off-season, plus a park use permit of $5 per day, $10 per week, or $20 per year. Senior discount available. Open year-round.

Directions: From Redding, drive west on Highway 299 for eight miles to the park entrance center. Turn left at the visitor center (Kennedy Memorial Drive) and drive five miles to the campground entrance road on the right. Turn right and drive a short distance to the camp.

Contact: Whiskeytown National Recreation Area, 530/242-3400, fax 530/246-5154.

145 PREMIERE RV RESORT

Rating: 2

In Redding.
Map 2.4, page 111

If you're stuck with no place to go, this large park could be your savior, but expect very hot weather in the summer. Nearby recreation options include a waterslide park and the Turtle Bay Museum and Exploration Park on the Sacramento River. In addition, Whiskeytown Lake is nearby to the west and Shasta Lake to the north. Some campers may remember this park as KOA of Redding; they are no longer associated. The park was renovated in 2002.

Campsites, facilities: There are 111 sites for RVs, most with full hookups and some with partial hookups, a small area for tents, and two yurts. Picnic tables and fire grills are provided. Drinking water, flush toilets, showers, playground, seasonal swimming pool, coin laundry, RV dump station, satellite TV hookups, a convenience store, propane gas, and recreation room are available. Leashed pets are permitted.

Reservations, fees: Reservations are accepted. The fee is $22–30.80 per night, $3 per person per night for more than two people. Major credit cards accepted. Senior discount available. Open year-round.

Directions: In Redding, drive north on I-5 to the Lake Boulevard/Burney-Alturas exit. Turn west (left) on Lake Boulevard and drive a quarter mile to North Boulder Drive. Turn right (north) on North Boulder Drive and drive one block to the campground on the right.

Contact: Premiere RV Resort, 888/710-8450 or 530/246-0101, fax 530/246-0123, website: www.premiererresort.com.

146 MARINA RV PARK

Rating: 6

On the Sacramento River.
Map 2.4, page 111

The riverside setting is a highlight here, with the Sacramento River providing relief from the dog days of summer. An easy, paved walking and bike trail is available nearby at the Sacramento River Parkway, providing river views and sometimes a needed breeze on hot summer evenings. A miniature golf course is nearby. It is also two miles away from the Turtle Bay Museum, and close to a movie theater.

Campsites, facilities: There are 42 sites, most with full hookups, for RVs. Picnic tables, restrooms, hot showers, a coin laundry, small store, seasonal swimming pool, spa, boat ramp, and RV dump station are on park grounds. Leashed pets are permitted.

Reservations, fees: Reservations are accepted. The fee is $22 per night, $2 per person for more than two people. Monthly rates available. Senior discount available. Open year-round.

Directions: In Redding, turn west on Highway 299 and drive 1.5 miles to Park Marina Drive. At Park Marina Drive turn left (south) and drive one mile to the park.

Contact: Marina RV Park, 530/241-4396.

147 SACRAMENTO RIVER RV PARK

Rating: 7

South of Redding.
Map 2.4, page 111

This makes a good headquarters for a fall fishing trip on the Sacramento River, where the salmon come big from August through October. In the summer trout fishing is very good from this area as well, but a boat is a must. No problem; there's a boat ramp at the park. In addition, you can hire fishing guides who launch from here daily. The park is open year-round, and if you want to stay close to home, a three-acre pond with bass, bluegill, and perch is also available at the park. You also get great long-distance views of Mt. Shasta and Mt. Lassen.

Campsites, facilities: There are 140 sites, including some drive-through sites, with full hookups for RVs and 20 sites for tents in a shaded grassy area. Picnic tables, restrooms, hot showers, grocery store, coin laundry, RV dump station, cable TV, bait, propane gas, boat launch, two tennis courts, and a large seasonal swimming pool are available. A clubhouse is available by reservation. Some facilities are wheelchair-accessible. Leashed pets are permitted.

Reservations, fees: Reservations are accepted. The fee is $11–21 per night. Major credit cards accepted. Open year-round.

Directions: From Redding, drive south on I-5 for five miles to the Knighton Road exit. Turn west (right) and drive a short distance to Riverland Drive. Turn left on Riverland Drive and drive two miles to the park at the end of the road.

Contact: Sacramento River RV Park, 530/365-6402, fax 530/365-2601.

148 DEERLICK SPRINGS

Rating: 8

On Browns Creek in Shasta-Trinity National Forest.
Map 2.4, page 111

It's a long, twisty drive to this remote and primitive camp set on the edge of the Chanchelulla Wilderness in the transition zone where the valley's oak grasslands give way to conifers. This quiet little spot is set along Browns Creek. A trailhead just north of camp provides a streamside walk. The elevation is 3,100 feet.

Campsites, facilities: There are 13 sites for tents or RVs up to 20 feet long. Picnic tables and fire grills are provided. Vault toilets are available. No drinking water is available. Leashed pets are permitted.

Reservations, fees: Reservations are not accepted. There is no fee for camping. Open May through October.

Directions: From Red Bluff, turn west on Highway 36 (very twisty) and drive to the Forest Service ranger station in Platina. In Platina, turn north on Harrison Gulch Road and drive 10 miles to the campground on the left.

Contact: Shasta-Trinity National Forest, Yolla Bolly Ranger Station, 530/352-4211, fax 530/352-4312.

149 BEEGUM GORGE

Rating: 8

In Shasta-Trinity National Forest.
Map 2.4, page 111

If you want to get the heck away from anything and everything, this spot should be your calling. The camp is set along little Beegum Creek. The road to this camp dead-ends another mile down the road (west) at a trailhead for a hike that is routed along the creek for nearly five miles to North Fork Beegum campground. Another route heads up nearby Little Red Mountain, but it involves a 2,000-foot climb, often across dry, hot terrain. The payoffs include incredible views of the Yolla Bolly-Middle Eel Wilderness and spectacular wildflower displays in the spring. The elevation at the camp is 2,200 feet.

Campsites, facilities: There are two sites for tents only. Picnic tables and fire grills are provided. Vault toilets are available. No drinking water is available. Garbage must be packed out. Leashed pets are permitted.

Reservations, fees: Reservations are not accepted. There is no fee for camping. Open May through October.

Directions: From Red Bluff, turn west on Highway 36 and drive to Platina. In Platina, turn south on Forest Road 29N06 and drive 6.5 miles to the campground.

Contact: Shasta-Trinity National Forest, Yolla

Bolly Ranger Station, 530/352-4211, fax 530/352-4312.

150 BASIN GULCH

Rating: 5

In Shasta-Trinity National Forest.
Map 2.4, page 111

This is one of three little-known campgrounds in the vicinity that rarely gets much use. A trail out of this camp climbs Noble Ridge, eventually rising to a good lookout at 3,933 feet, providing sweeping views of the north valley. Of course, you could also just drive there, taking a dirt road out of Platina. There are many backcountry Forest Service roads in the area so your best bet is to get a Shasta-Trinity National Forest map, which details the roads. The elevation is 2,600 feet. There is evidence in the area of a wildfire that occurred in 2001.

Campsites, facilities: There are 13 sites for tents or RVs up to 20 feet long. Picnic tables and fire grills are provided. Vault toilets are available. No drinking water is available. Leashed pets are permitted.

Reservations, fees: Reservations are not accepted. The fee is $6 per night. Senior discount available. Open May through October.

Directions: From Red Bluff, drive about 45 miles west on Highway 36 to the Yolla Bolly District Ranger Station. From the ranger station, turn south on Stuart Gap Road and drive two miles to the campground on the left.

Contact: Shasta-Trinity National Forest, Yolla Bolly Ranger Station, 530/352-4211, fax 530/352-4312.

151 BEND RV PARK AND FISHING RESORT

Rating: 7

On the Sacramento River.
Map 2.4, page 111

Here's a spot for RV cruisers to rest their rigs

for a while. Big Bend RV Park and Fishing Resort is open year-round and is set beside the Sacramento River. The salmon average 15–25 pounds in this area, and anglers typically have the best results from mid-August through October. In recent years, the Bureau of Reclamation has been raising the gates of the Red Bluff Diversion Dam in early September. When that occurs, huge numbers of salmon charge upstream from Red Bluff to Anderson, holding in each deep river hole. Expect very hot weather in July and August.

Campsites, facilities: There are 18 sites with full or partial hookups for RVs up to 40 feet long. In addition, there is a separate area for tents only. Picnic tables are provided. Drinking water, showers, flush toilets, grocery store, bait and tackle shop, boat ramp, boat dock, coin laundry, and RV dump station are available. Some facilities are wheelchair-accessible. Leashed pets are permitted.

Reservations, fees: Reservations are accepted. The fee is $14–20 per night. Open year-round.

Directions: From I-5 in Red Bluff, drive four miles north on I-5 to the Jelly's Ferry Road exit. Take that exit and turn northeast on Jelly's Ferry Road and drive 2.5 miles to the resort at 21795 Bend Ferry Road.

Contact: Bend RV Park and Fishing Resort, 530/527-6289.

152 O'NITE PARK

Rating: 4

Near the Sacramento River.

Map 2.4, page 111

O'Nite Park is set within a mobile home park with many full-time tenants. Pluses are easy access from the highway, nearby supermarkets and restaurants, and many side trips. The park is only one block from the Sacramento River, which gets a big salmon run from mid-August through October. It's about a 45-minute drive east to Lassen Park. The elevation is approximately 300 feet and temperatures are typically in the 100s from mid-June through August.

Campsites, facilities: There are 74 sites, including some drive-through sites, with full hookups for RVs, and a separate area for tents. Picnic tables are provided. Restrooms, coin showers, seasonal swimming pool, modem access, a coin laundry, propane gas, and ice are available. Some facilities are wheelchair-accessible. Leashed pets are permitted.

Reservations, fees: Reservations are accepted. The fee is $11–19 per night. Open year-round.

Directions: From I-5 and the junction of Highways 99 and 36 (in Red Bluff), drive west on Highway 36/Antelope Boulevard for one block to Gilmore Road. Turn south on Gilmore Road and drive one block to the camp.

Contact: O'Nite Park, 530/527-5868.

153 LAKE RED BLUFF

Rating: 6

On the Sacramento River near Red Bluff.

Map 2.4, page 111

Lake Red Bluff is created by the Red Bluff Diversion Dam on the Sacramento River, and water-skiing, bird-watching, hiking, and fishing are the most popular activities. It has become a backyard swimming hole for local residents in the summer when the temperatures reach the high 90s and low 100s almost every day. In early September, the Bureau of Reclamation raises the gates at the diversion dam to allow migrating salmon an easier course on the upstream journey, and in the process, Lake Red Bluff reverts to its former self as the Sacramento River.

Campsites, facilities: There are 30 sites with no hookups for tents or RVs (Sycamore Camp), a group camp (Camp Discovery) with six screened cabins that can accommodate a maximum of 48 campers, and 30 picnic shelters. Drinking water, showers, vault and flush toilets, picnic areas, two boat ramps, and a fish-viewing plaza are available. There are two large barbecues, electrical outlets, lockable storage, five large picnic tables, comfort station with showers and sinks, and an amphitheater in the group camp area. Some facilities are wheelchair-accessible. Leashed pets are permitted.

Reservations, fees: Reservations are required only for the group camp. The fee is $10 per night for individual sites and the group camp per night is $100 for up to 50 people, $150 for 51–75 people, and $200 for 76–100 people. Senior discount available. Open April through October.

Directions: From I-5 at Red Bluff, turn east on Highway 36 and drive 100 yards to the first turnoff at Sale Lane. Turn right (south) on Sale Lane. Turn right and drive 1.5 miles to the campground at the end of the road.

Contact: Mendocino National Forest, Corning Work Station, 530/824-5196, fax 530/824-6034.

154 WHITE ROCK

Rating: 4

In Shasta-Trinity National Forest.
Map 2.4, page 111

There's a reason why there's no charge to camp here: usually nobody's around. It's primitive, little known, and likely to be empty. If you don't want to see anybody, you've found the right place. The big attraction here is watching the turtles swim at nearby White Rock Pond. A trailhead is available nearby out of Stuart Gap, which provides access to the North Yolla Bolly Mountains.

Campsites, facilities: There are three tent sites. Picnic tables and fire grills are provided. Vault toilets are available. No drinking water is available. Garbage must be packed out. Leashed pets are permitted.

Reservations, fees: Reservations are not accepted. There is no fee for camping. Open late June through mid-September, weather permitting.

Directions: From Red Bluff, drive about 45 miles west on Highway 36 to the Yolla Bolly

ranger office. Continue west for about eight miles to Wild Mad River Road/Forest Road 30. Turn left on Forest Road 30 and drive nine miles to Pine Ridge Saddle Road/Forest Road 35. Turn left and drive nine miles (on a gravel road, very twisty) to the campground.

Contact: Shasta-Trinity National Forest, Yolla Bolly Ranger Station, 530/352-4211, fax 530/352-4312.

155 TOMHEAD SADDLE

Rating: 4

In Shasta-Trinity National Forest.
Map 2.4, page 111

This one is way out there in remote wildlands. Little known and rarely visited, it's primarily a jump-off point for ambitious backpackers. The camp is on the edge of the Yolla Bolly-Middle Eel Wilderness. A trailhead here is routed to the South Fork of Cottonwood Creek, a trek that entails hiking eight miles in dry, hot terrain. The elevation is 5,700 feet.

Campsites, facilities: There are five sites for tents or RVs. Picnic tables and fire grills are provided. Vault toilets are available. No drinking water is available. Garbage must be packed out. A horse corral is also available. Leashed pets are permitted.

Reservations, fees: Reservations are not accepted. There is no fee for camping. Open late June to mid-September, weather permitting.

Directions: From I-5 in Red Bluff, turn west on Highway 36 and drive about 13 miles to Cannon Road. Turn left on Cannon Road and drive about five miles to Pettyjohn Road. Turn west on Pettyjohn Road, drive to Saddle Camp and Forest Road 27N06. Turn south on Forest Road 27N06 and drive three miles to the campground on the left. It is advisable to obtain a map of Shasta-Trinity National Forest.

Contact: Shasta-Trinity National Forest, Yolla Bolly Ranger Station, 530/352-4211, fax 530/352-4312.

© JEFFREY PATTY

Chapter 3
Lassen and Modoc

Chapter 3—Lassen and Modoc

Mount Lassen and its awesome volcanic past seem to cast a shadow everywhere you go in this region. At 10,457 feet, the mountain's domed summit is visible for more than 100 miles in all directions. It blew its top in 1914, with continuing eruptions through 1918. Although now dormant, the volcanic-based geology dominates the landscape everywhere you look.

Of all the areas covered in this book, this region has the least number of romantic getaway spots. It caters instead primarily to outdoors enthusiasts. And Lassen Volcanic National Park is one of the best places to lace up the hiking boots or spool new line on a reel. It's often off the radar scope of vacationers, making it one of the few national parks where you can enjoy the wilderness in relative solitude.

The national park is easily explored along the main route, the Lassen Park Highway. Along the way, you can pick a few trails for adventure. The best hikes are the Summit Climb (moderate to challenging), best done first thing in the morning, and Bumpass Hell (easy and great for kids) to see the sulfur vents and boiling mud pots. Another favorite for classic alpine beauty is the Shadow Lake Trail.

Unique features of the region include its pumice boulders, volcanic rock, and spring-fed streams from the underground lava tubes. The highlights include the best still-water canoeing and fly fishing at Fall River, Big Lake, and Ahjumawi State Park. Access at Ahjumawi is by canoe or powerboat only, a great boat-in campground with access to a matrix of clear, cold waters with giant trout.

Nearby is Burney Falls State Park, along with the Pit River and Lake Britton, which together make up one of Northern California's best recreation destinations for families. This is also one of the best areas for fly-fishing, especially at Hat Creek, Pit River, Burney Creek, and Manzanita Lake. For more beautiful settings, you can visit Lake Almanor and Eagle Lake, both of which provide lakeside campgrounds and excellent fishing and boating recreation.

And there's more. In remote Modoc County, you'll find Lava Beds National Monument and the South Warner Wilderness. Lava Beds is a stark, pretty, and often lonely place. It's sprinkled with small lakes full of trout, is home to large-antlered deer that migrate in after the first snow (and after the hunting season has closed), and features a unique volcanic habitat with huge flows of obsidian (dark, smooth, natural glass formed by the cooling of molten lava) and dacite (gray, craggy volcanic flow). Lava Beds National Monument boasts 445 caves and lava tubes, including the 6,000-foot Catacomb tunnel. Nearby is pretty Medicine Lake, formed in a caldera, which provides good trout fishing, hiking, and exploring.

It seems no matter where you go, there are so many campgrounds that you can always find a match for what you desire.

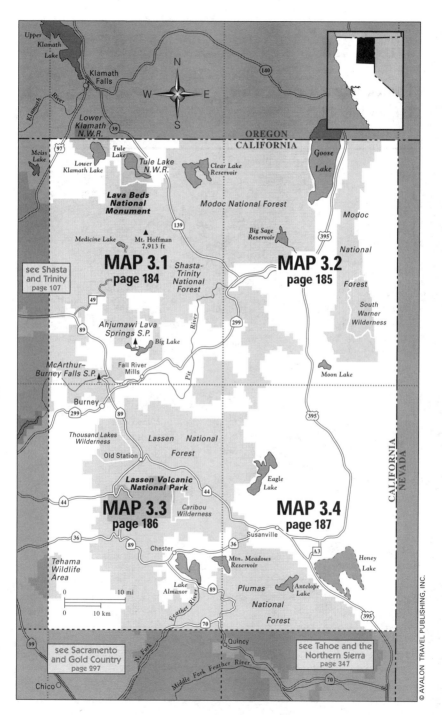

Map 3.1

Campgrounds 1–18
Pages 188–195

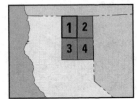

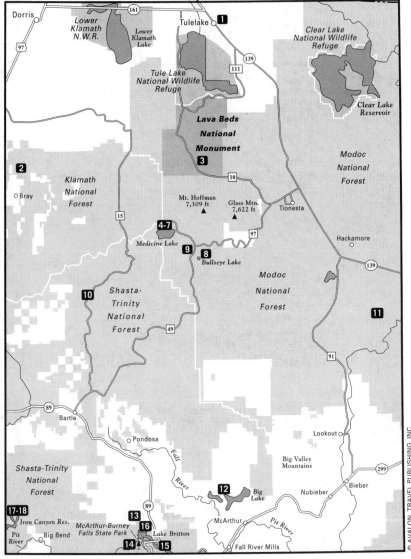

Map 3.2

Campgrounds 19–37
Pages 196–203

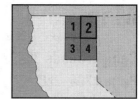

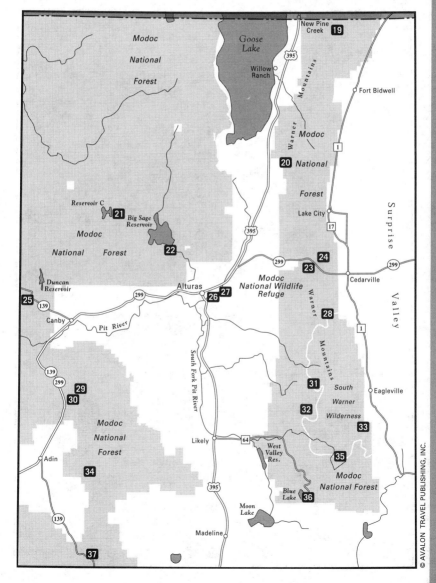

Map 3.3

Campgrounds 38–97
Pages 204–228

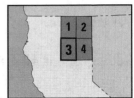

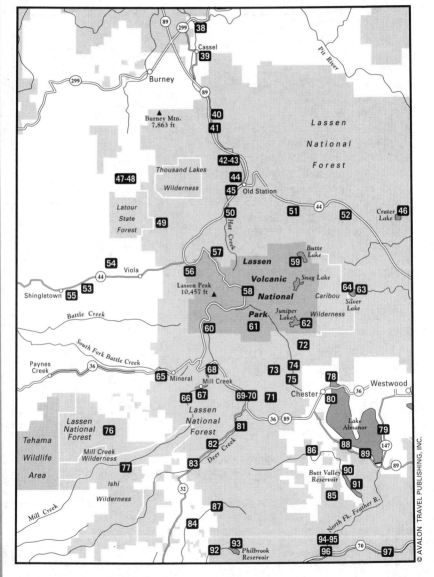

Map 3.4

Campgrounds 98–114
Pages 229–236

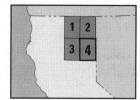

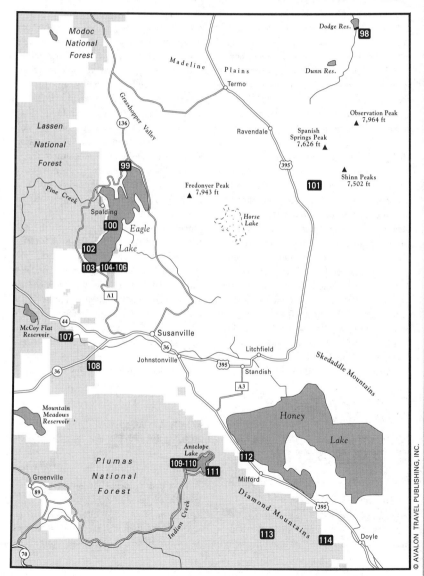

© AVALON TRAVEL PUBLISHING, INC.

1 SHADY LANE TRAILER PARK
🐕 🚐

Rating: 3

In Tulelake.

Map 3.1, page 184

There isn't much shade in some parts of Modoc County, but this private park manages to provide some. Good side trips include the Tule Lake Wildlife Refuge, one of the best places in America (during the winter) to see bald eagles and a good bet year-round for bird-watching. Nearby is Lava Beds National Monument, whose northern edge is an excellent place to see deer in late fall and early winter. There is also a network of lava tubes and ice caves, making for a great getaway adventure. The Tulelake unit of the Klamath National Wildlife Refuge is only four miles away, and the Lower Klamath Lake unit is eight miles away; both provide excellent waterfowl hunting in early fall.

Campsites, facilities: There are 60 RV sites with full hookups, some with long-term renters. Restrooms, showers, patios, and a coin laundry are available. Leashed pets are permitted.

Reservations, fees: Reservations are accepted. The fee is $15 per night. Open year-round.

Directions: From Redding, turn east on Highway 299 and drive to Canby and the junction with Highway 139. Turn left at Highway 139 (north) and drive 52 miles to Tulelake and the south exit of East West Road. Take that exit and drive 1.5 miles to Modoc Avenue. Turn left, and drive a short distance to the trailer park (795 Modoc Avenue).

Contact: Shady Lane Trailer Park, 795 Modoc Ave., Tulelake, CA 96134, 530/667-2617.

2 SHAFTER
🥾 🏊 🎣 🐕 5% 🚐 🏕

Rating: 4

In Klamath National Forest.

Map 3.1, page 184

This is a little-used camp with trout fishing at nearby Butte Creek for small rainbows, pri-

marily six- to eight-inchers. Little Orr Lake, about a 10-minute drive away on the southwest flank of Orr Mountain, provides fishing for bass and larger rainbow trout, 10- to 12-inchers, as well as a sprinkling of smaller brook trout. A boat ramp and restroom with vault toilets were opened in 2000. This camp is primitive and not well known, set in a juniper- and sage-filled landscape. A great side trip is to the nearby Orr Mountain Lookout, where there are spectacular views of Mt. Shasta. A Forest Service touch that is like gold in the summer is that the road adjacent to the campground is paved, which keeps the dust down.

Campsites, facilities: There are 14 sites for tents or small RVs. Picnic tables and fire grills are provided. Drinking water, a restroom, vault toilets, and boat ramp are available. Pack out all garbage. Leashed pets are permitted.

Reservations, fees: Reservations are not accepted. The fee is $6 per night. Senior discount available. Open year-round. Services available in summer only.

Directions: From Redding, drive north on I-5 to Weed and the exit for Highway 97. Take that exit, turn right at the stop sign, drive through Weed and bear right (north) on Highway 97 and drive 40 miles to Ball Mountain Road. Turn right at Ball Mountain Road and drive 2.5 miles to a T with Old State Highway 97. Turn right and drive 4.25 miles (crossing railroad tracks) to the campground on the right side of the road.

Contact: Klamath National Forest, Goosenest Ranger District, 530/398-4391, fax 530/398-5749.

3 INDIAN WELL
🥾 🐕 ♿ 🚐 🏕

Rating: 9

In Lava Beds National Monument.

Map 3.1, page 184

Lava Beds National Monument is a one-in-a-million spot with more than 400 lava tube caves, Schonchin Butte (a cinder cone with a hiking trail), Mammoth Crater, Native American pictographs, battlefields and campsites from the Modoc War, and wildlife overlooks of Tule Lake. After winter's first snow, this is one of the best places in the West to photograph deer. Nearby is Klamath National Wildlife Refuge, the largest bald eagle wintering area in the lower 48. If you are new to the outdoors, an interpretive center is available to explain it all to you.

Campsites, facilities: There are 42 sites for tents or RVs up to 30 feet long. Picnic tables, fire rings, and cooking grills are provided. From Memorial Day to Labor Day, water and flush toilets are available. Drinking water and flush toilets are always available in the B Loop and at the visitor center. Note that during the off-season in the A Loop, only pit toilets are available. Some facilities are wheelchair-accessible. The town of Tulelake (30 miles north) is the nearest supply station. Leashed pets are permitted in the campground and roads only.

Reservations, fees: Reservations are not accepted. The fee is $10 per night plus $5 per vehicle park entrance fee. Senior discount available. Open year-round.

Directions: From Redding, drive north on I-5 past Dunsmuir to Highway 89. Bear right (east) on Highway 89 and drive 28 miles. Turn left on Forest Road 15/Harris Springs Road (just past Bertel). Drive five miles to a fork with Forest Road 49 Medicine Lake Road. Bear right at the fork and drive 26 miles to the lake acccess road on the left. From Bartel, the route is signed.

Contact: Lava Beds National Monument, 530/667-2282, fax 530/667-2737.

4 MEDICINE

Rating: 7

On Medicine Lake in Modoc National Forest.

Map 3.1, page 184

Lakeside campsites tucked away in conifers make this camp a winner. Medicine Lake was

formed in the crater of an old volcano and is surrounded by lodgepole pine and fir trees. The lake is stocked with rainbow and brook trout in the summer, gets quite cold in the fall, and freezes over in winter. Many side trips are possible, including nearby Blanche Lake and Ice Caves (both signed and off the access road) and Lava Beds National Monument just 15 miles north. At 6,700 feet, temperatures can turn cold in summer and the season is short.

Campsites, facilities: There are 22 sites for tents or RVs up to 22 feet long. Picnic tables and fire grills are provided. Drinking water and vault toilets are available. A boat ramp is available nearby. A small restaurant for breakfast and lunch and with a bar is available in Bartle; otherwise, no supplies are available within an hour's drive. Leashed pets are permitted.

Reservations, fees: Reservations are not accepted. The fee is $7 per vehicle per night. Senior discount available. Open late May through early October, weather permitting.

Directions: From Redding, drive north on I-5 past Dunsmuir to Highway 89. Bear right (east) on Highway 89 and drive 28 miles. Turn left on Forest Road 15/Harris Springs Road (just past Bertel). Drive five miles to a fork with Forest Road 49 Medicine Lake Road. Bear right at the fork and drive 26 miles to the lake acccess road on the left. From Bartel, the route is signed.

Contact: Modoc National Forest, Doublehead Ranger District, 530/667-2246, fax 530/667-8609.

5 A. H. HOGUE

Rating: 7

On Medicine Lake in Modoc National Forest.

Map 3.1, page 184

This camp was created in 1990 when the original Medicine Lake Campground was divided in half. (For more information, see the entry for Medicine.)

Campsites, facilities: There are 24 sites for tents or RVs up to 22 feet long. Picnic tables and fire grills are provided. Drinking water and vault toilets are available. A boat ramp is available nearby. Leashed pets are permitted. A small restaurant for breakfast and lunch and with a bar is available in Bartle; otherwise, no supplies are available within an hour's drive.

Reservations, fees: Reservations are not accepted. The fee is $7 per vehicle per night. Senior discount available. Open late May through early October, weather permitting.

Directions: From Redding, drive north on I-5 past Dunsmuir to Highway 89. Bear right (east) on Highway 89 and drive 28 miles. Turn left on Forest Road 15/Harris Springs Road (just past Bertel). Drive five miles to a fork with Forest Road 49 Medicine Lake Road. Bear right at the fork and drive 26 miles to the lake access road on the left. From Bartel, the route is signed.

Contact: Modoc National Forest, Doublehead Ranger District, 530/667-2246, fax 530/667-8609.

⑥ HEMLOCK

Rating: 7

On Medicine Lake in Modoc National Forest.

Map 3.1, page 184

This is one in a series of campgrounds on Medicine Lake operated by the Forest Service. A special attraction at Hemlock is the natural sand beach. (For more information, see the entry for Medicine.)

Campsites, facilities: There are 19 sites for tents or RVs up to 22 feet long. Picnic tables and fire grills are provided. Drinking water and vault toilets are available. A boat ramp is available nearby. A small restaurant for breakfast and lunch and with a bar is available in Bartle; otherwise, no supplies are available within an hour's drive.

Reservations, fees: Reservations are not accepted. The fee is $7 per vehicle per night. Senior discount available. Open late May through early October, weather permitting.

Directions: From Redding, drive north on I-5 past Dunsmuir to Highway 89. Bear right (east) on Highway 89 and drive 28 miles. Turn left on Forest Road 15/Harris Springs Road (just past Bertel). Drive five miles to a fork with Forest Road 49 Medicine Lake Road. Bear right at the fork and drive 26 miles to the lake access road on the left. From Bartel, the route is signed.

Contact: Modoc National Forest, Doublehead Ranger District, 530/667-2246, fax 530/667-8609.

⑦ HEADQUARTERS

Rating: 7

On Medicine Lake in Modoc National Forest.

Map 3.1, page 184

This is one of four campgrounds set beside Medicine Lake. (For more information, see the entry for Medicine.)

Campsites, facilities: There are nine sites for tents and RVs up to 18 feet long. Picnic tables and fire grills are provided. Drinking water and vault toilets are available. A boat ramp is available nearby. A small restaurant for breakfast and lunch and with a bar is available in Bartle; otherwise, no supplies are available within an hour's drive.

Reservations, fees: Reservations are not accepted. The fee is $7 per vehicle per night. Senior discount available. Open late May through early October, weather permitting.

Directions: From Redding, drive north on I-5 past Dunsmuir to Highway 89. Bear right (east) on Highway 89 and drive 28 miles. Turn left on Forest Road 15/Harris Springs Road (just past Bertel). Drive five miles to a fork with Forest Road 49/ Medicine Lake Road. Bear right at the fork and drive 26 miles to the lake access road on the left. From Bartel, the route is signed.

Contact: Modoc National Forest, Doublehead Ranger District, 530/667-2246, fax 530/667-8609.

⑧ BULLSEYE LAKE

Rating: 7

Near Medicine Lake in Modoc National Forest.

Map 3.1, page 184

This tiny lake gets overlooked every year, mainly because of its proximity to nearby Medicine Lake. Bullseye Lake is shallow, but because snow keeps it locked up until late May or early June, the water stays plenty cold for small trout through July. It is stocked with just 750 six- to eight-inch rainbow trout, not much to crow about—or to catch, for that matter. Nearby are some ice caves, created by ancient volcanic action. The place is small, quiet, and pretty, but most of all, small. This camp is set at an elevation of 6,500 feet.

Campsites, facilities: There are a few primitive campsites. A vault toilet is available. No drinking water or other facilities are available. Garbage must be packed out. Supplies are available in McCloud. A small restaurant for breakfast and lunch and with a bar is available in Bartle; otherwise, no supplies are available within an hour's drive. Leashed pets are permitted.

Reservations, fees: Reservations are not accepted. There is no fee for camping. Open late May through early October, weather permitting.

Directions: From Redding, drive north on I-5 past Dunsmuir to Highway 89. Turn east on Highway 89 and drive 28 miles to Forest Road 49 (just past Bartle). Turn left on Forest Road 49 and drive 30 miles (if you reach Medicine Lake, you have gone about two miles too far) to the Bullseye Lake access road. Turn right at the Bullseye Lake access road and drive a short distance to the lake.

Contact: Modoc National Forest, Doublehead Ranger District, 530/667-2246, fax 530/667-8609.

⑨ PAYNE SPRINGS

Rating: 8

Near Medicine Lake in Modoc National Forest.

Map 3.1, page 184

This camp is set by a small spring in a very pretty riparian area. It's small, but it is special.

Campsites, facilities: There are six dispersed and primitive campsites for tents or RVs up to 20 feet long. A vault toilet is available. No drinking water is available. A small restaurant for breakfast and lunch and with a bar is available in Bartle; otherwise, no supplies are available within an hour's drive. Supplies are available in McCloud. Leashed pets are permitted.

Reservations, fees: Reservations are not accepted. There is no fee for camping. Open late May through early October, weather permitting.

Directions: From Redding, on I-5 drive past Dunsmuir to Highway 89. Turn east on Highway 89 and drive 28 miles to Forest Road 49 (just past Bartle). Turn left on Forest Road 49 and drive (it becomes Medicine Lake Road) 30 miles (.2 mile past the Bullseye Lake access road) to Payne Springs access road (if you reach Medicine Lake, you have gone too far). Turn left onto the Payne Springs access road and drive a short distance to the campground.

Contact: Modoc National Forest, Doublehead Ranger District, 530/667-2246, fax 530/667-8609.

⑩ HARRIS SPRINGS

Rating: 3

In Shasta-Trinity National Forest.

Map 3.1, page 184

This camp is a hidden spot in remote Shasta-Trinity National Forest, nestled in the long, mountainous ridge that runs east from Mt. Shasta to the Lava Beds National Monument. The camp is set at 4,800 feet, with a part-time fire station within a quarter mile on the opposite side of the access road. The area is best explored by four-wheel drive, venturing to a series of small buttes, mountaintops, and lookouts in the immediate area. A map of Shasta-Trinity National Forest is a must.

Campsites, facilities: There are 15 sites for tents or RVs up to 32 feet long. Picnic tables and fire grills are provided. Drinking water (spring water, not piped) and vault toilets are available. Garbage must be packed out. Leashed pets are permitted.

Reservations, fees: Reservations are not accepted. There is no fee for camping. Open late May to October, weather permitting.

Directions: From Redding, drive north on I-5 past Dunsmuir to the junction with Highway 89. Turn east on Highway 89 and drive 28 miles to Forest Road 49 (just past Bartle). Turn left on Forest Road 49 and drive five miles to the Y intersection with Harris Springs Road. Turn left at the Y on Harris Springs Road/Forest Road 15 and drive 12 miles to a junction with a forest road signed for the Harris Springs Ranger Station. Turn right and drive a short distance, and look for the campground entrance on the right side of the road.

Contact: Shasta-Trinity National Forest, McCloud Ranger District, 530/964-2184, fax 530/964-2938.

11 COTTONWOOD FLAT

Rating: 6

In Modoc National Forest.

Map 3.1, page 184

The camp is wooded and shady, set at 4,700 feet in elevation in the rugged and remote Devil's Garden area of Modoc National Forest. The region is known for large mule deer, and Cottonwood Flat is well situated as a base camp for a hunting trip in the fall. Temperatures can get extremely cold early and late in the season.

Campsites, facilities: There are 10 sites for tents or RVs up to 16 feet long. Picnic tables and

fire grills are provided. Drinking water (spring water) and vault toilets are available. Garbage must be packed out. Supplies are available within five miles in Canby. Leashed pets are permitted.

Reservations, fees: Reservations are not accepted. There is no fee for camping. Open June through September.

Directions: From Redding, drive east on Highway 299 for about 100 miles to Adin. Continue on Highway 299 for about 20 miles to the Canby Bridge at the Pit River and the junction with Forest Road 84. Turn left on Forest Road 84 and drive about eight miles to Forest Road 42N95. Turn right and drive a half mile to the campground entrance on the left side of the road. Note: the access road is not recommended for RVs longer than 14 to 16 feet.

Contact: Modoc National Forest, Devil's Garden Ranger District, 530/233-5811, fax 530/233-8709.

12 AHJUMAWI LAVA SPRINGS BOAT-IN

Rating: 9

At Big Lake.

Map 3.1, page 184

This is a one-of-a-kind boat-in camp set on Big Lake and connecting Horr Pond in the Fall River matrix of streams. Ahjumawi means "where the waters come together," named by the Pit River Native Americans who inhabit the area near the confluence of Big Lake, Tule River, Ja She Creek, Lava Creek, and Fall River. Together the waters form one of the largest freshwater springs in the world. Springs flowing from the lava are prominent along the shoreline. This is a place of exceptional and primeval beauty. Much of the land is covered by lava flows, including vast areas of jagged black basalt, along with lava tubes and spattercone and conic depressions. There are brilliant aqua bays, and for campers, peace and quiet. However, you may be joined on land by armies of mosquitoes in the spring; they're not so bad while on the water. Access is by boat only, ideal for canoes, and in addition, the lake is not well known outside of the region. Expert fly fishers try for giant but elusive rainbow trout, best in the early morning at the springs. Because of high water clarity, long leaders and perfect casts are essential. There are also nesting areas around the lake for bald eagles, ospreys, and blue herons and this park is considered a stellar habitat for bird-watching. A series of connecting trails are accessible from camp. The park is a wilderness area, covering 6,000 acres, and most of it is extremely rugged lava rock. There are many signs of this area's ancient past, with bedrock mortars, ceremonial sites, and prehistoric fish traps. There are also great herds of mule deer that forage through much of the park. Finally, there are magnificent views of Mt. Shasta, Mt. Lassen, and other peaks.

Campsites, facilities: There are nine boat-in sites. No motors are permitted on boats. Picnic tables and fire pits are provided. Vault toilets are available. No drinking water is available. Leashed pets are permitted.

Reservations, fees: Reservations are not accepted. The fee is $7 per night. Senior discount available. Open year-round, weather permitting.

Directions: From Redding, drive east on Highway 299 for 73 miles to McArthur. Turn left on Main Street and drive 3.5 miles (becomes a dirt road) to the Rat Farm boat launch at Big Lake. Launch boat and proceed by boat one to three miles to one of the nine boat-in campsites.

Contact: McArthur-Burney Falls Memorial State Park, 530/335-2777.

13 BURNEY FALLS TRAILER RESORT

🚶 ⛱ 🎣 🍴 🐕 🚐 ⛺

Rating: 5

Near Lake Britton.

Map 3.1, page 184

This is a year-round RV park near Lake Brit-

ton, Burney Creek, and the Pit River. McArthur-Burney Falls Memorial State Park, with its spectacular waterfall, is within a five-minute drive. The region is loaded with adventure, with Lassen Volcanic National Park, Hat Creek, and Fall River all within a 30-minute drive.

Campsites, facilities: There are 28 sites with full hookups for RVs or tents, 10 of which are long-term rentals. Picnic tables, restrooms, hot showers, a coin laundry, horseshoes, modem hookups, and a swimming pool (summer only) are available. Leashed pets are permitted.

Reservations, fees: Reservations are accepted. The fee is $18 per night, $1 per person per night for more than two people. Senior discount available. Monthly rates available. Open year-round.

Directions: From Redding, drive east on Highway 299 to Burney and continue for five miles to the junction with Highway 89. At Highway 89, turn left (north) and drive four miles to Clark Creek Road. Turn left on Clark Creek Road and drive a short distance to the campground entrance on the left.

Contact: Burney Falls Trailer Resort, 530/335-2781.

14 MCARTHUR-BURNEY FALLS MEMORIAL STATE PARK

🚶 ⛱ 🎣 🍴 🐕 ♿ 🚐 ⛺

Rating: 9

In McArthur-Burney Falls Memorial State Park.

Map 3.1, page 184

Burney Falls is a 129-foot waterfall, a beautiful cascade split at the top by a little grove of trees, with small trickles oozing and falling out of the adjacent moss-lined wall. Since it is fed primarily by a spring, it runs strong and glorious most of the year, producing 100 million gallons of water every day. The Headwaters Trail provides an outstanding hike, both to see the waterfall and Burney Creek, as well as for an easy adventure and fishing access to the stream. An excellent fly-fishing section of the Pit River is available below the dam. There are other stellar recreation options at this state park. At the end of the campground access road is a boat ramp for Lake Britton, with rentals available for canoes and paddleboats. This is a beautiful lake, with pretty canyon walls on its upper end, and good smallmouth bass (at rock piles) and crappie fishing (near the train trestle). There is also a good swimming beach. The Pacific Crest Trail is routed right through the park and provides an additional opportunity for a day hike, best explored downstream from the dam. Reservations for sites are essential during the summer. This park features 910 acres of forest and five miles of stream and lake shore. The park's landscape was created by volcanic activity, as well as erosion from weather and stream action.

Campsites, facilities: There are 128 sites for tents or RVs up to 35 feet long. Picnic tables and fire grills are provided. Drinking water, flush toilets, hot showers, and a RV dump station are available. Some facilities are wheelchair-accessible. A grocery/gift store and boat rentals are available in the summer. Leashed pets are permitted, except on the trails and the beach.

Reservations, fees: Reservations are accepted with a $7.50 reservation fee at 800/444-PARK (800/444-7275) and website www.Reserve America.com. The fee is $12 per night. Senior discount available. Open year-round.

Directions: From Redding, drive east on Highway 299 to Burney and then continue for five miles to the junction with Highway 89. At Highway 89, turn north (left) and drive six miles to the campground entrance on the left side of the road.

Contact: McArthur-Burney Falls State Park, 530/335-2777.

15 DUSTY CAMPGROUND

Rating: 8

On Lake Britton.
Map 3.1, page 184
This is one in a series of campgrounds near

the north shore of Lake Britton. (See the entry for Northshore for more information.) The camp is set at an elevation of 2,800 feet. It provides an option to the far more popular yet nearby state park.

Campsites, facilities: There are seven primitive sites for tents or RVs up to 20 feet long and two primitive group sites that can accommodate up to 25 people each. Fire rings are provided. Vault toilets are available. Drinking water is not available. Garbage must be packed out. Leashed pets are permitted.

Reservations, fees: Reservations are not accepted. The fee is $6 per night, $3 per night per extra vehicle, $7 per night per extra RV, $1 per pet per night, and $12 per night for group sites. Open year-round.

Directions: From Redding, drive east on Highway 299 to Burney and continue for five miles to the junction with Highway 89. Turn left (north) and drive 7.5 miles (past the state park entrance and over the Lake Britton Bridge) to the campground access road on the left (it will be confusing because the campground is on the right). Turn left and drive three-quarters of a mile (in the process crossing the highway) to the campground.

Contact: PG&E Land Projects, 916/386-5164, fax 916/923-7044, website: www.pge.com/recreation.

16 NORTHSHORE

Rating: 8

On Lake Britton.
Map 3.1, page 184
This peaceful campground is set among the woodlands near the shore of Lake Britton, directly across the lake from McArthur-Burney Falls Memorial State Park. Boating and fishing are popular here, and once the water warms up in midsummer, swimming is also a winner. The best trout fishing in the area is on the Pit River near Powerhouse Number Three, but skilled and aggressive wading is required. A

hot spring is available in Big Bend, about a 30-minute drive from camp.

Campsites, facilities: There are 30 sites for tents or RVs up to 30 feet long. Picnic tables and fire grills are provided. Drinking water and vault toilets are available. An unimproved boat ramp is available near the camp and an improved boat ramp is available in Burney Falls State Park (about four miles away). Supplies can be obtained in Fall River Mills or Burney. Leashed pets are permitted.

Reservations, fees: Reservations are not accepted. The fee is $13 per night, $1 per pet per night. Open mid-May to mid-September, weather permitting.

Directions: From Redding, drive east on Highway 299 to Burney and then continue for five miles to Highway 89. Turn left (north) and drive 9.7 miles (past the state park entrance and over the Lake Britton Bridge) to Clark Creek Road. Turn left (west) and drive about a mile to the camp access road. Turn left and drive one mile to the camp.

Contact: PG&E Land Projects, 916/386-5164, fax 916/923-7044, website: www.pge.com/recreation.

17 DEADLUN

Rating: 8

On Iron Canyon Reservoir in Shasta-Trinity National Forest.

Map 3.1, page 184

Deadlun is a pretty campground set in the forest, shaded and quiet, with a five-minute walk or one-minute drive to the Deadlun Creek arm of Iron Canyon Reservoir. Drive? If you have a canoe to launch or fishing equipment to carry, driving is the choice. Trout fishing is good here, both in April and May, then again in October and early November. One downer is that the shoreline is often very muddy here in March and early April. Because of an engineering error with the dam, the lake never fills completely, causing the lakeshore to be strewn with

stumps and quite muddy after spring rains and snowmelt.

Campsites, facilities: There are 30 sites for tents or RVs up to 24 feet long. Picnic tables and fire grills are provided. Vault toilets are available. No drinking water is available. A small boat ramp is available one mile from the camp. Leashed pets are permitted.

Reservations, fees: Reservations are not accepted. There is no fee for camping. Open year-round.

Directions: From Redding, drive east on Highway 299 for 37 miles to Big Bend Road. At Big Bend Road, turn left and drive 15.2 miles to the town of Big Bend. Continue for five miles to the lake, bearing right at the T intersection, and continue for two miles (past the boat launch turnoff) to the campground turnoff on the left side of the road. Turn left and drive one mile to the campground.

Contact: Shasta-Trinity National Forest, Shasta Lake Ranger District, 530/275-1587, fax 530/275-1512; Shasta Lake Visitor Center, 530/275-1589.

18 HAWKINS LANDING

Rating: 7

On Iron Canyon Reservoir.

Map 3.1, page 184

The adjacent boat ramp makes Hawkins Landing the better of the two camps at Iron Canyon Reservoir for campers with trailered boats (though Deadlun is far more secluded). Iron Canyon provides good fishing for trout, has a resident bald eagle or two, and also has nearby hot springs in the town of Big Bend. One problem with this lake is the annual drawdown in late fall, which causes the shoreline to be extremely muddy in the spring. The lake usually rises high enough to make the boat ramp functional by mid-April. This camp is set at an elevation of 2,700 feet.

Campsites, facilities: There are 10 sites for tents or RVs up to 30 feet long. Picnic tables and fire grills are provided. Drinking water, vault toilets, and a small boat ramp are available. Supplies can be obtained in Big Bend. Leashed pets are permitted.

Reservations, fees: Reservations are not accepted. The fee is $10 per night, $1 dog fee, $3 per night per extra vehicle, $7 per night for extra RV. Open Memorial Day weekend to Labor Day weekend, weather permitting.

Directions: From Redding, drive east on Highway 299 for 37 miles to Big Bend Road. At Big Bend Road turn left and drive 15.2 miles to the town of Big Bend. Continue for 2.1 miles to Forest Road 38N11. Turn left and drive 3.3 miles to the Iron Canyon Reservoir Spillway. Turn right and drive 1.1 miles to a dirt road. Turn left and drive .3 mile to the campground.

Contact: PG&E Land Projects, 916/386-5164.

19 CAVE LAKE

🏊 🛶 🚐 🐕 5% 🚙 ⛺

Rating: 8

In Modoc National Forest.

Map 3.2, page 185

A pair of lakes can be discovered out here in the middle of nowhere, with Cave Lake on one end and Lily Lake on the other. Together they make a nice set, very quiet, extremely remote, with good fishing for rainbow trout and brook trout. A canoe, pram, or float tube can be ideal. No motors are permitted and there is no boat ramp. Of the two lakes, it is nearby Lily Lake that is prettier and provides the better fishing. Cave Lake is set at 6,600 feet. By camping here, you become a member of the 5 Percent Club; that is, the 5 percent of campers who know of secret, isolated little spots such as this one.

Campsites, facilities: There are six sites for tents or RVs up to 15 feet long; trailers are not advised because of the steep access road. Picnic tables and fire grills are provided. Drinking water and vault toilets are available. Garbage must be packed out. Motors are prohibited on the lake, including electric. Supplies are available in New Pine Creek, Fort Bidwell, and Davis Creek. Leashed pets are permitted.

Reservations, fees: Reservations are not accepted. There is no fee for camping. Open July through September.

Directions: From Redding, drive east on Highway 299 for 146 miles to Alturas and U.S. 395. Turn north on U.S. 395 and drive 40 miles to Forest Road 2 (if you reach the town of New Pine Creek on the Oregon/California border, you have driven a mile too far). Turn right on Forest Road 2 (a steep dirt road—trailers are not recommended) and drive six miles to the campground entrance on the left side of the road, just beyond the Lily Lake picnic area.

Contact: Modoc National Forest, Warner Mountain Ranger, 530/279-6116, fax 530/279-8309.

20 PLUM VALLEY

🛶 🐕 🚙 ⛺

Rating: 7

Near the South Fork of Davis Creek in Modoc National Forest.

Map 3.2, page 185

This secluded and primitive camp is set near the South Fork of Davis Creek, at 5,600 feet elevation. Davis Creek provides for catch-and-release, barbless hook, no-bait fishing. You can, however, keep the brown trout. There are no other campgrounds within 15 miles.

Campsites, facilities: There are seven sites for tents or RVs up to 15 feet long. Picnic tables and fire grills are provided. A vault toilet is available. No drinking water is available. Garbage must be packed out. Supplies are available in Davis Creek, about 3.5 miles away. Leashed pets are permitted.

Reservations, fees: Reservations are not accepted. There is no fee for camping. Open May through September.

Directions: From Alturas drive north on U.S. 395 for 18 miles to the town of Davis Creek and County Road 11. Turn right on County Road 11 and drive two miles to a Y. Bear right on Forest Road 45N35 and drive one mile to the signed entrance to the campground on the left side of the road.

Contact: Modoc National Forest, Warner Mountain Ranger District, 530/279-6116, fax 530/279-8309.

21 RESERVOIR C

Rating: 6

Near Alturas in Modoc National Forest.

Map 3.2, page 185

It is one great adventure to explore the "alphabet lakes" in the remote Devil's Garden area of Modoc County. Reservoir C and Reservoir F provide the best of the lot, but the success can go up and down like a yo-yo, just like the water levels in the lakes. Reservoir C is stocked with both Eagle Lake trout and brown trout. A sidelight to this area is the number of primitive roads that are routed through Modoc National Forest, perfect for four-wheel-drive cowboys.

Campsites, facilities: There are six primitive sites for tents and self contained RVs. Picnic tables are provided. A vault toilet is available. No drinking water is available. Garbage must be packed out. Leashed pets are permitted.

Reservations, fees: Reservations are not accepted. There is no fee for camping. Open May through September.

Directions: From Alturas drive west on Highway 299 for three miles to Crowder Flat Road/County Road 73. Turn right on Crowder Flat Road and drive 9.5 miles to Triangle Ranch Road/Forest Road 43N18. Turn left on Triangle Ranch Road and drive seven miles to Forest Road 44N32. Turn right on Forest Road 44N32, drive a half mile, turn right on the access road for the lake and campground, and drive a half mile to the camp at the end of the road.

Contact: Modoc National Forest, Devil's Garden Ranger District, 530/233-5811, fax 530/233-8709.

22 BIG SAGE RESERVOIR

Rating: 6

In Modoc National Forest.

Map 3.2, page 185

This is a do-it-yourself camp; that is, pick your own spot, bring your own water, and don't expect to see any Forest Service rangers or, for that matter, anybody else. This camp is set along Big Sage Reservoir—that's right, sagebrush country at 5,100 feet elevation. It is a big lake, covering 5,000 acres, and a boat ramp is adjacent to the campground. This is one of the better bass lakes in Modoc County. Catfish and crappie are also here.

Campsites, facilities: There are primitive, dispersed sites for tents or RVs of any length. Picnic tables are provided. A vault toilet is available. Some facilities are wheelchair-accessible. No drinking water is available. Garbage must be packed out. A boat ramp is available nearby. Leashed pets are permitted. Supplies can be obtained in Alturas, about eight miles away.

Reservations, fees: Reservations are not accepted. There is no fee for camping. Open May through September.

Directions: From Alturas, drive west on Highway 299 for three miles to Crowder Flat Road/County Road 73. Turn right on Crowder Flat Road and drive about five miles to County Road 180. Turn right on County Road 180 and drive four miles. Turn left at the access road for the campground and boat ramp and drive a short distance to the camp on the left side of the road.

Contact: Modoc National Forest, Devil's Garden Ranger District, 530/233-5811, fax 530/233-8709.

23 CEDAR PASS

Rating: 5

On Cedar Pass in Modoc National Forest.

Map 3.2, page 185

Cedar Pass is at 5,900 feet, set on the ridge

between Cedar Mountain (8,152 feet) to the north and Payne Peak (7,618) to the south, high in the north Warner Mountains. Bear Creek enters Thomas Creek adjacent to the camp; both are small streams, but it's a pretty spot.

Campsites, facilities: There are 17 sites for tents or RVs up to 22 feet long. Picnic tables and fire grills are provided. Vault toilets are available. No drinking water is available. Garbage must be packed out. Supplies can be obtained in Cedarville or Alturas. Leashed pets are permitted.

Reservations, fees: Reservations are not accepted. There is no fee for camping. Open May through September.

Directions: From Redding drive east on Highway 299 to Alturas. In Alturas continue north on Highway 299/U.S. 395 for five miles to the split for Highway 299. Turn right on Highway 299 and drive about nine miles. Look for the signed entrance road on the right side of the road.

Contact: Modoc National Forest, Warner Mountain Ranger District, 530/279-6116, fax 530/279-8309.

24 STOWE RESERVOIR

Rating: 8

In Modoc National Forest.

Map 3.2, page 185

Stowe Reservoir looks like a large country pond where cattle might drink. You know why? Because it once actually was a cattle pond on a family ranch that has since been converted to Forest Service property. It is in the north Warner Mountains (not to be confused with the South Warner Wilderness), which features many back roads and remote four-wheel-drive routes. The camp is set at an elevation of 6,200 feet. Note that you may find this campground named "Stough Reservoir" on some maps and in previous editions of this book. The name is now officially spelled "Stowe Reservoir," after the family that originally owned the property.

Campsites, facilities: There are 14 sites for tents or RVs up to 22 feet long. Picnic tables and fire grills are provided. Drinking water and vault toilets are available. Garbage must be packed out. Leashed pets are permitted. Supplies can be obtained in Cedarville, six miles away.

Reservations, fees: Reservations are not accepted. There is no fee for camping. Open May to October.

Directions: From Redding, drive east on Highway 299 to Alturas. In Alturas, continue north on Highway 299/U.S. 395 for five miles to the split-off for Highway 299. Turn right on Highway 299 and drive about 12 miles (just past Cedar Pass). Look for the signed entrance road on the left side of the road. Turn left and drive one mile to the campground on the right side of the road.

Contact: Modoc National Forest, Warner Mountain Ranger District, 530/279-6116, fax 530/279-8309.

25 HOWARD'S GULCH

Rating: 6

Near Duncan Reservoir in Modoc National Forest.

Map 3.2, page 185

This is the nearest campground to Duncan Reservoir, three miles to the north and stocked with trout each year by the Department of Fish and Game. The camp is set in the typically sparse woods of Modoc National Forest, but a beautiful grove of aspen is three miles to the west on Highway 139, on the left side of the road. By the way, Highway 139 isn't much of a highway at all, but it is paved and will get you there. The elevation is 4,700 feet.

Campsites, facilities: There are 11 sites for tents or RVs up to 22 feet long. Picnic tables and fire grills are provided. Drinking water and vault toilets are available. Some facilities are wheelchair-accessible. Supplies are available within five miles in Canby. Leashed pets are permitted.

Reservations, fees: Reservations are not accepted. The fee is $6 per night. Senior discount available. Open May through October.

Directions: From Redding, drive east on Highway 299 for about 100 miles to Adin. Continue on Highway 299 for about 25 miles to Highway 139. Turn left (northwest) on Highway 139 and drive six miles to the campground on the left side of the road.

Contact: Modoc National Forest, Devil's Garden Ranger District, 530/233-5811, fax 530/233-8709.

26 BRASS RAIL

Rating: 4

Near Alturas.

Map 3.2, page 185

This private RV park has easy access from the highway. The elevation is 4,400 feet. Alturas is the biggest "small town" in Modoc County and offers a nice city park with a playground, museum, old-time saloon, and just south of town, the Modoc National Wildlife Refuge. The Warner Mountains to the distant east provide a backdrop.

Campsites, facilities: There are 70 RV sites, some with full hookups, and a separate tent area. Picnic tables are provided. Hot showers, flush toilets, RV dump station, coin laundry, ice, propane gas, playground, and tennis court are available. Some facilities are wheelchair-accessible. A restaurant is adjacent to the park. Supplies can be obtained in Alturas, less than a mile away. Leashed pets are permitted.

Reservations, fees: Reservations are accepted. The fee is $10.50–16 per night, $5.50 per person for more than two people, $3–5 per night for each extra vehicle. Major credit cards accepted. Open March through October.

Directions: In Alturas at the junction of Highway 299 and U.S. 395, turn east on U.S. 395 and drive a half mile to the signed campground entrance on the right.

Contact: Brass Rail Campground, 530/233-2906.

27 SULLY'S RV PARK

Rating: 4

Near Alturas.

Map 3.2, page 185

This privately operated park is next to the playground, the city park, and the Modoc County Museum, which details the history of the area. The surrounding Modoc National Wildlife Refuge is only a short drive away, either a mile southwest of town along the Pit River, or three miles east of town at Dorris Reservoir. Big Sage Reservoir provides another getaway. But alas, what gets most of the traffic is a casino, only one mile from Alturas. The area for tent camping here is grassy and separated from the RV camp.

Campsites, facilities: There are 25 RV sites with full hookups and picnic tables, including 10 drive-through sites, and a separate area for tents. Cable TV, modem hookups, showers, flush toilets, coin laundry, and horseshoe pits are available. Supplies can be obtained in Alturas one block away. Leashed pets are permitted.

Reservations, fees: Reservations are accepted. The fee is $10–17 per night. Monthly rates available. Open year-round.

Directions: In Alturas, at the junction of Highway 299 and U.S. 395, turn south on U.S. 395 and drive a half mile (look for the steam engine) to County Road 56. Turn east on County Road 56 and drive one block to the campground on the right.

Contact: Sully's RV Park, 530/233-5347, fax 530/233-2541.

28 PEPPERDINE

Rating: 5

In Modoc National Forest.

Map 3.2, page 185

This camp is outstanding for hikers planning a backpacking trip into the adjacent South

Warner Wilderness. The camp is at 6,680 feet, set along the south side of tiny Porter Reservoir, with a horse corral within walking distance. A trailhead out of camp provides direct access to the Summit Trail, the best hike in the South Warner Wilderness.

Campsites, facilities: There are five sites for tents or RVs up to 22 feet long. Picnic tables and fire grills are provided. Drinking water and vault toilets are available. Corrals are available with water for stock. Garbage must be packed out. Supplies are available in Cedarville or Alturas. Leashed pets are permitted.

Reservations, fees: Reservations are not accepted. There is no fee for camping. Open July through October.

Directions: In Alturas, drive south on U.S. 395 to the southern end of town and County Road 56. Turn left on County Road 56 and drive 13 miles to the Modoc Forest boundary and the junction with Parker Creek Road. Bear left on Parker Creek Road and continue for six miles to the signed campground access road on the right. Turn right and drive a half mile to the campground on the right side of the road.

Contact: Modoc National Forest, Warner Mountain Ranger District, 530/279-6116, fax 530/279-8309.

29 UPPER RUSH CREEK
🏃 🏊 🐴 🚐 🏕️

Rating: 8

In Modoc National Forest.
Map 3.2, page 185

Upper Rush Creek is a pretty campground, set along Rush Creek, a quiet, wooded spot that gets little use. It sits in the shadow of nearby Manzanita Mountain (7,036 feet elevation) to the east, where there is a Forest Service lookout for a great view. To reach the lookout, drive back toward Highway 299 and when you reach the paved road, County Road 198, turn left and drive one-half mile to Forest Road 22. Turn left on Forest Road 22 and head up the hill. One mile from the summit, turn left at a four-way junction and drive to the top. You get dramatic views of the Warm Springs Valley to the north and the Likely Flats to the east, looking across miles and miles of open country.

Campsites, facilities: There are 13 sites for tents or RVs up to 22 feet long, but Lower Rush Creek is better for trailers. Picnic tables and fire grills are provided. Drinking water and vault toilets are available. Supplies can be obtained in Adin or Canby. Leashed pets are permitted.

Reservations, fees: Reservations are not accepted. The fee is $6 per night. Senior discount available. Open May through September.

Directions: From Redding, turn east on Highway 299 and drive to Adin. Continue east on Highway 299 for about seven miles to a signed campground turnoff on the right side of the road. Turn right and drive to the junction with Forest Road 40N05. Turn left and drive 2.5 miles to the campground at the end of the road.

Contact: Modoc National Forest, Big Valley Ranger District, 530/299-3215, fax 530/299-8409.

30 LOWER RUSH CREEK
🏊 🏴 🚐 🏕️

Rating: 6

On Rush Creek in Modoc National Forest.
Map 3.2, page 185

This is one of two obscure campgrounds set a short distance from Highway 299 on Rush Creek in southern Modoc County. Lower Rush Creek is the first camp you will come to, with flat campsites surrounded by an outer fence and set along Rush Creek. This camp is better suited for trailers than the one at Upper Rush Creek. It is little known and little used. It's set at 4,400 feet in elevation.

Campsites, facilities: There are 10 sites for tents and five sites for RVs up to 22 feet long. Picnic tables and fire grills are provided. Drinking water and vault toilets are available. Supplies are available in Canby. Leashed pets are permitted.

Reservations, fees: Reservations are not accepted. The fee is $6 per night. Senior discount available. Open May through September.

Directions: From Redding, turn east on Highway 299 and drive to Adin. Continue east on Highway 299 for about seven miles to a signed campground turnoff on the right side of the road. Turn right and drive to the junction with Forest Road 40N05. Turn left and drive one mile to the campground on the right.

Contact: Modoc National Forest, Big Valley Ranger District, 530/299-3215, fax 530/299-8409.

31 SOUP SPRINGS

Rating: 8

In Modoc National Forest.

Map 3.2, page 185

This is a beautiful, quiet, wooded campground at a trailhead into the South Warner Wilderness. Soup Creek originates at Soup Springs in the meadow adjacent to the campground. The trailhead here is routed two miles into the wilderness, where it junctions with the Mill Creek Trail. From here, turn left for a beautiful walk along Mill Creek and into Mill Creek Meadow, an easy yet pristine stroll that can provide a serene experience. The elevation is 6,800 feet.

Campsites, facilities: There are six tent sites and eight sites for tents or RVs up to 22 feet long. Picnic tables and fire grills are provided. Drinking water and vault toilets are available. Corrals are also available. Supplies can be obtained in Likely. Leashed pets are permitted.

Reservations, fees: Reservations are not accepted. The fee is $6 per night. Senior discount available. Open June through September.

Directions: From Alturas, drive south on U.S. 395 for 17 miles to the town of Likely, where you'll come to Jess Valley Road. Turn left on Jess Valley Road/County Road 64 and drive nine miles to the fork. Bear left on West Warner Road/Forest Road 5 and go 4.5 miles to

Soup Loop Road. Turn right on Soup Loop Road/Forest Road 40N24 and continue on that gravel road for six miles to the campground entrance on the right.

Contact: Modoc National Forest, Warner Mountain Ranger District, 530/279-6116, fax 530/279-8309.

32 MILL CREEK FALLS

Rating: 9

In Modoc National Forest.

Map 3.2, page 185

This nice, wooded campground is a good base camp for a backpacking trip into the South Warner Wilderness. The camp is set on Mill Creek at 5,700 feet in elevation. To see Mill Creek Falls, take the trail out of camp and bear left at the Y. To enter the interior of the South Warner Wilderness, bear right at the Y, after which the trail passes Clear Lake, heads to Poison Flat and Poison Creek, and then reaches a junction. Left will take you to the Mill Creek Trail, right will take you up to the Summit Trail. Take your pick. You can't go wrong.

Campsites, facilities: There are 11 sites for tents and eight sites for tents or RVs up to 22 feet long. Picnic tables and fire grills are provided. Drinking water and vault toilets are available. Supplies are available in Likely. Leashed pets are permitted.

Reservations, fees: Reservations are not accepted. The fee is $6 per night. Senior discount available. Open May through October.

Directions: From Alturas drive 17 miles south on U.S. 395 to the town of Likely, where you'll come to Jess Valley Road. Turn left on Jess Valley Road/County Road 64 and drive nine miles to the fork. Bear left on West Warner Road/Forest Road 5 and drive 2.5 miles to Forest Road 40N46. Turn right on Forest Road 40N46 and drive two miles to the campground entrance at the end of the road.

Contact: Modoc National Forest, Warner

Mountain Ranger District, 530/279-6116, fax 530/279-8309.

33 EMERSON

Rating: 6

In Modoc National Forest.

Map 3.2, page 185

This tiny camp is virtually unknown, nestled at 6,000 feet on the eastern boundary of the South Warner Wilderness. Big alkali lakes and miles of the Nevada flats can be seen on the other side of the highway as you drive along the entrance road to the campground. A trailhead at this primitive setting is used by hikers and backpackers. Note that hitting the trail is a steep, sometimes wrenching climb for 4.5 miles to North Emerson Lake (poor to fair fishing). For many, this hike is a true butt-kicker.

Campsites, facilities: There are four sites for tents or RVs up to 16 feet long. Picnic tables and fire grills are provided. Vault toilets are available. No drinking water is available. Garbage must be packed out. Supplies can be obtained in Eagleville. Leashed pets are permitted.

Reservations, fees: Reservations are not accepted. There is no fee for camping. Open July through September.

Directions: From Alturas, drive north on U.S. 395/Highway 299 for about five miles to the junction with Highway 299. Turn right on Highway 299 and drive to Cedarville and County Road 1. Turn south on County Road 1 and drive to Eagleville. From Eagleville, continue south on County Road 1 for one mile to County Road 40. Turn right on County Road 40 and drive three miles to the campground at the end of the road. The access road is steep and very slick in wet weather. Trailers are not recommended.

Contact: Modoc National Forest, Warner Mountain Ranger District, 530/279-6116, fax 530/279-8309.

34 ASH CREEK

Rating: 7

In Modoc National Forest.

Map 3.2, page 185

This remote camp has stark beauty and is set at 4,800 feet along Ash Creek, a stream with small trout. This region of Modoc National Forest has an extensive network of backcountry roads, popular with deer hunters in the fall. Summer comes relatively late out here, and it can be cold and wet even in early June. Stash some extra clothes, just in case. That will probably guarantee nice weather.

Campsites, facilities: There are seven sites for tents or RVs up to 22 feet long. Picnic tables and fire grills are provided. Vault toilets are available. No drinking water is available. Garbage must be packed out. Supplies can be obtained in Adin. Leashed pets are permitted.

Reservations, fees: Reservations are not accepted. There is no fee for camping. Open May through September.

Directions: From Redding, turn east on Highway 299 and drive to Adin and Ash Valley Road. Turn right on Ash Valley Road/County Road 88/527 and drive eight miles. Turn left at the signed campground turnoff and drive a mile to the campground on the right side of the road.

Contact: Modoc National Forest, Big Valley Ranger District, 530/299-3215, fax 530/299-8409.

35 PATTERSON

Rating: 4

In Modoc National Forest.

Map 3.2, page 185

This once-beautiful landscape was burned by the Blue Fire of 2001, which enveloped 35,000 acres in the South Warners. There are both positives and negatives. The positives are a chance for much wider and longer views previously impossible, as well as the opportunity to watch the evolution of the landscape in a postfire setting, as has been the case in Yellowstone for years. The negatives are the tree skeletons. The most affected area is to the east, especially on the East Creek Trail, which rises through the burned area to a high, barren mountain rim. This camp is set across the road from Patterson Meadow at 7,200 feet in elevation. The camp is rarely open before July.

Campsites, facilities: There are five sites for tents or RVs up to 20 feet long. Picnic tables and fire grills are provided. Drinking water and vault toilets are available. Garbage must be packed out. Supplies are available in Likely or Eagleville. Leashed pets are permitted.

Reservations, fees: Reservations are not accepted. There is no fee for camping. Open late June through September, weather permitting.

Directions: From Alturas drive 17 miles south on U.S. 395 to the town of Likely. Turn left on Jess Valley Road/County Road 64 and drive nine miles to the fork. Bear right on Forest Road 64 and drive for 16 miles to the campground on the left.

Contact: Modoc National Forest, Warner Mountain Ranger District, 530/279-6116, fax 530/279-8309.

36 BLUE LAKE

Rating: 6

In Modoc National Forest.
Map 3.2, page 185

You won't believe this: the Blue Fire of 1991 burned 35,000 acres in this area, including the east and west slopes adjoining Blue Lake. Yet get this: the campground was untouched. It is a strange scene, a somewhat wooded campground (with some level campsites) near the shore of Blue Lake. The lake covers 160 acres and provides fishing for large brown trout and rainbow trout. A five-mph speed limit assures quiet water for small boats and canoes. A trail circles the lake and takes less than an hour to

hike. The elevation is 6,000 feet. A pair of nesting bald eagles lives here; in the last several years there have been several fledged chicks (up to eight by summer of 2002). While their presence negates year-round use of six campsites otherwise available, the trade-off is an unprecedented opportunity to view the national bird. This lake received national attention when it was uncovered that it received a special large stock of brown trout in the 30-inch class, a plant attributed to the fact that Blue Lake was the boyhood lake and still "secret" fishing spot of the director of Department of Fish and Game (and his brother).

Campsites, facilities: There are 48 sites for tents or RVs up to 25 feet long. Picnic tables and fire grills are provided. Drinking water and vault toilets are available. Some facilities are wheelchair-accessible, including a paved boat launch and fishing pier. Supplies are available in Likely. Leashed pets are permitted.

Reservations, fees: Reservations are not accepted. The fee is $7 per night. Senior discount available. Open June through October.

Directions: From Alturas, drive south on U.S. 395 for seven miles to the town of Likely, where you'll come to Jess Valley Road. Turn left on Jess Valley Road/County Road 64 and drive nine miles to the fork. At the fork, bear right on Forest Road 64 and drive seven miles to Forest Road 38N60. Turn right on Forest Road 38N60 and drive two miles to the campground.

Contact: Modoc National Forest, Warner Mountain Ranger District, 530/279-6116, fax 530/279-8309.

37 WILLOW CREEK

Rating: 7

In Modoc National Forest.
Map 3.2, page 185

This remote camp and picnic area is set at 5,200 feet along little Willow Creek amid pine, aspen, and willows. On the north side of the campground is Lower McBride Springs. To the southwest is a state game refuge, with access available by vehicle, and several four-wheel-drive routes near its border.

Campsites, facilities: There are eight sites for tents or RVs up to 22 feet long. Picnic tables and fire grills are provided. Drinking water and vault toilets are available. A wheelchair-accessible toilet is at the picnic area next to the campground. Leashed pets are permitted.

Reservations, fees: Reservations are not accepted. The fee is $6 per night. Senior discount available. Open May through October.

Directions: From Redding, drive east on Highway 299 to Adin and Highway 139. Turn right on Highway 139 and drive 14 miles to the campground on the left side of the road.

Contact: Modoc National Forest, Big Valley Ranger District, 530/299-3215, fax 530/299-8409.

38 PIT RIVER

Rating: 6

On the Pit River.
Map 3.3, page 186

Very few out-of-towners know about this hidden and primitive campground set along the Pit River. It can provide a good base camp for a fishing trip adventure. The best stretch of trout water on the Pit is near Powerhouse Number Three. In addition to fishing there are many other recreation options. A parking area and trail along Hat Creek are available where the Highway 299 bridge crosses Hat Creek. Baum Lake, Crystal Lake, and the Cassel section of Hat Creek are all within five miles of this camp.

Campsites, facilities: There are 10 sites for tents or RVs. Picnic tables and fire rings are provided. Vault toilets are available. No drinking water is available. Garbage service is provided only during summer. There are supplies and a coin laundry in Fall River Mills. Leashed pets are permitted.

Reservations, fees: Reservations are not ac-

cepted. There is no fee for camping. Open year-round, weather permitting.

Directions: From Redding, drive east on Highway 299 to Burney and continue for five miles to the junction with Highway 89. At the junction, continue straight on Highway 299, cross the Pit River Bridge, and drive about three miles to Pit One Powerhouse Road on the right. Just before the powerhouse, turn right (at the bend) and drive along the river for about a mile to the campground.

Contact: Bureau of Land Management, Alturas Field Office, 530/233-4666, fax 530/233-5696.

39 CASSEL

Rating: 8

On Hat Creek.
Map 3.3, page 186

This camp is set at 3,200 feet in the beautiful Hat Creek Valley. It is an outstanding location for a fishing trip base camp, with nearby Crystal Lake, Baum Lake, and Hat Creek (all set in the Hat Creek Valley) providing trout fishing. This section of Hat Creek is well known for its challenging fly-fishing, typically with an excellent evening hatch and surface rise. Long leaders and very small flies are critical. A good source of fishing information is Vaughn's Sporting Goods in Burney. Baum Lake is ideal for car-top boats with electric motors.

Campsites, facilities: There are 27 sites for tents or RVs up to 30 feet long. Picnic tables and fire grills are provided. Drinking water and vault toilets are available. Leashed pets are permitted.

Reservations, fees: Reservations are not accepted. The fee is $13 per night, $3 per night per extra vehicle, $7 per night per extra RV, $1 per pet per night. Open mid-April through October, weather permitting.

Directions: From Redding, drive east on Highway 299 to Burney and continue for five miles to the junction with Highway 89. At the junction, continue straight on Highway 299 for two miles to Cassel Road. At Cassel Road, turn right and drive 3.6 miles to the campground entrance on the left.

Contact: PG&E Land Projects, 916/386-5164, fax 916/923-7044, website: www.pge.com/recreation.

40 HAT CREEK HEREFORD RANCH RV PARK & CAMPGROUND

Rating: 8

Near Hat Creek.
Map 3.3, page 186

This privately operated campground is set in a working cattle ranch. Campers are not allowed near the cattle pasture or cattle. Fishing is available in Hat Creek or in the nearby stocked trout pond. Sight-seeing is excellent with Burney Falls, Lassen Volcanic National Park, and Subway Caves all within 30 miles.

Campsites, facilities: There are 40 tent sites and 40 RV sites, including some drive-through sites, with full or partial hookups. Restrooms, hot showers, RV dump station, coin laundry, playground, modem hookups, and a grocery store are available. Some facilities are wheelchair-accessible. Leashed pets are permitted.

Reservations, fees: Reservations are recommended. The fee is $17.45–22.45 per night, $2 per adult and $1.50 per child per night for more than two people, $.50 per night per pet. Major credit cards accepted. Open April through October.

Directions: From Redding, drive east on Highway 299 to Burney and continue for five miles to the junction with Highway 89. Turn right (south) on Highway 89 and drive 12 miles to the second Doty Road exit and the entrance to the campground.

Contact: Hat Creek Hereford Ranch RV Park & Campground, 877/459-9532 or 530/335-7171, website:www.hatcreekrv.com.

41 HONN

Rating: 7

On Hat Creek in Lassen National Forest.
Map 3.3, page 186

This primitive, tiny campground is set near the point where Honn Creek enters Hat Creek, at 3,400 feet elevation in Lassen National Forest. The creek is extremely pretty here, shaded by trees and flowing emerald green. The camp provides streamside access for trout fishing, though this stretch of creek is sometimes overlooked by the Department of Fish and Game in favor of stocking the creek at the more popular Cave and Bridge Campgrounds. (See the entry for Cave Camp for more information.)

Campsites, facilities: There are six tent sites. Picnic tables and fire grills are provided. Vault toilets are available. Drinking water is not available. A grocery store, coin laundry, and propane gas are also available nearby. Leashed pets are permitted.

Reservations, fees: Reservations are not accepted. The fee is $9 per night, $5 for each extra vehicle. Senior discount available. Open late April through October, weather permitting.

Directions: From Redding, drive east on Highway 299 to Burney and continue for five miles to the junction with Highway 89. Turn right (south) on Highway 89 and drive 15 miles to the campground entrance on the left side of the road.

Contact: Lassen National Forest, Hat Creek Ranger District, 530/336-5521, fax 530/336-5758.

42 BRIDGE CAMP

Rating: 7

On Hat Creek in Lassen National Forest.
Map 3.3, page 186

This camp is one of four along Highway 89 in the area along Hat Creek. It is set at 3,800 feet elevation, with shaded sites and the stream within very short walking distance. Trout are stocked on this stretch of the creek, with fishing access available out of camp, as well as at Rocky and Cave Camps to the south and Honn to the north. In one weekend, fishermen might hit all four.

Campsites, facilities: There are 25 sites for tents or RVs up to 22 feet long. Picnic tables and fire grills are provided. Drinking water and vault toilets are available. A grocery store and propane gas are available nearby. Leashed pets are permitted.

Reservations, fees: Reservations are not accepted. The fee is $12 per night, $5 for each extra vehicle. Senior discount available. Open late April through October, weather permitting.

Directions: From Redding, drive east on Highway 299 to Burney and continue for five miles to the junction with Highway 89. Turn right (south) on Highway 89 and drive 19 miles to the campground entrance on the right side of the road. If you reach Old Station, you have gone five miles too far.

Contact: Lassen National Forest, Hat Creek Ranger District, 530/336-5521, fax 530/336-5758.

43 ROCKY CAMP

Rating: 7

On Hat Creek in Lassen National Forest.
Map 3.3, page 186

This is a small, primitive camp along Hat Creek on Highway 89. It's usually a second choice for campers if nearby Cave and Bridge Camps are full. Streamside fishing access is a plus here, with this section of stream stocked with rainbow trout. (See the entry for Cave Camp for more information.)

Campsites, facilities: There are eight tent sites. Picnic tables and fire grills are provided. Vault toilets are available. No drinking water is available. A grocery store and propane gas are available nearby. Leashed pets are permitted.

Reservations, fees: Reservations are not accepted.

The fee is $9 per night, $5 for each extra vehicle. Senior discount available. Open late April through October, weather permitting.

Directions: From Redding, drive east on Highway 299 to Burney and continue for five miles to the junction with Highway 89. Turn right (south) on Highway 89 and drive 20 miles to the campground entrance on the right side of the road. If you reach Old Station, you have gone four miles too far.

Contact: Lassen National Forest, Hat Creek Ranger District, 530/336-5521, fax 530/336-5758.

44 CAVE CAMP

Rating: 7

On Hat Creek in Lassen National Forest.
Map 3.3, page 186

Cave Camp is set right along Hat Creek, with both easy access off Highway 89 and an anglers' trail available along the stream. This stretch of Hat Creek is planted with rainbow trout twice per month by the Department of Fish and Game, starting with the opening of trout season on the last Saturday of April. Nearby side trips include Lassen Volcanic National Park, about a 15-minute drive to the south on Highway 89, and Subway Caves (turn left at the junction just across the road from the campground). A rare bonus at this camp is that wheelchair-accessible fishing is available.

Campsites, facilities: There are 46 sites for tents or RVs up to 22 feet long. Picnic tables and fire grills are provided. Drinking water, flush toilets, and vault toilets are available. Some facilities are wheelchair-accessible. Supplies can be obtained in Old Station. Leashed pets are permitted.

Reservations, fees: Reservations are not accepted. The fee is $14 per night, $5 for each extra vehicle. Senior discount available. Open May through October.

Directions: From Redding, drive east on Highway 299 to Burney and continue for five miles to the junction with Highway 89. Turn right (south) on Highway 89 and drive 23 miles to the campground entrance on the right side of the road. If you reach Old Station, you have gone one mile too far.

Contact: Lassen National Forest, Hat Creek Ranger District, 530/336-5521, fax 530/336-5758.

45 HAT CREEK

Rating: 7

On Hat Creek in Lassen National Forest.
Map 3.3, page 186

This is one in a series of Forest Service camps set beside beautiful Hat Creek, a good trout stream stocked regularly by the Department of Fish and Game. The elevation is 4,400 feet. The proximity to Lassen Volcanic National Park to the south is a big plus. Supplies are available in the little town of Old Station one mile to the north.

Campsites, facilities: There are 73 sites for tents or RVs up to 22 feet long and three group camp loops, each of which accommodates 15–20 vehicles. Picnic tables and fire grills are provided. Drinking water, an RV dump station, and vault toilets are available. A grocery store, coin laundry, and propane gas are available nearby. Leashed pets are permitted.

Reservations, fees: Reservations are required with a $9 reservation fee only for campsites 1–9 and for group camps at 877/444-6777 or website www.ReserveUsa.com. The fee is $14 per night for family sites, $5 for each extra vehicle, $60–70 per night for group camps. Senior discount available. Open May through October.

Directions: From Redding, drive east on Highway 44 to the junction with Highway 89 (near the entrance to Lassen Volcanic National Park). Turn left (north) on Highway 89 and drive about 12 miles to the campground entrance on the left side of the road. Turn left and drive a short distance to the campground.

Contact: Lassen National Forest, Hat Creek

Ranger District, 530/336-5521, fax 530/336-5758.

46 CRATER LAKE

Rating: 8

In Lassen National Forest.
Map 3.3, page 186

This camp is set near Crater Lake at 6,800 feet in remote Lassen National Forest, just below Crater Mountain (that's it up there to the northeast at 7,420 feet). This primitive hideaway provides fishing, boating, and, if you can stand the ice-cold water, a quick dunk on warm summer days.

Campsites, facilities: There are 17 sites for tents. Picnic tables and fire grills are provided. Drinking water (from a well) and vault toilets are available. Leashed pets are permitted.

Reservations, fees: Reservations are not accepted. The fee is $12 per night. Senior discount available. Open June through October.

Directions: From Redding, drive east on Highway 44 to the junction with Highway 89 (near the entrance to Lassen Volcanic National Park). Turn north on Highway 89 and drive to Highway 44. Turn east on Highway 44 (right) and drive to the Bogard Work Center and adjacent rest stop. Turn left at Forest Road 32N08 (signed Crater Lake) and drive one mile to a T intersection. Bear right and continue on Forest Road 32N08 for six miles (including two hairpin left turns) to the campground on the left side of the road.

Contact: Lassen National Forest, Eagle Lake Ranger District, 530/257-4188, fax 530/252-5803.

47 OLD COW MEADOWS

Rating: 7

In Latour Demonstration State Forest.
Map 3.3, page 186

Nobody finds this campground without this

book. You want quiet? You don't want to be bugged by anybody? You want piped water, too? Well, two out of three ain't bad. This tiny camp, virtually unknown, is set at 5,900 feet in a wooded area along Old Cow Creek. Recreation options include all-terrain vehicle use on existing roads and walking the dirt roads that crisscross the area.

Campsites, facilities: There are three sites for tents or RVs. Picnic tables and fire grills are provided. Pit toilets are available. No drinking water is available. Leashed pets are permitted.

Reservations, fees: Reservations are not accepted. There is no fee for camping. Open June through October.

Directions: In Redding, turn east on Highway 44 and drive about 9.5 miles to Millville Road. Turn left on Millville Road and drive a half mile to the intersection of Millville Road and Whitmore Road. Turn right on Whitmore Road and drive 13 miles, through Whitmore, until Whitmore Road becomes Tamarac Road. Continue for one mile to a fork at Bateman Road. Take the right fork on Bateman Road, drive 3.5 miles (where the road turns to gravel), and then continue 12 miles to the entrance to the campground.

Contact: Latour Demonstration State Forest, 530/225-2438, fax 530/225-2514.

48 SOUTH COW CREEK MEADOWS
🚶 🐕 5% 🚐 ⛺

Rating: 6

In Latour Demonstration State Forest.
Map 3.3, page 186

This camp is set in a pretty, wooded area next to a small meadow along South Cow Creek. It's mostly used in the fall for hunting, with off-highway-vehicle use on the surrounding roads in the summer. The camp is set at 5,600 feet. If you want to get away from it all without leaving your vehicle, this is one way to do it. The creek is a reliable water source providing you use a water filtration pump.

Campsites, facilities: There are two sites for tents or RVs. Picnic tables and fire grills are provided. Pit toilets are available. No drinking water is available. Leashed pets are permitted.

Reservations, fees: Reservations are not accepted. There is no fee for camping. Open June through October.

Directions: In Redding, turn east on Highway 44 and drive about 9.5 miles to Millville Road. Turn left on Millville Road and drive one-half mile to the intersection of Millville Road and Whitmore Road. Turn right on Whitmore Road and drive 13 miles, through Whitmore, until Whitmore Road becomes Tamarac Road. Continue for one mile to the fork at Bateman Road. Take the right fork on Bateman Road, drive 3.5 miles (where the road turns to gravel), and then continue for 11 miles to South Cow Creek Road. Turn right (east) and drive one mile to the campground.

Contact: Latour Demonstration State Forest, 530/225-2438, fax 530/225-2514.

49 NORTH BATTLE CREEK RESERVOIR
🏊 🛶 🚙 🐕 🚐 ⛺

Rating: 7

On Battle Creek Reservoir.
Map 3.3, page 186

This little-known lake is at 5,600 feet in elevation, largely surrounded by Lassen National Forest. No gas engines are permitted on the lake, making it ideal for canoes, rafts, and car-top aluminum boats equipped with electric motors. When the lake level is up in early summer, it is a pretty setting with good trout fishing.

Campsites, facilities: There are 10 sites for tents or RVs and five walk-in tent sites. Picnic tables and fire grills are provided. Drinking water and vault toilets are available. A car-top boat launch is available nearby. Leashed pets are permitted.

Reservations, fees: Reservations are not accepted. The fee is $11 per night, $3 per night per extra vehicle, $7 per night per extra RV, $1 per pet per night. Open mid-May to mid-September, weather permitting.

Directions: From Redding, drive east on Highway 44 to Viola. From Viola, continue east for 3.5 miles to Forest Road 32N17. Turn left on Forest Road 32N17 and drive five miles to Forest Road 32N31. Turn left and drive four miles to Forest Road 32N18. Turn right and drive a half mile to the reservoir and the campground on the right side of the road.

Contact: PG&E Land Projects, 916/386-5164, website: www.pge.com/recreation.

50 BIG PINE CAMP

Rating: 7

On Hat Creek in Lassen National Forest.

Map 3.3, page 186

This campground is set on the headwaters of Hat Creek, a pretty spot amid ponderosa pines. A dirt road out of camp parallels Hat Creek, providing access for trout fishing. A great vista point is set on the highway, a mile south of the campground entrance road. It is only a 10-minute drive south to the Highway 44 entrance station for Lassen Volcanic National Park.

Campsites, facilities: There are 19 sites for tents or RVs up to 22 feet long. Picnic tables and fire grills are provided. Drinking water (at two hand pumps) and vault toilets are available. An RV dump station, grocery store, and propane gas are available nearby. Leashed pets are permitted.

Reservations, fees: Reservations are not accepted. The fee is $10 per night, $5 for each extra vehicle. Senior discount available. Open May to October, weather permitting.

Directions: From Redding, drive east on Highway 44 to the junction with Highway 89 (near the entrance to Lassen Volcanic National Park). Turn left (north) on Highway 89 and drive about eight miles (one mile past the vista point) to the campground entrance on the right side of the road. Turn right and drive a half mile to the campground.

Contact: Lassen National Forest, Hat Creek Ranger District, 530/336-5521, fax 530/336-5758.

51 BUTTE CREEK

Rating: 6

In Lassen National Forest.

Map 3.3, page 186

This primitive, little-known spot is just three miles from the northern boundary of Lassen Volcanic National Park, set on little Butte Creek. It is a four-mile drive south out of camp on Forest Road 18 to Butte Lake in Lassen Park and to the trailhead for a great hike up to the Cinder Cone (6,907 feet), with dramatic views of the Lassen wilderness.

Campsites, facilities: There are 10 unimproved sites for tents or RVs up to 22 feet long. Vault toilets are available. No drinking water is available. Garbage must be packed out. Leashed pets are permitted.

Reservations, fees: Reservations are not accepted. There is no fee for camping. Open May through October.

Directions: From Redding, drive east on Highway 44 to the junction with Highway 89 (near the entrance to Lassen Volcanic National Park). Turn north on Highway 89 and drive to Highway 44. Turn east (right) on Highway 44 and drive 11 miles to Forest Road 18. Turn right at Forest Road 18 and drive three miles to the campground on the left side of the road.

Contact: Lassen National Forest, Eagle Lake Ranger District, 530/257-4188, fax 530/252-5803.

52 BOGARD

Rating: 6

In Lassen National Forest.

Map 3.3, page 186

This little camp is set along Pine Creek, which flows through Pine Creek Valley at the foot of the Bogard Buttes. It is a relatively obscure camp that gets missed by many travelers. To the nearby west is a network of Forest Service roads, and beyond is the Caribou Wilderness.

Campsites, facilities: There are 13 sites for tents or RVs up to 28 feet long. Picnic tables and fire grills are provided. Drinking water and vault toilets are available. Leashed pets are permitted.

Reservations, fees: Reservations are not accepted. The fee is $10 per night. Senior discount available. Open May through September.

Directions: From Redding, drive east on Highway 44 to the junction with Highway 89 (near the entrance to Lassen Volcanic National Park). Turn north on Highway 89 and drive to Highway 44. Turn east on Highway 44 and drive to the Bogard Work Center (about seven miles past Poison Lake) and the adjacent rest stop. Continue east on Highway 44 for two miles to a gravel road on the right side of the road (Forest Road 31N26). Turn right on Forest Road 31N26 and drive two miles. Turn right on Forest Road 31N21 and drive a half mile to the campground at the end of the road.

Contact: Lassen National Forest, Eagle Lake Ranger District, 530/257-4188, fax 530/252-5803.

53 MT. LASSEN KOA

Rating: 6

Near Lassen Volcanic National Park.

Map 3.3, page 186

This popular KOA camp is 14 miles from the entrance of Lassen Volcanic National Park and has pretty, wooded sites. Location is always the critical factor on vacations, and this park is set up perfectly for launching trips to the nearby east. Hat Creek provides trout fishing along Highway 89, and just inside the Highway 44 entrance station at Lassen Park is Manzanita Lake, providing good fishing and hiking.

Campsites, facilities: There are 45 sites for tents or RVs, including some drive-through sites, with full or partial hookups, and five cabins. Picnic tables and fire grills are provided. Flush toilets, hot showers, playground, heated pool

(summer only), an RV dump station, groceries, ice, wood, coin laundry, video arcade and rec room, and propane gas are available. Leashed pets are permitted.

Reservations, fees: Reservations are accepted with a deposit at 800/562-3403. The fee is $20–33 per night, $2 per person for more than two people. Major credit cards accepted. Open year-round.

Directions: From Redding, turn east on Highway 44 and drive to Shingletown. In Shingletown, continue east for four miles and look for the park entrance on the right (signed KOA).

Contact: Mt. Lassen KOA, 530/474-3133, website: www.koa.com.

54 MACUMBER RESERVOIR

Rating: 7

On Macumber Reservoir.

Map 3.3, page 186

Here's a small lake, easy to reach from Redding, that is little known and rarely visited. Macumber Reservoir is set at 3,500 feet and is stocked with 6,000 rainbow trout each year, providing fair fishing. No gas motors are permitted here. That's fine—it guarantees quiet, calm water, ideal for car-top boats: prams, canoes, rafts, and small aluminum boats.

Campsites, facilities: There are seven sites for tents or RVs and five walk-in sites. Picnic tables and fire grills are provided. Drinking water and vault toilets are available. Leashed pets are permitted.

Reservations, fees: Reservations are not accepted. The fee is $13 per night, $3 per night for extra vehicles, $7 per night for extra RV, $1 per pet per night. Open mid-May to mid-September, weather permitting.

Directions: In Redding, turn east on Highway 44 and drive toward Viola to Lake Macumber Road (if you reach Viola, you have gone four miles too far). Turn left at Lake Macumber Road and drive two miles to the reservoir and campground.

Contact: PG&E Land Projects, 916/386-5164, fax 916/923-7044, website: www.pge.com/recreation.

55 MILL CREEK PARK

Rating: 7

Near Shingletown.

Map 3.3, page 186

Mill Creek Park is a year-round park set up primarily for RVs, yet it has sites for tents as well as cabins. It is set amid conifers on the western slopes of Mt. Lassen. A creek and pond for fishing are a plus. Its proximity to Lassen Volcanic National Park is a key attraction. The elevation is 4,000 feet. Note that adjacent to the park is a mobile home park with 10 sites for permanent residents.

Campsites, facilities: There are 16 sites with full or partial hookups for RVs, seven sites for tents, and four cabins. Picnic tables and fire rings are provided. Restrooms, drinking water, flush toilets, and showers are available. A coin laundry and RV dump station are on-site. Leashed pets are permitted.

Reservations, fees: Reservations are accepted. The fee is $14–18 per night. Monthly rates available. Major credit cards accepted. Open year-round.

Directions: From Redding, drive east on Highway 44 to Shingletown. Continue east on Highway 44 for two miles to the park on the right.

Contact: Mill Creek Park, 530/474-5384, fax 530/474-1236, website: www.MillCreekrv Park.org.

56 MANZANITA LAKE

Rating: 9

In Lassen Volcanic National Park.

Map 3.3, page 186

Manzanita Lake, set at 5,890 feet, is one of the prettiest lakes in Lassen Volcanic National Park and it has good catch-and-release trout

fishing for experienced fly fishers in prams and other nonpowered boats. This is no place for a dad, mom, and a youngster to fish from shore with Power Bait. Because of the great natural beauty of the lake, the campground is often crowded. Evening walks around the lake are beautiful. A museum, visitor center, and small store are available nearby. Ranger programs are offered in the summer.

Campsites, facilities: There are 179 sites for tents or RVs up to 35 feet long. Picnic tables, fire grills, and bearproof food lockers are provided. Drinking water and flush toilets are available. Propane gas, groceries, showers, an RV dump station, and a coin laundry are available nearby. A boat launch is also nearby (no motors are permitted on boats at Manzanita Lake). Some facilities are wheelchair-accessible. Leashed pets are permitted at campsites only.

Reservations, fees: Reservations are not accepted. The fee is $14 per night, $10 per vehicle park entrance fee. Major credit cards accepted. Open late May to late September, weather permitting (during the fall season, it's open without drinking water until the camp is closed by snow).

Directions: From Redding, drive east on Highway 44 to the junction with Highway 89. Turn right (south) on Highway 89 and drive one mile to the entrance station to Lassen Volcanic National Park (the state highway becomes Lassen Park Highway/Main Park Road). Continue a short distance on Lassen Park Highway/Main Park Road to the campground entrance road. Turn right and drive a half mile to the campground.

Contact: Lassen Volcanic National Park, 530/595-4444, fax 530/595-3262.

57 CRAGS

Rating: 8

In Lassen Volcanic National Park.

Map 3.3, page 186

Crags is sometimes overlooked as a prime spot

at Lassen Volcanic National Park because there is no lake nearby. No problem, because even though this campground is small compared to the giant complex at Manzanita Lake, the campsites are more spacious, do not fill up as quickly, and many are backed by forest. In addition, the Emigrant Trail runs out of camp, routing east and meeting pretty Lost Creek after a little more than a mile, a great short hike. Directly across from Crags are the towering Chaos Crags, topping out at 8,503 feet. The elevation here is 5,720 feet. Crags reopened in 2003 after being closed for one year for the removal of dead trees.

Campsites, facilities: There are 45 sites for tents or RVs up to 35 feet long. Picnic tables, fire rings, and bearproof food lockers are provided. Drinking water and vault toilets are available. Leashed pets are permitted in campground and on paved roads only.

Reservations, fees: Reservations are not accepted. The fee is $8 per night, $10 per vehicle park entrance fee. Senior discount available. Open late June to early September.

Directions: From Redding, drive east on Highway 44 for 42 miles to the junction with Highway 89. Turn right and drive one mile to the entrance station at Lassen Volcanic National Park (the state highway becomes Lassen Park Highway/Main Park Road). Continue on Lassen Park Highway/Main Park Road for about five miles to the campground on the left side of the road.

Contact: Lassen Volcanic National Park, 530/595-4444, fax 530/595-3262.

58 SUMMIT LAKE, NORTH AND SOUTH

Rating: 9

In Lassen Volcanic National Park.

Map 3.3, page 186

Summit Lake is a beautiful spot where deer often visit each evening on the adjacent meadow just east of the campground. The lake is

small, and since trout plants were suspended, it has been just about fished out. Evening walks around the lake are perfect for families. A more ambitious trail is routed out of camp and leads past lavish wildflower displays in early summer to a series of wilderness lakes. The campgrounds are set at an elevation of 6,695 feet.

Campsites, facilities: There are 94 sites for tents or RVs up to 35 feet long (only at North Summit). Picnic tables, fire rings, and bearproof food lockers are provided. Drinking water and toilets (flush toilets on the north side, vault toilets on the south side) are available. Some facilities are wheelchair-accessible. Ranger programs are available in summer. Leashed pets are permitted at campsites only.

Reservations, fees: Reservations are not accepted. The fee is $12 (South) to $14 (North) per night, $10 per vehicle park entrance fee. Major credit cards accepted. Senior discount available. Open late June to mid-September, weather permitting.

Directions: From Redding, drive east on Highway 44 to the junction with Highway 89. Turn south on Highway 89 and drive one mile to the entrance station to Lassen Volcanic National Park (where the state highway becomes Lassen Park Highway/Main Park Road). Continue on Lassen Park Highway/Main Park Road for 12 miles to the campground entrance on the left side of the road.

Contact: Lassen Volcanic National Park, 530/595-4444, fax 530/595-3262.

59 BUTTE LAKE

Rating: 9

In Lassen Volcanic National Park.

Map 3.3, page 186

Butte Lake campground is situated in an open, volcanic setting with a sprinkling of lodgepole pine. The contrast of the volcanics against the emerald greens of the lake is beautiful and memorable. The Cinder Cone Trail can provide an even better look. The trailhead is near the boat launch area, and it's a strenuous hike involving a climb of 800 feet over the course of two miles to the top of the Cinder Cone. The footing is often loose because of volcanic pebbles. At the rim, you can peer inside the Cinder Cone, as well as be rewarded with lake views and a long-distance vista. Trout fishing is poor at Butte Lake, as at nearly all the lakes at this national park, because trout have not been planted for years. The elevation is 6,100 feet.

Campsites, facilities: There are 42 sites for tents or RVs up to 35 feet long. No hookups. Picnic tables, fire rings, and bearproof food lockers are provided. Drinking water and flush and vault toilets are available. A boat ramp is nearby. Leashed pets are permitted at campsites only. No motors are permitted on the lake.

Reservations, fees: Reservations are not accepted. The fee is $12 per night, $10 per vehicle park entrance fee. Senior discount available. Open late May to late September, weather permitting.

Directions: From Redding, drive east on Highway 44 to the junction with Highway 89. Bear north on Highway 89/44 and drive 13 miles to Old Station. Just past Old Station, turn right (east) on Highway 44 and drive 10 miles to Forest Road 32N21/Butte Lake Road. Turn right and drive six miles to the campground.

Contact: Lassen Volcanic National Park, 530/595-4444, fax 530/595-3262.

60 SOUTHWEST WALK-IN

Rating: 8

In Lassen Volcanic National Park.

Map 3.3, page 186

Just taking the short walk required to reach this camp will launch you into an orbit beyond most of the highway cruisers visiting Lassen. In addition, the nearby trail to Bumpass Hell will put you into a different universe. The trail is about five miles north of the campground on the Lassen Park Highway/Main Park Road on the right side of the road. The route will

take you past steam vents and boiling mud pots, all set in prehistoric-looking volcanic rock. The elevation at the campground is 6,700 feet.

Campsites, facilities: There are 21 walk-in tent sites, and a large parking lot available for RVs. Picnic tables, fire pits, and bearproof food lockers are provided. Drinking water and flush toilets are available in summer. Ranger-led programs are available in summer. Leashed pets are permitted in campground only.

Reservations, fees: Reservations are not accepted. The fee is $12 per night for tent campers, $8 per night for RV parking, plus $10 per vehicle park entrance fee. Senior discount available. Open year-round, weather permitting.

Directions: From Red Bluff, take Highway 36 east for 48 miles to the junction with Highway 89. Turn left on Highway 89 (becomes Lassen Park Highway/Main Park Road) and drive to the park's entrance. Just after passing through the park entrance gate, look for the camp parking area on the right side of the road.

Contact: Lassen Volcanic National Park, 530/595-4444, fax 530/595-3262.

61 WARNER VALLEY

Rating: 10

On Hot Springs Creek in Lassen Volcanic National Park.

Map 3.3, page 186

Lassen is one of the great national parks of the West, yet it gets surprisingly little use compared to Yosemite, Sequoia, and Kings Canyon National Parks. This campground gets overlooked because of its remote access out of Chester. The camp is set along Hot Springs Creek at 5,650 feet. The best hike here is the 2.5-mile walk out to the unique Devil's Kitchen Geothermal Area. Another option here is a another 2.5-mile hike, this one with an 800-foot climb to Drake Lake. It's also a good horseback riding area. The Drakesbad Resort, where reservations are about as difficult to get as finding Bigfoot, is near the campground. The only chance is to sign up on a cancellation list, and then spend years waiting for the call.

Campsites, facilities: There are 18 tent sites. RVs and trailers are not recommended because of road conditions. Picnic tables, food lockers, and fire rings are provided. Drinking water and vault toilets are available. Leashed pets are permitted in the campground only.

Reservations, fees: Reservations are not accepted. The fee is $12 per night, $10 per vehicle park entrance fee. Senior discount available. Open June to late October, weather permitting, with no water from mid-September to snow closure.

Directions: From Red Bluff, take Highway 36 east for 44 miles to the junction with Highway 89 (do not turn left, or north, on Highway 89 to Lassen Volcanic National Park entrance, as signed). Continue east on Highway 36/89 to Chester and Feather River Drive. Turn left (north) on Feather River Drive (Warner Valley Road) and drive three-quarters of a mile to County Road 312. Bear left and drive six miles to Warner Valley Road. Turn right and drive 11 miles to the campground on the right. Note: the last 3.5 miles is unpaved and there is one steep hill that can be difficult to climb for large or underpowered RVs, or if you are towing a trailer).

Contact: Lassen Volcanic National Park, 530/595-4444, fax 530/595-3262.

62 JUNIPER LAKE
🏃 🛖 ⛺

Rating:10

In Lassen Volcanic National Park.
Map 3.3, page 186

This pretty spot is on the eastern shore of Juniper Lake, at an elevation of 6,792 feet. It is far distant from the busy Lassen Park Highway/Main Park Road (Highway 89) corridor that is routed through central Lassen Volcanic National Park. From the north end of the lake, a great side trip is to make the half-mile, 400-foot climb to Inspiration Point, which provides

a panoramic view of the park's backcountry. Since no drinking water is provided, it is critical to bring a water purification pump or plenty of bottled water.

Campsites, facilities: There are 18 sites. Fire rings and bearproof food lockers are provided. Vault toilets are available. Drinking water is not available. Leashed pets are permitted in the campground only.

Reservations, fees: Reservations are not accepted. The fee is $10 per night, $10 per vehicle park entrance fee. Senior discount available. Open late June to early October.

Directions: From Red Bluff, take Highway 36 east for 44 miles to the junction with Highway 89 (do not turn left, or north, on Highway 89 to Lassen Volcanic National Park entrance, as signed). Continue east on Highway 36/89 to Chester and Feather River Drive. Turn left (north) on Feather River Drive and drive three-quarters of a mile to the Y and the junction for County Road 318. Bear right (marked for Juniper Lake) on County Road 318 and drive 11 miles to the campground on the right, set along the east side of the lake. Note: this is a very rough dirt road; RVs and trailers are not recommended.

Contact: Lassen Volcanic National Park, 530/595-4444, fax 530/595-3262.

63 ROCKY KNOLL
🏃 ≈ 🎣 🛖 🐾 🚐 ⛺

Rating: 7

On Silver Lake in Lassen National Forest.
Map 3.3, page 186

This is one of two camps at pretty Silver Lake, set at 6,400 feet elevation at the edge of the Caribou Wilderness. The other camp is Silver Bowl to the nearby north, which is larger and provides better access for hikers. This camp, however, is closer to the boat ramp, which is set at the south end of the lake. Silver Lake provides a good summer fishery for campers.

Campsites, facilities: There are seven tent sites and 11 sites for RVs up to 27 feet long. Picnic tables and fire grills are provided. Drinking water and vault toilets are available. Leashed pets are permitted.

Reservations, fees: Reservations are not accepted. The fee is $11 per night. Senior discount available. Open late May through October, weather permitting.

Directions: From Red Bluff, drive east on Highway 36 to the junction with Highway 89. Continue east on Highway 89/36 past Lake Almanor to Westwood. In Westwood, turn left on County Road A21 and drive 12.5 miles to Silver Lake Road. Turn left (west) on Silver Lake Road/County Road 110 and drive 8.5 miles north to Silver Lake. At Silver Lake, turn left and drive a short distance to the campground.

Contact: Lassen National Forest, Almanor Ranger District, 530/258-2141, fax 530/258-5194.

64 SILVER BOWL

Rating: 7

On Silver Lake in Lassen National Forest.
Map 3.3, page 186

Silver Lake is a pretty lake set at 6,400 feet elevation at the edge of the Caribou Wilderness. There is an unimproved boat ramp at the southern end of the lake. It is occasionally planted by the Department of Fish and Game with Eagle Lake trout and brown trout, which provides a summer fishery for campers. A trailhead from adjacent Caribou Lake is routed west into the wilderness, with routes available both to Emerald Lake to the northwest, and Betty, Trail, and Shotoverin Lakes nearby to the southeast.

Campsites, facilities: There are 18 sites for tents or RVs. Picnic tables and fire grills are provided. Drinking water and vault toilets are available. Leashed pets are permitted.

Reservations, fees: Reservations are not accepted. The fee is $11 per night. Senior discount available. Open late May through October, weather permitting.

Directions: From Red Bluff, drive east on Highway 36 to the junction with Highway 89. Continue east on Highway 89/36 past Lake Almanor to Westwood. In Westwood, turn left on County Road A21 and drive 12.5 miles to Silver Lake Road. Turn left on Silver Lake Road/County Road 110 and drive 8.5 miles north to Silver Lake. At Silver Lake, turn right and drive a short distance to the campground.

Contact: Lassen National Forest, Almanor Ranger District, 530/258-2141, fax 530/258-5194.

65 BATTLE CREEK

Rating: 7

On Battle Creek in Lassen National Forest.
Map 3.3, page 186

This pretty spot offers easy access and streamside camping along Battle Creek. The trout fishing can be good in May, June, and early July, when the creek is stocked by the Department of Fish and Game, which plants 23,000 rainbow trout and 2,000 smaller brook trout. Many people drive right by without knowing there is a stream here and that the fishing can be good. The elevation is 4,800 feet.

Campsites, facilities: There are 12 tent sites and 38 sites for tents or RVs. Picnic tables and fire grills are provided. Drinking water, flush and vault toilets, and a day-use picnic area are available. Supplies can be obtained in the town of Mineral. Leashed pets are permitted.

Reservations, fees: Reservations are not accepted. The fee is $14 per night. Senior discount available. Open late April through October, weather permitting.

Directions: From Red Bluff, turn east on Highway 36 and drive 39 miles to the campground (if you reach Mineral, you have gone two miles too far).

Contact: Lassen National Forest, Almanor Ranger District, 530/258-2141, fax 530/258-5194.

66 HOLE-IN-THE-GROUND
🏃 🛶 🐕 🚐 ⛰

Rating: 8

On Mill Creek in Lassen National Forest.
Map 3.3, page 186

This is one of two campgrounds set along Mill Creek at 4,300 feet. Take your pick. The highlight here is a trail that follows along Mill Creek for many miles; it provides good fishing access. Rules mandate the use of artificials with a single barbless hook, and catch-and-release. The result is a challenging but quality wild trout fishery. Another option is to drive two more miles to the end of the Forest Service road, where there is a parking area for a trail that is routed downstream along Mill Creek and into a state game refuge. To keep things easy, obtain a map of Lassen National Forest that details the recreational opportunities.

Campsites, facilities: There are four tent sites and nine sites for tents or RVs. Picnic tables and fire grills are provided. Drinking water and vault toilets are available. Supplies are available in Mineral. Leashed pets are permitted.

Reservations, fees: Reservations are not accepted. The fee is $11 per night. Senior discount available. Open late April through October, weather permitting.

Directions: From Red Bluff, drive 43 miles east on Highway 36 to the town of Mineral and the junction with Highway 172. Turn right on Highway 172 and drive six miles to the town of Mill Creek. In Mill Creek, turn south onto a Forest Service road (signed) and drive five miles to the campground access road. Turn left and drive a quarter mile to the camp.

Contact: Lassen National Forest, Almanor Ranger District, 530/258-2141, fax 530/258-5194.

67 MILL CREEK RESORT
🏃 🛶 🐕 ♿ 🚐 ⛰

Rating: 7

On Mill Creek near Lassen National Forest.
Map 3.3, page 186

This is a great spot, surrounded by Lassen National Forest and within close range of the southern Highway 89 entrance to Lassen Volcanic National Park. It is set at 4,800 feet along oft-bypassed Highway 172. A highlight here is Mill Creek (to reach it, turn south on the Forest Service road in town and drive to a parking area at the end of the road along the stream), where there is a great easy walk along the stream and fair trout fishing.

Campsites, facilities: There are 16 sites for tents or RVs up to 22 feet long, eight with full hookups. About half are taken by long-term rentals. Nine one- and two-bedroom cabins are also available. Picnic tables and fire rings are provided. Drinking water and vault toilets are available. Showers, coin laundry, small grocery store, and a café are also available. Some facilities are wheelchair-accessible. Leashed pets are permitted.

Reservations, fees: Reservations are accepted. The fee is $12–20 per night. Campsites are open May through October. Cabins are available year-round.

Directions: From Red Bluff, drive 43 miles east on Highway 36 to the town of Mineral and the junction with Highway 172. Turn right and drive six miles to the town of Mill Creek. In Mill Creek, look for the sign for Mill Creek Resort on the right side of the road.

Contact: Mill Creek Resort, 888/595-4449 or 530/595-4449, website: www.millcreekresort.net.

68 CHILDS MEADOW RESORT
🏃 🛶 🐕 🚐 ⛰

Rating: 8

Near Mill Creek.
Map 3.3, page 186

Childs Meadow Resort is an 18-acre resort set

at 5,000 feet elevation. It features many recreation options, including catch-and-release fishing one mile away at Mill Creek. There are also a number of trails nearby for horseback riding. The trailhead for the Spencer Meadow Trail is just east of the resort along Highway 36. The trail provides a 12-mile route (one-way) to Spencer Meadow and an effervescent spring that is the source of Mill Creek.

Campsites, facilities: There are 26 sites, 12 drive-through sites with full hookups for RVs, and 14 sites for tents, with facilities available for groups. Picnic tables and fire rings are provided. Restrooms, drinking water, flush toilets, and showers are available. A coin laundry, store, restaurant, group picnic area, meeting room, and horseshoes are on-site. Leashed pets are permitted.

Reservations, fees: Reservations are accepted. The fee is $15–20 per night. Major credit cards accepted. Open mid-May through October, weather permitting.

Directions: From Red Bluff, drive east on Highway 36 for 43 miles to the town of Mineral. Continue east on Highway 36 for 10 miles to the resort on the left.

Contact: Childs Meadow Resort, 530/595-3383, website: www.ChildsMeadowResort.com.

69 GURNSEY CREEK GROUP CAMP

Rating: 7

In Lassen National Forest.
Map 3.3, page 186
This group camp is an ideal spot for a Scout troop. (For more information, see the entry for the adjacent Gurnsey Creek.)

Campsites, facilities: This group campground can accommodate up to 100 people, with 20 sites for tents or RVs. Picnic tables and fire grills are provided. Drinking water and vault toilets are available. A large community fireplace is centrally located for group use. Supplies are available in Mineral or Chester. Leashed pets are permitted.

Reservations, fees: Reservations are required. The fee is $112 per night for sites 31–37, $224 for sites 38–51, and $336 for sites 31–51, with a 50 percent deposit and two-night minimum stay required. Reserve at 877/444-6777 ($9 reservation fee) or website: www.ReserveUsa.com. The deposit is refundable if cancellation notice is given 10 days before the reservation date. Open May through October, weather permitting.

Directions: From Red Bluff, drive east on Highway 36 for 55 miles (five miles east of Childs Meadow). Turn left at the campground entrance road and drive a short distance to the campground.

Contact: Lassen National Forest, Almanor Ranger District, 530/258-2141, fax 530/258-5194.

70 GURNSEY CREEK

Rating: 7

In Lassen National Forest.
Map 3.3, page 186
This camp is set at 5,000 feet in Lassen National Forest, with extremely easy access off Highway 36. The camp is on the headwaters of little Gurnsey Creek, a highlight of the surrounding Lost Creek Plateau. Gurnsey Creek runs downstream and pours into Deer Creek, a good trout stream with access along narrow, winding Highway 32 to the nearby south.

Campsites, facilities: There are 30 sites for tents or RVs. Picnic tables and fire grills are provided. Drinking water and vault toilets are available. Supplies are available in Mineral. Leashed pets are permitted.

Reservations, fees: Reservations are not accepted. The fee is $12 per night. Senior discount available. Open May through October, weather permitting.

Directions: From Red Bluff, drive east on Highway 36 for 55 miles (five miles east of Childs Meadow). Turn left at the campground entrance road and drive a short distance to the campground.

Contact: Lassen National Forest, Almanor Ranger District, 530/258-2141, fax 530/258-5194.

71 WILLOW SPRINGS

Rating: 6

Near Lost Creek Spring in Lassen National Forest.

Map 3.3, page 186

This is a primitive, undeveloped camp set on the southwest flank of North Stover Mountain (6,035 feet), used primarily by hunters during the fall deer season and ignored the rest of the time. A network of Forest Service roads in the area provides vehicle access. Though there is no drinking water available, Lost Creek Spring to the east of camp and Lost Creek are viable water sources during wet years. The headwaters of Lost Creek run by the camp, flowing downstream into nearby Deer Creek to the south.

Campsites, facilities: There are 15 primitive sites for tents. Picnic tables and fire grills are provided. A vault toilet is available. Garbage must be packed out. No drinking water is available.

Reservations, fees: Reservations are not accepted. The fee is $10 per night. Senior discount available. Open late May through October, weather permitting.

Directions: From Red Bluff, drive east on Highway 36 for about 55 miles (two miles past Childs Meadows parking area) to Wilson Lake Road. Turn left on Wilson Lake Road/Forest Road 29N19 and drive 1.5 miles to Forest Road 29N19. Turn right on Forest Road 29N19 and drive about 3.5 miles to the campground on the left side of the road.

Contact: Lassen National Forest, Almanor Ranger District, 530/258-2141, fax 530/258-5194. For a map, send $6 to U.S. Forest Service, Attn: Map Sales, P.O. Box 9035, Prescott, AZ 86313, 928/443-8285 with credit card, website: www.fs.fed.us/maps/.

72 BENNER CREEK

Rating: 7

On Benner Creek in Lassen National Forest.

Map 3.3, page 186

Benner Creek is just outside the remote eastern border of Lassen Volcanic National Park and its stellar but primitive Juniper Lake Campground. If that national park camp is full, this provides a nearby option. For drivers of RVs, this camp is preferable to navigating the rough road to Juniper Lake. In the fall, the camp gets occasional use by deer hunters.

Campsites, facilities: There are nine sites for tents or RVs up to 20 feet long. Picnic tables and fire grills are provided. Vault toilets are available. No drinking water is available. Leashed pets are permitted.

Reservations, fees: Reservations are not accepted. The fee is $10 per night. Senior discount available. Open late May through October, weather permitting.

Directions: From Red Bluff, take Highway 36 east to Chester and Feather River Drive. Turn left on Feather River Drive and drive one mile to County Road 318/Juniper Lake Road (at the fork). Bear right on Juniper Lake Road and drive seven miles to Benner Creek Campground on the right.

Contact: Lassen National Forest, Almanor Ranger District, 530/258-2141, fax 530/258-5194.

73 DOMINGO SPRINGS

Rating: 7

In Lassen National Forest.

Map 3.3, page 186

This camp is named after a spring adjacent to the site. It is a small fountain that pours into the headwaters of the North Fork Feather River, a good trout stream. The Pacific Crest Trail is routed from this camp north for four miles to Little Willow Lake and the southern border of Lassen Volcanic National Park. The elevation is 5,200 feet.

Campsites, facilities: There are nine sites for tents and nine sites for tents or RVs. Picnic tables and fire grills are provided. Drinking water and vault toilets are available. Leashed pets are permitted.

Reservations, fees: Reservations are not accepted. The fee is $11 per night. Senior discount available. Open late May through October, weather permitting.

Directions: From Red Bluff, take Highway 36 east to Chester and Feather River Drive. Turn left on Feather River Drive and drive three-quarters of a mile to County Road 312. Bear left and drive five miles to the Y with County Road 311 and County Road 312. Bear left on County Road 311 and drive two miles to the campground entrance road on the left.

Contact: Lassen National Forest, Almanor Ranger District, 530/258-2141, fax 530/258-5194.

74 WARNER CREEK

Rating: 6

In Lassen National Forest.
Map 3.3, page 186

Some people find this camp by accident. They are driving to the Warner/Drakesbad entrance of Lassen Volcanic National Park and discover the small, primitive camp on the way in, always an option during crowded weekends. It is set at 5,000 feet in elevation along little Warner Creek, a tributary of the North Fork Feather River. Warner Valley is two miles to the north, and the entrance to Lassen Park is another six miles.

Campsites, facilities: There are 13 sites for tents or RVs up to 22 feet long. Picnic tables and fire grills are provided. Vault toilets are available. No drinking water is available. Leashed pets are permitted.

Reservations, fees: Reservations are not accepted. The fee is $10 per night. Senior dis-

count available. Open late May through October, weather permitting.

Directions: From Red Bluff, take Highway 36 east to Chester. In Chester, turn left on Feather River Drive and drive three-quarters of a mile to County Road 312. Bear left and drive 5.5 miles to a fork. Bear right (still on County Road 312) and drive one mile to the campground on the right.

Contact: Lassen National Forest, Almanor Ranger District, 530/258-2141, fax 530/258-5194.

75 HIGH BRIDGE

Rating: 8

On the North Fork of the Feather River in Lassen National Forest.
Map 3.3, page 186

This camp is set at an elevation of 5,200 feet, near where the South Cascades meets the North Sierra, and is ideal for many people. The result is that it is often full in July and August. The payoff includes a pretty, adjacent trout stream, the headwaters of the North Fork Feather. Trout fishing is often good here, including some rare large brown trout, a surprise considering the relatively small size of the stream. Nearby access to the Warner Valley/Drakesbad entrance of Lassen Volcanic National Park provides a must-do side trip. The area is wooded and the road dusty.

Campsites, facilities: There are 12 sites for tents or RVs. Picnic tables and fire grills are provided. Drinking water and vault toilets are available. Groceries and propane gas are available nearby. Leashed pets are permitted.

Reservations, fees: Reservations are not accepted. The fee is $11 per night. Senior discount available. Open late May through October, weather permitting.

Directions: From Red Bluff, take Highway 36 east to Chester and Feather River Drive. Turn left on Feather River Drive and drive three-quarters of a mile to County Road 312. Bear left and drive five miles to the campground entrance road on the left.

Contact: Lassen National Forest, Almanor Ranger District, 530/258-2141, fax 530/258-5194.

76 SOUTH ANTELOPE
🏃 🏕 5% ⛺

Rating: 6

Near the eastern edge of the Ishi Wilderness.
Map 3.3, page 186

This primitive campsite is for visitors who want to explore the Ishi Wilderness without an extensive drive (compared to other camps in the wilderness here). The South Fork of Antelope Creek runs west from the camp and provides an off-trail route for the ambitious. For easier hikes, trailheads along Ponderosa Way provide access into the eastern flank of the Ishi. The best nearby trail is the Lower Mill Creek Trail, with the trailhead eight miles south at Black Rock.

Campsites, facilities: There are four sites for tents only. Picnic tables and fire pits are provided. A vault toilet is available. No drinking water is available. All garbage must be packed out. Leashed pets are permitted.

Reservations, fees: Reservations are not accepted. There is no fee for camping. Open year-round, weather permitting.

Directions: From Red Bluff, drive east on Highway 36 for about 35 miles to the town of Paynes Creek and Plum Creek Road. Turn right (south) on Plum Creek Road and drive two miles to Ponderosa Way. Turn right (south) and continue for nine miles to the campground on the right. Note: the road is rough and only vehicles with high clearance are advised. No RVs or trailers are allowed.

Contact: Lassen National Forest, Almanor Ranger District, 530/258-2141, fax 530/258-5194. For a map, send $6 to U.S. Forest Service, Attn: Map Sales, P.O. Box 9035, Prescott, AZ 86313, 928/443-8285 with credit card, website: www.fs.fed.us/maps/.

77 BLACK ROCK
🏃 🏕 5% ⛺

Rating: 7

On the eastern edge of the Ishi Wilderness.
Map 3.3, page 186

This remote, primitive camp is set at the base of the huge, ancient Black Rock, one of the oldest geological points in Lassen National Forest. A bonus is that Mill Creek runs adjacent to the sites, providing a water source. This is the edge of the Ishi Wilderness, where remote hiking in solitude is possible without a wilderness permit and without venturing to high mountain elevations; a campfire permit is required for overnight use by backpackers. A trailhead is available right out of the camp. The trail here is routed downstream along Mill Creek, extending five miles into the Ishi Wilderness, downhill all the way.

Campsites, facilities: There are five tent sites. Picnic tables and fire pits are provided. A vault toilet is available. No drinking water is available. Mill Creek is adjacent to the camp and is a viable water source through early summer. Leashed pets are permitted.

Reservations, fees: Reservations are not accepted. The fee is $9 per night. Senior discount available. Open year-round, weather permitting.

Directions: From Red Bluff, drive east on Highway 36 for about 35 miles to the town of Paynes Creek and Plum Creek Road. Turn right (south) on Plum Creek Road and drive two miles to Ponderosa Way. Turn right (south) and continue for 16 miles to the campground on the right. Note: the road is rough and only vehicles with high clearance are advised. No RVs or trailers are allowed.

Contact: Lassen National Forest, Almanor Ranger District, 530/258-2141, fax 530/258-5194. For a map, send $6 to U.S. Forest Service, Attn: Map Sales, P.O. Box 9035, Prescott, AZ 86313, 928/443-8285 with credit card, website: www.fs.fed.us/maps/.

78 LAST CHANCE CREEK

Rating: 7

Near Lake Almanor.

Map 3.3, page 186

This secluded camp is set at 4,500 feet, adjacent to where Last Chance Creek empties into the north end of Lake Almanor. It is an unpublicized PG&E camp that is known primarily by locals and gets missed almost every time by out-of-towners. The adjacent lake area is a breeding ground in the spring for white pelicans, and the beauty of these birds in large flocks can be extraordinary.

Campsites, facilities: There are 12 sites for tents or RVs up to 30 feet long, and 13 group campsites. Picnic tables and fire grills are provided. Drinking water and vault toilets are available. Leashed pets are permitted.

Reservations, fees: Reservations are required for the group camp. The fee is $15 per night for individual sites, $20 for group sites, $1 per dog per night. Group sites require a two-night minimum stay and a three-night stay on holidays. Open mid-May through September, weather permitting.

Directions: From Red Bluff, take Highway 36 east to Chester and continue for two miles over the causeway (at the north end of Lake Almanor). About a quarter mile after crossing the causeway, turn left on the campground access road and drive 2.1 miles to the campground.

Contact: PG&E Land Projects, 916/386-5164, fax 916/923-7044, website: www.pge.com/recreation.

79 LASSEN VIEW RESORT

Rating: 8

At Lake Almanor east of Red Bluff.

Map 3.3, page 186

This is a classic fishing camp, designed from start to finish with fishing in mind, yet with other facilities and recreation available. It is near one of the best fishing spots on the entire lake, Big Springs, at the mouth of the Hamilton Branch. After launching a boat or renting one at Lassen View, Big Springs is just a five-minute ride, "right around the corner," as they say here. This is where salmon congregate in the spring, and big brown and rainbow trout show up in the fall to feed on the lake's huge supply of pond smelt. The camp is rustic but friendly, and the folks here can help put you on to the fish. Lake Almanor is a big, beautiful lake set at 4,600 feet, ringed by conifers, and kept full most of the year. Note that the RV sites are often completely booked for the entire summer with long-term rentals.

Campsites, facilities: There are 59 sites, including 10 drive-through sites, with full or partial hookups, including cable TV, for RVs or tents, and 13 cabins. Picnic tables and fire rings are provided. Drinking water, showers, and flush toilets are available. A small store, tackle shop, a small marina, boat rentals, boat dock, and a fish-cleaning facility are also available. A fishing guide can be hired through the store. Volleyball and horseshoes are available on-site, and a swimming area is nearby. Leashed pets are permitted.

Reservations, fees: Reservations are recommended. The fee is $22–25 per night, $3 per extra vehicle, $5 per pet per day. Long-term rentals available. Major credit cards accepted. Open May through October.

Directions: From Red Bluff, take Highway 36 east for 44 miles to the junction with Highway 89. Continue east on Highway 36/89 to Chester and drive through Chester to the junction with County Road A13. Turn right (south) and drive about four miles to the junction with Highway 147. Turn right on Highway 147 and drive.9 mile to the well-signed camp entrance on the right.

Contact: Lassen View Resort, 530/596-3437, fax 530/596-4437.

80 NORTHSHORE CAMPGROUND

Rating: 7

On Lake Almanor.

Map 3.3, page 186

This is a large, privately developed park on the northern shoreline of beautiful Lake Almanor. The park has 37 acres, with the camp set amid pine tree cover.

Campsites, facilities: There are 94 sites, including a few drive-through sites, with partial hookups for RVs up to 40 feet long, and 34 tent sites. About 35 of the RV sites are summer rentals. Picnic tables and fire rings are provided. Drinking water, showers, flush toilets, a boat ramp, and a dock are available. A playground and lending library are nearby. Leashed pets are permitted.

Reservations, fees: Reservations are accepted. The fee is $21–24 per night, $5 per person for more than two people. Monthly rentals available. Major credit cards accepted. Open April through October.

Directions: From Red Bluff, take Highway 36 east for 44 miles to the junction with Highway 89. Drive east on Highway 36/89; the camp is two miles past Chester on the right.

Contact: Northshore Campground, 530/258-3376, fax 530/258-2838, website: www.northshore campground.com.

81 ELAM

Rating: 7

On Deer Creek in Lassen National Forest.

Map 3.3, page 186

Of the campgrounds set on Deer Creek along Highway 32, Elam gets the most use. It is the first stopping point visitors arrive at while heading west on narrow, curvy Highway 32, and it has an excellent day-use picnic area available. The stream here is stocked with rainbow trout in late spring and early summer, with good access for fishing. It is a pretty area, set where

Elam Creek enters Deer Creek. A Forest Service Information Center is nearby in Chester. If the camp has too many people to suit your style, consider other more distant and primitive camps downstream on Deer Creek. The elevation here is 4,600 feet.

Campsites, facilities: There are 17 sites for tents or RVs. Picnic tables and fire grills are provided. Drinking water and vault toilets are available. Leashed pets are permitted.

Reservations, fees: Reservations are not accepted. The fee is $12 per night. Senior discount available. Open mid-April through October, weather permitting.

Directions: From Red Bluff, take Highway 36 east for 44 miles to the junction with Highway 89. Continue east on Highway 36/89 to the junction with Highway 32. Turn south on Highway 32 and drive three miles to the campground on the right side of the road. Trailers are not recommended.

Contact: Lassen National Forest, Almanor Ranger District, 530/258-2141, fax 530/258-5194.

82 ALDER

Rating: 7

On Deer Creek in Lassen National Forest.

Map 3.3, page 186

Deer Creek is a great little trout stream that runs along Highway 32. Alder is one of four camps set along Highway 32 with streamside access; this one is at 3,900 feet elevation, set near where both Alder Creek and Round Valley Creek pour into Deer Creek. The stream's best stretch of trout water is from here on upstream to Elam.

Campsites, facilities: There are five tent sites. Picnic tables and fire grills are provided. Vault toilets are available. No drinking water is available. Leashed pets are permitted.

Reservations, fees: Reservations are not accepted. The fee is $10 per night. Senior discount available. Open late March through October, weather permitting.

Directions: From Red Bluff, take Highway 36 east for 44 miles to the junction with Highway 89. Continue east on Highway 36/89 to the junction with Highway 32. Turn south on Highway 32 and drive eight miles to the campground on the right side of the road. Trailers are not recommended.

Contact: Lassen National Forest, Almanor Ranger District, 530/258-2141, fax 530/258-5194.

83 POTATO PATCH

Rating: 7

On Deer Creek in Lassen National Forest.
Map 3.3, page 186

You get good hiking and fishing at this camp. It is set beside Deer Creek at 3,400 feet elevation, with good access for trout fishing. This is a wild trout stream in this area, and the use of artificials with a single barbless hook and catch-and-release are required along much of the river; check DFG regulations. An excellent fisherman's trail is available along the river.

Campsites, facilities: There are 20 sites for tents and 12 sites for tents or RVs. Picnic tables and fire grills are provided. Drinking water and vault toilets are available. Leashed pets are permitted.

Reservations, fees: Reservations are not accepted. The fee is $12 per night. Senior discount available. Open April through October, weather permitting.

Directions: From Red Bluff, take Highway 36 east for 44 miles to the junction with Highway 89. Continue east on Highway 36/89 to the junction with Highway 32. Turn south on Highway 32 and drive 11 miles to the campground on the right side of the road. Trailers are not recommended.

Contact: Lassen National Forest, Almanor Ranger District, 530/258-2141, fax 530/258-5194.

84 BUTTE MEADOWS

Rating: 6

On Butte Creek in Lassen National Forest.
Map 3.3, page 186

On hot summer days, when a cold stream sounds even better than a cold drink, Butte Meadows provides a hideout in the national forest east of Chico. This is a summer camp situated along Butte Creek, which is stocked with 5,000 rainbow trout by the Department of Fish and Game. Nearby Doe Mill Ridge and the surrounding Lassen National Forest can provide a good side trip adventure. The camp elevation is 4,600 feet.

Campsites, facilities: There are 13 sites for tents or RVs. Fire grills and picnic tables are provided. Drinking water and vault toilets are available. Supplies are available in Butte Meadows. Leashed pets are permitted.

Reservations, fees: Reservations are not accepted. The fee is $10 per night. Senior discount available. Open late April through October, weather permitting.

Directions: From Chico, drive about 15 miles north on Highway 32 to the town of Forest Ranch. Continue on Highway 32 for another nine miles. Turn right on Humboldt Road and drive five miles to Butte Meadows.

Contact: Lassen National Forest, Almanor Ranger District, 530/258-2141, fax 530/258-5194.

85 YELLOW CREEK

Rating: 8

In Humbug Valley.
Map 3.3, page 186

Yellow Creek is one of Cal Trout's pet projects. It's a beautiful stream for fly fishers, demanding the best from skilled anglers: approaching with complete stealth, making delicate casts with long leaders and small dry flies during the evening rise. This camp is set at

4,400 feet in Humbug Valley and provides access to this stretch of water. An option is to fish Butt Creek, much easier fishing for small, planted rainbow trout, with access available along the road on the way in.

Campsites, facilities: There are 10 sites for tents or RVs. Picnic tables and fire grills are provided. Drinking water and vault toilets are available. Leashed pets are permitted.

Reservations, fees: Reservations are not accepted. The fee is $13 per night, $3 per night per extra vehicle and $7 per night per extra RV, $1 per pet per night. Open May through September.

Directions: From Oroville, drive north on Highway 70 to Belden. At Belden, turn left on Forest Road 26N26 and drive north about 11 miles to the campground entrance road on the left side of the road.

Contact: PG&E Land Projects, 916/386-5164, fax 916/923-7044, website: www.pge.com/recreation.

86 SOLDIER CREEK

Rating: 7

On Soldier Creek in Lassen National Forest.
Map 3.3, page 186

This camp is little known and primitive and is used primarily by fishermen and hunters in season. The campsites here are shaded, set in forest on the edge of meadows, and near a stream. The latter is Soldier Creek, which is stocked with trout by the Department of Fish and Game. In the fall, early storms can drive deer through this area on their annual migration to their wintering habitat in the valley, making this a decent base camp for hunters. However, no early storms often mean no deer.

Campsites, facilities: There are 15 sites for tents or RVs. Picnic tables and fire rings are provided. Vault toilets are available. No drinking water is available. Leashed pets are permitted.

Reservations, fees: Reservations are not accepted. The fee is $10 per night. Senior dis-

count available. Open late May through October, weather permitting.

Directions: From Chester, drive south on Highway 89 to Humboldt Road. Turn right on Humboldt Road and drive one mile, bear right at the fork, and continue five more miles to the intersection at Fanani Meadows. Turn right and drive one mile to the campground on the left.

Contact: Lassen National Forest, Almanor Ranger District, 530/258-2141, fax 530/258-5194.

87 CHERRY HILL

Rating: 7

On Butte Creek in Lassen National Forest.
Map 3.3, page 186

The camp is set along little Butte Creek at the foot of Cherry Hill, just downstream from the confluence of Colby Creek and Butte Creek. It is also on the western edge of the alpine zone in Lassen National Forest. A four-mile drive to the north, much of it along Colby Creek, will take visitors to the Colby Mountain Lookout at 6,002 feet for a dramatic view of the Ishi Wilderness to the west. Nearby to the south is Philbrook Reservoir.

Campsites, facilities: There are six walk-in tent sites and 19 sites for tents or RVs. Picnic tables and fire grills are provided. Drinking water and vault toilets are available. Supplies are available in the town of Butte Meadows. Leashed pets are permitted.

Reservations, fees: Reservations are not accepted. The fee is $11 per night. Senior discount available. Open May through September, weather permitting.

Directions: From Chico, drive north on Highway 32 to the junction with Humboldt Road (well past the town of Forest Ranch). Turn right and drive five miles to Butte Meadows. Continue on Humboldt Road for three miles to the campground on the right side of the road.

Contact: Lassen National Forest, Almanor Ranger District, 530/258-2141, fax 530/258-5194.

88 LAKE ALMANOR CAMPGROUND

Rating: 7

On Lake Almanor.
Map 3.3, page 186

What you get here is a series of four campgrounds along the southwest shore of Lake Almanor provided by PG&E as mitigation for its hydroelectric activities on the Feather River system. The camps are set upstream from the dam, with boat ramps available on each side of the dam. This is a pretty spot, with giant Almanor ringed by lodgepole pine and firs. The lake is usually full, or close to it, well into summer, with Mt. Lassen set in the distance to the north—bring your camera. Though it can take a day or two to find the fish, once that effort is made, fishing is good for large trout and salmon in the spring and fall and for smallmouth bass in the summer.

Campsites, facilities: There are 131 sites for tents or RVs up to 30 feet long. Picnic tables and fire grills are provided. Drinking water, vault toilets, and a RV dump station are available. Leashed pets are permitted.

Reservations, fees: Reservations are not accepted. The fee is $15 per night, $3 per night per extra vehicle, $7 per night per extra RV, $1 per pet per night. Open May through September.

Directions: From Red Bluff, take Highway 36 east for 44 miles to the junction with Highway 89. Continue east on Highway 36/89 to Lake Almanor and the next junction with Highway 89 (two miles before reaching Chester). Turn right on Highway 89 and drive eight miles to the southwest end of Lake Almanor. Turn left at your choice of four campground entrances.

Contact: PG&E Land Projects, 916/386-5164, fax 916/923-7044, website: www.pge.com/recreation.

89 ALMANOR NORTH AND SOUTH

Rating: 8

On Lake Almanor in Lassen National Forest.
Map 3.3, page 186

This is one of Lake Almanor's best-known and most popular Forest Service campgrounds. It is set along the western shore of beautiful Almanor at 4,519 feet elevation, directly across from the beautiful Almanor Peninsula. There is an excellent view of Mt. Lassen to the north, along with gorgeous sunrises. A 10-mile recreation trail runs right through the campground and is excellent for biking or hiking. This section of the lake provides good fishing for smallmouth bass in the summer, best using live crickets for bait. There are two linked campgrounds, named North and South.

Campsites, facilities: There are 101 sites for tents and RVs, including 15 sites for tents only, and a group camp for up to 100 people or 20 RVs. Picnic tables and fire grills are provided. Drinking water and vault and pit toilets are available. A boat ramp and beach area is available nearby. Some facilities are wheelchair-accessible. Leashed pets are permitted.

Reservations, fees: Reservations are accepted with a $9 reservation fee for some sites at 877/444-6777 or website www.ReserveUsa.com. The other sites are available on a first-come, first-served basis. The fee is $15 per night. Senior discount available. Reservations are required for the group camp, $88 per night. Open May through October, weather permitting.

Directions: From Red Bluff, take Highway 36 east for 44 miles to the junction with Highway 89. Continue east on Highway 36/89 to Lake Almanor and the next junction with Highway 89 (two miles before reaching Chester). Turn right on Highway 89 and drive six miles to County Road 310. Turn left on County Road 310 and drive one mile to the campground.

Contact: Lassen National Forest, Almanor Ranger District, 530/258-2141, fax 530/258-5194.

90 PONDEROSA FLAT
🏊 🎣 🚤 🐕 🚐 ⛺

Rating: 7

On Butt Lake.

Map 3.3, page 186

This camp is set at the north end of Butt Lake, the little brother to nearby Lake Almanor. It is a fairly popular camp, with the boat ramp a prime attraction, allowing campers/anglers a lakeside spot with easy access. Technically, Butt is the "afterbay" for Almanor, fed by a four-mile-long pipe with water from Almanor. What occurs is that pond smelt from Almanor get ground up in the Butt Lake powerhouse, providing a huge amount of feed for trout at the head of the lake; that's why the trout often get huge at Butt Lake. The one downer here is that lake drawdowns are common, exposing tree stumps.

Campsites, facilities: There are 63 sites for tents or RVs. Picnic tables and fire grills are provided. Drinking water, vault toilets, and a boat ramp are available. Leashed pets are permitted.

Reservations, fees: Reservations are not accepted. The fee is $15 per night, $3 per extra vehicle per night, $7 per extra RV per night, $1 per pet per night. Open May through October, weather permitting.

Directions: From Red Bluff, take Highway 36 east for 44 miles to the junction with Highway 89. Continue east on Highway 36/89 to Lake Almanor and the next junction with Highway 89 (two miles before reaching Chester). Turn right on Highway 89 and drive about seven miles to Butt Valley Road. Turn right on Butt Valley Road and drive 3.2 miles to the campground on the right side of the road.

Contact: PG&E Land Projects, 916/386-5164, fax 916/923-7044, website: www.pge.com/recreation.

91 COOL SPRINGS
🏊 🎣 🚤 🐕 🚐 ⛺

Rating: 7

On Butt Lake.

Map 3.3, page 186

One of two camps at Butt Lake, Cool Springs is set about midway down the lake on its eastern shore, 2.5 miles south of Ponderosa Flat. Cool Springs Creek enters the lake near the camp. (For more information about Butt Lake, see the entry for Ponderosa Flat.)

Campsites, facilities: There are 25 sites for tents or RVs, and five walk-in sites. Picnic tables and fire grills are provided. Drinking water, vault toilets, and a boat ramp are available. Leashed pets are permitted.

Reservations, fees: Reservations are not accepted. The fee is $15 per night, $3 per extra vehicle per night, $7 per extra RV per night, $1 per pet per night. Open May through October, weather permitting.

Directions: From Red Bluff, take Highway 36 east for 44 miles to the junction with Highway 89. Continue east on Highway 36/89 to Lake Almanor and the next junction with Highway 89 (two miles before reaching Chester). Turn right on Highway 89 and drive about seven miles to Butt Valley Road. Turn right on Butt Valley Road and drive 5.7 miles to the campground on the right side of the road.

Contact: PG&E Land Projects, 916/386-5164, fax 916/923-7044, website: www.pge.com/recreation.

92 WEST BRANCH
🎣 🐕 🚐 ⛺

Rating: 6

On the Feather River in Lassen National Forest.

Map 3.3, page 186

This is a small and remote campground set on the West Branch Feather River, 5,000 feet elevation, just upstream from where Philbrook Creek joins the Feather. It is set on the western edge of Lassen National Forest, with a network of backcountry roads in the area. Nearby destinations include Spring Valley Lake, Snag Lake, and Snow Mountain; several roads are accessible only to four-wheel-drive vehicles. Because of its proximity to Philbrook Reservoir, two miles to the east, this camp is often overlooked.

Campsites, facilities: There are eight sites for tents and seven sites for tents or RVs. Picnic tables and fire grills are provided. Drinking water and vault toilets are available. Leashed pets are permitted.

Reservations, fees: Reservations are not accepted. The fee is $10 per night. Senior discount available. Open late May through October, weather permitting.

Directions: At Orland on I-5, take the Highway 32/Chico exit and drive to Chico and the junction with Highway 99. Turn south on Highway 99 and drive to Skyway Road/Paradise (in south Chico). Turn east on Skyway Road and drive through Paradise and continue for 27 miles to Humbug Summit Road. Turn right and drive two miles to Philbrook Road and the campground access road on the right. Turn right and drive a half mile to the campground.

Contact: Lassen National Forest, Almanor Ranger District, 530/258-2141, fax 530/258-5194.

93 PHILBROOK RESERVOIR
Rating: 7

In Lassen National Forest.
Map 3.3, page 186

Philbrook Reservoir is set at 5,600 feet on the western mountain slopes above Chico, on the southwest edge of Lassen National Forest. It is a pretty lake, though subject to late-season drawdowns, with a scenic lookout a short distance from camp. The lake is loaded with small trout—a dink here, a dink there, a dink everywhere.

Campsites, facilities: There are 20 sites for tents

or RVs up to 30 feet long. Picnic tables and fire grills are provided. Drinking water and vault toilets are available. Trailer and car-top boat launches are available. Leashed pets are permitted.

Reservations, fees: Reservations are not accepted. The fee is $15 per night, $3 per night for extra vehicle, $7 per night for extra RV, $1 per pet per night. Open May through September.

Directions: At Orland on I-5, take the Highway 32/Chico exit and drive to Chico and the junction with Highway 99. Turn south on Highway 99 and drive to Skyway Road/Paradise (in south Chico). Turn east on Skyway Road, drive through Paradise, and continue for 27 miles to Humbug Summit Road. Turn right and drive two miles to Philbrook Road. Turn right and drive 3.1 miles to the campground entrance road. Turn right and drive one-half mile to the campground.

Contact: PG&E Land Projects, 916/386-5164, fax 916/923-7044, website: www.pge.com/recreation.

94 QUEEN LILY
Rating: 7

On the North Fork of the Feather River in Plumas National Forest.
Map 3.3, page 186

The North Fork Feather River is a prime destination for camping and trout fishing, especially for families. This is one of three camps along the river on Caribou Road. This stretch of river is well stocked. Insider's note: the first 150 yards of river below the dam at Caribou typically have large but elusive trout.

Campsites, facilities: There are 12 sites for tents or RVs up to 26 feet long. Picnic tables and fire grills are provided. Drinking water and vault toilets are available. A grocery store and coin laundry are available within three miles. Leashed pets are permitted.

Reservations, fees: Reservations are not accepted. The fee is $14 per night. Senior discount available. Open May through September.

Directions: From Oroville, drive north on Highway 70 to Caribou Road (two miles past Belden). Turn left on Caribou Road and drive about three miles to the campground on the left side of the road.

Contact: Northwest Park Management, 530/283-5559, fax 530/283-0159; Plumas National Forest, Mt. Hough Ranger District, 530/283-0555, fax 530/283-1821.

95 NORTH FORK

Rating: 7

On the North Fork of the Feather River in Plumas National Forest.

Map 3.3, page 186

This camp is between Queen Lily to the nearby north and Gansner Bar camp to the nearby south, all three set on the North Fork Feather River. The elevation is 2,600 feet. Fishing access is good and trout plants are decent, making for a good fishing/camping trip. Note: all three camps are extremely popular on summer weekends.

Campsites, facilities: There are 20 sites for tents or RVs up to 32 feet long. Picnic tables and fire grills are provided. Drinking water and flush toilets are available. A grocery store and coin laundry are available within three miles. Leashed pets are permitted.

Reservations, fees: Reservations are not accepted. The fee is $14 per night. Senior discount available. Open May through September.

Directions: From Oroville, drive north on Highway 70 to Caribou Road (two miles past Belden at Gansner Ranch Ranger Station). Turn left on Caribou Road and drive about two miles to the campground on the left side of the road.

Contact: Northwest Park Management, 530/283-5559, fax 530/283-0159; Plumas National Forest, Mt. Hough Ranger District, 530/283-0555, fax 530/283-1821.

96 GANSNER BAR

Rating: 7

On the North Fork of the Feather River in Plumas National Forest.

Map 3.3, page 186

Gansner Bar is the first of three camps along Caribou Road, which runs parallel to the North Fork Feather River. Of the three, this one receives the highest trout stocks of rainbow trout in the 10- to 12-inch class. Caribou Road runs upstream to Caribou Dam, with stream and fishing access along almost all of it. The camps often fill on summer weekends.

Campsites, facilities: There are 14 sites for tents or RVs up to 30 feet long. Picnic tables and fire grills are provided. Drinking water and flush toilets are available. A grocery store and coin laundry are available within one mile. Some facilities are wheelchair-accessible. Leashed pets are permitted.

Reservations, fees: Reservations are not accepted. The fee is $14 per night. Senior discount available. Open April through October.

Directions: From Oroville, drive north on Highway 70 to Caribou Road (two miles past Belden). Turn left on Caribou Road and drive a short distance to the campground on the left side of the road.

Contact: Northwest Park Management, 530/283-5559, fax 530/283-0159; Plumas National Forest, Mt. Hough Ranger District, 530/283-0555, fax 530/283-1821.

97 HALLSTED

Rating: 7

On the North Fork of the Feather River in Plumas National Forest.

Map 3.3, page 186

Easy highway access and a pretty trout stream right alongside have made this an extremely popular campground. It typically fills on summer weekends. Hallsted is set on the East

Branch North Fork Feather River at 2,800 feet elevation. The river is stocked with trout by the Department of Fish and Game.

Campsites, facilities: There are 20 sites for tents or RVs up to 30 feet long. Picnic tables and fire grills are provided. Drinking water and vault toilets are available. A grocery store is available within a quarter mile. Leashed pets are permitted.

Reservations, fees: Reservations are accepted with a $9 reservation fee at 877/444-6777 and website www.ReserveUsa.com. The fee is $14 per night. Senior discount available. Open May through September.

Directions: From Oroville, drive northeast on Highway 70 to Belden. Continue past Belden for about 12 miles to the campground entrance on the right side of the road. Turn right and drive a quarter mile to the campground.

Contact: Northwest Park Management, 530/283-5559, fax 530/283-0159; Plumas National Forest, Mt. Hough Ranger District, 530/283-0555, fax 530/283-1821.

98 DODGE RESERVOIR

Rating: 6

Near Ravendale.

Map 3.4, page 187

This camp is set at 5,735 feet near Dodge Reservoir, remote and little used. The lake covers 400 acres and is stocked with Eagle Lake trout. Those who know of this lake feel like they know a secret, since the limit is two at Eagle Lake itself, yet it is five here. Small boats can be launched from the shoreline here, and though it can be windy, mornings are usually calm, ideal for canoes. The surrounding hillsides are sprinkled with sage and juniper. This camp is also popular with hunters who get drawn in the annual DFG lottery for tags for this zone.

Campsites, facilities: There are 12 sites for tents or RVs. Picnic tables and fire pits are provided. A vault toilet is available. No drinking water is available. There is no boat ramp, but hand-launched boats are permitted. Leashed pets are permitted.

Reservations, fees: Reservations are not accepted. There is no fee for camping, but donations are accepted. Open year-round, weather permitting.

Directions: From Susanville, drive north on U.S. 395 for 54 miles to Ravendale and County Road 502. Turn right on County Road 502 (Mail Route) and drive 12 miles to County Road 506. Turn right and drive 5.5 miles to a T intersection. Turn left on County Road 506 and continue for six miles to the Dodge Reservoir access road. Turn left and drive one mile to the campground at the end of the road.

Contact: Bureau of Land Management, Eagle Lake Field Office, 530/257-0456, fax 530/257-4831.

99 NORTH EAGLE LAKE

Rating: 8

On Eagle Lake.

Map 3.4, page 187

This camp provides direct access in the fall to the best fishing area of huge Eagle Lake. When the weather turns cold, the population of big Eagle Lake trout migrate to their favorite haunts just outside the tules, often in water only five to eight feet deep. From shore, try fishing with inflated nightcrawlers near the lake bottom, just outside the tules. A boat ramp is about 1.5 miles to the southwest on Stone Road. From there, troll a Needlefish along the tules, or anchor or tie up and use a nightcrawler for bait under a slip bobber. In the summer this area is quite exposed and the lake can be hammered by west winds, which can howl from midday to sunset. The elevation is 5,100 feet.

Campsites, facilities: There are 20 sites for tents or RVs. Picnic tables and fire grills are provided. Drinking water and vault toilets are available. A private RV dump station and boat ramp are available within 1.5 miles. Leashed pets are permitted.

Chapter 3 • Lassen and Modoc   229

Reservations, fees: Reservations are not accepted. The fee is $8 per night. Senior discount available. Open Memorial Day through mid-November.

Directions: From Red Bluff, drive east on Highway 36 to Susanville. In Susanville, turn left (north) on Highway 139 and drive 29 miles to County Road A1. Turn left at County Road A1 and drive a half mile to the campground.

Contact: Bureau of Land Management, Eagle Lake Field Office, 530/257-0456, fax 530/257-4831.

100 EAGLE LAKE RV PARK

Rating: 7

Near Susanville.

Map 3.4, page 187

Eagle Lake RV Park has become something of a headquarters for anglers in pursuit of Eagle Lake trout, which typically range 18–22 inches. A nearby boat ramp provides access to Pelican Point and Eagle Point, where the fishing is often best in the summer. In the fall, the north end of the lake provides better prospects (see North Eagle Lake Campground). This RV park has all the amenities, including a small store. That means no special trips into town, just vacation time, lounging beside Eagle Lake, maybe catching a big trout now and then. One downer: the wind typically howls here most summer afternoons. Resident deer can be like pets here on late summer evenings, including bucks with spectacular racks.

Campsites, facilities: There are 69 RV sites with full hookups, including some drive-through sites, a separate grassy area for tents only, and cabin and RV rentals. Picnic tables and fire grills are provided. Restrooms, showers, coin laundry, satellite TV hookups, RV dump station, grocery store, propane gas, diesel, RV supplies, wood, and recreation room are available. A boat ramp and dock are available nearby. Some facilities are wheelchair-accessible. Leashed pets are permitted.

Reservations, fees: Reservations are recommended. The fee is $19–25 per night, $1 per pet per day. Major credit cards accepted. Open late May to late November, weather permitting.

Directions: From Red Bluff, drive east on Highway 36 toward Susanville. Just before reaching Susanville, turn left on County Road A1 and drive to County Road 518 near Spalding Tract. Turn right on County Road 518 and drive through a small neighborhood to Strand Way (the lake frontage road). Turn right on Strand Way and drive about eight blocks to Palmetto Way and the entrance to the store and the RV park entrance at 687-125 Palmetto Way. Register at the store.

Contact: Eagle Lake RV Park, 530/825-3133, website: www.eaglelakeandrv.com.

101 RAMHORN SPRINGS

Rating: 3

South of Ravendale.

Map 3.4, page 187

This camp is not even three miles off the biggest state highway in northeastern California, yet it feels remote and is little known. It is way out in Nowhere Land, near the flank of Shinn Peak (7,562 feet). There are large numbers of antelope in the area, along with a sprinkling of large mule deer. Though being drawn for tags for this area is nearly impossible, the hunters lucky enough to get a deer tag can use this camp for their base in the fall. It is also popular for upland game hunters in search of sage grouse.

Campsites, facilities: There are 12 sites for tents or RVs up to 28 feet long. Picnic tables and fire grills are provided. Vault toilets and a horse corral are available. There is no drinking water. Leashed pets are permitted.

Reservations, fees: Reservations are not accepted. There is no fee for camping, but, donations are accepted. Open year-round, weather permitting.

Directions: From Red Bluff, drive east on Highway 36 to Susanville. In Susanville, turn north on U.S. 395 and drive 45 miles to Post Camp Road. Turn right on Post Camp Road and drive 2.5 miles east to the campground.

Contact: Bureau of Land Management, Eagle Lake Field Office, 530/257-0456, fax 530/257-4831.

102 CHRISTIE

Rating: 9

On Eagle Lake in Lassen National Forest.
Map 3.4, page 187

This camp is set along the southern shore of Eagle Lake at 5,100 feet. Eagle Lake is well known for its big trout (yea) and big winds (boo). The camp offers some protection from the north winds. Its location is also good for seeing osprey with the Osprey Management Area, which covers a six-mile stretch of shoreline, just two miles to the north above Wildcat Point. A nearby resort is a bonus. The nearest boat ramp is at Aspen Grove Campground.

Campsites, facilities: There are 69 sites for tents or RVs up to 50 feet long. Picnic tables and fire grills are provided. Drinking water and flush toilets are available. Some facilities are wheelchair-accessible. A grocery store is nearby. An RV dump station is two miles away at Merrill Campground. Leashed pets are permitted.

Reservations, fees: Reservations are accepted with a $9 reservation fee at 877/444-6777 and website www.ReserveUsa.com. The fee is $14 per night. Open May through September.

Directions: From Red Bluff, drive east on Highway 36 toward Susanville. Three miles before Susanville turn left on Eagle Lake Road/County Road A1 and drive 15.5 miles to County Road 231. Turn right on County Road 231 and drive four miles to the campground on the right side of the road.

Contact: Lassen National Forest, Eagle Lake Ranger District, 530/257-4188, fax 530/252-5803.

103 MERRILL

Rating: 9

On Eagle Lake in Lassen National Forest.
Map 3.4, page 187

This is one of the largest, most developed Forest Service campgrounds in the entire county. It is set along the southern shore of huge Eagle Lake at 5,100 feet. The nearest boat launch is adjacent to Aspen Grove Campground.

Campsites, facilities: There are 180 sites for tents or RVs up to 32 feet long. Picnic tables and fire grills are provided. Drinking water, flush toilets, and a RV dump station are available. Some facilities are wheelchair-accessible. A grocery store and boat ramp are available nearby. Leashed pets are permitted.

Reservations, fees: Reservations are accepted with a $9 reservation fee at 877/444-6777 and website www.ReserveUsa.com. The fee is $14–15 per night. Senior discount available. Open May through November.

Directions: From Red Bluff, drive east on Highway 36 toward Susanville. Three miles before Susanville, turn left on Eagle Lake Road/County Road A1 and drive 15.5 miles to County Road 231. Turn right on County Road 231 and drive one mile to the campground on the right side of the road.

Contact: Lassen National Forest, Eagle Lake Ranger District, 530/257-4188, fax 530/252-5803.

104 ASPEN GROVE

Rating: 9

On Eagle Lake in Lassen National Forest.
Map 3.4, page 187

Eagle Lake is one of the great trout lakes in California, producing the fast-growing and often huge Eagle Lake trout, which are common in the 18- to 22-inch class. This camp is one of three at the south end of the lake and is a popular choice for anglers, with a boat ramp available adjacent to the campground. The one problem with Eagle Lake is the wind, which can whip the huge but shallow lake into a froth in the early summer. It is imperative that anglers/boaters get on the water early, and then get back to camp early, with the fishing for the day often done by 10:30 A.M. There have been many days where limits of 20-inch trout are in the boat before the sun rises. A bonus here is a good chance to see bald eagles and osprey.

Campsites, facilities: There are 25 tent sites. Picnic tables and fire grills are provided. Drinking water and flush toilets are available. A boat ramp is available nearby. Leashed pets are permitted

Reservations, fees: Reservations are not accepted. The fee is $13 per night. Senior discount available. Open May through September.

Directions: From Red Bluff, drive east on Highway 36 toward Susanville. Three miles before Susanville, turn left on Eagle Lake Road/County Road A1 and drive 15.5 miles to County Road 231. Turn right on County Road 231 and drive two miles to the campground on the left side of the road.

Contact: Lassen National Forest, Eagle Lake Ranger District, 530/257-4188, fax 530/252-5803.

105 WEST EAGLE GROUP CAMPS

Rating: 9

On Eagle Lake in Lassen National Forest.
Map 3.4, page 187

If you are coming in a big group to Eagle Lake, you'd better get on the telephone first and reserve this camp. Then you can have your own private slice of solitude along the southern shore of Eagle Lake. Bring your boat; the Aspen boat ramp is only about a mile away.

Campsites, facilities: There are two group camps for tents and RVs up to 35 feet long. Picnic tables and fire grills are provided. Drinking water, flush toilets, and picnic areas are available. A grocery store and boat ramp are near-

by. The campground capacity is limited to 100 people for Camp One and 75 people for Camp Two. Leashed pets are permitted.

Reservations, fees: Reservations are accepted with a $9 reservation fee at 877/444-6777 and website www.ReserveUsa.com. The fee is $125 per night for Camp One, $100 per night for Camp Two. Open from Memorial Day weekend to October, weather permitting.

Directions: From Red Bluff, drive east on Highway 36 toward Susanville. Three miles before Susanville, turn left on Eagle Lake Road/County Road A1 and drive 15.5 miles to County Road 231. Turn right on County Road 231 and drive a quarter mile to the campground on the left side of the road.

Contact: Lassen National Forest, Eagle Lake Ranger District, 530/257-4188, fax 530/252-5803.

106 EAGLE

Rating: 9

On Eagle Lake in Lassen National Forest.
Map 3.4, page 187

Eagle is set just up the road from Aspen Grove; the latter is more popular because of the adjacent boat ramp. (For information about Eagle Lake, see the entry for Aspen Grove.)

Campsites, facilities: There are 49 sites for tents or RVs up to 32 feet long. Picnic tables and fire grills are provided. Drinking water and flush toilets are available. Some facilities are wheelchair-accessible. There is a boat launch nearby at Aspen Grove. Leashed pets are permitted.

Reservations, fees: Reservations are accepted with a $9 reservation fee at 877/444-6777 and website www.ReserveUsa.com. The fee is $14 per night. Senior discount available. Open May through September.

Directions: From Red Bluff, drive east on Highway 36 toward Susanville. Three miles before Susanville, turn left on Eagle Lake Road/County Road A1 and drive 15.5 miles to County

Road 231. Turn right and drive a half mile to the campground on the left side of the road.
Contact: Lassen National Forest, Eagle Lake Ranger District, 530/257-4188, fax 530/252-5803.

107 GOUMAZ

Rating: 7

On the Susan River in Lassen National Forest.

Map 3.4, page 187

This camp is set beside the Susan River, adjacent to the historic Bizz Johnson Trail, a former route for a rail line that has been converted to a 25-mile trail. The trail runs from Susanville to Westwood, but this section provides access to many of its prettiest and most remote stretches as it runs in a half circle around Pegleg Mountain (7,112 feet) to the east. It is an outstanding route for biking, hiking, and horseback riding in the summer and cross-country skiing in the winter.

Campsites, facilities: There are five sites for tents or RVs up to 30 feet long. Picnic tables and fire grills are provided. Drinking water and vault toilets are available. Leashed pets are permitted.

Reservations, fees: Reservations are not accepted. The fee is $10 per night. Senior discount available. Open May through September.

Directions: From Red Bluff, drive east on Highway 36 past Lake Almanor to the junction with Highway 44. Turn west on Highway 44 and drive six miles (one mile past the Worley Ranch) to Goumaz Road/Forest Road 30N08. Turn left on Goumaz Road and drive about five miles to the campground entrance road on the right.

Contact: Lassen National Forest, Eagle Lake Ranger District, 530/257-4188, fax 530/252-5803.

108 ROXIE PECONOM WALK-IN

Rating: 5

In Lassen National Forest.

Map 3.4, page 187

This small camp is set next to Willard Creek, a seasonal stream in eastern Lassen National Forest. It's shaded and quiet. The best nearby recreation is the Bizz Johnson Trail, with a trailhead on Highway 44 (two miles east) at a parking area on the left side of the highway. This is an outstanding biking and hiking route. The camp requires only about a 100-foot walk.

Campsites, facilities: There are 10 tent sites. Picnic tables and fire rings are provided. Drinking water and flush toilets are available. Leashed pets are permitted.

Reservations, fees: Reservations are not accepted. There is no fee for camping. Open May through September.

Directions: From Red Bluff, drive east on Highway 36 past Lake Almanor and continue past Fredonyer Pass for three miles to Forest Road 29N03 on the right. Turn right and drive two miles to the campground parking area on the left. Park and walk 100 feet to the campground.

Contact: Lassen National Forest, Eagle Lake Ranger District, 530/257-4188, fax 530/252-5803.

109 BOULDER CREEK

Rating: 7

At Antelope Lake in Plumas National Forest.

Map 3.4, page 187

Antelope Lake is a pretty mountain lake circled by conifers with nice campsites and good trout fishing. It is set at 5,000 feet in remote eastern Plumas National Forest, far enough away so the marginally inclined never make the trip. Campgrounds are at each end of the lake (this one is just north of Lone Rock at the north end), with a boat ramp at Lost Cove on the east side of the lake. The lake isn't huge, but it is big enough, with 15 miles of shoreline and little islands, coves, and peninsulas to give it an intimate feel.

Campsites, facilities: There are 70 sites for tents or RVs. Picnic tables and fire grills are provided. Drinking water and vault toilets are available. An RV dump station, boat ramp, and grocery store are nearby. Leashed pets are permitted.

Reservations, fees: Reservations are accepted with a $9 reservation fee at 877/444-6777 and website www.ReserveUsa.com. The fee is $14 per night, lakeshore sites are $16 per night, $4 for an extra vehicle per night. Senior discount available. Open May through October.

Directions: From Red Bluff, drive east on Highway 36 to Susanville and U.S. 395. Turn south on U.S. 395 and drive about 10 miles (one mile past Janesville) to County Road 208. Turn right on County Road 208 (signed Antelope Lake) and drive about 15 miles to a Y (one mile before Antelope Lake). Turn left at the Y and drive four miles to the campground entrance on the right side of the road (on the northwest end of the lake).

Contact: Northwest Park Management, 530/283-5559, fax 530/283-0159; Plumas National Forest, Mt. Hough Ranger District, 530/283-0555, fax 530/283-1821.

110 LONE ROCK

Rating: 9

At Antelope Lake in Plumas National Forest.
Map 3.4, page 187

This camp provides an option to nearby Boulder Creek, to the immediate north at the northwest shore of Antelope Lake. (For more information, see the entry for Boulder Creek.) The elevation is 5,000 feet. Campfire programs are offered in the summer at the onsite amphitheater.

Campsites, facilities: There are 86 sites for tents or RVs up to 30 feet long. Picnic tables and fire grills are provided. Drinking water and vault toilets are available. An RV dump station, boat ramp, and grocery store are nearby. Leashed pets are permitted.

Reservations, fees: Reservations are accepted with a $9 reservation fee at 877/444-6777 and website www.ReserveUsa.com. The fee is $14–16 per night, $4 for an extra vehicle per night. Senior discount available. Open May through October.

Directions: From Red Bluff, drive east on Highway 36 to Susanville and U.S. 395. Go south on U.S. 395 and drive about 10 miles (one mile past Janesville) to County Road 208. Turn right on County Road 208 (signed Antelope Lake) and drive about 15 miles to a Y (one mile before Antelope Lake). Turn left at the Y and drive three miles to the campground entrance on the right side of the road (on the northwest end of the lake).

Contact: Northwest Park Management, 530/283-5559, fax 530/283-0159; Plumas National Forest, Mt. Hough Ranger District, 530/283-0555, fax 530/283-1821.

111 LONG POINT

Rating: 7

At Antelope Lake in Plumas National Forest.
Map 3.4, page 187

Long Point is a pretty camp set on a peninsula that extends well into Antelope Lake, facing Lost Cove. The lake's boat ramp is at Lost Cove, a three-mile drive around the northeast shore. Trout fishing is often good here, with a wide variety of sizes, from the little stocked Slim Jim rainbow trout on up to some large brown trout, and there is a nature trail. A group campground is set within this campground.

Campsites, facilities: There are 38 sites for tents or RVs up to 30 feet long, and four group units for up to 25 people at each. Picnic tables and fire grills are provided. Drinking water and vault toilets are available. A grocery store, boat ramp, and RV dump stations are nearby. Leashed pets are permitted.

Reservations, fees: Reservations are accepted with a $9 reservation fee at 877/444-6777 and website www.ReserveUsa.com. The fee is $14–16 per night, $40 per night for group sites. Senior discount available. Open May through October.

Directions: From Red Bluff, drive east on Highway 36 to Susanville and U.S. 395. Go south on U.S. 395 and drive about 10 miles (one mile past Janesville) to County Road 208. Turn right on County Road 208 (signed Antelope Lake) and drive about 15 miles to a Y (one mile before Antelope Lake). Turn right at the Y and drive one mile to the campground entrance on the left side of the road.

Contact: Northwest Park Management, 530/283-5559, fax 530/283-0159; Plumas National Forest, Greenville Work Center, Mt. Hough Ranger District, 530/284-7126, fax 530/284-6211.

112 HONEY LAKE CAMPGROUND

Rating: 4

Near Milford.

Map 3.4, page 187

For newcomers, Honey Lake is a strange-looking place—a vast, shallow lake set on the edge of the desert of the Great Basin. The campground is set at 4,385 feet and covers 30 acres, most of it overlooking the lake. There are a lot of junipers, and a few aspens and pines nearby, and a waterfowl management area is along the north shore of the lake. Fishing is pretty much zilch. The lake is 26 miles across, and on rare flat calm evenings, the sunsets are spectacular here.

Campsites, facilities: There are 62 sites, all drive-through, for tents or RVs, most with full or partial hookups, plus 19 mobile homes and trailers available. Picnic tables are provided. Restrooms, showers, laundry room, RV dump station, propane gas, grocery store, playground, ice, modem hookups, and a game room are available. Some facilities are wheelchair-accessible. Leashed pets are permitted.

Reservations, fees: Reservations are accepted. The fee is $12.50–19.95 per night, $2.50 per person per night for more than two people. Long-term rentals available. Senior discount available. Open year-round, weather permitting.

Directions: From Susanville on U.S. 395, drive 17 miles south (if you reach Milford, you have gone two miles too far) to the campground on the west side of the highway. It is 65 miles north of Reno.

Contact: Honey Lake Campground, 530/253-2508, website: www.honeylakecampground.com.

113 CONKLIN PARK

Rating: 4

On Willow Creek in Plumas National Forest.

Map 3.4, page 187

This camp is along little Willow Creek on the northeastern border of the Dixie Mountain State Game Refuge. Much of the area is recovering from a fire that burned during the summer of 1989. Although the area has greened up, there remains significant evidence of the fire. The campground is little known, primitive, rarely used, and is not likely to change any time soon. The elevation is 5,900 feet.

Campsites, facilities: There are nine sites for tents or RVs up to 22 feet long. Picnic tables and fire grills are provided. Vault toilets are available. No drinking water is available. Garbage must be packed out. Leashed pets are permitted.

Reservations, fees: Reservations are not accepted. There is no fee for camping. Open May through October.

Directions: From Susanville on U.S. 395, drive south for 24 miles to Milford. In Milford turn right (east) on County Road 336 and drive about four miles to a Y. Bear to the right on Forest Road 70/26N70 and drive three miles. Turn right at the bridge at Willow Creek, turn left on Forest Road 70 (now paved), and drive three miles to the camp entrance road on the left side.

Contact: Plumas National Forest, Beckwourth

Ranger District, 530/836-2575, fax 530/836-0493.

114 MEADOW VIEW

Rating: 6

Near Little Last Chance Creek in Plumas National Forest.

Map 3.4, page 187

This little-known, primitive camp is set along the headwaters of Little Last Chance Creek, along the eastern border of the Dixie Mountain State Game Refuge. The access road continues along the creek and connects with primitive roads that enter the interior of the game refuge. Side-trip options include Frenchman Lake to the south and the drive up to Dixie Mountain, at 8,323 feet in elevation. The camp elevation is 6,100 feet.

Campsites, facilities: There are six sites for tents or RVs up to 30 feet. Picnic tables and fire grills are provided. Vault toilets are available. No drinking water is available. Garbage must be packed out. Leashed pets are permitted.

Reservations, fees: Reservations are not accepted. There is no fee for camping. Open May through October.

Directions: From Reno, drive north on U.S. 395 for 43 miles to Doyle. At Doyle, turn west on Doyle Grade Road/County Road 331 (a dirt road most of the way) and drive 7.5 miles to the campground.

Contact: Plumas National Forest, Beckwourth Ranger District, 530/836-2575, fax 530/836-0493.

© JEFFREY PATTY

Chapter 4
Mendocino and
Wine Country

Chapter 4—Mendocino and Wine Country

For many people, this region offers the best possible combination of geography, weather, and outdoor activities around. The Mendocino coast is dramatic and remote, with several stellar state parks for hiking, while Sonoma Valley, in the heart of wine country, produces some of the most popular wines in the world. Add in the self-indulgent options of mud baths and hot springs at Calistoga and a dash of mainstream recreation at Clear Lake, Lake Berryessa, or any other lake, and you have a capsule summary of why the Mendocino coast and the wine country have turned into getaway favorites.

But it's like two worlds, and the twain do not meet.

For many, this area is where people go for romance, fine cuisine, great wine, mineral springs, and anything else that comes to mind spur-of-the-moment. Such is a vacation in the Napa-Sonoma wine country, or on the beautiful Sonoma and Mendocino coast.

This region wouldn't be the best of both worlds if there weren't options on the other end of spectrum. Campgrounds set up primarily for family recreation are available at Clear Lake, Lake Berryessa, and Blue Lakes. If the shoe fits—and for many, it does—you can have a great time fishing, boating, and water-skiing.

The coast features a series of romantic hideaways and excellent adventuring and hiking. The Fort Bragg area alone has three state parks, all with outstanding recreation, including several easy hikes, many amid redwoods and along pretty streams. Reservations are always required here far in advance for a chance at getting a campsite at a state park on a summer weekend. Fort Bragg also offers excellent fishing out of Noyo Harbor.

The driving tour of Highway 1 along the coast here is the fantasy of many, and it can live up to that fantasy if you don't mind the twists and turns of the road. Along the way, there are dozens of hidden beaches and untouched coastline where you can stop and explore and maybe play tag with the waves. The prize spots are MacKerricher State Park, Salt Point State Park, and Anchor Bay.

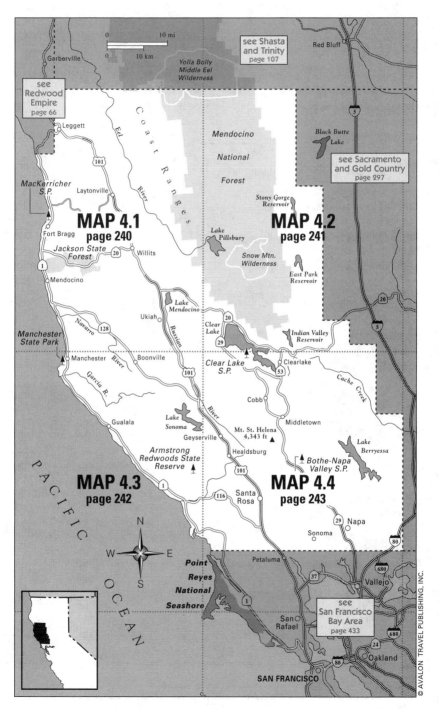

see Shasta
and Trinity
page 107

see
Redwood
Empire
page 66

see Sacramento
and Gold Country
page 297

see
San Francisco
Bay Area
page 433

0   10 mi

0   10 km

Garberville

Red Bluff

Yolla Bolly
Middle Eel
Wilderness

Leggett

Black Butte
Lake

MacKerricher
S.P.

Laytonville

Mendocino

National

Forest

Stony Gorge
Reservoir

MAP 4.1
page 240

MAP 4.2
page 241

Fort Bragg

Jackson State
Forest

Willits

Lake
Pillsbury

Snow Mtn.
Wilderness

East Park
Reservoir

Mendocino

Lake
Mendocino

Ukiah

Clear
Lake

Indian Valley
Reservoir

Manchester
State Park

Navarro

Boonville

Manchester

Garcia R.

Clear Lake
S.P.

Clearlake

Cache Creek

Gualala

Lake
Sonoma

Geyserville

Cobb

Mt. St. Helena
4,343 ft

Middletown

Lake
Berryessa

Armstrong
Redwoods State
Reserve

Healdsburg

Bothe-Napa
Valley S.P.

MAP 4.3
page 242

MAP 4.4
page 243

Santa
Rosa

Napa

Sonoma

N
W   E
S

Point
Reyes
National
Seashore

Petaluma

Vallejo

San
Rafael

Oakland

SAN FRANCISCO

PACIFIC OCEAN

Coast Ranges

Eel River

Russian River

© AVALON TRAVEL PUBLISHING, INC.

Map 4.1

Campgrounds 1–35
Pages 244–258

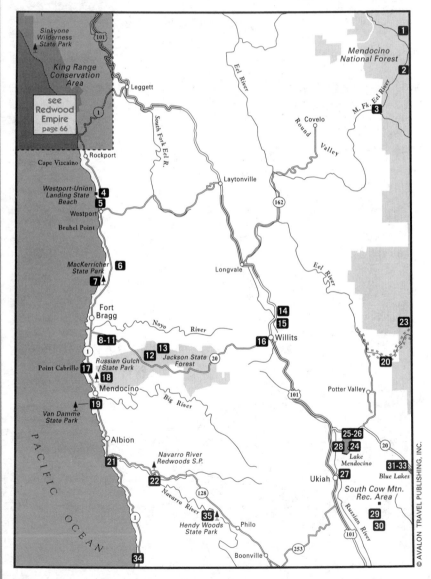

Sinkyone Wilderness State Park

King Range Conservation Area

see Redwood Empire page 66

Leggett

Rockport

Cape Vizcaino

Westport-Union Landing State Beach **4**
5
Westport

Bruhel Point

MacKerricher State Park **6**
7

Fort Bragg

8–11

Russian Gulch State Park

Point Cabrillo **17**
18

Mendocino

12 **13** Jackson State Forest
16 Willits

Van Damme State Park

19

Albion

21

22

Navarro River Redwoods S.P.

Navarro River

Hendy Woods State Park **35**

Philo

Boonville

34

Mendocino National Forest **1**
2

M. Fk. Eel River **3**

Eel River

Covelo

Round Valley

Laytonville

162

Longvale

Eel River

14
15

23

20

Potter Valley

25–26
28 **24**
Lake Mendocino
27

Ukiah

20

31–33
Blue Lakes

South Cow Mtn. Rec. Area

29
30

PACIFIC OCEAN

© AVALON TRAVEL PUBLISHING, INC.

Map 4.2

Campgrounds 36–67
Pages 259–272

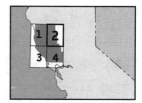

4.1
4.4

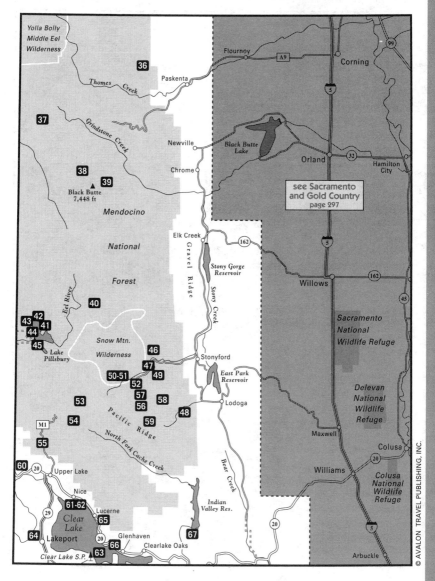

© AVALON TRAVEL PUBLISHING, INC.

Map 4.3

Campgrounds 68–87
Pages 273–282

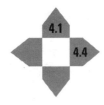

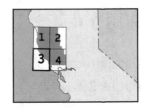

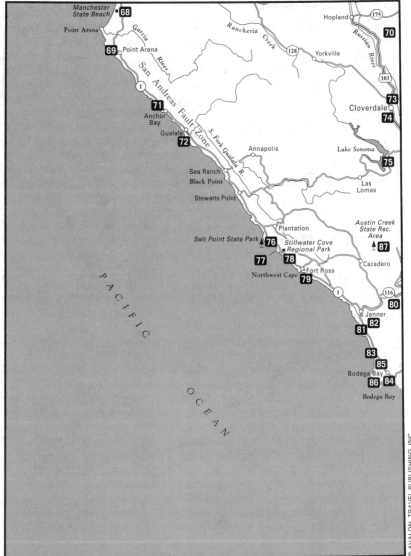

© AVALON TRAVEL PUBLISHING, INC.

Map 4.4

Campgrounds 88–111
Pages 283–293

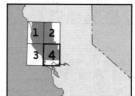

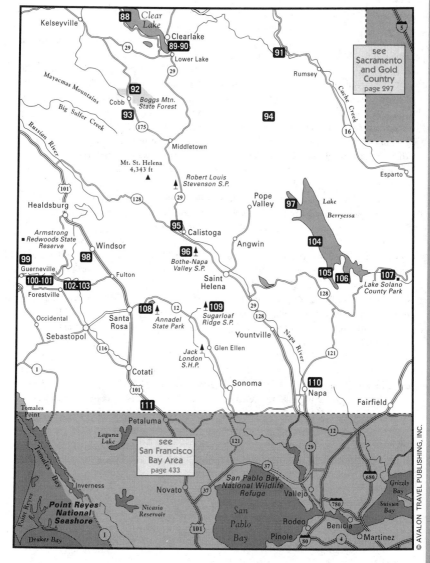

1 HAMMERHORN LAKE

Rating: 7

Near Covelo in Mendocino National Forest.

Map 4.1, page 240

Obscure and hidden, this is a veritable dot of a lake, just five acres, set at 3,500 feet in Mendocino National Forest. There is a spring for drinking water at the south end of the lake; go out of the camp and hike along the edge of the lake—you can hear the water running out of the pipe often before you see it. The lake is set near the border of the Yolla Bolly Wilderness, with the Green Springs Trailhead nearby to the northeast. A great side trip is the drive up to Anthony Peak.

Campsites, facilities: There are eight sites for tents or RVs up to 16 feet long, including one wheelchair-accessible site. Picnic tables and fire grills are provided. Drinking water and vault toilets are available. No water is available in fall and winter. Garbage must be packed out. Some facilities are wheelchair-accessible. Supplies are available in Covelo. Leashed pets are permitted.

Reservations, fees: Reservations are not accepted. The fee is $6 per night. Senior discount available. Open May through November.

Directions: From Willits, drive north on U.S. 101 for 13 miles to Longvale and the junction with Highway 162. Turn northeast on Highway 162 and drive to Covelo. Continue east on Highway 162 to the Eel River Bridge. Turn left at the bridge on Forest Road M1 and drive about 17 miles to Forest Road M21. Turn right and drive one mile to the campground entrance.

Contact: Mendocino National Forest, Covelo Ranger District, 707/983-6118, fax 707/983-8004. For a map, send $6 to U.S. Forest Service, Attn: Map Sales, P.O. Box 9035, Prescott, AZ 86313, 928/443-8285 with credit card, website: www.fs.fed.us/maps/.

2 LITTLE DOE

Rating: 5

Near Howard Lake in Mendocino National Forest.

Map 4.1, page 240

Little Howard Lake is tucked deep in the interior of Mendocino National Forest between Espee Ridge to the south and Little Doe Ridge to the north, at elevation 3,600 feet. For a drive-to lake, it is surprisingly remote and provides fair trout fishing, primitive camping, and an opportunity for car-top boating. Side trips include Hammerhorn Lake, about six miles away, and several four-wheel-drive roads that allow you to explore the area.

Campsites, facilities: There are 13 tent sites. Fire pits are provided. No drinking water is available. All garbage must be packed out. Supplies are available in Covelo, 12 miles away. Leashed pets are permitted.

Reservations, fees: Reservations are not accepted. There is no fee for camping. Open May through November.

Directions: From Willits, drive north on U.S. 101 for 13 miles to Longvale and the junction with Highway 162. Turn northeast on Highway 162 and drive to Covelo. Continue east on Highway 162 to the Eel River Bridge. Turn left at the bridge on Forest Road M1 and drive about 11 miles to the campground.

Contact: Mendocino National Forest, Covelo Ranger District, 707/983-6118, fax 707/983-8004. For a map, send $6 to U.S. Forest Service, Attn: Map Sales, P.O. Box 9035, Prescott, AZ 86313, 928/443-8285 with credit card, website: www.fs.fed.us/maps/.

3 EEL RIVER

Rating: 8

In Mendocino National Forest.

Map 4.1, page 240

This is a little-known spot, set in oak woodlands at the confluence of the Middle Fork of the Eel River and Black Butte River. The elevation is 1,500 feet, and it's often extremely hot in summer. Eel River is an ancient Native American campsite and a major archaeological site. For this reason restoration has been limited and at times the camp is overgrown and weedy. Who cares, though? After all, you're camping.

Campsites, facilities: There are 16 sites for tents or RVs up to 21 feet long. Picnic tables and fire grills are provided. Drinking water and vault toilets are available. Garbage must be packed out. Leashed pets are permitted.

Reservations, fees: Reservations are not accepted. The fee is $6 per night. Senior discount available. Open May through October.

Directions: From Willits, drive north on U.S. 101 for 13 miles to Longvale and the junction with Highway 162. Turn northeast on Highway 162 and drive to Covelo. Continue east on Highway 162 for 13 miles to the campground.

Contact: Mendocino National Forest, Covelo Ranger District, 707/983-6118, fax 707/983-8004.

4 WESTPORT UNION LANDING STATE BEACH

🏊 🏕 ♿ 🚐 ⛺

Rating: 8

Overlooking the Pacific Ocean.
Map 4.1, page 240

The northern Mendocino coast is remote, beautiful, and gets far less people pressure than the Fort Bragg area. That is the key to its appeal. The campsites are on an ocean bluff. It can get windy here, but the reward is the view. This park covers more than three miles of rugged and scenic coastline. There are magnificent views, sunsets, and tree-covered mountains that can provide great opportunities for photos. Several small sandy beaches, and one large beach at the mouth of Howard Creek, provide some good spots for surf fishermen. Several species of rockfish and abalone can be taken

when tides and ocean conditions are right. But note that the surf here can surge, discouraging all but the hardy. The park was named for two early-day communities, Westport and Union Landing, settlements famous for supply lumber and rail ties.

Campsites, facilities: There are 100 primitive sites for tents or RVs of any length. Picnic tables and fire rings are provided. Drinking water and vault toilets are available. A grocery store is nearby. Leashed pets are permitted.

Reservations, fees: Reservations are not accepted. The fee is $7 per night. Senior discount available. Open year-round.

Directions: From Fort Bragg, drive north on Highway 1 to Westport. In Westport, continue north on Highway 1 for three miles to the campground entrance on the west side of the road.

Contact: Westport Union Landing State Beach, 707/937-5804, fax 707/937-2953.

5 WAGES CREEK BEACH CAMPGROUND

🏊 🏕 🏕 ♿ 🚐 ⛺

Rating: 8

Overlooking the Pacific Ocean.
Map 4.1, page 240

Wages Creek Beach Campground is set above the beach near the mouth of Wages Creek, with creekside sites available, some offering glimpses of the ocean. You will notice as you venture north from Fort Bragg that the number of vacationers in the area falls way off, providing a chance for quiet beaches and serene moments. The best nearby hiking is to the north out of the trailhead for the Sinkyone Wilderness. This campground was completely renovated in 2002.

Campsites, facilities: There are 75 sites for RVs with full hookups, some drive-through, 22 sites for tents only, and a two-bedroom house for rent. Picnic tables and fire rings are provided. Drinking water, coin-operated showers, flush toilets, RV dump station, wood, and ice are available. Some facilities are wheelchair-accessible. Leashed pets are permitted.

Reservations, fees: Reservations are accepted. The fee is $22–27 per night for RV sites, $18 per night for tent sites, $1 per pet per night. Major credit cards accepted. Open year-round.

Directions: From Fort Bragg, drive north on Highway 1 to Westport. In Westport, continue north on Highway 1 for a half mile to the campground entrance on the west side of the highway.

Contact: Wages Creek Beach Campground, 707/964-2964, fax 707/964-8185.

6 HIDDEN VALLEY CAMPGROUND

Rating: 5

North of Willits.
Map 4.1, page 240

The privately operated park is in a pretty valley, primarily oak/bay woodlands with a sprinkling of conifers. The most popular nearby recreation option is taking the Skunk Train in Willits for the ride out to the coast at Fort Bragg. There are also two golf courses within six miles.

Campsites, facilities: There are 50 sites, 16 with full hookups and 19 with partial hookups, for RVs up to 45 feet and tents. Picnic tables, fire grills, and modem access are provided, and some sites provide satellite TV. Restrooms, ice, horseshoes, a coin laundry, RV dump station, and showers are available. Leashed pets are permitted.

Reservations, fees: Reservations are accepted. The fee is $17.50–23 per night for two campers, $3 per person for more than two people. Open year-round.

Directions: From Willits on U.S. 101, drive north for 6.5 miles on U.S. 101 to the campground on the east side (right) of the road.

Contact: Hidden Valley Campground, 707/459-2521.

7 MACKERRICHER STATE PARK

Rating: 9

Overlooking the Pacific Ocean.
Map 4.1, page 240

MacKerricher is a beautiful park on the Mendocino coast, a great destination for adventure and exploration. The camps are set in a coastal forest, with gorgeous walk-in sites. Nearby is a small beach, great tidepools, a rocky point where harbor seals hang out in the sun, a small lake (Cleone) with trout fishing, a great bike trail, and outstanding short hikes. The short jaunt around little Cleone Lake has many romantic spots, often tunneling through vegetation, then emerging for lake views. The coastal walk to the point to see seals and tidepools is equally captivating. For wheelchair users, there is a wheelchair-accessible trail to Laguna Point and also a route on a raised boardwalk that runs halfway around Cleone Lake, a former tidal lagoon. This park covers more than 1,530 acres of beach, bluff, headlands, dune, forest, and wetlands. That diverse landscape provides habitat for more than 90 species of bird, most in the vicinity of Cleone Lake. In winter and spring, the headland provides a good lookout for whale-watching.

Campsites, facilities: There are 142 sites for tents or RVs up to 35 feet long and 10 walk-in sites. Picnic tables, fire rings, and food lockers are provided. Drinking water, flush toilets, coin-operated showers, and RV dump station are available. Some facilities are wheelchair-accessible. Leashed pets are permitted.

Reservations, fees: Reservations are accepted with a $7.50 reservation fee at 800/444-PARK (800/444-7275) and website www.Reserve America.com. The fee is $12 per night. Senior discount available. Open year-round.

Directions: From Fort Bragg, drive north on Highway 1 for three miles to the campground entrance on the left side of the road.

Contact: MacKerricher State Park, 707/964-

9112; Mendocino District, 707/937-5804, fax 707/937-2953.

8 WOODSIDE RV PARK AND CAMPGROUND

Rating: 7

In Fort Bragg.
Map 4.1, page 240

This privately operated park is set up primarily for RVs. It covers nine acres, is somewhat wooded, and provides access to nearby Fort Bragg and the ocean. Note that about half of the RV sites are long-term rentals.

Campsites, facilities: There are 86 sites, some drive-through, with full or partial hookups for RVs to 40 feet long or tents, 18 sites for tents only, and a group site. Picnic tables and fire rings are provided. Restrooms, coin showers, recreation room, sauna, RV dump station, cable TV, modem access, RV supplies, ice, wood, and a fish-cleaning table are available. Boating and fishing access are available within one mile. Leashed pets are permitted.

Reservations, fees: Reservations are accepted at 800/207-8772. The fee is $18–25.50 per night, $5 per person per night for more than two people, $1 per pet per night. Major credit cards accepted.

Directions: In Fort Bragg at the junction of Highway 1 and Highway 20, drive south on Highway 1 for one mile to the campground on the west side of the highway.

Contact: Woodside RV Park and Campground, 707/964-3684, website: www.infortbrag.com/woodsiderv.

9 DOLPHIN ISLE MARINA

Rating: 7

On the Noyo River in Fort Bragg.
Map 4.1, page 240

Noyo Harbor is the headquarters of Fort Bragg—the place where everything begins in this area.

For vacationers that includes wharfside restaurants, fishing trips, boat docks, and a chance for a nice stroll out to the Noyo Harbor jetty. This RV park is right at the marina, providing an ideal jump-off point for all of those adventures. Beach access is available one mile away. Note that half of the sites are booked for the entire summer season.

Campsites, facilities: There are 84 sites with full or partial hookups for RVs. Picnic tables are provided. Restrooms, hot showers (coin-operated), RV dump station, a coin laundry, cable TV, delicatessen, propane gas, marina with gas and diesel, bait and tackle, boat ramp, and a dock are available. Some facilities are wheelchair-accessible. Leashed pets are permitted.

Reservations, fees: Reservations are accepted. The fee is $15–25 per night, $1 per person for more than two people, $6 for a second vehicle, $1 per pet per night. Long-term rates available. Major credit cards accepted. Open year-round.

Directions: In Fort Bragg at the junction of Highway 1 and Highway 20, drive east on Highway 20 for a quarter mile to South Harbor Drive. Turn left on South Harbor Drive and drive a quarter mile to Basin Street. Turn right on Basin Street and drive one mile to the campground at the end of the road.

Contact: Dolphin Isle Marina, 707/964-4113, fax 707/964-7136.

10 FORT BRAGG LEISURE TIME RV PARK

Rating: 5

In Fort Bragg.
Map 4.1, page 240

This privately operated park offers horseshoes, badminton, and a covered group picnic area. The drive from Willits to Fort Bragg on Highway 20 is always a favorite, a curving two-laner through redwoods, not too slow, not too fast, best seen from the saddle of a Harley-Davidson.

At the end of it is the coast, and just three miles inland is this campground in the sunbelt, said to be out of the fog by breakfast. Within short drives are Noyo Harbor in Fort Bragg, Russian Gulch State Park, Mendocino to the south, and MacKerricher State Park to the north. In fact, there's so much in the area, you could explore for days.

Campsites, facilities: There are 82 sites, all drive-through, many with full or partial hookups, for tents or RVs up to 40 feet long. Picnic tables and fire rings are provided. Restrooms, coin showers, satellite TV, modem access, RV dump station, and a coin laundry are available. Some facilities are wheelchair-accessible. Leashed pets are permitted.

Reservations, fees: Reservations are accepted at 800/700-8542. The fee is $19.50–27.50 per night, $1 per extra vehicle per night, $1 per pet per night. Major credit cards accepted. Open year-round.

Directions: In Fort Bragg at the junction of Highway 1 and Highway 20, turn east on Highway 20 and drive 2.5 miles to the campground entrance on the right side of the road.

Contact: Fort Bragg Leisure Time RV Park, 707/964-5994.

11 POMO CAMPGROUND AND RV PARK

Rating: 7

In Fort Bragg.

Map 4.1, page 240

This park covers 17 acres of lush, native vegetation near the ocean, one of several camps on the Fort Bragg and Mendocino coast. Nearby Noyo Harbor offers busy restaurants, deep-sea fishing, a boat ramp, harbor, and a nice walk out to the Noyo Harbor jetty. Huckleberry picking is also an option. Many of the RV spaces are quite wide at this park.

Campsites, facilities: There are 94 sites, a few drive-through, with full or partial hookups for RVs, and 30 sites for tents. Picnic tables and

fire rings are provided. Restrooms, hot showers (coin-operated), cable TV hookups, convenience store, firewood, ice, RV supplies, modem access, propane gas, coin laundry, RV dump station, fish-cleaning table, horseshoe pits, and large grass playing field are available. Leashed pets are permitted.

Reservations, fees: Reservations are recommended in the summer. The fee is $22–30 per night, $3–10 per person for more than two people, $1 per pet per night. Open year-round.

Directions: In Fort Bragg at the junction of Highway 1 and Highway 20, drive south on Highway 1 for one mile to Tregoning Lane. Turn left (east) and drive a short distance to the park at the end of the road (17999 Tregoning Lane).

Contact: Pomo Campground and RV Park, 707/964-3373, fax 707/964-0619, website: www.infortbragg.com/pomorvpark.

12 JACKSON DEMONSTRATION STATE FOREST, CAMP 1

Rating: 7

Near Fort Bragg.

Map 4.1, page 240

Primitive campsites set in a vast forest of redwoods and Douglas fir are the prime attraction at Jackson Demonstration State Forest. Even though Highway 20 is a major connecting link to the coast in the summer, these camps get bypassed because they are primitive and largely unknown. Why? Because reaching them requires driving on dirt roads sometimes frequented by logging trucks, and there are no campground signs along the highway. This camp features lots of tree cover, with oaks, redwoods, and madrones. Some of the campsites are along the Noyo River, well-known among locals, but completely missed by most others. A one-mile trail circles the campground. A DFG hatchery is next to the campground, but note that no fishing is permitted in the river.

Campsites, facilities: There are 50 primitive

sites for tents or RVs up to 27 feet long, and one group site for up to 50 people with a minimum of 20. Picnic tables and fire pits are provided. Pit toilets are available. No drinking water is available. Leashed pets are permitted.

Reservations, fees: Reservations are accepted only for the group site. There is no fee for camping. A camping permit is required and a campground map is needed. Both can be obtained from the State Department of Forestry office at 802 N. Main St. (Highway 1) in Fort Bragg, or with a group-site reservation from the campground host in Jackson Demonstration State Forest. Open April to October, weather permitting. Call ahead for status.

Directions: From Willits on U.S. 101, turn west on Highway 20 and drive 27 miles to Forest Road 350 (near the six-mile marker). Turn right and drive 1.3 miles (bear right at the forks on the road) to the campground.

Contact: Jackson Demonstration State Forest, 707/964-5674, fax 707/964-0941.

13 JACKSON DEMONSTRATION STATE FOREST, CAMP 20

Rating: 6

Near Fort Bragg.

Map 4.1, page 240

A highlight of Jackson Demonstration Forest is a 50-foot waterfall on Chamberlain Creek. Set in a steep canyon amid giant firs and redwoods, it can be reached with a 10-minute walk. There are also extensive logging roads that are good yet challenging for mountain biking. What to do first? Get a map from the State Forestry Department. For driving, the roads are extremely dusty in summer and muddy in winter. Some locals calls this campground "Dunlap Camp."

Campsites, facilities: There are 18 primitive sites for tents or RVs up to 27 feet long, and six equestrian sites across the road. Picnic tables and fire rings are provided. Pit toilets are available. No drinking water is available. There

is a camp host from Memorial Day to October. Leashed pets are permitted.

Reservations, fees: Reservations are not accepted. There is no fee for camping. A camping permit is required and a campground map is needed. Both can be obtained from the State Department of Forestry office at 802 N. Main St. (Highway 1) in Fort Bragg, or from the campground host in Jackson Demonstration State Forest from Memorial Day to October. Reservations accepted for equestrian sites only. Open year-round, but subject to closures, especially in winter because of muddy roads. Call ahead for status.

Directions: From Willits on U.S. 101, turn west on Highway 20 and drive 17 miles. At the 16.9-mile marker (just past the Chamberlain Bridge) at Road 200 turn left on Road 200 (the entrance for Jackson State Forest) and Camp 20/Dunlap. Obtain a camping permit and a map from the camp host on the premises at Camp 20.

Contact: Jackson Demonstration State Forest, 707/964-5674, fax 707/964-0941.

14 SLEEPY HOLLOW RV PARK

Rating: 5

North of Willits.

Map 4.1, page 240

This year-round, privately operated park provides easy access off the highway. A nearby recreation option is the Skunk Train in Willits.

Campsites, facilities: There are six sites for tents and 24 RV sites (six drive-through) with full or partial hookups. Picnic tables are provided. Restrooms, showers, a small pond, recreation room, and RV dump station are available. Leashed pets are permitted.

Reservations, fees: Reservations are accepted. The fee is $11–15 per night, $1 per person for more than two people. Open year-round.

Directions: From Willits on U.S. 101, drive north for 8.5 miles to the 55.5-mile marker (.2 mile beyond the Shimmins Ridge Road sign). At the beginning of the divided four-lane highway, turn right at the signed campground access road and drive to the entrance.

Contact: Sleepy Hollow RV Park, 707/459-0613.

15 QUAIL MEADOWS RV PARK & CAMPGROUND

Rating: 3

In Willits.

Map 4.1, page 240

This is one of several RV parks in the Willits area. Nearby is Lake Emily, set near the Brook Trails development, which is stocked in the spring and early summer with trout by the Department of Fish and Game. It's like a backyard fishing hole for the folks around here. Another recreation option is the Skunk Train, which runs from Willits to Fort Bragg. Note that of the 49 sites, only 10 are available for overnighters, as the rest are rented for the summer.

Campsites, facilities: There are 49 sites, most drive-through, with full or partial hookups for RVs, and a separate area for tents only. Picnic tables are provided. Patios, restrooms, showers, RV dump station, coin laundry, propane gas, ice, and TV hookups are available. Leashed pets are permitted.

Reservations, fees: Reservations are accepted. The fee is $24–26 per night, $3 per person for more than two people. Senior discount available. Open year-round.

Directions: In Willits at the junction of U.S. 101 and Highway 20, drive north on U.S. 101 for one mile to the campground on the east side of the road.

Contact: Quail Meadows RV Park & Campground, 707/459-6006.

16 WILLITS KOA

Rating: 3

Near Willits.

Map 4.1, page 240

This is an ideal spot to park your RV if you plan on taking the Skunk Train west to Fort Bragg. A depot for the train is within walking distance of the campground. The campground also offers nightly entertainment in summer. The elevation is 1,377 feet. Tickets are available here for the Skunk Train.

Campsites, facilities: There are 21 sites for tents and 50 RV sites (27 drive-through) with full or partial hookups. Group sites and 12 cabins are available. Picnic tables are provided. Drinking water, flush toilets, modem access, showers, a playground, swimming pool (heated in summer), hay rides, minigolf, basketball, volleyball, fishing pond, grocery store, RV supplies, coin laundry, and RV dump station are available. Leashed pets are permitted.

Reservations, fees: Reservations are accepted at 800/562-8542. The fee is $15–23 per night, $3–4 per person per night for more than two people. Major credit cards accepted. Open year-round.

Directions: From Willits at the junction of U.S. 101 and Highway 20, turn west on Highway 20 and drive 1.5 miles to the campground on the left.

Contact: Willits KOA, 707/459-6179, fax 707/459-1489, website: www.koa.com.

17 CASPAR BEACH RV PARK

Rating: 8

Near Mendocino.

Map 4.1, page 240

This privately operated park has ocean frontage and opportunities for beachcombing, fishing, abalone and scuba diving, and good lookouts for whale-watching. The park is somewhat wooded, with a small, year-round creek running behind it. The park is about midway between Fort Bragg and Mendocino, with Fort Bragg five miles to the north. Note that a 30-site mobile home park is adjacent to this park.

Campsites, facilities: There are 59 sites, some drive-through, with full or partial hookups for RVs, and 30 sites for tents only. Picnic tables and fire rings are provided. Cable TV, modem access, flush and pit toilets, showers (coin-operated), and RV dump station are available. A convenience store, firewood, playground, video arcade, and a coin laundry are available nearby. Some facilities are wheelchair-accessible. Leashed pets are permitted.

Reservations, fees: Reservations are accepted. The fee is $22–29.50 per night, $3–5 per person for more than two people, $2 per pet per night. Monthly rates available. Major credit cards accepted. Open year-round.

Directions: From Mendocino on Highway 1, drive north for 3.5 miles to the Point Cabrillo exit. Turn west on Point Cabrillo Drive and continue three-quarters of a mile to the campground on the left.

From Fort Bragg on Highway 1, drive south for 4.5 miles. Turn right on Point Cabrillo Drive and continue three-quarters of a mile to the campground.

Contact: Caspar Beach RV Park, 707/964-3306, fax 707/964-0526, website: www. caspar beachrvpark.com.

⑱ RUSSIAN GULCH STATE PARK

🥾 🚲 🛶 🏊 🐕 🚻 ♿ 🚐 ⛺

Rating: 9

Near the Pacific Ocean.

Map 4.1, page 240

Russian Gulch State Park is set near some of California's most beautiful coastline, but the camp speaks to the woods, not the water, with the campsites set in a wooded canyon. They include some of the prettiest and most secluded drive-in sites available on the Mendocino coast. There is a great hike here, an easy hourlong walk to Russian Gulch Falls, a wispy 36-foot waterfall that falls into a rock basin. While it's always pretty, it's awesome in late winter. Much of the route is accessible by bicycle, with a rack available where the trail narrows and turns to dirt. The park covers more than 1,100 acres with about 1.5 miles of ocean frontage, with its rugged headlands thrusting into the Pacific. It rivals Point Lobos

for coastal beaty. And yet the park is better known for its heavily forested canyon, Russian Gulch Creek Canyon, and a headland that features the Devil's Punchbowl. The latter is a large collapsed sea cove with churning water that acts as a blow-hole. It was created by the pounding of waves against the coastal headlands, gouging a 200-foot tunnel that ends where the earth caved away. That forms a hole 100 feet across and 60 feet deep, called Devil's Punchbowl, where one can look right into it and watch the surge. A beach offers tidepool exploring, swimming, diving, and rock fishing. There are miles of trails, with the best family outing being the three-mile bicycle trail called the North Boundary Trail.

Campsites, facilities: There are 30 sites for tents or RVs up to 24 feet long, one hike-in/bike-in site, and one group site. Picnic tables, fire grills, and food lockers are provided. Drinking water, coin showers, and flush toilets are available. A day-use picnic area, beach access, and recreation hall are available nearby. Some facilities are wheelchair-accessible. Leashed pets are permitted.

Reservations, fees: Reservations are accepted with a $7.50 reservation fee at 800/444-PARK (800/444-7275) and website www.Reserve America.com. The fee is $12 per night for campsites, $30 for the group site (up to 40 people), and $1 per night for hike-in, bike-in site. Senior discount available. Open mid-March to mid-October.

Directions: From Mendocino, drive two miles north on Highway 1 to the campground entrance on the west side of the highway.

Contact: Russian Gulch State Park, 707/937-4296; Mendocino District, 707/937-5804, fax 707/937-2953.

⑲ VAN DAMME STATE PARK

🥾 🚲 🛶 🏕 🐕 ♿ 🚐 ⛺

Rating:10

Near Mendocino.

Map 4.1, page 240

The campsites at Van Damme are extremely

popular, usually requiring reservations, but with a bit of planning your reward is a base of operations in a beautiful park with redwoods and a remarkable fern understory. The hike-in sites on the Fern Canyon Trail are perfectly situated for those wishing to take one of the most popular hikes in the Mendocino area, with the trail crossing the Little River several times and weaving among old trees. Just across from the entrance of the park is a small but beautiful coastal bay with a pretty beach, ideal for launching sea kayaks. The park covers 1,831 acres. A sidelight is the Pygmy Forest, where mature cone-bearing cypress and pine trees are only six inches to eight feet tall. Another favorite is the Cabbage Patch, where skunk cabbage grows in abundance, most striking when seen in May and June. The park has 10 miles of trails along the fern-carpeted canyon along the Little River. A paved road is used by joggers and bicyclists. The beach is popular with abalone divers. Kayak tours are available at the beach parking lot in the summer.

Campsites, facilities: There are 74 sites for tents or RVs up to 35 feet long, 10 primitive environmental sites, one hike-in/bike-in site, and one group campsite for up to 50 people. Picnic tables and fire grills are provided. Drinking water, flush toilets, RV dump station, and coin showers are available. A grocery store, coin laundry, and propane gas are available nearby. Leashed pets are permitted at campsites, but not in environmental sites.

Reservations, fees: Reservations are accepted with a $7.50 reservation fee at 800/444-PARK (800/444-7275) and website www.Reserve America.com. The fee is $12 per night, $7 per night for environmental sites, $37 per night for group site, $1 per night per person for hike-in site. Senior discount available. Open year-round.

Directions: From Mendocino on Highway 1, drive south for three miles to the town of Little River and the park entrance road on the left (east) side of the road.

Contact: Mendocino District, State Parks, 707/937-5804, fax 707/937-2953.

20 TROUT CREEK

Rating: 7

Near East Van Arsdale Reservoir.
Map 4.1, page 240

This is a spot that relatively few campers know about. Most others looking over this area are setting up shop at nearby Lake Pillsbury to the east. But if you like to watch the water roll by, this could be your port of call since it sits at the confluence of Trout Creek and the Eel River (not far from the East Van Arsdale Reservoir). Insider's note: nearby in Potter Valley to the south, the East Fork Russian River (Cold Creek) is stocked with trout during the summer. The elevation is 1,500 feet.

Campsites, facilities: There are 14 sites for tents and one double site for tents or RVs. Fire grills and picnic tables are provided. Drinking water and vault toilets are available. Leashed pets are permitted.

Reservations, fees: Reservations are not accepted. The fee is $10 per night, $3 per night per extra vehicle and $7 per night per extra RV, $1 per pet per night. Open May through October.

Directions: From Ukiah on U.S. 101, drive north to the junction with Highway 20. Turn east (right) on Highway 20 and drive five miles. Turn northwest on East Potter Valley Road toward Lake Pillsbury. Drive 5.9 miles to the town of Potter Valley. Continue on east Potter Valley Road to Eel River Road. Turn right and drive 4.5 miles to the Eel River Bridge. From the bridge, continue two miles to the campground entrance.

Contact: PG&E Land Services, 916/386-5164, fax 916/923-7044, website: www.pge.com/recreation.

21 NAVARRO BEACH

Rating: 6

Near the mouth of the Navarro River.

Map 4.1, page 240

Navarro Beach is primitive campground that can bail out drivers stuck for a night without a spot. It is small and open, with no tree cover, set near the ocean and the Navarro River. The camps are just south of the Navarro River Bridge.

Campsites, facilities: There 10 primitive sites for tents and RVs up to 35 feet long. Picnic tables and fire grills are provided. No drinking water. Pit toilets are available. Leashed pets are permitted.

Reservations, fees: Reservations are not accepted. The fee is $5 per night. Senior discount available. Open year-round.

Directions: Drive on U.S. 101 to the turnoff for Highway 128 (two miles north of Cloverdale). Turn west on Highway 128 and drive 55 miles to Highway 1. Turn south on Highway 1 and almost immediately, take the exit for Navarro Bluffs Road. Drive a short distance on Navarro Bluffs Road to the campground (on the south side of the Navarro River Bridge).

Contact: Navarro River Redwoods State Park, c/o Hendy Woods, 707/895-3141; Mendocino District, 707/937-5804, fax 707/937-2953.

22 PAUL M. DIMMICK

Rating: 7

On the Navarro River in Navarro River Redwoods State Park.

Map 4.1, page 240

A pretty grove of second-growth redwood trees and the nearby Navarro River are the highlights of this campground at Navarro River Redwoods State Park. It's a nice spot but, alas, lacks any significant hiking trails that could make it an overall spectacular destination; all the trailheads along Highway 128 turn out to be just little spur routes from the road to the river. That is because the park consists of an 11-mile "redwood tunnel" along the Navarro River in its course to the ocean. The river provides swimming in summer, but is better suited for easy kayaking and canoeing in later winter and spring.

Campsites, facilities: There are 27 sites for tents or RVs up to 30 feet long. Picnic tables and fire grills are provided. Drinking water (summer only) and vault toilets are available. Leashed pets are permitted.

Reservations, fees: Reservations are not accepted. The fee is $7 per night. Senior discount available. Open March through October.

Directions: From Cloverdale on U.S. 101, drive north for two miles to Highway 128. Turn west on Highway 128 and drive 49 miles. Look for the signed campground entrance on the left side of the road.

Contact: Navarro River Redwoods State Park, c/o Hendy Woods State Park, 707/895-3141; Mendocino District, 707/987-5804, fax 707/937-2953.

23 POGIE POINT

Rating: 7

On Lake Pillsbury in Mendocino National Forest.

Map 4.1, page 240

This camp is set beside Lake Pillsbury in Mendocino National Forest, in the back of a cove at the lake's northwest corner. When the lake is full, this spot is quite pretty. A boat ramp is about a quarter mile to the south, a bonus. The elevation is 1,900 feet.

Campsites, facilities: There are 50 sites for tents or RVs. Picnic tables and fire grills are provided. Drinking water and vault toilets are available. Some facilities are wheelchair-accessible. Leashed pets are permitted.

Reservations, fees: Reservations are not accepted. The fee is $12 per night, $3 per extra vehicle, $7 extra RV, $1 per pet per night. Open May through October.

Directions: From Ukiah on U.S. 101, drive north to the junction with Highway 20. Turn east (right) on Highway 20 and drive five miles. Turn northwest on East Potter Valley Road toward Lake Pillsbury. Drive 5.9 miles to the town of Potter Valley. Continue on east Potter Valley Road to Eel River Road. Turn right and drive 15 miles to the Eel River Information Kiosk at Lake Pillsbury. Continue for two miles to the campground access road. Turn right and drive a short distance to the campground.

Contact: Mendocino National Forest, Upper Lake Ranger District, 707/275-2361, fax 707/275-0676; PG&E Land Services, 916/386-5164, fax 916/923-7044, website: www.pge.com/recreation.

24 MITI BOAT-IN/HIKE-IN

Rating: 7

On Lake Mendocino.
Map 4.1, page 240
One of several campgrounds on the north end of Lake Mendocino. Boat ramps are at Kyen at the north end of the lake and at Che-Ka-Ka at the south end of the lake. The north ramp (Marina Drive off Highway 20) is open 24 hours; the south ramp closes at night.

Campsites, facilities: There are 17 boat-in sites for tents only. Picnic tables, fire rings, and lantern holders are provided. Vault toilets are available. No drinking water is available. Garbage must be packed out. Leashed pets are permitted.

Reservations, fees: Reservations are not accepted. The fee is $5 per night, one-time $2 boat launch fee. Senior discount available. Open April through September, weather permitting. (Some sites may be flooded in the spring.)

Directions: From Ukiah, drive north on U.S. 101 to the Highway 20 turnoff. For boat-in campers: drive east on Highway 20 to Marina Drive. Turn right and drive to the north boat ramp of the lake. The campground is approximately one mile by water.

For hike-in campers: drive five miles east on Highway 20. Just after crossing the Russian River bridge, turn left (Inlet Road) and drive approximately one mile to the Bu-Shay Ranger Station. Park and hike two miles to the campground.

Contact: U.S. Army Corps of Engineers, Lake Mendocino, 707/462-7581, fax 707/462-3372.

25 BU-SHAY

Rating: 7

At Lake Mendocino.
Map 4.1, page 240
Bu-Shay, on the northeast end of Lake Mendocino, is set on a point that provides a pretty southern exposure when the lake is full. The lake is five miles long and one mile wide. It offers fishing for striped bass, largemouth bass, catfish, and bluegill, as well as water-skiing and power boating. A nearby visitor center features exhibits of local Native American history. The elevation is 750 feet. (For more information about Lake Mendocino, see the entry for Che-Ka-Ka.)

Campsites, facilities: There are 164 sites for tents or RVs up to 35 feet long. There are three group sites for up to 120 people each. Picnic tables, fire rings, and lantern holders are provided. Drinking water, restrooms, showers, playground (in the adjacent day-use area), and RV dump station are available. The boat ramp is two miles from camp near Ky-En Campground. Some facilities are wheelchair-accessible. Leashed pets are permitted.

Reservations, fees: Reservations are accepted with a $9 reservation fee at 877/444-6777 and website www.ReserveUsa.com. The fee is $16 per night, group sites are $110–190 per night. Senior discount available. Open mid-April through September.

Directions: From Ukiah, drive north on U.S. 101 for five miles to the Highway 20 turnoff. Drive five miles east on Highway 20. Just after crossing the Russian River bridge, turn left (Inlet Road) and drive approximately one mile to the campground.

Contact: U.S. Army Corps of Engineers, Lake Mendocino, 707/462-7581, fax 707/462-3372.

26 KY-EN

Rating: 7

At Lake Mendocino.

Map 4.1, page 240

This camp is on the north shore of Lake Mendocino. With the access road off Highway 20 instead of U.S. 101 (as with Che-Ka-Ka), it can be overlooked by newcomers. A nearby boat ramp makes it especially attractive. (For more information, see the entry for Che-Ka-Ka.)

Campsites, facilities: There are 101 sites for tents or RVs up to 35 feet long. Picnic tables, fire grills, and lantern holders are provided. Restrooms, coin-operated showers, playground (in the adjacent day-use area), RV dump station, a boat ramp, boat rentals, and limited supplies are available at the nearby marina. Some facilities are wheelchair-accessible. Leashed pets are permitted.

Reservations, fees: Reservations are accepted with a $9 reservation fee at 877/444-6777 and website www.ReserveUsa.com. The fee is $16-18 per night. Senior discount available. Open year-round.

Directions: From Ukiah, drive north on U.S. 101 for five miles to the Highway 20 turnoff. Drive east on Highway 20 to Marina Drive. Turn right and drive 200 yards (past the boat ramp) to the campground.

Contact: U.S. Army Corps of Engineers, Lake Mendocino, 707/462-7581, fax 707/462-3372.

27 MANOR OAKS RV PARK

Rating: 2

In Ukiah.

Map 4.1, page 240

Manor Oaks RV Park is a drive-in park in an urban setting for U.S. 101 motor-home cruisers. Nearby Lake Mendocino provides a nearby side-trip option, with access to boating, water-skiing, and fishing. Note that about half of the sites are long-term rentals for the summer.

Campsites, facilities: There are 53 sites, 15 drive-through, with full hookups for RVs. Picnic tables and fire grills are provided. Restrooms, showers, heated swimming pool (in summer), a coin laundry, and ice are available. Some facilities are wheelchair-accessible. Leashed pets are permitted.

Reservations, fees: Reservations are accepted at 800/357-8772. The fee is $22 per night, $1 per person for more than two people. Open year-round.

Directions: From U.S. 101 in Ukiah, take the Central Ukiah/Gobbi Street exit and drive east for a short distance to 700 E. Gobbi St. on the left.

Contact: Manor Oaks RV Park, 707/462-0529.

28 CHE-KA-KA

Rating: 7

At Lake Mendocino.

Map 4.1, page 240

Lake Mendocino is known for good striped bass fishing, water-skiing, and boating. Nearby, upstream of the lake, is Potter Valley and the East Fork Russian River (also called Cold Creek), which provides trout fishing in the summer. A boat ramp adjacent to the dam is a bonus. The elevation is 750 feet. This campground sits beside the dam at the south end of Lake Mendocino.

Campsites, facilities: There are 22 sites for tents or RVs up to 35 feet long. Picnic tables and fire grills are provided. Drinking water, vault toilets, and lantern holders are available. A boat ramp is available nearby. Leashed pets are permitted.

Reservations, fees: Reservations are accepted with a $9 reservation fee at 877/444-6777 and website www.ReserveUsa.com. The fee is $10 per night. Senior discount available. Open mid-April through September.

Directions: From Ukiah, drive north on U.S. 101 to Lake Mendocino Drive. Exit right on Lake Mendocino Drive and continue to the first stoplight. Turn left on North State Street and drive to the next stoplight. Turn right (which will put you back on Lake Mendocino Drive) and drive about one mile to the signed entrance to the campground at Coyote Dam.

Contact: U.S. Army Corps of Engineers, Lake Mendocino, 707/462-7581, fax 707/462-3372.

29 RED MOUNTAIN

Rating: 3

Near Ukiah.

Map 4.1, page 240

Like Mayacmus, this camp is also set in the Cow Mountain area east of Ukiah. But be forewarned: it is a popular spot for off-highway motorcycles. If you don't like bikes, go to the other camp. Besides motorcycle trails, there are opportunities for hiking, horseback riding, and hunting.

Campsites, facilities: There are 10 tent sites. Picnic tables and fire grills are provided. No drinking water. Vault toilets are available. Leashed pets are permitted but not advised.

Reservations, fees: Reservations are not accepted. There is no fee for camping. Open year-round, weather permitting.

Directions: From Ukiah on U.S. 101, drive to Talmage Road. Turn east and drive 1.5 miles to Eastside Road. Turn right and drive a short distance to Mill Creek Road. Turn left and drive seven miles to the campground entrance road on the right. Turn right and drive a quarter mile to the campground.

Contact: Bureau of Land Management, Ukiah Field Office, 707/468-4000, fax 707/468-4027.

30 MAYACMUS

Rating: 5

Near Ukiah.

Map 4.1, page 240

This campground is set within the Cow Mountain Recreation Area on the slopes of Cow Mountain, the oft-overlooked wild region east of Ukiah. The primitive area is ideal for hiking and horseback riding. In the fall, it is a popular hunting area as well, for the few who know of it. This section of the recreation area is quiet, with hiking on the Mayacmus Trail providing access to Willow Creek, Mill Creek, and several overlooks of Clear Lake to the south. The flora is chaparral and oak/bay grasslands, and the weather is extremely hot in the summer. By the way, off-highway vehicles frequent the southern part of the recreation area, but not this immediate region.

Campsites, facilities: There are five tent sites. Picnic tables and fire grills are provided. Vault toilets are available. No drinking water is available. Garbage must be packed out. Leashed pets are permitted.

Reservations, fees: Reservations are not accepted. There is no fee for camping. Stay limit is 14 days. Open year-round, weather permitting.

Directions: From U.S. 101 in Ukiah, turn east on Talmage Road and drive 1.5 miles to Eastside Road. Turn right and drive a quarter mile to Mill Creek Road. Turn left and drive three miles (just beyond Mill Creek County Park) to the sign for North Cow Mountain sign at Mendo Rock Road. Turn left and drive five miles to a Y intersection with the campground access road. Bear left and drive one mile to the campground.

Contact: Bureau of Land Management, Ukiah District, 707/468-4000, fax 707/468-4027.

31 LE TRIANON RESORT

Rating: 6

On Lower Blue Lake.

Map 4.1, page 240

Le Trianon Resort is the biggest of the camps on the Blue Lakes, the overlooked lakes not far from giant Clear Lake. It is an angler's special with good trout fishing in spring and no water-skiing permitted. The better fishing is in Upper Blue Lake, which is stocked with 28,000 trout per year and where the water is much clearer than at the lower lake. The best fishing is in the spring, in April, May, and June.

Campsites, facilities: There are 200 sites for tents or RVs with partial hookups, and 14 cabins. Picnic tables are provided. Flush toilets, showers, RV dump station, playground, boat ramp, boat rentals, fishing supplies, coin laundry, snack bar, and convenience store are available. No pets. No skateboards.

Reservations, fees: Reservations are not accepted. The fee is $25 per night, $5 per child. Senior discount available. Major credit cards accepted. Open April through October.

Directions: From Ukiah, drive north on U.S. 101 for five miles to the junction with Highway 20. Turn east on Highway 20 and drive 12 miles to the resort on the right (5845 W. Hwy. 20).

Contact: Le Trianon Resort, 707/275-2262, fax 707/275-9416.

32 PINE ACRES BLUE LAKE RESORT

Rating: 8

On Upper Blue Lake.

Map 4.1, page 240

Because of their proximity to Clear Lake, the Blue Lakes are often overlooked. But these lovely lakes offer good fishing for trout, especially in spring and early summer on Upper Blue Lake, and a decent chance the rest of the year. With a speed limit (5 mph) in place, quiet boating is the rule. Swimming is good here. For tent camping, a lawn area is available here.

Campsites, facilities: There are 30 sites, two drive-through, with full or partial hookups for RVs, a lawn area for dispersed tent camping, five cabins, and six lodge rooms. Picnic tables and fire grills are provided. Flush toilets, coin showers, RV dump station, clubhouse for groups, boat rentals, boat launching, moorings, boat ramp, convenience store, fishing supplies, and lake frontage sites are available. Leashed pets are permitted.

Reservations, fees: Reservations are accepted for RV sites, cabins, and lodge rooms, not for tent camping. The fee is $18–25 per night, $2 per person for more than two people, $2 per pet per night. Major credit cards accepted. Open year-round.

Directions: From Ukiah, drive north on U.S. 101 for five miles to the junction with Highway 20. Turn east on Highway 20 and drive about 13 miles to Irvine Street. Turn right on Irvine Street and drive one block to Blue Lakes Road. Turn right and drive a short distance to the resort on the right.

Contact: Pine Acres Blue Lakes Resort, 707/275-2811, website: www.bluelakepineacres.com.

33 NARROWS RESORT

Rating: 8

On Upper Blue Lake.

Map 4.1, page 240

This is one of four campgrounds in the immediate vicinity at Blue Lakes. This campground is a good fish camp with boat docks and a fishing cleaning station. The Blue Lakes are often overlooked because of their proximity to Clear Lake, but they are a quiet and pretty alternative, with good trout fishing in the spring and early summer, and decent prospects year-round.

Campsites, facilities: There are 48 sites with full or partial hookups for RVs or tents, five park-model cabins and 14 motel rooms. Picnic tables are provided. Flush toilets, showers, RV dump station, modem access, recreation room, boat rentals, pier, boat ramp, fishing supplies, picnic area, propane, and ice are available. Leashed pets are allowed, but not in motel rooms or cabins.

Reservations, fees: Reservations are accepted at 800/476-2776. The fee is $22–33 per night, $3 per person for more than two people, $3 per pet per night. Major credit cards accepted. Open year-round.

Directions: From Ukiah, drive north on U.S. 101 for five miles to the junction with Highway 20. Turn east on Highway 20 and drive about 11.5 miles to Blue Lakes Road. Turn right and drive one mile to the resort (5690 Blue Lakes Road).

Contact: Narrows Lodge Resort, 707/275-2718.

34 MANCHESTER BEACH KOA

Rating: 7

North of Point Arena at Manchester State Beach.

Map 4.1, page 240

This is a privately operated KOA park set beside Highway 1 and near the beautiful Manchester State Beach. A great plus here is the cute little log cabins, complete with electric heat. They can provide a great sense of privacy, and after a good sleep, campers are ready to explore the adjacent state park.

Campsites, facilities: There are 100 tent sites and 43 sites with full or partial RV hookups. There are also two cottages and 24 cabins. Picnic tables and fire rings are provided. Drinking water, restrooms, flush toilets, showers, modem access, heated pool (seasonal), hot tub and spa, recreation room, playground, RV dump station, a convenience store, ice, firewood, a coin laundry, and propane gas are available. Some facilities are wheelchair-accessible. Leashed pets are permitted.

Reservations, fees: Reservations are accepted at 800/562-4188. The fee is $29–43 per night, $3–5 per person for more than two people. Major credit cards accepted. Open year-round.

Directions: On U.S. 101 north of Santa Rosa, turn west on River Road and drive 13 miles to Guerneville and Highway 116. Continue west on Highway 116 and drive about 20 miles to Highway 1 at Jenner. Turn north on Highway 1 and drive 55 miles to Point Arena. From Point Arena, continue north about six miles to the park on the left (west) side of the road.

Contact: Manchester Beach KOA, 707/882-2375, fax 707/882-3104, website: www.manchester beachkoa.com.

35 HENDY WOODS STATE PARK

Rating: 7

Near Boonville.

Map 4.1, page 240

This is a remarkable setting where the flora changes from open valley grasslands and oaks to a cloaked redwood forest with old growth, as if you had waved a magic wand. The campsites are set in the forest, with a great trail routed amid the old redwoods and up to the Hermit Hut (a fallen redwood stump covered with branches), where a hobo lived for 18 years. No, it wasn't me. The park features two virgin redwood groves, Big Hendy (80 acres with a self-guided discovery trail available), and Little Hendy (20 acres). The headwaters of the Navarro River run through the length of the park, but note fishing is forbidden in the park and that catch-and-release fishing is the law from the bridge at the park entrance on downstream; check regulations. The park is in the middle of the Anderson Valley wine district, which will at first seem an unlikely place to find a 845-acre redwood park, far warmer and less foggy than the redwood parks along the coast.

Campsites, facilities: There are 92 sites for tents or RVs up to 35 feet long, two hike-in/bike-in sites, and four cabins. Picnic tables, food lockers, and fire grills are provided. Drinking water, flush toilets, coin showers, firewood, and RV dump station are available. A seasonal junior ranger program with nature walks, campfire programs, and exhibits is also available. A grocery store and propane gas station are available nearby. Some facilities are wheelchair-accessible. Leashed pets are permitted.

Reservations, fees: Reservations are accepted with a $7.50 reservation fee at 800/444-PARK (800/444-7275) and website www.Reserve America.com. The fee is $12 per night for campsites, $1 per person for hike-in/bike-in sites. Open year-round.

Directions: From Cloverdale on U.S. 101, turn northwest on Highway 128 and drive about 35 miles to Philo Greenwood Road. Turn left on Philo Greenwood Road and drive one-half mile to the park entrance.

Contact: Hendy Woods State Park, 707/895-3141; Mendocino District, 707/937-5804, fax 707/937-2953.

36 WHITLOCK

Rating: 4

In Mendocino National Forest.
Map 4.2, page 241

This obscure Forest Service camp is often empty or close to it. It is set at 4,300 feet, where conifers have taken over from the valley grasslands to the nearby east. The camp is situated amid good deer range and makes a good hunting base camp in the fall, with a network of Forest Service roads in the area. It is advisable to obtain a Forest Service map.

Campsites, facilities: There are three sites for tents or RVs up to 22 feet long. Picnic tables, fire grills, and stoves are provided. Drinking water and a vault toilet are available. Note that a vault toilet is not always available; call if of concern. Garbage must be packed out. Leashed pets are permitted.

Reservations, fees: Reservations are not accepted. There is no fee for camping. Open June through October.

Directions: From Corning on I-5, turn west onto County Road A9/Corning Road and drive 20 miles to Paskenta and Toomes Camp Road/County Road 122. Turn right (north) on Toomes Camp Road/County Road 122 and drive 14 miles to the campground on the right.

Contact: Mendocino National Forest, Grindstone Ranger District, Corning Work Center, 530/824-5196, fax 530/824-6034.

37 WELLS CABIN

Rating: 6

In Mendocino National Forest.
Map 4.2, page 241

You'll join the 5 Percent Club when you reach this spot. It is one mile from Anthony Peak Lookout (6,900 feet) where, on a clear day, you can get great views all the way to the Pacific Ocean and sweeping views of the Sacramento Valley to the east. This campground is hardly used during the summer and often provides a cool escape from the heat of the valley. The elevation is 6,300 feet.

Campsites, facilities: There are 25 sites for tents only. Picnic tables and fire rings are provided. Vault toilets are available. Drinking water is not available in winter. Garbage must be packed out. Leashed pets are permitted.

Reservations, fees: Reservations are not accepted. There is no fee for camping. Open July through October.

Directions: From Corning on I-5, turn west on County Road A9 and drive 20 miles to Paskenta and Forest Road M4. Turn west on Forest Road M4 and drive to the junction with Forest Road 23N16. Turn north and drive three miles the campground.

Contact: Mendocino National Forest, Grindstone Ranger District, Corning Work Center, 530/824-5196, fax 530/824-6034.

38 MASTERSON GROUP CAMP
🏃 🚤 🐕 ⛺

Rating: 5

Near Plaskett Lakes in Mendocino National Forest.

Map 4.2, page 241

This is a group camp only. It is just a half mile away from the Plaskett Lakes, two small lakes set at 6,000 feet and surrounded by a mixed conifer forest. No swimming or motors are permitted at either lake. It is advisable to obtain a map of Mendocino National Forest, which details nearby streams, lakes, and hiking trails. One notable trail is the Black Butte Trail. (For more information, see the entry for Plaskett Meadows.)

Campsites, facilities: This group camp has 20 tent sites for up to 75 people. Fire grills and picnic tables are provided. Drinking water and vault toilets are available. Leashed pets are permitted.

Reservations, fees: Reservations are required. The fee is $35 group fee per night. Open mid-June through mid-October.

Directions: In Willows on I-5, turn west on Highway 162 and drive toward the town of Elk Creek. Just after crossing the Stony Creek Bridge, turn north on County Road 306 and drive four miles. Turn left on Alder Springs Road/Forest Highway 7 and drive 31 miles to the camp on the right.

Contact: Mendocino National Forest, Grindstone Ranger District, Stonyford Work Center, 530/963-3128, fax 530/963-3173.

39 PLASKETT MEADOWS
🏃 🚤 🐕 5% 🚐 ⛺

Rating: 7

In Mendocino National Forest.

Map 4.2, page 241

This is a little-known camp in the mountains near Plaskett Lakes, a pair of connected dot-sized mountain lakes that form the headwaters of little Plaskett Creek. Trout fishing is best at the westernmost of the two lakes. No motors are permitted in the lakes and swimming is not recommended. The camp is set at an elevation of 6,000 feet. Note that Plaskett Lakes were drained to kill weeds and were first restocked with trout in summer of 2002.

Campsites, facilities: There are 35 sites for tents or RVs up to 16 feet long. Fire grills and picnic tables are provided. Drinking water and vault toilets are available. Leashed pets are permitted.

Reservations, fees: Reservations are not accepted. The fee is $5 per night. Open mid-June through mid-October.

Directions: In Willows on I-5, turn west on Highway 162 and drive toward the town of Elk Creek. Just after crossing the Stony Creek Bridge, turn north on County Road 306 and drive four miles. Turn left on Alder Springs Road/Forest Highway 7 and drive 31 miles to the campground on the left.

Contact: Mendocino National Forest, Grindstone Ranger District, Stonyford Work Center, 530/963-3128, fax 530/963-3173.

40 LOWER NYE
🏃 🐕 5% 🚐 ⛺

Rating: 8

In Mendocino National Forest.

Map 4.2, page 241

This camp is on the northern border of the Snow Mountain Wilderness. It is a good jump-off point for backpackers, or a spot for folks who don't want to be bugged by anybody. It is set at 3,300 feet on Skeleton Creek near the Eel River. It is advisable to obtain a detailed USGS topographic map.

Campsites, facilities: There are six sites for tents or RVs. Picnic tables and fire grills are provided. Vault toilets are available. No drinking water is available. Leashed pets are permitted.

Reservations, fees: Reservations are not accepted. There is no fee for camping. Open year-round, weather permitting.

Directions: From Ukiah on U.S. 101, drive

north to the junction of Highway 20. Turn east on Highway 20 and drive to the town of Upper Lake and to Elk Mountain Road. Turn left on Elk Mountain Road (which becomes Forest Road 1N02) and drive 17 miles to Forest Road 18N01/Bear Creek Road. Turn right on Forest Road 18N01/Bear Creek Road and drive seven miles to Forest Road 18N04/Rice Creek Road. Turn north on Forest Road 18N04/Rice Creek Road and drive 14 miles to the campground.

Contact: Mendocino National Forest, Upper Lake Ranger District, 707/275-2361, fax 707/275-0676.

41 SUNSET CAMPGROUND

Rating: 7

On Lake Pillsbury in Mendocino National Forest.
Map 4.2, page 241

This camp is on the northeast corner of Lake Pillsbury, with a boat ramp available at the mouth of Squaw Creek Cove less than a quarter mile to the south. The Lakeshore Trail, an adjacent designated nature trail along the shore of the lake here, is accessible to hikers and equestrians only—no bikes. The surrounding national forest offers side-trip possibilities.

Campsites, facilities: There are 54 sites for tents or RVs. Picnic tables and fire grills are provided. Drinking water and vault toilets are available. A boat ramp is nearby. Leashed pets are permitted.

Reservations, fees: Reservations are not accepted. The fee is $12 per night, $3 per extra vehicle, $1 per pet. Senior discount available. Open May through October.

Directions: From Ukiah on U.S. 101, drive north to the junction with Highway 20. Turn east (right) on Highway 20 and drive five miles. Turn northwest on East Potter Valley Road toward Lake Pillsbury. Drive 5.9 miles to the town of Potter Valley. Continue on East Potter Valley Road to Eel River Road. Turn right

and drive 15 miles to the Eel River Information Kiosk at Lake Pillsbury. Continue east for 4.1 miles to Lake Pillsbury and the junction with Hall Mountain Road. Turn right and drive three miles to the camp entrance.

Contact: Mendocino National Forest, Upper Lake Ranger District, 707/275-2361, fax 707/275-0676; PG&E Land Services, 916/386-5164.

42 OAK FLAT

Rating: 6

On Lake Pillsbury in Mendocino National Forest.
Map 4.2, page 241

This primitive camp provides an option if Lake Pillsbury's other camps are full. It is set at 1,850 feet near the north shore of Lake Pillsbury in the heart of Mendocino National Forest. Nearby trails leading into the backcountry are detailed on a Forest Service map.

Campsites, facilities: There are 12 primitive sites for tents or RVs. Picnic tables and fire grills are provided. Vault toilets are available. No drinking water is available. Garbage must be packed out during the winter. Leashed pets are permitted.

Reservations, fees: Reservations are not accepted. There is no fee for camping. Open year-round.

Directions: From Ukiah on U.S. 101, drive north to the junction with Highway 20. Turn east (right) on Highway 20 and drive five miles to East Potter Valley Road. Turn northwest on East Potter Valley Road toward Lake Pillsbury and drive 5.9 miles to the town of Potter Valley. Continue on East Potter Valley Road to Eel River Road. Turn right and drive 15 miles to the Eel River Information Kiosk at Lake Pillsbury. Continue for four miles around the north end of the lake and look for the camp entrance on the right side of the road.

Contact: Mendocino National Forest, Upper Lake Ranger District, 707/275-2361, fax 707/275-0676.

43 NAVY CAMP

🚶 🏊 🚌 🐕 ♿ 🚐 ⛺

Rating: 7

On Lake Pillsbury in Mendocino National Forest.

Map 4.2, page 241

When Lake Pillsbury is full of water, this is one of the most attractive of the many camps here. It is set in the lake's north cove, sheltered from north winds. Surrounded by forest, the camp is in a pretty setting. However, when the lake level is down, as is common in the fall, it can seem as if the camp is on the edge of a dust bowl.

Campsites, facilities: There are 20 sites for tents or RVs. Picnic tables are provided. Drinking water and vault toilets are available. A boat ramp is nearby. Some facilities are wheelchair-accessible. Leashed pets are permitted.

Reservations, fees: Reservations are not accepted. The fee is $12 per night, $3 for extra vehicle per night, $1 per pet per night. Senior discount available. Open Memorial Day weekend through Labor Day weekend.

Directions: From Ukiah on U.S. 101, drive north to the junction with Highway 20. Turn east (right) on Highway 20 and drive five miles to East Potter Valley Road. Turn northwest on East Potter Valley Road toward Lake Pillsbury and drive 5.9 miles to the town of Potter Valley. Continue on East Potter Valley Road to Eel River Road. Turn right and drive 15 miles to the Eel River Information Kiosk at Lake Pillsbury. Continue for four miles around the north end of the lake and look for the campground entrance on the right side of the road. The campground is on the north shore, just west of Oak Flat Camp.

Contact: Mendocino National Forest, Upper Lake Ranger District, 707/275-2361, fax 707/275-0676. For a map send $6 to Upper Lake Ranger Station, 10025 Elk Mountain Rd., Upper Lake, CA 95485, and ask for Mendocino National Forest area.

44 FULLER GROVE AND FULLER GROVE GROUP CAMP

🚶 🏞 🏊 🚌 🐕 🚐 ⛺

Rating: 7

On Lake Pillsbury in Mendocino National Forest.

Map 4.2, page 241

This is one of several campgrounds bordering Lake Pillsbury, which at 2,000 acres is by far the largest lake in Mendocino National Forest. It has lakeside camping, good boat ramps, and in the spring, good fishing for trout, and in the warmer months for bass. This camp is set along the northwest shore of the lake, with a boat ramp only about a quarter mile away to the north. There are numerous backcountry roads in the area, which provide access to a state game refuge to the north and the Snow Mountain Wilderness to the east.

Campsites, facilities: There are 30 sites for tents or RVs up to 22 feet long, and one group site for up to 100 people. Picnic tables and fire grills are provided. Drinking water and vault toilets are available. A boat ramp is nearby. Leashed pets are permitted.

Reservations, fees: Reservations are accepted for the group site only at 916/386-5164. The fee is $13 per night for single sites, $3 per extra vehicle, $1 per pet, and $100 per night for the group site. Open May through October.

Directions: From Ukiah on U.S. 101, drive north to the junction with Highway 20. Turn east (right) on Highway 20 and drive five miles to East Potter Valley Road. Turn northwest on East Potter Valley Road toward Lake Pillsbury and drive 5.9 miles to the town of Potter Valley. Continue on East Potter Valley Road to Eel River Road. Turn right and drive 15 miles to the Eel River Information Kiosk at Lake Pillsbury. Continue for 2.2 miles to the campground access road. Turn right and drive a quarter mile to the campground.

Contact: Mendocino National Forest, Upper Lake Ranger District, 707/275-2361, fax 707/275-0676; PG&E Land Services, 916/386-5164.

45 LAKE PILLSBURY RESORT

Rating: 6

On Lake Pillsbury.

Map 4.2, page 241

This is a pretty spot beside the shore of Lake Pillsbury in the heart of Mendocino National Forest. It can be headquarters for a vacation involving boating, fishing, water-skiing, or exploring the surrounding national forest. A boat ramp, small marina, and full facilities make this place a prime attraction in a relatively remote location. This is the only resort on the lake that accepts reservations, and it has some lakefront sites.

Campsites, facilities: There are 35 sites for tents or RVs, and eight cabins. A snack bar, restrooms, flush toilets, coin showers, boat rentals, fuel, dock, fishing supplies, and small marina are available. Leashed pets are permitted.

Reservations, fees: Reservations are recommended. The fee is $15.50 per night, $4 per pet per night. Call for cabin prices. Major credit cards accepted. Open May through November.

Directions: From Ukiah on U.S. 101, drive north to the junction with Highway 20. Turn east (right) on Highway 20 and drive five miles to East Potter Valley Road (toward Lake Pillsbury). Turn northwest on East Potter Valley Road and drive 5.9 miles to the town of Potter Valley. Continue on East Potter Valley Road to Eel River Road. Turn right and drive 15 miles to Lake Pillsbury and Forest Road 301F. Turn right at Forest Road 301F and drive two miles to the resort.

Contact: Lake Pillsbury Resort, 707/743-1581, fax 707/743-2666.

46 NORTH FORK

Rating: 2

On Stony Creek in Mendocino National Forest.

Map 4.2, page 241

This primitive camp was largely wiped out by a forest fire. Facilities have been restored, but vegetation was burned and surrounding trees killed. It is set at 1,700 feet at the confluence of the north, south, and middle forks of Stony Creek. There are many trailheads for hiking in the area, within a few miles of the Snow Mountain Wilderness, but none at this camp. There are great views of St. John Mountain and Snow Mountain. (See entry for Mill Creek for additional information.) The elevation is 1,700 feet.

Campsites, facilities: There are six tent sites. Picnic tables and stoves are provided. Vault toilets are available. No drinking water is available. Garbage must be packed out. Leashed pets are permitted.

Reservations, fees: Reservations are not accepted. There is no fee for camping. Open year-round.

Directions: From I-5 at Maxwell, turn west on Maxwell-Sites Road and drive to Sites. Turn left on Sites-Lodoga Road and continue to Lodoga and Lodoga-Stonyford Road. Turn right on Lodoga-Stonyford Road and loop around East Park Reservoir to reach Stonyford and Fouts Springs Road. Turn west on Fouts Springs Road/Forest Road M10 and drive about eight miles to Forest Road 18N03. Turn right on Forest Road 18N03 and drive two miles to the campground on the right.

Contact: Mendocino National Forest, Grindstone Ranger District, Stonyford Work Center, 530/963-3128, fax 530/963-3173.

47 FOUTS AND SOUTH FORK

Rating: 1

On Stony Creek in Mendocino National Forest.

Map 4.2, page 241

These two adjoining camps are in a designated off-highway-vehicle area and are used primarily by dirt bikers. So if you're looking for quiet, these camps are not for you. The landscape was largely vanquished by forest fire, though facilities have been restored, including drinking water at Fouts. Several OHV trails are nearby—North Fork, South Fork, and Mill Creek. To the west is the Snow Mountain Wilderness and excellent hiking trails; to the south is an extensive Forest Service road and OHV trail network. The elevation is 1,700 feet.

Campsites, facilities: There are 11 dispersed sites for tents or RVs up to 16 feet long at Fouts; there are five dispersed tent sites at South Fork. Picnic tables and fire grills are provided. Vault toilets are available. Drinking water is available at Fouts, but no drinking water is available at South Fork. Some facilities are wheelchair-accessible. Leashed pets are permitted.

Reservations, fees: Reservations are not accepted. There is no fee for camping. Open year-round.

Directions: From I-5 at Maxwell, turn west on Maxwell-Sites Road and drive to Sites. Turn left on Sites-Lodoga Road and continue to Lodoga. Turn right on Lodoga-Stonyford Road and loop around East Park Reservoir to reach Stonyford. From Stonyford, turn west on Fouts Springs Road/County Road M10 and drive about eight miles. Turn right (north) on Forest Road 18N03 and drive one mile to the campgrounds on your right.

Contact: Mendocino National Forest, Grindstone Ranger District, Stonyford Work Center, 530/963-3128, fax 530/963-3173.

48 LITTLE STONY CAMPGROUND
🏕️ 🏊 🐕 ♿ 🚐 ⛺

Rating: 7

On Little Stony Creek in Mendocino National Forest.

Map 4.2, page 241

This pretty spot is set in Little Stony Canyon, beside Little Stony Creek at 1,500 feet. Very few people know of the place, and you will find it is appropriately named: it is little, it is stony, and the little trout amid the stones fit right in. The camp provides streamside access and, with Goat Mountain Road running along

most of the stream, it is easy to fish much of this creek in an evening. Expect heavy OHV use from fall through spring.

Campsites, facilities: There are seven sites for tents or small RVs, and two small group sites. Picnic tables and fire grills are provided. Vault toilets are available. No drinking water is available. Most facilities are wheelchair-accessible. Leashed pets are permitted.

Reservations, fees: Reservations are not accepted. There is no fee for camping. Open year-round.

Directions: From I-5 at Maxwell, turn west on Maxwell-Sites Road and drive to Sites. Turn left on Sites-Lodoga Road and continue to where the road crosses Stony Creek. Just after the bridge, turn left on Goat Mountain Road and drive four miles (a rough county road) to the campground on the left.

Contact: Mendocino National Forest, Grindstone Ranger District, Stonyford Work Center, 530/963-3128, fax 530/963-3173.

49 MILL CREEK
🏕️ 🏊 🐕 ⛺

Rating: 3

In Mendocino National Forest.

Map 4.2, page 241

It's a strange experience at this camp, like a camping island. That is because this area, including five of the campsites, was burned by a forest fire. While most of the facilities have been restored, you are still amid the scene of a largely burned-out landscape. It is set beside Mill Creek near Fouts Springs at the southeastern boundary of the Snow Mountain Wilderness. A nearby trailhead, a mile to the west, provides a hiking route into the wilderness that connects along Trout Creek, a great little romp. Mill Creek is quite pretty in the late spring, but by late summer the flow drops way down. The elevation is 1,700 feet. Expect heavy off-highway-vehicle use from October through May; Fouts Springs/Davis Flat is an OHV staging area.

Campsites, facilities: There are six tent sites. Picnic tables, stoves, and barbecues are provided. Vault toilets are available. No drinking water is available. Leashed pets are permitted.

Reservations, fees: Reservations are not accepted. There is no fee for camping. Open year-round.

Directions: From I-5 at Maxwell, turn west on Maxwell-Sites Road and drive to Sites. Turn left on Sites-Lodoga Road and continue to Lodoga. Turn right on Lodoga-Stonyford Road and loop around East Park Reservoir to reach Stonyford. From Stonyford, turn west on Fouts Springs Road/Forest Road M10 and drive about 8.5 miles to the campground entrance on the right.

Contact: Mendocino National Forest, Grindstone Ranger District, Stonyford Work Center, 530/963-3128, fax 530/963-3173.

50 GRAY PINE GROUP CAMP

Rating: 1

In Mendocino National Forest.

Map 4.2, page 241

Similar to Fouts Campground, Gray Pine is set in an area of burned-out forest with many OHV trails nearby. It is near (but not on) Stony Creek. (See Fouts campground for additional information.)

Campsites, facilities: There is one group site that can accommodate 15 to 70 campers with tents or RVs up to 16 feet long. Picnic tables, fire rings, drinking water, a vault toilet, a group barbecue grill, and an amphitheater are available. Leashed pets are permitted.

Reservations, fees: Make reservations at 530/963-3128, no fee. Open year-round.

Directions: From I-5 at Maxwell, turn west on Maxwell-Sites Road and drive to Sites. Turn left on Sites-Lodoga Road and continue to Lodoga. Turn right on Lodoga-Stonyford Road and loop around East Park Reservoir to reach Stonyford. From Stonyford, turn west on Fouts Springs Road/County Road M10 and drive

about eight miles. Turn right on Forest Road 18N03 and drive less than a mile to the campground on your right.

Contact: Mendocino National Forest, Grindstone Ranger District, Stonyford Work Center, 530/963-3128, fax 530/963-3173.

51 DAVIS FLAT

Rating: 1

In Mendocino National Forest.

Map 4.2, page 241

This camp was also a victim to the forest fire that swept through this area in August 2001. It is across the road from Fouts and South Fork campgrounds. All three are in a designated off-highway-vehicle area, so expect OHVers, especially in the winter. This isn't the quietest camp around, but there is some good hiking in the area to the immediate west in the Snow Mountain Wilderness. The elevation is 1,700 feet.

Campsites, facilities: There are 70 dispersed sites for tents or RVs of any length. Picnic tables and fire grills are provided. Drinking water and vault toilets are available. Leashed pets are permitted.

Reservations, fees: Reservations are not accepted. There is no fee for camping. Open year-round.

Directions: From I-5 at Maxwell, turn west on Maxwell-Sites Road and drive to Sites. Turn left on Sites-Lodoga Road and continue to Lodoga. Turn right on Lodoga-Stonyford Road and loop around East Park Reservoir to reach Stonyford. From Stonyford, turn west on Fouts Springs Road/County Road M10 and drive about eight miles. Turn right on Forest Road 18N03 and drive one mile to the campground on your left.

Contact: Mendocino National Forest, Grindstone Ranger District, Stonyford Work Center, 530/963-3128, fax 530/963-3173.

52 DIXIE GLADE HORSE CAMP
🐕 ♿ 🚐 ⛺

Rating: 6

Near the Snow Mountain Wilderness in Mendocino National Forest.

Map 4.2, page 241

Got a horse who likes to tromp? No? Then take a pass on this one. Yes? Then sign right up, because this is a trailhead camp for people preparing to head north by horseback into the adjacent Snow Mountain Wilderness.

Campsites, facilities: This camp has single sites in dispersed area with space for up to 50 people in tents or RVs. Picnic tables and fire grills are provided. Vault toilets are available. No drinking water is available. Garbage must be packed out. Some facilities are wheelchair-accessible. A horse corral, hitching rack, and water in a horse trough is available. Leashed pets are permitted.

Reservations, fees: Reservations are not accepted. There is no fee for camping. Open year-round.

Directions: From I-5 at Maxwell, turn west on Maxwell-Sites Road and drive to Sites and Sites-Lodgoa Road. Turn left on Sites-Lodoga Road and continue to Lodoga and Lodoga-Stonyford Road. Turn right on Lodoga-Stonyford Road and loop around East Park Reservoir to reach Stonyford and Fouts Spring Road. Turn west on Fouts Springs Road/County Road M10 and drive 13 miles to the camp on the left side of the road.

Contact: Mendocino National Forest, Grindstone Ranger District, Stonyford Work Center, 530/963-3128, fax 530/963-3173. For a map, send $6 to U.S. Forest Service, Attn: Map Sales, P.O. Box 9035, Prescott, AZ 86313, 928/443-8285 with credit card, website: www.fs.fed.us/maps/. Ask for Mendocino National Forest.

53 BEAR CREEK CAMPGROUND
🥾 🎣 🐕 5% 🚐 ⛺

Rating: 7

In Mendocino National Forest.

Map 4.2, page 241

This campground is a primitive spot out in the boondocks of Mendocino National Forest, set at 2,000 feet. It's a pretty spot, too, set beside Bear Creek near its confluence with Blue Slides Creek. Trout fishing can be good here. It's about a 10-minute drive to the Summit Springs trailhead at the southern end of the Snow Mountain Wilderness. There are also numerous OHV roads in this region.

Campsites, facilities: There are 16 sites for tents or small RVs. Picnic tables and fire grills are provided. Vault toilets are available. No drinking water is available. Leashed pets are permitted.

Reservations, fees: Reservations are not accepted. There is no fee for camping. Open year-round, weather permitting.

Directions: From Ukiah on U.S. 101, drive north to the junction with Highway 20. Turn east on Highway 20 and drive to the town of Upper Lake and Mendenhall Road. Turn left on Mendenhall Avenue (which becomes Forest Road M1) and drive 17 miles (the latter stretch is extremely twisty) to Forest Road M10. Turn east on Forest Road M10 and drive eight miles to the campground on the right side of the road.

Contact: Mendocino National Forest, Upper Lake Ranger District, 707/275-2361, fax 707/275-0676. Call for road conditions.

54 DEER VALLEY CAMPGROUND
🥾 🐕 5% 🚐 ⛺

Rating: 4

In Mendocino National Forest.

Map 4.2, page 241

This one is way out there. It is used primarily in summer by OHV enthusiasts and in the fall by deer hunters. It is set at 3,700 feet in Deer

Valley, about five miles from the East Fork of Middle Creek.

Campsites, facilities: There are 13 sites for tents or RVs. Picnic tables and fire grills are provided. Vault toilets are available. No drinking water is available. Leashed pets are permitted.

Reservations, fees: Reservations are not accepted. There is no fee for camping. Open year-round, weather permitting.

Directions: From Ukiah on U.S. 101, drive north to the junction with Highway 20. Turn east on Highway 20 and drive to the town of Upper Lake and Mendenhall Road. Turn left on Mendenhall Avenue (which becomes Forest Road M1) and drive 17 miles (the latter stretch is extremely twisty) to Forest Road 16N01. Turn right on Forest Road 16N01 and drive about three miles to the campground.

Contact: Mendocino National Forest, Upper Lake Ranger District, 707/275-2361, fax 707/275-0676.

55 MIDDLE CREEK CAMPGROUND

Rating: 6

In Mendocino National Forest.
Map 4.2, page 241

This camp is not widely known, but it's known well enough as an off-highway-vehicle staging area. Some call it "CC Camp." It is set at 2,000 feet at the confluence of the West and East Forks of Middle Creek.

Campsites, facilities: There are 23 sites for tents or small RVs. Picnic tables and fire grills are provided. Drinking water and vault toilets are available. Leashed pets are permitted.

Reservations, fees: Reservations are not accepted. The fee is $4 single sites, $8 double sites per night, $2 for an extra vehicle. Open year-round.

Directions: From Ukiah on U.S. 101, drive north to the junction with Highway 20. Turn east on Highway 20 and drive to the town of Upper Lake and Mendenhall Road. Turn left on Mendenhall Avenue (which becomes Forest

Road M1) and drive eight miles to the camp on the right side of the road.

Contact: Mendocino National Forest, Upper Lake Ranger District, 707/275-2361, fax 707/275-0676.

56 LETTS LAKE COMPLEX

Rating: 9

In Mendocino National Forest.
Map 4.2, page 241

Not too many folks know about Letts Lake, a 30-acre, spring-fed lake set in a mixed conifer forest at 4,500 feet just south of the Snow Mountain Wilderness. There are four main loops, each with a separate campground, Main, Stirrup, Saddle, and Spillway. The complex is set on the east side of the lake. No motors are allowed at Letts Lake, making it ideal for canoes, rafts, and float tubes. This lake is stocked with rainbow trout in the early summer and is known also for black bass. It's a designated historical landmark, the site where the homesteaders known as the Letts brothers were murdered. While that may not impress you, the views to the north of the Snow Mountain Wilderness will. In addition, there are several natural springs that can be fun to hunt up. By the way, after such a long drive to get here, don't let your eagerness cause you to stop at Lily Pond (on the left, one mile before reaching Letts Lake), because there are no trout in it.

Campsites, facilities: There are four campgrounds with 44 sites for tents or RVs up to 20 feet long. Picnic tables and fire rings are provided. Drinking water and vault toilets are available. A wheelchair-accessible fishing pier is available. There is also an 11-unit picnic area with tables and barbecues on the left side of the lake, open during the day only. Leashed pets are permitted.

Reservations, fees: Reservations are not accepted. The fee is $8 per night and there is a 14-day limit. Senior discount available. Open mid-April through October.

Directions: From I-5 at Maxwell, turn west on Maxwell-Sites Road and drive to Sites and Sites-Lodgoa Road. Turn left on Sites-Lodoga Road and continue to Lodoga and Lodoga-Stonyford Road. Turn right on Lodoga-Stonyford Road and loop around East Park Reservoir to reach Stonyford and Fouts Spring Road. Turn west on Fouts Springs Road/County Road M10 and drive about 17 miles into national forest (where the road becomes Forest Service 17N02) to the campground on the east side of Letts Lake.

Contact: Mendocino National Forest, Grindstone Ranger District, Stonyford Work Center, 530/963-3128, fax 530/963-3173.

57 MILL VALLEY

Rating: 5

Near Letts Lake in Mendocino National Forest.

Map 4.2, page 241

This camp is set beside Lily Pond, a little, teeny guy, with larger Letts Lake just a mile away. Since Lily Pond does not have trout and Letts Lake does, this camp gets far less traffic than its counterpart. The area is crisscrossed with numerous creeks, OHV routes, and Forest Service roads, making it a great adventure for owners of four-wheel drives. The elevation is 4,200 feet.

Campsites, facilities: There are 15 sites for tents or RVs up to 18 feet long. Picnic tables and fire stoves are provided. Vault toilets are available. Drinking water is available seasonally. Leashed pets are permitted.

Reservations, fees: Reservations are not accepted. Fees range from free to $5 per night, depending upon water availability. Senior discount available. Open mid-April through October, weather permitting.

Directions: From I-5 at Maxwell, turn west on Maxwell-Sites Road and drive to Sites and Sites-Lodgoa Road. Turn left on Sites-Lodoga Road and continue to Lodoga and Lodoga-

Stonyford Road. Turn right on Lodoga-Stonyford Road and loop around East Park Reservoir to reach Stonyford and Fouts Spring Road. Turn west on Fouts Springs Road/County Road M10 and drive about 16 miles into national forest (where the road becomes Forest Service 17N02) to the camp access road on the left. Turn left and drive a half mile to the camp.

Contact: Mendocino National Forest, Grindstone Ranger District, Stonyford Work Center, 530/963-3128, fax 530/963-3173.

58 OLD MILL

Rating: 5

Near Mill Creek in Mendocino National Forest.

Map 4.2, page 241

Little known and little used, this camp is set at 3,700 feet amid a mature stand of pine and fir on Trough Spring Ridge. It's at the site of—guess what? An old mill. Expect some OHV company.

Campsites, facilities: There are eight sites for tents and two sites for tents or RVs up to 16 feet long (poor access road for RVs.) Picnic tables and fire stoves are provided. Vault toilets are available. No drinking water is available. All garbage must be packed out. Leashed pets are permitted.

Reservations, fees: Reservations are not accepted. There is no fee for camping. Open May through October.

Directions: From I-5 at Maxwell, turn west on Maxwell-Sites Road and drive to Sites and Sites-Lodgoa Road. Turn left on Sites-Lodoga Road and continue to Lodoga and Lodoga-Stonyford Road. Turn right on Lodoga-Stonyford Road and loop around East Park Reservoir to reach Stonyford and Fouts Spring Road. Turn west on Fouts Springs Road/County Road M10 and and drive about six miles to Forest Road M5. Turn left on Forest Road M5/Trough Springs Road and drive 7.5 miles on a narrow road to the campground on your right.

Contact: Mendocino National Forest, Grindstone Ranger District, Stonyford Work Center, 530/963-3128, fax 530/963-3173.

59 CEDAR CAMP

Rating: 6

In Mendocino National Forest.

Map 4.2, page 241

This camp is set at 4,300 feet elevation, just below Goat Mountain (6,121 feet) to the west about a mile away. Why did anybody decide to build a campground way out here? Because a small spring starts nearby, creating a trickle that runs into the nearby headwaters of Little Stony Creek.

Campsites, facilities: There are five sites for tents or small RVs (the access road is poor for trailers). Picnic tables and fire grills are provided. A vault toilet is available. No drinking water is available. Garbage must be packed out. Leashed pets are permitted.

Reservations, fees: Reservations are not accepted. There is no fee for camping. Open mid-June through mid-October.

Directions: From I-5 at Maxwell, turn west on Maxwell-Sites Road and drive to Sites and Sites-Lodgoa Road. Turn left on Sites-Lodoga Road and continue to Lodoga and Lodoga-Stonyford Road. Turn right on Lodoga-Stonyford Road and loop around East Park Reservoir to reach Stonyford and Fouts Spring Road. Turn west on Fouts Springs Road/County Road M10 and drive about six miles to County Road M5. Turn left on County Road M5 (Trough Springs Road) and drive 13 miles to the campground on your right.

Contact: Mendocino National Forest, Grindstone Ranger District, Stonyford Work Center, 530/963-3128, fax 530/963-3173.

60 KELLY'S FAMILY KAMPGROUND & RV PARK

Rating: 6

On Scotts Creek near Clear Lake.

Map 4.2, page 241

This privately operated park is set beside Scotts Creek, within short driving range of Blue Lakes to the north on Highway 20 and the north end of Clear Lake to the south.

Campsites, facilities: There are 75 sites for tents or RVs, many with partial hookups. Picnic tables, fire pits, and barbecues are provided. Flush toilets, coin showers, RV dump station, coin laundry, ice, and a small camp store are available. Leashed pets are permitted.

Reservations, fees: Reservations are accepted. The fee is $19.25 per night, $2 per night for additional vehicle, $1 per pet per night. Open April through October.

Directions: From Ukiah on U.S. 101, drive north to the junction with Highway 20. Turn east and drive 14 miles (five miles from Upper Lake) to Scotts Valley Road. Turn right (south) and drive to the park on the left (at 8220 Scotts Valley Road).

Contact: Kelly's Family Kampground & RV Park, 707/263-5754.

61 SANDPIPER RV PARK

Rating: 7

On Clear Lake.

Map 4.2, page 241

Sandpiper provides boating access to the northern end of Clear Lake. Fishing for catfish is good near here, both in Rodman Slough and just outside the mouth of the slough. This is where the legendary Catfish George Powers caught 4,000 to 5,000 catfish per year, using dead minnows for bait. In addition, the old submerged pilings in this area provide good bass fishing for boaters casting spinner baits. Several beaches are also available at the north end of the lake. Note that most sites are filled with long-term rentals, with 6–10 sites available for overnighters.

Campsites, facilities: There are 30 sites with full or partial hookups for RVs, and three cabins. Picnic tables are provided. Drinking water, restrooms, flush toilets, showers, and coin laundry are available. Moorings, pier, and boat ramp are available nearby. Leashed pets are permitted.

Reservations, fees: Reservations are accepted. The fee is $17–21 per night, $3 for each additional vehicle, $2–3 per person for more than two people. Open year-round.

Directions: From Ukiah on U.S. 101, drive north to the junction with Highway 20. Turn east on Highway 20 and drive to the town of Nice and Hammond Avenue. Turn right on Hammond Avenue and drive a half mile to Lakeshore Boulevard. Turn left and drive a short distance to 2630 Lakeshore Boulevard.

Contact: Sandpiper RV Park, 707/274-4448.

62 HOLIDAY HARBOR RV PARK & MARINA

Rating: 7

On Clear Lake.

Map 4.2, page 241

This is one of the most popular resorts at the north end of Clear Lake. It is ideal for boaters, with marina gas and a major docking complex. Fishing for bass is good in this area, along old docks and submerged pilings. Water-skiing just offshore is also good, with the north end of the lake often more calm than the water to points south. The elevation is about 2,000 feet. Unlike in several privately owned campgrounds in this area, no long-term rentals are permitted, a plus for vacationers.

Campsites, facilities: There are 30 sites, some drive-through, with full or partial hookups for RVs. Picnic tables are provided. Restrooms, showers, recreation room, modem access, RV dump station, a coin laundry, and ice are available. An enclosed marina with 150 boat slips, boat ramp, and an adjacent beach are also available. Leashed pets are permitted.

Reservations, fees: Reservations are accepted. The fee is $18–19.50 per night, $2.50 per person per night for more than two people. Open year-round.

Directions: From north of Ukiah on U.S. 101, drive north to the junction with Highway 20. Turn east on Highway 20 and drive to the town of Nice and Howard Avenue. Turn left on Howard Avenue and drive 200 feet to the park at the end of the road.

Contact: Holiday Harbor RV Park, 707/274-1136, website: www.sojourner2000.com/clc/hh.

63 CLEAR LAKE STATE PARK

Rating: 9

In Kelseyville at Clear Lake.

Map 4.2, page 241

If you have fallen in love with Clear Lake and its surrounding oak woodlands, it is difficult to find a better spot than at Clear Lake State Park. It is set on the western shore of Clear Lake, and though the oak woodlands flora means you can seem quite close to your camping neighbors, the proximity to quality boating, water sports, and fishing makes the lack of privacy worth it. Reservations are a necessity in summer. That stands to reason, with excellent bass fishing from boats beside a tule-lined shoreline near the park and good catfishing in the sloughs that run through the park. Some campsites have water frontage. The elevation is 2,000 feet. Clear Lake is California's largest natural freshwater lake within state borders. Despite its name, the lake is not clear but green, and in late summer, rather soupy with algae and water grass. The high nutrients in the lake give rise to a flourishing aquatic food chain. With that comes the highest number of large bass of any lake in Northern California. A few short hiking trails are also available at the park. The self-guided Indian Nature Trail passes through the site of what was once a Pomo village. Rangers here are friendly, helpful, and provide reliable fishing information. Junior ranger programs and guided walks for bird and flower identification are also available.

Campsites, facilities: There are 147 sites for tents or RVs up to 35 feet long in four campgrounds, and two hike-in/bike-in sites. Picnic tables and fire rings are provided. Drinking water, restrooms, showers, flush toilets, and RV dump station are available. A boat ramp, dock, fish-cleaning station, and swimming beach are available nearby. A grocery store, coin laundry, propane gas, restaurant, and gas station are available within three miles. The boat ramp, picnic area, and some campsites are wheelchair-accessible. Leashed pets are permitted.

Reservations, fees: Reservations are accepted with a $7.50 reservation fee at 800/444-PARK (800/444-7275) and website www.Reserve America.com. The fee is $12 per night, $1 per person per night for hike-in/bike-in sites. Senior discount available. Open year-round.

Directions: From Vallejo, drive north on Highway 29 to Lower Lake. Turn left on Highway 29 and drive seven miles to Soda Bay Road. Turn right on Soda Bay Road and drive 11 miles to the park entrance on the right side of the road.

From Kelseyville on Highway 29, take the Kelseyville exit and turn north on Main Street. Drive a short distance to State Street. Turn right and drive one-quarter mile to Gaddy Lane. Turn right on Gaddy Lane and drive about two miles to Soda Bay Road. Turn right and drive one mile to the park entrance on the left.

Contact: Clear Lake State Park, 707/279-4293.

64 U-WANNA CAMP

Rating: 3

Near Clear Lake.
Map 4.2, page 241

Whether U-Wanna or not, this could be where you end up if you're hunting for a site on a good-weather summer weekend. The camp is set about two miles from Clear Lake, with a boat ramp at nearby Lakeport. A small fishing pond here is a plus. Note that there are 10 permanent rentals.

Campsites, facilities: There are 30 sites, four drive-through and all with partial hookups for RVs or tents. Picnic tables and fire rings are provided. Drinking water, restrooms, flush toilets, showers, RV dump station, coin laundry, and two playgrounds are available. A fishing pond, horseshoes, basketball, shuffleboard, and ping-pong are available. Leashed pets are permitted.

Reservations, fees: Reservations are accepted at 888/892-6622. The fee is $18–20 per night, $1–2 per person for more than two people, $1 for each extra vehicle, $1 per pet per night. Major credit cards accepted. Open year-round.

Directions: From Highway 29 in Lakeport, go to 11th Street. Turn west and drive a half mile to Riggs Road. Turn left and go three-quarters of a mile to Scotts Creek Road. Turn right and go three-quarters of a mile to the camp on the left (2699 Scotts Creek Road).

Contact: U-Wanna Camp, 707/263-6745.

65 ARROW RV PARK AND MARINA

Rating: 6

On Clear Lake.
Map 4.2, page 241

Lucerne is known for its harbor and its long stretch of well-kept public beaches along the shore of Clear Lake. The town offers a shopping district, restaurants, and cafes. In summer, crappie fishing is good at night from the boat docks, as long as there are bright lights to attract gnats, which in turn attract minnows, the prime food for crappie. Some sites here are filled with long-term rentals.

Campsites, facilities: There are 18 sites, two drive-through and many with full or partial hookups for RVs. Picnic tables, barbecues, restrooms, showers, coin laundry, moorings, fishing supplies, fish-cleaning station, boat ramp, convenience store, and ice are available. Leashed pets are permitted.

Reservations, fees: Reservations are accepted. The fee is $18 per night. Weekly and monthly rates available. Senior discount available. Open year-round.

Directions: From north of Ukiah on U.S. 101 (or from Williams on I-5), turn on Highway 20 and drive to the town of Lucerne. Continue on Highway 20 to the east side of Lucerne and the campground at 6720 E. Hwy. 20.

Contact: Arrow RV Park and Marina, 707/274-7715.

66 GLENHAVEN BEACH CAMP AND MARINA

Rating: 6

On Clear Lake.

Map 4.2, page 241

This makes a good base camp for all boaters, water-skiers, and anglers. It is set on a peninsula on the eastern shore of Clear Lake, with nearby Indian Beach providing a good recreation and water-play spot. In addition, it is a short boat ride out to Anderson Island, Weekend Island, and Buckingham Point, where bass fishing can be excellent along shaded tules.

Campsites, facilities: There are 21 sites with full or partial hookups for RVs up to 26 feet long and tents. Picnic tables and fire rings are provided. Drinking water, restrooms, showers, flush toilets, and a recreation room are available. A boat ramp and boat rentals are available nearby. Leashed pets are permitted.

Reservations, fees: Reservations are accepted. The fee is $16–18 per night, $1 per person for more than two people. Major credit cards accepted. Open February through November.

Directions: From north of Ukiah on U.S. 101 (or I-5 at Williams), turn on Highway 20 and drive to Clear Lake and the town of Glenhaven (four miles northwest of Clearlake Oaks). In Glenhaven, continue on Highway 20 to the camp (lakeside) at 9625 E. Hwy. 20.

Contact: Glenhaven Beach Camp and Marina, 707/998-3406, website: www.glenhaven beach.ohgolly.com.

67 BLUE OAK

Rating: 7

At Indian Valley Reservoir.

Map 4.2, page 241

Indian Valley Reservoir is kind of like an ugly dog that you love more than anything because inside beats a heart that will never betray you. The camp is out in the middle of nowhere in oak woodlands, about a mile from the dam. It is primitive and little known. For many, that kind of isolation is perfect. While there are good trails nearby, it is the outstanding fishing for bass and bluegill at the lake every spring and early summer that is the key reason to make the trip. In addition, in the spring, there is a great variety of wildflowers in and around the campground.

Campsites, facilities: There are six sites for tents or RVs. Picnic tables and fire grills are provided. Drinking water and vault toilets are available. Leashed pets are permitted.

Reservations, fees: Reservations are not accepted. There is no fee for camping. There is a 14-day stay limit. Open year-round, weather permitting.

Directions: From Williams on I-5, turn west on Highway 20 and drive 25 miles into the foothills to Walker Ridge Road. Turn north (right) on Walker Ridge Road (a dirt road) and drive north for about four miles to a "major" intersection of two dirt roads. Turn left and drive about 2.5 miles toward the Indian Valley Dam. The Blue Oak campground is just off the road on the right, about 1.5 miles from Indian Valley Reservoir.

Contact: Bureau of Land Management, Ukiah Field Office, 707/468-4000, fax 707/468-4027. A detailed map is available from the BLM.

68 MANCHESTER STATE PARK

Rating: 8

Near Point Arena.

Map 4.3, page 242

Manchester State Park is a beautiful park on the Sonoma coast, set near the Garcia River with the town of Point Arena to the nearby north providing a supply point. If you hit it during one of the rare times when the skies are clear and the wind is down, the entire area will seem aglow in magical sunbeams. The park features 760 acres of beach, sand dunes, and grasslands, with 18,000 feet of ocean frontage and five miles of gentle sandy beach stretching southward toward the Point Arena Lighthouse. The beach curves to form a catch basin for sea debris, which explains the high volume of driftwood here. The Alder Creek Trail is a great hike here, routed north along beachfront to the mouth of Alder Creek and its beautiful coastal lagoon. This is where the San Andreas Fault heads off from land and into the sea. In winter, the main attraction is steelhead fishing in the Garcia River. In spring and early summer, there is a variety of coastal wildflowers, including sea pinks, poppies, lupines, baby blue eyes, and blue iris. The park provides habitat for tundra swans. The region near the park is grazing land for sheep and cattle.

Campsites, facilities: There are 46 sites for tents or RVs up to 35 feet long, 10 environmental sites, and one group site for up to 40 people and RVs up to 21 feet long. Picnic tables and fire grills are provided. Drinking water, vault toilets, and RV dump station are available. Leashed pets are permitted. No dogs in environmental sites.

Reservations, fees: Reservations are accepted with a $7.50 reservation fee at 800/444-PARK (800/444-7275) and website www.Reserve America.com. The fee is $12 per night, $7 per night for environmental sites, $30 per night for group site. Senior discount available. Open year-round.

Directions: On U.S. 101 north of Santa Rosa, turn west on River Road and drive 16 miles to Guerneville and Highway 116. Continue west on Highway 116 and drive about 20 miles to Highway 1 at Jenner. Turn north on Highway 1 and drive 55 miles to Point Arena. From Point Arena, continue north about five miles to Kinney Lane. Turn left and drive one mile to the campground entrance on the right.

Contact: Manchester State Beach, Mendocino District, 707/937-5804, fax 707/937-2953.

69 ROLLERVILLE JUNCTION

Rating: 7

Near Point Arena.

Map 4.3, page 242

This privately operated campground has gone through recent renovation, including a new restaurant in 2002. Its location makes it an attractive spot, with the beautiful Manchester State Beach, Alder Creek, and Garcia River all available nearby on one of California's most attractive stretches of coastline. Point Arena Lighthouse and a fishing pier are also nearby. The elevation of the camp is 220 feet.

Campsites, facilities: There are 34 sites, some drive-through, with full hookups for RVs, 10 tent sites, five sleeping cabins, and two park-model cabins. Picnic tables and fire rings are provided. Drinking water, restrooms, flush toilets, hot showers, hot tub, heated swimming pool (seasonal), cable TV hookups, modem access, RV dump station, coin laundry, restaurant, small store, and propane gas are available. Some facilities are wheelchair-accessible. Leashed pets are permitted.

Reservations, fees: Reservations are accepted at 800/910-4317. The fee is $26–32 per night, $3–5 per person for more than two people. Major credit cards accepted. Open year-round.

Directions: On U.S. 101 north of Santa Rosa, turn west on River Road and drive 16 miles to Guerneville and Highway 116. Continue west on Highway 116 and drive about 20 miles to Highway 1 at Jenner. Turn north on Highway 1 and drive 55 miles to Point Arena. From Point Arena, continue north for 1.5 miles to Point Arena Lighthouse Road and the campground on the left (west side).

Contact: Rollerville Junction, 707/882-2440, fax 707/882-3049, website: www.rvdestinations .com /rollerville.

70 SHELDON CREEK

Rating: 3

Near Hopland.

Map 4.3, page 242

Only the locals know about this spot, and hey, there aren't a lot of locals around. The camp is set amid rolling hills, grasslands, and oaks along little Sheldon Creek. It is pretty and quiet in the spring when the hills have greened up, but hot in the summer. Recreational possibilities include hiking, and in the fall, hunting.

Campsites, facilities: There are six sites for tents. Picnic tables and fire grills are provided. Vault toilets are available. No drinking water is available. Garbage must be packed out. Leashed pets are permitted.

Reservations, fees: Reservations are not accepted. There is no fee for camping. Open year-round, weather permitting.

Directions: From Santa Rosa on U.S. 101, drive north to Hopland and the junction with Highway 175. Turn east on Highway 175 and drive three miles to Old Toll Road. Turn right on Old Toll Road and drive eight miles to the camp.

Contact: Bureau of Land Management, Ukiah Field Office, 707/468-4000, fax 707/468-4027.

71 ANCHOR BAY CAMPGROUND

Rating: 8

Near Gualala.

Map 4.3, page 242

This is a quiet and beautiful stretch of California coast. The campground is on the ocean side of Highway 1 north of Gualala, with sites set at ocean level as well as amid trees—take your pick. Nearby Gualala Regional Park, six miles to the south, provides an excellent easy hike, the headlands-to-beach loop with coastal views, a lookout of the Gualala River, and many giant cypress trees. In winter, the nearby Gualala River attracts large but elusive steelhead.

Campsites, facilities: There are 26 sites, three with partial hookups, for tents or RVs. Picnic tables and fire rings are provided. Drinking water, restrooms, flush toilets, coin showers, firewood, and RV dump station are available. Leashed pets are permitted.

Reservations, fees: Reservations are accepted. The fee is $27–38, $2–5 per person for more than two people, $10–20 for additional vehicles, $1 per pet per night. Major credit cards accepted. Open year-round.

Directions: On U.S. 101 north of Santa Rosa, turn west on River Road and drive 16 miles to Guerneville and Highway 116. Continue west on Highway 116 and drive about 20 miles to Highway 1 at Jenner. Turn north on Highway 1 and drive 38 miles to Gualala. Continue four miles north on Highway 1 to the campground on the left (west) side of the road.

Contact: Anchor Bay Campground, 707/884-4222, website: www.abcamp.com.

72 GUALALA POINT PARK

Rating: 8

At Sonoma County Regional Park.

Map 4.3, page 242

This is a dramatic spot right on the ocean, adjacent to the mouth of the Gualala River. A trail along the bluff provides an easy hiking adventure; on the west side of the highway other trails to the beach are available.

Campsites, facilities: There are 15 sites for tents and RVs up to 25 feet long, five walk-in tent sites, and one hike-in/bike-in site. Picnic tables and fire rings are provided. Drinking water, restrooms, flush toilets, coin-operated showers,

RV dump station, and wood are available. Some facilities are wheelchair-accessible. Leashed pets are permitted.

Reservations, fees: Reservations are accepted with a $7 reservation fee on weekdays at 707/656-2267. The fee is $16 per night, $3 per person per night for hike-in/bike-in site, $5 per extra vehicle per night, $1 per pet per night. Open year-round.

Directions: On U.S. 101 north of Santa Rosa, turn west on River Road and drive 16 miles to Guerneville and Highway 116. Continue west on Highway 116 and drive about 20 miles to Highway 1 at Jenner. Turn north on Highway 1 and drive 38 miles to Gualala. Turn right at the park entrance (a day-use area is on the west side of the highway).

Contact: Gualala Point, 707/785-2377, website: www.sonoma-county.org.

73 CLOVERDALE KOA

Rating: 7

Near the Russian River.

Map 4.3, page 242

This KOA campground is set just above the Russian River in the Alexander Valley wine country, just south of Cloverdale. The park is both rustic and tidy, with little camping cabins and lodges a great bonus. In addition, a fishing pond is stocked with largemouth bass, bluegill, catfish, and, when water temperatures are cool enough, trout. On moonless nights, this is a great place for stargazing. The nearby Russian River is an excellent beginner's route in an inflatable kayak or canoe. The nearby winery in Asti makes for a popular side trip.

Campsites, facilities: There are 98 sites, six drive-through, with full hookups for RVs, 49 sites for tents, 14 cabins, and three lodges. Picnic tables and fire grills are provided. Flush toilets, showers, modem access, solar-heated swimming pool, playground, RV dump station, coin laundry, recreation room, minigolf, nature trails, catch-and-release fishpond, nightly entertainment on weekends in the summer, and a grocery and gift store are available. Leashed pets are permitted.

Reservations, fees: Reservations are accepted at 800/562-4042. The fee is $32–42 per night, $6 per person for more than two people, $2 per night for extra vehicle. Major credit cards accepted. Open year-round.

Directions: From Cloverdale on U.S. 101, take the Central Cloverdale exit, which puts you on Asti Road. Drive straight on Asti Road to 1st Street. Turn right (east) and drive a short distance to River Road. Turn right (south) and drive four miles to KOA Road. Turn left and drive to the campground entrance.

In summer/fall: south of Cloverdale on U.S. 101, take the Asti exit and drive a short distance to Asti Road. Turn right (south) and drive 1.5 miles to Washington School Road. Turn left (east) and drive 1.5 miles to KOA Road. Turn right and drive to the campground entrance. (Note: this route is open Memorial Day Weekend to late November, when a seasonal bridge is in place.) Both routes are well signed.

Contact: Cloverdale KOA, 707/894-3337. Reservations only at 800/368-4558.

74 DUTCHER CREEK RV PARK AND CAMPGROUND

Rating: 6

Near Lake Sonoma.

Map 4.3, page 242

This privately operated campground provides a layover for U.S. 101 cruisers. It has both native and seasonal plant displays, exceptional opportunities for native bird-watching, and the nearby Asti Vineyard provides a side trip. It is set on 25 acres. Lake Sonoma is seven miles to the west, with the best access provided to the south out of Dry Creek Road (see listing for Lake Sonoma). The elevation is 385 feet. Note that new owners took over in 2001, added a swimming pool—a plus—but majority of sites are long-term rentals, with some mobile homes on the premises—a downer.

Campsites, facilities: There are 38 sites, two drive-through, most with full hookups for RVs up to 36 feet long, and six tent sites. Picnic tables are provided. Drinking water, restrooms, flush toilets, showers, heated swimming pool (seasonal), RV dump station, pay phone, and coin laundry are available. Leashed pets are permitted.

Reservations, fees: Reservations are accepted. The fee is $25–35 per night, $4 per person for more than two people. Open year-round.

Directions: From Santa Rosa, drive north on U.S. 101 beyond Healdsburg to the Dutcher Creek exit (just south of Cloverdale). Take the Dutcher Creek exit, drive west on Theresa Drive under the freeway, continue a half mile to the end of Theresa Drive, and follow signs to the park office at 230 Theresa Drive.

Contact: Dutcher Creek RV Park and Camp, 707/894-4829, fax 707/894-4196.

75 LAKE SONOMA RECREATION AREA

Rating: 8

Near Healdsburg.
Map 4.3, page 242

Lake Sonoma is one of the best weekend vacation sites for Bay Area campers. The developed campground (Liberty Glen) is fine for car campers, but the boat-in sites are ideal for folks who desire a quiet and pretty lakeside setting. This is a big lake, extending nine miles north on the Dry Creek arm and four miles west on the Warm Springs Creek arm. There is an adjacent 8,000-acre wildlife area, as well as 40 miles of hiking trails. The water-skier versus angler conflict has been resolved by limiting high-speed boats to specified areas. Laws are strictly enforced, making this lake excellent for either sport. The best fishing is in the protected coves of the Warm Springs and Dry Creek arms of the lake; use live minnows for bass, which are available at the Dry Creek Store

on the access road south of the lake. The visitor center is adjacent to a public fish hatchery. Steelhead come to spawn from the Russian River between late December and late March.

Campsites, facilities: There are 109 primitive boat-in sites around the lake, several hike-in sites, four group sites (two of which are boat-in), and 95 tent sites and two group sites at Liberty Glen Campground 2.5 miles from the lake. Picnic tables, fire grills, and vault toilets are provided at the primitive sites, but no drinking water is available. At Liberty Glen, picnic tables and fire rings are provided, flush toilets, lantern holders, solar-heated showers, and RV dump station are available. As of late 2002, Liberty Glen had no drinking water. A new well to provide drinking water is planned for 2003. A boat ramp and boat rentals are available nearby. Saturday night campfire talks are held at an amphitheater during the summer. Some facilities are wheelchair-accessible. Campsites have limited facilities in winter. Leashed pets are permitted.

Reservations, fees: Reservations are accepted at 877/444-6777 or website www.ReserveUsa.com. The fee is $16 per night, $10 for primitive sites, $80 per night for group campsites. A camping permit is required from the visitor center for boat-in sites. Open year-round.

Directions: From Santa Rosa, drive north on U.S. 101 to Healdsburg. In Healdsburg, take the Dry Creek Road exit, turn left, and drive northwest for 11 miles. After crossing a small bridge, the visitor center will be on your right.

Contact: Visitor Center, U.S. Army Corps of Engineers, Lake Sonoma, 707/433-9483, fax 707/431-1031, website: www.spn.usace.army.mil; Lake Sonoma Marina, 707/433-2200.

76 SALT POINT STATE PARK

Rating: 9

Near Fort Ross.
Map 4.3, page 242

This is a gorgeous piece of Sonoma coast,

highlighted by Fisk Mill Cove, inshore kelp beds, outstanding short hikes, and abalone diving. There is an underwater reserve for divers. In fact, this is one of the finest diving areas for red abalone in the state. Unfortunately there are also diving accidents that are due the occasional large surf, strong currents, and rocky shoreline. There are two campgrounds here, Gerstle Cove Campground and the much larger Woodside Campground. Great hikes include the Bluff Trail and Stump Beach Trail (great views). During abalone season, this is one of the best and most popular spots on the Northern California coast. The Kruse Rhododendron Reserve is within the park and definitely worth the stroll. This is a 317-acre conservation reserve that features second-growth redwoods, Douglas firs, tan oak, and many rhododendrons, with five miles of hiking trails. After the fall rains, this area is popular for mushroom hunters. Mushroom hunters must park in the area open to picking and be limited to five pounds per day. Of course, this can be a dangerous hobby; only eat mushrooms you can identify as safe. But you knew that, right?

Campsites, facilities: At Gerstle Cove Campground, there are 30 sites for tents or RVs up to 31 feet long. At Woodside Campground, there are 79 sites for tents or RVs up to 31 feet long, 20 walk-in tent sites (about a 300-yard walk), 10 hike-in/bike-in sites, a group site that can accommodate up to 40 people, and a primitive overflow area for self-contained vehicles. Picnic tables and fire rings are provided. Drinking water and flush toilets are available. Summer interpretive programs are also available; firewood is available for purchase. The picnic area and one hiking trail are wheelchair-accessible. Leashed pets are permitted, except on trails.

Reservations, fees: Reservations are accepted with a $7.50 reservation fee at 800/444-PARK (800/444-7275) and website www.Reserve America.com. The fee is $12 per night, $1 per night for hike-in/bike-in sites, $50 for the group site, and $10 per night for overflow sites. Senior discount available. Open year-round.

Directions: On U.S. 101 north of Santa Rosa, turn west on River Road and drive 16 miles to Guerneville and Highway 116. Continue west on Highway 116 and drive about 20 miles to Highway 1 at Jenner. Turn north on Highway 1 and drive about 20 miles to the park entrance; Woodside Campground on the right and Gerstle Cove on the left.

Contact: Salt Point State Park, 707/847-3221; Duncan Mills District, 707/865-2391, fax 707/847-3843.

77 OCEAN COVE CAMPGROUND

Rating: 8

On the ocean five miles north of Fort Ross.

Map 4.3, page 242

The highlights here are the campsites on a bluff overlooking the ocean. Alas, it can be foggy during the summer. A good side trip is to Fort Ross, with a stellar easy hike available on the Fort Ross Trail, which features a walk through an old colonial fort as well as great coastal views, excellent for whale-watching. There is also excellent hiking at Stillwater Cove Regional Park, just a mile to the south off Highway 1.

Campsites, facilities: There are 125 drive-through sites for tents or RVs. Picnic tables and fire grills are provided. Drinking water, chemical toilets, and coin showers are available. A boat launch, grocery store, fishing supplies, and diving gear sales are available nearby. Leashed pets are permitted.

Reservations, fees: Reservations are not accepted. The fee is $14 per night per vehicle, $1 per pet per night. Major credit cards accepted. Open April through November.

Directions: On U.S. 101 north of Santa Rosa, turn west on River Road and drive 16 miles to Guerneville and Highway 116. Continue west on Highway 116 and drive about 20 miles to Highway 1 at Jenner. Turn north on Highway 1 and drive 17 miles north on Highway 1 (five miles north of Fort Ross) to the campground entrance on the left.

Contact: Ocean Cove Campground, 707/847-3422, website: www.ocean-cove.com.

78 STILLWATER COVE REGIONAL PARK
🚶 🚴 🛶 🐕 ⛺ ♿ 🚐 ⛰

Rating: 8

Near Fort Ross.

Map 4.3, page 242

Stillwater Cove has a dramatic rock-strewn cove and sits on a classic chunk of Sonoma coast. The campground is sometimes overlooked, since it is a county-operated park and not on the state park reservation system. One of the region's great hikes is available here: the Stockoff Creek Loop, with the trailhead at the day-use parking lot. In a little over a mile, the trail is routed through forest with both firs and redwoods, and then along a pretty stream. To get beach access, you will need to cross Highway 1 and then drop to the cove.

Campsites, facilities: There are 20 sites for tents or RVs up to 35 feet long, and a hike-in/bike-in site. Picnic tables and fire rings are provided. Drinking water, flush toilets, coin showers, firewood for purchase, and RV dump station are available. Supplies can be obtained in Ocean Cove (one mile north) and Fort Ross. Some facilities are wheelchair-accessible. Leashed pets are permitted.

Reservations, fees: Reservations are accepted with a $7 reservation fee at 707/565-2267 on weekdays. The fee is $16 per night, $5 per night for each additional vehicle, $3 per night for the hike-in/bike-in site, and $1 per pet per night. Open year-round.

Directions: On U.S. 101 north of Santa Rosa, turn west on River Road and drive 16 miles to Guerneville and Highway 116. Continue west on Highway 116 and drive about 20 miles to Highway 1 at Jenner. Turn north on High-

way 1 and drive 16 miles north on Highway 1 (four miles north of Fort Ross) to the park entrance.

Contact: Stillwater Cove Regional Park, Sonoma County, 707/847-3245, website: www.sonoma-county.org.

79 FORT ROSS REEF
🚶 🛶 🐕 ♿ 🚐 ⛰

Rating: 8

At Fort Ross State Historic Park.

Map 4.3, page 242

Fort Ross is just as it name announces: an old fort, in this case, an old Russian fort from 1812. The campground is two miles south of the north entrance station, less than a quarter-mile from the ocean. Some redwoods and pines provide cover, and some sites are open. The privacy and beauty of the campsites vary as much as any state park camp in California. The sites at the end of the road fill up very quickly. Though the weather is relatively benign, tents are needed for moisture from fog. From camp, a trail leads down to a beach, more rocky than sandy, and a quarter-mile trail leads to the fort. As a destination site, Fort Ross is known as a popular abalone diving spot, with the best areas below the campground and also at nearby Reef Terrace. It also provides good, easy hikes amid its 3,386 acres. The park features a museum in the visitor center, which is always a must-see for campers making the tour up Highway 1.

Campsites, facilities: There are 20 sites for tents or RVs up to 17 feet long. No hookups. Picnic tables and fire rings are provided. Drinking water and flush toilets are available. Supplies can be obtained nearby. A visitor center and guided tours and programs are available. Some facilities are wheelchair-accessible. Leashed pets are permitted.

Reservations, fees: Reservations are not accepted. The fee is $12 per night. Open April through November, weather permitting.

Directions: On U.S. 101 north of Santa Rosa, turn west on River Road and drive 16 miles to Guerneville and Highway 116. Continue west on Highway 116 and drive about 20 miles to Highway 1 at Jenner. Turn north on Highway 1 and drive 10 miles north on Highway 1 to the Fort Ross State Park. The campground entrance is two miles north of the main state park entrance.

Contact: Fort Ross State Historic Park, 707/847-3286 or 707/847-3708.

80 CASINI RANCH FAMILY CAMPGROUND

Rating: 8

On the Russian River.

Map 4.3, page 242

Woods and water—this campground has both, with sites set near the Russian River in both sun-filled and shaded areas. Its location on the lower river makes a side trip to the coast easy, with the Sonoma Coast State Beach about a 15-minute drive to the nearby west. No long-term rentals available.

Campsites, facilities: There are 225 sites, some drive-through and many with full or partial hookups, for tents and RVs. Picnic tables and fire grills are provided. Flush toilets, showers, playground, RV dump station, coin laundry, cable TV, video arcade, game arcade, boat and canoe rentals, propane gas, and a grocery store are available. Some facilities are wheelchair-accessible. Leashed pets are permitted.

Reservations, fees: Reservations are accepted. The fee is $24–32 per night, $3 per person for more than two people. Weekly and monthly rates available. Senior discount available. Major credit cards accepted. Open year-round.

Directions: On U.S. 101 north of Santa Rosa, turn west on River Road and drive 16 miles to Guerneville and Highway 116. Continue west on Highway 116 and drive seven miles to Duncan Mills and Moscow Road. Turn left (southeast) on Moscow Road and drive .7 mile to the campground on the left.

Contact: Casini Ranch Family Campground,

800/451-8400 (reservations) or 707/865-2255, fax 707/865-0147.

81 WRIGHTS BEACH

Rating: 8

In Sonoma Coast State Beach.

Map 4.3, page 242

This park provides for more than its share of heaven and hell. This state park campground is at the north end of a beach that stretches south for several miles, yet to the north it is steep and rocky. The campsites are considered a premium because of their location next to the beach. Because the campsites are often full, a key plus is an overflow area available for self-contained vehicles. The beach actually consists of a series of beaches that are separated by rock bluffs and headlands and extends for 17 miles from Bodega Head to Vista Trail (four miles north of Jenner). You can reach the beach from more than a dozen points along the highway. There are many excellent side trips. The best is to the north, where you can explore dramatic Shell Beach (the turnoff is on the west side of Highway 1), or take the Pomo Trail (the trailhead is on the east side of the highway, across from Shell Beach) up the adjacent foothills for sweeping views of the coast. That's the heaven. Now for the hell: more than 125 people have drowned here. Wrights Beach is not for swimming because of rip currents, heavy surf, surprise rogue waves that can make even surf play dangerous. Many rescues are made each year. The bluffs and coastal rocks can also be unstable and unsafe for climbing. Got it? 1. Stay clear of the water. 2. Don't climb the bluffs. Now it's up to you to get it right.

Campsites, facilities: There are 30 sites for tents or RVs up to 27 feet long, with a limit of eight people per site, and an overflow area for self-contained vehicles. Picnic tables and fire rings are provided. Drinking water and flush toilets are available. Showers are available at nearby

Bodega Dunes Campground. Leashed pets are permitted.

Reservations, fees: Reservations are accepted with a $7.50 reservation fee at 800/444-PARK (800/444-7275) and website www.Reserve America.com. The fee is $12 per night. Senior discount available. Open year-round, weather permitting.

Directions: In Petaluma on U.S. 101, take the East Washington exit and turn west (this street becomes Bodega Avenue). Drive west through Petaluma and continue for 17 miles to Highway 1. Turn right (north) on Highway 1 and drive nine miles to Bodega Bay. From Bodega Bay, continue north for six miles to the campground entrance.

Contact: Sonoma Coast State Beach, 707/875-3483.

82 POMO CANYON/WILLOW CREEK WALK-IN

Rating: 10

In Sonoma Coast State Beach.

Map 4.3, page 242

This is a gorgeous camp, well hidden, and offering a great trailhead and nearby beach access. The camp is actually not on the coast at all, but on the east-facing slope of Pomo Canyon (just over the ridge from the coast), where the campsites are set within a beautiful second-growth redwood forest and among fern understory. A trail is routed through the redwoods (with many cathedral trees) and up to the ridge, where there are divine views of the mouth of the Russian River, Goat Rock, and the beautiful Sonoma coast. The trail continues for three miles, all the way to Shell Beach, where you can spend hours poking around and beachcombing. The camp's seclusion and proximity to the Bay Area make it a rare winner. Now get this: a camping option is provided at nearby Willow Creek hike-in sites. Willow Creek Campground is nestled in trees, adjacent to open meadow, next to the Russian River.

Campsites, facilities: At Pomo Canyon, there are 21 walk-in tent sites. Picnic tables and fire grills are provided. Drinking water and pit toilets are available. No pets are permitted. At Willow Creek, there are 11 hike-in sites. No drinking wates. Pit toilets are available, otherwise no facilities. No pets are permitted.

Reservations, fees: Reservations are not accepted. The fee is $7 per night. Open year-round, weather permitting. Occasionally closed in winter because of heavy rain.

Directions: In Petaluma on U.S. 101, take the East Washington exit and turn west (this street becomes Bodega Avenue). Drive west through Petaluma and continue for 17 miles to Highway 1. Turn right (north) on Highway 1 and drive nine miles to Bodega Bay, then continue north for nine miles to Willow Creek Road. To reach Pomo Canyon Campground, turn right on Willow Creek Road and drive about three miles to the campground parking. Park and walk to the campsites, requiring a one- to five-minute walk. To reach Willow Creek Campground, turn right on Willow Creek Road and drive 1.5 miles to campground parking on the left. Hike to the camp.

Contact: Sonoma Coast State Beach, 707/875-3483.

83 BODEGA BAY RV PARK

Rating: 8

In Bodega Bay.

Map 4.3, page 242

Bodega Bay RV Park is one of the oldest RV parks in the state, and there are few coastal destinations better than Bodega Bay. Excellent seafood restaurants are available within five minutes, and some of the best deep-sea fishing is available out of Bodega Bay Sportfishing. In addition, there is a great view of the ocean at nearby Bodega Head to the west. It is a 35-minute walk from the park to the beach.

Campsites, facilities: There are 85 sites, some drive-through and most with full hookups for

RVs, and one trailer rental. Picnic tables and fire rings are provided. Drinking water, flush toilets, and showers are available. Coin laundry, horseshoes, video arcade, boccie ball, modem access, and cable TV hookups are available. Some facilities are wheelchair-accessible. Leashed pets are permitted.

Reservations, fees: Reservations are recommended and may be made at 800/201-6864. The fee is $25–31 per night for two people, $2 for each additional person. Senior discount available in off-season. Major credit cards accepted. Open year-round.

Directions: In Petaluma on U.S. 101, take the East Washington exit and turn west (this street becomes Bodega Avenue). Drive west through Petaluma and continue for 17 miles to Highway 1. Turn right (north) on Highway 1 and drive nine miles to Bodega Bay. In Bodega Bay, continue north for two miles to the RV park on the left.

Contact: Bodega Bay RV Park, 707/875-3701, website: www.bodegabayrv.com.

84 DORAN REGIONAL PARK

Rating: 7

On Bodega Bay.

Map 4.3, page 242

This campground is set beside Doran Beach on Bodega Bay, which offers complete fishing and marina facilities. In season, it's also a popular clamming and crabbing spot. Salmon fishing is often excellent during the summer at the Whistle Buoy offshore from Bodega Head, and rock fishing is good year-round at Cordell Bank. Fishing is also available off the rock jetty in the park.

Campsites, facilities: There are 10 sites for tents and 122 sites for tents or RVs. Picnic tables and fire grills are provided. Drinking water, flush toilets, coin showers, RV dump stations, fish-cleaning station, and a boat ramp are available. Some facilities are wheelchair-accessible. Supplies can be obtained in Bodega Bay. Leashed pets are permitted.

Reservations, fees: Reservations are accepted with a $7 reservation fee on weekdays at 707/565-2267. The fee is $16 per night, $1 per pet per night. Open year-round.

Directions: In Petaluma on U.S. 101, take the East Washington exit and turn west (this street becomes Bodega Avenue). Drive west through Petaluma and continue for 17 miles to Highway 1. Turn right (north) on Highway 1 and drive toward Bodega Bay and look for the campground entrance on the right. If you reach the town of Bodega Bay, you have gone a mile too far.

Contact: Sonoma County Parks Department, 707/875-3540, website: www.sonoma-county.org.

85 BODEGA DUNES

Rating: 8

In Sonoma Coast State Beach.

Map 4.3, page 242

Sonoma Coast State Beach features several great campgrounds, and if you like the beach, this one rates high. It is set at the end of a beach that stretches for miles, providing stellar beach walks and excellent beachcombing during low tides. For some campers, a foghorn sounding repeatedly through the night can make sleep difficult. The quietest sites here are among the dunes. A day-use area includes a wheelchair-accessible boardwalk that leads out to a sandy beach. In summer, campfire programs and junior ranger programs are often available. To the nearby south is Bodega Bay, including a major deep-sea sportfishing operation, crowned by often excellent salmon fishing, best in July. The town of Bodega Bay offers a full marina and restaurants. This beach is far safer than Wrights Beach. (See that listing for details about Sonoma Coast State Beach.)

Campsites, facilities: There are 98 sites for tents or RVs up to 31 feet long, with a limit of eight people per site, and one hike-in/bike-in site. Picnic tables and fire grills are provided. Drinking water, flush toilets, coin showers, and RV dump station are available. Laundry facilities, supplies, and horse rentals are available within one mile. Some facilities are wheelchair-accessible. Leashed pets are permitted at the campsites only.

Reservations, fees: Reservations are accepted with a $7.50 reservation fee at 800/444-PARK (800/444-7275) and website www.Reserve America.com. The fee is $12 per night, $1 per pet per night. Senior discount available. Open year-round, weather permitting.

Directions: In Petaluma on U.S. 101, take the East Washington exit and turn west (this street becomes Bodega Avenue). Drive west through Petaluma and continue for 17 miles to Highway 1. Turn right (north) on Highway 1 and drive nine miles to Bodega Bay. In Bodega Bay, drive one-half mile north to the campground entrance on the left (west).

Contact: Sonoma Coast State Beach, 707/875-3483.

86 WESTSIDE REGIONAL PARK

Rating: 7

On Bodega Bay.

Map 4.3, page 242

This campground is on the west shore of Bodega Bay. One of the greatest boat launches on the coast is nearby to the south, providing access to prime fishing waters. Salmon fishing is excellent from mid-June through August. A small, protected beach (for kids to dig in the sand and wade) is available at the end of the road beyond the campground.

Campsites, facilities: There are 43 sites for tents or RVs. Picnic tables and fire grills are provided. Drinking water, flush toilets, coin showers, RV dump station, fish-cleaning station, and a boat ramp are available. Supplies can be obtained in Bodega Bay, less than one mile away. Some facilities are wheelchair-accessible. Leashed pets are permitted.

Reservations, fees: Reservations are accepted with a $7 reservation fee on weekdays at 707/565-

2267. The fee is $16 per night, $1 per pet per night. Open year-round.

Directions: In Petaluma on U.S. 101, take the East Washington exit and turn west (this street becomes Bodega Avenue). Drive west through Petaluma and continue for 17 miles to Highway 1. Turn right (north) on Highway 1 and drive nine miles to Bodega Bay. In Bodega Bay, continue north to Bay Flat Road. Turn left on Bay Flat Road and drive two miles (looping around the bay) to the campground on the right.

Contact: Westside Regional Parks, Sonoma County Parks Department, 707/875-3540, website: www.sonoma-county.org.

87 AUSTIN CREEK STATE RECREATION AREA

Rating: 7

Near the Russian River.

Map 4.3, page 242

Austin Creek State Recreation Area and Armstrong Redwoods State Reserve are actually coupled, forming 7,000 acres of continuous parkland. Most visitors prefer the redwood park. The campground is called Bullfrog Pond, set near a pond with bluegill. The landscape features open woodlands and foothills with 22 miles of trails. The rugged topography provides a sense of isolation. The highlight at the recreation area is a system of hiking trails that lead to a series of small creeks: Schoolhouse Creek, Gilliam Creek, and Austin Creek. They involve pretty steep climbs, and in the summer it's hot here, with temperatures occasionally exceeding 100°F, so plan accordingly. Elevations range from 150–1,900 feet on Marble Mine Ridge. All of the park's trails are open to horses and horseback riding rentals are available in adjacent Armstrong Redwoods State Park. There are many attractive side-trip possibilities, including the adjacent Armstrong Redwoods, of course, but also canoeing on the Russian River (3.5 miles away), fishing (smallmouth bass in summer, steelhead in winter), and wine-tasting. Annual winter rainfall often exceeds 50 inches. In late summer and fall, the park is sometimes closed because of fire danger.

Campsites, facilities: There are 24 sites for tents only and three hike-in sites. No trailers are allowed. (The access road is very narrow.) Picnic tables and fire grills are provided. Drinking water and flush toilets are available. Some facilities are wheelchair-accessible. Leashed pets are permitted at the main campground only. There are also three primitive, hike-in, backcountry campsites (requiring a hike of 2.5–5 miles) with picnic tables, fire rings, and pit toilets, but no drinking water is available and no pets are permitted. Obtain a backcountry camping permit from the office.

Reservations, fees: Reservations are not accepted. The fee is $12 per night, $1 for hike-in sites, $1 per pet. Open year-round.

Directions: On U.S. 101 north of Santa Rosa, turn west on River Road and drive 15 miles to Guerneville and Armstrong Woods Road. Turn right and drive 2.5 miles to the entrance of Armstrong Redwoods State Park. Continue 3.5 miles through Armstrong Redwoods to Austin Creek State Recreation Area to the campground. The final 2.5 miles are steep and narrow and no trailers, towed vehicles, or vehicles over 20 feet are permitted.

Contact: Austin Creek State Recreation Area, 707/869-2015, fax 707/869-5629.

88 EDGEWATER RESORT AND RV PARK

🏊 🐟 🚤 🐕 🚐 ⛺

Rating: 7

On Clear Lake.

Map 4.4, page 243

Soda Bay is one of Clear Lake's prettiest and most intimate spots, and this camp provides excellent access. Both water-skiing and fishing for bass and bluegill are excellent in this part of the lake, sheltered from north winds for quiet water, with a tule-lined shore from Henderson

Point all the way around to Dorn Bay—nearly three miles of prime fishing territory. This resort specializes in groups and gatherings.

Campsites, facilities: There are 61 sites with full hookups for RVs and tents, and eight cabins (sleep 4–12 people) with air conditioning and heat, kitchenettes, color TV, and cable. Picnic tables and fire grills are provided. Some sites have cable TV. Restrooms, showers, modem access, game room, general store, coin laundry, swimming pool, horseshoes, volleyball, and Ping-Pong are available. A seasonal swimming beach, boat ramp, fishing pier, boat docking, fish-cleaning station, and watercraft rentals are available on premises. Firewood is available for purchase. Leashed pets are permitted. There is a dog run at the beach.

Reservations, fees: Reservations are accepted at 800/396-6224. The fee is $28–38 per night, $5 per person per night for more than two people, $2.50 per pet per night. Major credit cards accepted. Open year-round.

Directions: In Kelseyville on Highway 29, take the Merritt Road exit and drive on Merritt Road for two miles (it becomes Gaddy Lane) to Soda Bay Road. Turn right on Soda Bay Road and drive three miles to the campground entrance on the left.

Contact: Edgewater Resort and RV Park, 707/279-0208, fax 707/279-0138, website: www.edgewaterresort.net.

89 SHAW'S SHADY ACRES

🏊 🐟 🚤 🐕 🚐 ⛺

Rating: 7

On Cache Creek.

Map 4.4, page 243

Shaw's Shady Acres is set beside Cache Creek, just south of Clear Lake. The fishing for catfish is often quite good on summer nights in Cache Creek, a deep green, slow-moving water that looks more like a slough in a Mississippi bayou than a creek. Waterfront campsites with scattered walnut, ash, and oak trees are available. Clear Lake (the lake, not the town) is a short drive to the north.

Campsites, facilities: There are 13 sites, six with full hookups, seven with partial hookups, for RV up to 38 feet and tents. Picnic tables and fire grills are provided. Restrooms, showers, RV dump station, pier, boat rentals, boat ramp, coin laundry, swimming pool (seasonal), recreation patio, beer and wine bar, fishing supplies, and a convenience store are available. Pets must be leashed and may not be left unattended in camp.

Reservations, fees: Reservations are recommended. The fee is $18 per night, $3 per person per night for more than two people, $.50 per pet per night. Open year-round.

Directions: From the town of Lower Lake, drive north on Highway 53 for 1.3 miles to Old Highway 53. Turn left on Old Highway 53 and then almost immediately you will arrive at Cache Creek Way. Turn left and drive a quarter mile to the park entrance.

Contact: Shaw's Shady Acres, 707/994-2236.

90 FUNTIME RV PARK & WATERSPORTS

🏊 🎣 🛶 🐕 ♿ 🚐 ⛺

Rating: 7

On Clear Lake.

Map 4.4, page 243

This is one of several privately operated parks near the mouth of Cache Creek at the southern end of Clear Lake. The park offers sites for tents as well as RVs, many near Cache Creek, which actually looks more like a slough— deep, wide, green, and slow-moving. Some may remember this park as "Garner's Resort." It was purchased and renamed in 2002. Note that a mobile home park is on the premises.

Campsites, facilities: There are 40 sites, most drive-through, with full hookups for RVs, 25 tent sites, four park-model cabins. and two cabins. Picnic tables, barbecues, and cable TV are provided at some sites. Flush toilets, showers, RV dump station, boat rentals, pier,

boat ramp, fish-cleaning station, swimming pool (seasonal), wading pool, fishing supplies, coin laundry, and a convenience store are available. Some facilities are wheelchair-accessible. Leashed pets are permitted.

Reservations, fees: Reservations are accepted. The fee is $18–25 per night, $2 per person per night for more than two people. Senior discount available. Major credit cards accepted. Open year-round.

Directions: From the town of Lower Lake, drive north on Highway 53 for 1.3 miles to Old Highway 53. Turn left on Old Highway 53 and drive 1.2 miles to the resort entrance on the left.

Contact: Funtime RV Park, 707/994-6267, fax 707/994-6248, website: www.funtimervparks.com.

91 CACHE CREEK CANYON REGIONAL PARK

🚶 🎣 🐕 ♿ 🚐 ⛺

Rating: 7

Near Rumsey.

Map 4.4, page 243

This is the best campground in Yolo County, yet it's known by few out-of-towners. It is set at 1,300 feet beside Cache Creek, which is the closest river to the Bay Area that provides white-water rafting opportunities. This section of river features primarily Class I and II water, ideal for inflatable kayaks and overnight trips. One rapid, Big Mother, is sometimes considered Class III, though that might be a stretch. Occasionally, huge catfish are caught in this area.

Campsites, facilities: There are 45 sites for tents or RVs and three group sites that can accommodate 20–30 people. Picnic tables and fire rings are provided. Drinking water, flush toilets, and RV dump station are available. Some facilities are wheelchair-accessible. Leashed pets are permitted.

Reservations, fees: Reservations are not accepted. The fee is $15–17 per night, $5 per night per extra vehicle, $2 per pet per night. Group sites $150 per night, $25 deposit. Senior discount available. Open year-round.

Directions: From Vacaville on I-80, turn north on I-505 and drive 21 miles to Madison and the junction with Highway 16 west. Turn northwest on Highway 16 and drive northwest for about 45 miles to the town of Rumsey. From Rumsey, continue west on Highway 16 for five miles to the park entrance on the left.

Contact: Cache Creek Canyon Regional Park, 530/666-8115, fax 530/666-8837.

92 BOGGS MOUNTAIN DEMONSTRATION STATE FOREST

Rating: 5

Near Middletown.

Map 4.4, page 243

This overlooked spot is set in a state forest that covers 3,500 acres of pine and Douglas fir. There are two adjoining campgrounds here. This is a popular destination for the region's equestrians. There are numerous trails for horses, hikers, and bikers, and there have been some trail conflicts between the groups. Remember: equestrians have the right of way over hikers and bikers, and hikers have the right of way over bikers. Got it? Apparently not, because too many mountain bikers are not yielding out here, and there have been some shouting matches over close calls. Note that in early fall, this area is open to deer hunting, and everybody yields to the guys with rifles. Boggs is one of nine state forests managed with the purpose of demonstrating economical forest management, which means there is logging along with compatible recreation. There is a 14-mile trail system available that started as a series of hand-built fire lines.

Campsites, facilities: There are 20 sites for tents or RVs up to 22 feet long. No drinking water is available. Picnic tables and fire pits are provided. Vault toilets are available. Garbage must be packed out. Coin laundry, pizza parlor, and gas station are available within two miles. Horses are permitted. Leashed pets are permitted.

Reservations, fees: Reservations are not ac-cepted. There is no fee for camping. Self-registration required. Open year-round.

Directions: From Vallejo, drive north on Highway 29 past Calistoga to Middletown and the junction with Highway 175. Turn left (north) on Highway 175 and drive seven miles (through the town of Cobb) to Forestry Road. Turn right and drive one mile to the campgrounds on the left.

Contact: Boggs Mountain Demonstration State Forest, 707/928-4378.

93 BEAVER CREEK RV PARK

Rating: 7

Near Cobb Mountain.

Map 4.4, page 243

This camp has a trout creek, a pond with canoes and kayaks in summer, plus plenty of hiking and bird-watching opportunities. In addition, horseback riding and hot air balloon rides are available nearby. This is one of the few campgrounds in California with tepees. This camp is set near Highway 175 between Middletown and Clear Lake, and while there is a parade of vacation traffic on Highway 29, relatively few people take the longer route on Highway 175. Cobb Mountain looms nearby.

Campsites, facilities: There are 97 sites, most drive-through and all with full hookups for RVs, 10 tent sites, four cabins, and two tepees. Picnic tables and fire rings are provided. Drinking water, restrooms, showers, group area, coin laundry, modem access, pool, kayaks and paddleboats, boating pond, playground, horseshoes, recreation hall, and a store are available. Some facilities are wheelchair-accessible. Leashed pets are permitted.

Reservations, fees: Reservations are accepted at 800/307-2267. The fee is $19–24 per night, $2 per person per night for more than two people. Tepees are $25 per night. Senior discount available. Major credit cards accepted. Open year-round.

Directions: From Vallejo, drive north on Highway 29 past Calistoga to Middletown and the junction with Highway 175. Turn north on

Highway 175 and drive 8.5 miles to Bottle Rock Road. Turn left and drive three miles to the campground entrance on the left side of the road.

Contact: Beaver Creek RV Park, 707/928-4322, fax 707/928-5341, website: www.campbeaver creek.com.

94 LOWER HUNTING CREEK

🏃 🐴 🚐 ⛺

Rating: 4

Near Lake Berryessa.

Map 4.4, page 243

This little-known camp might seem as if it's out in the middle of nowhere for the folks who wind up here accidentally (as we did), and it turns out that it is. If you plan on spending a few days here, it's advisable to get information or a map of the surrounding area from the Bureau of Land Management before your trip. There are about 25 miles of trails for off-highway-vehicle exploration on the surrounding lands. In the fall, the area provides access for deer hunting with generally poor to fair results.

Campsites, facilities: There are five sites for tents or RVs. Picnic tables and fire grills are provided. Shade shelters and vault toilets are available. No drinking water. Garbage must be packed out. Leashed pets are permitted.

Reservations, fees: Reservations are not accepted. There is no fee for camping. Open year-round.

Directions: In Lower Lake on Highway 29, turn southeast on Morgan Valley Road/Berryessa-Knoxville Road and drive 15 miles to Devilhead Road. Turn south and drive two miles to the campground.

Contact: Bureau of Land Management, Ukiah District, 707/468-4000, fax 707/468-4027.

95 NAPA COUNTY FAIRGROUNDS

🌊 🐴 ♿ 🚐 ⛺

Rating: 2

In Calistoga.

Map 4.4, page 243

What this really is, folks, is just the county fairgrounds, converted to an RV park. It is open year-round, including when the county fair is in progress. Who knows, maybe you can win a stuffed animal. What is more likely, of course, is that you have come here for the health spas, with great natural hot springs, mud baths, and assorted goodies at the health resorts in Calistoga. Nearby parks for hiking include Bothe-Napa Valley and Robert Louis Stevenson State Parks.

Campsites, facilities: There are 78 sites, some drive-through, with partial or full hookups for RVs, and a lawn area for tents. Group sites are available by reservation only with a 10-vehicle minimum. Restrooms, showers, and RV dump station are available. No fires are permitted. A nine-hole golf course is adjacent to the campground area. Some facilities are wheelchair-accessible. Leashed pets are permitted.

Reservations, fees: Reservations are accepted and required for groups. The fee is $10-25 per night. Major credit cards accepted. Open year-round.

Directions: From Napa on Highway 29, drive north to Calistoga, turn right on Lincoln Avenue, and drive four blocks to Fairway. Turn left and drive about four blocks to the end of the road to the campground.

Contact: Napa County Fairgrounds, 707/942-5221 (reservations) or 707/942-5111, fax 707/942-5125, website: www.napacountyfairgrounds.com.

96 BOTHE-NAPA VALLEY STATE PARK

🏃 🚲 🏊 🐴 ♿ 🚐 ⛺

Rating: 7

Near Calistoga.

Map 4.4, page 243

It's always a stunner for newcomers to discover this beautiful park with redwoods and a pretty stream so close to the Napa Valley wine and spa country. Though the campsites are relatively exposed, they are set beneath a pretty oak/bay/madrone forest, with trailheads for hiking nearby. One trail is routed south from the day-use parking lot for 1.1 mile to the restored Bale Grist Mill, a giant partially restored waterwheel on a pretty creek. Weekend tours of the Bale Grist Mill are available in summer. Another, more scenic, route, the Redwood Trail, heads up Ritchey Canyon, amid redwoods and towering Douglas fir, and along Ritchey Creek, all of it beautiful and intimate. The park covers 2,000 acres. Most of it is rugged, with elevations ranging from 300 feet to 2,000 feet. In summer, temperatures can reach the 100s, which is why finding a redwood grove can be stunning. The park has 10 miles of trails. Those who explore will find that the forests are on the north-facing slopes while the south-facing slopes tend to be brushy. The geology here is primarily volcanic, yet the vegetation hides most of it. Bird-watchers will note that this is one of the few places where you can see six species of woodpeckers, including the star of the show, the pileated woodpecker (the size of a crow).

Campsites, facilities: There are 40 sites for tents or RVs up to 31 feet long, one hike-in/bike-in site, and one group tent site for up to 30 people. Picnic tables and fire grills are provided. Drinking water, flush toilets, coin-operated showers, and a swimming pool in the summer are available. Some facilities are wheelchair-accessible. Supplies can be obtained four miles away in Calistoga. Leashed pets are permitted.

Reservations, fees: Reservations are accepted with a $7.50 reservation fee at 800/444-PARK (800/444-7275) and website www.Reserve America.com. The fee is $12 per night, $1 for hike-in/bike-in site, $22 for the group site, $1 pool fee (free for children 16 and under). Senior discount available. Open year-round.

Directions: From Napa on Highway 29, drive north to St. Helena and continue north for five miles (one mile past the entrance to Bale Grist Mill State Park) to the park entrance road on the left.

Contact: Bothe-Napa Valley State Park, 707/942-4575.

97 PUTAH CREEK RESORT

Rating: 7

On Lake Berryessa.

Map 4.4, page 243

This campground is set at 400 feet elevation on the northern end of Lake Berryessa. The Putah Creek arm provides very good bass fishing in the spring and trout trolling in the summer. The north end of the lake has a buoy line that keeps powerboats out, but it can still be explored by paddling a canoe, which allows you to fish in relatively untouched waters and see deer during the evening on the eastern shore. In the fall, usually by mid-October, the trout come to the surface and provide excellent fishing at the mouth of Pope Creek or Putah Creek for anglers drifting live minnows. The resort also has a small, rustic motel. There is a two-week camping limit in season.

Campsites, facilities: There are 175 sites for tents, 55 sites with full or partial hookups, some drive-through, for RVs, and a motel. Picnic tables and barbecues are provided. Restrooms, showers, RV dump station, coin laundry, two boat ramps, rowboat rentals, snack bar, motel, cocktail lounge, restaurant, propane gas, ice, and convenience store are available. Leashed pets are permitted; no pit bulls or rottweilers.

Reservations, fees: Reservations are accepted. The fee is $21–26 per night, $21 for a second vehicle, $2 per pet per night. Major credit cards accepted. Open year-round.

Directions: From Vallejo, drive north on I-80 to the Suisun Valley Road exit. Take Suisun Valley Road and drive north to Highway 121. Turn north on Highway 121 and drive five miles to Highway 128. Turn left on Highway 128, drive five miles to Berryessa-Knoxville Road, and continue 13 miles to 7600 Knoxville Road.

Contact: Putah Creek Resort, 707/966-0794 (reservations) or 707/966-2116, fax 707/966-0593.

98 WINDSORLAND RV PARK

Rating: 3

Near Santa Rosa.

Map 4.4, page 243

This developed park is close to the Russian River, the wine country to the east, redwoods to the west, and Lake Sonoma to the northwest. But with a swimming pool, playground, and recreation room, many visitors are content to stay right here, spend the night, then head out on their vacation. Note that some sites are long-term rentals.

Campsites, facilities: There are 55 sites with full hookups for RVs up to 35 feet long, and a separate area for tents. Patios are provided. Flush toilets, showers, heated swimming pool (seasonal), RV dump station, coin laundry, recreation room, picnic area, and a playground are available. Leashed pets are permitted.

Reservations, fees: Reservations are accepted. The fee is $25–30 per night. Monthly rates available. Senior discount available. Open year-round.

Directions: From Santa Rosa on U.S. 101, drive north for nine miles to Windsor. Take the Windsor exit, turn north on Old Redwood Highway, and drive a half mile to the park on the right (9290 Old Redwood Highway).

Contact: Windsorland RV Park, 800/864-3407 or 707/838-4882.

99 FAERIE RING CAMPGROUND

Rating: 7

Near the Russian River.

Map 4.4, page 243

If location is everything, then this privately operated campground is set right in the middle of the best of it in the Russian River region. It is one-half mile north of the Russian River and a half mile south of Armstrong Redwoods State Park.

Campsites, facilities: There are 33 sites for tents, nine sites with full or partial hookups for RVs up to 35 feet long, and several lodging rooms. Picnic tables and fire rings are provided. Drinking water, flush toilets, coin-operated showers, and RV dump station are available. A clubhouse with exercise area and meeting room with kitchen facilities are available for groups. Leashed pets are permitted.

Reservations, fees: Reservations are accepted. The fee is $20–25 per night, $3–5 per person for more than two people, $2 per pet per night. Group and monthly rates available. Major credit cards accepted. Open year-round.

Directions: On U.S. 101 north of Santa Rosa, turn west on River Road and drive 15 miles to Guerneville and Armstrong Woods Road. At Armstrong Woods Road, turn right and drive 1.5 miles to the campground on the right.

Contact: Faerie Ring Campground, 707/869-2746.

100 HILTON PARK FAMILY CAMPGROUND

Rating: 6

On the Russian River.

Map 4.4, page 243

This lush, wooded park is set on the banks of the Russian River, with a choice of open or secluded sites. The highlight of the campground is a large, beautiful beach that offers access for swimming, fishing, and canoeing. The folks here are very friendly, and you get a choice of many recreation options in the area.

Campsites, facilities: There are 20 tent sites and five sites for RVs up to 33 feet long, with no hookups. Picnic tables and fire rings are provided. Restrooms, coin showers, dishwashing area, arcade, playground, firewood, and ice are available. A beach is available nearby. Canoe rentals are available within three miles. Leashed pets are permitted.

Reservations, fees: Reservations are recommended. The fee is $25 per night, $5 per person per night for more than three people. Pets

$5 per night. Senior discount available. Open year-round.

Directions: From U.S. 101 north of Santa Rosa, take the River Road/Guerneville exit. Drive west for 11.5 miles (one mile after the metal bridge) to the campground on the left side of the road (just before the Russian River Pub).

Contact: Hilton Park, 707/887-9206.

101 BURKE'S CANOE TRIPS

Rating: 7

On the Russian River.
Map 4.4, page 243

The catch here is that if you want to camp, you have go on a canoe trip. That's just the deal you might be looking for, a fantastic overnighter for many. Burke's is the long-established canoe rental service and campground on the Russian River. The favorite trip is the 10-miler from Burke's in Forestville to Guerneville, which is routed right through the heart of the area's redwoods, about a 3.5-hour paddle trip with plenty of time in the day for sunbathing, swimming, or anything else you can think of. The cost is $42, including a return by shuttle. Many other trips are available.

Campsites, facilities: There are 60 sites for tents or RVs. Picnic tables and fire rings are provided. Flush toilets, showers, wood, and canoe rentals are available. Pets are not allowed.

Reservations, fees: Reservations are required. The fee is $18 per night, $9 per person per night for more than two people. Open May through mid-October.

Directions: From the Bay Area, drive north on U.S. 101 to the junction with Highway 116 West (just north of Petaluma). Take Highway 116 West and drive 15 miles to Forestville and Mirabel Road (at the gas station). Turn right and drive 1.5 miles until it dead-ends at Burke's and the Russian River.

Contact: Burke's Canoe Trips, 707/887-1222, website: www.burkescanoetrips.com.

102 SCHOOLHOUSE CANYON CAMPGROUND

Rating: 8

In the Russian River Valley.
Map 4.4, page 243

This campground comprises 210 acres and features a mile of river access along the Russian River, campsites in a grove of large redwoods, and a parklike setting on land originally homesteaded in the 1850s. A scenic hiking trail, two miles round-trip, is routed up to a ridge for some nice views of the countryside. This overlooks Korbel Winery and vineyards, with long-distance views of four counties. Touring the adjacent Korbel Winery is a popular side trip.

Campsites, facilities: There are 65 sites, some with partial hookups, for tents or RVs up to 25 feet long. Picnic tables and fire grills are provided. Drinking water, flush toilets, coin showers, and firewood are available. Some facilities are wheelchair-accessible. Leashed pets are permitted.

Reservations, fees: Reservations are accepted. The fee is $25 per night for two people, $5 for each additional person, $5 per night for additional vehicle, $4 per pet per night. Open May through October.

Directions: From Santa Rosa, drive north on U.S. 101 about 2.5 miles and take the River Road/Guerneville exit. Drive to the stop sign, turn left on River Road, and drive 12.5 miles to the campground entrance (next to Korbel Winery) on the right.

Contact: Schoolhouse Canyon Campground, 707/869-2311.

103 MIRABEL TRAILER PARK AND CAMP

Rating: 7

On the Russian River.
Map 4.4, page 243

The big attraction here during the summer is

swimming and paddling around in canoes or kayaks. The campsites are shaded by redwood, pine, and bay trees. This privately operated park is set near the Russian River, but in the summer the "river" is actually a series of small lakes, with temporary dams stopping most of the water flow. In winter, out come the dams, up comes the water, and in come the steelhead, migrating upstream past this area. Armstrong Redwoods State Park just north of Guerneville provides a nearby side trip. Note that about half of the sites are booked for entire summer.

Campsites, facilities: There are 125 sites with full or partial hookups for RVs up to 35 feet and tents. Picnic tables and fire grills are provided. Flush toilets, showers, coin laundry, RV dump station, horseshoes, shuffleboard, a small video arcade, and canoe and kayak rentals are available. Leashed pets, except pit bulls (which are prohibited), are allowed.

Reservations, fees: Reservations are recommended. The fee is $20–33 per night, $3 per person per night for more than two people, $3 per additional vehicle per night, $3 per pet per night. Open March through October.

Directions: North of Santa Rosa on U.S. 101, take the River Road exit and head west. Drive eight miles to the campground on the right at 8400 River Road.

Contact: Mirabel Trailer Park and Camp, tel./fax 707/887-2383.

104 LAKE BERRYESSA MARINA RESORT

🏊 🚤 🛶 🏕 ♿ 🚐 ⛺

Rating: 7

On Lake Berryessa.
Map 4.4, page 243

Lake Berryessa is the Bay Area's backyard water recreation headquarters, the number one lake (in the greater Bay Area) for water-skiing, loafing, and fishing. This resort is set on the west shore of the main lake, one of several resorts at the lake. The addition of park-model cabins is a great plus here.

Campsites, facilities: There are 73 sites for tents, 45 sites with partial hookups for RVs up to 40 feet, and 15 park-model cabins. Flush toilets, showers, RV dump station, coin laundry, snack bar, complete marina facilities, RV supplies, and convenience store are available. Leashed pets are permitted at RV sites (prohibited at tent sites and cabins).

Reservations, fees: Reservations are recommended. The fee is $20–29 per night, $9 per night for additional vehicle, $1 per pet per night. Major credit cards accepted. Open year-round.

Directions: From Vallejo, drive north on I-80 to the Suisun Valley Road exit. Take Suisun Valley Road and drive north to Highway 121. Turn north on Highway 121 and drive five miles to Highway 128. Turn left on Highway 128, drive five miles to Berryessa-Knoxville Road, turn right, and continue nine miles to 5800 Knoxville Road.

Contact: Lake Berryessa Marina Resort, 707/966-2161, fax 707/966-0761, website: www.lake berryessa.com.

105 SPANISH FLAT RESORT

🏊 🚤 🛶 🏕 ♿ 🚐 ⛺

Rating: 7

On Lake Berryessa.
Map 4.4, page 243

This is one of several lakeside camps at Lake Berryessa. As at Lake Berryessa Marina Resort, the addition of park-model cabins has given this resort a nice touch. This is one of the most popular because many of the sites are on the waterfront. That makes it a natural gathering place for water-skiers and power boaters, and on summer weekends, particularly holidays, it can get rowdy here. Berryessa, considered the Bay Area's backyard fishing hole, is the third largest man-made lake in Northern California (Lakes Shasta and Oroville are larger). Trout fishing is good, trolling deep in the summer in Skier's Cove from dawn to mid-morning, or drifting with minnows in fall and winter. The elevation is approximately 500 feet. There is a camping limit of two weeks.

Campsites, facilities: There are 120 sites, a few with partial hookups, for tents or RVs up to 37 feet, two yurts, and 12 park-model cabins. Picnic tables and fire grills are provided. Restrooms, drinking water, flush toilets, showers, boat launch, complete marina facilities, boat rentals, and convenience store are available. A deli and grill is open on summer weekends. Coin laundry, restaurant, and RV supplies are available within 1.5 miles. Some facilities are wheelchair-accessible. Leashed pets are permitted.

Reservations, fees: Reservations are accepted. The fee is $22 per night, $45 per night for yurts, $5 for boat launching, $2 per pet per night. Major credit cards accepted. Open year-round.

Directions: From Vallejo, drive north on I-80 to the Suisun Valley Road exit. Take Suisun Valley Road and drive north to Highway 121. Turn north on Highway 121 and drive five miles to Highway 128. Turn north on Highway 128 and drive five miles to Berryessa-Knoxville Road. Turn right on Berryessa-Knoxville Road and continue four miles to 4290 Knoxville Road.

Contact: Spanish Flat Resort, 707/966-7700, fax 707/966-7704; Spanish Flat Marina, 707/966-7708, website: www.spanishflatresort.com.

106 PLEASURE COVE RESORT

Rating: 7

On Lake Berryessa.

Map 4.4, page 243

Pleasure Cove is set deep in a extended lake arm on the south end of Lake Berryessa. This park is family-oriented. Of the resorts at Berryessa, this one is sometimes overlooked because of its off-the-beaten-path location. It is an excellent area of the lake for trout and bass fishing. Top spots that are nearby include the near Monticello Dam and the narrows, as well as beyond to the north at Skier's Cove for

trout and salmon, and to the south at the back of the coves of the Markley Cove arm for bass.

Campsites, facilities: There are 105 sites, most with partial hookups, for RVs or tents, and five park-model cabins. Picnic tables, fire rings, and barbecues are provided. Restrooms, showers, ice, restaurant, bar, marina, bait and tackle, boat ramp, propane gas, RV dump station, and store are available. Some facilities are wheelchair-accessible. Pets are not permitted.

Reservations, fees: Reservations are accepted. The fee is $20–24 per night per vehicle. Major credit cards accepted. Open year-round.

Directions: From Vallejo, drive north on I-80 about 10 miles to the Suisun Valley Road exit. Take Suisun Valley Road and drive north another 10 miles to Highway 121. Turn north (right) on Highway 121 and drive about eight miles to the end of Highway 121 and the junction with Highway 128. Bear right (southeast) on Highway 128 and proceed four miles to Wragg Canyon Road. Turn left and continue three miles to the resort entrance at the end of the road.

Contact: Pleasure Cove Resort, 707/966-2172, fax 707/966-0320.

107 LAKE SOLANO COUNTY PARK

Rating: 6

Near Lake Berryessa.

Map 4.4, page 243

Lake Solano provides a low-pressure option to nearby Lake Berryessa. It is a long, narrow lake set below the outlet at Monticello Dam at Lake Berryessa, technically called the afterbay. Compared to Berryessa, life here moves at a much slower pace and some people prefer it. The lake has fair trout fishing in the spring, and it is known among Bay Area anglers as the closest fly-fishing spot for trout in the region. No motors, including electric motors, are permitted on boats at the lake. The park covers 177 acres along the river. A swimming pond is available in summer.

Campsites, facilities: There are 50 sites for tents or RVs, and 40 sites, some drive-through, with partial hookups for RVs up to 38 feet long and tents. Picnic tables and fire grills are provided. Drinking water, flush toilets, two RV dump stations, showers, boat ramp (summer weekends only), and boat rentals are available. A grocery store is within walking distance, and firewood and ice are sold on the premises. Some facilities are wheelchair-accessible. Leashed pets are accepted in camping area only.

Reservations, fees: Reservations are recommended with a two-night minimum. The fee is $8–18 per night, $5 for second vehicle, $1 per pet per night. Senior discount available. Major credit cards accepted. Open year-round.

Directions: In Vacaville, turn north on I-505 and drive 11 miles to the junction of Highway 128. Turn west on Highway 128 and drive about five miles (past Winters) to Pleasant Valley Road. Turn left on Pleasant Valley Road and drive to the park at 8685 Pleasant Valley Rd. (well signed).

Contact: Lake Solano County Park, 530/795-2990, fax 530/795-1408.

108 SPRING LAKE REGIONAL PARK

Rating: 6

At Spring Lake near Santa Rosa.

Map 4.4, page 243

Spring Lake is one of the few lakes in the greater Bay Area that provides lakeside camping. Not only that, Spring Lake is stocked twice each month in late winter and spring with rainbow trout by the Department of Fish and Game. Only nonpowered boats are permitted on this small, pretty lake, which keeps things fun and quiet for everybody. An easy trail along the west shore of the lake to the dam, then into adjoining Howarth Park, provides a pleasant evening stroll. This little lake is where a 24-pound world-record bass was reportedly caught, a story taken as a hoax by nearly all anglers.

Campsites, facilities: There are 30 sites for tents

or RVs up to 44 feet long. Picnic tables and fire grills are provided. Drinking water, restrooms with flush toilets, showers, RV dump station, boat ramp (no gas-powered motorboats), and boat rentals (in summer) are available. Some facilities are wheelchair-accessible. A grocery store, coin laundry, firewood, and propane gas are available within five minutes. Leashed pets are permitted with proof of rabies vaccination. There is a 10-day camping limit, with a limit of eight people and two vehicles per campsite.

Reservations, fees: Reservations are accepted at 707/565-2267. The fee is $16 per night, $5 per night for second vehicle, $1 per pet per night. Open daily from mid-May through mid-September and on weekends and holidays only during off-season.

Directions: From Santa Rosa on U.S. 101, turn east on Highway 12 (it will become Hoen Avenue) and continue about a half mile to Newanga Avenue. Turn left and drive a quarter mile to the park at the end of the road.

Contact: Spring Lake Regional Park, Sonoma County Parks, 707/539-8092 or 707/565-2041.

109 SUGARLOAF RIDGE STATE PARK

Rating: 5

Near Santa Rosa.

Map 4.4, page 243

Sugarloaf Ridge State Park is a perfect example of a place that you can't make a final judgment about from your first glance. Your first glance will lead you to believe that this is just hot foothill country, with old ranch roads set in oak woodlands for horseback riding and sweaty hiking or biking. A little discovery here, however, is that a half-mile walk off the Canyon Trail will lead you to 25-foot waterfall, beautifully set in a canyon, complete with a redwood canopy. A shortcut to this waterfall is available off the south side of the park's entrance road. Otherwise, it can be a long, hot, and challenging hike. In all, there are 25 miles of trail here for hikers and equestrians. Hikers planning for a day of it should leave early, wear a hat, and bring plenty of water. Rangers report that some unprepared hikers have suffered heat stroke in summer, and many others have just plain suffered. In the off-season, when the air is cool and clear, the views from the ridge are eye-popping—visitors can see the Sierra Nevada, Golden Gate, and a thousand other points of scenic beauty from the top of Bald Mountain at 2,769 feet. For the less ambitious, a self-guided nature trail along Sonoma Creek begins at the campground.

Campsites, facilities: There are 47 sites for tents or RVs up to 27 feet long, and one group site for tents only for up to 50 people. Picnic tables and fire grills are provided. Drinking water and flush toilets are available. Leashed pets are permitted in campsites only.

Reservations, fees: Reservations are accepted with a $7.50 reservation fee at 800/444-PARK (800/444-7275) and website www.Reserve America.com. The fee is $12 per night, $37 per night for group site. Senior discount available. Open year-round.

Directions: From Santa Rosa on U.S. 101, turn east on Highway 12 and drive seven miles to Adobe Canyon Road. Turn left and drive 3.5 miles to the park entrance at the end of the road.

Contact: Sugarloaf Ridge State Park, 707/833-5712.

110 NAPA VALLEY EXPOSITION RV PARK

Rating: 2

In Napa.

Map 4.4, page 243

This RV park is directly adjacent to the Napa County Fairgrounds. When the fair is in operation in early August, it is closed for 10 days. The rest of the year it is simply a RV parking area, and it can come in handy.

Campsites, facilities: There are 100 sites, 40 drive-through, with partial hookups for RVs and a grassy area for up to 100 self-contained RVs. Picnic tables, restrooms, showers, coin laundry, and RV dump station are available. A camp host is on-site. A grocery store and restaurant are within walking distance. Leashed pets are permitted.

Reservations, fees: Reservations are not accepted. The fee is $20 per night, $5 per night for extra vehicle, $1 per pet per night. Reservations required for groups. Open year-round.

Directions: From Napa on Highway 29, drive to the Napa/Lake Berryessa exit. Turn east and drive to 3rd Street. Turn right and drive 1.5 blocks to Burnell Street and the campground entrance on the left.

Contact: Napa Valley Exposition, 707/253-4900, fax 707/253-4943, website: www.napa valleyexpo.com.

111 SAN FRANCISCO NORTH/PETALUMA KOA

Rating: 3

Near Petaluma.

Map 4.4, page 243

This campground is less than a mile from U.S. 101, yet it has a rural feel in a 60-acre farm setting. It's a good base camp for folks who require some quiet mental preparation before heading south to the Bay Area or to the nearby wineries, redwoods, and the Russian River. The big plus here is that this KOA has the cute log cabins called "Kamping Kabins," providing privacy for those who want it. There are recreation activities and live music on-site in summer.

Campsites, facilities: There are 312 sites, 161 drive-through, most with full or partial hookups, for RVs or tents, and 34 cabins. Picnic tables and fire grills are provided. Flush toilets, showers, cable TV hookups, modem access, RV dump station, playground, recreation rooms, heated swimming pool (seasonal), whirlpool, petting farm, shuffleboard, coin laundry, propane gas, and a convenience

store are available. Some facilities are wheelchair-accessible. Leashed pets are permitted.
Reservations, fees: Reservations are accepted at 800/562-1233. The fee is $27–49 per night, $4–7 per person for more than two people. Major credit cards accepted. Open year-round.

Directions: From Petaluma on U.S. 101, take the Penngrove exit and drive west for a quarter mile on Petaluma Boulevard to Stony Point Road. Turn right (north) on Stony Point Road and drive a quarter mile to Rainsville Road. Turn left (west) on Rainsville Road and drive a short distance to the park entrance (signed, 20 Rainsville Road).

Contact: San Francisco North/Petaluma KOA, 707/763-1492, fax 707/763-2668, website: www.koa.com.

© TOM STIENSTRA

Chapter 5
Sacramento and
Gold Country

Chapter 5—Sacramento and Gold Country

From a distance, this section of the Sacramento Valley looks like flat farmland extending into infinity, with a sprinkling of cities and towns interrupting the view. But a closer look reveals a landscape filled with Northern California's most significant rivers—the Sacramento, Feather, Yuba, American, and Mokelumne. All of these provide water recreation, in both lakes and rivers, as well as serve as the lifeblood for a series of wildlife refuges.

This is an area for California history buffs, with Malakoff Diggins State Historic Park and Placerville KOA in the center of some of the state's most extraordinary history: the gold rush era. In addition, Malakoff Diggins has the lowest-cost cabin rentals in the state that we could find—$10 a night. Another great deal is the Lake Oroville Floating Camps, which can sleep 15 and cost only $42 a night.

The highlight of the foothill country for lake recreation is the series of great lakes for water sports and fishing. These include Camanche, Rollins, Oroville, and many others. Note that the mapping we use for this region extends up to Bucks Lake, which is set high in Plumas National Forest, the northern start to the Gold Country.

Timing is everything in love and the great outdoors, and so it is in the Central Valley and the nearby foothills. Spring and fall are gorgeous here, along with many summer evenings. But there are always periods of 100-plus temperatures in the summer.

But that's what gives the lakes and rivers such appeal, and in turn, why they are treasured. Take your pick: Lake Oroville in the northern Sierra, Folsom Lake outside Sacramento. .. the list goes on. On a hot day, jumping into a cool lake makes water more valuable than gold, a cold drink on ice worth more than silver. These have become top sites for boating-based recreation and fantastic areas for water sports and fishing.

In the Mother Lode country, three other lakes—Camanche, Amador, and Pardee—are outstanding for fishing. The guidebook *Foghorn Outdoors California Fishing* ranks three of this chapter's lakes among the top 10 lakes for fishing in the state—Lake Oroville and Lake Camanche make the list for bass and Lake Amador makes it for bluegill and catfish—no small feat considering the 381 other lakes they were up against.

For touring, the state capital and nearby Old Sacramento are favorites. Others prefer reliving the gold-mining history of California's past or exploring the foothill country, including Malakoff Diggins State Historic Park.

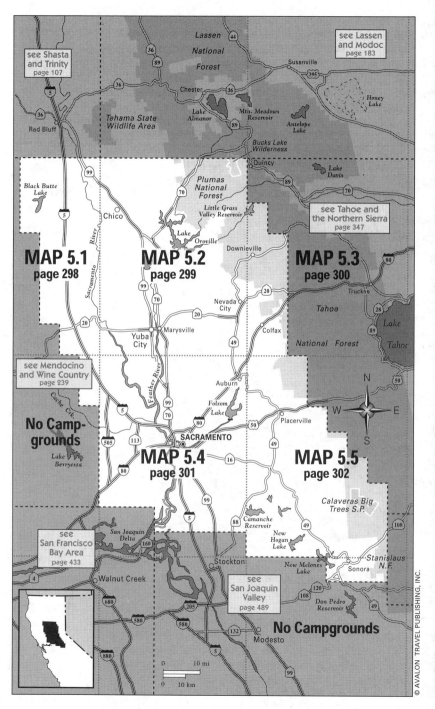

Map 5.1

Campgrounds 1–7
Pages 303–305

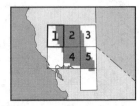

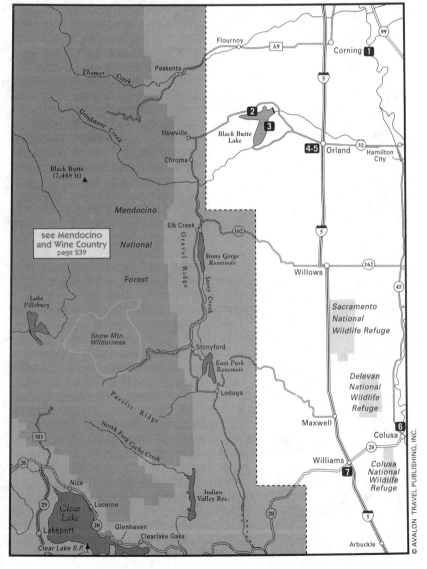

Map 5.2

Campgrounds 8–37
Pages 305–318

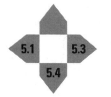

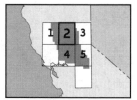

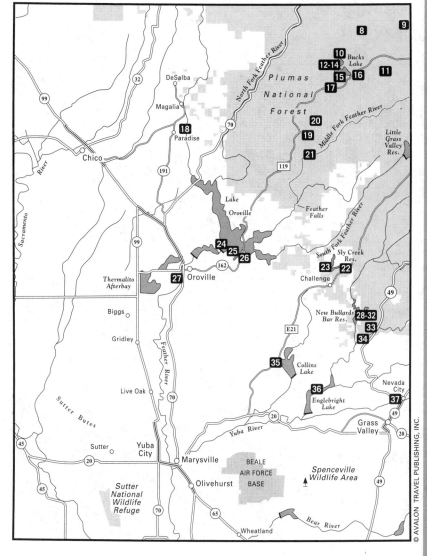

Map 5.3

Campgrounds 38–62
Pages 319–329

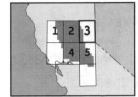

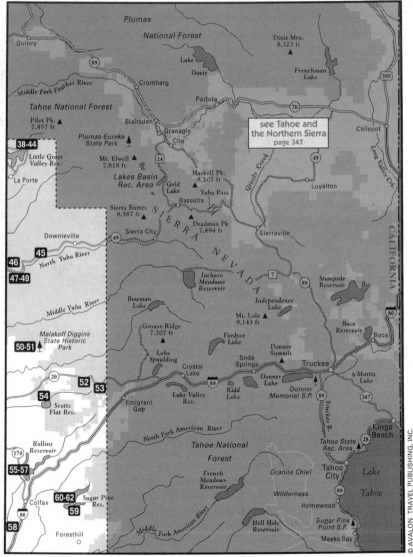

© AVALON TRAVEL PUBLISHING, INC.

Map 5.4

Campgrounds 63–73
Pages 330–334

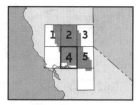

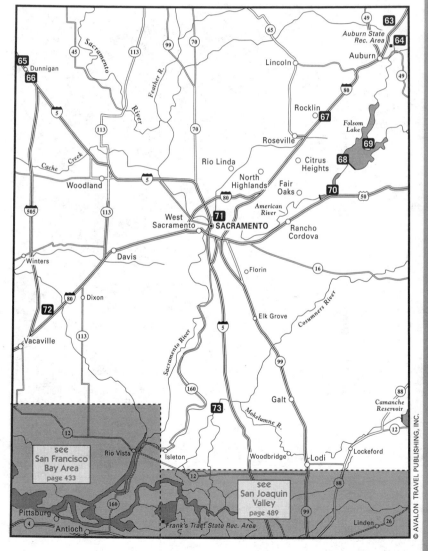

Map 5.5

Campgrounds 74–92
Pages 335–343

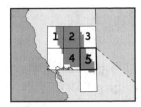

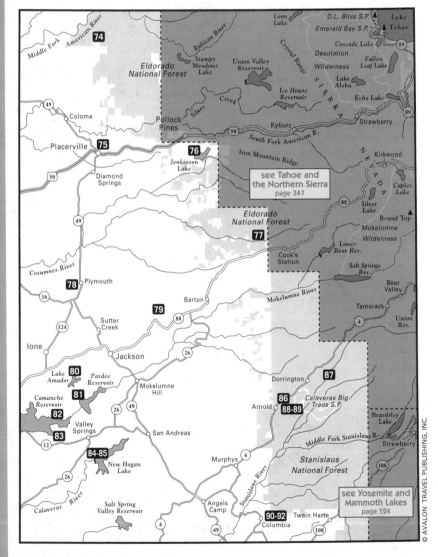

© AVALON TRAVEL PUBLISHING, INC.

◼1 WOODSON BRIDGE STATE RECREATION AREA

Rating: 7

On the Sacramento River.

Map 5.1, page 298

This campground features direct access to the Sacramento River, and a boat ramp makes it an ideal spot for campers with trailered boats. The boat ramp is across the road in the county park, providing easy access for water sports. This is a 328-acre preserve with a dense, native riparian forest, with a sand and gravel beach on the river. The junglelike grove displays some of the last remaining virgin riparian habitat on the 400-mile length of the Sacramento River. In June, the nearby Tehama Riffle is one of the best spots on the entire river for shad. By mid-August, salmon start arriving, en route to their spawning grounds. Summer weather here is hot, with high temperatures commonly 85–100°F and up. In winter, it is home to bald eagles, and in summer, provides a nesting site for the yellow bill cuckoo.

Campsites, facilities: There are 37 sites for tents or RVs up to 31 feet long and five boat-in sites. One group site is available. Picnic tables and fire grills are provided. Drinking water, showers, flush toilets, and boat launch (across the street) are available, and there is a camp host. Some facilities are wheelchair-accessible, but the restrooms are not. Leashed pets are permitted.

Reservations, fees: Reservations are accepted with a $7.50 reservation fee at 800/444-PARK (800/444-7275) and website www.Reserve America.com. The fee is $10 per night. Senior discount available. $30 for the group camp. Open year-round.

Directions: From I-5 in Corning, take the South Avenue exit and drive nine miles east to the campground on the left.

Contact: Woodson Bridge State Recreation Area, 530/839-2112; North Buttes District,

530/538-2200; Bidwell Mansion Visitor Center, 530/895-6144.

◼2 BUCKHORN

Rating: 7

On Black Butte Lake.

Map 5.1, page 298

Black Butte Lake is set in the foothills of the north valley at 500 feet. It is one of the 10 best lakes in Northern California for crappie, best in spring. There can also be good fishing for largemouth, smallmouth, and spotted bass, channel catfish, bluegill, and sunfish. Recreation options include power boating, sailboating, windsurfing, and hiking nearby. For dirt bikers, an off-highway motorcycle park is available at the Buckhorn Recreation Area.

Campsites, facilities: There are 65 sites for tents or RVs up to 35 feet long. Picnic tables and fire grills are provided. Drinking water, flush toilets, RV dump station, showers, and a playground are available. A boat ramp, propane gas, and a grocery store are within walking distance. Some facilities are wheelchair-accessible. Leashed pets are permitted.

Reservations, fees: Make reservations at 877/444-6777 or website: www.ReserveUsa.com, $14 per night. Senior discount available. Open year-round.

Directions: From I-5 in Orland, take the Black Butte Lake exit. Drive about 12 miles west on Road 200/Newville Road to Buckhorn Road. Turn left and drive a short distance to the campground on the north shore of the lake.

Contact: Black Butte Lake, U.S. Army Corps of Engineers, 530/865-4781, fax 530/865-5283.

◼3 ORLAND BUTTES

Rating: 7

On Black Butte Lake.

Map 5.1, page 298

Black Butte Lake isn't far from I-5, but a lot

of campers zoom right by it. The prime time to visit is in late spring and early summer, when the bass and crappie fishing can be quite good. Three self-guided nature trails are in the immediate area. (See entry for Buckhorn Camp for more information.) Note: in late winter and early spring, this area is delightful as spring arrives. But from mid-June through August, expect very hot, dry weather.

Campsites, facilities: There are 35 sites for tents or RVs up to 35 feet long. Picnic tables and fire grills are provided. Drinking water, restrooms, showers, boat ramp, a public telephone, and RV dump station are available. Leashed pets are permitted.

Reservations, fees: Make reservations at 877/444-6777 or website: www.ReserveUsa.com, $14 per night. Senior discount available. Open April through mid-July.

Directions: From I-5 in Orland, take the Black Butte Lake exit. Drive west on Road 200/Newville Road for eight miles to Road 206. Turn left and drive three miles to the camp entrance on the left.

Contact: Black Butte Lake, U.S. Army Corps of Engineers, 530/865-4781, fax 530/865-5283.

4 GREEN ACRES RV PARK

Rating: 3

Near Orland.
Map 5.1, page 298

This is a layover spot near I-5 in the Central Valley, set in the heart of olive and almond country. It's a restful setting, but hot in summer, at times unbearable without air conditioning. Salmon fishing is available on the nearby Sacramento River, best from mid-August through October.

Campsites, facilities: There are 68 sites, most drive-through, with partial or full hookups for RVs, and 24 tent sites. A store, coin laundry, RV dump station, barbecues, recreation room, modem access, seasonal swimming pool, and ice are available. Leashed pets are permitted.

Reservations, fees: Reservations are recommended. The fee is $15–20 per night, $3 per person for more than two people. Senior discount available. Monthly rates available. Open year-round.

Directions: From Orland on I-5, take the Highway 32 exit and drive a half mile west to the campground at 4515 County Road H.

Contact: Green Acres RV Park, 800/468-9452 or 530/865-9188.

5 OLD ORCHARD RV PARK

Rating: 4

Near Orland.
Map 5.1, page 298

Most folks use this as a layover spot while on long trips up or down I-5 in the Central Valley. If you're staying longer than a night, there are two side trips that have appeal for anglers. Nearby Black Butte Lake to the west, with crappie in the early summer, and the Sacramento River to the east, with salmon in the late summer and early fall, can add some spice to your trip. The elevation is 250 feet.

Campsites, facilities: There are 52 sites, all drive-through, with partial or full hookups for RVs up to 60 feet long, and a large separate site for tents only. Showers, RV dump station, coin laundry, modem access, clubhouse, and a small store are available. Some facilities are wheelchair-accessible. Leashed pets are permitted.

Reservations, fees: Reservations are accepted. The fee is $15–24 per night, $2 per person for more than two people. Major credit cards accepted. Open year-round.

Directions: From I-5 at Orland, take the Chico/Highway 32 exit west. Drive west one block to County Road HH. Turn right on County Road HH and drive one block to the park on the right at 4490 County Road HH.

Contact: Old Orchard RV Park, 877/481-9282, fax 530/865-5335.

6 COLUSA-SACRAMENTO RIVER STATE RECREATION AREA

Rating: 5

Near Colusa.

Map 5.1, page 298

This region of the Sacramento Valley is well known as a high-quality habitat for birds. This park covers 67 acres and features great bird-watching opportunities. Nearby Delevan and Colusa National Wildlife Refuges are outstanding destinations for wildlife-viewing as well, and they provide good duck hunting in December. In summer the nearby Sacramento River is a bonus with shad fishing in June and July, salmon fishing from August through October, sturgeon fishing in the winter, and striped bass fishing in the spring. The landscape here features cottonwoods and willows along the Sacramento River.

Campsites, facilities: There are 14 sites for tents or RVs up to 30 feet long, and one group site for a minimum of 10 people and maximum of 40 people. Picnic tables and barbecues are provided. Drinking water, flush toilets, hot showers, and RV dump station are available. Some facilities are wheelchair-accessible. A grocery store, restaurant, gas station, tackle shop, and coin laundry are nearby (within three blocks). A boat ramp for small boats is available. Leashed pets are permitted.

Reservations, fees: Reservations are accepted with a $7.50 reservation fee at 800/444-PARK (800/444-7275) and website www.Reserve America.com. The fee is $10 per night, $30 per night for the group site. Senior discount available. Open year-round.

Directions: In Williams, at the junction of I-5 and Highway 20, drive east on Highway 20 for 10 miles to the town of Colusa. Turn north (straight ahead) on 10th Street and drive two blocks, just over the levee, to the park.

Contact: Colusa-Sacramento River State Recreation Area, tel./fax 530/458-4927; North Buttes District, 530/538-2200.

7 ALMOND GROVE MOBILE HOME PARK

Rating: 1

In Williams.

Map 5.1, page 298

The town of Williams is set in the middle of the Sacramento Valley, a popular spot to stop and grab a bite at its outstanding delicatessen and restaurant, Granzella's, where there is a gigantic stuffed polar bear in a room filled with about 100 wildlife mounts.

Campsites, facilities: There are seven pull-through RV sites with full hookups. Picnic tables are provided. Restrooms, showers, cable TV (included with hookup), and a coin laundry are available. Some facilities are wheelchair-accessible. A store is nearby (within six blocks). Leashed pets are permitted.

Reservations, fees: Reservations are accepted. The fee is $14 per night. Open year-round.

Directions: In the Sacramento Valley on I-5, drive to Williams and the Central Williams exit. Take that exit and drive west on E Street for eight blocks to 12th Street. Turn left on 12th Street and drive three blocks to the entrance at 880 12th Street.

Contact: Almond Grove Mobile Home Park, 530/473-5620.

8 SILVER LAKE

Rating: 8

In Plumas National Forest.

Map 5.2, page 299

While tons of people go to Bucks Lake for the great trout fishing and lakeside camps, nearby Silver Lake gets little attention despite great natural beauty, good hiking, decent trout fishing, and a trailhead to the Bucks Lake Wilderness. The camp is at the north end of the lake, 5,800 feet elevation, a primitive and secluded spot. No powerboats (or swimming) are allowed on Silver Lake, which makes it ideal for canoes and rafts. The lake has lots of small brook trout. The Pacific Crest Trail is routed on the ridge above the lake, skirting past Mt. Pleasant (6,924 feet) to the nearby west.

Campsites, facilities: There are eight tent sites. Picnic tables and fire grills are provided. Vault toilets are available. Garbage must be packed out. No drinking water is available. Leashed pets are permitted.

Reservations, fees: Reservations are not accepted. There is no fee for camping. Open May through October.

Directions: From Oroville, drive north on Highway 70 to the junction with Highway 89. Turn south on Highway 89/70 and drive 11 miles to Quincy and Bucks Lake Road. Turn right at Bucks Lake Road and drive west for nine miles to Silver Lake Road. Turn right and drive seven miles to the campground at the north end of the lake.

Contact: Northwest Park Management, 530/283-5559, website: www.ucampwithus.com; Plumas National Forest, Mt. Hough Ranger District, 530/283-0555, fax 530/283-1821.

9 SNAKE LAKE

Rating: 8

In Plumas National Forest.

Map 5.2, page 299

Snake Lake is a rarity in the northern Sierra, a mountain lake that has bass, catfish, and bluegill. That is because it is a shallow lake, set at 4,200 feet in Plumas National Forest. The camp is on the west shore. A road that circles the lake provides a good bicycle route for youngsters. A side trip to the nearby north is Smith Lake, about a five-minute drive, with the Butterfly Valley Botanical Area bordering it.

Campsites, facilities: There are seven tent sites. Picnic tables and fire grills are provided. Vault toilets are available. No drinking water is available. Garbage must be packed out. Leashed pets are permitted.

Reservations, fees: Reservations are not accepted. There is no fee for camping. Open May through October.

Directions: From Oroville, drive north on Highway 70 to the junction with Highway 89. Turn south on Highway 89/70 and drive 11 miles to Quincy and Bucks Lake Road. Turn right at Bucks Lake Road and drive five miles to County Road 422. Turn right and drive two miles to the Snake Lake access road. Turn right and drive one mile to the campground on the right.

Contact: Northwest Park Management, 530/283-5559, website: www.ucampwithus.com; Plumas National Forest, Mt. Hough Ranger District, 530/283-0555, fax 530/283-1821.

10 MILL CREEK

Rating: 7

At Bucks Lake in Plumas National Forest.

Map 5.2, page 299

When Bucks Lake is full, this is one of the prettiest spots on the lake. The camp is set deep in Mill Creek Cove, adjacent to where Mill Creek enters the northernmost point of Bucks Lake. A boat ramp is a half mile away to the south, providing boat access to one of the better trout fishing spots at the lake. Unfortunately, when the lake level falls, this camp is left high and dry, some distance from the water. The elevation is 5,200 feet.

Campsites, facilities: There are eight sites for tents or RVs up to 27 feet long and two walk-in tent sites. Picnic tables and fire grills are provided. Drinking water and vault toilets are available. Groceries are available within five miles. Leashed pets are permitted.

Reservations, fees: Reservations are not accepted. The fee is $16 per night. Senior discount available. Open mid-May through September, weather permitting.

Directions: From Oroville, drive north on Highway 70 to the junction with Highway 89. Turn south on Highway 89/70 and drive 11 miles to

Quincy. In Quincy, turn right at Bucks Lake Road and drive 17 miles to Bucks Lake and the junction with Bucks Lake Dam Road/Forest Road 33. Turn right, drive around the lake, cross over the dam, and continue for about three miles to the campground.

Contact: Northwest Park Management, 530/283-5559, website: www.ucampwithus.com; Plumas National Forest, Mt. Hough Ranger District, 530/283-0555, fax 530/283-1821.

11 DEANES VALLEY

Rating: 5

On Rock Creek in Plumas National Forest.
Map 5.2, page 299

This secret spot is set on South Fork Rock Creek, deep in a valley at an elevation of 4,400 feet in Plumas National Forest. The trout here are very small natives. If you want a pure, quiet spot, great. If you want great fishing, not great. The surrounding region has a network of backcountry roads, including routes passable only by four-wheel-drive vehicles; to explore these roads, get a map of Plumas National Forest.

Campsites, facilities: There are seven sites for tents or RVs. Picnic tables and fire grills are provided. Vault toilets are available. No drinking water is available. Garbage must be packed out. Leashed pets are permitted.

Reservations, fees: Reservations are not accepted. There is no fee for camping. Open April through October.

Directions: From Oroville, drive north on Highway 70 to the junction with Highway 89. Turn south on Highway 89/70 and drive 11 miles to Quincy and Bucks Lake Road. Turn right at Bucks Lake Road and drive 3.5 miles to Forest Road 24N28. Turn left and drive seven miles to the campground on the left.

Contact: Northwest Park Management, 530/283-5559, website: www.ucampwithus.com; Plumas National Forest, Mt. Hough Ranger District, 530/283-0555, fax 530/283-1821.

12 SUNDEW

Rating: 7

On Bucks Lake in Plumas National Forest.
Map 5.2, page 299

Sundew Camp is set on the northern shore of Bucks Lake, just north of Bucks Lake Dam. A boat ramp is about two miles north at Sandy Point Day Use Area at the Mill Creek Cove, providing access to one of the better trout spots on the lake. You want fish? At Bucks Lake you can get fish—it's one of the state's top mountain trout lakes. Sunrises are often spectacular from this camp, with the light glowing on the lake's surface.

Campsites, facilities: There are 20 sites for tents or RVs up to 27 feet long. Picnic tables and fire grills are provided. Drinking water and vault toilets are available. Leashed pets are permitted. There is a boat ramp two miles north of the camp.

Reservations, fees: Reservations are not accepted. The fee is $14 per night, $16 for lakeside sites. Senior discount available. Open mid-May through September, weather permitting.

Directions: From Oroville, drive north on Highway 70 to the junction with Highway 89. Turn south on Highway 89/70 and drive 11 miles to Quincy. In Quincy, turn right at Bucks Lake Road and drive 17 miles to Bucks Lake and the junction with Bucks Lake Dam Road/Forest Road 33. Turn right, drive around the lake, cross over the dam, continue for a half mile, and turn right at the campground access road.

Contact: Northwest Park Management, 530/283-5559, website: www.ucampwithus.com; Plumas National Forest, Mt. Hough Ranger District, 530/283-0555, fax 530/283-1821.

13 HUTCHINS GROUP CAMP

Rating: 6

Near Bucks Lake in Plumas National Forest.
Map 5.2, page 299

This is a prime spot for a Scout outing or for

any other large group that would like a pretty spot. An amphitheater is available. It is set at 5,200 feet near Bucks and Lower Bucks Lakes. (For more information, see the entries for the following nearby campgrounds: Lower Bucks, Haskins Valley, and Sundew.)

Campsites, facilities: There are three group sites for tents or RVs, each with a maximum of 25 people and eight vehicles. Picnic tables and fire grills are provided. Drinking water and vault toilets are available. A boat ramp is available. Leashed pets are permitted.

Reservations, fees: Reservations are required at 877/444-6777 or website www.ReserveUsa.com. The fee is $45 per night. Open May through October.

Directions: From Oroville, drive north on Highway 70 to the junction with Highway 89. Turn south on Highway 89/70 and drive 11 miles to Quincy and Bucks Lake Road. Turn right at Bucks Lake Road and drive 17 miles to Bucks Lake and the junction with Bucks Lake Dam Road/Forest Road 33. Turn right, drive around the lake, cross over the dam, continue for a short distance, and turn right. Drive a half mile, cross the stream (passing an intersection), and continue straight for a half mile to the campground.

Contact: Northwest Park Management, 530/283-5559, website: www.ucampwithus.com; Plumas National Forest, Mt. Hough Ranger District, 530/283-0555, fax 530/283-1821.

14 LOWER BUCKS

Rating: 7

On Lower Bucks Lake in Plumas National Forest.

Map 5.2, page 299

This camp is on Lower Bucks Lake, which is actually the afterbay for Bucks Lake, set below the Bucks Lake Dam. It is a small, primitive, and quiet spot that is often overlooked because it is not on the main lake.

Campsites, facilities: There are six sites for RVs

only up to 26 feet long. Picnic tables and fire rings are provided. No drinking water or toilets are available. Leashed pets are permitted.

Reservations, fees: Reservations are not accepted. The fee is $10 per night. Senior discount available. Open May through October.

Directions: From Oroville, drive north on Highway 70 to the junction with Highway 89. Turn south on Highway 89/70 and drive 11 miles to Quincy and Bucks Lake Road. Turn right at Bucks Lake Road and drive 17 miles to Bucks Lake and the junction with Bucks Lake Dam Road/Forest Road 33. Turn right and drive four miles around the lake, cross over the dam, drive a quarter mile, and then turn left on the campground entrance road.

Contact: Northwest Park Management, 530/283-5559, website: www.ucampwithus.com; Plumas National Forest, Mt. Hough Ranger District, 530/283-0555, fax 530/283-1821.

15 HASKINS VALLEY

Rating: 7

On Bucks Lake.

Map 5.2, page 299

This is the biggest and most popular of the campgrounds at Bucks Lake, a pretty alpine lake with excellent trout fishing and clean campgrounds. A boat ramp is available to the nearby north, along with Bucks Lodge. This camp is set deep in a cove at the extreme south end of the lake, where the water is quiet and sheltered from north winds. Bucks Lake, 5,200 feet elevation, is well documented for excellent fishing for rainbow and Mackinaw trout, with high catch rates of rainbow trout and lake records in the 16-pound class.

Campsites, facilities: There are 65 sites for tents or RVs. Picnic tables and fire grills are provided. Drinking water and vault toilets are available. RV dump station and boat ramp are available nearby. Leashed pets are permitted.

Reservations, fees: Reservations are not accepted. The fee is $15 per night, $3 per extra vehicle per night, $7 per extra RV per night, $1 per pet per night. Open May through October, weather permitting.

Directions: From Oroville, drive north on Highway 70 to the junction with Highway 89. Turn south on Highway 89/70 and drive 11 miles to Quincy. In Quincy, turn right at Bucks Lake Road and drive 16.5 miles to the campground entrance on the right side of the road.

Contact: PG&E Land Services, 916/386-5164, fax 916/923-7044, website: www.pge.com/recreation.

16 WHITEHORSE

Rating: 7

Near Bucks Lake in Plumas National Forest.
Map 5.2, page 299

This campground is set along Bucks Creek, about two miles from the boat ramps and south shore concessions at Bucks Lake. The trout fishing can be quite good at Bucks Lake, particularly on early summer evenings. The elevation is 5,200 feet. (For more information, see the entry for Haskins Valley.)

Campsites, facilities: There are 20 sites for tents or RVs up to 27 feet long. Picnic tables and fire grills are provided. Drinking water and vault toilets are available. A grocery store and coin laundry are available within five miles. Leashed pets are permitted.

Reservations, fees: Reservations are not accepted. The fee is $14 per night. Senior discount available. Open June through September.

Directions: From Oroville, drive north on Highway 70 to the junction with Highway 89. Turn south on Highway 89/70 and drive 11 miles to Quincy and Bucks Lake Road. Turn right at Bucks Lake Road and drive 14.5 miles to the campground entrance on the right side of the road.

Contact: Northwest Park Management, 530/283-5559, website: www.ucampwithus.com; Plumas National Forest, Mt. Hough Ranger District, 530/283-0555, fax 530/283-1821.

17 GRIZZLY CREEK

Rating: 4

Near Bucks Lake in Plumas National Forest.
Map 5.2, page 299

This is an alternative to the more developed, more crowded campgrounds at Bucks Lake. It is a small, primitive camp set near Grizzly Creek at 5,400 feet in elevation. Nearby Bucks Lake provides good trout fishing, resorts, and boat rentals.

Campsites, facilities: There are eight sites for tents or RVs up to 35 feet long. Picnic tables and fire grills are provided. Drinking water and vault toilets are available. A boat ramp is available at Bucks Lake. A grocery store and coin laundry are available within five miles. Leashed pets are permitted.

Reservations, fees: Reservations are not accepted. The fee is $14 per night. Senior discount available. Open June through October.

Directions: From Oroville, drive north on Highway 70 to the junction with Highway 89. Turn south on Highway 89/70 and drive 11 miles to Quincy and Bucks Lake Road. Turn right at Bucks Lake Road and drive 17 miles to Bucks Lake and the junction with Bucks Lake Dam Road/Forest Road 33. Turn right and drive one mile to the junction with Oroville-Quincy Road/Forest Road 36. Bear left and drive one mile to the campground on the right side of the road.

Contact: Northwest Park Management, 530/283-5559, website: www.ucampwithus.com; Plumas National Forest, Mt. Hough Ranger District, 530/283-0555, fax 530/283-1821.

18 QUAIL TRAILS VILLAGE

Rating: 4

Near Paradise.
Map 5.2, page 299

This is a rural motor home campground, set near the west branch of the Feather River, with nearby Lake Oroville as the feature attraction. The Lime Saddle section of the Lake Oroville State Recreation Area is nearby, with a beach, boat launching facilities, and concessions. Note: some sites are taken by long-term rentals here.

Campsites, facilities: There are 20 sites, all drive-through, with full hookups for RVs, and five tent sites. Picnic tables are provided. Restrooms, hot showers, and coin laundry are available. Some facilities are wheelchair-accessible. Leashed pets are permitted.

Reservations, fees: Reservations are accepted. The fee is $12.50–18 per night, $2 per person for more than two people. Open year-round.

Directions: From Oroville, drive north on Highway 70 to Highway 191/Clark Road on the left. Turn left on Highway 191 and drive to Paradise and Pearson Road (lighted intersection). Turn right and drive 4.5 miles to the end of the road at Pentz Road. Turn right and drive 1.5 miles south to the park on the left (5110 Pentz Road).

Contact: Quail Trails Village, 530/877-6581, fax 530/876-0516.

19 ROGERS COW CAMP

Rating: 4

In Plumas National Forest.

Map 5.2, page 299

First note that the Oroville-Quincy "Highway" is actually a twisty Forest Service road, a backcountry route that connects Oroville to Quincy and passes Lake Oroville and Bucks Lake in the process. The road is paved, but it can still put you way out there in no-man's-land, set in Plumas National Forest at 4,000 feet. You want quiet, you get it. You want water, you bring it yourself. The camp is set near the headwaters of Coon Creek. There are no other natural destinations in the area, and I'm not saying Coon Creek is anything to see. It's advisable to obtain a map of Plumas National Forest, which details all backcountry roads. There has been logging activity in the area.

Campsites, facilities: There are five sites for tents or RVs. Picnic tables and fire grills are provided. Vault toilets are available. No drinking water is available. Garbage must be packed out. Leashed pets are permitted.

Reservations, fees: Reservations are not accepted. There is no fee for camping. Open May through September.

Directions: In Oroville, drive east on Highway 162 /Oroville-Quincy Highway for 26.5 miles to the Brush Creek Work Center. Continue on Oroville-Quincy Highway for eight miles to the campground entrance road on the left side of the road. Turn left and drive a short distance to the camp.

Contact: Plumas National Forest, Feather River Ranger District, 530/534-6500, fax 530/532-1210.

20 LITTLE NORTH FORK

Rating: 7

On the Middle Fork of the Feather River in Plumas National Forest.

Map 5.2, page 299

Guaranteed quiet? You got it. This is a primitive camp in the outback that few know of. It is set along the Little North Fork of the Middle Fork of the Feather River at 4,000 feet. The surrounding backcountry of Plumas National Forest features an incredible number of roads, giving four-wheel drive owners a chance to get so lost they'll need this camp. Instead, get a map of Plumas National Forest before venturing out.

Campsites, facilities: There are eight sites for tents or RVs up to 16 feet long. Picnic tables and fire grills are provided. Vault toilets are available. No drinking water is available. Garbage must be packed out. Leashed pets are permitted.

Reservations, fees: Reservations are not accepted. There is no fee for camping. Open May through October.

Directions: From Oroville, turn east on Highway 162/Oroville-Quincy Highway and drive 26.5 miles to the Brush Creek Work Center. Continue northeast on Oroville-Quincy Highway for about six miles to Forest Road 60. Turn right and drive about eight miles to the campground entrance road on the left side of the road. Turn left and drive a quarter mile to the campground. Note: this route is long, twisty, bumpy, and narrow for most of the way.

Contact: Plumas National Forest, Feather River Ranger District, 530/534-6500, fax 530/532-1210.

21 MILSAP BAR

Rating: 8

On the Middle Fork of the Feather River in Plumas National Forest.

Map 5.2, page 299

Among white-water river rafters, Milsap Bar is a well-known access point to the Middle Fork Feather River. This river country features a deep canyon, beautiful surroundings, and is formally recognized as the Feather Falls Scenic Area (named after the awesome 640-foot waterfall). Note that while no commercial raft companies are permitted to run this section of the Feather, private groups or individual use are permitted. The elevation is 1,600 feet.

Campsites, facilities: There are 20 sites for tents or RVs up to 16 feet long. Picnic tables and fire grills are provided. Vault toilets are available. No drinking water is available. Garbage must be packed out. Leashed pets are permitted.

Reservations, fees: Reservations are not accepted. There is no fee for camping. Open May through September.

Directions: In Oroville, drive east on Highway 162/Oroville-Quincy Highway for 26.5 miles to the Brush Creek Work Center and Bald Rock Road. Turn right on Bald Rock Road and drive for about a half mile to Forest Road 22N62/Milsap Bar Road. Turn left and drive

eight miles to the campground (a narrow, steep, mountain dirt road).

Contact: Plumas National Forest, Feather River Ranger District, 530/534-6500, fax 530/532-1210.

22 STRAWBERRY

Rating: 7

On Sly Creek Reservoir in Plumas National Forest.

Map 5.2, page 299

Sly Creek Reservoir is a long, narrow lake set in western Plumas National Forest. There are two campgrounds on opposite ends of the lake, with different directions to each. This camp is set in the back of a cove on the lake's eastern arm at an elevation of 3,530 feet, with a nearby boat ramp available. This is a popular lake for trout fishing in the summer. You must bring your own drinking water. The water source (such as at the fish-cleaning station) has a high mineral content and strong smell.

Campsites, facilities: There are 17 sites for tents, trailers, or RVs. Picnic tables and fire grills are provided. No drinking water. Vault toilets are available. A car-top boat launch and fish-cleaning station (do not drink the water here) are available on Sly Creek Reservoir. Leashed pets are permitted.

Reservations, fees: Reservations are not accepted. The fee is $14 per night. Senior discount available. Open late April to mid-October, weather permitting.

Directions: From Oroville, drive east on Highway 162 for about eight miles to the junction signed Challenge/LaPorte. Bear right and drive east on LaPorte Road past Challenge and continue for about 14 miles to a signed turnoff on the left for Sly Creek Reservoir. Turn left and drive one mile to the campground on the eastern end of the lake.

Contact: Plumas National Forest, Feather River Ranger District, 530/534-6500, fax 530/532-1210.

23 SLY CREEK

🏊 🎣 🚤 🐕 ♿ 🚐 ⛺

Rating: 7

On Sly Creek Reservoir in Plumas National Forest.

Map 5.2, page 299

Sly Creek Camp is set on Sly Creek Reservoir's southwestern shore near Lewis Flat, with a boat ramp about a mile to the north. Both camps are well situated for campers/anglers. This camp provides direct access to the lake's main body, with good trout fishing well upstream on the main lake arm. You get quiet water and decent fishing.

Campsites, facilities: There are 31 sites for tents, trailers, or RVs up to 40 feet long. Five walk-in tent cabins are also available. Picnic tables and fire grills are provided. Drinking water and vault toilets are available. A car-top boat launch and fish-cleaning stations are available on Sly Creek Reservoir. Leashed pets are permitted.

Reservations, fees: Reservations are not accepted. The fee is $14 per night. Senior discount available. Open late April to mid-October, weather permitting.

Directions: From Oroville, drive east on Highway 162 for about eight miles to the junction signed Challenge/LaPorte. Bear right (toward LaPorte) and drive east on LaPorte Road past Challenge and continue for 10 miles to Forest Road 16 (a signed turnoff on the left). Turn left and drive 4.5 miles to the campground.

Contact: Plumas National Forest, Feather River Ranger District, 530/534-6500, fax 530/532-1210.

24 LAKE OROVILLE BOAT-IN AND FLOATING CAMPS

🚶 🏊 🎣 🚤 🐕 ♿ 🚐 ⛺

Rating: 10

On Lake Oroville.

Map 5.2, page 299

It doesn't get any stranger than this, and for those who have tried, it doesn't get any better. We're talking about the double-decker floating camps at Lake Oroville, along with the great boat-in sites. The floating camps look like giant patio boats. They sleep 15 people and they include picnic table, sink, food locker, garbage can, vault toilet, and propane barbecue, and for $42 a night, it might be the best family camping deal in the state. There are also a series of dispersed boat-in campsites around the lake, which are particularly excellent in the spring and early summer, when the water level at the lake is high. In late summer, when the lake level drops, it can be a fair hike up the bank to the campsites, and in addition, if the water drops quickly, your boat can be left sitting on the bank; it can be quite an effort to get it back in the water. Oroville is an outstanding lake for water sports, with warm water and plenty of room, and also with excellent bass fishing, especially in the spring.

Campsites, facilities: There are dispersed boat-in sites, one group boat-in site (Bloomer) for up to 75 people, and 10 boat-in Floating Camps. Picnic tables, food lockers, and fire grills are provided. Vault toilets are available. No drinking water is provided. Leashed pets are permitted, except on trails or beaches; pets must be enclosed at night.

Reservations, fees: Reservations are accepted with a $7.50 reservation fee only for Floating Camps at 800/444-PARK (800/444-7275) or website www.ReserveAmerica.com. The fee is $42 per night, individual boat-in sites are $7 per night, and the group boat-in site is $30 per night. Open year-round.

Directions: From Oroville, drive east on Oroville Dam Road/Highway 162 for seven miles to Canyon Drive. Turn left and drive two miles to Oroville Dam. Turn left and drive over the dam to the spillway parking lot at the end of the road. Register at the entrance station. Boats can be launched from this area.

Contact: Lake Oroville State Recreation Area, 530/538-2200; Lake Oroville Visitor Center, 530/538-2219.

25 BIDWELL CANYON

Rating: 7

On Lake Oroville.

Map 5.2, page 299

Bidwell Canyon is a major destination at giant Lake Oroville as the campground is near a major marina and boat ramp. It is set along the southern shore of the lake, on a point directly adjacent to the massive Oroville Dam to the west. Many campers use this spot for boating headquarters. Lake Oroville is created from the tallest earth-filled dam in the country, rising 770 feet above the streambed of the Feather River. It creates a huge reservoir, with Oroville covering 28,450 acres when full. It is popular for water-skiing, as the water is warm enough in the summer for all water sports, and there is enough room for both fishermen and water-skiers. Recent habitat work has given the bass fishing a big help, with 30- and 40-fish days possible in the spring, casting plastic worms in the backs of coves where there is floating wood debris. What a lake—there are even floating toilets here (imagine that!). It is very hot in midsummer, with high temperatures ranging from the mid-80s to the low 100s. The area has four distinct seasons—spring is quite beautiful with many wildflowers and greenery. A must-see is the view from the 47-foot tower using the high-powered telescopes, where there is a panoramic view of the lake, Sierra Nevada, valley, foothills, and the Sutter Buttes. The Feather River Hatchery is nearby.

Campsites, facilities: There are 75 sites with full hookups for tents or RVs up to 40 feet long and trailers up to 31 feet long (including boat trailers). Picnic tables and fire grills are provided. Drinking water, flush toilets, and showers are available. A grocery store and propane gas are available within two miles. Leashed pets are permitted, except on trails or beaches; pets must be enclosed at night.

Reservations, fees: Reservations are accepted with a $7.50 reservation fee at 800/444-PARK (800/444-7275) and website www.Reserve America.com. The fee is $16 per night. Senior discount available. Open year-round.

Directions: From Oroville, drive east on Oroville Dam Road/Highway 162 for eight miles to Kelly Ridge Road. Turn north on Kelly Ridge Road and drive 1.5 miles to Arroyo Drive. Turn right and drive one-quarter mile to the campground.

Contact: Lake Oroville State Recreation Area, 530/538-2200; Lake Oroville Visitor Center, 530/538-2219.

26 LOAFER CREEK GROUP CAMPS AND EQUESTRIAN CAMPS

Rating: 7

On Lake Oroville.

Map 5.2, page 299

These are three different campground areas that are linked, designed for individual use, groups, and equestrians, respectively. The camps are just across the water at Lake Oroville from Bidwell Canyon, but campers come here for more spacious sites. It's also a primary option for campers with boats, with the Loafer Creek boat ramp one mile away. So hey, this spot is no secret. Bonus here includes an extensive equestrian trail system right out of camp.

Campsites, facilities: There are 137 sites for tents and RVs up to 40 feet long and trailers to 31 feet long (including boat trailers), 15 equestrian sites with a two-horse limit per site. Picnic tables and fire grills are provided. Drinking water, flush toilets, showers, and RV dump station are available. A tethering and feeding station is near each site for horses, and a horse-washing station is provided. Some facilities are wheelchair-accessible. Propane, groceries, and a boat ramp are available nearby. Leashed pets are permitted, but not on trails or beaches.

Reservations, fees: Reservations are accepted with a $7.50 reservation fee at 800/444-PARK (800/444-7275) and website www.Reserve America.com. The fee is $10 per night for single sites, $20 per night for group sites, $16 per night for equestrian sites. Senior discount available. Open year-round.

Directions: From Oroville, drive east on Oroville Dam Road/Highway 162 to Kelly Ridge Road. Continue on Highway 162 for two miles to the signed campground entrance on the left.

Contact: Lake Oroville State Recreation Area, 530/538-2200; Lake Oroville Visitor Center, 530/538-2219.

27 DINGERVILLE USA

Rating: 3

Near Oroville.

Map 5.2, page 299

You're right, they thought of this name all by themselves, needed no help. It is an RV park set in the Oroville foothill country—hot, dry, and sticky in the summer, but with a variety of side trips available nearby. It is adjacent to a wildlife area and the Feather River and within short range of Lake Oroville and the Thermalito Afterbay for boating, water sports, and fishing. In the fall, the Duck Club in nearby Richvale is one of the few privately owned properties that offers duck hunting on a single-day basis. The RV park is a clean, quiet campground with easy access from the highway. Half of the sites are long-term renters.

Campsites, facilities: There are 29 sites, all drive-through, with full hookups for RVs. Picnic tables are provided. Restrooms, showers, modem access, cable TV, swimming pool, coin laundry, horseshoe pit, and a nine-hole executive golf course are available. Some facilities are wheelchair-accessible. Leashed pets are permitted.

Reservations, fees: Reservations are recommended. The fee is $20 per night. Major credit cards accepted. Open year-round.

Directions: From Oroville, drive south on Highway 70 to the second Pacific Heights Road turnoff. Turn right at Pacific Heights Road

and drive less than one mile to the campground on the left.

From Marysville, drive north on Highway 70 to Palermo-Welsh Road. Turn left on Palermo-Welsh Road and drive to Pacific Heights Road. Turn north on Pacific Heights Road and drive a half mile to the campground entrance on the right.

Contact: Dingerville USA, 5813 Pacific Heights Rd., Oroville, CA 95965, 530/533-9343.

28 GARDEN POINT BOAT-IN

Rating: 8

On Bullards Bar Reservoir.

Map 5.2, page 299

Bullards Bar Reservoir is one of the few lakes in the Sierra Nevada to offer boat-in camping at developed boat-in sites and to allow boaters to create their own primitive sites anywhere along the lake's shoreline. A chemical toilet is required gear for boat-in shoreline camping. Garden Point Boat-In is on the western shore of the northern Yuba River arm. This lake provides plenty of recreation options, including good fishing for kokanee salmon, water-skiing, and many coves for playing in the water.

Campsites, facilities: There are 16 sites (12 single and four double sites) accessible by boat only. Picnic tables and fire grills are provided. Vault toilets are available. No drinking water is available. You must burn or pack out your garbage. Some facilities are wheelchair-accessible. Supplies are available at the Emerald Cove Marina. Leashed pets are permitted.

Reservations, fees: Reservations are required from Emerald Cove Resort. The fee is $14 per night. Open mid-April to mid-October.

Directions: From Marysville, drive northeast on Highway 20 to Marysville Road. Turn north at Marysville Road (signed Bullards Bar Reservoir) and drive about 10 miles to Old Marysville Road. Turn right and drive 14 miles to reach the Cottage Creek Launch Ramp and the marina (turn left just before the dam).

To reach the Dark Day boat ramp, continue over the dam and drive four miles, turn left on Dark Day Road, and continue to the ramp. From the boat launch, continue to the campground on the northwest side.

Contact: Emerald Cove Resort and Marina, 530/692-3200; Tahoe National Forest, North Yuba/Downieville Ranger District, 530/288-3231, fax 530/288-0727.

29 DARK DAY WALK-IN

Rating: 8

On Bullards Bar Reservoir.

Map 5.2, page 299

Along with Schoolhouse, this is the only car-accessible camping area at Bullards Bar Reservoir with direct shoreline access. You park in a central area and then walk a short distance to the campground. The lake is a very short walk beyond that. Bullards Bar is a great camping lake, pretty and large with several lake arms and good fishing for kokanee salmon (as long as you have a boat). It is set at 2,000 feet in the foothills, like a silver dollar in a field of pennies. A bonus at Bullards Bar is that there is never a charge for day use, parking, or boat launching.

Campsites, facilities: There are 16 walk-in tent sites, including single, double, and triple sites. Picnic tables and fire pits are provided. Drinking water and flush and vault toilets are available. A boat ramp is available nearby, and supplies are available at Emerald Cove Marina. Leashed pets are permitted.

Reservations, fees: Reservations are required from Emerald Cove Resort. The fee is $14 per night per site. Open mid-April to mid-October.

Directions: From Marysville, drive northeast on Highway 20 to Marysville Road. Turn north at Marysville Road (signed Bullards Bar Reservoir) and drive about 10 miles to Old Marysville Road. Turn right, drive 14 miles, and continue over the dam for four miles to Dark Day Road. Turn left and drive past the boat launch

to the campground on the northwest side of the lake.

Contact: Emerald Cove Resort and Marina, 530/692-3200; Tahoe National Forest, North Yuba/Downieville Ranger District, 530/288-3231, fax 530/288-0727.

30 SHORELINE CAMP BOAT-IN

Rating: 8

On Bullards Bar Reservoir.

Map 5.2, page 299

There are two boat-in campgrounds on Bullards Bar Reservoir, but another option is to throw all caution to the wind and just head out on your own, camping wherever you want. It is critical to bring a shovel to dig a flat site for sleeping, a large tarp for sun protection, and of course, plenty of water or a water purification pump. This is a big, beautiful lake, with good trolling for kokanee salmon. Note: a portable chemical toilet and campfire permit are required.

Campsites, facilities: Boaters may choose their own primitive campsite anywhere on the shore of Bullards Bar Reservoir. Garbage must be packed out. Supplies are available at Emerald Cove Marina. Leashed pets are permitted.

Reservations, fees: Reservations and a shoreline camping permit are required from Emerald Cove Resort. The fee is $14 per night. Open mid-April to mid-October.

Directions: From Marysville, drive east on Highway 20 for 12 miles to Marysville Road. Turn left on Marysville Road (look for the sign for Bullards Bar Reservoir) and drive 10 miles to Old Marysville Road. Turn right on Old Marysville Road and drive 14 miles to the Cottage Creek Launch Ramp (turn left just before the dam). To reach the boat launch, continue to the campgrounds on the west side.

Contact: Emerald Cove Resort and Marina, 530/692-3200; Tahoe National Forest, North Yuba/Downieville Ranger District, 530/288-3231, fax 530/288-0727.

31 MADRONE COVE BOAT-IN

🏊 🚣 🛥️ 🐕 5% 🏕️

Rating: 8

On Bullards Bar Reservoir.

Map 5.2, page 299

This is one of two boat-in campgrounds at Bullards Bar Reservoir. It is set on the main Yuba River arm of the lake, along the western shore. This is a premium boat-in site. The elevation is 2,000 feet.

Campsites, facilities: There are 10 sites, accessible by boat only. Picnic tables and fire grills are provided. Vault toilets are available. No drinking water is available. Garbage must be packed out. Supplies are available at the marina. Leashed pets are permitted.

Reservations, fees: Reservations and a shoreline camping permit are required from Emerald Cove Resort. The fee is $14 per night. Open mid-April to mid-October.

Directions: From Marysville, drive east on Highway 20 for 12 miles to Marysville Road (signed Bullards Bar Reservoir). Turn left at Marysville Road and drive 10 miles to Old Marysville Road. Turn right on Old Marysville Road and drive 14 miles to reach the Cottage Creek Launch Ramp and the marina (turn left just before the dam). To reach the ramp, continue over the dam, drive four miles to Dark Day Road, turn left and continue to the ramp. From the boat launch, continue to the campground on the west side.

Contact: Emerald Cove Resort and Marina, 530/692-3200; Tahoe National Forest, North Yuba/Downieville Ranger District, 530/288-3231, fax 530/288-0727.

32 SCHOOLHOUSE

🚶 🏊 🚣 🛥️ 🐕 🚐 🏕️

Rating: 7

On Bullards Bar Reservoir.

Map 5.2, page 299

Bullards Bar Reservoir is one of the better lakes in the Sierra Nevada for camping, primarily because the lake levels tend to be higher here than at many other lakes. The camp is set on the southeast shore, with a trail available out of the camp to a beautiful lookout of the lake. Bullards Bar is known for good fishing for trout and kokanee salmon, water-skiing, and all water sports. A three-lane concrete boat ramp is to the south at Cottage Creek. Boaters should consider the special boat-in camps at the lake. The elevation is 2,200 feet.

Campsites, facilities: There are 56 sites (one triple, 11 double, and 44 single sites) for tents or RVs. Single sites accommodate six people, double sites accommodate 12, and triple sites hold up to 18 people. Picnic tables and fire rings are provided. Drinking water and flush and vault toilets are available. A boat ramp is nearby. Supplies are available in North San Juan, Camptonville, Dobbins, and at the marina. Leashed pets are permitted.

Reservations, fees: Reservations and a shoreline camping permit are required from Emerald Cove Resort. The fee is $14 per night. Open mid-April to mid-October.

Directions: From Marysville, drive east on Highway 20 for 12 miles to Marysville Road (signed Bullards Bar Reservoir). Turn left on Marysville Road and drive 10 miles to Old Marysville Road. Turn right on Old Marysville Road and drive 14 miles to the dam, then continue three miles to the campground entrance road on the left.

Contact: Emerald Cove Resort and Marina, 530/692-3200; Tahoe National Forest, North Yuba/Downieville Ranger District, 530/288-3231, fax 530/288-0727.

33 HORNSWOGGLE GROUP CAMP

🏊 🚣 🛥️ 🐕 🚐 🏕️

Rating: 7

On Bullards Bar Reservoir in Tahoe National Forest.

Map 5.2, page 299

This camp is designed for group use. A three-lane concrete boat ramp is two miles north at the Dark Day Picnic Area. (For information about family campgrounds and boat-in sites, see the listings for Bullards Bar Reservoir in the Sacramento and Gold Country chapter.)

Campsites, facilities: There are five 25-person group sites and one 50-person group site for tents or RVs up to 50 feet long. Picnic tables and fire grills are provided. Drinking water and flush and vault toilets are available. A boat ramp is nearby. Supplies are available at the marina. Leashed pets are permitted.

Reservations, fees: Reservations are required from Emerald Cove Resort. The fee is $50–100 per night. Open April to mid-October.

Directions: From Auburn, drive north on Highway 49 to Nevada City and continue for 17 miles through the town of North San Juan. Continue on Highway 49 for approximately eight miles to Marysville Road. Turn left on Marysville Road and drive approximately five miles to the campground on the left.

Contact: Emerald Cove Resort and Marina, 530/692-3200; Tahoe National Forest, North Yuba/Downieville Ranger District, 530/288-3231, fax 530/288-0727.

34 MOONSHINE CAMPGROUND

Rating: 7

Near the Yuba River and Bullards Bar Reservoir.

Map 5.2, page 299

This campground features shaded sites and a swimming hole on the nearby Middle Fork Yuba River. Both are needed, with the weather hot here in the summer, at 1,430 feet in the Sierra foothills. It's a seven-mile drive to a three-lane boat ramp at Dark Day Picnic Area at Bullards Bar Reservoir, the feature side trip.

Campsites, facilities: There are 25 sites with hookups for water and electricity, for tents or RVs up to 30 feet. Picnic tables and fire rings are provided. Drinking water, vault toilets, ice, and firewood are available. Some facilities are wheelchair-accessible. A grocery store and propane gas are available about three miles away in North San Juan. Leashed pets are permitted.

Reservations, fees: Reservations are required. The fee is $20–25 per night, $2 per person per night for more than four people. Open May through early October.

Directions: From Auburn, drive north on Highway 49 to Nevada City and continue for 17 miles through the town of North San Juan. Continue on Highway 49 and cross a bridge over the Middle Fork Yuba River to Moonshine Road. Turn left on Moonshine Road and drive three-quarters of a mile to the campground.

Contact: Moonshine Campground, 530/288-3585, website: www.moonshinecampground.com.

35 COLLINS LAKE RECREATION AREA

Rating: 8

Near Marysville on Collins Lake.

Map 5.2, page 299

Collins Lake is set in the foothill country east of Marysville at 1,200 feet in elevation, ideal for the camper, boater, and angler. We counted 52 campsites set near the lakefront. This lake is becoming known as an outstanding destination for trophy-sized trout, especially in late spring through early summer, though fishing is often good year-round for know-hows. The lake has 12 miles of shoreline and is quite pretty. In summer, warm water makes the lake exceptional for water-skiing (permitted from May 15 through September 30). There is a marina adjacent to the campground, and farther south is a swimming beach and boat ramp. Bonuses for anglers: no personal watercraft are allowed on the lake. A weekly fishing report is available at the camp's website.

Campsites, facilities: There are 184 sites, including some drive-through, many with partial hookups and a few with full hookups, for RVs or tents, three trailer rentals, and a large overflow camping area. Picnic tables and fire grills are provided. Restrooms, drinking water, flush toilets, RV dump station, coin-operated showers, boat ramp, boat rentals, sandy swimming beach, volleyball, marina, three group picnic areas, convenience store, coin laundry, wood, ice, and propane gas are available. Some facilities are wheelchair-accessible. Leashed pets are permitted.

Reservations, fees: Reservations are recommended. The fee is $18–32 per night, $2 per person for more than two people, $6 per night for a second vehicle. Major credit cards accepted. Open year-round.

Directions: From Marysville, drive east on Highway 20 for about 12 miles to Marysville Road. Turn north and drive approximately eight miles to the recreation area entrance road on the right. Turn right, drive a mile to the entrance station, and then continue to the campground.

Contact: Collins Lake Recreation Area, 800/286-0576 or 530/692-1600, fax 530/692-1607, website: www.collinslake.com.

36 ENGLEBRIGHT LAKE BOAT-IN

Rating: 8

Near Marysville.

Map 5.2, page 299

Englebright Lake is an outstanding destination for boat-in camping, fishing, and water-skiing. Remember this place. It always seems to have plenty of water, and there are more developed boat-in campsites along its 24 miles of shoreline than at any other lake in California. The lake looks like a huge water snake, long and narrow, set in the Yuba River Canyon at 520 feet in elevation. In summer, it is a water-skiing mecca, with warm and calm water. Trout fishing is good on the upper end of the lake, where water-skiing is prohibited year-round.

Campsites, facilities: There are 100 boat-in sites along the shores of Englebright Lake and a group camping area that accommodates 50 people (by reservation only). Picnic tables, fire grills, and lantern hangers are provided. Vault

toilets are available. Two boat ramps are available on either side of Skippers Cove (and more boat-in campsites). Drinking water is available at each boat launch and at the marina. Boat rentals (including houseboats), mooring, fuel dock, and groceries are available. Leashed pets are permitted.

Reservations, fees: Reservations are accepted for groups only. The fee is $10 per night for boat-in sites, $25–50 per night for group site. Open year-round.

Directions: From Auburn, drive north on Highway 49 to Grass Valley and the junction with Highway 20. Turn west on Highway 20 and drive to Mooney Flat Road (if you reach Smartville, you have gone a mile too far). Turn right on Mooney Flat and drive three miles to the entrance for the Narrows Recreation Area. Continue a half mile to the entrance to Skipper's Cove Marina on the left.

Contact: U.S. Army Corps of Engineers, Sacramento District, Englebright Lake, 530/639-2342 (reservations), fax 530/639-2175; Skippers Cove concessionaire, 530/639-2272.

37 NEVADA COUNTY FAIRGROUNDS

Rating: 6

At the fairgrounds near Grass Valley.

Map 5.2, page 299

The motto here is "California's Most Beautiful Fairgrounds," and that's right. The area is set at 2,300 feet in the Sierra foothills, with a good number of pines sprinkled about. The park is adjacent to the fairgrounds, and even though the fair runs for a week every August, the park is open year-round. A caretaker at the park is available to answer any questions. Kids can fish at a small lake nearby. The Draft Horse Classic is held here every September and a country Christmas Faire is held Thanksgiving Weekend.

Campsites, facilities: There are 105 sites, 15 with full hookups and 80 with water and electricity, for RVs, and a open dirt and grassy area with no hookups available as an overflow area. Two RV dump stations, showers, and flush toilets are available. A building with kitchen facilities and space for up to 50 people is available for rent. Some facilities are wheelchair-accessible. Leashed pets are permitted.

Reservations, fees: Reservations are accepted. The fee is $17-20 per night. A 14-day limit is enforced. Major credit cards accepted. Open year-round.

Directions: From Auburn, drive north on Highway 49 to Grass Valley. Take either the Mc-Knight Way or Empire Street exit and follow the signs to the Nevada County Fairgrounds on the west side of Highway 49.

Contact: Nevada County Fairgrounds, 11228 McCourtney Rd., Grass Valley, CA 95949, 530/273-6217, fax 530/273-1146, website: www.nevadacountyfair.com.

38 BLACK ROCK

Rating: 7

On Little Grass Valley Reservoir in Plumas National Forest.

Map 5.3, page 300

This is the only campground on the west shore of Little Grass Valley Reservoir, with an adjacent boat ramp making it an attractive choice for anglers. The lake is set at 5,000 feet in Plumas National Forest and provides lakeside camping and decent fishing for rainbow trout and kokanee salmon. If you don't like the company, there are seven other camps to choose from at the lake, all on the opposite eastern shore.

Campsites, facilities: There are 10 walk-in tent sites and 20 sites for tents or RVs up to 22 feet long. Picnic tables and fire grills are provided. Drinking water, vault toilets, and a fish-cleaning station are available. RV dump station, boat ramp, and grocery store are nearby. Leashed pets are permitted.

Reservations, fees: Reservations are not accepted. The fee is $14 per night. Senior discount available. Open June through October.

Directions: From Oroville, drive east on Highway 162 for about eight miles to the junction signed Challenge/LaPorte. Bear right and drive east past Challenge and Strawberry Valley to LaPorte. Continue two miles past LaPorte to the junction with County Road 514/Little Grass Valley Road. Turn left and drive about five miles to the campground access road on the west side of the lake. Turn right on the access road and drive a quarter mile to the campground.

Contact: Plumas National Forest, Feather River Ranger District, 530/534-6500, fax 530/532-1210.

39 HORSE CAMP

Rating: 7

On Little Grass Valley Reservoir in Plumas National Forest.

Map 5.3, page 300

This camp is reserved for equestrians only and thus it gets low use. This is a high-country forested campground set near Little Grass Valley Reservoir, but there is no lake view because of tree cover. Several trails are accessible from the campground, including the Pacific Crest Trail and Lakeshore Trail, as well as access to Bald Mountain (6,255 feet). The elevation at camp is 5,060 feet.

Campsites, facilities: There are 10 sites for tents or RVs up to 35 feet long available for equestrian campers only. Picnic tables and fire grills are provided. Vault toilets are available. No drinking water is available. Hitching posts are available and a wheelchair-accessible mounting rack is available. A restaurant and deli are available five miles away in LaPorte. Leashed pets are permitted.

Reservations, fees: Reservations are recommended with a $9 reservation fee at 877/444-6777 or website www.ReserveUsa.com. The fee is $13 per night. Credit cards accepted. Senior discount available. Open June through September.

Directions: From Oroville, drive east on Highway 162 for about eight miles to the junction signed Challenge/LaPorte. Bear right (to LaPorte) and drive east past Challenge and Strawberry Valley to LaPorte. Continue on County Road 512 (which becomes County Road 514/Little Grass Valley Road) for three miles to Forest Road 22N57. Turn right and drive four miles (cross the bridge) to the campground on the left.

Contact: Plumas National Forest, Feather River Ranger District, 530/534-6500, fax 530/532-1210.

40 PENINSULA TENT

🏕️ 🏊 🎣 ⛵ 🐕 ⛺

Rating: 9

On Little Grass Valley Reservoir in Plumas National Forest.

Map 5.3, page 300

This camp is exceptional in that most of the campsites provide views of Little Grass Valley Reservoir, a pretty lake set at 5,060 feet in national forest. The fishing can be excellent, especially for rainbow trout, brown trout, and kokanee salmon. The camp gets moderate use, and it is a pretty site with tents sprinkled amid white fir and pine. A good family campground, tents only. A 13-mile hiking trail circles the lake.

Campsites, facilities: There are 25 sites for tents only. Picnic tables and fire rings are provided. Drinking water and flush toilets are available. A boat launch, fish-cleaning station, and a swimming beach are available nearby. Leashed pets are permitted.

Reservations, fees: Reservations are not accepted. The fee is $14 fee per night. Senior discount available. Open Memorial Day weekend through mid-October, weather permitting.

Directions: From Oroville, drive east on Highway 162 for about eight miles to the junction signed Challenge/LaPorte. Bear right (to La-

Porte) and drive east past Challenge and Strawberry Valley to LaPorte. Continue on County Road 512 (which becomes County Road 514/Little Grass Valley Road) for three miles to Forest Road 22N57. Continue on Forest Road 514 for one mile to the campground entrance on right. Turn right and drive a quarter mile to the campground.

Contact: Plumas National Forest, Feather River Ranger District, 530/534-6500, fax 530/532-1210.

41 RUNNING DEER

🏕️ 🏊 🎣 ⛵ 🐕 🚐 ⛺

Rating: 7

On Little Grass Valley Reservoir in Plumas National Forest.

Map 5.3, page 300

Little Grass Valley Reservoir is a pretty mountain lake set at 5,060 feet in Plumas National Forest, providing lakeside camping, boating, and fishing for rainbow trout and kokanee salmon. Looking straight north from the camp is a spectacular view, gazing across the water and up at Bald Mountain, 6,255 feet in elevation. One of seven campgrounds on the eastern shore, this one is on the far northeastern end of the lake. A trailhead for the Pacific Crest Trail is available nearby at little Fowler Lake about four miles north of Little Grass Valley Reservoir. Note that while no fish-cleaning station is available at Running Deer, there is one available nearby at Little Beaver.

Campsites, facilities: There are 40 sites for tents or RVs up to 40 feet long. Picnic tables and fire rings are provided. Drinking water, flush toilets, and a nearby fish-cleaning station are available. A boat ramp, grocery store, and RV dump station are nearby. Leashed pets are permitted.

Reservations, fees: Reservations are accepted with a $9 reservation fee at 877/444-6777 and website www.ReserveUsa.com. The fee is $14–16 per night. Senior discount available. Open June through September.

Directions: From Oroville, drive east on Highway 162 for about eight miles to the junction signed Challenge/LaPorte. Bear right (to LaPorte) and drive east past Challenge and Strawberry Valley to LaPorte. Continue on County Road 512 (which becomes County Road 514/Little Grass Valley Road) for three miles to Forest Road 22N57. Turn right and drive three miles to the campground on the left.

Contact: Plumas National Forest, Feather River Ranger District, 530/534-6500, fax 530/532-1210.

42 WYANDOTTE

Rating: 8

On Little Grass Valley Reservoir in Plumas National Forest.

Map 5.3, page 300

Of the eight camps on Little Grass Valley Reservoir, this is the favorite. It is set on a small peninsula at 5,100 foot elevation that extends well into the lake, with a boat ramp nearby. (For more information, see the entry for Running Deer.)

Campsites, facilities: There are 28 sites for tents or RVs up to 22 feet long. Picnic tables and fire rings are provided. Drinking water and flush toilets are available. RV dump station, boat ramp, fish-cleaning station, and grocery store are nearby. Leashed pets are permitted.

Reservations, fees: Reservations are not accepted. The fee is $14 per single site, $24 per double site, per night. Senior discount available. Open May through September.

Directions: From Oroville, drive east on Highway 162 for about eight miles to the junction signed Challenge/LaPorte. Bear right (to LaPorte) and drive east past Challenge and Strawberry Valley to LaPorte. Continue two miles past LaPorte to the junction with County Road 514/Little Grass Valley Road. Turn left and drive one mile to a junction. Turn left and drive one mile to the campground entrance road on the right.

Contact: Plumas National Forest, Feather River Ranger District, 530/534-6500, fax 530/532-1210.

43 LITTLE BEAVER

Rating: 7

On Little Grass Valley Reservoir in Plumas National Forest.

Map 5.3, page 300

This is one of eight campgrounds on Little Grass Valley Reservoir, set at 5,060 feet. Take your pick. (For more information, see the entry for Running Deer.)

Campsites, facilities: There are 120 sites for tents or RVs up to 40 feet long. Picnic tables and fire rings are provided. Drinking water and flush toilets are available. A grocery store, RV dump station, a fish-cleaning station, and boat ramp are nearby. Leashed pets are permitted.

Reservations, fees: Reservations are not accepted. The fee is $14–16 per night. Senior discount available. Open June through October.

Directions: From Oroville, drive east on Highway 162 for about eight miles to the junction signed Challenge/LaPorte. Bear right (to LaPorte) and drive east past Challenge and Strawberry Valley to LaPorte. Continue two miles past LaPorte to the junction with County Road 514/Little Grass Valley Road. Turn left and drive one mile to a junction. Turn right and drive two miles to the campground entrance road on the left.

Contact: Plumas National Forest, Feather River Ranger District, 530/534-6500, fax 530/532-1210.

44 RED FEATHER CAMP

Rating: 7

On Little Grass Valley Reservoir in Plumas National Forest.

Map 5.3, page 300

This camp is well developed and popular, set on the eastern shore of Little Grass Valley

Reservoir, just south of Running Deer and just north of Little Beaver. (For more information, see the entry for Running Deer.)

Campsites, facilities: There are 60 sites for tents or RVs up to 22 feet long. Picnic tables and fire rings are provided. Drinking water and flush toilets are available. RV dump station, boat ramp, fish- cleaning station, and grocery store are nearby. Leashed pets are permitted.

Reservations, fees: Reservations are accepted with a $9 reservation fee at 877/444-6777 and website www.ReserveUsa.com. The fee is $14–16 per night. Senior discount available. Open June through October.

Directions: From Oroville, drive east on Highway 162 for about eight miles to the junction signed Challenge/LaPorte. Bear right (to La-Porte) and drive east past Challenge and Strawberry Valley to LaPorte. Continue two miles past LaPorte to the junction with County Road 514/Little Grass Valley Road. Turn left and drive one mile to a junction. Turn right and drive three miles to the campground entrance road on the left.

Contact: Plumas National Forest, Feather River Ranger District, 530/534-6500, fax 530/532-1210.

45 RAMSHORN

Rating: 7

On the North Yuba River in Tahoe National Forest.

Map 5.3, page 300

This camp is set on Ramshorn Creek, just across the road from the North Yuba River. It's one in a series of camps on this stretch of the beautiful North Yuba River. One mile east is a famous access point for white-water rafting trips on the Yuba. The camp's elevation is 2,600 feet.

Campsites, facilities: There are nine tent sites and seven sites for tents or RVs up to 22 feet long. Picnic tables and fire grills are provided. Drinking water and vault toilets are avail-

able. Supplies are available in Downieville. Leashed pets are permitted.

Reservations, fees: Reservations are not accepted. The fee is $13 per night. Senior discount available. Open year-round.

Directions: From Auburn, take Highway 49 north to Nevada City and continue (the road jogs left, then narrows) to Camptonville. Drive 15 miles north to the campground entrance on the left.

Contact: Tahoe National Forest, North Yuba/Downieville Ranger District, 530/288-3231, fax 530/288-0727.

46 CARLTON/CAL-IDA

Rating: 7

On the North Yuba River in Tahoe National Forest.

Map 5.3, page 300

Carlton is on the North Yuba River, and Cal-Ida is across the road. Both are right next door to Fiddle Creek. (For more information, see the entry for Fiddle Creek.)

Campsites, facilities: There are two undeveloped camping areas for tents and small, self-contained RVs. Picnic tables and fire grills are provided. Drinking water and vault toilets are available. Some facilities are wheelchair-accessible. Some supplies are available at the Indian Valley Outpost nearby. Leashed pets are permitted.

Reservations, fees: Reservations are not accepted. The fee is $13 per night. Senior discount available. Open mid-April through November.

Directions: From Auburn, take Highway 49 north to Nevada City and continue (the road jogs left, then narrows) to Camptonville. Continue northeast for nine miles to the campground entrance. The camping area at Carlton is one mile northeast of the Highway 49 bridge at Indian Valley. The camping area at Cal-Ida is just east of the Indian Valley Outpost on the Cal-Ida Road.

Contact: Tahoe National Forest, North Yuba/Downieville Ranger District, 530/288-3231, fax 530/288-0727.

47 FIDDLE CREEK

Rating: 7

On the North Yuba River in Tahoe National Forest.

Map 5.3, page 300

This camp is situated on the North Yuba River along Highway 49 in a quiet, forested area. This is a beautiful river, one of the prettiest to flow westward out of the Sierra Nevada, with deep pools and miniature waterfalls. It is popular for rafting out of Goodyears Bar, and if you can stand the cold water, there are many good swimming holes along Highway 49. It's set at 2,200 feet. There are a series of campgrounds on this stretch of the Yuba River. The Fiddle Creek Ridge Trail starts across the highway on Cal-Ida Road and is routed out to Indian Rock.

Campsites, facilities: There are 15 tent sites. Picnic tables and fire rings are provided. Drinking water and vault toilets are available. Limited supplies are available nearby at the Indian Valley Outpost. Some facilities are wheelchair-accessible, including a paved trail to the Yuba River. Leashed pets are permitted.

Reservations, fees: Reservations are not accepted. The fee is $13 per night. Senior discount available. Open April to November.

Directions: From Auburn, take Highway 49 north to Nevada City and continue (the road jogs left, then narrows) to Camptonville. Continue northeast for 9.5 miles to the campground entrance on the right.

Contact: Tahoe National Forest, North Yuba/Downieville Ranger District, 530/288-3231, fax 530/288-0727.

48 INDIAN VALLEY

Rating: 7

On the North Yuba River in Tahoe National Forest.

Map 5.3, page 300

This is an easy-to-reach spot set at 2,200 feet beside the North Yuba River. Highway 49 runs adjacent to the Yuba River for miles eastward, providing easy access to the river in many areas. There are several other campgrounds in the immediate area (see the entries for Fiddle Creek and Cal-Ida, both within a mile).

Campsites, facilities: There are nine tent sites and eight sites for RVs up to 22 feet long. Picnic tables and fire grills are provided. Drinking water and vault toilets are available. Limited supplies are available nearby at the Indian Valley Outpost. Leashed pets are permitted.

Reservations, fees: Reservations are not accepted. The fee is $13 per night. Senior discount available. Open year-round.

Directions: From Auburn, take Highway 49 north to Nevada City and continue (the road jogs left, then narrows) to Camptonville. Drive 10 miles to the camp entrance on the right.

Contact: Tahoe National Forest, North Yuba/Downieville Ranger District, 530/288-3231, fax 530/288-0727.

49 ROCKY REST

Rating: 7

On the North Yuba River in Tahoe National Forest.

Map 5.3, page 300

This is one in a series of campgrounds set at streamside on the North Yuba River. The elevation is 2,200 feet. A footbridge crosses the North Yuba River and provides an outstanding seven-mile hike.

Campsites, facilities: There are 10 dispersed camping sites for tents and small, self-contained RVs. Picnic tables and fire grills are provided. Drinking water and vault toilets are available. Limited supplies are available at the Indian Valley Outpost nearby. Leashed pets are permitted.

Reservations, fees: Reservations are not accepted. The fee is $13 per night. Senior discount available. Open mid-April through November.

Directions: From Auburn, take Highway 49 north to Nevada City and continue (the road jogs left, then narrows) to Camptonville. Continue on Highway 49 for 10 miles to the campground entrance on the right.

Contact: Tahoe National Forest, North Yuba/Downieville Ranger District, 530/288-3231, fax 530/288-0727.

50 MALAKOFF DIGGINS STATE HISTORIC PARK

Rating: 7

Near Nevada City.

Map 5.3, page 300

This camp is set near a small lake in the park, but the main attraction of the area is the gold mining history. Tours of the numerous historic sites are available during the summer. The elevation is 3,400 feet. A trip here is like a walk through history. Malakoff Diggins State Historic Park is the site of California's largest "hydraulic" mine. Huge cliffs have been carved by mighty streams of water, a gold-mining technique involving the washing away of entire mountains to find the precious metal. This practice began in the 1850s and continued for many years. Several major gold-mining operations combined hydraulic mining with giant sluice boxes. Hydraulic mining was a scourge to the land, of course, and legal battles between mine owners and downstream farmers eventually ended this method of mining.

The park also contains a 7,847-foot bedrock tunnel that served as a drain. The visitor center has exhibits on life in the old mining town

of North Bloomfield. Tours of the numerous historic sites are available during the summer.

The cabins here are set near a small lake in the park and are the cheapest deal in California at $10 a night.

Campsites, facilities: There are 30 sites for tents or RVs up to 24 feet long, four cabins, and one group tent site for up to 50 people. Picnic tables and fire grills are provided. Drinking water and flush toilets (except mid-November through February) are available. Leashed pets are permitted.

Reservations, fees: Reservations are accepted Memorial Day through Labor Day with a $7.50 reservation fee at 800/444-PARK (800/444-7275) or website www.ReserveAmerica.com. The fee is $10 per night, $37 for the group site. Senior discount available. Open year-round.

Directions: From Auburn, drive north on Highway 49 to Nevada City and continue 11 miles to the junction of Tyler Foote Crossing Road. Turn right and drive 16 miles (in the process the road changes names: Cruzon Grade, Back Bone Road, Der Bec Road, North Bloomfield Road) to the entrance on the right. The route is well-signed; the last two miles are quite steep and the last mile is dirt.

Contact: California State Parks, Goldrush District, tel./fax 530/265-2740.

51 SOUTH YUBA

Rating: 7

Near the Yuba River.

Map 5.3, page 300

This little-known BLM camp is set next to where little Kenebee Creek enters the Yuba River. The Yuba is about a mile away, with some great swimming holes and evening trout fishing spots to explore. A good side trip is to nearby Malakoff Diggins State Historic Park and the town of North Bloomfield (about a 10-minute drive to the northeast on North Bloomfield Road), which is being completely restored to its 1850s character. Let's hope that does not include the food. The 12-mile-long South Yuba Trail begins at the state park and features outstanding spring wildflower blooms. The elevation is 2,600 feet.

Campsites, facilities: There are 16 sites for tents or RVs up to 27 feet long. Picnic tables and fire grills are provided. Drinking water and vault toilets are available. Some facilities are wheelchair-accessible. Leashed pets are permitted.

Reservations, fees: Reservations are not accepted. The fee is $5 per night. Senior discount available. Open April through October, weather permitting.

Directions: From Auburn, turn north on Highway 49, drive to Nevada City, and then continue a short distance to North Bloomfield Road. Turn right and drive 10 miles to the one-lane bridge at Edward's Crossing. Cross the bridge and continue 1.5 miles to the campground on the right side of the road (the road becomes quite rough).

Alternate route for RVs or vehicles with trailers: From Auburn turn north on Highway 49 to Nevada City and continue to Tyler Foote Crossing Road. Turn right and drive to Grizzly Hills Road (just past North Columbia). Turn right and drive three miles to North Bloomfield Road. Turn left and drive to the campground on the right.

Contact: The Bureau of Land Management, Folsom Field Office, 916/985-4474, fax 916/985-3259.

52 WHITE CLOUD

Rating: 5

In Tahoe National Forest.
Map 5.3, page 300

This camp is set along the historic Pioneer Trail, which has turned into one of the top mountain-bike routes in the Sierra Nevada, easy and fast. The trail traces the route of the first wagon road opened by emigrants and gold seekers in 1850. It is best suited for mountain biking, with a lot of bikers taking the one-way

downhill ride (with an extra car for a shuttle ride) from Bear Valley to Lone Grave. The Omega Overlook is the highlight, with dramatic views of granite cliffs and the Yuba River. The elevation is 4,200 feet.

Campsites, facilities: There are 46 sites for tents or RVs up to 26 feet long. Picnic tables and fire grills are provided. Drinking water and vault toilets are available. Leashed pets are permitted.

Reservations, fees: Reservations are accepted with a $9 reservation fee at 877/444-6777 and website www.ReserveUsa.com. The fee is $13 per night, $6 per extra vehicle. Senior discount available. Open May through October.

Directions: From Sacramento, drive east on I-80 to Emigrant Gap. Take the off-ramp and then head north on the short connector road to Highway 20. Turn west on Highway 20 and drive about 15 miles to the campground entrance on the left.

Contact: Tahoe National Forest, Nevada City Ranger District, 530/265-4531, fax 530/478-6109; Big Bend Visitor's Center, 530/426-3609, fax 530/426-1744.

53 SKILLMAN GROUP CAMP

Rating: 5

In Tahoe National Forest.
Map 5.3, page 300

Skillman Group Camp is set at 4,400 feet, on a loop access road just off Highway 20, and the historic Pioneer Trail runs right through it. (See the entry for White Cloud for more information.)

Campsites, facilities: This group campsite can accommodate up to 75 people. Picnic tables and fire grills are provided. Vault toilets are available. No drinking water is available. Horse corrals, tie rails, troughs, and stock water are available. Leashed pets are permitted.

Reservations, fees: Reservations are required. The fee is $15–35 per night. Open May through October, weather permitting.

Directions: From Sacramento, drive east on I-80 past Emigrant Gap to Highway 20. Turn west on Highway 20 and drive 12 miles to the campground entrance on the left.

Contact: Tahoe National Forest, Nevada City Ranger District, 530/265-4531, fax 530/478-6109; Sierra Recreation Managers, 209/295-4512; Big Bend Visitor's Center, 530/426-3609, fax 530/426-1744.

54 SCOTTS FLAT LAKE RECREATION AREA

Rating: 8

Near Grass Valley.

Map 5.3, page 300

Scotts Flat Reservoir (at 3,100 feet in elevation) is shaped like a large teardrop and is one of the prettier lakes in the Sierra foothills, with 7.5 miles of shoreline circled by forest. Rules prohibiting personal watercraft keep the place sane. The camp is set on the lake's north shore, largely protected from spring winds and within short range of the marina and one of the lake's two boat launches. Trout fishing is good here in the spring and early summer. When the lake heats up, water-skiing and power-boating become more popular. Sailing is also good during spring afternoon winds.

Campsites, facilities: There are 185 sites for tents or RVs up to 35 feet long. Restrooms, coin showers, coin laundry, and RV dump station are provided. A general store, bait and tackle shop, boat rentals, boat ramp, and a playground are also available. Some facilities are wheelchair-accessible. Leashed pets are permitted.

Reservations, fees: Reservations are recommended in the summer. The fee is $16–27 per night, $5 per night for a second vehicle, $1 per person per night for more than four people, $3 per pet per night, with a 14-day maximum stay. Major credit cards accepted. Open year-round, weather permitting.

Directions: From Auburn, drive north on Highway 49 to Nevada City and the junction with

Highway 20. Turn right on Highway 20 and drive five miles (east) to Scotts Flat Road. Turn right and drive four miles to the camp entrance road on the right (on the north shore of the lake).

Contact: Scotts Flat Lake Recreation Area, 530/265-8861.

55 LONG RAVINE

Rating: 7

On Rollins Lake near Colfax.

Map 5.3, page 300

Long Ravine is one of three campgrounds at Rollins Lake, a popular lake for fishing (bass and trout) and water-skiing. The lake, in the Sierra foothills at 2,100 feet, has two extensive lake arms covering 26 miles of shoreline. It also has long stretches of open water near the lower end of the lake, making it excellent for water-skiing, with water surface temperatures ranging 75–80°F in the summer.

Campsites, facilities: There are 84 sites, including some drive-through, for tents or RVs. Flush toilets, picnic tables, and barbecues or fire pits are provided. Hot showers, parking pads, hiking trails, and RV dump station are available. A full-service marina with floating gas dock, boat rentals, stores, restaurant, and a swimming beach and water slide are nearby. Some facilities are wheelchair-accessible. Leashed pets are permitted.

Reservations, fees: Reservations are recommended. The fee is $22–26 per night, $10 per night for extra vehicle, $3 per pet per night. Major credit cards accepted. Open year-round. Major credit cards accepted.

Directions: From Auburn, drive northeast on I-80 for about 20 miles to Colfax/Highway 174. Turn north on Highway 174 (a winding, two-lane road) and drive about two miles to Rollins Lake. Turn right on Rollins Lake Road and drive 1.5 miles the campground on the left at 26909 Rollins Lake Road.

Contact: Long Ravine, 530/346-6166, website: www.longravineresort.com.

56 ORCHARD SPRINGS

Rating: 7

On Rollins Lake.

Map 5.3, page 300

Orchard Springs is set on the shore of Rollins Lake in the Sierra Nevada foothills among pine, oak, and cedar trees. The summer heat makes the lake excellent for water-skiing, boating, and swimming, and the spring and fall are great for trout and bass fishing.

Campsites, facilities: There are 19 sites, including two drive-through, with full hookups for tents or RVs, and 90 tent sites. Picnic tables, fire rings, and barbecues are provided. Drinking water, restrooms, flush toilets, showers, launch ramp, boat rentals, dock space rentals, bait and tackle, swimming beach, group picnic area, and a convenience store are available. A restaurant nearby overlooks Rollins Lake. Some facilities are wheelchair-accessible. Leashed pets are permitted.

Reservations, fees: Reservations are accepted at 530/346-2212. The fee is $20–30 per night, $10 for additional vehicles unless towed, $5.75 per boat per night, $3 per pet per night. Major credit cards accepted. Open year-round.

Directions: From Auburn, drive northeast on I-80 for about 20 miles to Colfax and Highway 174. Turn north on Highway 174 (a winding, two-lane road) and drive 3.7 miles (bear left at Giovanni's Restaurant) to Orchard Springs Road. Turn right on Orchard Springs Road and drive a half mile to the road's end. Turn right at the gatehouse and continue to the campground.

Contact: Orchard Springs; 530/346-2837.

57 PENINSULA CAMPGROUND

Rating: 8

On Rollins Lake.

Map 5.3, page 300

Peninsula Campground is set on a point that extends into Rollins Lake, flanked on each side by two sprawling lake arms. If you like boating, water-skiing, or swimming, you'll definitely like this place in the summer. This is a family-oriented campground, with lots of youngsters on summer vacation. If you want trout, prospects are best in April and May. After that the fast boats take over, though there is a good bass bite at dawn and dusk. The boat ramp was remodeled in 2002 and now features two lanes.

Campsites, facilities: There are 69 sites for tents or self-contained RVs up to 38 feet long. No RV hookups. Groups can be accommodated by reservation. Picnic tables and fire rings are provided. Restrooms with flush toilets and hot showers, drinking water, modem access, RV dump station, boat rentals (fishing boats, patio boats, canoes, and kayaks), boat ramp, fish-cleaning station, swim beach, and a convenience store are available. Leashed pets are permitted.

Reservations, fees: Reservations are recommended. The fee is $19–25 per night, $10 for extra vehicle per night, $2 per pet per night, $5 for RV dump station. Major credit cards accepted. Open mid-April to September.

Directions: From Auburn, drive northeast on I-80 for about 20 miles to Colfax and Highway 174. Turn north on Highway 174 and drive about eight miles (a winding, two-lane road) to You Bet Road. Turn right and drive 4.3 miles (turning right again to stay on You Bet Road), and continue another 3.1 miles to the campground entrance at the end of the road.

Contact: Peninsula Campground; 866/4MY-CAMP (866/469-2267) or 530/477-9413, website: www.penresort.com.

58 BEAR RIVER CAMPGROUND

Rating: 7

Near Colfax on Bear River.

Map 5.3, page 300

This RV park is set in the Sierra foothills at 1,800 feet, near Bear River, featuring riverfront campsites. The park covers 200 acres, offers five miles of hiking trails, and is set right on the Placer and Nevada County lines. Wow! (Hey, try writing 1,600 of these). It fills up on weekends and is popular with both locals and out-of-towners. In the spring, when everything is greened up, it can be a gorgeous landscape. Fishing is OK for trout, noncommercial gold panning is permitted, and some rafting is popular on the river. A 14-day maximum stay is enforced.

Campsites, facilities: There are 25 sites for tents or RVs, and one group site for up to 100 people. Picnic tables and fire rings are provided. Drinking water and pit toilets are available. Supplies are available within five miles in Colfax or Bowman. Leashed pets are permitted.

Reservations, fees: Reservations are accepted only for group sites at 530/889-7750 with a $5 reservation fee. The fee is $10 per night, $2 for each additional vehicle, $1 per pet, and $40–75 for group site. Open year-round.

Directions: From Sacramento, drive east on I-80 east of Auburn to West Weimar Crossroads exit. Take that exit on to Weimar Cross Road and drive north for 1.5 miles to Placer Hills Road. Turn right and drive 2.5 miles to Plum Tree Road. Turn left and drive one mile to the campground on the left. The access road is steep and narrow.

Contact: Bear River Campground, Placer County Facilities Services, 530/889-7750, fax 530/889-6809, website: www.placer.ca.gov.

59 FORBES CREEK GROUP CAMP

Rating: 7

On Sugar Pine Reservoir in Tahoe National Forest.

Map 5.3, page 300

The boat launch is nearby, but note: a 10-mph speed limit is the law. That makes for quiet water, perfect for anglers, canoeists, and other small boats. A paved trail circles the lake. (For more information see Giant Gap entry.)

Campsites, facilities: There are two group campsites, Madrone and Rocky Ridge, each of which can accommodate up to 50 people in tents or RVs up to 45 feet long. Picnic tables and fire grills are provided. Drinking water and vault toilets are available, and there is a camp host. Some facilities are wheelchair-accessible. A campfire circle, central parking area, RV dump station, and a boat ramp are available nearby. Supplies can be obtained in Foresthill. Leashed pets are permitted.

Reservations, fees: Reservations are accepted with a $9 reservation fee at 877/444-6777 and website www.ReserveUsa.com. The fee is $65 per night. Open May through mid-October.

Directions: From Sacramento, drive east on I-80 to the north end of Auburn and the Foresthill Road exit. Take that exit and drive east for 20 miles to Foresthill. Drive through Foresthill (road changes to Foresthill Divide Road) and continue for eight miles to Sugar Pine Road/Forest Road 10. Turn left and drive five miles to the lake and campground.

Contact: Tahoe National Forest, Foresthill Ranger District, 530/367-2224, fax 530/367-2992.

60 GIANT GAP

Rating: 7

On Sugar Pine Reservoir in Tahoe National Forest.

Map 5.3, page 300

This is a lakeside spot along the western shore of Sugar Pine Reservoir at 3,500 feet in elevation in Tahoe National Forest. For boaters, there is a ramp on the south shore. Note that a 10-mph speed limit is the law, making this lake ideal for anglers in search of quiet water. Other recreation notes: there's a little less than a mile of paved trail, which goes through the day-use area. Big Reservoir, five miles to the east, is the only other lake in the region and also has a campground. The trout fishing at Sugar Pine is fair, not usually great, not usually bad.

Campsites, facilities: There are 30 sites for tents or RVs up to 30 feet long. Picnic tables and fire grills are provided. Drinking water and vault toilets are available, and there is a camp host. Some facilities are wheelchair-accessible. An RV dump station and boat ramp are available on the south shore. Supplies can be obtained in Foresthill. Leashed pets are permitted.

Reservations, fees: Reservations are accepted with a $9 reservation fee at 877/444-6777 and website www.ReserveUsa.com. The fee is $12 for a single, $24 for a double, per night. Senior discount available. Open May through mid-October.

Directions: From Sacramento, drive east on I-80 to the north end of Auburn and the Foresthill Road exit. Take that exit and drive east for 20 miles to Foresthill. Drive through Foresthill (road changes to Foresthill Divide Road) and continue for eight miles to Sugar Pine Road. Turn left and drive five miles to a fork. Turn right and drive one mile to the campground.

Contact: Tahoe National Forest, Foresthill Ranger District, 530/367-2224, fax 530/367-2992.

61 SHIRTTAIL CREEK

Rating: 7

On Sugar Pine Reservoir in Tahoe National Forest.
Map 5.3, page 300

This camp is set near the little creek that feeds into the north end of Sugar Pine Reservoir. The boat ramp is all the way around the south side of the lake, near Forbes Creek Group Camp. (For recreation information, see the entry for Giant Gap.)

Campsites, facilities: There are 30 sites for tents or RVs up to 30 feet long (double and triple sites are available). Picnic tables and fire grills are provided. Drinking water and vault toilets are available, and there is a camp host. Some facilities are wheelchair-accessible. An RV dump station and boat ramp are available on the

south shore. Supplies can be obtained in Foresthill. Leashed pets are permitted.

Reservations, fees: Reservations are accepted with a $9 reservation fee at 877/444-6777 and website www.ReserveUsa.com. The fee is $12 for single sites, $24 for double sites, $35 for triple site, per night. Senior discount available. Open May through mid-October.

Directions: From Sacramento, drive east on I-80 to the north end of Auburn and the Foresthill Road exit. Take that exit and drive east for 20 miles to Foresthill. Drive through Foresthill (road changes to Foresthill Divide Road) and continue for eight miles to Sugar Pine Road. Turn left and drive five miles to the campground access road. Turn right (signed) and drive to the campground.

Contact: Tahoe National Forest, Foresthill Ranger District, 530/367-2224, fax 530/367-2992.

62 BIG RESERVOIR

Rating: 7

On Big Reservoir in Tahoe National Forest.
Map 5.3, page 300

Here's a quiet lake, commonly called Morning Star Lake, where no boat motors are allowed. That makes it ideal for canoeists, row boaters, and tube floaters who don't like the idea of having to dodge water-skiers. The lake is stocked with rainbow trout. Big Reservoir is quite pretty and a nice beach is available not far from the resort. The elevation is 4,100 feet.

Campsites, facilities: There are 100 sites for tents or RVs up to 25 feet long. Picnic tables and fire grills are provided. Drinking water and vault toilets are available. Firewood is limited. There is a small store near the campground and supplies are also available in Foresthill. Leashed pets are permitted.

Reservations, fees: Reservations are accepted at 530/367-2129. The fee is $15 per night. Senior discount available. Open May through October.

Directions: From Sacramento, drive east on I-80 to the north end of Auburn and the Foresthill Road exit. Take that exit and drive east for 20 miles to Foresthill. Drive through Foresthill (road changes to Foresthill Divide Road) and continue for eight miles to Sugar Pine Road. Turn left and drive about three miles to Forest Road 24 (signed Big Reservoir). Bear right on Forest Road 24 and drive about five miles to the campground entrance road on the right.

Contact: Tahoe National Forest, Foresthill Ranger District, 530/367-2224, fax 530/367-2992.

63 AUBURN KOA

Rating: 4

Near Auburn.

Map 5.4, page 301

This year-round KOA park is set at 1,250 feet and has all the amenities. Hey, a swimming pool is always a bonus in Auburn. An 18-hole golf course is within one-half mile.

Campsites, facilities: There are 66 sites with full and partial hookups, including some drive-through, for RVs up to 40 feet, and 10 tent sites, two cabins, and a rental trailer. Picnic tables and fire rings are provided. Restrooms, drinking water, flush toilets, showers, RV dump station, a playground, seasonal swimming pool, whirlpool, recreation room, fishing pond, basketball, horseshoes, volleyball, grocery store, coin laundry, and propane gas are available. Some facilities are wheelchair-accessible. Leashed pets are permitted.

Reservations, fees: Reservations are accepted at 800/562-6671. The fee is $25–36 per night. Major credit cards accepted. Open year-round.

Directions: From Auburn, drive north on Highway 49 for 3.5 miles to Rock Creek Road (one block past Bell Road). Turn right on Rock Creek Road and drive a short distance to the KOA entrance on the left.

Contact: Auburn KOA, 530/885-0990.

64 AUBURN STATE RECREATION AREA

Rating: 8

Near Auburn.

Map 5.4, page 301

This state park is a jewel in the valley foothill country, covering more than 35,000 acres along 40 miles of the North and Middle Forks of the American River. This area once teemed with thousands of gold miners, but it is now a natural area offering a wide variety of recreational opportunities and wildlife. The Auburn SRA is actually made up of land set aside for the Auburn Dam, consisting of 20 miles along two forks of the American River. There are two drive-in campgrounds, Mineral Bar and Rucky-A-Chucky, and two boat-in campgrounds at Lake Clementine. The American River runs through the park, offering visitors opportunities to fish, boat, and raft. In addition, there are more than 100 miles of hiking and horseback riding trails. Lake Clementine offers fishing (not stocked) and water-skiing, with a boat limit of 25 boats per day; the quota is reached every day on summer weekends. White-water rafting is extremely popular, with more than 30 private outfitters licensed for trips in sections of river through the park.

Campsites, facilities: Mineral Camp provides 16 campsites. Rucky-A-Chucky provides 15 campsites for tents and self-contained RVs up to 20 feet. There are two boat-in campgrounds at Lake Clementine with 20 boat-in sites. Picnic tables and fire grills are provided. Pit toilets are available. No drinking water is available. Garbage must be packed out. Leashed pets are permitted, except at lake Clementine.

Reservations, fees: Reservations are accepted at 800/444-PARK (800/444-7275) or website: www.ReserveAmerica.com ($7.50 reservation fee), $7 per night, $9–13 per night for premium boat-in sites at Lake Clementine. Senior discount available. Tent sites open year-round.

Boat-in sites open Memorial Day weekend through Labor Day weekend.

Directions to Mineral Bar Camp: From I-80 in Auburn, drive east for 15 miles to Colfax. Take the Colfax exit and turn right on the frontage road and drive one-half mile to Iowa Hill Road. Turn left and drive 2.5 miles to the campground on the left.

Directions to Rucky-A-Chucky Camp: From I-80 in Auburn, take the Foresthill Road exit on to Foresthill Road. Continue on Foresthill Road for seven miles to Drivers Flat Road. Turn right and drive 2.8 miles (becomes Rucky-A-Chucky Road) to the campground on the right.

Directions to Lake Clementine boat-in camps: From I-80 at Auburn, take the Foresthill exit on to Foresthill Road. Continue northeast on Foresthill Road for two miles to Lake Clementine Road. Turn left and drive 2.5 miles to the boat launch. After launching, cruise by boat 1.5 miles northeast to the boat-in campgrounds.

Contact: Auburn State Recreation Area, 530/885-4527, fax 530/885-2798.

65 CAMPERS INN & GOLF COURSE

Rating: 1

Near Dunnigan.

Map 5.4, page 301

This private park has a rural valley atmosphere and provides a layover for drivers cruising I-5. The Sacramento River to the east is the closest body of water, but this section of river is hardly a premium side-trip destination. There are no nearby lakes.

Campsites, facilities: There are 13 tent sites and 72 RV sites (44 drive-through) with full or partial hookups. Picnic tables are provided. Restrooms, flush toilets, showers, modem access, seasonal pool, clubhouse, horseshoes, nine-hole golf course, coin laundry, propane gas, ice, and groceries are available. Some facilities are wheelchair-accessible. Leashed pets are permitted.

Reservations, fees: Reservations are accepted. The fee is $16–24 per night, $2 per person per night for more than four people. Major credit cards accepted. Open year-round.

Directions: From I-5, take the Dunnigan exit (just north of the I-505 cutoff). Drive west on County Road E4 for a mile to County Road 88. Turn right and drive for 1.5 miles to the park.

Contact: Campers Inn, 800/79-GOLF3 (800/794-6533) or 530/724-3350, fax 530/724-3110, website: www.campersinnrv.com.

66 HAPPY TIME RV PARK

Rating: 1

Near Dunnigan.

Map 5.4, page 301

If you are cruising I-5 and are exhausted or need to take a deep breath before hitting the Bay Area or Sacramento, this private park can provide a respite and, to be honest, not a whole lot more. Restaurants are available in nearby Dunnigan. About one-third of the sites here are long-term rentals.

Campsites, facilities: There are 67 sites with full hookups, including many drive-through, for RVs, and a grassy area for a few tents. Picnic tables are provided. Restrooms, flush toilets, showers, modem access, playground, coin laundry, and a seasonal swimming pool are available. Some facilities are wheelchair-accessible. Leashed pets are permitted.

Reservations, fees: Reservations are accepted. The fee is $22 for RVs, $10 for tents. Senior discount available. Major credit cards accepted. Open year-round.

Directions: From I-5 near the I-505 intersection, take the County Road 8 exit. Drive east on County Road 8 for a short distance to Road 99W. Turn left on Road 99W and drive to the first driveway (less than one block) and park entrance on the left.

Contact: Happy Time RV Park, 530/724-3336.

67 LOOMIS RV

⊠ 🏠 🐕 🚶 ♿ 🚐 ⛺

Rating: 2

In Loomis.

Map 5.4, page 301

This park is set in the Sierra foothills, which are known for hot summer weather. The sites are on level gravel and some are shaded. The elevation is 600 feet. Note that about half the sites are long-term rentals.

Campsites, facilities: There are 74 sites, most with full hookups, for RVs up to 40 feet long, a separate tent area, and two one-room cabins. Picnic tables and fire grills are provided. Drinking water, restrooms, flush toilets, showers, RV dump station, a playground, seasonal swimming pool, recreation room, horseshoes, convenience store, coin laundry, and propane gas are available. Some facilities are wheelchair-accessible. Leashed pets are permitted.

Reservations, fees: Reservations are accepted. The fee is $21–30 per night, $2 per person for more than two people. Senior discount available. Major credit cards accepted. Open year-round.

Directions: From Sacramento, drive east on I-80 to Loomis and the junction of Sierra College Boulevard. Take Sierra College Boulevard and drive north for a half mile to Taylor Road. Turn east and drive a half block to the camp on the right.

Contact: Loomis RV, 916/652-6737.

68 BEAL'S POINT

🚶 🚴 ⊠ 🛶 🚐 🐕 ♿ 🚐 ⛺

Rating: 6

In Folsom Lake State Recreation Area.

Map 5.4, page 301

Folsom Lake State Recreation Area is Sacramento's backyard vacation spot, a huge lake covering about 18,000 acres with 75 miles of shoreline, which means plenty of room for boating, water-skiing, fishing, and suntanning. This camp is set on the lake's south-west side, just north of the dam, with a boat ramp nearby at Granite Bay. The lake has a productive trout fishery in the spring, a fast-growing population of kokanee salmon, and good prospects for bass in late spring and early summer. By summer water-skiers usually take over the lake each day by about 10 A.M. One problem with this lake is that a minor water drawdown can cause major amounts of shoreline to become exposed on its upper arms. There are opportunities for hiking, biking, running, picnics, and horseback riding. A 32-mile-long trail connects Folsom Lake with many Sacramento County parks before reaching Old Sacramento. This trail is outstanding for family biking and roller blading. Summers are hot and dry. Note that before 2003, there were 15 sites with full hookups for RVs. These hookups were discontinued.

Campsites, facilities: There are 69 sites for tents or RVs up to 31 feet long. Picnic tables and fire grills are provided. Drinking water, flush toilets, showers, and RV dump station are available. A bike path and horseback riding facilities are available nearby. Camping, picnicking, and fishing areas are wheelchair-accessible. There are boat rentals, moorings, summer snack bar, ice, and bait and tackle available at the Folsom Lake Marina. Leashed pets are permitted.

Reservations, fees: Reservations are accepted April through September with a $7.50 reservation fee at 800/444-PARK (800/444-7275) or website www.ReserveAmerica.com. The fee is $12 per night. Senior discount available. Open year-round.

Directions: From Sacramento, drive east on U.S. 50 to the Folsom Boulevard exit. Turn left at the stop sign and continue on Folsom Boulevard for 3.5 miles, following the road as it curves onto Leidesdorff Street. Head east on Leidesdorff Street for a half mile until it dead-ends into Riley Street. Turn left onto Riley Street and proceed over the bridge to Folsom-Auburn Road. Turn right and on Folsom-

Auburn Road and drive north for 3.5 miles to the park entrance on the right.

Contact: Folsom Lake State Recreation Area, 916/988-0205, fax 916/988-9062.

69 PENINSULA

Rating: 6

In Folsom Lake State Recreation Area.

Map 5.4, page 301

This is one of the big camps at Folsom Lake, but it is also more remote than the other camps, requiring a circuitous drive. It is set on the peninsula on the northeast shore, right where the North Fork American River arm of the lake enters the main lake area. A nearby boat ramp, marina, and boat rentals make this a great weekend spot. Fishing for bass and trout is often quite good in spring and early summer, and water-skiing is popular in the hot summer.

Campsites, facilities: There are 100 sites for tents or RVs. Picnic tables and fire grills are provided. Drinking water, restrooms, flush toilets, and showers are available. A bike path is available nearby. Boat rentals, moorings, snack bar, ice, and bait and tackle are available at the Folsom Lake Marina. Leashed pets are permitted.

Reservations, fees: Reservations are accepted with a $7.50 reservation fee at 800/444-PARK (800/444-7275) and website www.Reserve America.com. The fee is $12 per night. Senior discount available. Open year-round.

Directions: From Placerville, drive east on U.S. 50 to the Spring Street/Highway 49 exit. Turn north on Highway 49 (toward the town of Coloma) and continue 8.3 miles into the town of Pilot Hill and Rattlesnake Bar Road. Turn left on Rattlesnake Bar Road and drive nine miles to the end of the road and the park entrance.

Contact: Folsom Lake State Recreation Area, 916/988-0205, fax 916/988-9062.

70 NEGRO BAR GROUP CAMP

Rating: 6

In Folsom Lake State Recreation Area.

Map 5.4, page 301

Lake Natoma is the afterbay for Folsom Lake, but it is nothing like Folsom Lake. Natoma is comparatively small (500 acres), very narrow instead of wide, with cold water instead of warm. This camp is set at the head of the lake on the northern shore, with an adjacent boat ramp available. Negro Bar used to have family sites but these were eliminated when the bridge crossing at Lake Natoma was built. Beal's Point increased its family sites in compensation. Lake Natoma is popular for crew races, sailing, kayaking, and other aquatic sports.

Campsites, facilities: There are three group sites that can accommodate 25–50 people each. Picnic tables and fire grills are provided. Drinking water, restrooms, and flush toilets are available. A bike path is available nearby. Boat rentals, moorings, snack bar, ice, and bait and tackle are available at the Folsom Lake Marina. Leashed pets are permitted.

Reservations, fees: Reservations are accepted May through September with a $7.50 reservation fee at 800/444-PARK (800/444-7275) or website www.ReserveAmerica.com. Reserve at 916/988-0205 from October through April. The fee is $18–37 per night. Open year-round.

Directions: From I-80 north of Sacramento, take the Douglas Boulevard exit and head east for five miles to Auburn-Folsom Road. Turn right on Auburn-Folsom Road and drive south for six miles until the road dead-ends into Greenback Lane. Turn right on Greenback Lane and merge immediately into the left lane. The park entrance is approximately .2 mile on the left.

Contact: Folsom Lake State Recreation Area, 916/988-0205, fax 916/988-9062.

71 SACRAMENTO-METRO KOA

Rating: 1

Downtown Sacramento.
Map 5.4, page 301

This is the choice of car and RV campers touring California's capital and looking for a layover spot. It is in downtown Sacramento near the Capitol building, the railroad museum, Sutter's Fort, Old Sacramento, Crocker Museum, and shopping.

Campsites, facilities: There are 95 sites with full or partial hookups, most drive-through, for RVs up to 40 feet long, 27 tent sites, and 12 cabins. Restrooms, flush toilets, showers, modem access, cable TV, playground, fishing pond, seasonal swimming pool, coin laundry, firewood, propane gas, and convenience store are available. Some facilities are wheelchair-accessible. Leashed pets are permitted.

Reservations, fees: Reservations are recommended and may be made at 800/562-2747. The fee is $26–36 per night, $5 per person for more than two people. Major credit cards accepted. Open year-round.

Directions: From Sacramento, drive west on I-80 about four miles to the West Capitol Avenue exit. Exit and turn left onto West Capitol Avenue, going under the freeway to the first stoplight and the intersection with Lake Road. Turn left onto Lake Road and continue a half block to the camp on the right at 3951 Lake Road.

Contact: Sacramento-Metro KOA, 916/371-6771 or 800/545-KAMP (800/545-5267).

72 NEIL'S VINEYARD RV PARK

Rating: 2

In Vacaville.
Map 5.4, page 301

This is one of two privately operated parks in the area set up primarily for RVs. It is in a eucalyptus grove, with clean, well-kept sites. If you are heading to the Bay Area, it is late in the day, and you don't have your destination set, this spot offers a chance to hole up for the night and formulate your travel plans. Note that about half of the sites are long-term rentals and the park doesn't take credit cards.

Campsites, facilities: There are 110 sites with full hookups, including 26 drive-through, for RVs up to 40 feet. Picnic tables are provided. Restrooms, flush toilets, showers, modem access, swimming pool, coin laundry, RV dump station, putting green, pay phones, and ice are available. Some facilities are wheelchair-accessible. Leashed pets are permitted.

Reservations, fees: Reservations are recommended. The fee is $30.75 per night, $2 per person per night for more than two people, $1 per pet per night. Open year-round.

From Vacaville on I-80, turn north on I-505 and drive three miles to Midway Road. Turn right (east) on Midway Road and travel a half mile to the second campground on the left at 4985 Midway Road.

Contact: Neil's Vineyard RV Park, 707/447-8797.

73 NEW HOPE LANDING

Rating: 6

On the Mokelumne River north of Stockton.
Map 5.4, page 301

New Hope Landing is a privately operated resort set along the Mokelumne River in the upper San Joaquin Delta. There's a marina available, which provides access to 1,000 miles of Delta waterways via the Mokelumne River. The Lower Mokelumne is often an excellent area to troll for striped bass in April and to water-ski in summer. In late summer, water hyacinth is sometimes a problem farther upstream.

Campsites, facilities: There are 52 sites with full hookups for RVs, and 12 sites for tents. Restrooms, showers, ice, bait, propane gas, and a marina are available. Some facilities are wheelchair-accessible. Leashed pets are permitted.

Reservations, fees: Reservations are accepted for tent sites only. The fee is $17.50–24.50 per night, $3.50 for each additional person, $3.50–5 for extra vehicle. Open year-round.

Directions: From Stockton, drive north on I-5 for 25 miles to the Thornton exit. Take that exit, turn west on Walnut Grove Road, and drive 3.3 miles to the campground entrance on the left.

Contact: New Hope Landing, tel./fax 209/794-2627.

74 DRU BARNER EQUESTRIAN CAMP

Rating: 7

Near Georgetown in Eldorado National Forest.
Map 5.5, page 302

This camp, set at 3,200 feet in an area of pine and fir, is ideal for horses; there are miles of equestrian trails. (For more information see the entries for Stumpy Meadows and Black Oak Group Camp.)

Campsites, facilities: There are 48 sites for tents or RVs up to 35 feet long. Picnic tables and fire grills are provided. Drinking water and vault toilets are available. Two stock troughs are also available. Garbage must be packed out. Leashed pets are permitted.

Reservations, fees: Reservations are not accepted. The fee is $6 per night. Senior discount available. Open year-round.

Directions: From Sacramento on I-80, drive east to the north end of Auburn and Elm Avenue. Turn left on Elm Avenue and drive about .1 mile to High Street. Turn left on High Street and drive through the signal that marks the continuation of High Street as Highway 49 and drive 3.5 miles on Highway 49 to the bridge. Turn right over the bridge and drive 2.5 miles into the town of Cool and Georgetown Road/Highway 193. Turn left and drive 14 miles into Georgetown to a four-way stop at Main Street. Turn left on Main Street and drive 5.5 miles (the road becomes Georgetown-Wentworth Springs Road/Forest Road 1) to Bottle Hill Bypass Road. Turn left on Bottle Hill Bypass Road and drive about a mile to the campground on the left.

Contact: Eldorado Information Center, 530/644-6048; Eldorado National Forest, Georgetown Ranger District, 530/333-4312, fax 530/333-5522.

75 PLACERVILLE KOA

Rating: 7

Near Placerville.
Map 5.5, page 302

This is a classic KOA campground, complete with the cute little log cabins KOA calls "Kamping Kabins." The location of this camp is ideal for many, set near U.S. 50 in the Sierra foothills, the main route up to South Tahoe. Nearby is Apple Hill, where from September to November it is a popular tourist attraction, when the local ranches and orchards sell produce and crafts, often with live music. In addition, the Marshall Gold Discovery Site is 10 miles north, where gold was discovered in 1848, setting off the 1849 gold rush. White-water rafting and gold panning are popular on the nearby American River.

Campsites, facilities: There are 70 sites, 46 with full hookups and 24 with partial hookups, for RVs, 14 tent sites, including eight with electricity, 20 sites for tents or RVs, and eight cabins. Picnic tables and barbecues are provided. Restrooms, drinking water, flush toilets, showers, RV dump station, pay phone, cable TV, modem access, recreation room, seasonal swimming pool, spa, playground, video arcade, basketball courts, 19-hole miniature golf course, convenience store, snack bar, dog run, petting zoo, fishing pond, bike rentals, pavilion cooking facilities, volleyball court, and horseshoe pits are available. Some facilities are wheelchair-accessible. Leashed pets are permitted.

Reservations, fees: Reservations are accepted at 800/562-4197. The fee is $5–38 for RV sites, $22–25 for tent sites, $3 per person per night for more than two people. Major credit cards accepted. Open year-round.

Directions: From U.S. 50 west of Placerville, take the Shingle Springs Drive exit (and not the Shingle Springs/Ponderosa Road exit). Drive one block to Rock Barn Road. Turn left and drive one-half mile to the campground at the end of the road.

Contact: Placerville KOA, 530/676-2267, website: www.koa.com.

76 SLY PARK RECREATION AREA

Rating: 7

On Jenkinson Lake.

Map 5.5, page 302

Jenkinson Lake is set at 3,500 feet in elevation in the lower reaches of Eldorado National Forest, with a climate that is perfect for water-skiing and fishing. The lake covers 640 acres and features eight miles of forested shoreline. Participants of both sports get along, with most water-skiers motoring around the lake's main body, while anglers head upstream into the Hazel Creek arm of the lake for trout (in the spring) and bass (in the summer). Good news for anglers: personal watercraft are not permitted. More good news: this is one of the better lakes in the Sierra for brown trout. The boat ramp is in a cove on the southwest end of the lake, about two miles from the campground. The area also has several hiking trails, and the lake is good for swimming. There are nine miles of trails available for hiking, biking, and equestrians; an equestrian trail also circles the lake. A group camp is available for visitors with horses, complete with riding trails, hitching posts, and corrals. Note: no pets or babies with diapers are allowed on the lake.

Campsites, facilities: There are 155 sites with no hookups for tents or RVs up to 40 feet long. Picnic tables, fire rings, and barbecues are pro-

vided. Drinking water and vault toilets are available. Two boat ramps are available nearby. Some facilities are wheelchair-accessible. There are five group sites that can accommodate 50–100 people and an equestrian camp called Black Oak, which has 12 sites and two youth-group areas. A grocery store, snack bar, RV dump station, bait, and propane gas are available nearby. Firewood is sold on-site. Leashed pets are permitted.

Reservations, fees: Reservations are recommended and may be made at 530/644-2792. The fee is $16–21 per night, $2 per person for more than two people, $2 per pet per night, $9 for each additional vehicle, $3–6 boat-launch fee, and $160 for up to 50 people for the group site. Senior discount available. Check out by 2 P.M. Open year-round.

Directions: From Sacramento, drive east on U.S. 50 to Pollock Pines and take the exit for Sly Park Road. Drive south for five miles to Jenkinson Lake and the campground access road. Turn left and drive one mile to the campground.

Contact: Sly Park Recreation Area, El Dorado Irrigation District, 530/644-2545, website: www.eid.org.

77 PIPI

Rating: 7

On the Middle Fork of the Cosumnes River in Eldorado National Forest.

Map 5.5, page 302

This place is far enough out of the way to get missed by most campers. It is beside the Middle Fork of the Cosumnes River at 4,100 feet. There are some good swimming holes in the area, but the water is cold in early summer (after all, it's snowmelt). A trail/boardwalk along the river is wheelchair-accessible. Several sites border a pretty meadow in the back of the camp. This is also a gateway to a vast network of Forest Service roads to the north in Eldorado National Forest.

Campsites, facilities: There are 51 sites for tents or RVs up to 40 feet long, including three double-family sites. Picnic tables and fire grills are provided. Drinking water and vault toilets are available. There is wheelchair access to some camping areas, restrooms, and pathways. Leashed pets are permitted.

Reservations, fees: Reservations are accepted with a $9 reservation fee for some sites at 877/444-6777 or website www.ReserveUsa.com. The fee is $11 per night. Senior discount available. Open May through mid-November, weather permitting.

Directions: From Jackson, drive east on Highway 88 to Pioneer and continue for nine miles to Omo Ranch Road. Turn left and drive .8 mile to North-South Road/Forest Road 6. Turn right and drive 5.9 miles to the campground on the left side of the road.

Contact: Eldorado Information Center, 530/644-6048, fax 530/295-5624; Eldorado National Forest, Amador Ranger District, 209/295-4251, fax 209/295-5994.

78 FAR HORIZONS 49ER VILLAGE

Rating: 4

In Plymouth.

Map 5.5, page 302

This is the granddaddy of RV parks, set in the heart of the gold country 40 miles east of Stockton and Sacramento. It is rarely crowded and offers warm pools, a huge spa, and a friendly staff.

Campsites, facilities: There are 329 sites with full hookups, including 15 drive-through, for RVs only, 10 park-model cabins, four RV rentals. Restrooms, flush toilets, showers, RV dump station, playground, two heated swimming pools, hot tub, recreation room, TV lounge, pool room, cable TV, modem access, coin laundry, delicatessen, propane gas, and a general store are available. Some facilities are wheelchair-accessible. Leashed pets are permitted.

Reservations, fees: Reservations are recommended. The fee is $28–50 per night, $2 per night for extra vehicle. Major credit cards accepted. Open year-round.

Directions: From Sacramento, drive east on U.S. 50 to Watt Avenue. Turn south on Watt Avenue and drive to Highway 16. Turn east on Highway 16 and drive to Highway 49. Turn north on Highway 49 and drive a mile to the campground on the left side of the road at 18265 Hwy. 49. Note: this is a mile south of Main Street in Plymouth.

Contact: Far Horizons 49er Trailer Village, 209/245-6981 or 800/339-6981, website: www.49ervillage.com.

79 INDIAN GRINDING ROCK STATE HISTORIC PARK

Rating: 7

Near Jackson.

Map 5.5, page 302

Visiting this park is like entering a time machine. It offers a reconstructed Miwok village with petroglyphs, bedrock mortars, a cultural center, a two-mile nature trail, and interpretive talks for groups, by reservation. One unique element is that you will discover *Chaw-fe* (grinding rock) signs about the park. The camp is set at 2,500 feet in the Sierra foothills, about 10 miles from Jackson. It covers 135 acres and is nestled in a small valley with open meadows and large valley oaks. There is a large outcropping of marbleized limestone with 1,185 mortar holes, the largest collection of bedrock mortars in North America. Ceremonies are scheduled several times a year by local Native Americans, including the Acorn Harvest Thanksgiving in September. Summers are warm and dry, with temperatures often exceeding 90°F. Spring and fall are ideal, with winters cool, often right on the edge of snow (a few times) and rain (mostly) during most storms.

Campsites, facilities: There are 23 sites for tents or RVs, with some sites available for RVs up to 27 feet long, and seven bark houses.

Picnic tables, fire grills, and food lockers are provided. Drinking water, flush toilets, and coin-operated hot showers are available. Some facilities are wheelchair-accessible. Leashed pets are permitted.

Reservations, fees: Reservations are not accepted. The fee is $12 per night. Reservations required for bark houses and groups. Open year-round.

Directions: From Jackson, drive east on Highway 88 for 11 miles to Pine Grove-Volcano Road. Turn left on Pine Grove-Volcano Road and drive 1.75 miles to the campground on the left.

Contact: Indian Grinding Rock State Historic Park, 209/296-7488.

80 LAKE AMADOR RECREATION AREA

Rating: 7

Near Stockton.
Map 5.5, page 302

Lake Amador is set in the foothill country east of Stockton at an elevation of 485 feet, covering 425 acres with 13 miles of shoreline. Everything here is set up for fishing, with large trout stocks from winter through late spring and the chance for huge bass; plus, water-skiing and personal watercraft are prohibited. The largest two-man bass limit in California was caught here (80 pounds), and the lake record bass weighed 17 pounds, 1.25 ounces. The Carson Creek arm and Jackson Creek arm are the top spots.

Campsites, facilities: There are 150 sites, including 72 with full hookups, for tents or RVs up to 30 feet, and 12 group sites. Picnic tables and fire grills are provided. Drinking water, restrooms, showers, RV dump station, boat ramp, boat rentals, fishing supplies (including bait and tackle), restaurant, grocery store, propane gas, swimming pond, and a playground are available. Some facilities are wheelchair-accessible. Leashed pets are permitted.

Reservations, fees: Reservations are accepted seven days in advance in the summer. The fee is $18–23 per night for each vehicle. Major credit cards accepted. Open year-round.

Directions: From Stockton, turn east on Highway 88 and drive 24 miles to Clements. Just east of Clements, bear left on Highway 88 and drive 11 miles to Jackson Valley Road. Turn right (well signed) and drive four miles to Lake Amador Drive. Turn right and drive over the dam to the campground office.

Contact: Lake Amador Recreation Area, 209/274-4739, website: www.lakeamador.com.

81 LAKE PARDEE MARINA

Rating: 7

On Pardee Reservoir.
Map 5.5, page 302

Many people think that Pardee is the prettiest lake in the Mother Lode country; it's a big lake covering 2,257 acres with 37 miles of shoreline. It is a beautiful sight in the spring when the lake is full and the surrounding hills are green and glowing. Water-skiing, personal watercraft, and swimming are prohibited at the lake; it is set up expressly for fishing, with high catch rates for rainbow trout and kokanee salmon. During hot weather, attention turns to bass, both smallmouth and largemouth, as well as catfish.

Campsites, facilities: There are 99 sites with no hookups for tents or RVs to 40 feet long, 12 sites with full hookups for RVs. Picnic tables and fire grills are provided. Drinking water, restrooms, showers (in the RV section), RV dump station, boat ramp, boat rentals, coin laundry, grocery store, propane gas, RV and boat storage, wading pool, and a seasonal swimming pool are available. Some facilities are wheelchair-accessible. Leashed pets are permitted.

Reservations, fees: Reservations are accepted for full-hookup RV sites only. The fee is $16–22 per night, $8 per night for second vehicle, $1 per pet per night. Major credit cards accepted. Open February through October.

Directions: From Stockton, drive east on Highway 88 for 24 miles to the town of Clements. Just east of Clements, bear left on Highway 88 and drive 11 miles to Jackson Valley Road. Turn right and drive to a four-way stop sign at Buena Vista. Turn right and drive for three miles to Stony Creek Road on the left. Turn left and drive a mile to the campground on the right.

Contact: Pardee Recreation Area, 209/772-1472, fax 209/772-0985, website: www.lakepardee.com.

82 LAKE CAMANCHE NORTH

Rating: 7

On Camanche Reservoir.

Map 5.5, page 302

The sites at North Shore feature grassy spots with picnic tables set above the lake, and though there are few trees and the sites seem largely exposed, the lake view is quite pretty. The lake will beckon you for water sports and is excellent for boat owners and all water sports, with a full-service marina available. The warm, clean waters make for good water-skiing (in specified areas), and fishing for trout in spring, bass in early summer, and crappie, bluegill, and catfish in summer. There are five miles of hiking and equestrian trails.

Campsites, facilities: There are 219 sites, no hookups, for tents or RVs, 22 cottages, and some motel rooms. Picnic tables and fire grills are provided. Restrooms, drinking water, showers, RV dump station, boat ramp, boat rentals, laundry room, grocery store, cafe, and a playground are available. Some facilities are wheelchair-accessible. Leashed pets are permitted.

Reservations, fees: Reservations recommended, $18 per night, $9 per night for each extra vehicle, $6 boat launch fee, $1 per pet per night. Major credit cards accepted. Open year-round.

Directions: From Stockton, drive east on Highway 88 for 24 miles to Clements. Just east of

Clements, bear left on Highway 88 and drive six miles to Camanche Parkway. Turn right and drive seven miles to the Camanche North Shore entrance gate.

Contact: Lake Camanche North, 209/763-5121, fax 209/763-5789, website: www.camanche recreation.com.

83 LAKE CAMANCHE SOUTH

Rating: 7

On Camanche Reservoir.

Map 5.5, page 302

Camanche Reservoir is a huge, multifaceted facility, covering 7,700 acres with 53 miles of shoreline, set in the foothills east of Lodi at 325 feet in elevation. It is the number one recreation lake for water-skiing and personal watercraft (in specified areas), as well as swimming. In the spring and summer, it provides outstanding fishing for bass, trout, crappie, bluegill, and catfish. There are two campgrounds at the lake, and both have boat ramps nearby and full facilities. This one at South Shore has a large, but exposed, overflow area for camping, a way to keep from getting stuck for a spot on popular weekends.

Campsites, facilities: There are 263 sites for tents and self-contained RVs, 120 sites with full hookups for RVs, and seven cottages. Picnic tables and fire grills are provided. Drinking water, restrooms, showers, RV dump station, trout pond, boat ramp, boat rentals, coin laundry, snack bar, and a grocery store are available. Some facilities are wheelchair-accessible. Leashed pets are permitted.

Reservations, fees: Reservations recommended, $18–25 per night, $9 per night for each extra vehicle, $6 boat launch fee, $1 per pet per night. Major credit cards accepted. Open year-round.

Directions: From Stockton, drive east on Highway 88 for 24 miles to Clements. Just east of Clements continue east on Highway 12 and drive six miles to South Camanche Parkway. Turn left and drive six miles to the entrance gate.

Contact: Lake Camanche South, 209/763-5178, fax 209/763-5724, website: www.camanche recreation.com.

84 OAK KNOLL

🏞 🏊 🎣 🚤 🐕 🚐 ⛺

Rating: 7

At New Hogan Reservoir.

Map 5.5, page 302

This is one of three camps at New Hogan Reservoir. The reservoir was created by an Army Corps of Engineers dam project on the Calaveras River. (See the entry for Acorn West and Acorn East for more information.)

Campsites, facilities: There are 50 sites for tents or RVs. Fire grills and picnic tables are provided. Drinking water and vault toilets are available. Groceries, propane gas, RV dump station, and a four-lane boat ramp are available nearby. Leashed pets are permitted.

Reservations, fees: Reservations are accepted at 877/444-6777 or website www.ReserveUsa.com. The fee is $10 per night. Senior discount available. Open May to early September.

Directions: From Stockton, drive east on Highway 26 for about 35 miles to Valley Springs and Hogan Dam Road. Turn right and drive 1.5 miles to Hogan Parkway. Turn left and drive one mile to South Petersburg Road. Turn left and drive one-half mile to the campground on the right (adjacent to Acorn campgrounds).

Contact: U.S. Army Corps of Engineers, Sacramento District, 209/772-1343, fax 209/772-9352.

85 ACORN WEST AND ACORN EAST

🏞 🏊 🎣 🚤 🐕 🚐 ⛺

Rating: 7

At New Hogan Reservoir.

Map 5.5, page 302

New Hogan is a big lake in the foothill country east of Stockton, set at an elevation of 680 feet and covering 4,000 acres with 50 miles of shoreline. Acorn West and Acorn East are two campgrounds on the lake operated by the Army Corps of Engineers. Boaters might also consider boat-in sites near Deer Flat on the eastern shore. Boating and water-skiing are popular here. Fishing for largemouth bass is off-and-on, best in the spring up the Bear Creek and Whiskey Creek arms, and again in the fall when the striped bass come to life, chasing bait fish on the surface. Fishing for largemouth bass can be exceptional in spring and summer. An interpretive trail below the dam is worth checking out.

Campsites, facilities: At Acorn West there are 58 sites for tents or RVs. At Acorn East there are 69 sites for tents or RVs. Fire pits and picnic tables are provided. Drinking water, flush toilets, showers, pay telephones, fish-cleaning station, and RV dump station are available. A two-lane, paved boat ramp is in Acorn East Campground. Groceries, a restaurant, and propane gas are available within three miles. Leashed pets are permitted.

Reservations, fees: Reservations are accepted at 877/444-6777 or website www.ReserveUsa.com. The fee is $12–16 per night. Senior discount available. Major credit cards accepted.

Directions: From Stockton, drive east on Highway 26 for about 35 miles to Valley Springs and Hogan Dam Road. Turn right and drive 1.5 miles to Hogan Parkway. Turn left and drive one mile to South Petersburg Road. Turn left and drive one-quarter mile to the campground on the right.

Contact: U.S. Army Corps of Engineers, Sacramento District, 209/772-1343, fax 209/772-9352.

86 GOLDEN PINES RV RESORT AND CAMP

🏞 🏊 🐕 🛶 ♿ 🚐 ⛺

Rating: 6

Near Arnold.

Map 5.5, page 302

This is a privately operated park set at 5,800 feet

on the slopes of the Sierra Nevada near Stanislaus National Forest, the North Stanislaus River, and Calaveras Big Trees State Park (two miles away). The latter features 150 giant sequoias, along with the biggest stump you can imagine, and two easy hikes, one routed through the North Grove, another through the South Grove. Note that about half the sites here are long-term rentals.

Campsites, facilities: There are 62 sites with full hookups for RVs, four sites with partial hookups for RVs, 40 tent sites, and three cabins. Picnic tables, fire pits, and barbecues are provided at all RV sites and most tent sites. Drinking water, restrooms, showers, recreation room, seasonal swimming pool, playground, convenience store, coin laundry, and propane gas are available. Some facilities are wheelchair-accessible. Leashed pets are permitted.

Reservations, fees: Reservations are recommended. The fee is $16–29 per night, $2 per person per night for more than four people, $1 per night for each extra vehicle. Senior discount available. Major credit cards accepted. Open year-round.

Directions: From Angels Camp, turn northeast on Highway 4 and drive 22 miles to Arnold. Continue for seven miles to the campground entrance on the left.

Contact: Golden Pines RV Resort and Camp, 209/795-2820, fax 209/795-7432, website: www.goldenpinesrvresort.com.

87 BOARDS CROSSING

Rating: 8

On the North Fork of the Stanislaus River in Stanislaus National Forest.

Map 5.5, page 302

One of the oldest campgrounds in the Western United States, Boards Crossing is near a historic one-way bridge that crosses the North Fork Stanislaus River. It is a small, primitive camp set along the river at 3,800 feet in elevation, with Beaver Creek three miles to the east (continue on the access road after crossing the bridge). This place is just far enough off Highway 4 to be overlooked by most campers.

Campsites, facilities: There are five tent sites. Picnic tables and fire rings are provided. Vault toilets are available. No drinking water is available. Garbage must be packed out. You can buy groceries and propane gas nearby. Leashed pets are permitted.

Reservations, fees: Reservations are not accepted. There is no fee for camping. Campfire permits are required (free). Open June through September.

Directions: From Angels Camp, drive east on Highway 4 and pass Arnold to Dorrington and Boards Crossing Road on the right. Turn right and drive about two miles to the campground entrance road on the right. Turn right and drive about a mile to the campground on the right.

Contact: Stanislaus National Forest, Calaveras Ranger District, 209/795-1381, fax 209/795-6849.

88 NORTH GROVE

Rating: 7

In Calaveras Big Trees State Park.

Map 5.5, page 302

This is one of two campgrounds at Calaveras Big Trees State Park, the state park known for its two groves of giant sequoias (Sierra redwoods). The park covers 6,500 acres, preserving the extraordinary North Grove of giant Sequoias. The grove includes the Discovery Tree. Over the years, additional acreage surrounding the grove has been added, providing a mixed conifer forest as a buffer around the giant sequoias. The trailhead for a hike on the North Grove Loop is here; it's an easy 1.5-mile walk that is routed among 150 sequoias, where the sweet fragrance of the huge trees fills the air. These trees are known for their massive diameter, not for their height, as is the case with coastal redwoods. Another hike, a five-miler, is in the South Grove, where the park's two largest sequoias (the Agassiz Tree and the Palace Hotel Tree) can be seen on a spur trail. A visitor center is open during peak periods, offering exhibits on the giant sequoia and natural history. The North Fork Stanislaus River runs near Highway 4, providing trout fishing access. The Stanislaus (near the bridge) and Beaver Creek (about 10 miles away) are stocked with trout in late spring and early summer. In the winter this is a popular spot for cross-country skiing and snowshoeing. The elevation is 4,800 feet.

Campsites, facilities: There are 27 sites for tents, 29 sites for RVs up to 30 feet long, five hike-in sites, and two sites designed for wheelchair use. Two group sites are also available for 40–60 people each. Fire grills, food lockers, and picnic tables are provided. Drinking water, flush toilets, firewood for purchase, coin-operated showers, and RV dump station are available. Some facilities are wheelchair-accessible, including a nature trail and exhibits. No bicycles are allowed on the paths, but they are permitted on fire roads and paved roads. Leashed pets are permitted, but not on trails.

Reservations, fees: Reservations are accepted with a $7.50 reservation fee at 800/444-PARK (800/444-7275) and website www.Reserve America.com. The fee is $12 per night, $30–45 group fee, and $11 for hike-in sites. Senior discount available. Open year-round, with 12 sites available in winter.

Directions: From Angels Camp, drive east on Highway 4 for 23 miles to Arnold and then continue another four miles to the park entrance on the right.

Contact: Calaveras Big Trees State Park, 209/795-2334; Columbia State Park, 209/532-0150.

89 OAK HOLLOW

Rating: 7

In Calaveras Big Trees State Park.
Map 5.5, page 302
This is one of two campgrounds at Calaveras Big Trees State Park. (See the entry for North Grove for recreation information.)
Campsites, facilities: There are 23 sites for tents

only, and 18 sites for RVs up to 30 feet long. Picnic tables, fire rings, and food lockers are provided. Drinking water, flush toilets, and coin-operated showers are available. An RV dump station is available four miles away at North Grove. You can buy supplies in Dorrington. Some facilities are wheelchair-accessible, including a nature trail and exhibits. Leashed pets are permitted, except on trails.

Reservations, fees: Reservations are accepted with a $7.50 reservation fee at 800/444-PARK (800/444-7275) and website www.Reserve America.com. The fee is $12 per night. Senior discount available. Open May through September.

Directions: From Angels Camp, drive east on Highway 4 for 23 miles to Arnold and then continue another four miles to the park entrance on the right. Continue another four miles to the campground on the right.

Contact: Calaveras Big Trees State Park, 209/795-2334; Columbia State Park, 209/532-0150.

90 49ER RV RANCH

Rating: 6

Near Columbia.
Map 5.5, page 302
This historic ranch/campground was originally built in 1852 as a dairy farm. Several original barns are still standing. The place has been brought up to date, of course, with a small store on the property providing last-minute supplies. Location is a plus, with the Columbia State Historic Park only a half mile away, and the Stanislaus River arm of New Melones Lake within a five-minute drive. The elevation is 2,100 feet. Note that there is a separate mobile home park on the premises and that there are long-term rentals in the RV park in the summer.
Campsites, facilities: There are 42 sites with full hookups for trailers and RVs up to 40 feet. Picnic tables and barbecues are provided. Restrooms, drinking water, hot showers, coin laundry, convenience store, RV dump station, cable

TV, modem access, propane gas, and a large barn for group or club activities are available. Some facilities are wheelchair-accessible. Leashed pets are permitted.

Reservations, fees: Reservations are accepted. The fee is $22.50–28.50 per night, $2.50 per person for more than two people. Long-term rates and group rates available. Senior discount available. Open year-round.

Directions: From Sonora, turn north on Highway 49 for 2.5 miles to Parrots Ferry Road. Turn right and drive 1.7 miles to Columbia Street. Turn right and drive .4 mile to Pacific Street. Turn left and drive a block to Italian Bar Road. Turn right and drive a half mile to the campground on the right.

Contact: 49er RV Ranch, 209/532-4978, website: www.49rv.com.

91 MARBLE QUARRY RV PARK

Rating: 6

Near Columbia.
Map 5.5, page 302

This is a family-oriented RV park set at 2,100 feet in the Mother Lode country, within nearby range of several adventures. A quarter-mile trail leads directly to Columbia State Historic Park, and the Stanislaus River arm of New Melones Lake is only five miles away.

Campsites, facilities: There are 85 sites, including 35 with full hookups and 50 with partial hookups for RVs, a small area for tents, and three sleeping cabins. Drinking water and picnic tables are provided. Restrooms, showers, seasonal swimming pool, coin laundry, modem access, convenience store, RV dump station, playground, two clubhouses, reading/TV room, two full kitchens, satellite TV, and propane gas are available. Some facilities are wheelchair-accessible. Leashed pets are permitted.

Reservations, fees: Reservations are accepted. The fee is $21–32 per night, $3 per person for more than two people. Senior discount available. Major credit cards accepted. Open year-round.

Directions: From Sonora, turn north on Highway 49 and drive 2.5 miles to Parrotts Ferry Road (stop sign). Bear right on Parrotts Ferry Road and drive 1.5 miles to Columbia Street. Turn right and drive a short distance to Jackson Street. Turn right on Jackson Street and drive a quarter mile (becomes Yankee Hill Road) to the campground on the right (at 11551 Yankee Hill Road).

Contact: Marble Quarry RV Park, 209/532-9539, website: www.marblequarry.com.

92 SUGARPINE RV PARK

Rating: 5

In Twain Harte.
Map 5.5, page 302

Twain Harte is a beautiful little town, right at the edge of the snow line in winter, and right where pines take over the alpine landscape. This park is at the threshold of mountain country, with Pinecrest, Dodge Ridge, and Beardsley Reservoir nearby. It sits on 15 acres and features several walking paths. It has a separate 64-site mobile home park for long-term renters.

Campsites, facilities: There are 13 sites with full hookups for RVs, 13 tent sites, three park-model cabins, and three RV rentals. Picnic tables are provided. Restrooms, showers, playground, seasonal pool, video games in summer, coin laundry, cable TV, and a convenience store are available. Some facilities are wheelchair-accessible. Leashed pets are permitted.

Reservations, fees: Reservations are accepted. The fee is $20–35 per night, $3 per vehicle for more than one vehicle, with exception for towed vehicles. There is a pet fee. Senior discount available. Major credit cards accepted. Open year-round.

Directions: From Sonora, drive east on Highway 108 for 17 miles to the park on the right side of the road.

Contact: Sugarpine RV Park, tel./fax 209/586-4631, website: www.surgarpinerv.com.

© TOM STIENSTRA

Chapter 6
Tahoe and the
Northern Sierra

Chapter 6—Tahoe and the Northern Sierra

Mount Tallac affords a view across Lake Tahoe like no other: a cobalt blue expanse of water bordered by mountains that span miles of Sierra wildlands. The beauty is stunning. Lake Tahoe is one of the few places on earth where people feel an emotional response just by looking at it. Yosemite Valley, the giant Sequoias, the Grand Canyon, a perfect sunset on the Pacific Ocean . . . these are a few other sights that occasionally can evoke the same response. But Tahoe often seems to strike the deepest chord. It can resonate inside you for weeks, even after a short visit.

"What about all the people?" you ask. It's true that people come here in droves. But we found many spots that we shared only with the chipmunks. You can enjoy these spots, too, if you're willing to read our books, hunt a bit, and most important, time your trip to span Monday through Thursday.

This area has the widest range and number of campgrounds in California—a stunning 193 different campgrounds!

Tahoe and the northern Sierra feature hundreds of lakes, including dozens you can drive to. The best for scenic beauty are Echo Lakes, Donner, Fallen Leaf, Sardine, Caples, Loon, Union Valley . . . well, we could go on and on. It is one of the most beautiful regions anywhere on earth.

The north end of the North Sierra starts near Bucks Lake, a great lake for trout fishing, and extends to Bear River Canyon (and Caples Lake, Silver Lake, and Bear River Reservoir). In between are the Lakes Basin Recreation Area (containing Gold, Sardine, Packer, and other lakes) in southern Plumas County, the Crystal Basin (featuring Union Valley Reservoir and Loon Lake, among others) in the Sierra foothills west of Tahoe, Lake Davis (with the highest catch rates for trout) near Portola, and the Carson River Canyon and Hope Valley south of Tahoe.

You could spend weeks exploring any of these places, having the time of your life, and still not get to Tahoe's magic. But it is Tahoe where the adventure starts for many, especially in the surrounding Tahoe National Forest and Desolation Wilderness.

One of California's greatest day trips from Tahoe is to Echo Lakes, where you can take a hiker's shuttle boat across the two lakes to the Pacific Crest Trail, then hike a few miles into Desolation Wilderness and Aloha Lakes. Yet with so many wonderful ways to spend a day in this area, this day trip is hardly a blip on the radar scope.

With so many places and so little time, this region offers what can be the ultimate adventureland.

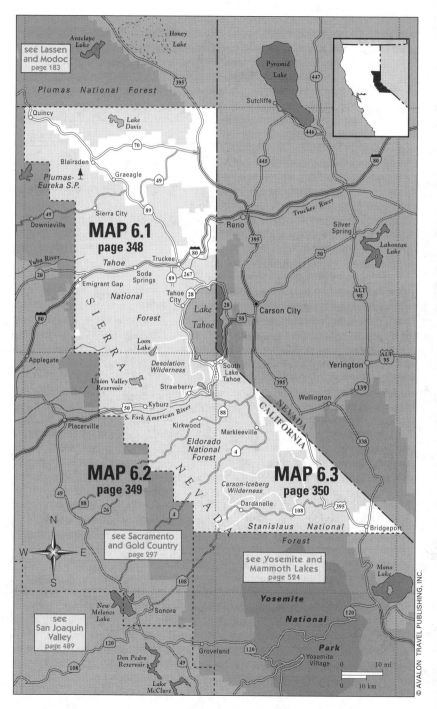

Map 6.1

**Campgrounds 1–90
Pages 351–388**

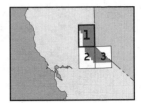

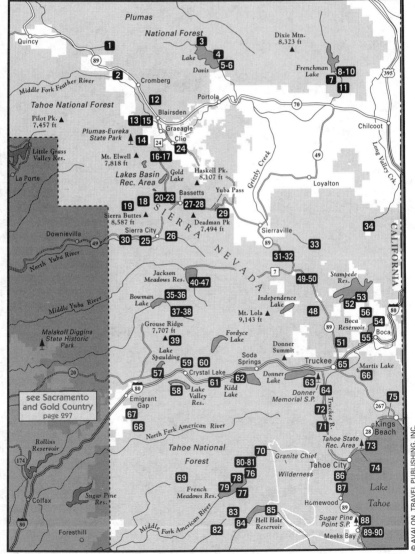

© AVALON TRAVEL PUBLISHING, INC.

Map 6.2

Campgrounds 91–141
Pages 388–410

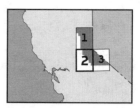

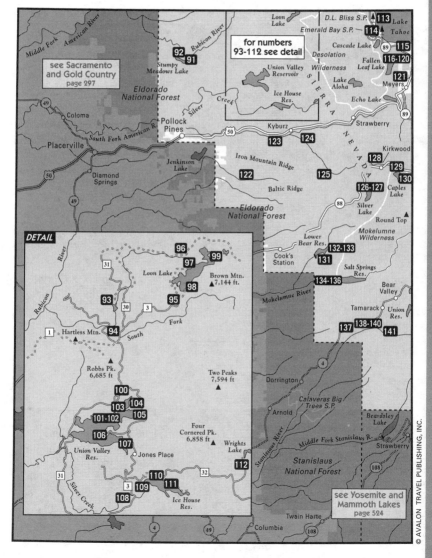

Map 6.3

Campgrounds 142–186
Pages 410–429

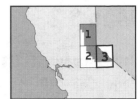

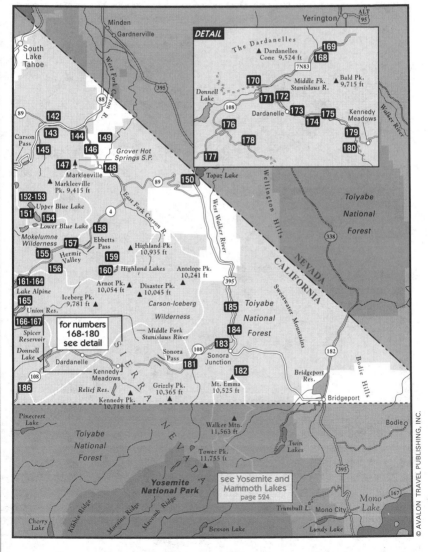

◼1 BRADY'S CAMP

Rating: 4

On Pine Creek in Plumas National Forest.

Map 6.1, page 348

Don't expect much company here. This is a tiny, little-known, primitive camp near Pine Creek, at roughly 7,000 feet in elevation. A side trip is to make the half-mile drive up to Argentine Rock (7,209 feet) for a lookout onto this remote forest country. To the east are many miles of national forest, accessible by vehicle, although there is significant logging activity in parts of the forest.

Campsites, facilities: There are four tent sites. Picnic tables and fire grills are provided. Vault toilets are available. No drinking water is available. Garbage must be packed out. Leashed pets are permitted.

Reservations, fees: Reservations are not accepted. There is no fee for camping. Open May through October.

Directions: From Oroville, drive north on Highway 70 to the junction with Highway 89. Turn south on Highway 89/70 and drive 11 miles to Quincy. In Quincy, continue on Highway 89/70 for six miles to Squirrel Creek Road. Turn left and drive seven miles (after two miles bear right at the Y) to Forest Road 25N29. Turn left and drive one mile to the campground on the right side of the road.

Contact: Plumas National Forest, Mt. Hough Ranger District, 530/283-0555, fax 530/283-1821 or 530/283-0159.

◼2 GOLDEN COACH RV RESORT

Rating: 6

Near the Feather River.

Map 6.1, page 348

This is a good layover spot for RV cruisers looking to hole up for the night. The park is wooded and set near the Feather River. You'll find mostly older adults here. Some spots at this park are booked for the entire summer.

Campsites, facilities: There are 57 sites, including some drive-through sites, with full hookups for RVs, and two group campgrounds for 10–20 people. Picnic tables are provided. Restrooms, showers, modem access, a coin laundry, wood, convenience store, café, and propane gas are available. Leashed pets are permitted.

Reservations, fees: Reservations are recommended. Fees are $15–20 per night, $2 per person for more than two people. Long-term rates available. Major credit cards accepted. Open May through mid-October.

Directions: In Truckee, at the junction of Highway 80 and Highway 89, take Highway 89 north to the junction with Highway 70. Drive north on Highway 89/Highway 70 for 6.5 miles to Cromberg and look for the signed entrance to the campground on the left at 59704 Highway 70.

Contact: Golden Coach RV Resort, 800/327-0933 or 530/836-2426.

◼3 LIGHTNING TREE

Rating: 7

On Lake Davis in Plumas National Forest.

Map 6.1, page 348

Lightning Tree campground is set near the shore of Lake Davis. This camp was closed in 2001 and 2002 because of low lake levels but will be reopened when the water rises, perhaps spring of 2003. Davis is a good-sized lake, with 30 miles of shoreline, set high in the northern Sierra at 5,775 feet. Lake Davis is one of the top mountain lakes for fishing in California, with large rainbow trout in the early summer and fall. This camp is perfectly situated for a fishing trip. It is at Lightning Tree Point on the lake's remote northeast shore, directly across the lake from Freeman Creek, one of the better spots for big trout. This lake is famous for the botched poisoning job in the 1990s by the Department of Fish and Game, and then, in turn, the biggest trout plants in

California history at a single lake: more than 1 million trout! It receives lots of snow and often freezes over in the winter. Since pike have reappeared, this future of this lake is one of the biggest environmental timebombs in California; if pike escape downstream, they could invade the Delta and wipe out salmon and other species. There are three boat ramps on the lake.

Campsites, facilities: There are 40 sites for RVs up to 50 feet long. Vault toilets and garbage service are available from May to October. No drinking water is available. An RV dump station and a car-top boat launch are nearby. Leashed pets are permitted.

Reservations, fees: Reserve at 877/444-6777 ($9 reservation fee) or website: www.Reserve Usa.com; $6 per night, $10 for a double site. Senior discount available. Open May to October.

Directions: From Truckee, turn north on Highway 89 and drive to Sattley and County Road A23. Turn right on County Road A23 and drive 13 miles to Highway 70. Turn left on Highway 70 and drive one mile to Grizzly Road. Turn right on Grizzly Road and drive about six miles to Lake Davis. Continue north on Lake Davis Road along the lake's east shore and drive about five miles to the campground entrance on the left side of the road.

Contact: Plumas National Forest, Beckwourth Ranger District, 530/836-2575, fax 530/836-0493.

◢ GRASSHOPPER FLAT

Rating: 7

On Lake Davis in Plumas National Forest.
Map 6.1, page 348

Grasshopper Flat provides a nearby alternative to Grizzly at Lake Davis, with the nearby boat ramp at adjacent Honker Cove a primary attraction for campers with trailered boats for fishing. The camp is on the southeast end of the lake, at 5,800 feet elevation. Lake Davis is known for its large rainbow trout that bite best in early summer and fall.

Campsites, facilities: There are 70 sites for tents or RVs up to 32 feet long. Picnic tables and fire grills are provided. Drinking water and vault toilets are available. A boat ramp, grocery store, and RV dump station are nearby. Leashed pets are permitted.

Reservations, fees: Reservations are accepted for some sites. Fees are $13 per night. Senior discount available. Open May through October.

Directions: From Truckee, turn north on Highway 89 and drive to Sattley and County Road A23. Turn right on County Road A23 and drive 13 miles to Highway 70. Turn left on Highway 70 and drive one mile to Grizzly Road. Turn right on Grizzly Road and drive about six miles to Lake Davis. Continue north on Lake Davis Road for a mile (just past Grizzly) to the campground entrance on the left side of the road.

Contact: Plumas National Forest, Beckwourth Ranger District, 530/836-2575, fax 530/836-0493.

◢ CROCKER

Rating: 5

In Plumas National Forest.
Map 6.1, page 348

Even though this camp is just four miles east of Lake Davis, it is little known and little used since there are three lakeside camps close by. This camp is set in Plumas National Forest at 5,800 feet elevation, and it is about a 15-minute drive north to the border of the Dixie Mountain State Game Refuge.

Campsites, facilities: There are 10 sites for tents or RVs up to 32 feet long. Picnic tables and fire grills are provided. Vault toilets are available. No drinking water is available. Garbage must be packed out. Leashed pets are permitted.

Reservations, fees: Reservations are not accepted. There is no fee for camping. Open May through October.

Directions: From Reno, drive north on U.S. 395 to the junction with Highway 70. Turn west on Highway 70 and drive to Beckwourth and County Road 111/Beckwourth-Genessee Road. Turn right on County Road 111 and drive six miles to the campground on the left side of the road.

Contact: Plumas National Forest, Beckwourth Ranger District, 530/836-2575, fax 530/836-0493.

6 GRIZZLY

Rating: 7

On Lake Davis in Plumas National Forest.
Map 6.1, page 348

This is one of the better developed campgrounds at Lake Davis and is a popular spot for camping anglers. Its proximity to the Grizzly Store, just over the dam to the south, makes getting last-minute supplies a snap. In addition, a boat ramp is to the north in Honker Cove, providing access to the southern reaches of the lake, including the island area, where trout trolling is good in early summer and fall.

Campsites, facilities: There are 55 sites for tents or RVs up to 32 feet long. Picnic tables and fire grills are provided. Drinking water and vault toilets are available. A boat ramp, grocery store, and RV dump station are nearby. Leashed pets are permitted.

Reservations, fees: Reservations are accepted for some sites. Fees are $13 per night. Senior discount available. Open May through October.

Directions: From Truckee, turn north on Highway 89 and drive to Sattley and County Road A23. Turn right on County Road A23 and drive 13 miles to Highway 70. Turn left on Highway 70 and drive one mile to Grizzly Road. Turn right on Grizzly Road and drive about six miles to Lake Davis. Continue north on Lake Davis Road for less than a mile to the campground entrance on the left side of the road.

Contact: Plumas National Forest, Beckwourth Ranger District, 530/836-2575, fax 530/836-0493.

7 COTTONWOOD SPRINGS

Rating: 7

Near Frenchman Lake in Plumas National Forest.
Map 6.1, page 348

Cottonwood Springs, elevation 5,700 feet, is largely an overflow camp at Frenchman Lake. It is the only camp at the lake with a group site. The more popular Frenchman, Big Cove, and Spring Creek camps are along the southeast shore of the lake near a boat ramp.

Campsites, facilities: There are 20 sites for tents or RVs up to 50 feet long and two group camping areas, which can accommodate up to 25 and 50 people, respectively. Picnic tables and fire rings are provided. Drinking water and flush toilets are available. Some facilities are wheelchair-accessible. A boat ramp and RV dump station are nearby. Leashed pets are permitted.

Reservations, fees: Reserve at 877/444-6777 ($9 reservation fee) or website: www.Reserve Usa.com; $13 per night, $44–87 per night for groups. Senior discount available. Open May through October.

Directions: From Reno, drive north on U.S. 395 to the junction with Highway 70. Turn west on Highway 70 and drive to Chilcoot and the junction with Frenchman Lake Road. Turn right on Frenchman Lake Road and drive nine miles to the lake and to a Y. At the Y, turn left and drive 1.5 miles to the campground on the left side of the road.

Contact: Plumas National Forest, Beckwourth Ranger District, 530/836-2575, fax 530/836-0493.

8 BIG COVE

Rating: 7

At Frenchman Lake in Plumas National Forest.
Map 6.1, page 348

Big Cove is one of four camps at the southeastern

end of Frenchman Lake, with a boat ramp available about a mile away near the Frenchman and Spring Creek camps. (See the entry for Frenchman for more information.) A trail from the campground leads to the lakeshore. Another trail connects to the Spring Creek Campground, a walk of a half mile.

Campsites, facilities: There are 38 sites for tents or RVs up to 50 feet long (19 are multiple-family units; 10 are wheelchair-accessible). Picnic tables and fire rings are provided. Drinking water and flush toilets are available. Some facilities are wheelchair-accessible. A boat ramp, RV dump station, grocery store (seven miles away), and propane gas are available nearby. Leashed pets are permitted.

Reservations, fees: Reserve at 877/444-6777 ($9 reservation fee) or website: www.ReserveUsa.com; $13–26 per night. Senior discount available. Open May through September.

Directions: From Reno, drive north on U.S. 395 to the junction with Highway 70. Turn west on Highway 70 and drive to Chilcoot and the junction with Frenchman Lake Road. Turn right on Frenchman Lake Road and drive nine miles to the lake and to a Y. At the Y, turn right and drive two miles to Forest Road 24N01. Turn left and drive a short distance to the campground entrance on the left side of the road (on the east side of the lake).

Contact: Plumas National Forest, Beckwourth Ranger District, 530/836-2575, fax 530/836-0493.

9 SPRING CREEK

Rating: 7

On Frenchman Lake in Plumas National Forest.

Map 6.1, page 348

Frenchman Lake is set at 5,500 feet elevation, on the edge of high desert to the east and forest to the west. This camp is on the southeast end of the lake, where there are three other campgrounds, including a group camp and a

boat ramp. The lake provides good fishing for stocked rainbow trout, best in the cove near the campgrounds. Trails lead out from the campground, one heading a quarter mile to the Frenchman Campground, the other routed a half mile to Big Cove Campground.

Campsites, facilities: There are 35 sites for tents or RVs up to 55 feet long. Picnic tables and fire grills are provided. Drinking water and vault toilets are available. A boat ramp and RV dump station are nearby. Leashed pets are permitted.

Reservations, fees: Reserve at 877/444-6777 ($9 reservation fee) or website: www.ReserveUsa.com; $13 per night. Senior discount available. Open May through October.

Directions: From Reno, drive north on U.S. 395 to the junction with Highway 70. Turn west on Highway 70 and drive to Chilcoot and the junction with Frenchman Lake Road. Turn right on Frenchman Lake Road and drive nine miles to the lake and to a Y. At the Y, turn right and drive two miles to the campground on the left side of the road.

Contact: Plumas National Forest, Beckwourth Ranger District, 530/836-2575, fax 530/836-0493.

10 FRENCHMAN

Rating: 7

On Frenchman Lake in Plumas National Forest.

Map 6.1, page 348

Frenchman Lake is set at 5,500 feet in elevation, on the edge of high desert to the east and forest to the west. This camp is on the southeast end of the lake, where there are three other campgrounds, including a group camp and a boat ramp. The lake provides good fishing for stocked rainbow trout. The best fishing is in the cove near the campgrounds and the two inlets, one along the west shore and one at the head of the lake. The proximity to Reno, only 35 miles away, keeps gambling in the back of the minds of many anglers. Because of water demands downstream, the lake often drops significantly by the end of summer. A trail from camp is routed a quarter mile to the Spring Creek Campground.

Campsites, facilities: There are 38 sites for tents or RVs. Picnic tables and fire grills are provided. Drinking water and vault toilets are available. An RV dump station and boat ramp are nearby. Leashed pets are permitted.

Reservations, fees: Reserve at 877/444-6777 ($9 reservation fee) or website: www.Reserve Usa.com; $13 per night. Senior discount available. Open May through October.

Directions: From Reno, drive north on U.S. 395 to the junction with Highway 70. Turn west on Highway 70 and drive to Chilcoot and the junction with Frenchman Lake Road. Turn right on Frenchman Lake Road and drive nine miles to the lake and to a Y. At the Y, turn right and drive 1.5 miles to the campground on the left side of the road.

Contact: Plumas National Forest, Beckwourth Ranger District, 530/836-2575, fax 530/836-0493.

11 CHILCOOT

Rating: 7

On Little Last Chance Creek in Plumas National Forest.

Map 6.1, page 348

This small camp is set along Little Last Chance Creek at 5,400 feet in elevation, about three miles downstream from Frenchman Lake. The stream provides good trout fishing, but access can be difficult at some spots because of brush.

Campsites, facilities: There are 35 sites for tents or RVs up to 45 feet long, and five walk-in sites for tents. Two sites are wheelchair-accessible. Picnic tables and fire rings are provided. Drinking water and flush toilets are available. Some facilities are wheelchair-accessible. A boat ramp, grocery store, and RV dump station are nearby. Leashed pets are permitted.

Reservations, fees: Reserve at 877/444-6777 ($9 reservation fee) or website: www.Reserve Usa.com; $13 per night. Senior discount available. Open May through October.

Directions: From Reno, drive north on U.S. 395 to the junction with Highway 70. Turn west on Highway 70 and drive to Chilcoot and the junction with Frenchman Lake Road. Turn right on Frenchman Lake Road and drive six miles to the campground on the left side of the road.

Contact: Plumas National Forest, Beckwourth Ranger District, 530/836-2575, fax 530/836-0493.

12 SIERRA SPRINGS TRAILER RESORT

Rating: 5

Near Blairsden.

Map 6.1, page 348

This privately operated park is centrally located near fishing, golf, and hiking. A hiking trail is behind the resort. A railroad museum is nearby in Portola. Other possible side trips include the Feather River Park, four miles away in the town of Blairsden. The elevation is 5,000 feet. About half the sites are reserved by long-term tenants for the summer.

Campsites, facilities: There are 40 sites, including some drive-through and 30 with full hookups for RVs up to 40 feet, and four tent sites. Picnic tables and fire rings are provided at some sites. Drinking water, flush toilets, showers, RV dump station, coin laundry, cable TV, modem access, playground, picnic area, horseshoes, recreation room, and volleyball net are available. Leashed pets are permitted.

Reservations, fees: Reservations are accepted. Fees are $17–19.50 per night, $2.50 per person per night for more than two people. Open April through October.

Directions: From Truckee, drive northwest on Highway 89 about 50 miles to Blairsden and the junction with Highway 70. Turn right and drive 3.5 miles east to Sierra Springs Drive.

Turn left on Sierra Springs Drive and drive a short distance to the resort entrance on the left at 70099 Sierra Springs Road.

Contact: Sierra Springs Trailer Resort, 530/836-2747, fax 530/836-2559, website: www.psln.com/osstr.

13 LITTLE BEAR RV PARK

Rating: 7

On the Feather River.

Map 6.1, page 348

This is a privately operated RV park set near the Feather River. Nearby destinations include Plumas-Eureka State Park and the Lakes Basin Recreation Area. The elevation is 4,300 feet. About half of the sites are taken by full-season rentals.

Campsites, facilities: There are 91 sites, including half taken by full-season rentals, 80 with full hookups for RVs up to 40 feet, and 10 sleeping cabins. Picnic tables and fire rings are provided. Drinking water, showers, flush toilets, coin laundry, convenience store, and ice are available. An RV dump station, clubhouse, ping-pong, shuffleboard, and horseshoes are also available. Leashed pets are permitted.

Reservations, fees: Reservations are recommended. Fees are $22–24 per night, $4–6 per person for more than two people, $1 per night. Open mid-April to late October.

Directions: In Truckee, drive north on Highway 89 to Blairsden and the junction with Highway 70. Turn north (left) and drive one mile to Little Bear Road. Turn left on Little Bear Road and drive a short distance to the campground on the right.

Contact: Little Bear RV Park, tel./fax 530/836-2774.

14 PLUMAS-EUREKA STATE PARK

Rating: 9

Near Graeagle.

Map 6.1, page 348

Plumas-Eureka State Park is a beautiful chunk of parkland, featuring great hiking, a pretty lake, and this well-maintained campground. For newcomers to the area, Jamison Camp at the southern end of the park makes for an excellent first stop. So does the nearby hike to Grass Lake, a first-class tromp that takes about two hours and features a streamside walk along Jamison Creek, with the chance to take a five-minute cutoff to see 40-foot Jamison Falls. A historic mine, park museum, blacksmith shop, stable, and stamp mill are also here, with campers provided free admission to the museum. Other must-see destinations in the park include Eureka Lake, and from there, the 1,100-foot climb to Eureka Peak (formerly known as Gold Mountain), 7,447 feet, for a dramatic view of all the famous peaks in this region. Camp elevation is 5,200 feet. The park covers 5,500 acres. Fishing opportunities feature Madora and Eureka Lakes and Jamison Creek, best in May and June. The visitor center was originally constructed as a bunkhouse for miners. More than $8 million of gold was mined here.

Campsites, facilities: There are 67 sites for tents, trailers, or RVs up to 30 feet long, and one group for up to 50 people for tent campers only. Picnic tables, food lockers, and fire rings are provided. Drinking water, flush toilets, and showers are available. An RV dump station is available nearby. The group camp is wheelchair-accessible. A grocery store, coin laundry, and propane gas are available within five miles. Leashed pets are permitted.

Reservations, fees: Reservations are not accepted. The fee is $12 per night. Senior discount available. Reservations required for group site, $100 per night. Open mid-May to mid-October, weather permitting.

Directions: In Truckee, drive north on Highway 89 to Graeagle. Just after passing Graeagle (one mile from the junction of Highway 70) turn left on County Road A14/Graeagle-Johnsville Road and drive west for about five miles to the park entrance on the left.

Contact: Plumas-Eureka State Park, 530/836-2380, fax 530/836-0498.

15 MOVIN' WEST RV PARK

Rating: 5

In Graeagle.

Map 6.1, page 348

This RV area is set within a mobile home park. This has become a very popular park and about half of the sites are rented for the full summer. A nine-hole golf course is across the road. The elevation is 4,300 feet.

Campsites, facilities: There are 51 sites, including some drive-through, with full or partial hookups for RVs, three tent sites, and two cabins. Picnic tables and fire rings are provided. Drinking water, flush toilets, showers, pay phone, cable TV, modem access, and a coin laundry are available. Propane gas, a nine-hole golf course, swimming pond, horse stable, and minigolf are nearby. Leashed pets are permitted.

Reservations, fees: Reservations are recommended. Fees are $21.50–24.50 per night, $3–5 per person for more than two people. Open Maythrough October.

Directions: From Truckee, drive northwest on Highway 89 about 50 miles to Graeagle. Continue just past Graeagle to County Road A14 (Graegle-Johnson Road). Turn left and drive a quarter mile northwest to the campground on the left.

Contact: Movin' West RV Park, 530/836-2614.

16 LAKES BASIN GROUP CAMP

Rating: 8

In Plumas National Forest.

Map 6.1, page 348

This is a Forest Service group camp that is ideal for Boy and Girl Scouts. It is set at 6,400 feet in elevation, just a short drive from the trailhead to beautiful Frazier Falls, and also near Gold Lake, Little Bear Lake, and 15 lakes set below nearby Mt. Elwell.

Campsites, facilities: This group tent camp can accommodate up to 25 people. Picnic tables and fire grills are provided. Drinking water and vault toilets are available. Supplies are available in Graeagle. Leashed pets are permitted.

Reservations, fees: Reserve at 877/444-6777 ($9 reservation fee) or website: www.Reserve Usa.com; $45 group fee per night. Open June through October.

Directions: From Truckee, drive north on Highway 89 toward Graeagle to the Gold Lake Highway (one mile before reaching Graeagle). Turn left on the Gold Lake Highway and drive about seven miles to the campground.

Contact: Plumas National Forest, Beckwourth Ranger District, 530/836-2575, fax 530/836-0493.

17 LAKES BASIN

Rating: 8

In Plumas National Forest.

Map 6.1, page 348

Since its renovation in the late 1990s, this camp is now far more accessible to small RVs and trailers and is a great location for a base camp to explore the surrounding Lakes Basin Recreation Area. From nearby Gold Lake or Elwell Lodge, there are many short hikes to small pristine lakes. A must-do trip is the easy hike to Frazier Falls, only a mile round-trip to see the spectacular 176-foot waterfall, though the trail is crowded during the middle of the day. The trail to this waterfall was paved in 2001 and is wheelchair-accessible. The camp elevation is 6,400 feet.

Campsites, facilities: There are 24 sites for tents or small RVs. Picnic tables and fire grills are provided. Drinking water and vault toilets are available. Some facilities are wheelchair-accessible. Supplies are available in Graeagle. Leashed pets are permitted.

Reservations, fees: Reserve at 877/444-6777 ($9 reservation fee) or website: www.Reserve Usa.com; $12 per night. Senior discount available. Open June through October.

Directions: From Truckee, drive north on Highway 89 toward Graeagle to the Gold Lake Highway (one mile before reaching Graeagle). Turn left on the Gold Lake Highway and drive about seven miles to the campground.

Contact: Plumas National Forest, Beckwourth Ranger District, 530/836-2575, fax 530/836-0493.

18 BERGER CREEK

Rating: 6

In Tahoe National Forest.
Map 6.1, page 348

Berger Creek provides an overflow alternative to nearby Diablo, which is also extremely primitive. On busy summer weekends, when an open campsite can be difficult to find at a premium location in the Lakes Basin Recreation Area, these two camps provide a safety valve to keep you from being stuck for the night. Nearby are Packer Lake, the trail to the Sierra Buttes, Sardine Lakes, and Sand Pond, all excellent destinations. The elevation is 5,900 feet.

Campsites, facilities: There are 10 sites for tents or RVs up to 16 feet long. Picnic tables and fire grills are provided. Vault toilets are available. No drinking water is available. Supplies are available in Bassetts and Sierra City. Leashed pets are permitted.

Reservations, fees: Reservations are not accepted. The fee is $6 per night. Open June through October.

Directions: From Truckee, turn north on Highway 89 and drive 20 miles to Sierraville. At Sierraville, turn left on Highway 49 and drive about 10 miles to the Bassetts Store. Turn right on Gold Lake Road and drive 1.5 miles to Packer Lake Road. Turn left, drive a short distance, bear right at the fork, and drive two miles to the campground on the left.

Contact: Tahoe National Forest, North Yuba/Downieville Ranger District, 530/288-3231, fax 530/288-0727.

19 PACKSADDLE

Rating: 6

Near Packer Lake in Tahoe National Forest.
Map 6.1, page 348

Packsaddle is a Forest Service site about a half mile from Packer Lake, with an additional 15 lakes within a five-mile radius, and one of America's truly great hiking trails nearby. The trail to the Sierra Buttes features a climb of 2,369 feet over the course of five miles. It is highlighted by a stairway with 176 steps that literally juts into open space and crowned by an astounding view for hundreds of miles in all directions. Packer Lake, 6,218 feet, is at the foot of the dramatic Sierra Buttes and has lakefront log cabins, good trout fishing, and low-speed boating.

Campsites, facilities: There are 12 sites for tents or RVs. Vault toilets are available. Drinking water (hand-pumped) is available. Pack and saddle animals are permitted and corrals and hitching rails are available. Supplies are available in Bassetts and Sierra City. Leashed pets are permitted.

Reservations, fees: Reservations are not accepted. The fee is $13 per night. Senior discount available. Open June through October.

Directions: From Truckee, turn north on Highway 89 and drive 20 miles to Sierraville. At Sierraville, turn left on Highway 49 and drive about 10 miles to the Bassetts Store. Turn right on Gold Lake Road and drive 1.5 miles to Packer Lake Road. Turn left, drive a short distance, bear right at the fork, and drive 2.5 miles to the campground on the left.

Contact: Tahoe National Forest, North Yuba/Downieville Ranger District, 530/288-3231, fax 530/288-0727.

20 SNAG LAKE

Rating: 8

In Tahoe National Forest.
Map 6.1, page 348

Snag Lake is an ideal little lake for camping

anglers with canoes. There are no boat ramps and you can have the place virtually to yourself. It is set at 6,600 feet in elevation, an easy-to-reach lake in the Lakes Basin Recreation Area. Trout fishing is only fair, as in fair numbers and fair size, mainly rainbow trout in the 10- to 12-inch class. Note that campers here must provide their own drinking water.

Campsites, facilities: There are 16 sites for tents or RVs up to 16 feet long. Picnic tables and fire grills are provided. Vault toilets are available. No drinking water is available. Only hand boat launching is allowed. Supplies are available in Bassetts and Sierra City. Leashed pets are permitted.

Reservations, fees: Reservations are not accepted. There is no fee for camping. Open June through October.

Directions: From Truckee, turn north on Highway 89 and drive 20 miles to Sierraville. At Sierraville, turn left on Highway 49 and drive about 10 miles to the Bassetts Store. Turn right on Gold Lake Road and drive five miles to the campground on the left.

Contact: Tahoe National Forest, North Yuba/Downieville Ranger District, 530/288-3231, fax 530/288-0727.

21 DIABLO

Rating: 8

On Packer Creek in Tahoe National Forest.
Map 6.1, page 348

This is a developed camping area set on Packer Creek, about two miles from Packer Lake. This area is extremely beautiful with several lakes nearby, including the Sardine Lakes and Packer Lake, and this camp provides an overflow area when the more developed campgrounds have filled.

Campsites, facilities: There is a camping area with dispersed, nondesignated sites for tents and RVs up to 40 feet long. Picnic tables, fire rings, and vault toilets are available. No drinking water is available. Supplies are available in

Bassetts and Sierra City. Leashed pets are permitted.

Reservations, fees: Reservations are not accepted. The fee is $6 per night. Open June through October.

Directions: From Truckee, turn north on Highway 89 and drive 20 miles to Sierraville. At Sierraville, turn left on Highway 49 and drive about 10 miles to the Bassetts Store. Turn right on Gold Lake Road and drive 1.5 miles to Packer Lake Road. Turn left, drive a short distance, bear right at the fork, and drive one mile to thecampground on the right side of the road.

Contact: Tahoe National Forest, North Yuba/Downieville Ranger District, 530/288-3231, fax 530/288-0727.

22 SALMON CREEK

Rating: 9

In Tahoe National Forest.
Map 6.1, page 348

This campground is set at the confluence of Packer and Salmon Creeks, 5,800 feet in elevation, with easy access off the Gold Lakes Highway. It is near the Lakes Basin Recreation Area, with literally dozens of small lakes within five miles, plus great hiking, fishing, and low-speed boating.

Campsites, facilities: There are 31 sites for tents or RVs up to 22 feet long. Picnic tables and fire grills are provided. Drinking water and vault toilets are available. Supplies and a coin laundry are available in Sierra City. Leashed pets are permitted.

Reservations, fees: Reservations are not accepted. The fee is $13 per night. Senior discount available. Open June through October.

Directions: From Truckee, turn north on Highway 89 and drive 20 miles to Sierraville and Highway 49. Turn left on Highway 49 and drive about 10 miles to the Bassetts Store and Gold Lake Road. Turn right on Gold Lake Road and drive two miles to the campground on the left side of the road.

Contact: Tahoe National Forest, North Yuba/Downieville Ranger District, 530/288-3231, fax 530/288-0727.

23 SARDINE LAKE

Rating: 8

In Tahoe National Forest.

Map 6.1, page 348

Lower Sardine Lake is a jewel set below the Sierra Buttes, one of the prettiest settings in California. The campground is actually about a mile east of the lake. Nearby is the beautiful Sand Pond Interpretive Trail. A great hike is routed along the shore of Lower Sardine Lake to a hidden waterfall (in spring) that feeds the lake, and ambitious hikers can explore beyond and discover Upper Sardine Lake. Trout fishing is excellent in Lower Sardine Lake, with a primitive boat ramp available for small boats. The speed limit and small size of the lake keeps boaters slow and quiet. A small marina and boat rentals are available.

Campsites, facilities: There are 29 sites for tents or RVs up to 22 feet long. Picnic tables and fire grills are provided. Drinking water and vault toilets are available. Some facilities are wheelchair-accessible. Limited supplies are available at the Sardine Lake Lodge or in Bassetts. Leashed pets are permitted.

Reservations, fees: Reservations are not accepted. The fee is $13 per night. Senior discount available. Open June through October.

Directions: From Truckee, drive north on Highway 89 for 20 miles to Sierraville. Turn left on Highway 49 and drive about 10 miles to the Bassetts Store. Turn right on Gold Lake Road and drive 1.5 miles to Packer Lake Road. Turn left, drive a short distance, then bear left at the fork (signed) and drive a half mile to the campground on the left.

Contact: Tahoe National Forest, North Yuba/Downieville Ranger District, 530/288-3231, fax 530/288-0727.

24 CLIO'S RIVER'S EDGE RV PARK

Rating: 7

On the Feather River.

Map 6.1, page 348

This is a giant RV park set adjacent to a pretty and easily accessible stretch of the Feather River. There are many possible side-trip destinations, including Plumas-Eureka State Park, Lakes Basin Recreation Area, and several nearby golf courses. The elevation is about 4,500 feet.

Campsites, facilities: There are 220 sites, including some drive-through, with full hookups for RVs. Picnic tables are provided. Drinking water, flush toilets, coin-operated showers, coin laundry, modem access, and cable TV are available. Some facilities are wheelchair-accessible. A grocery store is within three miles. Leashed pets are permitted.

Reservations, fees: Reservations are accepted. The fee is $24 per night, $3–5 per person for more than two people, $1 for extra vehicles not towed. Open mid-April through mid-October.

Directions: From Truckee, drive north on Highway 89 toward Graeagle and Blairsden. Near Clio (4.5 miles south of Highway 70 at Blairsden), look for the campground entrance on the right.

Contact: Clio's River's Edge, 530/836-2375, fax 530/836-2378; website: www.riversedge rvpark.net.

25 LOGANVILLE

Rating: 8

On the North Yuba River in Tahoe National Forest.

Map 6.1, page 348

Nearby Sierra City is only two miles away, meaning you can make a quick getaway for a prepared meal or any food or drink you may need to add to your camp. Loganville is set on the North Yuba River, elevation 4,200 feet. It offers a good stretch of water in this region for trout fishing, with many pools set below miniature waterfalls.

Campsites, facilities: There are 20 sites for tents or RVs up to 22 feet long. Picnic tables and fire grills are provided. Drinking water and vault toilets are available. Supplies and a coin laundry are available in Sierra City. Leashed pets are permitted.

Reservations, fees: Reservations are not accepted. The fee is $13 per night. Senior discount available. Open May through October.

Directions: From Auburn, take Highway 49 north to Nevada City and continue (the road jogs left, then narrows) to Downieville. Drive 12 miles east to the campground entrance on the right (two miles west of Sierra City).

Contact: Tahoe National Forest, North Yuba/Downieville Ranger District, 530/288-3231, fax 530/288-0727.

26 WILD PLUM

Rating: 8

On Haypress Creek in Tahoe National Forest.
Map 6.1, page 348

This popular Forest Service campground is set on Haypress Creek at 4,400 feet. There are several hidden waterfalls in the area, which makes this a popular camp for the people who know of them. There's a scenic hike up the Haypress Trail, which goes past a waterfall to Haypress Valley. Two other nearby waterfalls are Loves Falls (on the North Yuba on Highway 49 two miles east of Sierra City) and Hackmans Falls (remote, set in a ravine one mile south of Sierra City; no road access).

Campsites, facilities: There are a total of 47 sites, 26 for tents and 21 for RVs up to 22 feet long. Picnic tables and fire grills are provided. Drinking water and vault toilets are available. Supplies and a coin laundry are available in Sierra City. Leashed pets are permitted.

Reservations, fees: Reservations are not accepted. The fee is $13 per night. Senior discount available. Open May through October.

Directions: From Auburn, take Highway 49 north to Nevada City and continue (the road jogs left, then narrows) past Downieville to Sierra City at Wild Plum Road. Turn right on Wild Plum Road and drive two miles to the campground entrance road on the right.

Contact: Tahoe National Forest, North Yuba/Downieville Ranger District, 530/288-3231, fax 530/288-0727.

27 CHAPMAN CREEK

Rating: 8

On the North Yuba River in Tahoe National Forest.
Map 6.1, page 348

This campground is set along Chapman Creek at 6,000 feet, just across the highway from where it enters the North Yuba River. A good side trip is to hike the Chapman Creek Trail, which leads out of camp to Beartrap Meadow or to Haskell Peak (8,107 feet).

Campsites, facilities: There are a total of 29 sites, 15 for tents and 14 for RVs up to 22 feet long. Picnic tables and fire grills are provided. Drinking water and vault toilets are available. Supplies are available in Bassetts. Leashed pets are permitted.

Reservations, fees: Reservations are not accepted. The fee is $13 per night. Senior discount available. Open June through October.

Directions: From Truckee, turn north on Highway 89 and drive 20 miles to Sierraville. At Sierraville, turn left on Highway 49, drive over Yuba Pass, and continue for four miles to the campground on the right.

Contact: Tahoe National Forest, North Yuba/Downieville Ranger District, 530/288-3231, fax 530/288-0727.

28 SIERRA

Rating: 7

On the North Yuba River in Tahoe National Forest.

Map 6.1, page 348

This is an easy-to-reach spot set along the North Yuba River, used primarily as an overflow area from nearby Chapman Creek (a mile upstream). Nearby recreation options include the Chapman Creek Trail, several waterfalls (see Wild Plum), and the nearby Lakes Basin Recreation Area to the north off the Gold Lake Highway. The elevation is 5,600 feet. Note: bring your own drinking water.

Campsites, facilities: There are nine sites for tents and seven sites for tents or RVs up to 22 feet long. Picnic tables and fire rings are provided. Vault toilets are available. No drinking water is available. Supplies are available in Bassetts. Leashed pets are permitted.

Reservations, fees: Reservations are not accepted. The fee is $10 per night. Senior discount available. Open June through October.

Directions: From Truckee, turn north on Highway 89 and drive 20 miles to Sierraville. At Sierraville, turn left on Highway 49 and drive over Yuba Pass. Continue for five miles to the campground on the left side of the road.

Contact: Tahoe National Forest, North Yuba/Downieville Ranger District, 530/288-3231, fax 530/288-0727.

29 YUBA PASS

Rating: 6

In Tahoe National Forest.

Map 6.1, page 348

This camp is set right at Yuba Pass at an elevation of 6,700 feet. In the winter, the surrounding area is a Sno-Park, which gives it an unusual look in summer. Yuba Pass is a popular bird-watching area in the summer.

Campsites, facilities: There are 20 sites for tents or RVs up to 22 feet long. Picnic tables and fire grills are provided. Drinking water and vault toilets are available. Supplies are available at Bassetts. Leashed pets are permitted.

Reservations, fees: Reserve at 877/444-6777 ($9 reservation fee) or website: www.Reserve Usa.com; $13 per night. Senior discount available. Open late June through October.

Directions: From Truckee, drive north on Highway 89 past Sattley to the junction with Highway 49. Turn west on Highway 49 and drive about six miles to the campground on the left side of the road.

Contact: Tahoe National Forest, Sierraville Ranger District, 530/994-3401, fax 530/994-3143.

30 UNION FLAT

Rating: 8

On the North Yuba River in Tahoe National Forest.

Map 6.1, page 348

Of all the campgrounds on the North Yuba River along Highway 49, this one has the best swimming. The camp has a nice swimming hole next to it if you can stand the cold. Recreational mining is also an attraction here. The elevation is 3,400 feet.

Campsites, facilities: There are 11 sites for tents or RVs up to 35 feet long. Picnic tables and fire grills are provided. Drinking water and vault toilets are available. Some facilities are wheelchair-accessible. Supplies are available in Downieville. Leashed pets are permitted.

Reservations, fees: Reservations are not accepted. The fee is $13 per night. Senior discount available. Open May through October.

Directions: From Auburn, take Highway 49 north to Nevada City and continue (the road jogs left, then narrows) to Downieville. Drive six miles east to the campground entrance on the right.

Contact: Tahoe National Forest, North

Yuba/Downieville Ranger District, 530/288-3231, fax 530/288-0727.

31 COLD CREEK

Rating: 8

In Tahoe National Forest.
Map 6.1, page 348

There are four small campgrounds along Highway 89 between Sierraville and Truckee, all within close range of side trips to Webber Lake, Independence Lake, and Campbell Hot Springs in Sierraville. Cold Creek is set just downstream of the confluence of Cottonwood Creek and Cold Creek, at 5,800 feet in elevation.

Campsites, facilities: There are 13 sites for tents or RVs up to 22 feet long. Picnic tables and fire grills are provided. Drinking water and vault toilets are available. Supplies are available in Sierraville. Leashed pets are permitted.

Reservations, fees: Reserve at 877/444-6777 ($9 reservation fee) or website: www.Reserve Usa.com; $10 per night, $5 for an extra vehicle. Open May through October.

Directions: From Truckee, drive north on Highway 89 for about 20 miles to the campground on the left side of the road. If you reach Sierraville, you have gone five miles too far.

Contact: Tahoe National Forest, Truckee Ranger District, 530/587-3558, fax 530/587-6914; California Land Management, 530/544-0426.

32 COTTONWOOD CREEK

Rating: 7

In Tahoe National Forest.
Map 6.1, page 348

This camp sits beside Cottonwood Creek at 5,800 feet elevation. An interpretive trail starts at the camp and makes a short loop, and there are several nearby side-trip options, including trout fishing on the Little Truckee River to the nearby south, visiting the Sierra Valley Hot Springs out of Sierraville to the nearby north,

or venturing into the surrounding Tahoe National Forest.

Campsites, facilities: There are 21 sites for tents and 24 sites for tents or RVs up to 22 feet long. Picnic tables and fire grills are provided. Drinking water and vault toilets are available. Supplies are available in Sierraville. Leashed pets are permitted.

Reservations, fees: Reserve at 877/444-6777 ($9 reservation fee) or website: www.Reserve Usa.com; $11 per night. Open May through October, weather permitting.

Directions: From Truckee, drive north on Highway 89 for about 20 miles to the campground entrance road on the right (a half mile past Cold Creek Camp). Turn right and drive a quarter mile to the campground.

Contact: Tahoe National Forest, Sierraville Ranger District, 530/994-3401, fax 530/994-3143.

33 BEAR VALLEY

Rating: 7

On Bear Valley Creek in Tahoe
National Forest.
Map 6.1, page 348

The surrounding national forest land was largely burned by the historic Cottonwood Fire of 1994, but the camp itself was saved. It is set on the headwaters of Bear Valley Creek, 6,700 feet in elevation, with a spring adjacent to the campground. The road leading southeast out of camp is routed to Sardine Peak (8,134 feet), where there is a dramatic view of the burned region. There is an 18-mile loop OHV trail across the road from the campground. Note: camp spaces are too small for all trailers and all but the smallest RVs.

Campsites, facilities: There are 10 tent sites. Picnic tables and fire grills are provided. Drinking water and vault toilets are available. Supplies are available in Sierraville. Leashed pets are permitted.

Reservations, fees: Reservations are not accepted.

There is no fee for camping. Open June through October.

Directions: From Truckee, drive north on Highway 89 about 17 miles. Turn right on County Road 451 and drive northeast about six miles to the campground entrance on the right.

Contact: Tahoe National Forest, Sierraville Ranger District, 530/994-3401, fax 530/994-3143.

34 LOOKOUT

Rating: 4

In Humboldt-Toiyabe National Forest.
Map 6.1, page 348

This primitive camp is set in remote country near the California/Nevada border at 6,700 feet. It is a former mining site, and the highlight here is a quartz crystal mine a short distance from the campground. Stampede Lake provides a side-trip option, about 10 miles to the southwest, over the rough dirt Henness Pass Road.

Campsites, facilities: There are 15 sites for tents and four sites for tents or RVs up to 22 feet long, plus a group campground for up to 16 people. Picnic tables and fire grills are provided. Drinking water and vault toilets are available. Leashed pets are permitted.

Reservations, fees: Reservations are not accepted. The fee is $6 per night. Group site $20 per night. Senior discount available. Open June through September.

Directions: From Truckee on I-80, drive east across the state line into Nevada to Verdi. Take the Verdi exit and drive north through town to Old Dog Valley Road. Drive north on Old Dog Valley Road for 11 miles to the campground.

Contact: Humboldt-Toiyabe National Forest, Carson Ranger District, 775/882-2766, fax 775/884-8199.

35 JACKSON CREEK

Rating: 7

Near Bowman Lake in Tahoe National Forest.
Map 6.1, page 348

This primitive campground is at 5,600 feet, adjacent to Jackson Creek, a primary feeder stream to Bowman Lake to the nearby west. There are several lakes within a five-mile radius, including Bowman Lake, Jackson Meadow Reservoir, Sawmill Lake (private), and Faucherie Lake. A trailhead is available a mile south (on the right side of the road) at the north end of Sawmill Lake. The trail is routed to a series of pretty Sierra lakes to the west of Haystack Mountain (7,391 feet).

Campsites, facilities: There are 14 primitive tent sites. Picnic tables and fire grills are provided. Vault toilets are available. No drinking water is available. Garbage must be packed out. Leashed pets are permitted.

Reservations, fees: Reservations are not accepted. There is no fee for camping. Open June through October, weather permitting.

Directions: From Sacramento, drive east on I-80 past Emigrant Gap to Highway 20. Head west on Highway 20 and drive to Bowman Road/Forest Road 18. Turn right and drive about 16 miles to Bowman Lake (much of the road is quite rough), then continue for four miles east of the lake to the campground.

Contact: Tahoe National Forest, Nevada City Ranger District, 530/265-4531, fax 530/478-6109.

36 BOWMAN LAKE

Rating: 8

In Tahoe National Forest.
Map 6.1, page 348

Bowman is a sapphire jewel set in Sierra granite at 5,568 feet, extremely pretty and ideal for campers with car-top boats. There is no boat ramp (you wouldn't want to trailer a boat on the access road anyway), but there are lots of small rainbow trout that are eager to please during the evening bite. The camp is set on the eastern end of the lake, just below where Jackson Creek pours in. The lake is flanked by Bowman Mountain (7,392 feet) and Red Hill (7,075 feet) to the south and Quartz Hill (7,025 feet) to the north.

Campsites, facilities: There are seven primitive tent sites. Vault toilets are available. No drinking water is available. Garbage must be packed out. Leashed pets are permitted.

Reservations, fees: Reservations are not accepted. There is no fee for camping. Open June through October.

Directions: From Sacramento, drive east on I-80 past Emigrant Gap to Highway 20. Head west on Highway 20 and drive to Bowman Road/Forest Road 18. Turn right and drive about 16 miles (much of the road is quite rough) to Bowman Lake and the campground on the right side of the road at the head of the lake.

Contact: Tahoe National Forest, Nevada City Ranger District, 530/265-4531, fax 530/478-6109; Big Bend Visitor Center, 530/426-3609, fax 530/426-1744.

37 FAUCHERIE LAKE GROUP CAMP

Rating: 7

Near Bowman Lake in Tahoe National Forest.

Map 6.1, page 348

Faucherie Lake is the kind of place that most people believe can only be reached by long, difficult hikes with a backpack. Guess again: here it is, set in Sierra granite at 6,100 feet in elevation, quiet and pristine, a classic Alpine lake. It is ideal for car-top boating and has decent fishing for both rainbow and brown trout. This is a group camp on the lake's northern shore, a prime spot, with the outlet creek nearby. Note: road washouts may require four-wheel drive.

Campsites, facilities: There is a large group

camp for tents or RVs up to 22 feet long. The camp accommodates up to 25 campers. Picnic tables and fire grills are provided. Vault toilets are available. No drinking water is available. Garbage must be packed out. Leashed pets are permitted.

Reservations, fees: Reserve at 877/444-6777 ($9 reservation fee) or website: www.Reserve Usa.com; $50 per night. Open June through October.

Directions: From Sacramento, drive east on I-80 past Emigrant Gap to Highway 20. Head west on Highway 20 and drive to Bowman Road/Forest Road 18. Turn right and drive about 16 miles (much of the road is quite rough) to Bowman Lake and continue four miles to a Y. Bear right at the Y and drive about three miles to the campground at the end of the road.

Contact: Tahoe National Forest, Nevada City Ranger District, 530/265-4531, fax 530/478-6109; Big Bend Visitor Center, 530/426-3609, fax 530/426-1744.

38 CANYON CREEK

Rating: 6

Near Faucherie Lake in Tahoe National Forest.

Map 6.1, page 348

This pretty spot is at 6,000 feet in Tahoe National Forest, a mile from Sawmill Lake (which you pass on the way in) and a mile from pretty Faucherie Lake. It is set along Canyon Creek, the stream that connects those two lakes. Of the two, Faucherie provides better fishing and, because of that, there are fewer people at Sawmill. Take your pick. A trailhead is available at the north end of Sawmill Lake with a hike to several small Alpine lakes, a great day or overnight backpacking trip.

Campsites, facilities: There are 20 sites for tents. Picnic tables and fire grills are provided. Vault toilets are available. No drinking water is available. Garbage must be packed out. Leashed pets are permitted.

Reservations, fees: Reservations are not accepted. There is no fee for camping. Open June through October.

Directions: From Sacramento, drive east on I-80 to Emigrant Gap. Take the off-ramp and head north on the short connector road to Highway 20. Turn west on Highway 20 and drive four miles to Bowman Road/Forest Road 18. Turn right and drive about 16 miles (nine of these miles are paved, but the rest is quite rough) to Bowman Lake and continue four miles to a Y. Bear right at the Y and drive about two miles to the campground on the right side of the road.

Contact: Tahoe National Forest, Nevada City Ranger District, 530/265-4531, fax 530/478-6109; Big Bend Visitor Center, 530/426-3609, fax 530/426-1744.

39 GROUSE RIDGE

Rating: 6

Near Bowman Lake in Tahoe National Forest.

Map 6.1, page 348

Grouse Ridge is set at 7,400 feet at the gateway to some beautiful hiking country filled with small high Sierra lakes. The camp is primarily used as a trailhead and jump-off point, not as a destination itself. The closest hike is the half-mile tromp up to the Grouse Ridge Lookout, 7,707 feet, which provides a spectacular view to the north of this area and its many small lakes. As you hike north, the trail passes Round Lake (to the left) in the first mile and Middle Lake (on the right) two miles later, with opportunities to take cutoff trails on either side of the ridge to visit numerous other lakes.

Campsites, facilities: There are nine sites for tents only. Picnic tables and fire grills are provided. Vault toilets are available. No drinking water is available. Garbage must be packed out. Leashed pets are permitted.

Reservations, fees: Reservations are not ac-

cepted. There is no fee for camping. Open June through October.

Directions: From Sacramento, drive east on I-80 past Emigrant Gap to Highway 20. Turn west on Highway 20 and drive to Bowman Road/Forest Road 18. Turn north on Bowman Road and drive five miles to Grouse Ridge Road. Turn right on Grouse Ridge Road and drive six miles on rough gravel to the campground.

Contact: Tahoe National Forest, Nevada City Ranger District, 530/265-4531, fax 530/478-6109; Big Bend Visitor Center, 530/426-3609, fax 530/426-1744.

40 SILVER TIP GROUP CAMP

Rating: 7

At Jackson Meadow Reservoir in Tahoe National Forest.

Map 6.1, page 348

This group camp is set on the southwest edge of Jackson Meadow Reservoir at 6,200 feet, in a pretty area with pine forest, high meadows, and the trademark granite look of the Sierra Nevada. A boat ramp and swimming beach are nearby at Woodcamp. (For more information, see the entry for Woodcamp.)

Campsites, facilities: There are two 25-person group sites for tents or RVs up to 22 feet long. Picnic tables and fire grills are provided. Drinking water and vault toilets are available. Obtain supplies in Truckee or Sierraville. A boat ramp is nearby. Leashed pets are permitted.

Reservations, fees: Reserve at 877/444-6777 ($9 reservation fee) or website: www.Reserve Usa.com; $55 group fee per night. Open June through October.

Directions: From Truckee, drive north on Highway 89 for 17.5 miles to Forest Road 7. Turn left on Forest Road 7 and drive 16 miles to Jackson Meadow Reservoir. At the lake, continue across the dam around the west shoreline and then turn left at the campground access road. The entrance is on the right just before the Woodcamp boat ramp.

Contact: Tahoe National Forest, Sierraville Ranger District, 530/994-3401, fax 530/994-3143.

41 WOODCAMP

Rating: 7

At Jackson Meadow Reservoir in Tahoe National Forest.

Map 6.1, page 348

Woodcamp and Pass Creek are the best camps for boaters at Jackson Meadow Reservoir because each is directly adjacent to a boat ramp. That is critical because fishing is far better by boat here than from shore, with a good mix of both rainbow and brown trout. The camp is set at 6,100 feet along the lake's southwest shore, in a pretty spot with a swimming beach and short interpretive hiking trail nearby. This is a beautiful lake in the Sierra Nevada, complete with pine forest and a classic granite backdrop.

Campsites, facilities: There are 10 sites for tents and 10 sites for tents or RVs up to 22 feet long. Picnic tables and fire grills are provided. Drinking water and vault toilets are available. Supplies are available in Truckee or Sierraville. A boat ramp is adjacent to the camp. Leashed pets are permitted.

Reservations, fees: Reservations are accepted. The fee is $13 per night, $5 for each additional vehicle. Senior discount available. Open June through October.

Directions: From Truckee, drive north on Highway 89 for 17.5 miles to Forest Road 7. Turn left on Forest Road 7 and drive 16 miles to Jackson Meadow Reservoir. At the lake, continue across the dam around the west shoreline and then turn left at the campground access road. The entrance is on the right just before the Woodcamp boat ramp.

Contact: Tahoe National Forest, Sierraville Ranger District, 530/994-3401, fax 530/994-3143.

42 FIR TOP

Rating: 7

At Jackson Meadow Reservoir in Tahoe National Forest.

Map 6.1, page 348

Jackson Meadow is a great destination for a short vacation, and that's why there are so many campgrounds available; it's not exactly a secret. This camp is set on a cove on the lake's southwest shore, less than a mile from a boat ramp near Woodcamp. (See the entries for Woodcamp and Pass Creek for more information.) The elevation is 6,200 feet.

Campsites, facilities: There are 12 sites for tents or RVs up to 22 feet long. Picnic tables and fire grills are provided. Drinking water, vault toilets, and RV dump station (on the east side) are available. Supplies are available in Truckee or Sierraville. A boat ramp is nearby. Some facilities are wheelchair-accessible. Leashed pets are permitted.

Reservations, fees: Reserve at 877/444-6777 ($9 reservation fee) or website: www.Reserve Usa.com; $13 per night. Senior discount available. Open June through November.

Directions: From Truckee, drive north on Highway 89 for 17.5 miles to Forest Road 7. Turn left on Forest Road 7 and drive 16 miles to Jackson Meadow Reservoir. Continue across the dam and around the lake to the west side. Turn left at the campground access road. The campground entrance is on the right across from the entrance to the Woodcamp Picnic Area.

Contact: Tahoe National Forest, Sierraville Ranger District, 530/994-3401, fax 530/994-3143.

43 FINDLEY

Rating: 7

At Jackson Meadow Reservoir in Tahoe National Forest.

Map 6.1, page 348

Findley is set near Woodcamp Creek, a

quarter mile from where it pours into Jackson Meadow Reservoir. Though it is not a lakeside camp, it is quite pretty just the same, and within a half mile of the boat ramp near Woodcamp. It is set at 6,200 feet. This is one of several camps at the lake.

Campsites, facilities: There are 14 sites for tents or RVs up to 22 feet long. Picnic tables and fire grills are provided. Drinking water and vault toilets are available. Supplies are available in Truckee or Sierraville. A boat ramp is nearby. Some facilities are wheelchair-accessible. Leashed pets are permitted.

Reservations, fees: Reserve at 877/444-6777 ($9 reservation fee) or website: www.Reserve Usa.com; $13 per night. Senior discount available. Open late June through October.

Directions: From Truckee, drive north on Highway 89 for 17.5 miles to Forest Road 7. Turn left on Forest Road 7 and drive 16 miles to Jackson Meadow Reservoir. Continue across the dam around the lake to the west side. Turn left at the campground access road and drive about a quarter mile to the entrance on the left.

Contact: Tahoe National Forest, Sierraville Ranger District, 530/994-3401, fax 530/994-3143.

44 JACKSON POINT BOAT-IN

Rating: 10

At Jackson Meadow Reservoir in Tahoe National Forest.

Map 6.1, page 348

This is one of the few boat-in camps available anywhere in the high Sierra. The gorgeous spot is situated on the end of a peninsula that extends from the east shore of Jackson Meadow Reservoir. Small and primitive, it's the one place at the lake where you can gain entry into the 5 Percent Club. From the point, there is a spectacular view of the Sierra Buttes. Because the lake levels are kept near full all summer, this boat-in camp is doubly appealing. The elevation is 6,100 feet.

Campsites, facilities: There are 10 tent sites. Picnic tables and fire grills are provided. Vault toilets are available. No drinking water is available. Garbage must be packed out. Supplies are available in Truckee or Sierraville. Leashed pets are permitted.

Reservations, fees: Reservations are not accepted. There is no fee for camping. Open June through September.

Directions: From Truckee, drive north on Highway 89 for 17.5 miles to Forest Road 7. Turn left on Forest Road 7 and drive 16 miles to Jackson Meadow Reservoir. Drive to Pass Creek and boat launch (on the left at the north end of the lake). Launch your boat and cruise a half mile south to Jackson Point and the boat-in campsites.

Contact: Tahoe National Forest, Sierraville Ranger District, 530/994-3401, fax 530/994-3143.

45 PASS CREEK

Rating: 7

At Jackson Meadow Reservoir in Tahoe National Forest.

Map 6.1, page 348

This is the premium campground at Jackson Meadow Reservoir, a developed site with water, concrete boat ramp, swimming beach nearby at Aspen Creek Picnic Area, and access to the Pacific Crest Trail a half mile to the east (you'll pass it on the way in). This lake has the trademark look of the high Sierra, and the bonus here is that lake levels are often kept higher than at other reservoirs on the western slopes of the Sierra Nevada. Trout stocks are excellent, with 85,000 rainbow and brown trout planted each summer after ice-out. The elevation is 6,100 feet.

Campsites, facilities: There are 15 sites for tents and 15 sites for RVs up to 22 feet long. Picnic tables and fire grills are provided. Drinking water, vault toilets, and RV dump station are available. A boat ramp is nearby. Supplies are available in Truckee or Sierraville. Leashed pets are permitted.

Reservations, fees: Reserve Reserve at 877/444-6777 ($9 reservation fee) or website: www .ReserveUsa.com; $13 per night, $3 for an extra vehicle. Senior discount available. Open June through October.

Directions: From Truckee, drive north on Highway 89 for 17.5 miles to Forest Road 7. Turn left on Forest Road 7 and drive 16 miles to Jackson Meadow Reservoir; the campground is on the left at the north end of the lake.

Contact: Tahoe National Forest, Sierraville Ranger District, 530/994-3401, fax 530/994-3143.

46 EAST MEADOW

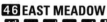

Rating: 7

At Jackson Meadow Reservoir in Tahoe National Forest.
Map 6.1, page 348

This camp is in a beautiful setting on the east side of Jackson Meadow Reservoir, on the edge of a sheltered cove. The Pacific Crest Trail passes right by camp, providing access for a day trip, though no stellar destinations are on this stretch of the PCT. The nearest boat ramp is at Pass Creek, two miles away. The elevation is 6,100 feet.

Campsites, facilities: There are 20 tent sites and 26 sites for tents or RVs. (Some sites can accommodate RVs 40 feet in length, most can accommodate 22 feet). Picnic tables and fire grills are provided. Drinking water and vault toilets are available. An RV dump station and boat ramp are available at Pass Creek. Supplies are available inTruckee or Sierraville. Some facilities are wheelchair-accessible. Leashed pets are permitted.

Reservations, fees: Reserve at 877/444-6777 ($9 reservation fee) or website: www.Reserve Usa.com; $13 per night, $3 for an extra vehicle. Senior discount available. Open June through October.

Directions: From Truckee, drive north on Highway 89 for 17.5 miles to Forest Road 7. Turn left on Forest Road 7 and drive 15 miles to the campground entrance road on the left (if you reach Pass Creek, you have gone too far). Turn left and drive a mile to the campground on the right.

Contact: Tahoe National Forest, Sierraville Ranger District, 530/994-3401, fax 530/994-3143.

47 ASPEN GROUP CAMP

Rating: 7

At Jackson Meadow Reservoir in Tahoe National Forest.
Map 6.1, page 348

A boat ramp and easy access to adjacent Jackson Meadow Reservoir make this a premium group camp. The elevation is 6,100 feet.

Campsites, facilities: There are two 25-person group sites and a 50-person group site for tents or RVs up to 22 feet long. Picnic tables and fire grills are provided. Drinking water, vault toilets, RV dump station, and a campfire circle are available. There is a boat ramp nearby at Pass Creek. Supplies are available in Truckee or Sierraville. Leashed pets are permitted.

Reservations, fees: Reserve at 877/444-6777 ($9 reservation fee) or website: www.Reserve Usa.com; $55 per night for 25-person sites, $110 per night for 50-person site. Open June through October.

Directions: From Truckee, drive north on Highway 89 for 17.5 miles to Forest Road 7. Turn left on Forest Road 7 and drive 16 miles (a mile past Pass Creek) to the campground entrance on the right.

Contact: Tahoe National Forest, Sierraville Ranger District,530/994-3401, fax 530/994-3143.

48 SAGEHEN CREEK

🏃 🎣 🐕 🚙 ⛺

Rating: 7

In Tahoe National Forest.

Map 6.1, page 348

This is a small, primitive camp set at 6,500 feet beside little Sagehen Creek, just north of a miniature mountain range called the Sagehen Hills, which top out at 7,707 feet. Sagehen Creek provides an option when the camps along Highway 89 and at Stampede, Boca, and Prosser Creek have filled. In the fall, it is popular with campers as a base camp.

Campsites, facilities: There are 10 sites for tents or RVs up to 16 feet long. Vault toilets are available. No drinking water is available. Garbage must be packed out. Leashed pets are permitted.

Reservations, fees: Reservations are not accepted. There is no fee for camping. Open June through October.

Directions: From Truckee, drive 8.5 miles north on Highway 89 to Sagehen Summit Road on the left. Turn left and drive four miles to the campground.

Contact: Tahoe National Forest, Truckee Ranger District, 530/587-3558, fax 530/587-6914.

49 UPPER LITTLE TRUCKEE

🏃 🎣 🐕 🚙 ⛺

Rating: 7

On the Little Truckee River in Tahoe National Forest.

Map 6.1, page 348

This camp is set along the Little Truckee River at 6,100 feet. The Little Truckee is a pretty trout stream, with easy access not only from this campground, but also from another three miles northward along Highway 89, then from another seven miles to the west along Forest Road 7, the route to Webber Lake. It is only about a 10-minute drive from this camp to reach Stampede Lake to the east.

Campsites, facilities: There are 26 sites for tents or RVs up to 22 feet long. Picnic tables and fire grills are provided. Drinking water and vault toilets are available. Supplies are available in Sierraville. Leashed pets are permitted.

Reservations, fees: Reserve at 877/444-6777 ($9 reservation fee) or website: www.Reserve Usa.com; $10 per night, $5 for an extra vehicle. Senior discount available. Open May through October.

Directions: From Truckee, drive north on Highway 89 for about 11 miles to the campground on the left, a short distance beyond Lower Little Truckee Camp.

Contact: Tahoe National Forest, Sierraville Ranger District, 530/994-3401, fax 530/994-3143; High Sierra Campground Management, 530/544-0426.

50 LOWER LITTLE TRUCKEE

🎣 🐕 🚙 ⛺

Rating: 7

On the Little Truckee River in Tahoe National Forest.

Map 6.1, page 348

This pretty camp is set along Highway 89 and the Little Truckee River at 6,000 feet. (For more information, see the entry for Upper Little Truckee.)

Campsites, facilities: There are 15 sites for tents or RVs up to 22 feet long. Picnic tables and fire grills are provided. Drinking water and vault toilets are available. Supplies are available in Sierraville. Leashed pets are permitted.

Reservations, fees: Reserve at 877/444-6777 ($9 reservation fee) or website: www.Reserve Usa.com; $10 per night, $5 for an extra vehicle. Senior discount available. Open May through October.

Directions: From Truckee, drive north on Highway 89 for about 12 miles to the campground on the left. If you reach Upper Little Truckee Camp, you have gone a half mile too far.

Contact: Tahoe National Forest, Sierraville Ranger District, 530/994-3401, fax 530/994-3143; High Sierra Campground Management, 530/544-0426.

51 LAKESIDE

Rating: 7

On Prosser Creek Reservoir in Tahoe National Forest.

Map 6.1, page 348

This primitive camp is in a deep cove in the northwestern end of Prosser Creek Reservoir, near the lake's headwaters. It is a gorgeous lake, set at 5,741 feet, and a 10-mph speed limit keeps the fast boats out. The adjacent shore is decent for hand-launched, car-top boats, providing the lake level is up, and a concrete boat ramp is a mile down the road. Lots of trout are stocked here every year, including 100,000 rainbow trout fingerlings added in an experiment by the Department of Fish and Game to see how fast they will grow. The trout fishing is often quite good after the ice breaks up in late spring; the lake is also popular with ice fishermen in the winter. Sound perfect? Unfortunately for many, the Prosser ORV Park is nearby and can be noisy.

Campsites, facilities: There are 30 sites for tents or RVs up to 33 feet long and one group site. Drinking water and vault toilets are available. A boat ramp is available nearby. Leashed pets are permitted.

Reservations, fees: Reservations are not accepted. The fee is $12 per night. Senior discount available. Open June through October.

Directions: From Truckee, drive north on Highway 89 for three miles to the campground entrance road on the right. Turn right and drive less than a mile to the campground.

Contact: Tahoe National Forest, Truckee Ranger District, 530/587-3558, fax 530/587-6914; California Land Management, 530/544-0426.

52 LOGGER

Rating: 7

At Stampede Lake in Tahoe National Forest.

Map 6.1, page 348

Stampede Lake is a huge lake by Sierra standards, covering 3,400 acres, the largest lake in the region after Lake Tahoe. It is set at 6,000 feet, surrounded by Sierra granite mountains and pines, and is big, and on days when the wind is down, quite beautiful. The campground is also huge, set along the lake's southern shore, a few minutes' drive from the Captain Roberts Boat Ramp. This camp is ideal for campers, boaters, and anglers. The lake is becoming one of the top fishing lakes in California for kokanee salmon (which can be caught only by trolling), and it also has some large Mackinaw trout and a sprinkling of planter-sized rainbow trout. One problem at Stampede is receding water levels from midsummer through fall, a real pain, which puts the campsites some distance from the lake. Even when the lake is full, there are only a few "lakeside" campsites. However, the boat ramp has been extended to assist boaters during drawdowns.

Campsites, facilities: There are 252 sites for tents or RVs up to 32 feet long. Picnic tables and fire rings are provided. Drinking water, vault toilets, and RV dump station are available. A concrete boat ramp is available one mile from camp. A small convenience store is within seven miles. Some facilities are wheelchair-accessible. Leashed pets are permitted.

Reservations, fees: Reserve at 877/444-6777 ($9 reservation fee) or website: www.Reserve Usa.com; $15 per night, $5 for an extra vehicle. Senior discount available. Open May through October.

Directions: From Truckee, drive east on I-80 for seven miles to the Boca-Hirschdale/County Road 270 exit. Take that exit and drive north on County Road 270 for about seven miles (past Boca Reservoir) to the junction with County Road S261 on the left. Turn left and drive 1.5 miles to the campground on the right.

Contact: Tahoe National Forest, Truckee Ranger District, 530/587-3558, fax 530/587-6914; High Sierra Campground Management, 530/544-0426.

53 EMIGRANT GROUP CAMP

Rating: 7

At Stampede Lake in Tahoe National Forest.
Map 6.1, page 348

Emigrant Group Camp is set at a beautiful spot on Stampede Lake, near a point along a cove on the southeastern corner of the lake. There is a beautiful view of the lake from the point, and a boat ramp is two miles to the east. Elevation is 6,000 feet. (See the entry for Logger for more information.)

Campsites, facilities: There are two 25-person group sites and two 50-person group sites for tents or RVs up to 32 feet long. Picnic tables and fire grills are provided. Drinking water and vault toilets are available. Bring your own firewood. A three-lane concrete boat ramp is available. Some facilities are wheelchair-accessible. Leashed pets are permitted.

Reservations, fees: Reservations required at 877/444-6777 ($9 reservation fee) or website: www.ReserveUsa.com; $63.25–126.50 group fee per night. Open May through September.

Directions: From Truckee, drive east on I-80 for seven miles to the Boca-Hirschdale/County Road 270 exit. Take that exit and drive north on County Road 270 for about seven miles (past Boca Reservoir) to the junction with County Road S261 on the left. Turn left and drive 1.5 miles to the campground access road on the right. Turn right and drive one mile to the camp on the left.

Contact: Tahoe National Forest, Truckee Ranger District, 530/587-3558, fax 530/587-6914; California Land Management, 530/544-0426.

54 BOCA REST CAMPGROUND

Rating: 7

On Boca Reservoir in Tahoe National Forest.
Map 6.1, page 348

The Boca Dam faces I-80, so the lake is out of sight of the zillions of highway travelers who would otherwise certainly stop here. Those who do stop find that the lake is very pretty, set at 5,700 feet in elevation and covering 1,000 acres with deep, blue water. This camp is on the lake's northeastern shore, not far from the inlet to the Little Truckee River. The boat ramp is some distance away.

Campsites, facilities: There are 31 sites for tents or RVs up to 22 feet long. Picnic tables and fire grills are provided. Drinking water and vault toilets are available. A hand-launch boat ramp is also available. A concrete boat ramp is three miles away on the southwest shore of Boca Reservoir. A convenience store is four miles away. Leashed pets are permitted.

Reservations, fees: Reservations are not accepted. The fee is $12 per night, $5 for an extra vehicle. Senior discount available. Open May through October.

Directions: From Truckee, travel east on I-80 for seven miles to the Boca-Hirschdale exit. Take that exit and drive north on County Road 270 for about 2.5 miles to the campground on the right side of the road.

Contact: Tahoe National Forest, Truckee Ranger District, 530/587-3558, fax 530/587-6914; California Land Management, 530/544-0426.

55 BOCA

Rating: 7

On Boca Reservoir in Tahoe National Forest.
Map 6.1, page 348

Boca Reservoir is known as a "big fish factory," with some huge but rare brown trout and rainbow trout sprinkled among a growing fishery for kokanee salmon. The lake is set at 5,700 feet amid a few sparse pines. While the surrounding landscape is not in the drop-dead beautiful class, the lake can still seem a Sierra gem on a windless dawn, out on a boat. It is within a few miles of I-80. The camp is the best choice for anglers/boaters, with a launch ramp set just down from the campground.

Campsites, facilities: There are 22 sites for tents

or RVs up to 16 feet long. Picnic tables and fire grills are provided. Vault toilets are available. No drinking water is available. A concrete boat ramp is north of the campground on Boca Reservoir. Truckee is the nearest place for telephones and supplies. Leashed pets are permitted.

Reservations, fees: Reservations are not accepted. The fee is $12 per night, $5 for an extra vehicle. Senior discount available. Open May through October.

Directions: From Truckee, drive east on I-80 for seven miles to the Boca-Hirschdale exit. Take that exit and drive north for a short distance to County Road 73. Turn left and continue for one mile to the campground on the right side of the road.

Contact: Tahoe National Forest, Truckee Ranger District, 530/587-3558, fax 530/587-6914; California Land Management, 530/544-0426.

56 BOYINGTON MILL

Rating: 7

On the Little Truckee River in Tahoe National Forest.

Map 6.1, page 348

Boyington Mill is a little Forest Service camp set between Boca Reservoir to the nearby south and Stampede Lake to the nearby north, along a small inlet creek to the adjacent Little Truckee River. Though open all summer, it is most often used as an overflow camp when lakeside campsites at Boca, Stampede, and Prosser have already filled. The elevation is 5,700 feet.

Campsites, facilities: There are 10 sites for tents or RVs up to 32 feet long. Picnic tables are provided. Vault toilets are available. No drinking water is available. Leashed pets are permitted.

Reservations, fees: Reservations are not accepted. The fee is $12 per night, $5 for an extra vehicle. Senior discount available. Open May through October.

Directions: From Truckee, go east on I-80 for seven miles. Take the Boca-Hirschdale exit and

drive north on County Road 270 for four miles (past Boca Reservoir) to the campground.

Contact: Tahoe National Forest, Truckee Ranger District, 530/587-3558, fax 530/587-6914; California Land Management, 530/544-0426.

57 LAKE SPAULDING

Rating: 8

Near Emigrant Gap.

Map 6.1, page 348

Lake Spaulding is set at 5,000 feet in the Sierra Nevada, complete with huge boulders and a sprinkling of conifers. Its clear, pure, very cold water has startling effects on swimmers. The lake is extremely pretty, with the Sierra granite backdrop looking as if it has been cut, chiseled, and smoothed. Just one problem. There's no lake view from the campground. In fact, the lake is about a half mile from the campground. The drive here is nearly a straight shot up I-80, the boat ramp is fine for small aluminum boats, and if there is any problem here, it is that there will be plenty of company at the campground. Fishing for kokanee salmon and rainbow trout is often good, as well as fishing for trout at the nearby South Fork Yuba River. There are many other lakes set in the mountain country to the immediate north that can make for excellent side trips, including Bowman, Weaver, and Faucherie Lakes.

Campsites, facilities: There are 25 sites for tents or RVs up to 20 feet long. Picnic tables and fire grills are provided. Drinking water, vault toilets, and five day-use picnic sites are available. A boat ramp is available nearby. Supplies are available in Nevada City. Leashed pets are permitted.

Reservations, fees: Reservations are not accepted. The fee is $13 per night, $3 per night per extra vehicle, $7 per night per extra RV, $1 per night. Open mid-May through September, weather permitting.

Directions: From Sacramento, drive east on I-80 past Emigrant Gap to Highway 20. Drive

west on Highway 20 for 2.3 miles to Lake Spaulding Road. Turn right on Lake Spaulding Road and drive one-half mile to the campground.
Contact: PG&E Land Projects, 916/386-5164; Big Bend Visitor's Center, 530/426-3609, fax 530/426-1744.

58 LODGEPOLE

Rating: 8

On Lake Valley Reservoir in Tahoe National Forest.
Map 6.1, page 348

Lake Valley Reservoir is set at 5,786 feet and covers 300 acres. It is gorgeous when full, its shoreline sprinkled with conifers and boulders. The lake provides decent results for anglers, who have the best luck while trolling. A speed limit prohibits water-skiing and personal watercraft, and that keeps the place quiet and peaceful. The camp is about a quarter mile from the lake's southwest shore and two miles from the boat ramp on the north shore. A trailhead from camp leads south up Monumental Ridge and to Monumental Creek (three miles, one way) on the northwestern flank of Quartz Mountain (6,931 feet).
Campsites, facilities: There are 35 sites for tents or RVs up to 20 feet long. Picnic tables and fire grills are provided. Drinking water and vault toilets are available. A boat ramp is available nearby. Supplies can be obtained off I-80. Leashed pets are permitted.
Reservations, fees: Reservations are not accepted. The fee is $15 per night, $3 per night per extra vehicle, $7 per night per extra RV, $1 per night. Open late May through September, weather permitting.
Directions: From I-80, take the Yuba Gap exit and drive south for .4 mile to Lake Valley Road. Turn right on Lake Valley Road and drive for 1.2 miles until the road forks. Bear right and continue for 1.5 miles to the campground entrance road to the right on another fork.
Contact: PG&E Land Projects, 916/386-5164, fax 916/386-5164; website: www.pge.com/recreation.

59 INDIAN SPRINGS

Rating: 7

Near the Yuba River in Tahoe National Forest.
Map 6.1, page 348

The camp is easy to reach from I-80 yet is in a beautiful setting at 5,600 feet along the South Fork Yuba River. This is a gorgeous stream, running deep blue-green and pure through a granite setting, complete with giant boulders and beautiful pools. Trout fishing is fair. There is a small beach nearby where you can go swimming, though the water is cold. There are also several lakes in the vicinity.
Campsites, facilities: There are 35 sites for tents or RVs up to 25 feet long. Picnic tables and fire grills are provided. Drinking water and vault toilets are available. A grocery store and propane gas are available nearby. Leashed pets are permitted.
Reservations, fees: Reservations are not accepted. The fee is $13 per night, $6 for each additional vehicle. Senior discount available. Open June through October.
Directions: From Sacramento, drive east on I-80 to Yuba Gap and continue for about three miles to the Eagle Lakes exit. Head north on Eagle Lakes Road for a mile to the campground on the left side of the road.
Contact: Tahoe National Forest, Nevada City Ranger District, 530/265-4531, fax 530/478-6109; Sierra Recreation Managers, 209/295-4512; Big Bend Visitor's Center, 530/426-3609, fax 530/426-1744.

60 WOODCHUCK

Rating: 8

On Rattlesnake Creek in Tahoe National Forest.
Map 6.1, page 348

This small camp is only a few miles from I-80, but it is quite obscure and little known to most travelers. It is set on Rattlesnake Creek at 6,300 feet in Tahoe National Forest, at the threshold of some great backcountry and four-wheel-drive roads that lead to many beautiful lakes. To explore, a map of Tahoe National Forest is a must.

Campsites, facilities: There are eight sites for tents or RVs up to 16 feet long. Picnic tables and fire grills are provided. Vault toilets are available. No drinking water is available. Garbage must be packed out. A grocery store and propane gas are available nearby. Leashed pets are permitted.

Reservations, fees: Reservations are not accepted. There is no fee for camping. Open June through October.

Directions: From Sacramento, drive east on I-80 to Yuba Gap and continue for about four miles to the Cisco Grove exit north. Take that exit, turn left on the frontage road, and drive a short distance on Rattlesnake Road. Turn right and continue on Rattlesnake Road (gravel, steep, and curvy; trailers not recommended) and drive three miles to the campground on the right.

Contact: Tahoe National Forest, Nevada City Ranger District, 530/265-4531, fax 530/478-6109; Big Bend Visitor's Center, 530/426-3609, fax 530/426-1744.

61 HAMPSHIRE ROCKS

Rating: 8

On the Yuba River in Tahoe National Forest.
Map 6.1, page 348

This camp sits along the South Fork of the Yuba River at 5,900 feet in elevation, with easy access off I-80 and a nearby Forest Service visitor information center. Fishing for trout is fair. There are some swimming holes, but the water is often very cold. Nearby lakes that can provide side trips include Sterling and Fordyce Lakes (drive-to) to the north, and the Loch Leven Lakes (hike-to) to the south.

Campsites, facilities: There are 31 sites for tents

or RVs up to 22 feet long. Picnic tables and fire grills are provided. Drinking water and vault toilets are available. A grocery store, restaurant, and propane gas are available nearby. Leashed pets are permitted.

Reservations, fees: Reserve at 877/444-6777 ($9 reservation fee) or website: www.Reserve Usa.com; $13 per night, $6 per night for each extra vehicle. Senior discount available. Open June through October.

Directions: From Sacramento, drive east on I-80 to Cisco Grove and continue for a mile to the Big Bend exit. Take that exit (remaining just south of the highway), then turn left on the frontage road and drive east for 1.5 miles to the campground.

Contact: Tahoe National Forest, Nevada City Ranger District, 530/265-4531, fax 530/478-6109; Big Bend Visitor's Center, 530/426-3609, fax 530/426-1744.

62 KIDD LAKE GROUP CAMP

Rating: 7

West of Truckee.
Map 6.1, page 348

Kidd Lake is one of four lakes bunched in a series along the access road just south of I-80. It is set in the northern Sierra's high country, at 6,750 feet, and gets loaded with snow every winter. In late spring and early summer, always call ahead for conditions on the access road. The fishing is frustrating, consisting of a lot of tiny brook trout. Only car-top boats are permitted on Kidd Lake. The camp is set just northeast of the lake, within walking distance of the shore. It features three group sites that can accommodate 100 people when reserved together.

Campsites, facilities: Three are three group sites for up to 50 people in tents only. Picnic tables and fire grills are provided. Drinking water, restrooms, and vault toilets are available. An unimproved boat ramp is available. Supplies are available in Truckee. Leashed pets are permitted.

Reservations, fees: Reservations are required. Sites 1–5 are $23 per night for up to 50 people, Sites 6–7 are $18 per night for up to 20 people, Sites 8–10 are $18 per night for up to 30 people; two night minimum,except for three-night minimum on holidays, $1 per night. Open June to mid-September, weather permitting.

Directions: From Sacramento, drive east on I-80 toward Truckee. Take the Norden/Soda Springs exit, drive a short distance, turn south on Soda Springs Road, and drive .8 mile to Pahatsi Road. Turn right and drive two miles. When the road forks, bear right and drive a mile to the campground entrance road on the left.

Contact: PG&E Land Projects, 916/386-5164.

63 DONNER MEMORIAL STATE PARK

Rating: 9

On Donner Lake.
Map 6.1, page 348

The remarkable beauty of Donner Lake often evokes a deep, heartfelt response. Nearly everybody has looked down and seen it, passing by from nearby I-80. The lake is big, three miles long and three-quarters of a mile wide, gem-like blue, and set near the Sierra crest at 5,900 feet. The area is well developed, with a number of cabins and access roads, and this state park is the feature destination. Along the southeastern end of the lake, it is extremely pretty, but the campsites are set in forest, not along the lake. Fishing is good here (typically only in the early morning), trolling for kokanee salmon or rainbow trout, with big Mackinaw and brown trout providing wild cards. The park features more than three miles of frontage of Donner Creek and Donner Lake, with 2.5 miles of hiking trails. The lake is open to power- and sailboats, and there is no boat launch at the park; a public ramp is available in the northwest corner of the lake. In the summer a wind often comes up in the early afternoon. In the winter a good cross-country ski trail is avail-

able. Campers get free admission to Emigrant Trail Museum.

Campsites, facilities: There are 147 sites for tents or RVs up to 28 feet long and trailers up to 24 feet long, and two hike-in/bike-in sites. Picnic tables and fire grills are provided. Drinking water and vault toilets are available. Supplies are available about one mile away in Truckee. Some facilities are wheelchair-accessible. Leashed pets are permitted.

Reservations, fees: Reserve at 800/444-PARK (800/444-7275) or website: www.Reserve America.com ($7.50 reservation fee); $12 per night, $1 per person for hike-in or bike-in sites. Senior discount available. Open mid-May to mid-October, weather permitting.

Directions: From Auburn, drive east on I-80 just past Donner Lake to the Donner State Park exit. Take that exit and turn south (right) on Donner Pass Road and drive a half mile to the park entrance on the left at the southeast end of the lake.

Contact: Donner Memorial State Park, 530/582-7892 or 530/582-7894, fax 530/550-2347. For boat launching info, call 530/582-7720.

64 GRANITE FLAT

Rating: 6

On the Truckee River in Tahoe National Forest.
Map 6.1, page 348

This camp is set along the Truckee River at 5,800 feet, in an area known for a ton of traffic on adjacent Highway 89, as well as decent trout fishing and, in the spring and early summer, rafting. It is about a 15-minute drive to Squaw Valley or Lake Tahoe. A bike route is also available along the Truckee River out of Tahoe City.

Campsites, facilities: There are 68 sites for tents or RVs and seven walk-in tent sites. Picnic tables and fire grills are provided. Drinking water and vault toilets are available. Some facilities are wheelchair-accessible. Leashed pets are permitted.

Reservations, fees: Reserve at 877/444-6777 ($9 reservation fee) or website: www.Reserve Usa.com; $14 per night, $5 for an extra vehicle. Senior discount available. Open May through October.

Directions: From Truckee, drive south on Highway 89 for 1.5 miles to the campground entrance on the right.

Contact: Tahoe National Forest, Truckee Ranger District, 530/587-3558, fax 530/587-6914; California Land Management, 530/544-0426.

65 COACHLAND RV PARK

Rating: 6

In Truckee.

Map 6.1, page 348

Truckee is the gateway to recreation at North Tahoe. Within minutes are Donner Lake, Prosser Creek Reservoir, Boca Reservoir, Stampede Lake, and the Truckee River. Squaw Valley is a short distance to the south off Highway 89, and Northstar is just off Highway 267. The park is set in a wooded area near the junction of I-80 and Highway 89, providing easy access. The downtown Truckee area (with restaurants) is a half mile away. This is one of the only parks in the area that is open year-round. The elevation is 6,000 feet. One problem: only 25 of the 131 sites are available for overnighters, with the rest taken by long-term rentals.

Campsites, facilities: There are 131 sites, including many drive-through and 25 sites available for overnighters, for trailers or RVs up to 40 feet long. Picnic tables, restrooms, showers, coin laundry, cable TV, modem access, and propane are available. Some facilities are wheelchair-accessible. Leashed pets are permitted.

Reservations, fees: Reservations are recommended. The fee is $31 per night, $1 per night for each extra vehicle. Monthly rates available. Major credit cards accepted. Open year-round.

Directions: From Truckee, drive north on High-

way 89 for a short distance to the park at 10500 Hwy. 89 on the left side of the road.

Contact: Coachland RV Park, 530/587-3071, fax 530/587-6976.

66 MARTIS CREEK LAKE

Rating: 7

Near Truckee.

Map 6.1, page 348

If only this lake weren't so often windy in the afternoon, it would be heaven to fly fishers in float tubes, casting out with sinking lines and leech patterns, using a strip retrieve. To some it's heaven anyway, with Lahontan cutthroat trout growing to 25 inches here. This is a special catch-and-release fishery where anglers are permitted to use only artificial lures with single, barbless hooks. The setting is somewhat sparse and open—a small lake on the eastern edge of the Martis Valley. No motors are permitted at the lake, making it ideal (when the wind is down) for float tubes or prams. The lake level can fluctuate daily, which along with the wind, can be frustrating for those who show up expecting automatic perfection; that just isn't the way it is out there. At times, the lake level can even be very low. The elevation is 5,800 feet.

Campsites, facilities: There are 25 sites, including some drive-through, for tents or RVs. Picnic tables and fire grills are provided. Drinking water, vault toilets, tent pads, and pay phones are available. Some facilities are wheelchair-accessible. Supplies are available six minutes away in Truckee. Leashed pets are permitted.

Reservations, fees: No reservations accepted except for the wheelchair-accessible sites. Rates are $10 per night. Open May through mid-November, weather permitting.

Directions: From Truckee, drive south on Highway 267 for about three miles (past the airport) to the entrance road to the lake on the left. Turn left and drive another 2.5 miles to the campground at the end of the road.

Contact: U.S. Army Corps of Engineers, Sacramento District, 530/639-2342, fax 530/639-2175.

67 NORTH FORK

🚶 🏊 ⛵ 🐕 🚐 ⛺

Rating: 7

On the North Fork of the American River in Tahoe National Forest.

Map 6.1, page 348

This is gold mining country, and this camp is set along the Little North Fork of the North Fork American River at 4,400 feet in elevation, where you might still find a few magic gold flecks. Unfortunately, they are probably fool's gold, not the real stuff. This feeder stream is small and pretty, and the camp is fairly remote and overlooked by most. It is set on the edge of a network of back-country Forest Service roads. To explore them, a map of Tahoe National Forest is a must.

Campsites, facilities: There are 17 sites for tents or RVs up to 16 feet long. Picnic tables and fire grills are provided. Drinking water and vault toilets are available. Supplies are available at Emigrant Gap, Cisco Grove, and Soda Springs. Leashed pets are permitted.

Reservations, fees: Reservations are not accepted. The fee is $13 per night, $6 per night for each extra vehicle. Senior discount available. Open June through October.

Directions: From Sacramento, drive east on I-80 to the Emigrant Gap exit. Take that exit and drive south for a quarter mile to Texas Hill Road/Forest Road 19. Turn right and drive about five miles to the camp on the right.

Contact: Tahoe National Forest, Nevada City Ranger District, 530/265-4531, fax 530/478-6109; Big Bend Visitor's Center, 530/426-3609, fax 530/426-1744.

68 TUNNEL MILL GROUP CAMP

🚶 🏊 ⛵ 🐕 🚐 ⛺

Rating: 7

On the North Fork of the American River in Tahoe National Forest.

Map 6.1, page 348

This is a good spot for a Boy or Girl Scout camp-out. It's a rustic, quiet group camp set all by itself along the (take a deep breath) East Fork of the North Fork of the North Fork of the American River (whew). (See North Fork for more recreation information.) The elevation is 4,400 feet.

Campsites, facilities: There is one group site for tents or RVs up to 16 feet long for up to 50 people. Picnic tables and fire grills are provided. Vault toilets are available. No drinking water is available. Supplies are available at the Nyack exit of Emigrant Gap. Leashed pets are permitted.

Reservations, fees: Reserve at 877/444-6777 ($9 reservation fee) or website: www.Reserve Usa.com; call for fees. Open from June through October.

Directions: From Sacramento, drive east on I-80 to the Emigrant Gap exit. Drive south for a quarter mile to Texas Hill Road/Forest Road 19. Turn right and drive about seven miles to the campground on the right side of the road.

Contact: Tahoe National Forest, Nevada City Ranger District, 530/265-4531, fax 530/478-6109; Big Bend Visitor's Center, 530/426-3609, fax 530/426-1744.

69 ROBINSON FLAT

🚶 🐕 ⛺

Rating: 5

Near French Meadows Reservoir in Tahoe National Forest.

Map 6.1, page 348

This camp is set at 6,800 feet in remote Tahoe National Forest, on the eastern flank of Duncan Peak (7,116 feet), with a two-mile drive south to Duncan Peak Lookout (7,182 feet).

A trail out of camp follows along a small stream, a fork to Duncan Creek, in Little Robinsons Valley. French Meadows Reservoir is 15 miles southeast. In 2002, an equestrian camp was added to this campground with four sites. Drinking water is also available, another addition from past years when this campground was maintained in a more primitive fashion.

Campsites, facilities: There are six tent sites, plus an equestrian camp with four sites. Picnic tables and fire grills are provided. Drinking water and vault toilets are available. Garbage must be packed out. Supplies are available in Foresthill. Leashed pets are permitted.

Reservations, fees: Reservations are not accepted. There is no fee for camping. Open mid-May through October, weather permitting.

Directions: From Sacramento, drive east on I-80 to the north end of Auburn and the Foresthill Road exit. Take that exit, Foresthill Divide Road, and drive east to Foresthill and continue northeast (the road is narrow and curvy) for 27 miles to the junction with County Road 43. The campground is at the junction.

Contact: Tahoe National Forest, Foresthill Ranger District, 530/367-2224, fax 530/367-2992.

70 TALBOT

Rating: 7

On the Middle Fork of the American River in Tahoe National Forest.

Map 6.1, page 348

Talbot camp is set at 5,600 feet along the Middle Fork of the American River, primarily used as a trailhead camp for backpackers heading into the Granite Chief Wilderness. The trail is routed along the Middle Fork American River, turning south into Picayune Valley, flanked by Needle Peak (8,971 feet), Granite Chief (9,886 feet), and Squaw Peak to the east, then beyond to connect with the Pacific Crest Trail. The nearby trailhead has 10 stalls for horses and pack stock trailer parking. Hitching rails are

available at the trailhead. No horses are allowed at the campground.

Campsites, facilities: There are five tent sites. Picnic tables and fire grills are provided. Vault toilets are available. No drinking water is available. Supplies are available in Foresthill. The camp is within a state game refuge and no firearms are permitted. Leashed pets are permitted.

Reservations, fees: Reservations are not accepted. There is no fee for camping. Open June through October, weather permitting.

Directions: From Sacramento, drive east on I-80 to the north end of Auburn and the Foresthill Road exit. Take that exit and drive east to Foresthill and Mosquito Ridge Road (Forest Road 96). Turn right (east) and drive 40 miles (curvy) to Anderson Dam and to a junction. Turn left (still Mosquito Ridge Road) and then continue along the southern shoreline of French Meadows Reservoir for four miles (road turns into dirt) and continue four more miles to the campground.

Contact: Tahoe National Forest, Foresthill Ranger District, 530/367-2224, fax 530/367-2992.

71 SILVER CREEK

Rating: 8

On the Truckee River in Tahoe National Forest.

Map 6.1, page 348

This pretty campground is set near where Silver Creek enters the Truckee River. The trout fishing is often good in this area. This is one of three campgrounds along Highway 89 and the Truckee River, between Truckee and Tahoe City. The elevation is 5,800 feet. Those who camped here in the past may remember the trailhead at this camp; that trail is closed, the trailhead shut down.

Campsites, facilities: There are 21 sites for tents or RVs up to 40 feet long and seven walk-in sites. Picnic tables and fire grills are provided. Drinking water and vault toilets are available.

Supplies are available in Truckee and Tahoe City. Leashed pets are permitted.

Reservations, fees: Reserve at 877/444-6777 ($9 reservation fee) or website: www.Reserve Usa.com; $12 per night, $5 for an extra vehicle. Open June through September.

Directions: From Truckee, drive south on Highway 89 for six miles to the campground entrance on the river side of the highway.

Contact: Tahoe National Forest, Truckee Ranger District, 530/587-3558, fax 530/587-6914; California Land Management, 530/544-0426.

72 GOOSE MEADOWS

Rating: 6

On the Truckee River in Tahoe National Forest.

Map 6.1, page 348

There are three campgrounds set along the Truckee River off Highway 89 between Truckee and Tahoe City. Goose Meadows provides good fishing access with decent prospects, despite the high number of vehicles roaring past on the adjacent highway. This stretch of river is also popular for rafting. The elevation is 5,800 feet.

Campsites, facilities: There are 24 sites for tents or RVs up to 30 feet long. Picnic tables and fire grills are provided. Drinking water and vault toilets are available. Supplies are available in Truckee and Tahoe City. Leashed pets are permitted.

Reservations, fees: Reserve at 877/444-6777 ($9 reservation fee) or website: www.Reserve Usa.com; $12 per night, $5 for an extra vehicle. Senior discount available. Open May through October, weather permitting.

Directions: From Truckee, drive south on Highway 89 for four miles to the campground entrance on the left (river) side of the highway.

Contact: Tahoe National Forest, Truckee Ranger District, 530/587-3558, fax 530/587-6914; California Land Management, 530/544-0426.

73 TAHOE STATE RECREATION AREA

Rating: 9

On Lake Tahoe.

Map 6.1, page 348

This is a popular summer-only campground at the north shore of Lake Tahoe. The Tahoe State Recreation Area covers a large area just west of Highway 28 near Tahoe City. There are opportunities for hiking and horseback riding nearby (though not right at the park). It is also near shopping, restaurants, and unfortunately, traffic jams in Tahoe City. A boat ramp is two miles to the northwest at nearby Lake Forest, and bike rentals are available in Tahoe City for rides along Highway 89 near the shore of the lake. For a more secluded site nearby at Tahoe, get reservations instead for Sugar Pine Point State Park, 11 miles south on Highway 89.

Campsites, facilities: There are 38 sites for tents or RVs up to 24 feet long. Picnic tables, food lockers, barbecues, and fire pits are provided. Drinking water, vault toilets, and coin-operated showers are available. Firewood, other supplies, and a coin laundry are available within walking distance. Leashed pets are permitted.

Reservations, fees: Reserve at 800/444-PARK (800/444-7275) or website: www.Reserve America.com ($7.50 reservation fee); $12 per night. Senior discount available. Open May through October, weather permitting.

Directions: From Truckee, drive south on Highway 89 through Tahoe City. Turn north on Highway 28 and drive .9 mile to the campground entrance on the right side of the road.

Contact: Tahoe State Recreation Area, 530/583-3074 or 530/525-7232.

74 LAKE FOREST CAMPGROUND

Rating: 8

On Lake Tahoe.

Map 6.1, page 348

The north shore of Lake Tahoe provides beautiful lookouts and excellent boating access. The latter is a highlight of this camp, with a boat ramp nearby. From here it is a short cruise to Dollar Point and around the corner north to Carnelian Bay, one of the better stretches of water for trout fishing. The elevation is 6,200 feet. There is a 10-day camping limit.

Campsites, facilities: There are 20 sites for tents or RVs up to 20 feet long. Picnic tables and fire grills are provided. Drinking water and vault toilets are available. Some facilities are wheelchair-accessible. A grocery store, coin laundry, and propane gas are available within four miles.

Reservations, fees: Reservations are not accepted. The fee is $15 per night. Open April through October, weather permitting.

Directions: From Truckee, drive south on Highway 89 through Tahoe City to Highway 28. Bear north on Highway 28 and drive four miles to the campground entrance road (Lake Forest Road) on the right.

Contact: Tahoe City Public Utility District, Parks and Recreation, 530/583-3796, ext. 7, fax 530/583-8452.

75 SANDY BEACH CAMPGROUND

Rating: 8

On Lake Tahoe.

Map 6.1, page 348

Sandy Beach Campground is set at 6,200 feet near the northwest shore of Lake Tahoe. A nearby boat ramp provides access to one of the better fishing areas of the lake for Mackinaw trout. A public beach is across the road. But the water in Tahoe is always cold, and though a lot of people will get suntans on beaches next to the lake, swimmers need to be members of the Polar Bear Club. A short drive to the east will take you past the town of Kings Beach and into Nevada, where there are some small casinos near the shore of Crystal Bay.

Campsites, facilities: There are 44 sites, including some drive-through and some rented for the full summer, with full or partial hookups for tents or RVs up to 40 feet long. Picnic tables and fire rings are provided. Drinking water, showers, flush toilets, and coin laundry are available. A free public boat ramp is available half a block away. A grocery store and propane gas are available nearby. Leashed pets are permitted.

Reservations, fees: Reservations are recommended. Fees are $20–25 per night for up to six people with two vehicles, two-dog limit. For weeklong stays, seventh night is free. Major credit cards accepted. Open May through October.

Directions: From Truckee, drive south on Highway 267 to Highway 28. Turn right and drive one mile to the park on the right side of the road (entrance well signed).

Contact: Sandy Beach Campground, 530/546-7682.

76 COYOTE GROUP CAMP

Rating: 6

On French Meadows Reservoir, in Tahoe National Forest.

Map 6.1, page 348

This group camp is set right at the head of French Meadows Reservoir, at 5,300 feet in elevation. A boat ramp is two miles to the south, just past Lewis on the lake's north shore. (For recreation options, see the entries for Poppy Hike-In/Boat-In and French Meadows.)

Campsites, facilities: There are three 25-person group sites and a 50-person group site for tents or RVs up to 35 feet long. Picnic tables and fire grills are provided. Drinking water and vault toilets are available. A campfire circle and central parking area are also available.

Supplies are available in Foresthill. Leashed pets are permitted.

Reservations, fees: Reserve at 877/444-6777 ($9 reservation fee) or website: www.Reserve Usa.com; $50–65 group fee per night or $1 per person. Open May through October.

Directions: From Sacramento, drive east on I-80 to the north end of Auburn and the Foresthill Road exit. Take that exit and drive east to Foresthill and Mosquito Ridge Road (Forest Road 96). Turn right (east) and drive 40 miles (curvy) to Anderson Dam and to a junction. Turn left (still Mosquito Ridge Road) and then continue along the southern shoreline of French Meadows Reservoir for five miles along the southern shoreline to French Meadows Reservoir and a fork at the head of the lake. Bear left at the fork and drive a half mile to the camp on the left side of the road.

Contact: Tahoe National Forest, Foresthill Ranger District, 530/367-2224, fax 530/367-2992.

77 FRENCH MEADOWS

Rating: 7

On French Meadows Reservoir in Tahoe National Forest.

Map 6.1, page 348

The nearby boat launch makes this the choice for boating campers. The camp is on French Meadows Reservoir at 5,300 feet. It is set on the lake's southern shore, with the boat ramp about a mile to the south (you'll see the entrance road on the way in). This is a big lake set in remote Tahoe National Forest in the North Fork American River Canyon with good trout fishing. The lake level often drops in late summer, and then a lot of stumps and boulders start poking through the lake surface. This creates navigational hazards for boaters, but it also makes it easier for the anglers to know where to find the fish. If the fish don't bite here, boaters should make the nearby side trip to pretty Hell Hole Reservoir to the south.

Campsites, facilities: There are 75 sites for tents or RVs up to 35 feet long. Picnic tables and fire grills are provided. Drinking water and vault toilets are available. Some facilities are wheelchair-accessible. A concrete boat ramp is nearby. Supplies are available in Foresthill. Leashed pets are permitted.

Reservations, fees: Reserve at 877/444-6777 ($9 reservation fee) or website: www.Reserve Usa.com; $12 per night. Senior discount available. Open June through October.

Directions: From Sacramento, drive east on I-80 to the north end of Auburn and the Foresthill Road exit. Take that exit and drive east to Foresthill and Mosquito Ridge Road (Forest Road 96). Turn right (east) and drive 40 miles (curvy) to Anderson Dam and to a junction. Turn left (still Mosquito Ridge Road) and then continue along the southern shoreline of French Meadows Reservoir for four miles to the campground.

Contact: Tahoe National Forest, Foresthill Ranger District, 530/367-2224, fax 530/367-2992; American Land & Leisure, 800/342-2267.

78 LEWIS

Rating: 7

On French Meadows Reservoir in Tahoe National Forest.

Map 6.1, page 348

This camp is not right at lakeside but is just across the road from French Meadows Reservoir. It is still quite pretty, set along a feeder creek near the lake's northwest shore. A boat ramp is available only a half mile to the south, and the adjacent McGuire Picnic Area has a trailhead that is routed along the lake's northern shoreline. This lake is big (2,000 acres) and pretty, created by a dam on the Middle Fork American River, with good fishing for rainbow trout.

Campsites, facilities: There are 40 sites for tents or RVs up to 35 feet long. Picnic tables and fire grills are provided. Drinking water and vault toilets are available. A concrete boat ramp is nearby. Supplies are available in Foresthill. Leashed pets are permitted.

Reservations, fees: Reserve at 877/444-6777 ($9 reservation fee) or website: www.Reserve Usa.com; $12 per night. Senior discount available. Open May through October.

Directions: From Sacramento, drive east on I-80 to the north end of Auburn and the Foresthill Road exit. Take that exit and drive east to Foresthill and Mosquito Ridge Road (Forest Road 96). Turn right (east) and drive 40 miles (curvy) to Anderson Dam and to a junction. Turn left (still Mosquito Ridge Road) and then continue along the southern shoreline of French Meadows Reservoir for five miles along the southern shoreline to French Meadows Reservoir and a fork at the head of the lake. Bear left at the fork and drive a half mile to the camp on the right side of the road.

Contact: Tahoe National Forest, Foresthill Ranger District, 530/367-2224, fax 530/367-2992.

79 POPPY HIKE-IN/BOAT-IN

Rating:10

On French Meadows Reservoir in Tahoe National Forest.

Map 6.1, page 348

This camp is on the north side of French Meadows Reservoir, about midway along the lake's shore. It can be reached only by boat or on foot, supplying a great degree of privacy compared to the other camps on this lake. A trail that is routed along the north shore of the reservoir runs right through the camp, providing two different trailhead access points, as well as a good side-trip hike. The lake is quite big, covering nearly 2,000 acres when full, at 5,300 feet in elevation on a dammed-up section of the Middle Fork American River. It is stocked with rainbow trout but also has prime habitat for brown trout, and big ones are sometimes caught by surprise.

Campsites, facilities: There are 12 tent sites,

accessible by boat or by a mile-long foot trail from McGuire Boat Ramp. Picnic tables and fire grills are provided. Vault toilets are available. No drinking water is available. Garbage must be packed out. Supplies are available in Foresthill. Leashed pets are permitted.

Reservations, fees: Reservations are not accepted. There is no fee for camping. Open May through October.

Directions: From Sacramento, drive east on I-80 to the north end of Auburn and the Foresthill Road exit. Take that exit and drive east to Foresthill and Mosquito Ridge Road (Forest Road 96). Turn right (east) and drive 40 miles (curvy) to French Meadows Reservoir Dam and to a junction. Turn left (still Mosquito Ridge Road) and continue for three miles to the lake and campground. Note: if the gate is locked early or late in the season, an option is to drive around the lake and hike in a mile from the McGuire Picnic Area.

Contact: Tahoe National Forest, Foresthill Ranger District, 530/367-2224, fax 530/367-2992.

80 AHART

Rating: 7

Near French Meadows Reservoir in Tahoe National Forest.

Map 6.1, page 348

This camp is a mile north of French Meadows Reservoir near where the Middle Fork of the American River enters the lake. It is on the Middle Fork and is primarily used for campers who would rather camp near this river than French Meadows Reservoir. Note: this is bear country in the summer.

Campsites, facilities: There are 12 sites for tents or RVs up to 22 feet long. Picnic tables and fire grills are provided. Vault toilets are available. No drinking water is available. Supplies are available in Foresthill. Leashed pets are permitted.

Reservations, fees: Reservations are not accepted.

The fee is $10 per night. Senior discount available. Open June through October.

Directions: From Sacramento, drive east on I-80 to the north end of Auburn and the Foresthill Road exit. Take that exit and drive east to Foresthill and Mosquito Ridge Road (Forest Road 96). Turn right (east) and drive 40 miles (curvy) to Anderson Dam and to a junction. Turn left (still Mosquito Ridge Road) and then continue along the southern shoreline of French Meadows Reservoir for seven miles.

Contact: Tahoe National Forest, Foresthill Ranger District, 530/367-2224, fax 530/367-2992.

81 GATES GROUP CAMP

Rating: 7

On the North Fork of the American River in Tahoe National Forest.

Map 6.1, page 348

This group camp is well secluded along the North Fork American River, just upstream from where it pours into French Meadows Reservoir. (For recreation options, see the entries for French Meadows, Lewis, and Coyote Group Camp.)

Campsites, facilities: There are two 25-person group sites and a 75-person group site for tents or RVs up to 35 feet long. Picnic tables and fire grills are provided. Drinking water, vault toilets, central parking, and a campfire circle are available. Obtain supplies in Foresthill. Leashed pets are permitted.

Reservations, fees: Reserve at 877/444-6777 ($9 reservation fee) or website: www.Reserve Usa.com; $50–60 fee per night. Open May through October.

Directions: From Sacramento, drive east on I-80 to the north end of Auburn and the Foresthill Road exit. Take that exit and drive east to Foresthill and Mosquito Ridge Road (Forest Road 96). Turn right (east) and drive 40 miles (curvy) to Anderson Dam and to a junction. Turn left (still Mosquito Ridge Road) and con-

tinue along the southern shoreline of French Meadows Reservoir for five miles to a fork at the head of the lake. Bear left at the fork (Forest Road 68) and drive a mile to the camp at the end of the road.

Contact: Tahoe National Forest, Foresthill Ranger District, 530/367-2224, fax 530/367-2992; American Land & Leisure, 800/342-2267.

82 MIDDLE MEADOWS GROUP CAMP

Rating: 7

On Long Canyon Creek in Eldorado National Forest.

Map 6.1, page 348

This group camp is within range of several adventures. To the nearby east is Hell Hole Reservoir (you'll need a boat here to do it right), and to the nearby north is French Meadows Reservoir (you'll drive past the dam on the way in). Unfortunately, there isn't a heck of a lot to do at this camp other than watch the water flow by on adjacent Long Canyon Creek.

Campsites, facilities: There are two group sites for tents or small RVs. Picnic tables and fire grills are provided. Drinking water and flush and vault toilets are available. Supplies can be obtained in Foresthill. Leashed pets are permitted.

Reservations, fees: Reserve at 877/444-6777 ($9 reservation fee) or website: www.Reserve Usa.com; $25–50 per night. Open June through September.

Directions: From Sacramento, drive east on I-80 to the north end of Auburn. Take the Elm Avenue exit and turn left at the first stoplight onto Elm Avenue. Drive .1 mile, turn left on High Street, and continue through the signal where High Street merges with Highway 49. Travel on Highway 49 for about 3.5 miles, turn right over the bridge, and drive about 2.5 miles into the town of Cool. Turn left on Georgetown Road/Highway 193 and drive about 14 miles into Georgetown. At the four-way stop turn left on Main Street (which becomes Wentworth Springs/Forest Road 1) and drive about 25 miles. Turn left on Forest Road 2 and drive 19 miles to the campground on the right.

Contact: Eldorado Information Center, 530/644-6048, fax 530/295-5624; Eldorado National Forest, Georgetown Ranger District, 530/333-4312, fax 530/333-5522.

83 BIG MEADOWS

Rating: 7

Near Hell Hole Reservoir in Eldorado National Forest.

Map 6.1, page 348

This camp sits on a meadow near the ridge above Hell Hole Reservoir (which is about two miles away). (For more information, see the entry for Hell Hole.)

Campsites, facilities: There are 54 sites for tents or RVs, including some sites for RVs up to 60 feet long. Picnic tables and fire grills are provided. Drinking water and flush and vault toilets are available. One wheelchair-accessible campsite and toilet are available. Leashed pets are permitted.

Reservations, fees: Reservations are not accepted. The fee is $8 per night. Senior discount available. Open May through October.

Directions: From Sacramento, drive east on I-80 to the north end of Auburn. Take the Elm Avenue exit and turn left at the first stoplight onto Elm Avenue. Drive .1 mile, turn left on High Street, and continue through the signal where High Street merges with Highway 49. Travel on Highway 49 for about 3.5 miles, turn right over the bridge, and drive about 2.5 miles into the town of Cool. Turn left on Georgetown Road/Highway 193 and drive about 14 miles into Georgetown. At the four-way stop turn left on Main Street (which becomes Wentworth Springs/Forest Road 1) and drive about 25 miles. Turn left on Forest Road 2 and drive 21 miles to the campground on the left.

Contact: Eldorado Information Center, 530/644-6048, fax 530/295-5624; Eldorado National Forest, Georgetown Ranger District, 530/333-4312, fax 530/333-5522.

84 HELL HOLE

Rating: 8

Near Hell Hole Reservoir in Eldorado National Forest.

Map 6.1, page 348

Hell Hole is a mountain temple with sapphire blue water. For the most part, there is limited bank access because of its granite-sculpted shore, and that's why there are no lakeside campsites. This is the closest drive-to camp at Hell Hole Reservoir, about a mile away with a boat launch nearby. Be sure to bring a boat and then enjoy the scenery while you troll for kokanee salmon, brown trout, Mackinaw trout, and a sprinkling of rainbow trout. This is a unique fishery compared to the put-and-take rainbow trout at so many other lakes. The lake elevation is 4,700 feet; the camp elevation is 5,200 feet.

Campsites, facilities: There are 10 sites for tents or RVs. Picnic tables and fire grills are provided. Drinking water and vault toilets are available. Supplies can be obtained in Georgetown. A boat launch is available nearby at the reservoir. Leashed pets are permitted.

Reservations, fees: Reservations are not accepted. The fee is $8 per night in the summer season. Senior discount available. Open May through mid-November, weather permitting.

Directions: From Sacramento, drive east on I-80 to the north end of Auburn. Take the Elm Avenue exit and turn left at the first stoplight onto Elm Avenue. Drive .1 mile, turn left on High Street, and continue through the signal where High Street merges with Highway 49. Travel on Highway 49 for about 3.5 miles, turn right over the bridge, and drive about 2.5 miles into the town of Cool. Turn left on Georgetown Road/Highway 193 and drive about 14 miles into Georgetown. At the four-way stop

turn left on Main Street (which becomes Wentworth Springs/Forest Road 1) and drive about 25 miles. Turn left on Forest Road 2 and drive about 22 miles to the campground on the left.
Contact: Eldorado Information Center, 530/644-6048, fax 530/295-5624; Eldorado National Forest, Georgetown Ranger District, 530/333-4312, fax 530/333-5522.

85 UPPER HELL HOLE WALK-IN

Rating:10

On Hell Hole Reservoir in Eldorado National Forest.

Map 6.1, page 348

This is a beautiful spot, set on the southern shore at the upper end of Hell Hole Reservoir in remote national forest seen by relatively few people. Getting here requires a 3.5-mile walk on a trail routed along the southern edge of the lake overlooking Hell Hole. The trail's short rises and falls can tire you out on a hot day—bring plenty of water. You arrive at this little trail camp, ready to explore onward the next day into the Granite Chief Wilderness, or just do nothing except enjoy adjacent Buck Meadow, the lake's headwaters, and the paradise you have discovered.

Campsites, facilities: There are 15 tent sites, accessible by trail or boat only. Picnic tables and fire grills are provided. Vault toilets are available. No drinking water is available. Garbage must be packed out. A boat launch is available at the reservoir and the camp can be reached by boat, but low water levels during August and September can make passage difficult or impossible. Supplies can be obtained in Georgetown. Leashed pets are permitted.

Reservations, fees: Reservations are not accepted. There is no fee for camping. Open May through October.

Directions: From Sacramento, drive east on I-80 to the north end of Auburn. Take the Elm Avenue exit and turn left at the first stoplight onto Elm Avenue. Drive .1 mile, turn left on

High Street, and continue through the signal where High Street merges with Highway 49. Travel on Highway 49 for about 3.5 miles, turn right over the bridge, and drive about 2.5 miles into the town of Cool. Turn left on Georgetown Road/Highway 193 and drive about 14 miles into Georgetown. At the four-way stop turn left on Main Street (which becomes Wentworth Springs/Forest Road 1) and drive about 25 miles. Turn left on Forest Road 2 and drive about 23 miles (a mile past the Hell Hole Campground access road) to the parking area at the boat ramp. From the trailhead hike 3.5 miles to the camp.

Contact: Eldorado Information Center, 530/644-6048, fax 530/295-5624; Eldorado National Forest, Georgetown Ranger District, 530/333-4312, fax 530/333-5522.

86 WILLIAM KENT

Rating: 8

Near Lake Tahoe in the Lake Tahoe Basin.

Map 6.1, page 348

William Kent camp is a little pocket of peace set near the busy traffic of Highway 89 on the western shore corridor. It is on the west side of the highway, meaning visitors have to cross the highway to get lakeside access. The elevation is 6,300 feet, and the camp is wooded with primarily lodgepole pines. The drive here is awesome or ominous, depending on how you look at it, with the view of incredible Lake Tahoe to the east, the deepest blue in the world. But you often have a lot of time to look at it, since traffic rarely moves quickly.

Campsites, facilities: There are 55 tent sites and 36 sites for RVs up to 40 feet long. Picnic tables and fire grills are provided. Drinking water, flush toilets, and RV dump station are available. A grocery store, coin laundry, and propane gas are available nearby. Leashed pets are permitted.

Reservations, fees: Reserve at 877/444-6777 ($9 reservation fee) or website: www.ReserveUsa.com;

$15 per night, $5 per night for each extra vehicle. Senior discount available. Open June through September.

Directions: From Truckee, drive south on Highway 89 to Tahoe City. Turn south on Highway 89 and drive three miles to the campground entrance on the right side of the road.

Contact: Lake Tahoe Basin Management Unit, Visitor Center, 530/573-2674, fax 530/573-2693; California Land Management, 530/583-3642.

87 KASPIAN

Rating: 7

On Lake Tahoe.

Map 6.1, page 348

As gorgeous and as huge as Lake Tahoe is, there are relatively few camps or even restaurants with lakeside settings. This is one of the few. Kaspian is set along the west shore of the lake at 6,235 feet in elevation, near the little town of Tahoe Pines. A Forest Service road (03) is available adjacent to the camp on the west side of Highway 89, routed west into national forest (becoming quite rough) to a trailhead. From there you can hike up to Barker Peak (8,166 feet) for incredible views of Lake Tahoe, as well as access to the Pacific Crest Trail.

Campsites, facilities: There are 10 sites for tents. RVs up to 20 feet long may use the parking lot on a space-available basis. Picnic tables and fire grills are provided. Drinking water and vault toilets are available. A grocery store, coin laundry, and propane gas are available nearby. Leashed pets are permitted.

Reservations, fees: Reserve at 877/444-6777 ($9 reservation fee) or website: www.Reserve Usa.com.; $14 per night, $5 per night for each extra vehicle (unless towed). Senior discount available. Open May through September.

Directions: From Truckee, drive south on Highway 89 to Tahoe City. Turn south on Highway 89 and drive four miles to the campground (signed) on the east side of the road.

Contact: Lake Tahoe Basin Management Unit,

Visitor Center, 530/573-2674, fax California Land Management, 530/583-3642.

88 SUGAR PINE POINT STATE PARK

Rating: 10

On Lake Tahoe.

Map 6.1, page 348

This is one of three beautiful and popular state parks on the west shore of Lake Tahoe. It is just north of Meeks Bay on General Creek, with almost two miles of lake frontage available, though the campground is on the opposite side of Highway 89. General Creek, a feeder stream to Lake Tahoe here, is one of the clearest streams imaginable. A pretty trail is routed seven miles along the creek up to Lost Lake, just outside the northern boundary of the Desolation Wilderness. This stream also provides trout fishing from mid-July to mid-September. This park contains one of the finest remaining natural areas at Lake Tahoe. The park features dense forests of pine, fir, aspen, and junipers, covering more than 2,000 acres of beautiful landscape. There are many hiking trails, a swimming beach, and in winter, 20 kilometers of cross-country skiing trails and a heated restroom. There is also evidence of occupation of Washoe Indians, with bedrock mortars, or grinding rocks, near the Ehrman Mansion. The elevation is 6,200 feet.

Campsites, facilities: There are 175 sites for tents or RVs up to 32 feet long and trailers up to 26 feet long. There are also 10 group sites available. Picnic tables and fire rings are provided. Drinking water, restrooms, flush toilets, coin-operated showers (except in winter), RV dump station, a day-use area, and nature center with bird display are available. A grocery store, coin laundry, and propane gas are available nearby. Some facilities are wheelchair-accessible. Leashed pets are permitted.

Reservations, fees: Reserve at 800/444-PARK

(800/444-7275) or website: www.Reserve America.com ($7.50 reservation fee); $12 per night, $37 per night group sites. Senior discount available. Open year-round.

Directions: From Truckee, drive south on Highway 89 through Tahoe City. Continue south on Highway 89 and drive 9.3 miles to the campground (signed) on the right (west) side of the road.

Contact: Sugar Pine Point State Park, 530/525-7982 or 530/525-7232.

89 MEEKS BAY

Rating: 9

On Lake Tahoe.

Map 6.1, page 348

Meeks Bay is a beautiful spot along the western shore of Lake Tahoe. A bicycle trail is available nearby and is routed along the lake's shore, but it requires occasionally crossing busy Highway 89.

Campsites, facilities: There are 40 sites for tents or RVs up to 20 feet long. Picnic tables and fire grills are provided. Drinking water and vault toilets are available. Coin laundry and groceries are available nearby. Leashed pets are permitted.

Reservations, fees: Reserve at 877/444-6777 ($9 reservation fee) or website: www.Reserve Usa.com; $18–26 per night, $5 per night for each extra vehicle (if not towed). Senior discount available. Open May through September.

Directions: In South Lake Tahoe at the junction of Highway 89 and U.S. 50, turn north on Highway 89 and drive 17 miles to the campground (signed) on the east side of Highway 89.

Contact: Lake Tahoe Basin Management Unit, Visitor Center, 530/573-2674 or fax 530/573-2693; California Land Management, 530/583-3642.

90 MEEKS BAY RESORT & MARINA

Rating: 7

On Lake Tahoe.

Map 6.1, page 348

Prime access for boating makes this a camp of choice for the boater/camper at Lake Tahoe. This campground is extremely popular and often booked well ahead of time for July and August. A boat launch is not only nearby, but access to Rubicon Bay and beyond to breathtaking Emerald Bay is possible, a six-mile trip one way for boats. The resort is adjacent to a 20-mile paved bike trail, with a swimming beach also nearby. A 14-day stay limit is enforced.

Campsites, facilities: There are 10 sites, including some drive-through, with full hookups for RVs of any length, 24 sites for tents, plus lodge rooms, cabins, and houses for rent. Showers, flush toilets, picnic tables, and fire grills are provided. Coin laundry, snack bar, gift shop, and groceries are available. A boat ramp, boat rentals (kayaks, canoes, and paddle boats), and boat slips are also available. No pets are allowed.

Reservations, fees: Reservations are accepted. The fee is $20–30 per night, $7 day-use fee, $25 per night for boat slips, $1 per shower. Major credit cards accepted. Open May through October.

Directions: In South Lake Tahoe at the junction of Highway 89 and U.S. 50, turn north on Highway 89 and drive 17 miles to the campground on the right.

Contact: Meeks Bay Resort & Marina, 530/525-6946 or 877/326-3357 (reservations), website: www.meeksbayresort.com.

91 BLACK OAK GROUP CAMP

Rating: 7

Near Stumpy Meadows Lake in Eldorado National Forest.

Map 6.2, page 349

This group camp is set directly adjacent to

Stumpy Meadows Campground. (For more information, see the entry for Stumpy Meadows.) The boat ramp for the lake is just south of the Mark Edson Dam, near the picnic area. The elevation is 4,400 feet.

Campsites, facilities: There are three group sites for tents and one group site for RVs up to 16 feet long. Picnic tables and fire grills are provided. Drinking water and vault toilets are available. A boat ramp is nearby. Leashed pets are permitted.

Reservations, fees: Reserve at 877/444-6777 ($9 reservation fee) or website: www.Reserve Usa.com; $55 group-use fee. Open April through September.

Directions: From Sacramento on I-80, drive east to the north end of Auburn. Turn left on Elm Avenue and drive about .1 mile. Turn left on High Street and drive through the signal that marks the continuation of High Street as Highway 49. Drive 3.5 miles on Highway 49, turn right over the bridge, and drive 2.5 miles into the town of Cool. Turn left on Georgetown Road/Highway 193 and drive 14 miles into Georgetown. At the four-way stop, turn left on Main Street, which becomes Georgetown-Wentworth Springs Road/Forest Road 1. Drive about 18 miles to Stumpy Meadows Lake, and then continue for two miles to the north shore of the lake and the campground entrance road on the right.

Contact: Eldorado Information Center, 530/644-6048, fax 530/295-5624; Eldorado National Forest, Georgetown Ranger District, 530/333-4312, fax 530/333-5522.

92 STUMPY MEADOWS

Rating: 7

On Stumpy Meadows Lake in Eldorado National Forest.

Map 6.2, page 349

This is the camp of choice for visitors to Stumpy Meadows Lake. The first thing visitors notice is the huge ponderosa pine trees, noted for

their distinctive mosaiclike bark. The lake is set at 4,400 feet in Eldorado National Forest and covers 320 acres with water that is cold and clear. The lake has both rainbow and brown trout, and in the fall provides good fishing for big browns (they move up into the head of the lake, near where Pilot Creek enters).

Campsites, facilities: There are 40 sites for tents or RVs, with some sites available for RVs up to 60 feet. Two of the sites are double units. Picnic tables and fire grills are provided. Drinking water and vault toilets are available. A boat ramp is nearby. Leashed pets are permitted.

Reservations, fees: Reserve at 877/444-6777 ($9 reservation fee) or website: www.Reserve Usa.com; $13 per night, $26 for double-unit sites. Senior discount available. Open April through October.

Directions: From Sacramento on I-80, drive east to the north end of Auburn. Turn left on Elm Avenue and drive about .1 mile. Turn left on High Street and drive through the signal that marks the continuation of High Street as Highway 49. Drive 3.5 miles on Highway 49, turn right over the bridge, and drive 2.5 miles into the town of Cool. Turn left on Georgetown Road/Highway 193 and drive 14 miles into Georgetown. At the four-way stop, turn left on Main Street, which becomes Georgetown-Wentworth Springs Road/Forest Road 1. Drive about 18 miles to Stumpy Meadows Lake. Continue about a mile and turn right into Stumpy Meadows campground.

Contact: Eldorado Information Center, 530/644-6048, fax 530/295-5624; Eldorado National Forest, Georgetown Ranger District, 530/333-4312, fax 530/333-5522.

93 GERLE CREEK

Rating: 7

On Gerle Creek Reservoir in Eldorado National Forest.

Map 6.2, page 349

This is a small, pretty, but limited spot set

along the northern shore of little Gerle Creek Reservoir at 5,231 feet in elevation. The lake is ideal for canoes or other small boats because no motors are permitted and no boat ramp is available. That makes for quiet water. It is set in the Gerle Creek Canyon, which feeds into the South Fork Rubicon River. No trout plants are made at this lake, and fishing is correspondingly poor. A network of Forest Service roads to the north can provide great exploring. A map of Eldorado National Forest is a must.

Campsites, facilities: There are 50 sites for tents or RVs up to 22 feet long. Picnic tables and fire grills are provided. Drinking water and vault toilets are available. Wheelchair-accessible trails and fishing pier are available nearby. Leashed pets are permitted.

Reservations, fees: Reserve at 877/444-6777 ($9 reservation fee) or website: www.Reserve Usa.com; $15 per night. Senior discount available. Open late May to early September.

Directions: From Sacramento, drive east on U.S. 50 to Riverton and the junction with Ice House Road/Soda Springs-Riverton Road. Turn north and drive 27 miles (past Union Valley Reservoir) to a fork with Forest Road 30. Turn left, drive two miles, bear left on the campground entrance road, and drive a mile to the campground.

Contact: Eldorado Information Center, 530/644-6048, fax 530/295-5624; Eldorado National Forest, Pacific Ranger District, 530/644-2349, fax 530/647-5405.

94 SOUTH FORK

Rating: 8

On the South Fork of the Rubicon River in Eldorado National Forest.
Map 6.2, page 349

This primitive national forest camp sits alongside the South Fork Rubicon River, just over a mile downstream from the outlet at Gerle Creek Reservoir. Trout fishing is fair, the water

tastes extremely sweet (always pump filter with a water purifier), and there are several side trips available. These include Loon Lake (eight miles to the northeast), Gerle Creek Reservoir (to the nearby north), and Union Valley Reservoir (to the nearby south).

Campsites, facilities: There are 15 sites for tents or RVs up to 22 feet long. Picnic tables and fire grills are provided. Vault toilets are available. No drinking water is available. Leashed pets are permitted.

Reservations, fees: Reservations are not accepted. There is no fee for camping. Open June through October.

Directions: From Sacramento, drive east on U.S. 50 to Riverton and the junction with Ice House Road/Soda Springs-Riverton Road. Turn north and drive about 25 miles to the junction with Forest Road 13N28 (3.5 miles past Union Valley Reservoir). Bear left on Forest Road 13N28 and drive two miles to the campground entrance on the right.

Contact: Eldorado Information Center, 530/644-6048, fax 530/295-5624; Eldorado National Forest, Pacific Ranger District, 530/644-2349, fax 530/647-5405.

95 RED FIR GROUP CAMP

Rating: 6

On Loon Lake in Eldorado National Forest.
Map 6.2, page 349

This is a pretty, wooded camp, ideal for medium-sized groups. It is across the road from the water, offering a secluded, quiet spot. Lake access is a short hike away. (See the entry for Loon Lake Northshore for more information.) The elevation is 6,500 feet.

Campsites, facilities: This group site will accommodate up to six vehicles and 25 people with tents or self-contained RVs. Drinking water, vault toilets, fire rings, and grills are provided. Leashed pets are permitted.

Reservations, fees: Reserve at 877/444-6777 ($9 reservation fee) or website: www.ReserveUsa.com;

$35 per night, $5 for an extra vehicle. Open June through September.

Directions: From Sacramento, drive east on U.S. 50 to Riverton and the junction with Ice House Road/Soda Springs-Riverton Road on the left. Turn left and drive 34 miles to a fork at the foot of Loon Lake. Turn left and drive three miles to the campground (just beyond the Loon Lake Northshore Camp).

Contact: Eldorado Information Center, 530/644-6048, fax 530/295-5624; Eldorado National Forest, Pacific Ranger District, 530/644-2349, fax 530/644-5405.

96 WENTWORTH SPRINGS FOUR-WHEEL DRIVE

Rating: 7

Near Loon Lake in Eldorado National Forest.

Map 6.2, page 349

There is one reason people come here: to set up a base camp for an OHV adventure, whether they are the owners of four-wheel drives, all-terrain vehicles, or dirt bikes. A network of roads leads from this camp, passable only by these vehicles; these roads would flat-out destroy your average car. The camp is set deep in Eldorado National Forest, at 6,200 feet in elevation. While the north end of Loon Lake is a mile to the east, the road there is extremely rough (perfect, right?). The road is gated along the lake, preventing access to this camp for those who drive directly to Loon Lake.

Campsites, facilities: There are eight tent sites. Picnic tables and fire grills are provided. Vault toilets are available. No drinking water is available. Garbage must be packed out. Leashed pets are permitted.

Reservations, fees: Reservations are not accepted. There is no fee for camping. Open June through October.

Directions: From Sacramento, drive east on U.S. 50 to Riverton and the junction with Ice House Road/Soda Springs-Riverton Road on

the left. Turn left and drive 30 miles to the junction with Forest Road 30. Bear left and drive 3.5 miles to Forest Road 33. Turn right and drive seven miles to the campground on the left side of the road. (The access road is suitable for four-wheel-drive vehicles and off-highway motorcycles only.)

Contact: Eldorado Information Center, 530/644-6048, fax 530/295-5624; Eldorado National Forest, Pacific Ranger District, 530/644-2349, fax 530/644-5405.

97 LOON LAKE NORTHSHORE

Rating: 8

On Loon Lake in Eldorado National Forest.

Map 6.2, page 349

This camp is for tents or small self-contained RVs, where the waterfront sites provide an extremely pretty setting on the northwestern shore of Loon Lake, even though there are few facilities and no boat ramp—the boat ramp is near the Loon Lake campground and picnic area at the south end of the lake. (For more information about Loon Lake, see the entries for Pleasant Hike-In/Boat-In and Loon Lake.)

Campsites, facilities: There are 15 sites for tents or self-contained RVs. Picnic tables, fire rings, and grills are provided. Vault toilets are available. No drinking water is available. Leashed pets are permitted.

Reservations, fees: Reservations are not accepted. The fee is $5 per night, $5 for an extra vehicle. Senior discount available. Open June through September.

Directions: From Sacramento, drive east on U.S. 50 to Riverton and the junction with Ice House Road/Soda Springs-Riverton Road on the left. Turn left and drive 34 miles to a fork at the foot of Loon Lake. Turn left and drive three miles to the campground.

Contact: Eldorado Information Center, 530/644-6048, fax 530/295-5624; Eldorado National Forest, Pacific Ranger District, 530/644-2349, fax 530/644-5405.

98 LOON LAKE

🥾 🚣 🎣 🛥 🐴 ♿ 🚐 ⛰

Rating: 9

In Eldorado National Forest.

Map 6.2, page 349

Loon Lake is set near the Sierra crest at 6,400 feet, covering 600 acres with depths up to 130 feet. This is the lake's primary campground, and it is easy to see why, with a picnic area, beach (includes a small unit to change your clothes in), and boat ramp adjacent to the camp. The lake provides good trout fishing, and once the access road is clear of snow, the lake can be stocked every week of summer. Afternoon winds drive anglers off the lake but are cheered by sailboarders. An excellent trail is also available here, with the hike routed along the lake's eastern shore to Pleasant Hike-In/Boat-In where there's a trailhead for the Desolation Wilderness.

Campsites, facilities: There are 53 sites for tents or RVs up to 50 feet long. Picnic tables and fire grills are provided. Drinking water and vault toilets are available. A boat ramp and swimming beach are nearby. Some facilities are wheelchair-accessible. Leashed pets are permitted.

Reservations, fees: Reserve at 877/444-6777 ($9 reservation fee) or website: www.Reserve Usa.com; $15 per night (single), $20 per night (double), $5 for a third vehicle. Open June through early September.

Directions: From Sacramento, drive east on U.S. 50 to Riverton and the junction with Ice House Road/Soda Springs-Riverton Road on the left. Turn left and drive 34 miles to a fork at the foot of Loon Lake. Turn right and drive one mile to the Loon Lake Picnic Area or boat ramp.

Contact: Eldorado Information Center, 530/644-6048, fax 530/295-5624; Eldorado National Forest, Pacific Ranger District, 530/644-2349, fax 530/644-5405.

99 PLEASANT HIKE-IN/BOAT-IN

🥾 🚣 🎣 🛥 🐴 ⛰

Rating: 9

On Loon Lake in Eldorado National Forest.

Map 6.2, page 349

This premium Sierra camp, hike-in or boat-in only, is set on the remote northeast shore of Loon Lake at 6,378 feet in elevation. In many ways this makes for a perfect short vacation. After you reach the camp, a trail is available routed east for four miles past Buck Island Lake (6,436 feet) and Rockbound Lake (6,529 feet), set just inside the northern border of the Desolation Wilderness. When the trail is clear of snow, this makes for a fantastic day hike; a wilderness permit is required if staying overnight inside the wilderness boundary.

Campsites, facilities: There are 10 boat-in or hike-in tent sites. Picnic tables and fire rings are provided. Vault toilets are available. No drinking water is available. Garbage must be packed out. The camp is accessible by boat or trail only. Leashed pets are permitted.

Reservations, fees: Reservations are not accepted. There is no fee for camping. Open June through October.

Directions: From Sacramento, drive east on U.S. 50 to Riverton and the junction with Ice House Road/Soda Springs-Riverton Road on the left. Turn left and drive 34 miles to a fork at the foot of Loon Lake. Turn right and drive a mile to the Loon Lake Picnic Area or boat ramp. Either hike or boat 2.5 miles to the campground on the northeast shore of the lake.

Contact: Eldorado Information Center, 530/644-6048, fax 530/295-5624; Eldorado National Forest, Pacific Ranger District, 530/644-2349, fax 530/644-5405.

100 BIG SILVER GROUP CAMP

Rating: 7

On Big Silver Creek in Eldorado
National Forest.

Map 6.2, page 349

This camp was built along the Union Valley bike trail, less than a mile from Union Valley Reservoir. The paved bike trail stretches for miles both north and south of the campground and is wheelchair-accessible. It's a classic Sierra forest setting, with plenty of ponderosa pine on the north side of Big Silver Creek.

Campsites, facilities: There is a large group site for tents or RVs, with some sites for RVs up to 50 feet long. Picnic tables and fire grills are provided. Vault toilets are available. No drinking water is available. Garbage must be packed out. There is also a group kitchen area with pedestal grills. Some facilities are wheelchair-accessible. Leashed pets are permitted.

Reservations, fees: Reserve at 877/444-6777 ($9 reservation fee) or website: www.Reserve Usa.com; $50 per night. Open late May to mid-October.

Directions: From Sacramento, drive east on U.S. 50 to Riverton and the junction with Ice House Road/Soda Springs-Riverton Road. Turn left and drive about 17 miles to the campground entrance road (three miles past the turnoff for Sunset Camp).

Contact: Eldorado Information Center, 530/644-6048, fax 530/295-5624; Eldorado National Forest, Pacific Ranger District, 530/644-2349, fax 530/647-5405.

101 WOLF CREEK

Rating: 9

On Union Valley Reservoir in Eldorado
National Forest.

Map 6.2, page 349

Wolf Creek Camp is on the north shore of Union Valley Reservoir. Listen up? Notice that

it's quieter? Yep. That's because there are not as many water-skiers in the vicinity. Why? There's no boat ramp in the immediate area. This camp opened in the summer of 1998 and was an immediate hit–hey, maybe it's time to create a major low-speed zone for this lake. The view of the Crystal Range from the campground is drop-dead gorgeous. The elevation is 4,900 feet.

Campsites, facilities: There are 42 sites for tents or RVs up to 50 feet long, and four double sites. Picnic tables and fire grills are provided. Drinking water and vault toilets are available. Some facilities are wheelchair-accessible. A boat ramp is three miles away at the campground at Yellowjacket. Leashed pets are permitted.

Reservations, fees: Reserve at 877/444-6777 ($9 reservation fee) or website: www.Reserve Usa.com; $15 for a single site per night, $30 for a double, $5 for a third vehicle. Senior discount available. Open early-May through October, weather permitting.

Directions: From Sacramento, drive east on U.S. 50 to Riverton and the junction with Ice House Road/Soda Springs-Riverton Road. Turn left and drive 21 miles to Union Valley Road (at the head of Union Valley Reservoir). Turn left and drive 2.5 miles to the campground.

Contact: Eldorado Information Center, 530/644-6048, fax 530/295-5624; Eldorado National Forest, Pacific Ranger District, 530/644-2349, fax 530/647-5405.

102 CAMINO COVE

Rating:10

On Union Valley Reservoir in Eldorado
National Forest.

Map 6.2, page 349

Camino Cove Camp opened in the summer of 2000, and right off, it proved to be the nicest spot at Union Valley Reservoir, a slam dunk. It is set at the north end of the lake on a peninsula, absolutely beautiful, a tree-covered landscape and yet with sweeping views of the Crystal Basin. The nearest boat ramp is 1.5 miles to the west at West Point. If this camp is full, there is a small camp at West Point, with just eight sites. The elevation is 4,900 feet.

Campsites, facilities: There are 32 sites for tents or RVs, with some sites for RVs up to 50 feet long. Fire rings are provided. Vault toilets are available. No drinking water is available. A swimming beach is nearby and a boat ramp is 1.5 miles away at the campground at West Point. Leashed pets are permitted.

Reservations, fees: Reservations are not accepted. There is no fee for camping. Open early-May through October, weather permitting.

Directions: From Sacramento, drive east on U.S. 50 to Riverton and the junction with Ice House Road/Soda Springs-Riverton Road. Turn north on Ice House Road and drive seven miles to Peavine Ridge Road. Turn left and drive three miles to Bryant Springs Road. Turn right and drive five miles north past the West Point boat ramp, and continue 1.5 miles east to the campground entrance on the right.

Contact: Eldorado Information Center, 530/644-6048, fax 530/295-5624; Eldorado National Forest, Pacific Ranger District, 530/644-2349, fax 530/647-5405.

103 YELLOWJACKET

🏊 🛶 🚐 🏕️ 🚙 ⛺

Rating: 8

On Union Valley Reservoir in Eldorado National Forest.

Map 6.2, page 349

The camp is set at 4,900 feet on the north shore of gorgeous Union Valley Reservoir. A boat launch adjacent to the camp makes this an ideal destination for trout-angling campers with boats. Union Valley Reservoir, a popular weekend destination for campers from the Central Valley, is stocked with brook trout and rainbow trout by the Department of Fish and Game.

Campsites, facilities: There are 40 sites for tents or RVs, with some sites for RVs up to 45 feet long. Picnic tables and fire rings are provided. Drinking water and vault toilets are available. A boat ramp is nearby. Leashed pets are permitted.

Reservations, fees: Reserve at 877/444-6777 ($9 reservation fee) or website: www.Reserve Usa.com; $15 for a single site per night, $30 for a double, $5 for a third vehicle. Senior discount available. Open Memorial Day weekend through Labor Day weekend.

Directions: From Sacramento, drive east on U.S. 50 to Riverton and the junction with Ice House Road/Soda Springs-Riverton Road. Turn left and drive 21 miles to Union Valley Road (at the head of Union Valley Reservoir). Turn left and drive a mile to the campground entrance road. Turn left and drive a mile to the campground.

Contact: Eldorado Information Center, 530/644-6048, fax 530/295-5624; Eldorado National Forest, Pacific Ranger District, 530/644-2349, fax 530/647-5405.

104 WENCH CREEK

🏃 🛶 🚐 🏕️ 🐕 🚙 ⛺

Rating: 7

On Union Valley Reservoir in Eldorado National Forest.

Map 6.2, page 349

Wench Creek is on the northeast shore of Union Valley Reservoir. (For more information, see the entries for Jones Fork and Sunset.) The elevation is 4,900 feet.

Campsites, facilities: There are 100 sites for tents or RVs, with some sites for RVs up to 55 feet long. There are also two group sites for up to 50 people each. Picnic tables and fire grills are provided. Drinking water and vault toilets are available. A boat ramp is three miles away at the campground at Yellowjacket. Leashed pets are permitted.

Reservations, fees: No reservations accepted for family sites. The fee is $15 for a site per night, $5 for a third vehicle. Senior discount available. Reserve group sites at 877/444-6777 ($9 reservation fee) or website: www.ReserveUsa.com; $80 group fee. Open mid-May through September.

Directions: From Sacramento, drive east on U.S. 50 to Riverton and the junction with Ice House Road/Soda Springs-Riverton Road. Turn left and drive 19 miles to the campground entrance road (four miles past the turnoff for Sunset Camp). Turn left and drive a mile to the campground at the end of the road.

Contact: Eldorado Information Center, 530/644-6048, fax 530/295-5624; Eldorado National Forest, Pacific Ranger District, 530/644-2349, fax 530/647-5405.

105 AZALEA COVE HIKE-IN/BOAT-IN

Rating: 7

On Union Valley Reservoir in Eldorado National Forest.

Map 6.2, page 349

On the shores of Union Valley Reservoir at 4,900 feet in elevation, there is access to 4.5 miles of bike trail in addition to boating and fishing activities. The distance to the campsite is less than a half mile by boat or by trail. The trail to this camp can be closed in early summer if a bald eagle nest in the vicinity is active, and there is consideration of delaying opening the camp as well. (For additional information, see the entries for Wench Creek and Peninsula Recreation Area.)

Campsites, facilities: There are 10 sites for tents only. Picnic tables and fire grills are provided. Vault toilets are available. No drinking water is available. Garbage must be packed out. Leashed pets are permitted.

Reservations, fees: Reservations are not accepted. There is no fee for camping. Open June through September.

Directions: From Sacramento, drive east on U.S. 50 to Riverton and the junction with Ice House Road/Soda Springs-Riverton Road. Turn left and drive about 17 miles to the camp-

ground entrance road (three miles past the turnoff for Sunset Camp). Park and then hike or boat less than one mile to the campground.

Contact: Eldorado Information Center, 530/644-6048, fax 530/295-5624; Eldorado National Forest, Pacific Ranger District, 530/644-2349, fax 530/647-5405.

106 PENINSULA RECREATION AREA

Rating: 8

On Union Valley Reservoir in Eldorado National Forest.

Map 6.2, page 349

The two campgrounds here, Sunset and Fashoda, are the prettiest of all the camps at Union Valley Reservoir, set at the eastern tip of the peninsula that juts into the lake at the mouth of Jones Fork. A nearby boat ramp (you'll see it on the left on the way in) is a big plus, along with a picnic area and beach. The lake has decent trout fishing, with brook trout, brown trout, rainbow trout, mackinaw, kokanee salamon, and smallmouth bass. The place is gorgeous, set at 4,900 feet in the Sierra Nevada.

Campsites, facilities: There are 131 sites for tents or RVs up to 50 feet long at Sunset Camp and 30 walk-in tent sites at Fashoda Camp. Picnic tables, fire rings, and fire grills are provided. Drinking water and vault toilets are available. A boat ramp and RV dump station are available. Some facilities are wheelchair-accessible. Leashed pets are permitted.

Reservations, fees: Reserve at 877/444-6777 ($9 reservation fee) or website: www.Reserve Usa.com; $15 for a single site per night, $30 for a double, $5 for a third vehicle. Open late May to early September.

Directions: From Sacramento, drive east on U.S. 50 to Riverton and the junction with Ice House Road/Soda Springs-Riverton Road. Turn left and drive 15 miles to the campground entrance road (a mile past the turnoff for Jones

Fork Camp). Turn left and drive 1.5 miles to the campground at the end of the road.

Contact: Eldorado Information Center, 530/644-6048, fax 530/295-5624; Eldorado National Forest, Pacific Ranger District, 530/644-2349, fax 530/647-5405.

107 JONES FORK

Rating: 7

On Union Valley Reservoir in Eldorado National Forest.

Map 6.2, page 349

The Crystal Basin Recreation Area is the most popular backcountry region for campers from the Sacramento area, and Union Valley Reservoir is the centerpiece. The area gets its name from the prominent granite Sierra ridge, which looks like crystal when it is covered with frozen snow. This is a big lake, set at 4,900 feet in elevation, with 10 lakeside campgrounds and three boat ramps providing access. This is the first camp you will arrive at, set at the mouth of the Jones Fork Cove.

Campsites, facilities: There are 10 sites for tents or RVs up to 25 feet long. Picnic tables and fire rings are provided. Vault toilets are available. No drinking water is available. Leashed pets are permitted.

Reservations, fees: Reservations are not accepted. The fee is $5 per night, $5 for a third vehicle. Senior discount available. Open June through October.

Directions: From Sacramento, drive east on U.S. 50 to Riverton and the junction with Ice House Road/Soda Springs-Riverton Road. Turn left and drive 14 miles to the campground entrance road on the left (at the south end of Union Valley Reservoir). Turn left and drive a half mile to the campground.

Contact: Eldorado Information Center, 530/644-6048, fax 530/295-5624; Eldorado National Forest, Pacific Ranger District, 530/644-2349, fax 530/647-5405.

108 SILVER CREEK

Rating: 5

Near Ice House Reservoir in Eldorado National Forest.

Map 6.2, page 349

Silver Creek might be a pretty spot at 5,200 feet in elevation, but it is rarely the destination of campers. Rather, it is primarily used as an overflow spot if the camps at nearby Ice House Reservoir are full. Ice House is only two miles north, and Union Valley Reservoir is four miles north. Note: not recommended for RVs or trailers. Either bring your own drinking water or bring a water filtration pump for stream water.

Campsites, facilities: There are 12 tent sites. Picnic tables and fire grills are provided. Vault toilets are available. No drinking water is available. Leashed pets are permitted.

Reservations, fees: Reservations are not accepted. The fee is $6. Senior discount available. Open June through October.

Directions: From Sacramento, drive east on U.S. 50 to Riverton and the junction with Ice House Road/Soda Springs-Riverton Road. Turn left and drive about seven miles to the campground entrance road on the left (if you reach the junction with Forest Road 3, you have gone a quarter mile too far). Turn left and drive a quarter mile to the campground.

Contact: Eldorado Information Center, 530/644-6048, fax 530/295-5624; Eldorado National Forest, Pacific Ranger District, 530/644-2349, fax 530/647-5405.

109 ICE HOUSE

Rating: 8

On Ice House Reservoir in Eldorado National Forest.

Map 6.2, page 349

Along with Loon Lake and Union Valley Reservoir, Ice House Reservoir is a feature destination in the Crystal Basin Recreation Area.

Ice House gets most of the fishermen and Union Valley gets most of the campers. The camp here is set on the lake's northwestern shore, 5,500 feet in elevation, just up from the dam and adjacent to the lake's boat ramp. The lake was created by a dam on South Fork Silver Creek and covers 650 acres, with the deepest spot about 130 feet deep. It is stocked with rainbow trout, brook trout, and brown trout.

Campsites, facilities: There are 17 sites for tents and 66 sites for tents or RVs up to 50 feet long. Three sites are wheelchair-accessible. Picnic tables and fire grills are provided. Drinking water, vault toilets, boat ramp, and RV dump station are available. Leashed pets are permitted.

Reservations, fees: Reserve at 877/444-6777 ($9 reservation fee) or website: www.ReserveUsa.com; $15 for a single site per night, $30 for a double, $5 for a third vehicle. Senior discount available. Open June through October.

Directions: From Sacramento, drive east on U.S. 50 to Riverton and the junction with Ice House Road/Soda Springs-Riverton Road. Turn left and drive about 11 miles to the junction with Forest Road 3 and Ice House Road. Turn right on Ice House Road and drive two miles to the campground access road on the right.

Contact: Eldorado Information Center, 530/644-6048, fax 530/295-5624; Eldorado National Forest, Pacific Ranger District, 530/644-2349, fax 530/647-5405.

110 NORTHWIND

Rating: 7

On Ice House Reservoir in Eldorado National Forest.

Map 6.2, page 349

This camp sits on the north shore of Ice House Reservoir. It is slightly above the reservoir, offering prime views. (See the entry for Ice House for more information.)

Campsites, facilities: There are nine sites for tents or RVs up to 25 feet long, and one double site. Picnic tables and fire grills are pro-

vided. Vault toilets are available. No drinking water is available. Leashed pets are permitted.

Reservations, fees: Reservations are not accepted. The fee is $5 per night, $5 for a third vehicle. Senior discount available. Open June through October.

Directions: From Sacramento, drive east on U.S. 50 to Riverton and the junction with Ice House Road/Soda Springs-Riverton Road. Turn left and drive about 11 miles to the junction with Forest Road 3 and Ice House Road. Turn right on Ice House Road and drive about three miles (two miles past the boat ramp) to the campground access road on the right.

Contact: Eldorado Information Center, 530/644-6048, fax 530/295-5624; Eldorado National Forest, Pacific Ranger District, 530/644-2349, fax 530/647-5405.

111 STRAWBERRY POINT

Rating: 7

On Ice House Reservoir in Eldorado National Forest.

Map 6.2, page 349

This camp is set on the north shore of Ice House Reservoir, 5,400 feet in elevation. (For more information, see the entry for Ice House.)

Campsites, facilities: There are 10 sites for tents or RVs up to 50 feet long. Picnic tables and fire grills are provided. Vault toilets are available. No drinking water is available. Leashed pets are permitted.

Reservations, fees: Reservations are not accepted. The fee is $5 per night, $5 for a third vehicle. Senior discount available. Open March through December, weather permitting.

Directions: From Sacramento, drive east on U.S. 50 to Riverton and the junction with Ice House Road/Soda Springs-Riverton Road. Turn left and drive about 11 miles to the junction with Forest Road 3 and Ice House Road. Turn right on Ice House Road and drive about four miles (three miles past the boat ramp) to the campground access road on the right.

Contact: Eldorado Information Center, 530/644-6048, fax 530/295-5624; Eldorado National Forest, Pacific Ranger District, 530/644-2349, fax 530/647-5405.

112 WRIGHTS LAKE

Rating: 9

In Eldorado National Forest.

Map 6.2, page 349

This high mountain lake (7,000 feet) has shoreline camping and good fishing and hiking. There is no boat ramp, plus rules do not permit motors, so it is ideal for canoes, rafts, prams, and people who like quiet. Fishing is fair for both rainbow trout and brown trout. It is a classic Alpine lake, though small (65 acres), with a trailhead for the Desolation Wilderness at its north end. From here it is only a three-mile hike to the beautiful Twin Lakes and Island Lake, set on the western flank of Mt. Price (9,975 feet).

Campsites, facilities: There are 35 sites for tents and 36 sites for tents or RVs up to 50 feet long. Picnic tables and fire grills are provided. Drinking water and vault toilets are available. Leashed pets are permitted.

Reservations, fees: Reserve at 877/444-6777 ($9 reservation fee) or website: www.Reserve Usa.com; $13 per night (single), $20 per night (double), $5 for a third vehicle. Senior discount available. Open late June to early October, weather permitting.

Directions: From Sacramento, drive east on U.S. 50 about 20 miles beyond Placerville. Turn left on Ice House Road and drive north 11.5 miles to Ice House Reservoir. Turn east on Road 32 and drive 10 miles. Turn left on Wrights Lake Road and drive two miles to the campground on the right side of the road.

Contact: Eldorado Information Center, 530/644-6048, fax 530/295-5624; Eldorado National Forest, Pacific Ranger District, 530/644-2349, fax 530/644-5405.

113 D. L. BLISS STATE PARK

Rating:10

On Lake Tahoe.

Map 6.2, page 349

D. L. Bliss State Park is set on one of Lake Tahoe's most beautiful stretches of shoreline, from Emerald Point at the mouth of Emerald Bay on northward to Rubicon Point, spanning about three miles. The camp is at the north end of the park, the sites nestled amid pine trees, with 80 percent of the campsites within a half mile to mile of the beach. The grandeur of this park and landscape is the result of successive upheavals of the mountain-building process that raised the Sierra Nevada range. The park is named for a pioneering lumberman, railroad owner, and banker of the region, whose family donated this 744-acre parcel to California in 1929. There are two great easy hiking trails. The Rubicon Trail is one of Tahoe's most popular easy hikes, a meandering path just above the southwest shore of Lake Tahoe, wandering through pine, cedars, and firs, with breaks for fantastic panoramas of the lake, as well as spots where you can see nearly 100 feet into the lake. Don't be surprised if you are joined by a chipmunk circus, many begging, sitting upright, hoping for their nut for the day. While this trail is beautiful and solitary at dawn, by noon it can be crowded by hikers and chipmunks alike. Another trail, a great hike for youngsters, is the Balancing Rock Trail, just a half mile romp, where after about 40 yards you arrive at this 130-ton, oblong granite boulder that is set on a tiny perch, and the whole thing seems to defy gravity. Some day it has to fall, right? Not yet. The Rubicon Trail runs all the way past Emerald Point to Emerald Bay. One major downer: all water must be pump-filtered or boiled before drinking or other use.

Campsites, facilities: There are 165 sites for tents or RVs up to 18 feet long and trailers up to 15 feet long, one hike-in or bike-in site, and a group site for up to 50 people. Picnic tables, fire grills, and food lockers are provided. Restrooms, coin showers, and flush toilets are available. All water must be pump filtered or boiled before use. Leashed pets are permitted at campsites only.

Reservations, fees: Reserve at 800/444-PARK (800/444-7275) or website: www.Reserve America.com ($7.50 reservation fee); $12 per night, $37 per night for group site, $3 per night for hike-in site. Senior discount available. Open May through mid-October, weather permitting.

Directions: In South Lake Tahoe at the junction of Highway 89 and U.S. 50, turn north on Highway 89 and drive 10.5 miles to the state park turnoff on the right side of the road. Turn right (east) and drive to the park entrance. (If arriving from the north, drive from Tahoe City south on Highway 89 for 17 miles to park entrance road).

Contact: D. L. Bliss State Park, 530/525-7232, fax 530/525-7277.

114 EMERALD BAY STATE PARK AND BOAT-IN

Rating:10

On Lake Tahoe.

Map 6.2, page 349

This is one of the most beautiful and popular state parks on the planet. The campground is set at Eagle Point, near the mouth of Emerald Bay on Lake Tahoe, a place of rare, divine beauty. Although the high number of people at Lake Tahoe, and at this park in particular, present inevitable problems, there are remarkable solutions: 20 boat-in sites and two hike-in sites. There may be no more beautiful place anywhere to run a boat than in Emerald Bay, with its deep cobalt-blue waters, awesome surrounding ridgelines, glimpses of Lake Tahoe out the mouth of the bay, and even a little island. The park also has several short hiking trails. Emerald Bay is a designated underwater park. It features Fanette Island,

Tahoe's only island. The park also features Vikingsholm, one of the finest examples of Scandinavian architecture in North America; tours are available and very popular, and the hike here features a two-mile round trip with 500-foot drop in elevation to the "castle." The boat-in camps are on the northern side of Emerald Bay at the site of the old Emerald Bay Resort.

Campsites, facilities: There are 100 sites for tents or RVs up to 21 feet long and trailers up to 18 feet long, two hike-in sites, and 22 boat-in sites. Picnic tables and fire grills are provided. Drinking water, restrooms, flush toilets, and coin-operated showers are available. At boat-in sites, water and toilets are available. Leashed pets are permitted in campground and on asphalt.

Reservations, fees: Reserve at 800/444-PARK (800/444-7275) or website: www.Reserve America.com ($7.50 reservation fee); $12 per night. No reservations for boat-in sites, $10 per night; $3 per night for hike-in sites. Senior discount available. Open late May through early September.

Directions: In South Lake Tahoe at the junction of Highway 89 and U.S. 50, turn north on Highway 89 and drive 6.5 miles to the state park entrance turnoff on the right side of the road.

Contact: Emerald Bay State Park, 530/541-3030 or 530/525-7277.

115 CAMP RICHARDSON RESORT

Rating: 7

On Lake Tahoe.

Map 6.2, page 349

Camp Richardson Resort is within minutes of boating, biking, gambling and, in the winter, skiing. It's a take-your-pick deal. With cabins, restaurant, and live music (often nightly in summer) also on the property, this is a place that offers one big package. The campsites are set in the woods, not on the lake itself. From here you can gain access to an excellent bike route that runs for three miles, then loops around by the lake for another three miles, most of it flat and easy, all of it beautiful. Expect company. The elevation is 6,300 feet.

Campsites, facilities: There are 223 sites for tents, 112 sites with full or partial hookups, including some drive-through, for RVs up to 35 feet, cabins, and hotel rooms. Picnic tables and fire pits are provided. Restrooms, drinking water, showers, flush toilets, RV dump station, and playground are available. A boat ramp, boat rentals, groceries, restaurant, ice cream parlor, and propane gas are available nearby. A swimming beach and bike rentals are also available. Some facilities are wheelchair-accessible. No pets are allowed.

Reservations, fees: Reservations are recommended. Fees are $17–25 per night, $5 for each additional vehicle. Major credit cards accepted. Open June through October.

Directions: In South Lake Tahoe at the junction of Highway 89 and U.S. 50, turn north on Highway 89 and drive 2.5 miles to the resort on the right side of the road.

Contact: Camp Richardson Resort, 800/544-1801 (reservations) or 530/541-1801, fax 530/541-1802, website: www.camprichardson.com.

116 CAMP SHELLEY
🚴 🏊 🛶 🚤 🐕 ♿ 🚙 ⛺

Rating: 7

Near Lake Tahoe in the Lake Tahoe Basin.
Map 6.2, page 349

This campground is set near South Lake Tahoe within close range of an outstanding bicycle trail. The camp is set in the woods, with campfire programs available on Saturday night in summer. Nearby to the west is the drive to Inspiration Point and the incredible lookout of Emerald Bay, as well as the parking area for the short hike to Eagle Falls. Nearby to the east are Fallen Leaf Lake and the south shore of Lake Tahoe.

Campsites, facilities: There are 26 sites for tents

or RVs up to 22 feet long. Picnic tables and fire grills are provided. Drinking water and vault toilets are available. Some facilities are wheelchair-accessible. A boat ramp, groceries, and propane gas are available nearby at Camp Richardson. Leashed pets are permitted.

Reservations, fees: Reservations can be made in person, Monday through Friday, 9 A.M. to 4 P.M. at the Livermore Recreation and Park District Office, 71 Trevarno Rd., Livermore, CA 94550. Reservations can also be made at the campground office, which is intermittently staffed during the season; $25 fee per night, ($18 for Livermore residents), $5 extra vehicle. Open mid-June through Labor Day Weekend.

Directions: In South Lake Tahoe at the junction of U.S. 50 and Highway 89, turn north on Highway 89, drive 2.5 miles to Camp Richardson, and then continue for 1.3 miles to the sign for Mt. Tallac. Turn left on Mt. Tallac Trailhead Road and drive to the campground on the right.

Contact: Camp Shelley, 530/541-6985; Livermore Area Recreation and Park District, 925/373-5700.

117 FALLEN LEAF CAMPGROUND
🏊 🛶 🚤 🐕 🚙 ⛺

Rating: 7

In the Lake Tahoe Basin.
Map 6.2, page 349

This is a large "tent city" near the north shore of Fallen Leaf Lake, set at 6,337 feet. The lake is almost as deep blue as nearby Lake Tahoe. It's a big lake, three miles long, and also quite deep, 430 feet at its deepest point. The campground is operated by the concessionaire, which provides a variety of recreational opportunities, including a boat ramp and horseback riding rentals. Fishing is best in the fall for kokanee salmon. Because Fallen Leaf Lake is circled by forest and much of it is private property, you will need a boat to fish or explore the lake. A visitor center is north of the Fallen Leaf Lake turnoff on Highway 89.

Campsites, facilities: There are 75 sites for tents and 130 sites for tents or RVs up to 40 feet long. Picnic tables and fire grills are provided. Drinking water and vault toilets are available. A boat ramp, coin laundry, and supplies are available nearby. Leashed pets are permitted.

Reservations, fees: Reserve at 877/444-6777 ($9 reservation fee) or website: www.Reserve Usa.com; $16 per night, $5 per night for each extra vehicle (unless towed). Senior discount available. Open May through October, weather permitting.

Directions: In South Lake Tahoe at the junction of U.S. 50 and Highway 89, turn north on Highway 89 and drive two miles to the Fallen Leaf Lake turnoff. Turn left and drive 1.5 miles to the campground.

Contact: Lake Tahoe Basin Management Unit, Visitor Center, 530/573-2674, fax 530/573-2693; California Land Management, 530/544-0426.

118 TAHOE VALLEY CAMPGROUND

Rating: 5

Near Lake Tahoe.
Map 6.2, page 349

This is a massive, privately operated park near South Lake Tahoe. The nearby attractions include five golf courses, horseback riding, casinos and, of course, "The Lake."

Campsites, facilities: There are 305 sites, including some drive-through, with full or partial hookups for RVs, and 77 sites for tents. Picnic tables and fire grills are provided. Restrooms, showers, modem access, RV dump station, coin laundry, seasonal heated swimming pool, playground, tennis courts, grocery store, RV supplies, propane gas, ice, firewood, cable TV, and a recreation room are available. Some facilities are wheelchair-accessible. Leashed pets are permitted.

Reservations, fees: Reservations are recommended. Fees are $24–40 per night. Monthly rates available. Major credit cards accepted. Open year-round.

Directions: Entering South Lake Tahoe on U.S. 50, drive east on U.S. 50 to Meyers. Continue on U.S. 50 about five miles beyond Meyers to the signed entrance on the right.

Contact: Tahoe Valley Campground, 530/541-2222, fax 530/541-1825.

119 CHRIS HAVEN MOBILE HOME AND RV PARK

Rating: 5

Near South Lake Tahoe.
Map 6.2, page 349

This is an RV-only park that is set within the boundaries of a mobile home park, within close range of the casinos to the east. About 75 percent of the campsites are long-term rentals for the summer.

Campsites, facilities: There are 30 sites with full hookups, including some drive-through, for RVs up to 40 feet. Patios, restrooms, showers, modem access and telephone hookups, cable TV, and a coin laundry are available. Some facilities are wheelchair-accessible. Leashed pets are permitted.

Reservations, fees: Reservations are recommended. Fees are $28–30 per night. Monthly rates available. Major credit cards accepted. Open year-round.

Directions: Entering South Lake Tahoe on U.S. 50, drive east to E Street (a half mile south of the junction of U.S. 50 and Highway 89). Turn left on E Street and drive one block to the park on the right.

Contact: Chris Haven Mobile Home and RV Park, 530/541-1895, fax 530/541-4248, website: www.chrishaven.com

120 CAMPGROUND BY THE LAKE

Rating: 5

Near Lake Tahoe.
Map 6.2, page 349

This city-operated campground provides an

option at South Lake Tahoe. It is set at 6,200 feet, across the road from the lake, with pine trees and views of the lake.

Campsites, facilities: There are 170 sites, including some drive-through and some with partial hookups, for tents or RVs up to 32 feet long, and one cabin. Picnic tables and fire grills are provided. Drinking water, flush toilets, showers, RV dump station, playground, and a boat ramp are available. An indoor ice skating rink and a public indoor heated pool is available nearby (fee for access). Some facilities are wheelchair-accessible. Supplies and a coin laundry are nearby. Pets are permitted with proof of vaccinations.

Reservations, fees: Reservations are accepted. The fee is $18–25 per night fpr up to four people with two-night minimum on holidays, $2 for each additional vehicle, $1 per night. Major credit cards accepted. Open April through October.

Directions: Entering South Lake Tahoe on U.S. 50, drive east on U.S. 50 to Rufus Allen Boulevard. Turn right and drive a quarter mile to the campground on the right side of the road.

Contact: Campground by the Lake, City of South Lake Tahoe, 530/542-6096 or 530/542-6055, website: www.ci.south-lake-tahoe.ca.us.

121 KOA SOUTH LAKE TAHOE

Rating: 5

Near Lake Tahoe.

Map 6.2, page 349

Like so many KOA camps, this one is on the outskirts of a major destination area, in this case, South Lake Tahoe. It is within close range of gambling, fishing, hiking, and bike rentals. The camp is set at 6,300 feet.

Campsites, facilities: There are 40 sites with full hookups, including some drive-through, for RVs up to 30 feet long, and 16 sites for tents and self-contained RVs. Picnic tables and fire grills are provided. Restrooms, showers, RV dump station, recreation room, seasonal swimming pool, cable TV, and a playground

are available, weather permitting. Coin laundry, groceries, RV supplies, and propane gas are also available. Leashed pets are permitted.

Reservations, fees: Reservations are recommended at 800/562-3477; $28–36 per night, $3.50 per person for more than two people, $3.50 per additional vehicles, $3.50 per night. Open April through mid-October.

Directions: From Sacramento, take U.S. 50 and drive east over the Sierra Nevada past Echo Summit to Meyers. As you enter Meyers, it will be the first campground on the right. Turn right and enter the campground.

Contact: KOA South Lake Tahoe, 530/577-3693, website: www.laketahoekoa.com.

122 CAPPS CROSSING

Rating: 7

On the North Fork of the Consumes River in Eldorado National Forest.

Map 6.2, page 349

This camp is set out in the middle of nowhere along the North Fork of the Cosumnes River. It's a primitive spot that doesn't get much use. This camp is in the western reaches of a vast number of backcountry Forest Service roads. A map of Eldorado National Forest is a must to explore them. The elevation is 5,200 feet.

Campsites, facilities: There are 11 tent sites. Picnic tables and fire grills are provided. Drinking water and vault toilets are available. Leashed pets are permitted.

Reservations, fees: Reservations are not accepted. The fee is $12 per night. Senior discount available. Open June through October.

Directions: From Sacramento, drive east on U.S. 50 to Placerville and continue for 12 miles to the Sly Park Road exit. Turn right and drive about six miles to the Mormon Emigrant Trail/Forest Road 5. Turn left on Mormon Emigrant Trail and drive about 13 miles to North-South Road/Forest Road 6. Turn right (south) on North-South Road and drive about six miles to the campground on the left side of the road.

Contact: Eldorado Information Center, 530/644-6048; Eldorado National Forest, Placerville Ranger District, 530/644-6048, fax 530/295-5994.

123 SAND FLAT

Rating: 7

On the South Fork of the American River in Eldorado National Forest.

Map 6.2, page 349

This first-come, first-served campground often gets filled up by U.S. 50 travelers. And why not? You get easy access, a well-signed exit, and a nice setting on the South Fork of the American River. The elevation is 3,900 feet. The river is very pretty here, but fishing is often poor. In winter the snow level usually starts just a few miles uphill.

Campsites, facilities: There are 29 sites for tents or RVs up to 40 feet. Picnic tables and fire grills are provided. Drinking water and vault toilets are available. Groceries, restaurant, and gas are available nearby. Leashed pets are permitted.

Reservations, fees: Reservations are not accepted. The fee is $11 per night, $5 per night for each extra vehicle. Senior discount available. Open year-round.

Directions: From Sacramento, drive east on U.S. 50 to Placerville and then continue 28 miles to the campground on the right.

Contact: Eldorado Information Center, 530/644-6048, fax 530/295-5624; Eldorado National Forest, Placerville Ranger District, 530/644-2324, fax 530/295-5994.

124 CHINA FLAT

Rating: 7

On the Silver Fork of the American River in Eldorado National Forest.

Map 6.2, page 349

China Flat sits across the road from the Silver Fork American River, with a nearby access road that is routed along the river for a mile. This provides access for fishing, swimming, gold panning, and exploring. The camp feels far off the beaten path, even though it is only five minutes from that parade of traffic on U.S. 50.

Campsites, facilities: There are 18 sites and one double site for tents or RVs up to 60 feet long. Picnic tables and fire grills are provided. Drinking water and vault toilets are available. Some facilities are wheelchair-accessible. Leashed pets are permitted.

Reservations, fees: Reservations are not accepted. The fee is $12 per night, $24 per night for the double site, $5 per night for each extra vehicle. Senior discount available. Open May through October.

Directions: From Sacramento, drive east on U.S. 50 to Kyburz and Silver Fork Road. Turn right and drive three miles to the campground on the right side of the road.

Contact: Eldorado Information Center, 530/644-6048, fax 530/295-5624; Eldorado National Forest, Placerville Ranger District, 530/644-2324, fax 530/295-5994.

125 SILVER FORK

Rating: 7

On the Silver Fork of the American River in Eldorado National Forest.

Map 6.2, page 349

The tons of vacationers driving U.S. 50 along the South Fork American River always get frustrated when they try to fish or camp, because there are precious few opportunities for either, with about zero trout and camps alike. But, just 20 minutes off the beaten path, you can find both at Silver Fork Camp. The access road provides many fishing opportunities and is stocked with rainbow trout by the state. The camp is set right along the river, at 5,500 feet in elevation, in Eldorado National Forest.

Campsites, facilities: There are 35 sites for tents or RVs up to 65 feet long and four double-family sites. Picnic tables and fire grills are provided. Drinking water and vault toilets are available. Some of the facilities are wheelchair-accessible. Leashed pets are permitted.

Reservations, fees: Reservations are not accepted. The fee is $12 per night, $24 for double-family sites. Senior discount available. Open May through October.

Directions: From Sacramento, drive east on U.S. 50 to Kyburz and Silver Fork Road. Turn right and drive eight miles to the campground on the right side of the road.

Contact: Eldorado Information Center, 530/644-6048; Eldorado National Forest, Placerville Ranger District, 530/644-6048, fax 530/295-5994.

126 SILVER LAKE WEST

Rating: 9

On Silver Lake in Eldorado National Forest.
Map 6.2, page 349

The Highway 88 corridor provides access to three excellent lakes: Lower Bear River Reservoir, Silver Lake, and Caples Lake. Silver Lake is difficult to pass by, with cabin rentals, pretty campsites, decent trout fishing, and excellent hiking. The lake is set at 7,200 feet in a classic granite cirque just below the Sierra ridge. This camp is on the west side of Highway 88, across the road from the lake. A great hike starts at the trailhead on the east side of the lake, a two-mile tromp to little Hidden Lake, one of several nice hikes in the area. In addition, horseback riding rentals are available nearby at Plasse's Resort.

Campsites, facilities: There are 42 sites for tents or RVs up to 30 feet long. Picnic tables and fire pits are provided. Vault toilets are available. No drinking water is available. Leashed pets are permitted. Maximum of six people and two pets per site.

Reservations, fees: Reservations are not accepted. The fee is $13 per night, $9 per night for each extra vehicle, $1 per night. Senior dis-

count available. Open Memorial Day Weekend through October, weather permitting.

Directions: From Jackson, drive east on Highway 88 for 50 miles (to the north end of Silver Lake) to the campground entrance road on the left.

Contact: Eldorado Irrigation District, 530/644-1960, fax 530/644-5155.

127 EAST SILVER LAKE

Rating: 7

In Eldorado National Forest.
Map 6.2, page 349

Silver Lake is an easy-to-reach Alpine lake set at 7,200 feet, which provides a beautiful setting, good trout fishing, and hiking. This camp is on the northeast side of the lake, with a boat ramp nearby. (See the entry for Silver Lake West for more information.)

Campsites, facilities: There are 28 sites for tents and 34 sites for tents or RVs. Picnic tables and fire grills are provided. Drinking water and vault toilets are available. A grocery store, boat rentals, boat ramp, and propane gas are nearby. Leashed pets are permitted.

Reservations, fees: Reserve at 877/444-6777 ($9 reservation fee) or website: www.Reserve Usa.com; $13 per night. Senior discount available. Open June through October.

Directions: From Jackson, drive east on Highway 88 for 50 miles (to the north end of Silver Lake) to the campground entrance road on the right.

Contact: Eldorado Information Center, 530/644-6048, fax 530/295-5624; Eldorado National Forest, Amador Ranger District, 209/295-4251, fax 209/295-5994.

128 KIRKWOOD LAKE

Rating: 8

In Eldorado National Forest.
Map 6.2, page 349

Little Kirkwood Lake is in a beautiful Sierra

setting, with good shoreline access, fishing for small rainbow trout, and quiet water. Despite that, it is often overlooked in favor of nearby Silver Lake and Caples Lake along Highway 88. Nearby Kirkwood Ski Resort stays open all summer and offers excellent opportunities for horseback riding, hiking, and meals. The elevation is 7,600 feet. Note: no trailers. The access road is too narrow.

Campsites, facilities: There are 12 sites for tents and small RVs. Picnic tables and fire grills are provided. Drinking water and vault toilets are available. Leashed pets are permitted.

Reservations, fees: Reservations are not accepted. The fee is $12 per night, $5 per extra vehicle per night. Senior discount available. Open June through October.

Directions: From Jackson, drive east on Highway 88 for 60 miles (four miles past Silver Lake) to the campground entrance road on the left (if you reach the sign for Kirkwood Ski Resort, you have gone a half mile too far). Turn left and drive a quarter mile (road not suitable for large RVs and trailers are not allowed) to the campground on the left.

Contact: Eldorado Information Center, 530/644-6048, fax 530/295-5624; Eldorado National Forest, Amador Ranger District, 209/295-4251, fax 209/295-5994.

129 CAPLES LAKE

Rating: 8

In Eldorado National Forest.
Map 6.2, page 349
Caples Lake, here in the high country at 7,800 feet, is a pretty lake right along Highway 88. It covers 600 acres, has a 10-mph speed limit, and provides good trout fishing and excellent hiking terrain. The camp is set across the highway (a little two-laner) from the lake, with the Caples Lake Resort and boat rentals nearby. There is a parking area at the west end of the lake, and from here you can begin a great 3.5-mile hike to Emigrant Lake, in the Mokelumne

Wilderness on the western flank of Mt. Round Top (10,310 feet).

Campsites, facilities: There are 20 sites for tents and 15 sites for tents or RVs up to 22 feet long. Picnic tables and fire grills are provided. Drinking water and vault toilets are available. Groceries, propane gas, boat ramp, and boat rentals are nearby. Leashed pets are permitted.

Reservations, fees: Reservations are not accepted. The fee is $12 per night, $6 per night for additional vehicle, $24 per night for a double site. Senior discount available. Open June through October.

Directions: From Jackson, drive east on Highway 88 for 63 miles (one mile past the entrance road to Kirkwood Ski Area) to the camp entrance road on the left.

Contact: Eldorado Information Center, 530/644-6048, fax 530/295-5624; Eldorado National Forest, Amador Ranger District, 209/295-4251, fax 209/295-5994.

130 WOODS LAKE

Rating: 9

In Eldorado National Forest.
Map 6.2, page 349
Woods Lake is only two miles from Highway 88, yet it can provide campers the feeling of visiting a far-off land. It is a small but beautiful lake in the granite backdrop of the high Sierra, set at 8,200 feet near Carson Pass. Boats with motors are not permitted, making it ideal for canoes and rowboats. Trout fishing is fair. A great trailhead is available here, a three-mile loop hike to little Round Top Lake and Winnemucca Lake (twice the size of Woods Lake) and back. They are set on the northern flank of Mt. Round Top (10,310 feet).

Campsites, facilities: There are 25 tent sites and a multiple-family unit. Picnic tables and fire rings are provided. Drinking water (hand-pumped) and vault toilets are available. Groceries and propane gas are available within five miles. Leashed pets are permitted.

Reservations, fees: Reservations are not accepted. The fee is $12 per night, $5 for additional vehicle per night, $24 for double site. Senior discount available. Open June through October, weather permitting.

Directions: From Jackson, drive east on Highway 88 to Caples Lake and continue for a mile to the Woods Lake turnoff on the right (two miles west of Carson Pass). Turn south and drive a mile to the campground on the right (trailers and RVs are not recommended).

Contact: Eldorado Information Center, 530/644-6048, fax 530/295-5624; Eldorado National Forest, Amador Ranger District, 209/295-4257, fax 209/295-5998.

131 SOUTH SHORE

Rating: 7

On Bear River Reservoir in Eldorado National Forest.

Map 6.2, page 349

Bear River Reservoir is set at 5,900 feet, which means it becomes ice-free earlier in the spring than its uphill neighbors to the east, Silver Lake and Caples Lake. It is a good-sized lake—725 acres—and cold and deep, too. It gets double-barreled trout stocks, receiving fish from the state and from the operator of the lake's marina and lodge. This campground is on the lake's southern shore, just east of the dam. Explorers can drive south for five miles to Salt Springs Reservoir, which has a trailhead and parking area on the north side of the dam for a great day hike along the lake.

Campsites, facilities: There are 13 sites for tents and nine sites for tents or RVs. There are four two-family sites. Picnic tables and fire grills are provided. Drinking water and vault toilets are available. A boat ramp, grocery store, boat rentals, and propane gas are available at nearby Bear River Lake Resort. Leashed pets are permitted.

Reservations, fees: Reservations are not accepted. The fee is $11 per night, $22 per night for two-family sites. Senior discount available. Open June through October.

Directions: From Stockton, drive east on Highway 88 for about 80 miles to the lake entrance on the right side of the road (well signed). Turn right and drive four miles (past the dam) to the campground entrance on the right side of the road.

Contact: Eldorado Information Center, 530/644-6048, fax 530/295-5624; Eldorado National Forest, Amador Ranger District, 209/295-4251, fax 209/295-5994.

132 BEAR RIVER GROUP CAMP

Rating: 6

On Bear River Reservoir in Eldorado National Forest.

Map 6.2, page 349

This is a group camp set near Bear River Reservoir, a pretty lake that provides power boating and trout fishing. (See the entry for South Shore, which is just a mile from this camp.)

Campsites, facilities: There are three group sites for tents; two sites can accommodate 25 people each and one site can accommodate 50 people. Picnic tables and fire grills are provided. Drinking water, vault toilets, and wash racks are available. A grocery store, boat ramp, boat rentals, and propane gas are available nearby. Leashed pets are permitted.

Reservations, fees: Reservations are required. Fees are $50-100 per night. Open mid-June through mid-September, weather permitting.

Directions: From Stockton, drive east on Highway 88 for about 80 miles to the lake entrance on the right side of the road (well signed). Turn right and drive five miles (past the dam) to the campground entrance on the left side of the road.

Contact: Eldorado Information Center, 530/644-6048, fax 530/295-5624; Eldorado National Forest, Amador Ranger District, 209/295-4251, fax 209/295-5994.

133 BEAR RIVER LAKE RESORT

Rating: 8

On Bear River Reservoir.

Map 6.2, page 349

Bear River Lake Resort is a complete vacation service lodge, with everything you could ask for. A lot of people have been asking in recent years, making this a popular spot that often requires a reservation. The resort also sponsors fishing derbies in the summer and sweetens the pot considerably by stocking exceptionally large rainbow trout. The resort is set at 6,000 feet. The lake freezes over in the winter. (For more information about Bear River Reservoir, see the entry for South Shore.)

Campsites, facilities: There are 150 sites, all with partial hookups, for tents or RVs up to 35 feet, and eight lodging units. Picnic tables and fire grills are provided. Restrooms, drinking water, coin showers, RV dump station, boat ramp, boat rentals, firewood, ice, propane gas, coin laundry, modem access, pay phone, restaurant and cocktail lounge, and a grocery store are available. Some facilities are wheelchair-accessible. Leashed pets are permitted at campsites. No pets in lodging units.

Reservations, fees: Reservations are recommended. The fee is $22 per night, $5 per extra vehicle per night, $5 one-time pet fee. Major credit cards accepted. Open year-round (call for access in winter).

Directions: From Stockton, drive east on Highway 88 for about 80 miles to the lake entrance on the right side of the road (well signed). Turn right and drive 2.5 miles to a junction (if you pass the dam, you have gone a quarter mile too far). Turn left and drive a half mile to the campground entrance on the right side of the road.

Contact: Bear River Reservoir, 209/295-4868, fax 209/295-4585, website: www.bearriver lake.com.

134 WHITE AZALEA

Rating: 7

On the Mokelumne River in Eldorado National Forest.

Map 6.2, page 349

Out here in the remote Mokelumne River Canyon are three primitive camps set on the Mokelumne's North Fork. White Azalea, 3,500 feet in elevation, is the closest of the three to Salt Springs Reservoir, the prime recreation destination. It's about a three-mile drive to the dam and an adjacent parking area for a wilderness trailhead for the Mokelumne Wilderness. This trail makes a great day hike, routed for four miles along the north shore of Salt Springs Reservoir to Blue Hole at the head of the lake.

Campsites, facilities: There are six tent sites. Vault toilets are provided. No drinking water is available. Garbage must be packed out. Leashed pets are permitted.

Reservations, fees: Reservations are not accepted. There is no fee for camping. Open year-round, weather permitting.

Directions: From Jackson, drive east on Highway 88 to Pioneer and then continue for 18 miles to Ellis Road/Forest Road 92 (78 miles from Jackson), at a signed turnoff for Lumberyard Campground. Turn right on Ellis Road and drive 12 miles to Salt Springs Road (Forest Road 9). Turn left, cross Bear River, and continue for three miles to the campground on the right. The road is steep, narrow, and curvy in spots, not good for RVs or trailers.

Contact: Eldorado Information Center, 530/644-6048, fax 530/295-5624; Eldorado National Forest, Amador Ranger District, 209/295-4251, fax 209/295-5994.

135 MOORE CREEK

🏊 🛶 🐕 🏕

Rating: 7

On the Mokelumne River in Eldorado National Forest.

Map 6.2, page 349

This camp is set at 3,200 feet elevation on little Moore Creek, a feeder stream to the nearby North Fork Mokelumne River. It's one of three primitive camps within two miles. (See the entry for White Azalea for more information.)

Campsites, facilities: There are eight tent sites. Vault toilets are provided, and some sites have picnic tables. No drinking water is available. Garbage must be packed out. Leashed pets are permitted.

Reservations, fees: Reservations are not accepted. There is no fee for camping. Open year-round, weather permitting.

Directions: From Jackson, drive east on Highway 88 to Pioneer and then continue for 18 miles to Ellis Road/Forest Road 92 (78 miles from Jackson), at a signed turnoff for Lumberyard Campground. Turn right on Ellis Road and drive 12 miles to Salt Springs Road (Forest Road 9). Turn right and drive 2.5 miles, cross the bridge over the Mokelumne River, and turn right on the campground entrance road. Drive a quarter mile to the campground on the right. The road is steep, narrow, and winding in spots—not good for RVs or trailers.

Contact: Eldorado Information Center, 530/644-6048, fax 530/295-5624; Eldorado National Forest, Amador Ranger District, 209/295-4251, fax 209/295-5994.

136 MOKELUMNE

🏊 🛶 🐕 🚐 🏕

Rating: 7

On the Mokelumne River in Eldorado National Forest.

Map 6.2, page 349

This primitive spot is set beside the Mokelumne River at 3,200 feet in elevation, one of three primitive camps in the immediate area. (See the entry for White Azalea for more information.) There are some good swimming holes nearby. Fishing is fair, with the trout on the small side.

Campsites, facilities: There are five tent sites and eight sites for tents or RVs. Vault toilets are provided. No drinking water is available. Garbage must be packed out (it is occasionally serviced in summer). Leashed pets are permitted.

Reservations, fees: Reservations are not accepted. There is no fee for camping. Open year-round, weather permitting.

Directions: From Jackson, drive east on Highway 88 to Pioneer and then continue for 18 miles to Ellis Road/Forest Road 92 (78 miles from Jackson), at a signed turnoff for Lumberyard Campground. Turn right on Ellis Road and drive 12 miles to Salt Springs Road (Forest Road 9). Turn right and drive 2.5 miles to the campground on the left side of the road (at the Mokelumne River).

137 WA KA LUU HEP YOO

🥾 🛶 🐕 ♿ 5% 🚐 🏕

Rating: 8

On the Stanislaus River in Stanislaus National Forest.

Map 6.2, page 349

This is a riverside Forest Service campground that provides good trout fishing on the Stanislaus River and a put-in for white-water rafting. The highlight for most is the fishing, one of the best spots on the Stanislaus, stocked monthly by Fish and Game, and good for rainbow, brook, and brown trout. It is four miles downstream of Dorrington, and was first opened in 1999 as part of the Sourgrass Recreation Complex. There are cultural sites and preserved artifacts, such as grinding rocks. It is a pretty streamside spot, with ponderosa pine and black oak providing good screening. A wheelchair-accessible trail is available along the stream. The camp is set at an elevation of 3,900 feet, but it feels higher. By the way, if anybody knows what the name of this campground means, please enlighten me; so far, nobody has a clue.

Campsites, facilities: There are 49 sites for tents or RVs up to 40 feet long. No RV hookups. Picnic tables and fire grills are provided. Restrooms, drinking water, showers, and flush and vault toilets are available. A camp host is onsite in summer. Some facilities are wheelchair-accessible. Leashed pets are permitted.

Reservations, fees: Reservations are not accepted. The fee is $13 per night. Free campfire permits are required. Senior discount available. Open Memorial Day weekend through September, weather permitting.

Directions: From Angels Camp, drive east on Highway 4, past Arnold to Dorrington and Boards Crossing Road. Turn right and drive four miles to the campground on the left (just before the bridge that crosses the Stanislaus River).

Contact: Stanislaus National Forest, Calaveras Ranger District, 209/795-1381, fax 209/795-6849.

138 BIG MEADOWS AND BIG MEADOWS GROUP CAMP

Rating: 5

In Stanislaus National Forest.

Map 6.2, page 349

Big Meadows is set at 6,460 feet on the western slopes of the Sierra Nevada. There are a number of recreation attractions nearby, the most prominent being the North Fork Stanislaus River two miles to the south in national forest (see Sand Flat), with access available from a four-wheel-drive road just east of camp, or on Spicer Reservoir Road (see Stanislaus River). Lake Alpine, a pretty, popular lake for trout fishing, is nine miles east on Highway 4.

Campsites, facilities: There are 65 sites for tents or RVs, including 23 sites for trailers, and an adjacent group campsite for tents or RVs. Picnic tables and fire grills are provided. Drinking water and vault toilets are available. Groceries,

a coin laundry, and propane gas are within five miles. Leashed pets are permitted.

Reservations, fees: Reserve at 877/444-6777 ($9 reservation fee) or website: www.ReserveUsa.com; $11 per night for single sites; $50 per group of 25 people per night, $2 per additional camper. Open May through September.

Directions: From Angels Camp on Highway 49, turn east on Highway 4 and drive about 30 miles (three miles past Ganns Meadows) to the campground on the right.

Contact: Stanislaus National Forest, Calaveras Ranger District, 209/795-1381, fax 209/795-6849.

139 BIG MEADOW

Rating: 5

Near the Stanislaus River in Stanislaus National Forest.

Map 6.2, page 349

Big Meadow is set at 6,460 feet and features a number of nearby recreation options. The most prominent is the North Fork Stanislaus River, with access available at Sand Flat and Stanislaus River campgrounds. In addition, Lake Alpine is nine miles to the east, and three mountain reservoirs, Spicer, Utica, and Union, are all within a 15-minute drive. Big Meadow is also a good base camp for hunters.

Campsites, facilities: There are 42 sites for tents and 23 sites for RVs up to 27 feet long. Picnic tables and fire grills are provided. Drinking water and vault toilets are available. Groceries, a coin laundry, and propane gas are within five miles. Leashed pets are permitted.

Reservations, fees: Reserve at 877/444-6777 ($9 reservation fee) or website: www.Reserve Usa.com; $11 per night. Senior discount available. Open June through October.

Directions: From Angels Camp on Highway 49, turn east on Highway 4 and drive about 30 miles (three miles past Ganns Meadows) to the campground on the right.

Contact: Stanislaus National Forest, Calaveras

Ranger District, 209/795-1381, fax 209/795-6849.

 140 SAND FLAT

Rating: 7

On the Stanislaus River in Stanislaus National Forest.

Map 6.2, page 349

This one is for four-wheel-drive cowboys who want to carve out a piece of the Sierra Nevada wildlands for themselves. It is set at 5,900 feet on the North Fork Stanislaus River, where there is decent fishing for small trout, with the fish often holding right where white water runs into pools. The tiny, primitive camp, where you won't get bugged by anyone, was named for the extensive sandy flat on the south side of the river. The access road is steep and often rough.

Campsites, facilities: There are four tent sites. Picnic tables and fire rings are provided. Vault toilets are available. No drinking water is available. Garbage must be packed out. Leashed pets are permitted.

Reservations, fees: Reservations are not accepted. There is no fee for camping. Free campfire permits are required. Open June through August.

Directions: From Angels Camp on Highway 49, turn east on Highway 4, drive about 30 miles (3.5 miles past Ganns Meadows), and then continue a half mile past Big Meadows Group Camp to a dirt/gravel road on the right. Turn right and drive two miles on a steep, unimproved road (four-wheel drive required).

Contact: Stanislaus National Forest, Calaveras Ranger District, 209/795-1381, fax 209/795-6849.

141 STANISLAUS RIVER

Rating: 8

In Stanislaus National Forest.

Map 6.2, page 349

As you might figure from its name, this camp provides excellent access to the adjacent North Fork Stanislaus River. The elevation is 6,200 feet, with timbered sites and the river just south of camp.

Campsites, facilities: There are 25 sites for tents or RVs up to 16 feet long. Fire grills and picnic tables are provided. Drinking water and vault toilets are available. Supplies are available in Tamarack. Leashed pets are permitted.

Reservations, fees: Reservations are not accepted. The fee is $8 per night. Senior discount available. Open June through September.

Directions: From Angels Camp on Highway 49, turn east on Highway 4 and drive about 32 miles (five miles past Ganns Meadows) to Spicer Reservoir Road on the right. Turn right and drive four miles to the campground on the right side of the road.

Contact: Stanislaus National Forest, Calaveras Ranger District, 209/795-1381, fax 209/795-6849.

142 KIT CARSON

Rating: 8

On the West Fork of the Carson River in Humboldt-Toiyabe National Forest.

Map 6.3, page 350

This is one in a series of pristine, high Sierra camps set along the West Fork of the Carson River. There's good trout fishing, thanks to regular stocks from the Department of Fish and Game. This is no secret, however, and the area from the Highway 89 bridge on downstream gets a lot of fishing pressure. The elevation is 6,900 feet.

Campsites, facilities: There are 12 sites for tents or RVs up to 22 feet long. Picnic tables and fire grills are provided. Drinking water and vault toilets are available. Leashed pets are permitted.

Reservations, fees: Reservations are not accepted. The fee is $9 per night. Senior discount available. Open late-May through mid-September.

Directions: From Sacramento, drive east on U.S. 50 to the junction with Highway 89. Turn south on Highway 89 and drive over Luther Pass to the junction with Highway 88. Turn left and drive a mile to the campground on the left side of the road.

From Jackson, drive east on Highway 88 over Carson Pass and to the junction with Highway 89 and then continue for a mile to the campground on the left side of the road.

Contact: Humboldt-Toiyabe National Forest, Carson Ranger District, 775/882-2766, fax 775/884-8199.

143 SNOWSHOE SPRINGS

Rating: 8

On the West Fork of the Carson River in Humboldt-Toiyabe National Forest.

Map 6.3, page 350

Take your pick of this or the other three streamside camps on the West Fork of the Carson River. This one is at 6,600 feet. Trout are plentiful but rarely grow very large.

Campsites, facilities: There are 13 tent sites. Picnic tables and fire grills are provided. Drinking water and vault toilets are available. Leashed pets are permitted.

Reservations, fees: Reservations are not accepted. The fee is $10 per night. Senior discount available. Open June through September.

Directions: From Sacramento, drive east on U.S. 50 to the junction with Highway 89. Turn south on Highway 89 and drive over Luther Pass to the junction with Highway 88. Turn left (east) and drive two miles to the campground on the right side of the road.

From Jackson, drive east on Highway 88 over Carson Pass to the junction with Highway 89 and continue for two miles to the campground on the right side of the road.

Contact: Humboldt-Toiyabe National Forest, Carson Ranger District, 775/882-2766, fax 775/884-8199.

144 CRYSTAL SPRINGS

Rating: 8

On the West Fork of the Carson River in Humboldt-Toiyabe National Forest.

Map 6.3, page 350

For many people, this camp is an ideal choice. It is set at an elevation of 6,000 feet, right alongside the West Fork of the Carson River. This stretch of water is stocked with trout by the Department of Fish and Game. Crystal Springs is easy to reach, just off Highway 88, and supplies can be obtained in nearby Woodfords or Markleeville. Grover Hot Springs State Park makes a good side trip destination.

Campsites, facilities: There are 20 sites for tents or RVs up to 22 feet long. Picnic tables and fire grills are provided. Drinking water and vault toilets are available. Leashed pets are permitted.

Reservations, fees: Reservations are not accepted. The fee is $10 per night. Senior discount available. Open late April through September.

Directions: From Sacramento, drive east on U.S. 50 to the junction with Highway 89. Turn south on Highway 89 and drive over Luther Pass to the junction with Highway 88. Turn left (east) and drive 4.5 miles to the campground on the right side of the road.

From Jackson, drive east on Highway 88 over Carson Pass to the junction with Highway 89 and continue for 4.5 miles to the campground on the right side of the road.

Contact: Humboldt-Toiyabe National Forest, Carson Ranger District, 775/882-2766, fax 775/884-8199.

145 HOPE VALLEY

Rating: 7

Near the Carson River in Humboldt-Toiyabe National Forest.

Map 6.3, page 350

The West Fork of the Carson River runs right

through Hope Valley, a pretty trout stream with a choice of four streamside campgrounds. Trout stocks are made near the campgrounds during summer. The campground at Hope Valley is just east of Carson Pass, at 7,300 feet in elevation, in a very pretty area. A trailhead for the Pacific Crest Trail is three miles south of the campground. The primary nearby destination is Blue Lakes, about a 10-minute drive away. An insider's note is that little Tamarack Lake, set just beyond the turnoff for Lower Blue Lake, is excellent for swimming.

Campsites, facilities: There are 20 sites for tents or RVs up to 22 feet long and a group area for up to 16 people. Picnic tables and fire grills are provided. Drinking water and vault toilets are available. Leashed pets are permitted.

Reservations, fees: Reserve at 877/444-6777 ($9 reservation fee) or website: www.Reserve Usa.com; $10 per night, $18 group camp fee per night. Senior discount available. Open June through September.

Directions: From Sacramento, drive east on U.S. 50 to the junction with Highway 89. Turn south on Highway 89 and drive over Luther Pass to the junction with Highway 88. Turn right (west) and drive two miles to Blue Lakes Road. Turn left (south) and drive 1.5 miles to the campground on the right side of the road.

From Jackson, drive east on Highway 88 over Carson Pass and continue east for five miles to Blue Lakes Road. Turn right (south) and drive 1.5 miles to the campground on the right side of the road.

Contact: Humboldt-Toiyabe National Forest, Carson Ranger District, 775/882-2766, fax 775/884-8199.

146 TURTLE ROCK PARK

Rating: 5

Near Woodfords.

Map 6.3, page 350

This pretty, wooded campground, set at 6,000 feet, gets missed by a lot of folks—but not by mountain bikers. It gets missed by vacationers because it is administered at the county level and also because most vacationers want the more pristine beauty of the nearby camps along the Carson River. (If it snows, it closes, so call ahead if you're planning an autumn visit.) But it doesn't get missed by mountain bikers, who travel here for the "Death Ride," an event held July 1 each year, a wild ride over several mountain passes. This camp always fills for this riding event. Nearby side trips include Grover Hot Springs and the hot springs in Markleeville.

Campsites, facilities: There are 28 sites for tents or RVs up to 35 feet long. Picnic tables and fire grills are provided. Drinking water and vault toilets are available. A recreation building is available for rent. A camp host is onsite. Coin laundry, groceries, and propane gas are available within two miles. Leashed pets are permitted.

Reservations, fees: Reservations are not accepted. The fee is $8 per night, $3 per night for each additional vehicle. Senior discount available. Open May to mid-October, weather permitting.

Directions: From Sacramento, drive east on U.S. 50 to the junction with Highway 89. Turn south on Highway 89 and drive over Luther Pass to the junction with Highway 88. Turn left (east) and drive to Woodfords and the junction with Highway 89. Turn south and drive 4.5 miles to the park entrance on the right side of the road.

Contact: Alpine County Parks, 530/694-2140.

147 GROVER HOT SPRINGS STATE PARK

Rating: 8

Near Markleeville.

Map 6.3, page 350

This is a famous spot for folks who like the rejuvenating powers of a hot spring. Some say they feel a glow about them for weeks. When touring the South Tahoe/Carson Pass area, many vacationers take part of a day to make the trip to the hot springs. This park is set in alpine meadow at 5,900 feet on the east side of the Sierra at the edge of the Great Basin, and it is surrounded by peaks that top 10,000 feet. The hot springs are green because of the mineral deposits at the bottom of the pools. The landscape is primarily pine forest and sagebrush. It is well known for the great fluctuations in weather, from major blizzards to dry scorchers, from warm, clear nights to awesome rim-rattling thunderstorms. High winds are occasional but legendary. During thunderstorms, the hot springs pools close because of the chance of lightning strikes. Yet they remain open in snow, even blizzards, when it can be a euphoric experience to sit in the steaming water. A forest fire near here remains in evidence. Side-trip options include a nature trail in the park and driving to the Carson River (where the water is a mite cooler) and fishing for trout.

Campsites, facilities: There are 26 sites for tents, 50 sites for tents or RVs up to 27 feet long and trailers up to 24 feet long. Picnic tables, fire rings, and food lockers are provided. Restrooms, drinking water, flush toilets, coin-operated showers (except in the winter), hot springs pool with wheelchair access, and swimming pool are available. A grocery store and coin laundry are nearby. Leashed pets are permitted.

Reservations, fees: Reserve at 800/444-PARK (800/444-7275) or website: www.Reserve America.com ($7.50 reservation fee); $12 per night; pool fees are $2 per adult, $1 per child 16 or under. Open year-round.

Directions: From Sacramento, drive east on U.S. 50 to the junction with Highway 89. Turn south on Highway 89 and drive over Luther Pass to the junction with Highway 88. Turn left and drive to Woodfords and the junction with Highway 89. Turn right (south) and drive six miles to Markleeville and the junction with Hot Springs Road. Turn right and drive four miles to the park entrance.

Contact: Grover Hot Springs State Park, 530/694-2248 or 530/525-7232, fax 530/694-2502.

148 MARKLEEVILLE

Rating: 7

On Markleeville Creek in Humboldt-Toiyabe National Forest.

Map 6.3, page 350

This is a pretty, streamside camp set at 5,500 feet along Markleeville Creek, a mile from the East Fork of the Carson River. The trout here are willing, but alas, are dinkers. This area is the transition zone where high mountains to the west give way to the high desert to the east. The hot springs in Markleeville and Grover Hot Springs State Park provide good side trips.

Campsites, facilities: There are 10 sites for tents or RVs up to 20 feet long. Trailers are prohibited because of road conditions. Picnic tables and fire grills are provided. Drinking water and vault toilets are available. A grocery store and restaurant are nearby. Leashed pets are permitted.

Reservations, fees: Reservations are not accepted. The fee is $10 per night. Senior discount available. Open late April through September.

Directions: From Sacramento, drive east on U.S. 50 to the junction with Highway 89. Turn south on Highway 89 and drive over Luther Pass to the junction with Highway 88. Turn left and drive to Woodfords and the junction with Highway 89. Turn south, drive six miles to Markleeville, and continue for a half mile to the campground on the left side of the highway.

Contact: Humboldt-Toiyabe National Forest, Carson Ranger District, 775/882-2766, fax 775/884-8199.

149 INDIAN CREEK RECREATION AREA

Rating: 10

Near Indian Creek Reservoir and Markleeville.

Map 6.3, page 350

This beautiful campground is set amid sparse

pines near Indian Creek Reservoir, elevation 5,600 feet. This is an excellent lake for trout fishing, and the nearby Carson River is managed as a trophy trout fishery. The lake covers 160 acres, with a maximum speed for boats on the lake set at 10 mph. There are several good hikes in the vicinity as well. The best is a short trek, a one-mile climb to Summit Lake, with scenic views of the Indian Creek area. Summers are dry and warm here, with high temperatures typically in the 80s, and nights cool and comfortable. Bears provide an occasional visit. The lake freezes over in winter. It is about 35 miles to Carson City, Nevada, and seven miles to Markleeville.

Campsites, facilities: There are 19 sites for RVs up to 30 feet long or tents, a secondary area with 10 walk-in sites for tents only, and a group site for up to 40 people. Picnic tables and fire grills are provided. Restrooms with drinking water, flush toilets, and showers are available. A boat ramp is nearby. Leashed pets are permitted.

Reservations, fees: Reservations are not accepted. The fee is $12 per night per vehicle, $8 per night for walk-in sites, $35 per night for group site. Senior discount available. Open early May through September.

Directions from Sacramento: From Sacramento, drive east on U.S. 50 over Echo Summit to Meyers and Highway 89. Turn south on Highway 89 and drive to Highway 88. Turn left (east) on Highway 88/89 and drive six miles to Woodfords and Highway 89. Turn right (south) on Highway 89 and drive about four miles to Airport Road. Turn left on Airport Road and drive four miles to Indian Creek Reservoir. At the fork, bear left and drive to the campground on the west side of the lake.

Directions from Markleeville: From Markleeville, drive north on Highway 89 for about four miles to Airport Road. Turn right on Airport Road and drive about three miles to Indian Creek Reservoir. At the fork, bear left and drive to the campground on the west side of the lake.

Contact: Bureau of Land Management, Carson City Field Office, 5665 Morgan Mill Road, Carson City, NV 89701, 775/885-6000.

150 TOPAZ LAKE RV PARK

Rating: 6

On Topaz Lake, near Markleeville.
Map 6.3, page 350

Topaz Lake, set at 5,000 feet, is one of the hidden surprises for California anglers. The surprise is the size of the rainbow trout, with one of the highest rates of 15- to 18-inch trout of any lake in the mountain country. The setting is hardly pretty, a good-sized lake on the edge of barren high desert which also serves as the border between California and Nevada. Wind is a problem for small boats, especially in the early summer. Some of the sites here are rented for the entire summer.

Campsites, facilities: There are 54 sites, including some drive-through, with full hookups for RVs up to 40 feet. Picnic tables and cable TV are provided. Restrooms, coin showers, coin laundry, propane gas, small grocery store, and modem access are available. A 40-boat marina with courtesy launch and boat trailer storage is available at lakeside. Some facilities are wheelchair-accessible. Leashed pets are permitted.

Reservations, fees: Reservations are accepted. The fee is $20–22 per night, $2 per person for more than two people. Monthly rates available. Major credit cards accepted. Open March through mid-October, weather permitting; owners request a call before visits in the off-season.

Directions: From Carson City, drive south on U.S. 395 for 45 miles to Topaz Lake and the campground on the left side of the road.

From Bridgeport, drive north on U.S. 395 for 45 miles to the campground on the right side of the road (.3 mile south of the California/Nevada border).

Contact: Topaz Lake RV Park, 530/495-2357, fax 530/495-2118.

151 MIDDLE CREEK

Rating: 7

Near Carson Pass and Blue Lakes.

Map 6.3, page 350

This is a tiny, captivating spot set along the creek that connects Upper and Lower Blue Lakes, providing a take-your-pick deal for anglers. (See the entry for Lower Blue Lake for more information.) The elevation is 8,100 feet.

Campsites, facilities: There are five sites for tents or RVs. Picnic tables and fire grills are provided. Drinking water and vault toilets are available. Leashed pets are permitted.

Reservations, fees: Reservations are not accepted. The fee is $15 per night, $3 for each extra vehicle per night, $7 for each extra RV per night, $1 per pet per night. Open June through September, weather permitting.

Directions: From Sacramento, drive east on U.S. 50 to the junction with Highway 89. Turn south on Highway 89 and drive over Luther Pass to the junction with Highway 88. Turn right and drive 2.5 miles to Blue Lakes Road. Turn left and drive 11 miles (road becomes dirt) to a junction at the south end of Lower Blue Lake. Turn right and drive 1.5 miles to the campground on the left side of the road.

From Jackson, drive east on Highway 88 over Carson Pass and continue east for five miles to Blue Lakes Road. Turn right (south) and drive 11 miles (road becomes dirt) to a junction at the south end of Lower Blue Lake. Turn right and drive 1.5 miles to the campground on the left side of the road.

Contact: PG&E Land Projects, 916/386-5164, fax 916/923-7044, website: www.pge.com/recreation.

152 UPPER BLUE LAKE

Rating: 7

Near Carson Pass.

Map 6.3, page 350

This is one of two camps set along Upper Blue Lake and one of four camps in the immediate area. The trout fishing is usually quite good here in early summer. (See the entry for Lower Blue Lake for more information.) This camp is 1.3 miles past the Lower Blue Lake Dam Campground. The elevation is 8,100 feet.

Campsites, facilities: There are 32 sites for tents. Picnic tables and fire grills are provided. Drinking water and vault toilets are available. Leashed pets are permitted.

Reservations, fees: Reservations are not accepted. The fee is $15 per night, $3 per night for each extra vehicle, $7 per night for each extra RV, $1 per pet per night. Open June through September, weather permitting.

Directions: From Sacramento, drive east on U.S. 50 to the junction with Highway 89. Turn south on Highway 89 and drive over Luther Pass to the junction with Highway 88. Turn right and drive 2.5 miles to Blue Lakes Road. Turn left and drive 11 miles (the road becomes dirt) to a junction at the south end of Lower Blue Lake. Turn right and drive three miles to the campground on the left side of the road.

From Jackson, drive east on Highway 88 over Carson Pass and continue east for five miles to Blue Lakes Road. Turn right (south) and drive 11 miles (the road becomes dirt) to a junction at the south end of Lower Blue Lake. Turn right and drive three miles to the campground on the left side of the road.

Contact: PG&E Land Projects, 916/386-5164, fax 916/923-7044, website: www.pge.com/recreation.

153 UPPER BLUE LAKE DAM

🏕️ 🚣 🛥️ 🐕 ⛰️

Rating: 8

Near Carson Pass.

Map 6.3, page 350

This is one of four camps at the Blue Lakes, at 8,200 feet in elevation south of Carson Pass. A boat ramp is near this camp. (For recreation options, see the entry for Lower Blue Lake.)

Campsites, facilities: There are 25 tent sites. Picnic tables and fire grills are provided. Drinking water and vault toilets are available. Leashed pets are permitted.

Reservations, fees: Reservations are not accepted. The fee is $15 per night, $3 for each extra vehicle per night, $7 for each extra RV per night, $1 per pet per night. Open June through September, weather permitting.

Directions: From Sacramento, drive east on U.S. 50 to the junction with Highway 89. Turn south on Highway 89 and drive over Luther Pass to the junction with Highway 88. Turn right and drive 2.5 miles to Blue Lakes Road. Turn left and drive 11 miles to a junction at the south end of Lower Blue Lake. Turn right and drive two miles to the campground next to the dam.

From Jackson, drive east on Highway 88 over Carson Pass and continue east for five miles to Blue Lakes Road. Turn right and drive 11 miles (the road becomes dirt) to a junction at the south end of Lower Blue Lake. Turn right and drive two miles to the campground next to the dam.

Contact: PG&E Land Projects, 916/386-5164, fax 916/923-7044, website: www.pge.com/recreation.

154 LOWER BLUE LAKE

🏕️ 🏊 🚣 🛥️ 🐕 🚐 ⛰️

Rating: 7

Near Carson Pass.

Map 6.3, page 350

This is the high country, 8,100 feet, where the terrain is stark and steep and edged by volcanic ridgelines, and where the deep blue-green hue of lake water brightens the landscape. Lower Blue Lake provides a popular trout fishery, with rainbow trout, brook trout, and cutthroat trout all stocked regularly. The boat ramp is adjacent to the campground. The access road crosses the Pacific Crest Trail, providing a route to a series of small, pretty, hike-to lakes just outside the edge of the Mokelumne Wilderness.

Campsites, facilities: There are 16 sites for tents or RVs to 30 feet. Picnic tables and fire grills are provided. Drinking water and vault toilets are available. Leashed pets are permitted.

Reservations, fees: Reservations are not accepted. The fee is $15 per night, $3 per additional vehicle per night, $1 per night, 14-day occupancy limit. Open June through September, weather permitting.

Directions: From Sacramento, drive east on U.S. 50 to the junction with Highway 89. Turn south on Highway 89 and drive over Luther Pass to the junction with Highway 88. Turn right and drive 2.5 miles to Blue Lakes Road. Turn left and drive 11 miles (road becomes dirt) to a junction at the south end of Lower Blue Lake. Turn right and drive a short distance to the campground on the left side of the road.

From Jackson, drive east on Highway 88 over Carson Pass and continue east for five miles to Blue Lakes Road. Turn right (south) and drive 11 miles (the road becomes dirt) to a junction at the south end of Lower Blue Lake. Turn right and drive a short distance to the campground on the left.

Contact: PG&E Land Projects, 916/386-5164, fax 916/923-7044; website: www.pge.com/recreation.

155 MOSQUITO LAKE

🏕️ 🚣 🐕 ⛰️

Rating:10

At Mosquito Lake in Stanislaus National Forest.

Map 6.3, page 350

Mosquito Lake is in a pristine Sierra setting

at 8,260 feet, presenting remarkable beauty for a place that can be reached by car. Most people believe that Mosquito Lake is for day-use only, and that's why they get crowded into nearby Alpine Campground. But it's not just for day-use, and this camp is often overlooked because it is about a mile west of the little lake, and on the opposite side of the road. The lake is small, a pretty emerald green, and even has a few small trout in it. The camp provides a few dispersed sites.

Campsites, facilities: There are a few sites for tents. Picnic tables and fire grills are provided. Vault toilets are available. No drinking water is available. Garbage must be packed out. Leashed pets are permitted.

Reservations, fees: Reservations are not accepted. The fee is $5 per night. Senior discount available. A freecampfire permit is required from the district office. Open mid-May through September.

Directions: From Angels Camp, drive east on Highway 4 to Lake Alpine and continue for about six miles to the campground on the left side of the road.

Contact: Stanislaus National Forest, Calaveras Ranger District, 209/795-1381, fax 209/795-6849. For a map, send $6 to U.S. Forest Service, Attn: Map Sales, P.O. Box 9035, Prescott, AZ 86313, 928/443-8285 with credit card, website: www.fs.fed.us/maps/.

156 PACIFIC VALLEY

Rating: 7

Overlooking Pacific Creek in Stanislaus National Forest.

Map 6.3, page 350

This is a do-it-yourself special; that is, more of a general area for camping than a campground, set up for backpackers heading out on expeditions into the Carson-Iceberg Wilderness to the south. It is set at 7,600 feet along Pacific Creek, a tributary to the Mokelumne River.

The landscape here is an open lodgepole forest with nearby meadow and a small stream. The trail from camp is routed south and reaches three forks within two miles. The best is routed deep into the wilderness, flanking Hiram Peak (9,760 feet), Airola Peak (9,938 feet), and Iceberg Peak (9,720 feet).

Campsites, facilities: There are nine sites for tents or small self-contained RVs and a large area for dispersed camping. Trailers are not recommended because of the rough roads. Picnic tables and fire grills are provided. Vault toilets are available. No drinking water is available. Leashed pets are permitted.

Reservations, fees: Reservations are not accepted. There is no fee for camping. A free campfire permit is required from the district office. Open June through September.

Directions: From Angels Camp, drive east on Highway 4 to Lake Alpine and continue for eight miles to a dirt road. Turn east and drive about a half mile to the campground.

Contact: Stanislaus National Forest, Calaveras Ranger District, 209/795-1381, fax 209/795-6849. For a map, send $6 to U.S. Forest Service, Attn: Map Sales, P.O. Box 9035, Prescott, AZ 86313, 928/443-8285 with credit card, website: www.fs.fed.us/maps/.

157 HERMIT VALLEY

Rating: 8

In Stanislaus National Forest.

Map 6.3, page 350

This tiny, remote, little-known spot is set near the border of the Mokelumne Wilderness near where Grouse Creek enters the Mokelumne River, at 7,100 feet in elevation. Looking north, there is a good view into Deer Valley. A primitive road, a half mile west of camp, is routed through Deer Valley north for six miles to the Blue Lakes. On the opposite (south) side of the road from the camp there is a little-traveled hiking trail that is routed up Grouse Creek to Beaver Meadow and Willow Meadow near the border of the Carson-Iceberg Wilderness.

Campsites, facilities: There is a large area for dispersed camping in tents or self-contained RVs. Vault toilets are available. No drinking water is available. Leashed pets are permitted.

Reservations, fees: Reservations are not accepted. There is no fee for camping. A free campfire permit is required from the district office. Open June through September.

Directions: From Angels Camp, drive east on Highway 4 to Lake Alpine and continue for about nine miles to the campground on the left side of the road (just east of the Mokelumne River Bridge).

Contact: Stanislaus National Forest, Calaveras Ranger District, 209/795-1381, fax 209/795-6849. For a map, send $6 to U.S. Forest Service, Attn: Map Sales, P.O. Box 9035, Prescott, AZ 86313, 928/443-8285 with credit card, website: www.fs.fed.us/maps/.

158 SILVER CREEK

Rating: 6

In Humboldt-Toiyabe National Forest.
Map 6.3, page 350

This pretty spot, set near Silver Creek, has easy access from Highway 4 and, in years without washouts, good fishing in early summer for small trout. It is in the remote high Sierra, east of Ebbetts Pass. A side trip to Ebbetts Pass features Kinney Lake, Pacific Crest Trail access, and a trailhead at the north end of the lake (on the west side of Highway 4) for a mile hike to Lower Kinney Lake. No bikes are permitted on the trails. The elevation is 6,800 feet.

Campsites, facilities: There are 22 sites for tents or RVs up to 22 feet long. Picnic tables and fire grills are provided. Drinking water and vault toilets are available. Leashed pets are permitted.

Reservations, fees: Reserve at 877/444-6777 ($9 reservation fee) or website: www.Reserve Usa.com; $10 per night. Senior discount available. Open late May to early September.

Directions: From Angels Camp, drive east on

Highway 4 all the way over Ebbetts Pass and continue for about six miles to the campground.

From Markleeville, drive south on Highway 89 to the junction with Highway 4. Turn west on Highway 4 (steep and winding) and drive about five miles to the campground.

Contact: Humboldt-Toiyabe National Forest, Carson Ranger District, 775/882-2766, fax 775/884-8199.

159 BLOOMFIELD

Rating: 7

In Stanislaus National Forest.
Map 6.3, page 350

This is a primitive and little-known camp set at 7,800 feet near Ebbetts Pass. The North Fork Mokelumne River runs right by the camp, with good stream access for about a mile on each side of the camp. The access road continues south to Highland Lakes, a destination that provides car-top boating, fair fishing, and trailheads for hiking into the Carson-Iceberg Wilderness.

Campsites, facilities: There are 20 sites for tents or RVs. Trailers are not recommended because of road conditions. Picnic tables and fire rings are provided. Drinking water and vault toilets are available. Facilities and supplies are available at Lake Alpine Lodge, 25 minutes away. Leashed pets are permitted.

Reservations, fees: Reservations are not accepted. The fee is $8 per night. A free campfire permit is required from the district office. Open June through October.

Directions: From Angels Camp, drive east on Highway 4 to Lake Alpine and continue for about 15 miles to Forest Road 8N01 on the right side of the road (1.5 miles west of Ebbetts Pass). Turn right and drive two miles to the campground on the right side of the road.

Contact: Stanislaus National Forest, Calaveras Ranger District, 209/795-1381, fax 209/795-6849. For a map, send $6 to U.S. Forest Service, Attn: Map Sales, P.O. Box 9035, Prescott,

AZ 86313, 928/443-8285 with credit card, website: www.fs.fed.us/maps/.

160 UPPER AND LOWER HIGHLAND LAKES

Rating: 9

In Stanislaus National Forest.

Map 6.3, page 350

This camp is set between Upper and Lower Highland Lakes, two beautiful Alpine ponds that offer good fishing for small brook trout as well as spectacular panoramic views. The elevation at this campground is 8,600 feet, with Hiram Peak (9,760 feet) looming to the nearby south. Several great trails are available from this camp. Day hikes include up Boulder Creek and Disaster Creek. For overnight backpacking, a trail that starts at the north end of Highland Lakes (a parking area is available) is routed east for two miles to Wolf Creek Pass, where it connects with the Pacific Crest Trail; from there, turn left or right—you can't lose. The access road is not recommended for trailers or large RVs.

Campsites, facilities: There are 35 sites for tents or small RVs, including five sites for equestrians. Picnic tables and fire grills are provided. Drinking water and vault toilets are available. Leashed pets are permitted.

Reservations, fees: Reservations are not accepted. The fee is $8 per night. Senior discount available. Open mid-June through September.

Directions: From Angels Camp, drive east on Highway 4 to Arnold, past Lake Alpine, and continue for 14.5 miles to Forest Road 8N01 (one mile west of Ebbetts Pass). Turn right and drive 7.5 miles to the campground on the right side of the road. Trailers are not recommended.

Contact: Stanislaus National Forest, Calaveras Ranger District, 209/795-1381, fax 209/795-6849.

161 PINE MARTEN

Rating: 8

Near Lake Alpine in Stanislaus National Forest.

Map 6.3, page 350

Lake Alpine is a beautiful Sierra lake surrounded by granite and pines and set at 7,320 feet, just above where the snowplows stop in winter. This camp is on the northeast side, about a quarter mile from the shore. Fishing for rainbow trout is good in May and early June, before the summer crush. Despite the long drive to get here, the lake is becoming better known for its beauty, camping, and hiking. A trailhead out of nearby Silver Valley Camp provides a two-mile hike to pretty Duck Lake and beyond into the Carson-Iceberg Wilderness.

Campsites, facilities: There are 33 sites for tents or RVs up to 22 feet long. Picnic tables and fire grills are provided. Restrooms, drinking water, flush toilets, and a boat ramp are available. A grocery store, propane gas, and coin laundry are nearby. Leashed pets are permitted.

Reservations, fees: Reservations are not accepted. The fee is $15 per night. A free campfire permit is required. Senior discount available. Open June to mid-October.

Directions: From Angels Camp, drive east on Highway 4 to Arnold and continue for 29 miles to Lake Alpine. Drive to the northeast end of the lake to the campground entrance on the right side of the road.

Contact: Stanislaus National Forest, Calaveras Ranger District, 209/795-1381, fax 209/795-6849.

162 SILVER VALLEY

Rating: 8

On Lake Alpine in Stanislaus National Forest.

Map 6.3, page 350

This is one of four camps at Lake Alpine.

Silver Valley is on the northeast end of the lake at 7,400 feet in elevation, with a trailhead nearby that provides access to the Carson-Iceberg Wilderness. (For recreation information, see the entry for Pine Marten.)

Campsites, facilities: There are 21 sites for tents or RVs up to 22 feet long. Picnic tables and fire grills are provided. Drinking water and vault toilets are available. A boat launch is available. Some facilities are wheelchair-accessible. A grocery store, propane gas, and a coin laundry are nearby. Leashed pets are permitted.

Reservations, fees: Reservations are not accepted. The fee is $15 per night. A free campfire permit is required. Senior discount available. Open June through mid-October.

Directions: From Angels Camp, drive east on Highway 4 to Arnold and continue for 29 miles to Lake Alpine. Drive to the northeast end of the lake to the campground entrance on the right side of the road. Turn right and drive a half mile to the campground.

Contact: Stanislaus National Forest, Calaveras Ranger District, 209/795-1381, fax 209/795-6849.

163 ALPINE CAMPGROUND

Rating: 8

On Lake Alpine in Stanislaus National Forest.
Map 6.3, page 350

This is the campground that is in the greatest demand at Lake Alpine, and it is easy to see why. It is very small, a boat ramp is adjacent to the camp, you can get supplies at a small grocery store within walking distance, and during the evening rise you can often see the jumping trout from your campsite. Lake Alpine is one of the prettiest lakes you can drive to, set at 7,320 feet amid pines and Sierra granite. A trailhead out of nearby Silver Valley Camp provides a two-mile hike to pretty Duck Lake and beyond into the Carson-Iceberg Wilderness.

Campsites, facilities: There are 25 sites for tents or RVs up to 22 feet long. Picnic tables and fire grills are provided. Restrooms, drinking water, flush and vault toilets, and a boat launch are available. A grocery store, propane gas, and a coin laundry are nearby. Some facilities are wheelchair-accessible. Leashed pets are permitted.

Reservations, fees: Reservations are not accepted. The fee is $15 per night. Senior discount available. Open June through October.

Directions: From Angels Camp, drive east on Highway 4 to Arnold and continue for 29 miles to Lake Alpine. Just before reaching the lake turn right and drive a quarter mile to the campground on the left.

Contact: Stanislaus National Forest, Calaveras Ranger District, 209/795-1381, fax 209/795-6849.

164 SILVER TIP

Rating: 6

Near Lake Alpine in Stanislaus National Forest.
Map 6.3, page 350

This camp is just over a half mile from the shore of Lake Alpine at an elevation of 7,350 feet. Why then would anyone camp here when there are campgrounds right at the lake? Two reasons: one, those lakeside camps are often full on summer weekends. Two, Highway 4 is snowplowed to this campground entrance, but not beyond. So in big snow years when the road is still closed in late spring and early summer, you can park your rig here to camp, then hike in to the lake. In the fall, it also makes for a base camp for hunters. (See the entry for Alpine campground for more information.)

Campsites, facilities: There are 24 sites for tents or RVs up to 22 feet long. Picnic tables and fire grills are provided. Restrooms, drinking water, and flush toilets are available. A boat launch is about a mile away. A grocery store, propane gas, a coin laundry, and coin showers are nearby. Leashed pets are permitted.

Reservations, fees: Reservations are not accepted. The fee is $15 per night. Senior discount available. Open July through September, weather permitting.

Directions: From Angels Camp, drive east on Highway 4 to Arnold and continue for 29 miles to Lake Alpine. A mile before reaching the lake (adjacent to the Bear Valley/Mt. Reba turnoff), turn right at the campground entrance on the right side of the road.

Contact: Stanislaus National Forest, Calaveras Ranger District, 209/795-1381, fax 209/795-6849.

165 UNION RESERVOIR WALK-IN

Rating: 10

Northeast of Arnold in Stanislaus National Forest.

Map 6.3, page 350

Union Reservoir is set in Sierra granite at 6,850 feet, a beautiful and quiet lake that is kept that way with rules that mandate a 5-mph speed limit and walk-in camping only. Most of the sites provide lakeside views. Fishing is often good, trolling for kokanee salmon, but you need a boat. The setting is great, especially for canoes or other small boats. This camp was once a secret, but now it fills up quickly on weekends. Those who visit usually keep the noise down so everybody can enjoy a pristine experience.

Campsites, facilities: There are 15 primitive walk-in tent sites. A vault toilet is available, along with a signboard explaining lake rules and camp policies. No drinking water is available. Garbage must be packed out. A boat ramp is available nearby.

Reservations, fees: Reservations are not accepted. There is no fee for camping. Open June through September, weather permitting.

Directions: From Angels Camp, drive east on Highway 4 for about 32 miles to Spicer Reservoir Road. Turn right and travel east for about seven miles to Forest Road 7N75. Turn left

and drive three miles to Union Reservoir. There are four designated parking areas for the walk-in camps along the road.

Contact: Stanislaus National Forest, Calaveras Ranger District, 209/795-1381, fax 209/795-6849. For a map, send $6 to U.S. Forest Service, Attn: Map Sales, P.O. Box 9035, Prescott, AZ 86313, 928/443-8285 with credit card, website: www.fs.fed.us/maps/.

166 SPICER RESERVOIR GROUP CAMP

Rating: 7

Near Spicer Reservoir in Stanislaus National Forest.

Map 6.3, page 350

Set at 6,418 feet, Spicer Reservoir isn't big by reservoir standards, covering only 227 acres, but it is quite pretty from a boat and is surrounded by canyon walls. The beauty is added to by good trout fishing. A boat ramp is available near the campground. A trail links the east end of Spicer Reservoir to the Summit Lake trailhead, with the route bordering the north side of the reservoir. Note: this area can really get hammered with snow in big winters, so in the spring and early summer, always check for access conditions before planning a trip.

Campsites, facilities: There is one group site for up to 75 people. Picnic tables and fire grills are provided. Drinking water, vault toilets, food preparation area, primitive amphitheater, and a group parking area are available. A boat ramp is available a mile away. Some facilities are wheelchair-accessible. Leashed pets are permitted.

Reservations, fees: Reservations are required. To reserve phone 877/444-6777 ($9 reservation fee); $90 per night. Open June through September, weather permitting.

Directions: From Angels Camp, drive east on Highway 4 for about 32 miles to Spicer Reservoir Road/Forest Road 7N01. Turn right, drive seven miles, bear right at a fork with a sharp right turn, and drive a mile to the campground at the west end of the lake.

Contact: Stanislaus National Forest, Calaveras Ranger District, 209/795-1381, fax 209/795-6849. For a map, send $4 to the USDA Forest Service, U.S. Forest Map Sales, 1323 Club Dr., Vallejo, CA 94592.

167 SPICER RESERVOIR

Rating: 8

Near Spicer Reservoir in Stanislaus National Forest.

Map 6.3, page 350

Spicer Reservoir, set at 6,200 feet, isn't big by reservoir standards, covering 227 acres, but it is surrounded by canyon walls and is quite pretty from a boat. The beauty is added to by good trout fishing, even awesome, trolling gold Cripplures. A boat ramp is available near the campground. Trails along much of the lake provide a day-hiking option. Note: this area can really get hammered with snow in big winters, so in the spring and early summer, always check for access conditions before planning a trip.

Campsites, facilities: There are 60 family sites, two double-family sites, and a triple-family site, all suitable for tents or RVs. Picnic tables and fire grills are provided. Drinking water, vault toilets, and a phone are available. Some facilities are wheelchair-accessible. A boat ramp is available nearby. Leashed pets are permitted.

Reservations, fees: Reservations are not accepted. The fee is $12 per night. Senior discount available. Open June through September, weather permitting.

Directions: From Angels Camp, drive east on Highway 4 for about 32 miles to Spicer Reservoir Road/Forest Road 7N01. Turn right, drive seven miles, bear right at a fork with a sharp right turn, and drive a mile to the campground at the west end of the lake.

Contact: Stanislaus National Forest, Calaveras Ranger District, 209/795-1381, fax 209/795-

6849. For a map, send $6 to U.S. Forest Service, Attn: Map Sales, P.O. Box 9035, Prescott, AZ 86313, 928/443-8285 with credit card, website: www.fs.fed.us/maps/.

168 CLARK FORK AND CLARK FORK HORSE

Rating: 8

On the Clark Fork of the Stanislaus River in Stanislaus National Forest.

Map 6.3, page 350

Clark Fork borders the Clark Fork of the Stanislaus River and is used both by drive-in vacationers and backpackers. A trailhead for hikers is a quarter mile away on the north side of Clark Fork Road (a parking area is available here). From here the trail is routed up along Arnot Creek, skirting between Iceberg Peak on the left and Lightning Mountain on the right, for eight miles to Wolf Creek Pass and the junction with the Pacific Crest Trail. (For another nearby trailhead, see the entry for Sand Flat.)

Campsites, facilities: There are 88 sites for tents or RVs up to 22 feet long, and at an adjacent area, 14 equestrian sites with water troughs. Picnic tables and fire grills are provided. Drinking water, flush toilets, and RV dump station are available. At the equestrian site, no drinking water is available. Some facilities are wheelchair-accessible. You can buy supplies in Dardanelle. Leashed pets are permitted.

Reservations, fees: Reservations are not accepted. The fee is $11–12 per night for family sites, horse camp fee is $6 per night, $5 for an extra vehicle. Senior discount available. Open May through mid-October, weather permitting.

Directions: From Sonora, drive east on Highway 108 past the town of Strawberry to Clark Fork Road. Turn left, drive five miles, turn right again, and drive a half mile to the campground entrance on the right side of the road.

Contact: Stanislaus National Forest, Summit

Ranger District, 209/965-3434, fax 209/965-3372. For a map, send $6 to U.S. Forest Service, Attn: Map Sales, P.O. Box 9035, Prescott, AZ 86313, 928/443-8285 with credit card, website: www.fs.fed.us/maps/.

169 SAND FLAT

Rating: 7

On the Clark Fork of the Stanislaus River in Stanislaus National Forest.

Map 6.3, page 350

Sand Flat Campground, at 6,200 feet, is only three miles (by vehicle on Clark Fork Road) from an outstanding trailhead for the Carson-Iceberg Wilderness. The camp is used primarily by late-arriving backpackers who camp for the night, get their gear in order, then head off on the trail. The trail is routed out of Iceberg Meadow, with a choice of heading north to Paradise Valley (unbelievably green and loaded with corn lilies along a creek) and onward to the Pacific Crest Trail, or east to Clark Fork and upstream to Clark Fork Meadow below Sonora Peak. Two choices, both winners.

Campsites, facilities: There are 53 sites for tents or RVs and 15 walk-in sites. Picnic tables and fire grills are provided. Drinking water and vault toilets are available. You can buy supplies in Dardanelle. Leashed pets are permitted.

Reservations, fees: Reservations are not accepted. The fee is $8 per night per vehicle. Senior discount available. Open May through September.

Directions: From Sonora, drive east on Highway 108 past the town of Strawberry to Clark Fork Road. Turn left on Clark Fork Road and drive six miles to the campground entrance on the right side of the road.

Contact: Stanislaus National Forest, Summit Ranger District, 209/965-3434, fax 209/965-3372.

170 FENCE CREEK

Rating: 4

Near the Middle Fork of the Stanislaus River in Stanislaus National Forest.

Map 6.3, page 350

Fence Creek is a feeder stream to Clark Fork, which runs a mile downstream and joins with the Middle Fork Stanislaus River en route to Donnells Reservoir. The camp sits along little Fence Creek, 5,600 feet in elevation. Fence Creek Road continues east for another nine miles to an outstanding trailhead at Iceberg Meadow on the edge of the Carson-Iceberg Wilderness.

Campsites, facilities: There are 38 sites for tents or RVs up to 22 feet long. Picnic tables and fire grills are provided. Vault and pit toilets are available. No drinking water is available. You can buy supplies in Pinecrest about 10 miles away. Leashed pets are permitted.

Reservations, fees: Reservations are not accepted. The fee is $5 per night. Senior discount available. Open May through mid-October, weather permitting.

Directions: From Sonora, drive east on Highway 108 about 49 miles to Clark Ford Road. Turn left and drive a mile to Forest Road 6N06. Turn left again and drive a half mile to the campground on the right.

Contact: Stanislaus National Forest, Summit Ranger District, 209/965-3434, fax 209/965-3372.

171 BOULDER FLAT

Rating: 7

Near the Middle Fork of the Stanislaus River in Stanislaus National Forest.

Map 6.3, page 350

You want camping on the Stanislaus River? As you drive east on Highway 108, this is the first in a series of campgrounds along the Middle Fork Stanislaus. Boulder Flat is set at 5,600 feet and offers easy access off the highway. Here's another bonus: this stretch of river is stocked with trout.

Campsites, facilities: There are 20 sites for tents or RVs up to 22 feet long, and one double site. Picnic tables and fire grills are provided. Drinking water and vault toilets are available. You can buy supplies in Dardanelle. Leashed pets are permitted.

Reservations, fees: Reservations are not accepted. The fee is $14 per night, $16 per night for a double site, $5 for an extra vehicle. Senior discount available. Open May through September.

Directions: From Sonora, drive east on Highway 108 past the town of Strawberry to Clark Fork Road. At Clark Fork Road, continue east on Highway 108 for a mile to the campground on the left side of the road.

Contact: Stanislaus National Forest, Summit Ranger District, 209/965-3434, fax 209/965-3372.

172 BRIGHTMAN FLAT

Rating: 7

On the Middle Fork of the Stanislaus River in Stanislaus National Forest.

Map 6.3, page 350

This camp is on the Middle Fork of the Stanislaus River at 5,700 feet elevation, a mile east of Boulder Flat and two miles west of Dardanelle. (For recreation options, see the entry for Pigeon Flat.)

Campsites, facilities: There are 33 sites for tents or RVs up to 22 feet long. Picnic tables and fire grills are provided. Vault toilets are available. No drinking water is available. You can buy supplies in Dardanelle. Leashed pets are permitted.

Reservations, fees: Reservations are not accepted. The fee is $11 per night, $5 per night for each extra vehicle. Senior discount available. Open May through mid-October, weather permitting.

Directions: From Sonora, drive east on Highway 108 past the town of Strawberry to Clark

Fork Road. At Clark Fork Road continue east on Highway 108 for two miles to the campground entrance on the left side of the road.

Contact: Stanislaus National Forest, Summit Ranger District, 209/965-3434, fax 209/965-3372.

173 DARDANELLE

Rating: 7

On the Middle Fork of the Stanislaus River in Stanislaus National Forest.

Map 6.3, page 350

This Forest Service camp is within walking distance of supplies in Dardanelle and is also right alongside the Middle Fork Stanislaus River. This section of river is stocked with trout by the Department of Fish and Game. The trail to see Columns of the Giants is just 1.5 miles to the east out of Pigeon Flat.

Campsites, facilities: There are 28 sites for tents or RVs up to 22 feet long, and three double sites. Picnic tables and fire grills are provided. Drinking water and vault toilets are available. You can buy supplies in Dardanelle. Leashed pets are permitted.

Reservations, fees: Reservations are not accepted. The fee is $16 per night for single sites, $20 per night for double sites, $5 for an extra vehicle. Senior discount available. Open May through October, weather permitting.

Directions: From Sonora, drive east on Highway 108 past Strawberry to Dardanelle and the campground on the left side of the road.

Contact: Stanislaus National Forest, Summit Ranger District, 209/965-3434, fax 209/965-3372.

174 PIGEON FLAT

Rating: 7

On the Middle Fork of the Stanislaus River in Stanislaus National Forest.

Map 6.3, page 350

The prime attraction at Pigeon Flat is the short

trail to Columns of the Giants, a rare example of columnar hexagonal rock, similar to the phenomenon at Devils Postpile near Mammoth Lakes. In addition, the camp is adjacent to the Middle Fork Stanislaus River; trout are small here and get fished hard. Supplies are available within walking distance in Dardanelle. The elevation is 6,000 feet.

Campsites, facilities: There are seven walk-in tent sites. Picnic tables and fire grills are provided. Vault toilets are available. No drinking water is available. You can buy supplies in Dardanelle. Leashed pets are permitted.

Reservations, fees: Reservations are not accepted. The fee is $9 per night, $5 for an extra vehicle. Senior discount available. Open May through October, weather permitting.

Directions: From Sonora, drive east on Highway 108 past the town of Strawberry to Dardanelle. Continue 1.5 miles east to the campground on the right side of the road, next to the Columns of the Giants Interpretive Site.

Contact: Stanislaus National Forest, Summit Ranger District, 209/965-3434, fax 209/965-3372.

175 EUREKA VALLEY

Rating: 8

On the Middle Fork of the Stanislaus River in Stanislaus National Forest.

Map 6.3, page 350

There are about a half dozen campgrounds on this stretch of the Middle Fork Stanislaus River near Dardanelle, at 6,100 feet in elevation. The river runs along two sides of this campground, making it quite pretty. This stretch of river is planted with trout by the Department of Fish and Game, but it is hit pretty hard despite its relatively isolated location. A good short and easy hike is to Columns of the Giants, accessible on a quarter-mile-long trail out of Pigeon Flat, a mile to the west.

Campsites, facilities: There are 28 sites for tents or RVs up to 30 feet long. Picnic tables and fire grills are provided. Drinking water and vault toilets are available. You can buy supplies in Dardanelle. Leashed pets are permitted.

Reservations, fees: Reservations are not accepted. The fee is $13 per night, $2 for an extra vehicle. Senior discount available. Open May through mid-October, weather permitting.

Directions: From Sonora, drive east on Highway 108 past the town of Strawberry to Dardanelle. Continue three miles east to the campground on the right.

Contact: Stanislaus National Forest, Summit Ranger District, 209/965-3434, fax 209/965-3372.

176 NIAGARA CREEK

Rating: 6

In Stanislaus National Forest.

Map 6.3, page 350

This camp is set beside Niagara Creek at 6,600 feet, high in Stanislaus National Forest on the western slopes of the Sierra. It provides direct access to a network of roads in national forest, including routes to Double Dome Rock and another to Eagle Meadows. So if you have a four-wheel-drive vehicle or dirt bike, this is the place to come.

Campsites, facilities: There are six sites for tents, five sites for RVs up to 22 feet long, and four walk-in sites. Picnic tables and fire grills are provided. A vault toilet is available. No drinking water is available. You can buy supplies in Pinecrest about 10 miles away. Leashed pets are permitted.

Reservations, fees: Reservations are not accepted. The fee is $5 per night. Senior discount available. Open May through mid-October, weather permitting.

Directions: From Sonora, drive east on Highway 108 to the town of Strawberry and continue for about 15 miles to Eagle Meadows Road/Forest Road 5N01 on the right. Turn right and drive one-half mile to the campground on the left.

Contact: Stanislaus National Forest, Summit Ranger District, 209/965-3434, fax 209/965-3372.

177 MILL CREEK

Rating: 7

On Mill Creek in Stanislaus National Forest.
Map 6.3, page 350

This pretty little camp is set along Mill Creek at 6,200 feet in elevation, high in Stanislaus National Forest, near a variety of outdoor recreation options. The camp is near the Middle Fork Stanislaus River, which is stocked with trout near Donnells. For hiking, there is an outstanding trailhead at Kennedy Meadow (east of Donnells). For fishing, both Beardsley Reservoir (boat necessary) and Pinecrest Lake (shoreline prospects fair) provide two nearby alternatives.

Campsites, facilities: There are 17 sites for tents or RVs. Picnic tables and fire grills are provided. Vault toilets are available. No drinking water is available. Leashed pets are permitted.

Reservations, fees: Reservations are not accepted. The fee is $5 per night. Senior discount available. Open May through mid-October, weather permitting.

Directions: From Sonora, drive east on Highway 108 to Strawberry. From Strawberry continue east on Highway 108 about 13 miles; turn right on Forest Road 5N21 and drive .1 mile to the campground access road (Forest Road 5N26) on the left.

Contact: Stanislaus National Forest, Summit Ranger District, 209/965-3434, fax 209/965-3372.

178 NIAGARA CREEK OFF-HIGHWAY VEHICLE

Rating: 6

On Niagara Creek in Stanislaus National Forest.
Map 6.3, page 350

This small, primitive camp along Niagara Creek is designed primarily for people with off-highway vehicles. Got it? It is set on Niagara Creek near Donnells Reservoir. The elevation is 6,600 feet.

Campsites, facilities: There are 10 sites for tents or RVs up to 22 feet long and two double sites. Picnic tables and fire grills are provided. A vault toilet is available. No drinking water is available. You can buy supplies in Pinecrest about 10 miles away. Leashed pets are permitted.

Reservations, fees: Reservations are not accepted. The fee is $5 per night. Senior discount available. Open May through mid-October, weather permitting.

Directions: From Sonora, drive east on Highway 108 to Strawberry and continue for about 15 miles to Eagle Meadows Road/Forest Road 5N01 on the right. Turn right and drive 1.5 miles to the campground on the left (just after crossing the bridge at Niagara Creek).

Contact: Stanislaus National Forest, Summit Ranger District, 209/965-3434, fax 209/965-3372.

179 BAKER

Rating: 7

On the Middle Fork of the Stanislaus River in Stanislaus National Forest.
Map 6.3, page 350

Baker lies at the turnoff for the well-known and popular Kennedy Meadow trailhead for the Emigrant Wilderness. The camp is set along the Middle Fork Stanislaus River, 6,200 feet elevation, downstream a short way from the confluence with Deadman Creek. The trailhead, with a nearby horse corral, is another two miles farther on the Kennedy Meadow access road. From here it is a 1.5-mile hike to a fork in the trail; right will take you two miles to Relief Reservoir, 7,226 feet, and left will route you up Kennedy Creek for five miles to pretty Kennedy Lake, just north of Kennedy Peak (10,716 feet).

Campsites, facilities: There are 44 sites for tents

or RVs up to 22 feet long. Picnic tables and fire grills are provided. Drinking water and vault toilets are available. You can buy supplies in Dardanelle. Leashed pets are permitted.

Reservations, fees: Reservations are not accepted. The fee is $13 per night, $5 for an extra vehicle. Senior discount available. Open May to mid-October, weather permitting.

Directions: From Sonora, drive east on Highway 108 past Strawberry to Dardanelle. From Dardanelle, continue 5.5 miles east to the campground on the right side of the road at the turnoff for Kennedy Meadow.

Contact: Stanislaus National Forest, Summit Ranger District, 209/965-3434, fax 209/965-3372.

180 DEADMAN

Rating: 7

On the Middle Fork of the Stanislaus River in Stanislaus National Forest.

Map 6.3, page 350

This is a popular trailhead camp and an ideal jump-off point for backpackers heading into the adjacent Emigrant Wilderness. The camp is a short distance from Baker (see the entry for Baker for hiking destinations).

Campsites, facilities: There are 17 sites for tents or RVs up to 22 feet long. Picnic tables and fire grills are provided. Drinking water and vault toilets are available. You can buy supplies in Dardanelle. Leashed pets are permitted.

Reservations, fees: Reservations are not accepted. The fee is $13 per night, $5 for an extra vehicle. Senior discount available. Open May through mid-October, weather permitting.

Directions: From Sonora, drive east on Highway 108 past the town of Strawberry to Dardanelle. From Dardanelle, continue 5.5 miles east to the Kennedy Meadow turnoff. Drive a mile on Kennedy Meadow Road to the campground, which is opposite the parking area for the Kennedy Meadow Trail.

Contact: Stanislaus National Forest, Summit Ranger District, 209/965-3434, fax 209/965-3372.

181 LEAVITT MEADOWS

Rating: 9

On the Walker River in Humboldt-Toiyabe National Forest.

Map 6.3, page 350

While Leavitt Meadows sits right aside Highway 108, a little winding two-laner, there are several nearby off-pavement destinations that make this camp a winner. The camp is set in the high eastern Sierra, east of Sonora Pass at 7,000 feet in elevation, where Leavitt Creek and Brownie Creek enter the West Walker River. There is a pack station for horseback riding nearby. For four-wheel-drive owners, the most popular side trip is driving four miles west on Highway 108, then turning south and driving four miles to Leavitt Lake, where the trout fishing is sometimes spectacular, trolling a gold Cripplure.

Campsites, facilities: There are 16 sites for tents or RVs up to 40 feet long. Picnic tables and fire grills are provided. Drinking water and vault toilets are available. Leashed pets are permitted.

Reservations, fees: Reservations are not accepted. The fee is $11 per night. Senior discount available. Open mid-April to mid-October, weather permitting.

Directions: From the junction of Highway 108 and U.S. 395 north of Bridgeport, turn west on Highway 108 and drive seven miles to the campground on the left side of the road.

Contact: Humboldt-Toiyabe National Forest, Bridgeport Ranger District, 760/932-7070, fax 760/932-1299.

182 OBSIDIAN

Rating: 6

On Molybdenite Creek in Humboldt-Toiyabe National Forest.

Map 6.3, page 350

This primitive, little-known camp at 7,800 feet in elevation is set up for backpackers, with an adjacent trailhead providing a jump-off point into the wilderness. The trail here is routed up the Molybdenite Creek drainage and into the Hoover Wilderness.

Campsites, facilities: There are 14 sites for tents or RVs up to 30 feet long. Picnic tables and fire grills are provided. Vault toilets are available. No drinking water is available. Garbage must be packed out. Leashed pets are permitted.

Reservations, fees: Reservations are not accepted. The fee is $7 per night. Senior discount available. Open early June to mid-October.

Directions: At the junction of U.S. 395 and Highway 108 (12 miles north of Bridgeport), drive south a short distance on U.S. 395 to an improved dirt road and a sign that says "Forest Service Campground." Turn west and drive four miles to the campground.

Contact: Humboldt-Toiyabe National Forest, Bridgeport Ranger District, 760/932-7070, fax 760/932-1299.

183 SONORA BRIDGE

Rating: 7

Near the Walker River in Humboldt-Toiyabe National Forest.

Map 6.3, page 350

The West Walker River is a pretty stream, flowing over boulders and into pools, and each year this stretch of river is well stocked with rainbow trout by the Department of Fish and Game. One of several campgrounds near the West Walker, Sonora Bridge is set at 6,800 feet, about a half mile from the river. The setting is in the transition zone from high mountains to high desert on the eastern edge of the Sierra Nevada.

Campsites, facilities: There are 23 sites for tents or RVs up to 40 feet long. Picnic tables and fire grills are provided. Drinking water and vault toilets are available. Leashed pets are permitted.

Reservations, fees: Reservations are not accepted. The fee is $11 per night. Senior discount available. Open May through mid-October.

Directions: From north of Bridgeport, at the

junction of U.S. 395 and Highway 108, turn west on Highway 108 and drive two miles to the campground.

Contact: Humboldt-Toiyabe National Forest, Bridgeport Ranger District, 760/932-7070, fax 760/932-1299.

184 CHRIS FLAT

Rating: 7

On the Walker River in Humboldt-Toiyabe National Forest.

Map 6.3, page 350

This is one of two campgrounds set along U.S. 395 next to the West Walker River, a pretty trout stream with easy access and good stocks of rainbow trout. The plants are usually made at two campgrounds, resulting in good prospects here at Chris Flat and west on Highway 108 at Sonora Bridge. The elevation is 6,600 feet.

Campsites, facilities: There are 15 sites for tents or RVs up to 40 feet long. Picnic tables and fire grills are provided. Drinking water and vault toilets are available. Leashed pets are permitted.

Reservations, fees: Reservations are not accepted. The fee is $11 per night. Senior discount available. Open late April through October.

Directions: From Carson City, drive south on U.S. 395 to Coleville and then continue south for 15 miles to the campground on the east side of the road (four miles north of the junction of U.S. 395 and Highway 108).

Contact: Humboldt-Toiyabe National Forest, Bridgeport Ranger District, 760/932-7070, fax 760/932-1299.

185 BOOTLEG

Rating: 6

On the Walker River in Humboldt-Toiyabe National Forest.

Map 6.3, page 350

Location is always a key, and easy access off

U.S. 395, the adjacent West Walker River, and good trout stocks in summer make this a popular spot. (See the entries for Chris Flat and Sonora Bridge for more information.) Note that this camp is on the west side of the highway, and that anglers will have to cross the road to gain fishing access. The elevation is 6,600 feet.

Campsites, facilities: There are 63 paved sites for tents or RVs up to 45 feet long. Picnic tables and fire grills are provided. Drinking water and flush toilets are available. Leashed pets are permitted.

Reservations, fees: Reservations are not accepted. The fee is $11 per night. Senior discount available. Open early May to mid-September.

Directions: From Carson City, drive south on U.S. 395 to Coleville and then continue south for 13 miles to the campground on the west side of the highway (six miles north of the junction of U.S. 395 and Highway 108).

Contact: Humboldt-Toiyabe National Forest, Bridgeport Ranger District, 760/932-7070, fax 760/932-1299.

186 CASCADE CREEK

Rating: 6

In Stanislaus National Forest.

Map 6.3, page 350

This campground is set along Cascade Creek at an elevation of 6,000 feet. A Forest Service road about a quarter mile west of camp on the south side of the highway provides a side trip three miles up to Pikes Peak, at 7,236 feet.

Campsites, facilities: There are 14 sites for tents or RVs up to 22 feet long. Picnic tables and fire rings are provided. Pit and vault toilets are available. No drinking water is available. Supplies are available in Dardanelle. Leashed pets are permitted.

Reservations, fees: Reservations are not accepted. The fee is $5 per night. Senior discount available. Open May through mid-October.

Directions: From Sonora, drive east on Highway 108 to Strawberry and continue for 11 miles to the campground on the left side of the road.

Contact: Stanislaus National Forest, Summit Ranger District, 209/965-3434, fax 209/965-3372.

© TOM STIENSTRA

Chapter 7
San Francisco Bay Area

Chapter 7—San Francisco Bay Area

It's ironic that many people who have chosen to live in the Bay Area are often the ones who complain the most about it. We've even heard some say, "Some day I'm going to get out of here and start having a good time."

We wish we could take anyone who has ever had these thoughts on a little trip in our airplane and circle the Bay Area at 3,000 feet. What you see is that despite strips of roadways and pockets of cities where people are jammed together, most of the region is wild, unsettled, and beautiful. There is no metropolitan area in the world that offers better and more diverse recreation and open space so close to so many.

The Bay Area has 150 significant parks (including 12 with redwoods), 7,500 miles of hiking and biking trails, 45 lakes, 25 waterfalls, 100 miles of coast, mountains with incredible lookouts, bays with islands, and in all, 1.2 million acres of greenbelt with hundreds of acres being added each year with land bought by money earmarked from property taxes. The land has no limit. Enjoy it.

Along with the unique recreation possiblities here come unique campgrounds. There are boat-in camps at Tomales Bay, ferry-in camps on Angel Island, and hike-in camps at Point Reyes National Seashore, the Marin Headlands, Sunol-Ohlone Wilderness, Butano Redwoods State Park, and Big Basin Redwoods State Park—along with a sprinkling of the more traditional drive-in sites at state, county, and regional parks throughout the region.

Note that proximity to a metropolitan area means two things: the demand is higher. So plan ahead. One shocker is that in spring and fall, there is a huge drop-off in use on weekdays, Sunday through Thursday.

There are many world-class landmarks to see while staying in the Bay Area. In San Francisco alone, there are the Golden Gate Bridge, Fisherman's Wharf, Alcatraz, Ghirardelli Square, Chinatown, Pacific Bell ballpark, the Crissy Field waterfront, cable cars, Fort Point, the Cliff House and Ocean Beach, and Fort Funston.

In fact, instead of going far away for a vacation, residents might consider what so many do from all over the world: stay and discover the treasures in your own backyard.

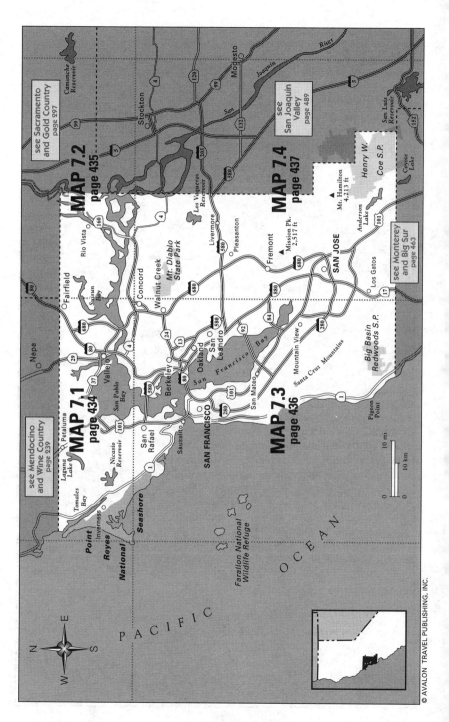

Map 7.1

Campgrounds 1–7
Pages 438–441

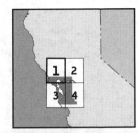

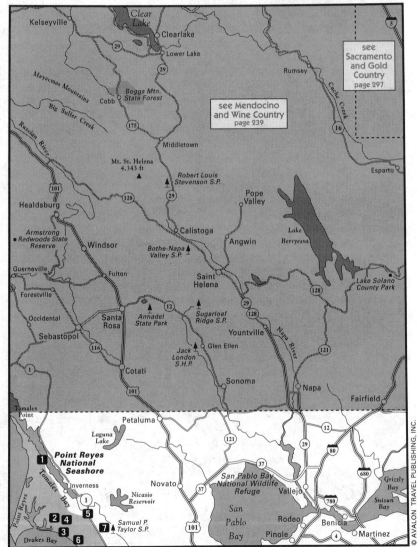

© AVALON TRAVEL PUBLISHING, INC.

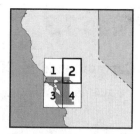

Map 7.2

Campgrounds 8–14
Pages 441–444

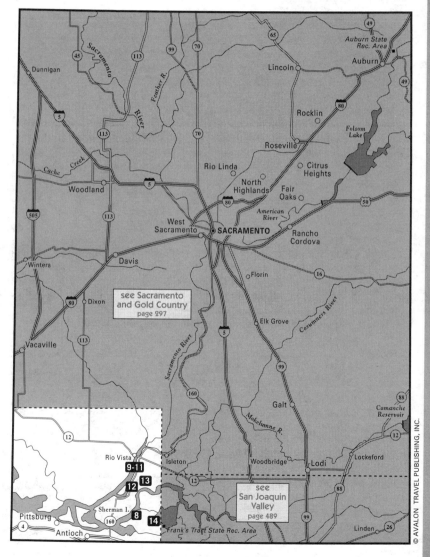

© AVALON TRAVEL PUBLISHING, INC.

Map 7.3

Campgrounds 15–34
Pages 445–455

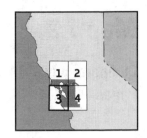

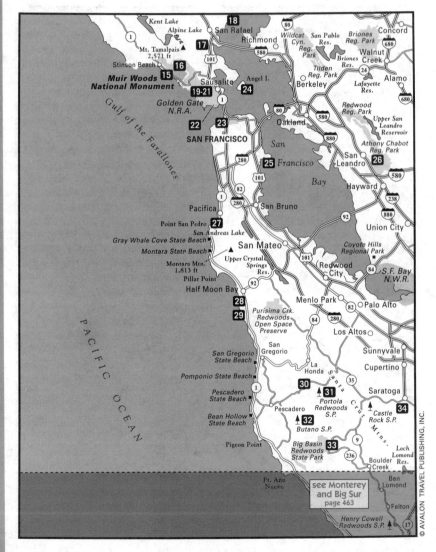

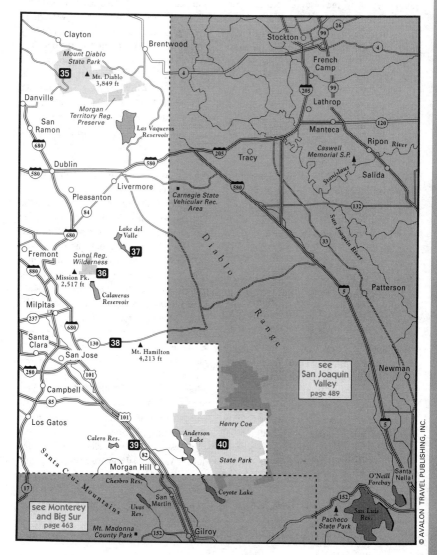

Map 7.4

Campgrounds 35–40
Pages 456–458

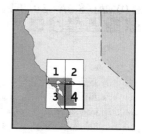

Clayton

Brentwood

Stockton

French Camp

Mount Diablo State Park

35 ▲ Mt. Diablo 3,849 ft

Danville

Morgan Territory Reg. Preserve

Las Vaqueros Reservoir

San Ramon

680

Dublin

580

580

Pleasanton

Livermore

84

680

Lake del Valle

37

Fremont

880

Sunol Reg. Wilderness

▲ Mission Pk. 2,517 ft **36**

Calaveras Reservoir

Milpitas

237

680

Santa Clara

130 **38**

San Jose

▲ Mt. Hamilton 4,213 ft

280

101

Campbell

85

Los Gatos

101

Calero Res. **39**

82

Morgan Hill

Santa Cruz Mountains

17

Chesbro Res.

San Martin

Uvas Res.

Mt. Madonna County Park

152

Gilroy

Carnegie State Vehicular Rec. Area

205

Tracy

580

Diablo Range

Henry Coe

Anderson Lake **40**

State Park

Coyote Lake

26

99

4

205

99

Lathrop

120

Manteca

Ripon *River*

Caswell Memorial S.P.

Stanislaus

Salida

132

33

San Joaquin River

5

Patterson

Newman

5

see San Joaquin Valley page 489

Santa Nella

O'Neill Forebay

152

Pacheco State Park

San Luis Res.

see Monterey and Big Sur page 463

© AVALON TRAVEL PUBLISHING, INC.

1 TOMALES BAY BOAT-IN

🏃 🏊 🚣 🛶 5% ⛺

Rating: 10

On Tomales Bay.

Map 7.1, page 434

Here is a little slice of paradise secreted away along the west shore of Tomales Bay. A series of dispersed boat-in camps are set along small, sandy coves along the bases of steep cliffs, set from just north of Indian Beach at Tomales Bay State Park on north all the way to Tomales Point. Note that boaters are required to bring portable toilets, and that reservations are often a necessity, especially on weekends. Tomales Bay is pretty, quiet, and protected from the coastal winds, and offers outstanding sea kayaking. Note that some spots that appear gorgeous during low tides can be covered by water during high tides, so pick your spot with care.

Campsites, facilities: There are 20 dispersed boat-in tent sites along the shore of Tomales Bay. Pits toilets are available only at Marshall Beach and Tomales/Kehoe Beach. No drinking water or other facilities are available. Garbage must be packed out. Boaters must bring portable toilets. No pets are allowed.

Reservations, fees: Reservations are strongly recommended, available Monday through Friday at 415/663-8054, $10–30 per night. Senior discount available. Open year-round, weather permitting.

Directions: Drive on U.S. 101 to Petaluma and the East Washington exit. Take that exit west and drive west (this street becomes Bodega Avenue) through Petaluma and continue to Highway 1. Turn left (south) on Highway 1 and drive 3.5 miles to the Miller County Park boat launch on the right (a half-mile before Blakes Landing). Launch your boat and paddle across Tomales Bay to the boat-in campsites along the Point Reyes National Seashore.

Contact: Point Reyes National Seashore, 415/464-5100, fax 415/464-5149.

2 SKY CAMP HIKE-IN

🏃 ⛺

Rating: 7

In Point Reyes National Seashore.

Map 7.1, page 434

Sky Camp is set on the western flank of Mt. Wittenberg on Inverness Ridge at 1,025 feet, right at the edge of the area in Point Reyes National Seashore that burned in the fall 1995 wildfire. In fact, this hike-in camp was right at the edge of the firebreak and was partially burned. To reach the camp, take the Bear Valley Trail from park headquarters and walk .2 mile to the Mt. Wittenberg Trail. Turn right (north) on the Mt. Wittenberg Trail and hike 2.2 miles to the Sky Trail. Turn right and hike .6 mile to the campground. From here you get a dramatic view of the burned area and the adjacent Marin coast. No wood fires and no pets are permitted. You must have a backcountry permit from the Bear Valley Visitor Center to camp here.

Campsites, facilities: There are 11 individual sites and a group site (walk-in only) which can accommodate up to six campers. Pit toilets and fire grills (charcoal only, no wood fires) are provided. Piped water is available, but it must be treated before use. Garbage must be packed out. No vehicles or pets are allowed.

Reservations, fees: Reservations required by phone Monday through Friday, or in person; $10 per night, $10–30 per night for the group site (maximum of 25 people); four-day maximum stay. Senior discount available. Open year-round.

Directions: From U.S. 101 in Marin, take the Sir Francis Drake Boulevard exit and drive west for about 20 miles to Highway 1 at Olema. Turn north on Highway 1 and drive a very short distance to Bear Valley Road. Turn left at Bear Valley Road and drive north for .7 mile to the visitor center road on the left (signed "Seashore Information"). Turn left and drive to the visitor center parking lot and the Bear Valley Trailhead.

Contact: Point Reyes camping line (reservations), 415/663-8054; Point Reyes National Seashore, 415/464-5100, fax 415/464-5149.

3 COAST CAMP HIKE-IN

Rating: 7

In Point Reyes National Seashore.

Map 7.1, page 434

This is a classic ocean-bluff setting, a hike-in camp set just above Santa Maria Beach on the Point Reyes National Seashore, providing an extended tour into a land of charm. It is a 2.8-mile hike to get here, the northernmost camp on the Coast Trail. (The complete Coast Trail is a 19-mile trip that is one of the best hikes in the Bay Area.) From Coast Camp, the trail contours south along the bluffs above the beach for 1.4 miles to Sculptured Beach, where there is a series of odd geologic formations, including caves, tunnels, and sea stacks. A backcountry permit is required. Note: this camp is set on the edge of the area that burned in the fall 1995 wildfire.

Campsites, facilities: There are 12 individual and two group hike-in sites. Picnic tables and fire grills are provided. Vault toilets are available. Piped water is available, but it must be treated before use. Charcoal or gas stoves are allowed, with backpacking stoves recommended for cooking. No wood fires permitted. Garbage must be packed out. No vehicles or pets are permitted.

Reservations, fees: Reservations are recommended and permits required; $10 per night, four-day maximum stay; $10–30 per night for group sites. Senior discount available. Open year-round.

Directions: From U.S. 101 in Marin, take the Sir Francis Drake Boulevard exit and drive about 20 miles to Highway 1 at Olema. Turn right on Highway 1 and drive a very short distance. Turn left at Bear Valley Road and drive north for two miles to Limantour Road. Turn left at Limantour Road and drive six miles to

the access road for the Point Reyes Hostel. Turn left and drive .2 mile to the trailhead on the right side of the road. A parking area is a short distance ahead and to the right.

Contact: Point Reyes camping line (reservations, permits), 415/663-8054; Point Reyes National Seashore, 415/464-5100, fax 415/464-5149.

4 GLEN CAMP HIKE-IN

Rating: 9

In Point Reyes National Seashore.

Map 7.1, page 434

Glen Camp Hike-In is set in the coastal foothills of Point Reyes National Seashore and is surrounded by forest. The hike to it starts at the Bear Valley Visitor Center, where you can obtain your backcountry permits and hiking information, and is routed on the popular Bear Valley Trail, a wide road made out of compressed rock. It is 1.6 miles to Divide Meadow, with a modest 215-foot climb, then another 1.6 miles through Bear Valley to the Glen Trail. Turn left on Glen Loop Trail and hike 1.4 miles, with the trail lateraling in and out of two canyons to reach the camp. It is secluded and quiet. Get a map, a permit, and bring everything you need.

Campsites, facilities: There are 12 hike-in sites. Picnic tables and fire grills are provided. Pit toilets are available. Water is usually available (check before arranging trip), but it must be treated before use. Charcoal or gas stoves are allowed, with backpacking stoves recommended for cooking. No wood fires permitted. Garbage must be packed out. No vehicles or pets are permitted.

Reservations, fees: Reservations recommended and permits are required; $10 per night, group sites $10–30 per night; four-day maximum stay. Open year-round.

Directions: From U.S. 101 in Marin, take the Sir Francis Drake Boulevard exit and drive west for about 20 miles to Highway 1 at Olema. Turn north on Highway 1 and drive a very short distance to Bear Valley Road. Turn left at Bear Valley Road and drive north for .7 mile to the visitor center road on the left (signed "Seashore Information"). Turn left and drive to the visitor center parking lot and the Bear Valley Trailhead. It is a 4.6-mile hike to the camp.

Contact: Point Reyes camping line (reservations, permits), 415/663-8054; Point Reyes National Seashore, 415/464-5100, fax 415/464-5149.

5 OLEMA RANCH CAMPGROUND

Rating: 4

In Olema.

Map 7.1, page 434

If location is everything, then this park should be rated a 10. It is set in Olema, in a valley amid Marin's coastal foothills, an ideal jumpoff spot for a Point Reyes adventure. It borders the Point Reyes National Seashore to the west and the Golden Gate National Recreation Area to the east, with Tomales Bay to the nearby north. There are several excellent trailheads available within a 10-minute drive along Highway 1 to the south. The campsites are small, tightly placed, and we have received complaint letters about the ambience of the place. In the past, when such problems are noted, we have found they are often quickly addressed.

Campsites, facilities: There are 225 sites, some with full or partial hookups, for tents or RVs. Picnic tables are provided. Drinking water, restrooms, showers, fire pits, RV dump station, coin laundry, modem access, arcade, and a recreation hall (for groups of 25 or more only) are available. Some facilities are wheelchair-accessible. Leashed pets are permitted.

Reservations, fees: Reservations are accepted, 800/655-CAMP (800/655-2267); $23–32 per night, $2 for second vehicle, $3 per person for more than two people. Major credit cards accepted. Open year-round.

Directions: From U.S. 101 in Marin, take the San Anselmo/Sir Francis Drake Boulevard exit and drive west for about 20 miles to Highway

1 at Olema. Turn north (right) on Highway 1 and drive a half mile to the campground on the left.

Contact: Olema Ranch Campground, 415/663-8001, fax 415/663-8832, website: www.camp grounds.com/olemaranch.

6 WILDCAT CAMP HIKE-IN

Rating: 10

In Point Reyes National Seashore.

Map 7.1, page 434

This backpack camp sits in a grassy meadow near a small stream that flows to the ocean, just above remote Wildcat Beach. From the Palomarin Trailhead, getting to this camp takes you on a fantastic 5.6-mile hike that crosses some of the Bay Area's most beautiful wildlands. The trail is routed along the ocean for about a mile, heads up in the coastal hills, turns left, and skirts past Bass Lake, Crystal Lake, and Pelican Lake and, ultimately, heads past Alamere Creek to this beautiful camp set on an ocean bluff. A fantastic side trip is to hike along the beach from Wildcat Camp on south, where you can get a full frontal view of Alamere Falls. It is a dramatic 40-foot freefall, one of the rare ocean bluff waterfalls anywhere.

Campsites, facilities: There are five individual and three group hike-in sites. Picnic tables and fire grills are provided. Vault toilets are available. Piped water is available, but it must be treated before use. Charcoal or gas stoves are allowed, with backpacking stoves recommended for cooking. No wood fires permitted. Garbage must be packed out. No vehicles or pets are permitted.

Reservations, fees: Reservations are recommended and permits required; $10 per night, group sites $10–30 per night; four-day maximum stay. Open year-round.

Directions: From U.S. 101 in Marin, take the Sir Francis Drake Boulevard exit and drive about 20 miles west on Sir Francis Drake Boulevard to the town of Olema and Highway 1.

Turn left on Highway 1 and drive 9.3 miles to Olema-Bolinas Road on the right (if the sign is missing—a common event—note that a white ranch house is opposite the turn). Turn right on Olema-Bolinas Road and drive 1.5 miles to Mesa Road. Turn right and drive six miles (past an area known as "The Towers" from all the antennas) to the parking area and Palomarin Trailhead. It is a 5.6-mile hike to the campground on the Coast Trail.

Contact: Point Reyes camping line (reservations, permits), 415/663-8054; Point Reyes National Seashore, 415/464-5100, fax 415/464-5149.

7 SAMUEL P. TAYLOR STATE PARK

Rating: 9

Near San Rafael.

Map 7.1, page 434

This is a beautiful park, with campsites set amid redwoods, complete with a babbling brook running nearby. The park covers more than 2,700 acres of wooded countryside in the steep and rolling hills of Marin County. This features unique contrasts of coast redwoods and open grassland. Hikers will find 20 miles of hiking trails, a hidden waterfall, and some good mountain biking routes on service roads. The paved bike path that runs through the park and parallels Sir Francis Drake Boulevard is a terrific, easy ride. Trees include redwood, Douglas fir, oak, and madrone, and native wildflowers include buttercups, milkmaids, and Indian paintbrush. The section of the park on the north side of Sir Francis Drake (the camp is on the south side) has the best hiking in the park.

Campsites, facilities: There are 25 sites for tents and 35 sites for tents or RVs up to 27 feet long, two group sites for 25 and 50 people, one hike-in/bike-in camp and one equestrian site with corrals at Devil's Gulch Horse Camp. Picnic tables, food lockers, and fire grills are provided. Drinking water and flush toilets are available. There is a small store and café two miles away in Lagunitas. Some facilities are wheelchair-accessible. Leashed pets are permitted in campsites only.

Reservations, fees: Reserve at 800/444-PARK (800/444-7275) or website: www.Reserve America.com ($7.50 reservation fee); $12 per night, group sites $18–37 per night, equestrian camp $10 per night, $1 per person per night for hike-in/bike-in site. Open year-round.

Directions: From U.S. 101 in Marin, take the Sir Francis Drake Boulevard exit and drive west for about 15 miles to the park entrance on the left side of the road.

Contact: Samuel P. Taylor State Park, 415/488-9897, fax 415/488-4315; California State Parks, Marin District, 415/893-1580, fax 415/893-1583.

8 EDDOS HARBOR AND RV PARK

Rating: 6

On the San Joaquin River Delta.

Map 7.2, page 435

This is an ideal spot for campers with boats. Eddos is set on the San Joaquin River, upstream of the Antioch Bridge, in an outstanding region for fishing, powerboating, and water-skiing. In summer, boaters have access to 1,000 miles of Delta waterways, with the best of them in a nearby spider web of rivers and sloughs off the San Joaquin to False River, Frank's Tract, and Old River. Hot weather and sheltered sloughs make this ideal for water-skiing. In the winter, a nearby fishing spot called Eddos Bar, as well as the mouth of the False River, attract striped bass.

Campsites, facilities: There are 40 sites with full hookups for RVs, and 10 tent sites. Picnic tables are provided. Flush toilets, hot showers, launch ramp, boat storage, fuel dock, coin laundry, modem access, and a small grocery store are available. Some facilities are wheelchair-accessible. Leashed pets are permitted.

Reservations, fees: Reservations are recommended. The fee is $19–22 per night and $1 per night. Major credit cards accepted. Open year-round.

Directions: In Fairfield on I-80, take the Highway 12 exit and drive 14 miles southeast to Rio Vista and continue three miles to Highway 160 (at the signal just after the bridge). Turn right on Highway 160 and drive five miles to Sherman Island/East Levee Road. Turn left on East Levee Road and drive five miles to the campground along the San Joaquin River. Note: if arriving by boat, the camp is adjacent to Light 21.

Contact: Eddos Harbor and RV Park, 925/757-5314, fax 925/757-6246, website: www.eddos resort.com.

9 SANDY BEACH COUNTY PARK

Rating: 6

On the Sacramento River.
Map 7.2, page 435

This is a surprisingly little-known park, especially considering it provides beach access to the Sacramento River. It is a popular spot for sunbathers in hot summer months, but in winter, it is one of the few viable spots where you can fish from the shore for sturgeon. It also provides outstanding boating access to the Sacramento River, including one of the best fishing spots for striped bass in the fall, the Rio Vista Bridge.

Campsites, facilities: There are 42 sites for tents or RVs. Picnic tables and fire grills are provided. Electricity, drinking water, flush toilets, showers, RV dump station, and a boat ramp are available. Some facilities are wheelchair-accessible. Supplies can be obtained nearby (within a mile). Pets are permitted with proof of rabies vaccination.

Reservations, fees: Reservations are accepted. The fee is $12–18 per night, $5 per night for each extra vehicle, maximum 10 people per site, senior discounts, $1 per night. Major credit cards accepted. Open year-round.

Directions: From I-80 in Fairfield, take the Highway 12 exit and drive southeast for 25 miles to Rio Vista and the intersection with Main Street. Turn right on Main Street and drive a short distance to 2nd Street. Turn right and drive a half mile to Beach Drive. Continue on Beach Drive to the park.

Contact: Solano County Parks, 707/374-2097, fax 707/374-4972; website: www.solano county.com.

10 DUCK ISLAND RV PARK

Rating: 6

On the Sacramento River.
Map 7.2, page 435

This pleasant rural park, set up for adults only, has riverside access that provides an opportunity for bank fishing on the Sacramento River. Note that half of the sites are long-term rentals and that this is an adults-only park. A boat ramp is available at the end of Main Street in Rio Vista. Hap's Bait Shop provides reliable fishing information as well as all gear needed for fishing.

Campsites, facilities: There are 51 RV sites with full hookups. Picnic tables are provided. A laundry and recreation room with a kitchen are available. Some facilities are wheelchair-accessible. A small store is available, with propane, bait, and RV supplies. Other supplies can be obtained in Rio Vista. Adults only. Leashed pets are permitted.

Reservations, fees: Reservations are accepted. The fee is $22 per night. Reservations required for groups. Major credit cards accepted. Open year-round.

Directions: In Fairfield on I-80, take the Highway 12 exit and drive 14 miles southeast to Rio Vista and continue to Highway 160 (at the signal after the bridge). Turn right on Highway 160 and drive just under a mile to the RV park on the right.

Contact: Duck Island RV Park, 800/825-3898 or 916/777-6663.

ELEVEN DELTA MARINA RV RESORT

Rating: 6

On the Sacramento River Delta.

Map 7.2, page 435

This is a prime spot for boat campers. Summers are hot and breezy, and water-skiing is popular on the nearby Sacramento River. From November to March, the striped bass fishing is quite good, often as close as just a half mile upriver at the Rio Vista Bridge. The boat launch at the harbor is a bonus.

Campsites, facilities: There are 25 sites with full hookups for RVs. Picnic tables and fire grills are provided. Restrooms, showers, coin laundry, playground, boat ramp, ice, and propane gas are available. Fuel is available 24 hours. Some facilities are wheelchair-accessible. Leashed pets (one pet per vehicle) are permitted.

Reservations, fees: Reservations are accepted. The fee is $18–25 per night. Major credit cards accepted. Open year-round.

Directions: From Fairfield on I-80, take the Highway 12 exit and drive southeast for 14 miles to Rio Vista and the intersection with Main Street. Take the Main Street exit and drive a short distance to 2nd Street. Turn right on 2nd Street and drive to Marina Drive. Turn left on Marina Drive, and continue another short distance to the harbor.

Contact: Delta Marina RV Resort, 707/374-2315, fax 707/374-6471, website: www.delta marina.com

TWELVE BRANNAN ISLAND STATE RECREATION AREA

Rating: 7

On the Sacramento River.

Map 7.2, page 435

This state park is perfectly designed for boaters, set in the heart of the Delta's vast waterways. You get year-round adventure: water-skiing and fishing for catfish are popular in the summer, and in the winter the immediate area is often good for striped bass fishing. The proximity of the campgrounds to the boat launch deserves a medal. What many people do is tow a boat here, launch it, and keep it docked, then return to their site and set up; this allows them to come and go as they please, boating, fishing, and exploring in the Delta. There is a six-lane boat ramp that provides access to a maze of waterways amid many islands, marshes, sloughs, and rivers. Day-use areas include the Windy Cove windsurfing area. Though striped bass in winter and catfish in summer are the most favored fish here, sturgeon, bluegill, perch, bullhead, and bass are also caught. Some sections of the San Joaquin Delta are among the best bass fishing spots in California.

Campsites, facilities: There are 102 sites for tents or RVs up to 36 feet long, and six group sites for up to 30 people each. Picnic tables and fire grills are provided. Drinking water, restrooms, coin showers (at campground and boat launch), boat berths, RV dump station, and a boat launch are available. Some facilities are wheelchair-accessible. Supplies can be obtained three miles away in Rio Vista. Leashed pets are permitted.

Reservations, fees: Reserve at 800/444-PARK (800/444-7275) or website: www.Reserve America.com ($7.50 reservation fee); $12 per night, $22.50 per night for group sites. Senior discount available. Open year-round.

Directions: In Fairfield on I-80, take the Highway 12 exit, drive southeast 14 miles to Rio Vista, and continue to Highway 160 (at the signal before the bridge). Turn right on Highway 160 and drive three miles to the park entrance on the left.

Contact: Brannan Island State Recreation Area, 916/777-6671; Goldfield District Office, 916/988-0205.

13 SNUG HARBOR MARINA AND RV CAMP/PARK

Rating: 9

Near Rio Vista.

Map 7.2, page 435

This year-round resort is an ideal resting place for families who enjoy water-skiing, boating, biking, swimming, and fishing. After the ferry ride, it is only a few minutes to Snug Harbor, a privately operated resort with a campground, RV hookups, and a separate area with cabins and a cottage. Some say that the waterfront sites with docks give the place the feel of a Louisiana bayou, yet everything is clean and orderly, including a full-service marina, a store, and all facilities—and an excellent location to explore the boating paradise of the Delta. Anglers will find good prospects for striped bass, black bass, blue gill, and catfish. The waterfront sites with docks make Snug Harbor a winner. Snug Harbor was awarded as the "2001 Best Small Park" by the California Travel Parks Association.

Campsites, facilities: There are 38 waterfront sites with docks and full hookups for RVs or tents, 15 inland sites with water hookups only, and 12 park-model cabins. Restrooms, hot showers, RV dump station, convenience store, barbecue, swimming beach, children's play area, boat launch, paddle boat rentals, propane gas, and a full-service marina are available. Some facilities are wheelchair-accessible.

Reservations, fees: Reservations are recommended. The fee is $27–30 per night, $4 per night for each extra vehicle, $4 per person per night for more than four people, $2 per night. Major credit cards accepted. Open year-round.

Directions: From the Bay Area, take I-80 to Fairfield and Highway 12. Turn east on Highway 12 and drive to Rio Vista and Front Street. Turn left on Front Street and drive under the bridge to River Road. Turn right on River Road and drive two miles to the Real McCoy Ferry (signed Ryer Island). Take the ferry (free) across the Sacramento River to Ryer Island and Levee Road. Turn right and drive 3.5 miles on Levee Road to Snug Harbor on the right.

From Sacramento, drive 26 miles south on I-5 to Highway 12. Drive west on Highway 12 about 20 miles to Rio Vista and then turn north on Route 84 for two miles to the Real McCoy Ferry to Ryer Island. Take the ferry across the Sacramento River (cars are allowed). On Ryer Island, drive 3.5 miles on Levee Road to Snug Harbor.

Contact: Snug Harbor Marina and RV Camp/Park, 916/775-1455, fax 916/775-1594, website: www.snugharbor.net; Fish Hooker Fishing Charters, 916/777-6498; Boat rentals at Waterflies (will deliver), 916/777-6431; Herman & Helen's, 209/951-4634.

14 LUNDBORG LANDING

Rating: 5

On the San Joaquin River Delta.

Map 7.2, page 435

This park is set on Bethel Island in the heart of the San Joaquin Delta. The boat ramp here provides immediate access to an excellent area for water-skiing, and it turns into a playland on hot summer days. In the fall and winter, the area often provides good striper fishing at nearby Frank's Tract, False River, and San Joaquin River. The fishing for largemouth bass at Frank's Tract is rated among the best in North America. Catfishing in surrounding slough areas is also good year-round. The Delta Sportsman Shop at Bethel Island has reliable fishing information. Live web camera pictures of Frank's Tract available on the website. Note that some sites are occupied by what appear to be permanent tenants.

Campsites, facilities: There are 76 sites, including some drive-through sites, with full hookups for RVs. Tents are permitted at some sites, and several cabins are available. Restrooms, laundry room, showers, RV dump station, propane gas, playground, boat ramp, and full restaurant and bar are available. Some facilities are wheelchair-accessible. Leashed pets are permitted.

Reservations, fees: Reservations and deposit are required. The rates are $16–23 per night. Long-term rates available. Open year-round.

Directions: From Antioch, turn east on Highway 4 and drive to Oakley and East Cypress Road. Turn left on East Cypress Road, drive over the Bethel Island Bridge, and continue a half mile to Gateway Road. Turn right on Gateway Road, drive two miles to the park entrance on the left (signed well, next to the tugboat).

Contact: Lundborg Landing, P.O. Box 220, Bethel Island, CA 94511, 925/684-9351, website: www.lundborglanding.com.

15 STEEP RAVINE ENVIRONMENTAL CAMPSITES

Rating: 10

In Mt. Tamalpais State Park.

Map 7.3, page 436

This is one of the most remarkable spots on the California coast, with primitive cabins/wood shacks set on a bluff on Rocky Point overlooking the ocean. It is primitive but dramatic, with passing ships, fishing boats, lots of marine birds, occasionally even whales, and a chance for heart-stopping sunsets. There is an easy walk to the north down to Redrock Beach, which is secluded, and just across the road (with a short jog to the right) is a trailhead for the Steep Ravine Trail on the slopes of Mt. Tamalpais. After a while you'll feel like you're a million miles from civilization.

Campsites, facilities: There are six walk-in sites for tents and 10 primitive cabins (also known as environmental sites), each with a wood stove, picnic table, and a flat wood surface for sleeping. At tent sites, picnic tables and fire grills are provided and pit toilets are available. Drinking water is nearby, and wood is available for purchase. No pets are permitted.

Reservations, fees: Reserve at 800/444-PARK

(800/444-7275) or website: www.Reserve America.com ($7.50 reservation fee); $7 per night for tent sites, $15 per night for environmental cabins, one vehicle per cabin, five people maximum per site. Senior discount available. Open year-round.

Directions: From U.S. 101 in Marin, take the Stinson Beach/Highway 1 exit. Drive west to the stoplight at the T intersection (Highway 1). Turn left on Highway 1 and drive about 11 miles to the gated access road on the left side of the highway at Rocky Point. (The gate lock combination will be provided when reservations are made.)

Contact: Steep Ravine Environmental Campsites, 415/388-2070; California State Parks, Marin District, 415/893-1580, fax 415/388-2968.

16 PANTOLL CAMPGROUND WALK-IN AND ALICE EASTWOOD GROUP CAMPS

Rating: 9

In Mt. Tamalpais State Park.

Map 7.3, page 436

When camping at Pantoll, you are within close range of the divine, including some of the best hiking, best lookouts, and just plain best places to be anywhere in the Bay Area. The camp is set in the woods on the western slopes of Mt. Tamalpais, which some say is a place of special power, with sensational hiking and trailheads. The walk to the Pantoll Campground can be as short as 100 feet, and as long as just over a quarter mile. This landscape is a mix of redwood groves, oak woodlands, and grasslands, providing both drop-dead beautiful views of the ocean nearby, as well as a trip into a lush redwood canyon with a stream. The Steep Ravine Trail is routed out of camp to the west into a wondrous gorge filled with redwoods and a stream with miniature waterfalls. It is best seen after a good rain, when everything is dripping with moisture. Another great hike from this camp is on the Matt Davis/Coast

Trail, which provides beautiful views of the coast. Another must is the nearby drive to the East Peak Lookout, where the entire world seems within reach. This park provides more than 50 miles of trails for hiking and biking, which in turn link to a network of 200 miles of other trails.

Campsites, facilities: There are 16 walk-in tent sites, and two group sites for 10–75 people. Picnic tables, food lockers, and fire grills are provided. Drinking water and vault toilets are available. Firewood is available for purchase. Leashed pets are permitted at campsites only.

Reservations, fees: Reservations are not accepted. The fee is $12 per night. Senior discount available. Make reservations for groups at 800/444-PARK (800/444-7275) or website: www.ReserveAmerica.com ($7.50 reservation fee; $18–37 per night. Open year-round.

Directions: From U.S. 101 in Marin, take the Stinson Beach/Highway 1 exit. Drive west to the stoplight at the T intersection for Highway 1. Turn left and drive about four miles uphill to the Panoramic Highway. Bear to the right on Panoramic Highway and continue for 5.5 miles to the Pantoll parking area. Turn left at the Pantoll parking area and ranger station. A 100- to 500-foot walk is required to reach the campground. To reach the group site, directions and the combination to the gate lock will be provided when reservations are made.

Contact: Pantoll Campground, 415/388-2070; California State Parks, Marin District, 415/893-1580, fax 415/388-2968.

17 MARIN PARK

Rating: 2

In Greenbrae.

Map 7.3, page 436

For out-of-towners with RVs, this can make an ideal base camp for Marin County adventures. To the west are Mt. Tamalpais State Park, Muir Woods National Monument, Samuel P. Taylor State Park, and Point Reyes National Seashore. To the nearby east is the Loch Lomond Marina on San Pablo Bay, where fishing trips can be arranged for striped bass and sturgeon; phone 415/456-0321. The park offers complete sight-seeing information and easy access to buses and ferry service to San Francisco.

Campsites, facilities: There are 89 RV sites with full hookups. Showers, coin laundry, modem access, swimming pool, and RV supplies are available. Some facilities are wheelchair-accessible. Leashed pets are permitted.

Reservations, fees: Reservations are recommended. The fee is $35 per night, $2 per person per night for more than two people. Six people maximum per site. Major credit cards accepted. Open year-round.

Directions: From the south: From the Golden Gate Bridge, drive north on U.S. 101 for 10 miles to Lucky Drive (south of San Rafael). Exit and turn left on Redwood Highway (no sign) and drive three blocks north to the park entrance.

From the north: From San Rafael, drive south on U.S. 101 to the Lucky Drive exit. Take that exit to the first light at Tamal Vista. Turn left and drive to Wornum. Turn left at Wornum and drive under the freeway to Redwood Highway (frontage road). Turn left and drive four blocks north to the park entrance.

Contact: Marin Park, 415/461-5199, fax 415/925-1584, website: www.campground.com.

18 CHINA CAMP STATE PARK WALK-IN

Rating: 10

On San Pablo Bay near San Rafael.

Map 7.3, page 436

This is one of the Bay Area's prettiest campgrounds. It is set in woodlands with a picturesque creek running past. The camps are shaded and sheltered. Directly adjacent to the camp is a meadow, marshland, and then San Pablo Bay. Deer can seem as tame as chipmunks. Hiking is outstanding here, either taking the Shoreline Trail for a pretty walk near the edge of San Pablo Bay, or the Bay View Trail for the climb up the ridge that borders the park, in the process gaining spectacular views of the bay and miles of charm. The landscape here includes an extensive intertidal salt marsh, and meadow and oak habitats. There are five miles of hiking trails, heavily used on spring and summer weekends. A sidelight is the China Camp Village, which depicts an early Chinese settlement.

Campsites, facilities: There are 30 walk-in tent sites and one hike-in/bike-in site. Picnic tables, food lockers, and fire grills are provided. Drinking water, showers, and a restroom are available. Leashed pets are permitted at the campground only.

Reservations, fees: Reserve at 800/444-PARK (800/444-7275) or website: www.Reserve America.com ($7.50 reservation fee); $12 per night, $1 per person per night for hike-in/bike-in site. Open year-round, weather permitting.

Directions: From San Francisco, drive north on U.S. 101 to San Rafael and take the North San Pedro Road exit. Drive east on North San Pedro Road for five miles to the Back Ranch Meadows Campground entrance on the right. Turn right and drive a short distance to the campground trailhead at the end of the road. Reaching the sites requires a one- to five-minute walk.

Contact: China Camp State Park Walk-In, 415/456-0766, fax 415/456-1743; California State Parks, Marin District, 415/893-1580, fax 415/388-2968.

19 BICENTENNIAL WALK-IN

Rating: 9

At Marin Headlands.
Map 7.3, page 436

Of the four hike-in campgrounds set at the Marin Headlands, it is Bicentennial Walk-In that is the easiest to reach. It is only a 100-yard walk from the parking area near Battery Wallace, just northwest of the parking area. This is a small camp with space for just three tents, with a maximum of two people per site.

Campsites, facilities: There are three tent sites. No more than two people and one tent per site. No facilities on site. Barbecues and picnic tables are available 100 yards away at Battery Wallace. Drinking water is available one mile away at the Marin Headlands Visitor Center.

Reservations, fees: Reservations required from the visitor center; no fee. Open year-round, weather permitting.

Directions: From San Francisco drive north on U.S. 101 over the Golden Gate Bridge, and into Marin to the Alexander Avenue exit. Take the Alexander Avenue exit and turn left underneath the highway. Take the wide paved road to the right (Conzelman Road, but there is no sign), and look for the Marin Headlands sign. Continue west for 3.5 miles (it becomes a one-way road) to the parking area on your left for Battery Wallace (on your right). Park and walk 100 yards north to the campground.

Contact: Marin Headlands Visitor Center, Golden Gate National Recreation Area, Bldg. 948, Fort Barry, Sausalito, CA 94965; 415/331-1540. A map/brochure is available at the Marin Headlands Visitor Center or by contacting the Golden Gate National Recreation Area, Marin Headlands, at the address listed. A detailed hiking map of the area is available for a fee from Olmsted Brothers Map Company, P.O. Box 5351, Berkeley, CA 94705.

20 HAWKCAMP HIKE-IN

Rating: 10

On Marin Headlands.
Map 7.3, page 436

This is the most remote of the campgrounds on the Marin Headlands. It is high above Gerbode Valley, requiring a hike of 3.5 miles, climbing much of the way from the parking lot and trailhead at Tennessee Valley. It is a small campground, with three sites and room for no more than four people per site. After parking at Tennessee Valley, take the trailhead for the Old Marincello Vehicle Road/Bobcat Trail. This route climbs in a counterclockwise direction around Mt. Vortac; after 1.7 miles you will reach a junction with the Mt. Vortac Trail. Do not turn at that junction. Continue straight on the Bobcat Trail for .7 mile to a junction with the Hawk Trail. Turn right and hike on the trail for one mile to Hawkcamp, set at an elevation of 750 feet. Below you to the southeast is Gerbode Valley.

Campsites, facilities: There are three tent sites. No more than four people per site. Picnic tables are provided and chemical toilets are available. No drinking water is available. No fires are permitted. Backpacking stoves required for cooking.

Reservations, fees: Reservations required from the visitor center; no fee. All three sites can be reserved by groups of up to 12 from November through March. Open year-round, weather permitting.

Directions: From U.S. 101 in Marin, take the Stinson Beach/Highway 1 exit. Drive .6 mile and turn left on Tennessee Valley Road. Drive two miles until the road dead-ends at the parking area and trailhead. Take the trailhead for Old Marincello Vehicle Road/Bobcat Trail and hike 3.5 miles.

Contact: Marin Headlands Visitor Center, Golden Gate National Recreation Area, Bldg. 948, Fort Barry, Sausalito, CA 94965; 415/331-1540. A map/brochure is available at the Marin Headlands Visitor Center or by contacting the Golden Gate National Recreation Area, Marin Headlands, at the address listed. A detailed hiking map of the area is available for a fee from Olmsted Brothers Map Company, P.O. Box 5351, Berkeley, CA 94705.

21 HAYPRESS HIKE-IN

🏃 ⛰️

Rating: 9

On Marin Headlands.

Map 7.3, page 436

Haypress Campground is set on the northern

outskirts of Tennessee Valley at the north end of the Marin Headlands. Reaching this camp is not difficult, just a three-quarter mile hike, departing from one of Marin's most popular trailheads in Tennessee Valley. Yet in just 20–30 minutes, hikers can create a world that seemingly belongs just to them at this camp. This is a primitive backpacking-style campground where you must supply everything you need.

Campsites, facilities: There are five tent sites. No more than four people per site. No facilities on site. No drinking water is available. No fires are permitted. Backpacking stoves required for cooking.

Reservations, fees: Reservations required from visitor center; no fee. All three sites can be reserved by groups of up to 12 from November through March. Open year-round, weather permitting.

Directions: From U.S. 101 in Marin, take the Stinson Beach/Highway 1 exit. Drive .6 mile to Tennessee Valley Road. Turn left on Tennessee Valley Road and drive two miles until the road dead-ends at the parking area and trailhead. Take the trailhead for Tennessee Valley (see directions above and map/brochure) and hike .7 miles to the campground.

Contact: Marin Headlands Visitor Center, Golden Gate National Recreation Area, Bldg. 948, Fort Barry, Sausalito, CA 94965; 415/331-1540. A map/brochure is available at the Marin Headlands Visitor Center or by contacting the Golden Gate National Recreation Area, Marin Headlands, at the address listed. A detailed hiking map of the area is available for a fee from Olmsted Brothers Map Company, P.O. Box 5351, Berkeley, CA 94705.

22 KIRBY COVE

🏃 ⛰️

Rating: 10

On Marin Headlands.

Map 7.3, page 436

Kirby Cove is nestled in a grove of cypress and eucalyputus trees in a stunning setting just west of the Golden Gate Bridge. It is one of the most beautiful campsites in any metropolitan area in North America. Yet it is small and pristine, with space for just four sites and restricted parking. The view from lookouts near the camp are drop-dead beautiful—sweeping views of the Golden Gate Bridge, San Francisco Headlands, and the mouth of the bay opening to the Pacific Ocean.

Campsites, facilities: There are four sites for tents. No more than 10 people per site. Picnic tables and fire rings/barbecue pits are provided. Pit toilets are available. No drinking water is available.

Reservations, fees: Reserve at 800/365-CAMP (800/365-2267) or website: reservations.nps.gov, $25 per night for up to three cars and 10 people. Open year-round.

Directions: From San Francisco drive north on U.S. 101 over the Golden Gate Bridge and into Marin to the Alexander Avenue exit. Take the Alexander Avenue exit and turn left underneath the highway. Take the wide paved road to the right (Conzelman Road, but there is no sign), and look for the Marin Headlands sign. Continue west on Conzelman about a quarter mile to Kirby Cove Road (the first turn on the left, a dirt road). Bear left and drive to the gate. When you get reservations, you will get the code for the gate. Unlock the gate and drive .9 miles to the campground.

Contact: Marin Headlands Visitor Center, Golden Gate National Recreation Area, Bldg. 948, Fort Barry, Sausalito, CA 94965; 415/331-1540. A map/brochure is available at the Marin Headlands Visitor Center or by contacting the Golden Gate National Recreation Area, Marin Headlands, at the address listed. A detailed hiking map of the area is available for a fee from Olmsted Brothers Map Company, P.O. Box 5351, Berkeley, CA 94705.

23 ROB HILL GROUP CAMP

Rating: 8

In San Francisco Presidio.

Map 7.3, page 436

Rob Hill Group Camp is a pretty spot set in a wooded area beneath cypress and eucalyptus canopy. It is well hidden in the Presidio in the San Francisco Headlands and is San Francisco's only campground with tent sites. Hiking is good in the vicinity. There are two group camps here. They are full all the time—a great spot for youth group camp. Parking is limited. From the parking area, it is a uphill climb of 150 feet to the camp. Free shuttle service is available from the Presidio, which can connect you to Muni bus service.

Campsites, facilities: There are two group sites, each with sites for up to 30 people. Picnic tables, stand-up grills, shared fire ring, and a pit toilet are available. No drinking water is available.

Reservations, fees: Reservations are required. The fee is $50 per night. Open April to October.

Directions: From the Peninsula, drive north on U.S. 101 into San Francisco and continue to Lombard Street. Get in the left lane and stay on Lombard (U.S. 101 and Doyle Drive go off to the right) and drive to Presidio Boulevard. Turn right on Presidio Boulevard and drive (it becomes Lincoln Boulevard) into the Presidio (past the Golden Gate Bridge toll plaza) to Kobbe Avenue. Turn left on Kobbe Avenue and drive to Washington Avenue. Turn right on Washington Avenue and drive to Central Magazine. Turn left on Central Magazine and drive to the first service road on the right. Turn right at that service road and park. Walk up the hill 150 feet to the campsite on the right.

From Marin, take U.S. 101 south over the Golden Gate Bridge and get in the right lane to the toll plaza. After the toll plaza, drive a very short distance to Merchant Street. Turn right and drive up the hill to the stop sign at Lincoln Boulevard. Turn right on Lincoln and drive to Kobbe Avenue. Turn left on Kobbe Avenue and drive to Washington Avenue. Turn right on Washington Avenue and drive to Central Magazine. Turn left on Central Magazine and drive to the first service road on the right. Turn right at that service road and park. Walk up the hill 150 feet to the campsite on the right.

Contact: Presidio/Rob Hill Camp information (reservations), 415/561-5444; Presidio Visitor Center, 415/561-4323; Golden Gate National Recreation Area, Fort Mason, Bldg. 201, San Francisco, CA 94123, 415/561-4700.

24 ANGEL ISLAND STATE PARK WALK-IN

Rating: 10

On Angel Island.

Map 7.3, page 436

Camping at Angel Island is one of the unique adventures in the Bay Area; the only catch is that getting to the campsites requires a ferry boat ride and then a walk of one to two miles. The payoff comes at 4:30 P.M., when all of the park's day visitors depart for the mainland, leaving the entire island to you. From start to finish, it's a great trip, featuring a ferry boat ride, a great hike in, and a private campsite, often with spectacular views of San Francisco Bay, the San Francisco waterfront and skyline, Marin Headlands, and Mt. Tamalpais. The tromp up to 798-foot Mt. Livermore includes a short, very steep stretch, but in return furnishes one of the most spectacular urban lookouts in America. Be ready for cold, foggy weather at night in midsummer. The park features more than 13 miles of trails, including Perimeter Road, a must-do for all avid hikers, with bikes permitted on the park's old road system. Angel Island has a stunning history, including being used from 1910 to 1940 to process thousands of immigrants as they entered America. One of the stupidest budget decisions in state park history occurred here in Marin County in the summer of 2002: the

Marin District closed the hike-in/bike-in camps at Tomales Bay State Park allegedly because of budget constraints, yet at the same time found the money to add 17 feet to Mt. Livermore, raising it from 781 feet to 798 feet.

Campsites, facilities: There are nine hike-in sites. Picnic tables, barbecues, and food lockers are provided. Drinking water and pit toilets are available. Garbage service is available. No pets are permitted. A seasonal café is on the island. No open wood campfires permitted; only charcoal allowed. Some facilities are wheelchair-accessible.

Reservations, fees: Reserve at 800/444-PARK (800/444-7275) or website: www.Reserve America.com ($7.50 reservation fee); $7 per night (limit eight people per site). Open year-round, with limited ferry service in winter.

Directions: Angel Island is in northern San Francisco Bay and can be reached by ferry from San Francisco and Oakland/Alameda, for schedule information, call 415/773-1188, website: www.blueandgoldfleet.com; and from Tiburon, for schedule information, call 415/435-2131, website: www.angelislandferry.com.

Contact: Angel Island State Park, 415/435-1915; California State Parks, Marin District, 415/893-1580, fax 415/893-1583; bike rentals, 415/897-7015, website: www.angelisland.com.

25 CANDLESTICK RV PARK

Rating: 6

In San Francisco.

Map 7.3, page 436

This RV park is set adjacent to Candlestick Park, with the Candlestick State Recreation Area on the other side. It is four miles from downtown San Francisco and an ideal destination for out-of-towners who want to explore the city without having to drive, because the park offers tours and inexpensive shuttles to the downtown area. In addition, there are good hiking opportunities along the shoreline of the bay. On summer afternoons, when the wind howls at 20 to 30 mph here, windsurfers rip by at 50 mph.

Campsites, facilities: There are 165 sites with full hookups for trailers or RVs. Restrooms, showers, coin laundry, modem access, grocery store, game room, and propane are available. Shuttles and bus tours are also available. Some facilities are wheelchair-accessible. A security officer is posted at the entry station at night. Small leashed pets are permitted.

Reservations, fees: Reservations are recommended. To make a reservation phone 800/888-CAMP (800/888-2267); $46–49 per night, $10 per night for each extra vehicle, $2 per person per night for more than two people. Major credit cards accepted. Open year-round.

Directions: From San Francisco on U.S. 101, take the Candlestick Park exit. Turn east on the stadium entrance road and drive around the parking lot to the far end of the stadium (Gate 4).

Contact: Candlestick RV Park, 415/822-2299, fax 415/822-7638; website: www.sanfrancsci rvparks.com.

26 ANTHONY CHABOT REGIONAL PARK

Rating: 7

Near Castro Valley.

Map 7.3, page 436

The campground at Chabot Regional Park is set on a hilltop sheltered by eucalyptus, with good views and trails available. The best campsites are the walk-in units, requiring a walk of only a minute or so. Several provide views of Lake Chabot to the south a half mile away. The lake provides good trout fishing in the winter and spring, and a chance for huge but elusive largemouth bass. The Huck Trail is routed down from the campground (near walk-in site 20) to the lake at Honker Bay, a good fishing area. There is also a good 12-mile bike ride around the lake. Boat rentals at a small marina are available.

Campsites, facilities: There are 43 sites for tents and small RVs, 12 sites with full hookups for RVs, and 10 walk-in sites for tent only. Picnic tables and fire grills are provided. Restrooms, drinking water, flush toilets, showers, and RV dump station are available. Leashed pets are permitted.

Reservations, fees: Reservations are accepted at 510/562-2267 ($6 reservation fee); $15–20 per night, $6 per night for each additional vehicle, $1 per night. Major credit cards accepted. Open year-round.

Directions: From I-580 in the Oakland hills, drive to the 35th Avenue exit. Take that exit, and at the stop sign, turn east on 35th Avenue and drive up the hill and straight across Skyline Boulevard, where 35th Avenue becomes Redwood Road. Continue on Redwood Road for eight miles to the park and Marciel Road (campground entrance road) on the right.

Contact: Regional Park Headquarters, 510/635-0135, ext. 2200, fax 510/569-4319; Anthony Chabot Regional Park, 510/639-4751.

27 SAN FRANCISCO RV RESORT

Rating: 8

In Pacifica.

Map 7.3, page 436

This has become the best RV park in the Bay Area. It is set on the bluffs just above the Pacific Ocean in Pacifica, complete with beach access, nearby fishing pier, and sometimes excellent surf fishing. There is also a nearby golf course and the chance for dramatic ocean sunsets. The park is kept clean and in good shape, and though there is too much asphalt, the proximity to the beach overcomes it. It is only 20 minutes from San Francisco. Many RV drivers will remember this park under its former name, Pacific Park RV. It was renamed and renovated in 2002.

Campsites, facilities: There are 182 sites with full hookups, including cable TV, for RVs.

Restrooms, showers, heated swimming pool, spa, a group-only recreation room, cable TV, grocery store, coin laundry, and propane gas are available. Some facilities are wheelchair-accessible. Leashed pets are permitted.

Reservations, fees: Reservations are recommended. The rates are $38–69 per night, $3.50 per person for more than two people, $3.50 pet fee. Major credit cards accepted. Open year-round.

Directions: From San Francisco, drive south on Highway 280 to Highway 1.Bear west on Highway 1 and drive into Pacifica and to the Manor Drive exit. Take that exit and drive to the stop sign (you will be on the west side of the highway). Continue straight ahead (the road becomes Palmetto Avenue) for about two blocks and look for the entrance to the park on the right side of the road at 700 Palmetto.

From the south, drive north on Highway 1 into Pacifica. Take the Manor Drive exit. At the stop sign, turn left on the frontage road (you will be on the east side of the highway) and drive a block to another stop sign. Turn left, drive a short distance over the highway to a stop sign at Manor/Palmetto, and turn left. Drive about two blocks to the park on the right.

Contact: Onterra San Francisco RV Resort, 800/992-0554, fax 650/355-7102, website: www.sanfranciscorv.com.

28 HALF MOON BAY STATE BEACH

Rating: 7

At Half Moon Bay.
Map 7.3, page 436

In summer, this park often fills to capacity with campers touring Highway 1. The campground has level, grassy sites for tents, a clean parking area for RVs, and a state beach available just a short walk away. The feature here is four miles of broad, sandy beaches with three access points with parking. A visitor center opened in 2002. Side trips include Princeton and Pillar Point Marina, seven miles north on Highway 1, where fishing and whale-watching trips are possible. Typical weather is fog in summer, clear days in spring and fall, and wet and windy in the winter–yet occasionally there are drop-dead beautiful days in winter between storms, warm, clear, and windless. Temperatures range from lows in the mid-40s in winter to highs in the mid-60s in fall. One frustrating point: the weekend traffic on Highway 1 up and down the coast here is often jammed, with absolute gridlock during festivals.

Campsites, facilities: There are 54 sites for tents or RVs up to 36 feet long, four hike-in or bike-in sites, and one group site two miles north of the main campground. Picnic tables, food lockers, and fire grills are provided. Restrooms, drinking water, flush toilets, coin showers, and RV dump station are available. Leashed pets are permitted.

Reservations, fees: Reservations are not accepted. The fee is $12 per night, $1 per person per night for hike-in or bike-in sites. Senior discount available. Reserve group site at 800/444-PARK (800/444-7275) or website: www.ReserveAmerica.com ($7.50 reservation fee); $37 per night. Open year-round.

Directions: Drive to Half Moon Bay to the junction of Highway 1 and Highway 92. Turn south on Highway 1 and drive one block to Kelly Avenue. Turn right on Kelly Avenue and drive one-half mile to the park entrance at the end of the road.

Contact: Half Moon Bay State Beach, 650/726-8820; Bay Area District, 415/330-6300.

29 PELICAN POINT RV PARK

Rating: 7

In Half Moon Bay.
Map 7.3, page 436

This park is in a rural setting on the southern outskirts of the town of Half Moon Bay, set on an extended bluff near the ocean. The sites consist of cement slabs with picnic tables. Note that half of RV sites are monthly rentals. All facilities are available nearby, with restaurants available in Half Moon Bay and 10 miles north in Princeton at Pillar Point Harbor. The harbor has an excellent boat launch, a fish-cleaning station, party boat trips for salmon and rockfish and, in the winter, whale-watching trips.

Campsites, facilities: There are 75 sites with full hookups and patios for RVs. Picnic tables are provided. Restrooms, showers, coin laundry, propane gas, small store, clubhouse, and RV dump station are available. Leashed pets are permitted.

Reservations, fees: Reservations are recommended. The rates are $34–38 per night, $2 per night for each extra vehicle, $3 per person per night for more than two people, $1 pet fee. Major credit cards accepted. Open year-round.

Directions: In Half Moon Bay, at the junction of Highway 1 and Highway 92, turn south on Highway 1 and drive 2.5 miles to Miramontes Point Road. Turn right and drive a short distance to the park entrance on the left.

Contact: Pelican Point RV Park, 650/726-9100.

30 MEMORIAL COUNTY PARK

Rating: 8

Near La Honda.
Map 7.3, page 436

This beautiful redwood park is set on the western slopes of the Santa Cruz Mountains, tucked in a pocket between the tiny towns of La Honda and Loma Mar. The campground features access to a nearby network of 50 miles of trails, with the best hike along the headwaters of Pescadero Creek. In late winter, it is sometimes possible to see steelhead spawn (no fishing permitted, of course). The trails link with others in nearby Portola State Park and Sam McDonald County Park, providing access to a vast recreation land. The camp is often filled on summer weekends, but the sites are spaced so it won't cramp your style.

Campsites, facilities: There are 156 sites for tents or RVs up to 35 feet long, two group sites for up to 75 people, and six youth areas for youth groups of up to 50 people. Picnic tables and fire grills are provided. Drinking water, showers, and flush toilets are available. An RV dump station is available from May through October. No pets are allowed.

Reservations, fees: Reservations are not accepted. The fee is $15 per night, $5 for each additional vehicle. Make reservations for groups at 650/363-4021, Monday through Thursday, $100. Open year-round.

Directions: Drive to Half Moon Bay at the junction of Highway 1 and Highway 92. Drive south on Highway 1 for 18 miles to the Pescadero Road exit. Turn left on Pescadero Road and drive about 10 miles to the park entrance.

Contact: Memorial County Park, 650/879-0212; San Mateo County Parks and Recreation, 650/363-4021, website: www.sanmateocounty parks.org.

31 PORTOLA REDWOODS STATE PARK

Rating: 9

Near Skyline Ridge.
Map 7.3, page 436

Portola Redwoods State Park is very secluded, since visitors are required to travel on an extremely slow and winding series of roads to reach it. The park features redwoods and a mixed evergreen and hardwood forest on the western slopes of the Santa Cruz Mountains, the headwaters of Pescadero Creek, and 18 miles of hiking trails. A literal highlight is a 300-foot-high redwood, one of the tallest trees in the Santa Cruz Mountains. In addition to redwoods, there are Douglas fir and live oak, as well as a riparian zone along the stream. A four-mile hike links up to nearby Pescadero Creek County Park (which, in turn, borders Memorial County Park). At times in the summer, a low fog will move in along the San Mateo coast, and from lookouts near Skyline, visitors can peer to the west at what seems like a pearlescent sea with little islands (hilltops) poking through (this view is available from the access road, not from campsites). Wild pigs are occasionally spotted here, with larger numbers at neighboring Pescadero Creek County park.

Campsites, facilities: There are 52 sites for tents or RVs up to 24 feet long, four walk-in/bike-in sites, one hike-in camp (three-mile hike), and four group sites for 25–50 people. Picnic tables and fire grills are provided. Drinking water, flush toilets, coin-operated showers, and firewood are available. There are nature hikes and campfire programs scheduled on weekends from Memorial Day through Labor Day. The nearest gas is 13 miles away. Leashed pets are permitted on paved surfaces only.

Reservations, fees: Reserve at 800/444-PARK (800/444-7275) or website: www.Reserve America.com ($7.50 reservation fee); $12 per night, $1 per person per night for walk-in/bike-in sites, $5 per person per night for hike-in site, $37–75 per night for group sites. Open March through November.

Directions: From Palo Alto on I-280, turn west on Page Mill Road and drive (slow and twisty) to Skyline Boulevard/Highway 35. Cross Skyline and continue west on Alpine Road (very twisty) for about three miles to Portola State Park Road. Turn left on Portola State Park Road and drive about three miles to the park entrance at the end of the road.

Contact: Portola Redwoods State Park, 650/948-9098; California State Parks, Santa Cruz District, 831/429-2850, fax 831/429-2876.

32 BUTANO STATE PARK

🏃 🐕 🚐 ⛺

Rating: 9

Near Pescadero.

Map 7.3, page 436

The campground at Butano is set in canyon filled with a redwood forest, so pretty and with such good hiking that it has become popular enough to make reservations a must. The rea-

son for its popularity is a series of exceptional hikes, including one to the Año Nuevo Lookout (well, the lookout is now blocked by trees, but there are glimpses of the ocean elsewhere along the way), the Mill Ox Loop, and, for the ambitious, the 11-mile Butano Rim Loop. The latter has a backpack camp with seven trail campsites (primitive with pit toilets available) requiring a 5.5-mile hike in the park's most remote area, where no water is available.

Campsites, facilities: There are 21 sites for tents or RVs, 18 walk-in sites, and seven hike-in (5.5 miles, with pit toilets available). Picnic tables, food lockers, and fire grills are provided. Restrooms, drinking water, and flush toilets are available. Leashed pets are permitted in campsites.

Reservations, fees: Reserve at 800/444-PARK (800/444-7275) or website: www.Reserve America.com ($7.50 reservation fee); $12 per night, $7 per night for hike-in trail sites. Senior discount available. Open year-round.

Directions: Drive to Half Moon Bay and the junction of Highway 1 and Highway 92. Drive south on Highway 1 for 18 miles to the Pescadero Road exit and Pescadero Road. Turn left on Pescadero Road and drive past the town of Pescadero to Cloverdale Road. Turn right and drive 4.5 miles to the park entrance on the left.

Contact: Butano State Park, 650/879-2040; California State Parks, Bay Area District, 415/330-6300, fax 415/330-6312.

33 BIG BASIN REDWOODS STATE PARK

🏃 🚻 ♿ 🚐 ⛺

Rating: 10

Near Santa Cruz.

Map 7.3, page 436

Big Basin is one of the best state parks in California, featuring giant redwoods near the park headquarters, secluded campsites set in forest, and rare opportunities to stay in a tent cabin or a backpacking trail site. The parks covers more than 18,000 acres of redwoods, much of it old-growth, including forest behemoths more than 1,000 years old. It is a great park for hikers, with two waterfalls, one close and one far, making for stellar destinations. The close one is Sempervirens Falls, a long, narrow, silvery stream, an easy 1.5-hour round-trip on the Sequoia Trail. The far one is the famous Berry Creek Falls, a spectacular 70-foot cascade set in a beautiful canyon, framed by redwoods. For hikers in good condition, figure two hours (4.7 miles) to reach Berry Creek Falls, five hours for the round-trip in and out, and six hours for the complete loop (12 miles) that extends into the park's most remote areas. There is also an easy nature loop trail near the park headquarters in the valley floor that is routed past several mammoth redwoods. This is California's oldest state park, established in 1902. It is home to the largest continuous stand of ancient coast redwoods south of San Francisco. There are more than 80 miles of trails with elevations varying from 2,000 feet at the eastern Big Basin Rim on down to sea level. Rainfall averages 48 inches per year, most arriving from December through mid-March.

Campsites, facilities: There are 31 sites for tents or RVs up to 27 feet long, 69 sites for tents only, 38 walk-in sites, 36 tent cabins (reservations required), 52 hike-in campsites, and four group sites for 40–50 people. Picnic tables, food lockers, and fire grills are provided. Restrooms, drinking water, flush toilets, coin-operated showers, RV dump station, and groceries are available. Some facilities are wheelchair-accessible. Leashed pets are allowed in campsites and on paved roads only.

Reservations, fees: Reserve at 800/444-PARK (800/444-7275) or website: www.Reserve America.com ($7.50 reservation fee); $12 for family sites and walk-in sites, $5 per person for hike-in sites, $60–75 per night for group sites. Senior discount available. Reserve tent cabins at 800/874-8368. Open year-round.

Directions: From Santa Cruz, turn north on Highway 9 and drive 12 miles to Boulder Creek and Highway 236 (signed Big Basin). Turn west

on Highway 236 and drive nine miles to the park headquarters.

Contact: Big Basin Redwoods State Park, 831/338-8860 or 831/338-8861, fax 831/338-8863; California State Parks, Santa Cruz District, 831/429-2851.

34 SANBORN-SKYLINE COUNTY PARK

Rating: 8

Near Pescadero.

Map 7.3, page 436

This is a pretty camp set in redwood forest, semiprimitive, but like a world in a different orbit compared to the asphalt of San Jose and the rest of the Santa Clara Valley. These campgrounds get heavy use on summer weekends, of course. This is headquarters for a 3,600-acre park that stretches from the foothills of Saratoga up to the Skyline Ridge. Many hiking trails are available, including a trailhead at camp, in all 15 miles of trails. Most explore lush wooded slopes, with redwoods and tan oak. Dogs are prohibited from walk-in sites, yet violation of this regulation has created an enforcement situation for rangers. Dogs are permitted, on the other hand, at the RV sites, the main park's grassy area, and day-use sites.

Campsites, facilities: There are 15 sites with full hookups for RVs up to 30 feet long, a separate walk-in campground with 33 sites for tents, and a youth group area. Picnic tables and fire pits are provided. Drinking water and flush toilets are available. A youth science center and one-mile nature trail gate close 30 minutes after sunset. Some facilities are wheelchair-accessible. Leashed pets are permitted in RV campground only.

Reservations, fees: Reservations for RV sites required, no reservations for walk-in sites; $25 per night, $8 per night for walk-in, $1 per night, $30 for youth group area for up to 30 people for first night and then $10 for each additional night. Major credit cards accepted. RV sites open year-round, walk-in sites open April to mid-October.

Directions: From Highway 17 in San Jose, drive south for six miles to Highway 9/Saratoga Avenue. Turn west and drive to Saratoga, then continue on Highway 9 for two miles to Sanborn Road. Turn left and drive one mile to the park on the right. Walk-in sites require a .1- to .5-mile walk from the parking area.

Contact: Sanborn-Skyline County Park, 408/867-9959, website: www.parkhere.org.

35 MT. DIABLO STATE PARK

Rating: 6

East of Oakland.

Map 7.4, page 437

Mount Diablo, elevation 3,849 feet, provides one of the most all-encompassing lookouts anywhere in America, an awesome 360° on clear mornings. On crystal-clear days you can see the Sierra Nevada and its white, snowbound crest. With binoculars, some claim to have seen Half Dome in Yosemite. The drive to the summit is a must-do trip, and the interpretive center right on top of the mountain is one of the best in the Bay Area. The camps at Mt. Diablo are set in foothill/oak grassland country, with some shaded sites. Winter and spring are good times to visit, when the weather is still cool enough for good hiking trips. Most of the trails require long hikes, often including significant elevation gains and losses. No alcohol is permitted in the park. The park offers extensive but challenging hiking, biking, and horseback riding. A museum, visitor center, and gift shop is perched on the Diablo summit. Summers are hot and dry, and in late summer the park can be closed because of fire danger. In winter, snow occasionally falls on the peak, according to my logbook, during the first full moon in February.

Campsites, facilities: There are 64 sites for tents or RVs up to 20 feet long (in three campgrounds), five group sites for 20–50 people, and one group

site is accessible for equestrian use with hitching posts and a water trough. Picnic tables and fire grills are provided. Drinking water and flush and vault toilets are available. Showers are available at Juniper and Live Oak campgrounds. Leashed pets are permitted.

Reservations, fees: Reserve at 800/444-PARK (800/444-7275) or website: www.Reserve America.com ($7.50 reservation fee); $12 per night, group sites are $15–37 per night. Senior discount available. Open year-round.

Directions: From Walnut Creek on I-680, take the Diablo Road exit. Turn east on Diablo Road and drive three miles to Mt. Diablo Scenic Boulevard. Turn left and continue 3.5 miles (the road becomes South Gate Road) to the park entrance station. Register at the kiosk, obtain a park map, and drive to the designated campground.

Contact: Mt. Diablo State Park, 925/837-2525 or 925/837-0904; district headquarters, 415/330-6300, website:www.dia.org.

36 SUNOL REGIONAL WILDERNESS WALK-IN

Rating: 7

South of Sunol.

Map 7.4, page 437

This is a very primitive camp set in the Sunol Regional Wilderness, an outstanding park for off-season hiking, camping, wildlife viewing, and wildflowers. The camps require walks of 25–75 yards, with wilderness-style camping also available requiring a hike of 3.4 miles or more. In the spring and early summer, it is one of the best of the 150 parks in the Bay Area to see wildflowers. It is also the home of more nesting golden eagles than anywhere else in the world, with a chance to see falcons and hawks as well. In addition, Alameda Creek in Little Yosemite forms several miniature pool-and-drop waterfalls in the spring and early summer. The park is set in rolling oak/bay grasslands. Some sites require hikes of 3.4 miles or longer, with access to the Ohlone Wilderness trail. It is extremely quiet and secluded, with a nearby spring developed to provide drinking water. This is also one of the Bay Area's most popular parks to bring dogs. No alcohol is permitted in the park, and it is subject to temporary closures in late summer because of fire danger.

Campsites, facilities: There are four primitive sites for tents requiring walks of 25 to 50 yards, a wilderness camp requiring hikes of 3.4 miles and longer, and two sites for horses requiring rides of 10 miles. Picnic tables and fire grills are provided. Drinking water and vault toilets are available. No dogs are permitted in the wilderness.

Reservations, fees: Reservations are required at 510/562-2267; ($6 reservation fee); $11 per night, $1 pet fee. Major credit cards accepted. Open year-round, weather permitting.

Directions: In the East Bay on I-680, drive to Sunol and the Highway 84/Calaveras Road exit. Turn south on Calaveras and drive four miles to Geary Road. Turn left on Geary Road and drive two miles to the park entrance.

Contact: East Bay Regional Park District Headquarters, 510/635-0135, ext. 2200, fax 510/569-4319; Sunol Regional Wilderness, 925/862-2244.

37 DEL VALLE REGIONAL PARK

Rating: 7

Near Livermore.
Map 7.4, page 437

Of the 50 parks in the East Bay Regional Park District, it is Del Valle that provides the greatest variety of recreation at the highest quality. Del Valle Reservoir is the centerpiece, a long narrow lake that fills a canyon, providing a good boat launch for powerboating and fishing for trout, striped bass, and catfish. The sites are somewhat exposed because of the grassland habitat, but they fill anyway on most weekends and three-day holidays. A trailhead south of the lake provides access to the Ohlone Wilderness Trail, and for the well conditioned,

there is the 5.5-mile butt-kicker of a climb to Murietta Falls, gaining 1,600 feet in 1.5 miles. Murietta Falls is the Bay Area's highest waterfall, 100 feet tall, though its thin, silvery wisp is difficult to view directly and rarely evokes much emotional response after such an intense climb.

Campsites, facilities: There are 150 sites, including 21 with partial hookups for tents or RVs. Picnic tables and fire grills are provided. Drinking water, flush toilets, hot showers, RV dump station, full marina, and a boat launch are available. Pets are permitted.

Reservations, fees: Reservations are required, 510/562-2267 ($6 reservation fee);$15–18 per night, $3 boat launch fee, $1 pet fee. Major credit cards accepted. Open year-round.

Directions: From I-580 East at Livermore, take the North Livermore Avenue exit and turn right. Drive south for 3.5 miles (the road becomes Tesla Road) to Mines Road. Turn right on Mines Road and drive 3.5 miles to Del Valle Road. Continue on Del Valle Road for three miles to the park entrance.

Contact: East Bay Regional Park District, 510/635-0135, ext. 2200; Del Valle Regional Park, 925/373-0332.

38 JOSEPH GRANT COUNTY PARK

Rating: 7

Near San Jose.
Map 7.4, page 437

Grant Ranch is a great, wild playland covering 9,000 acres in the foothills of nearby Mt. Hamilton to the east. It features 40 miles of hiking trails (horses permitted), 20 miles of old ranch roads that are perfect for mountain biking, a pretty lake (Grant Lake), and miles of foothills, canyons, and grasslands. The campground is set amid oak grasslands, is shaded, and can be used as a base camp for planning the day's recreation. The best hikes are to Halls Valley, especially in the winter and spring when there are many secret little creeks and miniature waterfalls in hidden canyons, the Hotel Trail, and Cañada de Pala Trail, which drops to San Felipe Creek, the prettiest stream in the park. A great side trip is the slow, curvy drive east to Lick Observatory for great views of the Santa Clara Valley. Wood fires are often banned in summer.

Campsites, facilities: There are 40 sites for tents or RVs up to 28 feet long. Picnic tables and fire grills are provided. Drinking water, hot showers, RV dump station, and toilets are available. Pets are permitted.

Reservations, fees: Reservations are not accepted. The fee is $15 per night for individual sites, $6 per night for each extra vehicle, eight-person maximum per campsite, $1 per night. Reservations for group sites only at 408/355-2201. Check-in required before sunset; gates are locked. Open weekends in March, then daily from April through November.

Directions: In San Jose at the junction of I-680 and U.S. 101, take I-680 north to the Alum Rock Avenue exit. Turn east and drive four miles to Mt. Hamilton Road. Turn right and drive eight miles to the park headquarters entrance on the right side of the road.

Contact: Santa Clara County Parks Department, 408/274-6121, fax 408/270-4808, website: www.parkhere.org.

39 PARKWAY LAKES RV PARK

Rating: 3

Near Morgan Hill.

Map 7.4, page 437

This RV park provides a spot to park on the southern outskirts of the San Francisco Bay Area. It gets its name from nearby Parkway Lake (408/629-9111), a pay-to-fish lake where for $12 you get a chance to catch rainbow trout up to 10 pounds in the winter and spring, and catfish and sturgeon in the summer. There are several other reservoirs in the nearby foothills, including Coyote, Anderson, Chesbro, Uvas, and Calero. The best nearby source for fish-

ing and recreation is Coyote Discount Bait and Tackle at 408/463-0711.

Campsites, facilities: There are 113 sites, including 12 drive-through, with electricity for RVs. Restrooms, drinking water, showers, RV dump station, heated swimming pool, modem access, coin laundry, and a recreation room are available. Some facilities are wheelchair-accessible. Leashed pets under 20 pounds are permitted.

Reservations, fees: Reservations are required. The fee is $36 per night, $3 per person for more than two people, $1 per night. Major credit cards accepted. Senior discount available. Open year-round.

Directions: From San Jose, drive south about 12 miles on U.S. 101 to the Cochrane-Monterey Road exit. Turn right on Cochrane Road and continue about 1.5 miles to the Monterey Highway turnoff. Drive south (right) on Monterey Highway about 3.5 miles to Ogier Road. Turn right on Ogier Road and drive to 100 Ogier Rd. on the right.

Contact: Parkway Lakes RV Park, 408/779-0244, fax 408/778-7647.

40 HENRY W. COE STATE PARK

Rating: 8

Near Gilroy.

Map 7.4, page 437

This is the Bay Area's backyard wilderness, with 100,000 acres of wildlands, including a 23,300-acre wilderness area. There are more than 100 miles of ranch roads and 300 miles of hiking trails, a remarkable network that provides access to 140 ponds and small lakes, hidden streams, and a habitat that is paradise for fish, wildlife, and wild flora. The best camping introduction is at drive-in campsites at park headquarters, set at a hilltop at 2,600 feet that is ideal for stargazing and watching meteor showers. That provides a taste. If you like it, then come back for the full meal. It is the wilderness hike-in and bike-in sites where you will get the full flavor of the park. Before setting out for the outback, always consult with the rangers here—the ambitious plans of many hikers cause them to suffer dehydration and heatstroke. For wilderness trips, the best jump-off point is Coyote Creek and Hunting Hollow trailheads upstream of Coyote Reservoir near Gilroy. The park has excellent pond-style fishing but requires extremely long hikes (typically 10- to 25-mile round-trips) to reach the best lakes, including Mustang Pond, Jackrabbit Lake, Coit Lake, and Mississippi Lake. Expect hot weather in the summer; spring and early summer are the prime times. Even though the park may appear to be 120 square miles of oak foothills, the terrain is often steep, and making ridges often involves climbs of 1,500 feet. There are many great secrets to be discovered here, including Rooster Comb and Coyote Creek. At times on spring days, wild pigs seem to be everywhere. Golden eagles are also abundant. Bring a water purifier for hikes because there is no drinking water in the outback.

Campsites, facilities: There are 10 sites for tents and 10 sites for tents or RVs. There are also eight equestrian campsites, 82 hike-in/bike-in sites, and 10 group sites for 10–50 people. At the drive-in site at park headquarters, picnic tables and fire grills are provided. Drinking water and vault toilets are available. Leashed pets are permitted at the drive-in campground only. At the horse camps, corrals and water troughs are available. At hike-in/bike-in sites, vault toilets are provided, but no drinking water is available. Garbage must be packed out at hike-in/bike-in camps.

Reservations, fees: Reserve at 800/444-PARK (800/444-7275) or website: www.Reserve America.com ($7.50 reservation fee); $10 per night. No reservation for hike-in/bike-in or horse sites, $12 per night for horse sites, $1 for hike-in/bike-in sites. For hike-in/bike-in or horse sites, a wilderness permit is required from park headquarters. Make reservations for group site at 408/779-2728, $15 per night. Open year-round.

Directions: From Morgan Hill on U.S. 101, take the East Dunne Avenue exit. Turn east and drive 13 miles (including over the bridge at Anderson Lake, then very twisty and narrow) to the park entrance.

Contact: Henry W. Coe State Park, 408/779-2728 or 408/848-4006; California State Parks, Four Rivers District, 209/826-1196, website: www.coepark.parks.ca.gov.

© TOM STIENSTRA

Chapter 8
Monterey and Big Sur

Chapter 8—Monterey and Big Sur

The scenic charm seems to extend to infinity from the seaside towns of Santa Cruz, Monterey, Big Sur, and San Simeon. The primary treasure is the coast, which is rock-strewn and sprinkled with inshore kelp beds, where occasionally you can find sea otters playing Pop Goes the Weasel. The sea here is a color like no other, often more of a tourmaline than a straight green or blue.

From Carmel to Lucia alone, touring the Big Sur on Highway 1 is one of the most captivating drives anywhere. The inland strip along Highway 1 provides access to state parks, redwoods, coastal streams, Los Padres National Forest, and the Ventana Wilderness. As you explore farther south on the Pacific Coast Highway, you will discover a largely untouched coast.

Most vacations to this region include several must-do trips, often starting in Monterey with a visit to Fisherman's Wharf and its domesticated sea lions, and then to the nearby Monterey Bay Aquarium.

From there, most head south to Big Sur to take in a few brush strokes of nature's canvas, easily realizing why this area is beloved around the world. At first glance, however, it's impossible not to want the whole painting. That is where the campgrounds come in. They provide both the ideal getaway and a launch point for adventure.

At Big Sur, the campgrounds are what many expect: small hideaways in the big redwoods. Most are in a variety of settings, some near Big Sur River, others set in the forest.

Other good opportunities are available in Los Padres National Forest and the adjacent Ventana Wilderness, which provides outstanding camping and hiking in the off-season, when the Sierra is buried in snow.

One note of caution: the state park campgrounds on Highway 1 are among the most popular in North America. Reservations far in advance are required all summer, even weekdays. They are always the first to fill on the state's reservation system. So get the game wired to get your site.

During the summer, only the fog on the coast and the intense heat just 10 miles inland keep this region from attaining perfection.

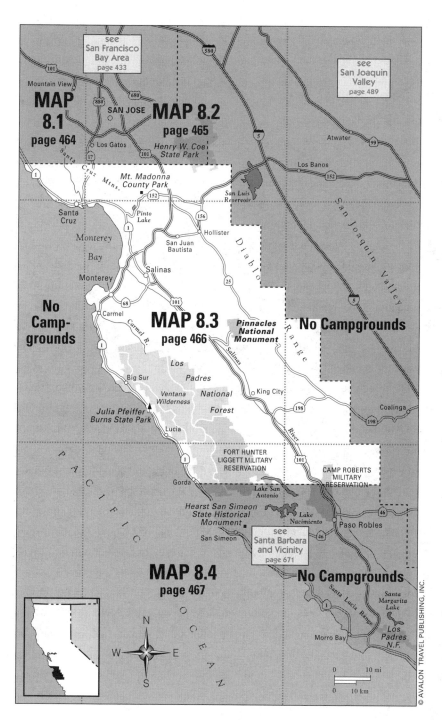

see
San Francisco
Bay Area
page 433

see
San Joaquin
Valley
page 489

101

Mountain View

MAP 8.1
page 464

880 680

SAN JOSE

MAP 8.2
page 465

5

Los Gatos

17

101

Atwater

99

Henry W. Coe
State Park

Los Banos

152

Mt. Madonna
County Park

Santa
Cruz
Mtns.

152

San Luis
Reservoir

1

Santa
Cruz

Pinto
Lake

156

Monterey

1

Hollister

Bay

San Juan
Bautista

Salinas

25

Monterey

68

101

Carmel

Carmel R.

MAP 8.3
page 466

**Pinnacles
National
Monument**

No Campgrounds

Diablo

**No
Camp-
grounds**

1

Los

Padres

Salinas

Big Sur

Ventana
Wilderness

National

Forest

King City

198

Range

Coalinga

198

Julia Pfeiffer
Burns State Park

Lucia

P

A

C

I

F

I

C

1

Gorda

FORT HUNTER
LIGGETT MILITARY
RESERVATION

101

River

CAMP ROBERTS
MILITARY
RESERVATION

46

Lake San
Antonio

Hearst San Simeon
State Historical
Monument

Lake
Nacimiento

Paso Robles

see
Santa Barbara
and Vicinity
page 671

San Simeon

46

MAP 8.4
page 467

No Campgrounds

O

C

E

A

N

Santa Lucia Range

Santa
Margarita
Lake

1

Los
Padres
N.F.

Morro Bay

N

W   E

S

© AVALON TRAVEL PUBLISHING, INC.

0   10 mi

0   10 km

Map 8.1

**Campgrounds 1–4
Pages 468–469**

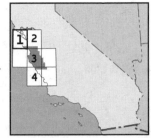

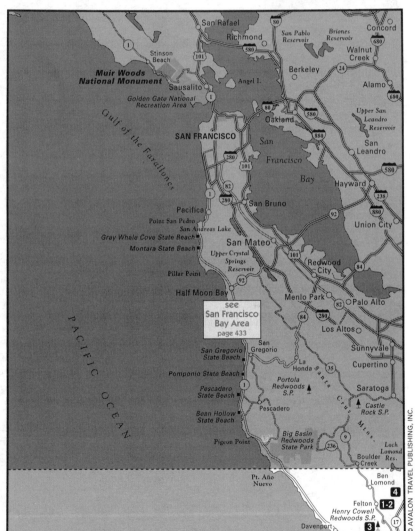

Map 8.2

Campgrounds 5–7
Pages 469–470

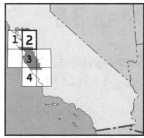

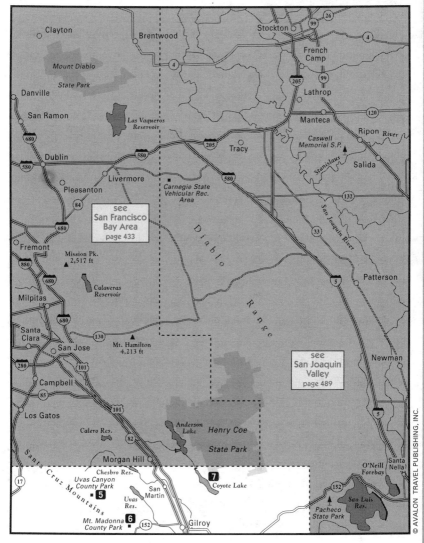

Map 8.3

Campgrounds 8–42
Pages 471–485

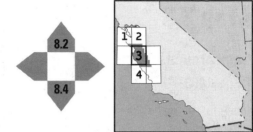

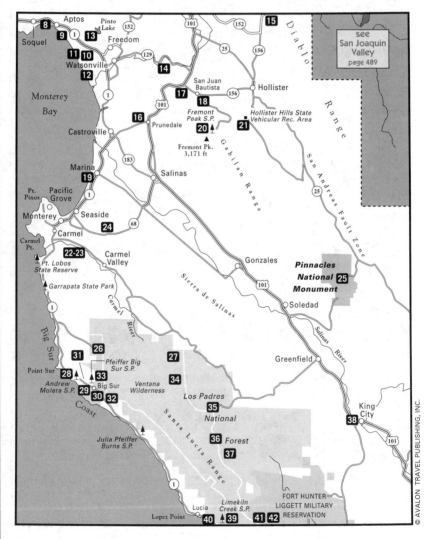

8.2

8.4

see
San Joaquin
Valley
page 489

8
Aptos
9
1
13
Soquel
Pinto
Lake
(152)
Freedom
15
Diablo
11
10
Watsonville
129
14
12

Monterey
Bay
1
16
Castroville
Prunedale
17
San Juan
Bautista
156
Hollister
18
156
Fremont
Peak S.P.
20
Hollister Hills State
Vehicular Rec. Area
21
Fremont Pk.
3,171 ft
183
Salinas
Gabilan Range
San Andreas Fault Zone

Pt.
Pinos
Pacific
Grove
19
Marina
1
Monterey
Seaside
24
Carmel
68
22-23
Carmel Pt.
Pt. Lobos
State Reserve
Carmel
Valley
Garrapata State Park
Sierra de Salinas
Carmel River
Gonzales
101
Pinnacles
National
Monument
25
Soledad
Salinas River
Big Sur
1
26
31
Pfeiffer Big
Sur S.P.
27
Point Sur
28
33
Big Sur
34
Greenfield
Andrew
Molera S.P.
29
30
32
Ventana
Wilderness
Los Padres
35
King
City
38
Julia Pfeiffer
Burns S.P.
National
36
Forest
37
Coast
Santa Lucia Range
Lucia
Limekiln
Creek S.P.
40
39
41
42
FORT HUNTER
LIGGETT MILITARY
RESERVATION
Lopez Point

© AVALON TRAVEL PUBLISHING, INC.

Map 8.4

Campgrounds 43–44
Pages 485–486

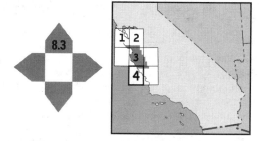

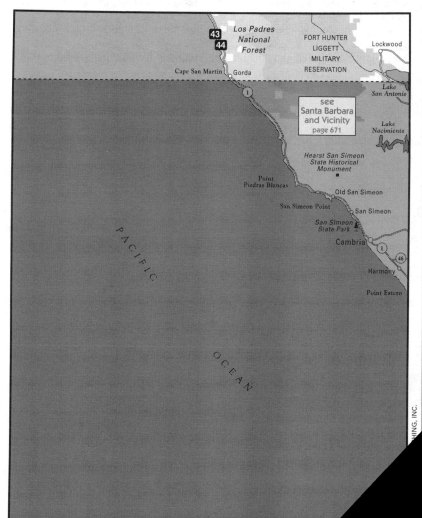

1 COTILLION GARDENS RV PARK

Rating: 6

Near Santa Cruz.

Map 8.1, page 464

This is a pretty place with several possible side trips. It is set on the edge of the Santa Cruz Mountain redwoods, near Henry Cowell Redwoods State Park and the San Lorenzo River. Monterey Bay is only about a 10-minute drive from the park. Other side trips include the steam engine ride along the San Lorenzo River out of Roaring Camp Train Rides in Felton and visiting Loch Lomond Reservoir near Ben Lomond for hiking, boat rentals, or fishing. There is a mix of both overnighters and some long-term rentals at this park.

Campsites, facilities: There are 80 sites, including one drive-through, with partial or full hookups, including cable TV, for RVs, three sites for tents, and five camping cabins. Picnic tables and fire grills are provided. Restrooms, showers, recreation room, heated swimming pool, and a convenience store are available. Some facilities are wheelchair-accessible. Leashed pets are permitted.

Reservations, fees: Reservations are recommended. The fee is $34 per night, $5 per person per night for more than two people with a maximum of six. No pet fee if clean. Major credit cards accepted. Open year-round.

Directions: From Los Gatos, drive west on Highway 17 for 20 miles toward Santa Cruz to the Mt. Hermon Road exit/Scotts Valley (second exit in Scotts Valley). Take the Mt. Hermon Road exit to the stoplight at Mt. Hermon Road. Turn right on Mt. Hermon [Road and drive 3.5 miles to Fe]lton and Gra-[ham Hill Road. Turn right on] Graham Hill [Road and drive 50 feet to Hig]hway 9. Turn [left on Highway 9 and drive 1.]5 miles to the

[park entrance on the left.]

[Contact: Cotillion Gardens RV] Park, 300 Old [San Jose Rd., 8]31/335-7669.

2 SMITHWOODS RV PARK

Rating: 6

Near Felton.

Map 8.1, page 464

You get a pretty redwood setting at this privately operated park with its many side-trip possibilities. Henry Cowell Redwoods State Park (good) and Big Basin Redwoods State Park (better) are two nearby parks that provide hiking opportunities. The narrow-gauge train ride through the area is fun, too; it is in Felton at Roaring Camp Train Rides.

Campsites, facilities: There are 142 RV sites with full hookups. No tent camping is allowed. Picnic tables and fire pits are provided. Restrooms, showers, a recreation room, a swimming pool, a playground, modem access in Rec Hall, and a convenience store are available. Some facilities are wheelchair-accessible. Leashed pets are permitted.

Reservations, fees: Reservations are recommended. The fee is $36 per night, $2 per person for more than two people, with a maximum of six, $1 per night. Open year-round.

Directions: From Los Gatos, drive west on Highway 17 for 20 miles toward Santa Cruz to the Mt. Hermon Road exit/Scotts Valley (second exit in Scotts Valley). Take Mt. Hermon Road exit to the stoplight. Turn right on Mt. Hermon Road and drive 3.5 miles to Felton and Graham Hill Road. Turn right on Graham Hill Road and drive 50 feet to Highway 9. Turn left on Highway 9 and drive 1.5 miles to the park entrance on the left.

Contact: Smithwoods RV Park, 831/335-4321.

3 HENRY COWELL REDWOODS STATE PARK

Rating: 8

Near Santa Cruz.

Map 8.1, page 464

This is a redwood state park near Santa Cruz

with good hiking, good views, and a chance of fishing in the winter for steelhead. The park features a 1,750-acre grove of old-growth redwoods, 20 miles of trails in the forest, where the old-growth redwoods estimated at 1,400–1,800 years old. One great easy hike is a 15-minute walk to a great lookout platform over Santa Cruz and the Pacific Ocean; the trailhead is near campsite 49. Another good hike is the Eagle Creek Trail, a three-mile walk that heads along Eagle Creek and the San Lorenzo River, running through a classic redwood canyon. In winter, there is limited steelhead fishing in the San Lorenzo River. A side-trip option is taking the Roaring Camp Big Trees Railroad, which is adjacent to camp, 408/335-4484.

Campsites, facilities: There are 111 sites for tents or RVs up to 40 feet long and trailers up to 31 feet long, and one hike-in/bike-in site. Picnic tables and fire grills are provided. Drinking water, flush toilets, and coin-operated showers are available. Some facilities are wheelchair-accessible. A nature center, book store, and picnic area are available. Leashed pets are permitted and must be kept inside tents or vehicles at night.

Reservations, fees: Reservations accepted mid-March through October; reserve at 800/444-PARK (800/444-7275) or website: www.ReserveAmerica.com ($7.50 reservation fee); $12 per night (maximum of eight people), $1 per person per night for hike-in, bike-in site. Senior discount available. Open mid-February through November.

Directions: In Scotts Valley on Highway 17, take the Mt. Hermon Road exit and drive west toward Felton to Lockwood Lane. Turn left on Lockwood Lane and drive about one mile to Graham Hill Road. Turn left on Graham Hill Road and drive a half mile to the campground on the right.

Contact: Henry Cowell Redwoods State Park, 831/335-4598 or 831/438-2396.

4 CARBONERO CREEK TRAILER PARK

Rating: 5

Near Scotts Valley.

Map 8.1, page 464

This camp is just a short hop from Santa Cruz and the shore of Monterey Bay. There are many side-trip options, making this a prime location for vacationers cruising the California coast. In Santa Cruz there are several quality restaurants, plus fishing trips and boat rentals at Santa Cruz Wharf, as well as the famous Santa Cruz Boardwalk and amusement park. Note: open fires are prohibited in the campground.

Campsites, facilities: There are 104 sites with full or partial hookups for RVs and 10 sites for tents. Restrooms, showers, cable TV, coin laundry, modem access (toll-free numbers only), recreation room, hot tub, whirlpool, and a seasonal swimming pool are available. Leashed pets are permitted at the RV sites only.

Reservations, fees: Reservations are recommended. The fee is $31–35 per night, $3 per person for more than two people, $10 per night for each extra vehicle. Major credit cards accepted. Open year-round.

Directions: From Santa Cruz, at the junction of Highways 1 and 17 north, turn east on Highway 17 north and drive four miles to the Mt. Hermon/Big Basin exit. Take that exit north onto Mt. Hermon Road and drive to Scotts Valley Drive. Turn right and drive to Disc Drive. Turn right and continue to 917 Disc Drive.

Contact: Carbonero Creek Trailer Park, 831/438-1288, 800/546-1288, fax 831/438-2877, website: www.campersworld.com.

5 UVAS CANYON COUNTY PARK

Rating: 6

Near Morgan Hill.

Map 8.2, page 465

This county park has a stunning array of waterfalls that can be reached with short hikes, including Triple Falls, Black Rock Falls, and several others, making for stellar hikes in winter and spring. But Uvas is even better known for its lake, Uvas Reservoir, which provides some of the better black bass and crappie fishing in the Bay Area. Prospects are best by far during the spring, when the lake is also stocked with rainbow trout. Call Coyote Discount Bait and Tackle at 408/463-0711 for the latest fishing tips. Notethat the gate to the campground is locked at sunset.

Campsites, facilities: There are 25 sites for tents only. There is a youth group area with five tent sites. Picnic tables and fire grills (charcoal fires only) are provided. Drinking water and flush toilets are available. There is a boat ramp at the reservoir six miles away. Some facilities are wheelchair-accessible. Leashed pets are permitted.

Reservations, fees: Reservations are not accepted for individual sites. The fee is $15 per night, $6 for each additional vehicle, $1 pet fee. Call to reserve the youth group area, 831/355-2201.

Directions: From U.S. 101 in San Jose, drive west on Bernal Avenue and then south on Santa Teresa Boulevard to Bailey Avenue. Drive west on Bailey Avenue to McKean Road. Go south on McKean Road, which becomes Uvas Road. Continue on Uvas Road to Croy Road. Turn right on Croy Road and drive 4.5 miles to the park.

Contact: Uvas Canyon County Park, 408/779-9232, fax 408/779-3315, website: www.parkhere.org.

⑥ MT. MADONNA COUNTY PARK

Rating: 7

Between Watsonville and Gilroy.

Map 8.2, page 465

It's a twisty son-of-a-gun road to reach the top of Mt. Madonna, but the views on clear days of Monterey Bay to the west and Santa Clara Valley to the east always make it worth the trip. In addition, a small herd of white deer are kept protected in a pen near the parking area for a rare chance to see unique wildlife. There are many good hiking trails in the park; the best is the Bayview Loop. Elevation in the park reaches 1,896 feet. Insider's notes: campsite 5 at Valley View is the only drive-through site. While no credit cards are accepted in person, there is a self-pay machine that accepts credit cards, a nice touch.

Campsites, facilities: There are 117 sites for tents or RVs. Picnic tables and fire grills are provided. Drinking water, coin showers, and flush toilets are available. Some facilities are wheelchair-accessible. Leashed pets are permitted.

Reservations, fees: Reservations are not accepted. The fee is $15–25 per night, $6 per night for each extra vehicle, $1 per night. Major credit cards accepted at self-serve machine. Open year-round.

Directions: From U.S. 101 in Gilroy, take the Hecker Pass Highway/Highway 152 exit west. Drive west seven miles to the park entrance on the right.

From Highway 1 in Watsonville, turn east onto Highway 152 and drive about 12 miles east to the park entrance on the left.

Contact: Call Mt. Madonna County Park, 408/842-2341, fax 408/842-6642, website: www.parkhere.org.

⑦ COYOTE LAKE COUNTY PARK

Rating: 7

Near Gilroy.

Map 8.2, page 465

Coyote Lake is a pretty surprise to newcomers, a long, narrow lake set in a canyon just over the ridge east of U.S. 101. It covers 688 acres and is stocked with a total of 24,000 trout on a biweekly basis from late winter through spring; the lake also provides a decent fishery for bass. The campground is nestled in oaks, furnishing some much-needed shade. Note: if you continue east about four miles on the access road that runs past the lake to the Coe State Park Hunting Hollow entrance, you'll come to two outstanding trailheads (one at a parking area, one at the Coyote Creek gate) into that park's wildlands. Wildlife is abundant, including deer and wild turkey.

Campsites, facilities: There are 75 drive-through sites for tents or self-contained RVs. Picnic tables and fire grills are provided. Drinking water, flush toilets, and a boat ramp are available. A visitor center and firewood for sale are also available. Some facilities are wheelchair-accessible. Leashed pets are permitted.

Reservations, fees: Make reservations at 408/355-2201 or 408/358-3751; $15 per night, $6 for a second vehicle, $4 for boat launching plus $5 for gas motor, $1 per night. Major credit cards accepted. Open year-round.

Directions: Drive on U.S. 101 to Gilroy and Leavesley Road. Take that exit and drive east on Leavesley Road to New Avenue. Turn left on New Avenue and drive to Roop Road. Turn right on Roop Road and drive to Coyote Lake Road. Turn left on Coyote Lake Road and drive to the campground. The park is a total of 5.5 miles from Gilroy.

Contact: Coyote Lake County Park, 408/842-7800, fax 408/842-6439, website: www.parkhere.org.

8 NEW BRIGHTON STATE BEACH

Rating: 10

Near Capitola.
Map 8.3, page 466

This is one in a series of state park camps set on the bluffs overlooking Monterey Bay. They are among the most popular and in-demand state campgrounds in California. Reservations are a necessity. This camp is set near a forest of Monterey pine and live oak. The summer is often foggy and cool, especially in the morning. Beachcombing, swimming, and surf fishing for perch provide recreation options, and skiff rentals are available at the nearby Capitola Wharf. The San Lorenzo River enters the ocean nearby.

Campsites, facilities: There are 112 sites for

tents or RVs up to 36 feet long, and one hike-in/bike-in site. Picnic tables, fire rings, and food lockers are provided. Drinking water, coin-operated showers, and flush toilets are available. RV dump station, propane gas, groceries, coin laundry, restaurant, and gas station are available within 2.5 miles. Leashed pets are permitted.

Reservations, fees: Reservations are recommended from mid-March through October. Reserve at 800/444-PARK (800/444-7275) or website: www.ReserveAmerica.com ($7.50 reservation fee); $12 per night, $1 per person per night for hike-in/bike-in site. Senior discount available. Open year-round, weather permitting.

Directions: From Santa Cruz, drive south on Highway 1 for about five miles to the Park Avenue exit. Take that exit and turn right on Park Avenue and drive a short distance to McGregor Drive. Turn left and drive a short distance to the park entrance on the right.

Contact: New Brighton State Beach, 831/464-6330 or 831/464-6329; California State Parks, Santa Cruz District, 831/429-2851, fax 831/429-2876.

9 SEACLIFF STATE BEACH

Rating: 10

Near Santa Cruz.
Map 8.3, page 466

Here is a very pretty spot on a beach along Monterey Bay. Beach walks are great, especially on clear evenings for dramatic sunsets. An interpretive center is available in the summer. This is a popular layover for vacationers touring Highway 1 in the summer, but the best weather is from mid-August to early October. This is a popular beach for swimming and sunbathing, with a long stretch of sand backed by coastal bluffs. A structure called the "old cement ship" by many nearby provides some fascination, but visitors are no longer allowed to walk on it for safety reasons. It is actually an old concrete freighter, the *Palo Alto*. Fishing is often good adjacent to the ship.

Campsites, facilities: There are 26 sites with hookups for RVs up to 40 feet long, and an overflow area for RVs up to 30 feet long. Picnic tables and fire grills are provided. Restrooms, drinking water, flush toilets, and coin-operated showers are available. Propane gas, groceries, covered picnic area, and a coin laundry are available nearby. Some facilities are wheelchair-accessible. Leashed pets are permitted in the camping area and on the beach.

Reservations, fees: Reserve at 800/444-PARK (800/444-7275) or website: www.Reserve America.com ($7.50 reservation fee); $18 per night. Senior discount available. Open year-round.

Directions: From Santa Cruz, drive south on Highway 1 about six miles to State Park Drive/Seacliff Beach exit. Take that exit, turn west, and drive a short distance to the park entrance.

Contact: Seacliff State Beach, 831/685-6500; California State Parks, Santa Cruz District, 831/429-2851, fax 831/429-2876.

10 SANTA CRUZ KOA

Rating: 8

Near Watsonville.
Map 8.3, page 466

Bike rentals and nearby access to Manresa State Beach make this KOA campground a winner. The little log cabins are quite cute, and security is first class. For those who have been here, it is a popular layover spot and weekend vacation destination. The only downer is the amount of asphalt, with everything paved right up to your cabin doorstep.

Campsites, facilities: There are 180 sites, including five drive-through, with full or partial hookups, six sites for tents only, 50 camping cabins, and two camping lodges. Picnic tables and fire grills are provided. Restrooms, showers, RV dump station, modem access (free at store), swimming pool, hot tub, wading pool, playground, recreation room, bicycle rentals, miniature golf, store, and propane gas are available. Some facilities are wheelchair-accessible. Leashed pets are permitted.

Reservations, fees: Reservations are advised. To make a reservation call 800/562-7701. Rates are $41–54 per night for two adults, $3 each child, and $6 each additional adult. Major credit cards accepted. Open year-round.

Directions: From Santa Cruz, drive 12 miles southeast on Highway 1. Take the San Andreas Road exit and head southwest for 3.5 miles to 1186 San Andreas Road.

Contact: Santa Cruz KOA, 831/722-0551, fax 831/722-0989; website: www.koa.com.

11 MANRESA STATE BEACH WALK-IN

Rating: 10

On the Pacific Ocean.
Map 8.3, page 466

This is a beautiful and extremely popular state park, with the campground set on uplands overlooking the Pacific Ocean. Many sites have ocean views; others are set back in a secluded grove of pine and cypress trees. The walk to the campsites is 20–120 yards from a vehicle unloading zone. There is beach access for fishing, swimming, and surfing. Santa Cruz and Monterey are each a short drive away and offer endless recreation possibilities.

Campsites, facilities: There are 64 walk-in tent sites, and one hike-in/bike-in site. Picnic tables and fire grills are provided. Restrooms, drinking water, flush toilets, and coin-operated showers are available. Some facilities are wheelchair-accessible. Leashed pets are permitted.

Reservations, fees: Reserve at 800/444-PARK (800/444-7275) or website: www.Reserve America.com ($7.50 reservation fee); $12 per night, $1 per person per night for hike-in/bike-in site. Open April through October.

Directions: From Santa Cruz, drive 12 miles

southeast on Highway 1 to the San Andreas Road exit. Take that exit south and drive five miles to Sand Dollar Drive. Turn right and drive a short distance to the park entrance on the left. The parking area is about 1,000 yards from the camping area. A 20-minute unloading zone is available within 20–150 yards of the sites.

Contact: Manresa Beach State Park, 831/761-1795; California State Parks, Santa Cruz District, 831/429-2851, fax 831/429-2876.

12 SUNSET STATE BEACH

Rating: 9

Near Watsonville.

Map 8.3, page 466

On clear evenings, the sunsets here look as if they are imported from Hawaii. The camp is set on a bluff along Monterey Bay. While there are no ocean views from the campsites, the location makes for easy, short walks down to the beach for beautiful shoreline walks. The beachfront features pine trees, bluffs, and expansive sand dunes. The park is bordered by large agricultural fields. This area was once a good spot for clamming, but they've just about been fished out. The best weather is in late summer and fall. Spring can be windy here, and early summer is often foggy. Reservations are often needed well in advance to secure a spot.

Campsites, facilities: There are 90 sites for tents or RVs up to 31 feet long, one hike-in/bike-in site, and one group site for up to 50 people. Picnic tables, food lockers, and fire grills are provided. Restrooms, drinking water, flush toilets, and coin-operated showers are available. Some facilities are wheelchair-accessible. Firewood is available for purchase. Leashed pets are permitted, except on the beach.

Reservations, fees: Reserve at 800/444-PARK (800/444-7275) or website: www.Reserve America.com ($7.50 reservation fee); $12 per night, $1 per person per night for hike-in/bike-

in site, $75 per night for group site. Senior discount available. Open year-round.

Directions: From Highway 1 near Watsonville, take the Riverside Drive exit toward the ocean to Beach Road. Drive 3.5 miles on Beach Road to the San Andreas Road exit. Turn right on San Andreas Road and drive about three miles to the beach on the left.

Contact: Sunset State Beach, 831/763-7063; California State Parks, Santa Cruz District, 831/429-2851, fax 831/429-2876.

13 PINTO LAKE PARK

Rating: 7

Near Watsonville.

Map 8.3, page 466

Pinto Lake can be a real find. Of the seven lakes in the nine Bay Area counties that offer camping, it is the only one where the RV campsites are actually near the lake. For the few who know about it, it's an offer that can't be refused. But note that no tent camping is permitted. From winter to early summer, the Department of Fish and Game stocks the lake twice a month with rainbow trout. A 5-mph speed limit has been established for boaters, and no swimming is permitted. The leash law for dogs is strictly enforced here.

Campsites, facilities: There are 28 sites with full hookups for RVs. Drinking water, sewer hookups, modem access, and electricity are available. A boat ramp and boat rentals are available nearby in the summer. Leashed pets are permitted. Most facilities are wheelchair-accessible.

Reservations, fees: Reservations are accepted. The fee is $25 per night, $2 for extra vehicles, $2 per night.

Directions: From Santa Cruz, drive 17 miles south on Highway 1 to the exit for Watsonville/Gilroy-Highway 152. Take that exit and immediately turn left on Green Valley Road and drive 2.7 (a half mile past Holohan intersection) to the entrance for the lake and campground.

From Monterey, drive north on Highway 1 to the Green Valley Road exit. Take that exit and turn right at the Green Valley Road and drive 2.7 miles (a half mile past the Holohan intersection) to the entrance for the lake and campground.

Contact: Pinto Lake Park, 831/722-8129, website: www.pintolake.com.

14 MCALPINE LAKE AND PARK

Rating: 5

Near San Juan Bautista.
Map 8.3, page 466

This is the only privately operated campground in the immediate region that has any spots for tenters. The two camping cabins here look like miniature log cabins, quite cute and comfortable. In addition, the park has a 40-foot-deep lake stocked with trout and catfish. Other highlights of the park are its proximity to Mission San Juan Bautista and the relatively short drive to the Monterey-Carmel area.

Campsites, facilities: There are 40 sites for tents only, 27 sites with partial hookups for tents or RVs, and 14 sites with full hookups for RVs, and two cabins. Picnic tables and fire grills are provided. Flush toilets, showers, RV dump station, recreation room, swimming pool, coin laundry, propane gas, and groceries are available. Some facilities are wheelchair-accessible. Leashed pets are permitted.

Reservations, fees: Reservations are accepted. The fee is $28-34 per night, $2-4 per person for more than two people, $5 per night for each extra vehicle. Major credit cards accepted.

Directions: On U.S. 101, drive to the Highway 129 exit. Take Highway 129 west and drive 100 feet to Searle Road (frontage road). Turn left onto Searle Road and drive to the stop sign at Anzar. Turn left again on Anzar and drive under the freeway to the park entrance on the left (900 Anzar Road).

Contact: McAlpine Lake and Park, 831/623-4263, fax 831/623-4559, website: www.mcalpine lake.com.

15 CASA DE FRUTA ORCHARD RESORT

Rating: 1

Near Pacheco Pass.
Map 8.3, page 466

This 80-acre RV park has a festival-like atmosphere to it, with country music and dancing every weekend in the summer and barbecues on Sunday. Huge, but sparse, San Luis Reservoir is 20 miles to the east.

Campsites, facilities: There are 300 drive-through sites, all with water and electric hookups and some with sewer connections, for RVs. Picnic tables are provided. Flush toilets, showers, RV dump station, cable TV, satellite TV, coin laundry, playground, swimming pool, wading pool, outdoor dance floor, horseshoes, volleyball courts, baseball diamonds, wine and cheese tasting room, candy factory, bakery, fruit stand, petting zoo, 24-hour restaurant, gift shop, and a minimart are available. Leashed pets are permitted. Some facilities are wheelchair-accessible.

Reservations, fees: Reservations are accepted. The fee is $30-32 per night, $2 per person per night for more than two people, $3 per pet per night. Major credit cards accepted. Open year-round.

Directions: Drive on U.S. 101 to the junction with Highway 152 (near Gilroy). Take Highway 152 east and drive 13 miles to Highway 156. Turn left (north) on Highway 156 and drive one mile to the park entrance on the right (well signed).

Contact: Casa de Fruta Orchard Resort, 408/842-9316, fax 831/848-3793, website: www.casade fruta.com.

16 CABANA HOLIDAY

Rating: 2

Near Salinas.

Map 8.3, page 466

If Big Sur, Monterey, and Carmel are packed, this spot provides some overflow space. It's about a half-hour drive from the Monterey area.

Campsites, facilities: There are 96 sites, including some drive-through, with full or partial hookups for RVs. Picnic tables are provided. Restrooms, showers, recreation room, swimming pool (heated and open mid-May to mid-October), playground, and a coin laundry are available. Leashed pets are permitted. Some facilities are wheelchair-accessible.

Reservations, fees: Reservations are recommended. The fee is $35 per night. Major credit cards accepted.

Directions: From Salinas, drive north on U.S. 101 for seven miles to Highway 156 West. Take the exit for Highway 156 West and drive over the overpass .2 mile to Prunedale North Road to the campground entrance at the intersection.

Contact: Cabana Holiday, 800/541-0085 (reservations) or 831/663-2886, fax 831/663-1660, website: www.reynoldsresorts.com.

17 MONTEREY VACATION RV PARK

Rating: 5

Near San Juan Bautista.

Map 8.3, page 466

This RV park has an ideal location for many vacationers. It's a 10-minute drive to San Juan Bautista, 30 minutes to the Monterey Bay Aquarium, and 40 minutes to Monterey's Fisherman's Wharf. It's set in an attractive spot with some trees, but the nearby attractions are what make it a clear winner. The park is well landscaped.

Campsites, facilities: There are 88 drive-through sites for RVs with full hookups and a few tent

sites. Flush toilets, showers, hot tub, swimming pool, coin laundry, modem access (in office), and propane gas are available. Some facilities are wheelchair-accessible. Leashed pets up to 40 pounds are permitted.

Reservations, fees: Reservations are recommended for three-day holiday weekends; $29 per night, $1 per night. Major credit cards accepted (except on discounts).

Directions: On U.S. 101, drive toward San Juan Bautista (between Gilroy and Salinas). The park is on U.S. 101 two miles south of the Highway 156/San Juan Bautista exit at 1400 Hwy. 101.

Contact: Monterey Vacation RV Park, 831/726-9118, fax 831/726-1841.

18 MISSION FARM RV PARK

Rating: 5

Near San Juan Bautista.

Map 8.3, page 466

The primary appeal of this RV park is that it is within easy walking distance of San Juan Bautista. The park is set beside a walnut orchard.

Campsites, facilities: There are four sites for tents and 165 RV sites with full hookups and picnic tables. Flush toilets, showers, barbecue area, RV dump station, coin laundry, and propane gas are available. Leashed pets are permitted; a dog run is available.

Reservations, fees: Reservations are recommended. Rates are $25–28 per night, $5 per night for each extra vehicle, $6 per person per night for more than two people, $1 pet fee. Major credit cards accepted. Open year-round.

Directions: From U.S. 101, drive three miles east on Highway 156. Turn right on The Alameda and drive a block. Turn left on San Juan-Hollister Road and drive a quarter mile to the campground at 400 San Juan-Hollister Road.

Contact: Mission Farm RV Park, 831/623-4456.

19 MARINA DUNES RV PARK

🏊 🎣 🐕 ♿ 🚐 ⛺

Rating: 5

Near Monterey Bay.

Map 8.3, page 466

This is a popular park for RV cruisers who are touring Highway 1 and want a layover spot near Monterey. This place fills the bill, open all year and in Marina, just a short drive from the many side-trip opportunities available in Monterey and Carmel. It is set in the sand dunes, about 300 yards from the ocean.

Campsites, facilities: There are 65 sites, including 61 with full hookups and 10 sites for tents. Picnic tables are provided. Restrooms, drinking water, showers, laundry room, cable TV (some RV sites), modem access, recreation room, and groceries are available. Leashed pets are permitted. Some facilities are wheelchair-accessible.

Reservations, fees: Reservations are recommended. Rates are $35–65 per night. Major credit cards accepted.

Directions: From Highway 1 in Marina, drive to the Reservation West Road exit. Take that exit and drive a short distance to Dunes Drive. Turn right on Dunes Drive and drive to the end of the road and the park entrance on the right.

Contact: Marina Dunes RV Park, 831/384-6914, fax 831/384-0285, website: www.marina dunesrv.com.

20 FREMONT PEAK STATE PARK

🥾 🐕 ♿ 🚐 ⛺

Rating: 7

Near San Juan Bautista.

Map 8.3, page 466

Most vacationers in this region are heading to Monterey Bay and the surrounding environs. That's why Fremont Peak State Park is missed by a lot of folks. It is on a ridge (2,900 feet) with great views of Monterey Bay available on the trail going up Fremont Peak (3,169 feet) in the Gavilan Range. An observatory with a 30-inch telescope at the park is open to the public on specified Saturday evenings. There are views of the San Benito Valley, Salinas Valley, and the Santa Lucia Mountains east of Big Sur. A picnic is held in the park each April to commemorate Captain John C. Frémont, his expeditions, and his raising of the U.S. flag in defiance of the Mexican government. Note: there is no access from this park to the adjacent Hollister Hills State Vehicular Recreation Area.

Campsites, facilities: There are 25 primitive sites for tents or RVs up to 26 feet long and trailers up to 18 feet long, and one group site for up to 25 people. Picnic tables and fire grills are provided. Drinking water and vault toilets are available. Some facilities are wheelchair-accessible. Leashed pets are permitted.

Reservations, fees: Reserve at 800/444-PARK (800/444-7275) or website: www.Reserve America.com ($7.50 reservation fee); $7 per night, $50 per night for group site for up to 50 people. Senior discount available. Open year-round.

Directions: From Highway 156 in San Juan Bautista, drive to San Juan Canyon Road. Turn south on San Juan Canyon Road and drive 11 miles (narrow, twisty, not recommended for vehicles longer than 25 feet) to the park.

Contact: Fremont Peak State Park, 831/623-4255; Monterey State Park District, Gavilan Sector, 831/623-4526; observatory, 831/623-2465.

21 HOLLISTER HILLS STATE VEHICULAR RECREATION AREA

🥾 🚲 🐕 🚐 ⛺

Rating: 4

Near Hollister.

Map 8.3, page 466

This unique park was designed for off-highway-vehicle enthusiasts. It provides 80 miles of trails for motorcycles and 40 miles of trails for four-wheel-drive vehicles. Some of the trails are accessible directly from the campground. All trails close at sunset. Note that there is no direct access to the Fremont Peak State Park, bordering directly to the west. Elevations at the park range 800–2,600 feet. Visitors are advised to always call in advance in planning a trip because the area is sometimes closed for special events. A sidelight is that a 288-acre area is set aside for hiking and mountain biking. In addition, a self-guided natural history walk is routed into Azalea Canyon and along the San Andreas Fault.

Campsites, facilities: There are four campgrounds with a total of 125 sites for tents or RVs, and group sites for up to 300 people. Picnic tables and fire rings are provided. Drinking water, flush toilets, showers, and a camp store are available. Leashed pets are permitted.

Reservations, fees: Reservations are not accepted. The fee is $6 per night, group site $6 per vehicle. Senior discount available. Open year-round.

Directions: From Highway 156 northwest of Hollister, drive to Union Road. Turn south on Union Road and drive three miles to Cienega Road. Turn left (south) on Cienega Road and drive five miles to the park on the right.

Contact: Hollister Hills State Vehicular Recreation Area, 831/637-3874, 831/637-8186; Pit Stop, park store, 831/637-3138.

22 CARMEL BY THE RIVER RV PARK

Rating: 8

On the Carmel River.
Map 8.3, page 466

Location, location, location. That's what vacationers want. Well, this park is set on the Carmel River, minutes away from Carmel, Cannery Row, the Monterey Bay Aquarium, golf courses, and the beach. Each RV site is separated by hedges and flowers.

Campsites, facilities: There are 35 sites with full hookups, including cable TV, for RVs. Restrooms, showers, modem access, recreational cabana, game room with pool tables, barbe-

cue area, horseshoes, basketball courts, and a river beach are available. A grocery store, coin laundry, and propane gas are nearby. Some facilities are wheelchair-accessible. Leashed pets are permitted.

Reservations, fees: Reservations are accepted for two or more nights; $45–50 per night, $1 per night with a limit of three dogs. Open year-round.

Directions: In Carmel on Highway 1 drive to Carmel Valley Road. Take Carmel Valley Road southeast and drive 4.5 miles to Schulte Road. Turn right and drive to the end of the road (27680 Schulte Rd. in Carmel).

Contact: Carmel by the River RV Park, 831/624-9329, fax 831/624-8416, website: www.carmel rv.com.

23 SADDLE MOUNTAIN RECREATION PARK

Rating: 6

Near the Carmel River.
Map 8.3, page 466

This pretty park is set about 100 yards from the Carmel River amid a grove of oak trees. The park offers hiking trails, and if you want to make a buyer's swing into Carmel, it's only a five-mile drive. Note: the Carmel River is reduced to a trickle most of the year.

Campsites, facilities: There are 25 tent sites and 25 sites with full hookups for RVs up to 40 feet. Picnic tables, food lockers, and fire grills are provided. Restrooms, drinking water, flush toilets, and showers are available. A swimming pool, playground, horseshoe pits, volleyball net, basketball court, and a game room are available nearby. Some facilities are wheelchair-accessible. Leashed pets are permitted in the RV area only.

Reservations, fees: Reservations are accepted for weekends only. Rates are $30–45 per night, $5 per person for more than two people. Open year-round.

Directions: In Carmel on Highway 1 drive to Carmel Valley Road. Take Carmel Valley Road southeast and drive 4.5 miles to Schulte Road. Turn right and drive to the park at the end of the road.

Contact: Saddle Mountain Recreation Park, 831/624-1617, fax 831/624-4470.

24 LAGUNA SECA RECREATION AREA

Rating: 5

Near Monterey.
Map 8.3, page 466

This campground is just minutes away from the sights in Monterey and Carmel. It is situated in oak woodlands overlooking the world-famous Laguna Seca Raceway. It is also near a OHV area.

Campsites, facilities: There are 175 sites, many with partial hookups, for tents or RVs. Picnic tables and fire grills are provided. Restrooms, showers, RV dump station, pond, rifle and pistol range, clubhouse, and group camping facilities are available. Some facilities are wheelchair-accessible. Leashed pets are permitted; maximum stay of two nights.

Reservations, fees: Reservations accepted at 831/755-4899 or 888/588-2267 ($3.50 reservation fee); $18-22 per night, $10 per extra vehicle, $1 pet fee. Major credit cards accepted. Open year-round.

Directions: From Monterey, drive east on Highway 68 for nine miles to the park entrance on the left.

Contact: Laguna Seca Recreation Area, 831/758-3604 or tel./fax 831/758-6818, website: www.co.monterey.ca.us/parks.

25 PINNACLES CAMPGROUND

Rating: 7

Near Pinnacles National Monument.
Map 8.3, page 466

This is the only camp at the Pinnacles National Monument; a once-great hike-in site was closed by flooding. This private one has always received a lot more use—it has more facilities, the access road is in better shape, and the campground is closer to Bear Gulch Caves, a prime destination. The jagged pinnacles for which the park was named were formed by the erosion of an ancient volcanic eruption. The Pinnacles National Monument is like a different planet. It's a 16,000-acre park with volcanic clusters and strange caves, all great for exploring. In addition, expansion is imminent. If you are planning to stay a weekend in the spring, arrive early on Friday evening to be sure you get a campsite. In the summer, beware of temperatures in the 90s and 100s. Also note that caves can be closed to access; always check with rangers. Note that a ban on wood fires is in effect. Duraflame logs are permitted as a substitute.

Campsites, facilities: There are 78 sites for tents or RVs, 36 sites with partial hookups for RVs, and 13 group sites. Picnic tables and fire grills are provided. Drinking water, flush toilets, electricity, modem access, RV dump station, showers, store, and a swimming pool are available. Some facilities are wheelchair-accessible. Leashed pets are permitted, except on trails.

Reservations, fees: Reservations ($7 reservation fee) are available by phone, limited hours daily, and at the website: www.co .monterey.ca.us/parks, and required for group sites; $7 per person per night for a family site, $3 for extra vehicle, $10 leash deposit; for group site, $6 per person per night with a $60 minimum. Major credit cards accepted. Open year-round, weather permitting.

Directions: From Hollister, drive south on Highway 25 for 32 miles to Highway 146 (signed Pinnacles). Take Highway 146 and drive 2.5 miles to the campground.

Contact: Pinnacles Campground, 831/389-4462, fax 775/258-7141, website: www.pinncamp.com.

26 BOTTCHER'S GAP WALK-IN

Rating: 6

In Los Padres National Forest.

Map 8.3, page 466

Here is a surprise for all the Highway 1 cruisers who never leave the highway. Just inland is this little-known camp, set in beautiful Palo Colorado (redwood) Canyon. It's a good jump-off spot for a hiking trip; the trail leading out of camp is routed all the way into the Ventana Wilderness. Compared to the RV parks near Monterey and Carmel, this place is truly a world apart. The elevation is 2,100 feet.

Campsites, facilities: There are 11 walk-in sites. Picnic tables and fire grills are provided. Vault toilets are available. No drinking water is available. Leashed pets are permitted.

Reservations, fees: Reservations are not accepted. The fee is $12 per night. Senior discount available. Open year-round.

Directions: From Carmel, drive south on Highway 1 for about 10 miles to Palo Colorado Road/County Road 5012. Turn left and drive nine miles to the campground.

Contact: Los Padres National Forest, Monterey Ranger District, 831/385-5434, fax 831/385-0628; Parks Management Company, 805/434-1996, website: www.campone.com.

27 WHITE OAKS

Rating: 7

On Chews Ridge in Los Padres National Forest.

Map 8.3, page 466

This camp is set at 4,000 feet, near Anastasia Creek, and there's a surprisingly remote feel to the area despite its relative proximity to Carmel Valley. You can get some unexpected adventures around here. On one trip, I kept meeting these bald guys and asking them about the hiking possibilities. They just shook their heads. Turns out they were from a religious group on a one-week vigil of silence. Either that or they wanted to keep their favorite hikes secret. Well, there is a good one that starts about a mile from the camp and is routed into the Ventana Wilderness. Several backcountry trail camps are also available.

Campsites, facilities: There are seven tent sites. There is no drinking water. Picnic tables and fire grills are provided. Vault toilets are available. Leashed pets are permitted.

Reservations, fees: No reservations are accepted. A $5 day-use Adventure Pass (or $30 annual fee) is required. Open year-round, weather permitting.

Directions: From Highway 1 in Carmel, drive to Carmel Valley road. Turn east on Carmel Valley Road and drive about 22 miles to Tassajara Road/County Road 5007. Turn right (south) on Tassajara Road/County Road 5007 and drive eight miles to the campground on the left.

Contact: Los Padres National Forest, Monterey Ranger District, 831/385-5434, fax 831/385-0628.

28 ANDREW MOLERA STATE PARK WALK-IN

Rating: 7

In Big Sur.

Map 8.3, page 466

Considering the popularity and grandeur of Big Sur, some campers might find it hard to believe that any primitive campgrounds are available. Believe it. This park offers walk-in sites amid some beautiful coastal terrain. One of the highlights is a great trail that leads one mile to a beautiful beach. It is part of a trail system that features miles of trails routed through meadows, beaches, and to hill tops. One downer: the campsites are too close together, and if you don't like your neighbor, you're in for a long night. In 2003, this campground was converted from a dispersed camping area that was often overcrowded to a more intimate 12-site campground. It may soon be placed on the state parks reservation system, which would increase the fee to $12 per night.

Campsites, facilities: There are 12 sites for tents, with picnic tables and fire grills provided. Drinking water and flush toilets are available. Reservations are not accepted, and the fee is $1 per night. Bring your own wood. Leashed pets are permitted.

Reservations, fees: Reservations are not accepted. The fee is $1 per night per person. There is a three-day limit. Open year-round, weather permitting.

Directions: From Carmel, drive 21 miles south on Highway 1 to the park camping lot on the right. Park and walk 150 yards to the camp.

Contact: Andrew Molera State Park, 831/667-2315; California State Parks, Monterey District, 831/649-2836.

29 RIVERSIDE CAMPGROUND & CABINS

Rating: 8

On the Big Sur River.
Map 8.3, page 466

This is one in a series of privately operated camps designed for Highway 1 cruisers touring the Big Sur area. This camp is set amid redwoods. Side trips include expansive beaches with sea otters playing on the edge of kelp beds (Andrew Molera State Park), redwood forests and waterfalls (Julia Pfeiffer Burns State Park), and several quality restaurants, including Nepenthe for those on a budget, and the Ventana Inn for those who can light cigars with $100 bills.

Campsites, facilities: There are 46 sites, including 14 with partial hookups, for tents or RVs. Picnic tables and fire grills are provided. Restrooms and coin showers are available. Leashed pets are permitted.

Reservations, fees: Reservations are recommended ($3 reservation fee); $28–38 per night, $6 per person per night for more than two peo-

ple, $6 per night for each extra vehicle, $3 per night. Major credit cards accepted. Open April through October.

Directions: From Carmel, drive 25 miles south on Highway 1 to the campground on the right.

Contact: Riverside Campground, tel./fax 831/667-2414; website: www.riversidecampground.com.

30 FERNWOOD PARK

Rating: 7

On the Big Sur River.
Map 8.3, page 466

This RV park is on the banks of the Big Sur River in the redwoods of the beautiful Big Sur coast. Many of the sites are set along the river. A highlight is that there is live music on Friday and Saturday nights in season. You can crown your trip with a dinner at the Ventana Inn (first-class—bring your bank with you).

Campsites, facilities: There are 38 sites for tents only and 28 sites with partial hookups for RVs. Fire grills and picnic tables are provided. Restrooms with showers, grocery store, restaurant, and a bar are available. Leashed pets are permitted.

Reservations, fees: Reservations are accepted. The fee is $24–27 per night, $4 per person for more than two people (to maximum of six), $5 per night for each extra vehicle, $3 per night. Group rates available. Major credit cards accepted. Open year-round.

Directions: From Carmel, drive 26 miles south on Highway 1 to the campground on the right.

Contact: Fernwood Park, 831/667-2422, fax 831/667-2663.

31 BIG SUR CAMPGROUND AND CABINS

Rating: 8

On the Big Sur River.
Map 8.3, page 466

This camp is in the redwoods near the Big Sur

River. Campers can stay in the redwoods, hike on great trails through the forest at nearby state parks, or explore nearby Pfeiffer Beach. Nearby Los Padres National Forest and Ventana Wilderness in the mountains to the east provide access to remote hiking trails with ridgetop vistas. Cruising Highway 1 south to Lucia and back offers endless views of breathtaking coastal scenery.

Campsites, facilities: There are 40 sites for RVs with water and electrical hookups, 40 sites for tents or RVs, 13 cabins, and four tent cabins. Picnic tables and fire grills are provided. Restrooms, drinking water, flush toilets, showers, RV dump station, playground, convenience store, and a laundry room are available. Some facilities are wheelchair-accessible. Leashed pets are permitted at campsites. No pets in cabins.

Reservations, fees: Reservations are recommended. Rates are $26–29 per night, $4 per person for more than two people, $8 per night for each extra vehicle, $4 per night. Major credit cards accepted. Open year-round.

Directions: From Carmel, drive 27 miles south on Highway 1 to the campground on the right side of the road (two miles north of the state park).

Contact: Big Sur Campground and Cabins, 831/667-2322, fax 831/667-0456.

32 VENTANA CAMPGROUNDS

Rating: 10

In Big Sur.

Map 8.3, page 466

This rustic camp has wooded sites and is set in an ideal location for many. The campsites are private and extremely beautiful, set in the redwoods with a small creek running through camp, with a few small waterfalls nearby. Premium side trips are available, highlighted by the beautiful beach at Andrew Molera State Park (a one-mile hike is necessary), the majestic redwoods, a creek hike, and a bluff-top waterfall in Julia Pfeiffer Burns State Park.

Campsites, facilities: There are 80 sites for tents or self-contained RVs up to 22 feet. Picnic tables and fire grills are provided. A restroom, drinking water, showers, and flush toilets are available. A small store is nearby with firewood and ice. Some facilities are wheelchair-accessible. Leashed pets are permitted.

Reservations, fees: Reservations are accepted. The fee is $25–35 per night, $4 per person per night for more than two people, $5 per night for each extra vehicle. Three-day minimum stay on holidays. Major credit cards accepted. Open year-round; call to confirm, may be closed in winter.

Directions: From Carmel, drive 28 miles south on Highway 1 to Big Sur and the campground entrance on the left.

Contact: Ventana Campgrounds, 831/667-2712, website: www.ventanawildernesscampground.com.

33 PFEIFFER BIG SUR STATE PARK

Rating: 10

In Big Sur.

Map 8.3, page 466

This stretch of coast is one of the most beautiful anywhere. This is one of the most popular state parks in California, and it's easy to see why. You can have it all: fantastic coastal vistas along Highway 1, redwood forests and waterfalls in the Julia Pfeiffer Burns State Park (11.5 miles to the south), expansive beaches with sea otters playing on the edge of kelp beds in the Andrew Molera State Park (4.5 miles north), great restaurants such as Ventana Inn (a few miles south), and private, patrolled sites. Reservations are a necessity. Some campsites in this park are set along the Big Sur River. The park features 800 acres of redwoods, conifers, oaks, sycamores, cottonwoods, maples, alders, and willows, plus open meadows—just about everything, in other words. Wildlife includes wild boar, raccoons, skunk, and many birds, among them water ouzels and belted kingfishers. A number of loop trails provide spectacular views of the Pacific Ocean and the Big Sur Gorge. Big Sur Lodge is within the park.

Campsites, facilities: There are 218 sites for tents or RVs up to 32 feet long, two hike-in or bike-in sites, and two group sites for up to 35 people. Picnic tables and fire grills are provided. Restrooms, drinking water, showers, and flush toilets are available. Groceries, a café, and propane gas are available nearby. Some facilities are wheelchair-accessible. Leashed pets are permitted in the campground only.

Reservations, fees: Reserve at 800/444-PARK (800/444-7525) or website: www.Reserve America.com ($7.50 reservation fee); $12 per night, $26 per night for group sites, $1 per person per night for hike-in or bike-in sites. Open year-round, weather permitting.

Directions: From Carmel, drive 26 miles south on Highway 1 to the park on the left (east side of highway).

Contact: Pfeiffer Big Sur State Park, 831/667-2315, fax 831/667-2886; California State Parks, Monterey District, 831/649-2836.

34 CHINA CAMP

Rating: 6

On Chews Ridge in Los Padres National Forest.

Map 8.3, page 466

A lot of folks might find it difficult to believe that a spot that feels so remote can be so close to the manicured Carmel Valley. But here it is, one of two camps on Tassajara Road at an elevation of 4,500 feet. This one has a trail out of camp that is routed into the Ventana Wilderness. Tassajara Hot Springs is seven miles away at the end of Tassajara Road. And keep a lookout for the gents with shaved heads. I kept asking them for all the secret spots, but they'd never talk. Turned out they were on a vigil of silence.

Campsites, facilities: There are six sites for tents only. Picnic tables and fire grills are provided. Vault toilets are available. No drinking water is available. Leashed pets are permitted.

Reservations, fees: No reservations are accepted. A $5 day-use Adventure Pass (or $30 annual fee) is required. Open April through November, weather permitting.

Directions: From Highway 1 in Carmel, turn east on Carmel Valley Road and drive about 22 miles. Turn right (south) on Tassajara Road/County Road 5007 and drive 10 miles to the campground on the right.

Contact: Los Padres National Forest, Monterey Ranger District, 831/385-5434, fax 831/385-0628.

35 ARROYO SECO

Rating: 8

Along Arroyo Seco River in Los Padres National Forest.

Map 8.3, page 466

This pretty spot near Arroyo Seco River is just outside the northern border of the Ventana Wilderness. The elevation is 900 feet. Arroyo Seco Group Camp is available to keep the pressure off this campground.

Campsites, facilities: There are 48 sites for tents or RVs up to 26 feet long, plus a group site for 25–50 people. Picnic tables and fire grills are provided. Restrooms, drinking water, flush toilets, and coin-operated showers are available. Leashed pets are permitted.

Reservations, fees: Reservations are not accepted. The fee is $16 per night. Senior discount available. Reserve group site at 877/444-6777 ($9 reservation fee) or website: www.ReserveUsa.com; $50 group fee per night. Open year-round.

Directions: Drive on U.S. 101 to the town of Greenfield and Greenfield-Arroyo Seco Road. Turn west on Greenfield-Arroyo Seco Road/County Roads G16 and 3050 and drive 19 miles to the camp at the end of the road.

Contact: Los Padres National Forest, Monterey Ranger District, 831/385-5434, fax 831/385-0628.

36 ESCONDIDO

Rating: 6

In Los Padres National Forest.

Map 8.3, page 466

This is a prime jump-off spot for backpackers heading into the Ventana Wilderness. The camp is set at an elevation of 2,300 feet at a trailhead that connects to a network of other trails. The only catch is you have to plan on walking up, steeply at times, for a climb of more than 1,000 feet to reach the ridge.

Campsites, facilities: There are nine tent sites. Picnic tables and fire grills are provided. Vault toilets are available. No drinking water is available. Leashed pets are permitted.

Reservations, fees: No reservations are accepted. A $5 day-use Adventure Pass (or $30 annual fee) is required. Open April through November.

Directions: From U.S. 101 in King City, turn south on County Route G14 and drive 18 miles. Turn north on Mission Road and drive six miles. Turn left on Del Venturi-Milpitas Road/Indian Road and drive 20 miles to the campground on the left.

Contact: Los Padres National Forest, Monterey Ranger District, 831/385-5434, fax 831/385-0628.

37 MEMORIAL PARK

Rating: 6

In Los Padres National Forest.

Map 8.3, page 466

This is one of two backcountry camps in the area. The highlights are a trailhead and the vicinity of the Arroyo Seco River. The camp has a trailhead that provides access to the Ventana Wilderness trail network. The elevation is 2,000 feet, which gives hikers a nice head start on the climb. Be sure to pack plenty of drinking water for the trail and, even in spring, expect warm, dry conditions.

Campsites, facilities: There are eight tent sites. Picnic tables and fire grills are provided. Vault toilets are available. No drinking water is available. Leashed pets are permitted.

Reservations, fees: No reservations are accepted. A $5 day-use Adventure Pass (or $30 annual fee) is required. Open year-round.

Directions: From U.S. 101 in King City, turn south on County Route G14 and drive 18 miles. Turn north on Mission Road and drive six miles. Turn left on Del Venturi-Milpitas Road/County Road 4050 and drive 16 miles to the campground on the right.

Contact: Los Padres National Forest, Monterey Ranger District, 831/385-5434, fax 831/385-0628.

38 SAN LORENZO COUNTY PARK

Rating: 3

In King City.

Map 8.3, page 466

A lot of folks cruising up and down the state on U.S. 101 can underestimate their travel time and find themselves caught out near King City, a small city about midpoint between Northern and Southern California. Well, don't sweat it, because San Lorenzo County Park offers a spot to overnight. It's set near the Salinas River, which isn't exactly the Mississippi, but it'll do. A museum and visitor center capture the rural agricultural life of the valley. The park covers 200 acres, featuring a playground and ball fields.

Campsites, facilities: There are 99 sites, including 65 drive-through, with partial hookups for tents or RVs. Picnic tables and fire grills are provided. An RV dump station, restrooms, flush toilets, showers, and laundry facilities are available. Leashed pets are permitted.

Reservations, fees: Reservations are accepted at 888/588-2267; $16–21 per night, $2 per night. Group rates available. Open year-round.

Directions: From King City on U.S. 101, turn left at the Broadway exit and drive to the park at 1160 Broadway.

Contact: San Lorenzo County Park, 831/385-5964.

39 LIMEKILN STATE PARK
🏃 🏕 ♿ 🚐 ⛺

Rating: 9

On the Pacific Ocean.

Map 8.3, page 466

Limekiln State Park provides breathtaking views of the Big Sur Coast. This camp provides a great layover spot in the Big Sur area of Highway 1, with drive-in campsites set up both near the beach and the redwoods—take your pick. Several hiking trails are nearby, including one that is routed past some historic lime kilns, which were used in the late 1800s to make cement and bricks. Want more? A short rock hop on a spur trail (just off the main trail) leads to dramatic 100-foot Limekiln Falls, a gorgeous waterfall. This camp was originally called Limekiln Beach Redwoods and was privately operated. It became a state park in 1995. One remaining problem: parking is limited.

Campsites, facilities: There are 18 sites for tents or RVs up to 24 feet long and trailers up to 15 feet long, and 15 sites for tents. Picnic tables and fire grills are provided. Restrooms, drinking water, showers, flush toilets, and firewood are available. Leashed pets are allowed, except on trails.

Reservations, fees: Make reservations ($7.50 reservation fee) at 800/444-PARK (800/444-7275) or website: www.ReserveAmerica.com; $12 per night. Senior discount available. Major credit cards accepted. Open year-round.

Directions: From Big Sur, drive south on Highway 1 for 35 miles (past Lucia) to the park on the left.

Contact: Limekiln State Park, 831/667-2403; California State Parks, Monterey District, 831/649-2836.

40 KIRK CREEK
🏃 🚲 🏊 🛶 🐕 🚐 ⛺

Rating: 8

Near the Pacific Ocean in Los Padres National Forest.

Map 8.3, page 466

This pretty camp is set along Kirk Creek as it empties into the Pacific Ocean. There is beach access through a footpath. Another trail from camp branches north through the Ventana Wilderness, which is sprinkled with little-used, hike-in, backcountry campsites. For gorgeous scenery without all the work, a quaint little café in Lucia provides open-air dining on a cliff-top deck, with a dramatic sweeping lookout over the coast.

Campsites, facilities: There are 33 sites for tents or RVs up to 26 feet long. Picnic tables and fire grills are provided. Drinking water and flush toilets are available. Leashed pets are permitted.

Reservations, fees: Reservations are not accepted. The fee is $16 per night, $5 per night for bicyclists. Senior discount available. Open year-round.

Directions: From Monterey, drive south on Highway 1 to Lucia. From Lucia, continue south on Highway 1 for four miles to the campground on the right.

Contact: Parks Management Company, 805/434-1996, fax 805/434-1986; Los Padres National Forest, Monterey Ranger District, 831/385-5434, fax 831/385-0628.

41 NACIMIENTO
🏃 🛶 🐕 🚐 ⛺

Rating: 5

In Los Padres National Forest.

Map 8.3, page 466

This little-known spot is set near the Nacimiento River at 1,600 feet elevation. Most campers will head up Nacimiento-Ferguson Road to camp on a Friday night and get up Saturday morning to head off on a hiking or backpacking trip in the nearby Ventana Wilderness.

Campsites, facilities: There are nine sites for tents and eight sites for tents or RVs up to 24 feet long. Picnic tables and fire grills are provided. Vault toilets are available. No drinking water is available. Leashed pets are permitted.
Reservations, fees: Reservations are not accepted. The fee is $5 per night. Open year-round.
Directions: From Monterey, drive south on Highway 1 to Lucia. From Lucia, continue south on Highway 1 for four miles to Nacimiento Road. Turn east (left) on Nacimiento Road and drive 11 winding miles to the campground on the right.
Contact: Parks Management Company, 805/434-1996, fax 805/434-1986; Los Padres National Forest, Monterey Ranger District, 831/385-5434, fax 831/385-0628.

42 PONDEROSA

Rating: 4

In Los Padres National Forest.
Map 8.3, page 466
As soon as you turn off Highway 1, you leave behind the crowds and enter a land that is largely unknown to people. This camp is set at 1,500 feet elevation in Los Padres National Forest, not far from the border of the Ventana Wilderness (good hiking and backpacking) and the Hunter Liggett Military Reservation (wild pig hunting is allowed there with a permit). It is one in a series of small camps on Nacimiento-to-Ferguson Road.
Campsites, facilities: There are 23 sites for tents or RVs up to 32 feet long. Picnic tables and fire grills are provided. Vault toilets are available. No drinking water is available. Leashed pets are permitted.
Reservations, fees: Reservations are not accepted. The fee is $13 per night. Senior discount available. Open year-round.
Directions: From Monterey, drive south on Highway 1 to Lucia. From Lucia, continue south on Highway 1 for four miles to Nacimiento-to-Ferguson Road. Turn left on Nacimiento-

to-Ferguson Road and drive about 12 miles to the campground on the right.
Contact: Parks Management Company, 805/434-1996, fax 805/434-1986, website: www.camp one.com; Los Padres National Forest, Monterey Ranger District, 831/385-5434, fax 831/385-0628.

43 PLASKETT CREEK

Rating: 8

Overlooking the Pacific Ocean in Los Padres National Forest.
Map 8.4, page 467
This is a premium coastal camp for Highway 1 cruisers, set at an elevation of just 100 feet along little Plaskett Creek above the Pacific Ocean. The campground provides access to Sand Dollar Beach. It gets overlooked by many for two reasons: it is not listed with a reservation service, and it is farther south of Big Sur than most are willing to drive. A little café in Lucia provides open-air dining with a dramatic lookout over the coast.
Campsites, facilities: There are 45 sites for tents or RVs up to 26 feet long. Picnic tables and fire grills are provided. Drinking water and flush toilets are available. Leashed pets are permitted.
Reservations, fees: Reservations are not accepted. The fee is $16 per night, $5 for bicyclists. Senior discount available. Open year-round.
Directions: From Monterey, drive south on Highway 1 to Lucia. From Lucia, continue south on Highway 1 for 9.5 miles to the campground on the left.
Contact: Parks Management Company, 805/434-1996, fax 805/434-1986, website: www.camp one.com; Los Padres National Forest, Monterey Ranger District, 831/385-5434, fax 831/385-0628.

44 PLASKETT CREEK GROUP CAMP

🏃 🏊 🚣 🐕 🚐 ⛺

Rating: 8

Overlooking the Pacific Ocean in Los Padres National Forest.

Map 8.4, page 467

This is one of two prime coastal camps in the immediate area along Highway 1, which is one of the prettiest drives in the West. The camp is for small groups and is set beside little Plaskett Creek. For a premium day trip, drive north five miles to Nacimiento-Ferguson Road, turn east, and drive into Los Padres National Forest and to the border of the Ventana Wilderness. Coastal views and hikes are first-class.

Campsites, facilities: There are three group sites for tents or RVs up to 26 feet long. Picnic tables and fire grills are provided. Drinking water and vault toilets are available. Leashed pets are permitted.

Reservations, fees: Reserve at 877/444-6777 ($9 reservation fee) or website: www.Reserve Usa.com; $60 group fee per night. Open year-round.

Directions: From Monterey, drive south on Highway 1 to Lucia. From Lucia, continue south on Highway 1 for 9.5 miles to the campground on the left.

Contact: Parks Management Company, 805/434-1996, fax 805/434-1986, website: www.camp one.com; Los Padres National Forest, Monterey Ranger District, 831/385-5434, fax 831/385-0628.

© JEFFREY PATTY

Chapter 9
San Joaquin Valley

Chapter 9—San Joaquin Valley

This section of the San Joaquin Valley is noted for its searing weather all summer long. But that is also when the lakes in the foothills become something like a Garden of Eden for boating and water sports enthusiasts. The region also offers many settings in the Sierra foothills, which can serve as launch points for short drives into the alpine beauty of Yosemite, Sequoia, and Kings Canyon National Parks.

Most of the campgrounds in this region are family-oriented. Many of them are on access roads to Yosemite. A bonus is that most have lower prices than their counterparts in the park, and as we said, are more hospitable to children.

The lakes are the primary recreation attraction, with the refreshing, clean water revered as a tonic against the valley heat all summer long. When viewed from the air, the closeness of these lakes to the Sierra Nevada mountain range is surprising to many. Their proximity to the high country results in cool, high-quality water—the product of snowmelt sent down river canyons on the western slope. Some of these lakes are among the best around for water-skiing and powerboat recreation, including Lake Don Pedro east of Modesto, Bass Lake near Oakhurst, Lake McClure near Merced, Pine Flat Reservoir east of Fresno, and Lake Kaweah near Visalia.

In addition, Lake Don Pedro, Pine Flat Reservoir, and Lake Kaweah are among the best fishing lakes in the entire Central Valley; some anglers rate Don Pedro as the number-one all-around fishing lake in the state. The nearby Sierra rivers that feed these lakes (and others) also offer the opportunity to fly-fish for trout. In particular, the Kaweah and Kings Rivers boast many miles of ideal pocket water for fly fishers. While the trout on these streams are only occasionally large, the catch rates are often high and the rock-strewn beauty of the river canyons is exceptional.

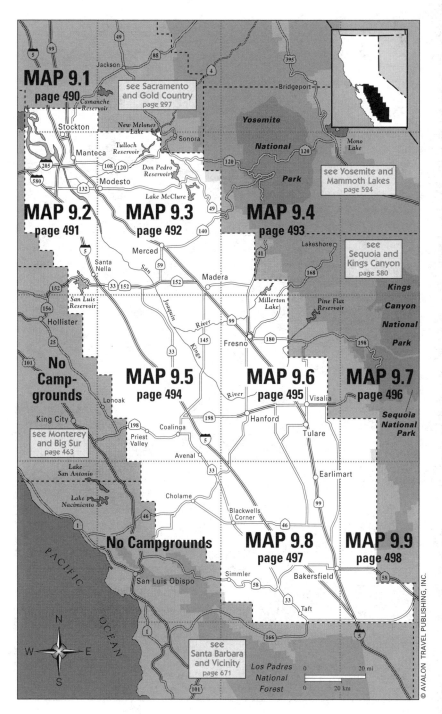

Map 9.1

**Campgrounds 1–3
Page 499**

9.2

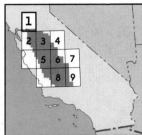

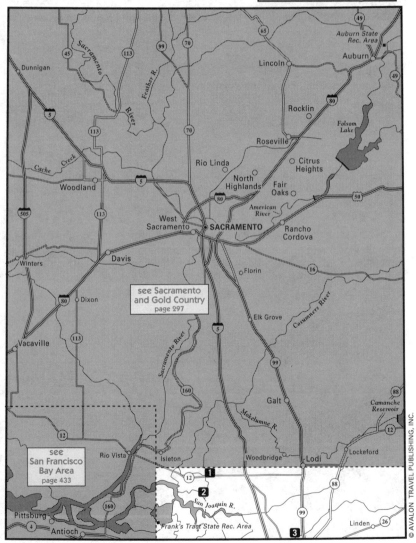

Map 9.2

Campgrounds 4–12
Pages 500–503

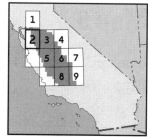

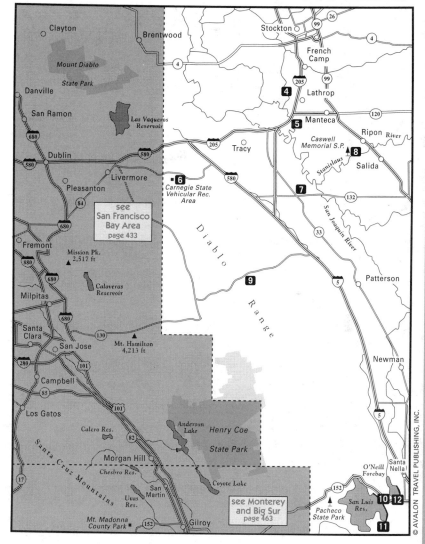

Clayton

Brentwood

Stockton

French Camp

Mount Diablo State Park

Danville

San Ramon

Lathrop

Manteca

Ripon

Caswell Memorial S.P.

Salida

Las Vaqueros Reservoir

Dublin

Tracy

Stanislaus

Livermore

Pleasanton

Carnegie State Vehicular Rec. Area

see San Francisco Bay Area page 433

Diablo

San Joaquin River

Fremont

Mission Pk. 2,517 ft

Calaveras Reservoir

Milpitas

Patterson

Range

Santa Clara

San Jose

Mt. Hamilton 4,213 ft

Newman

Campbell

Los Gatos

Calero Res.

Anderson Lake

Henry Coe State Park

Santa Cruz Mountains

Morgan Hill

Chesbro Res.

San Martin

Coyote Lake

O'Neill Forebay

Santa Nella

Uvas Res.

see Monterey and Big Sur page 463

Pacheco State Park

San Luis Res.

Mt. Madonna County Park

Gilroy

Map 9.3

**Campgrounds 13–31
Pages 504–512**

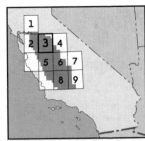

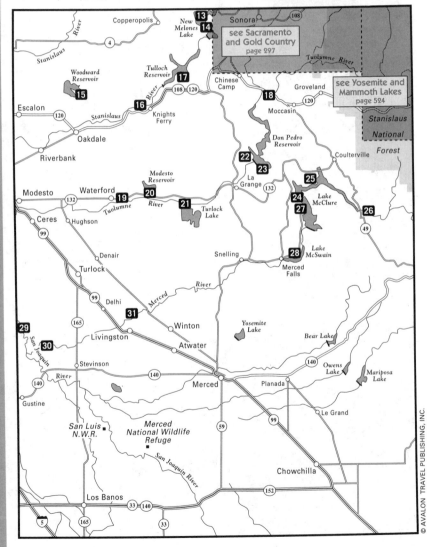

see Sacramento and Gold Country page 297

see Yosemite and Mammoth Lakes page 524

© AVALON TRAVEL PUBLISHING, INC.

Map 9.4

Campgrounds 32–34
Pages 512–513

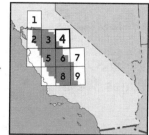

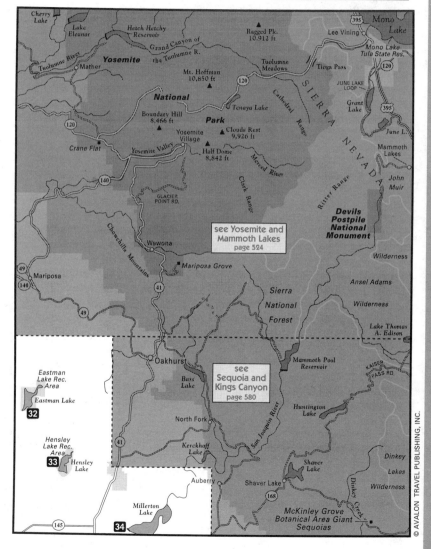

Cherry Lake
Lake Eleanor
Hetch Hetchy Reservoir
Grand Canyon of the Tuolumne R.
Ragged Pk. 10,912 ft
Lee Vining
Mono Lake
Tuolumne River
Mather
Yosemite
Mt. Hoffman 10,850 ft
Tuolumne Meadows
Tioga Pass
Mono Lake Tufa State Res.
120
JUNE LAKE LOOP
395
National
Boundary Hill 8,466 ft
Tenaya Lake
Cathedral Range
Grant Lake
June L.
120
Park
Yosemite Village
Clouds Rest 9,926 ft
Crane Flat
Yosemite Valley
Half Dome 8,842 ft
Merced River
Mammoth Lakes
140
John Muir
GLACIER POINT RD.
Clark Range
Ritter Range
Devils Postpile National Monument
Wawona
see Yosemite and Mammoth Lakes page 524
49
Mariposa
140
Mariposa Grove
41
Sierra
National
Forest
Wilderness
Ansel Adams Wilderness
Lake Thomas A. Edison
49
Oakhurst
see Sequoia and Kings Canyon page 580
Mammoth Pool Reservoir
KAISER PASS RD.
Eastman Lake Rec. Area
Eastman Lake
32
Bass Lake
Huntington Lake
Hensley Lake Rec. Area
33
Hensley Lake
41
North Fork
Kerckhoff Lake
San Joaquin River
Shaver Lake
Dinkey Lakes
Auberry
145
Millerton Lake
34
Shaver Lake
168
McKinley Grove Botanical Area Giant Sequoias
Dinkey Creek Wilderness
© AVALON TRAVEL PUBLISHING, INC.

Map 9.5

Campgrounds 35–37
Pages 514–515

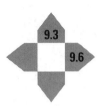

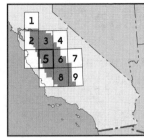

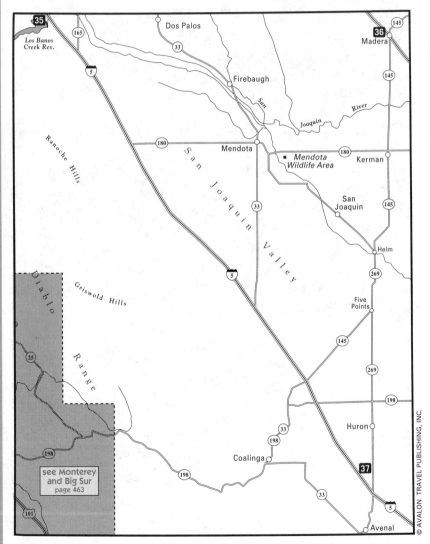

Map 9.6

Campgrounds 38–40
Pages 515–516

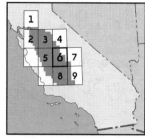

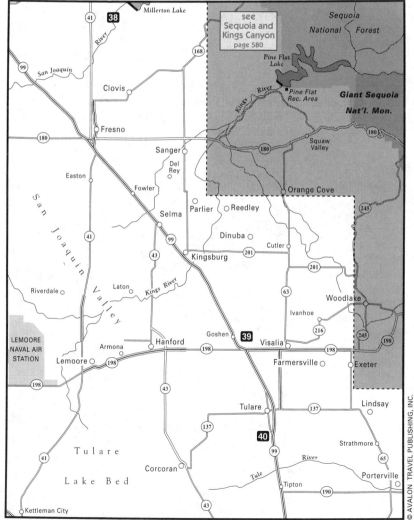

Map 9.7

**Campgrounds 41–42
Pages 516–517**

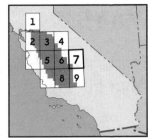

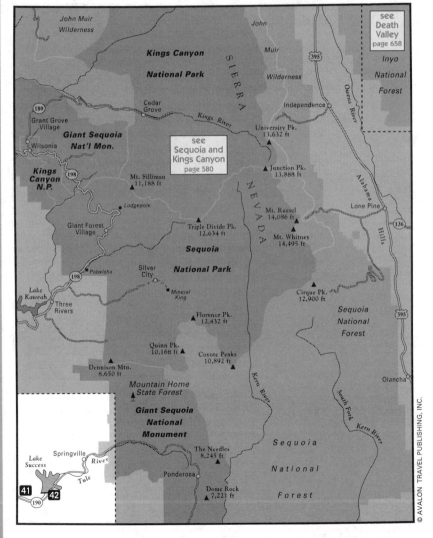

© AVALON TRAVEL PUBLISHING, INC.

Map 9.8

Campgrounds 43–48
Pages 517–519

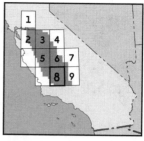

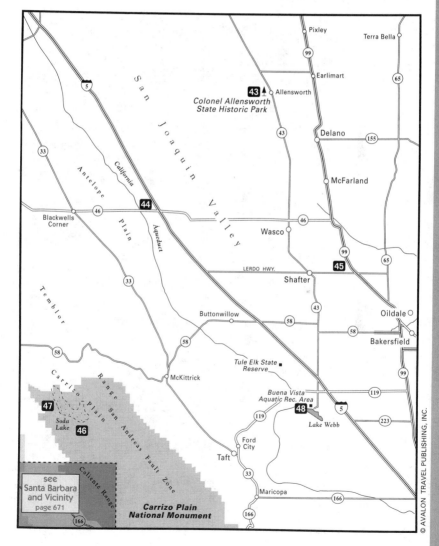

Map 9.9

**Campground 49
Page 520**

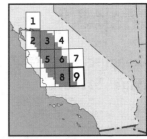

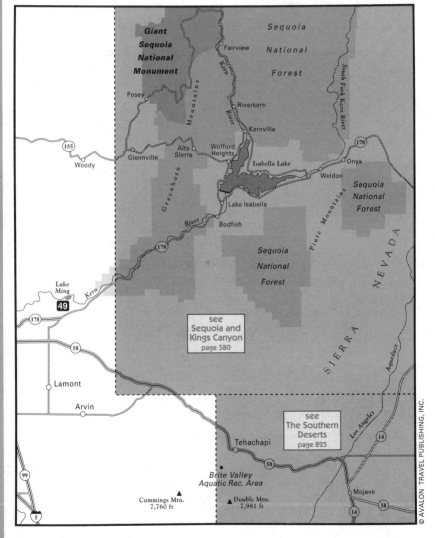

❶ WESTGATE LANDING COUNTY PARK

🏊 🚣 🚐 🐕 ♿ 🚍 ⛺

Rating: 6

In the San Joaquin River Delta near Stockton.

Map 9.1, page 490

Summer temperatures typically reach the high 90s and low 100s here, and this county park provides a little shade and boating access to the South Fork Mokelumne River. On hot summer nights, some campers will stay up late and night fish for catfish. Between storms in winter, the area typically gets smothered in dense fog. For RV drivers, the sites are not drive-through but semicircles, which work nearly as well.

Campsites, facilities: There are 14 sites for tents or RVs up to 32 feet. Picnic tables and barbecues are provided. Drinking water and flush toilets are available. Groceries and propane gas are nearby. There are 24 boat slips available. Leashed pets are permitted.

Reservations, fees: Reservations are accepted with a $10 reservation fee at least three weeks in advance. Less than three weeks, sites are first-come, first-served. The fee is $10 per night, $5 per night for each extra vehicle, boat slips $10, $1 per night. Open year-round.

Directions: On I-5, drive to Lodi and Highway 12. Take Highway 12 west and drive about five miles to Glasscock Road. Turn right and drive about a mile to the park.

Contact: San Joaquin County Parks Department, 209/953-8800.

❷ TOWER PARK MARINA AND RESORT

🚣 🚐 🐕 👨‍👩‍👧 ♿ 🚍 ⛺

Rating: 6

Near Stockton.

Map 9.1, page 490

This huge resort is ideal for boat-in campers who desire a full-facility marina. The camp is set on Little Potato Slough near the Mokelumne River. In the summer, this is a popular water-skiing area. Some hot weekends are like a continuous party. While there are no drive-through sites, access for large RVs is still easy when the adjacent campsite is not taken.

Campsites, facilities: There are 500 sites, most with full hookups for RVs or tents, and park-model cabins. Picnic tables and barbecues are provided. Restrooms, showers, RV dump station, pavilion, boat rentals, overnight boat slips, double boat launch, playground, restaurant, coin laundry, gift shop, store, ice, and propane gas are available. Some facilities are wheelchair-accessible. Leashed pets are permitted.

Reservations, fees: Reservations are recommended. The fee is $19–27 per night, maximum six people per site, $2 per night. Major credit cards accepted. Open year-round. No tent camping in winter.

Directions: On I-5, drive to Lodi and Highway 12. Take Highway 12 west and drive about five miles to Tower Park Way (before first bridge). Turn left and drive a short distance to the park.

Contact: Tower Park Marina and Resort, 209/369-1041, fax 209/943-5656, website: www.westrec.com.

❸ STOCKTON-LODI KOA

🏊 🏕 🐕 👨‍👩‍👧 ♿ 🚍 ⛺

Rating: 1

In Lodi.

Map 9.1, page 490

This KOA camp is in the heart of the San Joaquin Valley. The proximity to I-5 and Highway 99 makes it work for long-distance vacationers looking for a spot to park the rig for the night. The San Joaquin Delta is 15 miles to the west, with best access provided off Highway 12 to Isleton and Rio Vista; it's also a pretty drive.

Campsites, facilities: There are 102 sites, most drive-through and many with full hookups, for RVs or tents, and two cabins. Picnic tables are provided. Restrooms, showers, RV dump station, store, propane gas, coin laundry, modem access, recreation room, seasonal swimming pool, and a playground are available. Some facilities are wheelchair-accessible. Leashed pets are permitted.

Reservations, fees: Reservations are accepted at 800/562-1229. The fee is $23–29 per night. Major credit cards accepted. Open year-round.

Directions: On I-5, drive to Eight Mile Road (five miles north of Stockton). Turn east and drive five miles to the campground at 2851 E. Eight Mile Road.

Contact: Stockton-Lodi KOA, 209/941-2573 (from Stockton), 209/334-0309 (from Lodi), or tel./fax 209/941-2573.

🄳 DOS REIS COUNTY PARK
🏊 ⛵ 🐕 ♿ 🚐 ⛺

Rating: 6

On the San Joaquin River near Stockton.
Map 9.2, page 491

This is a 90-acre county park that has a quarter mile of San Joaquin River frontage, boat ramp, and nearby access to the eastern Delta near Stockton. The sun gets scalding hot here in the summer, branding everything in sight. That's why boaters make quick work of getting in the water, then cooling off with water sports. In the winter, this area often has zero visibility from tule fog.

Campsites, facilities: There are 26 sites with full hookups for RVs and tents. Picnic tables and fire grills are provided. Restrooms, showers, and a boat ramp are available. A store, coin laundry, and propane gas are within three miles. Leashed pets are permitted with a limit of two.

Reservations, fees: Reservations are accepted up to four weeks in advance. The fee is $15 per night, $5 per night for additional vehicle, $1 per night. Open year-round.

Directions: Drive on I-5 to Stockton and the Lathrop exit. Turn north on Lathrop and drive 1.5 blocks to Manthy Road. Turn north and drive a half mile to Dos Rios Road. Turn left

and drive to the campground at the end of the road.

Contact: San Joaquin County Parks Department, 209/953-8800, fax 209/331-2012, website: www.co.san-joaquin.ca.us/parks.

🄵 OAKWOOD LAKE RESORT & MANTECA WATERSLIDES

Rating: 2

Near Stockton.
Map 9.2, page 491

This is a huge, privately operated "water theme" park that covers 375 acres and offers a wide array of water-related recreation. It is a great place for families to cool off and have fun on hot summer days, with youngsters lining up for trips down the water slides.

Campsites, facilities: There are 196 sites with full hookups for RVs, 111 sites for tents, and 74 sites with partial hookups for RVs or tents. Picnic tables are provided. Restrooms, showers, RV dump station, store, coin laundry, propane gas, swimming lagoon, water slides, organized activities, and a stocked 75-acre lake are available. The facilities are wheelchair-accessible. Leashed pets are permitted.

Reservations, fees: Reservations are accepted at 209/239-2500, ext. 308, 301, or 313. The fee is $28–32 per night, $15 per person per night for more than four people. The fee is $2 per night. Open year-round.

Directions: Drive on Highway 120 to Airport Way (two miles east of Manteca). Turn south on Airport Way and drive a half mile to Woodward Way. Turn right and drive two miles to the park entrance.

Contact: Oakwood Lake Resort, 209/239-9566, fax 209/239-2060, website: www.oakwood lake.com.

6 CARNEGIE STATE VEHICULAR REC AREA

Rating: 2

Carnegie State Vehicular Rec Area near Tracy.

Map 9.2, page 491

This is a major state-run OHV area, with mainly dirt bikes. Don't show up without one, or its equivalent. This area is barren, ugly, and extremely noisy on weekends. It can get hot, windy, and dusty as well. But that's just what dirt bikers want, and they have it all to themselves. There is an overflow area, so no one need fear being turned away, but the main campsite almost never fills. The area covers 1,500 acres with challenging hill-type trail riding and a professionally designed motocross track. There is also a four-wheel-drive obstacle course. Elevations here rise to 1,800 feet, with summer temperatures peaking at 105°F. Winters are mild.

Campsites, facilities: There are 19 tent and RV sites with no length limit. No hookups. Picnic tables and fire rings are provided. Restrooms, drinking water, flush toilets, and outdoor cold showers are available, but note that the drinking water (high in iron) tastes terrible, and you are advised to bring bottled water. Nearest supplies are 10 miles away. Leashed pets are permitted.

Reservations, fees: Reservations are not accepted. The fee is $6 fee per night. Senior discount available. Open year-round, weather permitting.

Directions: From I-580 (south of Tracy), drive to Corral Hollow Road. Take that exit and drive southwest for six miles to the campground on the left.

Contact: Carnegie State Vehicular Rec Area, 925/447-9027; Carnegie Sector Office, 925/447-0426.

7 ORCHARD RV PARK

Rating: 5

Near Stockton.

Map 9.2, page 491

The huge swimming pool and water slides here make this a popular campground for families. Temperatures in the 100-degree range in the summer keep both in constant use. This privately operated park is set up primarily for owners of RVs. Its location near I-5 makes it a winner for many of them.

Campsites, facilities: There are 12 tent sites and 88 drive-through RV sites with full hookups. Picnic tables and fire grills are provided. Restrooms, showers, laundry room, RV dump station, swimming pool, propane, ice, and horseshoe pits are available. A restaurant is next door. A store, post office, and weekend flea market are nearby. Some facilities are wheelchair-accessible. Leashed pets are permitted with a two-dog limit.

Reservations, fees: Reservations are accepted. The fee is $20 per night. Open year-round.

Directions: Drive on I-5 to Vernalis and Highway 132. Turn east on Highway 132 and drive three miles to the signed campground entrance at 2701 E. Hwy. 132.

Contact: Orchard RV Park, 209/836-2090.

8 CASWELL MEMORIAL STATE PARK

Rating: 7

On the Stanislaus River near Stockton.

Map 9.2, page 491

Caswell Memorial State Park features shoreline frontage along the Stanislaus River, along with an additional 250 acres of parkland. The Stanislaus provides shoreline fishing for catfish on summer nights. Bass and crappie are also occasionally caught. Other recreation options here include a visitor center, an interpretive nature trail, and swimming. Bird-watching is popular; look for red-shouldered and red-tail hawks. During warm months, bring mosquito repellent.

Campsites, facilities: There are 64 sites for tents or RVs up to 24 feet long, and one group site for up to 50 people. Picnic tables, food lockers, and fire grills are provided. Drinking water, flush toilets, showers, firewood, a swimming beach, and nature trails are available. Some facilities are wheelchair-accessible. Weekend interpretive programs and junior ranger programs are available in the summer. Leashed pets are permitted.

Reservations, fees: Reservations are accepted. The fee is $12 per night; groups with up to 12 vehicles, $37 per night. Senior discount available. Open year-round.

Directions: Drive on Highway 99 to Austin Road (1.5 miles south of Manteca). Turn south on Austin Road and drive four miles to the park entrance at the end of the road.

Contact: Caswell Memorial State Park, 209/599-3810; California State Parks, Four Rivers District, 209/826-1197, fax 209/826-0284.

9 FRANK RAINES REGIONAL PARK
🏃 🐎 🛶 ♿ 🚐 ⛺

Rating: 4

Near Modesto.

Map 9.2, page 491

This park is primarily a riding area for folks with dirt bikes and three- and four-wheel OHVs who take advantage of the rough-terrain riding course available here. A side-trip option is to visit Minniear Park, directly to the east, which is a day-use wilderness park with hiking trails and a creek. This area is very pretty in the spring when the foothills are still green and many wildflowers are blooming.

Campsites, facilities: There are 34 sites, some drive-through and some with full hookups, for RVs or tents. Fire grills and picnic tables are provided. Restrooms, drinking water, showers, and a playground are available. Some facilities are wheelchair-accessible. Pets are permitted.

Reservations, fees: Reservations are not accepted. The fee is $12–16 per night, $6–8 per night for each extra vehicle, $2 fee for rough-terrain vehicles, $2 per night. Disabled vets with proof of disability from the Veterans Administration can camp free for 15 days; others with disabilities get a 50 percent discount. Open year-round.

Directions: On I-5, drive to the Patterson exit (south of the junction of I-5 and I-580). Turn west on Patterson and drive to Del Puerto Canyon Road. Turn west and drive 16 miles to the park.

Contact: Frank Raines Regional Park, 209/256-6750 or 408/897-3127, fax 408/897-3127.

10 SAN LUIS CREEK
🏃 🏊 🛶 🍽 🐕 🚐 ⛺

Rating: 5

On San Luis Reservoir.

Map 9.2, page 491

San Luis Campground is on Los Banos Creek near San Luis Reservoir. It is one in a series of camps operated by the state in the San Luis Reservoir State Recreation Area, adjacent to the reservoir and O'Neill Forebay, home of the biggest striped bass in California, including the world record for landlocked stripers.

Campsites, facilities: There are 53 sites for tents or RVs with electrical and water hookups, and two group sites for up to 30–60 people. Picnic tables and fire pits are provided. Drinking water, pit toilets, and RV dump station are available. Leashed pets are permitted.

Reservations, fees: Reservations are accepted with a $7.50 reservation fee at 800/444-PARK (800/444-7275) or website: www.Reserve America.com. The fee is $12–14 per night, $20–45 per night for group sites. Senior discount available. Open year-round.

Directions: Drive on Highway 152 to San Luis Reservoir (12 miles west of Los Banos) and the signed campground entrance road (15 miles west of Los Banos). Turn and drive two miles to the campground on the left.

Contact: San Luis Reservoir State Recreation Area, 209/826-1196; Four Rivers District, 209/826-1197, fax 209/826-0284.

11 BASALT

Rating: 5

On San Luis Reservoir.

Map 9.2, page 491

San Luis Reservoir is a huge, man-made lake, covering 13,800 acres with 65 miles of shoreline, developed among stark foothills to provide a storage facility along the California Aqueduct. It fills by late winter and is used primarily by anglers, water-skiers, and windsurfers. When the Sacramento River Delta water pumps take the water, they also take the fish, filling this lake up with both. Striped bass fishing is best in the fall when the stripers chase schools of bait fish on the lake surface. Spring and early summer can be quite windy, but that makes for good windsurfing. The adjacent O'Neill Forebay is the best recreation bet because of the boat launch and often good fishing. There is a visitor center at the Romero Overlook. The elevation is 575 feet. Summer temperatures can occasionally exceed 100°F, but evenings are usually pleasant. During winter, tule fog is common. Note that in spring and early summer, it can turn windy very quickly. Warning lights mark several spots at the reservoir and forebay.

Campsites, facilities: There are 79 sites for tents or RVs. Picnic tables and fire grills are provided. Drinking water, flush toilets, coin showers, RV dump station, and a boat ramp are available. A store, coin laundry, gas station, restaurant, and propane gas are nearby (about 1.5 miles away). Some facilities are wheelchair-accessible. Leashed pets are permitted.

Reservations, fees: Reservations are accepted with a $7.50 reservation fee at 800/444-PARK (800/444-7275) or website: www.ReserveAmerica.com. The fee is $12–14 per night. Senior discount available. Open year-round.

Directions: Drive on Highway 152 to San Luis Reservoir (12 miles west of Los Banos) and the Basalt Campground entrance road. Turn south and drive a short distance to Gonzaga Road. Drive straight on Gonzaga Road and continue 2.5 miles (the road becomes Basalt Road) to the campground on the left.

Contact: San Luis Reservoir State Recreation Area, 209/826-1196; Four Rivers District, 209/826-1197, fax 209/826-0284.

12 MEDEIROS

Rating: 5

On O'Neill Forebay near Santa Nella.

Map 9.2, page 491

This is a vast, primitive campground set on the stark expanse of foothill country near O'Neill Forebay near Santa Nellsa and San Luis Reservoir. Some of the biggest striped bass in California history have been caught here at the forebay. It is best known for wind in the spring, hot weather in the summer, and low water levels in the fall. Striped bass fishing is best in the fall when the wind is down and stripers will corral schools of bait fish near the lake surface. The campground elevation is 225 feet. (See listing for Basalt Campground for more information about San Luis.) Note that the location of the boat ramp caused it to be closed in 2002 for security reasons. Its future as an access point is uncertain.

Campsites, facilities: There are 350 primitive sites for tents or RVs. Some shaded ramadas with fire grills and picnic tables are available. Drinking water and chemical toilets are available. A boat ramp is nearby. Leashed pets are permitted.

Reservations, fees: Reservations are not accepted. The fee is $7 per night. Senior discount available. Open year-round.

Directions: Drive on Highway 152 to Highway 33 (located about three miles west of Los

Banos). Turn north (right) on Highway 33 and drive one-quarter mile to the campground entrance on the left.

Contact: San Luis Reservoir State Recreation Area, 209/826-1196; Four Rivers District, 209/826-1197, fax 209/826-0284.

13 GLORY HOLE

Rating: 7

At New Melones Lake.

Map 9.3, page 492

Glory Hole encompasses both Big Oak and Ironhorse campgrounds. This is one of two major recreation areas on New Melones Lake in the Sierra Nevada foothills, a popular spot with a boat ramp nearby for access to outstanding water-skiing and fishing. (See the entry for Tuttletown Recreation Area.) Some may remember a baseball field that was once here. No more. It was reconstructed into an amphitheater where campfire programs are often available in summer.

Campsites, facilities: Big Oak has 55 sites for tents or RVs, Ironhorse has 89 sites for tents or RVs; 20 sites are for tents only. Picnic tables and fire grills are provided. Drinking water, flush toilets, showers, marina, boat rentals, amphitheater, playground, and horseshoes are available. Some facilities are wheelchair-accessible. Leashed pets are permitted.

Reservations, fees: Reservations are not accepted. The fee is $14 per night. Senior discount available. Open year-round.

Directions: From Sonora, drive north on Highway 49 for about 15 miles (Glory Hole Market will be on the left side of the road) to Glory Hole Road. Turn left and drive five miles to the campground, with sites on both sides of the road.

Contact: U.S. Department of Reclamation, 209/536-9094, fax 209/536-9652.

14 TUTTLETOWN RECREATION AREA

Rating: 7

At New Melones Lake.

Map 9.3, page 492

Here is a mammoth camping area set on the giant New Melones Lake in the Sierra Nevada foothills, a beautiful sight when the lake is full. Tuttletown encompasses three campgrounds (Acorn, Manzanita, and Chamise) and two group camping areas (Oak Knoll and Fiddleneck). New Melones is a huge reservoir that covers 12,250 acres and offers 100 miles of shoreline and good fishing. Water-skiing is permitted in specified areas; a boat ramp is near camp. Although the lake's main body is huge, the better fishing is well up the lake's Stanislaus River arm (for trout) and in its coves (for bass and bluegill), where there are submerged trees providing perfect aquatic habitat. Trolling for kokanee salmon also has become popular. The lake level often drops dramatically in the fall.

Campsites, facilities: At Acorn there are 69 sites for tents or RVs, at Chamise there are 36 sites for tents or RVs, and at Manzanita there are 55 sites for tents or RVs, 13 walk-in tent sites; Oak Knoll group site holds up to 80 people, and Fiddleneck group site up to 60 people. Picnic tables and fire grills are provided. Drinking water, flush toilets, RV dump station, showers, playground, and a boat ramp are available. Some facilities are wheelchair-accessible. Leashed pets are permitted.

Reservations, fees: Reservations are not accepted. The fee is $84–140 per night. Senior discount available. Open year-round.

Directions: From Sonora, drive north on Highway 49 to Reynolds Ferry Road. Turn left and drive about two miles to the entrance road to the campgrounds.

Contact: U.S. Department of Reclamation, 209/536-9094, fax 209/536-9652.

15 WOODWARD RESERVOIR COUNTY PARK

Rating: 7

Near Oakdale.
Map 9.3, page 492

Woodward Reservoir is a large lake covering 2,900 acres with 23 miles of shoreline, set in the rolling foothills just north of Oakdale. It is a good lake for both water-skiing and bass fishing, with minimal conflict between the two sports. Alas, just when peace was at hand, rentals of personal watercraft are now available here. Two large coves on the south and east ends of the lake, as well as the area behind Whale Island, are for low-speed boats only. That makes for good fishing, while the speedboats have the main lake body to let her rip.

Campsites, facilities: There are 155 sites, 115 with partial hookups and 40 with full hookups, for RVs or tents. Picnic tables and fire grills are provided. Drinking water, flush toilets, showers, RV dump station, three boat ramps, mooring, dry boat storage, a store, bait, fishing licenses, and some equestrian facilities are available. Some facilities are wheelchair-accessible. Leashed pets are permitted.

Reservations, fees: Reservations are not accepted. The fee is $12–16 per night, $5 boat launch fee, $2 pet fee. Open year-round.

Directions: Drive on Highway 120 to Oakdale (the road becomes Highway 108/120) and the junction with County Road J14/26 Mile Road. Turn left on 26 Mile Road and drive four miles to the park entrance at Woodward Reservoir (14528 26 Mile Road).

Contact: Woodward Reservoir County Park, 209/847-3304 or 209/525-6750, website: www.co.stanislaus.ca.us.

16 KNIGHTS FERRY RESORT

Rating: 7

On the Stanislaus River.
Map 9.3, page 492

This is a privately run campground in the small historic town of Knights Ferry. The campground has a good number of trees. A nice touch is a restaurant overlooking the Stanislaus River. Side trips include tours of the covered bridge ("the longest west of the Mississippi") and several historic buildings and homes, all within walking distance of the park. River access and hiking trails are available at the east end of town. Raft and canoe rentals are also available nearby.

Campsites, facilities: There are 21 sites for tents or RVs. A community fire pit, restrooms, showers, and a restaurant are available. Some facilities are wheelchair-accessible. No pets permitted.

Reservations, fees: Reservations are accepted with a deposit. The fee is $20–23 per night. There is a two-night minimum stay on weekends and a three-night minimum on holidays. Major credit cards accepted. Open year-round.

Directions: From Manteca, drive east on Highway 120 to Oakdale (the road becomes Highway 108/120). Continue east on Highway 108 for 12 miles to Knight's Ferry and Kennedy Road. Turn left and drive to a bridge, cross the bridge, and continue a short distance to Sonora Road/Main Street. Turn left and drive to the campground entrance at the Knights Ferry Restaurant.

Contact: Knights Ferry Resort, 209/881-3349.

17 LAKE TULLOCH RV CAMP AND MARINA

Rating: 8

On the south shore of Lake Tulloch.
Map 9.3, page 492

This camp features tons of waterfront on Lake Tulloch, including 20 RV sites with partial hookups, a dispersed tent area, and cabins with direct beach access. Unlike so many reservoirs in the foothill country, this one is nearly always full of water. In addition, it is one of the rare places where fishermen and water-skiers live in harmony. That is due to the many coves and a six-mile-long arm with an enforced 5-mph speed limit. It's a big lake, shaped like a giant "X" with extended lake arms adding up to 55 miles of shoreline. The campground features mature oak trees that provide shade to most of the developed sites. A secret at Tulloch is that fishing is also good for crawdads. The elevation is 500 feet.

Campsites, facilities: There are 120 sites, including 51 with full hookups and boat sites, 45 with partial hookups for RVs or tents, a large area for lakefront tent camping and self-contained RVs, and 10 waterfront cabins. Picnic tables and fire grills are provided. Drinking water, flush toilets, showers, laundry room, store, RV dump station, propane gas, playground, restaurant, volleyball, horseshoes, tetherball, ping pong, marina, boat rentals, boat launch, and a boat ramp are available. Some facilities are wheelchair-accessible, including three cabins. Group sites and rates are available. Leashed pets are permitted.

Reservations, fees: Reservations are accepted. The fee is $20–30 per night. No boat berth charge for campers. Credit cards accepted. Open year-round.

Directions: From Manteca, drive east on Highway 120 (it becomes Highway 108/120) to Oakdale. Continue east for 13 miles to Tulloch Road on the left. Turn left and drive 4.6 miles to the campground entrance and gatehouse at the south shore of Lake Tulloch.

Contact: Lake Tulloch RV Camp and Marina, 14448 Tulloch Dam Rd., Jamestown, CA 95327, 209/881-0107, website: www.laketullochcampground.com.

18 MOCCASIN POINT

Rating: 7

At Don Pedro Reservoir.
Map 9.3, page 492

This camp is at the north end of Don Pedro Reservoir, adjacent to a boat ramp. Moccasin Point juts well into the lake, directly across from where the major Tuolumne River arm enters the lake. Don Pedro is a giant lake, with nearly 13,000 surface acres and 160 miles of shoreline, but it is subject to drawdowns from midsummer through early fall. At different times, fishing is excellent for salmon, trout, or bass. Houseboating and boat-in camping (bring sunscreen) provide options.

Campsites, facilities: There are 65 sites for tents and 15 sites with full hookups for RVs. Picnic tables, food lockers, and barbecue units are provided at all sites. Drinking water, restrooms, showers, store, RV dump station, propane gas, ice, snack bar, boat ramp, motorboat and houseboat rentals, fuel, moorings, and bait and tackle are available. Some facilities are wheelchair-accessible. Campfires are prohibited. No pets are permitted.

Reservations, fees: Reservations are accepted. The fee is $15–22 per night, $5 per night for each extra vehicle. Major credit cards accepted. Open year-round.

Directions: From Manteca, drive east on Highway 120 (it becomes Highway 108/120) for 30 miles to the Highway 120/Yosemite exit. Bear right on Highway 120 and drive 11 miles to Jacksonville Road. Turn left on Jacksonville Road and drive a short distance to the campground on the right.

Contact: Moccasin Point, 209/852-2396, website: www.donpedrolake.com.

19 BIG BEAR

Rating: 5

On the Tuolumne River near Modesto.
Map 9.3, page 492

Big Bear once was well known as a water park designed for families with young children. In fact, some have instant recognition of the name "Big Bear Water Park." The water park was discontinued in 2002 and may never be restarted. The arcade is also gone. A miniature train ride now operates only on holidays and weekends. In addition, some long-term rentals were permitted to take campsites once reserved for overnighters. The park is set at 2,500 feet in the foothill country east of Modesto. The Tuolumne River runs right alongside the campground. Nearby side trips include Modesto Reservoir, Turlock Lake, and Don Pedro Reservoir.

Campsites, facilities: There are 116 sites, most with full hookups, for RVs, and 96 sites for tents. Drinking water, restrooms, showers, RV dump station, coin laundry, modem access, ice, small store, three clubhouses, and a playground are available. Some facilities are wheelchair-accessible. Leashed pets are permitted in RV section only.

Reservations, fees: Reservations are accepted. The fee is $21–25 per night, $3 per person for more than four people, $3 per night. Major credit cards accepted. Open year-round.

Directions: From Modesto, drive east on Highway 132 for 12 miles to the town of Waterford (where the road becomes Yosemite Boulevard) and drive to the park at 13400 Yosemite Boulevard.

Contact: Big Bear, 209/874-4000, fax 209/874-4544.

20 MODESTO RESERVOIR REGIONAL PARK

Rating: 7

On Modesto Reservoir.

Map 9.3, page 492

Modesto Reservoir is not well known, but it is a surprisingly big lake, at 2,700 acres with 31 miles of shoreline, set in the hot foothill country. It is one of the first recreation lakes in the Central Valley to advertise "MTBE-free waters." To keep it that way, boaters must buy gas that does not contain MTBE. Some gas stations provide gas that does not contain MBTE. You must show proof that the gas in your boat comes from such a station. Water-

skiing is excellent in the main lake body. Anglers head to the southern shore of the lake, which is loaded with submerged trees and coves and is also protected by a 5-mph speed limit. Fishing for bass is good, though the fish are often small.

Campsites, facilities: There are 150 sites with full hookups for RVs and 38 tent sites. Picnic tables and fire grills are provided. Drinking water, flush toilets, RV dump station, showers, two boat ramps, marina, a store, and propane gas are available. Some facilities are wheelchair-accessible. No pets are allowed.

Reservations, fees: Reservations are not accepted. The fee is $12–16 per night, $2 surcharge per vehicle on holidays. Senior discount available in winter. Open year-round.

Directions: From Modesto, drive east on Highway 132 for 16 miles past Waterford to Reservoir Road. Turn left and drive to the campground at 18143 Reservoir Road.

Contact: Modesto Reservoir Regional Park, 209/874-9540, fax 209/874-4513, website: www.co.stanislaus.ca.us.

21 TURLOCK LAKE STATE RECREATION AREA

Rating: 6

East of Modesto.

Map 9.3, page 492

This campground is on the shady south shore of the Tuolumne River, about one mile from Turlock Lake. Turlock Lake warms to 65–74°F in the summer, cooler than many Central Valley reservoirs, since the water entering this lake is released from the bottom of Don Pedro Reservoir. It often seems just right for boating and all water sports on hot summer days. The lake covers 3,500 surface acres and offers 26 miles of shoreline. A boat ramp is available near the camp, making it ideal for boaters/campers. Bass fishing is fair in the summer. In the late winter and spring, the lake is quite cold, fed by snowmelt from the Tuolumne

River. Trout fishing is good year-round as a result. The elevation is 250 feet. The park is bordered by ranches, orchards, and mining tailings along the river.

Campsites, facilities: There are 48 sites for tents or RVs up to 27 feet long, 15 sites for tents, and one hike-in/bike-in site. Picnic tables, fire grills, and food lockers are provided. Drinking water, flush toilets, coin showers, a swimming beach, and a boat ramp are available. The boat facilities are wheelchair-accessible. Leashed pets are permitted.

Reservations, fees: Reservations are accepted with a $7.50 reservation fee at 800/444-PARK (800/444-7275) or website: www.Reserve America.com. The fee is $12 per night, $1 for hike-in/bike-in site. Senior discount available. Open year-round.

Directions: From Modesto, drive east on Highway 132 for 14 miles to Waterford, then continue eight miles on Highway 132 to Roberts Ferry Road. Turn right and drive one mile to Lake Road. Turn left and drive two miles to the campground on the left.

Contact: Turlock Lake State Recreation Area, 209/874-2008 or 209/874-2056, fax 209/874-2611.

22 BLUE OAKS

Rating: 7

At Don Pedro Reservoir.
Map 9.3, page 492

Blue Oaks is between the dam at Don Pedro Reservoir and Fleming Meadows. The on-site boat ramp to the east is a big plus here. (See the entries for Fleming Meadows and Moccasin Point for more information.)

Campsites, facilities: There are 117 sites, including 29 sites with partial hookups and one drive-through, for RVs or tents. Picnic tables, food lockers, and barbecue units are provided. Drinking water, flush toilets, showers, and RV dump station are available. Some facilities are wheelchair-accessible. A store, coin laun-

dry, and propane gas are nearby at Fleming Meadows Marina. No ground fires are permitted. No pets are permitted.

Reservations, fees: Reservations are accepted. The fee is $17–22 per night, $5 per night for more than one vehicle. Major credit cards accepted. Open Memorial Day weekend through Labor Day weekend.

Directions: From Manteca, take Highway 120 east to Oakdale (the road becomes Highway 120/108). Continue east on Highway 108 for 20 miles to La Grange Road/J59 (signed Don Pedro Reservoir). Turn right on La Grange Road and drive 10 miles to Bonds Flat Road. Turn left on Bonds Flat Road and drive a half mile to the campground on the left.

Contact: Blue Oaks, 209/852-2396, website: www.donpedrolake.com.

23 FLEMING MEADOWS

Rating: 7

On Don Pedro Reservoir.
Map 9.3, page 492

Fleming Meadows is set on the shore of Don Pedro Reservoir at its extreme south end, just east of the dam. A boat ramp is available in the campground on the southeast side of the dam. This is a big camp at the foot of a giant lake, where hot weather, warm water, water-skiing, and bass fishing make for weekend vacations. Don Pedro has many extended lake arms, providing 160 miles of shoreline and nearly 13,000 surface acres when full.

Campsites, facilities: There are 173 sites, including six drive-through, for tents or RVs, and 89 sites with full hookups, including eight drive-through, for RVs. Picnic tables, food lockers, and barbecues are provided. Restrooms, drinking water, flush toilets, showers, and RV dump station are available. A coin laundry, store, ice, snack bar, restaurant, bait and tackle, motorboat and houseboat rentals, boat ramp, berths, engine repairs, and propane gas are nearby. Some facilities are wheelchair-accessible. Ground fires are prohibited. No pets are permitted.

Reservations, fees: Reservations are accepted. The fee is $17–25 per night, $5 per night for more than one vehicle. Major credit cards accepted. Open year-round.

Directions: From Manteca, take Highway 120 east to Oakdale (the road becomes Highway 120/108). Continue east on Highway 108 for 20 miles to La Grange Road/J59 (signed Don Pedro Reservoir). Turn right on La Grange Road and drive 10 miles to Bonds Flat Road. Turn left on Bonds Flat Road and drive 2.5 miles to the campground on the left.

Contact: Fleming Meadows, 209/852-2396, website: www.donpedrolake.com.

24 BARRETT COVE RECREATION AREA

Rating: 7

On Lake McClure.

Map 9.3, page 492

Lake McClure is shaped like a giant "H," with its lake arms providing 81 miles of shoreline. This camp is on the left side of the "H," that is, on the western shore, within a park that provides a good boat ramp. This is the largest in a series of camps on Lake McClure. (See Horseshoe Bend Recreation Area, McClure Point Recreation Area, and Bagby Recreation Area for more information.)

Campsites, facilities: There are 275 sites, 65 with full hookups and two drive-through, for RVs or tents. Picnic tables are provided. Restrooms, showers, boat ramps, RV dump station, swimming lagoon, and playground are available. A store, coin laundry, boat and houseboat rentals, and propane gas are also available on-site. Some facilities are wheelchair-accessible. Leashed pets are permitted.

Reservations, fees: Reservations are accepted. The fee is $16–22 per night, $8 per night for each extra vehicle, $2 per night. Major credit cards accepted. Open year-round.

Directions: From Modesto, drive east on Highway 132 for 31 miles to La Grange and then continue for about 11 miles (toward Coulterville) to Merced Falls Road. Turn right and drive three miles to the campground entrance on the left. Turn left and drive a mile to the campground on the left side of the road.

Contact: Barrett Cove Recreation Area, 800/468-8889 or 209/378-2521, fax 209/378-2519, website: www.lakemcclure.com.

25 LAKE MCCLURE/HORSESHOE BEND RECREATION AREA

Rating: 7

On Lake McClure.

Map 9.3, page 492

Lake McClure is a unique, horseshoe-shaped lake in the foothill country west of Yosemite. It adjoins smaller Lake McSwain, connected by the Merced River. McClure is shaped like a giant "H," with its lake arms providing 81 miles of shoreline, warm water for water-skiing, and fishing for bass (on the left half of the "H" near Cotton Creek) and for trout (on the right half of the "H"). There is a boat launch adjacent to the campground. It's one of four lakes in the immediate area; the others are Don Pedro Reservoir to the north and Modesto Reservoir and Turlock Lake to the west. The elevation is 900 feet.

Campsites, facilities: There are 110 sites, including 35 with partial hookups, for tents or RVs. Picnic tables are provided. Restrooms, showers, RV dump station, a boat ramp, store, and coin laundry are available. Some facilities are wheelchair-accessible. Leashed pets are permitted.

Reservations, fees: Reservations are accepted at 800/468-8889. The fee is $16–22 per night, $8 per night for each extra vehicle. The fee is $2 per night. Major credit cards accepted. Open year-round.

Directions: From Modesto, drive east on Highway 132 for 31 miles to La Grange and then continue for about 17 miles (toward Coulterville) to the north end of Lake McClure and the campground entrance road on the right side of the road. Turn right and drive a half mile to the campground.

Contact: Horseshoe Bend Recreation Area, 209/878-3452, fax 209/378-2519, website: www.lakemcclure.com.

26 BAGBY RECREATION AREA

Rating: 7

On upper Lake McClure.
Map 9.3, page 492

This is the most distant and secluded camp on Lake McClure. It is set near the Merced River as it enters the lake, way up adjacent to the Highway 49 Bridge, nearly an hour's drive from the dam. Trout fishing is good in the area, and it makes sense; when the lake heats up in summer, the trout naturally congregate near the cool incoming flows of the Merced River.

Campsites, facilities: There are 30 sites, 10 with partial hookups, for RVs and tents. Drinking water, restrooms with flush toilets and coin showers, small store, and a boat ramp are available. Leashed pets are permitted.

Reservations, fees: Reservations are accepted. The fee is $15–21 per night, $8 per night for extra vehicle, $2 per night. Open year-round.

Directions: From Modesto, drive east on Highway 132 for 31 miles to La Grange and then continue for 20 miles to Coulterville and the junction with Highway 49. Turn south on Highway 49, drive about 12 miles, cross the bridge, and look for the campground entrance on the left side of the road. Turn left and drive a quarter mile to the campground.

Contact: Bagby Recreation Area, 800/468-8889 or 209/378-2521, fax 209/378-2519, website: www.lakemcclure.com.

27 MCCLURE POINT RECREATION AREA

Rating: 7

On Lake McClure.
Map 9.3, page 492

McClure Point Recreation Area is the campground of choice for campers/boaters coming from the Turlock and Merced areas. It is a well-developed facility with an excellent boat ramp that provides access to the main body of Lake McClure. This is the best spot on the lake for water-skiing. For large RVs, the best accessible spots are drive-through sites in what is called the G Loop.

Campsites, facilities: There are 100 sites, all drive-through and many with partial hookups, for tents or RVs up to 40 feet long. Picnic tables are provided. Restrooms, showers, boat ramp, marina, and a laundry room are available. A store is nearby. Leashed pets are permitted.

Reservations, fees: Reservations are accepted. The fee is $14–18 per night, $2 pet fee. Open year-round.

Directions: From Turlock, drive east on County Road J16 for 19 miles to the junction with Highway 59. Continue east on Highway 59/County Road J16 for 4.5 miles to Snelling and bear right at Lake McClure Road. Drive seven miles to Lake McSwain Dam and continue for seven miles to the campground at the end of the road.

Contact: McClure Point Recreation Area, 800/468-8889 or 209/378-2521, fax 209/378-2519, website: www.lakemcclure.com.

28 LAKE MCSWAIN RECREATION AREA

Rating: 7

Near McSwain Dam on the Merced River.
Map 9.3, page 492

Lake McSwain is actually the afterbay for adjacent Lake McClure, and this camp is near the McSwain Dam on the Merced River. If you have a canoe or car-top boat, this lake is preferable to Lake McClure because water-skiing is not allowed. In terms of size, McSwain is like a puddle compared to the giant McClure, but unlike McClure, the water levels are kept up almost year-round at McSwain. The water is cold here and trout stocks are good in the spring.

Campsites, facilities: There are 112 sites for tents or RVs up to 40 feet long. Picnic tables and electrical connections are provided. Drinking water, RV dump station, restrooms, showers, boat ramp, boat rentals, coin laundry, and a playground are available. A store and propane gas are available nearby. Leashed pets are permitted.

Reservations, fees: Reservations are accepted. The fee is $16–22 per night, $2 pet fee. Open year-round.

Directions: From Turlock, drive east on County Road J16 for 19 miles to the junction with Highway 59. Continue east on Highway 59/County Road J16 for 4.5 miles to Snelling. Continue straight ahead to Lake McClure Road and drive seven miles to the campground turnoff on the right.

Contact: Lake McSwain Recreation Area, 800/468-8889 or 209/378-2521, fax 209/378-2519, website: www.lakemcclure.com.

29 FISHERMAN'S BEND RIVER CAMP

Rating: 5

On the San Joaquin River.

Map 9.3, page 492

This small, privately operated campground is set along the San Joaquin River on the southern outskirts of the San Joaquin Delta country. The park offers shaded sites and direct river access for boaters. This section of river provides fishing for catfish on hot summer nights.

Campsites, facilities: There are 38 sites, all drive-through, with full hookups for RVs, and 20 sites for tents only. Picnic tables and fire grills are provided. Drinking water, restrooms,

showers, RV dump station, laundry room, modem access (in office), boat ramp, fish-cleaning station, seasonal swimming pool, playground, and horseshoe pits are available. Some facilities are wheelchair-accessible. Leashed pets are permitted.

Reservations, fees: Reservations are accepted at 800/862-3731. The fee is $20–28 per night, $3 per person per night for more than three people. Major credit cards accepted. Open year-round.

Directions: Drive on I-5 to the exit for Newman/Stuhr Road (south of the junction of I-5 and I-580). Take that exit and turn east on County Road J18/Stuhr Road and drive 6.5 miles to Hills Ferry Road. Turn left and drive a mile to River Road. Turn left on River Road and drive to 26836 River Road.

Contact: Fisherman's Bend River Camp, 209/862-3731, fax 209/862-1684.

30 GEORGE J. HATFIELD STATE RECREATION AREA WALK-IN

Rating: 5

Near Newman.

Map 9.3, page 492

This is a small state park set in the heart of the San Joaquin Valley, near the confluence of the Merced River and the San Joaquin River, well known for hot summer days and foggy winter nights. The park has many trees. Swimming is popular in the summer. Fishing is good for catfish in the summer here, and some folks will stay up late hoping a big channel catfish will take their bait. During the peak migration from late fall through winter and early spring, there can also be a good number of striped bass in the area. This park is more popular for day-use than for camping. The campsites require a walk of about 100 feet.

Campsites, facilities: There are 21 walk-in sites for tents, and a large group site for tents or RVs. The group site has an electrical hookup and can accommodate up to 40 people. Picnic tables and fire grills are provided. Drinking water and flush toilets are available. Supplies can be obtained in Newman, five miles away. Leashed pets are permitted.

Reservations, fees: Reservations are accepted for groups only with a $7.50 reservation fee at 800/444-PARK (800/444-7275) or website: www.ReserveAmerica.com. The fee is $12 per night, $30 per night for groups. Senior discount available. Open year-round.

Directions: Drive on I-5 to the exit for Newman/Stuhr Road (south of the junction of I-5 and I-580). Take that exit and turn east on County Road J18/Stuhr Road and drive to Newman and the junction with Highway 33. Continue straight on Stuhr Road for 1.5 miles to Hills Ferry Road. Turn left and drive three miles to the park entrance on the right (just past the bridge over the San Joaquin River).

Contact: George J. Hatfield State Recreation Area, 209/632-1852; Four Rivers District, 209/826-1199, fax 209/826-0284.

31 MCCONNELL STATE RECREATION AREA

🏊 🛶 🎣 🚐 🏕

Rating: 6

On the Merced River.

Map 9.3, page 492

The weather gets scorching hot around these parts in the summer, and a lot of out-of-towners would pay a bunch for a little shade and a river to sit next to. That's what this park provides, with the Merced River flowing past, along with occasional mermaids on the beach. The park covers 70 acres. Fishing is popular for catfish, black bass, and panfish. In high-water years the Merced River attracts salmon (in the fall).

Campsites, facilities: There are 20 sites for tents and RVs up to 30 feet, and two group sites for tents only. Picnic tables, fire grills, and food lockers are provided. Drinking water, flush toilets, coin showers, and a swimming beach are available. Group sites have an electrical hookup.

Firewood is available for purchase. Supplies can be obtained in Delhi, five miles away. Leashed pets are permitted.

Reservations, fees: Reservations are accepted with a $7.50 reservation fee at 800/444-PARK (800/444-7275) or website: www.Reserve America.com. The fee is $12 per night for family sites, $18–37 per night for group sites. Senior discount available. Open year-round.

Directions: From Modesto or Merced, drive on Highway 99 to Delhi and the Shanks Road exit. Take that exit and turn east on Shanks Road and drive a short distance to Vincent Road. Turn right (south) and drive one-quarter mile to El Capitan Way. Turn left on El Capitan Way and drive three miles to Pepper Street. Turn right and drive one mile to 2nd Avenue. Turn left and drive a half mile to McConnell Road. Turn right and drive .2 mile to the park entrance at the end of the road.

Contact: McConnell State Recreation Area, 209/394-7755; Four Rivers District, California State Parks, 209/826-1197, fax 209/826-0284.

32 CODORNIZ RECREATION AREA

🚶 🚴 🎣 🛶 🚤 🐕 🚐 🏕

Rating: 6

On Eastman Lake.

Map 9.4, page 493

Eastman Lake provides relief on your typical 90- and 100-degree summer day out here. It is tucked in the foothills of the San Joaquin Valley at an elevation of 650 feet and covers 1,800 surface acres. Shade shelters have been added at 12 of the more exposed campsites, a big plus. The warm water in summer makes it good spot for a dip, and it is thus a favorite for water-skiing, swimming and, in the spring, for fishing. The DFG has established a trophy bass program here, and fishing can be good in the appropriate season for rainbow trout, catfish, bluegill, and sunfish. Check fishing regulations, posted on all bulletin boards. The lake is also a designated "Watchable Wildlife" site with 163 species of birds, and it is home to a nesting pair of bald eagles. A small area near the upper end of the lake is closed to boating to protect a bald eagle nest site. Some may remember the problem that Eastman Lake had with hydrilla, an invasive weed. The problem has been largely solved, with one closed area remaining below Chapman Creek, more than a mile upstream from the main body of the lake. Mild winter temperatures are a tremendous plus at this lake.

Campsites, facilities: There are 62 sites for tents or RVs, 15 with full hookups, three group sites for up to 200 people, and three equestrian sites. Picnic tables and fire grills are provided. Drinking water, flush toilets, showers, RV dump station, and a boat ramp are available. An equestrian staging area is available for overnight use, and there are seven miles of hiking, biking, and equestrian trails. Leashed pets are permitted.

Reservations, fees: Reservations are accepted with a $9 reservation fee at 877/444-6777 or website: www.ReserveUsa.com. The fee is $14–20 per night, $55–75 per night for group sites, and $8–25 per night for equestrian sites. Senior discount available. Open year-round.

Directions: Drive on Highway 99 to Chowchilla and the Avenue 26 exit. Take that exit and drive east for 17 miles to County Road 29. Turn left (north) on County Road 29 and drive eight miles to the lake.

Contact: U.S. Army Corps of Engineers, Sacramento District, Eastman Lake, 559/689-3255, fax 559/689-3408.

33 HIDDEN VIEW

Rating: 5

North of Fresno on Hensley Lake.

Map 9.4, page 493

Hensley Lake is one of two lakes just east of Madera (the other is Millerton Lake). Hensley covers 1,500 surface acres with 24 miles of shoreline and, as long as water levels are maintained, makes for a wonderful water playland. Swimming is good, with the best spot at

Buck Ridge on the east side of the lake, where there are picnic tables and trees for shade. The reservoir was created by a dam on the Fresno River. A nature trail is also here. The elevation is 500 feet.

Campsites, facilities: There are 55 sites for tents or RVs, some with electric hookups, and two group sites for 25–100 people. Picnic tables and fire grills are provided. Restrooms, drinking water, flush toilets, showers, RV dump station, playground, and a boat ramp are available. Leashed pets are permitted.

Reservations, fees: Reservations are accepted for groups only with a $9 reservation fee at 877/444-6777 or website: www.ReserveUsa.com. The fee is $14–20 per night for individual sites, $50 for group sites, plus a $3 boat launch fee. Groups can also reserve the Wakalumi Primitive Area at 559/673-5151. Open year-round.

Directions: From Madera, drive northeast on Highway 145 for about six miles to County Road 400. Bear left on County Road 400 and drive to County Road 603 below the dam. Turn left and drive about two miles on County Road 603 to County Road 407. Turn right on County Road 407 and drive a half mile to the campground.

Contact: U.S. Army Corps of Engineers, Sacramento District, Hensley Lake, 559/673-5151, fax 559/673-2044.

34 MILLERTON LAKE STATE RECREATION AREA

Rating: 6

Near Madera.

Map 9.4, page 493

As the temperature gauge goes up in the summer, the value of Millerton Lake increases at the same rate. The lake is set at 578 feet in the foothills of the San Joaquin Valley, and the water is like gold here. The campground and recreation area are set on a peninsula along the north shore of the lake; there are sandy beach areas on both sides of the lake with boat ramps available near the campgrounds. It's a big lake, with 43 miles of shoreline, from a narrow lake inlet extending to an expansive main lake body. The irony at Millerton is that when the lake is filled to the brim, the beaches are covered, so ideal conditions are actually when the lake level is down a bit, typically from early summer on. Fishing can be good here in spring for bass. Catfish are popular for shoreliners on summer evenings. Water-skiing is very popular in summer, of course. During winter, boat tours are available to view bald eagles. A note of history: the original Millerton County Courthouse, built in 1867, is in the park.

Campsites, facilities: There are 148 sites, 26 with full hookups, for tents or RVs up to 31 feet long, three boat-in sites, and two group sites for 45–75 people. Picnic tables and fire grills are provided. Drinking water, flush toilets, coin-operated showers, RV dump station, and boat ramps are available. Some facilities are wheelchair-accessible. You can buy supplies in Friant. Leashed pets are permitted.

Reservations, fees: Reservations are accepted with a $7.50 reservation fee at 800/444-7275 or website: www.ReserveAmerica.com. The fee is $12–18 per night, $7 for boat-in sites, $30–56 for group sites. Senior discount available. Open year-round.

Directions: Drive on Highway 99 to Madera at the exit for Highway 145 East. Take that exit east and drive on Highway 145 for 22 miles (six miles past the intersection with Highway 41) to the park entrance on the right.

Contact: Millerton Lake State Recreation Area, 559/822-2332, fax 559/822-2319.

35 LOS BANOS CREEK RESERVOIR

🏊 🚣 🚐 🐕 🚌 ⛺

Rating: 6

Near Los Banos.

Map 9.5, page 494

Los Banos Creek Reservoir is set in a long, narrow valley, covering 410 surface acres with 12 miles of shoreline. It provides a smaller,

more low-key setting (a 5-mph speed limit is enforced) compared to the nearby giant, San Luis Reservoir. In spring, it can be quite windy and is a popular spot for sailboarding. It is also stocked with trout in late winter and spring. The elevation is 400 feet.

Campsites, facilities: There are 15 sites for tents or RVs up to 30 feet long. Picnic tables and fire grills are provided. Chemical toilets are available. No drinking water is available. A boat ramp is available nearby. Leashed pets are permitted.

Reservations, fees: Reservations are not accepted. The fee is $7 per night. Senior discount available. Open year-round.

Directions: Drive on Highway 152 to Volta Road (five miles west of Los Banos). Turn south on Volta Road and drive about a mile to Pioneer Road. Turn left on Pioneer Road and drive a mile to Canyon Road. Turn south (right) onto Canyon Road and drive about five miles to the park.

Contact: San Luis Reservoir State Recreation Area, 209/826-1196; Four Rivers District, 209/826-1197, fax 209/826-0284.

36 COUNTRY LIVING MOBILE HOME AND RV PARK

🏊 🐕 ♿ 🚐

Rating: 1

In Madera.

Map 9.5, page 494

It can be a dry piece of life driving this country on a hot summer afternoon, when you're ready to stop but know of nowhere to go. This RV park gives you an option, one of the scant few on Highway 99 in this region of the San Joaquin Valley. The ambience of the place has been helped by the planting of 34 trees in spring of 2000, along with the removal of 64 dead trees (killed by bug infestation).

Campsites, facilities: There are 49 sites, 25 drive-through and many with partial hookups, for RVs. Picnic tables are provided at some sites. Restrooms, drinking water, showers, and coin laundry are available. A swimming pool and hot tub are open in the summer only. A store is available within 1.5 miles. Leashed pets are permitted.

Reservations, fees: Reservations are accepted. The fee is $15–23 per night, $2 per person for more than two people. Open year-round.

Directions: Drive on Highway 99 to Madera and the Avenue 16 exit west. Take that exit and drive west .4 mile to the park entrance on the right (24833 Ave. 16).

Contact: Country Living Mobile Home and RV Park, tel./fax 559/674-5343.

37 TRAVELER'S RV PARK

Rating: 2

Near Kettleman City.

Map 9.5, page 494

Being stuck in Kings County looking for a place to park an RV is no picnic. Unless, that is, you are lucky enough to know about Kettleman City RV Park. The spaces are wide open with long-distance views of the Sierra. It's literally the "only game in town"; in fact, it's the only camp in the entire county. Another claim to fame: it's eight hours to the Mexican border. Visitors will find access to miles of open paths and roads for hiking or running. Some may remember this park as "Kettleman City RV Park." New owners arrived in 2002, new name, too, and an improved attitude with it.

Campsites, facilities: There are 46 sites, all drive-through, with full or partial hookups for RVs and tents. Picnic tables are provided. Restrooms, showers, playgrounds, swimming pool, RV dump station, dog run, and propane gas are available. A restaurant and snack bar are nearby. Leashed pets are permitted. Some facilities are wheelchair-accessible.

Reservations, fees: Reservations are accepted at 800/258-0537. The fee is $20 per night. The fee is $5 per night for extra vehicle. Major credit cards accepted. Open year-round.

Directions: Drive on I-5 to the junction with Highway 41 (Kettleman Junction). Take Highway 41 north and drive a half mile to Hubert Way. Turn left on Hubert Way and drive to Cyril Place. Turn right on Cyril Place to the park entrance (30000 Cyril Place).

Contact: Traveler's RV Park, 559/386-0583, fax 559/386-0585.

38 LOST LAKE

Rating: 7

On lower San Joaquin River.

Map 9.6, page 495

Lost Lake Campground is part of a Fresno County park. It is set in the foothills of the San Joaquin Valley, at an elevation of about 500 feet, along the lower San Joaquin River. The campground is broken out into two areas, with about half along the river. Many think this park is quite pretty. There is a lot of wildlife at this park, especially birds and deer. A self-guided hiking trail is routed into a nature study area. Easy canoeing is a plus, with no power boats permitted.

Campsites, facilities: There are 42 sites for tents, with most accessible for self-contained RVs, and one group site. Picnic tables and fire rings are provided. Drinking water and flush toilets are available. An RV dump station is one mile away. A restaurant and store are two miles away in Friant. Leashed pets are permitted.

Reservations, fees: No reservations except for the group site which is $80 per night. Family sites are $11 per night, $5 per extra vehicle with maximum of two. Senior discount available. Open year-round.

Directions: From Fresno, drive north on Highway 41 for 24 miles to the first exit for Friant Road. Take that exit and drive 12 miles to the entrance road for Lost Lake. Turn left and drive a short distance to the campground.

Contact: Fresno County Parks Department, 559/488-3004, fax 559/488-1988.

39 VISALIA/FRESNO SOUTH KOA

Rating: 1

West of Visalia.

Map 9.6, page 495

This is a layover spot for Highway 99 cruisers. If you're looking for a spot to park your rig for the night, you can't get too picky around these parts.

Campsites, facilities: There are 48 sites, all drive-through, with full or partial hookups, 38 sites for tents or RVs, and 30 sites for tents only. Restrooms, showers, swimming pool, laundry facilities, playground, recreation room, store, RV dump station, and propane gas are available. Leashed pets are permitted.

Reservations, fees: Reservations are accepted at 800/562-0544. The fee is $20–28 per night. The fee is $2–4 per person for more than two people. Major credit cards accepted. Open year-round.

Directions: From Visalia, drive west on Highway 198 to the Plaza exit. Turn right on Plaza and drive five miles to Goshen Road. Turn left on Goshen Road and drive a quarter mile to Road 76. Turn right and drive to the camp entrance (well signed).

Contact: Visalia-Fresno KOA, 559/651-0544, website: www. koa.com.

40 SUN AND FUN RV PARK

Rating: 1

Near Tulare.

Map 9.6, page 495

This RV park is just off Highway 99, exactly halfway between San Francisco and Los Angeles. Are you having fun yet? Anybody making the long drive up or down the state on Highway 99 will learn what a dry piece of life the San Joaquin Valley can seem. That's why the swimming pool at this RV park can be a lifesaver.

Campsites, facilities: There are 62 sites with full hookups for RVs. Picnic tables and barbecues are provided. Restrooms, drinking water, showers, modem access, RV dump station, playground, swimming pool, spa, laundry facilities, and a recreation room are available. Some facilities are wheelchair-accessible. A golf course, restaurant, and store are nearby. Leashed pets are permitted.

Reservations, fees: Reservations are accepted. The fee is $25–28 per night. Open year-round.

Directions: From Tulare, drive south on Highway 99 for three miles to the Avenue 200 exit. Take Avenue 200 west and drive a short distance to the park (1000 Ave. 200).

Contact: Sun and Fun RV Park, 559/686-5779.

41 EAGLE'S NEST ROOST

Rating: 4

Near Lake Success.

Map 9.7, page 496

This campground is in a parklike setting with trees and flowers. It is two miles from Lake Success. A small, stocked fishing pond is available, and pet geese and ducks are often wandering around. (For information on Lake Success, see the entry for Tule 2.)

Campsites, facilities: There are 250 sites, with full or partial hookups, for RVs or tents. Picnic tables and barbecues are provided at some sites. Restrooms, showers, recreation room, playground, swimming pool, fishing facilities, laundry room, store, ice, firewood, RV dump station, dog-walking area, and propane gas are available. Quiet, well-mannered, leashed pets are permitted.

Reservations, fees: Reservations are accepted. The fee is $16–24 per night, $3–6 per person for more than two people. Major credit cards accepted. Open year-round.

Directions: Drive on Highway 65 to Porterville and the junction with Highway 190. Turn east on Highway 190 and drive five miles to the park on the left (27798 Hwy. 190).

Contact: Eagle's Nest Roost, 559/784-3948.

42 TULE 2

Rating: 7

On Success Lake.

Map 9.7, page 496

Success Lake is a big lake with many arms, providing 30 miles of shoreline and making the place seem like a dreamland for boaters on hot summer days. The lake is set in the foothill country, at an elevation of 650 feet, where day after day of 100-degree summer temperatures are common. That is why boating, water-skiing, and personal watercraft are so popular—anything to get wet. In the winter and spring, fishing for trout and bass is good, including the chance for giant bass. No beaches are developed for swimming because of fluctuating water levels, though the day-use area has a decent sloped stretch of shore that is good for swimming. The wildlife area along the west side of the lake is worth exploring, and there is a nature trail below the dam. The campground is the centerpiece of the Tule Recreation Area.

Campsites, facilities: There are 104 sites, some with electrical hookups, for tents or RVs up to 35 feet long. Picnic tables and fire grills are provided. Restrooms, flush toilets, RV dump station, and a playground are available. A store, marina, boat ramp, boat and water-ski rentals, bait and tackle, propane gas, restaurant, and gas station are available nearby. Leashed pets are permitted.

Reservations, fees: Reservations are accepted with a $9 reservation fee at 877/444-6777 or website: www.ReserveUsa.com. The fee is $16–21 per night. Senior discount available. Open year-round.

Directions: Drive on Highway 65 to Porterville and the junction with Highway 190. Turn east on Highway 190 and drive eight miles to Success Lake and the campground entrance on the left.

Contact: U.S. Army Corps of Engineers, Sacramento District, 559/784-0215, fax 559/784-5469; Success Marina, 559/781-2078.

43 COLONEL ALLENSWORTH STATE HISTORIC PARK

Rating: 3

Near Earlimart.

Map 9.8, page 497

What you have here is the old town of Allensworth, which has been restored as a historical park dedicated to the African-American pioneers who founded it with Colonel Allen Allensworth. He was the highest-ranking army chaplain of his time. Allensworth is the only town in California to founded, funded, and governed by African Americans. One museum is available at the school here and another is at the colonel's house with a 30-minute movie on the history of Allensworth. Tours are available by appointment. One frustrating element here is that railroad tracks run alongside the park and it can be disruptive. There can be other problems: very hot weather in the summer, and since it is an open area, the wind can blow dust and sand. Are we having fun yet? One nice touch is the addition of shade ramadas at some campsites. A history note: this small farming community was founded in 1908, but a drop in the water table led to its demise.

Campsites, facilities: There are 15 sites for tents or RVs up to 35 feet long. Picnic tables and fire grills are provided. Restrooms, drinking water, flush toilets, coin showers, RV dump station, a visitor center, and picnic area are available. A store and coin laundry are 12 miles away in Delano. Leashed pets are permitted.

Reservations, fees: Reservations are accepted with a $7.50 reservation fee at 800/444-PARK (800/444-7275) or website: www.Reserve America.com. The fee is $8 per night. Senior discount available. Open year-round.

Directions: From Fresno, drive south on Highway 99 about 60 miles to Earlimart and the Alpaugh Road exit. Take that exit and drive to Avenue 56. Turn right (west) on Avenue 56 and drive eight miles to the Highway 43 turnoff. Turn left on Highway 43 and drive two miles to Palmer Avenue. Turn right (and drive over the railroad tracks) to the park entrance.

Contact: Colonel Allensworth State Historic Park, 661/849-3433; San Joaquin South Sector, 661/634-3795.

44 LOST HILLS KOA

Rating: 4

Near Kern National Wildlife Refuge.
Map 9.8, page 497

The pickings can get slim around these parts when you're cruising north on I-5 so if it's late, you'll likely be happy to find this KOA camp. The cabin that sleeps four is a nice plus. The nearby Kern National Wildlife Refuge, about a 15-minute drive away, offers a side-trip possibility. It's a waterfowl reserve that attracts ducks, geese, and other waterfowl in the fall and winter.

Campsites, facilities: There are 79 sites, all drive-through, with full hookups for RVs, nine sites for tents only, an overflow area with 20 sites for tents and self-contained RVs, and one cabin. Picnic tables are provided. Restrooms, drinking water, showers, satellite TV, swimming pool, laundry facilities, store, video room, and propane gas are available. Some facilities are wheelchair-accessible. Restaurants are nearby. Leashed pets are permitted.

Reservations, fees: Reservations are accepted at 800/562-2793. The fee is $24–28 per night. Major credit cards accepted. Open year-round.

Directions: Drive on I-5 to the junction with Highway 46 (41 miles south of Avenal near Lost Hills). Turn west on Highway 46 and drive a short distance to the park entrance (near the Carl's Jr.).

Contact: Lost Hills KOA, 661/797-2719, website: www.koa.com.

45 KOA BAKERSFIELD

Rating: 1

North of Bakersfield.
Map 9.8, page 497

If you're stuck in the southern valley and the temperature feels like you're sitting in a cauldron, well, this spot provides a layover for the night near the town of Shafter. It's not exactly a hotbed of excitement.

Campsites, facilities: There are 12 tent sites and 62 RV sites with full or partial hookups. Picnic tables are provided. Restrooms, drinking water, showers, swimming pool (summer only), laundry room, store, RV dump station, and propane gas are available. Leashed pets are permitted. Some facilities are wheelchair-accessible.

Reservations, fees: Reservations are accepted at 800/562-1633. The fee is $24–29 per night. The fee is $4 per person per night for more than two people. Major credit cards accepted. Open year-round.

Directions: From Bakersfield, drive north on Highway 99 for 12 miles to the Shafter-Lerdo Highway exit. Take that exit west and drive a mile west on Lerdo Highway to the park (5101 Lerdo Hwy. in Shafter).

Contact: KOA Bakersfield, 661/399-3107, fax 661/399-8981, website: www. koa.com.

46 KCL

Rating: 6

At the Carrizo Plain, northeast of San Luis Obispo.
Map 9.8, page 497

KCL is the name of the old ranch headquarters in the Carrizo, of which remains an old broken-down barn, a water wagon, and not much else. At least there are some trees here (in comparison, there are none at nearby Selby camp). The Carrizo Plain is best known for providing a habitat for many rare species of plants, in addition to furnishing the winter nesting sites at Soda Lake for the awesome migration of giant sandhill cranes. Occasionally these huge birds will fly down the valley and are visible here.

Campsites, facilities: This is a primitive camping area with no designated sites. Picnic tables and fire pits are provided. A pit toilet and corrals are available. No drinking water is available. Garbage must be packed out. Leashed pets are permitted.

Reservations, fees: Reservations are not accepted. There is no fee for camping. Open year-round.

Directions: From Bakersfield, drive west on Highway 58 for about 30 miles to McKittrick (where Highway 33 merges with Highway 58). Stay on Highway 58/33 for about another 10 miles to Seven-Mile Road. Turn west on Seven-Mile Road, and drive seven miles (six miles will be on gravel road) to Soda Lake Road. Turn left on Soda Lake Road and drive six miles to the entrance of the Carrizo Plains Natural Area. Continue about 15 miles to the KCL camping area on your right.

Contact: Bureau of Land Management, Bakersfield Field Office, 661/391-6000, fax 661/391-6040.

47 SELBY

Rating: 6

At the Carrizo Plain, northeast of San Luis Obispo.

Map 9.8, page 497

The Carrizo Plain is California's largest nature preserve, but because of its remote location, primitive setting, and lack of recreational lakes and streams, it remains largely unknown and is explored by few people. The feature attraction is to visit Soda Lake in the winter to see flocks of the endangered sandhill crane; the lake is a nesting area for the huge bird with a seven-foot wingspan. Selby is a primitive camping area at the base of the Caliente Mountain Range, known for its scorching hot (hey, after all, "Caliente") temperatures during the sum-

mer. The top hiking destination in the region is Painted Rock, a 55-foot rock with Indian pictographs.

Campsites, facilities: This is a primitive camping area with no designated sites. Picnic tables and fire pits are provided. A pit toilet is available. No drinking water is available. Garbage must be packed out. Leashed pets are permitted.

Reservations, fees: Reservations are not accepted. There is no fee for camping. Open year-round.

Directions: From Bakersfield, drive west on Highway 58 for about 30 miles to McKittrick (where Highway 33 merges with Highway 58). Stay on Highway 58/33 for about another 10 miles to Seven-Mile Road. Turn west on Seven-Mile Road, and drive seven miles (six miles will be on gravel road) to Soda Lake Road. Turn left on Soda Lake Road and drive about six miles to the Selby camping area on your right.

Contact: Bureau of Land Management, Bakersfield Field Office, 661/391-6000, fax 661/391-6040.

48 BUENA VISTA AQUATIC RECREATION AREA

Rating: 6

Near Bakersfield.

Map 9.8, page 497

Buena Vista is actually two connected lakes fed by the West Side Canal, little Lake Evans to the west and larger Lake Webb to the east. Be certain to know the difference between the two: Lake Webb (875 acres) is open to all boating including personal watercraft, and fast boats towing skiers are a common sight in designated ski areas. The speed limit is 45 mph. Lake Evans (85 acres) is small, quiet, and has a strictly enforced 5-mph speed limit, an ideal lake for family water play and fishing. The elevation is 330 feet on the outskirts of Bakersfield.

Campsites, facilities: There are 112 sites with full hookups for RVs or tents. Picnic tables and fire grills are provided. Restrooms, drinking water, flush toilets, showers, playground, three boat ramps, store, RV dump station, and propane gas are available. Two swimming lagoons, marina, snack bar, fishing supplies, and groceries are available nearby. A PGA-rated golf course is two miles west. Leashed pets are permitted.

Reservations, fees: Reservations are accepted at 661/868-7050 Monday through Friday. The fee is $21–32 per night, $10 per night for extra vehicle. The fee is $3 per night. Major credit cards accepted. Open year-round.

Directions: From I-5 just south of Bakersfield, take Highway 119 west and drive two miles to Highway 43. Turn south (left) on Highway 43 and drive two miles to the campground at road's end.

Contact: Buena Vista Aquatic Recreation Area, 661/763-1526, website: www.co.kern.ca.us/parks/index.htm.

49 KERN RIVER

Rating: 7

At Lake Ming.

Map 9.9, page 498

The campground is set at Lake Ming, a small but exciting place. The lake covers just 205 surface acres, and with the weather so hot, the hot jet boats can make it a wild affair here. It's become a popular spot for southern valley residents, only a 15-minute drive from Bakersfield. It is so popular for water sports that every year the lake is closed to the public one weekend per month for private boat races and water-skiing competitions. Sailing and windsurfing are permitted on the second weekend of every month and on Tuesday and Thursday afternoons. All motorized boating, including water-skiing, is permitted on the remaining days. All boats are required to have a permit; boaters may buy one at the park. Swimming is not allowed. The elevation is 450 feet. Maximum stay is 10 days.

Campsites, facilities: There are 50 sites for tents or RVs up to 28 feet long. Picnic tables and fire rings are provided. Restrooms, drinking water, flush toilets, coin showers, RV dump station, playground, and a boat ramp are available. Some facilities are wheelchair-accessible. A store is nearby. Leashed pets are permitted.

Reservations, fees: Reservations are not accepted. The fee is $18 per night, $9 per night for each extra vehicle (15-person maximum per site), $3 pet fee. Open year-round.

Directions: From Bakersfield, drive east on Highway 178 to Alfred Harrell Highway. Turn left (north) on Alfred Harrell Highway and follow the signs to Lake Ming Road. Turn right on Lake Ming Road and follow the signs to the campground on the right.

Contact: Kern County Parks Department, 661/868-7000.

© JEFFREY PATTY

Chapter 10
Yosemite and
Mammoth Lakes

Chapter 10—Yosemite and Mammoth Lakes

Some of nature's most perfect artwork has been created in Yosemite and the adjoining eastern Sierra near Mammoth Lakes, as well as some of the most profound natural phenomena imaginable.

Yosemite Valley is the world's greatest showpiece. It is also among the most highly visited and well-known destinations on earth. Many of the campgrounds listed in this section are set within close driving proximity of Yosemite National Park. When it comes to cabin rentals in this region, the variety is extraordinary.

Anything in Yosemite, or in its sphere of influence, is going to be in high demand almost year-round, and the same is true near Mammoth Mountain.

Many family recreation opportunities exist at lake-based settings, including at Lake Alpine, Pinecrest Lake on the western slopes of the Sierra, and at June Lake, Silver Lake, Lake Mary, Twin Lakes, Convict Lake, and Rock Creek Lake on the eastern Sierra. We noticed that the demand is very reasonable in the vicinity of Highway 4 and Calaveras Big Trees, and Highway 108 and Pinecrest. That's what happens when you're competing with Yosemite.

Of course, most visits to this region start with a tour of Yosemite Valley. It is framed by El Capitan, the Goliath of Yosemite, on one side and the three-spired Cathedral Rocks on the other. As you enter the valley, Bridalveil Falls comes to view, a perfect free fall over the south canyon rim, then across a meadow. To your left you'll see the two-tiered Yosemite Falls, and finally, Half Dome, the single most awesome piece of rock in the world.

The irony is that this is all most people ever see of the region, even though it represents but a fraction of the fantastic land of wonder, adventure, and unparalleled natural beauty. Though 24,000 people jam into five square miles of Yosemite Valley each summer day, the park is actually 90 percent wilderness. Other landmark areas you can reach by car include the Wawona Grove of Giant Sequoias, Tenaya Lake, Tuolumne Meadows, and Hetch Hetchy.

But that's still only scratching the surface. For those who hike, another world will open up: Yosemite has 318 lakes, dozens of pristine streams, the Grand Canyon of the Tuolumne River, Matterhorn Peak, Benson Lake (with the largest white sand beach in the Sierra), and dozens of spectacular waterfalls.

If you explore beyond the park boundaries, the adventures just keep getting better. Over Tioga Pass, outside the park and just off Highway 120, are Tioga Lake, Ellery Lake, and Saddlebag Lake (10,087 feet), the latter of which is the highest lake in California accessible by car. To the east is Mono Lake and its weird tufa spires, which create a stark moonscape.

The nearby June Lake Loop and Mammoth Lakes area is a launch point to another orbit. Both have small lakes with on-site cabin rentals, excellent fishing, and great hiking for all levels. In addition, just east of Mammoth Lakes airport is a series of hot springs, including a famous spot on Hot Creek, something of a legend in these parts.

More hiking (and fishing) opportunities abound at Devils Postpile National Monument, where you can hike to Rainbow Falls. At nearby Agnew Meadows, you'll find a trail that hugs the pristine San Joaquin River up to Thousand Island Lake and leads to the beautiful view from Banner and Ritter Peaks in the Ansel Adams Wilderness.

If you didn't already know, many of California's best lakes for a chance to catch giant rainbow and brown trout are in this region. They include Bridgeport Reservoir, Twin Lakes, June Lake, Convict Lake, and Crowley Lake in the eastern Sierra, and Beardsley and Spicer Meadows in the western Sierra.

This region has it all: beauty, variety, and a chance at the hike or fish of a lifetime. There is nothing else like it on earth.

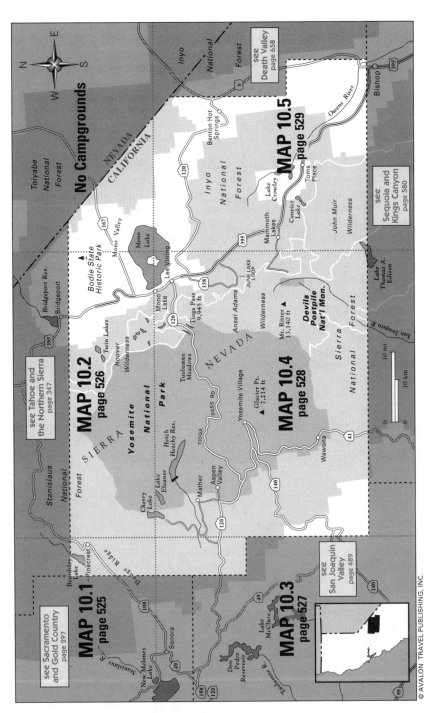

Map 10.1

Campgrounds 1–3
Page 530

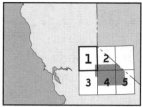

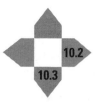

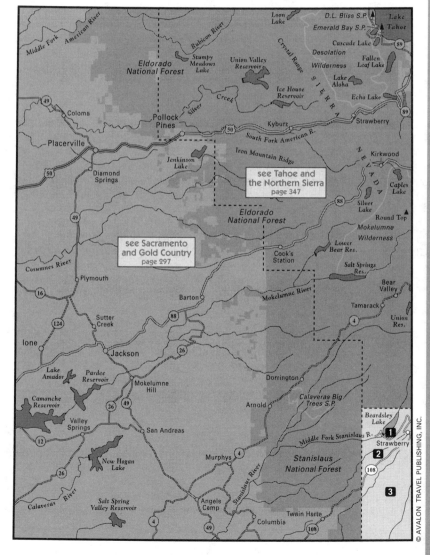

© AVALON TRAVEL PUBLISHING, INC.

Map 10.2

Campgrounds 4–17
Pages 531–536

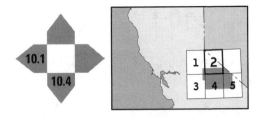

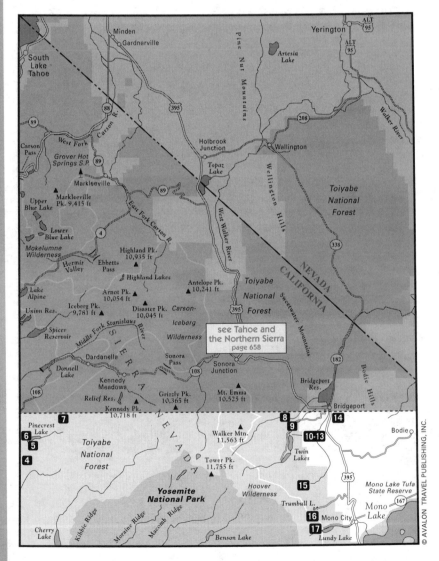

Map 10.3

Campgrounds 18–22
Pages 536–538

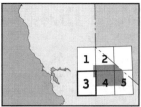

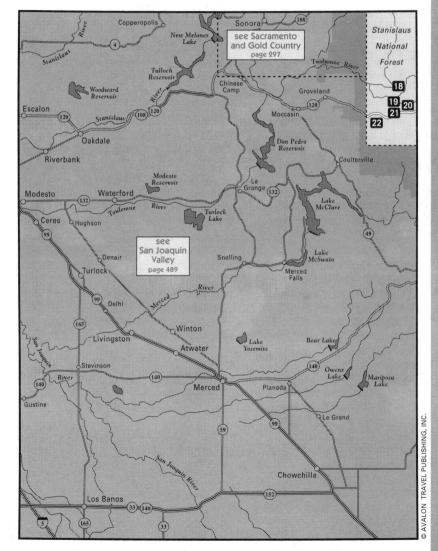

Map 10.4

Campgrounds 23–80
Pages 538–564

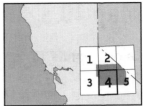

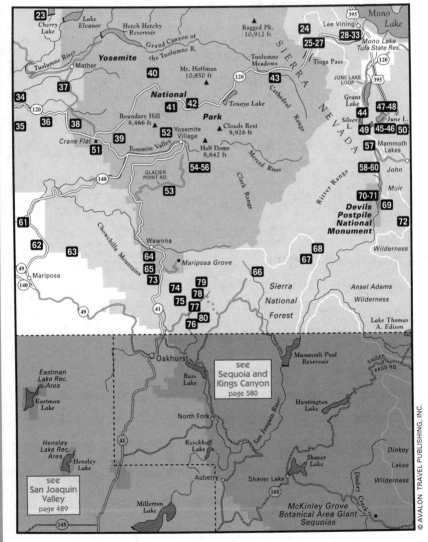

Map 10.5

Campgrounds 81–108
Pages 564–575

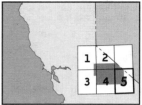

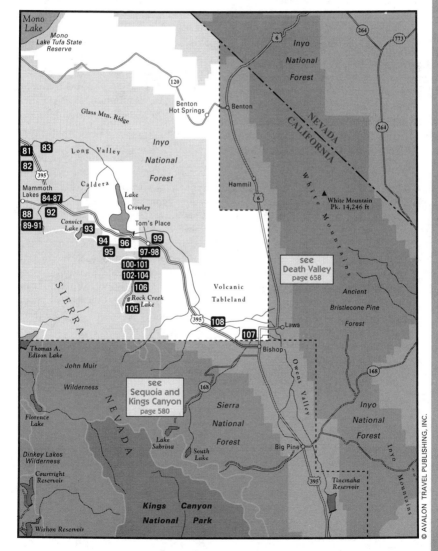

1 BEARDSLEY
🚶 🏊 🎣 🛶 🐴 🚐 ⛺

Rating: 6

At Beardsley Lake in Stanislaus
National Forest.

Map 10.1, page 525

For years people wondered why there was no
campground at Beardsley Reservoir. In fact,
some started parking their campers and creating their own. Well, that's why this primitive
site is here, used primarily as a base camp for
people fishing for trout at Beardsley Reservoir.
It is often an outstanding fishery early in the
season for brown trout, and then once planted, good for limits of hatchery fish during the
evening bite. In winter and spring, as soon as
the gate is opened to the boat ramp access
road, the fishing is best when the wind blows,
believe it or not; let it push your boat while
you drift half a nightcrawler behind a set of
Half Fast Flashers. The wind always comes up
here out of the west, but this is what gets the
fish biting. The camp is set at 3,400 feet, but
because it is near the bottom of the lake canyon,
it actually feels much higher in elevation. Bonus:
there is more fishing nearby on the Middle
Fork of the Stanislaus.

Campsites, facilities: There are 26 sites for tents
or RVs up to 22 feet long. Fire rings are provided. Vault toilets are available. No drinking
water is available. Leashed pets are permitted.

Reservations, fees: Reservations are not accepted. There is no fee for camping. Open year-
round, weather permitting (the road is often
gated at the top of the canyon, when the boat
ramp road at lake level is iced over).

Directions: From Sonora, drive east on Highway 108 for about 25 miles to Strawberry and
the turnoff for Beardsley Reservoir/Forest Road
52. Turn left and drive seven miles to Beardsley Dam. Continue for a quarter mile past the
dam to the campground.

Contact: Stanislaus National Forest, Summit
Ranger District, 209/965-3434, fax 209/965-
3372.

2 FRASER FLAT
🎣 🐴 ♿ 🚐 ⛺

Rating: 7

On the South Fork of the Stanislaus River in
Stanislaus National Forest.

Map 10.1, page 525

This camp is set along the South Fork of the
Stanislaus River. If the fish aren't biting, a
short side trip via Forest Service roads will
route you north into the main canyon of the
Middle Fork Stanislaus. A map of Stanislaus
National Forest is required for this adventure.
Fraser Flat also provides an overflow if the
campgrounds at Pinecrest or up at Clark Fork
and the upper Highway 108 corridor are filled.

Campsites, facilities: There are 38 sites for tents
or RVs up to 22 feet long. Picnic tables and
fire grills are provided. Drinking water and
vault toilets are available. Some facilities are
wheelchair-accessible. A grocery store and
propane gas are nearby. A camping and fishing site for wheelchair use is provided. Leashed
pets are permitted.

Reservations, fees: Reservations are not accepted. The fee is $13 per night, $5 per night
for each extra vehicle for more than two vehicles. Senior discount available. Open May
through October, weather permitting.

Directions: From Sonora, drive east on Highway 108 to Long Barn. Continue east for six
miles to Spring Gap Road/Forest Road 4N01.
Turn left and drive three miles to the campground on the left side of the road.

Contact: Stanislaus National Forest, Mi-Wok
Ranger District, 209/586-3234, fax 209/586-
0643.

3 HULL CREEK
🐴 🚐 ⛺

Rating: 7

In Stanislaus National Forest.

Map 10.1, page 525

This obscure camp borders little Hull Creek
(too small for trout fishing), at 5,600 feet ele-

vation in Stanislaus National Forest. This is a good spot for those wishing to test out four-wheel-drive vehicles, with an intricate set of Forest Service roads available to the east. To explore that area, a map of Stanislaus National Forest is essential.

Campsites, facilities: There are 17 sites for tents or RVs up to 22 feet long. Picnic tables and fire grills are provided. Drinking water and vault toilets are available. Leashed pets are permitted.

Reservations, fees: Reservations are not accepted. The fee is $5 per night. Senior discount available. Open May through October, weather permitting.

Directions: From Sonora, drive east on Highway 108 to Long Barn and the Long Barn Fire Station and a signed turnoff for the campground at Road 31/Forest Road 3N01. Turn right and drive 12 miles to the campground on the left side of the road.

Contact: Stanislaus National Forest, Mi-Wok Ranger District, 209/586-3234, fax 209/586-0643.

◪ MEADOWVIEW
Rating: 7

Near Pinecrest Lake in Stanislaus National Forest.

Map 10.2, page 526

No secret here, folks. This camp is one mile from Pinecrest Lake, a popular weekend vacation area (and there's a trail that connects the camp with the town). Pinecrest Lake is set at 5,621 feet, covers 300 acres, is stocked with rainbow trout, and has a 20-mph speed limit for boaters. This is a family-oriented vacation center, and a popular walk is the easy hike around the lake. If you want something more ambitious, there is a cutoff on the north side of the lake that is routed one mile up to little Catfish Lake. The Dodge Ridge Ski Area is nearby, with many privately owned cabins in the area.

Campsites, facilities: There are 100 sites for tents or RVs up to 22 feet long. Picnic tables and fire grills are provided. Drinking water and flush toilets are available. A grocery store, coin laundry, boat ramp, pay showers (in summer only), and propane gas are nearby. Leashed pets are permitted.

Reservations, fees: Reservations are not accepted. The fee is $13 per night. Senior discount available. Open May to mid-October.

Directions: From Sonora, drive east on Highway 108 for about 30 miles to the signed road for Pinecrest Lake. Turn right at the sign and drive a half mile to Pinecrest/Dodge Ridge Road. Turn right and drive about 200 yards to the campground entrance on the right side of the road.

Contact: Stanislaus National Forest, Summit Ranger District, 209/965-3434, fax 209/965-3372.

◫ PIONEER TRAIL GROUP CAMP
Rating: 8

Near Pinecrest Lake in Stanislaus National Forest.

Map 10.2, page 526

If you're going to Pinecrest Lake with a Scout troop, this is the spot, since it is set up specifically for groups. You get beautiful creek and lake views, with the camp set at an elevation of 5,800 feet. (For recreation information, see the entry for nearby Meadowview.)

Campsites, facilities: Sites can accommodate tents and self-contained RVs. There are also three group sites for up to 50 people and 25 vehicles per site. Picnic tables and fire grills are provided. Drinking water and vault toilets are available. A grocery store, coin laundry, boat ramp, pay showers (in summer only), and propane gas are nearby. Leashed pets are permitted.

Reservations, fees: Reserve at 877/444-6777 ($9 reservation fee) or website: www.ReserveUsa.com; $55–70 group fee per night. Open May to mid-October, weather permitting.

Directions: From Sonora, drive east on Highway

108 for about 30 miles to the signed road for Pinecrest Lake. Turn right at the sign and drive one-half mile to the signed road for Pinecrest/Dodge Ridge Road. Turn right and drive about a mile to the campground entrance on the left.

Contact: Stanislaus National Forest, Summit Ranger District, 209/965-3434, fax 209/965-3372.

6 PINECREST

Rating: 7

Near Pinecrest Lake in Stanislaus National Forest.

Map 10.2, page 526

This monster-sized Forest Service camp is set near Pinecrest Lake. In early summer, there is good fishing for stocked rainbow trout. A launch ramp is available, and a 20-mph speed limit is enforced on the lake. A trail circles the lake and also branches off to nearby Catfish Lake. The elevation is 5,600 feet. Winter camping is allowed near the Pinecrest Day-Use Area.

Campsites, facilities: There are 200 sites for tents or RVs up to 22 feet long. Picnic tables and fire grills are provided. Drinking water and toilets are available. There are two winterized restrooms with flush toilets and sinks. A grocery store, coin laundry, pay showers (in summer only), boat ramp, and propane gas are nearby. Leashed pets are permitted.

Reservations, fees: Reservations required from mid-May to mid-September at 877/444-6777 ($9 reservation fee) or website: www.ReserveUsa.com; $19 per night. Senior discount available. Open April to mid-October, weather permitting.

Directions: From Sonora, drive east on Highway 108 for about 30 miles to the signed turn for Pinecrest Lake on the right. Turn right and drive to the access road (.7 mile past the turnoff signed Pinecrest) for the campground. Turn right and drive a short distance to the campground.

Contact: Stanislaus National Forest, Summit Ranger District, 209/965-3434, fax 209/965-3372.

7 HERRING RESERVOIR

Rating: 8

At Herring Lake in Stanislaus National Forest.

Map 10.2, page 526

This is a pretty little spot, a rustic campground set near Herring Creek as it enters Herring Lake, set at an elevation of 7,350 feet. There is no boat ramp, but hand-launched boats, such as canoes, rafts, prams, and float tubes, are ideal. The lake is shallow, with fair fishing for brook trout and rainbow trout. No horses are permitted here.

Campsites, facilities: There are 42 sites for tents and RVs. Fire rings are provided. Vault toilets are available. No drinking water is available. Leashed pets are permitted.

Reservations, fees: This campground does not take reservations and there is no fee, although donations are accepted. Open May through October, weather permitting.

Directions: From Sonora, drive east on Highway 108 for about 25 miles to Strawberry. Continue past Strawberry for two miles to Herring Creek Road/Forest Road 4N12. Turn right and drive seven miles to Hamill Canyon Road/Forest Road 4N12. Bear right and drive a quarter mile to Herring Creek Reservoir. Continue another quarter mile (cross the bridge) and turn right to the campground. The road is rough and not recommended for RVs or low-clearance vehicles.

Contact: Stanislaus National Forest, Summit Ranger District, 209/965-3434, fax 209/965-3372.

8 BUCKEYE

Rating: 8

Near Buckeye Creek in Humboldt-Toiyabe National Forest.

Map 10.2, page 526

Here's a little secret: a two-mile hike out of

camp heads to the undeveloped Buckeye Hot Springs. That is what inspires campers to by-pass the fishing at nearby Robinson Creek (three miles away) and Twin Lakes (six miles away). The camp feels remote and primitive, set at 7,000 feet on the eastern slope of the Sierra near Buckeye Creek. Another secret is that brook trout are planted at the little bridge that crosses Buckeye Creek near the campground. A trail that starts near camp is routed through Buckeye Canyon and into the Hoover Wilderness.

Campsites, facilities: There are 65 paved sites for tents or RVs up to 45 feet long. There is one group site available. Picnic tables and fire grills are provided. Drinking water and flush toilets are available. Leashed pets are permitted.

Reservations, fees: Reservations are not accepted for individual sites. The fee is $11 per night. Senior discount available. Group site reservations at 877/444-6777 ($9 reservation fee) or website: www.ReserveUsa.com; $50 per night. Open early May to mid-October.

Directions: On U.S. 395, drive to Bridgeport and the junction with Twin Lakes Road. Turn west and drive seven miles to Buckeye Road. Turn north on Buckeye Road (dirt, often impassable when wet) and drive 3.5 miles to the campground.

Contact: Humboldt-Toiyabe National Forest, Bridgeport Ranger District, 760/932-7070, fax 760/932-1299.

9 HONEYMOON FLAT

Rating: 8

On Robinson Creek in Humboldt-Toiyabe National Forest.

Map 10.2, page 526

The camp is set beside Robinson Creek at 7,000 feet in elevation, in the transition zone between the Sierra Nevada range to the west and the high desert to the east. It is easy to reach on the access road to Twin Lakes, only three miles farther. The lake is famous for occasional huge brown trout. However, the fishing at Robin-

son Creek is also often quite good, thanks to the more than 50,000 trout planted each year by the Department of Fish and Game.

Campsites, facilities: There are 35 sites for tents or RVs up to 45 feet long. Picnic tables and fire grills are provided. Drinking water and vault toilets are available. Leashed pets are permitted.

Reservations, fees: Reserve at 877/444-6777 ($9 reservation fee) or website: www.Reserve Usa.com; $11 per night. Senior discount available. Open mid-April through October.

Directions: On U.S. 395, drive to Bridgeport and the junction with Twin Lakes Road. Turn west and drive eight miles to the campground.

Contact: Humboldt-Toiyabe National Forest, Bridgeport Ranger District, 760/932-7070, fax 760/932-1299.

10 PAHA

Rating: 8

Near Twin Lakes in Humboldt-Toiyabe National Forest.

Map 10.2, page 526

This is one in a series of camps near Robinson Creek and within close range of Twin Lakes. The elevation at the camp is 7,000 feet. (See the entries for Lower Twin Lake and Honeymoon Flat for more information.)

Campsites, facilities: There are 22 paved sites for tents or RVs up to 40 feet long. Picnic tables and fire grills are provided. Drinking water and flush toilets are available. A boat launch, store, showers, and a coin laundry are available nearby at Twin Lakes Resort. Leashed pets are permitted.

Reservations, fees: Reserve at 877/444-6777 ($9 reservation fee) or website: www.Reserve Usa.com; $13 per night. Senior discount available. Open early May to late October, weather permitting.

Directions: On U.S. 395, drive to Bridgeport and the junction with Twin Lakes Road. Turn west and drive 10 miles to the campground.

Contact: Humboldt-Toiyabe National Forest,

Bridgeport Ranger District, 760/932-7070, fax 760/932-1299.

11 ROBINSON CREEK
🚶 ⛵ 🏊 🚤 🏕 🐕 ♿ 🚐 ⛺

Rating: 9

Near Twin Lakes in Humboldt-Toiyabe National Forest.

Map 10.2, page 526

This campground, one of a series in the area, is set at 7,000 feet on Robinson Creek, not far from Twin Lakes. (For recreation options, see the entries for Lower Twin Lake and Honeymoon Flat.)

Campsites, facilities: There are 54 paved sites for tents or RVs up to 45 feet long. Picnic tables and fire grills are provided. Drinking water and flush and vault toilets are available. Some facilities are wheelchair-accessible. An amphitheater is nearby. Leashed pets are permitted.

Reservations, fees: Reserve at 877/444-6777 ($9 reservation fee) or website: www.Reserve Usa.com; $13 per night. Senior discount available. Open mid-April through October.

Directions: On U.S. 395, drive to Bridgeport and the junction with Twin Lakes Road. Turn west and drive 10 miles to the campground.

Contact: Humboldt-Toiyabe National Forest, Bridgeport Ranger District, 760/932-7070, fax 760/932-1299.

12 CRAGS CAMPGROUND
🚶 🏊 🚤 🏕 🐕 ♿ 🚐 ⛺

Rating: 8

On Robinson Creek in Humboldt-Toiyabe National Forest.

Map 10.2, page 526

Crags Camp is set at 7,000 feet in the Sierra, one of a series of campgrounds along Robinson Creek near Lower Twin Lake. While this camp does not offer direct access to Lower Twin, home of giant brown trout, it is very close. (See the entries for Lower Twin Lake and Honeymoon Flat.)

Campsites, facilities: There are 27 sites for tents or RVs up to 45 feet long. Picnic tables and fire grills are provided. A lighted restroom, drinking water, and flush toilets are available. Some facilities are wheelchair-accessible. A boat launch (at Lower Twin Lake), store, a coin laundry, and showers are within a half mile. Leashed pets are permitted.

Reservations, fees: Reserve at 877/444-6777 ($9 reservation fee) or website: www.Reserve Usa.com; $13 per night. Senior discount available. Open early May to mid-October, weather permitting.

Directions: On U.S. 395, drive to Bridgeport and the junction with Twin Lakes Road. Turn west and drive 11 miles to a road on the left (just before reaching Lower Twin Lake). Turn left and drive over the bridge at Robinson Creek to another road on the left. Turn left and drive a short distance to the campground.

Contact: Humboldt-Toiyabe National Forest, Bridgeport Ranger District, 760/932-7070, fax 760/932-1299.

13 LOWER TWIN LAKE
🚶 ⛵ 🏊 🚤 🏕 🐕 🚐 ⛺

Rating: 9

In Humboldt-Toiyabe National Forest.

Map 10.2, page 526

The Twin Lakes are actually two lakes, set high in the eastern Sierra at 7,000 feet. The best of the two is Lower Twin, where a full resort, marina, boat ramp, and some of the biggest brown trout in the West can be found. The state record brown was caught here, 26.5 pounds and, in 1991, 11-year-old Micah Beirle of Bakersfield caught one that weighed 20.5 pounds, one of the great fish catches by a youngster anywhere in America. Of course, most of the trout are your typical 10- to 12-inch planted rainbow trout, but nobody seems to mind, with the chance of a true monster-sized fish always in the back of the minds of anglers. An option for campers is an excellent trailhead for hiking near Mono Village at the head of Upper

Twin Lake. Here you will find the Barney Lake Trail, which is routed up the headwaters of Robinson Creek, steeply at times, to Barney Lake, an excellent day hike.

Campsites, facilities: There are 15 paved sites for tents or RVs up to 40 feet long. Picnic tables and fire grills are provided. Drinking water and flush toilets are available. A boat launch, store, showers, and a coin laundry are available nearby. Leashed pets are permitted.

Reservations, fees: Reserve at 877/444-6777 ($9 reservation fee) or website: www.Reserve Usa.com; $13 per night. Senior discount available. Open early May to mid-October, weather permitting.

Directions: On U.S. 395, drive to Bridgeport and the junction with Twin Lakes Road. Turn west and drive 11 miles to the campground.

Contact: Humboldt-Toiyabe National Forest, Bridgeport Ranger District, 760/932-7070, fax 760/932-1299.

14 WILLOW SPRINGS TRAILER PARK

Rating: 6

Near Bridgeport.

Map 10.2, page 526

Willow Springs Trailer Park is set at 6,800 feet along U.S. 395, which runs along the eastern Sierra from Carson City south to Bishop and beyond to Lone Pine. The park is one mile from the turnoff to Bodie ghost town. A nice touch to the place is a central campfire than has been in place for 50 years. The country is stark here on the edge of the high Nevada desert, but there are many side trips that give the area life. The most popular destinations are to the nearby south: Mono Lake, with its tufa towers and incredible populations of breeding gulls and waterfowl, and the Bodie ghost town. For trout fishing, there's Bridgeport Reservoir to the north (good trolling) and downstream to the East Walker River (fly-fishing), both excellent destinations, as well as Twin

Lakes to the west (huge brown trout). Ken's Sporting Goods in Bridgeport provides excellent information.

Campsites, facilities: There are 25 sites with full hookups for RVs and a motel. Picnic tables are provided. Restrooms, showers, trout pond, coin laundry, and nightly campfires are available. A restaurant is within walking distance. Leashed pets are permitted.

Reservations, fees: Reservations are accepted. The fee is $20 per night, $4 per person per night for more than two people. Open May through October.

Directions: From Bridgeport on U.S. 395, drive five miles south to the park.

Contact: Willow Springs Trailer Park, 760/932-7725, fax 760/932-1145.

15 GREEN CREEK

Rating: 7

In Humboldt-Toiyabe National Forest.

Map 10.2, page 526

This camp is ideal for backpackers or campers who like to fish for trout in streams. That is because it is set at 7,500 feet, with a trailhead that leads into the Hoover Wilderness and to several high mountain lakes, including Green Lake, West Lake, and East Lake; the ambitious can hike beyond in remote northeastern Yosemite National Park. The camp is set along Green Creek, a fair trout stream with small rainbow trout.

Campsites, facilities: There are 11 sites for tents or RVs up to 22 feet long and two group sites for up to 20 and 25 people. Picnic tables and fire grills are provided. Drinking water and vault toilets are available. Leashed pets are permitted.

Reservations, fees: Reserve at 877/444-6777 ($9 reservation fee) or website: www.Reserve Usa.com; $11 per night per individual site. Senior discount available. Open mid-May to early October, weather permitting.

Directions: From Bridgeport, drive south on

U.S. 395 for four miles to Green Lakes Road (dirt). Turn right and drive seven miles to the campground.

Contact: Humboldt-Toiyabe National Forest, Bridgeport Ranger District, 760/932-7070, fax 760/932-1299.

16 TRUMBULL LAKE
🏃 ⛵ 🎣 🐕 🚐 ⛺

Rating: 8

In Humboldt-Toiyabe National Forest.
Map 10.2, page 526

This is a high-mountain camp (9,500 feet) at the gateway to a beautiful Sierra basin. Little Trumbull Lake is the first lake on the north side of Virginia Lakes Road, with Virginia Lakes set nearby, along with the Hoover Wilderness and access to many other small lakes by trail. A trail is available that is routed just north of Blue Lake, then leads west to Frog Lake, Summit Lake, and beyond into a remote area of Yosemite National Park. If you don't want to rough it, cabins, boat rentals, and a restaurant are available at Virginia Lakes Resort.

Campsites, facilities: There are 45 sites for tents or RVs up to 45 feet long. Picnic tables and fire grills are provided. Drinking water and vault toilets are available. A store is nearby at the resort. Leashed pets are permitted.

Reservations, fees: Reserve at 877/444-6777 ($9 reservation fee) or website: www.Reserve Usa.com; $11 per night. Senior discount available. Open mid-June to mid-October, weather permitting.

Directions: From Bridgeport, drive south on U.S. 395 for 13.5 miles to Virginia Lakes Road. Turn right on Virginia Lakes Road and drive 6.5 miles to the campground entrance road.

Contact: Humboldt-Toiyabe National Forest, Bridgeport Ranger District, 760/932-7070, fax 760/932-1299.

17 LUNDY CANYON CAMPGROUND
🏃 ⛵ 🚐 🐕 🚌 ⛺

Rating: 7

Near Lundy Lake.
Map 10.2, page 526

This camp is set high in the eastern Sierra at 7,800 feet in elevation along pretty Lundy Creek, the mountain stream that feeds Lundy Lake and then runs downhill, eventually joining other creeks on its trip to nearby Mono Lake. Nearby Lundy Lake is a long, narrow lake with good fishing for rainbow trout and brown trout. There is a trailhead just west of the lake that is routed steeply up into the Hoover Wilderness to several small pretty lakes, passing two waterfalls about two miles in. A must-do side trip is visiting Mono Lake and its spectacular Tufa Towers, best done at the Mono Lake Tufa State Reserve along the southern shore of the lake.

Campsites, facilities: There are 50 sites for tents or RVs up to 24 feet long. Pit toilets are available. No drinking water is available. You can buy supplies in Lee Vining, 8.5 miles away. Leashed pets are permitted.

Reservations, fees: Reservations are not accepted. The fee is $8 per night, with a limit of two vehicles and six people per site. Open May through October.

Directions: From Lee Vining, drive north on U.S. 395 for seven miles to Lundy Lake Road. Turn left and drive a short distance to the campground.

Contact: Mono County Public Works, 760/932-5252, fax 760/932-5248.

18 LUMSDEN BRIDGE
🎣 🐕 ⛺

Rating: 7

On the Tuolumne River in Stanislaus National Forest.
Map 10.3, page 527

This is one of three camps along this immediate stretch of the Tuolumne River, one of the best white-water rafting rivers in California. The camp is set at 1,500 feet on the north side of the river, accessible just after crossing the Lumsden Bridge, hence the name. (See the entry for Lumsden for more information.)

Campsites, facilities: There are nine tent sites. Picnic tables and fire grills are provided. Vault toilets are available. No drinking water is available. Garbage must be packed out. Leashed pets are permitted.

Reservations, fees: Reservations are not accepted. There is no fee for camping. Open April through October.

Directions: From Groveland, drive east on Highway 120 for about eight miles (just under a mile beyond County Road J132) to Ferretti Road. Turn left on Ferretti and drive to a Forest Service road intersection. Jog left, then right, and continue for 5.5 miles to the camp on the left side of the road.

Contact: Stanislaus National Forest, Groveland Ranger District, 209/962-7825, fax 209/962-7412. For a map, send $6 to U.S. Forest Service, Attn: Map Sales, P.O. Box 9035, Prescott, AZ 86313, 928/443-8285 with credit card, website: www.fs.fed.us/maps/.

19 LUMSDEN

Rating: 7

On the Tuolumne River in Stanislaus National Forest.

Map 10.3, page 527

This is one of the great access points for white-water rafting on the wild and scenic Tuolumne River and its premium stretch between Hetch Hetchy Reservoir in Yosemite and Don Pedro Reservoir in the Central Valley foothills. Unless you are an expert rafter, you are advised to attempt running this stretch of river only with a professional rafting company. The camp is set at 1,500 feet, just across the road from the river. The access road down the canyon is steep and bumpy. There are two other camps within a mile, South Fork and Lumsden Bridge.

Campsites, facilities: There are 11 tent sites. Picnic tables and fire grills are provided. Vault toilets are available. No drinking water is available. Leashed pets are permitted.

Reservations, fees: Reservations are not accepted. There is no fee for camping. Open April through October.

Directions: From Groveland, drive east on Highway 120 for about eight miles (just under a mile beyond County Road J132) to Ferretti Road. Turn left on Ferretti and drive to a Forest Service road intersection. Jog left, then right, and continue for four miles to the camp on the left side of the road.

Contact: Stanislaus National Forest, Groveland Ranger District, 209/962-7825, fax 209/962-7412. For a map, send $6 to U.S. Forest Service, Attn: Map Sales, P.O. Box 9035, Prescott, AZ 86313, 928/443-8285 with credit card, website: www.fs.fed.us/maps/.

20 SOUTH FORK

Rating: 6

Near the Tuolumne River in Stanislaus National Forest.

Map 10.3, page 527

South Fork camp is a half mile upstream from Lumsden and about a mile downstream from Lumsden Bridge. Why do we say "upstream" and "downstream" instead of east and west? Because this is a camp for white-water rafters, featuring the spectacular Tuolumne River and access to its most exciting stretches. You should attempt to run this river only with a professional rafting company. The elevation is 1,500 feet.

Campsites, facilities: There are eight tent sites. Picnic tables and fire grills are provided. Vault toilets are available. No drinking water is available. Leashed pets are permitted.

Reservations, fees: Reservations are not accepted. There is no fee for camping. Open April through October.

Directions: From Groveland, drive east on

Highway 120 for about eight miles (just under a mile beyond County Road J132) to Ferretti Road. Turn left on Ferretti and drive to a Forest Service road intersection. Jog left, then right, and continue for five miles to the camp on the left side of the road.

Contact: Stanislaus National Forest, Groveland Ranger District, 209/962-7825, fax 209/962-7412. For a map, send $6 to U.S. Forest Service, Attn: Map Sales, P.O. Box 9035, Prescott, AZ 86313, 928/443-8285 with credit card, website: www.fs.fed.us/maps/.

21 LOST CLAIM

Rating: 4

Near the Tuolumne River in Stanislaus National Forest.
Map 10.3, page 527

This is one in a series of easy-access camps off Highway 120 that provide overflow areas when all the sites are taken in Yosemite National Park to the east. A feeder stream to the Tuolumne River runs by the camp. The elevation is 3,100 feet.

Campsites, facilities: There are 10 sites for tents. Picnic tables and fire grills are provided. Vault toilets and drinking water are available. A convenience store is nearby. Leashed pets are permitted.

Reservations, fees: Reservations are not accepted. The fee is $10 per night. Senior discount available. Open May through Labor Day.

Directions: From Groveland, drive east on Highway 120 for 14 miles (1.5 miles past the Groveland District Office) to the campground on the left side of the road.

Contact: Stanislaus National Forest, Groveland Ranger District, 209/962-7825, fax 209/962-7412.

22 THE PINES

Rating: 4

In Stanislaus National Forest.
Map 10.3, page 527

The Pines Camp is set at 3,200 feet in elevation on the western edge of Stanislaus National Forest, only a half mile from the Groveland District Office and about five miles from the Tuolumne River (see Lumsden Campground). A Forest Service road is routed south of camp for two miles, climbing to Smith Peak Lookout (3,877 feet) and providing sweeping views to the west of the San Joaquin Valley foothills.

Campsites, facilities: There are 12 sites for tents or RVs up to 22 feet long. Picnic tables and fire grills are provided. Drinking water (May through October only) and vault toilets are available. A convenience store is nearby. Leashed pets are permitted.

Reservations, fees: Reservations are accepted for the group site only. Fees for the individual sites are $10 per night, $55 per night for group site. Senior discount available. Open year-round.

Directions: From Groveland, drive east on Highway 120 for nine miles (about a mile past the County Road J132 turnoff) to the signed campground entrance road on the right. Turn right onto the campground entrance road and drive a short distance to the camp.

Contact: Stanislaus National Forest, Groveland Ranger District, 209/962-7825, fax 209/962-6406.

23 CHERRY VALLEY

Rating: 8

On Cherry Lake in Stanislaus National Forest.
Map 10.4, page 528

Cherry Lake is a mountain lake surrounded by national forest at 4,700 feet in elevation, just outside the western boundary of Yosemite National Park. It is much larger than most people anticipate and provides much better trout fishing than anything in Yosemite. The camp is on the southwest shore of the lake, a very pretty spot, about a mile ride to the boat launch on the west side of the Cherry Valley Dam. The lake is bordered to the east by Kibbie Ridge; just on the other side are Yosemite Park and Lake Eleanor.

Campsites, facilities: There are 46 sites for tents or RVs of any length. Picnic tables and fire grills are provided. Drinking water and vault toilets are available. A boat ramp is nearby. Leashed pets are permitted.

Reservations, fees: Reservations are not accepted. The fee is $12 per night, $22 for double sites. Senior discount available. Open April through October.

Directions: From Groveland, drive east on Highway 120 for about 15 miles to Forest Road 1N07/Cherry Lake Road on the left side of the road. Turn left and drive 18 miles to the south end of Cherry Lake and the campground access road on the right. Turn right and drive one mile to the campground.

Contact: Stanislaus National Forest, Groveland Ranger District, 209/962-7825, fax 209/962-7412.

24 SADDLEBAG LAKE

Rating: 10

In Inyo National Forest.
Map 10.4, page 528

This camp is set in spectacular high country above tree line, the highest drive-to camp and lake in California; Saddlebag Lake sits at 10,087 feet. The camp is about a quarter mile from the lake, within walking range of the little store, boat rentals, and a one-minute drive for launching a boat at the ramp. The scenery is stark; everything is granite, ice, or water, with only a few lodgepole pines managing precarious toeholds, sprinkled across the landscape on the access road. An excellent trailhead is available for hiking, with the best hike routed out

past little Hummingbird Lake to Lundy Pass. Note that with the elevation and the high mountain pass, it can be windy and cold here, and some people find it difficult to catch their breath on simple hikes. In addition, RV users should note that level sites are extremely hard to come by.

Campsites, facilities: There are 20 sites for tents or RVs up to 30 feet long, and one group site for up to 25 people. Drinking water, fire grills, and picnic tables are provided. Vault toilets, boat rentals, and a boat launch are available. A grocery store is nearby. Leashed pets are permitted.

Reservations, fees: No reservations for single sites, $15 per night; reservations for the group site only at 877/444-6777 ($9 reservation fee) or website: www.ReserveUsa.com; $46 per night for the group site. Open July through September, weather permitting.

Directions: On U.S. 395, drive one-half mile south of Lee Vining and the junction with Highway 120. Turn west and drive about 11 miles to Saddlebag Lake Road. Turn right and drive 2.5 miles to the campground on the right.

From Merced, drive east on Highway 140 to the Arch Rock entrance station. Continue east to the Big Oak Flat Road junction (a half mile before entering Yosemite Valley). Turn left and drive 14 miles to Tioga Road. Turn right and drive about 65 miles (past Tuolumne Meadows) and through the Tioga Pass entrance station. Continue two miles to Saddlebag Lake Road. Turn left and drive 2.5 miles to the campground on the right.

Contact: Inyo National Forest, Mono Lake Visitor Center, 760-647-3044, fax 760/647-3046.

25 JUNCTION

Rating: 7

Near Ellery and Tioga Lakes in Inyo National Forest.
Map 10.4, page 528

Which way do you go? From Junction any way

you choose, you can't miss. Two miles to the north is Saddlebag Lake, the highest drive-to lake (10,087 feet) in California. Directly across the road is Ellery Lake, and a mile to the south is Tioga Lake, two beautiful, pristine waters with trout fishing. To the east is Mono Lake, and to the west is Yosemite National Park. From camp, it is a one-mile hike to Bennetville, a historic camp. Take your pick. Camp elevation is 9,600 feet.

Campsites, facilities: There are 13 sites for tents or RVs up to 30 feet long. Picnic tables and fire grills are provided. Vault toilets are available. No drinking water is available. Leashed pets are permitted.

Reservations, fees: Reservations are not accepted. The fee is $9 per night. Senior discount available. Open mid-May to mid-October, weather permitting.

Directions: On U.S. 395, drive to just south of Lee Vining and the junction with Highway 120. Turn west on Highway 120 and drive about 10 miles to Saddlebag Road and the campground on the right side of the road.

From Merced, drive east on Highway 140 to the Arch Rock entrance station. Continue east to the Big Oak Flat Road junction (a half mile before entering Yosemite Valley). Turn left and drive 14 miles to Tioga Road. Turn right and drive about 65 miles (past Tuolumne Meadows) and through the Tioga Pass entrance station. Continue two miles to Saddlebag Lake Road and the campground on the left side of the road.

Contact: Inyo National Forest, Mono Lake Visitor Center, 760/647-3044, fax 760/647-3046.

26 TIOGA LAKE

Rating: 9

In Inyo National Forest.
Map 10.4, page 528

Tioga Lake is a dramatic sight, with gemlike blue waters encircled by Sierra granite at 9,700 feet in elevation. Together with adjacent Ellery Lake, it makes up a pair of gorgeous waters with near-lake camping, trout fishing (stocked with rainbow trout), and access to Yosemite National Park and Saddlebag Lake. The only downers: it can get windy here (no foolin'!) and the camps fill quickly from the overflow crowds at Tuolumne Meadows. (See the entry for Ellery Lake for more information.)

Campsites, facilities: There are 13 sites for tents or RVs up to 30 feet long. Picnic tables and fire grills are provided. Drinking water and vault toilets are available. Leashed pets are permitted.

Reservations, fees: Reservations are not accepted. The fee is $11 per night. Senior discount available. Open June through September, weather permitting.

Directions: On U.S. 395, drive to just south of Lee Vining and the junction with Highway 120. Turn west on Highway 120 and drive about 11 miles (just past Ellery Lake) to the campground on the left side of the road.

From Merced, drive east on Highway 140 to the Arch Rock entrance station. Continue east to the Big Oak Flat Road junction (a half mile before entering Yosemite Valley). Turn left and drive 14 miles to Tioga Road. Turn right and drive about 65 miles (past Tuolumne Meadows) and through the Tioga Pass entrance station. Continue one mile to the campground entrance road on the right side of the road.

Contact: Inyo National Forest, Mono Lake Visitor Center, 760/647-3044, fax 760/647-3046.

27 ELLERY LAKE

Rating: 9

In Inyo National Forest.
Map 10.4, page 528

Ellery Lake offers all the spectacular beauty of Yosemite but is two miles outside park borders. That means it is stocked with trout by the Department of Fish and Game (no lakes in Yosemite are planted, hence the lousy fishing). Just like neighboring Tioga Lake, here are deep-blue waters set in rock in the 9,500-

foot elevation range, one of the most pristine highway-access lake settings anywhere. Nearby Saddlebag Lake is a common side trip, the highest drive-to lake in California. Whenever Tuolumne Meadows fills in Yosemite, this camp fills shortly thereafter. Camp elevation is 9,600 feet.

Campsites, facilities: There are 12 sites for tents or RVs up to 30 feet long. Picnic tables and fire grills are provided. Drinking water and flush toilets are available. A grocery store is nearby. Leashed pets are permitted.

Reservations, fees: Reservations are not accepted. The fee is $11 per night. Open late May to mid-October, weather permitting.

Directions: On U.S. 395, drive to just south of Lee Vining and the junction with Highway 120. Turn west on Highway 120 and drive about 10 miles to the campground on the left side of the road.

From Merced, drive east on Highway 140 to the Arch Rock entrance station. Continue east to the Big Oak Flat Road junction (a half mile before entering Yosemite Valley). Turn left and drive 14 miles to Tioga Road. Turn right and drive about 65 miles (past Tuolumne Meadows) and through the Tioga Pass entrance station. Continue four miles to the campground entrance road on the right.

Contact: Inyo National Forest, Mono Lake Visitor Center, 760/647-3044, fax 760/647-3046.

28 LOWER LEE VINING CAMP

Rating: 7

Near Lee Vining.
Map 10.4, page 528

This camp and its neighboring camps—Cattleguard, Moraine, Aspen, Big Bend, and Boulder—can be a godsend for vacationers who show up at Yosemite National Park and make the discovery that there are no sites left, a terrible experience for some late-night arrivals. But these county campgrounds provide a great safety valve, even if they are extremely prim-

itive, on the edge of timber. Lee Vining Creek is the highlight, flowing right past the campgrounds along Highway 120, bound for Mono Lake to the nearby east. It is stocked weekly during the fishing season. A must-do side trip is venturing to the south shore of Mono Lake to walk amid the bizarre yet beautiful tufa towers. There is good rock-climbing and hiking in the area. Although sunshine is the norm, be prepared for all kinds of weather: it can snow every month of the year here. Short but lively thunderstorms are common in early summer. Other nearby trips are available to Mammoth Lakes, June Lake, and Bodie State Park.

Campsites, facilities: There are 59 sites for tents or RVs up to 40 feet long. Pit and portable toilets are available. No drinking water is available. You can buy supplies in Lee Vining (about two miles away). Leashed pets are permitted.

Reservations, fees: Reservations are not accepted. The fee is $8 per night. Open May through October, weather permitting.

Directions: On U.S. 395, drive to just south of Lee Vining and the junction with Highway 120. Turn west on Highway 120 and drive about 2.5 miles. Turn left into the campground entrance.

Contact: Mono County Public Works, 760/932-5252, fax 760/932-5248.

29 CATTLEGUARD CAMP

Rating: 7

Near Lee Vining.
Map 10.4, page 528

This camp is an alternative to Yosemite National Park. Though primitive, it has several advantages: it is quiet, gets more sun than the three neighboring camps (Lower Lee Vining, Moraine, and Boulder), and provides the best views of Dana Plateau. (For more information, see the entry for Lower Lee Vining camp.)

Campsites, facilities: There are 16 sites for tents or RVs up to 30 feet long. Portable toilets are available. No drinking water is available. You can buy supplies in Lee Vining (about two miles away). Leashed pets are permitted.

Reservations, fees: Reservations are not accepted. The fee is $8 per night. Open May through October.

Directions: On U.S. 395, drive to just south of Lee Vining and the junction with Highway 120. Turn west on Highway 120 and drive about three miles. Turn left into the campground entrance.

Contact: Mono County Public Works, 760/932-5252, fax 760/932-5248.

30 MORAINE CAMP

Rating: 7

Near Lee Vining.

Map 10.4, page 528

This camp provides an alternative to Yosemite National Park. (For more information, see the entry for Lower Lee Vining camp.)

Campsites, facilities: There are 30 sites for tents or RVs up to 30 feet long. Portable toilets are available. There is no drinking water, so bring your own. You can buy supplies in Lee Vining (about two miles away). Leashed pets are permitted.

Reservations, fees: Reservations are not accepted. The fee is $8 per night, limited to two vehicles and six people per site. Open May through October.

Directions: On U.S. 395, drive to just south of Lee Vining and the junction with Highway 120. Turn west on Highway 120 and drive 3.5 miles to Poole Power Plant Road. Exit left onto Poole Power Plant Road and drive a quarter mile to the campground entrance at the end of the road.

Contact: Mono County Public Works, 760/932-5252, fax 760/932-5248.

31 BOULDER CAMP

Rating: 7

Near Lee Vining.

Map 10.4, page 528

This camp provides an alternative to Yosemite

National Park. (For more information, see the entry for Lower Lee Vining.)

Campsites, facilities: There are 22 sites for tents or RVs up to 30 feet long. Portable toilets are available. No drinking water is available. You can buy supplies in Lee Vining (about two miles away). Leashed pets are permitted.

Reservations, fees: Reservations are not accepted. The fee is $8 per night, limited to two vehicles and six people per site. Open May through October.

Directions: On U.S. 395, drive to just south of Lee Vining and the junction with Highway 120. Turn west on Highway 120 and drive 3.5 miles to Poole Power Plant Road. Exit left and then make a quick right on Poole Power Plant Road and drive a half mile to the campground entrance on the left.

Contact: Mono County Public Works, 760/932-5451, fax 760/932-5458.

32 BIG BEND

Rating: 8

On Lee Vining Creek in Inyo National Forest.

Map 10.4, page 528

This camp is set in sparse but beautiful country along Lee Vining Creek at 7,800 feet elevation. It is an excellent bet for an overflow camp if Tuolumne Meadows in nearby Yosemite is packed. The view from the camp to the north features Mono Dome (10,614 feet) and Lee Vining Peak (11,691 feet).

Campsites, facilities: There are 17 sites for tents or RVs up to 30 feet long. Picnic tables and fire grills are provided. Drinking water and vault toilets are available. Leashed pets are permitted.

Reservations, fees: Reservations are not accepted. The fee is $15 per night. Senior discount available. Open late April to mid-October, weather permitting.

Directions: On U.S. 395, drive to just south of Lee Vining and the junction with Highway 120. Turn west on Highway 120 and drive about

3.5 miles to Poole Power Plant Road and signed campground access road on the right. Turn right and drive a short distance to the camp.
Contact: Inyo National Forest, Mono Lake Visitor Center, 760/647-3044, fax 760/647-3046.

ᴁᴂ ASPEN GROVE

Rating: 8

On Lee Vining Creek.
Map 10.4, page 528
This high-country, primitive camp is set along Lee Vining Creek at 7,500 feet, on the eastern slopes of the Sierra just east of Yosemite National Park. Take the side trip to moonlike Mono Lake, best seen at the south shore's Tufa State Reserve.
Campsites, facilities: There are 58 sites for tents or RVs up to 40 feet long. Pit and portable toilets are available. Drinking water is available from a wellhead at the entrance to the camp. You can buy supplies in Lee Vining. Leashed pets are permitted.
Reservations, fees: Reservations are not accepted. The fee is $7 per night, limit two vehicles and six people per site. Open May through October, weather permitting.
Directions: On U.S. 395, drive to just south of Lee Vining and the junction with Highway 120. Turn west on Highway 120 and drive about 3.5 miles. Exit onto Poole Power Plant Road. Turn left and drive about four miles west to the campground on the left.
Contact: Mono County Public Works, 760/932-5451, fax 760/932-5458; Inyo National Forest, Mono Lake Visitor Center, 760/647-3044, fax 760/647-3046.

ᴁᴃ SWEETWATER

Rating: 4

Near the South Fork of the Tuolumne River in Stanislaus National Forest.
Map 10.4, page 528
This camp is set at 3,000 feet, near the South

Fork Tuolumne River, one of several camps along Highway 120 that provide a safety valve for campers who can't find space in Yosemite National Park to the east.
Campsites, facilities: There are 13 sites for tents or RVs up to 22 feet long. Picnic tables and fire grills are provided. Drinking water and vault toilets are available. A convenience store is nearby. Leashed pets are permitted.
Reservations, fees: Reservations are not accepted. The fee is $12 per night. Senior discount available. Open April through October.
Directions: From Groveland, drive east on Highway 120 for about 18 miles (four miles past the Groveland District Office) to the campground on the left side of the road.
Contact: Stanislaus National Forest, Groveland Ranger District, 209/962-7825, fax 209/962-7412.

ᴁᴅ MOORE CREEK GROUP CAMP

Rating: 6

In Stanislaus National Forest.
Map 10.4, page 528
This group camp is set at 2,800 feet, just past where the Sierra alpine zone takes over from foothill oak woodlands. It is near the access route (Highway 120) to the Crane Flat entrance station of Yosemite National Park.
Campsites, facilities: There is a group campsite. Picnic tables and fire grills are provided. Vault toilets are available. No drinking water is available. Garbage must be packed out. Leashed pets are permitted.
Reservations, fees: Reservations are recommended. There is no fee. Open year-round, weather permitting.
Directions: From Groveland, drive east on Highway 120 about 12 miles to Forest Road 2S95. Turn right and drive 1.5 miles to the campground on the right.
Contact: Stanislaus National Forest, Groveland Ranger District, 209/962-7825, fax 209/962-7412.

36 YOSEMITE LAKES
🚶 🚲 🛶 🎣 🐕 🛝 🏇 ♿ 🚐 ⛺

Rating: 7

On Tuolumne River at Groveland.
Map 10.4, page 528

This is a 400-acre park set at 3,400 feet along the South Fork Tuolumne River in the Sierra foothills near Groveland. Its proximity to Yosemite National Park, just five miles from the west entrance station, make it ideal for many. The park is an affiliate of Thousand Trails, whose facilities usually are open only to members, but in this rare case, it is open to the general public. It is a family-oriented park with a large variety of recreation options and organized activities. Fishing and swimming are popular, and the river is stocked with trout. A plus is 24-hour security.

Campsites, facilities: There are 20 sites with full hookups for RVs and 25 sites for tents available to the public (more sites available to Thousand Trails members only), and cabins, cottages, yurts, rental trailers, and a hostel. Picnic tables and fire rings are provided. Restrooms, drinking water, showers, flush toilets, RV dump station, fish-cleaning station, and coin laundry are available. A store, weekend restaurant for breakfast and dinner, TV room, recreation lodge, playground with basketball, volleyball, and horseshoes, game room, and minigolf are on-site. Kayak rentals, pedalboats, inner tubes, and bicycles are available for rent. Horseback riding is nearby. Leashed pets are permitted.

Reservations, fees: Reservations are accepted at 800/533-1001. The fee is $30 per night for RVs, $22 per night for tents, $10 per extra vehicle unless towed. Major credit cards accepted. Open year-round, weather permitting.

Directions: Drive east on Highway 120 to Groveland. From Groveland, continue east for 18 miles to the entrance road (signed) for Yosemite Lakes on the right. Turn right and drive a short distance to the park.

Contact: Yosemite Lakes, 209/962-0121, website: www.ThousandTrails.com.

37 DIMOND "O"
🐕 ♿ 🚐

Rating: 7

In Stanislaus National Forest.
Map 10.4, page 528

Dimond "O" is set at 4,400 feet in elevation on the eastern side of Stanislaus National Forest—just two miles from the western border of Yosemite National Park.

Campsites, facilities: There are 38 sites suitable for trailers and RVs up to 33 feet long. Picnic tables and fire grills are provided. Drinking water and vault toilets are available. Some facilities are wheelchair-accessible. Leashed pets are permitted.

Reservations, fees: Reservations are not accepted. The fee is $13 per night. Senior discount available. Open April through October.

Directions: From Groveland, drive east on Highway 120 for 25 miles to Evergreen Road/Forest Road 12. Turn left on Evergreen Road and drive six miles to the campground.

Contact: Stanislaus National Forest, Groveland Ranger District, 209/962-7825, fax 209/962-7412.

38 HODGDON MEADOW
🐕 🚐 ⛺

Rating: 7

In Yosemite National Park.
Map 10.4, page 528

Hodgdon Meadow is on the outskirts of Yosemite, just inside the park's borders at the Big Oak Flat (Highway 120) entrance station, at 4,900 feet in elevation. It is near a small feeder creek to the South Fork Tuolumne River. It is about a 20-minute drive on Highway 120 to a major junction, where a left turn takes you on Tioga Road and to Yosemite's high country, including Tuolumne Meadows, and where staying on Big Flat Road routes you toward Yosemite Valley (25 miles from the camp).

Campsites, facilities: There are 105 family sites for tents or RVs up to 35 feet long. There are also four group sites for 13–30 people. Picnic tables and fire rings are provided. Drinking water and flush toilets are available. Leashed pets are permitted in the campground, but not on trails.

Reservations, fees: Reserve at 800/436-PARK (800/436-7275) or website: reservations.nps.gov. Reservations are required May through October; $18 per night May through October, $12 remainder of year, group campsite $40 per night, plus $20 park entrance fee per vehicle. Open year-round.

Directions: From Groveland, drive east on Highway 120 to the Big Oak Flat entrance station for Yosemite National Park. Just after passing the entrance station, turn left and drive a short distance to the campground on the right.

Contact: Yosemite National Park, 209/372-0200, for a touch-tone menu of recorded information.

39 TAMARACK FLAT

Rating: 7

On Tamarack Creek in Yosemite National Park.

Map 10.4, page 528

The road to this campground looks something like the surface of the moon. Then you arrive and find one of the few primitive drive-to camps in Yosemite National Park, at 6,300 feet in elevation. From the trailhead at camp, you can link up with the El Capitan Trail and then hike across Ribbon Meadow on up to the north valley rim at El Capitan, 7,569 feet in elevation. This is the largest single piece of granite in the world, and standing atop it for both the sensation and the divine view is a breathtaking experience. From camp, Yosemite Valley is 23 miles away.

Campsites, facilities: There are 52 sites for tents or small RVs up to 24 feet long (note difficult access road). Picnic tables and fire grills are provided. Vault toilets are available. No drinking water is available. No pets are allowed.

Reservations, fees: Reservations are not accepted. The fee is $8 per night, plus $20 park entrance fee per vehicle. Open late June through September.

Directions: From Merced, drive east on Highway 140 to the Arch Rock entrance station. Continue east to the Big Oak Flat Road junction (a half mile before entering Yosemite Valley). Turn left and drive 14 miles to Tioga Road. Turn right on Tioga Road and drive three miles to the campground entrance on the right side of the road. Turn right and drive 2.5 miles to the campground at the end of the road. Trailers and RVs are not advised.

Contact: Yosemite National Park, 209/372-0200, for a touch-tone menu of recorded information.

40 WHITE WOLF

Rating: 8

In Yosemite National Park.

Map 10.4, page 528

This is one of Yosemite National Park's prime mountain camps for people who like to hike, either for great day hikes in the immediate area and beyond, or for overnight backpacking trips. The day hike to Lukens Lake is an easy two-mile trip, the payoff being this pretty little alpine lake set amid a meadow, pines, and granite. Just about everybody who camps at White Wolf makes the trip. Backpackers (wilderness permit required) can make the overnight trip into the Ten Lakes Basin, set below Grand Mountain and Colby Mountain. Bears are common at this camp, so be certain to secure your food in the bearproof lockers. The elevation is 8,000 feet.

Campsites, facilities: There are 74 sites for tents or RVs up to 27 feet long. Picnic tables and fire grills are provided. Drinking water and flush toilets are available. Evening ranger programs are also available. A small store with a walk-up window and limited items is nearby. Leashed pets are permitted in the campground, but not on trails.

Reservations, fees: Reservations are not accepted. The fee is $12 per night, plus $20 park entrance fee per vehicle. Open July to early September.

Directions: From Merced, drive east on Highway 140 to the Arch Rock entrance station. Continue east to the Big Oak Flat Road junction (a half mile before entering Yosemite Valley). Turn left and drive 14 miles to Tioga Road. Turn right and drive 15 miles to White Wolf Road on the left. Turn left and drive a mile to the campground entrance road on the right.

Contact: Yosemite National Park, 209/372-0200, for a touch-tone menu of recorded information.

41 YOSEMITE CREEK

Rating: 9

On Yosemite Creek in Yosemite
National Park.

Map 10.4, page 528

This is the most remote drive-to camp in Yosemite National Park, a great alternative to camping in the valley or at Tuolumne Meadows, and the rough, curvy access road keeps many visitors away. It is set along Yosemite Creek at 7,659 feet, with poor trout fishing but a trailhead for a spectacular hike. If you arrange a shuttle ride, you can make a great one-way trip down to the north side of the Yosemite Canyon rim, skirting past the top of Yosemite Falls (a side trip to Yosemite Point is a must!), then tackling the unbelievable descent into the valley, emerging at Camp 4 Walk-In. Note: the narrow entrance road is a remnant of "Old Tioga Road."

Campsites, facilities: There are 75 tent sites. Picnic tables and fire grills are provided. Pit toilets are available. No drinking water is available. Leashed pets are permitted.

Reservations, fees: Reservations are not accepted. The fee is $8 per night, plus $20 park entrance fee per vehicle. Senior discount available. A 14-day stay limit is enforced. Open June through September.

Directions: From Merced, drive east on Highway 140 to the Arch Rock entrance station. Continue east to the Big Oak Flat Road junction (a half mile before entering Yosemite Valley). Turn left and drive 14 miles to Tioga Road. Turn right and drive about 30 miles (just beyond the White Wolf turnoff on the left) to Yosemite Creek Campground Road on the right. Turn right (RVs over 24 feet and trailers are not recommended) and drive five miles to the campground at the end of the road.

Contact: Yosemite National Park, 209/372-0200, for a touch-tone menu of recorded information.

42 PORCUPINE FLAT

Rating: 6

Near Yosemite Creek in Yosemite
National Park.

Map 10.4, page 528

Porcupine Flat, set at 8,100 feet, is southwest of Mt. Hoffman, one of the prominent nearby peaks along Tioga Road in Yosemite National Park. The trailhead for a hike to May Lake, set just below Mt. Hoffman, is about five miles away on a signed turnoff on the north side of the road. There are several little peaks above the lake where hikers can gain great views, including one of the back side of Half Dome.

Campsites, facilities: There are 52 sites for tents or RVs up to 35 feet long. There is limited RV space. Picnic tables and fire rings are provided. Pit toilets are available. No drinking water is available. No pets are allowed.

Reservations, fees: Reservations are not accepted. The fee is $8 per night, plus $20 park entrance fee per vehicle. Senior discount available. Open July to early September.

Directions: From Merced, drive east on Highway 140 to the Arch Rock entrance station. Continue east to the Big Oak Flat Road junction (a half mile before entering Yosemite Valley). Turn left and drive 14 miles to Tioga Road. Turn right and drive about 25 miles to the campground on the left side of the road (16 miles west from Tuolumne Meadows).

Contact: Yosemite National Park, 209/372-0200, for a touch-tone menu of recorded information.

43 TUOLUMNE MEADOWS

Rating: 8

In Yosemite National Park.

Map 10.4, page 528

This is Yosemite's biggest camp, and for the variety of nearby adventures, it might also be the best. It is set in the high country, at 8,600 feet, and can be used as a base camp for fishing, hiking, and horseback riding, or as a start-up point for a backpacking trip (wilderness permits required). This is one of the top trail-heads in North America. There are two outstanding and easy day hikes from here, one heading north on the Pacific Crest Trail for the near-level walk to Tuolumne Falls and Glen Aulin, the other heading south up Lyell Fork (toward Donohue Pass), with good fishing for small brook trout. With a backpack (wilderness permit required), either route can be extended for as long as desired into remote and beautiful country. The campground is huge, and neighbors are guaranteed, but it is well wooded and feels somewhat secluded even with all the RVs and tents. There are lots of food-raiding bears in the area, so use of the food lockers is required.

Campsites, facilities: There are 304 sites for tents or RVs up to 35 feet long. Picnic tables and fire grills are provided. There are also an additional 25 hike-in sites available for backpackers (no parking is available for backpacker campsites, usually reserved for those hiking the Pacific Crest Trail, for which a wilderness permit is required), and seven group sites that can accommodate 30 people each. Drinking water, flush toilets, and RV dump station are available. No RV hookups are available. Showers and groceries are nearby. Leashed pets are permitted.

Reservations, fees: Reserve at 800/436-PARK (800/436-7275) or website: reservations.nps.gov; half of the sites are available through reservations; the other half are first-come, first-served. There is a $18 fee per night for family sites, $5 per night per person for walk-in sites, and $40 per night for group sites, plus a $20 per vehicle park entrance fee. Open July through mid-September.

Directions: From Merced, drive east on Highway 140 to the Arch Rock entrance station. Continue east to the Big Oak Flat Road junction (a half mile before entering Yosemite Valley). Turn left and drive 14 miles to Tioga Road. Turn right and drive 46 miles to the campground on the right side of the road.

From just south of Lee Vining at the junction of U.S. 395 and Highway 120, turn west and drive to the Tioga Pass entrance station for Yosemite National Park. Continue for about 10 miles to the campground entrance on the left.

Contact: Yosemite National Park, 209/372-0200, for a touch-tone menu of recorded information.

44 SILVER LAKE

Rating: 9

In Inyo National Forest.

Map 10.4, page 528

Silver Lake is set at 7,200 feet, an 80-acre lake in the June Lake Loop with Carson Peak looming in the background. Boat rentals, fishing for trout at the lake, a beautiful trout stream (Rush Creek) next to the camp, and a nearby trailhead for wilderness hiking and horseback riding (rentals available) are the highlights. The camp is largely exposed and vulnerable to winds, the only downer. Within walking distance to the south is Silver Lake, always a pretty sight, especially when afternoon winds cause the lake surface to sparkle in crackling silvers. Just across the road from the camp is a great trailhead for the Ansel Adams Wilderness, with a two-hour hike available that climbs to pretty

Agnew Lake overlooking the June Lake basin; wilderness permit required for overnight use.

Campsites, facilities: There are 63 sites for tents or RVs up to 40 feet long. Picnic tables and fire grills are provided. Drinking water, flush toilets, and horseback riding facilities are available. A grocery store, coin laundry, motorboat rentals, boat ramp, bait, snack bar, boat fuel, and propane gas are available nearby. Leashed pets are permitted.

Reservations, fees: Reservations are not accepted. The fee is $13 per night. Senior discount available. Open late April to mid-November.

Directions: From Lee Vining on U.S. 395, drive south for six miles to the first Highway 158 North/June Lake Loop turnoff. Turn west (right) and drive nine miles (past Grant Lake) to Silver Lake. Just as you arrive at Silver Lake (a small store is on the right), turn left at the campground entrance.

Contact: Inyo National Forest, Mono Lake Visitor Center, 760/647-3044, fax 760/647-3046.

45 REVERSED CREEK

Rating: 6

In Inyo National Forest.

Map 10.4, page 528

This camp is set at 7,600 feet near pretty Reversed Creek, the only stream in the region that flows toward the mountains, not away from them. It is a small, tree-lined stream that provides decent trout fishing. The campsites are sheltered and set in a grove of aspen, but close enough to the road so you can still hear highway traffic. There are also cabins available for rent near here. Directly opposite the camp, on the other side of the road, is Gull Lake and the boat ramp. Two miles to the west, on the west side of the road, is the trailhead for the hike to Fern Lake on the edge of the Ansel Adams Wilderness, a little buttkicker of a climb.

Campsites, facilities: There are 17 sites for tents or RVs up to 30 feet long. Picnic tables and

fire grills are provided. Drinking water and flush toilets are available. A grocery store, coin laundry, and propane gas are nearby. Boating is available at nearby Silver Lake, two miles away. Leashed pets are permitted.

Reservations, fees: Reservations are not accepted. The fee is $13 per night. Senior discount available. Open mid-May to early November, weather permitting.

Directions: From Lee Vining, drive south on U.S. 395 (past the first Highway 158/June Lake Loop turnoff) to June Lake Junction (a gas station/store is on the west side of the road) and Highway 158 South. Turn west on Highway 158 South and drive three miles to the campground on the left side of the road (across from Gull Lake).

Contact: Inyo National Forest, Mono Lake Visitor Center, 760/647-3044, fax 760/647-3046.

46 JUNE LAKE

Rating: 9

In Inyo National Forest.

Map 10.4, page 528

There are three campgrounds at pretty June Lake; this is one of the two operated by the Forest Service (the other is Oh! Ridge). This one is on the northeast shore of the lake at 7,600 feet in elevation, a pretty spot with all supplies available just two miles to the south in the town of June Lake. The nearest boat launch is north of town. This is a good lake for trout fishing, receiving nearly 100,000 stocked trout per year.

Campsites, facilities: There are 28 sites, including 15 available by reservation, for tents or RVs up to 20 feet long. Picnic tables and fire grills are provided. Drinking water, flush toilets, and a boat ramp are available. A grocery store, coin laundry, boat and tackle rentals, moorings, and propane gas are available nearby. Leashed pets are permitted.

Reservations, fees: Reserve at 877/444-6777 ($9 reservation fee) or website: www.Reserve

Usa.com; $13 per night. Senior discount available. Open late April to early November, weather permitting.

Directions: From Lee Vining, drive south on U.S. 395 (passing the Highway 158 North) for 20 miles (six miles past Highway 158 North) to June Lake Junction (a sign is posted for "June Lake Village") and Highway 158 South. Turn west (right) on Highway 158 North and drive two miles to June Lake. Turn right (signed) and drive a short distance to the campground.

Contact: Inyo National Forest, Mono Lake Visitor Center, 760/647-3044, fax 760/647-3046.

47 OH! RIDGE

Rating: 8

On June Lake in Inyo National Forest.
Map 10.4, page 528
This is the largest of the campgrounds on June Lake. However, it is not the most popular since it is not right on the lakeshore, but back about a quarter mile or so from the north end of the lake. Regardless, it has the best views of the lake, with the ridge of the high Sierra providing a backdrop. The lake is a good one for trout fishing. The elevation is 7,600 feet.

Campsites, facilities: There are 148 sites, including 74 available for reservation, for tents or RVs up to 40 feet long. Picnic tables and fire grills are provided. Drinking water, flush toilets, and a playground are available. A grocery store, coin laundry, boat ramp, boat and tackle rentals, swimming beach, moorings, and propane gas are available nearby. Leashed pets are permitted.

Reservations, fees: Reserve at 877/444-6777 ($9 reservation fee) or website: www.Reserve Usa.com; $13 per night. Senior discount available. Open late April to early November.

Directions: From Lee Vining, drive south on U.S. 395 (past the first Highway 158/June Lake Loop turnoff) to June Lake Junction (a gas station/store is on the west side of the road)

and Highway 158 South. Turn west on Highway 158 South and drive two miles to Oh! Ridge Road. Turn right and drive a mile to the campground access road (signed). Turn left and drive to the campground.

Contact: Inyo National Forest, Mono Lake Visitor Center, 760/647-3044, fax 760/647-3046.

48 PINE CLIFF RESORT

Rating: 7

At June Lake.
Map 10.4, page 528
You found "kid heaven" at Pine Cliff Resort. This camp is in a pretty setting along the north shore of June Lake (7,600 feet in elevation), the feature lake among four in the June Lake Loop. The campsites are nestled in pine trees, designed so each site accommodates different-sized rigs and families, and the campground is set about a quarter-mile from June Lake. This is the only camp at June Lake Loop that has a swimming beach available. The landscape is a pretty one, with the lake set below snowcapped peaks. The bonus is that June Lake gets large numbers of trout plants each summer, making it extremely popular with anglers. Of the lakes in the June Lake Loop, this is the one that has the most of everything—the most beauty, the most fish, the most developed accommodations and, alas, the most people. This resort has been operated as a family business for nearly 50 years.

Campsites, facilities: There are 154 sites, including 15 drive-through, with full hookups for RVs, 55 sites for tents and small trailers (18 feet or shorter) only, and 17 sites with partial hookups for tents or RVs. Picnic tables and fire rings are provided. Restrooms, flush toilets, showers, drinking water, coin laundry, basketball, volleyball, tetherball and horseshoes, store, and propane gas are available. Some facilities are wheelchair-accessible. A primitive boat ramp, boat, fish-cleaning facilities, and fuel are available nearby. Leashed pets are permitted.

Reservations, fees: Reservations are recommended. The fee is $11–20 per night, $5 per extra vehicle. Open mid-April through October.

Directions: From Lee Vining, drive south on U.S. 395 (passing the first Highway 158 North/June Lake Loop turnoff) for 20 miles (six miles past Highway 158 North) to June Lake Junction (a sign is posted for "June Lake Village") and Highway 158 South. Turn right (west) on Highway 158 South and drive a mile to North Shore Drive (a sign is nearby for Pine Cliff Resort). Turn right and drive one-half mile to Pine Cliff Road. Turn left and drive one-half mile to the resort store on the right (route is well signed).

Contact: Pine Cliff Resort, 760/648-7558.

49 GULL LAKE

Rating: 8

In Inyo National Forest.

Map 10.4, page 528

Little Gull Lake, just 64 acres, is the smallest of the lakes on the June Lake Loop, but to many it is the prettiest. It is set at 7,600 feet, just west of June Lake and, with Carson Peak looming on the Sierra crest to the west, it is a dramatic and intimate setting. The lake is stocked with nearly 50,000 trout each summer, providing good fishing. A boat ramp is on the lake's southwest corner.

Campsites, facilities: There are 11 sites for tents or RVs up to 30 feet long. Drinking water, fire grills, and picnic tables are provided, and flush toilets are available. A grocery store, coin laundry, boat ramp, and propane gas are available nearby. Leashed pets are permitted.

Reservations, fees: Reservations are not accepted. The fee is $13 per night. Senior discount available. Open late April to early November, weather permitting.

Directions: From Lee Vining, drive south on U.S. 395 (past the first Highway 158/June Lake Loop turnoff) to June Lake Junction (a gas station/store is on the west side of the road) and Highway 158. Turn west on Highway 158 and drive three miles to the campground entrance on the right side of the road.

Contact: Inyo National Forest, Mono Lake Visitor Center, 760/647-3044, fax 760/647-3046.

50 HARTLEY SPRINGS

Rating: 8

In Inyo National Forest.

Map 10.4, page 528

Even though this camp is only a five-minute drive from U.S. 395, those five minutes will take you into another orbit. It is set in a forest of Jeffrey pine and has the feel of a remote, primitive camp, set in a high-mountain environment at an elevation of 8,400 feet. About two miles to the immediate north at elevation 8,611 feet is Obsidian Dome "Glass Flow," a craggy geologic formation that some people enjoy scrambling around and exploring; pick your access point carefully.

Campsites, facilities: There are 20 sites for tents or RVs up to 40 feet long. Picnic tables and fire grills are provided. Vault toilets are available. No drinking water is available. Leashed pets are permitted.

Reservations, fees: Reservations are not accepted. There is no fee for camping. Open late May to late September, weather permitting.

Directions: From Lee Vining, drive south on U.S. 395 (passing the first Highway 158/June Lake Loop turnoff) for 10 miles to June Lake Junction. Continue south on U.S. 395 for six miles to Glass Creek Road (a dirt road on the west side of the highway). Turn west (right) and drive two miles to the campground entrance road on the left.

Contact: Inyo National Forest, Mono Lake Visitor Center, 760/647-3044, fax 760/647-3046.

51 CRANE FLAT

Rating: 6

Near Tuolumne Grove of Big Trees in Yosemite National Park.

Map 10.4, page 528

Crane Flat is within a five-minute drive of the Tuolumne Grove of Big Trees, as well as the Merced Grove to the nearby west. This is the feature attraction in this part of Yosemite National Park, set near the western border in close proximity to the Big Oak Flat Entrance Station (Highway 120). The elevation is 6,200 feet. Yosemite Valley is about a 25-minute drive away.

Campsites, facilities: There are 166 sites for tents or RVs up to 35 feet long. Picnic tables and fire rings are provided. Drinking water and flush toilets are available. Groceries, propane gas, and a gas station are nearby.

Reservations, fees: Reserve at 800/436-PARK (800/436-7275) or website: reservations.nps.gov; $18 per night, plus $20 park entrance fee per vehicle. Senior discount available. Open June through September.

Directions: From Groveland, drive east on Highway 120 to the Big Oak Flat entrance station for Yosemite National Park. After passing through the entrance station, drive about 10 miles to the campground entrance road on the right. Turn right and drive a half mile to the campground.

Contact: Yosemite National Park, 209/372-0200, for a touch-tone menu of recorded information.

52 CAMP 4

Rating: 8

In Yosemite Valley in Yosemite National Park.

Map 10.4, page 528

The concept at Camp 4 was to provide a climber's bivouac near the base of El Capitan, and so it is. It has also worked as a walk-in alternative to drive-in camps that sometimes resemble combat zones. The sites here are jammed together, and six people will be placed in your site, whether you know them or not. Regardless, the camp is in a great location, within walking distance of Yosemite Falls. It has a view of Leidig Meadow and the southern valley rim, with Sentinel Rock directly across the valley. A trail is routed from camp to Lower Yosemite Fall. In addition, the trailhead for the Yosemite Falls Trail is a short distance away, a terrible, butt-kicking climb up Columbia Rock to the rim adjacent to the top of the falls, but providing one of most incredible views in all the world. Note: after originally being named Camp 4, the park once renamed this campground as "Sunnyside Walk-In." The name was switched back to the original, because after all, climbers never stopped calling it Camp 4.

Campsites, facilities: There are 35 walk-in tent sites. Six people are placed in each campsite, regardless of the number of people in each party. Picnic tables and fire pits are provided. Drinking water and flush toilets are available. A parking area, showers, groceries, and a coin laundry are nearby. No pets are allowed.

Reservations, fees: Reservations are not accepted. The fee is $5 per person per night, plus $20 park entrance fee per vehicle. There is a seven-day limit.

Directions: From Merced, drive east on Highway 140 to the Arch Rock entrance station. Continue east to the Big Oak Flat Road junction (a half mile before entering Yosemite Valley). Continue into Yosemite Valley, and drive past the chapel to a stop sign. Turn left, cross Sentinel Bridge, and drive one mile to another stop sign. Continue 1.5 miles and look for the large sign marking the parking area for Camp 4 Walk-In on the right (near the base of El Capitan).

Contact: Yosemite National Park, 209/372-0200, for a touch-tone menu of recorded information.

53 BRIDALVEIL CREEK

Rating: 10

Near Glacier Point in Yosemite National Park.

Map 10.4, page 528

There may be no better view in the world than the one from Glacier Point, looking down into Yosemite Valley, where Half Dome stands like nature's perfect sculpture. Then there are the perfect views of Yosemite Falls, Nevada Fall, Vernal Fall, and several hundred square miles of Yosemite's wilderness backcountry. This is the closest camp to Glacier Point's drive-to vantage point, but it is also the closest camp to the best day hikes in the entire park. Along Glacier Point Road are trailheads to Sentinel Dome (incredible view of Yosemite Falls) and Taft Point (breathtaking drop, incredible view of El Capitan), and McGurk Meadow (one of the most pristine spots on Earth). At 7,200 feet, the camp is more than 3,000 feet higher than Yosemite Valley. A good day hike out of camp leads you to Ostrander Lake, just below Horse Ridge.

Campsites, facilities: There are 110 sites for tents and RVs up to 35 feet long. Picnic tables and fire grills are provided. Drinking water and flush toilets are available. Leashed pets are permitted.

Reservations, fees: Reservations are not accepted. The fee is $12 per night, plus $20 park entrance fee per vehicle. A 14-day stay limit is enforced. Open July to early September.

Directions: From Merced, drive east on Highway 140 to the Arch Rock entrance station. Continue east (past Big Oak Flat Road junction) to the junction with Wawona Road/Highway 41 (just before Yosemite Valley). Turn right on Highway 41/Wawona Road and drive about 10 miles to Glacier Point Road. Turn left on Glacier Point Road and drive about five miles (a few miles past Badger Pass Ski Area) to Peregoy Meadow and the campground access road on the right. Turn right and drive a short distance to the campground.

Contact: Yosemite National Park, 209/372-0200, for a touch-tone menu of recorded information.

54 LOWER PINES

Rating: 9

In Yosemite Valley in Yosemite National Park.

Map 10.4, page 528

Lower Pines sits right along the Merced River, quite pretty, in the center of Yosemite Valley. Of course, the tents and RVs are jammed in quite close together. Within walking distance is the trail to Mirror Lake (a zoo on parade), as well as the trailhead at Happy Isles for the hike up to Vernal Fall and Nevada Fall. The park's shuttle bus picks up riders near the camp entrance.

Campsites, facilities: There are 60 sites for tents or RVs up to 40 feet long. Fire rings and picnic tables are provided. Drinking water and flush toilets are available. A grocery store, coin laundry, propane gas, recycling center, and horse, bike, and cross-country ski rentals are available nearby. Leashed pets are allowed.

Reservations, fees: Reserve at 800/436-PARK (800/436-7275) or website: reservations.nps.gov; $18 per night, plus $20 park entrance fee per vehicle. Senior discount available. Open April through October, weather permitting.

Directions: From Merced, drive east on Highway 140 to the Arch Rock entrance station. Continue east to the Big Oak Flat Road junction (a half mile before entering Yosemite Valley). Continue into Yosemite Valley, drive past Curry Village (on the right) to the campground entrance on the left side of the road (just before Clarks Bridge).

Contact: Yosemite National Park, 209/372-0200, for a touch-tone menu of recorded information.

55 UPPER PINES

🏃 🚴 🏊 🛶 🐕 🚐 ⛺

Rating: 9

In Yosemite Valley in Yosemite National Park.

Map 10.4, page 528

Of the campgrounds in Yosemite Valley, Upper Pines is the closest trailhead to paradise, providing you can get a campsite at the far south end of the camp. From here it is a short walk to the Happy Isles trailhead and with it the chance to hike to Vernal Fall on the Mist Trail (steep), or beyond to Nevada Fall (very steep) at the foot of Liberty Cap. But crowded this camp is, and you'd better expect it. People come from all over the world to camp here. Sometimes it appears as if they are from other worlds as well. The elevation is 4,000 feet.

Campsites, facilities: There are 238 sites for tents or RVs up to 40 feet long. Fire rings and picnic tables are provided. Drinking water, flush toilets, and RV dump station are available. A grocery store, coin laundry, propane gas, recycling center, and bike rentals are available nearby. Leashed pets are permitted in the campgrounds, but not on trails.

Reservations, fees: Reserve at 800/436-PARK (800/436-7275) or website: reservations.nps.gov; $18 per night, plus $20 park entrance fee per vehicle. Senior discount available. Open year-round.

Directions: From Merced, drive east on Highway 140 to the Arch Rock entrance station. Continue east to the Big Oak Flat Road junction (a half mile before entering Yosemite Valley). Continue into Yosemite Valley, drive past Curry Village (on the right) to the campground entrance on the right side of the road (just before Clarks Bridge).

Contact: Yosemite National Park, 209/372-0200, for a touch-tone menu of recorded information.

56 NORTH PINES

🏃 🚴 🏊 🛶 🐕 🚐 ⛺

Rating: 9

In Yosemite Valley in Yosemite National Park.

Map 10.4, page 528

North Pines is set along the Merced River. A trail out of camp heads east and links up the paved road/trail to Mirror Lake, a virtual parade of people. If you continue hiking past Mirror Lake you will get astounding views of Half Dome and then leave the masses behind as you enter Tenaya Canyon. The elevation is 4,000 feet.

Campsites, facilities: There are 80 sites for tents or RVs up to 40 feet long. Picnic tables and fire grills are provided. Drinking water and flush toilets are available. A grocery store, coin laundry, recycling center, propane gas, and bike rentals are available nearby. Leashed pets are allowed.

Reservations, fees: Reserve at 800/436-PARK (800/436-7275) or website: reservations.nps.gov; $18 per night, plus $20 park entrance fee per vehicle. Senior discount available. Open April through September.

Directions: From Merced, drive east on Highway 140 to the Arch Rock entrance station. Continue east to the Big Oak Flat Road junction (a half mile before entering Yosemite Valley). Continue into Yosemite Valley, drive past Curry Village (on the right), continue past Upper and Lower Pines Campgrounds, and drive over Clarks Bridge to a junction at the horse stables. Turn left at the horse stables and drive a short distance to the campground on the right.

Contact: Yosemite National Park, 209/372-0200, for a touch-tone menu of recorded information.

57 AGNEW MEADOWS
🥾 🏊 🐴 🚐 ⛺

Rating: 9

In Inyo National Forest.

Map 10.4, page 528

This is a perfect camp to use as a launching pad for a backpacking trip or day of fly-fishing for trout. It is set along the Upper San Joaquin River at 8,400 feet, with a trailhead for the Pacific Crest Trail available near the camp. From here you can hike seven miles to the gorgeous Thousand Island Lake, a beautiful lake sprinkled with islands set below Banner and Ritter Peaks in the spectacular Minarets. For day hikes, another choice is walking the River Trail, which is routed from Agnew Meadows along the San Joaquin, providing excellent fishing, though the trout are small.

Campsites, facilities: There are 21 sites for tents or RVs, most of which can accommodate RVs 46 feet in length and some up to 55 feet. A group camp is also available (reservations required for the group camp). Picnic tables and fire grills are provided. Drinking water, chemical toilets, and horseback riding facilities are available (three family sites have hitching racks where horse camping is permitted). Supplies can be obtained at Red's Meadows. Leashed pets are permitted.

Reservations, fees: Reservations are not accepted. The fee is $15 per night, plus $5 per person Reds Meadow/Agnew Meadows access fee. Senior discount available. For group camp and horse camping sites, reserve at 877/444-6777 ($9 reservation fee) or website: www .ReserveUsa.com; $30–50 per night. Open mid-June to early October.

Directions: On U.S. 395, drive to Mammoth Junction/Highway 203. Turn west on Highway 203 and drive four miles, through the town of Mammoth Lakes to Minaret Road (still Highway 203). Turn right and drive five miles to Minaret Station (past the Mammoth Mountain Ski Area). Continue for 2.6 miles to the campground entrance road on the right.

Turn right and drive just under a mile to the campground.

Access note: Noncampers are required to use a shuttle bus from the Shuttle Bus Terminal at Mammoth Mountain Main Lodge Gondola Station; 7 A.M. to 7:45 P.M. Space available for leashed dogs, bikes, and backpacks.

Contact: Inyo National Forest, Mammoth Lakes Visitor Center, 760/924-5500, fax 760/924-5547.

58 PUMICE FLAT
🥾 🏊 🐴 🚐 ⛺

Rating: 8

On the San Joaquin River in Inyo National Forest.

Map 10.4, page 528

Pumice Flat (7,700 feet in elevation) provides roadside camping within short range of several adventures. A trail out of camp links with the Pacific Crest Trail, where you can hike along the Upper San Joaquin River for miles, providing excellent access for fly-fishing, and head north into the Ansel Adams Wilderness. Devils Postpile National Monument is just two miles south, along with the trailhead for Rainbow Falls.

Campsites, facilities: There are 17 sites for tents or RVs, most of which can accommodate RVs 47 feet in length and some up to 55 feet. Picnic tables and fire grills are provided. Drinking water, flush toilets, and horseback riding facilities are available. Limited supplies are available at a small store, or full supplies in Mammoth Lakes. Leashed pets are permitted.

Reservations, fees: Reservations are not accepted. The fee is $15 per night, plus $5 per person Reds Meadow/Agnew Meadows access fee. Senior discount available. Open mid-June to late September.

Directions: On U.S. 395, drive to Mammoth Junction/Highway 203. Turn west on Highway 203 and drive four miles, through the town of Mammoth Lakes to Minaret Road (still Highway 203). Turn right and drive five miles to Minaret Station (past the Mammoth Mountain Ski Area). Continue for 5.1 miles to the campground on the right side of the road.

Access note: Noncampers are required to use a shuttle bus from the Shuttle Bus Terminal at Mammoth Mountain Main Lodge Gondola Station; 7 A.M. to 7:45 P.M. Space available for leashed dogs, bikes, and backpacks.

Contact: Inyo National Forest, Mammoth Lakes Visitor Center, 760/924-5500, fax 760/924-5547.

59 UPPER SODA SPRINGS

Rating: 8

On the San Joaquin River in Inyo National Forest.

Map 10.4, page 528

This is a premium location within earshot of the Upper San Joaquin River and within minutes of many first-class recreation options. The river is stocked with trout at this camp, with several good pools within short walking distance. Farther upstream, accessible by an excellent trail, are smaller wild trout that provide good fly-fishing prospects. Devils Postpile National Monument, a massive formation of ancient columnar jointed rock, is only three miles to the south. The Pacific Crest Trail passes right by the camp, providing a trailhead for access to numerous lakes in the Ansel Adams Wilderness. The elevation is 7,700 feet.

Campsites, facilities: There are 29 sites for tents or RVs, most of which can accommodate RVs 36 feet in length and some up to 55 feet. Picnic tables and fire grills are provided. Drinking water, flush toilets, and horseback riding facilities are available. You can buy supplies at Red's Meadows. Leashed pets are permitted.

Reservations, fees: Reservations are not accepted. The fee is $15 per night, plus $5 per person Reds Meadow/Agnew Meadows access fee. Senior discount available. Open mid-June to late September.

Directions: On U.S. 395, drive to Mammoth Junction/Highway 203. Turn west on Highway 203 and drive four miles, through the town of

Mammoth Lakes to Minaret Road (still Highway 203). Turn right and drive 4.5 miles to the entrance kiosk (adjacent to the Mammoth Mountain Ski Area). Continue for five miles to the campground entrance road on the right. Turn right and drive a quarter mile to the campground.

Access note: Noncampers are required to use a shuttle bus from the Shuttle Bus Terminal at Mammoth Mountain Main Lodge Gondola Station; 7 A.M. to 7:45 P.M. Space available for leashed dogs, bikes, and backpacks.

Contact: Inyo National Forest, Mammoth Lakes Visitor Center, 760/924-5500, fax 760/924-5547.

60 PUMICE FLAT GROUP CAMP

Rating: 6

On the San Joaquin River in Inyo National Forest.

Map 10.4, page 528

Pumice Flat Group Camp is set at 7,700 feet in elevation near the Upper San Joaquin River, adjacent to Pumice Flat. (For recreation information, see the entry for Pumice Flat.)

Campsites, facilities: There are four group sites for tents or RVs (check with ranger for information regarding acceptable RV lengths). Picnic tables and fire grills are provided. Drinking water, flush toilets, and horseback riding facilities are available. You can buy supplies in Mammoth Lakes. Leashed pets are permitted.

Reservations, fees: Reserve at 877/444-6777 ($9 reservation fee) or website: www.Reserve Usa.com; $50, $70, and $100 per night per group, plus $5 per person Reds Meadow/Agnew Meadows access fee. Open mid-June to late September.

Directions: On U.S. 395, drive to Mammoth Junction/Highway 203. Turn west on Highway 203 and drive four miles, through the town of Mammoth Lakes to Minaret Road (still Highway 203). Turn right and drive five miles to Minaret Station (past the Mammoth Mountain Ski Area). Continue for 5.1 miles to the campground on the left side of the road.

Access note: Noncampers are required to use a shuttle bus from the Shuttle Bus Terminal at Mammoth Mountain Main Lodge Gondola Station; 7 A.M. to 7:45 P.M. Space available for leashed dogs, bikes, and backpacks.

Contact: Inyo National Forest, Mammoth Lakes Visitor Center, 760/924-5500, fax 760/924-5547.

61 MERCED RECREATION AREA

🚶 🚴 🏊 🛶 🐕 🎣 ♿ 🚐 ⛺

Rating: 8

On the Merced River east of Briceburg.

Map 10.4, page 528

What a spot: the campsites are along one of the prettiest sections of the Merced River, where you can enjoy great hiking, swimming, and fishing, all on the same day. There are three campgrounds here: McCabe Flat, Willow Placer, and Railroad Flat. The access road out of camp leads downstream to the Yosemite Railroad Grade, which has been converted into a great trail. One of the best wildflower blooms anywhere in the Sierra foothills is found near here at Red Hills (just outside Chinese Camp), best usually in April. If you don't mind the cold water, swimming in the Merced River's pools can provide relief from summer heat. Evening fly-fishing is good in many of the same spots through July.

Campsites, facilities: There are 21 walk-in tent sites and nine sites for tents or RVs up to 18 feet long. Picnic tables and fire grills are provided. Vault and pit toilets are available. No drinking water is available (drinking water is available across from the Briceburg Bridge). Some facilities are wheelchair-accessible. Leashed pets are permitted. Supplies are available in Mariposa.

Reservations, fees: Reservations are not accepted. The fee is $10 per night. There is a 14-day limit. Senior discount available. Open April to mid-October, weather permitting.

Directions: From Merced, drive south on Highway 99 for just a few miles to its junction with Highway 140. Turn east on Highway 140 and drive 40 miles to Mariposa and continue another 15 miles to Briceburg and the Briceburg Visitor Center on the left. Turn left at a road that is signed "BLM Camping Areas" (the road remains paved for about 150 yards). Drive over the Briceburg suspension bridge and turn left, traveling downstream on the road, parallel to the river. Drive 2.5 miles to McCabe Flat, 3.8 miles to Willow Placer, and 4.8 miles to Railroad Flat.

Contact: Bureau of Land Management, Folsom Field Office, 916/985-4474, fax 916/985-3259.

62 YOSEMITE-MARIPOSA KOA

🏊 🐕 🚣 ♿ 🚐 ⛺

Rating: 7

Near Mariposa.

Map 10.4, page 528

A little duck pond, cute log cabins, swimming pool, and proximity to Yosemite National Park make this one a winner. The RV sites are lined up along the entrance road, edged by grass. A 10 P.M. "quiet time" helps ensure a good night's sleep. It's a one-hour drive to Yosemite Valley, and your best bet is to get there early to enjoy the spectacular beauty before the park is packed with people.

Campsites, facilities: There are 49 sites for RVs, including 28 with full hookups and 21 with partial hookups, 26 tent sites, and 12 cabins. Picnic tables and barbecues are provided. Restrooms, showers, RV dump station, modem access, coin laundry, store, propane gas, recreation room, swimming pool, and a playground are available. Leashed pets are permitted in sites for RVs and tents only.

Reservations, fees: Reservations are accepted. The fee is $27–39 per night. Major credit cards accepted. Open year-round.

Directions: From Merced, drive east on Highway 140 to Mariposa. Continue on Highway 140 for six miles to Midpines and the campground entrance on the left at 6323 Hwy. 140.

Contact: Yosemite-Mariposa KOA, 209/966-

2201 or 800/562-9391 (reservations only), website: www.koa.com.

63 JERSEYDALE

Rating: 5

In Sierra National Forest.

Map 10.4, page 528

This little camp gets overlooked by many visitors shut out of nearby Yosemite National Park simply because they don't realize it exists. Jerseydale is set southwest of the national park in Sierra National Forest, with two good side trips nearby. If you continue north on Jerseydale Road to its end (about six miles), you will come to a gated Forest Service road/trailhead that provides access east for miles along the South Fork of the Merced River, where there is often good fishing, swimming, and rafting. In addition, a dirt road from the camp is routed east for many miles into the Chowchilla Mountains.

Campsites, facilities: There are eight tent sites and two sites for tents or RVs up to 22 feet long. Picnic tables and fire grills are provided. Drinking water and vault toilets are available. Garbage must be packed out. Leashed pets are permitted.

Reservations, fees: Reservations are not accepted. There is no fee for camping. Open May through November.

Directions: From Mariposa, drive northeast on Highway 140 for about five miles to Triangle Road (if you reach Midpines, you have gone 1.5 miles too far). Turn right on Triangle Road and drive about six miles to Darrah and Jerseydale Road. Turn left and drive three miles to the campground on the left side of the road (adjacent to the Jerseydale Ranger Station).

Contact: Sierra National Forest, Bass Lake Ranger District, 559/877-2218, fax 559/877-3108.

64 WAWONA

Rating: 9

On the South Fork of the Merced River in Yosemite National Park.

Map 10.4, page 528

Wawona Camp is an attractive alternative to the packed camps in Yosemite Valley, providing you don't mind the relatively long drives to the best destinations. The camp is pretty, set along the South Fork Merced River, with the sites more spacious than at most other drive-to camps in the park. The nearest attraction is the Mariposa Grove of Giant Sequoias, but get your visit in early and be out by 9 A.M. because after that it turns into a zoo, complete with shuttle train. The best nearby hike is a strenuous eight-mile round-trip to Chilnualna Falls, the prettiest sight in the southern region of the park; the trailhead is at the east end of Chilnualna Road in North Wawona. It's a 45-minute drive to either Glacier Point or Yosemite Valley.

Campsites, facilities: There are 93 sites for tents or RVs up to 35 feet long and one group campsite. Picnic tables and fire grills are provided. Drinking water and flush toilets are available. Leashed pets are permitted in the campground, but not on trails. There are also some stock handling facilities for camping with pack animals; call for further information. A grocery store, propane gas, gas station, post office, restaurant, and horseback riding facilities are available nearby.

Reservations, fees: Reservations are required May to September. Reserve by calling 800/436-PARK (800/436-7275) or website: http://reservations.nps.gov; $18 per night, plus $20 park entrance fee per vehicle; group camp $40 per night. No reservations October to April, $12 per night. A seven-day camping limit is enforced. Open year-round.

Directions: From Oakhurst, drive north on Highway 41 to the Wawona entrance to Yosemite National Park. Continue north on Highway 41 past Wawona (golf course on the left) and drive one mile to the campground entrance on the left.

Contact: Yosemite National Park, 209/372-0200, for a touch-tone menu of recorded information.

65 SUMMIT CAMP

Rating: 5

In Sierra National Forest.
Map 10.4, page 528

The prime attraction of tiny Summit Camp is its proximity to the Wawona entrance of Yosemite National Park. It sits along a twisty Forest Service road, perched in the Chowchilla Mountains at 5,800 feet, about three miles from Big Creek. It's a little-known alternative when the park campgrounds at Wawona are packed.

Campsites, facilities: There are six tent sites. Picnic tables and fire grills are provided. Vault toilets are available. No drinking water is available. Garbage must be packed out. Leashed pets are permitted.

Reservations, fees: Reservations are not accepted. There is no fee for camping. Open June through October.

Directions: From Oakhurst, drive north on Highway 41 toward the town of Fish Camp and the gravel Forest Road 5S09X a mile before Fish Camp on the left. Turn left and drive six twisty miles to the campground on the left side of the road.

Contact: Sierra National Forest, Bass Lake Ranger District, 559/877-2218, fax 559/877-3108.

66 UPPER CHIQUITO

Rating: 7

On Chiquito Creek in Sierra National Forest.
Map 10.4, page 528

Upper Chiquito is set at 6,800 feet on a major access road to Sierra National Forest and the western region of the Ansel Adams Wilder-

ness, about 15 miles to the east. The camp is set on Upper Chiquito Creek. About a mile down the road (southwest) is a Forest Service spur road (turn north) that provides access to a trail that is routed up Chiquito Creek for three miles to gorgeous Chiquita Lake (another route with a longer drive and shorter hike is available out of Fresno Dome).

Campsites, facilities: There are 10 sites for tents only and 10 sites for tents or RVs up to 22 feet long. Picnic tables and fire grills are provided. Vault toilets are available. No drinking water is available. Garbage must be packed out. Leashed pets are permitted.

Reservations, fees: Reservations are not accepted. There is no fee for camping. Open from June through September.

Directions: From Fresno, drive north on Highway 41 for 50 miles to Yosemite Forks and County Road 222. Turn right on County Road 222 and drive six miles to Pines Village and Beasore Road. Turn left onto Beasore Road and drive 16 miles to the campground.

Contact: Sierra National Forest, Bass Lake Ranger District, 559/877-2218, fax 559/877-3108.

67 CLOVER MEADOW

Rating: 8

In Sierra National Forest.
Map 10.4, page 528

This is one of two excellent jump-off camps in the area for backpackers; the other is Granite Creek. The camp is set at 7,000 feet, adjacent to the Clover Meadow Ranger Station, where backcountry information is available. While a trail is available from camp heading east into the Ansel Adams Wilderness, most hikers drive about three miles farther northeast on Minarets Road to a trailhead for a five-mile hike to Cora Lakes.

Campsites, facilities: There are seven sites for tents or RVs up to 16 feet long. Picnic tables and fire grills are provided. Drinking water and vault toilets are available. Leashed pets are permitted.

Reservations, fees: Reservations are not accepted. There is no fee for camping. Open June through September.

Directions: From the town of North Fork (south of Bass Lake), drive east on Mammoth Pool Road/County Road 225 (which becomes Minarets Road/Forest Road 4S81). The road eventually will bear left (north) on Forest Road 4S81 to the campground entrance road. Turn and drive to the campground, adjacent to the Clover Meadow Ranger Station. The total distance from North Fork to the entrance road is about 63 miles; it's 20 miles north of the well-signed Mammoth Pool Reservoir on Minarets Road.

Contact: Sierra National Forest, Bass Lake Ranger District, 559/877-2218, fax 559/877-3108.

68 GRANITE CREEK

Rating: 6

In Sierra National Forest.

Map 10.4, page 528

This camp is a good jump-off point for backpackers since a trail from camp leads north for five miles to Cora Lakes in the Ansel Adams Wilderness, with the option of continuing to more remote wilderness. Note that nearby Clover Meadow may be more desirable because it has both drinking water to tank up your canteens and a ranger station to obtain the latest trail information. In addition, one-half of this campground is available for equestrians. The elevation is 6,900 feet.

Campsites, facilities: There are 20 tent sites, half available for equestrian use. Picnic tables and fire grills are provided. Vault toilets and a horse corral are available. No drinking water is available. Garbage must be packed out. Leashed pets are permitted.

Reservations, fees: Reservations are not ac-

cepted. There is no fee for camping. Open June through September.

Directions: From the town of North Fork (south of Bass Lake), drive east on Mammoth Pool Road/County Road 225 (which becomes Minarets Road/Forest Road 4S81). The road eventually will bear left (north) on Forest Road 4S81 to the campground entrance road. Turn and drive 3.5 miles (passing the Clover Meadow Ranger Station) to the campground. (The total distance from North Fork to the entrance road is about 66.5 miles; it's 23.5 miles north of Mammoth Pool Reservoir on the well-signed Minarets Road.)

Contact: Sierra National Forest, Bass Lake Ranger District, 559/877-2218, fax 559/877-3108.

69 RED'S MEADOW

Rating: 6

In Inyo National Forest.

Map 10.4, page 528

Red's Meadow has long been established as one of the best outfitters for horseback riding trips. To get the feel of it, three-mile round-trip rides are available to Rainbow Falls. Multiday trips into the Ansel Adams Wilderness on the Pacific Crest Trail are also available. A small restaurant is a bonus here, always a must-stop for long-distance hikers getting a shot to chomp their first hamburger in weeks, something like a bear finding a candy bar, quite a sight for the drive-in campers. The nearby Devils Postpile National Monument, Rainbow Falls, Minaret Falls, and San Joaquin River provide recreation options.

Campsites, facilities: There are 56 sites for tents or RVs, most of which can accommodate RVs 30 feet in length and some up to 55 feet. Picnic tables and fire grills are provided. Drinking water, flush toilets, and bear boxes are available. Natural hot springs, shower house, and horseback riding facilities are also available. You can buy limited supplies at a small store. Leashed pets are permitted.

Reservations, fees: Reservations are not accepted. The fee is $15 per night, plus $5 per person Reds Meadow/Agnew Meadows access fee. Senior discount available. Open mid-June to late October.

Directions: On U.S. 395, drive to Mammoth Junction/Highway 203. Turn west on Highway 203 and drive four miles, through the town of Mammoth Lakes to Minaret Road (still Highway 203). Turn right and drive five miles to Minaret Station (past the Mammoth Mountain Ski Area). Continue for 7.4 miles to the campground entrance on the left.

Access note: Noncampers are required to use a shuttle bus from the Shuttle Bus Terminal at Mammoth Mountain Main Lodge Gondola Station; 7 A.M. to 7:45 P.M. Space available for leashed dogs, bikes, and backpacks.

Contact: Inyo National Forest, Mammoth Lakes Visitor Center, 760/924-5500, fax760/924-5547.

70 MINARET FALLS

Rating: 8

On the San Joaquin River in Inyo National Forest.

Map 10.4, page 528

This camp has one of the prettiest settings of the series of camps along the Upper San Joaquin River and near Devils Postpile National Monument. It is set at 7,700 feet near Minaret Creek, across from where beautiful Minaret Falls pours into the San Joaquin River. Devils Postpile National Monument, one of the best examples in the world of hexagonal, columnar jointed rock, is less than a mile from camp, where there is also a trail to awesome Rainbow Falls. The Pacific Crest Trail runs right through this area as well, and if you hike to the south, there is excellent streamside fishing access.

Campsites, facilities: There are 27 sites for tents or RVs, most of which can accommodate RVs

up to 47 feet long and some up to 55 feet. Picnic tables and fire grills are provided. Drinking water and vault toilets are available. Chemical toilets and horseback riding facilities are available nearby. You can buy limited supplies at Red's Meadow Store, or all supplies in Mammoth Lakes. Leashed pets are permitted.

Reservations, fees: Reservations are not accepted. The fee is $15 per night, plus $5 per person Reds Meadow/Agnew Meadows access fee. Senior discount available. Open mid-June to late September.

Directions: On U.S. 395, drive to Mammoth Junction/Highway 203. Turn west on Highway 203 and drive four miles, through the town of Mammoth Lakes to Minaret Road (still Highway 203). Turn right and drive five miles to Minaret Station (past the Mammoth Mountain Ski Area). Continue for six miles to the campground entrance road on the right. Turn right and drive a quarter mile to the campground.

Access note: Noncampers are required to use a shuttle bus from the Shuttle Bus Terminal at Mammoth Mountain Main Lodge Gondola Station; 7 A.M. to 7:45 P.M. Space available for leashed dogs, bikes, and backpacks.

Contact: Inyo National Forest, Mammoth Lakes Visitor Center, 760/924-5500, fax 760/924-5547.

71 DEVILS POSTPILE NATIONAL MONUMENT

Rating: 9

Near the San Joaquin River.

Map 10.4, page 528

Devils Postpile is a spectacular and rare example of hexagonal, columnar jointed rock that look like posts, hence the name. The camp is set at 7,600 feet in elevation and provides nearby access for the easy hike to the Postpile. If you keep walking, it is a 2.5-mile walk to Rainbow Falls, a breathtaking 101-foot cascade that produces rainbows in its floating mist, seen only from the trail alongside the waterfall looking downstream. The camp is also adjacent to the Middle Fork San Joaquin River and the Pacific Crest Trail.

Campsites, facilities: There are 21 sites for tents or RVs. Picnic tables and fire grills are provided. Drinking water and flush toilets are available. Leashed pets are permitted.

Reservations, fees: Reservations are not accepted. The fee is $14 per night, plus $5 per person Reds Meadow/Agnew Meadows access fee. Senior discount available. Open mid-June to late October, weather permitting.

Directions: On U.S. 395, drive to Mammoth Junction/Highway 203. Turn west on Highway 203 and drive four miles, through the town of Mammoth Lakes to Minaret Road (still Highway 203). Turn right and drive five miles to Minaret Station (past the Mammoth Mountain Ski Area). Continue for nine miles to the campground entrance road on the right.

Access note: Noncampers are required to use a shuttle bus from the Shuttle Bus Terminal at Mammoth Mountain Main Lodge Gondola Station; 7 A.M. to 7:45 P.M. Space available for leashed dogs, bikes, and backpacks.

Contact: Devil Postpile National Monument, tel./fax 760/934-2289.

72 LAKE GEORGE

Rating: 8

In Inyo National Forest.

Map 10.4, page 528

The sites here have views of Lake George, a beautiful lake in a rock basin set below the spectacular Crystal Crag. Lake George is at 9,000 feet in elevation, a small lake fed by creeks coming from both Crystal Lake and TJ Lake. Both of the latter make excellent short hiking trips; TJ Lake is only about a 20-minute walk from the campground. Trout fishing at Lake George is decent—not great, not bad, but decent.

Campsites, facilities: There are 16 sites for tents or RVs, most of which can accommodate RVs up to 18 feet long and some up to 25 feet. Picnic tables and fire grills are provided. Drinking water and flush toilets are available. A grocery store, coin laundry, coin showers, and propane gas are available nearby. Leashed pets are permitted.

Reservations, fees: Reservations are not accepted. The fee is $14 per night with a seven-day limit. Senior discount available. Open mid-June to mid-September.

Directions: From Lee Vining on U.S. 395, drive south for 25 miles to Mammoth Junction and Highway 203/Minaret Summit Road. Turn west on Highway 203 and drive four miles to Lake Mary Road. Continue straight through the intersection and drive four miles to Lake Mary Loop Drive. Turn left and drive one-third of a mile to Lake George Road. Turn right and drive a half mile to the campground.

Contact: Inyo National Forest, Mammoth Lakes Visitor Center, 760/924-5500, fax 760/924-5547.

73 SUMMERDALE

Rating: 7

On the South Fork of the Merced River in Sierra National Forest.

Map 10.4, page 528

You can't get much closer to Yosemite National Park. This camp is within a mile of the Wawona entrance to Yosemite, about a five-minute drive to the Mariposa Grove. If you don't mind its proximity to the highway, this is a pretty spot in its own right, set along Big Creek, a feeder stream to the South Fork Merced River. Some good swimming holes are in this area. The elevation is 5,000 feet.

Campsites, facilities: There are 30 tent sites and nine sites for tents or RVs up to 22 feet long. Picnic tables and fire grills are provided. Drinking water and vault toilets are available. A grocery store is nearby (within one mile). Leashed pets are permitted.

Reservations, fees: Reserve at 877/444-6777 ($9 reservation fee) or website: www.Reserve

Usa.com; $16 per night. Senior discount available. Open May through September.

Directions: From Oakhurst, drive north on Highway 41 to Fish Camp and continue for one mile to the campground entrance on the left side of the road.

Contact: Sierra National Forest, Bass Lake Ranger District, 559/877-2218, fax 559/877-3108.

74 BIG SANDY

Rating: 7

On Big Creek in Sierra National Forest.
Map 10.4, page 528

It's only six miles from the highway and just eight miles from the southern entrance to Yosemite National Park. Add that up: right, when Wawona is full in southern Yosemite, this camp provides a much-needed option. It's a pretty camp set on Big Creek in the Sierra National Forest, one of two camps in the immediate area. The elevation is 5,800 feet. If you head into Yosemite for the tour of giant sequoias in Wawona, get there early, by 7:30 or 8:30 A.M., when the grove is still quiet and cool, and you will have the old, mammoth trees practically to yourself.

Campsites, facilities: There are 14 sites for tents only and four sites for tents or RVs up to 16 feet long. Picnic tables and fire grills are provided. Vault toilets are available. No drinking water is available. Leashed pets are permitted.

Reservations, fees: Reservations are not accepted. The fee is $13 per night, $5 for each additional vehicle. Senior discount available. Open from June through October.

Directions: From Oakhurst drive north on Highway 41 for 15 miles to Forest Road 6S07 (one mile before reaching Marriotts). Turn right on Forest Road 6S07 and drive about six miles (a slow, rough road) to the camp.

Contact: Sierra National Forest, Bass Lake Ranger District, 559/877-2218, fax 559/877-3108.

75 NELDER GROVE

Rating: 7

In Sierra National Forest.
Map 10.4, page 528

Nelder Grove is a primitive spot, also pretty, yet it is a camp that is often overlooked. It is set amid the Nelder Grove of giant sequoias, the majestic mountain redwoods. Since the southern entrance to Yosemite National Park is just 10 miles away, Nelder Grove is overshadowed by Yosemite's Wawona Grove. The elevation is 5,300 feet. A good option.

Campsites, facilities: There are seven sites for tents or RVs up to 22 feet long. Picnic tables and fire grills are provided. Vault toilets are available. No drinking water is available. Garbage must be packed out. Leashed pets are permitted.

Reservations, fees: Reservations are not accepted. There is no fee for camping. Open May through September.

Directions: From Fresno, drive north on Highway 41 for 46 miles to the town of Oakhurst. Continue north on Highway 41 for five miles to Sky Ranch Road/County Road 632. Turn northeast and drive about eight miles to the campground.

Contact: Sierra National Forest, Bass Lake Ranger District, 559/877-2218, fax 559/877-3108.

76 GREY'S MOUNTAIN

Rating: 7

On Willow Creek in Sierra National Forest.
Map 10.4, page 528

This is a small, primitive campground to keep in mind when all the campgrounds are filled at nearby Bass Lake. It is one of a series of campgrounds on Willow Creek. The elevation is 5,200 feet, set just below Sivels Mountain to the east at 5,813 feet.

Campsites, facilities: There are 26 sites for tents and RVs up to 22 feet long. Picnic tables and fire grills are provided. Vault toilets are available. No drinking water is available. Leashed pets are permitted.

Reservations, fees: Reservations are not accepted. The fee is $13 per night, $5 for each additional vehicle. Senior discount available. Open June through October.

Directions: From Oakhurst, drive north on Highway 41 for about 15 miles to Jackson Road/Forest Road 6S07. Turn right and drive four miles to the campground on the right.

Contact: Sierra National Forest, Bass Lake Ranger District, 559/877-2218, fax 559/877-3108.

77 SOQUEL

Rating: 7

On the North Fork of Willow Creek in Sierra National Forest.

Map 10.4, page 528

Soquel is at 5,400 feet in elevation on the North Fork of Willow Creek, an alternative to nearby Grey's Mountain in Sierra National Forest. When the camps are filled at Bass Lake, these two camps provide overflow areas as well as more primitive settings for those who are looking for more of a wilderness experience.

Campsites, facilities: There are 11 sites for tents and RVs up to 22 feet long. Picnic tables and fire grills are provided. Vault toilets are available. No drinking water is available. Leashed pets are permitted.

Reservations, fees: Reserve at 877/444-6777 ($9 reservation fee) or website: www.Reserve Usa.com; $13 per night, $5 for each additional vehicle. Open June through October.

Directions: From Fresno, drive north on Highway 41 for 46 miles to the town of Oakhurst. Continue north on Highway 41 for five miles to Sky Ranch Road/County Road 632. Turn east on County Road 632 and drive about five miles to Forest Road 6540. Turn right on For-

est Road 6540 and drive about three-quarters of a mile to the campground.

Contact: Sierra National Forest, Bass Lake Ranger District, 559/877-2218, fax 559/877-3108.

78 KELTY MEADOW

Rating: 6

On Willow Creek in Sierra National Forest.

Map 10.4, page 528

This primitive campground is often used by campers with horses. It is at Kelty Meadow by Willow Creek. Side-trip options feature nearby Fresno Dome, the Nelder Grove of giant sequoias and, of course, the southern entrance to nearby Yosemite National Park. The elevation is 5,800 feet.

Campsites, facilities: There are 11 sites for tents and RVs up to 22 feet long. Fire grills and picnic tables are provided. Vault toilets and stock-handling facilities are available. No drinking water is available. Leashed pets are permitted.

Reservations, fees: Reservations are not accepted. The fee is $11 per night, $5 for each additional vehicle. Reservations required for equestrians, 877/444-6777 ($9 reservation fee) or website: www.ReserveUsa.com. Senior discount available. Open June through October.

Directions: From Oakhurst on Highway 41, drive five miles north to Sky Ranch Road/County Road 632. Turn northeast on County Road 632 and drive about 10 miles to the campground.

Contact: Sierra National Forest, Bass Lake Ranger District, 559/877-2218, fax 559/877-3108.

79 FRESNO DOME

Rating: 7

On Big Creek in Sierra National Forest.

Map 10.4, page 528

This camp is named after nearby Fresno Dome to the east, at 7,540 feet the dominating feature in the surrounding landscape. The trailhead for a mile hike to its top is two miles curving down the road to the east. This camp is set at 6,400 feet on Big Creek in Sierra National Forest, a good option to nearby Yosemite National Park.

Campsites, facilities: There are 15 sites for tents or RVs up to 22 feet long. Picnic tables and fire grills are provided. Pit toilets are available. No drinking water is available. Garbage must be packed out. Leashed pets are permitted.

Reservations, fees: Reservations are not accepted. The fee is $13 per night, $5 for each additional vehicle. Senior discount available. Open June through mid-October.

Directions: From Oakhurst, drive north on Highway 41 about 15 miles to Jackson Road/Forest Road 6S07. Turn right and drive six miles to the campground on the left.

Contact: Sierra National Forest, Bass Lake Ranger District, 559/877-2218, fax 559/877-3108.

80 TEXAS FLAT GROUP CAMP

Rating: 5

On the North Fork of Willow Creek in Sierra National Forest.

Map 10.4, page 528

If you are on your honeymoon, this definitely ain't the place. Unless you like the smell of horses, that is. It's a pretty enough spot, set along the North Fork of Willow Creek, but the camp is primitive and designed for groups with horses. This camp is 15 miles from the south entrance of Yosemite National Park and 15 miles north of Bass Lake. The elevation is 5,500 feet.

Campsites, facilities: There are four sites for tents or RVs up to 22 feet long. Fire grills and picnic tables are provided. Vault toilets and stock-handling facilities are available. No drinking water is available. Leashed pets are permitted.

Reservations, fees: Reservations are required.

Reserve at 877/444-6777 ($9 reservation fee) or website: www. reserveusa.com; $44–66 per night. Open June through November.

Directions: From Fresno, drive about 52 miles north on Highway 41 to Sky Ranch Road/County Road 632. Turn east on Sky Ranch Road/County Road 632 and drive approximately five miles to Forest Road 6S40. Turn right on Forest Road 6S40 and drive about three-quarters of a mile to Forest 6538. Turn left on Forest Road 6538 and drive 2.5 miles to the campground.

Contact: Sierra National Forest, Bass Lake Ranger District, 559/877-2218, fax 559/877-3108.

81 GLASS CREEK

Rating: 5

In Inyo National Forest.

Map 10.5, page 529

This primitive camp is set along Glass Creek at 7,600 feet, about a mile from Obsidian Dome to the nearby west. A trail follows Glass Creek past the southern edge of the dome, a craggy, volcanic formation that tops out at 8,611 feet in elevation. That trail continues along Glass Creek, climbing to the foot of San Joaquin Mountain for a great view of the high desert to the east. Insider's note: the Department of Fish and Game stocks Glass Creek with trout just once each June, right at the camp.

Campsites, facilities: There are 50 sites for tents or RVs up to 40 feet long. Picnic tables and fire grills are provided. Vault toilets are available. No drinking water is available. Leashed pets are permitted.

Reservations, fees: Reservations are not accepted. There is no fee for camping. Open mid-May through October, weather permitting.

Directions: From Lee Vining, drive south on U.S. 395 (past the first Highway 158/June lake Loop turnoff) for 11 miles to June Lake Junction. Continue south on U.S. 395 for six miles to a Forest Service road (Glass Creek Road). Turn west (right) and drive a quarter mile to the camp access road on the right. Turn right and continue a half mile to the main camp at the end of the road. Two notes: 1. A primitive area with large RV sites can be used as an overflow area on the right side of the access road. 2. If arriving from the south on U.S. 395, a direct left turn to Glass Creek Road is impossible. Heading north you will pass the CalTrans Crestview Maintenance Station on the right. Continue north, make a U-turn when possible, and follow the above directions.

Contact: Inyo National Forest, Mono Lake Visitor Center, 760/647-3044, fax 760/647-3046.

82 DEADMAN/OBSIDIAN FLAT GROUP

Rating: 5

On Deadman Creek in Inyo National Forest.
Map 10.5, page 529
This little-known camp is set at 7,800 feet along little Deadman Creek. It is primitive and dusty in the summer, cold in the early summer and fall. From camp, hikers can drive west for three miles to the headwaters of Deadman Creek and to a trailhead for a route that runs past San Joaquin Mountain and beyond to little Yost Lake, a one-way hike of four miles.

Campsites, facilities: There are 30 sites for tents or RVs up to 40 feet long, and the group camp, Obsidian Flat, is nearby. Picnic tables and fire grills are provided. Vault toilets are available. No drinking water is available. Leashed pets are permitted.

Reservations, fees: No reservations are accepted and there is no fee at Deadman. Reservations required at Obsidian Group; reserve at 877/444-6777 ($9 reservation fee) or website: www.ReserveUsa.com; $20 per night per group site, no fee for individual sites. Open late May to mid-October, weather permitting.

Directions: From Lee Vining, drive south on U.S. 395 (past the first Highway 158/June Lake Loop turnoff) to June Lake Junction. Continue south for 6.5 miles to a Forest Service road (Deadman Creek Road) on the west (right) side of the road. Turn west (right) and drive two miles to the camp access road on the right. Turn right and drive a half mile to the camp. Note: if you are arriving from the south on U.S. 395 and you reach the CalTrans Crestview Maintenance Station on the right, you have gone one mile too far; make a U-turn when possible and return for access.)

Contact: Inyo National Forest, Mono Lake Visitor Center, 760/647-3044, fax 760/647-3046.

83 BIG SPRINGS

Rating: 5

On Deadman Creek in Inyo National Forest.
Map 10.5, page 529
Big Springs, at 7,300 feet, is set on the edge of the high desert on the east side of U.S. 395. The main attractions are Deadman Creek, which runs right by the camp, and Big Springs, which is set just on the opposite side of the river. There are several hot springs in the area, best reached by driving south on U.S. 395 to the Mammoth Lakes Airport and turning left on Hot Creek Road. As with all hot springs, use at your own risk.

Campsites, facilities: There are 26 sites for tents or RVs up to 40 feet long. Picnic tables and fire grills are provided. Vault toilets are available. No drinking water is available. Leashed pets are permitted.

Reservations, fees: Reservations are not accepted. There is no fee for camping. Open late April through early November, weather permitting.

Directions: From Lee Vining, drive south on U.S. 395 (past the first Highway 158/June lake Loop turnoff) to June Lake Junction. Continue south for about seven miles to Owens River Road. Turn east (left) and drive two miles to a fork. Bear left at the fork and drive a quarter mile to the camp on the left side of the road.

Contact: Inyo National Forest, Mono Lake Visitor Center, 760/647-3044, fax 760/647-3046.

84 PINE GLEN

Rating: 6

In Inyo National Forest.

Map 10.5, page 529

This is a well-situated base camp for several side trips. The most popular is the trip to Devils Postpile National Monument, with a shuttle ride from the Mammoth Ski Area. Other nearby trips include exploring Inyo Craters, Mammoth Lakes, and the hot springs at Hot Creek east of Mammoth Lakes Airport. The elevation is 7,800 feet.

Campsites, facilities: There are 11 family sites (used as overflow from Old Shady Rest and New Shady Rest campgrounds) and six group sites for tents or RVs. Most family sites will accommodate RVs up to 51 feet in length and some up to 55 feet. Picnic tables and fire grills are provided. Drinking water, flush toilets, and RV dump station are available. A grocery store, coin laundry, propane gas, and horseback riding facilities are nearby in Mammoth Lakes. Leashed pets are permitted.

Reservations, fees: Reservations are not accepted. The fee is $13 per night. Senior discount available. Reservations are required for group sites; reserve at 877/444-6777 ($9 reservation fee) or website: www.ReserveUsa.com; $35–50 for group sites. Open late May through September.

Directions: From Lee Vining on U.S. 395, drive south for 25 miles to Mammoth Junction and Highway 203/Minaret Summit Road. Turn west on Highway 203 and drive about three miles to the Mammoth Lakes Visitor Center. Just past the visitor center, turn right on Old Sawmill Road and drive a short distance to the campground.

Contact: Inyo National Forest, Mammoth Lakes Visitor Center, 760/924-5500, fax 760/924-5547.

85 NEW SHADY REST

Rating: 6

In Inyo National Forest.

Map 10.5, page 529

This easy-to-reach camp is set at 7,800 feet, not far from the Mammoth Mountain Ski Area. The surrounding Inyo National Forest provides many side-trip opportunities, including Devils Postpile National Monument by shuttle available from near the Mammoth Mountain Ski Area, Upper San Joaquin River, and the Inyo National Forest backcountry trails, streams, and lakes. The camp is open for walk-in, tent-only camping during the winter.

Campsites, facilities: There are 94 sites for tents or RVs, most of which will accommodate RVs up to 38 feet in length and some up to 55 feet. Picnic tables and fire grills are provided. Drinking water and flush toilets are available. RV dump station, playground, grocery store, coin laundry, and propane gas are available nearby. Leashed pets are permitted.

Reservations, fees: Reservations are not accepted. The fee is $13 per night with a 14-day limit. Senior discount available. Open late May to mid-October, weather permitting.

Directions: From Lee Vining on U.S. 395, drive south for 25 miles to Mammoth Junction and Highway 203/Minaret Summit Road. Turn west on Highway 203 and drive about three miles to the Mammoth Lakes Visitor Center. Just past the visitor center, turn right on Old Sawmill Road and drive a short distance to the campground.

Contact: Inyo National Forest, Mammoth Lakes Visitor Center, 760/924-5500, fax 760/924-5547.

86 OLD SHADY REST

Rating: 6

In Inyo National Forest.

Map 10.5, page 529

Names such as "Old Shady Rest" are usually

reserved for mom-and-pop RV parks. The Forest Service respected tradition in officially naming this park what the locals have called it all along. Like New Shady Rest, this camp is near the Mammoth Lakes Visitor Center, with the same side trips available. It is one of three camps in the immediate vicinity. The elevation is 7,800 feet.

Campsites, facilities: There are 51 sites for tents or RVs, most of which can accommodate RVs up to 40 feet in length and some up to 55 feet. Picnic tables and fire grills are provided. Drinking water and flush toilets are available. An RV dump station, playground, grocery store, coin laundry, and propane gas are available nearby. Leashed pets are permitted.

Reservations, fees: Reservations are not accepted. The fee is $13 per night with a 14-day limit. Senior discount available. Open mid-June through early September.

Directions: From Lee Vining on U.S. 395, drive south for 25 miles to Mammoth Junction and Highway 203/Minaret Summit Road. Turn west on Highway 203 and drive about three miles to the Forest Service Visitor Center. Just past the visitor center turn right and drive .3 mile to the campground.

Contact: Inyo National Forest, Mammoth Lakes Visitor Center, 760/924-5500, fax 760/924-5547.

87 MAMMOTH MOUNTAIN RV PARK

Rating: 6

Near Mammoth Lakes.
Map 10.5, page 529

This RV park is just across the street from the Forest Service Visitor Center. Got a question? Someone there has got an answer. This camp is open year-round, making it a great place to stay for a ski trip.

Campsites, facilities: There are 185 sites, some with full hookups, including cable TV, for tents and RVs. Fire grills are provided. Restrooms, drinking water, showers, picnic tables, modem

access (in office), RV dump station, coin laundry, swimming pool, RV supplies, and a whirlpool are available. Some facilities are wheelchair-accessible. Supplies can be obtained in Mammoth Lakes, a quarter-mile away. Leashed pets are permitted.

Reservations, fees: Reservations are accepted. The fee is $25–30 per night, $2 per night for each extra vehicle. Major credit cards accepted. Open year-round.

Directions: From Lee Vining on U.S. 395, drive south for 25 miles to Mammoth Junction and Highway 203. Turn west on Highway 203 and drive three miles to the park on the left.

From Bishop, drive 40 miles north on Highway 395 to Mammoth Lakes exit. Turn west on Highway 203, go under the overpass, and drive three miles to the park on the left.

Contact: Mammoth Mountain RV Park, 760/934-3822, fax 760/934-1896, website: www.camp grounds.com/mammoth.

88 TWIN LAKES

Rating: 8

In Inyo National Forest.
Map 10.5, page 529

From Twin Lakes, you can look west and see pretty Twin Falls, a wide cascade that runs into the head of upper Twin Lake. There are actually two camps here, one on each side of the access road, at 8,600 feet. Lower Twin Lake is a favorite for fly fishers in float tubes.

Campsites, facilities: There are 95 sites for tents and RVs, most of which can accommodate RVs up to 38 feet long and some up to 55 feet. Picnic tables and fire grills are provided. Drinking water, flush toilets, boat launch, and horseback riding facilities are available. A grocery store, coin laundry, coin showers, and propane gas are available nearby. Some facilities are wheelchair-accessible. Leashed pets are permitted.

Reservations, fees: Reservations are not accepted. The fee is $14 per night, seven-day limit.

Senior discount available. Open mid-May to late October.

Directions: From Lee Vining on U.S. 395, drive south for 25 miles to Mammoth Junction and Highway 203/Minaret Summit Road. Turn west on Highway 203 and drive four miles to Lake Mary Road. Continue straight through the intersection and drive 2.3 miles to Twin Lakes Loop Road. Turn right and drive a half mile to the campground.

Contact: Inyo National Forest, Mammoth Lakes Visitor Center, 760/924-5500, fax 760/924-5547.

89 LAKE MARY

Rating: 9

In Inyo National Forest.

Map 10.5, page 529

Lake Mary is the star of the Mammoth Lakes region. Of the 11 lakes in the area, this is the largest. It provides a resort, boat ramp, and boat rentals, and it receives the highest number of trout stocks. It is set at 8,900 feet in a place of incredible natural beauty, one of the few spots that literally has it all. Of course, that often includes quite a few other people. If there are too many for you, an excellent trailhead is available at nearby Coldwater camp.

Campsites, facilities: There are 48 sites for tents or RVs up to 30 feet long. Picnic tables and fire grills are provided. Drinking water and flush toilets are available. A grocery store, coin laundry, and propane gas are nearby. Leashed pets are permitted.

Reservations, fees: Reservations are not accepted. The fee is $14 per night with a 14-day limit. Senior discount available. Open mid-June to mid-September.

Directions: From Lee Vining on U.S. 395, drive south for 25 miles to Mammoth Junction and Highway 203/Minaret Summit Road. Turn west on Highway 203 and drive four miles to Lake Mary Road. Continue straight through the intersection and drive 3.6 miles to Lake

Mary Loop Drive. Turn right and drive a half mile to the campground entrance.

Contact: Inyo National Forest, Mammoth Lakes Visitor Center, 760/924-5500, fax 760/924-5547.

90 PINE CITY

Rating: 7

Near Lake Mary in Inyo National Forest.

Map 10.5, page 529

This camp is at the edge of Lake Mary at an elevation of 8,900 feet. This camp is popular for both families and fly fishers with float tubes.

Campsites, facilities: There are 10 sites for tents or RVs, most of which can accommodate RVs up to 40 feet in length and some up to 50 feet. Picnic tables and fire grills are provided. Drinking water and flush toilets are available. A grocery store, a coin laundry, and propane gas are available nearby. Some facilities are wheelchair-accessible. Leashed pets are permitted.

Reservations, fees: Reservations are not accepted. The fee is $14 fee per night. Senior discount available. Open late June to mid-September.

Directions: From Lee Vining on U.S. 395, drive south for 25 miles to Mammoth Junction and Highway 203/Minaret Summit Road. Turn west on Highway 203 and drive four miles to Lake Mary Road. Continue straight through the intersection and drive 3.6 miles to Lake Mary Loop Drive. Turn left and drive a quarter mile to the campground.

Contact: Inyo National Forest, Mammoth Lakes Visitor Center, 760/924-5500, fax 760/924-5547.

91 COLDWATER

Rating: 7

On Coldwater Creek in Inyo National Forest.

Map 10.5, page 529

While this camp is not the first choice of many simply because there is no lake view, it has a special attraction all its own. First, it is a two-minute drive from the campground to Lake

Mary, where there is a boat ramp, rentals, and good trout fishing. Second, at the end of the campground access road is a trailhead for two outstanding hikes. From the Y at the trailhead, if you head right, you will be routed up Cold-water Creek to Emerald Lake, a great little hike. If you head to the left, you will have a more ambitious trip to Arrowhead, Skelton, and Red Lakes, all within three miles. The elevation is 8,900 feet.

Campsites, facilities: There are 77 sites for tents or RVs, most of which can accommodate RVs up to 37 feet in length and some up to 50 feet. Picnic tables and fire grills are provided. Drinking water, flush toilets, and horse facilities are available. You can buy supplies in Mammoth Lakes. Leashed pets are permitted.

Reservations, fees: Reservations are not accepted. The fee is $14 per night with a 14-day limit. Senior discount available. Open mid-June to late September.

Directions: From Lee Vining on U.S. 395, drive south for 25 miles to Mammoth Junction and Highway 203/Minaret Summit Road. Turn west on Highway 203 and drive four miles to Lake Mary Road. Continue straight through the intersection and drive 3.6 miles to Lake Mary Loop Drive. Turn left and drive .6 mile to the camp entrance road.

Contact: Inyo National Forest, Mammoth Lakes Visitor Center, 760/924-5500, fax 760/924-5547.

92 SHERWIN CREEK

Rating: 7

In Inyo National Forest.

Map 10.5, page 529

This camp is set along little Sherwin Creek, at 7,600 feet in elevation, a short distance from the town of Mammoth Lakes. If you drive a mile east on Sherwin Creek Road, then turn right at the short spur road, you will find a trailhead for a hike that is routed up six miles to Valentine Lake in the John Muir Wilderness, set on the northwest flank of Bloody Mountain.

Campsites, facilities: There are 87 sites for tents or RVs, most of which can accommodate RVs up to 34 feet in length and some up to 50 feet, and 15 walk-in sites for tents only. Picnic tables and fire grills are provided. Drinking water and flush toilets are available. Leashed pets are permitted.

Reservations, fees: Reservations are accepted for 58 sites, including the 15 walk-in sites, $13 per night, 21-day limit. Senior discount available. Open mid-May through mid-September.

Directions: From Lee Vining on U.S. 395, drive south for 25 miles to Mammoth Junction and Highway 203/Minaret Summit Road. Turn west on Highway 203 and drive about three miles to the Mammoth Lakes Visitor Center and continue a short distance to Old Mammoth Road. Turn left and drive about a mile to Sherwin Creek. Turn south and drive two miles on largely unpaved road to the campground on the left side of the road.

Contact: Inyo National Forest, Mammoth Lakes Visitor Center, 760/924-5500, fax 760/924-5547.

93 CONVICT LAKE

Rating: 7

In Inyo National Forest.

Map 10.5, page 529

After driving in the stark desert on U.S. 395 to get here, it is always astonishing to clear the rise and see Convict Lake (7,583 feet) and its gemlike waters set in a mountain bowl beneath a back wall of high, jagged wilderness peaks. The camp is right beside Convict Creek, about a quarter mile from Convict Lake. Both provide very good trout fishing, including some rare monster-sized brown trout below the Convict Lake outlet. Fishing is often outstanding in Convict Lake, with a chance of hooking a 10- or 15-pound trout. A bonus is an outstanding resort with a boat launch, boat rentals, cabin rentals, small store, restaurant, and bar. Horseback rides and hiking are also available, with a trail routed along the north side of the lake, then along upper Convict Creek (a stream crossing is required about three miles in), and into the John Muir Wilderness. This is the most popular camp in the Mammoth area and it is frequently full. While the lake rates a 10 for scenic beauty, the camp itself is in a stark desert setting, out of sight of the lake, plus it can get windy and cold here because of the exposed sites.

Campsites, facilities: There are 88 sites for tents or RVs, most of which can accommodate RVs up to 41 feet in length and some up to 55 feet. Rental cabins are also available through the Convict Lake Resort. Picnic tables and fire grills are provided. Drinking water and flush toilets are available. RV dump station, boat ramp, store, restaurant, and horseback riding facilities are available nearby. Leashed pets are permitted.

Reservations, fees: Reservations are not accepted. The fee is $13 per night, seven-day limit. Senior discount available. For cabins, reservations advised, 800/992-2260. Open late April through October; cabins open year-round.

Directions: From Lee Vining on U.S. 395, drive south for 31 miles (five miles past Mammoth Junction) to Convict Lake Road (adjacent to Mammoth Lakes Airport). Turn west (right) on Convict Lake Road and drive two miles to Convict Lake. Cross the dam and drive a short distance to the campground entrance road on the left. Turn left and drive a quarter mile to the campground.

Contact: Inyo National Forest, Mammoth Lakes Visitor Center, 760/924-5500, fax 760/924-5537; Convict Lake Resort & Cabins, 800/992-2260.

94 MCGEE CREEK RV PARK

Rating: 6

Near Crowley Lake.
Map 10.5, page 529
This is a popular layover spot for folks visiting giant Crowley Lake. Crowley Lake is still one of the better lakes in the Sierra for trout fishing, with good prospects for large rainbow trout and brown trout, though the 20-pound brown trout that once made this lake famous are now mainly a legend. Beautiful Convict Lake provides a nearby side-trip option. It is also about nine miles to Rock Creek Lake, a beautiful high-mountain destination. The elevation is 7,000 feet.

Campsites, facilities: There are 31 sites with partial or full hookups for tents or RVs. Picnic tables and fire pits are provided. Restrooms, drinking water, showers, and flush toilets are available. Leashed pets are permitted.

Reservations, fees: Reservations are accepted. The fee is $20–30 per night, $4 for showers. Weekly and monthly rates available. Open late April through mid-October.

Directions: From the junction of U.S. 395 and Highway 203 (the Mammoth Lakes turnoff), drive south on U.S. 395 for 10 miles to the turnoff for McGee Creek Road. Take that exit and look for the park entrance on the left.

Contact: McGee Creek RV Park, 760/935-4233.

95 MCGEE CREEK

Rating: 7

In Inyo National Forest.
Map 10.5, page 529
This is a Forest Service camp at an elevation of 7,600 feet, set along little McGee Creek, a good location for fishing and hiking. The stream is stocked with trout, and a trailhead is just up the road. From here you can hike along upper McGee Creek and into the John Muir Wilderness.

Campsites, facilities: There are 28 sites for tents or RVs up to 22 feet long. Picnic tables and fire grills are provided. Drinking water and flush toilets are available. Some facilities are wheelchair-accessible. Leashed pets are permitted.

Reservations, fees: Reserve at 877/444-6777 ($9 reservation fee) or website: www.Reserve

Usa.com; $15 per night. Senior discount available. Open May through September.

Directions: From Mammoth Lakes at the junction of U.S. 395 and Highway 203, drive south on U.S. 395 for 8.5 miles to McGee Creek Road (signed). Turn right (toward the Sierra) and drive 1.5 miles to the campground.

Contact: Inyo National Forest, White Mountain Ranger District, 760/873-2500, fax 760/873-2563.

96 CROWLEY LAKE

Rating: 5

Near Crowley Lake.

Map 10.5, page 529

This large BLM camp is across U.S. 395 from the south shore of Crowley Lake. Crowley is the trout-fishing capital of the eastern Sierra, with the annual opener (the last Saturday in April) a great celebration. Though the trout fishing can go through a lull in midsummer, it can become excellent again in the fall when the lake's population of big brown trout heads up to the top of the lake and the mouth of the Owens River. The surroundings are fairly stark; the elevation is 6,800 feet.

Campsites, facilities: There are 47 sites for tents or RVs. Picnic tables and fire grills are provided. Vault toilets are available. No drinking water is available. A grocery store and boat ramp are nearby on Crowley Lake. Leashed pets are permitted.

Reservations, fees: Reservations are not accepted. There is no fee for camping. Open late April through October, weather permitting.

Directions: Drive on U.S. 395 to the Crowley Lake Road exit (21 miles north of Bishop). Take that exit west (toward the Sierra) to Crowley Lake Road and drive northwest for 5.5 miles (past Tom's Place) to the campground entrance on the left (well signed).

Contact: Bureau of Land Management, Bishop Field Office, 760/872-4881, fax 760/872-5050.

97 FRENCH CAMP

Rating: 5

On Rock Creek near Crowley Lake in Inyo National Forest.

Map 10.5, page 529

French Camp is just a short hop from U.S. 395 and Tom's Place, right where the high Sierra turns into high plateau country. Side-trip opportunities include boating and fishing on giant Crowley Lake and, to the west on Rock Creek Road, visiting little Rock Creek Lake 10 miles away. The elevation is 7,500 feet.

Campsites, facilities: There are six sites for tents only and 80 sites for tents or RVs up to 22 feet long. Picnic tables and fire grills are provided. Drinking water, flush toilets, and RV dump station are available. You can buy groceries nearby. Leashed pets are permitted.

Reservations, fees: Reservations are accepted for sites 1–30 and 73–86; reserve at 877/444-6777 ($9 reservation fee) or website: www.Reserve Usa.com; $15 per night. Senior discount available. Open late April through October.

Directions: From Mammoth Lakes at the junction of U.S. 395 and Highway 203, drive south on U.S. 395 for 15 miles to Tom's Place and Rock Creek Road. Turn right (toward the Sierra) at Rock Creek Road and drive a quarter mile to the campground on the right.

Contact: Inyo National Forest, White Mountain Ranger District, 760/873-2500, fax 760/873-2563.

98 HOLIDAY

Rating: 5

Near Crowley Lake in Inyo National Forest.

Map 10.5, page 529

There's a story behind every name. The story here is that this camp is open only on holiday weekends. It is near Rock Creek, not far from Crowley Lake. The elevation is 7,500 feet, with surroundings far more stark than the camps to the west on Rock Creek Road.

Campsites, facilities: There are 35 sites for tents or RVs up to 22 feet long. Picnic tables and fire grills are provided. Drinking water and flush toilets are available. You can buy groceries nearby. Leashed pets are permitted.

Reservations, fees: Reservations are not accepted. The fee is $15 per night. Senior discount available. Opened as necessary.

Directions: From Mammoth Lakes at the junction of U.S. 395 and Highway 203, drive south on U.S. 395 for 15 miles south to Tom's Place and Rock Creek Road. Turn right (toward the Sierra) and drive a half mile to the campground on the left.

Contact: Inyo National Forest, White Mountain Ranger District, 760/873-2500, fax 760/873-2563.

99 TUFF

Rating: 5

Near Crowley Lake in Inyo National Forest.
Map 10.5, page 529

Easy access off U.S. 395 makes this camp a winner, though it is not nearly as pretty as those up Rock Creek Road to the west of Tom's Place. The fact that you can get in and out of here quickly makes it ideal for campers planning fishing trips to nearby Crowley Lake. The elevation is 7,000 feet.

Campsites, facilities: There are 15 sites for tents only and 19 sites for tents or RVs up to 22 feet long. Picnic tables and fire grills are provided. Drinking water and flush toilets are available. Leashed pets are permitted.

Reservations, fees: Reserve at 877/444-6777 ($9 reservation fee) or website: www.Reserve Usa.com; $15 per night. Senior discount available. Open late April through mid-October.

Directions: From Mammoth Lakes at the junction of U.S. 395 and Highway 203, drive south on U.S. 395 for 15.5 miles (one mile north of

Tom's Place) to Rock Creek Road. Turn right (toward the Sierra) on Rock Creek Road and drive a half mile to the campground.

Contact: Inyo National Forest, White Mountain Ranger District, 760/873-2500, fax 760/873-2563.

100 ASPEN GROUP CAMP

Rating: 7

Near Crowley Lake in Inyo National Forest.
Map 10.5, page 529

This small group campground set on Rock Creek is used primarily as a base camp for anglers and campers heading to nearby Crowley Lake or venturing west to Rock Creek Lake. The elevation at the camp is 8,100 feet.

Campsites, facilities: There is one group camp for tents or RVs up to 16 feet long. Picnic tables and fire grills are provided. Drinking water and flush toilets are available. You can buy supplies in Tom's Place, three miles away. Leashed pets are permitted.

Reservations, fees: Reserve at 877/444-6777 ($9 reservation fee) or website: www.Reserve Usa.com; $55 group fee per night. Open mid-May through mid-October.

Directions: From Mammoth Lakes at the junction of U.S. 395 and Highway 203, drive south on U.S. 395 for 15 miles south to Tom's Place and Rock Creek Road. Turn right (toward the Sierra) at Rock Creek Road and drive three miles to the campground.

Contact: Inyo National Forest, White Mountain Ranger District, 760/873-2500, fax 760/873-2563.

101 IRIS MEADOW

Rating: 5

Near Crowley Lake in Inyo National Forest.
Map 10.5, page 529

Iris Meadow, at 8,300 feet elevation on the flank of Red Mountain (11,472 feet), is the first in a series of five Forest Service camps set near Rock Creek Canyon on the road leading from Tom's Place up to pretty Rock Creek Lake. Rock Creek is stocked with trout, and nearby Rock Creek Lake also provides fishing and boating for hand-launched boats. This camp also has access to a great trailhead for wilderness exploration.

Campsites, facilities: There are 14 sites for tents or RVs up to 22 feet long. Picnic tables and fire grills are provided. Drinking water and flush toilets are available. You can buy supplies in Tom's Place, three miles away. Leashed pets are permitted.

Reservations, fees: Reservations are not accepted. The fee is $12 per night. Open late June through early September.

Directions: From Mammoth Lakes at the junction of U.S. 395 and Highway 203, drive south on U.S. 395 for 15 miles south to Tom's Place and Rock Creek Road. Turn right (toward the Sierra) at Rock Creek Road and drive three miles to the campground.

Contact: Inyo National Forest, White Mountain Ranger District, 760/873-2500, fax 760/873-2563.

102 BIG MEADOW

Rating: 8

Near Crowley Lake in Inyo National Forest.
Map 10.5, page 529

This is a smaller, quieter camp in the series of campgrounds along Rock Creek. Beautiful Rock Creek Lake provides a nearby side trips. The elevation is 8,600 feet. In the fall, turning aspens here make for spectacular colors.

Campsites, facilities: There are five sites for tents only and six sites for tents or RVs up to 22 feet long. Picnic tables and fire grills are provided. Drinking water and flush toilets are available. You can buy supplies in Tom's Place, four miles away. Leashed pets are permitted.

Reservations, fees: Reservations are not accepted.

The fee is $16 per night. Senior discount available. Open late May through early September.

Directions: From Mammoth Lakes at the junction of U.S. 395 and Highway 203, drive south on U.S. 395 for 15 miles south to Tom's Place and Rock Creek Road. Turn right (toward the Sierra) at Rock Creek Road and drive four miles to the campground.

Contact: Inyo National Forest, White Mountain Ranger District, 760/873-2500, fax 760/873-2563.

103 PALISADE

Rating: 8

Near Crowley Lake in Inyo National Forest.
Map 10.5, page 529

This shoe might just fit. Palisade, a tiny campground, provides a pretty spot along Rock Creek at 8,600 feet in elevation, with many side-trip options. The closest is fishing for small trout on Rock Creek and at pretty Rock Creek Lake up the road to the west. The area is loaded with aspens.

Campsites, facilities: There are two sites for tents only and three sites for tents or RVs up to 22 feet long. Picnic tables and fire grills are provided. Drinking water and flush toilets are available. Horseback riding facilities are available nearby. You can buy supplies in Tom's Place, five miles away. Leashed pets are permitted.

Reservations, fees: Reservations are not accepted. The fee is $15 per night. Senior discount available. Open from late June through early September.

Directions: From Mammoth Lakes at the junction of U.S. 395 and Highway 203, drive south on U.S. 395 for 15 miles south to Tom's Place and Rock Creek Road. Turn right (toward the Sierra) at Rock Creek Road and drive five miles to the campground.

Contact: Inyo National Forest, White Mountain Ranger District, 760/873-2500, fax 760/873-2563.

104 EAST FORK

Rating: 8

Near Crowley Lake in Inyo National Forest.
Map 10.5, page 529

This is a beautiful, popular campground set along East Fork Rock Creek at 9,000 feet elevation. The camp is only three miles from Rock Creek Lake, where there's an excellent trailhead.

Campsites, facilities: There are 133 sites for tents or RVs up to 22 feet long. Picnic tables and fire grills are provided. Drinking water and flush toilets are available. You can buy supplies in Tom's Place and at Rock Creek Lake Resort. Leashed pets are permitted.

Reservations, fees: Reservations are accepted for sites 16–57 and 102–127; reserve at 877/444-6777 ($9 reservation fee) or website: www.Reserve Usa.com; $15 per night. Senior discount available. Open mid-May through October.

Directions: From Mammoth Lakes at the junction of U.S. 395 and Highway 203, drive south on U.S. 395 for 15 miles south to Tom's Place and Rock Creek Road. Turn right (toward the Sierra) at Rock Creek Road and drive five miles to the campground access road on the left.

Contact: Inyo National Forest, White Mountain Ranger District, 760/873-2500, fax 760/873-2563.

105 ROCK CREEK LAKE

Rating: 9

In Inyo National Forest.
Map 10.5, page 529

Rock Creek Lake, set at an elevation of 9,600 feet, is a small but beautiful lake that features cool, clear water, small trout, and a great trailhead for access to the adjacent John Muir Wilderness. The setting is drop-dead beautiful, hence the high rating for scenic beauty, but note that the campsites are set closely to-

gether, side by side, in a paved parking area. Note that at times, especially afternoons in late spring, winds out of the west can be cold and pesky at the lake. If this campground is full, the nearby Mosquito Flat walk-in campground provides an option. Note that Mosquito Flat has a limit of one night and is designed as a staging area for wilderness backpacking trips.

Campsites, facilities: There are 28 sites for tents or RVs up to 22 feet long, and one group site for up to 50 people. Picnic tables and fire grills are provided. Drinking water and flush toilets are available. You can buy supplies in Tom's Place and at the Rock Creek Lake Resort. Leashed pets are permitted.

Reservations, fees: Reservations are not accepted. The fee is $16 per night. Senior discount available. Reservations required for group site at 877/444-6777 ($9 reservation fee) or website: www.ReserveUsa.com; $45 per night. Open mid-May through October.

Directions: From the junction of U.S. 395 and Highway 203 (the Mammoth Lakes turnoff), drive 15 miles south on U.S. 395 to Tom's Place. Turn right (toward the Sierra) at Rock Creek Road and drive seven miles to the campground.

Contact: Inyo National Forest, White Mountain Ranger District, 760/873-2500, fax 760/873-2563.

106 PINE GROVE

Rating: 8

Near Crowley Lake in Inyo National Forest.
Map 10.5, page 529

Pine Grove is one of the smaller camps in the series of campgrounds along Rock Creek. Of the five camps in this canyon, this one is the closest to Rock Creek Lake, just a two-mile drive away (Rock Creek Lake Campground is closer, of course). The aspens here are stunning in September, when miles of mountains turn to shimmering golds. The elevation is 9,300 feet.

Campsites, facilities: There are five sites for tents only and six sites for tents or RVs up to

22 feet long. Picnic tables and fire grills are provided. Drinking water and flush toilets are available. Horseback riding facilities are available nearby. You can buy supplies in Tom's Place and at the Rock Creek Lake Resort. Leashed pets are permitted.

Reservations, fees: Reservations are not accepted. The fee is $15 per night. Senior discount available. Open mid-May through mid-October.

Directions: From Mammoth Lakes at the junction of U.S. 395 and Highway 203, drive south on U.S. 395 for 15 miles south to Tom's Place and Rock Creek Road. Turn right (toward the Sierra) at Rock Creek Road and drive seven miles to the campground.

Contact: Inyo National Forest, White Mountain Ranger District, 760/873-2500, fax 760/873-2563.

107 HIGHLANDS RV PARK

Rating: 3

Near Bishop.
Map 10.5, page 529

This is a privately operated RV park near Bishop that is set up for U.S. 395 cruisers. There is an Indian casino in town. A great side trip is up two-lane Highway 168 to Lake Sabrina. The elevation is 4,300 feet.

Campsites, facilities: There are 103 sites with full hookups, including cable TV, for RVs. Picnic tables are provided. Restrooms, drinking water, flush toilets, showers, RV dump station, modem access (in office), propane gas, ice, fish-cleaning station, and coin laundry are available. You can buy groceries nearby (about three blocks away). Leashed pets are permitted.

Reservations, fees: Reservations are recommended. The fee is $25 per night. Weekly and monthly rates available. Open year-round.

Directions: From Bishop, drive two miles north on U.S. 395/North Sierra Highway to the campground on the right at 2275 N. Sierra Highway.

Contact: Highlands RV Park, 760/873-7616.

108 PLEASANT VALLEY

Rating: 7

Near Pleasant Valley Reservoir.
Map 10.5, page 529

Pleasant Valley County Park is set adjacent to long, narrow Pleasant Valley Reservoir, created by the Owens River. It is east of the Sierra range in the high desert plateau country; the elevation is 4,200 feet. That makes it available for year-round fishing. The Owens River passes through the park, providing wild trout fishing, with most anglers practicing catch-and-release fly-fishing. This is also near a major jump-off point for hiking, rock-climbing, and wilderness fishing at the Bishop Pass area to the west. Major additional improvements to this campground were planned for 2003 and 2004. One of the first, implemented in late 2002, was replacing the old pit toilets with new vault toilets. People were lined up for miles to try them out.

Campsites, facilities: There are 200 sites for tents or RVs. Picnic tables and fire grills are provided. Drinking water (hand-pumped well water) and vault toilets are available. Leashed pets are permitted. No hookups.

Reservations, fees: Reservations are not accepted. The fee is $10 per night. Open year-round.

Directions: Drive on U.S. 395 to Pleasant Valley Road (seven miles north of Bishop) on the east side of the road. Turn east and drive one mile to the park entrance.

Contact: Inyo County Parks Department, 760/878-0272, fax 760/873-5599.

© TOM STIENSTRA

Chapter 11
Sequoia and
Kings Canyon

Chapter 11—Sequoia and Kings Canyon

There is no place on earth like the high Sierra, from Mt. Whitney north through Sequoia and Kings Canyon National Parks. This is a paradise filled with deep canyons, high peaks, and fantastic natural beauty, and sprinkled with groves of the largest living things in the history of the earth—giant sequoias.

Though the area is primarily known for the national parks, the campgrounds available span a great variety of settings. The most popular spots, though, are in the vicinity of Sequoia and Kings Canyon National Parks, or on the parks' access roads.

Sooner or later, everyone will want to see the biggest tree of them all—the General Sherman Tree, estimated to be 2,300–2,700 years old with a circumference of 102.6 feet. It is in the Giant Forest at Sequoia National Park. To stand in front of it is to know true awe. That said, we found the Grant Grove and the Muir Grove even more enchanting.

These are among the highlights of a driving tour through both parks. A must for most is taking in the view from Moro Rock, parking, and then making the 300-foot walk up a succession of stairs to reach the 6,725-foot summit. Here you can scan a series of mountain rims and granite peaks, highlighted by the Great Western Divide.

The drive out of Sequoia and into Kings Canyon features rim-of-the-world-type views as you first enter the Kings River canyon. You then descend to the bottom of the canyon, right along the Kings River, gaze up at the high glacial-carved canyon walls, and drive all the way out to Cedar Grove, the end of the road. The canyon rises 8,000 feet from the river to Spanish Peak, the deepest canyon in the continental United States.

Crystal Cave is another point of fascination. Among the formations are adjoined crystal columns that look like the sound pipes in the giant organ at the Mormon Tabernacle. Lights are placed strategically for perfect lighting.

This is only a start. Bears, marmot, and deer are abundant and are commonly seen in Sequoia, especially at Dorst Creek Campground. If you drive up to Mineral King and take a hike, it can seem like the marmot capital of the world.

But this region also harbors many wonderful secrets having nothing to do with the national parks. One of them, for instance, is the Muir Trail Ranch near Florence Lake. The ranch is set in the John Muir Wilderness and requires a trip by foot, boat, or horse to reach it. Other unique launch points for trips into the wilderness lie nearby.

On the western slopes of the Sierra, pretty lakes with good trout fishing include Edison, Florence, and Hume Lakes. Hidden spots in Sierra National Forest provide continual fortune hunts, especially up the Dinkey Creek drainage above Courtright Reservoir. On the eastern slopes, a series of small streams offers good vehicle access; here, too, you'll encounter the beautiful Rock Creek Lake, Sabrina and South Lakes (west of Bishop), and great wilderness trailheads at the end of almost every road.

The remote Golden Trout Wilderness on the southwest flank of Mt. Whitney is one of the most pristine areas in California. Yet it is lost in the shadow of giant Whitney, elevation 14,497.6 feet, the highest point in the continental United States, where hiking has become so popular that reservations are required at each trailhead for overnight use, and quotas are enforced to ensure an undisturbed experience for each visitor.

In the Kernville area, there are a series of campgrounds along the Kern River. Most choose this canyon for one reason: the outstanding white-water rafting and kayaking.

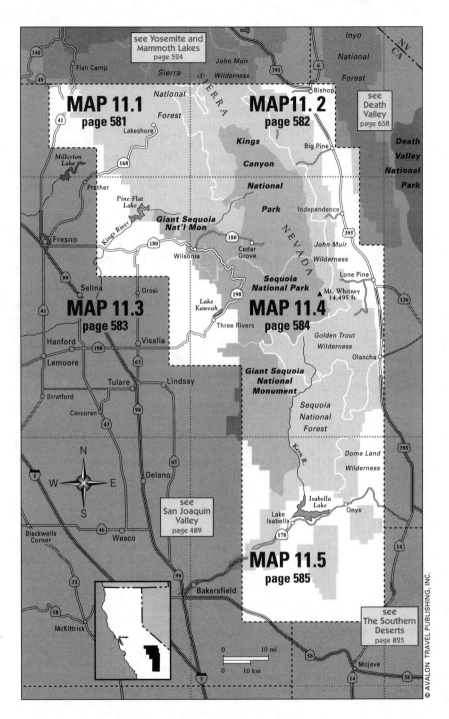

Map 11.1

**Campgrounds 1–36
Pages 586–600**

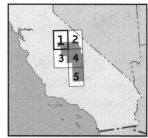

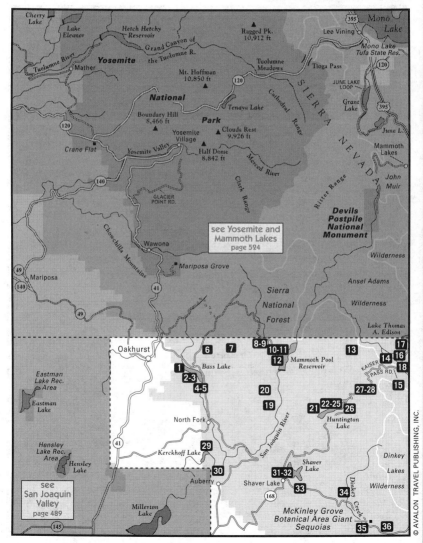

© AVALON TRAVEL PUBLISHING, INC.

Map 11.2

Campgrounds 37–63
Pages 600–610

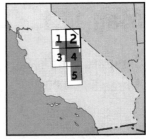

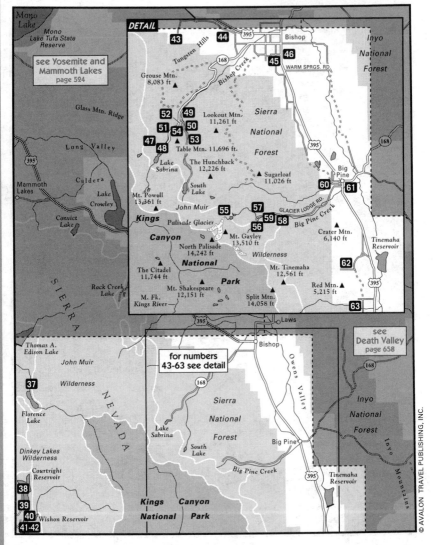

DETAIL

Mono Lake

Mono Lake Tufa State Reserve

see Yosemite and Mammoth Lakes
page 524

Glass Mtn. Ridge

Long Valley

Mammoth Lakes

Caldera

Lake Crowley

Convict Lake

Rock Creek Lake

SIERRA

43 44 **395** Bishop

168

46
45 WARM SPRGS. RD.

Inyo National Forest

Grouse Mtn. 8,083 ft

Tungsten Hills

Bishop Creek

Lookout Mtn. 11,261 ft

Sierra National Forest

52 49
51 50
47 54 53
48

Table Mtn. 11,696 ft.

The Hunchback 12,226 ft

395

168

Lake Sabrina

Mt. Powell 13,361 ft

South Lake

Sugarloaf 11,026 ft

Big Pine

John Muir

Kings

55 57
56 59 58

60
61

GLACIER LODGE RD.

Big Pine Creek

Crater Mtn. 6,140 ft

Tinemaha Reservoir

Palisade Glacier

Canyon

Mt. Gayley 13,510 ft

North Palisade 14,242 ft

Wilderness

The Citadel 11,744 ft

National

Park

Mt. Tinemaha 12,561 ft

62

395

M. Fk. Kings River

Mt. Shakespeare 12,151 ft

Split Mtn. 14,058 ft

Red Mtn. 5,215 ft

63

395 Laws

Thomas A. Edison Lake

John Muir

37

Wilderness

Florence Lake

Dinkey Lakes Wilderness

Courtright Reservoir

38
39
40
41-42

Wishon Reservoir

NEVADA

for numbers 43-63 see detail

Bishop

168

Lake Sabrina

South Lake

Sierra National Forest

Kings Canyon

National Park

Owens Valley

Big Pine Creek

Big Pine

395

Inyo National Forest

Inyo Mountains

Tinemaha Reservoir

see Death Valley page 658

168

© AVALON TRAVEL PUBLISHING, INC.

Map 11.3

Campgrounds 64–73
Pages 610–614

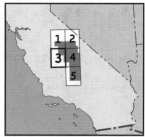

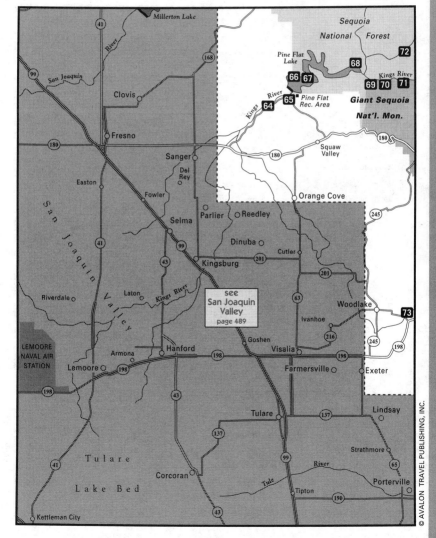

Map 11.4

Campgrounds 74–128
Pages 615–637

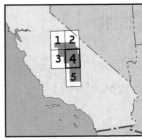

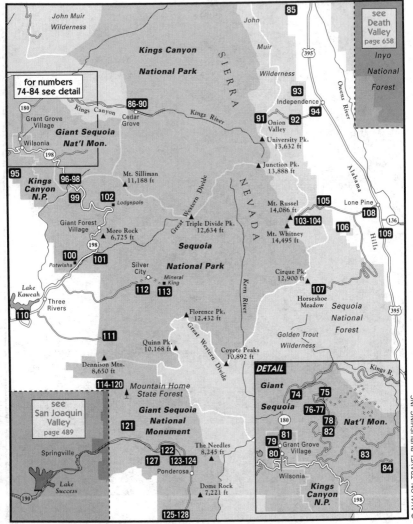

see Death Valley page 658

John Muir Wilderness

Kings Canyon National Park

for numbers 74-84 see detail

Grant Grove Village

Wilsonia

Giant Sequoia Nat'l Mon.

Kings Canyon N.P.

Cedar Grove

Kings Canyon

Kings River

Inyo National Forest

John Muir Wilderness

Independence

Onion Valley

University Pk. 13,632 ft

Owens River

Mt. Silliman 11,188 ft

Lodgepole

Giant Forest Village

Moro Rock 6,725 ft

Potwisha

Lake Kaweah

Three Rivers

Great Western Divide

Triple Divide Pk. 12,634 ft

Sequoia

National Park

Silver City

Mineral King

Junction Pk. 13,888 ft

Mt. Russel 14,086 ft

Mt. Whitney 14,495 ft

Lone Pine

Alabama Hills

Kern River

Cirque Pk. 12,900 ft

Horseshoe Meadow

Sequoia National Forest

Florence Pk. 12,432 ft

Great Western Divide

Quinn Pk. 10,168 ft

Coyote Peaks 10,892 ft

Golden Trout Wilderness

Dennison Mtn. 8,650 ft

Mountain Home State Forest

Giant Sequoia National Monument

see San Joaquin Valley page 489

Springville

The Needles 8,245 ft

Ponderosa

Dome Rock 7,221 ft

Lake Success

DETAIL

Giant Sequoia Nat'l Mon.

Grant Grove Village

Wilsonia

Kings Canyon N.P.

Kings R.

© AVALON TRAVEL PUBLISHING, INC.

Map 11.5

Campgrounds 129–167
Pages 637–653

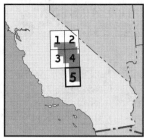

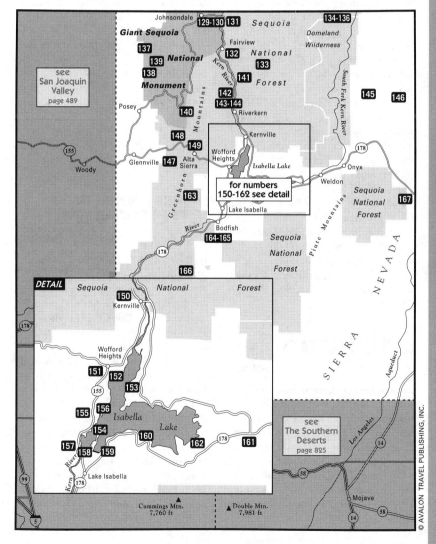

① CRANE VALLEY GROUP AND RECREATION POINT

🏃 🏊 🎣 🚤 🐕 🚐 ⛺

Rating: 8

On Bass Lake in Sierra National Forest.
Map 11.1, page 581

This is a group camp at Bass Lake. Bass Lake is a long, narrow, mountain lake set in the Sierra foothills at 3,400 feet. It's especially popular in the summer for water-skiers.

Campsites, facilities: There are four sites that hold 30–50 people each at Recreation Point Group Camp and seven sites that hold 30–50 people each at Crane Valley Camp. At Recreation Point, picnic tables and fire grills are provided. Drinking water and flush toilets are available. At Crane Valley, picnic tables and fire grills are provided. Vault toilets are available. No drinking water is available. A store is nearby. Leashed pets are permitted.

Reservations, fees: Reserve at 877/444-6777 ($9 reservation fee); $45–74 per night, $5 for each additional vehicle. Open year-round.

Directions: From Fresno, drive north on Highway 41 to Oakhurst and continue 2.5 miles to Yosemite Forks and Bass Lake Road/County Road 222. Turn right at Bass Lake Road and drive four miles to the campground.

Contact: Sierra National Forest, Bass Lake Ranger District, 559/877-2218, fax 559/877-3108.

② FORKS

🏃 🏊 🎣 🚤 🐕 🚐 ⛺

Rating: 8

On Bass Lake in Sierra National Forest.
Map 11.1, page 581

Bass Lake is set in a canyon. It's a long, narrow, deep lake that is popular for fishing in the spring and water-skiing in the summer. It's a pretty spot, set at 3,400 feet in the Sierra National Forest. This is one of several camps at the lake. Boats must be registered at the Bass Lake observation tower after launching. Note

that the only camp on Bass Lake that is open year-round is Lupine-Cedar, except for the group camp.

Campsites, facilities: There are 25 sites for tents only and six sites for tents or RVs up to 22 feet long. Picnic tables and fire grills are provided. Drinking water and flush toilets are available. A store and coin laundry are nearby. Leashed pets are permitted.

Reservations, fees: From Memorial Day through Labor Day, reserve at 877/444-6777 or website: www.ReserveUsa.com ($9 reservation fee); $18 per night, $5 for each additional vehicle. Senior discount available. Open May through September.

Directions: From Fresno, drive north on Highway 41 to Oakhurst and continue 2.5 miles to Yosemite Forks and Bass Lake Road/County Road 222. Turn right at Bass Lake Road and drive six miles (staying right at two forks) to the campground (on the south shore of Bass Lake).

Contact: Sierra National Forest, Bass Lake Ranger District, 559/877-2218, fax 559/877-3108.

③ LUPINE-CEDAR BLUFFS

🏃 🏊 🎣 🚤 🐕 ♿ 🚐 ⛺

Rating: 8

On Bass Lake in Sierra National Forest.
Map 11.1, page 581

This is the camping headquarters at Bass Lake and the only camp open year-round, except for the group camp. Bass Lake is a popular vacation spot, a pretty lake, long and narrow, covering 1,200 acres when full and surrounded by national forest. Most of the campgrounds are filled on weekends and three-day holidays. Fishing is best in the spring for rainbow trout and largemouth bass, and by mid-June water-skiers have usually taken over. Boats must be registered at the Bass Lake observation tower after launching.

Campsites, facilities: There are 113 sites for tents or RVs up to 40 feet long, and several double-family sites. Picnic tables and fire grills are provided. Drinking water and flush toilets are available. Some facilities are wheelchair-accessible. Groceries and a boat ramp are available nearby. Leashed pets are permitted.

Reservations, fees: Reserve at 877/444-6777 or website: www.ReserveUsa.com ($9 reservation fee); $18 per night, $30 per night for double-family sites, $5 for each additional vehicle. Senior discount available. Open year-round.

Directions: From Fresno, drive north on Highway 41 to Oakhurst and continue 2.5 miles to Yosemite Forks and Bass Lake Road/County Road 222. Turn right at Bass Lake Road and drive eight miles (staying right at two forks) to the campground (on the south shore of Bass Lake).

Contact: Sierra National Forest, Bass Lake Ranger District, 559/877-2218, fax 559/877-3108.

◪ SPRING COVE

Rating: 8

On Bass Lake in Sierra National Forest.
Map 11.1, page 581

This is one of the several camps beside Bass Lake, a long, narrow reservoir in the Sierra foothill country. Expect hot weather in the summer. Boats must be registered at the Bass Lake observation tower after launching. The elevation is 3,400 feet.

Campsites, facilities: There are 54 sites for tents only and 11 sites for RVs up to 30 feet long. Picnic tables and fire grills are provided. Drinking water and flush toilets are available. Groceries and a boat ramp are available nearby. Leashed pets are permitted.

Reservations, fees: From Memorial Day through Labor Day, reserve at 877/444-6777 or website: www.ReserveUsa.com ($9 reservation fee); $18 per night. Senior discount available. Open May through August.

Directions: From Fresno, drive north on Highway 41 to Oakhurst and continue 2.5 miles to Yosemite Forks and Bass Lake Road/County Road 222. Turn right at Bass Lake Road

and drive 8.5 miles (staying right at two forks) to the campground (on the south shore of Bass Lake).

Contact: Sierra National Forest, Bass Lake Ranger District, 559/877-2218, fax 559/877-3108.

◫ WISHON POINT

Rating: 9

On Bass Lake in Sierra National Forest.
Map 11.1, page 581

This camp on Wishon Point is the smallest, and many say the prettiest, of the camps at Bass Lake. The elevation is 3,400 feet.

Campsites, facilities: There are 47 sites for tents or RVs up to 30 feet long and several double-family sites. Picnic tables and fire grills are provided. Drinking water and flush toilets are available. Groceries and a boat ramp are nearby. Leashed pets are permitted.

Reservations, fees: From Memorial Day through Labor Day, reserve at 877/444-6777 or website: www.ReserveUsa.com ($9 reservation fee); $18 per night, $30 per night for double-family sites. Senior discount available. Open June through September.

Directions: From Fresno, drive north on Highway 41 to Oakhurst and continue 2.5 miles to Yosemite Forks and Bass Lake Road/County Road 222. Turn right at Bass Lake Road and drive nine miles (staying right at two forks) to the campground (on the south shore of Bass Lake).

Contact: Sierra National Forest, Bass Lake Ranger District, 559/877-2218, fax 559/877-3108.

◬ CHILKOOT

Rating: 7

Near Bass Lake in Sierra National Forest.
Map 11.1, page 581

A lot of people have heard of Bass Lake, but

only the faithful know about Chilcoot Creek. That's where this camp is, but it's just two miles from Bass Lake. It provides a primitive option to use either as an overflow area for Bass Lake or for folks who don't want to get jammed into one of the Bass Lake campgrounds on a popular weekend.

Campsites, facilities: There are 14 sites for tents and RVs up to 22 feet long. Picnic tables and fire grills are provided. Vault toilets are available. No drinking water is available. Groceries and a coin laundry are available at Bass Lake. Leashed pets are permitted.

Reservations, fees: Reserve at 877/444-6777 or website: www.ReserveUsa.com ($9 reservation fee); $13 per night, $5 for each additional vehicle. Senior discount available. Open May through August.

Directions: From Fresno, drive north on Highway 41 to Oakhurst and continue 2.5 miles to Yosemite Forks and Bass Lake Road/County Road 222. Turn right at Bass Lake Road and drive six miles to the town of Bass Lake and Beasore Road. Turn left at Beasore Road and drive 4.5 miles to the campground.

Contact: Sierra National Forest, Bass Lake Ranger District, 559/877-2218, fax 559/877-3108.

7 GAGGS CAMP
🏕 🐾 5% 🚗 ⛺

Rating: 7

In Sierra National Forest.
Map 11.1, page 581

The masses are not exactly beating a hot trail to this camp. It's a small, remote, and primitive spot, set along a little creek at 5,800 feet, deep in the interior of Sierra National Forest. A Forest Service map is advisable. With that in hand, you can make the three-mile drive to Little Shuteye Pass, where the road is often gated in the winter (the gate is open when the look-out station is staffed); from here it is a three-mile trip to Shuteye Peak, 8,351 feet, where there is a drop-dead gorgeous view of the surrounding landscape.

Campsites, facilities: There are 12 sites for tents or RVs up to 16 feet long. Picnic tables and fire grills are provided. Vault toilets are available. No drinking water is available. Garbage must be packed out. Leashed pets are permitted.

Reservations, fees: Reservations are not accepted. The fee is $14 per night, $5 for each extra vehicle. Senior discount available. Open June through October, weather permitting.

Directions: From Fresno, drive north on Highway 41 for about 25 miles to North Fork Road/County Road 200. Turn right and drive northeast for 17.5 miles to Auberry Road/County Road 222. Turn left (north) and drive one mile to the town of North Fork and Mammoth Pool Road. Turn right and drive a half mile to Malum Ridge Road/County Road 274. Turn left (north) and drive 4.5 miles to Central Camp Road/Forest Road 6S42. Turn right and drive 11.5 miles (narrow, winding road) to the campground on the right.

Contact: Sierra National Forest, Bass Lake Ranger District, 559/877-2218, fax 559/877-3108.

8 SODA SPRINGS
🏕 🏊 🚣 🚗 🐾 🚐 ⛺

Rating: 7

On the West Fork of Chiquito Creek in Sierra National Forest.
Map 11.1, page 581

Soda Springs is set at 4,400 feet on West Fork Chiquito Creek, about five miles from Mammoth Pool Reservoir, and is used primarily as an overflow area if the more developed camps with drinking water have filled up. As long as you remember that the camp is primitive, it is a good overflow option.

Campsites, facilities: There are 18 sites for tents or RVs up to 25 feet long. Picnic tables and fire grills are provided. Vault toilets are available. No drinking water is available. A store and boat ramp are nearby. Leashed pets are permitted.

Reservations, fees: Reservations are not accepted. The fee is $12 per night, $5 for each extra vehicle. Senior discount available. Open April through October, weather permitting.

Directions: From Fresno, drive north on Highway 41 for about 25 miles to North Fork Road/County Road 200. Turn right and drive northeast for 17.5 miles to Auberry Road/County Road 222. Turn left (north) and drive one mile to the town of North Fork and Mammoth Pool Road. Turn right and drive 1.5 miles to County Road 225 (still Mammoth Pool Road). Turn right and drive 35 miles (the road becomes Minarets Road/Forest Road 81) to the campground. The last 37 miles are on narrow winding roads.

Contact: Sierra National Forest, Bass Lake Ranger District, 559/877-2218, fax 559/877-3108.

⑨ LOWER CHIQUITO

Rating: 7

On Chiquito Creek in Sierra National Forest.
Map 11.1, page 581

Lower Chiquito is a small, little-known, primitive camp in Sierra National Forest, about eight miles from Mammoth Pool Reservoir. The elevation is 4,900 feet, with a very warm climate in summer. Note that Lower Chiquito is a long distance (a twisting, 30- to 40-minute drive) from Upper Chiquito, despite the similarity in names and streamside settings along the same creek.

Campsites, facilities: There are seven sites for tents or RVs up to 22 feet long. Picnic tables and fire grills are provided. Vault toilets are available. No drinking water is available. Leashed pets are permitted.

Reservations, fees: Reservations are not accepted. The fee is $13 per night, $5 for each additional vehicle. Senior discount available. Open May through September.

Directions: From the town of North Fork (south of Bass Lake), drive east on Mammoth Pool Road/County Road 225 (it becomes Minarets Road/Forest Road 4S81). Bear left (north, still Minarets Road/Forest Road 4S81) and drive to Forest Road 6S71. Turn left on Forest Road 6S71 and drive three miles to the campground. The distance is about 40 miles from North Fork.

Contact: Sierra National Forest, Bass Lake Ranger District, 559/877-2218, fax 559/877-3108.

⑩ PLACER

Rating: 7

Near Mammoth Pool Reservoir on Chiquito Creek in Sierra National Forest.
Map 11.1, page 581

This little camp is just three miles from Mammoth Pool Reservoir. With Forest Road access and a pretty setting along Chiquito Creek, it is one of the better campgrounds used as an overflow area for Mammoth Pool visitors. The elevation is 4,100 feet. (For more information, see the entry for Mammoth Pool.)

Campsites, facilities: There are seven tent sites. Picnic tables and fire grills are provided. Vault toilets are available. No drinking water is available. Leashed pets are permitted.

Reservations, fees: Reservations are not accepted. The fee is $13 per night. Senior discount available. Open April through October.

Directions: From Fresno, drive north on Highway 41 for about 25 miles to North Fork Road/County Road 200. Turn right and drive northeast for 17.5 miles to Auberry Road/County Road 222. Turn left (north) and drive one mile to the town of North Fork and Mammoth Pool Road. Turn right and drive 1.5 miles to County Road 225 (still Mammoth Pool Road.) Turn right and drive about 37 miles (the road becomes Minarets Road/Forest Road 81) to a junction. Bear right (still Mammoth Pool Road) and drive one mile to the campground on the right. The drive from North Fork takes 1.5–2 hours.

Contact: Sierra National Forest, Bass Lake Ranger District, 559/877-2218, fax 559/877-3108.

11 SWEETWATER

🏊 🛶 🚤 🎣 🚐 ⛺

Rating: 6

Near Mammoth Pool Reservoir on Chiquito Creek in Sierra National Forest.

Map 11.1, page 581

Sweetwater is small and primitive, but if the camp at Mammoth Pool Reservoir is filled up, this spot provides an alternative. It is set on Chiquito Creek, just a mile from the lake. The elevation is 3,800 feet. (See the entry for Mammoth Pool for more information.)

Campsites, facilities: There are five sites for tents only and five sites for RVs up to 16 feet long. Picnic tables and fire grills are provided. Vault toilets are available. No drinking water is available. A store and boat ramp are within 1.5 miles. Leashed pets are permitted.

Reservations, fees: Reservations are not accepted. The fee is $12 per night. Senior discount available. Open April through October.

Directions: From Fresno, drive north on Highway 41 for about 25 miles to North Fork Road/County Road 200. Turn right and drive northeast for 17.5 miles to Auberry Road/County Road 222. Turn left (north) and drive one mile to the town of North Fork and Mammoth Pool Road. Turn right and drive 1.5 miles to County Road 225 (still Mammoth Pool Road.) Turn right and drive about 37 miles (the road becomes Minarets Road/Forest Road 81) to a junction. Bear right (still Mammoth Pool Road) and drive 1.5 miles to the campground on the right. The drive from North Fork takes 1.5–2 hours.

Contact: Sierra National Forest, Bass Lake Ranger District, 559/877-2218, fax 559/877-3108.

12 MAMMOTH POOL

🏊 🛶 🚤 🎣 🚐 ⛺

Rating: 7

Near Mammoth Pool Reservoir in Sierra National Forest.

Map 11.1, page 581

Mammoth Pool was created by a dam in the San Joaquin River gorge, a steep canyon, resulting in a long, narrow lake with steep, high walls. The lake seems much higher than its official elevation of 3,330 feet, but that is because of the high ridges. This is the only drive-in camp at the lake, though there is a boat-in camp, China Camp, on the lake's upper reaches. Trout fishing can be good in the spring and early summer, with water-skiing dominant during warm weather. Get this: water sports are restricted from May 1 to June 15 because of deer migrating across the lake—that's right, swimming—but the campgrounds here are still open.

Campsites, facilities: There are 18 sites for tents only, 29 sites for tents or RVs up to 22 feet long, and five multifamily sites. Picnic tables and fire grills are provided. Drinking water and vault toilets are available. A store and boat ramp are within a mile. Leashed pets are permitted.

Reservations, fees: Reservations are not accepted. The fee is $13 per night, $24 multifamily site fee, $5 for each additional vehicle. Senior discount available. Open May through October.

Directions: From Fresno, drive north on Highway 41 for about 25 miles to North Fork Road/County Road 200. Turn right and drive northeast for 17.5 miles to Auberry Road/County Road 222. Turn left (north) and drive one mile to the town of North Fork and Mammoth Pool Road. Turn right and drive 1.5 miles to County Road 225 (still Mammoth Pool Road.) Turn right and drive about 37 miles (the road becomes Minarets Road/Forest Road 81) to a junction. Bear right (still Mammoth Pool Road) and drive three miles to Mammoth Pool Reservoir and the campground. The drive from North Fork takes 1.5–2 hours.

Contact: Sierra National Forest, Bass Lake Ranger District, 559/877-2218, fax 559/877-3108.

13 SAMPLE MEADOW

Rating: 7

On Kaiser Creek in Sierra National Forest.
Map 11.1, page 581

This is a pretty, secluded spot set at 7,800 feet along Kaiser Creek, with nearby trailheads available for backpackers. While there is a trail out of camp, most will drive a mile down Forest Road 80 to the Rattlesnake Parking Area. From here, one trail is routed three miles southwest to Kaiser Ridge and Upper and Lower Twin Lakes in the Kaiser Wilderness, a great hike. Another trail is routed north for three miles to Rattlesnake Creek, then enters the western slopes of the Ansel Adams Wilderness, with this section featuring a series of canyons, streams, and very few people.

Campsites, facilities: There are 16 sites for tents or small RVs up to 16 feet long. Picnic tables and fire grills are provided. Vault toilets are available. No drinking water is available. Garbage must be packed out. Leashed pets are permitted.

Reservations, fees: Reservations are not accepted. There is no fee for camping. Open June through September.

Directions: From Fresno, drive east on Highway 168 to Shaver Lake, then continue 21 miles to Huntington Lake and Kaiser Pass Road/Forest Road 80. Bear right on Forest Road 80 and drive eight miles to a fork with Forest Road 5. Turn left on Forest Road 5 and drive 3.5 miles to a fork with the campground entrance road. Bear left at the campground entrance road and drive a quarter mile to the campground. The road is narrow and curvy, with blind turns.

Contact: Sierra National Forest, High Sierra Ranger District, 559/855-5360, fax 559/855-5375.

14 PORTAL FOREBAY

Rating: 8

On Forebay Lake in Sierra National Forest.
Map 11.1, page 581

This small, primitive camp is set along the shore of little Forebay Lake at 7,200 feet. The camp is pretty and provides a good hiking option, with a trailhead near the camp that is routed up Camp 61 Creek and then to Mono Creek, with a ford of Mono Creek required about two miles in. Another side trip is visiting Mono Hot Springs about five miles to the east, just off the road to Lake Edison.

Campsites, facilities: There are 14 sites for tents or small RVs up to 16 feet long. Picnic tables and fire grills are provided. Vault toilets are available. No drinking water is available. Garbage must be packed out. Groceries are available nearby at Mono Hot Springs. Leashed pets are permitted.

Reservations, fees: Reservations are not accepted. The fee is $8 per night, $5 for each extra vehicle. Senior discount available. Open June through September.

Directions: From Fresno, drive east on Highway 168 to Shaver Lake, then continue to 21 miles to Huntington Lake and Kaiser Pass Road/Forest Road 80. Bear right on Forest Road 80 and drive eight miles to a fork with Forest Road 5. Stay right at the fork on Forest Road 80 and continue five miles to the campground entrance on the left. The road is narrow and curvy, with blind turns.

Contact: Sierra National Forest, High Sierra Ranger District, 559/855-5360, fax 559/855-5375.

15 BOLSILLO

Rating: 4

On Bolsillo Creek in Sierra National Forest.
Map 11.1, page 581

This tiny camp has many first-class bonuses.

It is set at 7,400 feet along Bolsillo Creek, just three miles by car to Mono Hot Springs and seven miles to Lake Edison. A trailhead out of camp provides the chance for a three-mile hike south, climbing along Bolsillo Creek and up to small, pretty Corbett Lake on the flank of nearby Mt. Givens, 10,648 feet.

Campsites, facilities: There are three tent sites. Picnic tables and fire grills are provided. Drinking water and vault toilets are available. Garbage must be packed out. You can buy supplies in Mono Hot Springs. Leashed pets are permitted.

Reservations, fees: Reservations are not accepted. There is no fee for camping. Open June through September.

Directions: From Fresno, drive east on Highway 168 to Shaver Lake, then continue 21 miles to Huntington Lake and Kaiser Pass Road/Forest Road 80. Bear right on Forest Road 80 and drive eight miles to a fork with Forest Road 5. Stay right on Forest Road 80 and drive seven miles (two miles past Portal Forebay) to the campground entrance on the right. The road is narrow and curvy, with blind turns.

Contact: Sierra National Forest, High Sierra Ranger District, 559/855-5360, fax 559/855-5375.

16 MONO HOT SPRINGS

Rating: 8

On the San Joaquin River in Sierra National Forest.

Map 11.1, page 581

The campground is set in the Sierra at 6,500 feet in elevation along the San Joaquin River directly adjacent to the Mono Hot Springs Resort. The hot springs are typically 104°F, with public pools (everybody wears swimming suits) available just above the river on one side, and the private resort (rock cabins available) with its private baths on the other. A small convenience store and excellent restaurant are avail-

able at the lodge. The best swimming lake in the Sierra Nevada, Dorris Lake, is a 15-minute walk past the lodge; the lake is clear, clean, and yet not too cold, with walls on one side for fun jumps into deep water. The one downer: the drive in is long, slow, and hellacious, with many blind corners in narrow sections.

Campsites, facilities: There are 26 sites for tents or RVs, and four sites for tents only. Picnic tables and fire grills are provided. Drinking water and vault toilets are available. You can buy supplies in Mono Hot Springs. Leashed pets are permitted.

Reservations, fees: Reserve at 877/444-6777 ($9 reservation fee) or website: www.Reserve Usa.com; $14 per night, $5 per night for each extra vehicle. Senior discount available. Open May through September.

Directions: From the town of Shaver Lake, drive east on Highway 168 for 21 miles to Kaiser Pass Road. Bear northeast on Kaiser Pass Road/Forest Road 80 (slow and curvy) to Mono Hot Springs Campground Road (signed). Turn left and drive a short distance to the campground.

Contact: Sierra National Forest, High Sierra Ranger District, 559/855-5360, fax 559/855-5375.

17 VERMILLION

Rating: 8

On Lake Edison in Sierra National Forest.

Map 11.1, page 581

Lake Edison is a premium vacation destination. It is a large, high-mountain camp set just a few miles from the border of the John Muir Wilderness. The elevation is 7,700 feet. A 15-mph speed limit on the lake guarantees quiet water, and trout fishing is often quite good in early summer, with occasionally huge brown trout hooked. A day-trip option is to hike the trail from the camp out along the north shore of Lake Edison for five miles to Quail Meadows, where it intersects with the Pacific Crest

Trail in the John Muir Wilderness. A lodge at the lake provides meals and supplies, with a hiker's boat shuttle available to the head of the lake. Hang out here for long and you are bound to see JMT hikers taking a break. Note that the drive in is long and extremely twisty on a narrow road.

Campsites, facilities: There are 11 tent sites and 20 sites for tents or RVs up to 16 feet. Picnic tables and fire grills are provided. Drinking water and vault toilets are available. A boat ramp and horseback riding facilities are nearby. A small store and restaurant are nearby. Leashed pets are permitted.

Reservations, fees: Reserve at 877/444-6777 ($9 reservation fee) or website: www.ReserveUsa.com; $14 per night, $5 per night for each extra vehicle. Open June through September.

Directions: From the town of Shaver Lake, drive east on Highway 168 for 21 miles to Kaiser Pass Road. Bear northeast on Kaiser Pass Road/Forest Road 80 (slow and curvy) to Mono Hot Springs (the road becomes Edison Lake Road). Continue on Kaiser Pass/Edison Lake Road for five miles to the campground. It is about a quarter mile from the west shore of Lake Edison.

Contact: Sierra National Forest, High Sierra Ranger District, 559/855-5360, fax 559/855-5375.

18 MONO CREEK

Rating: 5

Near Lake Edison in Sierra National Forest.
Map 11.1, page 581

Here's a beautiful spot in the forest near Mono Creek that makes for an overflow campground when the camps at Mono Hot Springs and Lake Edison are filled. The camp is set at 7,400 feet, is about three miles from Lake Edison, via a twisty and bumpy road. Edison has good evening trout fishing and a small restaurant. For side trips, the Mono Hot Springs Resort is three miles away (slow, curvy, and bumpy driving), and there are numerous trails near-

by into the backcountry. Always check if drinking water is available. Though drinking water is scheduled to be available at this camp, on our visits that was not the case. A camp host is on-site.

Campsites, facilities: There are 14 sites for tents or RVs up to 16 feet long. Picnic tables and fire grills are provided. Drinking water and vault toilets are available. Limited supplies and small restaurants are available at Lake Edison and Mono Hot Springs. Leashed pets are permitted.

Reservations, fees: Reserve at 877/444-6777 ($9 reservation fee) or website: www.Reserve Usa.com; $14 per night, $5 per night for each extra vehicle. Open June through August.

Directions: From the town of Shaver Lake, drive east on Highway 168 for 21 miles to Kaiser Pass Road. Bear northeast on Kaiser Pass Road/Forest Road 80 (slow and curvy) to Mono Hot Springs (the road becomes Edison Lake Road). Continue on Kaiser Pass/Edison Lake Road for three miles to the campground on the left.

Contact: Sierra National Forest, High Sierra Ranger District, 559/855-5360, fax 559/855-5375.

19 FISH CREEK

Rating: 6

In Sierra National Forest.
Map 11.1, page 581

This is a small, primitive camp set along Fish Creek at 4,600 feet in the Sierra National Forest. It's a nearby option to Rock Creek, both set on the access road to Mammoth Pool Reservoir.

Campsites, facilities: There are seven sites for tents or RVs up to 16 feet long. Picnic tables and fire grills are provided. Vault toilets are available. No drinking water is available. Leashed pets are permitted.

Reservations, fees: Reserve at 877/444-6777 or website: www.ReserveUsa.com ($9 reservation fee); $13 per night. Senior discount available. Open April through October, weather permitting.

Directions: From Fresno, drive north on Highway 41 for about 25 miles to North Fork Road/County Road 200. Turn right and drive northeast for 17.5 miles to Auberry Road/County Road 222. Turn left (north) and drive one mile to the town of North Fork and Mammoth Pool Road. Turn right and drive 1.5 miles to County Road 225 (still Mammoth Pool Road.) Turn right and drive about 21 miles (the road becomes Minarets Road/Forest Road 81) to the campground on the right.

Contact: Sierra National Forest, Bass Lake Ranger District, 559/877-2218, fax 559/877-3108.

20 ROCK CREEK
🏕 ⛵ 🎣 🚻 🚗 🏕

Rating: 6

In Sierra National Forest.

Map 11.1, page 581

Drinking water is the big bonus here. It's easier to live with than the no-water situation at Fish Creek, the other camp in the immediate area. It is also why this camp tends to fill up on weekends. A side trip is the primitive road that heads southeast out of camp, switchbacks as its heads east, and drops down the canyon near where pretty Aspen Creek feeds into Rock Creek. The elevation at camp is 4,300 feet. (Note that the best camp in the immediate region is at Mammoth Pool.)

Campsites, facilities: There are 18 sites for tents or RVs up to 32 feet long. Picnic tables and fire grills are provided. Drinking water and vault toilets are available. Leashed pets are permitted.

Reservations, fees: Make reservations at website: www.ReserveUsa.com; $16 per night. Senior discount available. Open April through October, weather permitting.

Directions: From Fresno, drive north on Highway 41 for about 25 miles to North Fork Road/County Road 200. Turn right and drive

northeast for 17.5 miles to Auberry Road/County Road 222. Turn left (north) and drive one mile to the town of North Fork and Mammoth Pool Road. Turn right and drive 1.5 miles to County Road 225 (still Mammoth Pool Road.) Turn right and drive about 25 miles (the road becomes Minarets Road/Forest Road 81) to the campground on the right.

Contact: Sierra National Forest, Bass Lake Ranger District, 559/877-2218, fax 559/877-3108.

21 UPPER AND LOWER BILLY CREEK
🏕 ⛵ 🎣 🚻 🐕 🚗 🏕

Rating: 8

On Huntington Lake in Sierra National Forest.

Map 11.1, page 581

Huntington Lake is at an elevation of 7,000 feet in the Sierra Nevada, and this is one of several camps here. These camps are at the west end of the lake along the north shore, where Billy Creek feeds the lake. Of these two adjacent campgrounds, Lower Billy Creek is smaller than Upper Billy and has lakeside sites available. The lake is four miles long and a half mile wide, with 14 miles of shoreline, five resorts, boat rentals, and a trailhead for hiking into the Kaiser Wilderness.

Campsites, facilities: Upper Billy has 57 sites for tents only and 20 sites for tents or RVs up to 25 feet long. Lower Billy has 11 sites for tents or RVs. Picnic tables and fire grills are provided. Drinking water and flush toilets and vault toilets are available. A small store is nearby. Leashed pets are permitted.

Reservations, fees: Reserve at 877/444-6777 or website: www.ReserveUsa.com ($9 reservation fee); $16 per night, $5 for each extra vehicle. Senior discount available. Open June through September.

Directions: From Fresno, drive east on Highway 168 to Shaver Lake, then continue 21 miles to Huntington Lake and Huntington Lake

Road. Turn left on Huntington Lake Road and drive about five miles to the campgrounds on the left.

Contact: Sierra National Forest, High Sierra Ranger District, 559/855-5360, fax 559/855-5375.

22 CATAVEE

Rating: 7

On Huntington Lake in Sierra National Forest.

Map 11.1, page 581

Catavee Camp is one of three camps in the immediate vicinity, set on the north shore at the eastern end of Huntington Lake. The camp sits near where Bear Creek enters the lake. Huntington Lake is a scenic, High Sierra Ranger District lake at 7,000 feet, where visitors can enjoy fishing, hiking, and sailing. Sailboat regattas take place here regularly during the summer. Nearby resorts offer boat rentals and guest docks, and a boat ramp is nearby. Tackle rentals and bait are also available. A trailhead near camp offers access to the Kaiser Wilderness.

Campsites, facilities: There are 26 sites for tents or RVs up to 25 feet long. Picnic tables and fire grills are provided. Drinking water and flush toilets are available. Horseback riding facilities and a small store are nearby. Some facilities are wheelchair-accessible. Leashed pets are permitted.

Reservations, fees: Reserve at 877/444-6777 or website: www.ReserveUsa.com ($9 reservation fee); $20 per night, $5 for each extra vehicle. Senior discount available. Open June through October.

Directions: From Fresno, drive east on Highway 168 to Shaver Lake, then continue 21 miles to Huntington Lake and Huntington Lake Road. Turn left on Huntington Lake Road and drive one mile (just past Kinnikinnick) to the campground on the left.

Contact: Sierra National Forest, High Sierra Ranger District, 559/855-5360, fax 559/855-5375.

23 KINNIKINNICK

Rating: 7

On Huntington Lake in Sierra National Forest.

Map 11.1, page 581

Flip a coin; there are three camps in the immediate vicinity on the north shore of the east end of Huntington Lake and, with a boat ramp nearby, they are all favorites. Kinnikinnick is set between Catavee and Deer Creek campgrounds. The elevation is 7,000 feet.

Campsites, facilities: There are 35 sites for tents or RVs up to 22 feet long. Picnic tables and fire grills are provided. Drinking water and flush toilets are available. Horseback riding facilities and a store are available nearby. Some facilities are wheelchair-accessible. Leashed pets are permitted.

Reservations, fees: Reserve at 877/444-6777 or website: www.ReserveUsa.com ($9 reservation fee); $20 per night, $5 for each extra vehicle. Senior discount available. Open June through August.

Directions: From Fresno, drive east on Highway 168 to Shaver Lake, then continue 21 miles to Huntington Lake and Huntington Lake Road. Turn left on Huntington Lake Road and drive one mile to the campground on the left.

Contact: Sierra National Forest, High Sierra Ranger District, 559/855-5360, fax 559/855-5375.

24 DEER CREEK

Rating: 8

On Huntington Lake in Sierra National Forest.

Map 11.1, page 581

This is one of the best camps at Huntington Lake, set near lakeside at Bear Cove with a boat ramp nearby. It is on the north shore of the lake's eastern end. Huntington Lake is four miles long and a half mile wide, with 14 miles of shoreline, five resorts, boat rentals, and a trailhead for hiking into the Kaiser Wilderness. Two other campgrounds are nearby.

Campsites, facilities: There are 34 sites for tents or RVs up to 22 feet long. Picnic tables and fire grills are provided. Drinking water and flush toilets are available. Some facilities are wheelchair-accessible. A store and propane gas are nearby. Leashed pets are permitted.

Reservations, fees: Reserve at 877/444-6777 or website: www.ReserveUsa.com ($9 reservation fee); $20–22 per night, $5 for each extra vehicle. Senior discount available. Open June through September.

Directions: From Fresno, drive east on Highway 168 to Shaver Lake, then continue 21 miles to Huntington Lake and Huntington Lake Road. Turn left on Huntington Lake Road and drive one mile to the campground entrance road on the left.

Contact: Sierra National Forest, High Sierra Ranger District, 559/855-5360, fax 559/855-5375.

25 COLLEGE

Rating: 7

On Huntington Lake in Sierra National Forest.

Map 11.1, page 581

College is a beautiful site along the shore of the northeastern end of Huntington Lake, at 7,000 feet elevation. This camp is close to a small store in the town of Huntington Lake.

Campsites, facilities: There are 11 sites for tents or RVs up to 22 feet long. Picnic tables and fire grills are provided. Drinking water and vault toilets are available. Horseback riding facilities, store, and propane gas are available nearby. Leashed pets are permitted.

Reservations, fees: Reserve at 877/444-6777 or website: www.ReserveUsa.com ($9 reservation

fee); $18 per night, $5 for each extra vehicle. Senior discount available. Open June through September.

Directions: From Fresno, drive east on Highway 168 to Shaver Lake, then continue 21 miles to Huntington Lake and Huntington Lake Road. Turn left on Huntington Lake Road and drive a half mile to the campground.

Contact: Sierra National Forest, High Sierra Ranger District, 559/855-5360, fax 559/855-5375.

26 RANCHERIA

Rating: 8

Near Huntington Lake in Sierra National Forest.

Map 11.1, page 581

This is the granddaddy of the camps at Huntington Lake, and also the easiest to reach. It is along the shore of the lake's eastern end. A bonus here is the nearby Rancheria Falls National Recreation Trail, which provides access to beautiful Rancheria Falls. Another side trip is the 15-minute drive to Bear Butte (the access road is across from the campground entrance) at 8,598 feet, providing a sweeping view of the lake below. The elevation at camp is 7,000 feet.

Campsites, facilities: There are 150 sites for tents or RVs up to 22 feet long. Picnic tables and fire grills are provided. Drinking water and flush toilets are available. A store and propane gas are available nearby. Leashed pets are permitted.

Reservations, fees: Reserve at 877/444-6777 or website: www.ReserveUsa.com ($9 reservation fee); $18 per night, $5 for each extra vehicle. Senior discount available. Open year-round.

Directions: From Fresno, drive east on Highway 168 to Shaver Lake, then continue 20 miles to Huntington Lake and the campground on the left.

Contact: Sierra National Forest, High Sierra Ranger District, 559/855-5360, fax 559/855-5375.

27 BADGER FLAT

Rating: 7

On Rancheria Creek in Sierra National Forest.

Map 11.1, page 581

This camp is a good launching pad for backpackers. It is set at 8,200 feet along Rancheria Creek. The trail leading out of the camp is routed into the Kaiser Wilderness to the north and Dinkey Lakes Wilderness to the south.

Campsites, facilities: There are 15 sites for tents or RVs up to 22 feet long. Fire grills and picnic tables are provided. Vault toilets and horseback riding facilities are available. No drinking water is available. Leashed pets are permitted.

Reservations, fees: Reservations are not accepted. The fee is $8 per night, $5 for each extra vehicle. Senior discount available. Open June through September.

Directions: From Fresno, drive east on Highway 168 to Shaver Lake, then continue 21 miles to Huntington Lake and Kaiser Pass Road/Forest Road 80. Turn right and drive seven miles to the campground.

Contact: Sierra National Forest, High Sierra Ranger District, 559/855-5360, fax 559/855-5375.

28 BADGER FLAT GROUP CAMP

Rating: 7

On Rancheria Creek in Sierra National Forest.

Map 11.1, page 581

Badger Flat is a primitive site along Rancheria Creek at 8,200 feet, about five miles east of Huntington Lake. It is a popular horse camp and a good jump-off spot for wilderness trekkers. A trail that passes through camp provides two options: head south for three miles to enter the Dinkey Lakes Wilderness, or head north for two miles to enter the Kaiser Wilderness.

Campsites, facilities: This campground will accommodate groups of up to 100 people in tents or RVs up to 25 feet long. Picnic tables and fire grills are provided. Vault toilets and horseback riding facilities are available. No drinking water is available. A store is nearby. Leashed pets are permitted.

Reservations, fees: Reserve at 877/444-6777 or website: www.ReserveUsa.com ($9 reservation fee); $200 per night per group. Open June through September.

Directions: From Fresno, drive east on Highway 168 to Shaver Lake, then continue 21 miles to Huntington Lake and Kaiser Pass Road/Forest Road 80. Turn right and drive six miles to the campground.

Contact: Sierra National Forest, High Sierra Ranger District, 559/855-5360, fax 559/855-5375.

29 SMALLEY COVE

Rating: 7

On Kerckhoff Reservoir near Madera.

Map 11.1, page 581

Kerckhoff Reservoir can get so hot that it might seem you could fry an egg on the rocks. Campers should be certain to have some kind of tarp they can set up as a sun screen. The lake is small and remote, and the use of motors on boats is prohibited. Most campers bring rafts or canoes, and there is a good swimming beach near the picnic area and campground. The elevation is 1,000 feet.

Campsites, facilities: There are five sites for tents or RVs. Picnic tables and fire grills are provided. Drinking water and vault toilets are available. Five group picnic sites are available. You can buy supplies in Auberry. Leashed pets are permitted.

Reservations, fees: Reservations are not accepted. The fee is $10 per night, $3 for each vehicle, $7 for extra RV, $1 per night. Open year-round.

Directions: From Fresno, take Highway 41 north for three miles to the exit for Highway

168 East. Take that exit and drive east on Highway 168 for about 22 miles to Auberry Road. Turn left and drive 2.8 miles to Powerhouse Road. Turn left and drive 8.4 miles to the campground.

Contact: PG&E Land Services, 916/386-5164.

30 SQUAW LEAP WALK-IN

Rating: 8

On the San Joaquin River.

Map 11.1, page 581

Not many folks know about this spot. It's a primitive setting, but it has some bonuses. For one thing, there's access to the San Joaquin River if you drive to the fishing access trailhead at the end of the road. From there, you get great views of the San Joaquin River Gorge. The camp is a trailhead for two excellent hiking and equestrian trails. Beautiful wildflower displays are highlights in the late winter and spring.

Campsites, facilities: There are five family sites and two group sites for tents. All are walk-in sites. Fire grills and picnic tables are provided. Vault toilets and a hitching post are available. No drinking water is available. You can buy supplies in Auberry. Leashed pets are permitted.

Reservations, fees: Reservations are not accepted. There is no fee for camping. Open year-round.

Directions: From Fresno, take Highway 41 north for three miles to the exit for Highway 168 East. Take that exit and drive east on Highway 168 for about 22 miles to Auberry Road. Turn left and drive 2.8 miles to Powerhouse Road. Turn left and drive two miles Smalley Road (signed Smalley Road and Squaw Leap Management Area). Turn left and drive four miles to the campground on the right.

Contact: Bureau of Land Management, Bakersfield Field Office, 661/391-6000, fax 661/391-6040.

31 CAMP EDISON

Rating: 8

On Shaver Lake.

Map 11.1, page 581

Camp Edison is the best camp at Shaver Lake, set on a peninsula along the lake's western shore, with a boat ramp and marina. The lake is at an elevation of 5,370 feet in the Sierra, a pretty area that has become popular for its calm, warm days and cool water. Boat rentals and bait and tackle are available at the marina. Newcomers with youngsters will discover that the best area for swimming and playing in the water is on the east side of the lake. Though more distant, this part of the lake offers sandy beaches rather than rocky drop-offs.

Campsites, facilities: There are 252 sites, 43 with full hookups for RVs or tents. Picnic tables, fire rings, and barbecues are provided. Restrooms, drinking water, flush toilets, cable TV, electrical connections, coin showers, RV dump station, coin laundry, marina, boat ramp, and horseback riding facilities are available. In winter, a minimum of 25 sites are kept open. Some facilities are wheelchair-accessible. Leashed pets are permitted.

Reservations, fees: Reservations are accepted. The fee is $22–40 per night, $5 for each extra vehicle with a maximum of eight people per site, $5 for a boat, $4 per night. Senior discount available. Open year-round with limited winter services.

Directions: From Fresno, drive east on Highway 168 to the town of Shaver Lake. Continue one mile on Highway 168 to the campground entrance road on the right. Turn right and drive to the campground on the west shore of Shaver Lake.

Contact: Camp Edison, 559/841-3134, fax 559/841-3193; website: www.sce.com/camp edison.com.

32 DORABELLE

Rating: 7

On Shaver Lake in Sierra National Forest.
Map 11.1, page 581

This is one of the few Forest Service camps in the state that is set up more for RVers than for tenters. The camp is along a long cove at the southwest corner of the lake, well-protected from winds out of the northwest. Shaver Lake is a popular lake for vacationers, and it is well stocked with trout during the summer. Boat rentals and bait and tackle are available at the nearby marina. This is also a popular snow-play area in the winter. The elevation is 5,400 feet.

Campsites, facilities: There are 68 sites for tents or RVs up to 30 feet long. Picnic tables and fire grills are provided. Drinking water and vault toilets are available. A store is nearby. Leashed pets are permitted.

Reservations, fees: Reserve at 877/444-6777 or website: www.ReserveUsa.com ($9 reservation fee); $18 per night, $5 for each extra vehicle. Senior discount available. Open May through September.

Directions: From Fresno, drive east on Highway 168 to Dorabelle Road (on the right just as entering the town of Shaver Lake). Turn right on Dorabelle Road and drive one mile to the campground at the southwest end of Shaver Lake.

Contact: Sierra National Forest, High Sierra Ranger District, 559/855-5360, fax 559/855-5375.

33 SWANSON MEADOW

Rating: 4

Near Shaver Lake in Sierra National Forest.
Map 11.1, page 581

This is the smallest and most primitive of the camps near Shaver Lake; it is used primarily as an overflow area if lakeside camps are full.

It is about two miles south of Shaver Lake at an elevation of 5,600 feet.

Campsites, facilities: There are 12 sites for tents or RVs up to 22 feet long. Picnic tables and fire grills are provided. Vault toilets are available. No drinking water is available. A store is nearby. Leashed pets are permitted.

Reservations, fees: Reservations are not accepted. The fee is $12 per night, $5 for each extra vehicle. Senior discount available. Open May through October.

Directions: From Fresno, drive east on Highway 168 to Dinkey Creek Road (on the right just as you enter the town of Shaver Lake). Turn right and drive three miles to the campground entrance road on the left. Turn left and drive a short distance to the campground.

Contact: Sierra National Forest, High Sierra Ranger District, 559/855-5360, fax 559/855-5375.

34 DINKEY CREEK

Rating: 7

In Sierra National Forest.
Map 11.1, page 581

This is a huge Forest Service camp set along Dinkey Creek at 5,700 feet, well in the interior of Sierra National Forest. It is a popular camp for anglers who take the trail and hike upstream along the creek for small-trout fishing in a pristine setting. Backpackers occasionally lay over here before driving on to the Dinkey Lakes Parking Area, for hikes to Mystery Lake, Swede Lake, South Lake, and others in the nearby Dinkey Lakes Wilderness.

Campsites, facilities: There are 128 sites for tents or RVs up to 30 feet long. Picnic tables and fire grills are provided. Drinking water, flush toilets, showers, and horseback riding facilities are available nearby. You can buy supplies in Dinkey Creek. Leashed pets are permitted.

Reservations, fees: From Memorial Day through Labor Day, reserve at 877/444-6777 or website: www.ReserveUsa.com ($9 reservation fee); $18 per night; 14-day stay limit. Senior discount available. Open from May through September.

Directions: From Fresno, drive east on Highway 168 to Dinkey Creek Road (on the right just as you enter the town of Shaver Lake). Turn right and drive 14 miles to the campground. A map of Sierra National Forest is advised.

Contact: Sierra National Forest, High Sierra Ranger District, 559/855-5360, fax 559/855-5375.

35 GIGANTEA

Rating: 7

On Dinkey Creek in Sierra National Forest.
Map 11.1, page 581

This primitive campground is set along Dinkey Creek adjacent to the McKinley Grove Botanical Area, which features a little-known grove of giant sequoias. The campground is set on a short loop spur road, and day visitors are better off stopping at the McKinley Grove Picnic Area. The elevation is 6,500 feet.

Campsites, facilities: There are 10 sites for tents or RVs up to 16 feet long. Picnic tables and fire grills are provided. Vault toilets are available. No drinking water is available. You can buy supplies in Dinkey Creek. Leashed pets are permitted.

Reservations, fees: Reservations are not accepted. The fee is $10 per night. Senior discount available. Open June through September.

Directions: From Fresno, drive east on Highway 168 to Dinkey Creek Road (on the right just as you enter the town of Shaver Lake). Turn right and drive 13 miles to McKinley Grove Road (Forest Road 40). Turn right and drive six miles to the campground.

Contact: Sierra National Forest, High Sierra Ranger District, 559/855-5360, fax 559/855-5375.

36 BUCK MEADOW

Rating: 7

On Deer Creek in Sierra National Forest.
Map 11.1, page 581

This is one of the three little-known, primitive camps in the area. It's set at 6,800 feet along Deer Creek, about seven miles from Wishon Reservoir, a more popular destination.

Campsites, facilities: There are five sites for tents only and five sites for tents or RVs up to 22 feet long. Picnic tables and fire grills are provided. Vault toilets are available. No drinking water is available. Leashed pets are permitted.

Reservations, fees: Reservations are not accepted. The fee is $10 per night. Senior discount available. Open June through September.

Directions: From Fresno, drive east on Highway 168 to Dinkey Creek Road (on the right just as you enter the town of Shaver Lake). Turn right and drive 13 miles to McKinley Grove Road (Forest Road 40). Turn right and drive eight miles to the campground.

Contact: Sierra National Forest, High Sierra Ranger District, 559/855-5360, fax 559/855-5375.

37 JACKASS MEADOW

Rating: 7

On Florence Lake in Sierra National Forest.
Map 11.2, page 582

Jackass Meadow is a pretty spot adjacent to Florence Lake, near the Upper San Joaquin River. There are good canoeing, rafting, and float-tubing possibilities, all high-Sierra style. The elevation is 7,200 feet. The lake is remote and can be reached only after a long, circuitous drive on a narrow road and many blind turns. A trailhead at the lake offers access to the wilderness and the John Muir Trail.

Campsites, facilities: There are 44 sites for tents or RVs up to 16 feet long. Picnic tables and fire grills are provided. Drinking water and vault toilets are available. A wheelchair-accessible fishing pier is available nearby. Leashed pets are permitted.

Reservations, fees: Reserve at 877/444-6777 ($9 reservation fee) or website: www.Reserve Usa.com; $14 per night, $5 per night for each extra vehicle. Senior discount available. Open June through September.

Directions: From the town of Shaver Lake, drive east on Highway 168 for 21 miles to Kaiser Pass Road. Bear northeast on Kaiser Pass Road/Forest Road 80 (slow and curvy) to a junction (left goes to Mono Hot Springs and Lake Edison) with Florence Lake Road. Bear right at the junction and drive five miles to the campground.

Contact: Sierra National Forest, High Sierra Ranger District, 559/855-5360, fax 559/855-5375.

38 TRAPPER SPRINGS

🚶 🏊 🎣 ⛵ 🐴 ♿ 🚐 ⛺

Rating: 8

On Courtright Reservoir in Sierra National Forest.

Map 11.2, page 582

Trapper Springs is on the west shore of Courtright Reservoir, set at 8,200 feet on the west slope of the Sierra. Courtright is a great destination, with excellent camping, boating, fishing, and hiking into the nearby John Muir Wilderness. A 15-mph speed limit makes the lake ideal for fishing, canoeing, and rafting. A trailhead a mile north of camp by car heads around the north end of the lake to a fork; to the left it is routed into the Dinkey Lakes Wilderness, and to the right it is routed to the head of the lake, then follows Dusy Creek in a long climb into spectacular country in the John Muir Wilderness. There are two driving routes to this lake, one from Shaver Lake and the other from Pine Flat Reservoir; both are very long, slow, and twisty drives.

Campsites, facilities: There are 75 sites for tents or RVs up to 22 feet long. Picnic tables and

fire grills are provided. Drinking water and vault toilets are available. A boat ramp is nearby. Some facilities are wheelchair-accessible. Leashed pets are permitted.

Reservations, fees: Reservations are not accepted. The fee is $16 per night, $7 for extra RV, $3 for extra vehicle, $1 per night. Senior discount available. Open June through September.

Directions: From Fresno, drive east on Highway 168 to Dinkey Creek Road (on the right just as you enter the town of Shaver Lake). Turn right and drive 13 miles to McKinley Grove Road (Forest Road 40). Turn right and drive 14 miles to Courtright Road. Turn left (north) and drive 12 miles to the campground entrance road on the right.

Contact: Sierra National Forest, High Sierra Ranger District, 559/855-5360, fax 559/855-5375.

39 MARMOT ROCK WALK-IN

🚶 🏊 🎣 ⛵ 🐴 ⛺

Rating: 8

On Courtright Reservoir in Sierra National Forest.

Map 11.2, page 582

Courtright Reservoir is in the high country at 8,200 feet. Marmot Rock Walk-In is set at the southern end of the lake, with a boat ramp nearby. This is a pretty Sierra lake that provides options for boaters and hikers. Trout fishing can also be good here. Boaters must observe a 15-mph speed limit, which makes for quiet water. There are two driving routes to this lake, one from Shaver Lake and the other from Pine Flat Reservoir; both are very long, slow, and twisty drives.

Campsites, facilities: There are 14 walk-in sites for tents only. Picnic tables and fire grills are provided. Vault toilets are available. No drinking water is available, but water is available three miles away at Trapper Springs Campground. A boat ramp is available nearby. Leashed pets are permitted.

Reservations, fees: Reservations are not accepted.

The fee is $16 per night, $7 for extra RV, $3 for extra vehicle, $1 per night. Senior discount available. Open June through September.

Directions: From Fresno, drive east on Highway 168 to Dinkey Creek Road (on the right just as you enter the town of Shaver Lake). Turn right and drive 13 miles to McKinley Grove Road (Forest Road 40). Turn right and drive 14 miles to Courtright Road. Turn left (north) and drive 10 miles to the campground entrance road on the right (on the south shore of the lake). Park and walk a short distance to the campground.

Contact: PG&E Land Services, 916/386-5164, fax 916/386-5388; Sierra National Forest, High Sierra Ranger District, 559/855-5360, fax 559/855-5375.

40 WISHON VILLAGE

🏃 🏊 🛶 🏄 🎣 🚐 ⛺

Rating: 7

Near Wishon Reservoir.
Map 11.2, page 582

This privately operated mountain park is set near the shore of Wishon Reservoir, about one mile from the dam. Trout stocks often make for good fishing in early summer, and anglers with boats love the 15-mph speed limit, which keeps personal watercraft off the water. Backpackers and hikers can find a great trailhead at the south end of the lake at Coolidge Meadow, where a trail awaits that is routed to the Woodchuck Creek drainage and numerous lakes in the John Muir Wilderness. The elevation is 6,500 feet.

Campsites, facilities: There are 96 sites with full hookups for RVs, 26 sites for tents. Picnic tables and fire pits are provided. Restrooms, drinking water, coin showers, electrical connections, and sewer hookups are available. Coin laundry, country store, bar, ice, boat ramp, motorboat rentals, bait and tackle, and propane gas are available nearby. Leashed pets are permitted.

Reservations, fees: Reservations are recommended. The fee is $30 per night for RV sites, $20 per night for tent sites, $2 for each additional person up to a six-camper limit per site. Open May through October.

Directions: From Fresno, drive east on Highway 168 to Dinkey Creek Road (on the right just as you enter the town of Shaver Lake). Turn right and drive 13 miles to McKinley Grove Road (Forest Road 40). Turn right and drive 15 miles to the park (66500 McKinley Grove Rd./Forest Road 40).

Contact: Wishon Village, 559/865-5361, fax 559/865-2000; website: www.wishonvillage.com.

41 LILY PAD

🏃 🏊 🛶 🏄 🎣 ♿ 🚐 ⛺

Rating: 7

Near Wishon Reservoir in Sierra
National Forest.
Map 11.2, page 582

This is the smallest of the three camps at Wishon Reservoir. It is set along the southwest shore at 6,500 feet, about a mile from both the lake and a good boat ramp. A 15-mph speed limit ensures quiet water, making this an ideal destination for families with canoes or a raft. There are two driving routes to this lake, one from Shaver Lake and the other from Pine Flat Reservoir; both are very long, slow, and twisty drives.

Campsites, facilities: There are six sites for tents only and 10 sites for tents or RVs up to 16 feet long. Picnic tables and fire grills are provided. Drinking water and vault toilets are available. Groceries, boat rentals, boat ramp, and propane gas are available nearby. Some facilities are wheelchair-accessible. There is also a group campsite nearby called Upper Kings River for up to 50 people. Leashed pets are permitted.

Reservations, fees: Reservations are not accepted. The fee is $16 per night, $7 for extra RV, $3 for extra vehicle, $1 per night. Senior discount available. Open May through October, weather permitting.

Directions: From Fresno, drive east on Highway 168 to Dinkey Creek Road (on the right just as entering the town of Shaver Lake). Turn right and drive 13 miles to McKinley Grove Road (Forest Road 40). Turn right and drive 16 miles to the campground on the right.

Contact: Sierra National Forest, High Sierra Ranger District, 559/855-5360, fax 559/855-5375; PG&E Land Services, 916/386-5164.

42 UPPER KINGS RIVER GROUP CAMP

Rating: 8

On Wishon Reservoir.

Map 11.2, page 582

Wishon Reservoir is a great place for a camping trip. When the lake is full, which is not often enough, the place has great natural beauty, set at 6,500 feet and surrounded by national forest. The fishing is fair enough on summer evenings, and a 15-mph speed limit keeps the lake quiet. A side-trip option is hiking from the trailhead at Woodchuck Creek, which within the span of a one-day hike takes you into the John Muir Wilderness and past three lakes—Woodchuck, Chimney, and Marsh. There are two driving routes to this lake, one from Shaver Lake and the other from Pine Flat Reservoir; both are very long, slow, and twisty drives.

Campsites, facilities: There is a group site for up to 50 people. Picnic tables and fire grills are provided. Drinking water and vault toilets are available. Leashed pets are permitted.

Reservations, fees: Reservations are required. The fee is $125 per night with a two-night minimum, $1 per night. Open May through October, weather permitting.

Directions: From Fresno, drive east on Highway 168 to Dinkey Creek Road (on the right just as you enter the town of Shaver Lake). Turn right and drive 13 miles to McKinley Grove Road (Forest Road 40). Turn right and drive to the Wishon Dam. The campground is near the base of the dam.

Contact: PG&E Land Services, 916/386-5164, fax 916/386-5388.

43 HORTON CREEK

Rating: 7

Near Bishop.

Map 11.2, page 582

This is a little-known, primitive BLM camp set along Horton Creek, northwest of Bishop. It can make a good base camp for hunters in the fall, with wild, rugged country to the west. The Inyo Mono Ecology Center is nearby. The elevation is 4,975 feet.

Campsites, facilities: There are 53 sites for tents or RVs. Picnic tables and fire grills are provided. Pit toilets and a dumpster are available. No drinking water is available. Leashed pets are permitted.

Reservations, fees: Reservations are not accepted. There is no fee for camping. Open late April through October, weather permitting.

Directions: Drive on U.S. 395 to Ed Powers Road (6.5 miles north of Bishop). Turn northwest (toward the Sierra) and drive a short distance to the campground (signed).

Contact: Bureau of Land Management, Bishop Field Office, 760/872-4881, fax 760/872-5050.

44 BROWN'S MILLPOND CAMPGROUND

Rating: 6

Near Bishop.

Map 11.2, page 582

This privately operated camp is adjacent to the Millpond Recreation Area, which offers ball fields, playgrounds, and a swimming lake. There is also the opportunity for sailing, archery, tennis courts, horseshoe games, and fishing.

Campsites, facilities: There are 75 sites, 16 with partial hookups, for tents or RVs. Picnic tables and fire grills are provided. Restrooms, drinking water, flush toilets, coin showers, and coin laundry are available. A concession stand is available nearby. Leashed pets are permitted.

Reservations, fees: Make reservations at 760/872-6911. Fees are $16–19 per night. Open March through October.

Directions: Drive on U.S. 395 to a road signed Millpond/County Park (just north of Bishop). Turn southwest (toward the Sierra) at that road (Ed Powers Road) and drive a quarter mile to Sawmill Road. Turn right and drive a quarter mile to Millpond Road, then turn left.

Contact: Brown's Millpond Campground, 760/873-5342.

45 BROWN'S TOWN SCHOBER LANE CAMP

Rating: 5

Near Bishop.

Map 11.2, page 582

This privately operated campground, one of several in the vicinity of Bishop, is the only one in the area that accepts tents. It's all shade and grass, and it's next to the golf course.

Campsites, facilities: There are 160 sites, 46 with partial hookups, for tents or RVs. Picnic tables are provided. Restrooms, drinking water, flush toilets, coin showers, cable TV at 10 sites, RV dump station, museum, store, and a snack bar are available. Leashed pets are permitted.

Reservations, fees: Reservations are accepted. The fee is $16–21 per night, one-vehicle limit per site. Major credit cards accepted. Open March through Thanksgiving, weather permitting.

Directions: Drive on U.S. 395 to Schober Lane (one mile south of Bishop) and the campground entrance. Turn northwest (toward the Sierra) and into the campground.

Contact: Brown's Town Schober Lane Camp, 760/873-8522; website: www.sierraweb.com.

46 SHADY REST TRAILER PARK

Rating: 3

In Bishop.

Map 11.2, page 582

This is an option for folks who want to find a layover in the Bishop area without going to much trouble to find it. This is a mobile home park with long-term rentals, with some sites available for overnighters. Possible side trips include the Indian Cultural Center in Bishop and the Pleasant Valley Reservoir, about a 15-minute drive from Shady Rest.

Campsites, facilities: There are 25 sites with full hookups for RVs. Restrooms, drinking water, flush toilets, showers, cable TV, and coin laundry are available. Leashed pets are permitted.

Reservations, fees: Reservations are recommended. The fee is $25 per night. Long-term rates available. Open year-round.

Directions: Drive on U.S. 395 to Bishop and Yaney Street. Turn southeast (away from the Sierra) and drive .7 mile to the park (399 E. Yaney Street).

Contact: Shady Rest Trailer Park, 760/873-3430.

47 NORTH LAKE

Rating: 8

On Bishop Creek near North Lake in Inyo National Forest.

Map 11.2, page 582

North Lake is a beautiful Sierra Lake set at an elevation of 9,500 feet, with good trout fishing much of the season and surrounded by beautiful aspens. The camp is set on the North Fork of Bishop Creek near North Lake and close to a trailhead that offers access to numerous lakes in the John Muir Wilderness and eventually connects with the Pacific Crest Trail. There is also an outstanding trailhead that leads to several small alpine lakes in the nearby John

Muir Wilderness for day hikes, or all the way up to Bishop Pass and Dusy Basin.

Campsites, facilities: There are 11 tent sites. Picnic tables and fire grills are provided. Drinking water and vault toilets are available. Horseback riding facilities are available nearby. Supplies are available in Bishop. Leashed pets are permitted.

Reservations, fees: Reservations are not accepted. The fee is $14 per night. Senior discount available. Open mid-May through September.

Directions: Drive on U.S. 395 to Bishop and Highway 168. Turn northwest (toward the Sierra) on Highway 168 and drive 17 miles to Forest Road 8S02 (signed North Lake). Turn right (north) on Forest Road 8S02 and drive for two miles to the campground.

Contact: Inyo National Forest, White Mountain Ranger District, 760/873-2500, fax 760/873-2563.

48 SABRINA

Rating: 8

Near Lake Sabrina in Inyo National Forest.
Map 11.2, page 582

You get the best of both worlds at this camp. It is set at 9,000 feet on Bishop Creek, just a half mile from Lake Sabrina, a beautiful High Sierra lake. In addition, trails nearby are routed into the high country of the John Muir Wilderness. Take your pick. Whatever your choice, it's a good one.

Campsites, facilities: There are 18 sites for tents or RVs up to 30 feet. Picnic tables and fire grills are provided. Drinking water and vault toilets are available. A boat ramp and boat rentals are available nearby. Supplies are available in Bishop. Leashed pets are permitted.

Reservations, fees: Reservations are not accepted. The fee is $14 per night. Senior discount available. Open mid-May through October.

Directions: Drive on U.S. 395 to Bishop and Highway 168. Turn northwest (toward the Sier-

ra) on Highway 168 and drive 17 miles (signed Lake Sabrina at a fork) to the campground.

Contact: Inyo National Forest, White Mountain Ranger District, 760/873-2500, fax 760/873-2563.

49 BIG TREES

Rating: 8

On Bishop Creek in Inyo National Forest.
Map 11.2, page 582

This is a small Forest Service camp on Bishop Creek at 7,500 feet in elevation. This section of the stream is stocked with small trout by the Department of Fish and Game. Both South Lake and Lake Sabrina are about 10 miles away.

Campsites, facilities: There are nine sites for tents or RVs. Picnic tables and fire grills are provided. Drinking water and flush toilets are available. Supplies are available in Bishop. Leashed pets are permitted.

Reservations, fees: Reservations are not accepted. The fee is $14 per night. Senior discount available. Open late April through September.

Directions: Drive on U.S. 395 to Bishop and Highway 168. Turn northwest (toward the Sierra) on Highway 168 and drive 11 miles to the campground access road on the left. Turn left and drive two miles on a dirt road to the campground.

Contact: Inyo National Forest, White Mountain Ranger District, 760/873-2500, fax 760/873-2563.

50 FOUR JEFFREY

Rating: 8

Near South Lake in Inyo National Forest.
Map 11.2, page 582

The camp is set on the South Fork of Bishop Creek at 8,100 feet, about four miles from South Lake. If you can arrange a trip in the fall, make sure you visit this camp. The fall colors are spectacular, with the aspen trees exploding in yellows and oranges. It is also the last camp on South Lake Road to be closed in the fall, and though nights are cold, it is well worth the trip. This is by far the largest of the Forest Service camps in the vicinity. There are three lakes in the area: North Lake, Lake Sabrina, and South Lake.

Campsites, facilities: There are 106 sites for tents or RVs up to 22 feet long. Picnic tables and fire grills are provided. Drinking water, vault toilets, and RV dump station are available. Some facilities are wheelchair-accessible. Supplies are available in Bishop. Leashed pets are permitted.

Reservations, fees: Reservations are not accepted. The fee is $14 per night. Senior discount available. Open mid-April through October.

Directions: Drive on U.S. 395 to Bishop and Highway 168. Turn northwest (toward the Sierra) on Highway 168 and drive 14 miles to South Lake Road. Turn left and drive a half mile to the campground.

Contact: Inyo National Forest, White Mountain Ranger District, 760/873-2500, fax 760/873-2563.

51 BISHOP PARK

Rating: 6

Near Lake Sabrina in Inyo National Forest.
Map 11.2, page 582

Bishop Park Camp is one in a series of camps along Bishop Creek. This one is set just behind the summer community of Aspendell. It is about two miles from Lake Sabrina, an ideal day trip or jump-off spot for a backpacking expedition into the John Muir Wilderness. The elevation is 8,400 feet.

Campsites, facilities: There are 20 sites for tents or RVs up to 22 feet long, and a group campsite for tents. Picnic tables and fire grills are provided. Drinking water and flush toilets are available. Horseback riding facilities are avail-

able at North Lake. Supplies are available in Bishop. Leashed pets are permitted.

Reservations, fees: Reservations are not accepted. The fee is $14 per night, $45 per night for groups. Senior discount available. Open mid-May through mid-October.

Directions: Drive on U.S. 395 to Bishop and Highway 168. Turn northwest (toward the Sierra) on Highway 168 and drive 15 miles to the campground.

Contact: Inyo National Forest, White Mountain Ranger District, 760/873-2500, fax 760/873-2563.

52 FORKS

Rating: 7

Near South Lake in Inyo National Forest.
Map 11.2, page 582

After a visit here, it's no mystery how the Forest Service named this camp. It is at the fork in the road, which gives you two options: you can turn south on South Lake Road and drive along the South Fork of Bishop Creek up to pretty South Lake, or you can keep driving on Highway 168 to another beautiful lake, Lake Sabrina, where hikers will find a trailhead that accesses the John Muir Wilderness. The elevation is 7,800 feet.

Campsites, facilities: There are eight sites for tents or RVs. Picnic tables and fire grills are provided. Drinking water and flush toilets are available. Horseback riding facilities are available nearby. Supplies are available in Bishop. Leashed pets are permitted.

Reservations, fees: Reservations are not accepted. The fee is $14 per night. Senior discount available. Open mid-April through October.

Directions: Drive on U.S. 395 to Bishop and Highway 168. Turn northwest (toward the Sierra) on Highway 168 and drive 14 miles to South Lake Road. Turn left and drive a quarter mile to the campground entrance on the right.

Contact: Inyo National Forest, White Mountain Ranger District, 760/873-2500, fax 760/873-2563.

53 CREEKSIDE RV PARK

Rating: 7

On the South Fork of Bishop Creek.

Map 11.2, page 582

This privately operated park in the high country is set up primarily for RVs. A lot of folks are surprised to find it here. North, Sabrina, and South Lakes are in the area. The elevation is 8,400 feet.

Campsites, facilities: There are 45 sites with full or partial hookups for RVs, four sites for tents, and rental trailers. Restrooms, drinking water, flush toilets, coin showers, store, and fish-cleaning facilities are available. A store and propane are available two blocks away. Leashed pets are permitted.

Reservations, fees: Reservations are accepted. The fee is $22–32 per night, $2 per night. Open May through October. Major credit cards accepted.

Directions: Drive on U.S. 395 to Bishop and Highway 168. Turn northwest (toward the Sierra) on Highway 168 and drive 14 miles to South Lake Road. Turn left and drive two miles to the campground entrance on the left (1949 South Lake Road).

Contact: Creekside RV Park, 760/873-4483.

54 INTAKE AND INTAKE WALK-IN

Rating: 7

On Sabrina Creek in Inyo National Forest.

Map 11.2, page 582

This small camp, set at 8,200 feet at a tiny reservoir on Bishop Creek, is about three miles from Lake Sabrina where a trailhead leads into the John Muir Wilderness. Nearby North Lake and South Lake provide side-trip options. All three are beautiful alpine lakes.

Campsites, facilities: There are eight sites for tents or RVs, and seven walk-in sites for tents. Picnic tables and fire grills are provided. Drinking water and flush toilets are available. Sup-

plies are available in Bishop. Leashed pets are permitted.

Reservations, fees: Reservations are not accepted. The fee is $12 per night. Senior discount available. The walk-in sites are open year-round, weather permitting. Drive-in sites are open mid-April through October.

Directions: Drive on U.S. 395 to Bishop and Highway 168. Turn northwest (toward the Sierra) on Highway 168 and drive 14.5 miles to the campground entrance.

Contact: Inyo National Forest, White Mountain Ranger District, 760/873-2500, fax 760/873-2563.

55 FIRST FALLS HIKE-IN CAMP

Rating:10

In Inyo National Forest.

Map 11.2, page 582

This high country hike-in camp is the first step for backpackers heading into the John Muir Wilderness. It is set at 8,300 feet on the South Fork of Big Pine Creek, with nearby Mt. Alice (11,630 feet) looming to the west. The hike in is about two miles to the campground.

Campsites, facilities: There are five tent sites. Picnic tables and fire grills are provided. Pit toilets are available. Garbage must be packed out. No drinking water is available. Leashed pets are permitted.

Reservations, fees: Reservations are not accepted. There is no fee for camping. Open May to mid-October.

Directions: Drive on U.S. 395 to Big Pine and Crocker Street/Glacier Lodge Road. Turn northwest (toward the Sierra) and drive 9.5 miles (it becomes Glacier Lodge Road) to the parking area. Park and hike two miles to the campground.

Contact: Inyo National Forest, White Mountain Ranger District, 760/873-2500, fax 760/873-2563.

56 BIG PINE CREEK

🏃 🛶 🐕 ♿ 🚐 ⛺

Rating: 8

In Inyo National Forest.

Map 11.2, page 582

This is another good spot for backpackers to launch a multiday trip. The camp is set along Big Pine Creek at 7,700 feet, with trails near the camp that are routed to the numerous lakes in the high country of the John Muir Wilderness.

Campsites, facilities: There are five sites for tents only and 25 sites for tents or RVs. Picnic tables and fire grills are provided. Drinking water and vault toilets are available. Some facilities are wheelchair-accessible. Leashed pets are permitted.

Reservations, fees: Reserve at 877/444-6777 or website: www. ReserveUsa.com ($9 reservation fee); $13 per night. Senior discount available. Open early May through October.

Directions: Drive on U.S. 395 to Big Pine and Crocker Street/Glacier Lodge Road. Turn northwest (toward the Sierra) and drive nine miles (it becomes Glacier Lodge Road) to the campground.

Contact: Inyo National Forest, White Mountain Ranger District, 760/873-2500, fax 760/873-2563.

57 PALISADE-CLYDE GROUP CAMP

🏃 🛶 🐕 🚐 ⛺

Rating: 8

On Big Pine Creek in Inyo National Forest.

Map 11.2, page 582

This is a trailhead camp set at 7,600 feet, most popular for groups planning to rock-climb the Palisades. This climbing trip is for experienced mountaineers only; it's a dangerous expedition where risk of life can be included in the bargain. Safer options include exploring the surrounding John Muir Wilderness.

Campsites, facilities: There is one group site for tents or RVs. Picnic tables and fire grills

are provided. Drinking water and vault toilets are available. Leashed pets are permitted.

Reservations, fees: Reserve at 877/444-6777 or website: www. ReserveUsa.com ($9 reservation fee); $35 per night. Open mid-April to mid-October.

Directions: Drive on U.S. 395 to Big Pine and Crocker Street/Glacier Lodge Road. Turn northwest (toward the Sierra) and drive 8.5 miles (it becomes Glacier Lodge Road) and drive 9.5 miles to the campground.

Contact: Inyo National Forest, White Mountain Ranger District, 760/873-2500, fax 760/873-2563.

58 SAGE FLAT

🏃 🛶 🐕 ♿ 🚐 ⛺

Rating: 8

On Big Pine Creek near Big Pine in Inyo National Forest.

Map 11.2, page 582

This camp, like the others in the immediate vicinity, is set up primarily for backpackers who are getting ready to head out on multiday expeditions into the nearby John Muir Wilderness. The trail is routed west past several lakes to the base of the Palisades, and beyond to the John Muir Trail. Your hike from here will begin with a steep climb from the trailhead at 7,600 feet elevation. The camp is set along Big Pine Creek, which is stocked with small trout.

Campsites, facilities: There are 28 sites for tents or RVs. Picnic tables and fire grills are provided. Drinking water and vault toilets are available. Some facilities are wheelchair-accessible. Leashed pets are permitted.

Reservations, fees: Reservations are not accepted. The fee is $13 per night. Senior discount available. Open mid-April through October.

Directions: Drive on U.S. 395 to Big Pine and Crocker Street/Glacier Lodge Road. Turn northwest (toward the Sierra) and drive eight miles (it becomes Glacier Lodge Road) to the campground.

Contact: Inyo National Forest, White Mountain Ranger District, 760/873-2500, fax 760/873-2563.

59 UPPER SAGE FLAT

Rating: 8

On Big Pine Creek in Inyo National Forest.
Map 11.2, page 582

This is one in a series of Forest Service camps in the area set up primarily for backpackers taking off on wilderness expeditions. Several trails are available near the camp that lead into the John Muir Wilderness. The trail is routed west past several lakes to the base of the Palisades, and beyond to the John Muir Trail. Even starting at 7,600 feet, expect a steep climb.

Campsites, facilities: There are 21 sites for tents or RVs. Picnic tables and fire grills are provided. Drinking water and vault toilets are available. Leashed pets are permitted.

Reservations, fees: Reserve at 877/444-6777 or website: www. ReserveUsa.com ($9 reservation fee); $11 per night. Senior discount available. Open mid-April through October.

Directions: Drive on U.S. 395 to Big Pine and Crocker Street/Glacier Lodge Road. Turn northwest (toward the Sierra) and drive 8.5 miles (it becomes Glacier Lodge Road) to the campground.

Contact: Inyo National Forest, White Mountain Ranger District, 760/873-2500, fax 760/873-2563.

60 BAKER CREEK CAMPGROUND

Rating: 4

Near Big Pine.
Map 11.2, page 582

Because this is a county-operated RV park, it is overlooked by many who usually consider only camps on reservations systems. That makes this a good option for cruisers touring the eastern Sierra on U.S. 395. It's ideal for a quick overnighter, with easy access from Big Pine. The camp is set along Baker Creek at 4,000

feet in the high plateau country of the eastern Sierra. An option is fair trout fishing during the evening bite on the creek.

Campsites, facilities: There are 45 sites for tents or RVs. Picnic tables and fire grills are provided. Vault toilets are available. No drinking water is available, but the stream can be hand-pumped with a water filter. You can buy supplies about 1.5 miles away in Big Pine. Leashed pets are permitted.

Reservations, fees: Reservations are not accepted. The fee is $10 per night. Open year-round, weather permitting.

Directions: Drive on U.S. 395 to Big Pine and Baker Creek Road. Turn northwest (toward the Sierra) on Baker Creek Road and drive a mile to the campground on the left.

Contact: Inyo County Parks Department, 760/878-0272, fax 760/873-5599, website: www.395.com\inyo\campgrounds.

61 BROWN'S GLACIER

Rating: 4

Near Big Pine.
Map 11.2, page 582

This is one of two county camps near the town of Big Pine, providing U.S. 395 cruisers with two options. The camp is set along the Big Pine Canal at 3,900 feet. It is owned by the county but operated by a concessionaire. Some may remember this campground once was named Triangle Campground; it has been renamed and improved for the 2003 season. Brown's runs five small campgrounds in the area named Glacier, Keough Hot Springs, Moll Pond, Brown's Owens River, and Brown's Town.

Campsites, facilities: There are 40 sites, some with partial hookups, for RVs or tents. Picnic tables and fire grills are provided. Restrooms, drinking water, flush toilets and coin showers are available. Supplies are available in Big Pine. Leashed pets are permitted.

Reservations, fees: Reservations are not accepted. The fee is $14 per night for tent sites, $17 for

RV sites with partial hookups. Open April through October.

Directions: Drive on U.S. 395 to the park entrance (a half mile north of Big Pine) on the southeast side of the road. Turn east (away from the Sierra) and enter the park.

Contact: Inyo County Parks Department, 760/872-6911, fax 760/873-5599.

62 TINEMAHA CREEK COUNTY PARK

Rating: 6

Near Big Pine.
Map 11.2, page 582

This primitive, little-known (to out-of-towners) county park campground is on Tinemaha Creek at 4,400 feet. The park's campground will be renovated over the course of several years, with small changes each year. Partial hookups for RVs should be in by summer of 2003.

Campsites, facilities: There are 55 sites, some with partial hookups, for RVs or tents. Picnic tables and fire grills are provided. Pit toilets are available. No drinking water. Stream water is available and must be boiled or pump-filtered before use. Leashed pets are permitted.

Reservations, fees: Reservations are not accepted. The fee is $10 per vehicle per night. Open year-round.

Directions: Drive on U.S. 395 to Tinemaha Creek Road (seven miles south of Big Pine and 20 miles north of Indepence). Turn west (toward the Sierra) on Tinemaha Creek Road anddrive two miles to the park on the left.

Contact: Inyo County Parks Department, 760/878-0272, fax 760/873-5599.

63 TABOOSE CREEK COUNTY CAMPGROUND

Rating: 4

Near Big Pine.
Map 11.2, page 582

The eastern Sierra is stark country, but this lit-

tle spot provides a stream (Taboose Creek) and some trees near the campground. There is an opportunity for trout fishing, fair, not spectacular. The easy access off U.S. 395 is a bonus. The elevation is 3,900 feet.

Campsites, facilities: There are 55 sites for tents or RVs. Picnic tables and fire grills are provided. Drinking water (hand-pumped from a well) and vault toilets are available. Supplies are available in Big Pine or Independence. Leashed pets are permitted.

Reservations, fees: Reservations are not accepted. The fee is $10 per night. Open year-round.

Directions: Drive on U.S. 395 to Taboose Creek Road (11 miles south of Big Pine). Turn west (toward the Sierra) on Taboose Creek Road and drive 2.5 miles to the campground (straight in).

Contact: Inyo County Parks Department, 760/878-0272, fax 760/873-5599.

64 CHOINUMNI

Rating: 7

On lower Kings River.
Map 11.3, page 583

This campground is set in the San Joaquin foothills on the Kings River, a pretty area. Since the campground is operated by Fresno County, it is off the radar scope of many visitors. Fishing, rafting, and hiking are popular. The elevation is roughly 1,000 feet, surrounded by a landscape of oak woodlands and grassland foothills. The park is roughly 33 miles east of Fresno.

Campsites, facilities: There are 36 sites for tents or self-contained RVS, and one group site for up to 75 people. Picnic tables and fire rings are provided. Drinking water, flush toilets, and RV dump station are available. No facilities within 10 miles. Leashed pets are permitted.

Reservations, fees: No reservations accepted, except for the group site, $11 per night, $5 per extra vehicle with maximum of two; for the group site, $80 per night for up to

75 people. Senior discount available. Open year-round.

Directions: From Fresno, drive east on Highway 180 for 17.5 miles to Piedra Road. Turn left on Piedra Road and drive eight miles to Trimmer Springs Road. Turn right on Trimmer Springs Road and drive one mile to Pine Flat Road. Turn right and drive 100 yards to camp entrance on the right.

Contact: Fresno County Parks Department, 559/488-3004, fax 559/488-1988.

65 PINE FLAT RECREATION AREA
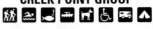

Rating: 7

On Pine Flat Reservoir.

Map 11.3, page 583

This is a county park that is open all year, set below the dam of Pine Flat Reservoir, actually not on the lake at all. As a county park campground, it is often overlooked by out-of-towners.

Campsites, facilities: There are 52 sites for tents or RVs. Fire grills and picnic tables are provided. Restrooms, drinking water, flush toilets, RV dump station, playground, and a wheelchair-accessible fishing area are available. A store, coin laundry, and propane gas are nearby (within a mile). Leashed pets are permitted.

Reservations, fees: Reservations are not accepted. The fee is $11 per night. Open year-round.

Directions: From Fresno, drive east on Highway 180 for 17.5 miles to Trimmer Springs Road. Turn left and drive eight miles to the town of Piedra. Continue on Trimmer Springs Road for one mile to Pine Flat Road. Turn right and drive three miles to the campground on the right.

Contact: Fresno County Parks Department, 559/488-3004, fax 559/488-1988.

66 ISLAND PARK AND DEER CREEK POINT GROUP

Rating: 7

On Pine Flat Reservoir.

Map 11.3, page 583

These are two of four Army Corps of Engineer campgrounds available at Pine Flat Reservoir, a popular lake set in the foothill country east of Fresno. When Pine Flat is full, or close to full, it is very pretty. The lake is 21 miles long with 67 miles of shoreline and 4,270 surface acres. Right: a big lake with unlimited potential. Because the temperatures get warm in spring here, then smoking hot in summer, the lake is like Valhalla for boating and water sports. The fishing for white bass is often excellent in late winter and early spring and, after that, conditions are ideal for water sports. The elevation is 1,000 feet.

Campsites, facilities: There are 52 sites for tents or self-contained RVs, 60 overflow sites (at Island Park), and two group sites for 50 people each for tents or RVs. Picnic tables and fire grills are provided. Restrooms, drinking water, flush toilets, coin showers, pay telephone, boat ramp, fish-cleaning station, and RV dump station are available. Some facilities are wheelchair-accessible. There is a seasonal store at the campground entrance. Boat rentals are available within five miles. Leashed pets are permitted.

Reservations, fees: Reservations for Island Park are available at 877/444-6777 ($9 reservation fee) or website: www.ReserveUsa.com; reservations for group sites required at 559/787-2589; $10–16 per night, $60 for group sites, $2 boat launch fee. Open year-round.

Directions: From Fresno, drive east on Highway 180 for 17.5 miles to Trimmer Springs Road. Turn left and drive eight miles to the town of Piedra. Continue on Trimmer Springs Road for one mile to Pine Flat Road. Turn right and drive a quarter mile to the park entrance (signed Island Park).

Contact: U.S. Army Corps of Engineers, Sacramento District, Pine Flat Field Office, 559/787-2589, fax 559/787-2773.

67 LAKERIDGE CAMPING AND BOATING RESORT

Rating: 7

On Pine Flat Reservoir.

Map 11.3, page 583

Pine Flat Reservoir is a big lake with seemingly unlimited recreation potential. It is in the foothills east of Fresno at 961 feet elevation, covering 4,270 surface acres with 67 miles of shoreline. The lake's proximity to Fresno has made it a top destination for boating and water sports. Fishing for white bass can also be excellent in the spring and early summer. Note: the one downer is that there are only a few sandy beaches.

Campsites, facilities: There are 108 sites, some with hookups, for tents or RVs up to 32 feet long. Picnic tables, restrooms, showers, modem access, coin laundry, convenience store, ice, pay phone, petting zoo, and houseboat rentals are available.

Reservations, fees: Reservations are recommended at 877/787-2260; $20 per night for tent sites and $25 per night for RV sites with hookups, $2.50 per person for more than two people, $2.50 per night. Major credit cards accepted.

Directions: From Fresno, drive east on Highway 180 for 17.5 miles to Trimmer Springs Road. Turn left and drive eight miles to the town of Piedra. Continue on Trimmer Springs Road for three miles to Sunnyslope Road. Turn right and drive one mile to the resort on the right.

Contact: Lakeridge Camping and Boating Resort, tel./fax 559/787-2260; marina, 559/787-2506.

68 KIRCH FLAT

Rating: 6

On the Kings River in Sierra National Forest.

Map 11.3, page 583

Kirch Flat is on the Kings River, about five miles from the head of Pine Flat Reservoir. This campground is a popular take-out spot for rafters running the Middle Kings, putting in at Garnet Dike dispersed camping area and then making the 10-mile run downstream to Kirch Flat, a Class III run. The camp is set in the foothill country at 1,100 feet in elevation, where the temperatures are often hot and the water cold.

Campsites, facilities: There are 17 sites for tents or RVs up to 22 feet long, and one group camp for up to 50 people. Picnic tables and fire grills are provided. Vault toilets are available. No drinking water is available. Leashed pets are permitted.

Reservations, fees: No reservations accepted, except for at the group site. There is no fee for individual sites, and the group camp fee is $50 per night, with a 50-person maximum. Open year-round.

Directions: From Fresno, drive east on Highway 180 for 17.5 miles to Trimmer Springs Road. Turn left and drive 28 miles to Trimmer. Continue east on Trimmer Springs Road (along the north shore of Pine Flat Reservoir) and drive 18 miles to the campground on the left.

Contact: Sierra National Forest, High Sierra Ranger District, 559/855-5360, fax 559/855-5375.

69 CAMP 4 1/2

Rating: 7

On the Kings River in Sequoia National Forest.

Map 11.3, page 583

We found five sites here, not "four and a half." This campground is small, primitive, and usually hot. It is one in a series of camps just east of Pine Flat Reservoir along the Kings River, primarily used for rafting access. (See the entries for Kirch Flat and Mill Flat campgrounds for more information.)

Campsites, facilities: There are five sites for tents only. Picnic tables and fire grills are provided. Vault toilets are available. No drinking water is available. Garbage must be packed out. Leashed pets are permitted.

Reservations, fees: Reservations are not accepted. There is no fee for camping. Open year-round.

Directions: From Fresno, drive east on Highway 180 for 17.5 miles to Trimmer Springs Road. Turn left and drive 28 miles to Trimmer. Continue east on Trimmer Springs Road (along the north shore of Pine Flat Reservoir) and drive 18 miles (it becomes Forest Road 11S12) to Forest Road 12S01 (crossing the river). Take Forest Road 12S01 for one mile (along the river) to a dirt road on the right (at the junction of the second bridge). Turn right (still Forest Road 12S01) and drive .7 mile to the campground. Not advised for trailers and large RVs.

Contact: Sequoia National Forest, Hume Lake Ranger District, 559/338-2251, fax 559/338-2131.

70 CAMP 4

Rating: 7

On the Kings River in Sequoia National Forest.

Map 11.3, page 583

This is one in a series of camps set on the Kings River upstream from Pine Flat Reservoir, a popular access point for rafters. The weather gets so hot that many take a dunk in the river on purpose; nonrafters had better bring a cooler stocked with ice and drinks. (See the entry for Mill Flat campground for information on a great hike to Garlic Falls.) Camp 4 is a mile from Mill Flat.

Campsites, facilities: There are five sites for

tents only. Picnic tables and fire grills are provided. Vault toilets are available. No drinking water is available. Garbage must be packed out. Leashed pets are permitted.

Reservations, fees: Reservations are not accepted. There is no fee for camping. Open year-round.

Directions: From Fresno, drive east on Highway 180 for 17.5 miles to Trimmer Springs Road. Turn left and drive 28 miles to Trimmer. Continue east on Trimmer Springs Road (along the north shore of Pine Flat Reservoir) and drive 18 miles (it becomes Forest Road 11S12) to Forest Road 12S01 (crossing the river). Take Forest Road 12S01 for one mile (along the river) to a dirt road on the right (at the junction of the second bridge). Turn right (still Forest Road 12S01) and drive 1.5 miles to the campground (on the south side of the river). Not advised for trailers and large RVs.

Contact: Sequoia National Forest, Hume Lake Ranger District, 559/338-2251, fax 559/338-2131.

71 MILL FLAT

Rating: 7

On the Kings River in Sequoia National Forest.

Map 11.3, page 583

This camp is on the Kings River at the confluence of Mill Flat Creek. It's a small, primitive spot that gets very hot in the summer. Rafters sometimes use this as an access point for trips down the Kings River. A side trip from this camp is driving east on the Forest Service access road for five miles to its end point at the Kings River National Recreational Trail, and then making the challenging seven-mile hike to the overlook of spectacular Garlic Falls. This is best in spring and early summer, when melting snow from the high country fills the river with water, and yet when temperatures are still cool enough for excellent hiking conditions.

Campsites, facilities: There are five sites for

tents only. Picnic tables and fire grills are provided. Vault toilets are available. No drinking water is available. Garbage must be packed out. Leashed pets are permitted.

Reservations, fees: Reservations are not accepted. There is no fee for camping. Open year-round.

Directions: From Fresno, drive east on Highway 180 for 17.5 miles to Trimmer Springs Road. Turn left and drive 28 miles to Trimmer. Continue east on Trimmer Springs Road (along the north shore of Pine Flat Reservoir) and drive 18 miles (it becomes Forest Road 11S12) to Forest Road 12S01 (crossing the river). Take Forest Road 12S01 for one mile (along the river) to a dirt road on the right (at the junction of the second bridge). Turn right (still Forest Road 12S01) and drive 2.5 miles to the campground (on the south side of the river). Not advised for trailers and large RVs.

Contact: Sequoia National Forest, Hume Lake Ranger District, 559/338-2251, fax 559/338-2131.

72 BLACK ROCK

Rating: 7

On Black Rock Reservoir in Sierra National Forest.

Map 11.3, page 583

Little Black Rock Reservoir is a little-known spot that can provide a quiet respite compared to the other big-time lakes and camps in the region. The camp is set near the outlet stream on the west end of the lake, created from a small dam on the North Fork Kings River at 4,200 feet elevation.

Campsites, facilities: There are seven sites for tents only and a trailer site. Picnic tables and fire grills are provided. Drinking water and vault toilets are available. Garbage must be packed out. Leashed pets are permitted.

Reservations, fees: Reservations are not accepted. The fee is $10 per night. Senior discount available. Open May through September.

Directions: From Fresno, drive east on Highway 180 for 17.5 miles to Trimmer Springs Road. Turn left and drive 28 miles to Trimmer. Continue east on Trimmer Springs Road (along the north shore of Pine Flat Reservoir) and drive 18 miles to Black Road. Turn left and drive 10 miles to the campground.

Contact: Sierra National Forest, High Sierra Ranger District, 559/855-5360, fax 559/855-5375.

73 LEMON COVE-SEQUOIA

Rating: 5

Near Lake Kaweah.

Map 11.3, page 583

This is a privately run, year-round campground set in the foothills just west of Lake Kaweah. Some use this park as a base camp for enjoying nearby Lake Kaweah or as a launch point for a trip into the mountains and Sequoia National Park. Compared to many towns in the San Joaquin Valley, Visalia is exceptionally clean, pretty, with greenery from the surrounding farms for many miles. This park is 18 miles from Visalia to the west and three miles from Lake Kaweah to the east (on Highway 198). By the way, the nearby groves of fruit trees along the highway provide a fantastic sideshow.

Campsites, facilities: There are 55 sites, many with partial hookups, for RVs or tents, and group camping facilities. Picnic tables, and drinking water are provided. Restrooms, showers, playground, swimming pool, laundry facilities, recreation room, cable TV, store, RV dump station, and propane gas are available. Leashed pets are permitted.

Reservations, fees: Reservations are accepted. The fee is $18–22 per night. Open year-round. Major credit cards accepted.

Directions: From Visalia, drive east on Highway 198 for 18 miles to the campground.

Contact: Lemon Cove-Sequoia, 559/597-2346, website: www.lemoncovesequoia.com.

74 PRINCESS

Rating: 7

On Princess Meadow in Giant Sequoia National Monument.

Map 11.4, page 584

This mountain camp is at 5,900 feet. It is popular because of its proximity to both Hume Lake and the star attractions at Kings Canyon National Park. Hume Lake is just four miles from the camp and the Grant Grove entrance to Kings Canyon National Park is only six miles away to the south, while continuing on Highway 180 to the east will take you into the heart of Kings Canyon.

Campsites, facilities: There are 50 sites for tents and 40 sites for tents or RVs up to 22 feet long. Picnic tables and fire grills are provided. Drinking water, vault toilets, and RV dump station are available. A store is four miles away at Hume Lake. Leashed pets are permitted.

Reservations, fees: Reserve at 877/444-6777 or website: www.ReserveUsa.com ($9 reservation fee); $14 per night, plus $10 per vehicle national park entrance fee, $28 per night for a double site, $5 for each extra vehicle. Senior discount available. Open May through September.

Directions: From Fresno, drive east on Highway 180 for 55 miles to the Big Stump Entrance Station at Sequoia-Kings Canyon National Park. Continue 1.5 miles to a junction (signed left for Grant Grove). Turn left and drive 1.5 miles to Grant Grove Village, then continue for 4.5 miles to the campground on the right.

Contact: Sequoia National Forest, Hume Lake Ranger District, 559/338-2251, fax 559/338-2131.

75 HUME LAKE

Rating: 8

In Giant Sequoia National Monument.

Map 11.4, page 584

For newcomers, Hume Lake is a surprise: a pretty lake, with great summer camps for teenagers. Canoeing and kayaking are excellent, and so is the trout fishing, especially near the dam. Another surprise is the adjacent religious camp center. The nearby entrances to Kings Canyon National Park add a bonus. The elevation is 5,200 feet.

Campsites, facilities: There are 60 tent sites and 14 sites for tents or RVs up to 22 feet long. Picnic tables and fire grills are provided. Drinking water and flush toilets are available. A store is nearby. Leashed pets are permitted.

Reservations, fees: Reservations are recommended for weekends and holidays; reserve at 877/444-6777 or website: www.ReserveUsa.com ($9 reservation fee); $16 per night, $5 for each extra vehicle. Senior discount available. Open May through August.

Directions: From Fresno, drive east on Highway 180 for 55 miles to the Big Stump Entrance Station at Sequoia-Kings Canyon National Park. Continue 1.5 miles to a junction (signed left for Grant Grove). Turn left and drive six miles to the Hume Lake Road junction. Turn right and drive three miles to Hume Lake and the campground entrance road. Turn right and drive a quarter mile to the campground on the left.

Contact: Sequoia National Forest, Hume Lake Ranger District, 559/338-2251, fax 559/338-2131.

76 ASPEN HOLLOW GROUP CAMP

Rating: 6

Near Hume Lake in Sequoia National Forest.

Map 11.4, page 584

This large group camp is set at 5,200 feet about a mile south of Hume Lake near a feeder to Tenmile Creek, the inlet stream to Hume Lake. Entrances to Kings Canyon National Park are nearby.

Campsites, facilities: This is a group campsite for up to 100 people. Picnic tables and fire grills are provided. Drinking water and vault toilets are available. A store is nearby. Leashed pets are permitted.

Reservations, fees: Reserve at 877/444-6777 or website: www. ReserveUsa.com ($9 reservation fee); $150 per night. Open May through August.

Directions: From Fresno, drive east on Highway 180 for 55 miles to the Big Stump Entrance Station at Sequoia-Kings Canyon National Park. Continue 1.5 miles to a junction (signed left for Grant Grove). Turn left and drive six miles to the Hume Lake Road junction. Turn right and drive three miles to Hume Lake and the campground entrance road. Turn right and drive around Hume Lake. Continue south one mile (past the lake) to the campground entrance road.

Contact: Sequoia National Forest, Hume Lake Ranger District, 559/338-2251, fax 559/338-2131.

77 LOGGER FLAT GROUP CAMP

Rating: 7

On Tenmile Creek in Giant Sequoia National Monument.

Map 11.4, page 584

This is the group-site alternative to Landslide campground. This camp is set near the confluence of Tenmile Creek and Landslide Creek, about two miles upstream from Hume Lake. (For more information, see the entry for Landslide.)

Campsites, facilities: This is one group campsite for up to 50 people. Picnic tables and fire grills are provided. Drinking water and vault toilets are available. A store is nearby. Leashed pets are permitted.

Reservations, fees: Reserve at 877/444-6777 or website: www. ReserveUsa.com ($9 reservation fee); $75 per night.

Directions: From Fresno, drive east on Highway 180 for 55 miles to the Big Stump Entrance Station at Sequoia-Kings Canyon National Park. Continue 1.5 miles to a junction (signed

left for Grant Grove). Turn left and drive six miles to the Hume Lake Road junction. Turn right and drive three miles to Hume Lake and the campground entrance road. Turn right and drive around Hume Lake to Tenmile Road. Continue south three miles to the campground entrance on the right.

Contact: Sequoia National Forest, Hume Lake Ranger District, 559/338-2251, fax 559/338-2131.

78 LANDSLIDE

Rating: 7

On Landslide Creek in Giant Sequoia National Monument.

Map 11.4, page 584

If you want quiet, you got it; few folks know about this camp. If you want a stream nearby, you got it; Landslide Creek runs right beside the camp. If you want a lake nearby, you got it; Hume Lake is just to the north. If you want a national park nearby, you got it; Kings Canyon National Park is nearby. Add it up: you got it. The elevation is 5,800 feet.

Campsites, facilities: There are six sites for tents only and three sites for tents or RVs up to 16 feet long. Picnic tables and fire grills are provided. Drinking water and vault toilets are available. A store is nearby. Leashed pets are permitted.

Reservations, fees: Reservations are not accepted. The fee is $12 per night, $5 per extra vehicle. Senior discount available. Open May through September.

Directions: From Fresno, drive east on Highway 180 for 55 miles to the Big Stump Entrance Station at Sequoia-Kings Canyon National Park. Continue 1.5 miles to a junction (signed left for Grant Grove). Turn right at Generals Highway and drive three miles to Hume Lake Road/Ten Mile Road (Forest Road 13S09). Turn left and drive about seven miles (past Tenmile Campground) to the campground on the right.

Contact: Sequoia National Forest, Hume Lake Ranger District, 559/338-2251, fax 559/338-2131.

79 AZALEA

Rating: 7

In Kings Canyon National Park.

Map 11.4, page 584

This camp is tucked just inside the western border of Sequoia National Park. It is set at 6,600 feet near the General Grant Grove of giant sequoias. (For information on several short, spectacular hikes among the giant sequoias, see the entry for Sunset.) Nearby Sequoia Lake is privately owned; no fishing, no swimming, no trespassing. To see the spectacular Kings Canyon, one of the deepest gorges in North America, reenter the park on Highway 180.

Campsites, facilities: There are 113 sites for tents or RVs up to 30 feet long. Picnic tables and fire grills are provided. Drinking water, flush toilets, and horseback riding facilities are available. Evening ranger programs are often available in the summer. Some facilities are wheelchair-accessible. A store is nearby. Showers are available in Grant Grove Village. Leashed pets are permitted, except on trails.

Reservations, fees: Reservations are not accepted. The fee is $14 per night, $10 per vehicle park entrance fee. Senior discount available. Open year-round.

Directions: From Fresno, drive east on Highway 180 for 55 miles to the Big Stump Entrance Station at Sequoia-Kings Canyon National Park. Continue 1.5 miles to a junction (signed left for Grant Grove). Turn left and drive 1.5 miles to Grant Grove Village, then continue for .7 mile to the campground entrance on the left.

Contact: Kings Canyon National Park, 559/565-3341.

80 SUNSET

Rating: 7

In Kings Canyon National Park.

Map 11.4, page 584

This is the biggest of the camps that are just inside the Sequoia National Park boundaries at Grant Grove Village, 6,600 feet in elevation. The nearby General Grant Grove of Giant Sequoias is the main attraction, with many short, easy walks among the sequoias, each breathtakingly beautiful. They include the Big Stump Trail, Sunset Trail, North Grove Loop, General Grant Tree, Manzanita and Azalea Loop, and Panoramic Point and Park Ridge Trail. Seeing the General Grant Tree is a rite of passage for newcomers; after a half-hour walk you arrive at a sequoia that is 1,800 years old, 107 feet in circumference, and 267 feet tall.

Campsites, facilities: There are 200 sites for tents or RVs up to 30 feet long. Picnic tables and fire grills are provided. Drinking water, flush toilets, and horseback riding facilities are available. Some facilities are wheelchair-accessible. In the summer, evening ranger programs are often available. A store is nearby. Showers are available in Grant Grove Village. Leashed pets are permitted, except on trails.

Reservations, fees: Reservations are not accepted. The fee is $14 per night, $10 per vehicle park entrance fee. Senior discount available. Open late May to mid-September.

Directions: From Fresno, drive east on Highway 180 for 55 miles to the Big Stump Entrance Station at Sequoia-Kings Canyon National Park. Continue 1.5 miles to a junction (signed left for Grant Grove). Turn left (still Highway 180) and drive one mile to the campground entrance (a half mile before reaching Grant Grove Village).

Contact: Kings Canyon National Park, 559/565-3341.

81 CRYSTAL SPRINGS
🧍🐕♿🚐⛺

Rating: 5

In Kings Canyon National Park.
Map 11.4, page 584

Directly to the south of this camp is the General Grant Grove and its giant sequoias. But continuing on Highway 180 provides access to the interior of Kings Canyon National Park, and this camp makes an ideal jump-off point. From here you can drive east, passing Cedar Grove Village, cruising along the Kings River, and finally coming to a dead-end loop, taking in the drop-dead gorgeous landscape of one of the deepest gorges in North America. One of the best hikes, but also the most demanding, is the 13-mile round-trip to Lookout Peak, out of the Cedar Grove Village area. It involves a 4,000-foot climb to 8,531 feet, and with it, a breathtaking view of Sierra ridges, Cedar Grove far below, and Kings Canyon.

Campsites, facilities: There are 62 sites for tents or RVs up to 22 feet long. Picnic tables and fire grills are provided. Drinking water, flush toilets, and horseback riding facilities are available. Evening ranger programs are often available in the summer. Some facilities are wheelchair-accessible. A store is nearby. Showers are available in Grant Grove Village. Leashed pets are permitted, except on trails.

Reservations, fees: Reservations are not accepted. The fee is $14 per night, $10 per vehicle park entrance fee. Senior discount available. Open mid-May to late September.

Directions: From Fresno, drive east on Highway 180 for 55 miles to the Big Stump Entrance Station at Sequoia-Kings Canyon National Park. Continue 1.5 miles to a junction (signed left for Grant Grove). Turn left and drive 1.5 miles to Grant Grove Village, then continue for .7 mile to the campground entrance on the right.

Contact: Kings Canyon National Park, 559/565-3341.

82 TENMILE
🏊🐕🚐⛺

Rating: 7

On Tenmile Creek in Giant Sequoia National Monument.
Map 11.4, page 584

This is one of three small, primitive campgrounds along Tenmile Creek south (and upstream) of Hume Lake. This one is about four miles from the lake at 5,800 feet in elevation. It provides an alternative to camping in nearby Kings Canyon National Park.

Campsites, facilities: There are 10 sites for tents or RVs up to 22 feet long. Picnic tables and fire grills are provided. Vault toilets are available. No drinking water is available. Leashed pets are permitted.

Reservations, fees: Reservations are not accepted. There is no fee for camping. Open May through September.

Directions: From Fresno, drive east on Highway 180 for 55 miles to the Big Stump Entrance Station at Sequoia-Kings Canyon National Park. Continue 1.5 miles to a junction (signed left for Grant Grove). Turn right at Generals Highway and drive three miles to Hume Lake Road/Tenmile Road (Forest Road 13S09). Turn left and drive about five miles to the campground on the left.

Contact: Sequoia National Forest, Hume Lake Ranger District, 559/338-2251, fax 559/338-2131.

83 BUCK ROCK
🐕🚐⛺

Rating: 4

Near Big Meadows Creek in Giant Sequoia National Monument.
Map 11.4, page 584

This is a remote camp that provides a little-known option to nearby Sequoia and Kings Canyon National Parks. If the national parks are full and you're stuck, this camp provides an insurance policy. The elevation is 7,500 feet.

Campsites, facilities: There are five primitive sites for tents or RVs up to 16 feet long. Picnic tables and fire grills are provided. Vault toilets are available. No drinking water is available. Leashed pets are permitted.

Reservations, fees: No reservations accepted and there is no fee. However, a $10 per vehicle national park entrance fee does apply. Open June through September.

Directions: From Fresno, drive east on Highway 180 for 55 miles to the Big Stump Entrance Station at Sequoia-Kings Canyon National Park. Continue 1.5 miles to a junction (signed left for Grant Grove). Turn right at Generals Highway and drive about five miles to Big Meadows Road/Forest Road 14S11. Turn left on Big Meadows Road and drive five miles to the campground entrance road on the left. Turn left and drive a short distance to the campground.

Contact: Sequoia National Forest, Hume Lake Ranger District, 559/338-2251, fax 559/338-2131.

84 BIG MEADOWS
Rating: 7

On Big Meadows Creek in Giant Sequoia National Monument.

Map 11.4, page 584

This primitive, high-mountain camp (7,600 feet) is beside little Big Meadows Creek. Backpackers can use this as a launching pad, with the nearby trailhead (one mile down the road to the west) leading to the Jennie Lake Wilderness. Kings Canyon National Park, only a 12-mile drive away, is a nearby side trip.

Campsites, facilities: There are numerous sites along Big Meadows Creek and Big Meadows Road for tents or RVs up to 22 feet long. Picnic tables and fire grills are provided. Vault toilets are available. No drinking water is available. Leashed pets are permitted.

Reservations, fees: No reservations accepted and there is no fee. There is a $10 per vehicle

national park entrance fee. Open June through September.

Directions: From Fresno, drive east on Highway 180 for 55 miles to the Big Stump Entrance Station at Sequoia-Kings Canyon National Park. Continue 1.5 miles to a junction (signed left for Grant Grove). Turn right at Generals Highway and drive about five miles to Big Meadows Road/Forest Road 14S11. Turn left on Big Meadows Road and drive five miles to the camp.

Contact: Sequoia National Forest, Hume Lake Ranger District, 559/338-2251, fax 559/338-2131.

85 GOODALE CREEK
Rating: 6

Near Independence.

Map 11.4, page 584

This obscure BLM camp is set along little Goodale Creek at 4,000 feet. It is a good layover spot for U.S. 395 cruisers heading north. In hot summer months, snakes are occasionally spotted near this campground.

Campsites, facilities: There are 62 sites for tents or RVs. Picnic tables and fire rings are provided. Pit toilets are available. No drinking water is available. Leashed pets are permitted.

Reservations, fees: Reservations are not accepted. There is no fee for camping. Open mid-April through October.

Directions: Drive on U.S. 395 to Aberdeen Road (12 miles north of Independence). Turn west (toward the Sierra) on Aberdeen Road and drive two miles to the campground on the left.

Contact: Bureau of Land Management, Bishop Field Office, 760/872-4881, fax 760/873-5050.

86 SENTINEL

Rating: 8

In Kings Canyon National Park.

Map 11.4, page 584

This camp provides a nearby alternative to Sheep Creek. They both tend to fill up quickly in the summer. It's a short walk to Cedar Grove Village, the center of activity in the park. The elevation is 4,600 feet. Hiking and trout fishing are excellent in the vicinity. The entrance road provides stunning rim-of-the-world views of Kings Canyon, and then drops down right along the Kings River.

Campsites, facilities: There are 82 sites for tents or RVs up to 30 feet long. Picnic tables and fire grills are provided. Restrooms, drinking water, flush toilets, and showers are available. Some facilities are wheelchair-accessible. A store, coin laundry, restaurant, and horseback riding facilities are nearby. Leashed pets are permitted.

Reservations, fees: Reservations are not accepted. The fee is $14 per night, $10 per vehicle park entrance fee. Senior discount available. Open late April through mid-November, weather permitting.

Directions: From Fresno, drive east on Highway 180 for 55 miles to the Big Stump Entrance Station at Sequoia-Kings Canyon National Park. Continue 1.5 miles to a junction (signed left for Grant Grove). Turn left and drive 32 miles to the campground entrance on the left (near Cedar Grove Village).

Contact: Kings Canyon National Park, 559/565-3341.

87 SHEEP CREEK

Rating: 8

In Kings Canyon National Park.

Map 11.4, page 584

This is one of the camps that always fills up quickly on summer weekends. It's a pretty spot and just a short walk from Cedar Grove Village. The camp is set along Sheep Creek at 4,600 feet.

Campsites, facilities: There are 111 sites for tents or RVs up to 30 feet long. Picnic tables and fire grills are provided. Restrooms, drinking water, flush toilets, and showers are available. A store, coin laundry, restaurant, and horseback riding facilities are available nearby. Leashed pets are permitted.

Reservations, fees: Reservations are not accepted. The fee is $14 per night, $10 per vehicle park entrance fee. Senior discount available. Open June through September.

Directions: From Fresno, drive east on Highway 180 for 55 miles to the Big Stump Entrance Station at Sequoia-Kings Canyon National Park. Continue 1.5 miles to a junction (signed left for Grant Grove). Turn left and drive 31.5 miles to the campground entrance on the left (near Cedar Grove Village).

Contact: Kings Canyon National Park, 559/565-3341.

88 CANYON VIEW

Rating: 8

In Kings Canyon National Park.

Map 11.4, page 584

This is another of several camps in the Cedar Grove Village area of the Kings Canyon National Park. The access road leads to dramatic views of the deep Kings River Canyon, one of the deepest gorges in North America. The elevation is 4,600 feet.

Campsites, facilities: There are 37 sites for tents. Picnic tables and fire grills are provided. Drinking water and flush toilets are available. Showers, horseback riding facilities, store, restaurant, and a coin laundry are nearby. Leashed pets are permitted.

Reservations, fees: Reservations are not accepted. The fee is $14 per night, $10 per vehicle park entrance fee. Senior discount available. Open June through September, weather permitting.

Directions: From Fresno, drive east on Highway 180 for 55 miles to the Big Stump Entrance Station at Sequoia-Kings Canyon National Park. Continue 1.5 miles to a junction (signed left for Grant Grove). Turn left and drive 32.5 miles to the campground entrance (a half mile past the ranger station, near Cedar Grove Village).

Contact: Kings Canyon National Park, 559/565-3341.

89 CANYON VIEW GROUP CAMP

Rating: 8

In Kings Canyon National Park.

Map 11.4, page 584

If it weren't for this spot, large groups wishing to camp together in Kings Canyon National Park would be out of luck. Reservations are a must. The elevation is 4,600 feet.

Campsites, facilities: There are four group sites for tents for a minimum of 20 people and a maximum of 40 people per site. Picnic tables and fire grills are provided. Drinking water and flush toilets are available. A store, coin laundry, showers, restaurant, and horseback riding facilities are nearby (within 1.5 miles). Leashed pets are permitted.

Reservations, fees: Reservations are required by mail at Canyon View Group Sites, P.O. Box 926, Kings Canyon National Park, CA 93633, or by fax at 559/565-0314 May through October, or by fax at 559/565-4391 November through April; $40 per night, plus $10 per vehicle park entrance fee. Open June through September, weather permitting.

Directions: From Fresno, drive east on Highway 180 for 55 miles to the Big Stump Entrance Station at Sequoia-Kings Canyon National Park. Continue 1.5 miles to a junction (signed left for Grant Grove). Turn left and drive 32.5 miles to the campground entrance (a half mile past the ranger station, near Cedar Grove Village).

Contact: For group camp information only,

559/565-3792 May through October, 559/565-4335 November through April; Kings Canyon National Park, 559/565-3341.

90 MORAINE

Rating: 8

In Kings Canyon National Park.

Map 11.4, page 584

This is one in a series of camps in the Cedar Grove Village area of Kings Canyon National Park. This camp is used only as an overflow area. Hikers should drive past the Cedar Grove Ranger Station to the end of the road at Copper Creek, a prime jump-off point for a spectacular hike. The elevation is 4,600 feet.

Campsites, facilities: There are 120 sites for tents or RVs. Picnic tables and fire grills are provided. Drinking water and flush toilets are available. Showers, horseback riding facilities, store, restaurant, and a coin laundry are nearby. Leashed pets are permitted.

Reservations, fees: Reservations are not accepted. The fee is $14 per night, $10 per vehicle park entrance fee. Senior discount available. Open June through September, weather permitting.

Directions: From Fresno, drive east on Highway 180 for 55 miles to the Big Stump Entrance Station at Sequoia-Kings Canyon National Park. Continue 1.5 miles to a junction (signed left for Grant Grove). Turn left and drive 33 miles to the campground entrance (one mile past the ranger station, near Cedar Village).

Contact: Kings Canyon National Park, 559/565-3341.

91 ONION VALLEY

Rating: 8

In Inyo National Forest.

Map 11.4, page 584

Onion Valley is one of the best trailhead camps for backpackers in the Sierra. The camp is set at 9,200 feet, and from here it's a 2,600-foot climb over the course of about three miles to awesome Kearsage Pass (11,823 feet). From there you can camp at the Kearsage Lakes, explore the Kearsage Pinnacles, or join the John Muir Trail and venture to your choice of many High Sierra Ranger District lakes. A wilderness map and a free wilderness permit (if obtained from the ranger station) are your passports to the high country from this camp. Note: bears frequent this camp almost every night of summer. Do not keep your food in your vehicle. Many cars have been severely damaged by bears. Use bearproof food lockers at the campground and parking area, or use bearproof food canisters. For backpackers, trailhead reservations are required.

Campsites, facilities: There are 29 sites for tents only. Picnic tables and fire grills are provided. Drinking water and vault toilets are available. Leashed pets are permitted.

Reservations, fees: Reservations are accepted at 877/444-6777 ($9 reservation fee) or website: www.ReserveUsa.com; $12 per night. Senior discount available. Open mid-June through September.

Directions: Drive on U.S. 395 to Independence and Onion Valley Road. Turn west (toward the Sierra) at Onion Valley Road and drive 15 miles to the campground at the road's end.

Contact: Inyo National Forest, Mt. Whitney Ranger District, 760/876-6200, fax 760/876-6202.

92 GRAY'S MEADOW

Rating: 6

On Independence Creek in Inyo National Forest.

Map 11.4, page 584

Gray's Meadow is one of two adjacent camps that are set along Independence Creek. The creek is stocked with small trout by the Department of Fish and Game. The highlight in the immediate area is the trailhead at the end

of the road at Onion Valley Camp. For U.S. 395 cruisers looking for a spot, this is a pretty alternative to the camps in Bishop.

Campsites, facilities: There are 52 sites for tents or RVs. Picnic tables and fire grills are provided. Drinking water and flush toilets are available. Supplies and a coin laundry are available in Independence. Leashed pets are permitted.

Reservations, fees: Reserve at 877/444-6777 or website: www. ReserveUsa.com ($9 reservation fee); $12 per night. Senior discount available. Open April through October.

Directions: Drive on U.S. 395 to Independence and Onion Valley Road. Turn west (toward the Sierra) at Onion Valley Road and drive five miles to the campground on the right.

Contact: Inyo National Forest, Mt. Whitney Ranger District, 760/876-6200, fax 760/876-6202.

93 OAK CREEK

Rating: 6

In Inyo National Forest.

Map 11.4, page 584

Oak Creek is in a series of little-known camps west of Independence that provide a jump-off spot for backpackers. This camp is set at 5,000 feet, with a trail from camp that is routed west (and up) into the California Bighorn Sheep Zoological Area, a rugged, stark region well above the tree line. Caution: plan on a terrible, long, butt-kicker of a climb up to the Sierra crest; stay on the trail. Note that half of the campsites are available by reservation, half first-come, first-served.

Campsites, facilities: There are 22 sites for tents or RVs. Picnic tables and fire grills are provided. Drinking water and vault toilets are available. Garbage must be packed out. Some facilities are wheelchair-accessible. Supplies and a coin laundry are available in Independence. Leashed pets are permitted.

Reservations, fees: Reservations are accepted at 877/444-6777. The fee is $12 per night. Senior discount available. Open year-round, weather permitting.

Directions: Drive on U.S. 395 to North Oak Creek Drive (two miles north of Independence). Turn west (toward the Sierra) at North Oak Creek Drive and drive three miles to the campground on the right.

Contact: Inyo National Forest, Mt. Whitney Ranger District, 760/876-6200, fax 760/876-6202.

94 INDEPENDENCE CREEK COUNTY CAMPGROUND

Rating: 4

In Independence.

Map 11.4, page 584

This unpublicized county park is often overlooked among U.S. 395 cruisers. It is set at 3,900 feet just outside of Independence, which is spiraling downward into something resembling a ghost town. True to form, maintenance is sometimes lacking here. Independence Creek (no fishing) runs through the campground and a museum is within walking distance. At the rate it's going, the whole town could be a museum.

Campsites, facilities: There are 25 sites for tents or RVs. Picnic tables are provided. Drinking water and vault toilets are available. Some facilities are wheelchair-accessible. Supplies and a coin laundry are available in Independence. Leashed pets are permitted.

Reservations, fees: Reservations are not accepted. The fee is $10 per night. Open year-round.

Directions: Drive on U.S. 395 to Independence and Market Street. Turn west (toward the Sierra) at Market Street and drive a half mile (outside the town limits) to the campground.

Contact: Inyo County Parks Department, 760/878-0272, fax 760/873-5599.

95 ESHOM CREEK

Rating: 7

On Eshom Creek in Giant Sequoia National Monument.

Map 11.4, page 584

The campground at Eshom Creek is just two miles outside the boundaries of Sequoia National Park. It is well hidden and a considerable distance from the crowds and sights in the park interior. It is set along Eshom Creek at an elevation of 4,800 feet. Many campers at Eshom Creek hike straight into the national park, with a trailhead at Redwood Saddle (just inside the park boundary) providing a route to see the Redwood Mountain Grove, Fallen Goliath, Hart Tree, and Hart Meadow in a sensational loop hike.

Campsites, facilities: There are 17 sites for tents or RVs up to 22 feet long, and seven group sites for up to 12 people each. Picnic tables and fire grills are provided. Drinking water and vault toilets are available. Leashed pets are permitted.

Reservations, fees: Reservations are not accepted. The fee is $14 per night, $28 per night for group site. Open May through September.

Directions: Drive on Highway 99 to Visalia and the exit for Highway 198 East. Take that exit and drive east on Highway 198 for 11 miles to Highway 245. Turn left (north) on Highway 245 and drive 18 miles to Badger and County Road 465. Turn right and drive eight miles to the campground.

Contact: Sequoia National Forest, Hume Lake Ranger District, 559/338-2251, fax 559/338-2131.

96 FIR GROUP CAMPGROUND

Rating: 6

Near Stony Creek in Giant Sequoia National Monument.

Map 11.4, page 584

This is the second of two large group camps in the area set along Stony Creek.

Campsites, facilities: This is a group campsite for up to 100 people in tents or self-contained RVs. Picnic tables and fire grills are provided. Drinking water and vault toilets are available. A store and coin laundry are nearby. Leashed pets are permitted.

Reservations, fees: Reserve at 877/444-6777 or website: www. ReserveUsa.com ($9 reservation fee); $75 per night, plus $10 per vehicle national park entrance fee. Open June through August.

Directions: From Fresno, drive east on Highway 180 for 55 miles to the Big Stump Entrance Station at Sequoia-Kings Canyon National Park. Continue 1.5 miles to a junction (signed left for Grant Grove). Turn right at Generals Highway and drive about 14 miles to the campground entrance on the right.

Contact: Sequoia National Forest, Hume Lake Ranger District, 559/338-2251, fax 559/338-2131.

97 STONY CREEK

Rating: 6

In Giant Sequoia National Monument.
Map 11.4, page 584

Stony Creek Camp provides a good option if the national park camps are filled. It is set at creekside at 6,400 feet elevation. Sequoia and Kings Canyon National Parks are nearby.

Campsites, facilities: There are 49 sites for tents and RVs up to 22 feet long. Picnic tables and fire grills are provided. Drinking water and flush toilets are available. A store and coin laundry are nearby. Leashed pets are permitted.

Reservations, fees: Reserve at 877/444-6777 or website: www. ReserveUsa.com ($9 reservation fee); $16 per night, plus $10 per vehicle park entrance fee, $5 for each extra vehicle. Senior discount available. Open June through August.

Directions: From Fresno, drive east on Highway 180 for 55 miles to the Big Stump Entrance Station at Sequoia-Kings Canyon National Park. Continue 1.5 miles to a junction (signed

left for Grant Grove). Turn right at Generals Highway and drive about 13 miles to the campground entrance on the right.

Contact: Sequoia National Forest, Hume Lake Ranger District, 559/338-2251, fax 559/338-2131.

98 COVE GROUP CAMP

Rating: 6

Near Stony Creek in Giant Sequoia National Monument.
Map 11.4, page 584

This large group camp is beside Stony Creek. The elevation is 6,500 feet.

Campsites, facilities: This is a group campsite for up to 50 people in tents or self-contained RVs. Picnic tables and fire grills are provided. Drinking water and vault toilets are available. A store and coin laundry are available nearby. Leashed pets are permitted.

Reservations, fees: Reserve at 877/444-6777 or website: www. ReserveUsa.com ($9 reservation fee); $50 per night, plus $10 per vehicle national park entrance fee. Open June through August.

Directions: From Fresno, drive east on Highway 180 for 55 miles to the Big Stump Entrance Station at Sequoia-Kings Canyon National Park. Continue 1.5 miles to a junction (signed left for Grant Grove). Turn right at Generals Highway and drive about 14 miles to the campground entrance on the right (just past Fir Group Campground).

Contact: Sequoia National Forest, Hume Lake Ranger District, 559/338-2251, fax 559/338-2131.

99 DORST CREEK

Rating: 7

On Dorst Creek in Sequoia National Park.
Map 11.4, page 584

Things that go bump in the night swing through Dorst all summer long. That's right, Mr. Bear (a whole bunch of them) makes food raids like a UPS driver on a pick-up route. There are so many bears raiding food here that some years rangers keep a running tally posted on the bulletin board. That's why keeping your food in a bearproof locker is not only a must, it's the law. The camp is set on Dorst Creek at 6,700 feet, near a trail that is routed into the backcountry and through Muir Grove. It is one in a series of big, popular camps in Sequoia National Park.

Campsites, facilities: There are 204 family sites for tents or RVs up to 30 feet long and five group sites. Picnic tables and fire grills are provided. Drinking water, flush toilets, RV dump station, and evening ranger programs are available. Some facilities are wheelchair-accessible. A store and a coin laundry are nearby. Leashed pets are permitted.

Reservations, fees: Reserve at 800/365-CAMP (800/365-2267) or website: reservations.nps.gov; $16 per night (includes reservation fee), plus $10 per vehicle park entrance fee, $38–57 for group sites. Open Memorial Day through Labor Day.

Directions: From Fresno, drive east on Highway 180 for 55 miles to the Big Stump Entrance Station at Sequoia-Kings Canyon National Park. Continue 1.5 miles to a junction (signed left for Grant Grove). Turn right at Generals Highway and drive about 17 miles to the campground entrance on the right.

Contact: Sequoia National Park, 559/565-3341.

100 POTWISHA

Rating: 7

On the Marble Fork of the Kaweah River in Sequoia National Park.

Map 11.4, page 584

This pretty spot on the Marble Fork of the Kaweah River is one of Sequoia National Park's smaller drive-to campgrounds. By looking at maps, newcomers may think it is a very short drive farther into the park to see the General Sherman Tree, Giant Forest, and the famous trailhead for the walk up Moro Rock. Nope. It's a slow, twisty drive, but with many pullouts for great views. A few miles east of the camp, visitors can find Buckeye Flat and a trail that is routed along Paradise Creek.

Campsites, facilities: There are 42 sites for tents or RVs up to 30 feet long. Picnic tables and fire grills are provided. Drinking water, flush toilets, RV dump station, and evening ranger programs are available. Some facilities are wheelchair-accessible. Leashed pets are permitted.

Reservations, fees: Reservations are not accepted. The fee is $14 per night, plus $10 per vehicle park entrance fee. Senior discount available. Open year-round.

Directions: From Visalia, drive east on Highway 198 for 36 miles to the Ash Mountain entrance station to Sequoia National Park. Continue into the park (the road becomes Generals Highway) and drive four miles to the campground on the left. Vehicles of 22 feet or longer are not advised on Generals Highway from Potwisha to Giant Forest Village and are advised to use Highway 180 through the Big Stump entrance station.

Contact: Sequoia National Park, 559/565-3341.

101 BUCKEYE FLAT

Rating: 8

On the Middle Fork of the Kaweah River in Sequoia National Park.

Map 11.4, page 584

In any big, popular national park like Sequoia, the smaller the campground, the better. Well, Buckeye Flat is one of the smaller ones here, set on the Middle Fork of the Kaweah River with a trail just south of camp that runs beside pretty Paradise Creek.

Campsites, facilities: There are 28 tent sites. Picnic tables and fire grills are provided. Drinking water and flush toilets are available. Leashed pets are permitted.

Reservations, fees: Reservations are not accepted.

The fee is $14 per night, plus $10 per vehicle park entrance fee. Senior discount available. Open April through Labor Day weekend, weather permitting.

Directions: From Visalia, drive east on Highway 198 for 36 miles to the Ash Mountain entrance station to Sequoia National Park. Continue into the park (the road becomes Generals Highway) and drive 6.2 miles to the turnoff (across from Hospital Rock) for Buckeye Flat Campground. Turn right and drive .6 mile to the campground. Vehicles of 22 feet or longer are not advised on Generals Highway from Potwisha to Giant Forest Village and are advised to use Highway 180 through the Big Stump entrance station.

Contact: Sequoia National Park, 559/565-3341.

102 LODGEPOLE
🚶 🐕 🚐 ⛺

Rating: 8

On the Marble Fork of the Kaweah River in Sequoia National Park.

Map 11.4, page 584

This giant, pretty camp on the Marble Fork of the Kaweah River is typically crowded. A bonus here is an excellent trailhead nearby that leads into the backcountry of Sequoia National Park. The elevation is 6,700 feet.

Campsites, facilities: There are 214 sites for tents or RVs up to 40 feet long. Picnic tables and fire grills are provided. Restrooms, drinking water, flush toilets, pay showers, RV dump station, horseback riding facilities, gift shop, and evening ranger programs are available. A store, deli, and a coin laundry are nearby. Leashed pets are permitted.

Reservations, fees: Reserve at 800/365-CAMP (800/365-2267) or website: reservations.nps.gov; $16 per night (includes reservation fee), plus $10 per vehicle park entrance fee. Senior discount available. Open year-round, with limited winter services.

Directions: From Fresno, drive east on Highway 180 for 55 miles to the Big Stump Entrance

Station at Sequoia-Kings Canyon National Park. Continue 1.5 miles to a junction (signed left for Grant Grove). Turn right at Generals Highway and drive about 25 miles to Lodgepole Village and the turnoff for Lodgepole Campground. Turn left and drive a quarter mile (past Lodgepole Village) to the campground.

Contact: Sequoia National Park, 559/565-3341.

103 WHITNEY TRAILHEAD HIKE-IN
🚶 🐕 ⛺

Rating: 9

In Inyo National Forest.

Map 11.4, page 584

If Whitney Portal is full (common for this world-class trailhead), this camp provides a hike-in option, backpacking in a quarter mile to an elevation of 8,300 feet. Reservations for the summit hike are required. That accomplished, this hike-in camp is an excellent choice for spending a day to become acclimated to the high altitude. The trailhead to the Mt. Whitney summit (14,495 feet) is nearby. Mt. Whitney is the beginning of the 211-mile John Muir Trail, which ends in Yosemite Valley. Food-raiding bears are a common problem here. Campers are required to use bearproof food lockers or food canisters.

Campsites, facilities: There are 10 tent sites at this walk-in campground. Picnic tables and fire grills are provided. Drinking water and pit toilets are available. Supplies are available in Lone Pine. Leashed pets are permitted.

Reservations, fees: Reservations are not accepted. The fee is $8 per night. Stays are limited to one night only. Senior discount available. Open late May to mid-October.

Directions: Drive on U.S. 395 to Lone Pine and Whitney Portal Road. Turn west (toward the Sierra) and drive 13 miles to the parking lot at Whitney Portal. Park and hike a quarter mile to the campground.

Contact: Inyo National Forest, Mt. Whitney Ranger District, 760/876-6200, fax 760/876-6202.

104 WHITNEY PORTAL AND WHITNEY PORTAL GROUP

🏃 🐕 ♿ 🚗 ⛰️

Rating: 9

Near Mt. Whitney in Inyo National Forest.
Map 11.4, page 584

This camp is home to a world-class trailhead. It is regarded as the number one jump-off spot for the hike to the top of Mt. Whitney, the highest spot in the continental United States, 14,497.6 feet, as well as the start of the 211-mile John Muir Trail from Mt. Whitney to Yosemite Valley. Hikers planning to scale the summit must have a wilderness permit, available by reservation at the Forest Service office in Lone Pine. The camp is at 8,000 feet, and virtually everyone staying here plans to make the trek to the Whitney summit, a climb of 6,500 feet over the course of 10 miles. The trip includes an ascent over 100 switchbacks (often snow-covered in early summer) to top Wotan's Throne and reach Trail Crest (13,560 feet). Here you turn right and take the Summit Trail, where the ridge is cut by huge notch windows providing a view down more than 10,000 feet to the little town of Lone Pine and the Owens Valley. When you sign the logbook on top, don't be surprised if you see my name in the registry. A plus at the campground is watching the JMT hikers arrive who are just finishing the trail from north to south, that is, from Yosemite to Whitney. There is no comparing the happy look of success when they drop their packs for the last time, head into the little store, and pick a favorite refreshment for celebration.

Campsites, facilities: There are 43 sites for tents or RVs up to 16 feet long, and three group sites. Picnic tables and fire grills are provided. Drinking water and flush toilets are available. Some facilities are wheelchair-accessible. Supplies are available in Lone Pine. Leashed pets are permitted.

Reservations, fees: Reservations are accepted for 60 percent of the sites. Reserve at 877/444-6777 or website: www. ReserveUsa.com ($9 reservation fee); $14 per night, $35 for group sites. Stays are limited to seven days. Senior discount available. Open late May to mid-October.

Directions: Drive on U.S. 395 to Lone Pine and Whitney Portal Road. Turn west (toward the Sierra) on Whitney Portal Road and drive 13 miles to the campground on the left.

Contact: Inyo National Forest, Mt. Whitney Ranger District, 760/876-6200, fax 760/876-6202.

105 LONE PINE AND LONE PINE GROUP

🏃 🚣 🐕 🚗 ⛰️

Rating: 8

Near Mt. Whitney in Inyo National Forest.
Map 11.4, page 584

This is an alternative for campers preparing to hike Mt. Whitney or start the John Muir Trail. It is set at 6,000 feet, 2,000 feet below Whitney Portal (the hiking jump-off spot), providing a lower-elevation location for hikers to acclimate themselves to the altitude. The camp is set on Lone Pine Creek, with decent fishing and spectacular views of Mt. Whitney. Because of its exposure to the east, there are also beautiful sunrises, especially in fall.

Campsites, facilities: There are 43 sites for tents or RVs, and one group site. Picnic tables and fire grills are provided. Drinking water and flush toilets are available. Supplies are available in Lone Pine. Leashed pets are permitted.

Reservations, fees: Reservations are accepted for 25 of the sites. Reserve at 877/444-6777 or website: www. ReserveUsa.com ($9 reservation fee); $12 per night, $30 for a group site. Stays are limited to 14 days. Open year-round, with no facilities from mid-October through late April.

Directions: Drive on U.S. 395 to Lone Pine and Whitney Portal Road. Turn west (toward the Sierra) on Whitney Portal Road and drive six miles to the campground on the left.

Contact: Inyo National Forest, Mt. Whitney Ranger District, 760/876-6200, fax 760/876-6202.

106 TUTTLE CREEK

Rating: 4

Near Mt. Whitney.

Map 11.4, page 584

This primitive BLM camp is set at the base of Mt. Whitney along Tuttle Creek at 5,120 feet and is shadowed by several impressive peaks (Mt. Whitney, Lone Pine Peak, and Mt. Williamson). It is often used as an overflow area if the camps farther up Whitney Portal Road are full. Note: this campground is often confused with a small county campground also on Tuttle Creek Road just off Whitney Portal Road.

Campsites, facilities: There are 85 sites for tents or RVs and one group picnic area. Picnic tables and fire rings are provided. Pit toilets are available. No drinking water. Supplies are available in Lone Pine. Leashed pets are permitted.

Reservations, fees: Reservations are not accepted. There is no fee for camping. Open from early March through October.

Directions: Drive on U.S. 395 to Lone Pine and Whitney Portal Road. Turn west (toward the Sierra) on Whitney Portal Road and drive 3.5 miles to Horseshoe Meadow Road. Turn left and drive 1.5 miles to Tuttle Creek Road and the campground entrance (a dirt road) on the right.

Contact: Bureau of Land Management, Bishop Field Office, 760/872-4881, fax 760/873-5050.

107 HORSESHOE MEADOW

Rating: 8

Near the John Muir Wilderness in Inyo National Forest.

Map 11.4, page 584

Horseshoe Meadow features three trailhead camps, remote and choice, for backpackers heading into the adjacent John Muir Wilderness and Golden Trout Wilderness. The three camps are Cottonwood Pass walk-in, Cottonwood Lakes walk-in, and Horseshoe Meadow Equestrian. The camps are set at 10,000 feet near the wilderness border, one of the highest trailheads and drive-to campgrounds in the state. Several trails lead out of camp. The best heads west through Horseshoe Meadow and along a creek, then rises steeply for four miles to Cottonwood Pass, where it intersects with the Pacific Crest Trail. From here backpackers can hike north on the PCT to Chicken Spring Lake to set up camp, a rewarding overnighter, or drop into Big Whitney Meadow in the Golden Trout Wilderness. Some use this camp as a starting point to climb Mt. Whitney from its back side (via Guitar lake). Trailhead reservations are required. Food-raiding bears mean that campers are required to use bearproof food lockers or bearproof food canisters. The drive in is one the most spectacular anywhere, with the access road following a cliff edge much of the way, with a 6,000-foot drop to the Owens Valley below. You will also pass fantastic volcanics, the site of many movie settings, including *Star Trek* with Captain Kirk (can you remember the episode? My kids, Jeremy and Kris could, who simulated a scene playing on the rocks here).

Campsites, facilities: Cottonwood Pass has 18 walk-in sites, Cottonwood Lakes walk-in has 12 sites, and Horseshoe Meadow Equestrian has 10 sites. Picnic tables and fire grills are provided. Drinking water and vault toilets are available. A pack station and horseback riding are also available at the equestrian camp. Leashed pets are permitted.

Reservations, fees: Reservations are not accepted. The fee is $6 per night for walk-in sites, $12 for equestrians. Senior discount available. Open from late May through mid-October.

Directions: Drive on U.S. 395 to Lone Pine and Whitney Portal Road. Turn west (toward the Sierra) on Whitney Portal Road and drive 3.5 miles to Horseshoe Meadows Road. Turn left on Horseshoe Meadows Road and drive 19 miles to the end of the road (nearly a 7,000-foot climb) and the parking area. Park and walk a short distance to the campground.

Contact: Inyo National Forest, Mt. Whitney Ranger District, 760/876-6200, fax 760/876-6202.

108 PORTAGEE JOE CAMPGROUND

Rating: 4

Near Lone Pine.
Map 11.4, page 584

This small, little-known county park provides an option for both Mt. Whitney hikers and U.S. 395 cruisers. It is about five miles from Diaz Lake, set on a small creek at 3,750 feet, near the base of Mt. Whitney. Very few out-of-towners know about this spot, a nice insurance policy if you find yourself stuck for a campsite in this region. Trout fishing at a small creek provides an recreation opportunity.

Campsites, facilities: There are 15 sites for tents or RVs. Picnic tables and fire grills are provided. Vault toilets are available. There is no drinking water, but water from the stream can be hand-pumped with a filter. Supplies and a coin laundry are available in Lone Pine. Leashed pets are permitted.

Reservations, fees: Reservations are not accepted. The fee is $10 per night. Open year-round.

Directions: Drive on U.S. 395 to Lone Pine and Whitney Portal Road. Turn west (toward the Sierra) on Whitney Portal Road and drive a half mile to Tuttle Creek Road and the campground entrance. Turn left at Tuttle Creek Road and drive 100 yards to the campground on the right.

Contact: Inyo County Parks Department, 760/878-0272, fax 760/873-5599.

109 DIAZ LAKE

Rating: 6

Near Lone Pine.
Map 11.4, page 584

Diaz Lake is set at 3,650 feet in the Owens Valley. It is sometimes overlooked by visitors to nearby Mt. Whitney. It's a small lake, just 85 acres, and it is popular for trout fishing in the spring, when a speed limit of 15 mph is enforced. In summer when hot weather takes over and the speed limit is bumped to 35 mph, you can say *adios* to the anglers and *hola* to water-skiers. It also becomes a good spot for swimming in the shallows. A 20-foot limit is enforced for boats. Major improvements were planned for this campground starting in 2003.

Campsites, facilities: There are 200 sites, some with partial hookups, for RVs or tents. Picnic tables and fire grills are provided. Restrooms, drinking water, flush toilets, solar shower, and a boat ramp are available. Supplies and a coin laundry are available in Lone Pine. Leashed pets are permitted.

Reservations, fees: Reservations are accepted for 50 sites at 760/876-5656; $10 per night. Open year-round.

Directions: Drive on U.S. 395 to the Diaz Lake entrance (two miles south of Lone Pine) on the west side of the road.

Contact: Inyo County Parks Department, 760/873-5577.

110 HORSE CREEK

Rating: 6

On Lake Kaweah.
Map 11.4, page 584

Lake Kaweah is a big lake, covering nearly 2,000 acres with 22 miles of shoreline. This camp is set on the southern shore of the lake. In the spring when the lake is full and the surrounding hills are green, you may even think you have found Valhalla. With such hot weather in the San Joaquin Valley, it's a boater's heaven, ideal for water-skiers. In spring, when the water is still too cool for water sports, anglers can have the lake to themselves with good bass fishing. By early summer, it's a zoo from the personal watercraft and ski boats. One problem is that the water level drops a great deal during late summer, as thirsty farms suck up every drop they can get, killing prospects of developing beaches for swimming and wading. The elevation is 300 feet.

Campsites, facilities: There are 80 sites for tents or RVs. Picnic tables and fire grills are provided. Restrooms, drinking water, flush toilets, showers, playground, and a RV dump station are available. Some facilities are wheelchair-accessible. Two paved boat ramps are available at Kaweah Recreation Area and Lemon Hill Recreation Area. A store, coin laundry, boat and water-ski rentals, ice, snack bar, restaurant, gas station, and propane gas are available nearby. Leashed pets are permitted.

Reservations, fees: Reservations are accepted with a $9 reservation fee at 877/444-6777 or website: www.ReserveUsa.com. The fee is $16 per night. Senior discount available. Major credit cards accepted. Open year-round.

Directions: From Visalia, drive east on Highway 198 for 25 miles to Lake Kaweah's south shore and the camp on the left.

Contact: U.S. Army Corps of Engineers, 559/597-2301, fax 559/597-2468.

111 SOUTH FORK

Rating: 7

On the South Fork of the Kaweah River in Sequoia National Park.

Map 11.4, page 584

The smallest developed camp in Sequoia National Park might just be what you're looking for. It is set at 3,650 feet on the South Fork of the Kaweah River, just inside the southwestern border of Sequoia National Park. While it is technically in the park, it is nothing like at the Giant Forest. Instead, the road in is twisty and slow, the landscape open and hot. A trail heads east from the camp and traverses Dennison Ridge, eventually leading to Hockett Lakes, a long, demanding overnight trip. This is black bear habitat so proper food storage is required.

Campsites, facilities: There are 10 sites for tents only. Picnic tables and fire grills are provided. Vault toilets are available. No drinking water is available. Leashed pets are permitted, except on trails.

Reservations, fees: Reservations are not accepted. The fee is $8 per night from May through October, no fee in other months, $10 per vehicle park entrance fee. Senior discount available. Open year-round.

Directions: From Visalia, drive east on Highway 198 for 35 miles to South Fork Road (one mile before reaching the town of Three Rivers). Turn right on South Fork Road and drive 13 miles to the campground (the road is dirt for the last four miles).

Contact: Sequoia National Park, 559/565-3341.

112 ATWELL MILL

Rating: 7

On Atwell Creek in Sequoia National Park.

Map 11.4, page 584

This small, pretty camp in Sequoia National Park is on Atwell Creek near the East Fork of the Kaweah River, at an elevation of 6,650 feet. While the road in is paved, it is slow and twisty, with many blind turns. The terrain in this canyon is open and dry, overlooking the East Fork Kaweah River well below. A trail at camp is routed south for a mile down to the Kaweah River, then climbs out of the canyon and along Deer Creek for another two miles through the East Fork Grove, an outstanding day hike.

Campsites, facilities: There are 21 tent sites; no trailers are permitted. Picnic tables and fire grills are provided. Drinking water and pit toilets are available. A small store is nearby. Leashed pets are permitted.

Reservations, fees: Reservations are not accepted. The fee is $8 per night, $10 per vehicle park entrance fee. Senior discount available. Open Memorial Day through October, weather permitting.

Directions: From Visalia, drive east on Highway 198 for 36 miles to the town of Three Rivers. Continue east for three miles to Mineral King Road. Turn right on Mineral King Road and drive 19 miles (slow, steep, narrow, and twisty, with blind curves) to the campground. RVs and trailers are not recommended.

Contact: Sequoia National Park, 559/565-3341.

113 COLD SPRINGS

Rating: 9

On the East Fork of the Kaweah River in Sequoia National Park.
Map 11.4, page 584

This high-country camp at Sequoia National Park is set at 7,500 feet on the East Fork of the Kaweah River. There is a stellar hiking trail from here, with the trailhead just west of the camp. The hike is routed south along Mosquito Creek, climbing over the course of about three miles to the pretty Mosquito Lakes, a series of four small, beautiful lakes set on the north flank of Hengst Peak (11,127 feet). At road's end, there are two wilderness trailheads for sensational hikes, including one routed out to the Great Western Divide. Outstanding meals are available at nearby Silver King Resort.

Campsites, facilities: There are 40 tent sites. Picnic tables and fire grills are provided. Drinking water and vault toilets are available. A store is nearby. Leashed pets are permitted.

Reservations, fees: Reservations are not accepted. The fee is $8 per night, $10 per vehicle park entrance fee. Senior discount available. Open from May to September.

Directions: From Visalia, drive east on Highway 198 for 36 miles to the town of Three Rivers. Continue east for three miles to Mineral King Road. Turn right on Mineral King Road and drive 23 miles (slow, steep, narrow, and twisty,

with blind curves) to the campground. RVs and trailers are not recommended.

Contact: Sequoia National Park, 559/565-3341.

114 BALCH PARK

Rating: 6

Near Mountain Home State Forest.
Map 11.4, page 584

Balch Park is surrounded by Mountain Home State Forest and Sequoia National Forest. A nearby grove of giant sequoias is a featured attraction. The elevation is 6,500 feet. Two fishing ponds are also a feature.

Campsites, facilities: There are 71 sites, a few drive-through, for RVs up to 40 feet long or tents. Picnic tables and fire grills are provided. Drinking water and flush toilets and vault toilets are available. Some facilities are wheelchair-accessible. Leashed pets are permitted.

Reservations, fees: Reservations are not accepted. The fee is $14 per night, $1 for each extra vehicle, $1 per night. Senior discount available. Open from May to late October.

Directions: From Porterville, drive east on Highway 190 for 19 miles (a mile past the town of Springville) to Balch Park Road. Turn left (north) at Balch Park Road and drive three miles to Bear Creek Road. Turn east (right) and drive 15 miles (extremely slow and curvy) to the campground (RVs not recommended). Alternate route for RV drivers: After turning north onto Balch Park Road, drive 40 miles (long and curvy) to the park.

Contact: Balch Park, Tulare County, 559/733-6291.

115 HIDDEN FALLS WALK-IN

Rating: 7

On the Tule River in Mountain Home State Forest.
Map 11.4, page 584

This small, quiet camp, set at 5,900 feet along

the Tule River near Hidden Falls, is one of the prettier camps in Mountain Home State Forest. It is remote and overlooked by all but a handful of insiders who know its qualities.

Campsites, facilities: There are eight walk-in sites for tents only. Picnic tables and fire grills are provided. Drinking water and pit toilets are available. Leashed pets are permitted.

Reservations, fees: Reservations are not accepted. There is no fee for camping. Open from June to October.

Directions: From Porterville, drive east on Highway 190 for 19 miles (a mile past the town of Springville) to Balch Park Road. Turn left (north) at Balch Park Road and drive about 23 miles to the Mountain Home State Forest sign. Continue on Balch Park Road (the road is long and twisty) and follow the signs to the State Forest Headquarters (where free forest maps are available). The campgrounds are well signed from this point. The trip from the Highway 190/Balch Road turnoff to the campground is about 45 miles.

Contact: Mountain Home State Forest, 559/539-2321 (summer) or 559/539-2855 (winter).

116 MOSES GULCH

Rating: 7

On the Tule River in Mountain Home State Forest.

Map 11.4, page 584

Obscure Moses Gulch sits near the Tule River in a canyon below Moses Mountain (9,331 feet) to the nearby north. A trailhead at the eastern end of the state forest provides access both north and south along the North Fork of the Middle Fork Tule River for a scenic hike. The elevation here is 5,400 feet. Mountain Home State Forest is surrounded by Sequoia National Forest. The cost? Free.

Campsites, facilities: There are 10 sites for tents. Picnic tables and fire grills are provided. Drinking water and vault toilets are available. Leashed pets are permitted.

Reservations, fees: Reservations are not accepted. There is no fee for camping. Open mid-May to early November, weather permitting.

Directions: From Porterville, drive east on Highway 190 for 19 miles (a mile past the town of Springville) to Balch Park Road. Turn left (north) at Balch Park Road and drive about 23 miles to the Mountain Home State Forest sign. Continue on Balch Park Road (the road is long and twisty) and follow the signs to the State Forest Headquarters (where free forest maps are available). The campgrounds are well signed from this point. The trip from the Highway 190/Balch Road turnoff to the campground is about 45 miles.

Contact: Mountain Home State Forest, 559/539-2321 (summer) or 559/539-2855 (winter).

117 FRAZIER MILL

Rating: 5

In Mountain Home State Forest.

Map 11.4, page 584

The prime attractions here are the obscurity, remoteness, and abundance of old-growth giant sequoias. The Wishon Fork of the Tule River is the largest of the several streams that pass through this forest. You can't beat the price.

Campsites, facilities: There are 46 sites for tents and a few sites for small RVs. Picnic tables and fire grills are provided. Drinking water and vault toilets are available. Leashed pets are permitted.

Reservations, fees: Reservations are not accepted. There is no fee for camping. Open from June to October.

Directions: From Porterville, drive east on Highway 190 for 19 miles (a mile past the town of Springville) to Balch Park Road. Turn left (north) at Balch Park Road and drive about 23 miles to the Mountain Home State Forest sign. Continue on Balch Park Road (the road is long and twisty) and follow the signs to the State Forest Headquarters (where free forest maps are available). The campgrounds are well signed from this point. The trip from the Highway 190/Balch Road turnoff to the campground is about 45 miles.

Contact: Mountain Home State Forest, 559/539-2321 (summer) or 559/539-2855 (winter).

118 SHAKE CAMP

Rating: 6

In Mountain Home State Forest.

Map 11.4, page 584

This is a little-known spot for horseback riding. Horses can be rented for the day, hour, or night. The camp is set at 6,500 feet and there's a trailhead here for trips into the adjoining Sequoia National Forest and beyond to the east into the Golden Trout Wilderness. Hikers should note that the Balch Park Pack Station, a commercial outfitter, is nearby, so you can expect horse traffic on the trail.

Campsites, facilities: There are 11 sites for tents or small RVs. Picnic tables and fire grills are provided. Drinking water and vault toilets are available. A public pack station with corrals is nearby. Leashed pets are permitted.

Reservations, fees: Reservations are not accepted. There is no fee for camping. Open from June to October.

Directions: From Porterville, drive east on Highway 190 for 19 miles (a mile past the town of Springville) to Balch Park Road. Turn left (north) at Balch Park Road and drive about 23 miles to the Mountain Home State Forest sign. Continue on Balch Park Road (the road is long and twisty) and follow the signs to the State Forest Headquarters (where free forest maps are available). The campgrounds are well signed from this point. The trip from the Highway 190/Balch Road turnoff to the campground is about 45 miles.

Contact: Mountain Home State Forest, 559/539-2321 (summer) or 559/539-2855 (winter).

119 HEDRICK POND

Rating: 6

In Mountain Home State Forest.

Map 11.4, page 584

Mountain Home State Forest is highlighted by giant sequoias, and Hedrick Pond provides a fishing opportunity, as it's stocked occasionally in summer with rainbow trout. This camp is set at 6,200 feet, one of five campgrounds in the immediate region. (See Methuselah Group Camp for recreation options.)

Campsites, facilities: There are 14 sites for tents or RVs. Picnic tables and fire grills are provided. Drinking water and vault toilets are available. Leashed pets are permitted.

Reservations, fees: Reservations are not accepted. There is no fee for camping. Open from June through October, weather permitting.

Directions: From Porterville, drive east on Highway 190 for 19 miles (a mile past the town of Springville) to Balch Park Road. Turn left (north) at Balch Park Road and drive about 23 miles to the Mountain Home State Forest sign. Continue on Balch Park Road (the road is long and twisty) and follow the signs to the State Forest Headquarters (where free forest maps are available). The campgrounds are well signed from this point. The trip from the Highway 190/Balch Road turnoff to the campground is about 45 miles.

Contact: Mountain Home State Forest, 559/539-2321 (summer) or 559/539-2855 (winter).

120 METHUSELAH GROUP CAMP

Rating: 6

In Mountain Home State Forest.

Map 11.4, page 584

This is one of the few group campgrounds anywhere in California that is free to users. But hey: remember to bring water. The elevation is 5,900 feet. Mountain Home State Forest is best known for its remoteness, old-growth giant sequoias (hence the name of this camp, Methuselah), trails that provide access to small streams, and horseback trips into the surrounding Sequoia National Forest.

Campsites, facilities: This group site can accommodate 20–100 people in tents or RVs. Fire grills and some picnic tables are provided. Vault toilets are available. No drinking water is available. Leashed pets are permitted. Garbage must be packed out.

Reservations, fees: Reservations are required, but there is no fee. Open from June to October.

Directions: From Porterville, drive east on Highway 190 for 19 miles (a mile past the town of Springville) to Balch Park Road. Turn left (north) at Balch Park Road and drive about 23 miles to the Mountain Home State Forest sign. Continue on Balch Park Road (the road is long and twisty) and follow the signs to the State Forest Headquarters (where free forest maps are available). The campgrounds are well signed from this point. The trip from the Highway 190/Balch Road turnoff to the campground is about 45 miles.

Contact: Mountain Home State Forest, 559/539-2321 (summer) or 559/539-2855 (winter).

121 WISHON

Rating: 8

On the Tule River in Giant Sequoia National Monument.

Map 11.4, page 584

Wishon Camp is set at 4,000 feet on the Middle Fork of the North Fork Tule River, just west of the Doyle Springs Summer Home Tract. Just down the road to the east, on the left side, is a parking area for a trailhead. The hike here is routed for a mile to the Tule River and then runs along the stream for about five miles, to Mountain Home State Forest.

Campsites, facilities: There are nine sites for tents only and 26 sites for tents or RVs up to 24 feet long. Picnic tables and fire grills are

provided. Drinking water and vault toilets are available. Leashed pets are permitted.

Reservations, fees: Reserve at 877/444-6777 or website: www. ReserveUsa.com ($9 reservation fee); $14 per night, $5 for each extra vehicle. Senior discount available. Open year-round.

Directions: From Porterville, drive east on Highway 190 for 25 miles to County Road 209/Wishon Drive. Turn left at County Road 208/Wishon Drive and drive 3.5 miles (narrow, curvy, RVs not advised).

Contact: Giant Sequoia National Monument, Tule River/Hot Springs Ranger District, 559/539-2607 or 661/548-6503, fax 559/539-2067.

122 BELKNAP

Rating: 7

On the South Fork of Middle Fork Tule River in Giant Sequoia National Monument.

Map 11.4, page 584

The groves of sequoias in this area are a highlight wherever you go. This camp is set on the South Fork of the Middle Fork Tule River near McIntyre Grove and Belknap Camp Grove, and a trail from camp is routed east for three miles through Wheel Meadow Grove to the junction with the Summit National Recreation Trail at Quaking Aspen Camp. The elevation is 4,800 feet.

Campsites, facilities: There are 15 sites for tents. RVs prohibited. Picnic tables and fire grills are provided. Drinking water and vault toilets are available. A store is nearby. Leashed pets are permitted.

Reservations, fees: Reserve at 877/444-6777 or website: www. ReserveUsa.com ($9 reservation fee); $14 per night, $5 for an extra vehicle. Senior discount available. Open from mid-April through mid-November.

Directions: From Porterville, drive east on Highway 190 for 34 miles to Camp Nelson and Nelson Drive. Turn right on Nelson Drive and drive one mile to the camp.

Contact: Giant Sequoia National Monument,

Tule River/Hot Springs Ranger District, 209/539-2607, fax 209/539-2067.

 QUAKING ASPEN

Rating: 2

In Giant Sequoia National Monument.

Map 11.4, page 584

Quaking Aspen sits at a junction of Forest Service roads at 7,000 feet in elevation, near the headwaters of Freeman Creek. A trailhead for the Summit National Recreation Trail runs right through camp; it's a popular trip on horseback, heading deep into Sequoia National Forest. Another trailhead is a half-mile away on Forest Road 21S50. This hike is routed east along Freeman Creek and reaches the Freeman Grove of sequoias in four miles. This camp is in the vicinity of the Sequoia forest fire, named the McNalley Fire, which burned more than 100,000 acres in this area in the summer of 2002. The fire started in the Kern River Canyon near Road's End Resort (which burned down) and then burned up the Kern Canyon north to Forks of the Kern and the surrounding environs. While 11 groves of giant sequoias here were saved, much of the surrounding forest to the east of the camps was burned.

Campsites, facilities: There are 32 sites for tents or RVs up to 24 feet long. Picnic tables and fire grills are provided. Drinking water and vault toilets are available. A store is nearby. Leashed pets are permitted. Some facilities are wheelchair-accessible.

Reservations, fees: Reservations are accepted at 877/444-6777. The fee is $14 per night, $5 per extra vehicle. Senior discount available. Open from May to mid-November, weather permitting.

Directions: From Porterville, drive east on Highway 190 for 34 miles to Camp Nelson. Continue east on Highway 190 for 11 miles to the campground on the right.

Contact: Giant Sequoia National Monument,

Tule River/Hot Springs Ranger District, 559/539-2607 or 661/548-6503, fax 559/539-2067.

QUAKING ASPEN GROUP CAMP

Rating: 2

At the headwaters of the South Fork of the Middle Fork Tule River in Giant Sequoia National Monument.

Map 11.4, page 584

For groups, here is an alternative to nearby Peppermint. (See the entry for Peppermint for recreation options.) The elevation is 7,000 feet. This camp is in the vicinity of the Sequoia forest fire, named the McNalley Fire, which burned more than 100,000 acres in this area in the summer of 2002. The fire started in the Kern River Canyon near Road's End Resort (which burned down) and then burned up the Kern Canyon north to Forks of the Kern and the surrounding environs. While 11 groves of giant sequoias here were saved, much of the surrounding forest to the east of the camps was burned.

Campsites, facilities: There are three group sites for up to 12 people, two group sites for up to 25 people, and two group sites for up to 50 people, suitable for tents only except for first three sites, which have space for RVs up to 24 feet. Picnic tables and fire grills are provided. Drinking water and vault toilets are available. A lodge with limited supplies is nearby. Leashed pets are permitted.

Reservations, fees: Reserve at 877/444-6777 or website: www. ReserveUsa.com ($9 reservation fee); $18–75 group fee per night, depending on group size. Open from mid-May to mid-November.

Directions: From Porterville, drive east on Highway 190 for 34 miles to Camp Nelson. Continue east on Highway 190 for 11 miles to the campground on the right.

Contact: Giant Sequoia National Monument, Tule River/Hot Springs Ranger District, 559/539-2607 or 661/548-6503, fax 559/539-2067.

125 HOLEY MEADOW

Rating: 7

On Double Bunk Creek in Giant Sequoia National Monument.

Map 11.4, page 584

Holey Meadow is set at 6,400 feet on the western slopes of the Sierra, near Redwood and Long Meadow. Parker Pass is a mile to the west, and if you drive on the Forest Service road over the pass, continue southwest (four miles from camp) to Cold Springs Saddle, and then turn east on the Forest Service spur road, it will take you two miles to Starvation Creek and the Starvation Creek Grove.

Campsites, facilities: There are 10 sites for tents or RVs up to 16 feet long, and a group site for up to 60 people. Drinking water, fire grills, and picnic tables are provided. Vault toilets are available. Leashed pets are permitted.

Reservations, fees: Reserve group site at 877/444-6777 ($9 reservation fee) or website: www .ReserveUsa.com; $12 per night, $75 per night for group site. Senior discount available. Open from June to October.

Directions: Drive on Highway 99 to Earlimart (about eight miles north of Delano) and the exit for Avenue 56/County Road J22. Take that exit east and drive 39 miles to the town of California Hot Springs and Parker Pass Road/County Road M50. Turn left on Parker Pass Road and drive 12 miles to Western Divide Highway/County Road M107. Turn left on Western Divide Highway and drive a half mile to the entrance.

Contact: Giant Sequoia National Monument, Tule River/Hot Springs Ranger District, 559/539-2607 or 661/548-6503, fax 559/539-2067.

126 REDWOOD MEADOW

Rating: 7

Near Parker Meadow Creek in Giant Sequoia National Monument.

Map 11.4, page 584

The highlight here is the half-mile Trail of the Hundred Giants, which is routed through a grove of giant sequoias and is accessible for wheelchair hikers. This is the site where President Clinton proclaimed the Giant Sequoia National Monument in 2000. The camp is set near Parker Meadow Creek at 6,500 feet elevation. Despite its remoteness, this has become a popular place.

Campsites, facilities: There are 15 sites for tents or RVs up to 16 feet long. Picnic tables and fire grills are provided. Drinking water and vault toilets are available. Leashed pets are permitted.

Reservations, fees: Reserve at 877/444-6777 or website: www. ReserveUsa.com ($9 reservation fee); $14 per night, $5 for each extra vehicle. Open from June to September.

Directions: Drive on Highway 99 to Earlimart (about eight miles north of Delano) and the exit for Avenue 56/County Road J22. Take that exit east and drive 39 miles to the town of California Hot Springs and Parker Pass Road/County Road M50. Turn left on Parker Pass Road and drive 12 miles to Western Divide Highway/County Road M107. Turn left on Western Divide Highway and drive three miles to the campground entrance.

Contact: Giant Sequoia National Monument, Tule River/Hot Springs Ranger District, 559/539-2607 or 661/548-6503, fax 559/539-2067.

127 COY FLAT

Rating: 4

In Giant Sequoia National Monument.

Map 11.4, page 584

Coy Flat is set between Coy Creek and Bear Creek, small forks of the Tule River, at 5,000 feet in elevation. The road out of camp is routed five miles (through Rogers' Camp, which is private property) to the Black Mountain Grove of redwoods, with some giant sequoias set just inside the border of the neighboring Tule River Indian Reservation. From camp, a hiking trail (Forest Trail 31S31) is routed east for two miles through the Belknap Camp Grove of sequoias and then turns and heads south for four miles to Slate Mountain, where it intersects with the Summit National Recreation Trail, a steep butt-kicker of a hike that tops out at over 9,000 feet.

Campsites, facilities: There are 20 sites for tents or RVs up to 24 feet long. Picnic tables and fire grills are provided. Drinking water and vault toilets are available. Leashed pets are permitted.

Reservations, fees: Reserve at 877/444-6777 or website: www. ReserveUsa.com ($9 reservation fee); $14 per night, $5 for each extra vehicle. Senior discount available. Open from mid-April through mid-November.

Directions: From Porterville, drive east on Highway 190 for 34 miles to Camp Nelson and Coy Flat Road. Turn right on Coy Flat Road and drive one mile to the campground.

Contact: Giant Sequoia National Monument, Tule River/Hot Springs Ranger District, 559/539-2607 or 661/548-6503, fax 559/539-2067.

128 LONG MEADOW GROUP CAMP

Rating: 8

In Giant Sequoia National Monument.

Map 11.4, page 584

Long Meadow is set on little Long Meadow Creek at an elevation of 6,500 feet, within a mile of the remote Cunningham Grove of redwoods one mile to the east. Note that Redwood Meadow is just one mile to the west, where the Trail of the Hundred Giants is a feature attraction.

Campsites, facilities: There is one group site for tents or RVs up to 16 feet long for up to 36 people. Picnic tables and fire grills are provided. Vault toilets are available. No drinking water is available. Leashed pets are permitted.

Reservations, fees: Reservations required at 877/444-6777 ($9 reservation fee) or website: www.ReserveUsa.com; $40 per night. Open from June to September.

Directions: Drive on Highway 99 to Earlimart (about eight miles north of Delano) and the exit for Avenue 56/County Road J22. Take that exit east and drive 39 miles to the town of California Hot Springs and Parker Pass Road/County Road M50. Turn left on Parker Pass Road and drive 12 miles to Western Divide Highway/County Road M107. Turn left on Western Divide Highway and drive four miles to the campground entrance.

Contact: Giant Sequoia National Monument, Tule River/Hot Springs Ranger District, 661/548-6503, fax 661/548-6236.

129 PEPPERMINT

Rating: 2

On Peppermint Creek in Giant Sequoia National Monument.

Map 11.5, page 585

This is one of two primitive campgrounds at Peppermint Creek, but a road does not directly connect the two camps. Several backcountry access roads snake throughout the area, as detailed on a Forest Service map, and exploring them can make for some self-styled fortune hunts. For the ambitious, hiking the two-mile trail at the end of nearby Forest Road 21S05 leads to a fantastic lookout at The Needles (8,245 feet). The camp elevation is 7,100 feet. This camp is in the vicinity of the Sequoia forest fire, named the McNalley Fire, which burned more than 100,000 acres in this area in the summer of 2002. The fire started in the Kern River Canyon near Road's End Resort (which burned down) and then burned up the Kern Canyon north to Forks of the Kern and the surrounding environs. While 11 groves of giant sequoias here were saved, much of the surrounding forest to the east of the camps was burned.

Campsites, facilities: There is dispersed camping for tents or RVs up to 32 feet long and trailers up to 24 feet long. Picnic tables are provided. Vault toilets are available. No drinking water is available. A lodge with limited supplies is nearby. Leashed pets are permitted.

Reservations, fees: Reservations are not accepted. There is no fee for camping. A fire permit is required. Open from May to October.

Directions: From Porterville, drive east on Highway 190 for 34 miles to Camp Nelson. Continue east on Highway 190 for 15 miles to the campground entrance road.

Contact: Giant Sequoia National Monument, Tule River/Hot Springs Ranger District, 559/539-2607 or 661/548-6503, fax 559/539-2067.

130 LOWER PEPPERMINT

Rating: 2

In Giant Sequoia National Monument.

Map 11.5, page 585

This is a little-known camp in Sequoia National Forest, set along Peppermint Creek at 5,300 feet. This area has a vast network of backcountry roads, which are detailed on a Forest Service map. This camp is in the vicinity of the Sequoia forest fire, named the McNalley Fire, which burned more than 100,000 acres in this area in the summer of 2002. The fire started in the Kern River Canyon near Road's End Resort (which burned down) and then burned up the Kern Canyon north to Forks of the Kern and the surrounding environs. While 11 groves of giant sequoias here were saved, much of the surrounding forest to the east of the camps was burned.

Campsites, facilities: There are 17 sites for tents or RVs up to 16 feet long. Picnic tables and fire grills are provided. Drinking water and vault toilets are available. Leashed pets are permitted.

Reservations, fees: Reservations are not ac-

cepted. The fee is $14 per night. Senior discount available. Open from June to October.

Directions: From Bakersfield, drive east on Highway 178 for 40 miles to the town of Lake Isabella and Highway 155/Burlando Way. Turn left (north) and drive 10 miles to Kernville and Sierra Way. Turn (north) and drive 24 miles to Johnsondale and Forest Road 22S82/Lloyd Meadow Road. Turn right and drive about 10.5 miles (paved road) to the campground.

Contact: Giant Sequoia National Monument, Tule River/Hot Springs Ranger District, 559/539-2607 or 661/548-6503, fax 559/539-2067.

131 LIMESTONE

Rating: 1

On the Kern River in Sequoia National Forest.

Map 11.5, page 585

Set deep in the Sequoia National Forest at 3,800 feet, Limestone is a small campground along the Kern River, fed by snowmelt from Mt. Whitney. This stretch of the Kern is extremely challenging and sensational for white-water rafting, with cold water and many of the rapids rated Class IV and Class V, for experts with guides only. The favored put-in is at the Johnsondale Bridge, and from here it's a 21-mile run to Kernville. The river pours into Lake Isabella many miles later. Two sections are unrunnable: Fairview Dam (mile 2.5) and Salmon Falls (mile 8). For nonrafters, South Creek Falls provides a side trip, one mile to the west. This campground was one of two burned in the McNalley Fire in the summer of 2002. The first started near Road's End Lodge (which burned down), 16 miles up the Kern River Highway. Other campgrounds to the south of that were not burned. Even though the canyon has been blackened and left with tree skeletons from the start of the fire on north past Forks of the Kern, the river can still provide an outstanding rafting experience. The sight of the damage from the fire, however, is shocking.

Campsites, facilities: There are 12 sites for tents only and 10 sites for tents or RVs up to 30 feet long. Picnic tables and fire grills are provided. Vault toilets are available. No drinking water is available. Supplies and a coin laundry are available in Kernville. Leashed pets are permitted.

Reservations, fees: Reservations are not accepted. The fee is $12 per night, $5 for an extra vehicle. Senior discount available. Open from April through November.

Directions: From Bakersfield, drive east on Highway 178 for about 40 miles to the town of Lake Isabella and Highway 155/Burlando Way. Turn left (north) and drive 10 miles to Kernville and the Kern River Highway/Sierra Way. Turn left on the Kern River Highway and drive 20 miles (two miles past Fairview) to the campground entrance.

Contact: Sequoia National Forest, Cannell Meadow Ranger District, 760/376-3781, fax 760/376-3795.

132 FAIRVIEW

Rating: 1

On the Kern River in Sequoia National Forest.

Map 11.5, page 585

Fairview is one of six campgrounds set on the Upper Kern River above Lake Isabella and adjacent to the Kern River, one of the prime rafting rivers in California. This camp sits at 3,500 feet. Many of the rapids are rated Class IV and Class V, for experts with guides only. The favored put-in is at the Johnsondale Bridge, and from here it's a 21-mile run to Kernville. The river eventually pours into Lake Isabella. Two sections are unrunnable, Fairview Dam (Mile 2.5) and Salmon Falls (Mile Eight). This campground was one of two burned in the McNally Fire in the summer of 2002. The first started near Road's End Lodge (which burned down), 16 miles up the Kern River Highway. Other campgrounds to the south of that were

not burned. Even though the canyon has been blackened and left with tree skeletons from the start of the fire on north past Forks of the Kern, the river can still provide an outstanding rafting experience. The sight of the damage from the fire, however, is shocking.

Campsites, facilities: There are 55 sites for tents or RVs up to 45 feet long. Picnic tables and fire grills are provided. Drinking water and vault toilets are available. Some facilities are wheelchair-accessible. Supplies and a coin laundry are available in Kernville. Leashed pets are permitted.

Reservations, fees: Reserve at 877/444-6777 or website: www. ReserveUsa.com ($9 reservation fee); $14–16 per night, $5 for an extra vehicle. Senior discount available. Open from May to October.

Directions: From Bakersfield, drive east on Highway 178 for about 40 miles to the town of Lake Isabella and Highway 155/Burlando Way. Turn left (north) and drive 10 miles to Kernville and the Kern River Highway/Sierra Way. Turn left on the Kern River Highway and drive 18 miles to the town of Fairview. Continue to the north end of town to the campground entrance.

Contact: Sequoia National Forest, Cannell Meadow Ranger District, 760/376-3781, fax 760/376-3795.

133 HORSE MEADOW

Rating: 8

On Salmon Creek in Sequoia National Forest.

Map 11.5, page 585

This is a little-known spot set along Salmon Creek at 7,600 feet. It is a region known for big meadows, forests, backcountry roads, and plenty of horses. It is just west of the Dome Land Wilderness, and there is a series of three public pastures for horses in the area, as well as trails ideal for horseback riding. From camp, one such trail follows along Salmon Creek to the west to Salmon Falls, a favorite for the few who know of it. A more popular overnight trip is to head to a trailhead about five miles east, which provides a route to Manter Meadows in the Dome Lands.

Campsites, facilities: There are 26 sites for tents only and 15 sites for tents or RVs up to 22 feet long. Picnic tables and fire grills are provided. Drinking water and vault toilets are available. Garbage must be packed out. Leashed pets are permitted.

Reservations, fees: Reservations are not accepted. The fee is $5 per night. Senior discount available. Open from June to November.

Directions: From Bakersfield, drive east on Highway 178 for about 40 miles to the town of Lake Isabella and Highway 155/Burlando Way. Turn left (north) and drive 10 miles to Kernville and the Kern River Highway/Sierra Way. Turn left on the Kern River Highway for about 20 miles to Sherman Pass Road (signed "Highway 395/Black Rock Ranger Station") Make a sharp right on Sherman Pass Road and drive about 6.5 miles to Cherry Hill Road/Forest Road 22512 (there is a green gate with a sign that says "Horse Meadow/Big Meadow"). Turn right and drive about four miles (the road becomes dirt) and continue for another three miles (follow the signs) to the campground entrance road.

Contact: Sequoia National Forest, Cannell Meadow Ranger District, 760/376-3781, fax 760/376-3795.

134 TROY MEADOWS

Rating: 7

On Fish Creek in Sequoia National Forest.
Map 11.5, page 585

Obscure? Yes, but what the heck, it gives you an idea of what is possible out in the boondocks. The camp is set at 7,800 feet right along Fish Creek. An information station is available two miles northwest. You are advised to stop there before any backcountry trips. Note

that off-highway vehicles (OHVs) are allowed in this area. Also note that the Jackass National Recreation Trail is a short drive to the east; it runs north aside Jackass Creek to its headwaters just below Jackass Peak (9,245 feet). The camp was closed and renovated in 2002 and reopened in 2003.

Campsites, facilities: There are 63 sites for tents and 10 sites for RVs up to 24 feet long. Picnic tables and fire grills are provided. Drinking water and vault toilets are available. Garbage must be packed out. Leashed pets are permitted.

Reservations, fees: Reservations are not accepted. The fee is $5 per night. Senior discount available. Open from May to November.

Directions: Drive on U.S. 395 to Ninemile Canyon Road (four miles north of the town of Pearsonville, 48 miles south of Lone Pine). Turn west on Ninemile Canyon Road and drive 31 miles (the road becomes Sherman Pass Road) to the campground.

Contact: Sequoia National Forest, Cannell Meadow Ranger District, 760/376-3781, fax 760/376-3795.

135 FISH CREEK

Rating: 8

In Sequoia National Forest.
Map 11.5, page 585

This is a pretty spot set at the confluence of Fish Creek and Jackass Creek. The elevation is 7,400 feet. The nearby trails are used by off-highway vehicles and can make this a noisy campground during the day.

Campsites, facilities: There are 27 sites for tents and 12 sites for RVs up to 24 feet long. Picnic tables and fire grills are provided. Drinking water and vault toilets are available. Garbage must be packed out. Leashed pets are permitted.

Reservations, fees: Reservations are not accepted. The fee is $5 per night. Senior discount available. Open from May to November.

Directions: Drive on U.S. 395 to Ninemile Canyon Road (four miles north of the town of Pearsonville, 48 miles south of Lone Pine). Turn west on Ninemile Canyon Road and drive 28 miles (the road becomes Sherman Pass Road) to the campground.

Contact: Sequoia National Forest, Cannell Meadow Ranger District, 760/376-3781, fax 760/376-3795.

136 KENNEDY MEADOW

Rating: 8

On the South Fork of the Kern River in Sequoia National Forest.

Map 11.5, page 585

This is a pretty Forest Service campground set amid piñon pine and sage country, with the Pacific Crest Trail running by the camp. That makes it a great trailhead camp, as well as a refreshing stopover for PCT-through hikers. A highlight is the nearby South Fork Kern River, which provides fishing for rainbow trout. The camp receives moderate use and is a lifesaver for PCT-through hikers.

Campsites, facilities: There are 23 sites for tents, and 15 for tents or RVs up to 30 feet long. Picnic tables and fire rings are provided. Drinking water (seasonal) and vault toilets are available. Garbage must be packed out. Leashed pets are permitted.

Reservations, fees: Reservations are not accepted. The fee is $5 fee per night. Senior discount available. Open year-round, weather permitting.

Directions: Drive on U.S. 395 to Ninemile Canyon Road (four miles north of the town of Pearsonville, 48 miles south of Lone Pine). Turn west on Ninemile Canyon Road and drive 21 miles to a small store. Bear right at the store (still Ninemile Canyon Road) and continue for three miles to the campground.

Contact: Sequoia National Forest, Cannell Meadow Ranger District, 760/376-3781, fax 760/376-3795.

137 LEAVIS FLAT

Rating: 7

On Deer Creek in Giant Sequoia National Monument.

Map 11.5, page 585

Leavis Flat is just inside the western border of Sequoia National Forest along Deer Creek, at an elevation of 3,100 feet. The highlight here is the adjacent California Hot Springs.

Campsites, facilities: There are five sites for tents only and four sites for RVs up to 16 feet long. Picnic tables and fire grills are provided. Drinking water and vault toilets are available. A store, coin laundry, and propane gas can be found nearby. Leashed pets are permitted.

Reservations, fees: Reservations are accepted at 877/444-6777. The fee is $14 per night, $5 for each extra vehicle. Senior discount available. Open year-round.

Directions: Drive on Highway 99 to Earlimart (about eight miles north of Delano) and the exit for Avenue 56/County Road J22. Take that exit east and drive 39 miles to the town of California Hot Springs and the campground.

Contact: Giant Sequoia National Monument, Tule River/Hot Springs Ranger District, 559/539-2607 or 661/548-6503, fax 559/539-2067.

138 FROG MEADOW

Rating: 6

Near Giant Sequoia National Monument.

Map 11.5, page 585

This small, primitive camp, set near Tobias Creek at 7,500 feet, is in the center of a network of Forest Service roads that explore the surrounding Sequoia National Forest. The nearby feature destination is the Tobias Peak Lookout (8,284 feet), two miles directly south of the camp.

Campsites, facilities: There are 10 sites for tents or RVs up to 16 feet long. Picnic tables and fire grills are provided. Vault toilets are available. No drinking water is available.

Leashed pets are permitted. Garbage must be packed out.

Reservations, fees: Reservations are not accepted. There is no fee for camping. Open from June to October, weather permitting.

Directions: Drive on Highway 99 to Delano and the exit for Highway 155. Take that exit and drive east for about 40 miles to Jack Ranch Road (just west of Glennville). Turn left on Jack Ranch Road and drive about four miles to White River Road/Sugarloaf Drive. Turn right on Sugarloaf Drive and drive 4.5 miles to Guernsey Mill/Sugarloaf Drive. Continue on Sugarloaf Road/Forest Road 23S16 for about seven miles to Forest Road 24S50 (a dirt road). Turn left on Forest Road 24S50 and drive four miles to Frog Meadow and the campground. The route is long, slow, and circuitous. A map of Sierra National Forest is required.

Contact: Giant Sequoia National Monument, Tule River/Hot Springs Ranger District, 559/539-2607 or 661/548-6503, fax 559/539-2067.

139 WHITE RIVER

Rating: 7

In Giant Sequoia National Monument.
Map 11.5, page 585

White River is set at 4,000 feet, on the White River near where little Dark Canyon Creek enters it. A trail from camp follows downstream along the White River to the west for three miles, dropping into Ames Hole and Cove Canyon. The region's hot springs are about a 10-minute drive away to the north.

Campsites, facilities: There are eight sites for tents and four sites for RVs up to 16 feet long. Picnic tables and fire grills are provided. Drinking water and vault toilets are available. Leashed pets are permitted.

Reservations, fees: Reserve at 877/444-6777 or website: www. ReserveUsa.com ($9 reservation fee); $14 per night, $5 for each extra vehicle. Senior discount available. Open from May to October.

Directions: Drive on Highway 99 to Delano and the exit for Highway 155. Take that exit and drive east for about 40 miles to Jack Ranch Road (just west of Glennville). Turn left on Jack Ranch Road and drive about four miles to White River Road/Sugarloaf Drive. Turn right and drive 1.5 miles to Forest Road 24S05. Bear left and drive three-quarters of a mile to Idlewild, and continue (on this dirt road) for six miles to the campground.

Contact: Giant Sequoia National Monument, Tule River/Hot Springs Ranger District, 559/539-2607 or 661/548-6503, fax 559/539-2067.

140 PANORAMA

Rating: 7

In Giant Sequoia National Monument.
Map 11.5, page 585

This pretty spot is set at 7,200 feet in elevation in a region of Sequoia National Forest filled with a network of backcountry roads. This camp is set in an inconspicuous spot and is easy to miss. A good side trip is to drive two miles south, turn left, and continue a short distance to a trailhead on the right side of the road for Portuguese Peak (a Forest Service map is strongly advised). From here, it's a one-mile butt-kicker to the top of Portuguese Peak, 7,914 feet in elevation.

Campsites, facilities: There are 10 sites for tents or RVs up to 40 feet long. Picnic tables and fire grills are provided. Vault toilets are available. No drinking water is available. Garbage must be packed out. Leashed pets are permitted.

Reservations, fees: Reservations are not accepted. There is no fee for camping. Open from June to September.

Directions: Drive on Highway 99 to Delano and the exit for Highway 155. Take that exit and drive east for about 40 miles to Jack Ranch Road (just west of Glennville). Turn left on Jack Ranch Road and drive about four miles to White River Road/Sugarloaf Drive. Turn right on Sugarloaf Drive and drive 4.5 miles

to Guernsey Mill/Sugarloaf Drive. Continue on Sugarloaf Road/Forest Road 23S16 for about six miles to the campground (paved all the way).
Contact: Giant Sequoia National Monument, Tule River/Hot Springs Ranger District, 559/539-2607 or 661/548-6503, fax 559/539-2067.

141 GOLDLEDGE

Rating: 7

On the Kern River in Sequoia National Forest.

Map 11.5, page 585

This is another in the series of camps on the Kern River north of Lake Isabella. This one is set at 3,200 feet.

Campsites, facilities: There are 37 sites for tents or RVs up to 30 feet long. Picnic tables and fire grills are provided. Drinking water and vault toilets are available. Supplies and a coin laundry are available in Kernville. Leashed pets are permitted.

Reservations, fees: Reserve at 877/444-6777 or website: www. ReserveUsa.com ($9 reservation fee); $14 per night, $5 for an extra vehicle. Open from May to September.

Directions: From Bakersfield, drive east on Highway 178 for about 40 miles to the town of Lake Isabella and Highway 155/Burlando Way. Turn left (north) and drive 10 miles to Kernville and the Kern River Highway/Sierra Way. Turn left on the Kern River Highway and drive 10 miles to the campground.

Contact: Sequoia National Forest, Cannell Meadow Ranger District, 760/376-3781, fax 760/376-3795.

142 HOSPITAL FLAT

Rating: 8

On the North Fork of the Kern River in Sequoia National Forest.

Map 11.5, page 585

It's kind of like the old shell game, trying to pick the best of the campgrounds along the North Fork of the Kern River. This one is seven miles north of Lake Isabella. The elevation is 2,800 feet. (For information on rafting on the Kern River, see the entry for Fairview.)

Campsites, facilities: There are 40 sites for tents or RVs up to 30 feet long. Picnic tables and fire grills are provided. Drinking water and vault toilets are available. Some facilities are wheelchair-accessible. Supplies and a coin laundry are available in Kernville. Leashed pets are permitted.

Reservations, fees: Reserve at 877/444-6777 or website: www. ReserveUsa.com ($9 reservation fee); $14 per night, $5 for an extra vehicle. Senior discount available. Open from May to September.

Directions: From Bakersfield, drive east on Highway 178 for about 40 miles to the town of Lake Isabella and Highway 155/Burlando Way. Turn left (north) and drive 10 miles to Kernville and the Kern River Highway/Sierra Way. Turn left on the Kern River Highway and drive seven miles to the campground.

Contact: Sequoia National Forest, Cannell Meadow Ranger District, 760/376-3781, fax 760/376-3795.

143 CAMP 3

Rating: 9

On the North Fork of the Kern River in Sequoia National Forest.

Map 11.5, page 585

This is the second in a series of camps along the Kern River north of Lake Isabella (in this case, five miles north of the lake). If you don't like this spot, Hospital Flat is just two miles upriver and Headquarters is just one mile downriver. The camp elevation is 2,800 feet.

Campsites, facilities: There are 52 sites for tents or RVs up to 30 feet long. Picnic tables and fire grills are provided. Drinking water and vault toilets are available. Supplies and a coin laundry are available in Kernville. Leashed pets are permitted.

Reservations, fees: Reserve at 877/444-6777 or website: www. ReserveUsa.com ($9 reservation fee); $14 per night, $5 for an extra vehicle. Senior discount available. Open from May to September.

Directions: From Bakersfield, drive east on Highway 178 for about 40 miles to the town of Lake Isabella and Highway 155/Burlando Way. Turn left (north) and drive 10 miles to Kernville and the Kern River Highway/Sierra Way. Turn left on the Kern River Highway and drive five miles to the campground.

Contact: Sequoia National Forest, Cannell Meadow Ranger District, 760/376-3781, fax 760/376-3795.

144 HEADQUARTERS

Rating: 8

On the North Fork of the Kern River in Sequoia National Forest.

Map 11.5, page 585

As you head north from Lake Isabella on Sierra Way, this is the first in a series of Forest Service campgrounds from which to take your pick, all of them set along the North Fork of the Kern River. The North Fork Kern is best known for offering prime white water for rafting. The elevation is 2,700 feet.

Campsites, facilities: There are 44 sites for tents or RVs up to 27 feet long. Picnic tables and fire grills are provided. Drinking water and vault toilets are available. Some facilities are wheelchair-accessible. Supplies and a coin laundry are available in Kernville. Leashed pets are permitted.

Reservations, fees: Reserve at 877/444-6777 or website: www. ReserveUsa.com ($9 reservation fee); $14 per night, $5 for an extra vehicle. Senior discount available. Open year-round.

Directions: From Bakersfield, drive east on Highway 178 for about 40 miles to the town of Lake Isabella and Highway 155/Burlando Way. Turn left (north) and drive 10 miles to Kernville and the Kern River Highway/Sier-

ra Way. Turn left on the Kern River Highway and drive three miles to the campground.

Contact: Sequoia National Forest, Cannell Meadow Ranger District, 760/376-3781, fax 760/376-3795.

145 LONG VALLEY

Rating: 5

Near the Dome Land Wilderness.

Map 11.5, page 585

This one is way out there. It's set at road's end in Long Valley, a mile from the border of the Dome Land Wilderness to the east, and the camp is used primarily as a jump-off spot for hikers. A trail from camp leads 2.5 miles west, climbing along a small stream and reaching the South Fork of the Kern River, in rugged and remote country. The elevation is 5,200 feet.

Campsites, facilities: There are 13 tent sites. Picnic tables and fire grills are provided. Pit toilets are available. No drinking water is available. Garbage must be packed out. Leashed pets are permitted.

Reservations, fees: No reservations are accepted and there is no fee, but donations encouraged. Open year-round.

Directions: Drive on U.S. 395 to Ninemile Canyon Road (four miles north of the town of Pearsonville, 48 miles south of Lone Pine). Turn west on Ninemile Canyon Road and drive 11 miles to the BLM Work Station and Cane Brake Road. Turn left on Cane Brake Road (the dirt road opposite the BLM station) and drive six miles to Long Valley Road. Turn right and drive eight miles to the campground entrance road on the left. Turn left and drive one mile to the campground.

Contact: Bureau of Land Management, Bakersfield Field Office, 661/391-6000, fax 661/391-6040.

146 CHIMNEY CREEK

Rating: 5

On the Pacific Crest Trail.

Map 11.5, page 585

This BLM camp is set at 5,900 feet along the headwaters of Chimney Creek, on the southern flank of Chimney Peak (7,990 feet) two miles to the north. This is a trailhead camp for the Pacific Crest Trail, one of its relatively obscure sections. The PCT heads north from camp and in 10 miles it skirts the eastern border of Dome Land Wilderness.

Campsites, facilities: There are 36 sites for tents or RVs up to 25 feet long. Picnic tables and fire grills are provided. Vault toilets are available. No drinking water is available. Garbage must be packed out. Leashed pets are permitted.

Reservations, fees: Reservations are not accepted. There is no fee for camping. Open year-round.

Directions: Drive on U.S. 395 to Ninemile Canyon Road (four miles north of the town of Pearsonville, 48 miles south of Lone Pine). Turn west on Ninemile Canyon Road and drive 11 miles to the BLM Work Station and Cane Brake Road. Turn left on Cane Brake Road (the dirt road opposite the BLM station) and drive three miles to the camp on the left.

Contact: Bureau of Land Management, Bakersfield Field Office, 661/391-6000, fax 661/391-6040.

147 ALDER CREEK

Rating: 7

In Sequoia National Forest.

Map 11.5, page 585

This primitive camp is just inside the western border of Sequoia National Forest, an obscure spot that requires traversing a very twisty and, at times, rough road. It is set at 3,900 feet, just a quarter of a mile upstream from where Alder Creek meets Slick Rock Creek. There is a trail out of the camp that runs north for two miles along Slick Rock Creek.

Campsites, facilities: There are 12 sites for tents or RVs up to 20 feet long. Picnic tables and fire grills are provided. Vault toilets are available. No drinking water is available. Garbage must be packed out. Leashed pets are permitted.

Reservations, fees: Reservations are not accepted. There is no fee for camping. Open from May to November.

Directions: Drive on Highway 99 to Delano and the exit for Highway 155. Take that exit and drive east on Highway 155 for 41 miles to Glennville. Continue east for eight miles to Alder Creek Road. Turn right on Alder Creek Road and drive three miles to the campground.

Contact: Sequoia National Forest, Greenhorn Ranger District, 760/379-5646, fax 760/379-8597.

148 CEDAR CREEK

Rating: 7

In Sequoia National Forest.

Map 11.5, page 585

This is a little-known Forest Service camp set at 4,800 feet on the southwest flank of Sequoia National Forest, right along little Cedar Creek, with easy access off Highway 155. Greenhorn Mountain Park and Alder Creek provide nearby alternatives.

Campsites, facilities: There are 10 sites for tents only. Picnic tables and fire grills are provided. Drinking water (from May to October only) and vault toilets are available. Garbage must be packed out. Leashed pets are permitted.

Reservations, fees: Reservations are not accepted. There is no fee for camping. Open year-round.

Directions: Drive on Highway 99 to Delano and the exit for Highway 155. Take that exit and drive east on Highway 155 for 41 miles to Glennville. Continue east for nine miles to the campground.

Contact: Sequoia National Forest, Greenhorn Ranger District, 760/379-5646, fax 760/379-8597.

149 GREENHORN MOUNTAIN PARK

🚶 ❄ 🐕 🚐 ⛺

Rating: 7

Near Shirley Meadows.

Map 11.5, page 585

This county campground is near the Shirley Meadows Ski Area, a small ski park open on weekends in winter when there is sufficient snow. Greenhorn Mountain Park covers 160 acres, set at 6,000 feet in elevation. The region is filled with a spider-web network of Forest Service roads, detailed on a map of Sequoia National Forest. Lake Isabella is a 15-minute drive to the east.

Campsites, facilities: There are 70 sites for tents or RVs up to 24 feet long. Picnic tables and fire grills are provided. Restrooms, drinking water, flush toilets, and two showers are available. Leashed pets are permitted.

Reservations, fees: No reservations accepted, except for groups. Rates are $20 per night, $4 for extra vehicle, $4 per night. Senior discount available. Open spring through fall, weather permitting.

Directions: From Bakersfield, drive east on Highway 178 for about 40 miles to the town of Lake Isabella and Highway 155/Burlando Way. Turn left (north) and drive six miles to Wofford Heights. Turn left (west) on Highway 155 and drive 10 miles to the park on the left.

Contact: Kern County Parks, 661/868-7000, website: www.co.kern.ca.us/parks/index.htm.

150 RIVERNOOK CAMPGROUND

🏊 🚣 🚗 🐕 ♿ 🚐 ⛺

Rating: 7

On the North Fork of the Kern River.

Map 11.5, page 585

This is a large, privately operated park set near Lake Isabella a few miles from the head of the lake. Boat rentals are available at one of the nearby marinas. An optional side trip is to visit Keysville, the first town to become established on the Kern River during the gold rush days. The elevation is 2,665 feet.

Campsites, facilities: There are 30 drive-through sites with full hookups for RVs, 41 sites with partial hookups for RVs, and 59 sites for tents. Picnic tables and drinking water are provided. Restrooms, showers, RV dump station, and cable TV are available. Leashed pets are permitted. Some facilities are wheelchair-accessible.

Reservations, fees: Reservations are recommended. The fee is $25 per night for RVs with full hookups, $19 per night for tents. Major credit cards accepted. Open year-round.

Directions: From Bakersfield, drive east on Highway 178 for about 40 miles to the town of Lake Isabella and Highway 155/Burlando Way. Turn left (north) and drive 10 miles to Kernville and the Kern River Highway/Sierra Way. Turn left on Sierra Way and a half mile to the park entrance (14001 Sierra Way).

Contact: Rivernook Campground, 760/376-2705, fax 760/376-2595.

151 LIVE OAK NORTH AND SOUTH

🏊 🚣 🚗 🐕 🚐 ⛺

Rating: 8

On Lake Isabella.

Map 11.5, page 585

This is one of two camps set in the immediate area on Lake Isabella's northwest side; the other is Tillie Creek. Live Oak is on the west side of the road, Tillie Creek on the eastern, lake side of the road. (For recreation information, see the entry for Tillie Creek.)

Campsites, facilities: There are 150 sites for tents or RVs up to 30 feet long and one group site. Picnic tables and fire grills are provided. Drinking water, showers, and flush toilets are available. Supplies and a coin laundry are available in nearby Wofford Heights. Leashed pets are permitted.

Reservations, fees: Reservations are required for group sites; reserve at 877/444-6777 ($9 reservation fee) or website: www. reserveusa.com; $16 per night, $5 for an extra vehicle; $200 per night for group site for up to 200 people. Open from May through September.

Directions: From Bakersfield, drive east on Highway 178 for about 40 miles to the town of Lake Isabella and Highway 155/Burlando Way. Turn left (north) and drive 5.5 miles to the campground entrance road on the left (a half mile before reaching Wofford Heights).

Contact: Sequoia National Forest, Greenhorn Ranger District, 760/379-5646, fax 760/379-8597.

152 TILLIE CREEK

Rating: 9

On Lake Isabella.

Map 11.5, page 585

This is one of two camps (the other is Live Oak) near where Tillie Creek enters Lake Isabella, set on the northwest shore of the lake near the town of Wofford Heights. Lake Isabella is the largest freshwater lake in Southern California, covering 11,400 acres, and with it comes a dynamic array of campgrounds, marinas, and facilities. It is set at 2,605 feet in the foothills east of Bakersfield, fed by the Kern River, and dominated by boating sports of all kinds.

Campsites, facilities: There are 155 family sites and four group sites for tents or RVs up to 45 feet long. Picnic tables and fire grills are provided. Restrooms, drinking water, showers, and flush toilets are available. RV dump station, playground, amphitheater, and a fish-cleaning station are available nearby. Some facilities are wheelchair-accessible. Supplies are nearby in Wofford Heights. Leashed pets are permitted.

Reservations, fees: Reservations are required for group sites; reserve at 877/444-6777 ($9 reservation fee) or website: www. reserveusa.com; $16 per night, $5 for an extra vehicle; $100–175 per night for group sites. Senior discount available. Open year-round.

Directions: From Bakersfield, drive east on Highway 178 for about 40 miles to the town of Lake Isabella and Highway 155/Burlando Way. Turn left (north) and drive five miles to the campground (one mile before reaching Wofford Heights).

Contact: Sequoia National Forest, Greenhorn Ranger District, 760/379-5646, fax 760/379-8597.

153 CAMP 9

Rating: 8

On Lake Isabella.

Map 11.5, page 585

This campground is primitive and sparsely covered, but it has several bonus features. It is set along the northwest shore of Lake Isabella, known for good boating, water-skiing in the summer, and fishing in the spring. Other options include great rafting waters along the North Fork of the Kern River (north of the lake), a good bird-watching area at the South Fork Wildlife Area (along the northeast corner of the lake), and an off-highway-motorcycle park across the road from this campground. The elevation is 2,650 feet.

Campsites, facilities: There are 109 primitive sites for tents or RVs. Drinking water, flush toilets, RV dump station, boat launch, and a fish-cleaning station are available. Supplies and a coin laundry are available nearby in Kernville. Leashed pets are permitted.

Reservations, fees: Reservations are not accepted. The fee is $8 per night, $5 for each additional vehicle. Group reservations at 760/376-3008. Senior discount available. Open year-round.

Directions: From Bakersfield, drive east on Highway 178 for about 40 miles to the town of Lake Isabella and Highway 155/Burlando Way. Turn right (south) and drive six miles to the campground entrance on the right (on the northeast shore of Lake Isabella). The campground entrance is just south of the small airport at Lake Isabella.

Contact: Sequoia National Forest, Greenhorn Ranger District, 760/379-5646, fax 760/379-8597.

154 FRENCH GULCH GROUP CAMP

Rating: 9

On Lake Isabella.

Map 11.5, page 585

This is a large group camp on Lake Isabella at the southwest end of the lake about two miles north of Pioneer Point and the spillway. (For recreation information, see the entry for Pioneer Point.) The elevation is 2,700 feet.

Campsites, facilities: There is one large group campsite for up to 100 people with tents or RVs. Picnic tables and fire grills are provided. Drinking water, flush toilets, and solar-heated showers are available. A store, coin laundry, and propane gas are nearby. Leashed pets are permitted.

Reservations, fees: Reserve at 877/444-6777 or website: www. ReserveUsa.com ($9 reservation fee); $200 group fee per night. Open year-round.

Directions: From Bakersfield, drive east on Highway 178 for about 40 miles to the town of Lake Isabella and Highway 155/Burlando Way. Turn left (north) and drive three miles to the campground entrance on the right.

Contact: Sequoia National Forest, Greenhorn Ranger District, 760/379-5646, fax 760/379-8597.

155 HUNGRY GULCH

Rating: 9

On Lake Isabella, in Sequoia National Forest.

Map 11.5, page 585

Hungry Gulch is on the western side of Lake Isabella, but across the road from the shore. Nearby Boulder Gulch, directly across the road, is an option. There are no boat ramps in the immediate area. (For details about Lake Isabella, see the entry for Pioneer Point.)

Campsites, facilities: There are 78 sites for tents, RVs, or trailers up to 30 feet long. Picnic tables and fire grills are provided. Restrooms, drinking water, showers, and flush toilets are available. A playground is available nearby. Supplies and a coin laundry are available in Lake Isabella. Leashed pets are permitted.

Reservations, fees: Reserve at 877/444-6777 or website: www. ReserveUsa.com ($9 reservation fee); $16 per night, $5 for each additional vehicle. Open from April through September.

Directions: From Bakersfield, drive east on Highway 178 for about 40 miles to the town of Lake Isabella and Highway 155/Burlando Way. Turn left (north) and drive four miles north on Highway 155 to the campground.

Contact: Sequoia National Forest, Greenhorn Ranger District, 760/379-5646, fax 760/379-8597.

156 BOULDER GULCH

Rating: 8

On Lake Isabella.

Map 11.5, page 585

Boulder Gulch lies fairly near the western shore of Lake Isabella, across the road from Hungry Gulch. Take your pick. Isabella is the biggest lake in Southern California and a prime destination point for Bakersfield area residents. Fishing for trout and bass is best in the spring. By the dog days of summer, when people are bow-wowin' at the heat, water-skiers take over, along with folks just looking to cool off. Like a lot of lakes in the valley, Isabella is subject to drawdowns. The elevation is 2,650 feet. (For more information, see the entry for Pioneer Point.)

Campsites, facilities: There are 78 sites for tents, trailers, or RVs up to 45 feet long. Picnic tables and fire grills are provided. Restrooms, drinking water, flush toilets, showers, playground, and a fish-cleaning station are available. Some facilities are wheelchair-accessible. Supplies and a coin laundry are available in the town of Lake Isabella. Leashed pets are permitted.

Reservations, fees: Reserve at 877/444-6777 or website: www. ReserveUsa.com ($9 reservation fee); $16 per night, $5 for each additional vehicle. Senior discount available. Open from April through September.

Directions: From Bakersfield, drive east on Highway 178 for about 40 miles to the town of Lake Isabella and Highway 155/Burlando Way. Turn left (north) and drive four miles to the campground entrance.

Contact: Sequoia National Forest, Greenhorn Ranger District, 760/379-5646, fax 760/379-8597.

157 PIONEER POINT

Rating: 9

On Lake Isabella, in Sequoia National Forest.

Map 11.5, page 585

Lake Isabella is the largest freshwater lake in Southern California, covering 11,400 acres, and with it comes a dynamic array of campgrounds, marinas, and facilities. It is set at 2,605 feet in the foothills east of Bakersfield, fed by the Kern River, and dominated by boating sports of all kinds. This camp is at the lake's southwest corner, between the spillway and the main dam, with a boat ramp available a mile to the east. Another camp is nearby, Main Dam. Isabella is a first-class lake for water-skiing, but in the spring and early summer windsurfing is also excellent, best just east of the Auxiliary Dam. Boat rentals of all kinds are available at several marinas.

Campsites, facilities: There are 78 sites for tents, RVs, or trailers up to 30 feet long. Picnic tables and fire grills are provided. Restrooms, drinking water, showers, and flush toilets are available. A playground and a fish-cleaning station are available nearby. A boat ramp is three miles from camp. Supplies and a coin laundry

are available in the town of Lake Isabella. Leashed pets are permitted.

Reservations, fees: Reserve at 877/444-6777 or website: www. ReserveUsa.com ($9 reservation fee); $16 per night, $5 for each additional vehicle. Senior discount available. Open year-round.

Directions: From Bakersfield, drive east on Highway 178 for about 40 miles to the town of Lake Isabella and Highway 155/Burlando Way. Turn left (north) and drive 2.5 miles north on Highway 155 to the campground.

Contact: Sequoia National Forest, Greenhorn Ranger District, 760/379-5646, fax 760/379-8597.

158 MAIN DAM

Rating: 8

On Lake Isabella.

Map 11.5, page 585

This camp is on the south shore of Lake Isabella, just east of Pioneer Point and within a mile of a boat ramp. (For recreation information, see the entry for Pioneer Point.)

Campsites, facilities: There are 82 sites for tents, trailers, or RVs up to 30 feet long. Picnic tables and fire grills are provided. Drinking water and flush toilets are available. An RV dump station is available nearby. Supplies and a coin laundry are available in the town of Lake Isabella. Leashed pets are permitted with proof of shots.

Reservations, fees: Reserve at 877/444-6777 or website: www. ReserveUsa.com ($9 reservation fee); $14 per night, $5 for each additional vehicle. Senior discount available. Open May to September.

Directions: From Bakersfield, drive east on Highway 178 for about 40 miles to the town of Lake Isabella and Highway 155/Burlando Way. Turn left (north) and drive 1.5 miles to the campground.

Contact: Sequoia National Forest, Greenhorn Ranger District, 760/379-5646, fax 760/379-8597.

159 AUXILIARY DAM

Rating: 8

On Lake Isabella.
Map 11.5, page 585

This primitive camp was designed to be an overflow area if other camps at Lake Isabella are packed. It's the only camp directly on the shore of the lake, and many people like it. In addition, a boat ramp is just a mile north for good lake access, and the windsurfing prospects adjacent to the campground are the best of the entire lake. The winds come up and sail right over the dam, creating a steady breeze in the afternoon that is not gusty.

Campsites, facilities: There are a number of primitive, undesignated sites for tents or RVs. A restroom, drinking water, flush toilets, and a shower are available. Supplies and a coin laundry are available in the town of Lake Isabella. Leashed pets are permitted.

Reservations, fees: Reservations are not accepted. The fee is $5 per night or $35 for a season pass. Senior discount available. Open year-round.

Directions: From Bakersfield, drive east on Highway 178 for about 40 miles to the town of Lake Isabella. Continue east on Highway 178 for one mile to the campground entrance.

Contact: Sequoia National Forest, Greenhorn Ranger District, 760/379-5646, fax 760/379-8597.

160 PARADISE COVE

Rating: 6

On Lake Isabella.
Map 11.5, page 585

Paradise Cove is on the southeast shore of Lake Isabella. A boat ramp is about two miles away to the east, near the South Fork Picnic Area. While the camp is not directly at the lakeshore, it does overlook the broadest expanse of the lake. This part of the lake is relatively undeveloped compared to the areas near Wofford Heights and the dam.

Campsites, facilities: There are 58 sites for tents or RVs, some with picnic tables and fire grills. Flush toilets, showers, and a fish-cleaning station are available. Some facilities are wheelchair-accessible. Supplies, RV dump station, and a coin laundry are available in Mountain Mesa. Leashed pets are permitted.

Reservations, fees: Reserve at 877/444-6777 or website: www. ReserveUsa.com ($9 reservation fee); $16 per night, $5 for each additional vehicle. Senior discount available. Open year-round.

Directions: From Bakersfield, drive east on Highway 178 for about 40 miles to the town of Lake Isabella. Continue east on Highway 178 for six miles to the campground entrance.

Contact: Sequoia National Forest, Greenhorn Ranger District, 760/379-5646, fax 760/379-8597.

161 LAKE ISABELLA RV RESORT

Rating: 5

Near Lake Isabella.
Map 11.5, page 585

This quiet, privately operated park set up for RVs is across the street from Lake Isabella. It is one of many camps at the lake, so plan on plenty of company. There is a free public boat ramp 200 yards away within Sequoia National Forest and a full-service marina with watercraft rentals two miles west of the resort. (For details on the immediate area, see the entry for the nearby Forest Service camps, Auxiliary Dam and Paradise Cove.) The elevation is 2,600 feet.

Campsites, facilities: There are 91 sites with full hookups for RVs, including some permanent residents. Picnic tables and barbecues are provided. Restrooms, showers, swimming pool, modem access, clubhouse, billiards, cable TV, laundry facilities, and a fish-cleaning station are available. Some facilities are wheelchair-accessible. Leashed pets are permitted.

Reservations, fees: Reservations are accepted. The fee is $24 per night. Major credit cards accepted. Open year-round.

Directions: From Bakersfield, drive east on Highway 178 for about 40 miles to the town of Lake Isabella. Continue east on Highway 178 for six miles to the campground entrance on the right (signed).

Contact: Lake Isabella RV Resort, 800/787-9920, website: www.lakeisabellarv.com.

162 KOA LAKE ISABELLA

Rating: 4

On Lake Isabella.
Map 11.5, page 585

This KOA camp provides a good, clean option to the Forest Service camps on the southern end of Lake Isabella, Southern California's largest lake. It is set in South Fork Valley (elevation 2,600 feet), east of the lake off Highway 178. The nearest boat ramp is at South Fork Picnic Area (about a five-minute drive to the west), where there is also a good view of the lake.

Campsites, facilities: There are 104 sites with full or partial hookups for RVs or tents. Picnic tables are provided. Restrooms, drinking water, flush toilets, showers, playground, swimming pool, laundry facilities, store, RV dump station, and propane gas are available. Leashed pets are permitted.

Reservations, fees: Reservations are accepted. The fee is $25–35 per night for RVs, $23 per night for tents. Major credit cards accepted. Open May through September.

Directions: From Bakersfield, drive east on Highway 178 for about 40 miles to the town of Lake Isabella. Continue east on Highway 178 for 10 miles to the campground entrance on the left (well signed).

Contact: KOA Lake Isabella, 760/378-2001.

163 EVANS FLAT

Rating: 4

In Sequoia National Forest.
Map 11.5, page 585

Evans Flat is an obscure campground in the southwest region of Sequoia National Forest, about 10 miles west of Lake Isabella, with no other camps in the vicinity. You have to earn this one, but if you want solitude, Evans Flat can provide it. It is set at 6,200 feet, with Woodward Peak a half mile to the east. A natural spring is east of camp within walking distance.

Campsites, facilities: There are 20 sites for tents or RVs up to 16 feet long. Fire grills and picnic tables are provided. A portable restroom is available. No drinking water is available. Garbage must be packed out. Four corrals with water troughs (though water for the troughs is not always available) and a pasture area are provided for horses. Leashed pets are permitted.

Reservations, fees: Reservations are not accepted. There is no fee for camping. Open from May to October.

Directions: From Bakersfield, drive east on Highway 178 for about 40 miles to the town of Lake Isabella and Highway 155/Burlando Way. Turn left (north) and drive six miles to Wofford Heights. Turn left (west) on Highway 155 and drive 5.5 miles to Rancheria Road. Turn left and drive 8.3 miles (first paved, then dirt) to the campground.

Contact: Sequoia National Forest, Greenhorn Ranger District, 760/379-5646, fax 760/379-8597.

164 SANDY FLAT

Rating: 6

On the Kern River in Sequoia National Forest.
Map 11.5, page 585

This camp was opened in the mid-1990s as an overflow camp in case Hobo was filled. It is about a mile from Hobo. It is a low-use campground, with less shade than Hobo; some sites shaded, others, well, nope. It is used primarily as a boat launch area for kayakers and rafters. Fishing is fair for catfish, bass, and rainbow trout. The river is stocked with trout in the summer.

Campsites, facilities: There are 38 sites for tents and for RVs. Fire rings and picnic tables are provided. Water is provided some of the time; call ahead for details. Vault toilets are available. Some facilities are wheelchair-accessible. Leashed pets are permitted.

Reservations, fees: Reservations are recommended. Reserve at 877/444-6777 ($9 reservation fee) or website: www. reserveusa.com; $14 per night for the first vehicle, $5 per night for each additional vehicle. Senior discount available. There is no fee when there is no water at the camp. Open from May through September.

Directions: From Bakersfield, drive east on Highway 178 for 35 miles to Borel Road (five miles from Lake Isabella). Turn right (south) at Borel Road and drive .3 mile to Old Kern Road. Turn right and drive one mile to the campground on your right.

Contact: Sequoia National Forest, Greenhorn Ranger District, 760/379-5646, fax 760/379-8597.

165 HOBO

Rating: 7

On the Kern River in Sequoia National Forest.

Map 11.5, page 585

The secret is out about Hobo: it is set adjacent to a mineral hot springs, that is, an open-air springs, with room for about 10 people at once. The camp is also situated along the lower Kern River, about 10 miles downstream of the dam at Lake Isabella. Rafters sometimes use this camp as a put-in spot for an 18-mile run to the takeout at Democrat Picnic Area, a challenging Class IV run. The elevation is 2,300 feet.

Campsites, facilities: There are 25 sites for tents and 10 sites for RVs up to 16 feet long. Fire grills and picnic tables are provided. Water is provided some of the time; call ahead for details. Vault toilets and showers are available. Leashed pets are permitted. Some facilities are wheelchair-accessible.

Reservations, fees: Reservations are recommended. Reserve at 877/444-6777 ($9 reservation fee) or website: www. reserveusa.com; $14 per night for the first vehicle, $5 per night for each additional vehicle. Senior discount available. There is no fee when there is no water at the camp. Open from May through September.

Directions: From Bakersfield, drive east on Highway 178 for 35 miles to Borel Road (five miles from Lake Isabella). Turn right (south) at Borel Road and drive .3 mile to Old Kern Road. Turn right and drive two miles to the campground on your right.

Contact: Sequoia National Forest, Greenhorn Ranger District, 760/379-5646, fax 760/379-8597.

166 BRECKENRIDGE

Rating: 7

In Sequoia National Forest.

Map 11.5, page 585

This is a popular spot for people to visit with sport utility vehicles. It is a tiny, primitive camp set at 7,100 feet near Breckenridge Mountain (a good lookout here) in a little-traveled southwest sector of the Sequoia National Forest. From camp, it's a two-mile drive south up to the lookout, with sweeping views afforded in all directions. There are no other camps in the immediate area.

Campsites, facilities: There are eight tent sites. Picnic tables and fire grills are provided. A portable toilet is available. No drinking water is available. Garbage must be packed out. Leashed pets are permitted.

Reservations, fees: Reservations are not accepted. There is no fee for camping. Open from May to October.

Directions: From Bakersfield, drive east on Highway 178 for about 40 miles to the town of Lake Isabella and Lake Isabella Boulevard. Turn right (south) on Lake Isabella Boulevard and drive two miles to a Y intersection with Kern River Canyon Road and Caliente Bodfish Road. Bear left on Caliente Bodfish Road and drive nine miles to the town of Havilah. Continue on Caliente Bodfish Road for two miles to Forest Road 28S06. Turn right and drive about 10 miles to the campground.

Contact: Sequoia National Forest, Greenhorn Ranger District, 760/379-5646, fax 760/379-8597.

167 WALKER PASS WALK-IN

Rating: 6

On the Pacific Crest Trail southwest of Death Valley National Park.

Map 11.5, page 585

Long-distance hikers on the Pacific Crest Trail treat this camp as if they were arriving at Valhalla. That's because it is set right on the trail and, better yet, drinking water is available. Out here in the desert there aren't many places where you can act like a camel and suck up all the liquid you can hold. The camp is set at 5,200 feet, southwest of Death Valley National Park. And if you guessed it was named for Joe Walker, the West's greatest trailblazer and one of my heroes, well, right you are. If you arrive by car instead of on the PCT, use this spot as a base camp. Because of its desert remoteness, very few hikers start trips from this location.

Campsites, facilities: There are two sites for tents and RVs with limited parking and 11 walk-in sites for tents only. Picnic tables and fire rings are provided. Drinking water (spring through fall) and pit toilets are available. Hitching racks and corrals are available. Garbage must be packed out. Leashed pets are allowed.

Reservations, fees: Reservations are not accepted. There is no fee for camping. A 14-day stay limit is enforced. Open year-round.

Directions: From Bakersfield, drive east on Highway 178 for about 40 miles to the town of Lake Isabella. Continue east on Highway 178 to Onyx and continue 14 miles to Walker Pass and the right side of the road (where a sign is posted for the Pacific Crest Trail). Park and walk a quarter mile to the campground.

Contact: Bureau of Land Management, Bakersfield Field Office, 661/391-6000, fax 661/391-6040.

© ROBERT HOLMES/CALTOUR

Chapter 12
Death Valley

Chapter 12—Death Valley

What good are Death Valley, the Panamint Range, and the nearby desert environs?

The answer is that this country is good for looking at. On a fall evening, you can take a seat on a ridge, overlooking hundreds of square miles of landscape, and just watch. Every few minutes, you'll find, the view changes. It is like watching the face of someone you care for, one minute joyous, the next pensive, then wondrous, then mysterious.

The desert is like this, always changing the way it looks, just as the sunlight changes. The reason is because as the sun passes through the sky, its azimuth is continuously changing. In turn, that causes a continuous transformation in the way sunlight is refracted through the atmosphere and across the vast landscape. So every few minutes, especially at dawn and dusk in spring and fall, the desert looks different from minute to minute. For those who appreciate this subtlety, the desert calls for them in a way that many others do not understand.

There are other appeals. It is often warm even on the fringe of winter, the wildflowers are small but can be spectacular in spring, and the highways—and everything else—are wide open, at times without another soul for miles in all directions. This region is huge, with Death Valley the largest national park in California, yet there are only 10 campgrounds. Because of the sparse nature of the land, campers should arrive self-contained, that is, equipped with everything they need.

Some of the highlights include the lowest point in the United States, 282 feet below sea level, at Badwater in Death Valley National Park. Yet also in the park is Telescope Peak, towering at 11,048 feet. Crazy? Oh yeah.

When viewed from a distance, in between is a vast terrain that seems devoid of vegetation. The sub-sea-level salt flats can seem indeed like a bunch of nothing. But they are linked to barren, rising mountains, Eureka Dunes, and surrounding vastness everywhere.

Camping is good at the developed campsites, but better if you strike out on your own and create your own site, do-it-yourself style. One key is to never camp at a water source or in the bottom of ravines. Instead, always camp a good distance from water sources and on shelves or flat spots above ravines. This is why: 1. If you camp at a water source, you may unintentionally block it from use by wildlife. In their case, it may be life or death, and yet you are in their way–so keep at wide berth from water sources at night. 2. Never camp at the bottom of ravines in the desert because you can drown. What? Yep. Thunderstorms with tremendous short-term rainfall are common in the desert. If the runoff is blocked, the water can back itself up like a small lake, and then suddenly break through with the force of a small flood. In turn, if you are camped at the bottom of a ravine, you can find yourself in the path of a surprise torrent of water–right in the middle of the desert, the driest place in the state.

Of course, summer is well known for the blazing temperatures, over 100 about every day and occasionally hitting 120 and up.

But that is not when people visit here. They visit in fall, winter, and spring. And if you see somebody sitting on an overlooking ridge at dusk, watching the changing colors of the landscape as if it were created from the palate of an artist, well, don't be surprised. When it comes to beautiful views, the changing colors of the emotion of the land, it doesn't get any better than this.

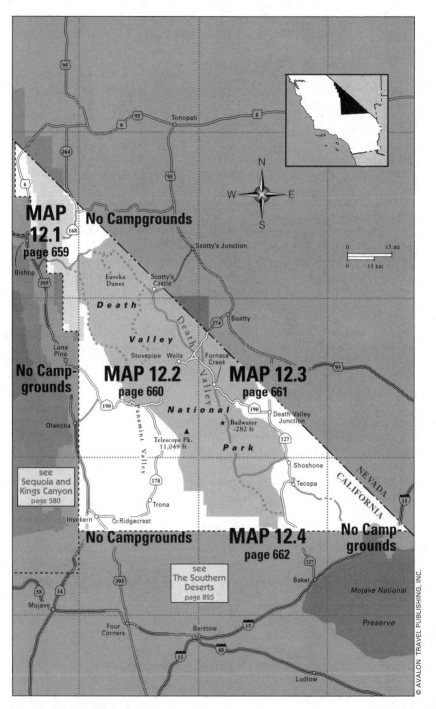

Map 12.1

**Campgrounds 1–5
Pages 663–664**

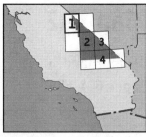

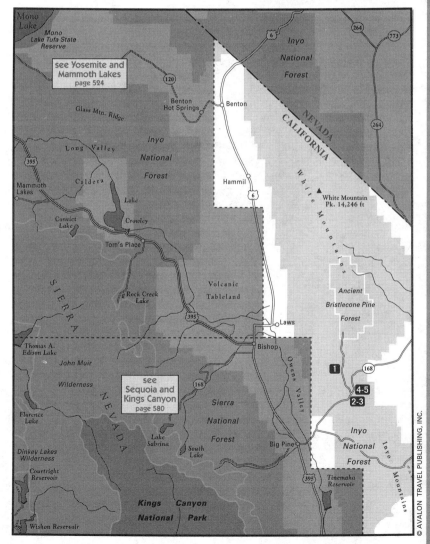

Map 12.2

Campgrounds 6–11
Pages 664–666

12.3

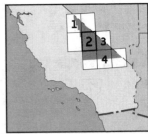

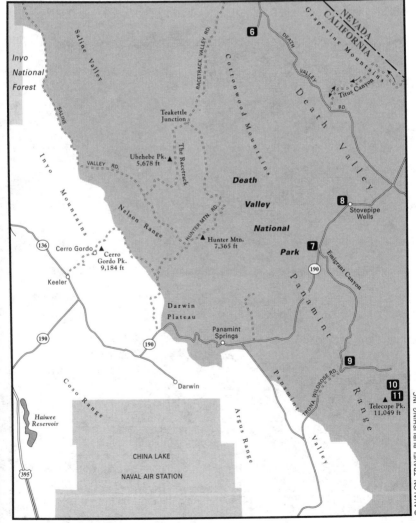

© AVALON TRAVEL PUBLISHING, INC.

Map 12.3

Campgrounds 12–14
Page 667

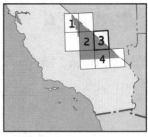

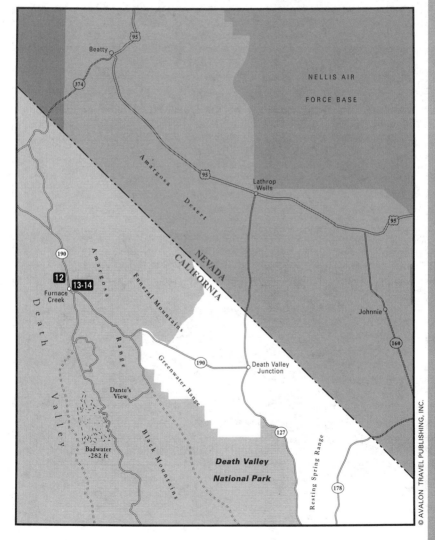

© AVALON TRAVEL PUBLISHING, INC.

Map 12.4

**Campground 15
Page 668**

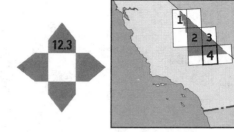

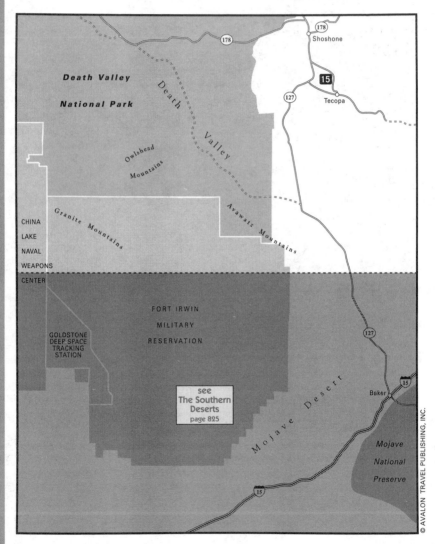

see
The Southern
Deserts
page 825

© AVALON TRAVEL PUBLISHING, INC.

1 GRANDVIEW

Rating: 6

Near Big Pine in Inyo National Forest.

Map 12.1, page 659

This is a primitive and little-known camp, and the folks who find this area earn their solitude. It is in the White Mountains east of Bishop at 8,600 feet along White Mountain Road. The road borders the Ancient Bristlecone Pine Forest to the east and leads north to jump-off spots for hikers heading up Mt. Barcroft (13,023 feet) or White Mountain (14,246 feet, the third-highest mountain in California). A trail out of the camp leads up to an old mining site.

Campsites, facilities: There are 26 sites for tents or RVs up to 22 feet long. Picnic tables and fire grills are provided. Vault toilets are available. No drinking water is available. Leashed pets are permitted.

Reservations, fees: Reservations are not accepted. There is no fee for camping. Open May through October.

Directions: From Big Pine on U.S. 395, turn east on Highway 168 and drive 13 miles. Turn north on White Mountain/Bristlecone Forest Road (Forest Road 4S01) and drive 5.5 miles to the campground.

Contact: Inyo National Forest, White Mountain Ranger District, 760/873-2500, fax 760/873-2563.

2 PIÑON GROUP CAMP

Rating: 5

Near Big Pine in Inyo National Forest.

Map 12.1, page 659

Piñon Group Camp is the first of four group camps set in the immediate area along Highway 168. It is a remote and stark setting, 7,200 feet in elevation, at the foot of the White Mountains on the east side of the Owens Valley. Most campers here will head to the Ancient Bristlecone Pine Forest (turn north on White Moun-

tain Road and drive 10 miles to Schulman Grove Visitor Center), where the oldest tree in the world, nearly 5,000 years old, has been documented. (It is unmarked so some idiot won't cut it down.) The road up here, by the way, provides sweeping views to the west of the Sierra. Hikers can get a similar view by taking the trail out of Cedar Flat to Black Mountain (9,038 feet), about a five-mile tromp one way, with the trail quite faint, often invisible, over the last mile.

Campsites, facilities: There are five sites for tents or RVs. Picnic tables are provided. Vault toilets are available. No drinking water is available. Leashed pets are permitted.

Reservations, fees: Reservations are accepted with a $9 reservation fee at 877/444-6777 or website: www.ReserveUsa.com. Open year-round.

Directions: From Big Pine on U.S. 395, head east on Highway 168 for 13 miles to the camp.

Contact: Inyo National Forest, White Mountain Ranger District, 760/873-2500, fax 760/873-2563.

3 FOSSIL GROUP CAMP

Rating: 5

Near Big Pine in Inyo National Forest.

Map 12.1, page 659

Fossil Group Camp is a primitive Forest Service group camp set at 7,220 feet in elevation, one of four in the immediate vicinity. (See the entry for Piñon Group Camp for side-trip options.)

Campsites, facilities: There are 11 sites for tents or RVs. Picnic tables are provided. Vault toilets are available. No drinking water is available. Leashed pets are permitted.

Reservations, fees: Reservations are accepted with a $9 reservation fee at 877/444-6777 or website: www.ReserveUsa.com. Open year-round.

Directions: From Big Pine on U.S. 395, head east on Highway 168 and drive 13 miles to the campground.

Contact: Inyo National Forest, White Mountain Ranger District, 760/873-2500, fax 760/873-2563.

4 POLETA GROUP CAMP
Rating: 5

Near Big Pine in Inyo National Forest.
Map 12.1, page 659

This is one of four camps in the immediate area, so take your pick. (For side-trip possibilities, see the entry for Piñon Group camp.)

Campsites, facilities: There are eight sites for tents or RVs. Picnic tables are provided. Vault toilets are available. No drinking water is available. Leashed pets are permitted.

Reservations, fees: Reservations are accepted with a $9 reservation fee at 877/444-6777 or website: www.ReserveUsa.com. Open year-round.

Directions: From Big Pine on U.S. 395, turn east on Highway 168 and drive 13 miles to the campground.

Contact: Inyo National Forest, White Mountain Ranger District, 760/873-2500, fax 760/873-2563.

5 JUNIPER GROUP CAMP
Rating: 5

Near Big Pine in Inyo National Forest.
Map 12.1, page 659

Juniper Camp is a nearby option to Poleta Camp for group campers. (See the entry for Piñon Group Camp for side-trip details.)

Campsites, facilities: There are five sites for tents. Picnic tables are provided. Vault toilets are available. No drinking water is available. Leashed pets are permitted.

Reservations, fees: Reservations are accepted with a $9 reservation fee at 877/444-6777 or website: www.ReserveUsa.com. Open year-round.

Directions: From Big Pine on U.S. 395, head

east on Highway 168 for 13 miles to the camp (signed "Cedar Flat Group Camps").

Contact: Inyo National Forest, White Mountain Ranger District, 760/873-2500, fax 760/873-2563.

6 MESQUITE SPRING
Rating: 7

In Death Valley National Park.
Map 12.2, page 660

Mesquite Spring is the northernmost and often the prettiest campground in Death Valley, providing you time it right. If you are a lover of desert beauty, then you must make this trip in late winter or early spring, when all kinds of tiny wildflowers can bring the stark valley floor to life. The key is soil moisture, courtesy of rains in November and December. The elevation is 1,800 feet. Mesquite Spring Campground is within short range of two side trips. It is five miles (past the Grapevine Entrance Station) to Ubehebe Crater, a scenic point, and four miles to Scotty's Castle, a historic building, where tours are available.

Campsites, facilities: There are 30 sites for tents or RVs. Picnic tables and fire grills are provided. Drinking water, flush toilets, and RV dump station are available. Some facilities are wheelchair-accessible. Leashed pets are permitted.

Reservations, fees: Reservations are not accepted. The fee is $10 per night, plus a $10 park entrance fee. Senior discount available. Visitors may pay the entrance fee and obtain a park brochure at the Furnace Creek, Grapevine, Stovepipe Wells, or Beatty Ranger Stations.

Directions: From Furnace Creek Visitor Center, drive north on Highway 190 for 19 miles to Scotty's Castle Road. Turn right and drive 33 miles (three miles before reaching Scotty's Castle) to the campground entrance road on the left. Turn left and drive two miles to the campground.

Contact: Death Valley National Park, 760/786-

3200; Furnace Creek Visitor Center, 760/786-3244, fax 760/786-3283.

7 EMIGRANT

Rating: 4

In Death Valley National Park.
Map 12.2, page 660

The key here is the elevation, and Emigrant, at 2,100 feet, is out of the forbidding subzero elevations of Death Valley. That makes it one of the more habitable camps. From the camp a good side trip is to drive south 21 miles on Emigrant Canyon Road, then turn east on Upper Wildrose Canyon Road for seven miles, the last two miles a rough dirt road. That done, you come to the trailhead for Wildrose Peak, on the left side of the road at the parking area for the Charcoal Kilns. The trail here climbs 4.2 miles to the peak, with awesome views in the last two miles; the last mile is a butt-kicker.

Campsites, facilities: There are 10 sites for tents. Picnic tables are provided. Drinking water and flush toilets are available. Leashed pets are permitted at campsites only.

Reservations, fees: No reservations are accepted and there is no camping fee, however, there is a $10 park entrance fee per vehicle. Open year-round.

Directions: In Stovepipe Wells Village, drive eight miles southwest on Highway 190 to the campground on the right.

Contact: Death Valley National Park, 760/786-3200; Furnace Creek Visitor Center, 760/786-3244, fax 760/786-3283.

8 STOVEPIPE WELLS

Rating: 4

In Death Valley National Park.
Map 12.2, page 660

Stovepipe Wells is on the major highway through Death Valley. The RV sites consist of an enormous asphalt area with sites simply marked on it. There is no shelter or shade. But note: get fuel here because prices are usually lower than at Furnace Creek. An unusual trail is available off the highway within a short distance; look for the sign for the Mosaic Canyon Trail parking area. From here you can take the easy one-mile walk up a beautiful canyon, where the walls are marble and seem as if they are polished. Rock scramblers can extend the trip for another mile. The elevation is at sea level on the edge of a large expanse of Death Valley below sea level.

Campsites, facilities: There are 18 sites for tents only and 200 sites for RVs. Drinking water, flush toilets, RV dump station, swimming pool, camp store, and gasoline are available. Evening ranger programs are available on winter weekends. Some facilities are wheelchair-accessible. Leashed pets are permitted at campsites only.

Reservations, fees: Reservations are not accepted. The fee is $10 per night, plus a $10 park entrance fee per vehicle. Senior discount available. Open mid-October to mid-April.

Directions: In Stovepipe Wells Village, drive west on Highway 190 through town to the signed entrance (just before the general store) on the right.

Contact: Death Valley National Park, 760/786-3200; Furnace Creek Visitor Center, 760/786-3244, fax 760/786-3283.

9 WILDROSE

Rating: 4

In Death Valley National Park.
Map 12.2, page 660

Wildrose is set on the road that heads out to the primitive country of the awesome Panamint Range, eventually coming within range of Telescope Peak, the highest point in Death Valley National Park (11,049 feet). The elevation at the camp is 4,100 feet.

Campsites, facilities: There are 23 sites for tents or RVs up to 25 feet long. Picnic tables are provided. Drinking water (April through November only) and pit toilets are available. Leashed pets are permitted at campsites only.

Reservations, fees: No reservations are accepted and there is no camping fee, however, there is a $10 park entrance fee per vehicle. Open year-round.

Directions: From Stovepipe Wells Village, drive 30 miles south on Highway 190 to Wildrose Canyon Road. Turn left and immediately enter the campground entrance road.

Contact: Death Valley National Park, 760/786-3200; Furnace Creek Visitor Center, 760/786-3244, fax 760/786-3283.

10 THORNDIKE FOUR-WHEEL DRIVE
🚶 🐕 5% ⛰️

Rating: 4

In Death Valley National Park.
Map 12.2, page 660

This is one of Death Valley National Park's little-known camps. It is set in the high country at 7,500 feet. It's free, of course. Otherwise they'd have to actually send somebody out to tend to the place. Nearby are century-old charcoal kilns that were built by Chinese laborers and tended by Shoshone Indians. The trailhead that serves Telescope Peak (11,049 feet), the highest point in Death Valley, can be found in nearby Mahogany Flat.

Campsites, facilities: This backcountry campground is accessible only by foot or four-wheel-drive vehicle and has six campsites for tents. Picnic tables and pit toilets are available. No drinking water is available. Leashed pets are permitted at campsites only.

Reservations, fees: No reservations are accepted and there is no camping fee, however, there is a $10 park entrance fee per vehicle.

Directions: In Death Valley at Stovepipe Wells Village, drive south on Highway 190 for 37 miles to Wildrose Canyon Road. Turn left and drive nine miles to the end of the road and the camp. (The road becomes extreme-ly rough; high-clearance four-wheel drive is required.)

Contact: Death Valley National Park, 760/786-3200; Furnace Creek Visitor Center, 760/786-3244, fax 760/786-3283.

11 MAHOGANY FLAT FOUR-WHEEL DRIVE
🚶 🐕 ⛰️

Rating: 5

In Death Valley National Park.
Map 12.2, page 660

This is one of two primitive, hard-to-reach camps (the other is Thorndike) set in the Panamint Range high country. It is one of the few shaded camps, offering beautiful piñon pines and junipers. What makes it popular, however, is the trail to Telescope Peak leading out from camp. Only the ambitious and well-conditioned should attempt the climb, a seven-mile trip one way with breathtaking (literally) views of both Panamint Valley and Death Valley. The elevation at the campground is 8,200 feet and Telescope Peak tops out at 11,049 feet, which translates to a climb of 2,849 feet.

Campsites, facilities: There are 10 sites for tents only. Picnic tables are provided. Pit toilets are available. No drinking water is available. The campground is accessible only by foot or four-wheel-drive vehicle. Leashed pets are permitted at campsites only.

Reservations, fees: No reservations are accepted and there is no camping fee, however, there is a $10 park entrance fee per vehicle. Open year-round, weather permitting.

Directions: From Stovepipe Wells Village, drive 38 miles south on Highway 190 to Wildrose Canyon Road, turn left, and drive to the end of the road and the camp.

Contact: Death Valley National Park, 760/786-3200; Furnace Creek Visitor Center, 760/786-3244, fax 760/786-3283.

 FURNACE CREEK

Rating: 5

In Death Valley National Park.

Map 12.3, page 661

This is a well-developed national park site that provides a good base camp for exploring Death Valley, especially for newcomers. The nearby visitor center includes Death Valley Museum and offers maps and suggestions for hikes and drives in this unique wildland. The elevation is 190 feet below sea level. This camp offers shady sites, a rarity in Death Valley. It's open all year, but keep in mind that the daytime summer temperatures commonly exceed 120∞F, making this area virtually uninhabitable in the summer.

Campsites, facilities: There are 136 sites for tents or RVs. Picnic tables are provided. Drinking water, flush toilets, RV dump station, and evening ranger programs are available. Some facilities are wheelchair-accessible. Leashed pets are permitted at campsites only.

Reservations, fees: Reservations are recommended mid-October through mid-April at 800/365-CAMP (800/365-2267) or website: reservationsnps.gov; $16 per night (includes reservation fee), plus a $10 park entrance fee per vehicle. Senior discount available. Open year-round.

Directions: From Furnace Creek Ranch, drive one mile north on Highway 190 to the signed campground entrance on the left.

Contact: Death Valley National Park, 760/786-3200; Furnace Creek Visitor Center, 760/786-3244, fax 760/786-3283.

13 TEXAS SPRING

Rating: 2

In Death Valley National Park.

Map 12.3, page 661

This camp is another enormous section of asphalt where the campsites consist of white lines as borders. There's no shade and no shelter.

It is open only in winter. The nearby visitor center, which features the Death Valley Museum, offers maps and suggestions for hikes and drives. The lowest point in the United States, Badwater, set 282 feet below sea level, is to the southwest. This camp has one truly unique feature: bathrooms that are listed on the National Historic Register. In summer, you could probably fry an egg on the asphalt here.

Campsites, facilities: There are 92 sites for tents or RVs, and two group sites for up to 10 vehicles and 40 people each. Picnic tables are provided. Drinking water, flush toilets, and a RV dump station are available. Some facilities are wheelchair-accessible. Leashed pets are permitted.

Reservations, fees: No reservations are accepted for individual sites. There is a $10 per night fee, plus a $10 park entrance fee per vehicle. Reservations are required for group camp at 800/365-CAMP (800/365-2267) or website: reservationsnps.gov; $50 per night (includes reservation fee), plus a $10 park entrance fee per vehicle. Senior discount available. Open mid-October to mid-April.

Directions: From Furnace Creek Ranch, drive south on Highway 190 for a quarter mile to the signed campground entrance on the left.

Contact: Death Valley National Park, 760/786-3200; Furnace Creek Visitor Center, 760/786-3244, fax 760/786-3283.

14 SUNSET

Rating: 4

In Death Valley National Park.

Map 12.3, page 661

This is one of several options for campers in the Furnace Creek area of Death Valley, with an elevation of 190 feet below sea level. It is advisable to make your first stop at the nearby visitor center for maps and suggested hikes (according to your level of fitness) and drives. Don't forget your canteen—and if you're backpacking, never set up a wilderness camp closer than 100 yards to water in Death Valley.

Campsites, facilities: There are 1,000 sites for RVs. Drinking water, flush toilets, and RV dump station are available. Some facilities are wheelchair-accessible. Leashed pets are permitted at campsites.

Reservations, fees: No reservations are accepted for individual sites. There is a $10 per night fee, plus a $10 park entrance fee per vehicle. Senior discount available. Open mid-October through mid-April.

Directions: From Furnace Creek Ranch, turn south on Highway 190 and drive a quarter mile to the signed campground entrance and turn left into the campground.

Contact: Death Valley National Park, 760/786-3200; Furnace Creek Visitor Center, 760/786-3244, fax 760/786-3283.

15 TECOPA HOT SPRINGS COUNTY CAMPGROUND

Rating: 3

North of Tecopa.

Map 12.4, page 662

This one is out there in no-man's-land, and if it weren't for the hot springs and the good rockhounding, all you'd see around here is a few skeletons. Regardless, it's quite an attraction in the winter, when the warm climate is a plus and the nearby mineral baths are worth taking a dunk in. Rockhounds will enjoy looking for amethysts, opals, and petrified wood in the nearby areas. The elevation is 1,500 feet. Nobody gets here by accident.

Campsites, facilities: There are 340 sites for tents or RVs, some with electrical hookups. No drive-through sites. Picnic tables and fire grills are provided. Drinking water, flush toilets, showers, and a RV dump station are available. Some facilities are wheelchair-accessible. Coin laundry, groceries, and propane gas are available nearby. Leashed pets are permitted.

Reservations, fees: Reservations are not accepted. The fee is $10–14, $5 per person for more than four people. Open year-round.

Directions: From Baker, drive north on I-15 for 52 miles to the Highway 127/Tecopa exit. Turn north on Highway 127 and drive to a county road signed Tecopa Hot Springs (south of the junction of Highway 178 and Highway 127). Turn right (east) and drive three miles to the park and campground entrance.

Contact: Inyo County Parks Department, 760/852-4264, fax 760/852-4243.

© TOM STIENSTRA

Chapter 13
Santa Barbara
and Vicinity

Chapter 13—Santa Barbara and Vicinity

For many, this region of California coast is like a dream, the best place to live on earth. Visitors, picking one or several of the 93 campgrounds in the region, can get a taste of why it is so special. What you will likely find, however, is that a taste will only whet your appetite. That's how it is here. Many keep coming back for more. Some eventually even move here.

The region is a unique mix of sun-swept sand beaches that stretch 200 miles and surprise inland coastal forests. The coast offers a series of stunning state beaches, where getting a campsite reservation can feel like winning the lottery. If you have a dream trip in mind in which you cruise the coast highway the entire length, you'd better have the reservation system wired from the start. These campsites go fast and are filled every night of the vacation season. There are many highlights on the coast: San Simeon, Hearst Castle, all the state beaches, the stunning towns of Cambria, Goleta, and Cayucos, and the Coast Highway that provides a route through all of it.

Yet as popular as the coast may seem, just inland lie many remote, hidden campsites and destinations. Los Padres National Forest spans a matrix of canyons with small streams, mountaintop lookouts, and wilderness trailheads. In fact, rangers reviewing the text for this book requested that we remove one of the trails highlighted from a campground because it was too primitive and difficult for most visitors to successfully follow to its end at a mountaintop. The landscape is a mix of pine, deep canyons, chaparral, and foothills.

Two of California's best recreation lakes also provide major destinations, Lake Nacimiento and San Antonio Reservoir. Nacimiento is one of the top family-oriented lakes for water sports, and it also provides sensational fishing for white bass and largemouth bass in the spring. San Antonio is a great lake for bass, at times even rating as one of the best in America, and tours to see bald eagles are also popular in the winter. Lake Cachuma and Lake Casitas near Santa Barbara have produced some of the largest bass caught in history.

The ocean is dramatic here, the backdrop for every trip on the Coast Highway, and it seems to stretch to forever. Maybe it does. For many visiting here, forever is how long they wish to stay here.

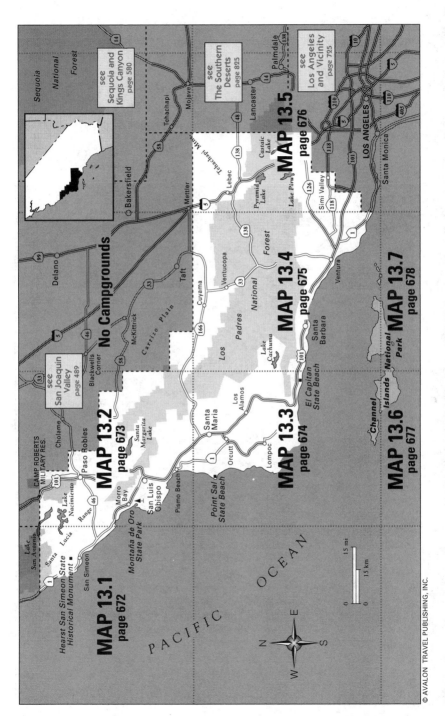

© AVALON TRAVEL PUBLISHING, INC.

Map 13.1

Campground 1
Page 679

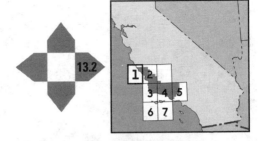

13.2

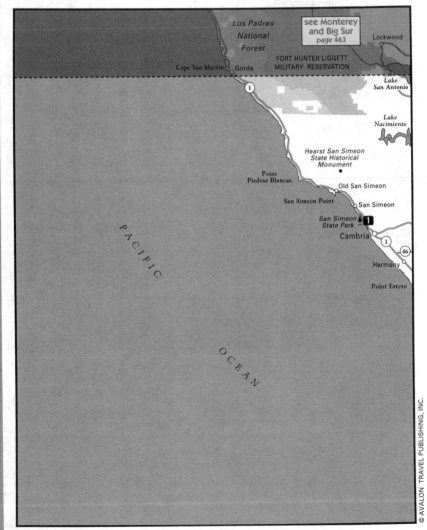

see Monterey
and Big Sur
page 463

Los Padres
National
Forest

Lockwood

Cape San Martin   Gorda

FORT HUNTER LIGGETT
MILITARY RESERVATION

Lake
San Antonio

Lake
Nacimiento

Hearst San Simeon
State Historical
Monument

Point
Piedras Blancas

Old San Simeon

San Simeon Point   San Simeon

San Simeon
State Park

Cambria

Harmony

Point Estero

PACIFIC

OCEAN

© AVALON TRAVEL PUBLISHING, INC.

Map 13.2

Campgrounds 2–22
Pages 679–688

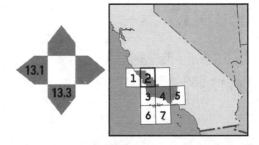

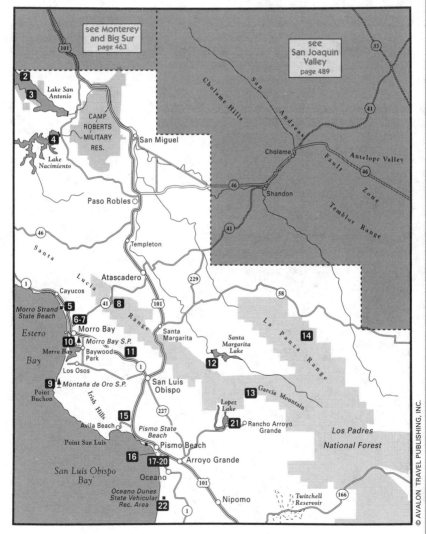

Map 13.3

Campgrounds 23–33
Pages 689–693

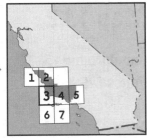

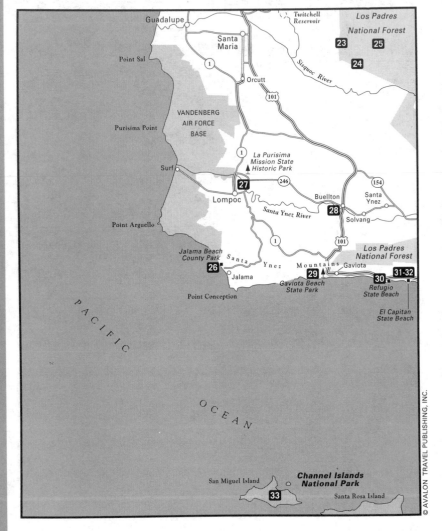

Map 13.4

Campgrounds 34–83
Pages 694–714

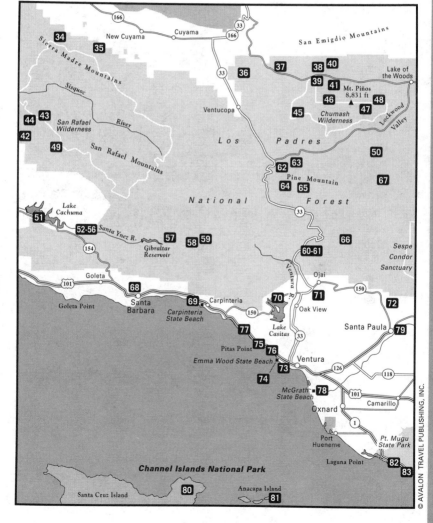

Map 13.5

Campgrounds 84–95
Pages 715–719

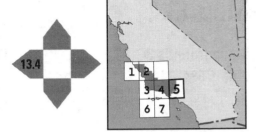

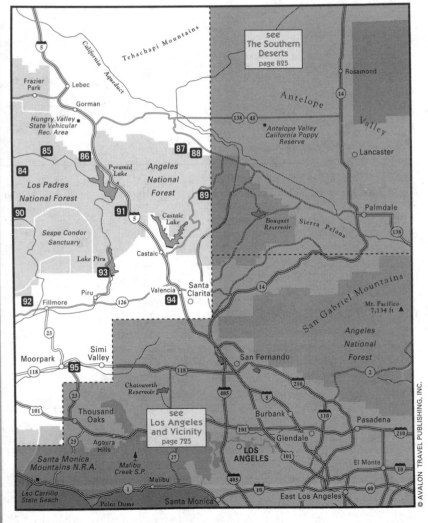

© AVALON TRAVEL PUBLISHING, INC.

Map 13.6

**Campground 96
Page 720**

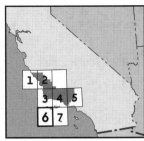

Map 13.7

Campground 97
Page 720

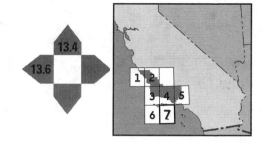

Santa Cruz Island

Santa Rosa Island

Channel Islands National Park

P A C I F I C

O C E A N

Santa Barbara Island [97]

San Nicolas Island

U.S. NAVAL RESERVATION

© AVALON TRAVEL PUBLISHING, INC.

❶ SAN SIMEON STATE PARK

🏃 🚲 🛶 🐕 ♿ 🚐 ⛺

Rating: 9

In San Simeon State Park.

Map 13.1, page 672

Hearst Castle is only five miles northeast, so San Simeon Creek is a natural for visitors planning to take the tour; for a tour reservation, phone 800/444-4445. San Simeon Creek Campground is set across the highway from the ocean, with easy access under the highway to the beach. San Simeon Creek, while not exactly the Mississippi, runs through the campground and adds a nice touch. Washburn Campground provides an option at this park, and while providing better views, the sites are exposed and can be windy. It is one mile inland on a plateau overlooking the Pacific Ocean and Santa Lucia Mountains. The best hike in the area is from Leffingwell Landing to Moonstone Beach, featuring sweeping views of the coast from ocean bluffs and a good chance to see passing whales. There are three preserves in the park, including a wintering site for moarch butterfly populations, and it has an archaeological site dating from more than 5,800 years ago. In the summer, junior ranger programs and interpretive programs are available.

Campsites, facilities: At San Simeon Creek Camp, there are 115 sites for tents or RVs up to 35 feet long, 14 sites for tents only, and two hike-in/bike-in sites. Picnic tables and fire grills are provided. Drinking water, restrooms, flush toilets, and coin showers are available. At Washburn Camp, there are 70 sites for tents or RVs up to 31 feet long. Picnic tables and fire grills are provided. Firewood is for sale from thee camp host. A pay phone and RV dump station are available. Some facilities are wheelchair-accessible. A grocery store, coin laundry, gas station, restaurants, and propane gas are two miles away in Cambria. Leashed pets are permitted.

Reservations, fees: Reserve at 800/444-PARK (800/444-7275) or website: www.Reserve America.com ($7.50 reservation fee); $12 per night at San Simeon Creek, $7 per night at Washburn, $1 per person for hike-in/bike-in sites. Senior discount available. Open year-round.

Directions: From Cambria, drive two miles north on Highway 1 to San Simeon Creek Road. Turn east and drive .2 mile to the park entrance on the right.

Contact: San Simeon State Park, 805/927-2035 or 805/927-2020.

❷ NORTH SHORE SAN ANTONIO

🏊 🛶 🚤 🐕 ♿ 🚐 ⛺

Rating: 7

On Lake San Antonio.

Map 13.2, page 673

Lake San Antonio makes a great year-round destination for adventure. It is a big, warm-water lake, long and narrow, set at an elevation of 775 feet in the foothills north of Paso Robles. The camp features four miles of shoreline camping, with the bonus of primitive sites along Pleyto Points. There are four miles of shoreline for camping at North Shore. The lake is 16 miles long, covers 5,500 surface acres, and has 60 miles of shoreline and average summer water temperatures in the 70s, making it an ideal place for fun in the sun. It is one of the top lakes in California for bass fishing, best in spring and early summer. It is also good for striped bass, catfish, crappie, sunfish, and bluegill. It also provides the best wintering habitat in the region for bald eagles, and eagle-watching tours are available from the south shore of the lake. Of course, the size of the lake, along with hot temperatures all summer, make water-skiing and water sports absolutely first-class. Note that boat rentals are not available here, but at South Shore.

Campsites, facilities: There are 200 sites for tents or self-contained RVs, 87 sites with electrical hookups for tents or RVs, 20 sites with full hookups for RVs, cabins, and rooms. Fire grills and tables are provided. Rest-rooms, drinking water, showers, RV dump station, boat ramp, stables, a grocery store, and fishing licenses are available. Leashed pets are permitted.

Reservations, fees: Reservations are accepted at 888/588-2267. The fee is $20–22 per night, $2 per night . Major credit cards accepted. Open year-round.

Directions: On U.S. 101, drive to Jolon Road/G14 exit (just north of King City). Take that exit and turn south on Jolon Road and drive 27 miles to Pleyto Road (curvy road). Turn right and drive three miles to the North Shore entrance of the lake. Note: when arriving from the south or east on U.S. 101 near Paso Robles, it is faster to take G18/Jolon Road exit.

Contact: North Shore, 805/472-2311, website: www.co.monterey.ca.us/parks.

🖪 SOUTH SHORE SAN ANTONIO
🚶 🚴 🏊 🛶 � 🎣 🐾 ♿ 🚐 ⛺

Rating: 7

On Lake San Antonio.

Map 13.2, page 673

Harris Creek, Redondo Vista, and Lynch are the three campgrounds set near each other along the south shore of Lake San Antonio, a 16-mile reservoir that provides good bass fishing in the spring and water-skiing in the summer. There are also 26 miles of good biking and hiking trails available nearby. There is a museum and visitor center available at the park's administration building. In the winter, the Monterey County Department of Parks offers a unique eagle-watching program here, which includes boat tours. (See the entry for North Shore for more details about the lake.) Note that South Shore has boat rentals, laundry facilities, and a playground.

Campsites, facilities: There are three campgrounds here: Redondo has 173 sites for tents and 86 sites with full hookups for RVs; Lynch has 52 sites for tents and 54 with full hookups for RVs; Harris Creek has 91 sites for tents and 26 with full hookups for RVs. Cabin and mobile home rentals are also available. Picnic

tables and fire grills are provided. Drinking water and flush toilets are available. Restrooms, showers, RV dump station, boat ramp, boat rentals, playground, recreation room, laundry facilities, a grocery store, and fishing licenses are available nearby. Leashed pets are permitted. Note than 20 sites are taken by reservation, the rest are first-come, first-served.

Reservations, fees: Reservations are accepted at 888/588-2267. The fee is $18–22 per night. The fee is $2 pet fee. Group reservations at 805/472-2311. Open year-round.

Directions: From the north, on U.S. 101 (just north of King City), take the Jolon Road/G14 exit. Turn south on Jolon Road and drive 20 miles to Lockwood and Interlake Road (G14). Turn right and drive 13 miles to San Antonio Lake Road. Turn left and drive three miles to the South Shore entrance of the lake.

From the south, drive on U.S. 101 to Paso Robles and the 24th Street exit (G14 West). Take that exit and drive 14 miles to Lake Nacimiento Drive. Turn right and drive across Lake Nacimiento Dam to Interlake Road. Turn left and drive seven miles to Lake San Antonio Road. Turn right and drive three miles to the South Shore entrance.

Contact: South Shore, 805/472-2311, website: www.co.monterey.ca.us/parks.

🖪 LAKE NACIMIENTO RESORT
🏊 🛶 🚐 🎣 🐾 ♿ 🚐 ⛺

Rating: 8

At Lake Nacimiento.

Map 13.2, page 673

This is the only game in town at Nacimiento, and the management plays it well. It's an outstanding operation, with headquarters for a great fishing or water sports trip. The fishing for white bass can be incredible, catching dozens, vertical jigging a Horizon jig. And the water play is also great, with such a big lake, 70-degree temperatures, and some of the best water-skiing in California. The lake has 165 miles of shoreline with an incredible number of arms and lakes, many ideal for bass fishing. Nacimiento hosts 25 fishing tournaments per year. Not only is bass fishing good, but there are also opportunities for trout (in cool months) and bluegill and catfish (in warm months). The resort has a great restaurant with a lake view, and the campsites provide limited tree cover with pines and oaks. Two camps are on the lake's shore, and the rest are set back about three-quarters of a mile from the lake. Lakeview lodging is also available. There are 72 campsites available by reservation and 272 sites that are run on a first-come, first-served basis.

Campsites, facilities: There are 297 campsites at a series of campgrounds operated by the resort at the southeast end of the lake, 19 lodges, eight trailer rentals, one RV rental, two mobile home rentals, and 12 group sites for 15–40 people. Oak Knoll Camp has 40 sites with full hookups for RVs. Picnic tables and fire grills are provided. Drinking water and flush toilets are available. Restrooms, showers, RV dump station, boat ramp, boat docks, boat rentals, playground, swimming pool, restaurant, recreation room, laundry facilities, a grocery store, and fishing licenses are available nearby. Swimming beaches, basketball and volleyball courts, and horseshoe pits are also available. Leashed pets are permitted.

Reservations, fees: Reservations are accepted. The fee is $25 per vehicle per night, pets $5 per night. Major credit cards accepted. Open year-round.

Directions: On U.S. 101, drive to Paso Robles and the 24th Street/Lake Nacimiento exit. Take that exit, turn west on 24th Street (becomes Lake Nacimiento Road/G14) and drive for nine miles. Bear right on Lake Nacimiento road for seven miles to the resort entrance on the left. Note: if you cross the Lake Nacimiento dam, you've gone too far.

Contact: Lake Nacimiento Resort, 800/323-3839 (ext. 1 for reservations) or 805/238-3256 (ext. 1 for reservations), website: www.nacimiento resort.com.

5 MORRO STRAND STATE BEACH

🏊 🎣 🐕 🚐 ⛺

Rating: 7

Near Morro Bay.

Map 13.2, page 673

A ton of Highway 1 cruisers plan to stay overnight at this state park. It is set along the ocean near Morro Bay, right on the beach, a pretty spot year-round. The park features a three-mile stretch of beach that connects the southern and northern entrances to the state beach. Fishing, jogging, windsurfing, and kite flying are popular. Side trips include the Morro Bay Wildlife Refuge, the Museum of Natural History, or an ocean fishing trip out of Morro Bay. (See the entry for Morro Bay State Park for more information.)

Campsites, facilities: There are 75 sites for tents or RVs up to 24 feet long. Picnic tables and fire grills are provided. Drinking water and flush toilets are available. Cold, outdoor showers are also available. Supplies and a coin laundry are available in Morro Bay. Leashed pets are permitted.

Reservations, fees: Reserve at 800/444-PARK (800/444-7275) or website: www.Reserve America.com ($7.50 reservation fee); $12 per night. Open year-round.

Directions: On Highway 1, drive to Morro Bay. Take the Yerba Buena Street/Morro Strand State Beach exit. Turn west on Yerba Buena Street and drive one block to the campground.

Contact: Morro Strand State Beach, 805/772-8812 or 805/772-2560, fax 805/772-7434; California State Parks, San Luis Obispo District, 805/549-3312, fax 805/541-4799.

6 RANCHO COLINA RV PARK

🐕 ♿ 🚐

Rating: 6

In Morro Bay.

Map 13.2, page 673

This privately operated RV park is one of several camping options in the Morro Bay area.

Folks who park here typically stroll the boardwalk, exploring the little shops. (For recreation, see the entry for Morro Bay State Park.) About 20 percent of the sites here are long-term rentals.

Campsites, facilities: There are 57 sites with full hookups for RVs. Picnic tables are provided. Restrooms, showers, laundry facilities, and a recreation room are available. You can buy supplies nearby. Leashed pets are permitted.

Reservations, fees: Reservations are accepted. The fee is $23 per night. Major credit cards accepted. Open year-round.

Directions: From Morro Bay on Highway 1, drive one mile east on Atascadero Road/Highway 41 to the park at 1045 Atascadero Road. **Contact:** Rancho Colina RV Park, 805/772-8420.

◢ MORRO DUNES TRAILER PARK AND CAMP

Rating: 6

In Morro Bay.

Map 13.2, page 673

A wide array of side-trip possibilities and great natural beauty make Morro Bay an attractive destination. Most visitors will walk the boardwalk, try at least one of the coastal restaurants, and then head to Morro Bay State Park for hiking or sea kayaking. Other folks will head straight to the port for fishing, or just explore the area before heading north to San Simeon for the Hearst Castle tour. (See the entry for Morro Bay State Park for more information.)

Campsites, facilities: There are 139 sites with full hookups including cable TV for RVs, and 43 sites for tents. Picnic tables and fire grills are provided. Restrooms, drinking water, showers, electrical connections, modem access, laundry facilities, store, wood, ice, and RV dump station are available. Propane gas can be obtained nearby. Leashed pets are permitted. Some facilities are wheelchair-accessible.

Reservations, fees: Reservations are accepted. The fee is $17–25 per night, $1 per night. Major credit cards accepted. Open year-round.

Directions: Drive on Highway 1 to Morro Bay and the exit for Highway 41. Take that exit and turn west on Atascadero Road/Highway 41 and drive a half mile to 1700 Embarcadero/Atascadero Road.

Contact: Morro Dunes Trailer Park and Camp, 805/772-2722, fax 805/772-2372, website: www.morrodunes.com.

◉ CERRO ALTO

Rating: 7

Near San Luis Obispo.

Map 13.2, page 673

This camp is set near Morro Creek, which runs most of the year but which in dry years can disappear in late summer. In addition, some sites are along the creek, nicely spaced, with sycamore and bay trees peppering the hillside. There are numerous hiking and mountain biking trails. The best of these is the Cerro Alto Trail, which is accessible from camp and then is routed four miles up to Cuesta Ridge for sweeping views of Morro Bay.

Campsites, facilities: There are 20 sites for tents or RVs up to 25 feet long. No hookups. Picnic tables and fire grills are provided. Drinking water and vault toilets are available. A camp host, amphitheater, and public phone are nearby. Some facilities are wheelchair-accessible. Leashed pets permitted.

Reservations, fees: Reservations are not accepted. The fee is $16 per night. Senior discount available. Open year-round, weather permitting.

Directions: From U.S. 101 at Atascadero, take the Highway 41 west exit. Drive west on Highway 41 for eight miles to the campground on the left.

Contact: Los Padres National Forest, Santa Lucia Ranger District, 805/925-9538, fax 805/961-5781.

9 MONTAÑA DE ORO STATE PARK

🚶 🚴 🛶 🐴 🚗 ⛺

Rating: 9

Near Morro Bay.

Map 13.2, page 673

This sprawling chunk of primitive land includes coastline, 8,500 acres of foothills, and Valencia Peak at 1,347 feet in elevation. The name means "Mountain of Gold," named for the golden widlfowers that bloom here in the spring. The camp is perched near a bluff, and while there are no sweeping views from campsites, they await nearby. The Bluffs Trail is one of the best easy coastal walks anywhere, offering stunning views of the ocean and cliffs and, in the spring, tons of wildflowers over the course of just 1.5 miles. Another hiking option at the park is to climb Valencia Peak, a little butt-kicker of an ascent that tops out at 1,373 feet, providing more panoramic coastal views. These are the two best hikes among 50 miles of trails for horses, mountain bikers, and hikers, with trails accessible right out of the campground.

Campsites, facilities: There are 50 sites for tents or RVs up to 27 feet long, four walk-in environmental sites, four equestrian sites, and two group equestrian sites for up to 50 people and 25 horses. Picnic tables and fire grills are provided. Vault toilets are available. Drinking water is available only at the main campground; stock water is available at the equestrian campground. There is limited corral space and single-site equestrian camps with two stalls each. Garbage from equestrian and environmental sites must be packed out. Supplies and a coin laundry are available five miles away in the town of Los Osos. Leashed pets are permitted.

Reservations, fees: Reserve at 800/444-PARK (800/444-7275) or website: www.Reserve America.com ($7.50 reservation fee); $7 per night, $12 for equestrian sites, $25 for group sites. Senior discount available. Open year-round.

Directions: From Morro Bay, drive two miles south on Highway 1. Turn on South Bay Boulevard and drive four miles to Los Osos. Turn right on Los Osos Valley Road and drive five miles (it becomes Pecho Valley Road) to the park.

Contact: Montaña de Oro State Park, 805/528-0513; San Luis Obispo District, 805/549-3312.

10 MORRO BAY STATE PARK

🚶 🚴 🛶 🛶 🚐 🐴 ♿ 🚗 ⛺

Rating: 9

In Morro Bay.

Map 13.2, page 673

Reservations are strongly advised at this popular campground. This is one of the premium stopover spots for folks cruising north on Highway 1. The park offers a wide range of activities and exhibits covering the natural and cultural history of the area. The park features lagoon and natural bay habitat. The most prominent feature is Morro Rock. A "morro" is a small volcanic peak, and there are nine of them along the local coast. The top hike at the park climbs one of them, Black Hill, and rewards hikers with sensational coastal views. The park has a marina and golf course, with opportunities for sailing, fishing, and bird-watching. Activities include beach walks, kayaking in Morro Bay, fishing the nearby ocean on a party boat, and touring Hearst Castle.

Campsites, facilities: There are 95 sites for tents or RVs up to 31 feet long, 30 sites with partial hookups for RVs, two hike-in/bike-in sites, and two group sites for 30–50 people. Picnic tables, food lockers, and fire rings are provided. Restrooms, drinking water, flush toilets, coin-operated showers, RV dump station, museum exhibits, and nature walks and interpretive programs are available. A coin laundry, grocery store, propane gas, boat ramp, mooring, rentals, gas stations, and food service are available in Morro Bay. Some facilities are wheelchair-accessible. Leashed pets are permitted.

Reservations, fees: Reserve at 800/444-PARK (800/444-7275) or website: www.Reserve America.com ($7.50 reservation fee); $12–18 per night, $1 per person per night for hike-in/bike-in sites, group sites $22–37 per night. Senior discount available. Open year-round.

Directions: On Highway 1, drive to Morro Bay and take the exit for Los Osos-Baywood Park/Morro Bay State Park. Turn south and drive one mile to State Park Road. Turn right and drive one mile to the park entrance on the right.

Contact: Morro Bay State Park, 805/772-7434, fax 805/772-5760; California State Parks, San Luis Obispo District, 805/549-3312, fax 805/541-4799.

11 EL CHORRO REGIONAL PARK

Rating: 6

Near San Luis Obispo.

Map 13.2, page 673

North of Morro Bay on the way to San Simeon and Hearst Castle, this can be a prime spot for RV travelers. Note that the campground isn't in the state park reservation system, which means there are times when coastal state parks can be jammed full and this regional park may still have space. Morro Bay, six miles away, provides many possible side trips. The park has full recreational facilities, including volleyball, horseshoe pits, softball, hiking trails, and botanical gardens. A golf course is nearby. Note that there's a men's prison about one mile away. For some people, this can be a real turnoff.

Campsites, facilities: There are 42 sites with full hookups for RVs up to 40 feet or tents and some undesignated overflow sites. Fire grills and picnic tables are provided. Restrooms, drinking water, flush toilets, showers, and recreational facilities are available. Supplies and a coin laundry are nearby in San Luis Obispo. Leashed pets are permitted.

Reservations, fees: Reservations are not accepted. The fee is $18–22 per night, $2 pet fee. Groups may reserve six or more sites three weeks before arrival. Major credit cards accepted. Open year-round.

Directions: From San Luis Obispo, drive 4.5 miles north on Highway 1 to the park entrance on the right side of the highway.

Contact: El Chorro Regional Park, 805/781-5930, website: www.slocountyparks.com.

12 SANTA MARGARITA KOA

Rating: 6

Near Santa Margarita Lake.

Map 13.2, page 673

Santa Margarita Lake should have a sign at its entrance that proclaims, "Fishing Only!" That's because the rules here do not allow water-skiing or any water contact, including swimming, wading, using float tubes, and windsurfing. The excellent prospects for bass fishing, along with the prohibitive rules, make this lake a favorite among anglers. Santa Margarita Lake covers nearly 800 acres, most of it long and narrow and set in a dammed-up valley in the foothill country at an elevation of 1,300 feet, just below the Santa Lucia Mountains. On weekends, this place can turn into another world: paintball war games are often held here, and on Saturday afternoons, a BMX track is popular.

Campsites, facilities: There are 54 sites, some with partial hookups and one drive-through, for RVs or tents, and 11 cabins. Picnic tables and fire grills are provided. Restrooms, drinking water, flush toilets, showers, modem access, swimming pool, playground, coin laundry, store, RV dump station, and propane gas are available. Leashed pets are permitted.

Reservations, fees: Make reservations at 800/562-5619. Fees are $25–31 per night, $3–4 per person for more than two people. Major credit cards accepted. Open year-round.

Directions: From San Luis Obispo, drive north on U.S. 101 for eight miles to the Highway 58/Santa Margarita exit. Take that exit, drive through the town of Santa Margarita to Entrada. Turn right on Entrada and drive seven miles (Entrada becomes Pozo Road) to Santa

Margarita Lake Road. Turn left and drive a half mile to the campground on the right.

Contact: Santa Margarita KOA, 805/438-5618, fax 805/438-3576; website: www.koacamp grounds.com.

13 HI MOUNTAIN

Rating: 4

In Los Padres National Forest.
Map 13.2, page 673

At an elevation of 2,800 feet, this is the highest point in the Santa Lucia Wilderness. A mile west you can drive to the Hi Mountain Lookout, with awesome 360-degree views from the 3,180-foot summit.

Campsites, facilities: There are 11 sites for tents or RVs up to 16 feet long (trailers not recommended). Picnic tables and fire grills are provided. Vault toilets are available. No drinking water is available. Leashed pets are permitted.

Reservations, fees: No reservations are accepted and there is no camping fee. There is a charge of $5 per day per parked vehicle or Adventure Pass ($30 annual fee). Open year-round (road may be closed during heavy rains).

Directions: From San Luis Obispo, drive eight miles north on U.S. 101. Turn east on Highway 58 and drive four miles (four miles past Santa Margarita). Turn southeast on Pozo Road and drive for 16 miles to the town of Pozo. Turn on Hi Mountain Road and drive four miles to the campground.

Contact: Los Padres National Forest, Santa Lucia Ranger District, 805/925-9538, fax 805/961-5781.

14 LA PANZA

Rating: 3

In Los Padres National Forest.
Map 13.2, page 673

This primitive spot sits at 2,400 feet in the La Panza Range, an oak woodland area that is crisscrossed by numerous trails and small streams. Some of the trails are not maintained. The Machesna Mountain Wilderness is to the south. Water is scarce.

Campsites, facilities: There are 15 sites for tents or RVs up to 16 feet long. Picnic tables and fire grills are provided. Vault toilets are available. No drinking water is available. Leashed pets are permitted.

Reservations, fees: No reservations; an Adventure Pass ($30 annual fee) or a $5 daily fee per parked vehicle is required. Open year-round.

Directions: From San Luis Obispo, drive eight miles north on U.S. 101. Turn east on Highway 58 and drive four miles (two miles past Santa Margarita). Turn southeast on Pozo Road and drive for 16 miles to the town of Pozo. Continue 11.5 miles east past Pozo on County Road M3093 to the campground.

Contact: Los Padres National Forest, Santa Lucia Ranger District, 805/925-9538, fax 805/961-5781.

15 AVILA VALLEY HOT SPRINGS SPA AND RV PARK

Rating: 6

On San Luis Obispo Bay.
Map 13.2, page 673

The hot mineral pool here is a featured attraction. This is a natural mineral hot springs with a artesian well that produces water directly into the spas at 105°F. A pizza kitchen and snack bar are available as well. Nearby recreation options include Avila State Beach and Pismo State Beach.

Campsites, facilities: There are 50 sites, seven drive-through, with full or partial hookups for RVs, and 25 tent sites in three areas. Picnic tables and fire grills (at some spots) are provided. Restrooms, showers, swimming pool, hot mineral pool, spa, cable TV, RV dump station, recreation room, arcade, massage service, golf course, grocery store, snack bar, and group barbecue pits are available.

Leashed pets are permitted. Some facilities are wheelchair-accessible.

Reservations, fees: Reservations are accepted at 800/332-2359. The fee is $30–40, $5 per night for each extra vehicle. Use of spas free with campsite. Major credit cards accepted. Open year-round.

Directions: From San Luis Obispo, drive south on U.S. 101 for nine miles to the Avila Beach Drive exit. Take that exit and drive to the park at 250 Avila Beach Drive.

Contact: Avila Valley Hot Springs Spa and RV Park, 805/595-2359, fax 805/595-2060, website: www.avilahotsprings.com.

16 NORTH BEACH

Rating: 7

In Pismo State Beach.

Map 13.2, page 673

Pismo State Beach is nationally renowned for its beaches, dunes, and, in the good old days, clamming. The adjacent tree-lined dunes make for great walks or, for kids, great rolls. The clamming on minus low tides was legendary. The beach is popular with bird-watchers, and the habitat supports the largest wintering colony of monarch butterflies in the United States. Plan on a reservation and having plenty of company in summer. This is an exceptionally popular state beach, either as an ultimate destination or as a stopover for folks cruising Highway 1. There are four restaurants and ATV rentals within two blocks. A trolley service provides a shuttle to the surrounding community. Poaching has devastated the clamming here, with no legal clams taken for years.

Campsites, facilities: There are 103 sites for tents or RVs up to 31 feet long and one hike-in/bike-in site. Fire grills, food lockers, and picnic tables are provided. Restrooms, drinking water, showers, flush toilets, and RV dump station are available. Horseback riding facilities, grocery store, ATV rentals, restaurants, coin

laundry, and propane gas are nearby. Some facilities are wheelchair-accessible, including a wheelchair-accessible fishing pier at Ocean Lagoon. Leashed pets are permitted.

Reservations, fees: Reserve at 800/444-PARK (800/444-7275) or website: www.Reserve America.com ($7.50 reservation fee); $12 per night. The hike-in/bike-in site is $1 per person per night. Open year-round.

Directions: On Highway 1 in Pismo Beach, take the North Beach/State Campground exit (well signed) and drive to the park entrance.

Contact: Pismo State Beach, 805/773-2334; California State Parks, San Luis Obispo District, 805/549-3312.

17 PISMO COAST VILLAGE RV RESORT

Rating: 7

In Pismo Beach.

Map 13.2, page 673

This big-time RV park gets a lot of use by Highway 1 cruisers. Its location is a plus, set near the ocean. Pismo Beach is famous for its clamming, sand dunes, and beautiful coastal frontage.

Campsites, facilities: There are 400 sites with full hookups including satellite TV and modem access for RVs. Picnic tables and fire grills are provided. Restrooms, showers, playgrounds, swimming pools, laundry facilities, store, firewood, ice, recreation room, propane gas, recreation programs, restaurant, and a miniature golf course are available. Leashed pets are permitted. Some facilities are wheelchair-accessible.

Reservations, fees: Reserve at 888/RV BEACH (888/782-3224). Fees are $29–40 per night. Group discounts available. Major credit cards accepted. Open year-round.

Directions: In Pismo Beach, drive on Highway 1 to the park at 165 S. Dolliver St./Hwy. 1.

Contact: Pismo Coast Village, 805/773-1811, fax 805/773-1507; website: www.pismocoastvillage.com.

18 LE SAGE RIVIERA

Rating: 6

Near Pismo State Beach.

Map 13.2, page 673

This is a year-round RV park that can serve as headquarters for folks who are interested in visiting several nearby attractions, including neighboring Pismo State Beach and Lopez Lake, 10 miles to the east. The park is set on the ocean side of Highway 1, 250 yards from the beach.

Campsites, facilities: There are 60 sites, half drive-through, with full hookups for RVs. No tent camping is permitted. Picnic tables are provided. Restrooms, drinking water, showers, and laundry facilities are available. Stores, restaurants, and golf courses are nearby. Some facilities are wheelchair-accessible. Leashed pets are permitted with size restrictions.

Reservations, fees: Reservations are accepted. The fee is $30–45 per night. Add $5–10 for holidays. Winter discount. Major credit cards accepted. Open year-round.

Directions: In Pismo Beach on Highway 1, drive south on Highway 1 for a half mile to the park on the right (west side) to 319 N. Hwy. 1 (in Grover Beach).

Contact: Le Sage Riviera, 805/489-5506, fax 805/489-2103.

19 OCEANO MEMORIAL CAMPGROUND

Rating: 7

In Oceano.

Map 13.2, page 673

This county park often gets overlooked because it isn't on the state reservation system. That's other folks' loss and your gain. The location is a bonus, set near Pismo State Beach, the site of great sand dunes and wide-open ocean frontage.

Campsites, facilities: There are 22 sites for tents or RVs up to 40 feet, with full hookups, and a group site. Picnic tables and fire grills are provided. Drinking water and flush toilets are available. A playground, coin laundry, grocery store, and propane gas are available nearby. Leashed pets are permitted with proof of vaccinations.

Reservations, fees: Reservations are not accepted. The fee is $23 per night, $5 per night for extra vehicle, $2 per night. Reservations required for groups. Open year-round.

Directions: From Pismo Beach, drive south on U.S. 101 to Grand Avenue exit west to Highway 1. Take that exit and turn south on Highway 1 and drive 1.5 miles to Pier Avenue. Turn right on Pier Avenue and drive a short distance. Turn left and drive to the campground on the right at 540 Air Park Drive.

Contact: Oceano Memorial Campground, 805/781-5930, fax 805/781-1102, website: www.slocountyparks.com.

20 OCEANO

Rating: 6

In Pismo State Beach.

Map 13.2, page 673

This is a prized state beach campground, with Pismo Beach and its sand dunes and coastal frontage a centerpiece for the state park system. Its location on the central coast on Highway 1, as well as its beauty and recreational opportunities, makes it extremely popular. It fills to capacity most nights, and reservations are usually a necessity. (For more information on Pismo State Beach, see the entry for North Beach campground.)

Campsites, facilities: There are 82 sites for tents, trailers, or RVs up to 31 feet long, 42 with partial hookups for trailers and RVs up to 36 feet long. There is also one primitive hike-in/bike-in site. Picnic tables, food lockers, and fire grills are provided. Restrooms, drinking water, flush toilets, and coin-operated showers are available. Horseback riding facilities, grocery store, coin laundry, RV dump station, restaurants, and gas stations are nearby. Leashed pets are permitted.

Reservations, fees: Reserve at 800/444-PARK (800/444-7275) or website: www.Reserve America.com ($7.50 reservation fee); $12–18 per night, $6 per night for a third vehicle, $1 per night per person for hike-in/bike-in sites. Senior discount available. Open year-round.

Directions: From Pismo Beach, drive two miles south on Highway 1 to Pier Avenue. Turn right and drive .2 mile to the campground entrance.

Contact: Pismo Beach State Park, 805/489-1869 or 805/473-7220.

21 LOPEZ LAKE RECREATION AREA

Rating: 7

Near Arroyo Grande.

Map 13.2, page 673

Lopez Lake has become an example of how to do something right, with special marked areas set aside exclusively for water-skiing, personal watercraft, and windsurfing, and the rest of the lake designated for fishing and low-speed boating. There are also reserved areas for swimming. That makes it perfect for just about everyone and, with good bass fishing, the lake has become very popular, especially on spring weekends when the bite is on. Lopez Lake is set amid oak woodlands southeast of San Luis Obispo. The lake is shaped something like a horseshoe, has 940 surface acres with 22 miles of shoreline when full, and gets excellent weather most of the year. Features of the park in summer are ranger-led hikes and campfire shows.

Campsites, facilities: There are 143 sites with full hookups for RVs, 211 sites partial hookups for RVs and tents, an overflow site for self-contained RVs of any length, and a group site. Picnic tables and fire rings are provided. Restrooms, showers, playground, laundry facilities, store, ice, snack bar, marina, boat ramp, mooring, boat fuel, tackle, boat rentals, and a water slide are available. Some facilities are wheelchair-accessible. Leashed pets are permitted.

Reservations, fees: Reservations are accepted by phone or website; $14–23 per night, $5 per night for each extra vehicle, $2 per night, $5 boat launch fee. Group rates available. Major credit cards accepted. Open year-round.

Directions: From Arroyo Grande on U.S. 101, take the Grand Avenue exit. Turn east and drive through Arroyo Grande. Turn northeast on Lopez Drive and drive 10 miles to the park.

Contact: Lopez Lake Recreation Area, 805/788-2381, website: www.slocountyparks.com.

22 OCEANO DUNES STATE VEHICULAR RECREATION AREA

Rating: 6

South of Pismo Beach.

Map 13.2, page 673

This is "National Headquarters" for all-terrain vehicles (ATVs)—you know, those three- and four-wheeled motorcycles that turn otherwise normal people into lunatics. The camps are along one to three miles of beach and 1,500 acres of open sand dunes, and since not many make the walk to the campsites, four-wheel drives or ATVs are needed for access. This is the only California state park where vehicles can be driven on the beach. The area covers 3,600 acres, including 5.5 miles of beach open for vehicles and 1,500 acres of sand dunes available for OHVs. They roam wild on the dunes here; that's the law, so don't go planning a quiet stroll. If you don't like 'em, you are strongly advised to go elsewhere. If this is your game, have fun and try to keep from killing yourself. Each fall, the "National Sand Drags" are held here. More than one million people visit here each year. High tides can limit access. A beach towing service for RVs and trailers is available. Surfing, swimming, surf fishing, horseback riding, bird-watching, and nut-case watching are also popular.

Campsites, facilities: There are 1,000 primitive sites. Chemical and vault toilets are provided. No drinking water. Drinking water, horseback riding facilities, grocery store, coin laundry, restaurants, gas stations, and RV dump station are available nearby. Leashed pets are permitted.

Reservations, fees: Reserve at 800/444-PARK (800/444-7275) or website: www.Reserve America.com ($7.50 reservation fee); $6 per night, $1 per person per night for hike-in sites. Senior discount available. Open year-round.

Directions: Drive on U.S. 101 to Arroyo Grande and take the Grand Avenue exit. Turn left (toward the beach) on Grand Avenue and drive four miles until the road ends at the North Entrance beach camping area. The South Entrance is one mile south. To get there from Highway 1, take Pier Avenue.

Contact: Oceano Dunes, 805/473-7230, fax 805/473-7234.

23 COLSON

Rating: 6

In Los Padres National Forest.

Map 13.3, page 674

Colson is set just a mile from the western border of Los Padres National Forest, making it far easier to reach than other Forest Service camps in this region. The camp is named after the canyon in which it sits, Colson Canyon. This area really has just two seasons when you should visit, spring and fall. In the summer, it's hot and dry, with no water available, and is scarcely fit for habitation. The elevation is 2,100 feet.

Campsites, facilities: There are five tent sites. Picnic tables and fire grills are provided. A pit toilet is available. No drinking water is available. Garbage must be packed out. Leashed pets are permitted.

Reservations, fees: No reservations are accepted and there is no camping fee. An Adventure Pass ($30 annual fee or $5 daily pass) per parked vehicle is required. Senior discount available. Open year-round.

Directions: From U.S. 101 in Santa Maria, take

the Betteravia Road exit east and drive eight miles southeast to a fork with Santa Maria Mesa Road. Bear left at the fork and drive southeast on Santa Maria Mesa Road to Tepusquet Road. Turn left on Tepusquet Road and drive 6.5 miles to Colson Canyon Road. Turn right on Colson Canyon Road/Forest Road 11N04 and drive four miles to the campground. Colson Canyon Road can be impassable when wet.

Contact: Los Padres National Forest, Santa Lucia Ranger District, 805/925-9538, fax 805/961-5781.

24 BARREL SPRINGS

Rating: 7

In Los Padres National Forest.

Map 13.3, page 674

This small, primitive camp sits at 1,000 feet in elevation along La Brea Creek and is shaded by the oaks in La Brea Canyon. It is named after nearby Barrel Springs, which forms a small creek and feeds into La Brea Creek.

Campsites, facilities: There are six tent sites. Picnic tables and fire grills are provided. Vault toilets are available. No drinking water is available. Garbage must be packed out. Leashed pets are permitted.

Reservations, fees: No reservations are accepted and there is no camping fee. An Adventure Pass ($30 annual fee or $5 daily pass) per parked vehicle is required. Senior discount available. Open year-round, but access roads may be closed during and after heavy rains.

Directions: From U.S. 101 in Santa Maria, take the Betteravia Road exit east and drive eight miles southeast to a fork with Santa Maria Mesa Road. Bear left at the fork and drive southeast on Santa Maria Mesa Road to Tepusquet Road. Turn left on Tepusquet Road and drive 6.5 miles to Colson Canyon Road. Turn right on Colson Canyon Road/Forest Road 11N04 and drive eight miles to the campground. Colson Canyon Road can be impassable when wet.

Contact: Los Padres National Forest, Santa Lucia Ranger District, 805/925-9538, fax 805/961-5781.

25 WAGON FLAT

Rating: 6

On the North Fork of La Brea Creek in Los Padres National Forest.

Map 13.3, page 674

Not many folks know about this obscure spot, and if it's a hot, late summer day, they're probably better off for it. The camp is set at an elevation of 1,400 feet, pretty in spring, but in summer often a hot, dry region of Los Padres National Forest. The bright spot is little La Brea Creek, which runs by the camp.

Campsites, facilities: There are three sites for tents. Picnic tables and fire grills are provided. Vault toilets are available. No drinking water is available. Garbage must be packed out. Leashed pets are permitted.

Reservations, fees: No reservations are accepted and there is no camping fee. An Adventure Pass ($30 annual fee or $5 daily pass) per parked vehicle is required. Senior discount available. Open year-round, but access roads may be closed during and after heavy rains.

Directions: From U.S. 101 in Santa Maria, take the Betteravia Road exit east and drive eight miles southeast to a fork with Santa Maria Mesa Road. Bear left at the fork and drive southeast on Santa Maria Mesa Road to Tepusquet Road. Turn left on Tepusquet Road and drive 6.5 miles to Colson Canyon Road. Turn right on Colson Canyon Road/Forest Road 11N04 and drive 10 miles to the campground. Colson Canyon Road can be impassable when wet.

Contact: Los Padres National Forest, Santa Lucia Ranger District, 805/925-9538, fax 805/961-5781.

26 JALAMA BEACH COUNTY PARK

Rating: 8

Near Lompoc on the Pacific Ocean.

Map 13.3, page 674

This is a pretty spot set where Jalama Creek empties into the ocean, about five miles north of Point Conception and just south of Vandenberg Air Force Base. The area is known for its sunsets and beachcombing, with occasional lost missiles washing up on the beach. The camp is so popular that a waiting list is common in summer.

Campsites, facilities: There are 110 sites, 29 with water hookups, for tents or RVs up to 35 feet long, and several group sites. Picnic tables and fire grills are provided. Restrooms, drinking water, flush toilets, showers, RV dump station, and a grocery store are available. Note that the nearest gas station is 20 miles away. Leashed pets are permitted. Some facilities are wheelchair-accessible.

Reservations, fees: No reservations are accepted except for groups. Fees are $16–22 per night, $8 for an extra vehicle (two-vehicle maximum per site), $2 per night. Group reservations required at 805/934-6211 ($25 reservation fee). Major credit cards accepted. Open year-round.

Directions: From Lompoc, drive about five miles south on Highway 1. Turn southwest on Jalama Road and drive 14 miles to the park.

Contact: Jalama Beach County Park, 805/736-6316, fax 805/736-8020 or 805/736-3504, website: www.slocountyparks.com or www.sbpark.org.

27 RIVER PARK

Rating: 4

In Lompoc.

Map 13.3, page 674

Before checking in here you'd better get a lesson in how to pronounce Lompoc. It's

"Lom-Poke." If you arrive and say, "Hey, it's great to be in Lom-Pock," they might just tell ya to get on back to the other cowpokes. The camp is set near the lower Santa Ynez River, which looks quite a bit different than it does up in Los Padres National Forest. A small fishing lake within the park is stocked regularly with trout. Side-trip possibilities include the nearby La Purisima Mission State Historic Park.

Campsites, facilities: There are 36 sites with full hookups for RVs and a large open area for tents. Restrooms, drinking water, flush toilets, coin showers, RV dump station, fishing pond, and a playground are available. Supplies and a coin laundry are nearby. Leashed pets are permitted.

Reservations, fees: Reservations are not accepted. The fee is $5–15 per night, $10 per night for extra vehicles, $5 per night for hike-in/bike-in sites, $1 per night. Reservations required for groups. Open year-round.

Directions: In Lompoc, drive to the junction of Highway 246 and Sweeney Road at the southwest edge of town and continue to the park at 401 E. Hwy. 246.

Contact: Lompoc Parks and Recreation Department, 805/736-6565, fax 805/736-5195, website: www.ci.lompoc.ca.us.

28 FLYING FLAGS RV PARK

Rating: 3

Near Solvang.

Map 13.3, page 674

This is one of the few privately operated parks in the area that welcomes tenters as well as RVers. Nearby side trips include the Santa Ynez Mission, just east of Solvang. The town of Solvang is of interest. It was originally a small Danish settlement that has expanded since the 1920s yet managed to keep its cultural heritage intact over the years. The town is spotless, with no trash of any kind in sight, and an example of how to do something right.

Campsites, facilities: There are 256 sites with full or partial hookups for RVs and 100 sites for tents. Picnic tables are provided. Restrooms, showers, playground, swimming pool, two hot therapy pools, laundry room, store, RV dump station, ice, recreation room, modem access, arcade, five clubhouses, and propane gas are available. Some facilities are wheelchair-accessible. A nine-hole golf course is nearby. Leashed pets are permitted.

Reservations, fees: Reservations are recommended. Fees are $18–28.50 per night, $3 per person for more than two people, $3 per night for extra vehicle, $1 per night. Open year-round. Major credit cards accepted.

Directions: From Santa Barbara, drive 45 miles north on U.S. 101 to Highway 246. Turn west (left) on Highway 246 and drive about a half mile to Avenue of the Flags (a four-way stop). Turn left on Avenue of the Flags and drive about one block to the campground entrance on the left at 180 Avenue of the Flags.

Contact: Flying Flags RV Park, 805/688-3716, fax 805/688-9245, website: www.flyingflags.com.

29 GAVIOTA STATE PARK

Rating: 10

Near Santa Barbara.

Map 13.3, page 674

This is the granddaddy, the biggest of the three state beaches along U.S. 101 northwest of Santa Barbara. Spectacular and beautiful, the park covers 2,700 acres, providing trails for hiking and horseback riding, as well as a mile-long stretch of stunning beach frontage. Gaviota means "seagull" and was first named by the soldiers of the Portola Expedition in 1769, who learned why you always wear a hat (or a helmet) when they are passing overhead. The ambitious can hike the beach to get more seclusion. Trails to Gaviota Overlook (1.5 miles) and Gaviota Peak (3.2 miles one way) provide lookouts with drop-dead gorgeous views of the coast and Channel Islands. Want more? There is also a half-mile trail to the hot springs. This park is known for being windy and for shade being hard to find. Unfortunately, a railroad trestle crosses above the day-use parking lot. You know what that means? Of course you do. It means trains run through here day and night, and with them, noise. This is a popular beach for swimming and surf fishing, as well as fishing from the pier.

Campsites, facilities: There are 42 sites for tents and RVs up to 27 feet long and an area with hike-in/bike-in sites. Picnic tables and fire grills are provided. Restrooms, drinking water, flush toilets, coin showers, summer lifeguard service, and a boat hoist are available. Some facilities are wheelchair-accessible. A convenience store (open summer only) is nearby. Leashed pets are permitted at campsites.

Reservations, fees: Reservations are not accepted. The fee is $10 per night, $1 per person per night for hike-in/bike-in sites. Senior discount available. Open year-round.

Directions: From Santa Barbara, drive north on U.S. 101 for 33 miles to the Gaviota State Beach exit. Take that exit and turn west and drive a short distance to the park entrance.

Contact: Gaviota State Park, Channel Coast District, 805/968-1033 or 805/899-1400.

30 REFUGIO STATE BEACH

Rating: 9

Near Santa Barbara.
Map 13.3, page 674

Refugio State Beach is the smallest of the three beautiful state beaches along U.S. 101 north of Santa Barbara. The others are Gaviota and El Capitan, which also have campgrounds. Palm trees planted close to Refugio Creek provide a unique look to this beach and campground. This is a great spot for family campers with bikes, with a paved two-mile bike trail connecting Refugio campground with El Cap-

itan. Fishing is often good in this area of the coast. As with all state beaches and private camps on the Coast Highway, reservations are strongly advised and often a necessity throughout the vacation season.

Campsites, facilities: There are 85 sites for tents or RVs up to 30 feet long, five hike-in/bike-in sites, and one group site for up to 80 people and 25 vehicles. Picnic tables and fire grills are provided. Restrooms, drinking water, flush toilets, coin-operated showers, summer lifeguard service, summer convenience store, and food services areavailable. An RV dump station is two miles away at El Capitan State Beach. Some facilities are wheelchair-accessible. Leashed pets are permitted at campsites.

Reservations, fees: Reserve at 800/444-PARK (800/444-7275) or website: www.Reserve America.com ($7.50 reservation fee); $12 per night, $1 per night per person for hike-in/bike-in sites, $60 per night for the group site. Senior discount available. Open year-round, weather permitting.

Directions: From Santa Barbara, drive northwest on U.S. 101 for 23 miles to the Refugio State Beach exit. Take that exit and turn west (left) and drive a short distance to the campground entrance.

Contact: Refugio State Beach, 805/899-1400; Channel Coast District, 805/968-1033.

31 EL CAPITAN CANYON

Rating: 8

Near Goleta.
Map 13.3, page 674

El Capitan Canyon is a unique campground where you do not bring your own tent, but rather rent permanent tents or cabins on site. The camp was remodeled and gone are personal sites for tents and RVs. The park covers 65 acres in the coastal foothills north of Santa Barbara and offers visitors the best of both worlds: there are 2,200 acres of public land near the camp with backcountry hiking and mountain biking trails, or for those who prefer the sand and surf, beach access is within walking distance and ocean kayaking and deep-sea fishing trips can be booked at the resort. In the summer live entertainment is available, including a concert series and the "Blues and Barbecue" event every Saturday night. Dogs are strictly prohibited in a mission here to stop the spread of non-native plants; this in turn has inspired a return of native habitat and the birds and wildlife that rely on it.

Campsites, facilities: There are 26 permanent tent sites and 96 cabins. Picnic tables and fire pits are provided. Bottled water is recommended. Restrooms, flush toilets, showers, swimming pool, children's playground, live music (on Saturday nights), volleyball, horseshoes, small store, and firewood are available. Some facilities are wheelchair-accessible. Pets are strictly prohibited.

Reservations, fees: Reservations are recommended. Fees are $20–25 per night, $5 per night for each extra vehicle, $5 per person per night for more than four people, $5 pet fee. Major credit cards accepted. Open year-round.

Directions: From Santa Barbara, drive about 20 miles northwest on U.S. 101 to the El Capitan State Beach exit. Go straight on the frontage road paralleling the freeway for about 100 yards. Turn right at the sign for El Capitan Canyon on the mountain side of the freeway.

Contact: El Capitan Canyon, 11560 Calle Real, Goleta, CA 93117, 805/685-3887, fax 805/968-6772, website: www.elcapitancanyon.com.

32 EL CAPITAN STATE BEACH
Rating:10

Near Santa Barbara.

Map 13.3, page 674

This is one in a series of beautiful state beaches along the Santa Barbara coast. The water is warm, the swimming good. A stairway descends from the bluffs to the beach, a beautiful setting. El Capitan has a sandy beach, rocky tide-

pools, and stands of sycamores and oaks along El Capitan Creek. A paved, two-mile bicycle trail is routed to Refugio State Beach, a great family trip. This is a perfect layover for Coast Highway vacationers, and reservations are usually required to assure a spot. Refugio State Beach to the north is another camping option.

Campsites, facilities: There are 142 sites for tents or RVs up to 30 feet long, seven hike-in/bike-in sites, and three group sites for tents only for 50–125 people. Picnic tables and fire grills are provided. Restrooms, drinking water, flush toilets, coin-operated showers, RV dump station, summer lifeguard service, and a summer convenience store are available. Leashed pets are permitted. Some facilities are wheelchair-accessible.

Reservations, fees: Reserve at 800/444-PARK (800/444-7275) or website: www.ReserveAmerica.com ($7.50 reservation fee); $12 per night; $1 per person per night for hike-in/bike-in sites, $37–93 per night for group sites. Senior discount available. Open year-round, weather permitting.

Directions: From Santa Barbara, drive north on U.S. 101 for 20 miles to the El Capitan State Beach exit. Turn west (left) and drive a short distance to the campground entrance.

Contact: El Capitan State Beach, 805/968-1033 or 805/899-1400.

33 SAN MIGUEL ISLAND BOAT-IN AND HIKE-IN
Rating:10

In Channel Islands National Park.

Map 13.3, page 674

There is no camping trip like this one anywhere in America. It starts with a five-hour boat ride, after which you arrive at San Miguel Island, the most unusual of the five Channel Islands. It is small, distant, and extremely rugged, and it is home to unique birds and much wildlife, including elephant seals and the largest sea lion rookery in California (on the south side of the island). Only rarely do people take advantage of this island paradise, limited to no more than 30 people at any one time on the entire island. To reach the campground start from Cuyler Harbor, where you will be dropped off, and then hike up Nidever Canyon and take the left fork. Bring plenty of water, warm clothes, and be prepared for the chance of fog and wind; the boat typically will not return to pick you up for several days. That's why camping here is like staking out your own personal island wilderness.

Campsites, facilities: There are nine primitive tent sites. Picnic tables and food lockers are provided. Pit toilets and windbreaks are available. No drinking water is available, and garbage must be packed out. No open fires are allowed; bring a camp stove for cooking. No pets are permitted.

Reservations, fees: Reserve by calling Island Packers at 805/642-1393 or Truth Aquatics at Sea Landing in Santa Barbara at 805/963-3564. After arranging transportation, you must obtain a camping reservation at 800/365-CAMP (800/365-2267) or website: reservations.nps.gov, $10 camping fee; round-trip boat transportation, $90 for adults, $80 for children. Open year-round, weather permitting.

Directions: Drive on U.S. 101 to south of Ventura and the Seaward exit. Take that exit and turn west on Seaward Avenue and drive one mile to Harbor Boulevard. Bear left on Harbor and drive about two miles to Spinnaker Drive. Turn right and drive a short distance to the harbor. The boat ride is about five hours each way.

Contact: Channel Islands National Park Visitor Information Line, 805/658-5730.

34 BATES CANYON
Rating: 7

In Los Padres National Forest.
Map 13.4, page 675

This camp is on the northeast flank of the Sierra Madre Mountains, along a small stream

in Bates Canyon, at 2,900 feet in elevation. Note that the primitive access road out of camp to the south is often gated; it leads to the Sierra Madre Ridge, where a road contours right along the ridge on the border of the San Rafael Wilderness, passing from peak to peak.

Campsites, facilities: There are six tent sites. Picnic tables and fire grills are provided. Vault toilets are available. No drinking water is available. Garbage must be packed out. Leashed pets are permitted.

Reservations, fees: No reservations are accepted and there is no camping fee. An Adventure Pass ($30 annual fee or $5 daily pass) per parked vehicle is required. Senior discount available. Open year-round. Note that access roads can be closed during and after heavy rains.

Directions: From Santa Maria, drive east on Highway 166 for 50 miles to Cottonwood Canyon Road. Turn right on Cottonwood Canyon Road and drive southwest for 7.5 miles to the campground.

Contact: Los Padres National Forest, Santa Lucia Ranger District, 805/925-9538, fax 805/961-5781.

35 ALISO PARK
Rating: 6

In Los Padres National Forest.
Map 13.4, page 675

This primitive, quiet camp is set at the foot of the Sierra Madre Mountains at 3,200 feet, directly below McPherson Peak (5,749 feet). It is just inside the northeast boundary of Los Padres National Forest, making it easily accessible from Highway 166.

Campsites, facilities: There are 10 sites for tents or RVs up to 22 feet long. Picnic tables and fire grills are provided. Pit toilets are available. No drinking water is available. Garbage must be packed out. Leashed pets are permitted.

Reservations, fees: No reservations are accepted

and there is no camping fee. An Adventure Pass ($30 annual fee or $5 daily pass) per parked vehicle is required. Senior discount available. Open year-round.

Directions: From Santa Maria, drive east on Highway 166 for 59 miles to Aliso Canyon Road/Forest Road 10N04. Turn right on Aliso Canyon Road/Forest Road 10N04 and drive south about six miles to the campground at the end of the road.

Contact: Los Padres National Forest, Mt. Piños Ranger District, 661/245-3731, fax 661/245-1526.

36 BALLINGER

Rating: 3

In Los Padres National Forest.

Map 13.4, page 675

Ballinger Camp is right inside the boundary of Los Padres National Forest in the Mt. Piños Ranger District, just six miles east of Highway 33. During the week, this camp receives very little use. On weekends, it gets moderate, even heavy use at times, from OHV owners. The camp is set at an elevation of 3,000 feet.

Campsites, facilities: There are 20 sites for tents or RVs up to 32 feet long. Picnic tables and fire grills are provided. Vault toilets are available. No drinking water is available. Garbage must be packed out. Leashed pets are permitted.

Reservations, fees: No reservations are accepted and there is no camping fee. An Adventure Pass ($30 annual fee or $5 daily pass) per parked vehicle is required. Senior discount available. Open year-round.

Directions: From Maricopa, drive southwest on Highway 166 about 14 miles to Highway 33. Turn south on Highway 33 and drive about 3.5 miles to Ballinger Canyon Road/Forest Road 9N10. Turn left (east) and drive three miles to the campground.

Contact: Los Padres National Forest, Mt. Piños Ranger District, 661/245-3731, fax 661/245-1526.

37 VALLE VISTA

Rating: 8

In Los Padres National Forest.

Map 13.4, page 675

The view of the southern San Joaquin Valley and the snow-capped Sierra is the highlight of this primitive camp. It is set at 4,800 feet, near the boundary of Los Padres National Forest. Visitors have an opportunity to view condors here, and you can usually spot a few buzzards, er, turkey vultures, circling around. If you don't bring your own water, they might just start circling you. Little-known fact: this camp sits exactly on the border of Kern County and Ventura County. Wow.

Campsites, facilities: There are seven sites for tents or RVs up to 22 feet long. Picnic tables and fire grills are provided. Pit toilets are available. No drinking water is available. Garbage must be packed out. Leashed pets are permitted.

Reservations, fees: No reservations are accepted and there is no camping fee. An Adventure Pass ($30 annual fee or $5 daily pass) per parked vehicle is required. Senior discount available. Open year-round.

Directions: From Maricopa, drive south on Highway 166 about nine miles to Cerro Noroeste Road. Turn left and drive 12 miles to the campground on the left.

Contact: Los Padres National Forest, Mt. Piños Ranger District, 661/245-3731, fax 661/245-1526.

38 CABALLO

Rating: 4

In Los Padres National Forest.

Map 13.4, page 675

Caballo is set at 5,850 feet on a small creek that is the headwaters for Santiago Creek, on the northern flank of Mt. Abel. The creek only flows about 10 days a year, usually before the opening of the campground, so do not count on it for water. It is one of several primitive camps in the immediate area—a take-your-pick offer. But it's an offer not many folks even know about.

Campsites, facilities: There are six sites for tents or RVs up to 16 feet long. Picnic tables and fire grills are provided. Pit toilets are available. No drinking water is available. Garbage must be packed out. Leashed pets are permitted.

Reservations, fees: No reservations are accepted and there is no camping fee. An Adventure Pass ($30 annual fee or $5 daily fee) per parked vehicle is required. Senior discount available. Open May through October.

Directions: Drive on I-5 to just south of Lebec to the Frazier Park exit. Take that exit and drive west on Frazier Mountain Road to the town of Lake of the Woods and Cuddy Valley Road. Turn right on Cuddy Valley Road and drive six miles to Mil Potrero Highway (sign says Pine Mountain Club). Turn right and drive 10 miles to Forest Road 9N27. Turn right and drive a short distance to the campground. Note: to reach Marian campground, continue for another mile.

Contact: Los Padres National Forest, Mt. Piños Ranger District, 661/245-3731, fax 661/245-1526.

39 TOAD SPRINGS

Rating: 8

In Los Padres National Forest.
Map 13.4, page 675

Toad Springs is set at 5,700 feet near Apache Saddle, on the northwest flank of Mt. Abel (8,286 feet). It is at the head of Quatal Canyon with a spectacular badlands landscape. No water or toilets are available, so forget this one for your honeymoon. Note that a landslide destroyed a primitive trail (about a mile out of camp) that once was routed south out of camp for six miles to Mesa Springs and a trail camp. It is considered too dangerous for use.

Campsites, facilities: There are five sites for tents or RVs up to 16 feet long. Picnic tables

and fire grills are provided. No drinking water is available. Garbage must be packed out. Leashed pets are permitted.

Reservations, fees: No reservations are accepted and there is no camping fee. An Adventure Pass ($30 annual fee or $5 daily fee) per parked vehicle is required. Senior discount available. Open May through October.

Directions: Drive on I-5 to just south of Lebec to the Frazier Park exit. Take that exit and drive west on Frazier Mountain Road to the town of Lake of the Woods and Cuddy Valley Road. Turn right on Cuddy Valley Road and drive six miles to Mil Potrero Highway (sign says Pine Mountain Club). Turn right and drive 10 miles to the campground on the left.

Contact: Los Padres National Forest, Mt. Piños Ranger District, 661/245-3731, fax 661/245-1526.

40 MARIAN

Rating: 4

In Los Padres National Forest.
Map 13.4, page 675

Marian is extremely primitive, set on the outskirts of Los Padres National Forest at 6,600 feet in elevation, between Brush Mountain to the immediate northwest and San Emigdio Mountain to the immediate southeast. A primitive route out of camp leads three miles to the San Emigdio summit, 7,495 feet in elevation. A network of Forest Service roads provides access to a number of other camps in the area, as well as Mt. Abel (8,286 feet) and Mt. Piños (8,831 feet). If the access gate is locked, reaching this camp requires a two-mile hike; nearby Toad Spring and Caballo are smaller but more easily accessible. Note that not only is no drinking water available, but there are no toilets either.

Campsites, facilities: There are five sites for tents or RVs up to 16 feet long. Picnic tables and fire grills are provided. No drinking water is available. Garbage must be packed out. Leashed pets are permitted.

Reservations, fees: No reservations are accepted and there is no camping fee. An Adventure Pass ($30 annual fee or $5 daily fee) per parked vehicle is required. Senior discount available. Open May through October.

Directions: Drive on I-5 to just south of Lebec to the Frazier Park exit. Take that exit and drive west on Frazier Mountain Road to the town of Lake of the Woods and Cuddy Valley Road. Turn right on Cuddy Valley Road and drive six miles to Mil Potrero Highway (sign says Pine Mountain Club). Turn right and drive 10 miles to Forest Road 9N27. Turn right and drive one mile (passing Caballo Campground) to the camp.

Contact: Los Padres National Forest, Mt. Piños Ranger District, 661/245-3731, fax 661/245-1526.

41 MIL POTRERO PARK

Rating: 5

Near Mt. Piños.
Map 13.4, page 675

This is one of the rare RV parks that provides equal billing for tents. It is set at 5,300 feet, with national forest generally surrounding the area. Nearby side trips worth noting are to the Big Trees of Pleito Canyon and also the drive on Forest Service roads to the summit of Frazier Mountain at 8,013 feet, where there is a lookout with drop-dead gorgeous 360-degree views.

Campsites, facilities: There are 43 sites for tents or RVs. Picnic tables and fire grills are provided. Restrooms, drinking water, flush toilets, showers, and horse corrals are available. Leashed pets are permitted.

Reservations, fees: Reservations are recommended. The fee is $15 per night, $10 for residents of Taft, 10-person maximum per site. Open year-round.

Directions: Drive on I-5 to just south of Lebec to the Frazier Park exit. Take that exit and

drive west on Frazier Mountain Road to the town of Lake of the Woods and Cuddy Valley Road. Bear right on Cuddy Valley Road and drive five miles to Mil Potrero Highway. Turn right and drive 5.5 miles to Pine Mountain Village Center. Continue 1.3 miles to the park entrance on the left.

Contact: Mil Potrero Park, 661/763-4246.

42 FIGUEROA

Rating: 7

In Los Padres National Forest.
Map 13.4, page 675

This is one of the more attractive camps in Los Padres National Forest. It is set at 4,000 feet beneath an unusual stand of oak and huge manzanita trees and offers a view of the Santa Ynez Valley. Nearby attractions include the Piño Alto Picnic Area, 2.5 miles away, offering a panoramic view of the adjacent wildlands with a half-mile, wheelchair-accessible nature trail. An exceptional view is also available from the nearby Figueroa fire lookout. Though it requires a circuitous 10-mile ride around Figueroa Mountain to get there, Nira to the east provides the best trailhead for the San Rafael Wilderness in this area.

Campsites, facilities: There are 33 sites for tents. Picnic tables and fire grills are provided. Drinking water and vault toilets are available. Garbage must be packed out. Leashed pets are permitted.

Reservations, fees: No reservations are accepted and there is no camping fee. An Adventure Pass ($30 annual fee or $5 daily pass) per parked vehicle is required. Senior discount available. Open year-round.

Directions: Drive on Highway 154 to Los Olivos and Figueroa Mountain Road. Turn northeast on Figueroa Mountain Road and drive 12.5 miles to the campground.

Contact: Los Padres National Forest, Santa Lucia Ranger District, 805/925-9538, fax 805/961-5781.

43 NIRA

Rating: 8

On Manzana Creek in Los Padres National Forest.

Map 13.4, page 675

Nira is a premium jump-off spot for back-packers, set at 2,100 feet along Manzana Creek, on the border of the San Rafael Wilderness. A primary wilderness trailhead is available, routed east into the San Rafael Wilderness through Lost Valley, along Fish Creek, and to Manzana Creek (and beyond), all in just six miles, with a series of hike-in camps available as the trail enters the wilderness interior. Today's history lesson? This camp was originally an NRA (National Recovery Act) camp during the Depression, hence the name Nira.

Campsites, facilities: There are 11 sites for tents or RVs up to 16 feet long. Picnic tables and fire grills are provided. Vault toilets and horse-hitching posts are available. No drinking water is available. Garbage must be packed out. Leashed pets are permitted.

Reservations, fees: No reservations are accepted and there is no camping fee. An Adventure Pass ($30 annual fee or $5 daily pass) per parked vehicle is required. Senior discount available. Open year-round, but access roads may be closed during and after heavy rains.

Directions: From U.S. 101 in Santa Barbara, take Highway 154 northeast and drive 22 miles to Armour Ranch Road. Turn right on Armour Ranch Road and drive 1.5 miles to Happy Canyon Road. Turn right on Happy Canyon Road and drive 11 miles to Cachuma Saddle. Continue straight (north) on Sunset Valley/Cachuma Road/Forest Road 8N09 for six miles to the campground.

Contact: Los Padres National Forest, Santa Lucia Ranger District, 805/925-9538, fax 805/961-5781.

44 DAVY BROWN

Rating: 7

On Davy Brown Creek in Los Padres National Forest.

Map 13.4, page 675

This is a pretty spot, set along little Davy Brown Creek at 4,000 feet, deep in Los Padres National Forest. The border of the San Rafael Wilderness and an excellent trailhead are just two miles down the road (along Davy Brown Creek) to the northeast at Nira (see for hiking options).

Campsites, facilities: There are 13 sites for tents and RVs up to 18 feet long. Picnic tables and fire grills are provided. Vault toilets are available. No drinking water is available. Garbage must be packed out. Leashed pets are permitted.

Reservations, fees: No reservations are accepted and there is no camping fee. An Adventure Pass ($30 annual fee or $5 daily pass) per parked vehicle is required. Senior discount available. Open year-round.

Directions: From U.S. 101 in Santa Barbara, take Highway 154 and drive northeast for 22 miles to Armour Ranch Road. Turn right on Armour Ranch Road and drive 1.5 miles to Happy Canyon Road. Turn right on Happy Canyon Road/County Route 3350 and drive 11 miles to Cachuma Saddle. Continue straight (north) on Sunset Valley/Cachuma Road/Forest Road 8N09 for four miles to the campground.

Contact: Los Padres National Forest, Santa Lucia Ranger District, 805/925-9538, fax 805/961-5781.

45 NETTLE SPRINGS

Rating: 4

In Los Padres National Forest.

Map 13.4, page 675

This remote camp borders the Chumash Wilderness, set near the end of a Forest Service road in Apache Canyon. A mile east of camp, via the access road, is a primitive trailhead on the left side. This trail is routed four miles to Mesa Springs and a trail camp. The elevation is 4,400 feet.

Campsites, facilities: There are seven sites for tents only and four sites for tents or RVs up to 22 feet long. Picnic tables and fire grills are provided. Pit toilets are available. No drinking water is available. Garbage must be packed out. Leashed pets are permitted.

Reservations, fees: No reservations are accepted and there is no camping fee. An Adventure Pass ($30 annual fee or $5 daily fee) per parked vehicle is required. Senior discount available. Open year-round.

Directions: From Maricopa, drive 14 miles south on Highway 166 to the Highway 33 exit. Turn south on Highway 33 and drive about 13 miles to Apache Canyon Road (Forest Road 8N06). Turn left and drive about 10 miles to the campground. Note: the last 10 miles are rough and high-clearance vehicles are advised.

Contact: Los Padres National Forest, Mt. Piños Ranger District, 661/245-3731, fax 661/245-1526.

46 CAMPO ALTO

Rating: 6

In Los Padres National Forest.

Map 13.4, page 675

Campo Alto means "High Camp," and you'll find that the name fits when you visit here. The camp is set high (8,250 feet) on Cerro Noroeste/Mt. Abel in Los Padres National Forest. Don't show up thirsty, as there's no drinking water. About half a mile from camp there is a trailhead on the southeast side of the road. From here, you can hike two miles to Grouse Mountain, and in another mile, reach remote, hike-in Sheep Camp.

Campsites, facilities: There are 17 sites for tents or RVs up to 22 feet long. Picnic tables and fire grills (stoves) are provided. Pit toilets are avail-

able. No drinking water is available. Garbage must be packed out. Leashed pets are permitted.

Reservations, fees: No reservations are accepted and there is no camping fee. An Adventure Pass ($30 annual fee or $5 daily fee) per parked vehicle is required. Senior discount available. Open May through October.

Directions: Drive on I-5 to just south of Lebec to the Frazier Park exit. Take that exit and drive west on Frazier Mountain Road to the town of Lake of the Woods and Cuddy Valley Road. Turn right on Cuddy Valley Road and drive six miles to Mil Potrero Highway (sign says Pine Mountain Club). Turn right and drive nine miles to Cerro Noroeste Road (Forest Road 9N07). Turn left and drive nine miles to the campground.

Contact: Los Padres National Forest, Mt. Piños Ranger District, 661/245-3731, fax 661/245-1526.

47 MT. PIÑOS

Rating: 7

In Los Padres National Forest.

Map 13.4, page 675

This camp is set at 7,800 feet, one of three camps on the eastern flank of Mt. Piños (8,831 feet). This is one of the few places on earth where it is possible to see flying California condors, the largest bird in North America. Note that a once-popular drive to the top of Mt. Piños for beautiful and sweeping views is now closed after being recognized as a Chumash holy site. There's access to the Mt. Piños summit trail 2.5 miles away on Mil Potrero Highway at the Chula Vista parking area. From there it's about two miles to the summit, which is a designated botanical area. July and August usually are the best months for wildflower displays. McGill provides a nearby camping alternative. Rangers hope to run a water line to this campground, but there is no commitment as to when this will occur.

Campsites, facilities: There are 19 sites for tents

or RVs up to 16 feet long. Picnic tables and fire grills are provided. No drinking water is available. Pit toilets are available. Leashed pets are permitted.

Reservations, fees: Reservations are not accepted. The fee is $10 per night. Senior discount available. Open late May through September.

Directions: Drive on I-5 to just south of Lebec to the Frazier Park exit. Take that exit and drive west on Frazier Mountain Road to the town of Lake of the Woods and Cuddy Valley Road. Turn right on Cuddy Valley Road and drive about six miles to Mt. Piños Highway. Bear left and drive four miles to the campground.

Contact: Los Padres National Forest, Mt. Piños Ranger District, 661/245-3731, fax 661/245-1526.

48 MCGILL
🚶 🚲 🐕 ♿ 🚐 ⛺

Rating: 6

Near Mt. Piños in Los Padres National Forest.

Map 13.4, page 675

The camp is set at 7,400 feet, about four miles from the top of nearby Mt. Piños. Although the road is closed to the top of Mt. Piños, there are numerous hiking and biking trails in the area that provide spectacular views. On clear days, there are vantage points to the high Sierra, the San Joaquin Valley, and Antelope Valley.

Campsites, facilities: There are 73 family sites for tents or RVs up to 16 feet long, and two group sites for 60 and 80 people. Picnic tables and fire grills are provided. Drinking water and flush toilets are available. Leashed pets are permitted. A note of caution: the water wells have been known to run dry in the summer, so bring your own water during the summer. Some facilities are wheelchair-accessible.

Reservations, fees: Reservations are required for group sites; reserve at 877/444-6777 ($9 group reservation fee); $8 per night for family sites, $75 for a group site. Senior discount available. Open late May through October.

Directions: Drive on I-5 to just south of Lebec to the Frazier Park exit. Take that exit and drive west on Frazier Mountain Road to the town of Lake of the Woods and Cuddy Valley Road. Turn right on Cuddy Valley Road and drive about six miles to Mt. Piños Highway. Turn left and drive about four miles to the campground on the right.

Contact: Los Padres National Forest, Mt. Piños Ranger District, 661/245-3731, fax 661/245-1526.

49 CACHUMA
🚶 🐕 ⛺

Rating: 6

Near Cachuma Creek in Los Padres National Forest.

Map 13.4, page 675

This camp is set at 2,200 feet along one of the major streams that feeds Lake Cachuma, just 10 miles downstream. A dirt road south of the camp follows the creek to the lake.

Campsites, facilities: There are five tent sites. Picnic tables and fire grills are provided. Vault toilets are available. No drinking water is available. Garbage must be packed out. Leashed pets are permitted.

Reservations, fees: No reservations are accepted and there is no camping fee. An Adventure Pass ($30 annual fee or $5 daily pass) per parked vehicle is required. Senior discount available. Open year-round.

Directions: From U.S. 101 in Santa Barbara, take Highway 154 and drive northeast for 22 miles to Armour Ranch Road. Turn right on Armour Ranch Road and drive 1.5 miles to Happy Canyon Road. Turn right on Happy Canyon Road/County Route 3350 and drive 9.5 miles to the campground.

Contact: Los Padres National Forest, Santa Barbara Ranger District, 805/967-3481, fax 805/967-7312.

50 PINE SPRINGS

Rating: 6

Near San Guillermo Mountain in Los Padres National Forest.

Map 13.4, page 675

This primitive camp is set at 5,800 feet in elevation on a short spur road that dead-ends on the east flank of San Guillermo Mountain (6,569 feet). Pine Springs feeds the tiny headwaters of Guillermo Creek at this spot. This is a quiet spot. It gets little use, primarily in the fall by hunters.

Campsites, facilities: There are 12 sites for tents or RVs up to 22 feet long. Picnic tables and fire grills are provided. Pit toilets are available. No drinking water is available. Garbage must be packed out. Leashed pets are permitted.

Reservations, fees: No reservations are accepted and there is no camping fee. An Adventure Pass ($30 annual fee or $5 daily fee) per parked vehicle is required. Senior discount available. Open May through September.

Directions: Drive on I-5 to just south of Lebec to the Frazier Park exit. Take that exit and drive west on Frazier Mountain Road to the town of Lake of the Woods and Lockwood Valley Road. Turn left on Lockwood Valley Road (take the left fork) and drive about 12 miles to Grade Valley Road (Forest Road 7N03). Turn left and drive 3.5 miles to Forest Road 7N03A. Turn right and drive one mile to the campground.

Contact: Los Padres National Forest, Mt. Piños Ranger District, 661/245-3731, fax 661/245-1526.

51 LAKE CACHUMA RECREATION AREA

Rating: 7

Near Santa Barbara.

Map 13.4, page 675

Cachuma has become one of the best lakes in America for fishing big bass, and the ideal climate makes it a winner for camping as well. Cachuma is set at 600 feet in the foothills northwest of Santa Barbara, a big, beautiful lake covering 3,200 acres. The rules are perfect for fishing: no water-skiing, personal watercraft, swimming, canoeing, kayaking, or windsurfing is permitted; for fishing boats there is a 5-mph speed limit in the coves and a 40-mph limit elsewhere. Yeah, let it rip on open water, then quiet down to sneak-fish the coves.

Campsites, facilities: There are 500 sites, some drive-through with full hookups, for tents or RVs, and three yurts. Picnic tables and fire pits are provided. Restrooms, drinking water, flush toilets, and showers are available. Playground, general store, propane gas, swimming pool, boat ramp, mooring, boat fuel, boat rentals, bicycle rentals, ice, and a snack bar are available nearby. Watercraft under 10 feet are prohibited on the lake. Leashed pets are permitted, but must be kept at least 50 feet from the lake.

Reservations, fees: Reservations are not accepted. The fee is $16–22 per night, $8 for a second vehicle, $2 per night. Group reservations available. Open year-round.

Directions: From Santa Barbara, drive 20 miles north on Highway 154 to the campground entrance on the right.

Contact: Lake Cachuma, 805/686-5053, website: www.cachuma.com.

52 FREMONT

Rating: 7

Near the Santa Ynez River in Los Padres National Forest.

Map 13.4, page 675

Traveling west to east, Fremont is the first in a series of Forest Service campgrounds near the Santa Ynez River. This one is just inside the boundary of Los Padres National Forest at 900 feet in elevation, nine miles east of Lake Cachuma to the west.

Campsites, facilities: There are 15 sites for tents or RVs up to 16 feet long. Picnic tables and fire grills are provided. Drinking water and flush toilets are available. Some facilities are wheelchair-accessible. Groceries are available within two miles and propane gas is available at Lake Cachuma nine miles away. Leashed pets are permitted.

Reservations, fees: Reservations are not accepted. The fee is $12 per night, $4 for a second vehicle. Senior discount available. Open April through September.

Directions: From Santa Barbara, drive northeast on Highway 154 for about 10 miles to Paradise Road/Forest Road 5N18. Turn right on Paradise Road/Forest Road 5N18 and drive 2.5 miles to the campground on the right.

Contact: Los Padres National Forest, Santa Barbara Ranger District, 805/967-3481, fax 805/967-7312.

53 LOS PRIETOS

Rating: 7

Near the Santa Ynez River in Los Padres National Forest.

Map 13.4, page 675

Los Prietos is set across from the Santa Ynez River at an elevation of 1,000 feet, just upstream from nearby Fremont campground to the west. There are several nice hiking trails nearby; the best starts near the Los Prietos Ranger Station, heading south for two miles to Wellhouse Falls (get specific directions and a map at the ranger station).

Campsites, facilities: There are 37 sites for tents or RVs up to 22 feet long. Picnic tables and fire grills are provided. Drinking water and flush toilets are available. Some facilities are wheelchair-accessible. Leashed pets are permitted.

Reservations, fees: Reservations are not accepted. The fee is $12 per night, $4 for a second vehicle. Senior discount available. Open April through September.

Directions: From Santa Barbara, take High-

way 154 and drive 10 miles northeast to Paradise Road/Forest Road 5N18. Turn right on Paradise Road/Forest Road 5N18 and drive 3.8 miles to the campground.

Contact: Los Padres National Forest, Santa Barbara Ranger District, 805/967-3481, fax 805/967-7312.

54 UPPER OSO

Rating: 7

Near the Santa Ynez River in Los Padres National Forest.

Map 13.4, page 675

This is one of the Forest Service campgrounds in the Santa Ynez Recreation Area. It is set in Oso Canyon at 1,100 feet, one mile from the Santa Ynez River. This is prime spot for equestrians, with horse corrals available and adjacent campsites. Note that at high water this campground can become inaccessible. A mile north of camp is the Santa Cruz trailhead for a hike that is routed north up Oso Canyon for a mile, then three miles up to Happy Hollow, and beyond that to a trail camp just west of Little Pine Mountain, elevation 4,508 feet. A trailhead into the San Rafael Wilderness is nearby, and once on the trail, you'll find many primitive sites in the backcountry.

Campsites, facilities: There are 28 sites for tents or RVs up to 22 feet long. Picnic tables and fire grills are provided. Drinking water and flush toilets are available. Some facilities are wheelchair-accessible. Horse corrals are also available. Leashed pets are permitted.

Reservations, fees: Reservations are not accepted. The fee is $12 per night, $4 for a second vehicle. Senior discount available. Reservation for sites with horse corrals at 800/444-6777 or website: www.ReserveUsa.com, ($9 reservation fee), $14 per night. Open year-round, weather permitting.

Directions: From Santa Barbara, take Highway 154 and drive 10 miles northeast to Paradise Road/Forest Road 5N18. Turn right on Paradise Road/Forest Road 5N18 and drive six miles to Upper Oso Road. Turn left on Upper Oso Road and drive one mile to the campground at the end of the road.

Contact: Los Padres National Forest, Santa Barbara Ranger District, 805/967-3481, fax 805/967-7312.

55 PARADISE

Rating: 7

Near the Santa Ynez River in Los Padres National Forest.

Map 13.4, page 675

Here is yet another option among the camps along the Santa Ynez River. As you drive east it is the second camp you will come to, just after Fremont. The best hiking trailheads nearby are at Upper Oso Camp and the Sage Hill Group Campground. Lake Cachuma is six miles to the west.

Campsites, facilities: There are 15 sites for tents or RVs up to 22 feet long. Picnic tables and fire grills are provided. Drinking water and flush toilets are available. Some facilities are wheelchair-accessible. Groceries are available nearby. Leashed pets are permitted.

Reservations, fees: Reserve at 877/444-6777 ($9 reservation fee) or website: www. reserve usa.com; $12 per night, $4 for a second vehicle. Open year-round.

Directions: From Santa Barbara, take Highway 154 and drive 10 miles northeast to Paradise Road/Forest Road 5N18. Turn right on Paradise Road/Forest Road 5N18 and drive three miles to the campground on the right.

Contact: Los Padres National Forest, Santa Barbara Ranger District, 805/967-3481, fax 805/967-7312.

56 SAGE HILL GROUP CAMP

Rating: 7

On the Santa Ynez River in Los Padres National Forest.

Map 13.4, page 675

This is another in the series of camps along the Santa Ynez River in Los Padres National Forest. This one, set at 2,000 feet, was designed for large groups as well as equestrians, with horse corrals available next to one group site. A 3.5-mile loop trail starts at the back end of Sage Hill Group Camp. The first mile is a self-guided interpretive trail.

Campsites, facilities: There are five group areas with sites for tents or RVs up to 32 feet long. Picnic tables and fire grills are provided. Drinking water and flush toilets are available. Horse corrals are in one group site. Leashed pets are permitted.

Reservations, fees: Reservations required for sites with horse corral; reserve at 877/444-6777 ($9 reservation fee) or website: www.Reserve Usa.com; $50–60 per group of 25–50 per night. Open year-round, weather permitting.

Directions: From Santa Barbara, take Highway 154 and drive 10 miles northeast to Paradise Road/Forest Road 5N18. Turn right on Paradise Road/Forest Road 5N18 and drive five miles to the ranger station and the campground entrance road. Turn left and drive a half mile to the campground.

Contact: Los Padres National Forest, Santa Barbara Ranger District, 805/967-3481, fax 805/967-7312.

57 MONO HIKE-IN

Rating: 7

On Mono Creek in Los Padres National Forest.

Map 13.4, page 675

Not many folks know about this spot. The camp is small and primitive, at elevation 1,500 feet on little Mono Creek. Also note that Little Caliente Hot Springs is one mile northeast of the campground. Mono Creek is a feeder to Gibraltar Reservoir, a long, narrow lake with no direct access available. Some may remember a great swimming hole on Mono Creek. Well, as is the case with all rivers, they get reshaped by nature and that swimming hole is gone.

Campsites, facilities: There are four tent sites. Picnic tables and fire grills are provided. Vault toilets are available. No drinking water is available. Garbage must be packed out. Leashed pets are permitted.

Reservations, fees: No reservations are accepted and there is no camping fee. An Adventure Pass ($30 annual fee or $5 daily pass) per parked vehicle is required. Senior discount available. Open year-round, weather permitting.

Directions: From U.S. 101 in Santa Barbara, take Highway 154 and drive northeast for eight miles to East Camino Cielo/Forest Road 5N12. Turn right on East Camino Cielo/Forest Road 5N12 and drive 18 miles to the end of the paved road at Camuesa Road/Forest Road 5N15 (a dirt road). Continue on Camuesa Road for five miles to the old Juncal Campground (closed). Turn left (still on Forest Road 5N15) and drive seven miles to the parking area for Mono Hike-In. Park and hike to the campground.

Contact: Los Padres National Forest, Santa Barbara Ranger District, 805/967-3481, fax 805/967-7312.

58 P-BAR FLAT

Rating: 7

On the Santa Ynez River in Los Padres National Forest.

Map 13.4, page 675

The best thing or the worst thing, depending on how you look at it, about P-Bar Flat is a trailhead that is routed north into the remote wildlands of Los Padres National Forest. The

camp is very small and primitive, set at 1,800 feet along the Santa Ynez River. The trail starts by heading up Horse Canyon along a creek, but eventually is routed 10 miles to Hildreth Peak, elevation 8,066 feet, a 6,000-foot buttkicker of a climb. A lot of guys in prison get less punishment.

Campsites, facilities: There are four tent sites. Picnic tables and fire grills are provided. Vault toilets are available. No drinking water is available. Garbage must be packed out. Leashed pets are permitted.

Reservations, fees: No reservations are accepted and there is no camping fee. An Adventure Pass ($30 annual fee or $5 daily pass) per parked vehicle is required. Senior discount available. Open year-round, weather permitting.

Directions: From U.S. 101 in Santa Barbara, take Highway 154 and drive northeast for eight miles to East Camino Cielo/Forest Road 5N12. Turn right on East Camino Cielo/Forest Road 5N12 and drive 18 miles to the end of the paved road at Camuesa Road/Forest Road 5N15 (a dirt road). Continue on Camuesa Road for five miles to the old Juncal Campground (closed). Turn left (still on Forest Road 5N15) and drive four miles to the campground.

Contact: Los Padres National Forest, Santa Barbara Ranger District, 805/967-3481, fax 805/967-7312.

59 MIDDLE SANTA YNEZ

Rating: 7

On the Santa Ynez River in Los Padres National Forest.

Map 13.4, page 675

There are four camps bordering the Santa Ynez River between Gibraltar Reservoir to the west and little Jameson Lake to the east. Look them over and pick the one you like best. This one is set at an elevation of 1,500 feet, about a half mile east of P-Bar Flat (see the P-Bar Flat entry for a trailhead there).

Campsites, facilities: There are nine tent sites. Picnic tables and fire grills are provided. Vault toilets are available. No drinking water is available. Garbage must be packed out. Leashed pets are permitted.

Reservations, fees: No reservations are accepted and there is no camping fee. An Adventure Pass ($30 annual fee or $5 daily pass) per parked vehicle is required. Senior discount available. Open year-round, weather permitting.

Directions: From U.S. 101 in Santa Barbara, take Highway 154 and drive northeast for eight miles to East Camino Cielo/Forest Road 5N12. Turn right on East Camino Cielo/Forest Road 5N12 and drive 18 miles to the end of the paved road at Camuesa Road/Forest Road 5N15 (a dirt road). Continue on Camuesa Road for five miles to the old Juncal Campground (closed). Turn left (still on Forest Road 5N15) and drive three miles to the campground.

Contact: Los Padres National Forest, Santa Barbara Ranger District, 805/967-3481, fax 805/967-7312.

60 HOLIDAY GROUP CAMP

Rating: 7

On Matilija Creek in Los Padres National Forest.

Map 13.4, page 675

This group site, set at 2,000 feet, is near the North Fork of the Matilija. It's only three miles uphill from Matilija Reservoir.

Campsites, facilities: There are eight sites for tents or RVs up to 22 feet long. Picnic tables and fire grills are provided. Drinking water and vault toilets are available. Leashed pets are permitted.

Reservations, fees: Reservations are required. Reserve at 877/444-6777 ($9 reservation fee) or website: www. reserveusa.com; $50 group fee per night. Open year-round.

Directions: From Ojai, drive northwest on Highway 33 for nine miles to the campground entrance on the right.

Contact: Los Padres National Forest, Ojai Ranger District, 805/646-4348, fax 805/646-0484.

61 WHEELER GORGE

Rating: 7

On Matilija Creek in Los Padres National Forest.

Map 13.4, page 675

This developed Forest Service camp is set at 2,000 feet and is one of the more popular spots in the area. The North Fork of the Matilija runs beside the camp and provides some fair trout fishing in the spring and good swimming holes in early summer. A camp host is on-site in summer. Interpretive programs are also available, a nice plus, and a nature trail is adjacent to the campground.

Campsites, facilities: There are 73 sites for tents or RVs up to 16 feet long. Picnic tables and fire grills are provided. Drinking water and pit toilets are available. Garbage must be packed out. Leashed pets are permitted. Some facilities are wheelchair-accessible.

Reservations, fees: Reserve at 877/444-6777 ($9 reservation fee) or website: www.Reserve Usa.com; $12–15 per night. Senior discount available. Open year-round.

Directions: From Ojai, drive northwest on Highway 33 for 8.5 miles to the campground entrance on the right.

Contact: Los Padres National Forest, Ojai Ranger District, 805/646-4348, fax 805/646-0484.

62 OZENA

Rating: 7

In Los Padres National Forest.

Map 13.4, page 675

This camp is set at 3,660 feet, about a mile from Reyes Creek and about 3.5 miles from Reyes Creek campground, the premium campground in this area. This camp gets light use and is known primarily by the locals. A Forest Service map is recommended.

Campsites, facilities: There are 10 sites for tents or RVs up to 22 feet long. Picnic tables and fire grills are provided. Vault toilets are available. No drinking water is available. Garbage must be packed out. You can buy groceries and propane gas about 30 minutes away in Ojai or Frazier Park. Leashed pets are permitted.

Reservations, fees: No reservations are accepted and there is no camping fee. An Adventure Pass ($30 annual fee or $5 daily pass) per parked vehicle is required. Senior discount available. Open year-round.

Directions: From Ojai, drive north on Highway 33 for 36 miles to Lockwood Valley Road. Turn right on Lockwood Valley Road and drive 1.5 miles to the campground on the right.

Contact: Los Padres National Forest, Mt. Piños Ranger District, 661/245-3731, fax 661/245-1526. For a map, send $6 to U.S. Forest Service, Attn: Map Sales, P.O. Box 9035, Prescott, AZ 86313, 928/443-8285 with credit card, website: www.fs.fed.us/maps/.

63 REYES CREEK

Rating: 7

In Los Padres National Forest.

Map 13.4, page 675

This developed Forest Service camp sits at the end of an old spur, Forest Road 7N11. The camp is set at 3,960 feet along Reyes Creek, which is stocked with trout in early summer. A trail is routed out of camp to the south and climbs three miles to Upper Reyes backpack camp, and beyond, up a ridge and down to Beartrap Creek and several trail camps along that creek.

Campsites, facilities: There are 24 sites for tents and six sites for tents or RVs up to 22 feet long. Picnic tables and fire grills are provided. Pit toilets and a corral are available. No drinking

water is available. Garbage must be packed out. A small store, bar, and café are nearby. Leashed pets are permitted.

Reservations, fees: No reservations are accepted and there is no camping fee. An Adventure Pass ($30 annual fee or $5 daily pass) per parked vehicle is required. Senior discount available. Open year-round.

Directions: From Ojai, drive north on Highway 33 for 36 miles to Lockwood Valley Road. Turn right on Lockwood Valley Road (Ozena Road) and drive about 3.5 miles to Forest Road 7N11. Turn right and drive about 1.5 miles to the village of Camp Scheideck to a T intersection. Bear left at the T intersection and drive one-quarter mile to the campground.

Contact: Los Padres National Forest, Mt. Piños Ranger District, 661/245-3731, fax 661/245-1526.

64 PINE MOUNTAIN

Rating: 6

In Los Padres National Forest.

Map 13.4, page 675

Pine Mountain, along with nearby Reyes Peak campground (a quarter mile to the east), is a tiny, primitive campground in a pretty setting with a few trailheads close at hand. The two best nearby hikes lead to springs. A trail is routed out of camp and into Boulder Canyon for a mile down the mountain, where it meets another trail that turns left and heads a quarter mile to McGuire Spring Trail camp (piped spring water is available there). It's advisable to obtain a Forest Service map. The elevation is 6,700 feet.

Campsites, facilities: There are six tent sites. Picnic tables and fire grills are provided. Pit toilets are available. No drinking water is available. Garbage must be packed out. Leashed pets are permitted.

Reservations, fees: No reservations are accepted and there is no camping fee. An Adventure Pass ($30 annual fee or $5 daily pass) per parked vehicle is required. Senior discount available. Open April through November, weather permitting (closed after first winter snow).

Directions: From Ojai, drive north on Highway 33 for 33 miles to Reyes Peak Road. Turn right on Reyes Peak Road and drive 2.5 miles to the campground on the left.

Contact: Los Padres National Forest, Ojai Ranger District, 805/646-4348, fax 805/646-0484.

65 REYES PEAK

Rating: 6

In Los Padres National Forest.
Map 13.4, page 675

Reyes Peak is a primitive camp set at 6,800 feet. Three short hikes in the immediate vicinity lead to trail camps. The closest is from a trailhead just to the west of camp, which provides an easy, half-mile hike north to Raspberry Spring (a backcountry camp is available there). Nearby Pine Mountain Campground provides an alternative.

Campsites, facilities: There are seven tent sites. Picnic tables and fire grills are provided. Vault toilets are available. No drinking water is available. Garbage must be packed out. Leashed pets are permitted.

Reservations, fees: No reservations are accepted and there is no camping fee. An Adventure Pass ($30 annual fee or $5 daily pass) per parked vehicle is required. Senior discount available. Open April through October.

Directions: From Ojai, drive north on Highway 33 for 33 miles to Reyes Peak Road. Turn right on Reyes Peak Road and drive five miles to the campground.

Contact: Los Padres National Forest, Ojai Ranger District, 805/646-4348, fax 805/646-0484.

66 ROSE VALLEY

Rating: 8

In Los Padres National Forest.
Map 13.4, page 675

The short walk to Rose Valley Falls, a 300-foot waterfall that provides a happy surprise, makes this camp a sure-thing winner in late winter and spring. The walk to the waterfall is just a half-mile round-trip; note that there are two views of it, a long-distance view of the entire waterfall, and then at the base, a view of just the lower tier. It is one of the scenic highlights in this section of Los Padres National Forest. The camp is set at 3,400 feet next to Rose Valley Creek, about two miles from Sespe Creek.

Campsites, facilities: There are nine sites for tents or RVs up to 16 feet long. Picnic tables and fire grills are provided. Drinking water and vault toilets are available. Horseback riding facilities are available nearby. Garbage must be packed out. Some facilities are wheelchair-accessible. Leashed pets are permitted.

Reservations, fees: No reservations are accepted and there is no camping fee. An Adventure Pass ($30 annual fee or $5 daily pass) per parked vehicle is required. Senior discount available. Open year-round, weather permitting.

Directions: From Ojai, drive north on Highway 33 for 15 miles to Sespe River Road/Rose Valley Road. Turn right on Sespe River Road/Rose Valley Road and drive 5.5 miles to the campground entrance.

Contact: Los Padres National Forest, Ojai Ranger District, 805/646-4348, fax 805/646-0484.

67 THORN MEADOWS

Rating: 7

On Piru Creek in Los Padres National Forest.
Map 13.4, page 675

The reward at Thorn Meadows is a small, quiet

spot along Piru Creek at 5,000 feet, deep in Los Padres National Forest. A trail out of camp leads three miles up to Thorn Point, a magnificent 6,935-foot lookout. It is by far the best view in the area, worth the 2,000-foot climb, and on a clear day you can see the Channel Islands.

Campsites, facilities: There are five sites for tents or RVs up to 16 feet long. Picnic tables and fire grills are provided. Pit toilets and a corral are available. No drinking water is available. Garbage must be packed out. Leashed pets are permitted.

Reservations, fees: No reservations are accepted and there is no camping fee. An Adventure Pass ($30 annual fee or $5 daily fee) per parked vehicle is required. Senior discount available. Open May through October.

Directions: Drive on I-5 to just south of Lebec and the Frazier Park exit. Take that exit and drive west on Frazier Mountain Road to the town of Lake of the Woods and Lockwood Valley Road. Turn left on Lockwood Valley Road and drive about 12 miles to Mutau Flat Road (Forest Road 7N03). Turn left and drive seven miles to Forest Road 7N03B. Turn right and drive one mile to the campground.

Contact: Los Padres National Forest, Mt. Piños Ranger District, 661/245-3731, fax 661/245-1526.

68 SANTA BARBARA SUNRISE RV PARK

Rating: 3

In Santa Barbara.
Map 13.4, page 675

Motor-home cruisers get a little of two worlds here. For one thing, the park is close to the beach; for another, the downtown shopping area isn't too far away, either. This is the only RV park in Santa Barbara.

Campsites, facilities: There are 33 sites, three drive-through, with full hookups and patios for RVs, and two tent sites. Restrooms, show-

ers, cable TV, and laundry facilities are available. A grocery store, golf course, tennis courts, and propane gas are nearby. Leashed pets are permitted.

Reservations, fees: Reservations are recommended. The fee is $35 per night and up (depending on size), $5 per night for each extra vehicle, $5 per night. Major credit cards accepted. Open year-round.

Directions: In Santa Barbara on U.S. 101 northbound, drive to the Salinas Street exit. Take that exit and drive to the park (well signed) to 516 S. Salinas Street.

In Santa Barbara on U.S. 101 southbound, drive to the Milpas Street exit. Take that exit and drive to the junction with Salinas Street (signed with blue camper signs).

Contact: Santa Barbara Sunrise RV Park, 805/966-9954, 800/345-5018, fax 805/966-7950.

69 CARPINTERIA STATE BEACH

Rating: 8

Near Santa Barbara.
Map 13.4, page 675

First, plan on reservations, and then, plan on plenty of neighbors. This state beach is one pretty spot, and a lot of folks cruising up the coast like the idea of taking off their cowboy boots here for awhile. This is an urban park; that is, it is within walking distance of downtown, restaurants, and shopping. You can love it or hate it, but this camp is almost always full. It features one mile of beach. Harbor seals can be seen December through May, along with an occasional passing gray whale. Tidepools here are protected and contain starfish, sea anemones, crabs, snails, octopus, and sea urchins. In the summer, the visitor center features a living tidepool exhibit. Other state beaches to the nearby north are El Capitan State Beach and Refugio State Beach, both with campgrounds.

Campsites, facilities: There are 82 sites for tents, 60 sites with full or partial hookups for

RVs up to 21 feet long, 119 sites for tents or RVs up to 30 feet long, one hike-in/bike-in site, two group sites for a maximum of 40 and 65 campers. Picnic tables and fire grills are provided. Restrooms, drinking water, flush toilets, and coin-operated showers are available. A convenience store, coin laundry, restaurants, and propane gas are nearby in the town of Carpinteria. Some facilities are wheelchair-accessible. Leashed pets are permitted, except on the beach.

Reservations, fees: Reserve at 800/444-PARK (800/444-7275) or website: www.Reserve America.com ($7.50 reservation fee); $12–18 per night, $1 per person per night for hike-in/bike-in sites, $50 for group sites. Senior discount available. Open year-round.

Directions: From Santa Barbara, drive south on U.S. 101 for 12 miles to the Casitas Pass exit. Take that exit and turn right on Casitas Pass Road and drive about a block to Carpinteria Avenue. Turn right and drive a short distance to Palm Avenue. Turn left and drive about six blocks to the campground at the end of Palm Avenue.

Contact: Carpinteria State Beach, 805/684-2811; Channel Coast District, 805/889-1400.

70 LAKE CASITAS RECREATION AREA

Rating: 7

North of Ventura.

Map 13.4, page 675

Lake Casitas is known as one of Southern California's world-class fish factories, with more 10-pound bass produced here than anywhere, and including the former state record, a bass that weighed 21 pounds, three ounces. The ideal climate in the foothill country gives the fish a nine-month growing season and provides excellent weather for camping. Casitas is north of Ventura at an elevation of 550 feet in the foothills bordering Los Padres National Forest. The lake has 32 miles of shoreline with a huge number

of sheltered coves, covering 2,700 acres. The lake is managed primarily for anglers. Waterskiing, personal watercraft, and swimming are not permitted, and only boats between 11 and 24 feet are allowed on the lake.

Campsites, facilities: There are 400 sites, 150 with partial hookups and 14 with full hookups, for RVs up to 50 feet long and tents. Picnic tables and fire grills are provided. Restrooms, drinking water, flush toilets, showers, two RV dump stations, seven playgrounds, grocery store, propane, ice, snack bar, water playground for children 12 and under, and a full-service marina (including boat ramps, boat rentals, slips, fuel, tackle, and bait) are available. Some facilities are wheelchair-accessible. Leashed pets are permitted.

Reservations, fees: Reservations are advised 14 days in advance and must be made 72 hours in advance at 805/649-1122; $24–42 per night for RVs, $16–18 for tents, $10 per night for each extra vehicle, $2 per night. Major credit cards accepted. Open year-round.

Directions: From Ventura, drive north on Highway 33 for 11 miles to Highway 150. Turn west on Highway 150 and drive about four miles to the campground entrance at 11311 Santa Ana Road.

Contact: Lake Casitas Recreation Area, 805/649-2233, fax 805/649-4661, website: www.casitas water.org.

71 CAMP COMFORT PARK

Rating: 2

On San Antonio Creek.

Map 13.4, page 675

This park gets missed by many. It's set in a residential area in the foothill country at 1,000 feet along San Antonio Creek in the Ojai Valley. Lake Casitas Recreation Area is 10 miles away.

Campsites, facilities: There are 43 sites for tents or RVs up to 34 feet long. Picnic tables and fire grills are provided. Restrooms, drinking water, flush toilets, showers, and a playground are available. Supplies and a coin laundry are nearby. Leashed pets are permitted.

Reservations, fees: Reservations are accepted. The fee is $16–22 per night, $1 pet fee. Open year-round, weather permitting.

Directions: From Ventura, take Highway 33 north to Highway 150. Turn west on Highway 150 and drive three miles to Creek Road. Turn right and drive one mile to the park.

Contact: Camp Comfort Park, 805/654-3951.

72 FAR WEST RESORT

Rating: 7

On Santa Paula Creek.

Map 13.4, page 675

Far West Resort is set near little Santa Paula Creek in the foothill country adjacent to Steckel County Park. For those who want a well-developed park with a lot of amenities, the shoe fits. Note that at one time the two campgrounds, Far West Resort and Steckel County Park, were linked. No more, and for good reason. Far West Resort is a tight ship where the gates close at 10 P.M. and quiet time assures campers of a good night's sleep. It is a good place to bring a family. Steckel County Park, on the other hand, has a campground with so many problems that we removed it from the book. Steckel is a beautiful place gone bad, crime-ridden and scary for most visitors, with wild partying, fights, and screaming. Clearly the rangers at Steckel have let down the public. So what do you do? Go next door to Far West where the inmates aren't running the asylum, and the days are fun and nights are peaceful.

Campsites, facilities: There are 72 sites, 15 with full hookups, the rest with partial hookups, for RVs or tents, three group sites for RVs, and a group tent site for up to 400 people. Picnic tables and fire grills are provided. Restrooms, drinking water, flush toilets, coin laundry, modem access, RV dump station, clubhouse, and horseshoes are available. Supplies and a coin laundry are nearby. Leashed pets are permitted.

Reservations, fees: Reservations are recommended. Fees are $15–22 per night, $1 per person per night for more than four people, $1 per night, group sites $3 per person per night. Major credit cards accepted. Open year-round for RVs and group tent site; individual tent sites closed in winter.

Directions: From Ventura, drive east on Highway 126 for 14 miles to Highway 150. Turn northwest on Highway 150 and drive four miles to the resort entrance on right.

Contact: Far West Resort, 805/933-3200, website: www.farwestresort.com.

73 VENTURA RIVER GROUP CAMP

Rating: 1

At Emma Wood State Beach near Ventura.

Map 13.4, page 675

This is an extremely noisy area and the campsites are also downright ugly. It is set near the freeway and railroad tracks, and you get a lot of noise from both. It's not popular either. What you have here is mainly a dry riverbed. It is saved somewhat by a freshwater marsh at the southwest end of the beach that attracts red-tailed hawks, songbirds, and raccoons.

Campsites, facilities: There are four group tent sites for up to 30 people each, one group RV site for up to 50 people, and five hike-in/bike-in sites. Picnic tables and fire rings are provided. Drinking water, chemical toilets, and cold showers are available. Leashed pets are permitted. Facilities are within one mile.

Reservations, fees: Reserve at 800/444-PARK (800/444-7275) or website: www.ReserveAmerica.com ($7.50 reservation fee); $22–62 per night, $1 per person per night for hike-in/bike-in sites. Open year-round.

Directions: On U.S. 101 in Ventura, take the Main Street exit and turn west. Drive one mile on Main Street to the campground on the left.

Contact: Ventura River Group Camp, 805/643-7532; Channel Coast State Park District, 805/899-1400.

74 EMMA WOOD STATE BEACH

Rating: 8

On the Pacific Ocean north of Ventura.

Map 13.4, page 675

This is more of a camping "area" than a campground with individual sites. And oh, what a place to camp: it is set along the ocean, a pretty spot with tidepools full of all kinds of little marine critters waiting to be discovered. It is also just a short drive from the town of Ventura and the Mission San Buenaventura. One downer, a big one for many: noise from passing trains.

Campsites, facilities: There are 94 primitive sites for tents and self-contained RVs. Chemical toilets are available. No drinking water is available. Supplies and a coin laundry are three miles away. Leashed pets are permitted.

Reservations, fees: Reservations are not accepted. The fee is $7 fee per night. Senior discount available. Open year-round.

Directions: From Ventura drive north on U.S. 101 for three miles to the State Beaches exit. Take that exit, drive under the freeway, and continue less than a mile to the park entrance on the left.

Contact: Emma Wood State Beach Group Camp, 805/648-4807; Channel Coast State Park District, 805/899-1400.

75 FARIA COUNTY PARK

Rating: 7

On the Pacific Ocean north of Ventura.

Map 13.4, page 675

This county park provides a possible base of operations for beach adventures. It is set along the ocean, with Emma Wood State Beach, San Buenaventura State Beach, and McGrath State Beach all within 10 miles of the park.

Campsites, facilities: There are 42 sites for tents or RVs up to 34 feet long. Picnic tables and fire grills are provided. Restrooms, drinking water, flush toilets, coin-operated showers, playground, and a snack bar are available. Pets are permitted.

Reservations, fees: Reservations are accepted. The fee is $22–35 per night, $1 per night. Open year-round.

Directions: From Ventura, drive north on U.S. 101 for three miles to the State Beaches exit. Take that exit and turn north on West Pacific Highway and drive four miles to the campground.

Contact: Ventura County Parks Department, 805/654-3951; website: www.ventura.org/gsa/c-srv.htm.

76 RINCON PARKWAY

Rating: 5

On the Pacific Ocean north of Ventura.

Map 13.4, page 675

This is basically an RV park near the ocean, where the sites are parking end-to-end along old Highway 1. It is not quiet. Passing trains across the highway vie for noise honors with the surf. Emma Wood State Beach, San Buenaventura State Beach, and McGrath State Beach are all within 10 miles.

Campsites, facilities: There are 127 RV sites for self-contained vehicles up to 34 feet long. An RV dump station and supplies are available nearby. Leashed pets are allowed, but not on the beach.

Reservations, fees: Reservations are not accepted. The fee is $18 per night, $3 per night for extra vehicle, $1 per night. Open year-round.

Directions: From Ventura, drive northwest on U.S. 101 for three miles to the State Beaches exit. Take that exit and turn north on West Pacific Highway and drive 4.5 miles to the campground on the left.

Contact: Ventura County Parks Department, 805/654-3951; website: www.ventura.org/gsa/c-srv.htm.

77 HOBSON COUNTY PARK

Rating: 6

On the Pacific Ocean north of Ventura.

Map 13.4, page 675

This county park is at the end of Rincon Parkway, kind of like a crowded cul-de-sac, with easy access to the beach and many side-trip possibilities. Emma Wood State Beach, San Buenaventura State Beach, and Mc-Grath State Beach are all within 11 miles of the park.

Campsites, facilities: There are 31 sites for tents or RVs up to 34 feet long. Picnic tables and fire grills are provided. Restrooms, drinking water, flush toilets, coin-operated showers, and a snack bar are available. Leashed pets are permitted, but not on the beach.

Reservations, fees: Reservations are accepted. The fee is $22–30 per night, $3 per night for extra vehicle, $1 per night. Open year-round.

Directions: From Ventura, drive northwest on U.S. 101 for three miles to the State Beaches exit. Take that exit and turn north on West Pacific Highway and drive five miles to the campground on the left.

Contact: Ventura County Parks Department, 805/654-3951; website: www.ventura.org/gsa/c-srv.htm.

78 MCGRATH STATE BEACH

Rating: 9

On the Pacific Ocean south of Ventura.

Map 13.4, page 675

This is a pretty spot just south of Ventura Harbor. Campsites are about 200 yards from the beach. This park features two miles of beach frontage, as well as lush riverbanks and sand dunes along the ocean shore. That gives rise to some of the best bird-watching in California. The north tip of the park borders the Santa Clara River Estuary Natural Preserve, where the McGrath State Beach Nature Trail provides an easy walk (wheelchair-accessible) along the Santa Clara River as it feeds into the estuary and then into the ocean. Rangers caution all considering swimming here to beware of strong currents and rip tides; they can be deadly. Ventura Harbor and the Channel Islands National Park Visitor Center are nearby side trips.

Campsites, facilities: There are 174 sites for tents or RVs up to 34 feet long (29 of the sites can be used as group sites), and a hike-in/bike-in site. Picnic tables and fire grills are provided. Restrooms, drinking water, flush toilets, coin-operated showers, RV dump station, and horseshoes are available. A lifeguard service is provided in summer. Supplies and a coin laundry are nearby. Some facilities are wheelchair-accessible. Leashed pets are permitted in campsites only.

Reservations, fees: Reserve at 800/444-PARK (800/444-7275) or website: www.Reserve America.com ($7.50 reservation fee); $12 per night, $1 per person for hike-in/bike-in sites. Senior discount available. Open year-round.

Directions: Drive on U.S. 101 to south of Ventura and the Seaward exit. Take that exit and turn west on Seaward Avenue and drive one mile to Harbor Boulevard. Bear left on Harbor and drive four miles to the park (signed).

Contact: McGrath State Beach, 805/654-4744 or 805/648-4127; Channel Coast State Park District, 805/899-1400.

79 MOUNTAIN VIEW RV PARK

Rating: 3

In Santa Paula.

Map 13.4, page 675

The town of Santa Paula is known for its excellent weather and nearby recreation options, including Los Padres National Forest and the beaches at Ventura. Lake Casitas and Lake Cachuma, both known for big Florida bass, are within reasonable driving range.

Campsites, facilities: There are 31 sites, 20 drive-through, with full hookups including cable TV for RVs. A swim spa (a giant hot tub, like a small swimming pool) is available. No showers. A coin laundry, restaurant, and shopping center are nearby. Leashed pets are permitted.

Reservations, fees: Reservations are required. The fee is $23–25 per night. Open year-round.

Directions: From Ventura, drive east on Highway 126 for 11 miles to Peck Drive exit. Take that exit and drive a short distance to Harvard Boulevard. Turn right and drive to the park at 714 West Harvard Boulevard.

Contact: Mountain View RV Park, 805/933-1942.

80 SANTA CRUZ ISLAND BOAT-IN
🚶 ≋ 🛶 5% ⛰

Rating: 10

In the Channel Islands.

Map 13.4, page 675

This is the largest of the Channel Islands, perfect for camping and multiday visits. It covers 96 square miles, features a 2,450-foot mountain (Devil's Peak), and boasts an incredible array of flora and fauna, sheltered canyons, and sweeping ocean views. The camp is set in a eucalyptus grove in a valley, with trailheads near camp that hikers can take to the surrounding ridgeline. A great hike is from Pelican Bay to Prisoner's Harbor, a three-miler that is routed through the interior of the island to a beautiful beach. Kayaking through sea caves is outstanding.

Campsites, facilities: There are 40 primitive campsites. Picnic tables and fire rings are provided. Pit toilets are available. No drinking water is available. Garbage must be packed out. No pets are permitted.

Reservations, fees: Reserve by calling Island Packers at 805/642-1393 or Truth Aquatics at Sea Landing in Santa Barbara at 805/963-3564. After arranging transportation, you must obtain a camping reservation at 800/365-CAMP (800/365-2267) or website: reservations.nps.gov, $10 camping fee; round-trip boat transportation, $54 for adult campers, $25 for child campers. Open year-round, weather permitting.

Directions: Drive on U.S. 101 to south of Ventura and the Seaward exit. Take that exit and turn west on Seaward Avenue and drive one mile to Harbor Boulevard. Bear left on Harbor and drive about two miles to Spinnaker Drive. Turn right and drive a short distance to the harbor. The boat ride is about 1.5 hours each way.

Contact: Channel Islands National Park Visitor Information Line, 805/658-5730.

81 ANACAPA ISLAND BOAT-IN AND HIKE-IN
🚶 ≋ 🛶 5% ⛰

Rating: 10

In Channel Islands National Park.

Map 13.4, page 675

Little Anacapa, long and narrow, is known for its awesome caves, cliffs, and sea lion rookeries that range near huge kelp beds. After landing on the island, you face a 154-step staircase trail that leaves you perched on an ocean bluff. From there, it is a half mile hike to the camp. Other trails venture past Inspiration Point and Cathedral Cove and provide vast views of the channel. The inshore waters are an ecological preserve loaded with marine life and seabirds and, with the remarkably clear water, this island makes a great destination for snorkeling and sea kayaking. Of the Channel Islands, the boat ride here is the shortest, only 75 minutes.

Campsites, facilities: There are seven primitive tent sites. Picnic tables are provided. Pit toilets are available. No drinking water is available. Garbage must be packed out. No open fires are allowed; bring a camp stove for cooking. No pets are permitted.

Reservations, fees: Reserve by calling Island Packers at 805/642-1393 or Truth Aquatics at Sea Landing in Santa Barbara at 805/963-3564. After arranging transportation, you must obtain a camping reservation at 800/365-CAMP (800/365-2267) or website: reservations.nps.gov, $10 camping fee. Round-trip boat transportation $48 for adult campers,

$20 for children campers. Open year-round, weather permitting.

Directions: Drive on U.S. 101 to south of Ventura and the Seaward exit. Take that exit and turn west on Seaward Avenue and drive one mile to Harbor Boulevard. Bear left on Harbor and drive about two miles to Spinnaker Drive. Turn right and drive a short distance to the harbor. The boat ride is about 75 minutes each way.

Contact: Channel Islands National Park Visitor Information Line, 805/658-5730.

82 POINT MUGU STATE PARK/THORNHILL BROOME AND LA JOLLA GROUP WALK-IN

🚶 🏊 🛶 🎣 ♿ 🚐 ⛺

Rating: 7

In Point Mugu State Park.

Map 13.4, page 675

Point Mugu State Park is known for its rocky bluffs, sandy beaches, rugged hills, and uplands. There are two major river canyons and wide grassy valleys sprinkled with sycamores, oaks, and a few native walnut trees. Of the campgrounds at Point Mugu, Thornehill Broome Campground is more attractive than Big Sycamore (see listing) for many visitors because it is on the ocean side of the highway (Big Sycamore is on the east side of the highway). While the beachfront is pretty and you can always just lie there in the sun and pretend you're a beached whale, the park's expanse on the east side of the highway in the Santa Monica Mountains provides more recreation. That includes two stellar hikes, the 9.5-mile Big Sycamore Canyon Loop and the seven-mile La Jolla Valley Loop. In all, the park covers 14,980 acres, far more than the obvious strip of beachfront. The park has more than 70 miles of hiking trails and five miles of ocean shoreline. Swimming, body surfing, and surf fishing are available on the beach.

Campsites, facilities: There are 60 primitive sites for tents or RVs up to 31 feet long, and one group site at La Jolla Group Walk-In for up to 50 people. Picnic tables and fire rings are provided. Drinking water and chemical toilets are available. Supplies can be obtained nearby. Some facilities are wheelchair-accessible. Leashed pets are permitted. Note that nearby Big Sycamore has a restroom with flush toilets and coin showers, RV dump station, and nature center.

Reservations, fees: Reserve at 800/444-PARK (800/444-7275) or website: www.Reserve America.com ($7.50 reservation fee); $7–12 per night, $37 per night for group site. Senior discount available. Open year-round.

Directions: From Oxnard, drive 15 miles south on Highway 1 to the camp entrance; on the right for Thornhill Broome, on the left for La Jolla Group.

Contact: Thornhill Broome State Beach, 818/880-0350, fax 818/880-6165.

83 POINT MUGU STATE PARK/BIG SYCAMORE CANYON

🚶 🚴 🏊 🛶 🎣 ♿ 🚐 ⛺

Rating: 6

In Point Mugu State Park.

Map 13.4, page 675

While this camp is across the highway from the ocean, it is also part of Point Mugu State Park, which covers 14,980 acres. That gives you plenty of options. One of the best is taking the Big Sycamore Canyon Loop, a long hiking route with great views that starts right at the camp. In all, it's a 9.5-mile loop that climbs to a ridge top and offers beautiful views of nearby canyons and long-distance vistas of the coast. Note: front gate closes at 10 P.M. and reopens at 8 A.M.

Campsites, facilities: There are 55 sites for tents or RVs up to 31 feet long (up to eight campers per site), and one hike-in/bike-in site. Picnic tables and fire grills are provided. Restrooms, drinking water, flush toilets, coin showers, and RV dump station are available. A nature center is within walking distance. Supplies can be obtained nearby. Some facilities are wheelchair-accessible. Leashed pets are permitted at campsites.

Reservations, fees: Reserve at 800/444-PARK (800/444-7275) or website: www.Reserve America.com ($7.50 reservation fee); $12 per night, $1 per person per night for hike-in/bike-in site. Senior discount available. Open year-round.

Directions: From Oxnard, drive south on Highway 1 for 16 miles to the camp on the left.

Contact: Big Sycamore Canyon, 818/880-0350, fax 818/880-6165.

84 TWIN PINES AND DUTCHMAN

Rating: 6

On Alamo Mountain in Los Padres National Forest.

Map 13.5, page 676

Twin Pines Camp is set at 6,600 feet on Alamo Mountain, a small, remote, and primitive spot—no picnic tables, no toilets, no drinking water. Dutchman Campground is nearby at 6,800 feet. These spots are best known by four-wheel-drive cowboys rumbling around the area. The big attraction here is access to the Miller Jeep Trail, a gnarly black-diamond route that can bend metal and alter minds. This camp also provides an alternative to the Hungry Valley State Vehicular Recreation Area to the nearby northeast.

Campsites, facilities: There are five tent sites at Twin Pines and eight primitive sites at Dutchman. Picnic tables and fire grills are provided. Pit toilets are available. No drinking water is available. Garbage must be packed out. Leashed pets are permitted.

Reservations, fees: No reservations are accepted and there is no camping fee. An Adventure Pass ($30 annual fee or $5 daily fee) per parked vehicle is required. Senior discount available. Open May through October.

Directions: Drive on I-5 to south of Gorman and the Gorman-Hungry Valley Road exit (the northern exit for the Hungry Valley Recreation Area). Take that exit and turn south on Hun-

gry Valley Road (Forest Road 8N01) and drive six miles to Gold Hill Road (Forest Road 8N01). Turn right and drive 13 miles to Twin Pines campground. To reach Dutchman, at Twin Pines campground, turn right at Forest Road 7N01 and drive three miles to the campground.

Contact: Los Padres National Forest, Mt. Piños Ranger District, 661/245-3731, fax 661/245-1526.

85 KINGS

Rating: 5

Near Piru Creek in Los Padres National Forest.

Map 13.5, page 676

The Hungry Valley State Vehicular Recreation Area is just five miles to the east. Figure it out: right, this is a primitive but well-placed camp for four-wheel-drive and off-highway vehicles. The camp is near Piru Creek, off a short spur road, so it feels remote yet is close to one of California's top off-road areas.

Campsites, facilities: There are seven sites for tents or RVs up to 16 feet long. Picnic tables and fire grills are provided. Vault toilets are available. No drinking water is available. Garbage must be packed out. Leashed pets are permitted.

Reservations, fees: No reservations are accepted and there is no camping fee. An Adventure Pass ($30 annual fee or $5 daily fee) per parked vehicle is required. Senior discount available. Open year-round.

Directions: Drive on I-5 to south of Gorman and the Gorman-Hungry Valley Road exit (the northern exit for the Hungry Valley Recreation Area). Take that exit and turn south on Hungry Valley Road (Forest Road 8N01) and drive six miles to Gold Hill Road (Forest Road 8N01). Turn right and drive six miles to Forest Road 18N01A. Turn left and drive three-quarters of a mile to the campground.

Contact: Los Padres National Forest, Mt. Piños Ranger District, 661/245-3731, fax 661/245-1526.

86 LOS ALAMOS

Rating: 4

Near Pyramid Lake in Angeles National Forest.

Map 13.5, page 676

Los Alamos is set at an elevation of 2,600 feet near the southern border of the Hungry Valley State Vehicular Recreation Area and about 2.5 miles north of Pyramid Lake. Pyramid Lake is a big lake, covering 1,300 acres with 20 miles of shoreline, and is extremely popular for water-skiing and fast boating, as well as for windsurfing (best at the northern launch point), fishing (best in the spring and early summer and in the fall for striped bass), and swimming (best at boat-in picnic sites).

Campsites, facilities: There are 93 family sites and several group sites for tents or RVs. Picnic tables and fire pits are provided. Drinking water and flush toilets are available. A boat ramp is at the Emigrant Landing Picnic Area. Leashed pets are permitted. Some facilities are wheelchair-accessible.

Reservations, fees: Reservations are not accepted. The fee is $12 per night. Group reservations required at 800/416-6992; $50 per night. Senior discount available. Open April through October.

Directions: Drive on I-5 to eight miles south of Gorman and the Smokey Bear Road exit. Take the Smokey Bear Road exit and drive west about three-quarters of a mile and follow the signs to the campground.

Contact: Angeles National Forest, Santa Clara/Mojave Rivers Ranger District, 661/296-9710, fax 661/296-5847.

87 SAWMILL

Rating: 7

On the Pacific Crest Trail in Angeles National Forest.

Map 13.5, page 676

This is a classic hiker's trailhead camp. It is set at 5,200 feet, right on the Pacific Crest Trail and just one mile from the junction with the Burnt Peak Canyon Trail. For a good day hike, head southeast on the Pacific Crest Trail for one mile to the Burnt Peak Canyon Trail, turn right (southwest), and hike just over a mile to Burnt Peak, elevation 5,788 feet. Note that this camp is inaccessible after the first snow. Nearby Upper Shake provides an alternative.

Campsites, facilities: There are eight sites for tents or RVs up to 16 feet long. Picnic tables and fire pits are provided. Vault toilets are available. No drinking water is available. Garbage must be packed out. Leashed pets are permitted.

Reservations, fees: No reservations are accepted and there is no camping fee. An Adventure Pass ($30 annual fee or $5 daily pass per parked vehicle) is required. Open May through October, weather permitting.

Directions: Drive on I-5 to the Tehachapis near the small town of Castaic and Lake Hughes Road. Turn northeast on Lake Hughes Road and drive 27 miles to the town of Lake Hughes and Pine Canyon Road/County Road N2. Turn left on Pine Canyon Road and drive 10 miles to Bushnell Summit Road. Turn left and drive two miles to the campground on the left.

Contact: Angeles National Forest, Santa Clara/Mojave Rivers Ranger District, 661/296-9710, fax 661/296-5847.

88 UPPER SHAKE

Rating: 7

Near the Pacific Crest Trail in Angeles National Forest.

Map 13.5, page 676

Upper Shake, like nearby Sawmill, is right on the Pacific Crest Trail. The elevation is 4,300 feet. Hikers who plan on heading to Burnt Peak are better off departing from Sawmill (less than two miles to the west). This camp is used primarily as a jump-off point for those heading east on the PCT; Lake Hughes is the nearest destination, less than four miles away, and a mile after that is Lake Elizabeth. The camp is inaccessible after the first snow.

Campsites, facilities: There are 18 sites for tents or RVs up to 22 feet long. Picnic tables and fire pits are provided. Vault toilets are available. No drinking water is available. Garbage must be packed out. Leashed pets are permitted.

Reservations, fees: No reservations are accepted and there is no camping fee. An Adventure Pass ($30 annual fee or $5 daily pass per parked vehicle) is required. Open May through October, weather permitting.

Directions: Drive on I-5 to the Tehachapis near the small town of Castaic and Lake Hughes Road. Turn northeast on Lake Hughes Road and drive 27 miles to the town of Lake Hughes and Pine Canyon Road/County Road N2. Turn left on Pine Canyon Road and drive about 5.5 miles to the entrance road on the left.

Contact: Angeles National Forest, Santa Clara/Mojave Rivers Ranger District, 661/296-9710, fax 661/296-5847.

89 COTTONWOOD

Rating: 5

Near the Warm Springs Mountain Lookout in Angeles National Forest.

Map 13.5, page 676

Cottonwood Camp is set at 2,680 feet in remote Angeles National Forest along a small stream. The camp is on the north flank of Warm Springs Mountain. A great side trip is to the Warm Springs Mountain Lookout (4,023 feet), about a five-mile drive. Drive south on Forest Road 7N09 for three miles, turn right (west) on Forest Road 6N32, and drive for 1.5 miles to Forest Road 7N13. Turn left (south) and drive a mile to the summit.

Campsites, facilities: There are 22 sites for tents or RVs up to 22 feet long. Picnic tables and fire pits are provided. Vault toilets are available. No drinking water is available. Supplies are available less than four miles away in the town of Lake Hughes. Leashed pets are permitted.

Reservations, fees: No reservations are accepted and there is no camping fee. An Adventure Pass ($30 annual fee or $5 daily pass per parked vehicle) is required. Open year-round.

Directions: Drive on I-5 to the Tehachapis near the small town of Castaic and Lake Hughes Road. Turn northeast on Lake Hughes Road and drive 25 miles to the campground on the right.

Contact: Angeles National Forest, Santa Clara/Mojave Rivers Ranger District, 661/296-9710, fax 661/296-5847.

90 HALF MOON

Rating: 7

Near Piru Creek in Los Padres National Forest.

Map 13.5, page 676

Half Moon is a primitive camp set along Piru Creek at 4,700 feet. Adjacent to camp, Forest Road 7N13 follows the creek for a few miles, then dead-ends at a trailhead that continues along more remote stretches of this little stream. Hikers should also consider the trail to nearby Thorn Point for a beautiful lookout (see the entry for Thorn Meadows for more information).

Campsites, facilities: There are 10 sites for tents or RVs up to 22 feet long. Picnic tables and fire grills are provided. Pit toilets are available. No drinking water is available. Garbage must be packed out. Leashed pets are permitted.

Reservations, fees: No reservations are accepted and there is no camping fee. An Adventure Pass ($30 annual fee or $5 daily fee) per parked vehicle is required. Senior discount available. Open May through October.

Directions: Drive on I-5 to just south of Lebec and the Frazier Park exit. Take that exit and drive west on Frazier Mountain Road to the town of Lake of the Woods and Lockwood Valley Road. Turn left on Lockwood Valley

Road and drive about 12 miles to Mutau Flat Road (Forest Road 7N03). Turn left and drive 11 miles to the campground on the left. Four-wheel-drive vehicles are recommended.

Contact: Los Padres National Forest, Mt. Piños Ranger District, 661/245-3731, fax 661/245-1526.

91 OAK FLAT

Rating: 3

Near Pyramid Lake in Angeles National Forest.

Map 13.5, page 676

Oak Flat is just a short drive from Pyramid Lake, at 2,800 feet near the southwestern border of Angeles National Forest. Pyramid is surrounded by national forest, quite beautiful, and is a favorite destination for folks with powerboats, especially those towing water-skiers. The lake covers 1,300 acres and has 20 miles of shoreline. Fishing for striped bass can be good in the spring and fall, but in summer warfare can practically break out between low-speed fishermen and high-speed skiers. (For more information on Pyramid Lake, see the entry for Los Alamos.)

Campsites, facilities: There are 27 sites for tents or RVs up to 32 feet long. Picnic tables and fire pits are provided. Vault toilets are available. No drinking water is available. Leashed pets are permitted.

Reservations, fees: No reservations are accepted and there is no camping fee. An Adventure Pass ($30 annual fee or $5 daily fee) per parked vehicle is required. Senior discount available. Open year-round.

Directions: Drive on I-5 to six miles north of Castaic to Templin Highway. Take Templin Highway west and drive three miles to the campground.

Contact: Angeles National Forest, Santa Clara/Mojave Rivers Ranger District, 661/296-9710, fax 661/296-5847.

92 KENNEY GROVE

Rating: 4

Near Fillmore.

Map 13.5, page 676

A lot of folks miss this spot, a park tucked away among orchards and eucalyptus groves. It's just far enough off the highway to allow for some privacy. Note that groups are given priority over family and individual campers.

Campsites, facilities: There are 33 sites with partial hookups for RVsand 19 sites for tents. Picnic tables and fire grills are provided. Drinking water, flush toilets, and a playground are available. Supplies and a coin laundry are nearby. Leashed pets are permitted.

Reservations, fees: Reservations are required. The fee is $15-20 per night, $2 for a second vehicle, $1 pet fee. Open year-round.

Directions: From Ventura, drive east on Highway 126 for 22 miles to Old Telegraph Road (before the town of Fillmore). Take the Old Telegraph Road exit and turn left and drive to 7th Street. Turn left and drive to Oak. Turn right on Oak and drive to the park on the left.

Contact: Kenney Grove, 805/524-0750.

93 LAKE PIRU RECREATION AREA

Rating: 7

On Lake Piru.

Map 13.5, page 676

Things can get crazy at Lake Piru, but it's usually a happy crazy, not an insane crazy. Lake Piru is shaped like a teardrop and covers 1,200 acres when full and is set at an elevation of 1,055 feet. This is a lake set up for water-skiing, with lots of fast boats. All others be forewarned: the rules prohibit boats under 12 feet or over 26 feet, as well as personal watercraft such as Jet Skis, Ski-Doos, and WaveRunners. Bass fishing can be quite good in the spring before the water-skiers take over. From Memorial Day Weekend through Labor Day Weekend, there is a designated swimming area, safe from the boats. The tent sites here consist of roughly 40-by-40 foot areas amid trees.

Campsites, facilities: There are 235 sites with electrical hookups for RVs or tents, five sites with full hookups for RVs, and two group camps. Fire pits and picnic tables are provided. Restrooms, drinking water, flush toilets, showers, RV dump station, snack bar, ice, bait, boat ramp, temporary mooring, boat fuel, motorboat rentals, and tackle are available. Some facilities are wheelchair-accessible. Leashed pets are permitted.

Reservations, fees: Reservations advised at least one week in advance (phone Monday through Thursday); $18–33, $2 per person for more than four people, $2 per night. Special conditions on holiday weekends. Reservations required for group camps; $214–318 per night. Major credit cards accepted. Open year-round.

Directions: From Ventura, drive east on Highway 126 for about 30 miles to the Piru Canyon Road exit. Take that exit and drive northeast on Piru Canyon Road for about six miles to the campground at the end of the road.

Contact: Lake Piru Recreation Area, 805/521-1500, website: www.lake-piru.org.

94 VALENCIA TRAVEL VILLAGE

Rating: 6

In Valencia.

Map 13.5, page 676

This huge RV park is in the scenic San Fernando foothills, just five minutes from Six Flags Magic Mountain. Lake Piru and Lake Castaic are only 15 minutes away. The camp was built on a 65-acre horse ranch. Some may remember that this park had a large tent camping area. In 2003, that was converted to add 66 new RV sites.

Campsites, facilities: There are 367 sites, most drive-through with full hookups for RVs. Fire pits are provided. A market and deli, two swimming pools, spa, lounge, video and games arcade, playground, shuffleboard, horseshoes, volleyball courts, laundry facilities, modem access, propane, and RV dump station are available. Some facilities are wheelchair-accessible.

Reservations, fees: Reservations are recommended at 888/LUV-TORV (888/588-8678); $37–47 per night, $2 per person per night for more than two people. Weekly and monthly rates are available. Major credit cards accepted. Open year-round.

Directions: Drive on I-5 to Santa Clarita and Highway 126/Henry Mayo Road. Take that exit and drive west on Highway 126 for one mile to the camp on the left.

Contact: Valencia Travel Village, 27946 Henry Mayo Rd. (Hwy. 126), Valencia, CA 91384, 661/257-3333, website: www.goodsam.com.

95 OAK PARK

Rating: 3

In Simi Valley near Moorpark.

Map 13.5, page 676

One of the frustrations of trying to find a camp for the night is that so many state and national park campgrounds are full from reservations, especially at the state beaches. The county parks often provide a safety valve, and Oak Park certainly applies. But not always, and that's the catch. This is an oft-overlooked county park set in the foothill country of Simi Valley. The park has many trails offering good hiking possibilities. The camp is somewhat secluded, more so than many expect. The catch? Sometimes the entire campground is rented to a single group. Note: gates close at dusk and reopen at 7 A.M.

Campsites, facilities: There are 16 sites with partial hookups for RVs, a group area for up to 22 RVs, and a large group tent area for up to 140 people. Picnic tables and fire grills are provided. Restrooms, drinking water, flush toilets, and RV dump station are available. Horseshoe pits, a playground, and basketball and volleyball courts are available nearby. Supplies and a coin laundry are within one mile. Leashed pets are permitted.

Reservations, fees: Reservations are accepted. The fee is $10 per night for tents, $12 per night with no hookups for RVs, $20 per night with partial hookups for RVs, $5 per person per night for more than two people, $1 per night. Open year-round, except Christmas Day.

Directions: From Ventura, drive south on U.S. 101 to Highway 23. Turn north on Highway 23 (which becomes Highway 118) and drive about three miles to the Collins Street exit. Continue straight through the intersection (it becomes Quismisa Drive) and drive 1.2 miles to the park entrance on the right.

Contact: Oak Park, 805/527-6886, website: www.ventura.org/gsa/parks.htm.

96 SANTA ROSA ISLAND BOAT-IN
🏃 🏊 🎣 5% ⛺

Rating:10

In Channel Islands National Park.
Map 13.6, page 677

Santa Rosa, the second-largest of the Channel Islands (the largest is Santa Cruz), is 10 miles wide and 15 miles long, and it holds many mysteries and adventures. A camping trip to Santa Rosa Island, available Friday through Sunday, will be an unforgettable experience even for those who think they've seen it all. The island is beautiful in the spring, when its grasslands turn emerald green and are sprinkled with wildflowers. There are many good hikes, the best the Cherry Canyon Trail into the island's interior with the likely chance of seeing wild goats, and the Lobo Canyon Trail descending to a Chumash village site and tidepools. Because the boat ride to Santa Rosa is approximately four hours, longer than the trip to Santa Cruz, this island often receives fewer visitors than its nearby neighbor, which makes it even more special. Bring plenty of fresh water and, because of the chance of fog and wind, warm clothes.

Campsites, facilities: There are 15 primitive tent sites. Picnic tables and windbreaks are provided. Pit toilets are available. No open fires are allowed; bring a camp stove for cooking. Garbage must be packed out. No pets are permitted.

Reservations, fees: Reserve by calling Island Packers at 805/642-1393 or Truth Aquatics at Sea Landing in Santa Barbara at 805/963-3564. After arranging transportation, you must obtain a camping reservation at 800/365-CAMP (800/365-2267) or website: reservations.nps.gov, $10 camping fee; round-trip boat transportation $80 for adult campers, $70 for children campers. Open year-round, weather permitting.

Directions: Drive on U.S. 101 to south of Ventura and the Seaward exit. Take that exit and turn west on Seaward Avenue and drive one mile to Harbor Boulevard. Bear left on Harbor and drive about two miles to Spinnaker Drive. Turn right and drive a short distance to the harbor. The boat ride is about four hours each way.

Contact: Channel Islands National Park Visitor Information Line, 805/658-5730.

97 SANTA BARBARA ISLAND BOAT-IN AND HIKE-IN
🏃 🏊 🎣 5% ⛺

Rating:10

In Channel Islands National Park.
Map 13.7, page 678

This is a veritable dot of an island, well to the south of the four others that make up the Channel Islands. It is best known for its five miles of hiking trails, solitude, snorkeling, swimming, and excellent viewing of marine mammals. It is a breeding ground for elephant seals, with dolphins, sea lions, and whales (in the winter), all common in the area. The snorkeling can be wonderful, as you dive amid playful seals. The only negative is the long boat ride, four hours from the mainland. After landing, it is a steep hike to the campground (no stairs up the bluff), covering about a half mile. Most campers treat this as a wilderness backpacking experience with a long boat ride instead of a long hike.

Campsites, facilities: There are eight primitive tent sites. Picnic tables are provided. Pit toilets are available. No drinking water is available. Garbage must be packed out. No open fires are allowed; bring a camp stove for cooking. No pets are permitted.

Reservations, fees: Reserve by calling Island Packers at 805/642-1393 or Truth Aquatics at Sea Landing in Santa Barbara at 805/963-3564. After arranging transportation, you must obtain a camping reservation at 800/365-CAMP (800/365-2267) or website: reservations.nps.gov, $10 camping fee. Round-trip boat transportation $75 for adult campers, $65 for children campers. Open year-round, weather permitting.

Directions: Drive on U.S. 101 to south of Ventura and the Seaward exit. Take that exit and turn west on Seaward Avenue and drive one mile to Harbor Boulevard. Bear left on Harbor and drive about two miles to Spinnaker Drive. Turn right and drive a short distance to the harbor. The boat ride is about four hours each way.

Contact: Channel Islands National Park Visitor Information Line, 805/658-5730.

Chapter 14
Los Angeles and Vicinity

Chapter 14—Los Angeles and Vicinity

The stereotypical image of the region you see on TV—the blonde in a convertible, the surfer with the movie-star jawline—is so flawed as to be ridiculous, pathetic, and laughable. And while there is some classic beach, lifeguards and all, the surrounding area for recreation spans some of the best opportunities in California.

In fact, there are 121 campgrounds in this region, more than any other in California's 16 geographic regions except for three: Tahoe/North Sierra (with 193), Sequoia and Kings Canyon (with 166) and Shasta and Trinity (with 149). It stuns some to learn that Los Angeles and its nearby forests provide more campgrounds than even the Yosemite area, and three times as many as the San Francisco Bay Area and its 1.2 million acres of greenbelt.

But for those of us who know this landscape, it does not come as a surprise. The area has a tremendous range of national forests, canyons, mountains, lakes, coast, and islands. In fact, there are so many hidden gems that it is like a giant fortune hunt for those who love the outdoors.

While most people first think of the coast, the highways, and the beaches when envisioning this region, it is the opportunities for camping and hiking in the national forests that surprise most. Angeles National Forest and San Bernardino National Forest provide more than one million acres, a thousand miles of trails, and dozens of hidden campgrounds, including remote sites set along the Pacific Crest Trail that make perfect launch points for weekend trips.

The mountaintop views are incredible, probably best from Mt. Baldy (10,064 feet), Mt. San Jacinto (10,804 feet), and Mt. San Gorgonio (11,490 feet). There are a series of great campgrounds nestled on the flanks of all three of these destinations. It is only a start.

Even more famous is the region's top recreation lake, Big Bear, for fishing and boating. Though the region is known for its high population, and Big Bear is no exception on weekends, the relatively few people on weekdays, especially Monday to Thursday mornings, can be stunning to discover. Other top lakes include Arrowhead, Castaic, and several smaller reservoirs.

Yet this is not even the best of it. Look over the opportunities and take your pick. People? What people?

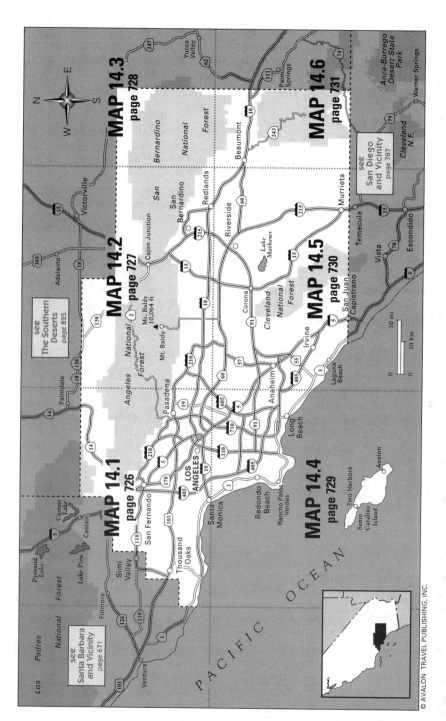

Map 14.1

Campgrounds 1–14
Pages 732–737

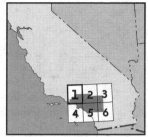

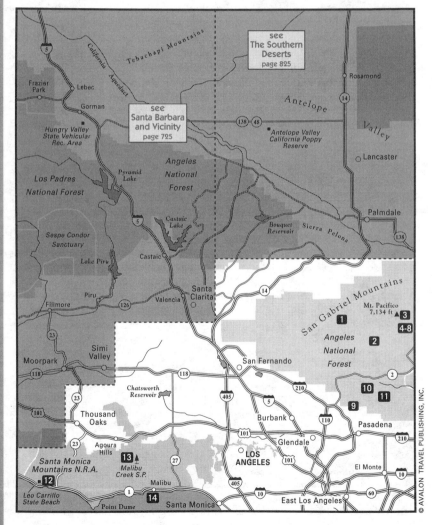

© AVALON TRAVEL PUBLISHING, INC.

Map 14.2

Campgrounds 15–52
Pages 737–754

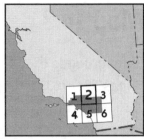

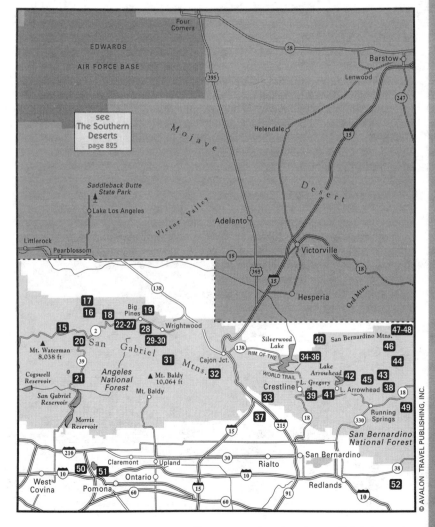

Map 14.3

Campgrounds 53–73
Pages 754–763

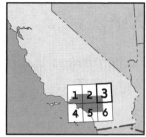

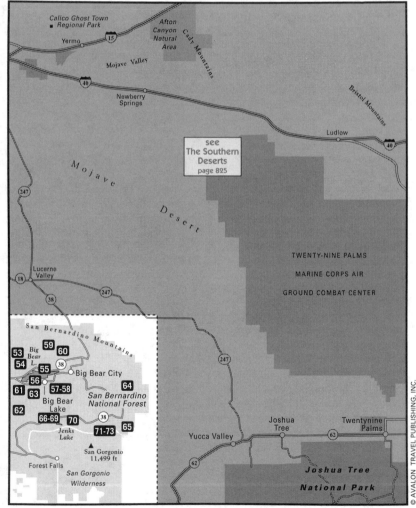

- Calico Ghost Town Regional Park
- Yermo
- Afton Canyon Natural Area
- Cady Mountains
- Mojave Valley
- Newberry Springs
- Bristol Mountains
- Ludlow
- Mojave Desert

see The Southern Deserts page 825

- Lucerne Valley
- TWENTY-NINE PALMS MARINE CORPS AIR GROUND COMBAT CENTER
- San Bernardino Mountains
- 53 54
- 59 60
- Big Bear L.
- 55
- Big Bear City
- 56
- 57-58
- 61 63
- 64
- San Bernardino National Forest
- 62
- Big Bear Lake
- 66-69 70
- 71-73 65
- Jenks Lake
- San Gorgonio 11,499 ft
- Forest Falls
- San Gorgonio Wilderness
- Joshua Tree
- Twentynine Palms
- Yucca Valley
- Joshua Tree National Park

© AVALON TRAVEL PUBLISHING, INC.

Map 14.4

Campgrounds 74–81
Pages 763–766

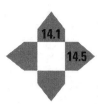

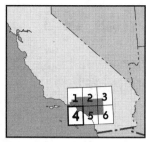

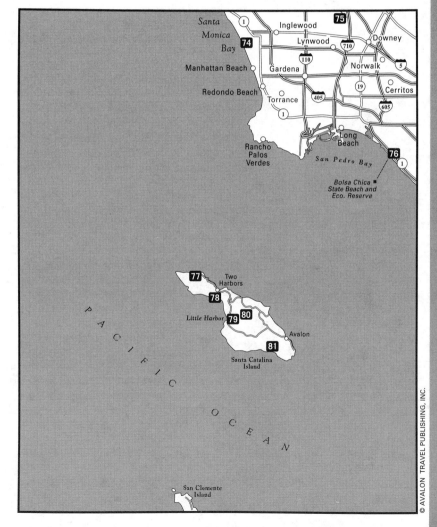

Map 14.5

Campgrounds 82–103
Pages 767–776

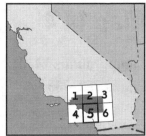

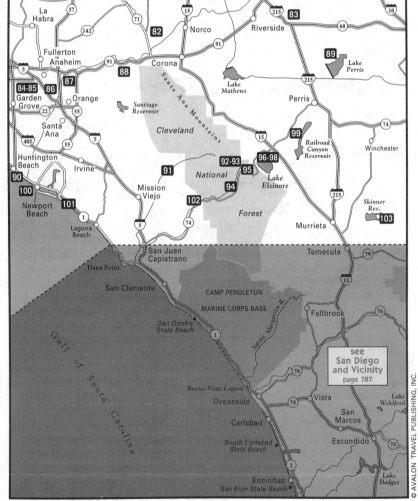

Map 14.6

Campgrounds 104–120
Pages 777–783

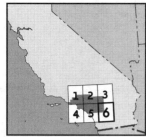

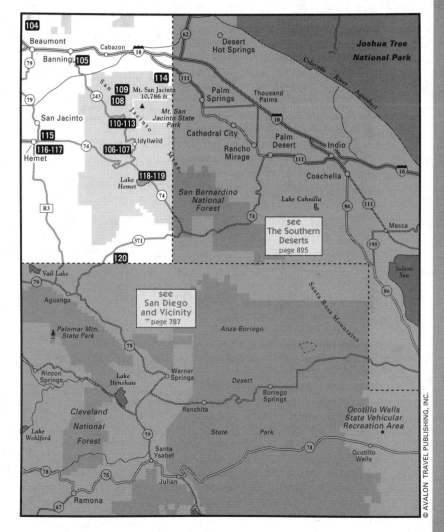

◼ MESSENGER FLATS
🚶 🐎 ⛺

Rating: 7

Near Mt. Gleason in Angeles National Forest.

Map 14.1, page 726

Messenger Flats is an ideal camp for many, a half mile east of Mt. Gleason (6,502 feet). The Pacific Crest Trail is routed through this camp, featuring a one-mile hike with a climb of 600 feet to reach Gleason's summit. The camp is at 5,500 feet, set in a flat area about a quarter mile east of an electronic transmitter at Messenger Peak.

Campsites, facilities: There are 10 tent sites. Picnic tables and fire grills are provided. Drinking water and vault toilets are available. Two horse corrals are also available. Leashed pets are permitted.

Reservations, fees: Reservations are not accepted. The fee is $5 per night. Senior discount available. Open April through November, weather permitting.

Directions: From Pasadena, drive north on I-210 for four miles to the exit for Highway 2/Angeles Crest Highway. Take that exit and drive north on Highway 2 for nine miles to Angeles Forest Highway/County Road N3. Turn left on Angeles Forest Highway and drive 12 miles to Santa Clara Divide Road. Turn left and drive 11 miles to the campground.

Contact: Angeles National Forest, Los Angeles River Ranger District, 818/899-1900, fax 818/896-6727.

◼ MONTE CRISTO
🚶 🏊 🐎 ♿ 🚐 ⛺

Rating: 7

On Mill Creek in Angeles National Forest.

Map 14.1, page 726

This is a Forest Service camp on Mill Creek at 3,600 feet, just west of Iron Mountain. The camp is situated under sycamore trees, which provide great color in the fall. In most years Mill Creek flows eight months out of the year.

Campsites, facilities: There are 19 sites for tents or RVs up to 30 feet long. Picnic tables and fire grills are provided. Drinking water and vault toilets are available. Some facilities are wheelchair-accessible. Leashed pets are permitted. There is no drinking water in dry years.

Reservations, fees: Reservations are not accepted. The fee is $8 per night, $2 for each additional vehicle. Reservations are available for sites with wheelchair facilities. Senior discount available. Open year-round.

Directions: From Pasadena, drive north on I-210 for four miles to the exit for Highway 2/Angeles Crest Highway. Take that exit and drive northeast on Highway 2 for nine miles to Angeles Forest Highway/County Road N3. Turn left on Angeles Forest Highway and drive about nine miles to the campground.

Contact: Angeles National Forest, Los Angeles River Ranger District, 818/899-1900, fax 818/896-6727.

◼ MT. PACIFICO
🚶 🐎 ⛺

Rating: 7

On the Pacific Crest Trail in Angeles National Forest.

Map 14.1, page 726

This is one of the great primitive camps in Angeles National Forest. It is set near the top of Mt. Pacifico at an elevation of 7,134 feet, with the Pacific Crest Trail running right through the camp. The views are outstanding, especially to the north of the sparse Antelope Valley and beyond. From here, the PCT is routed through a series of ravines and draws and up short ridges, pleasant but not inspiring.

Campsites, facilities: There are seven tent sites. Picnic tables and fire grills are provided. Vault toilets are available. No drinking water is available. Garbage must be packed out. Leashed pets are permitted.

Reservations, fees: No reservations are accepted. An Adventure Pass ($30 annual fee or $5 daily pass per vehicle) is required. Senior discount available. Open mid-May through mid-November.

Directions: From Pasadena, drive north on I-210 for four miles to the exit for Highway 2/Angeles Crest Highway. Take that exit and drive north on Highway 2 for nine miles to Angeles Forest Highway/County Road N3. Turn left on Angeles Forest Highway and drive about 12 miles to the intersection with Santa Clara Divide Road/County Road 3N17 (look for the Mill Creek Summit sign). Turn right and drive about five miles to Mt. Pacifico Road. Turn left on the dirt road and drive four miles to the campground.

Note that at Mill Creek Summit, the gate is locked from November 15 to May 15 and it will be necessary to hike from the gate. When Santa Clara Divide Road is impassable because of weather conditions, it will be necessary to hike from Alder Saddle.

Contact: Angeles National Forest, Los Angeles River Ranger District, 818/899-1900, fax 818/896-6727.

4 HORSE FLATS

Rating: 7

Near the San Gabriel Wilderness in Angeles National Forest.

Map 14.1, page 726

This is one of several options in the immediate area: Chilao, Bandido Group Camp, and Coulter Group Camp are the other three. Horse Flats is set at 5,700 feet along a national recreation trail and is close to the Chilao Visitor Center. Several trails into the San Gabriel Wilderness are nearby.

Campsites, facilities: There are 25 sites for tents or RVs up to 36 feet long. Picnic tables and fire pits are provided. Vault toilets, hitching rails, and horse corrals are available. No drinking water is available. Leashed pets are permitted.

Reservations, fees: Reservations are not accepted. The fee is $10 per night. Senior discount available. Open April through November.

Directions: From Pasadena, drive north on I-210 for four miles to the exit for Highway 2/Angeles Crest Highway. Take that exit and drive northeast on Highway 2 for 28 miles to Santa Clara Divide Road at Three Points (signed). Turn left and drive three miles to the campground (signed).

Contact: Angeles National Forest, Los Angeles River Ranger District, 818/899-1900, fax 818/896-6727.

5 BANDIDO GROUP CAMP

Rating: 6

Near the Pacific Crest Trail in Angeles National Forest.

Map 14.1, page 726

This is a base camp for groups preparing to hike off into the surrounding wilderness. A trail out of the camp heads north and intersects with the Pacific Crest Trail a little over one mile away at Three Points, a significant PCT junction. Before heading out most visitors check in with the rangers at nearby Chilao Visitor Center, two miles west of Three Points on Highway 2. The elevation is 5,840 feet.

Campsites, facilities: There are 25 sites for tents or RVs up to 40 feet long. The camp will accommodate up to 120 people. Picnic tables and fire rings are provided. Drinking water, vault toilets, corrals, and water troughs are available. Leashed pets are permitted. There is no drinking water in dry years.

Reservations, fees: Reservations are required. The fee is $100 per night with 60-person maximum, $200 per night with 120-person maximum. Open April through November.

Directions: From Pasadena, drive north on I-210 for four miles to the exit for Highway 2/Angeles Crest Highway. Take that exit and drive northeast on Highway 2 for 28 miles to Santa Clara Divide Road at Three Points (signed). Turn left and drive two miles to the campground on the left.

Contact: Angeles National Forest, Los Angeles

River Ranger District, 818/899-1900, fax 818/896-6727.

6 CHILAO

Rating: 6

Near the San Gabriel Wilderness in Angeles National Forest.

Map 14.1, page 726

This popular trailhead camp gets a lot of use. And it's easy to see why, with the Chilao Visitor Center nearby (have any questions—here's where you ask them) and a national recreation trail running right by the camp. Access to the Pacific Crest Trail is two miles north at Three Points, and parking is available there. The elevation is 5,300 feet.

Campsites, facilities: There are 110 sites for tents or RVs up to 36 feet long. Picnic tables and fire rings are provided. Drinking water and vault toilets are available. RV dump station is available at Charlton Flat Picnic Area. Leashed pets are permitted. There is no drinking water in dry years.

Reservations, fees: Reservations are not accepted. The fee is $12 per night. Senior discount available. Open May through October.

Directions: From Pasadena, drive north on I-210 for four miles to the exit for Highway 2/Angeles Crest Highway. Take that exit and drive northeast on Highway 2 for 26 miles to the campground entrance road (signed) on the left.

Contact: Angeles National Forest, Los Angeles River Ranger District, 818/899-1900, fax 818/896-6727.

7 COULTER GROUP CAMP

Rating: 6

Near the San Gabriel Wilderness in Angeles National Forest.

Map 14.1, page 726

This is a popular group camp set near both a visitor center and a trailhead for the Pacific Crest Trail. Access to the PCT is two miles north at Three Points, and parking is available there. The elevation is 5,200 feet. It is close to Chilao Campground.

Campsites, facilities: There is one group site for up to 50 people. Four picnic tables, a barbecue pit, fire ring, vault toilet, and drinking water are available. There is no drinking water in dry years.

Reservations, fees: Reservations are required. The fee is $100 per night. Open May through October.

Directions: From Pasadena, drive north on I-210 for four miles to the exit for Highway 2/Angeles Crest Highway. Take that exit and drive northeast on Highway 2 for 26 miles to the campground entrance road (signed) on the left.

Contact: Angeles National Forest, Los Angeles River Ranger District, 818/899-1900, fax 818/896-6727.

8 SULPHUR SPRINGS GROUP CAMP

Rating: 6

Near the Pacific Crest Trail in Angeles National Forest.

Map 14.1, page 726

This group camp is on the South Fork of Little Rock Creek, a short distance from a trailhead for the Pacific Crest Trail. It is set at 5,300 feet amid pines and is a popular jump-off point for group hikes. The nearby Chilao Visitor Center is a must-stop for newcomers.

Campsites, facilities: There is one group site for up to 80 people that can accommodate tents and self-contained RVs. Picnic tables and stoves are provided. Drinking water and pit toilets are available. A water trough is available for horses. Leashed pets are permitted. There is no drinking water in dry years.

Reservations, fees: Reservations are required. The fee is $100 fee per night. Open April through November.

Directions: From Pasadena, drive north on I-210 for four miles to the exit for Highway 2/Angeles

Crest Highway. Take that exit and drive northeast on Highway 2 for 28 miles to Santa Clara Divide Road at Three Points (signed). Turn left and drive five miles to the campground entrance road on the right (it will seem like the continuation of the road you're on).

Contact: Angeles National Forest, Los Angeles River Ranger District, 818/899-1900, fax 818/896-6727.

9 MILLARD

Rating: 8

Near Millard Falls in Angeles National Forest.

Map 14.1, page 726

This tiny, pretty camp, set near a creek amid oak and alder woodlands, is best known as the launching point for some excellent hikes. The best is the half-mile hike to Millard Falls, where you actually rock-hop your way upstream to the 60-foot waterfall, a drop-dead beautiful sight. On weekends, there can be lots of foot traffic through the campground with hikers on their way to the falls. Another trail out of camp leads to Inspiration Point and continues to San Gabriel Peak. It a short walk to the campsites.

Campsites, facilities: There are five tent sites. Picnic tables and fire pits are provided. Vault toilets are available. No drinking water is available. Leashed pets are permitted.

Reservations, fees: Reservations are not accepted. There is no fee for camping. Adventure Pass ($30 annual fee or $5 daily fee per vehicle) is required. Open year-round.

Directions: From Pasadena, drive north on I-10 to the exit for Lake Avenue. Take that exit north and drive 3.5 miles to Loma Alta Drive. Turn left (west) at Loma Alta Drive and drive one mile to Chaney Trail Road (at the flashing yellow light). Turn right at Chaney Trail and drive 1.5 miles (keep left at the fork) to the parking lot for the campground. It is a short walk on a fire road to the campground.

Contact: Angeles National Forest, Los Angeles River Ranger District, 818/899-1900, fax 818/896-6727.

10 VALLEY FORGE HIKE-IN

Rating: 8

On the San Gabriel River in Angeles National Forest.

Map 14.1, page 726

Valley Forge is a good camp for anglers or hikers who are looking for a short backpacking trip. A three-mile hike is required to reach this campground. For hikers, a national recreation trail passes close to the camp. For anglers, there are small but feisty trout. The elevation is 3,500 feet.

Campsites, facilities: There are 12 tent sites. Picnic tables and fire rings are provided. Vault toilets are available. No drinking water is available. Stream water can be used if it is boiled or pump-filtered. Garbage must be packed out. Leashed pets are permitted.

Reservations, fees: Reservations are not accepted. There is no fee for camping. Adventure Pass ($30 annual fee or $5 daily fee per vehicle) is required. Open year-round, weather permitting.

Directions: From Pasadena, drive north on I-210 for four miles to the exit for Highway 2/Angeles Crest Highway. Take that exit and drive north on Highway 2 for 14 miles to Mt. Wilson Road. Park in the lot there, walk in through the gate (on Red Box-Rincon Road) to the dirt road (not the paved one), and hike three miles to the campground.

Contact: Angeles National Forest, Los Angeles River Ranger District, 818/899-1900, fax 818/896-6727.

11 WEST FORK HIKE-IN

Rating: 8

On the West Fork of the San Gabriel River in Angeles National Forest.

Map 14.1, page 726

It takes a circuitous drive and a 4.5- to six-mile

hike to reach this camp, but for backpackers it is worth it. The camp is on the West Fork of the San Gabriel River amid pine woodlands, with two national recreation trails intersecting just south of here. The canyon is deep and the river is beautiful. The elevation is 3,100 feet.

Campsites, facilities: There are seven tent sites. Picnic tables and fire rings are provided. Vault toilets are available. No drinking water is available. Stream water can be used if it is boiled or pump-filtered. Garbage must be packed out. Leashed pets are permitted.

Reservations, fees: Reservations are not accepted. There is no fee for camping. Adventure Pass ($30 annual fee or $5 daily fee per vehicle) is required. Senior discount available. Open year-round.

Directions: From Pasadena, drive north on I-210 for four miles to the exit for Highway 2/Angeles Crest Highway. Take that exit and drive north on Highway 2 for 14 miles to Mt. Wilson Road. Park in the lot there, walk in through the gate (on Red Box-Rincon Road) to the dirt road (not the paved one), and hike six miles to the camp or use the rock stairway on the east side of the parking lot and take that trail to the campground.

Contact: Angeles National Forest, Los Angeles River Ranger District, 818/899-1900, fax 818/896-6727.

12 LEO CARRILLO STATE PARK

Rating: 8

North of Malibu.

Map 14.1, page 726

The camping area at this state park is set in a nearby canyon, and reservations are essential for these canyon sites during the summer. Giant sycamores shade the campsites. The Nicholas Flat Trail provides an excellent hike to the Willow Creek Overlook for beautiful views of the beach. In addition, a pedestrian tunnel provides access to a wonderful coastal spot with sea caves, tunnels, tidepools, and patches of beach. This park features 1.5 miles of beach for swimming, surfing, and surf fishing. In the summer, lifeguards are posted at the beach. Many will remember a beach camp that was once popular here. Well, that sucker is gone, wiped out by a storm.

Campsites, facilities: There are 127 sites for tents or RVs up to 31 feet long, one hike-in/bike-in site for up to 24 people, and one group tent site for up to 50 people. Picnic tables and fire rings are provided. Restrooms, drinking water, flush toilets, coin showers, RV dump station, visitor center, summer programs, and a summer convenience store are available. Some facilities are wheelchair-accessible. Leashed pets are permitted. Front gates close at 10 P.M. and reopen at 8 A.M.

Reservations, fees: Reserve at 800/444-PARK (800/444-7275) or website: www.Reserve America.com ($7.50 reservation fee); $12 per night, $1 per person per night for hike-in/bike-in site, $37 for group tent site. Senior discount available. Open year-round.

Directions: From Santa Monica, drive north on Highway 1 for 28 miles north to the park entrance (signed) on the right.

From Oxnard, drive south on Highway 1 for 20 miles to the park entrance (signed) on the left.

Contact: Leo Carrillo State Beach, 818/880-0350, fax 818/880-6165.

13 MALIBU CREEK STATE PARK

Rating: 9

Near Malibu.

Map 14.1, page 726

If you plan on staying here, be sure to get your reservation in early. This 6,600-acre state park is just a few miles out of Malibu between Highway 1 and U.S. 101, two major thoroughfares for vacationers. Despite its popularity, the park manages to retain a natural setting, with miles of trails for hiking, biking, and horseback riding, and inspiring scenic views. The park offers

15 miles of streamside trail through oak and sycamore woodlands and also some chaparral covered slopes. It is an ideal spot for a break on a coastal road trip. This park was once used as a setting for the filming of some movies and TV shows, including *Planet of the Apes* and *M*A*S*H.*

Campsites, facilities: There are 63 sites for tents or self-contained RVs up to 24 feet long and a group tent site for up to 50 people. Picnic tables are provided. No wood fires are permitted in the summer, but propane or charcoal barbecues are allowed. Restrooms, drinking water, flush toilets, and coin showers are available. Some facilities are wheelchair-accessible. Leashed pets are permitted, but only in the campground area.

Reservations, fees: Reserve at 800/444-PARK (800/444-7275) or website: www.Reserve America.com ($7.50 reservation fee); $12 per night, $45 per night for group site. Senior discount available. Open year-round.

Directions: From U.S. 101: Drive on U.S. 101 to the exit for Las Virgenes Canyon Road (on the western border of Calabasas). Take that exit south and drive on Las Virgenes Canyon Road/County Road N1 for four miles to the park entrance on the right.

From Highway 1: Drive on Highway 1 to Malibu and Malibu Canyon Road. Turn north on Malibu Canyon Road and drive north for 5.5 miles (the road becomes Las Virgenes Canyon Road/County Road N1) to the park entrance on the left.

Contact: Malibu Creek State Park, 818/880-0367, fax 818/880-6165.

14 MALIBU BEACH RV PARK

Rating: 7

In Malibu.

Map 14.1, page 726

This is one of the few privately developed RV parks in the region that provides some sites for tent campers as well. It's one of the nicer spots in the area, set on a bluff overlooking the Pacific Ocean, near both Malibu Pier (for fishing) and Paradise Cove. Each site has a view of either the ocean or adjacent mountains. Sites with ocean views are charged a small premium.

Campsites, facilities: There are 140 sites, five drive-through, with full or partial hookups for RVs and 50 sites for tents. Picnic tables and barbecue grills are provided. Restrooms, showers, hot tub, recreation room, playground, coin laundry, modem access, propane gas, ice, cable TV, RV dump station, and a store are available. Some facilities are wheelchair-accessible. Leashed pets are permitted, except in the tent area.

Reservations, fees: Reservations are recommended at 800/622-6052; $29–47 for RV sites, $20–23 for tent sites, $3 per person for more than two people. Reduced rates in winter. Major credit cards accepted. Open year-round.

Directions: Drive on Pacific Coast Highway/Highway 1 to the Malibu area. The park is two miles north of the intersection of Highway 1 and Malibu Canyon Road on the east side of the road.

Contact: Malibu Beach RV Park, 310/456-6052, fax 310/456-2532, website: www.MalibuRv.com.

15 BUCKHORN

Rating: 9

Near Snowcrest Ridge in Angeles National Forest.

Map 14.2, page 727

This is a prime jump-off spot for backpackers in Angeles National Forest. The camp is set at 6,300 feet among huge pine and cedar trees, along a small creek near Mt. Waterman (8,038 feet). A great day hike begins here, a tromp down to Cooper Canyon and the PCT; hikers will be rewarded by beautiful Cooper Falls on this three-hour round-trip. Want a weekend trip? Got it: the High Desert National Recreational Trail leads north from camp into the backcountry, over Burkhart Saddle, and west around Devil's Punchbowl County Park to South Fork Campground. Then it heads south to the Islip Trailhead, east past Eagle's Roost, and south again for the last mile back to Buckhorn. It's a 20-mile hike, with the South Fork Camp situated 10 miles out, perfect for a weekend trip.

Campsites, facilities: There are 38 sites for tents or RVs up to 18 feet long. Picnic tables and fire pits are provided. Drinking water and vault toilets are available, and there is a camp host. Leashed pets are permitted.

Reservations, fees: Reservations are not accepted. The fee is $14 per night. Senior discount available. Open May through November.

Directions: From Pasadena, drive north on I-210 for four miles to the exit for Highway 2/Angeles Crest Highway. Take that exit and drive northeast on Highway 2 for 34 miles northeast to the signed campground entrance.

Contact: Angeles National Forest, Los Angeles River Ranger District, 818/899-1900, fax 818/896-6727.

16 SOUTH FORK

Rating: 7

On Big Rock Creek in Angeles National Forest.

Map 14.2, page 727

This is an excellent trailhead camp set at 4,500 feet along South Fork Creek. One trail climbs 2.2 miles to the west to Devils Punchbowl County Park, topping out at Devils Chair (the trail includes a steep descent and climb). There are two other options. You can hike south along Big Rock Creek, and another hike heads east on the High Desert National Recreation Trail (also called the Manzanita Trail).

Campsites, facilities: There are 21 sites for tents or RVs up to 16 feet long. Picnic tables and fire rings are provided. Vault toilets are available. No drinking water is available. Leashed pets are permitted.

Reservations, fees: No reservations are accepted.

An Adventure Pass ($30 annual fee or a $5 daily fee per vehicle) is required. Senior discount available. Open May to November.

Directions: From Palmdale (at the junction of Highway 14 and Highway 138), take Highway 138 southeast and drive about 10 miles to Pearlblossom and Longview Road. Turn south (right) and drive a short distance to Avenue W/Valyermo Road. Turn left on Avenue W/Valyermo Road and drive about 20 miles into national forest (past the ranger station) to Big Rock Road. Turn right on Big Rock Road and drive about four miles up the canyon (past the Sycamore Flat campground entrance) to the South Fork campground entrance.

Contact: Angeles National Forest, Santa Clara/Mojave River Ranger District, 661/296-9710, fax 661/296-5847.

17 SYCAMORE FLAT

Rating: 7

On Big Rock Creek in Angeles National Forest.

Map 14.2, page 727

Sycamore Flat is a developed camp just inside the northern boundary of Angeles National Forest, set at 4,300 feet on the southwest flank of Piñon Ridge. While there are no trails leading out from this camp, a trailhead is at South Fork, which is two miles to the south.

Campsites, facilities: There are 11 sites for tents or RVs up to 22 feet long. Picnic tables and fire grills are provided. Drinking water and vault toilets are available. Leashed pets are permitted. There is no drinking water in dry years.

Reservations, fees: Reservations are not accepted. There is no fee for camping. Adventure Pass ($30 annual fee or a $5 daily fee per vehicle) is required. Senior discount available. Open year-round.

Directions: From Palmdale (at the junction of Highway 14 and Highway 138), take Highway 138 southeast and drive about 10 miles to Pearlblossom and Longview Road. Turn south (right) and drive a short distance to Avenue W/Valyermo Road. Turn left on Avenue W/Valyermo Road and drive about 20 miles into national forest (past the ranger station) to Big Rock Road. Turn right on Big Rock Road and drive about two miles to the campground entrance.

Contact: Angeles National Forest, Santa Clara/Mojave Rivers Ranger District, 661/296-9710, fax 661/296-5847.

18 BIG ROCK

Rating: 7

On Big Rock Creek in Angeles National Forest.

Map 14.2, page 727

This is a good spot for four-wheel-drive cowboys. It is a primitive Forest Service camp set at the head of Fenner Canyon along Big Rock Creek. Forest Road 4N11 to the southeast is a four-wheel-drive road that connects to a network of backcountry roads and hiking trails. A Forest Service map is essential. The elevation is 5,550 feet.

Campsites, facilities: There are eight sites for tents. Picnic tables and fire pits are provided. Vault toilets are available. No drinking water is available. Leashed pets are permitted.

Reservations, fees: Reservations are not accepted. There is no fee for camping. Adventure Pass ($30 annual fee or a $5 daily fee per vehicle) is required. Senior discount available. Open year-round.

Directions: From Palmdale (at the junction of Highway 14 and Highway 138), take Highway 138 southeast and drive about 10 miles to Pearlblossom and Longview Road. Turn south (right) and drive a short distance to Avenue W/Valyermo Road. Turn left on Avenue W/Valyermo Road and drive about 20 miles into national forest (past the ranger station) to Big Rock Road. Turn right on Big Rock Road and drive up the canyon (past the turnoff for South Fork Camp and past Camp Fenner) to the campground entrance road on the right.

Contact: Angeles National Forest, Santa Clara/Mojave Rivers Ranger District, 661/296-9710, fax 661/296-5847.

19 TABLE MOUNTAIN

Rating: 6

In Angeles National Forest.

Map 14.2, page 727

This is a family campground that accommodates both tents and RVs. The road leading in is a paved two-lane county road, easily accessible by any vehicle. The nearby Big Pines Visitor Information Center, one mile to the south, can provide maps and information on road conditions. The camp elevation is 7,200 feet. A rough road for four-wheel-drive rigs is available out of camp that leads north along the Table Mountain Ridge.

Campsites, facilities: There are 115 sites for tents or RVs up to 32 feet long. Picnic tables and fire pits are provided. Drinking water and vault toilets are available. Leashed pets are permitted.

Reservations, fees: Reserve at 877/444-6777 or website: www.ReserveUsa.com ($9 reservation fee); $14 per night. Senior discount available. Open May through September.

Directions: Drive on I-15 to Cajon Junction (north of San Bernardino) and the exit for Highway 138 West. Take that exit and drive west on Highway 138 to Angeles Crest Highway/Highway 2. Turn west on Angeles Crest Highway and drive five miles to Wrightwood, then continue for three miles to Big Pines and Table Mountain Road. Turn right on Table Mountain Road and drive one mile to the campground.

Contact: Angeles National Forest, Santa Clara/Mojave Rivers Ranger District, 661/296-9710, fax 661/296-5847.

20 DEER FLATS GROUP CAMP

Rating: 6

Near Crystal Lake in Angeles National Forest.

Map 14.2, page 727

This is an ideal spot to bring a troop of Boy or Girl Scouts. It is about a mile from little Crystal Lake, a small lake with decent shoreline bait-dunking for trout. This is a huge group camp with space for high numbers of tents, with nine group sites for 20–65 per site, and up to 300 total. This is for tents only. There is RV parking available at the parking lot near the campground, but there are no drive-in sites for RVs. A nearby trail leads north from camp and in two miles intersects with the Pacific Crest Trail, though most just make it to the junction of the PCT, enjoy the views, and return. The Crystal Lake Recreation Area has a network of excellent trails. Because of a dry year, this campground was temporarily closed in 2002. Its future will be reviewed each winter.

Campsites, facilities: There are nine group sites for tents for up to 20–65 people at each, with a total capacity of 300. Picnic tables and fire grills are provided. Drinking water and vault toilets are available. A visitor information center is nearby. Leashed pets are permitted. Note that in dry years, there is no drinking water and the campground is also subject to closure.

Reservations, fees: Reservations are required. The fee is $40–130 per night for a single site, $600 per night for all nine sites. Open mid-May to late September, weather permitting.

Directions: Drive on I-210 to Azusa and the exit for Azusa Canyon and San Gabriel Canyon Road/Highway 39. Take that exit and drive north on San Gabriel Canyon Road for 25 miles to the Crystal Lake Recreation Area and the campground.

Contact: Angeles National Forest, San Gabriel Ranger District, 626/335-1251, fax 626/914-3790.

21 COLDBROOK

Rating: 7

On the North Fork of the San Gabriel River in Angeles National Forest.

Map 14.2, page 727

This roadside camp is set along the North Fork San Gabriel River, with little Crystal Lake to the north. A secret waterfall is hidden off the road, about three miles north on Soldier Creek. To find it, park at the deep bending turn in the road at Soldier Creek, then hike uphill for less than a mile. It's just like a treasure hunt, and it's always a welcome surprise to find the waterfall. The elevation is 3,300 feet.

Campsites, facilities: There are 22 sites for tents or RVs up to 22 feet long. Picnic tables and fire rings are provided. Drinking water and vault toilets are available. Leashed pets are permitted.

Reservations, fees: Reservations are not accepted. The fee is $12 per night, $5 for each additional vehicle. Discounts available for those with Adventure Passes and for seniors. Open year-round.

Directions: Drive on I-210 to Azusa and the exit for Azusa Canyon and San Gabriel Canyon Road/Highway 39. Take that exit and drive north on San Gabriel Canyon Road for 18 miles to the campground entrance.

Contact: Angeles National Forest, San Gabriel River Ranger District, 626/335-1251, fax 626/914-3790.

22 JACKSON FLAT GROUP CAMP WALK-IN

Rating: 4

Near the Pacific Crest Trail in Angeles National Forest.

Map 14.2, page 727

This is a good spot for a group to overnight, assess themselves, and get information before heading out into the surrounding wildlands. The camp is set in the Angeles National Forest high country at 7,500 feet, near the end of a short spur road. It takes a 200-yard walk to reach this campground from the parking area. The Pacific Crest Trail passes just north of camp and can be reached by a short connecting link trail.

Campsites, facilities: There are five group sites for up to 40–50 people each. Picnic tables and fire pits are provided. Drinking water and vault toilets are available. Leashed pets are permitted.

Reservations, fees: Make reservations at 877/444-6777 or website: www.ReserveUsa.com ($9 reservation fee); $85–100 per night. Open Memorial Day through Labor Day.

Directions: Drive on I-15 to Cajon Junction (north of San Bernardino) and the exit for Highway 138 West. Take that exit and drive west on Highway 138 to Angeles Crest Highway/Highway 2. Turn west on Angeles Crest Highway and drive five miles to Wrightwood, then continue for three miles to Big Pines. Bear left (still on Angeles Crest Highway) and drive two miles to a Forest Service road (opposite the sign for Grassy Hollow Campground). Turn right and drive one mile to the campground parking lot. Walk 200 yards to the campground.

Contact: Angeles National Forest, Santa Clara/Mojave Rivers Ranger District, 661/296-9710, fax 661/296-5847.

23 CABIN FLAT

Rating: 7

On Prairie Fork Creek in Angeles National Forest.

Map 14.2, page 727

It takes a four-wheel drive to get here, but that done, you're guaranteed solitude along little Prairie Fork Creek, deep in the Angeles National Forest. Along the way, you will pass several other camps, including Guffy and Lupine. A short trail runs beside the stream for about a quarter mile. The elevation is 5,400 feet.

Campsites, facilities: There are 12 tent sites.

Picnic tables, fire pits, and vault toilets are provided. There is no drinking water, so bring your own. Leashed pets are permitted.

Reservations, fees: Reservations are not accepted. There is no fee for camping. Adventure Pass ($30 annual fee or a $5 daily fee per vehicle) is required. Senior discount available. Open June through September.

Directions: From I-15 near Cajon, take Highway 138 west. Turn west on Angeles Crest Highway/Highway 2 and drive five miles to Wrightwood. Continue for three miles to Big Pines. Bear left and continue on Angeles Crest Highway for 1.5 miles. Turn left (opposite Inspiration Point) on Blue Ridge Road and drive 12 miles to the campground (the road becomes a rough, dirt road after the first three miles).

Contact: Angeles National Forest, Santa Clara/Mojave Rivers Ranger District, 661/296-9710, fax 661/296-5847.

24 APPLE TREE

Rating: 6

Near Jackson Lake in Angeles National Forest.

Map 14.2, page 727

This is one of four camps set on Big Pines "Highway" near Jackson Lake. This "lake" is more of a pond and is about a half mile to the west, just up the road. Lake and Peavine camps are between Apple Tree and Jackson Lake, while Mountain Oak is just beyond the lake. Any questions? Rangers can answer them at the nearby Big Pines Visitor Information Center and ski complex. The elevation is 6,200 feet.

Campsites, facilities: There are eight tent sites. Picnic tables and fire rings are provided. Drinking water and vault toilets are available. Leashed pets are permitted. There is no drinking water in dry years.

Reservations, fees: Reservations are not accepted. There is no fee for camping. Adventure Pass ($30 annual fee or a $5 daily fee per vehicle) is required. Senior discount available. Open year-round.

Directions: Drive on I-15 to Cajon Junction (north of San Bernardino) and the exit for Highway 138 West. Take that exit and drive west on Highway 138 to Angeles Crest Highway/Highway 2. Turn west on Angeles Crest Highway and drive five miles to Wrightwood, then continue for three miles to Big Pines and Big Pines Highway/County Road N4. Bear right on Big Pines Highway and drive two miles to the campground.

Contact: Angeles National Forest, Santa Clara/Mojave Rivers Ranger District, 661/296-9710, fax 661/296-5847.

25 MOUNTAIN OAK

Rating: 4

Near Jackson Lake in Angeles National Forest.

Map 14.2, page 727

This is one of four camps within a mile of little Jackson Lake on Big Pines Highway. The others are Lake, Peavine, and Apple Tree. This camp is about a quarter mile northwest of the lake. The elevation is 6,200 feet.

Campsites, facilities: There are 17 sites for tents or RVs up to 18 feet long. Picnic tables and fire pits are provided. Drinking water and flush toilets are available. Groceries and propane gas are nearby. Leashed pets are permitted.

Reservations, fees: Reserve at 877/444-6777 or website: www.ReserveUsa.com ($9 reservation fee); $12 per night. Senior discount available. Open May through September.

Directions: Drive on I-15 to Cajon Junction (north of San Bernardino) and the exit for Highway 138 West. Take that exit and drive west on Highway 138 to Angeles Crest Highway/Highway 2. Turn west on Angeles Crest Highway and drive five miles to Wrightwood, then continue for three miles to Big Pines and Big Pines Highway/County Road N4. Bear right on Big Pines Highway and drive three miles to the campground.

Contact: Angeles National Forest, Santa Clara/Mojave Rivers Ranger District, 661/296-9710, fax 661/296-5847.

26 LAKE

Rating: 8

On Jackson Lake in Angeles National Forest.

Map 14.2, page 727

This is a pretty setting on the southeast shore of little Jackson Lake. Of the four camps within a mile, this is the only one right beside the lake. The elevation is 6,100 feet.

Campsites, facilities: There are eight sites for tents or RVs up to 18 feet long. Picnic tables and fire pits are provided. Drinking water and vault toilets are available. Leashed pets are permitted. Some facilities are wheelchair-accessible.

Reservations, fees: Reserve at 877/444-6777 or website: www.ReserveUsa.com ($9 reservation fee); $12 per night. Senior discount available. Open May through October.

Directions: Drive on I-15 to Cajon Junction (north of San Bernardino) and the exit for Highway 138 West. Take that exit and drive west on Highway 138 to Angeles Crest Highway/Highway 2. Turn west on Angeles Crest Highway and drive five miles to Wrightwood, then continue for three miles to Big Pines and Big Pines Highway/County Road N4. Bear right on Big Pines Highway and drive 2.5 miles to the campground.

Contact: Angeles National Forest, Santa Clara/Mojave Rivers Ranger District, 661/296-9710, fax 661/296-5847.

27 PEAVINE

Rating: 4

Near Jackson Lake in Angeles National Forest.

Map 14.2, page 727

This tiny camp is one of four in the immediate

area, just a half mile east of little eight-acre Jackson Lake. The elevation is 6,100 feet.

Campsites, facilities: There are four tent sites. Picnic tables and fire pits are provided. Drinking water and vault toilets are available. A store and propane gas are nearby. Leashed pets are permitted. There is no drinking water in dry years.

Reservations, fees: Reservations are not accepted. There is no fee for camping. Adventure Pass ($30 annual fee or a $5 daily fee per vehicle) is required. Open May through October.

Directions: Drive on I-15 to Cajon Junction (north of San Bernardino) and the exit for Highway 138 West. Take that exit and drive west on Highway 138 to Angeles Crest Highway/Highway 2. Turn west on Angeles Crest Highway and drive five miles to Wrightwood, then continue for three miles to Big Pines and Big Pines Highway/County Road N4. Bear right on Big Pines Highway and drive and drive 2.7 miles to the campground.

Contact: Angeles National Forest, Santa Clara/Mojave Rivers Ranger District, 661/296-9710, fax 661/296-5847.

28 BLUE RIDGE

Rating: 8

On the Pacific Crest Trail in Angeles National Forest.

Map 14.2, page 727

Blue Ridge is set high in Angeles National Forest at 8,000 feet and makes a jump-off spot for a multiday backpacking trip. The Pacific Crest Trail runs right alongside the camp. Guffy, also aside the PCT, provides an option two miles to the southeast, but it takes a four-wheel-drive vehicle to get there. There are a number of primitive four-wheel-drive routes in the area.

Campsites, facilities: There are eight sites for tents or RVs up to 16 feet long. Picnic tables and fire rings are provided. Vault toilets are available. No drinking water is available. Leashed pets are permitted.

Reservations, fees: Reservations are not accepted. There is no fee for camping. Adventure Pass ($30 annual fee or a $5 daily fee per vehicle) is required. Senior discount available. Open June through September.

Directions: Drive on I-15 to Cajon Junction (north of San Bernardino) and the exit for Highway 138 West. Take that exit and drive west on Highway 138 to Angeles Crest Highway/Highway 2. Turn west on Angeles Crest Highway and drive five miles to Wrightwood, then continue for three miles to Big Pines. Bear left (still on Angeles Crest Highway) and drive 1.5 miles to Blue Ridge Road (adjacent to Inspiration Point). Turn left on Blue Ridge Road and drive three miles to the campground.

Contact: Angeles National Forest, Santa Clara/Mojave Rivers Ranger District, 661/296-9710, fax 661/296-5847.

29 LUPINE

Rating: 7

On Prairie Fork Creek in Angeles National Forest.

Map 14.2, page 727

This little-known, hard-to-reach camp, set at 6,500 feet along Prairie Fork Creek, is used most often by campers with four-wheel-drive rigs. A challenging butt-kicker hike on a primitive trail starts here. The trail leads from the camp over Pine Mountain Ridge, down into a canyon, and then winds to the east up Dawson Peak—long, difficult, and completed by few.

Campsites, facilities: There are 11 tent sites. Picnic tables and fire pits are provided. Vault toilets are available. No drinking water is available. Leashed pets are permitted.

Reservations, fees: Reservations are not accepted. There is no fee for camping. Adventure Pass ($30 annual fee or a $5 daily fee per vehicle) is required. Senior discount available. Open June through September.

Directions: Drive on I-15 to Cajon Junction (north of San Bernardino) and the exit for Highway 138

West. Take that exit and drive west on Highway 138 to Angeles Crest Highway/Highway 2. Turn west on Angeles Crest Highway and drive five miles to Wrightwood, then continue for three miles to Big Pines. Bear left (still on Angeles Crest Highway) and drive 1.5 miles to Blue Ridge Road (adjacent to Inspiration Point). Turn left on Blue Ridge Road and drive 10 miles (rough road after the first three miles) to the campground.

Contact: Angeles National Forest, Santa Clara/Mojave Rivers Ranger District, 661/296-9710, fax 661/296-5847.

30 GUFFY

Rating: 7

On the Pacific Crest Trail in Angeles National Forest.

Map 14.2, page 727

A short trail right out of this camp connects with the Pacific Crest Trail, making Guffy a backpacker's special. The area is also popular for campers with four-wheel-drive rigs, because there are a number of primitive roads in the area. The elevation is 8,300 feet.

Campsites, facilities: There are six tent sites. Picnic tables and fire rings are provided. Vault toilets are available. No drinking water is available. Leashed pets are permitted.

Reservations, fees: No reservations are accepted. An Adventure Pass ($30 annual fee or a $5 daily fee per vehicle) is required. Open June through September.

Directions: From I-15 near Cajon, take Highway 138 west. Turn west on Angeles Crest Highway/Highway 2 and drive five miles to Wrightwood. Continue for three miles to Big Pines. Bear left and continue on Angeles Crest Highway for 1.5 miles. Turn left (opposite Inspiration Point) on Blue Ridge Road and drive six miles to the campground (it's a rough, dirt road after the first three miles).

Contact: Angeles National Forest, Santa Clara/Mojave Rivers Ranger District, 661/296-9710, fax 661/296-5847.

31 MANKER FLATS

Rating: 7

Near Mt. Baldy in Angeles National Forest.

Map 14.2, page 727

This camp is best known for its proximity to Mt. Baldy and the nearby trailhead to reach San Antonio Falls. The trail to San Antonio Falls starts at an elevation of 6,160 feet, .3 mile up the road on the left. From here, it's a 1.5-mile saunter on a ski park maintenance road to the waterfall, a pretty 80-footer. The wild and ambitious can continue six more miles and climb to the top of Mt. Baldy (10,064 feet) for breathtaking 360-degree views. Making this all-day butt-kicker is like a baptism for Southern California hikers.

Campsites, facilities: There are 21 sites for tents or RVs up to 16 feet long. Picnic tables and fire grills are provided. Drinking water and vault toilets are available. Leashed pets are permitted. There is no drinking water in dry years.

Reservations, fees: Reservations are not accepted. The fee is $12 per night, $4 for each additional vehicle. Discounts for those with Adventure Pass and for seniors. Open May through September.

Directions: Drive on I-10 to Ontario and the exit for Highway 83. Take that exit and drive north on Highway 83 to Mt. Baldy Road. Continue north on Mt. Baldy Road for nine miles to the campground.

Contact: Angeles National Forest, San Gabriel River Ranger District, 626/335-1251, fax 626/914-3790.

32 APPLE WHITE

Rating: 5

Near Lytle Creek in San Bernardino National Forest.

Map 14.2, page 727

Nothing like a little insiders' know-how, especially at this camp, set at 3,300 feet near Lytle

Creek. You can reach the Middle Fork of Lytle Creek by driving north from Fontana via Serra Avenue to the Lytle Creek area. To get to the stretch of water that is stocked with trout by the Department of Fish and Game, turn west on Middle Fork Road, which is 1.5 miles before the campground at Apple White. The first mile upstream is stocked in early summer.

Campsites, facilities: There are 42 sites for tents or RVs up to 30 feet long. Picnic tables and fire grills are provided. Restrooms, drinking water, and flush toilets are available. A store is nearby. Leashed pets are permitted. Some facilities are wheelchair-accessible.

Reservations, fees: Reservations are not accepted. The fee is $10 per night, $3 for each extra vehicle, $15 for double sites. Senior discount available. Open year-round.

Directions: Drive to Ontario and the junction of I-10 and I-15. Take I-15 north and drive 11 miles to the Sierra Avenue exit. Turn left, go under the freeway, and continue north for about nine miles (into national forest) to the campground on the right.

Contact: San Bernardino National Forest, Front Country Ranger District, 909/887-2576, fax 909/887-8197.

33 SAN BERNARDINO-CABLE CANYON KOA

Rating: 5

Near Silverwood Lake.

Map 14.2, page 727

This KOA camp provides space for tents as well as RVs. It is set at 2,200 feet and is virtually surrounded by national forest. Silverwood Lake to the east provides a nearby side trip. (For information on Silverwood Lake, see the entry for Mesa campground.)

Campsites, facilities: There are 155 sites, 65 drive-through, with full or partial hookups for RVs or tents, seven RV rentals, and two camping cabins. Picnic tables are provided. Restrooms, drinking water, flush toilets, showers,

coin laundry, modem access, playground, swimming pool, recreation room, store, and propane gas are available. Some facilities are wheelchair-accessible. Leashed pets are permitted.

Reservations, fees: Reservations accepted at 800/KOA-4155 (800/562-4155); $19 per night for tent sites, $49 per night for RV sites, $2–4 per person for more than two people. Weekday discounts. Major credit cards accepted. Open year-round.

Directions: From San Bernardino, drive north on I-215 for six miles to the exit for Devore and Devore Road (two miles south of the junction of I-15 and I-215). Take that exit to Devore Road. Turn right and drive to Santa Fe Road. Turn right and drive one block to Dement Road. Turn right on Dement Road (which becomes Cable Canyon Road) and continue to the park entrance (1707 Cable Canyon Road).

Contact: San Bernardino-Cable Canyon KOA, 909/887-4098; website: www.sanbernardino koa.com or www.koa.com.

34 MESA

Rating: 6

On Silverwood Lake.

Map 14.2, page 727

This state park campground is on the west side of Silverwood Lake at 3,355 feet in elevation, bordered by San Bernardino National Forest to the south and high desert to the north. The hot weather and proximity to San Bernardino make it a winner with boaters, who have 1,000 surface acres of water and 13 miles of shoreline to explore. It's a great lake for water-skiing (35-mph speed limit), water sports (5-mph speed limit in coves), and windsurfing, with afternoon winds usually strong in the spring and early summer. Note that the quota on boats is enforced, with a maximum of 175 boats per day, and that boat launch reservations are required on summer weekends and holidays. There are also designated areas for boating, water-skiing, and fishing, to reduce conflicts.

Fishing varies dramatically according to season, with trout planted in the cool months, and largemouth bass, bluegill, and striped bass occasionally caught the rest of the year. The park also has a modest trail system with both nature and bike trails. A bonus is that there are also some hike-in/bike-in campsites.

Campsites, facilities: There are 131 sites for tents or RVs up to 32 feet long (with a few for RVs up to 60 feet long), four hike-in/bike-in sites, and six group sites for 10–100 people. Picnic tables and fire rings are provided. Restrooms, drinking water, flush toilets, coin showers, RV dump station, boat ramp, marina, boat rentals, and store are available. Some facilities are wheelchair-accessible. Leashed pets are permitted.

Reservations, fees: Reserve at 800/444-PARK (800/444-7275) or website: www.Reserve America.com ($7.50 reservation fee); $8 per night, $1 per night per camper for hike-in/bike-in sites, $40–75 for group sites. Open year-round.

Directions: Drive on I-15 to Cajon Junction (north of San Bernardino) and the exit for Highway 138 East. Take that exit and drive east on Highway 138 for 13 miles to the park entrance on the right.

Contact: Silverwood Lake State Recreation Area, 760/389-2303 or 760/389-2281.

35 WEST FORK GROUP CAMPS

Rating: 6

At Silverwood Lake.

Map 14.2, page 727

There are three group camps at this site, Barranca, Rio, and Valle. This is a group camping option at Silverwood Lake. (For information on Silverwood Lake, see the entry for Mesa campground.) These group campgrounds are about 2.5 miles from the lake.

Campsites, facilities: There are three group camps for RVs and tents for up to 80 people each, and one equestrian site for up to four horses and 20 people. Picnic tables and fire rings are provided. Restrooms, drinking water,

flush toilets, and coin showers are available. Some facilities are wheelchair-accessible. A corral is available at the equestrian site. Picnic areas, fishing, hiking, swimming, boating, food service, and a store are available nearby. An RV dump station is available at Mesa Campground. Leashed pets are permitted.

Reservations, fees: Reserve at 800/444-PARK (800/444-7275) or website: www.Reserve America.com ($7.50 reservation fee); $40 group fee per night, $8 per night for equestrian site. Open April through October.

Directions: Drive on I-15 to Cajon Junction (north of San Bernardino) and the exit for Highway 138 East. Take that exit and drive east on Highway 138 for 13 miles to the park entrance on the right.

Contact: Silverwood Lake State Recreation Area, 760/389-2303 or 760/389-2281.

36 MILLER CANYON GROUP

Rating: 6

At Silverwood Lake.

Map 14.2, page 727

This group camp at Silverwood Lake is about a half mile from the lake. It is set in a pine and redwood forest, with good hiking and biking trails out of camp. The Pacific Crest Trail (no bikes permitted) runs nearby, ideal for hiking and horses. Silverwood Lake is set at 3,350 feet in elevation, bordered by San Bernardino National Forest to the south and high desert to the north. No fires are permitted.

Campsites, facilities: There are three group sites for RVs and tents for up to 80 people each. Picnic tables are provided. Restrooms, drinking water, flush toilets, coin showers, corral, snack bar, and convenience store are available. Some facilities are wheelchair-accessible. Leashed pets are permitted.

Reservations, fees: Reserve at 800/444-PARK (800/444-7275) or website: www.Reserve America.com ($7.50 reservation fee); $75 per night. Open April through October.

Directions: Drive on I-15 to Cajon Junction (north of San Bernardino) and the exit for Highway 138 East. Take that exit and drive east on Highway 138 for 15 miles to the exit for the campground on the left. Turn left and drive a short distance to the campground on the right.

Contact: Silverwood Lake State Recreation Area, 760/389-2303 or 760/389-2281.

37 GLEN HELEN REGIONAL PARK

Rating: 4

Near Cajon Pass.

Map 14.2, page 727

The centerpieces of Glen Helen Regional Park are two lakes and this campground. The park covers 1,340 acres in the rolling hills at the mouth of Cajon Pass. The ponds are stocked with trout in winter and with catfish in summer, and bass are also occasionally caught. Both lakes are set up for shore-fishing, with no boats allowed on the lakes, except for those little pedalboats, and no swimming or water contact is permitted. Two 350-foot water slides for kids are a great bonus. A major obtrusive problem is the location of the campground, actually set just across the street from the park, near both the freeway and railroad tracks. That's right, drivers in passing cars can actually see you, and at night, passing trains feel and sound like the world is ending. This park is home of the Renaissance Pleasure Faire in May and June. The Blockbuster Pavilion is the largest outdoor amphitheater in the United States and can accommodate up to 65,000 people at major events. A OHV park is also nearby.

Campsites, facilities: There are 48 sites, some drive-through, for tents or RVs, and two group sites for 50–200 people. Picnic tables and fire rings are provided. Restrooms, drinking water, flush toilets, showers, RV dump station, and pay phone are on site. Some facilities are wheelchair-accessible. A swimming lagoon, picnic area with shelters, bait and tackle, pedal boat

rentals, playground with volleyball, horseshoes, and water slides are available nearby on-site. A snack bar is available on weekends. A store and gas station is a half mile away. Leashed pets are permitted.

Reservations, fees: Reservations are not accepted. The fee is $10 per night, $1 per pet per night. Senior discount available. Maximum 14-day stay in any 30-day period. Reservations are accepted for group sites ($10 reservation fee), $3 three per person per night. Open year-round.

Directions: From San Bernardino, drive north on I-215 for nine miles to the exit for Devore Road. Take that exit and turn west on Devore Road and drive one mile to the campground and the park (adjacent to the interchange for I-15 and I-215).

Contact: Glen Helen Regional Park, 909/887-7540 (reservations), fax 909/887-1359; Blockbuster Pavilion, 909/880-6500 or 909/88-MUSIC (909/886-8742); OHV Park, 909/880-3090.

38 GREEN VALLEY

Rating: 7

Near Green Valley Lake in San Bernardino National Forest.

Map 14.2, page 727

This camp sits along pretty Green Valley Creek at an elevation of 7,000 feet. Little Green Valley Lake is a mile to the west. The lake is stocked with trout by the Department of Fish and Game and is also a good spot to take a flying leap and belly flop.

Campsites, facilities: There are 37 sites for tents or RVs up to 22 feet long. Picnic tables and fire grills are provided. Drinking water and flush toilets are available. A store and coin laundry are nearby. Leashed pets are permitted.

Reservations, fees: Reservations may be made at 877/444-6777 ($9 reservation fee) or website: www.ReserveUsa.com; $15 per night, $5 per night for each extra vehicle. Open May through October.

Directions: Drive on Highway 30 to the junction with Highway 330 (east of San Bernardino near Highland). Take Highway 330 North (signed "Mountain Resorts") and drive to Running Springs and the junction with Highway 18. Turn east on Highway 18 and drive to Green Valley Road. Turn left on Green Valley Road and drive three miles to Forest Road 3N16 (a dirt road). Turn left and drive four miles (you will cross two creeks that vary in depth depending on season; high clearance is recommended but is typically not necessary) to the campground (one mile past the town of Green Valley Lake).

Contact: San Bernardino National Forest, Mountaintop Ranger Station, 909/337-2444, fax 909/337-1104.

39 CAMP SWITZERLAND

Rating: 7

Near Lake Gregory.
Map 14.2, page 727

Well, it really doesn't look much like Switzerland, but this camp is set in a wooded canyon at 4,500 feet below the dam at little Lake Gregory. Since it is well below the dam, there are no lake views or even much of a sense that the lake is nearby. Yet it is only a short distance away. Lake Gregory covers just 120 acres, and while no privately owned boats are permitted here, boats can be rented at the marina. No gas motors are permitted at the lake, but electric motors are allowed. It is surrounded by the San Bernardino National Forest. A large swimming beach is available on the south shore (about three-quarters of a mile away) with a water slide and dressing rooms.

Campsites, facilities: There are 30 sites with full hookups for RVs, 10 sites for tents, and two cabins. Picnic tables are provided. Restrooms, drinking water, flush toilets, and coin showers are available. A store and propane gas are nearby. Leashed pets are permitted, with some restrictions.

Reservations, fees: Reservations are accepted. The fees for individual sites are $20–25 per night, $5 for each extra vehicle, $3 per night. Open year-round, weather permitting.

Directions: Drive on Highway 30 to San Bernardino and Highway 18 (two miles east of the junction of Highway 30 and Highway 259). Turn north on Highway 18/Rim of the World Highway and drive 14 miles to Crestline/Highway 138. Turn north (left) on Highway 138 and drive two miles to Lake Drive. Turn right and drive three miles to campground entrance (signed, just past the fire station, below the dam at the north end of Lake Gregory).

Contact: Camp Switzerland, P.O. Box 967, Crestline, CA 92325; 909/338-2731.

40 MOJAVE RIVER FORKS REGIONAL PARK

Rating: 5

Near Silverwood Lake.
Map 14.2, page 727

The bonuses here are for RV drivers, with the full hookups for RVs and the park's proximity to Silverwood Lake—which is only 15 minutes away but does not have any sites with hookups. The sites here are well spaced, but the nearby "river" is usually dry. The elevation is 3,000 feet.

Campsites, facilities: There are 25 sites, seven drive-through, with full hookups for RVs, 25 sites for RVs or tents, 30 sites for tents only, and four group sites. Picnic tables and fire grills are provided. Restrooms, drinking water, flush toilets, showers, and RV dump station are available. Leashed pets are permitted with proof of shots and/or current license.

Reservations, fees: Reservations are accepted for RV sites; tent sites are $10 per night, RV sites with hookups are $15 per night, $10 per night for each extra vehicle, $3 per night. Open year-round.

Directions: Drive on I-15 to Cajon Junction (north of San Bernardino) and the exit for

Highway 138. Take that exit east and drive nine miles to a fork with Highway 173. Bear left at the fork on Highway 173 and drive six miles to the park on the right.

Contact: Mojave River Forks Regional Park, 760/389-2322.

41 DOGWOOD

Rating: 6

Near Lake Arrowhead in San Bernardino National Forest.

Map 14.2, page 727

So close, but yet so far—that's the paradox between Lake Arrowhead and Dogwood. The lake is just a mile away, but no public boating or swimming is permitted and only extremely limited access for shore fishing is permitted, with the lake ringed by gated trophy homes, each worth millions. The elevation is 5,600 feet. Any questions? The rangers at the Arrowhead Ranger Station, about 1.5 miles down the road to the east, can answer them.

Campsites, facilities: There are 90 sites for tents or RVs up to 22 feet long. Picnic tables and fire grills are provided. Drinking water, flush toilets, coin showers, and RV dump station are available. Some facilities are wheelchair-accessible. A store and coin laundry are nearby. Leashed pets are permitted.

Reservations, fees: Reserve at 877/444-6777 or website: www.ReserveUsa.com ($9 reservation fee); $20 per night, $5 for each extra vehicle. Senior discount available. Open May through October.

Directions: Drive on Highway 30 to San Bernardino and Highway 18 (two miles east of the junction of Highway 30 and Highway 259). Turn north on Highway 18 and drive 15 miles to Rim of the World Highway. Continue on Highway 18 for .2 mile to Daley Canyon Road. Turn left on Daley Canyon Road and make an immediate right on the Daley Canyon access road. Drive a short distance to the campground entrance on the left.

Contact: San Bernardino National Forest, Mountaintop Ranger Station, 909/337-2444, fax 909/337-1104.

42 NORTH SHORE

Rating: 8

On Lake Arrowhead in San Bernardino National Forest.

Map 14.2, page 727

Of the two camps at Lake Arrowhead, this one is preferable. It is set at 5,300 feet near the northeastern shore of the lake, which provides decent trout fishing in the spring and early summer. To the nearby north, Deep Creek in San Bernardino National Forest is well worth exploring; a hike along the stream to fish for small trout or see a unique set of small waterfalls is highly recommended.

Campsites, facilities: There are 27 sites for tents or RVs up to 22 feet long. Picnic tables and fire rings are provided. Drinking water and flush toilets are available. Some facilities are wheelchair-accessible. A store and a coin laundry are nearby. Leashed pets are permitted.

Reservations, fees: Reserve at 877/444-6777 ($9 reservation fee) or website: www.Reserve Usa.com; $12 per night, $5 per night for each extra vehicle. Senior discount available. Open May through November.

Directions: Drive on Highway 30 to San Bernardino and Highway 18 (two miles east of the junction of Highway 30 and Highway 259). Turn north on Highway 18/Rim of the World Highway and drive 17 miles to Highway 173. Turn left on Highway 173 and drive north for 1.6 miles to the stop sign. Turn right (still on Highway 173) and drive 2.9 miles to Hospital Road. Turn right and continue .1 mile to the top of the small hill. Turn left just past the hospital entrance and you will see the campground.

Contact: San Bernardino National Forest, Mountaintop Ranger Station, 909/337-2444, fax 909/337-1104.

43 CRAB FLATS

Rating: 4

Near Crab Creek in San Bernardino National Forest.

Map 14.2, page 727

Four-wheel-drive cowboys and dirt-bike enthusiasts often make this a base camp, known as a staging area for off-highway vehicles. It is a developed Forest Service camp set at a fork in the road at 6,200 feet. A challenging jeep road and motorcycle trail is available from here, heading west into Deep Creek Canyon. Note that Tent Peg Group Camp is just a half mile to the west on Forest Road 3N34 (hiking trails are available there).

Campsites, facilities: There are 29 sites for tents or RVs up to 15 feet long. Drinking water, vault toilets, picnic tables, and fire rings are provided. Leashed pets are permitted.

Reservations, fees: Reserve at 877/444-6777 or website: www.ReserveUsa.com ($9 reservation fee); $15 per night. Senior discount available. Open mid-May through October.

Directions: Drive on Highway 30 to the junction with Highway 330 (east of San Bernardino near Highland). Take Highway 330 North (signed "Mountain Resorts") and drive to Running Springs and the junction with Highway 18. Turn east on Highway 18 and drive to Green Valley Road. Turn left on Green Valley Road and drive three miles to Forest Road 3N16 (a dirt road). Turn left and drive four miles (you will cross two creeks that vary in depth depending on season; high clearance is recommended but is typically not necessary) to an intersection. Bear left at the intersection and drive a very short distance to the campground entrance on the right.

Contact: San Bernardino National Forest, Mountaintop Ranger Station, 909/337-2444, fax 909/337-1104.

44 FISHERMAN'S HIKE-IN GROUP CAMP

Rating: 10

On Deep Creek in San Bernardino National Forest.

Map 14.2, page 727

Get here and you join the 5 Percent Club. Fisherman's Hike-In Group Camp is a secluded, wooded campground set deep in San Bernardino National Forest at 5,400 feet. Deep Creek runs alongside providing stream trout fishing and a beautiful setting. It's worth the significant effort required to get here. Once here, you will find a primitive route along the creek (which looks more like a deer trail than a hiking trail) that anglers use to tromp along the stream. The trout are small but well colored, and the first cast into the head of a pool often results in a strike.

Campsites, facilities: There are four group campsites for up to eight people per site. Picnic tables and fire grills are provided. Vault toilets are available. No drinking water is available. Garbage must be packed out. Leashed pets are permitted.

Reservations, fees: Reservations are required. The fee is $10 per site. Open mid-May to mid-October, weather permitting.

Directions: Drive on Highway 30 to the junction with Highway 330 (east of San Bernardino near Highland). Take Highway 330 North (signed "Mountain Resorts") and drive to Running Springs and the junction with Highway 18. Turn east on Highway 18 and drive to Green Valley Road. Turn left on Green Valley Road and drive three miles to Forest Road 3N16 (a dirt road). Turn left and drive four miles (you will cross two creeks that vary in depth depending on season; high clearance is recommended but is typically not necessary) to the campground (one mile past town of Green Valley Lake) to an intersection with Forest Road 3N34. Bear left on Forest Road 3N34 and drive west for 1.3 miles to Forest Service Trail 2W07 on your left. Park and take this hiking trail for 2.5 miles southwest to Deep Creek. The campground is on the other side of the creek.

Contact: San Bernardino National Forest, Mountaintop Ranger Station, 909/337-2444, fax 909/337-1104.

45 TENT PEG GROUP

Rating:10

Near the Pacific Crest Trail in San Bernardino National Forest.
Map 14.2, page 727

This camp would be a lot easier to reach with a helicopter than a vehicle. But that's why Tent Peg is a well-loved camp for the few who book it: it's a primitive camp for groups at 5,400 feet, complete with trailhead. A rough jeep road heads out of camp to the west and down into Deep Creek. In addition, there is a trailhead for a three-mile hike down the canyon to the south to Fisherman's Hike-In Group Campground, set along Deep Creek. The trout are small but willing, in a beautiful setting.

Campsites, facilities: There is one group camp that will accommodate 10–30 people and five cars. Picnic tables and fire grills are provided. Vault toilets are available. No drinking water is available. A store and coin laundry are five miles away. Leashed pets are permitted.

Reservations, fees: Reserve at 877/444-6777 or website: www.ReserveUsa.com ($9 reservation fee); $50 per night. Open mid-May through October.

Directions: Drive on Highway 30 to the junction with Highway 330 (east of San Bernardino near Highland). Take Highway 330 North (signed "Mountain Resorts") and drive to Running Springs and the junction with Highway 18. Turn east on Highway 18 and drive to Green Valley Road. Turn left on Green Valley Road and drive three miles to Forest Road 3N16 (a dirt road). Turn left and drive four miles (you will cross two creeks that vary in depth depending on season; high clearance is

recommended but is typically not necessary) to the campground (one mile past town of Green Valley Lake) to an intersection with Forest Road 3N34. Bear left on Forest Road 3N34 and drive one mile to the campground on the left.

Contact: San Bernardino National Forest, Mountaintop Ranger Station, 909/337-2444, fax 909/337-1104.

46 IRONWOOD GROUP CAMP

Rating: 7

In San Bernardino National Forest.
Map 14.2, page 727

This is a primitive and isolated group camp. It is set at 6,700 feet, nestled in huge pines amid an old-growth forest, and also close to a creek near a meadow. The last two miles of the access road can be rough going for cars.

Campsites, facilities: There is one group camp that can accommodate up to 25 people and five cars (no trailers or RVs). Picnic tables and fire grills are provided. Vault toilets are available. No drinking water is available. Leashed pets are permitted.

Reservations, fees: Reserve at 877/444-6777 or website: www.ReserveUsa.com ($9 reservation fee); $50 group fee per night. Open June through September.

Directions: Drive on Highway 30 to the junction with Highway 330 (east of San Bernardino near Highland). Take Highway 330 North (signed "Mountain Resorts") and drive 35 miles to the dam on Big Bear Lake and a fork with Highway 38. Turn left on Highway 38 and drive about four miles to the town of Fawnskin and Rim of the World Highway. Turn left and drive six miles (after a half mile it becomes Forest Road 3N14, a dirt road) to Forest Road 3N97. Turn left and drive two miles to the campground.

Contact: San Bernardino National Forest, Big Bear Ranger District Discovery Center, 909/866-3437, fax 909/866-1781.

47 BIG PINE FLATS

Rating: 6

In San Bernardino National Forest.

Map 14.2, page 727

This is a favorite staging area for OHV users, with many OHV trails nearby. It is a pretty spot set at 6,800 feet in San Bernardino National Forest and provides a little of both worlds: you are surrounded by wildlands near Redondo Ridge, yet you're not a long drive from Big Bear Lake to the south. Any questions? The firefighters at Big Pine Flats Fire Station, just across the road, can answer them.

Campsites, facilities: There are 17 sites for tents or RVs up to 32 feet long. Picnic tables and fire grills are provided. Vault toilets are available. No drinking water is available. Leashed pets are permitted.

Reservations, fees: Reservations are not accepted. The fee is $12 per night. Senior discount available. Open mid-May to mid-November.

Directions: Drive on Highway 30 to the junction with Highway 330 (east of San Bernardino near Highland). Take Highway 330 North (signed "Mountain Resorts") and drive 35 miles to the dam on Big Bear Lake and a fork with Highway 38. Turn left on Highway 38 and drive about four miles to the town of Fawnskin and Rim of the World Highway. Turn left and drive seven miles (after a half mile it becomes Forest Road 3N14, a dirt road) to Big Pine Flats Fire Station and the campground on the right.

Contact: San Bernardino National Forest, Big Bear Ranger District Discovery Center, 909/866-3437, fax 909/866-1781.

48 BIG PINE HORSE CAMP

Rating: 3

In San Bernardino National Forest.

Map 14.2, page 727

You might want to bring an apple or a carrot, or maybe some nose plugs. Of course, if you're a horse lover, none of that is a problem. That's because this is a camp for the horse packers adjacent to the Big Pine Flats Fire Station. A trailhead for the Pacific Crest Trail is about two miles to the southeast of the camp via Forest Road 3N14. The elevation is 6,700 feet.

Campsites, facilities: This camp is expressly for equestrians. There is one group camp that can accommodate up to 60 people and 15 cars or RVs up to 32 feet, and stock. Picnic tables and fire grills are provided. Vault toilets are available. No drinking water is available, but water is available for livestock. Leashed pets are permitted.

Reservations, fees: Reserve at 877/444-6777 or website: www.ReserveUsa.com ($9 reservation fee); $50 group fee per night. Open mid-May to mid-November.

Directions: Drive on Highway 30 to the junction with Highway 330 (east of San Bernardino near Highland). Take Highway 330 North (signed "Mountain Resorts") and drive 35 miles to the dam on Big Bear Lake and a fork with Highway 38. Turn left on Highway 38 and drive about four miles to the town of Fawnskin and Rim of the World Highway. Turn left and drive seven miles (after a half mile it becomes Forest Road 3N14, a dirt road) to Forest Road 3N16. Turn left and drive a quarter mile to the campground on the right.

Contact: San Bernardino National Forest, Big Bear Ranger District Discovery Center, 909/866-3437, fax 909/866-1781.

49 SHADY COVE GROUP WALK-IN

Rating: 7

Near the Children's Forest in
San Bernardino National Forest.

Map 14.2, page 727

The highlight here is the adjacent short looped trail that is routed through the Children's Forest. The camp is excellent for Boy Scout and

Girl Scout troops. The walk to the camp is about 100 yards. The elevation is 7,500 feet.

Campsites, facilities: There are two group campsites, which can accommodate a maximum of 30 at one site and 70 at the other. When reserved together, the two sites are allowed a maximum of 100 people with a limit of 15 cars (no trailers or RVs). Picnic tables and fire grills are provided. Drinking water and flush toilets are available. Note: the camp is gated for safety; groups are given a key. Leashed pets are permitted.

Reservations, fees: Reservations are required. The fee is $30 and $70 per night. Open May through September.

Directions: Drive on Highway 30 to San Bernardino and Highway 18 (two miles east of the junction of Highway 30 and Highway 259). Turn north on Highway 18/Rim of the World Highway and drive 17 miles to the Mountaintop Ranger Station, then continue east on Highway 18 for seven miles (past the town of Running Springs) to Keller Peak Road (just past Deer Lick Fire Station). Turn right (south) on Keller Peak Road and drive four miles to the Children's Forest. Bear left to the parking area. The sites are 100 yards from the parking area.

Contact: San Bernardino National Forest, Mountaintop Ranger Station, 909/337-2444, fax 909/337-1104.

50 POMONA-FAIRPLEX KOA

Rating: 4

In Pomona.

Map 14.2, page 727

This is what you might call an urban RV park. Then again, the L.A. County Fairgrounds are right across the street, and there's something going on there every weekend. Fishing at Bonelli Park is only 15 minutes away.

Campsites, facilities: There are 159 drive-through sites with full hookups for RVs and 27 sites with partial hookups for RVs. Restrooms, show-ers, heated pool and spa, convenience store, RV dump station, and coin laundry are available. Some facilities are wheelchair-accessible.

Reservations, fees: Reservations are accepted. The fee is $33–40 per night, $1 for each extra vehicle, $4 per person for more than two people. Major credit cards accepted. Open year-round.

Directions: Drive on I-10 to the exit for Fairplex (five miles west of Pomona). Take that exit north (toward the mountain) and drive two miles to McKinley Avenue. Turn right on McKinley Avenue and drive one mile to White Avenue. Turn left and drive about a half mile (.2 mile south of Arrow Street) to the park on the right (2200 N. White Avenue).

Contact: Pomona-Fairplex KOA, 909/865-4318 or 909/593-8915; website: www.fairplexkoa.com or www.koa.com.

51 EAST SHORE RV PARK

Rating: 7

At Puddingstone Lake.

Map 14.2, page 727

Considering how close Puddingstone Lake is to so many people, the quality of fishing and water-skiing might be a surprise to newcomers. The lake covers 250 acres and is an excellent recreation facility. For the most part, rules permit water-skiing between 10 A.M. and 4 P.M., making it an excellent lake for fishing for bass and trout (in season) during the morning and evening. In addition, even days are set for water-skiing and boating (but no personal watercraft), and odd days for personal watercraft. A ski beach is available on the north shore, and there is a large, sandy swimming beach on the southwest shore about a mile away. The lake is just south of Raging Waters in San Dimasand is bordered to the south by Bonelli Regional County Park; there is also golf course adjacent to the park.

Campsites, facilities: There are 519 sites, 14 drive-through, with full hookups for RVs, and

25 walk-in sites for tents. Restrooms, showers, recreation room, swimming pool, modem access, cable TV, store, propane gas delivery, and coin laundry are available. A hot tub facility is nearby. Leashed pets are permitted. Some facilities are wheelchair-accessible.

Reservations, fees: Reservations are accepted. The fee is $30–32 per night, $2 per person for more than two people, $2 per night. Major credit cards accepted. Open year-round.

Directions: Drive on I-10 to the exit for Fairplex (five miles west of Pomona). Take that exit north to Via Verde (the first traffic light). Turn left on Via Verde and drive to the first stop sign at Campers View. Turn right on Campers View and drive into the park.

Contact: East Shore RV Park, 909/599-8355 or 800/809-3778, fax 909/592-7481.

52 YUCAIPA REGIONAL PARK

Rating: 7

Near Redlands.

Map 14.2, page 727

This is a great family-oriented county park, complete with water slides and paddleboats for the kids and fishing access and hiking trails for adults. Three lakes are stocked weekly with catfish in the summer and trout in the winter, the closest thing around to an insurance policy for anglers. Spectacular scenic views of the Yucaipa Valley, the San Bernardino Mountains, and Mt. San Gorgonio are possible from the park. The park covers 885 acres in the foothills of the San Bernardino Mountains. A one-acre swimming lagoon and two 350-foot water slides make this a favorite for youngsters. The Yucaipa Adobe and Mousley Museum of Natural History is nearby.

Campsites, facilities: There are 26 sites, 18 drive-through and 11 with full hookups, for RVs, nine sites for tents, and nine group camps. Picnic tables and fire rings are provided. Restrooms, drinking water, flush toilets, and showers are available. A swimming lagoon, fishing

ponds, water slides, paddleboat rentals, aquacycle rentals, pay phone, snack bar, picnic shelter, playground with volleyball and horseshoes, and RV dump station are available nearby. The water slide is open Memorial Day weekend through Labor Day weekend. Some facilities are wheelchair-accessible. Leashed pets are permitted.

Reservations, fees: Reservations are accepted. The fee is $11 per night for tent sites, $20 per night for RV sites, $1 per night. Major credit cards accepted. Additional charges for fishing, swimming, and use of the water slide. Open year-round.

Directions: Drive on I-10 to Redlands and the exit for Yucaipa Boulevard. Take that exit and drive east on Yucaipa Boulevard to Oak Glen Road. Turn left and continue two miles to the park on the left.

Contact: Yucaipa Regional Park, 909/790-3127, fax 909/790-3121, website: www.co.san-bernardino.ca.us/parks.

53 HANNA FLAT

Rating: 8

Near Big Bear Lake in San Bernardino National Forest.

Map 14.3, page 728

This is one of the largest, best maintained, and most popular of the Forest Service camps in the Big Bear Lake District (Serrano Campground is the most popular). All the trees and vegetation provide seclusion for individual sites. There is great forest scenery with many hardwood trees, including oak and mountain mahogany. The camp is set at 7,000 feet on the slopes on the north side of Big Bear Lake, just under three miles from the lake. Big Bear is a beautiful mountain lake covering more than 3,000 acres, with 22 miles of shoreline and often excellent trout fishing and water-skiing. A trailhead for the Pacific Crest Trail is a mile by road north of the camp.

Campsites, facilities: There are 69 sites for tents

and 19 sites for tents or RVs up to 32 feet long. Picnic tables and fire grills are provided. Drinking water and flush toilets are available. Some facilities are wheelchair-accessible. Leashed pets are permitted.

Reservations, fees: Reserve at 877/444-6777 or website: www.ReserveUsa.com ($9 reservation fee); $15 per night, $5 for a second vehicle. Senior discount available. Open May through September.

Directions: Drive on Highway 30 to the junction with Highway 330 (east of San Bernardino near Highland). Take Highway 330 North (signed "Mountain Resorts") and drive 35 miles to the dam on Big Bear Lake and a fork for Highway 38. Take the left fork to Highway 38 and drive about four miles to the town of Fawnskin and Rim of the World Highway. Turn left and drive three miles (after a half mile, it becomes Forest Road 3N14, a dirt road) to the campground on the left.

Contact: San Bernardino National Forest, Big Bear Ranger District Discovery Center, 909/866-3437, fax 909/866-1781.

54 GRAY'S PEAK GROUP CAMP

Rating: 4

Near Big Bear Lake in San Bernardino National Forest.

Map 14.3, page 728

The appeal of this primitive group camp is its proximity to Big Bear Lake, with the camp just three miles northwest of the lake, set at 7,200 feet. Gray's Peak (7,952 feet) is about a mile south of the camp, but there is no direct access to the peak. The drive is not recommended for trailers or large RVs.

Campsites, facilities: There is one group campsite for up to 40 people and eight cars (limited use of trailers and RVs up to 32 feet). Picnic tables and fire grills are provided. Vault toilets are available. No drinking water is available. Leashed pets are permitted.

Reservations, fees: Reserve at 877/444-6777

or website: www.ReserveUsa.com ($9 reservation fee); $65 per night. Open June through September.

Directions: Drive on Highway 30 to the junction with Highway 330 (east of San Bernardino near Highland). Take Highway 330 North (signed "Mountain Resorts") and drive 35 miles to the dam on Big Bear Lake and a fork for Highway 38. Take the left fork to Highway 38 and drive about four miles to the town of Fawnskin and Rim of the World Highway. Turn left and drive 1.2 miles (after a half mile, it becomes Forest Road 3N14, a dirt road) to Forest Road 2N13. Turn left and drive about a mile to the campground on the right.

Contact: San Bernardino National Forest, Big Bear Ranger District Discovery Center, 909/866-3437, fax 909/866-1781.

55 SERRANO

Rating: 8

On Big Bear Lake in San Bernardino National Forest.

Map 14.3, page 728

This campground opened in the 1990s and became the first National Forest campground to offer state-of-the-art restrooms and hot showers. That is why it costs so much to camp here. Regardless, it has since become the most popular campground in the region. Location is also a big plus, as this is one of the few camps at Big Bear within walking distance of the lakeshore. It covers 60 acres, a big plus. Another bonus is a paved trail that is wheelchair-accessible. Want more? Big Bear is the jewel of Southern California lakes, the Lake Tahoe of the South, with outstanding trout fishing and water-skiing. A trailhead for the Pacific Crest Trail is nearby, and Canada is only 2,200 miles away. The elevation is 6,800 feet.

Campsites, facilities: There are 132 sites, 30 sites with full hookups, for RVs up to 36 feet long or tents. Picnic tables and fire rings are provided. Restrooms, drinking water, flush toilets, showers, and RV dump station are available. Some facilities are wheelchair-accessible. A store is nearby. Leashed pets are permitted.

Reservations, fees: Reserve at 877/444-6777 or website: www.ReserveUsa.com ($9 reservation fee); $20 per night, $40 per night for double sites. Senior discount available. Open mid-April to mid-November.

Directions: Drive on Highway 30 to the junction with Highway 330 (east of San Bernardino near Highland). Take Highway 330 North (signed "Mountain Resorts") and drive 35 miles to the dam on Big Bear Lake and a fork with Highway 38 and Highway 18. Bear left at Highway 38 and drive about 2.5 miles to Fawnskin and North Shore Lane (signed Serrano Campground). Turn on North Shore Lane and drive to the campground entrance.

Contact: San Bernardino National Forest, Big Bear Ranger District Discovery Center, 909/866-3437, fax 909/866-1781.

56 HOLLOWAY'S MARINA AND RV PARK

Rating: 6

On Big Bear Lake.
Map 14.3, page 728

This privately operated RV park (no tent sites) is a good choice at Big Bear Lake with boat rentals, ramp, and full marina available. Big Bear is the jewel of Southern California's lakes, covering more than 3,000 surface acres with 22 miles of shoreline. Its cool waters make for excellent trout fishing, and yet, by summer, it has heated up enough to make for superb water-skiing. A bonus in the summer is that a breeze off the lake keeps the temperature in the mid-80s.

Campsites, facilities: There are 100 sites with full hookups, two with partial hookups, and seven with no hookups for RVs. Picnic tables and fire grills are provided. Restrooms, drinking water, flush toilets, showers, RV dump station, cable TV, convenience store, ice, propane gas, coin laundry, playground, and a full ma-

rina with boat rentals are on the premises. Leashed pets are permitted.

Reservations, fees: Reservations are accepted. The fee is $25–40 per night, $5 for each extra vehicle. Major credit cards accepted. Open year-round, weather permitting.

Directions: Drive on Highway 30 to the junction with Highway 330 (east of San Bernardino near Highland). Take Highway 330 North (signed "Mountain Resorts") and drive 35 miles to the dam on Big Bear Lake and a fork with Highway 38 and Highway 18. Turn right at Highway 18 and drive three miles to Edgemoor Road (at a log cabin restaurant). Turn left at Edgemoor Road and drive one-half mile to the park on the left.

Contact: Holloway's Marina and RV Park, 909/866-5706 or 800/448-5335, fax 909/866-5436.

57 PINEKNOT

Rating: 6

Near Big Bear Lake in San Bernardino National Forest.
Map 14.3, page 728

This popular, developed Forest Service camp is set just east of Big Bear Lake Village (on the southern shore of the lake) about two miles from the lake. It is a popular spot for mountain biking, with several ideal routes available. Of the camps at Big Bear, this is the closest to supplies. The elevation is 7,000 feet.

Campsites, facilities: There are 52 sites for tents and RVs up to 45 feet long. Picnic tables and fire grills are provided. Drinking water and flush toilets are available. Some facilities are wheelchair-accessible. A store and coin laundry are nearby. Leashed pets are permitted.

Reservations, fees: Reserve at 877/444-6777 or website: www.ReserveUsa.com ($9 reservation fee); $18 per night. Senior discount available. Open mid-May through September.

Directions: Drive on Highway 30 to the junction with Highway 330 (east of San Bernardino near Highland). Take Highway 330 North (signed "Mountain Resorts") and drive 35 miles to the dam on Big Bear Lake and a fork with Highway 38 and Highway 18. Turn right at Highway 18 and drive about six miles to Summit Boulevard. Turn right and drive through the parking area to the road on the left (just before the gate to the ski area). Turn left and drive a quarter mile to the campground on the right.

Contact: San Bernardino National Forest, Big Bear Ranger District Discovery Center, 909/866-3437, fax 909/866-1781.

58 BUTTERCUP GROUP CAMP

Rating: 5

Near the town of Big Bear Lake in San Bernardino National Forest.

Map 14.3, page 728

This is a forested camp designed for large groups looking for a developed site near Big Bear Lake. It is about four miles from the southeast side of the lake, just outside the Snow Summit Ski Area. The elevation is 7,000 feet.

Campsites, facilities: There is one group campsite for up to 40 people and eight cars (limited use of trailers or RVs up to 32 feet long). Picnic tables and fire rings are provided. Drinking water and portable toilets are available. A store and coin laundry are nearby. Leashed pets are permitted.

Reservations, fees: Reservations are requested. Reserve at 877/444-6777 ($9 reservation fee) or website: www. reserveusa.com; $75 group fee per night. Open June through September.

Directions: Drive on Highway 30 to the junction with Highway 330 (east of San Bernardino near Highland). Take Highway 330 North (signed "Mountain Resorts") and drive 35 miles to the dam on Big Bear Lake and a fork with Highway 38 and Highway 18. Turn right at Highway 18 and drive about six miles to Summit Boulevard. Turn right and drive through the parking area to the road on the left (just before the gate to the ski area). Turn left and

drive a half mile (past Pineknot Camp) to the campground on the right.

Contact: San Bernardino National Forest, Big Bear Ranger District Discovery Center, 909/866-3437, fax 909/866-1781.

59 HOLCOMB VALLEY

Rating: 7

Near the Pacific Crest Trail in San Bernardino National Forest.

Map 14.3, page 728

This camp is set near the Holcomb Valley Historic Area, at 7,400 feet in the mountains about four miles north of Big Bear Lake. On the way in on Van Dusen Canyon Road you will pass a trailhead for the Pacific Crest Trail (two miles southeast of the camp.) From here you can make the two-mile climb southwest to Bertha Peak, 8,198 feet, overlooking Big Bear to the south.

Campsites, facilities: There are 19 sites for tents or RVs up to 32 feet long. Picnic tables and fire grills are provided. Pit toilets are available. No drinking water is available. Garbage service provided only in summer. Leashed pets are permitted.

Reservations, fees: Reservations are not accepted. The fee is $10 per night. Senior discount available. Open year-round, weather permitting.

Directions: Drive on Highway 30 to the junction with Highway 330 (east of San Bernardino near Highland). Take Highway 330 North (signed "Mountain Resorts") and drive 35 miles to the dam on Big Bear Lake and a fork with Highway 38. Take the left fork to Highway 38 and drive about 10 miles to Van Dusen Canyon Road/Forest Road 3N09. Turn left and drive three miles (a dirt road) to Forest Road 3N16. Turn left and drive to the campground on the right.

Contact: San Bernardino National Forest, Big Bear Ranger District Discovery Center, 909/866-3437, fax 909/866-1781.

60 TANGLEWOOD GROUP CAMP

🏕 🚐 🏖 ⛺

Rating: 4

On the Pacific Crest Trail in San Bernardino National Forest.

Map 14.3, page 728

This primitive group camp is off an old spur road with the Pacific Crest Trail trailhead the primary highlight. It is set at 7,400 feet in a flat but wooded area northeast of Big Bear Lake. It is about a 10- to 15-minute drive from Big Bear City.

Campsites, facilities: There is one group campsite for up to 40 people and eight cars (limited use of trailers or RVs up to 32 feet long). Picnic tables and fire grills are provided. Pit toilets are available. No drinking water is available. Leashed pets are permitted.

Reservations, fees: Reserve at 877/444-6777 or website: www.ReserveUsa.com ($9 reservation fee); $65 group fee per night. Open June through September.

Directions: Drive on Highway 30 to the junction with Highway 330 (east of San Bernardino near Highland). Take Highway 330 North (signed "Mountain Resorts") and drive 35 miles to the dam on Big Bear Lake and a fork for Highway 38. Take the left fork to Highway 38 and drive about 10 miles to Van Dusen Canyon Road/Forest Road 3N09. Turn left (dirt road) and drive four miles to Forest Road 3N16. Turn right and drive 1.7 miles to Forest Road 3N79. Turn right and drive a half mile to the campground. Trailers are not recommended.

Contact: San Bernardino National Forest, Big Bear Ranger District Discovery Center, 909/866-3437, fax 909/866-1781.

61 BLUFF MESA GROUP CAMP

🏕 🚐 ⛺

Rating: 7

Near Big Bear Lake in San Bernardino National Forest.

Map 14.3, page 728

Bluff Mesa Group Camp is one of several camps south of Big Bear Lake. A highlight here is the trailhead (signed on the access road on the way in) for the half-mile walk to the Champion Lodgepole Pine, the largest lodgepole pine in the world: 400 years old, 112 feet tall, with a circumference of 20 feet. Many Forest Service roads are available nearby for self-planned side trips. The elevation is 7,600 feet.

Campsites, facilities: There is one group campsite for up to 40 people and eight cars. Picnic tables and fire grills are provided. Pit toilets are available. No drinking water is available. Leashed pets are permitted.

Reservations, fees: Reservations are requested. Reserve at 877/444-6777 or website: www.ReserveUsa.com ($9 reservation fee); $50 group fee per night. Open June through September.

Directions: Drive on Highway 30 to the junction with Highway 330 (east of San Bernardino near Highland). Take Highway 330 North (signed "Mountain Resorts") and drive 35 miles to the dam on Big Bear Lake and a fork with Highway 38 and Highway 18. Turn right at Highway 18 and drive about four miles to Mill Creek Road. Turn right on Mill Creek Road and drive about 1.5 miles to the sign at the top of the hill and Forest Road 2N10. Turn right on Forest Road 2N10 and drive three miles (dirt road) to Forest Road 2N86. Turn right on Forest Road 2N86 and drive a quarter mile to the campground.

Contact: San Bernardino National Forest, Big Bear Ranger District Discovery Center, 909/866-3437, fax 909/866-1781.

62 SIBERIA CREEK HIKE-IN GROUP CAMP

🏕 🏊 🚐 5% ⛺

Rating: 7

In San Bernardino National Forest.

Map 14.3, page 728

This is a primitive area that requires a fairly steep three-mile hike. Your reward is solitude at a camp that will hold up to 40 people. The camp is set near the confluence of Siberia

Creek and larger Bear Creek. The latter is the major feeder stream into Big Bear Lake, and both provide a good opportunity to try sneak-fishing techniques for small rainbow trout. The elevation is 4,800 feet.

Campsites, facilities: There is one group campsite for up to 40 people. Fire rings are provided, but that's all. No drinking water is available. Garbage must be packed out. Leashed pets are permitted.

Reservations, fees: Reservations are required. There is no camping fee. An Adventure Pass ($30 annual fee or a $5 daily fee per vehicle) is required. Open June through September.

Directions: Drive on Highway 30 to the junction with Highway 330 (east of San Bernardino near Highland). Take Highway 330 North (signed "Mountain Resorts") and drive about 20 miles to the turnoff signed Camp Creek Trail (just past Snow Valley Ski Area). Take the Camp Creek Trail turnoff and follow the signs to the trailhead. Park and hike three miles to the camp.

Contact: San Bernardino National Forest, Big Bear Ranger District Discovery Center, 909/866-3437, fax 909/866-1781.

63 BOULDER GROUP CAMP
🐾 🚐 ⛺

Rating: 6

Near Big Bear Lake in San Bernardino National Forest.

Map 14.3, page 728

This is a primitive camp at 7,500 feet elevation, just far enough away from some prime attractions to make you wish you could move the camp to a slightly different spot. The headwaters of Metcalf Creek are hidden in the forest on the other side of the road, tiny Cedar Lake is about a half-mile drive north, and Big Bear Lake is about two miles north. You get the idea.

Campsites, facilities: There is one group campsite for up to 40 people and eight cars (limited use of trailers and RVs up to 32 feet). Picnic

tables and fire grills are provided. Pit toilets are available. No drinking water is available. A store and coin laundry are nearby. Leashed pets are permitted.

Reservations, fees: Reserve at 877/444-6777 or website: www.ReserveUsa.com ($9 reservation fee); $50 group fee per night. Open June through September.

Directions: Drive on Highway 30 to the junction with Highway 330 (east of San Bernardino near Highland). Take Highway 330 North (signed "Mountain Resorts") and drive 35 miles to the dam on Big Bear Lake and a fork with Highway 38 and Highway 18. Turn right at Highway 18 and drive about four miles to Mill Creek Road. Turn right on Mill Creek Road and drive about 1.5 miles to the sign at the top of the hill and Forest Road 2N10. Turn right on Forest Road 2N10 and drive about two miles to the campground entrance road (Forest Road 2M10B). Turn right and drive to the camp.

Contact: San Bernardino National Forest, Big Bear Ranger District Discovery Center, 909/866-3437, fax 909/866-1781.

64 JUNIPER SPRINGS GROUP CAMP
🐾 🚐 ⛺

Rating: 3

In San Bernardino National Forest.

Map 14.3, page 728

This is a little-known group camp, set at 7,700 feet in a desertlike area about 10 miles east of Big Bear Lake. It is little known because there are not a lot of reasons to camp here. You need to be creative. Got a Scrabble game? Want to watch the junipers grow? Or maybe watch the features of the land change colors as the day passes? You get the idea.

Campsites, facilities: There is one group camp for up to 40 people and eight cars (limited use of trailers and RVs up to 32 feet long). Picnic tables and fire grills are provided. Pit toilets are available. No drinking water is available. Leashed pets are permitted.

Reservations, fees: Reserve at 877/444-6777 or website: www.ReserveUsa.com ($9 reservation fee); $50 per night. Open June through September.

Directions: Drive on I-10 to Redlands and Highway 38. Take Highway 38 northeast and drive about 40 miles (1.5 miles past Onyx Summit) to Forest Road 2N01 on the right. Turn right (dirt road) and drive three miles to a Forest Service road (opposite the sign on the left posted Forest Road 2N04). Turn right and drive into the campground.

Contact: San Bernardino National Forest, Big Bear Ranger District Discovery Center, 909/866-3437, fax 909/866-1781.

65 COON CREEK CABIN GROUP CAMP

Rating: 4

On the Pacific Crest Trail in San Bernardino National Forest.

Map 14.3, page 728

Backpackers call this the "Coon Creek jump-off" because it is set on the Pacific Crest Trail at 8,200 feet and provides a "jump-off" for a trek on the PCT. The camp is set on Coon Creek, but the creek often runs dry by summer. Note that in the off-season the access road, Forest Road 1N02, can be gated; campers must hike or cross-country ski to the camp.

Campsites, facilities: There is one group camp for up to 40 people and 14 cars (no trailers or RVs). Picnic tables and fire grills are provided. Vault toilets are available. No drinking water is available. Leashed pets are permitted.

Reservations, fees: Reserve at 877/444-6777 or website: www.ReserveUsa.com ($9 reservation fee); $50 group fee per night. Open year-round.

Directions: Drive on I-10 to Redlands and Highway 38. Take Highway 38 northeast and drive 33.5 miles to Forest Road 1N02. Turn right and drive five miles to the campground entrance (dirt road).

Contact: San Bernardino National Forest, Big Bear Ranger District Discovery Center, 909/866-3437, fax 909/866-1781.

66 COUNCIL GROUP CAMP

Rating: 5

Near Jenks Lake and the San Gorgonio Wilderness in San Bernardino National Forest.

Map 14.3, page 728

This is a group camp in a pretty wooded area across the road from little Jenks Lake (there is a nice, easy walk around the lake) and a few miles north of the northern border of the San Gorgonio Wilderness. There are several other camps in the area.

Campsites, facilities: There is one group campsite for tents only for up to 50 people and 10 cars (no trailers or RVs). Picnic tables and fire rings are provided. Drinking water and vault toilets are available. Leashed pets are permitted.

Reservations, fees: Reserve at 877/444-6777 or website: www.ReserveUsa.com ($9 reservation fee); $100 group fee per night. Open May through November.

Directions: Drive on I-10 to Redlands and Highway 38. Take Highway 38 northeast and drive 26 miles to the campground on the left.

Contact: San Bernardino National Forest, Mill Creek Ranger Station, 909/794-1123, fax 909/794-1125.

67 BARTON FLATS

Rating: 7

Near Jenks Lake in San Bernardino National Forest.

Map 14.3, page 728

This is one of the more developed Forest Service camps in San Bernardino National Forest. The camp is set at 6,500 feet near the northwest end of Jenks Lake, a small, pretty lake with good hiking and a picnic area. Barton Creek, a small stream, runs nearby although it may be waterless in late summer. The San Gorgonio Wilderness, one mile to the south, is accessible via Forest Service roads to the wilderness area trailhead. Permits are required for overnight camping within the wilderness boundaries and are available at Forest Service ranger stations. For those driving in on Highway 38, stop at the Mill Creek Ranger Station in Redlands.

Campsites, facilities: There are 52 sites for RVs up to 55 feet long. Picnic tables and fire grills are provided. Drinking water and flush toilets are available. Some facilities are wheelchair-accessible. Leashed pets are permitted.

Reservations, fees: Reserve at 877/444-6777 or website: www.ReserveUsa.com ($9 reservation fee); $20 per night, $30 for multifamily sites, $5 for each additional vehicle. Senior discount available. Open mid-May through October.

Directions: Drive on I-10 to Redlands and Highway 38. Take Highway 38 northeast and drive 27.5 miles to the campground on the left.

Contact: San Bernardino National Forest, Mill Creek Ranger Station, 909/794-1123, fax 909/794-1125.

68 SAN GORGONIO

Rating: 7

Near the San Gorgonio Wilderness in San Bernardino National Forest.
Map 14.3, page 728

San Gorgonio is one in a series of Forest Service camps along Highway 38 near Jenks Lake. (See the entry for Barton Flats for details.) The elevation is 6,500 feet.

Campsites, facilities: There are 54 sites for RVs up to 55 feet long. Picnic tables and fire grills are provided. Restrooms, drinking water, flush toilets, and showers are available. Leashed pets are permitted. Some facilities are wheelchair-accessible.

Reservations, fees: Reserve at 877/444-6777 or website: www.ReserveUsa.com ($9 reservation fee); $20 per night, $30 for multifamily sites,

$5 for each additional vehicle. Senior discount available. Open mid-May through October.

Directions: Drive on I-10 to Redlands and Highway 38. Take Highway 38 northeast and drive 28 miles to the campground.

Contact: San Bernardino National Forest, Mill Creek Ranger Station, 909/794-1123, fax 909/794-1125.

69 OSO AND LOBO GROUP

Rating: 6

Near the San Gorgonio Wilderness in San Bernardino National Forest.
Map 14.3, page 728

Oso and Lobo Group Camps are set directly adjacent to each other at 6,600 feet elevation. The camps are about three-quarters of a mile from the Santa Ana River. Little Jenks Lake is two miles away to the west, and the northern border of the San Gorgonio Wilderness is just a few miles to the south.

Campsites, facilities: Oso will accept up to 100 people and 20 cars (limited use of trailers and RVs), and Lobo accepts up to 75 people and 15 cars. Picnic tables and fire grills are provided. Drinking water and flush toilets are available. Leashed pets are permitted.

Reservations, fees: Reserve at 877/444-6777 or website: www.ReserveUsa.com ($9 reservation fee); $150 per night for Lobo, $200 per night for Oso. Open April through October, weather permitting.

Directions: From I-10 in Redlands, drive 29 miles east on Highway 38 to the campground entrance road on the left.

Contact: San Bernardino National Forest, Mill Creek Ranger Station, 909/794-1123, fax 909/794-1125.

70 SOUTH FORK
🏊 🐕 🚐 ⛺

Rating: 7

Near the Santa Ana River in San Bernardino National Forest.

Map 14.3, page 728

This is an easy-access Forest Service camp just off Highway 38, set at 6,400 feet near the headwaters of the South Fork Santa Ana River. It is part of the series of camps in the immediate area, just north of the San Gorgonio Wilderness. This one is a four-mile drive from little Jenks Lake. (See the entry for Barton Flats for more details.)

Campsites, facilities: There are 24 sites for tents or RVs up to 30 feet long. Picnic tables and fire rings are provided. Drinking water and vault toilets are available. Leashed pets are permitted.

Reservations, fees: Reservations are not accepted. The fee is $15 per night, $5 for each additional vehicle. Open mid-May through mid-October.

Directions: Drive on I-10 to Redlands and Highway 38. Take Highway 38 northeast and drive 29.5 miles to the campground entrance road.

Contact: San Bernardino National Forest, Mill Creek Ranger Station, 909/794-1123, fax 909/794-1125.

71 SKYLINE GROUP CAMP
🥾 🐕 ⛺

Rating: 6

In San Bernardino National Forest.

Map 14.3, page 728

Skyline Group Camp is set at an elevation of 6,900 feet near Big Meadows. A trailhead at the end of a short spur road about a half mile to the north off the main road provides access to a great butt-kicker of a trail about eight or nine miles (one way) that runs along Wildhorse Creek and up to Sugarloaf Mountain, elevation 9,952 feet. Insider's note: a trail camp is set on Wildhorse Creek, just past the midway point on the trail to Sugarloaf Mountain.

Campsites, facilities: There is one group campsite for up to 25 people. Picnic tables and fire rings are provided. Drinking water and vault toilets are available. Leashed pets are permitted.

Reservations, fees: Reserve at 877/444-6777 or website: www.ReserveUsa.com ($9 reservation fee); $50 group fee per night. Open May through November.

Directions: Drive on I-10 to Redlands and Highway 38. Take Highway 38 northeast and drive 33.5 miles to Forest Road 1N02. Turn right and drive a mile to the campground (just behind Heart Bar Campground).

Contact: San Bernardino National Forest, Mill Creek Ranger Station, 909/794-1123, fax 909/794-1125.

72 HEART BAR FAMILY CAMP
🥾 🐕 ♿ 🚐 ⛺

Rating: 4

In San Bernardino National Forest.

Map 14.3, page 728

It's a good thing there is drinking water at this camp. Why? Because Heart Bar Creek often isn't much more than a trickle and can't be relied on for water. The camp is set at 6,900 feet near Big Meadows, the location of the Heart Bar Fire Station. A challenging butt-kicker of a hike has a trailhead about a half mile away to the north off a spur road, midway between the camp and the fire station. The trail here is routed along Wildhorse Creek to Sugarloaf Mountain (9,952 feet, about eight or nine miles one way to the top). Insider's note: just past the midway point on the trail to Sugarloaf Mountain is a trail camp on Wildhorse Creek.

Campsites, facilities: There are 95 sites for tents or RVs up to 50 feet long. Picnic tables and fire grills are provided. Drinking water and vault toilets are available. Some facilities are wheelchair-accessible. Leashed pets are permitted.

Reservations, fees: Reserve at 877/444-6777 or website: www.ReserveUsa.com ($9 reservation fee); $15 per night for single family sites, $25 for multifamily sites. Open May through November.

Directions: Drive on I-10 to Redlands and Highway 38. Take Highway 38 northeast and drive 33.5 miles to Forest Road 1N02. Turn right and drive a mile to the campground (adjacent to Skyline Group Campground).

Contact: San Bernardino National Forest, Mill Creek Ranger Station, 909/794-1123, fax 909/794-1125.

73 HEART BAR EQUESTRIAN GROUP AND WILD HORSE EQUESTRIAN

Rating: 5

In San Bernardino National Forest.

Map 14.3, page 728

You might not meet Mr. Ed here, but bring an apple anyway. Heart Bar is a horse camp on Heart Bar Creek, less than a mile east of Heart Bar Family Camp. Wild Horse is just .1 mile down the road. A good trail that leads into the San Gorgonio Wilderness starts four miles down the road at Fish Creek Meadows. It is routed west for three miles to Fish Creek and then up Grinnell Mountain to the north peak of the Ten Thousand Foot Ridge. A wilderness permit is required. The elevation is 7,000 feet.

Campsites, facilities: Heart Bar has one group campsite with 46 corrals for up to 65 people and 21 cars (limited use of trailers and RVs). Wild Horse has 11 equestrian sites. Picnic tables and fire grills are provided. Flush toilets are available. No drinking water is available. Water is available for horses. Leashed pets are permitted.

Reservations, fees: Reserve at 877/444-6777 or website: www.ReserveUsa.com ($9 reservation fee); $20 per night for family equestrian sites, $200 per night for group sites. At Wild Horse, $5 per night for each extra vehicle. Open May through November.

Directions: Drive on I-10 to Redlands and Highway 38. Take Highway 38 northeast and drive

33.5 miles to Forest Road 1N02. Turn right and drive a mile to the Heart Bar Group Campground on the right. Continue for .1 mile to the camp on the left.

Contact: San Bernardino National Forest, Mill Creek Ranger Station, 909/794-1123, fax 909/794-1125.

74 DOCKWEILER BEACH RV PARK

Rating: 6

On the Pacific Ocean near Manhattan Beach.

Map 14.4, page 729

This layover spot for coast cruisers is just a hop from the beach and the Pacific Ocean. There is access to a 26-mile-long coastal bike path.

Campsites, facilities: There are 117 sites, 82 with full hookups for RVs up to 35 feet long. Picnic tables and barbecue grills are provided. Flush toilets, hot showers, RV dump station, and coin laundry are available. Some facilities are wheelchair-accessible. You can buy supplies nearby. Leashed pets are permitted.

Reservations, fees: Reserve weekdays at 800/950-7275 ($7 reservation fee), $17–27 per night, $6 for more than one vehicle, $1 per night. Open year-round. Major credit cards accepted.

Directions: From Santa Monica and the junction of I-405 and I-10, take I-405 south and drive 12 miles to the exit for Imperial Highway West. Take that exit and drive west on Imperial Highway for four miles to the park (signed) on the left.

Contact: Dockweiler Beach, Los Angeles County, 800/950-7275 or 310/322-4951, fax 310/322-7036.

75 DEL RIO MOBILE HOME AND RV PARK

Rating: 1

Near Los Angeles.

Map 14.4, page 729

This privately operated, urban RV park is about

15 minutes from downtown Los Angeles and 20 minutes from Long Beach. The camp has half mobile homes, half campsites.

Campsites, facilities: There are 40 sites, six drive-through, with full hookups for RVs. Restrooms, drinking water, flush toilets, showers, recreation room, swimming pool, hot tub, and coin laundry are available. Leashed pets are permitted.

Reservations, fees: Reservations are accepted. The fee is $20 per night, $1 per person for more than two people. Open year-round.

Directions: Drive on I-710/Long Beach Freeway to the exit for Florence Avenue. Take that exit west and drive on Florence Avenue to the park (5246 E. Florence Ave.), eight miles south of the junction of U.S. 101, I-5, and I-710 in Los Angeles.

Contact: Del Rio Mobile Home and RV Park, 323/560-2895, fax 323/560-6476.

76 BOLSA CHICA STATE BEACH

Rating: 7

Near Huntington Beach.
Map 14.4, page 729

This state beach extends three miles from Seal Beach to Huntington Beach City Pier. A bikeway connects it with Huntington State Beach, seven miles to the south. Across the road from Bolsa Chica is the 1,000-acre Bolsa Chica Ecological Preserve, managed by the Department of Fish and Game. The campground consists of basically a beachfront parking lot, but a popular one at that. A great little walk is available at the adjacent Bolsa Chica State Reserve, a 1.5-mile loop that provides an escape from the parking lot and entry into the 530-acre nature reserve, complete with egrets, pelicans, and many shorebirds. Lifeguard service is available during the summer. This camp has a seven-day maximum stay during the summer, and a 14-day maximum stay during the winter. Surf fishing is popular here for perch, cabezon, small sharks, and croaker. There are also occasional runs of grunion, a small fish that

spawns in hordes on the sandy beaches of Southern California.

Campsites, facilities: There are sites with partial hookups available in a parking lot configuration for RVs up to 48 feet long. Fire rings are provided. Restrooms, drinking water, flush toilets, coin showers, RV dump station, picnic areas, bicycle trail, and food service (seasonal) are available. Some facilities are wheelchair-accessible, including a paved ramp for wheelchair access to the beach. Leashed pets are permitted at campsites.

Reservations, fees: Make reservations at 800/444-PARK (800/444-7275) or website: www.ReserveAmerica.com ($7.50 reservation fee); $18 per night. Senior discount available. Open year-round.

Directions: Drive on Highway 1 to the park entrance (1.5 miles north of Huntington Beach).

Contact: Bolsa Chica State Beach, 714/846-3460; Huntington State Beach, 714/536-1454.

77 PARSON'S LANDING HIKE-IN

Rating:10

On Catalina Island.
Map 14.4, page 729

This primitive campground is one of five on Catalina Island. It is set on the island's northern end, seven miles from the island's isthmus and the village of Two Harbors. If you want to try and avoid the crowds, this is the area to visit; forget Avalon and head instead to Two Harbors.

Campsites, facilities: There are nine tent sites, each for up to six campers. Picnic tables, barbecue and fire rings, and a locker with firewood and two gallons of drinking water are provided. Chemical toilets are available. Pets are not permitted.

Reservations, fees: Reservations are required at 310/510-2800; $12 per person per night, plus $9 first night for wood and water. The round-trip ferry ride to Avalon at Catalina Island is $36 from Newport, $40 from Long Beach,

$44.50 from Dana Point. Discounts for children. Check in at the visitor information booth to validate your camping permit and obtain locker key for water and wood. Open year-round, weather permitting.

Directions: Take ferry boat ride to Avalon. From Avalon, take shuttle bus to Two Harbors. At Two Harbors, check in at the visitor information booth to validate your camping permit and obtain locker key for water and wood. From Two Harbors, hike seven miles to campsites. Note: a shuttle boat is sometimes available from Two Harbors to Emerald Bay; from Emerald Bay, it is a 1.5-mile hike to the campground.

Contact: For ferry information, camp reservations, or general information: Avalon, 310/510-2800; Two Harbors, 310/510-0303; website: www.scico.com.

78 TWO HARBORS

Rating:10

On Catalina Island.

Map 14.4, page 729

This campground is only a quarter mile away from the village of Two Harbors. Nearby attractions include the Two Harbors Dive Station with snorkeling equipment, paddleboard rentals, and scuba tank fills to 3,000 psi. There are guided tours of the island and a scheduled bus service between Two Harbors and Avalon; the bus stops at all the interior campgrounds. An excellent hike is the nine-mile round-trip from Two Harbors to Emerald Bay, featuring a gorgeous coast and pretty valleys. A quarter-mile hike is required to reach this campground.

Campsites, facilities: There are 34 sites for tents, 13 tent cabins for up to six people, and two group sites for up to 25 people. Picnic tables and fire grills are provided. Drinking water, sun shades, cold showers, and chemical toilets are available. Firewood, charcoal, and propane are sold at the ranger station by advance order.

A general store, restaurant and saloon, snack bar, tennis courts, volleyball, coin laundry, and hot showers are available in the town of Two Harbors. Pets are not permitted.

Reservations, fees: Reservations are required at 310/510-2800; $12 per person per night. The round-trip ferry ride to Avalon at Catalina Island is $36 from Newport, $40 from Long Beach, $44.50 from Dana Point. Discounts for children. Check in at the visitor information booth to validate your camping permit and obtain locker key for water and wood. Open year-round, weather permitting.

Directions: Take ferry boat ride to Avalon. From Avalon, take shuttle bus to Two Harbors. At Two Harbors, check in at the visitor information booth to validate your camping permit and obtain locker key for water and wood. From Two Harbors, hike one-quarter mile to campground.

Contact: For ferry information, camp reservations, or general information: Avalon, 310/510-2800; Two Harbors, 310/510-0303; website: www.scico.com.

79 LITTLE HARBOR HIKE-IN

Rating:10

On Catalina Island.

Map 14.4, page 729

There is plenty to do: you can swim, dive, fish, or go for day hikes. There are two sandy beaches near this camp, both great for swimming and snorkeling. A Native American historic site is nearby. Two Harbors has several excellent hikes, including the nine-mile excursion to Emerald Bay. Of course, you could always take the shuttle bus. Many folks consider this to be the pick of the campgrounds on the island. It is a gorgeous place—small wonder that some big Hollywood flicks have been shot here.

Campsites, facilities: There are 16 tent sites. Picnic tables and fire rings are provided. Drinking water, cold showers, sun shades, pay telephone, shuttle bus service, and chemical toilets are available. A phone is available nearby. Wood, charcoal, and propane can be ordered in advance from the ranger station. Pets are not permitted.

Reservations, fees: Reservations are required at 310/510-2800; $12 per person per night. The round-trip ferry ride to Avalon at Catalina Island is $36 from Newport, $40 from Long Beach, $44.50 from Dana Point. Discounts for children. Check in at the visitor information booth to validate your camping permit and obtain locker key for water and wood. Open year-round, weather permitting.

Directions: Take ferry boat ride to Avalon. From Avalon, take shuttle bus to Little Harbor. Depart and hike a short distance to the campground.

Contact: For ferry information, camp reservations, or general information: Avalon, 310/510-2800; Two Harbors, 310/510-0303; website: www.scico.com.

80 BLACK JACK HIKE-IN
🏃 ≋ 🛶 5% ⛰

Rating: 7

On Catalina Island.

Map 14.4, page 729

This camp is named after Mt. Black Jack (2,008 feet) and is a great place to hunker down for a spell. It's also the site of the old Black Jack Mine. This is the least-popular campground on the island, viewed by most as a stopover site, not a base camp. From Black Jack Junction (accessible by shuttle bus), it is a one-mile hike to the camp. The camp is set at 1,500 feet in elevation. If you stand in just the right spot, you can see the mainland, but L.A. will seem like a million miles away.

Campsites, facilities: There are 11 tent sites with a maximum of six campers per site. Drinking water, picnic tables, fire pits, cold showers, and a locker with firewood are provided. Chemical toilets are available. A phone is available nearby. Propane, charcoal, and other rental equipment are not available November through March. Pets are not permitted.

Reservations, fees: Reservations are required at 310/510-2800; $12 per person per night. The round-trip ferry ride to Avalon at Catalina Island is $36 from Newport, $40 from Long Beach, $44.50 from Dana Point. Discounts for children. Check in at the visitor information booth to validate your camping permit and obtain locker key for water and wood. Open year-round, weather permitting.

Directions: Take ferry boat ride to Avalon. From Avalon, take the shuttle bus to Black Jack Junction. Depart the bus and hike one mile to the campground.

Contact: For ferry information, camp reservations, or general information: Avalon, 310/510-2800; Two Harbors, 310/510-0303; website: www.scico.com.

81 HERMIT GULCH
🏃 ≋ 🛶 ⛺ 5% ⛰

Rating:10

On Catalina Island.

Map 14.4, page 729

This is the closest campground to the town of Avalon, the gateway to Catalina. Reaching the camp requires a 1.25-mile hike up Avalon Canyon. If you're making a tourist trip, there are a ton of things to do here: visit Avalon's underwater city park, play the nine-hole golf course, rent a bicycle, or visit the famous casino. Fishing can be excellent, including angling for white seabass, yellowtail, and, in the fall, even marlin. The best hiking experience in the Avalon area is found by taking the shuttle bus to the Airport in the Sky and from there hiking along Empire Landing Road. The route traces the island's curving, hilly northern shore, providing great views of secluded beaches, coves, and rock formations, and a chance to see wildlife, at times even buffalo. Some may remember the tepees that were set up here for years. They have been permanently removed.

Campsites, facilities: There are 54 sites for tents and eight tent cabins. Picnic tables, fire rings, and barbecue pits are provided. Restrooms, drinking water, flush toilets, showers, ice, lockers, playground, coin microwave, vending machines, and a public phone are available. Some camping equipment is available for rent. Pets are not permitted.

Reservations, fees: Reservations are required at 310/510-2800; $12 per night, $20 for tent cabins. The round-trip ferry ride to Avalon at Catalina Island is $36 from Newport, $40 from Long Beach, $44.50 from Dana Point. Discounts for children. Check in at the visitor information booth to validate your camping permit and obtain locker key for water and wood. Open year-round, weather permitting.

Directions: Take ferry boat ride to Avalon. In Avalon at Sumner Avenue, walk up Avalon Canyon (follow the "Avalon Canyon Road" sign) for 1.25 miles to the campground. The camp is across from the picnic area.

Contact: For ferry information, camp reservations, or general information: Avalon, 310/510-2800; Two Harbors, 310/510-0303; website: www.scico.com.

82 PRADO REGIONAL PARK

Rating: 6

On Prado Park Lake near Corona.

Map 14.5, page 730

Prado Park Lake is the centerpiece of a 2,280-acre recreation-oriented park that features an equestrian center, athletic fields, shooting range, and a golf course. The lake is small and used primarily for paddling small boats and fishing, which is best in the winter and early spring when trout are planted, and then in early summer for catfish and bass. The shooting facility is outstanding, the site of the 1984 Olympic shooting venue.

Campsites, facilities: There are 35 sites, most drive-through, with full hookups for RVs, 15 tent sites, and 25 group sites. Picnic tables and fire pits are provided. Restrooms, coin laundry, showers, pay phone, snack bar, picnic area, playing fields, boat ramp, bait shop, and boat

rentals are available. A playing field with softball, soccer, and horseshoes is on site. Leashed pets are permitted. Some facilities are wheelchair-accessible.

Reservations, fees: Reservations accepted ($2 reservation fee); $16 per night, $1 per night. Long-term rates available. Proof of insurance for all vehicles is required. Open year-round. Major credit cards accepted.

Directions: Drive on Highway 91 to Highway 71 (west of Norco and Riverside). Take Highway 71 north and drive four miles to Highway 83/Euclid Avenue. Turn right on Euclid Avenue and drive a mile to the park entrance on the right.

Contact: Prado Regional Park, 909/597-4260, fax 909/393-8428; website: www.san-bernardino .ca.us/parks/prado.

83 RANCHO JURUPA COUNTY PARK

Rating: 4

Near Riverside.

Map 14.5, page 730

Lord, it gets hot in the summertime, but there is shade and grass here. The setting is amid cottonwood trees and meadows. In the cooler weather during spring, this county park stocks a fishing pond. That is also the best time to explore the park's hiking and equestrian trails. Shaded picnic sites are a plus. Summer visitors will find that the nearest lake for swimming and water sports is Lake Perris, about a 20-minute drive away. The elevation is 780 feet.

Campsites, facilities: There are 72 sites, 12 with full hookups, for RVs or tents. Picnic tables and fire grills are provided. Drinking water, flush toilets, showers, and RV dump station are available. Some facilities are wheelchair-accessible. Leashed pets are permitted.

Reservations, fees: Reservations are accepted at 800/234-7275; $16–18 per night, $5-per-rod fishing fee, $2 pet fee. Major credit cards accepted. Open year-round.

Directions: Drive on I-215 to Riverside and Highway 60. Take Highway 60 east and drive seven miles to Rubidoux Boulevard. Turn left on Rubidoux Boulevard and drive a half mile to Mission Boulevard. Turn left on Mission Boulevard and drive about a mile to Crestmore Road. Turn right and drive 1.5 miles to the park gate on the left (4800 Crestmore Road).

Contact: Rancho Jurupa County Park, 909/684-7032, fax 909/955-4305.

84 ANAHEIM VACATION PARK
🏊 🏕 🚐 ⛺

Rating: 1

Near Knott's Berry Farm.

Map 14.5, page 730

Some of the most popular RV parks in America are in this area, and it's easy to see why. Knott's Berry Farm is within walking distance (five blocks) and Disneyland is nearby. Plus, where else are you going to park your rig? The park has a western theme. This park will be under new ownership in 2003 with changes likely.

Campsites, facilities: There are 222 sites, all drive-through with full hookups for RVs up to 42 feet long, and seven sites for tents with barbecues. Restrooms, showers, spa, satellite TV, phone and modem access, swimming pool, coin laundry, store, recreation room, and propane gas are available. A round-trip shuttle service is available to Disneyland for $2. Leashed pets are permitted.

Reservations, fees: Reservations are recommended. The fee is $33–45 for RV sites, $25 for tent sites, $2.50 per person for more than two people. Major credit cards accepted. Open year-round.

Directions: Drive on I-5 to Anaheim and the Beach Boulevard exit. Take that exit south and drive south on Beach Boulevard for two miles to the park on the right.

Contact: Anaheim Vacation Park, 714/821-4311, fax 714/761-1743.

85 TRAVELERS WORLD RV PARK
🏊 🏕 🏕 ♿ 🚐 ⛺

Rating: 1

Near Disneyland.

Map 14.5, page 730

This is one of the most popular RV parks for visitors to Disneyland and other nearby attractions. It is easy to see why, with the park just a half mile from Disneyland. A shuttle service is a great bonus, with buses to Knott's Berry Farm, the Wax Museum, Universal Studios, Marineland, and the *Queen Mary.*

Campsites, facilities: There are 335 sites for tents or RVs with full hookups. Picnic tables and fire grills are provided. Restrooms, showers, playground, adult lounge/game room, swimming pool, coin laundry, store, RV dump station, ice, recreation room, RV wash rack, and propane gas are available. Leashed pets are permitted. Some facilities are wheelchair-accessible.

Reservations, fees: Reservations are required. The fee is $34–38 per night, $3 per person for more than two people, $2 pet fee. Major credit cards accepted. Open year-round.

Directions: Drive on I-5 to Anaheim and the exit for Ball Road. Take that exit east and drive to East Vermont Street (from this point, you will be driving in a square in order to make a right turn into the park). Turn right on Vermont and drive to Lemon Street. Turn right on Lemon Street and drive to Ball Road. Turn right at Ball Road and drive half block on Ball Road to the park on the right (at 333 W. Ball Road).

Contact: Travelers World RV Park, 714/991-0100, fax 714/991-4939, website: www.travel.to/rv.

86 C. C. CAMPERLAND
🏊 🏕 ♿ 🚐 ⛺

Rating: 1

Near Disneyland.

Map 14.5, page 730

Camperland is nine blocks south of Disneyland, and that right there is the number-one appeal. Knott's Berry Farm is also close by.

This park was renovated in 2002, with the RV sites reduced from 90 to 70, and in turn, sites have been enlarged and improved, now all with full hookups. An outdoor sink for washing dishes and a dog run are also new for 2003.

Campsites, facilities: There are 70 sites with full hookups for RVs or tents. Picnic tables are provided. Restrooms, showers, solar-heated swimming pool, coin laundry, RV dump station, and ice are available. Some facilities are wheelchair-accessible. Leashed pets are permitted, except in the tent area.

Reservations, fees: Reservations are accepted. The fee is $36–44 per night for RVs, $30 per night for tents, $2 per person for more than two people, $3 per night. Major credit cards accepted. Open year-round.

Directions: Drive on I-5 to Garden Grove and the exit for Harbor Boulevard south. Take that exit and drive south on Harbor Boulevard for 1.5 miles to the park on the left (12262 Harbor Boulevard).

Contact: C. C. Camperland, 714/750-6747.

87 ORANGELAND RV PARK

Rating: 1

Near Disneyland.

Map 14.5, page 730

This park is about five miles east of Disneyland. If the RV parks on West Street near Disneyland are filled, this is a useful alternative.

Campsites, facilities: There are 212 sites with full hookups for RVs. Picnic tables and fire grills are provided. Restrooms, showers, playground, swimming pool, therapy pool, exercise room, coin laundry, store, modem access, car wash, shuffleboard court, billiards, RV dump station, ice, and a recreation room are available. Some facilities are wheelchair-accessible. Leashed pets are permitted.

Reservations, fees: Reservations are recommended. The fee is $45–55 per night, $2 per person for more than two people, $1 per night. Major credit cards accepted. Open year-round.

Directions: Drive on I-5 to Anaheim and the exit for Katella Avenue. Take that exit east for Katella Avenue and drive two miles (Anaheim Stadium and the Santa Ana River) to Struck Avenue. Turn right and drive 200 yards to the park on the right (1600 W. Struck Avenue).

Contact: Orangeland RV Park, 714/633-0414, fax 714/633-9012; website: www.orangeland.com.

88 CANYON RV PARK

Rating: 6

At Featherly Regional Park.

Map 14.5, page 730

This RV park is in Featherly Regional Park, an Orange County Park that covers 795 acres. The campground is set in a mature grove of cottonwood and sycamore trees, with natural riparian wildland areas and open spaces nearby. It is near the Santa Ana River (swimming or wading at the lake or creek is prohibited). The Santa Ana River Bicycle Trail runs through this park, which runs from Orange in Riverside County to Huntington Beach and the Pacific Ocean. Side-trip possibilities include Chino Hills State Park to the north, Cleveland National Forest to the south, and Lake Matthews to the southeast. The park is also close to Disneyland and Knott's Berry Farm.

Campsites, facilities: There are 140 sites with partial hookups for RVs up to 40 feet long, 19 sites for tents, and three cabins. Picnic tables and fire grills are provided. Restrooms, flush toilets, hot showers, modem access, two RV dump stations, seasonal swimming pool, and a playground are available. A visitor center, summer campfire programs, guided nature walks are available, and two amphitheaters are on-site. A convenience store, coin laundry, and propane are also available. Restaurants are nearby. Leashed pets are permitted, with some restrictions. Some facilities are wheelchair-accessible.

Reservations, fees: Reservations are accepted. The fee is $20 for tent sites, $30 for RV sites, $5 for each additional vehicle, $2 per person for more than two people, $1 per night. Major credit cards accepted. Open year-round.

Directions: Drive on I-5 to Highway 91 in Anaheim. Take Highway 91 east and drive 13 miles to the exit for Gypsum Canyon Road. Take that exit to Gypsum Canyon Road. Turn left, drive under the freeway, and drive about one block to the park entrance on the left.

Contact: Canyon RV, 714/637-0210, fax 714/637-9317, website: www.canyonrvpark.com or www.ocparks.com.

89 LAKE PERRIS STATE RECREATION AREA

Rating: 7

On Lake Perris.

Map 14.5, page 730

Lake Perris is a great recreation lake with first-class fishing for spotted bass and, in the summer, it's an excellent destination for boating and water sports. It is set at 1,500 feet in Moreno Valley, just southwest of the Badlands foothills. The lake has a roundish shape, covering 2,200 acres, with an island that provides a unique boat-in picnic site. There are large ski beaches on the northeast and southeast shores and a designated sailing cove on the northwest side, an ideal spot for windsurfing and sailing. Swimming is also excellent, but it's allowed only at the developed beaches a short distance from the campground. The recreation area covers 8,300 acres and includes 11 miles of paved bike trails, including a great route that circles the lake, 15 miles of equestrian trails, and five miles of hiking trails. Summer campfire and junior ranger programs are available. There is also a special area for scuba diving, and a rock-climbing area is just south of the dam.

Campsites, facilities: There are 177 sites for tents only, 254 sites with partial hookups for tents or RVs up to 31 feet long, seven primitive horse camps with corrals and water troughs, six group sites for 25–85 people each, and one hike-in/bike-in site. There are no hookups in

the group area. Picnic tables and fire grills are available. Restrooms, drinking water, flush toilets, coin-operated showers, RV dump station, playground, convenience store, two swimming beaches, boat launch, mooring, and boat rentals are available. Some facilities are wheelchair-accessible. Leashed pets are permitted, except near the water.

Reservations, fees: Reserve at 800/444-PARK (800/444-7275) or website: www.Reserve America.com ($7.50 reservation fee) for individual sites and equestrian sites; $8–14 per night, $12 per night for equestrian sites, $1 per person per night for hike-in/bike-in site. Senior discount available. Reserve group sites at 909/657-0676, $60 per night. Open year-round.

Directions: From Riverside, drive southeast on Highway 215/60 for about five miles to the 215/60 split. Bear south on 215 at the split and drive six miles to Ramona Expressway. Turn left (east) and drive 3.5 miles to Lake Perris Drive. Turn left and drive three-quarters of a mile to the park entrance.

Contact: Lake Perris State Park, 909/657-0676 or 909/940-5603.

90 HUNTINGTON CITY BEACH

Rating: 7

On the Pacific Ocean.

Map 14.5, page 730

This RV park will reopen in fall of 2003, likely with major changes in store. One definite change is that partial hookups will be available for RVs, instead of the previous zilch. In the long term, this park is a helpful layover for Highway 1 cruisers. Bolsa Chica State Beach provides an alternative spot to park an RV. The best nearby adventure is the short loop walk at Bolsa Chica State Reserve (see the entry for Bolsa Chica State Beach for more information).

Campsites, facilities: There are 150 sites, 50 with partial hookups, for RVs up to 36 feet long and tents. Fire rings are provided. Drinking water, flush toilets, and RV dump station are available. Supplies are available within a mile. No pets are allowed.

Reservations, fees: Open starting fall of 2003. Call for reservations policy; $15 per night. Open November through April.

Directions: Drive on I-405 to Huntington Beach and the exit for Beach Boulevard. Take that exit west and drive on Beach Boulevard to Highway 1/Pacific Coast Highway. Turn right (north) and drive to 1st Street.Turn left and drive a short distance to the park entrance.

Contact: Huntington City Beach, city park headquarters, 714/536-5286.

91 O'NEILL REGIONAL PARK

Rating: 6

Near Cleveland National Forest.

Map 14.5, page 730

This park is just far enough off the main drag to get missed by most of the RV cruisers on I-5. It is set near Trabuco Canyon, adjacent to Cleveland National Forest to the east. About 70 percent of the campsites are set under a canopy of sycamore and oak, and in general, the park is heavily wooded. The park covers 3,800 acres and features 18 miles of trails, including those accessible by equestrians. Several roads near this park lead to trailheads into Cleveland National Forest. Occasional mountain lion warnings are posted by rangers. The elevation is 1,000 feet.

Campsites, facilities: There are 85 sites, eight drive-through, for RVs up to 35 feet long and tents, six equestrian sites for up to three horses per site, and two group camping areas for up to 150 people. Picnic tables and fire rings are provided. Restrooms, drinking water, flush toilets, showers, playground, picnic area, and RV dump station are available. Horse corral, water troughs, and an arena are available at equestrian sites. Firewood is sold on-site. A nature center is open on weekends. A store is nearby. Some facilities are wheelchair-accessible. Leashed pets are permitted.

Reservations, fees: Reservations are not accepted. The fee is $12 per night, $4 for extra vehicle, $2 per night, $3 per horse. Reservations accepted for group sites only ($10–25 reservation fee). Senior discount available. Open year-round.

Directions: From I-5 in Laguna Hills, take the County Road S18/El Toro Road exit and drive east (past El Toro) for 7.5 miles. Turn right onto Live Oak Canyon Road/County Road S19 and drive about three miles to the park on the right.

92 FALCON GROUP CAMPS

Rating: 4

In the Santa Ana Mountains in Cleveland National Forest.

Map 14.5, page 730

At an elevation of 3,300 feet, Falcon is near the trailheads for the San Juan and Chiquito Trails, which both lead into the backcountry wilderness and the Santa Ana Mountains. There are three group campgrounds here, with limited parking at Lupine and Yarrow campgrounds.

Campsites, facilities: There are three group campsites for tents or RVs. Sage Camp accommodates 30 people and RVs up to 40 feet, Lupine Camp accommodates 40 people and RVs up to 20 feet, and Yarrow Camp accommodates 70 people and RVs up to 30 feet. Picnic tables and fire rings are provided. Drinking water and pit toilets are available. A store is within five miles. Leashed pets are permitted.

Reservations, fees: Reserve at 877/444-6777 or website: www.ReserveUsa.com ($9 reservation fee); $50–100 per group per night. Open year-round, weather permitting.

Directions: Drive on I-15 to Lake Elsinore and the Central exit to Highway 74 west. Take that exit and drive west on Highway 74 for 12 miles to Forest Road 6S05 (North Main Divide Road). Turn right and drive about seven miles to the campground entrance on the left.

Contact: Cleveland National Forest, Trabuco Ranger District, 909/736-1811, fax 909/736-3002.

93 BLUE JAY

Rating: 4

In the Santa Ana Mountains in Cleveland National Forest.

Map 14.5, page 730

The few hikers who know of this spot like it and keep coming back, provided they time their hikes when temperatures are cool (near-by Upper San Juan Campground is also set near a great trailhead). The trailheads to the San Juan Trail and the Chiquito Trail, both of which lead into the backcountry wilderness and the Santa Ana Mountains, are adjacent to the camp. A Forest Service map is strongly advised. The elevation is 3,400 feet.

Campsites, facilities: There are 12 sites for tents only and 43 sites for tents or RVs up to 20 feet long. Picnic tables and fire rings are provided. Drinking water and vault toilets are available. A store is within five miles. Leashed pets are permitted.

Reservations, fees: Reservations are not accepted. The fee is $15 per night with a two-vehicle maximum. Senior discount available. Open year-round, weather permitting.

Directions: Drive on I-15 to Lake Elsinore and the Central exit to Highway 74 west. Take that exit and drive west on Highway 74 for 12 miles (the road circles the northwest end of Lake Elsinore, then turns right, away from the lake, to enter national forest) to Forest Road 6S05 (North Main Divide Road). Turn right and drive about seven miles to Falcon Group Camp. Continue a quarter mile to the campground entrance on the left.

Contact: Cleveland National Forest, Trabuco Ranger District, 909/736-1811, fax 909/736-3002.

94 UPPER SAN JUAN

Rating: 6

In Long Canyon in Cleveland National Forest.

Map 14.5, page 730

Two seasonal creeks run through this camp, set under an oak canopy in Cleveland National Forest at an elevation of 1,800 feet. Unfortunately, not all is sanguine. It is close enough to the highway that you can not only hear cars, but see them. Numerous hiking trails save the day. The San Juan Loop Trail is accessible from the campground. It runs 2.2 miles. That trail intersects with the Chiquito Trail, which extends 8.5 miles into national forest land.

Campsites, facilities: There are 18 sites for tents or RVs up to 18 feet long. Picnic tables and fire pits are provided. Drinking water and vault toilets are available. A small store is one mile away. Leashed pets are permitted. Some facilities are wheelchair-accessible.

Reservations, fees: Reservations are not accepted. The fee is $15 per night with a two-vehicle maximum. Senior discount available. Open year-round, weather permitting.

Directions: Drive on I-15 to Lake Elsinore and the Central exit to Highway 74 west. Take that exit and drive west on Highway 74 for 12 miles to Forest Road 6S05 (North Main Divide Road). Turn right and drive five miles to a Y junction with Long Canyon Road. Bear to the left on Long Canyon Road and drive .9 mile to the campground entrance on the right.

Contact: Cleveland National Forest, Trabuco Ranger District, 909/736-1811, fax 909/736-3002.

95 EL CARISO NORTH CAMPGROUND

Rating: 5

Near Lake Elsinore in Cleveland National Forest.

Map 14.5, page 730

This pretty, shaded spot at 2,600 feet is just inside the border of Cleveland National Forest with Lake Elsinore to the east. On the drive in there are great views to the east, looking down at Lake Elsinore and across the desert country. Hikers should head west to the Upper San Juan Campground.

Campsites, facilities: There are 24 sites for tents or RVs up to 22 feet long. Picnic tables and fire rings are provided. Drinking water and vault toilets are available. Leashed pets are permitted.

Reservations, fees: Reservations are not accepted. The fee is $15 per night with a two-vehicle maximum. Senior discount available. Open year-round, weather permitting.

Directions: Drive on I-15 to Lake Elsinore and the Central exit to Highway 74 west. Take that exit and drive west on Highway 74 for 12 miles (the road circles the northwest end of Lake Elsinore, then turns right, away from the lake, to enter national forest) to the campground.

Drive on I-5 to San Juan Capistrano and Highway 74/Ortega Highway. Turn east on the Ortega Highway and drive 24 miles northeast (into national forest) to the campground.

Contact: Cleveland National Forest, Trabuco Ranger District, 909/736-1811, fax 909/736-3002.

96 LAKE ELSINORE MARINA & RV RESORT

Rating: 7

On Lake Elsinore.

Map 14.5, page 730

This privately operated RV park is just a half

mile from Lake Elsinore. A nearby alternative RV park is Roadrunner, which used to be owned by the same folks. (For information about Lake Elsinore, see the entry for Lake Elsinore Recreation Area.)

Campsites, facilities: There are 195 sites with full hookups for RVs or tents. Picnic tables are provided. Restrooms, showers, RV dump station, horseshoe pit, clubhouse, convenience store, telephone hookups, cable TV hookups, and a boat ramp are available. Some facilities are wheelchair-accessible. Leashed pets are permitted, with some restrictions.

Reservations, fees: Reservations are accepted. The fee is $35 per night. Major credit cards accepted. Open year-round.

Directions: Drive to the junction of I-15 and Highway 74. At that junction, take Highway 74 west/Central Avenue and drive west for four miles to the entrance to the park on the left (32700 Riverside Drive).

Contact: Elsinore West Marina, 909/678-1300 or 800/328-6844, fax 909/678-6377.

97 ROADRUNNER RV PARK

Rating: 7

On Lake Elsinore.

Map 14.5, page 730

The Roadrunner, a privately operated park, features 600 feet of lakefront property along Lake Elsinore. This lake is best known for water-skiing, with hot weather to match, but only poor to fair fishing, with some bluegill, crappie, and catfish. Boat ramps are at both the north and south ends of the lake.

Campsites, facilities: There are 20 sites with full hookups for RVs and 21 sites for tents only. Picnic tables are provided. Restrooms, drinking water, flush toilets, coin showers, cable television, clubhouse, telephone hookups, coin laundry, RV dump station, and boat ramp are available. Leashed pets are permitted, with some restrictions.

Reservations, fees: Reservations are required.

The fee is $25–30 per night, $7 per person for more than four people, $3 for more than one vehicle, $2 per night. Senior discount available. Major credit cards accepted. Open year-round.

Directions: Drive to the junction of I-15 and Highway 74. At that junction, take Highway 74 west/Central Avenue and drive west for four miles to the entrance to the park on the left (.3 mile past the city park).

Contact: Roadrunner, 909/674-4900.

98 LAKE ELSINORE RECREATION AREA

Rating: 7

On Lake Elsinore.

Map 14.5, page 730

The weather is hot and dry enough in this region to make the water in Lake Elsinore more valuable than gold. Elsinore is a huge, wide lake, where water-skiers, personal watercraft, and windsurfers can find a slice of heaven. This camp is set along the north shore, where there are also several trails for hiking, biking, and horseback riding. There is a designated area near the campground for swimming and water play, with a gently sloping lake bottom a big plus here. If you like thrill sports, hang gliding and parachuting are also available at the lake and, as you scan across the water, you can often look up and see these daredevils soaring overhead. The recreation area covers 3,300 acres. While the lake is huge when full, an extremely low water level in early 2003 has caused problems with water quality, as well as leaving the boat ramps high and dry. This situation is unresolved, with two government entities blaming each other. Boaters planning to visit this lake should call first to get the latest on water levels and quality.

Campsites, facilities: There are 400 sites, many with hookups, for RVs up to 40 feet long or tents. Fire pits are provided. Picnic tables are provided at some sites. Restrooms, drinking water, flush toilets, showers, RV dump station, playground, coin laundry, and a store are available. Some facilities are wheelchair-accessible. Leashed pets are permitted.

Reservations, fees: Reservations are accepted at 800/416-6992. Fees are $20–25 per night, $2 per person for more than six people, $10 for more than two vehicles. Open year-round.

Directions: Drive to the junction of I-15 and Highway 74. At that junction, take Highway 74 west/Central Avenue and drive west for three miles to the park entrance on the left.

Contact: Elsinore Campground, 909/471-1212; city of Lake Elsinore, 909/674-3124, fax 909/245-9308.

99 PALM VIEW RV PARK

Rating: 5

Near Lake Elsinore.

Map 14.5, page 730

This privately operated RV park is in a quiet valley at 700 feet elevation. The sites are fairly rustic, with some shade trees. The park's recreation area offers basketball, volleyball, horseshoes, tetherball, and a playground, which should tell you everything you need to know. For you wonderful goofballs, bungy jumping and parachuting are available in the town of Perris.

Campsites, facilities: There are 50 sites, some drive-through and all with full hookups for RVs or tents. Restrooms, fire rings, RV dump station, recreation area, modem access, swimming pool, pond, laundry facilities, store, ice, and firewood are available. Leashed pets are permitted.

Reservations, fees: Reservations are accepted. The fee is $20–23 per night, $3 per person for more than four people. Open year-round.

Directions: Drive to the junction of I-15 and Highway 74. At that junction, take Highway 74/Central Avenue and drive east on Highway 74 for 4.5 miles to River Road. Turn right (south) and drive one mile to the park on the left (22200 River Road).

Contact: Palm View RV Park, 909/657-7791, fax 909/657-7673; website: www.palmview rvpark.com.

100 NEWPORT DUNES WATERFRONT RESORT

Rating: 9

In Newport Beach.
Map 14.5, page 730

This privately operated park is set in a pretty spot on the bay, with a beach, boat ramp, and storage area providing bonuses. It is situated on 100 acres of Newport Bay beach, beautiful and private, without public access. It features one mile of beach and a swimming lagoon, double-wide sites, and 24-hour security. Nearby to the west is Corona del Mar State Beach, and to the south, Crystal Cove State Park. The park is five minutes' walking distance from Balboa Island and is next to the largest estuary in California, the Upper Newport Bay Ecological Reserve.

Campsites, facilities: There are 406 sites with full hookups for tents or RVs up to 50 feet long. Picnic tables and fire grills are provided. Restrooms, showers, swimming pool and spa, waveless saltwater lagoon, 450-slip marina, satellite TV, planned activities, beach volleyball, coin laundry, store, waterfront restaurant, fitness room, and marina with boat launch ramp are available. Some facilities are wheelchair-accessible. Kayaking, windsurfing, and sailing lessons and rentals are also available. Leashed pets are permitted, with some restrictions.

Reservations, fees: Reserve at 800/765-7661 or 800/288-0770. Fees are $30–145 per night, $3 per person for more than two people, $7 for each additional vehicle. Major credit cards accepted. Open year-round.

Directions: Drive on I-405 to the exit for Highway 55. Take that exit south and drive on Highway 55 to Highway 73. Turn south on Highway 73 and drive three miles to the Jamboree Road exit. Take that exit and drive south on Jam-

boree Road for five miles to Back Bay Drive. Turn right and drive a short distance to the resort on the left.

Contact: Newport Dunes Resort, 949/729-3863, fax 949/729-1133, website: www.newport dunes.com.

101 CRYSTAL COVE STATE PARK HIKE-IN AND HORSE CAMP

Rating: 9

On the Pacific Ocean.
Map 14.5, page 730

First, get this straight: this park does not provide beach camping. The campsites are rather sites that require hikes of 3.5–4.5 miles. That known, this place is very special. This is a gorgeous park that covers 2,200 acres, featuring 3.5 miles of coast and a 1,140-acre underwater park that is popular with scuba divers and snorkelers. The inland acreage is popular with mountain bikers and hikers, and the beach is popular with swimmers and surfers. Of the hike-in camps, the two Moro camps are the most popular. The two Moro camps have a ridgetop vantage point and beautiful views of the ocean. Deer Canyon Camp is sheltered by a grove of oaks and offers privacy, but no views. El Moro Canyon is shady and tree-lined. Note that El Moro Creek flows only in the wet season. The camps are rarely full. Most of the park's backcountry is grass hills and some foothill woodlands. In winter, guided nature hikes are available.

Campsites, facilities: There are 32 hike-in/bike-in and equestrian sites at three environmental campgrounds, Lower Moro, Upper Moro, and Deer Canyon (horses are not allowed at Lower Moro). Picnic tables are provided. Pit toilets are available. No drinking water is available. No fires are permitted. Bring a backpacking stove for cooking. No pets are permitted.

Reservations, fees: Make reservations at 800/444-PARK (800/444-7275) or website: www.ReserveAmerica.com ($7.50 reservation fee); $7 per night. Registration at the visitor center is required. Senior discount available. Open year-round.

Directions: Drive on Highway 1 to the park entrance (three miles south of Corona del Mar) on the east side of the highway. Register at the visitor center. The Moro camps require a 3.5- to four-mile walk. The Deer Canyon Camp requires a 4.5-mile walk.

Contact: Crystal Cove State Park, 949/494-3539; Orange Coast District, San Clemente Sector, 949/492-0802, website: www.crystal covestatepark.com

102 CASPERS WILDERNESS PARK

Rating: 6

On the San Juan Creek.
Map 14.5, page 730

This is an 8,000-acre protected wilderness preserve that is best known for coastal stands of live oak and magnificent stands of California sycamore. Highway 74 provides access to this regional park. It is a popular spot for picnics and day hikes, and since the campground is not listed with any of the computer-based reservation services, it is overlooked by most out-of-town travelers. A highlight is 30 miles of trails. Much of the land is pristine and protected in its native state. It is bordered to the south by the San Juan Creek and to the east by the Cleveland National Forest and the San Mateo Canyon Wilderness, adding to its protection.

Campsites, facilities: There are 35 sites for tents or RVs, 22 sites for equestrian campers, six group sites, and 10 sites in an overflow area for RVs. Picnic tables and barbecues are provided. Drinking water, flush toilets, showers, RV dump station, corrals, stables, museum with interpretive programs, and a playground are available. Pets are not allowed. Some facilities are wheelchair-accessible.

Reservations, fees: Reservations are not accepted. The fee is $12 per night, $4 per extra vehicle, $3 for each horse per night. Reserva-

tions accepted for groups; group fees vary. Open year-round.

Directions: Drive on I-5 to San Juan Capistrano and Highway 74/Ortega Highway. Turn east on the Ortega Highway and drive 7.5 miles northeast to the signed park entrance on the left.

Contact: Caspers Wilderness Park, Orange County, 949/728-0235, fax 949/728-0346.

103 LAKE SKINNER RECREATION AREA

Rating: 7

On Lake Skinner.
Map 14.5, page 730

Lake Skinner is set within a county park at an elevation of 1,470 feet in sparse foothill country, where the water can sparkle, and it covers 1,200 surface acres. There is a speed limit of 10 mph. Unlike nearby Lake Elsinore, which is dominated by fast boats and water-skiers, no water contact sports are permitted here; hence no water-skiing, no swimming, no windsurfing. Afternoon winds make for great sailing, and you can count on consistent midday breezes. The fish can be good. Many fish are stocked at this lake, including trophy-sized bass and trout, along with catfish, crappie, and bluegill. The fish are stocked weekly November through May. The fishing records here include a 39.5-pound striped bass and 33-pound catfish. The recreation area also provides hiking and horseback riding trails.

Campsites, facilities: There are 257 sites, many drive-through with full hookups for RVs or tents, an overflow area, and a group camping area. Picnic tables and fire grills are provided. Restrooms, drinking water, flush toilets, coin showers, playground, store, ice, bait, RV dump station, swimming pool (in the summer), boat ramp, marina, mooring, boat rentals, and propane gas are available. Leashed pets are permitted. Some facilities are wheelchair-accessible.

Reservations, fees: Reservations are accepted at 800/234-7275. Fees are $15–18 per night, $10 per night for overflow area, $4 per night for each additional vehicle, six-person maximum per site, $2 per night. Open year-round. Major credit cards accepted.

Directions: Drive on I-15 to Temecula and the exit for Rancho California. Take that exit northeast and drive 9.5 miles to the park entrance on the right.

Contact: Lake Skinner Recreation Area, 909/926-1541, website: www.RiversideCountyParks.org.

104 BOGART COUNTY PARK

Rating: 4

In Cherry Valley.

Map 14.6, page 731

This county park is overlooked by many vacationers on I-10, and it is as pretty as it gets for this area. There are two miles of horse trails and some hiking trails for a recreation option during the cooler months. It covers 414 acres of Riverside County foothills set at the north end of Cherry Valley. The elevation is 2,800 feet.

Campsites, facilities: There are 38 sites for tents or RVs, a group campground, and an equestrian campground. Fire grills and picnic tables are provided. Drinking water, flush toilets, and a playground are available. Supplies are available in Beaumont. Leashed pets are permitted.

Reservations, fees: Reservations are not accepted. The fee is $12 per night, $2 per pets per night. Reservations are required for groups at 800/234-7275 ($6.50–12 reservation fee). Open year-round.

Directions: Drive on I-10 to Beaumont and the exit for Beaumont Avenue. Take that exit north and drive four miles to Brookside. Turn right and drive a half mile to Cherry Avenue. Turn left at Cherry Avenue and drive to the park on the right (9600 Cherry Avenue).

Contact: Bogart County Park, 909/845-3818.

105 STAGECOACH RV PARK

Rating: 2

In Banning.

Map 14.6, page 731

Banning may not seem like a hotbed of civilization at first glance, but this clean, comfortable park is a good spot to make camp while exploring some of the area's hidden attractions, including Agua Caliente Indian Canyons and the Lincoln Shrine. It is set at 2,400 feet, 22 miles from Palm Springs. A good side trip is to head south on curving "Highway" 240 up to Vista Point in the San Bernardino National Forest.

Campsites, facilities: There are 106 sites, most drive-through and many with full hookups, for RVs or tents. Picnic tables and fire grills are provided. Restrooms, showers, playground, swimming pool, coin laundry, modem access, cable TV store, RV dump station, ice, recreation room, horseshoes, video arcade, and propane gas are available. Leashed pets are permitted.

Reservations, fees: Reservations are accepted. Fees are $15–21.50 per night, $2 per person for more than two people, $1 for extra vehicle. Major credit cards accepted. Open year-round.

Directions: Drive on I-10 to Banning and the exit for Highway 243. Take that exit south and take 8th Avenue south for one block to Lincoln. Turn left on Lincoln and drive two blocks to San Gorgonio. Turn right and drive one mile to the park (1455 S. San Gorgonio Avenue).

Contact: Stagecoach RV Park, 909/849-7513, fax 909/849-7998.

106 IDYLLWILD COUNTY PARK

Rating: 6

Near San Bernardino National Forest.

Map 14.6, page 731

This county park covers 202 acres, set at 5,300 feet and surrounded by Mt. San Jacinto State Park, San Jacinto Wilderness, and the San Bernardino National Forest lands. That provides plenty of options for visitors. The park has equestrian trails and an interpretive trail. The top hike in the region is the ambitious climb up the western slopes to the top of Mt. San Jacinto (10,804 feet), a terrible challenge of a butt-kicker that provides one of the most astounding views in all the land. (The best route, however, is out of Palm Springs, taking the aerial tramway, which will get you to 8,516 feet in elevation before hiking out the rest.)

Campsites, facilities: There are 60 sites for tents or RVs up to 34 feet long, and 30 sites for RVs only. Fire grills and picnic tables are provided. Restrooms, drinking water, flush toilets, and showers are available. A store, coin laundry, and propane gas are nearby. Leashed pets are permitted. Some facilities are wheelchair-accessible. There is no drinking water in dry years.

Reservations, fees: Reservations are accepted at 800/234-PARK (800/234-7275) ($6.50 reservation fee); $15 per night, six-person-per-site maximum. Major credit cards accepted. Open year-round.

Directions: Drive on I-10 to Banning and Highway 243/Idyllwild Panoramic Highway. Turn south on Idyllwild Panoramic Highway and drive to Idyllwild and Riverside County Playground Road. Turn west on Riverside County Playground Road and drive a half mile (follow the signs) to the park entrance.

Contact: Idyllwild County Park, 909/659-2656.

107 IDYLLWILD

Rating: 8

In Mt. San Jacinto State Park.
Map 14.6, page 731

This is a prime spot for hikers and one of the better jump-off points for trekking in the area, set at 5,400 feet. There are no trails from this campground. But a half-mile north is the Deer Spring Trail, which is connected with the Pacific Crest Trail and then climbs on to Mt. San Jacinto (10,804 feet) and its astounding lookout.

Campsites, facilities: There are 11 sites for tents only, 10 sites for tents or RVs up to 18 feet long, 11 sites for RVs only up to 24 feet long, and one hike-in/bike-in site. Fire grills and picnic tables are provided. Piped water, flush toilets, and showers are available. Supplies and coin laundry (100 yards) are nearby. Leashed pets are permitted. Some facilities are wheelchair-accessible.

Reservations, fees: Reserve at 800/444-PARK (800/444-7275) or website: www.ReserveAmerica.com ($7.50 reservation fee); $12 per night, $1 per person for hike-in/bike-in site. Senior discount available. Open year-round.

Directions: In Idyllwild, drive to the north end of town on Highway 243 to the park entrance on the left (next to the fire station).

Contact: Mt. San Jacinto State Park, 909/659-2607, website: www.sanjac.statepark.org; Inland Empire District, 909/657-0676.

108 BOULDER BASIN

Rating: 8

Near the San Jacinto Wilderness in San Bernardino National Forest.
Map 14.6, page 731

This camp is on the top of the world for these parts, 7,300 feet, adjacent to the Black Mountain Fire Lookout with great views in all directions and highlighted by Tahquitz Peak (8,828 feet) 10 miles to the southeast. Boulder Basin is also near the San Jacinto Wilderness (to the northeast) and makes a good trailhead camp for hikers. A trail starting at Black Mountain Lookout leads west, dropping steeply into a canyon and also into a designated scenic area.

Campsites, facilities: There are 34 sites for tents or RVs up to 22 feet long (trailers are not recommended). Picnic tables and fire rings are provided. Drinking water and vault toilets are available. Leashed pets are permitted.

Reservations, fees: Reservations are accepted for half of the sites; reserve at 877/444-6777 or website: www.ReserveUsa.com ($9 reservation fee); $10 per night. Senior discount available. Open May to mid-October.

Directions: Drive on I-10 to Banning and Highway 243/Idyllwild Panoramic Highway. Turn south on Idyllwild Panoramic Highway and drive about 15 miles south to Forest Road 4S01. Turn left on Forest Road 4S01 and drive six miles (a narrow dirt road) to the campground on the right. RVs not advised.

Contact: San Bernardino National Forest, San Jacinto Ranger District, 909/659-2117, fax 909/659-2107.

109 BLACK MOUNTAIN GROUP CAMP

Rating: 6

Near Mt. San Jacinto in San Bernardino National Forest.

Map 14.6, page 731

This is a beautiful scenic area, particularly to the north on the edge of the San Jacinto Wilderness and to the east of Mt. San Jacinto State Park. The camp is set at 7,500 feet and is within a mile of a trailhead for the Pacific Crest Trail. Here you can turn southeast and hike along Fuller Ridge for another mile to the border of Mt. San Jacinto State Park. Note that Black Mountain Lookout is just a two-mile drive, close to Boulder Basin Camp.

Campsites, facilities: There is one group camp with tent sites for up to 100 people and 20 vehicles. Picnic tables and fire rings are provided. Drinking water and vault toilets are available. Leashed pets are permitted.

Reservations, fees: Reserve at 877/444-6777 or website: www.ReserveUsa.com ($9 reservation fee); $60–130 per night. Open May through September.

Directions: Drive on I-10 to Banning and Highway 243/Idyllwild Panoramic Highway. Turn south on Idyllwild Panoramic Highway and drive about 15 miles south to Forest Road 4S01. Turn left on Forest Road 4S01 and drive eight

miles (a narrow dirt road) to the campground on the right. RVs not advised.

Contact: San Bernardino National Forest, San Jacinto Ranger District, 909/659-2117, fax 909/659-2107.

110 DARK CANYON

Rating: 7

In the San Jacinto Mountains in San Bernardino National Forest.

Map 14.6, page 731

This pretty setting is on the slopes of the San Jacinto Mountains at 5,800 feet in elevation. Hikers can drive to the Seven Pines Trailhead less than a mile north of camp at the end of Forest Road 4S02. The trail leads east for three miles into Mt. San Jacinto State Park to Deer Springs, where there is a trail camp and a junction with the Pacific Crest Trail. A wilderness permit is required.

Campsites, facilities: There are 17 sites for tents or RVs up to 22 feet long. Picnic tables and fire grills are provided. Drinking water and vault toilets are available. Leashed pets are permitted.

Reservations, fees: Reservations are accepted for 12 sites. To reserve call 877/444-6777 or visit www.ReserveUsa.com ($9 reservation fee); $12 per night. Senior discount available. Open May to mid-October.

Directions: Drive on I-10 to Banning and Highway 243/Idyllwild Panoramic Highway. Turn south on Idyllwild Panoramic Highway and drive about 13 miles south to Forest Road 4S02. Turn left on Forest Road 4S02 and drive three miles (narrow paved road) to the campground.

Contact: San Bernardino National Forest, San Jacinto Ranger District, 909/659-2117, fax 909/659-2107.

111 MARION MOUNTAIN

Rating: 7

In San Bernardino National Forest.

Map 14.6, page 731

You get good lookouts and a developed campground at this spot. Nearby Black Mountain is a good side trip, including a drive-to scenic lookout point. In addition, there are several trailheads in the area. The best one starts near this camp and heads up the slopes to Marion Mountain and east into adjacent Mt. San Jacinto State Park. The elevation is 6,400 feet.

Campsites, facilities: There are 24 sites for tents or RVs up to 15 feet long. Picnic tables and fire grills are provided. Drinking water and vault toilets are available.

Reservations, fees: Reservations are accepted for 18 sites. To reserve call 877/444-6777 or visit www.ReserveUsa.com ($9 reservation fee); $10 per night. Open May to mid-October.

Directions: Drive on I-10 to Banning and Highway 243/Idyllwild Panoramic Highway. Turn south on Idyllwild Panoramic Highway and drive about 13 miles south to Forest Road 4S02. Turn left on Forest Road 4S02 and drive two miles (narrow paved road) to the campground.

Contact: San Bernardino National Forest, San Jacinto Ranger District, 909/659-2117, fax 909/659-2107.

112 FERN BASIN

Rating: 7

Near Mt. San Jacinto State Park in San Bernardino National Forest.

Map 14.6, page 731

This is a nearby alternative to Stone Creek (you'll pass it on the way in) and Dark Canyon (another three miles in). The Marion Mountain Trailhead is accessible within one-half mile of the campground by driving east on Forest Road 4S02.

Campsites, facilities: There are 22 sites for tents or RVs up to 15 feet long. Picnic tables and fire rings are provided. Drinking water and vault toilets are available. Leashed pets are permitted.

Reservations, fees: Reservations are accepted for half of the sites; reserve at 877/444-6777 or website: www.ReserveUsa.com ($9 reservation fee); $10 per night. Senior discount available. Open May through September.

Directions: Drive on I-10 to Banning and Highway 243/Idyllwild Panoramic Highway. Turn south on Idyllwild Panoramic Highway and drive about 13 miles south to Forest Road 4S02. Turn left on Forest Road 4S02 and drive one mile (narrow paved road) to the campground on the left.

Contact: San Bernardino National Forest, San Jacinto Ranger District, 909/659-2117, fax 909/659-2107.

113 STONE CREEK

Rating: 7

In Mt. San Jacinto State Park.

Map 14.6, page 731

This is a wooded camp set in Mt. San Jacinto State Park. The elevation is 5,900 feet, a quarter mile off the main road along Stone Creek, just outside the national forest boundary. It is less than a mile from Fern Basin and less than three miles from Dark Canyon. The best trailhead in the immediate area is the Seven Pines Trail out of Marion Mountain Camp, one-half mile from this camp.

Campsites, facilities: There are 26 sites for tents, 11 sites for tents or RVs up to 18 feet long, and 13 sites for RVs up to 24 feet long. Picnic tables and fire rings are provided. Drinking water and vault toilets are available. Some facilities are wheelchair-accessible. Supplies and coin laundry are three miles away in Pine Cove. Leashed pets are permitted.

Reservations, fees: Reserve at 800/444-PARK (800/444-7275) or website: www.Reserve America.com ($7.50 reservation fee); $7 per night. Senior discount available. Open year-round.

Directions: Drive on I-10 to Banning and Highway 243/Idyllwild Panoramic Highway. Turn south on Idyllwild Panoramic Highway and drive about 13 miles south to the park entrance on the left.

Contact: Mt. San Jacinto State Park, 909/659-2607, website: www.sanjac.statepark.org; Inland Empire District, 909/657-0676.

114 ROUND VALLEY AND TAMARACK VALLEY TRAM AND WALK-IN

Rating:10

Near Mt. San Jacinto.
Map 14.6, page 731

This is one of the most spectacular getaways in the Western United States. It includes a tram ride that will take you from 2,643 feet to 8,516 feet, with stunning views across the desert, especially heart-breaking sunsets. On clear days, you can see the Salton Sea 50 miles to the south. From the tram, you then hike two or 2.5 miles to one of the two camps, set at 9,100 feet, an ideal launch point for the hike to the Mt. San Jacinto summit, at 10,804 feet, the second-highest peak in Southern California. From Round Valley Camp, it is a 7.5-mile round-trip (just add another mile round-trip from Tamarack Valley). On clear days from the summit, you can see 100 miles, including the Channel Islands, Mexico, and Nevada. On summer weekends, these campgrounds are often filled for dates more than a month in advance.

Campsites, facilities: There are 28 tent sites at Round Valley and 12 tent sites at Tamarack Valley. Pit toilets are available. No drinking water is available (Round Valley Camp has seasonal stream water that must be boiled or pump filtered before use). No campfires are permitted. Bring a camp stove for cooking. Garbage must be packed out. Pets are not permitted.

Reservations, fees: Camping permit required, no fee, at least six days in advance by mail at Mt. San Jacinto State Park, P.O. Box 308, Idyllwild, CA 92549. An application is available at the website: www.sanjac.statepark.org. A required tram ride costs $20.80 for adults, $13.80 for children under 12. Open May through September.

Directions: From Banning, drive east on I-10 for 12 miles to the Highway 111/Palm Springs exit. Take that exit to Highway 111 and drive south nine miles to Tramway Road. Turn right and drive three miles to the parking area for Palm Springs Aerial Tramway. Ride the tram to Mountain Station. Hike two miles to Round Valley Camp, or continue from Round Valley Camp for another half-mile to Tamarack Valley Camp.

Contact: Mt. San Jacinto State Park, 909/659-2607, website: www.sanjac.statepark.org; Palm Springs Aerial Tramway, 818/515-8726 or 760/325-1391, website: www.pstramway.com.

115 GOLDEN VILLAGE PALMS RV RESORT

Rating: 5

In Hemet.
Map 14.6, page 731

This RV resort is for those ages 55 and over. It is the biggest RV park in Southern California, with major renovation planned for completion in 2003. The grounds are lush, with gravel pads for RVs. It is set near Diamond Valley Lake, about 10 miles south, a new lake that will become the largest reservoir in California. A golf course is nearby, Lake Hemet is 20 miles east, and winery tours are available in Temecula, a 30-minute drive. About 250 of the 1,019 sites are rented on a year-round basis.

Campsites, facilities: There are 1,019 sites, 60 drive-through, all with full hookups for RVs up to 45 feet long. No tent sites. Restrooms, drinking water, flush toilets, showers, cable TV, modem access, telephones, three swimming pools, recreation room, fitness center, billiard room, three spas, coin laundry, large clubhouse, banquet and meeting rooms, shuffleboard, nine-hole putting green, volleyball courts, and horseshoe pits are available.

A day-use area with propane barbecues is also available. Leashed pets are permitted.

Reservations, fees: Reservations are accepted at 800/323-9610. Fees are $33 per night, $10 per person for more than two people. Long-term rates available. Open year-round.

Directions: Drive to the junction of I-215 and Highway 74 (near Perris). At that junction, take Highway 74 east and drive 15 miles to Hemet (the highway becomes Florida Avenue in Hemet) and continue to the resort on the left.

Contact: Golden Village Palms RV Resort, 909/925-2518; website: www.GoldenVillage Palms.com.

116 CASA DEL SOL RV RESORT

Rating: 3

In Hemet.

Map 14.6, page 731

Hemet is a retirement town, so if you want excitement, the three lakes in the area are the best place to look for it: Lake Perris to the northwest, Lake Skinner to the south, and Lake Hemet to the east. Note that many of the sites are taken by year-round or long-term rentals.

Campsites, facilities: There are 358 sites with full hookups for RVs. Restrooms, drinking water, flush toilets, showers, cable TV, telephones, swimming pool, recreation room, exercise room, billiard room, hot tub, and coin laundry are available. Leashed pets are permitted.

Reservations, fees: Reservations are accepted at 888/925-2516. Fees are $25 per night, $15 for extra vehicle, $2.50 per person for more than two people. Open year-round.

Directions: Drive to the junction of I-215 and Highway 74 (near Perris). At that junction, take Highway 74 east and drive 15 miles to Hemet (the highway becomes Florida Avenue in Hemet) and drive to Kirby Avenue. Turn right (south) on Kirby Avenue and drive a half block to the resort (2750 W. Acacia Avenue).

Contact: Casa del Sol RV Resort, 909/925-2515; website: www.CasadelSolrvpark.com.

117 MOUNTAIN VALLEY RV PARK

Rating: 3

In Hemet.

Map 14.6, page 731

This is one of three RV parks in the Hemet area. Three lakes in the area provide side-trip possibilities: Lake Perris to the northwest, Lake Skinner to the south, and Lake Hemet to the east.

Campsites, facilities: There are 170 sites with full hookups for RVs. Restrooms, drinking water, flush toilets, showers, a fireside room, swimming pool, enclosed hot tub, coin laundry, satellite TV, recreation room, and telephone hookups are available. Some facilities are wheelchair-accessible. A store and propane gas are nearby. Leashed pets are permitted.

Reservations, fees: Reservations are accepted at 800/926-5593. Fees are $28 per night, $2 pet fee. Major credit cards accepted. Open year-round.

Directions: Drive to the junction of I-215 and Highway 74 (near Perris). At that junction, take Highway 74 east and drive 15 miles to Hemet (the highway becomes Florida Avenue in Hemet) and continue to Sanderson Avenue. Turn right on Sanderson Avenue and drive one block to Acadia. Turn left and drive to Lyon Avenue. Turn right on Lyon Avenue and drive to the park at the corner of Lyon and South Acacia (235 S. Lyon).

Contact: Mountain Valley RV Park, 909/925-5812, fax 909/658-6272, website: www.Mountain Valleyrvp.com.

118 LAKE HEMET

Rating: 7

Near Hemet.

Map 14.6, page 731

Lake Hemet covers 420 acres, is set at 4,340 feet, and sits near San Bernardino National Forest just west of Garner Valley. Many campsites have lake views. It provides a good camping/fishing destination, with stocks of 75,000 trout each year, a lot for a lake this size, and yep, catch rates are good. The lake also has bass, bluegill, and catfish. Boating rules prohibit boats under 10 feet, canoes, sailboats, inflatables, and swimming—no swimming or wading at Lake Hemet.

Campsites, facilities: There are 275 sites with full hookups for RVs, an open area for dispersed tent sites, and an open area for groups. Picnic tables and fire rings are provided. Restrooms, drinking water, flush toilets, coin showers, RV dump station, playground, pond, boat ramp, boat rentals, store, coin laundry, and propane gas are available. Some facilities are wheelchair-accessible. Leashed pets are permitted.

Reservations, fees: No reservations are accepted, except for groups of 20 an up. Fees are $15–18.25 per vehicle per night, $2.50 per person for more than two people, $1 per night. Major credit cards accepted. Open year-round.

Directions: From Palm Desert, drive southwest on Highway 74 for 32 miles (near Lake Hemet) to the campground entrance on the left. For directions if arriving from the west (several options), phone 909/659-2680, ext. 2.

Contact: Lake Hemet, 909/659-2680, website: www.lakehemet.com.

119 HURKEY CREEK COUNTY PARK

Rating: 5

Near Lake Hemet.
Map 14.6, page 731

This large county park is just east (across the road) of Lake Hemet, beside Hurkey Creek (which runs in winter and spring). The highlight, of course, is the nearby lake, known for good fishing in the spring. No swimming is permitted. The camp elevation is 4,800 feet. The park covers 59 acres.

Campsites, facilities: There are 107 family sites and 105 group sites for tents or RVs up to 35 feet long. Fire grills and picnic tables are provided. Drinking water, flush toilets,

and showers are available. Some facilities are wheelchair-accessible. An RV dump station is available at nearby Lake Hemet. Leashed pets are permitted.

Reservations, fees: Reserve at 800/234-PARK (800/234-7275) (reservation fee charged); $15 per night, $2 per night. Major credit cards accepted. Open year-round.

Directions: From Palm Desert, drive southwest on Highway 74 for 32 miles (near Lake Hemet) to the campground entrance on the right.

Contact: Hurkey Creek County Park, 909/659-2050, website: www.riversidecoparks.org.

120 KAMP ANZA RV RESORT

Rating: 4

Near Anza.
Map 14.6, page 731

This is a year-round RV park set at 4,100 feet, with many nearby recreation options. Lake Hemet is 11 miles away, with hiking, motorbiking, and jeep trails nearby in San Bernardino National Forest. Pacific Crest Trail hikers are welcome to clean up and to arrange for food and mail pick-up.

Campsites, facilities: There are 116 sites, including some drive-through and many with full hookups, for RVs or tents. Picnic tables and fire grills are provided. Restrooms, showers, playground, fishing pond, hot tub, horseshoe pits, coin laundry, store, RV dump station, ice, recreation room, modem access, and propane gas are available.

Reservations, fees: Reservations are accepted. The fee is $15–18 per night. Open year-round.

Directions: From Palm Desert, drive west on Highway 74 for 24 miles to Highway 371. Turn left on Highway 371 and drive west to the town of Anza and Kirby Road. Turn left on Kirby Road and drive 3.5 miles to the campground on the left at Terwilliger Road (look for the covered wagon out front).

Contact: Kamp Anza RV Resort, 909/763-4819, fax 909/763-0619.

© TOM STIENSTRA

Chapter 15
San Diego and Vicinity

Chapter 15—San Diego and Vicinity

S an Diego was picked as one of the best regions to live in America in an unofficial vote at a national conference for the Outdoors Writers Association of America.

It is easy to understand why: the weather, the ocean and beaches, the lakes and the fishing, Cleveland National Forest, the state parks, the Palomar Mountains, the hiking, biking, and water sports. What more could anyone ask for? For many, the answer is you don't ask for more, because it does not get any better than this.

The weather is near perfect. It fits a warm coastal environment with an azure-tinted sea that borders foothills and mountains. In a relatively small geographic spread, you get it all.

The ocean here is warm and beautiful, with 70 miles of beaches and often sensational fishing offshore for albacore, yellowtail, and marlin. The foothills provide canyon settings for many lakes, including Lower Otay, Morena, Barrett, El Capitan, Cuyamaca, San Vicente, Hodges, and Henshaw. . . and several more—with some of the biggest lake-record bass ever caught in the world.

Cleveland National Forest provides a surprise for many—remote mountains with more canyons, hidden streams, small campgrounds, and a terrain with a forest of fir, cedar, and hardwoods such as oak. A landmark is Palomar Mountain, with several campgrounds at Palomar State Park and nearby in national forest. This is a great family destination. Long-distance views, stargazing, and watching meteor showers are all among the best anywhere in the state from the 5,000-foot ridges and lookouts set on the edge of Anza-Borrego Desert to the nearby east.

For more urban pursuits, San Diego's Mission Bay Park offers a fantastic network of recreation, with trails for biking and rollerblading, and beaches and boating access.

Everywhere you go, you will find campgrounds and parks, from primitive to deluxe. Some of the more remote sections of Cleveland National Forest, as well as Cuyamaca Rancho State Park, provide access to wild lands and primitive campsites. Yet in the San Diego area are developed RV parks that cost as much as fine hotel rooms in other parts of the state, and they're worth it, like silver dollars in a sea of pennies.

The region is one of the few that provides year-round recreation at a stellar level.

If you could live anywhere in America, where would it be? Well, that's what makes it so special to explore and visit, camping along the way.

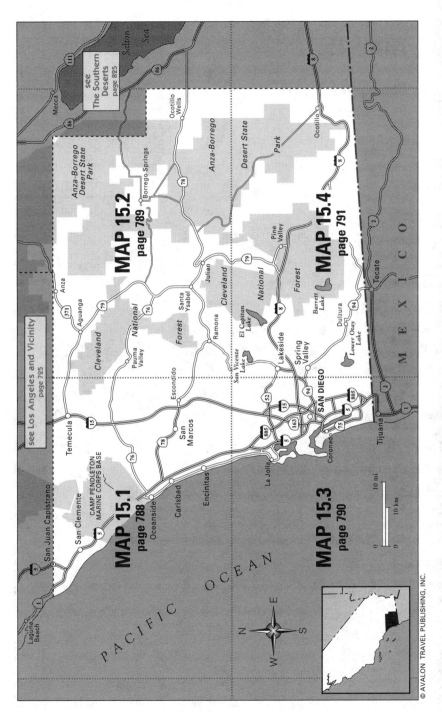

Map 15.1

Campgrounds 1–11
Pages 792–796

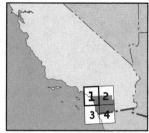

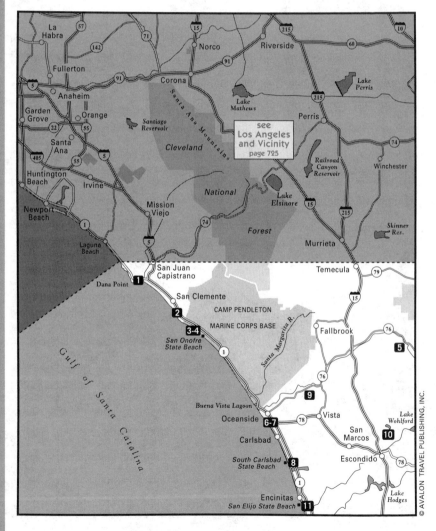

Map 15.2

Campgrounds 12–33
Pages 797–806

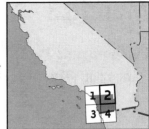

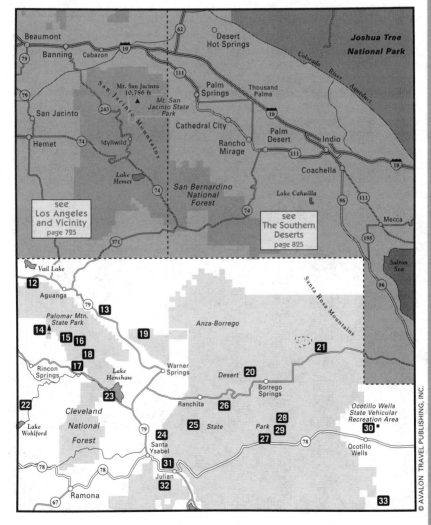

Map 15.3

Campgrounds 34–41
Pages 806–810

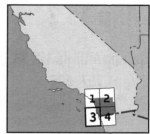

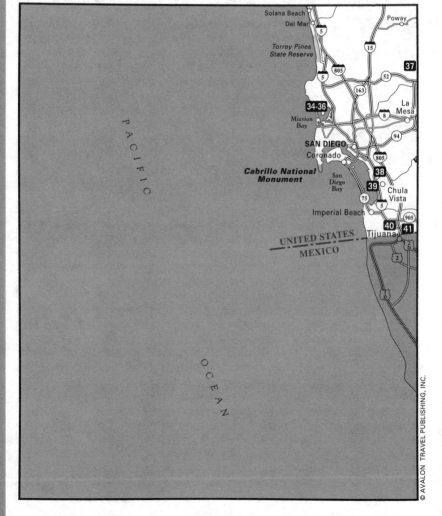

Map 15.4

Campgrounds 42–69
Pages 810–821

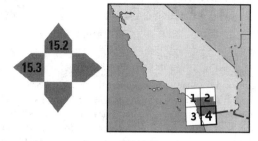

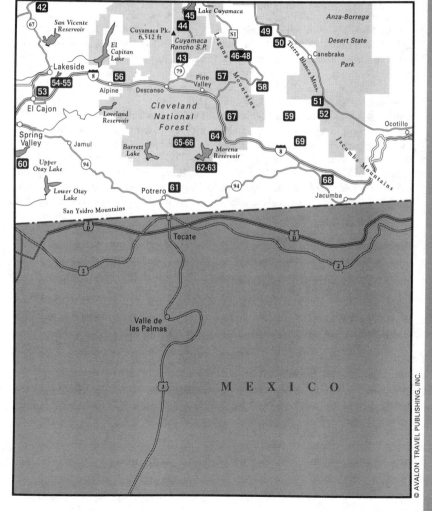

42

67
San Vicente
Reservoir

45 Lake Cuyamaca

Anza-Borrego

44
Cuyamaca Pk.
6,512 ft
Cuyamaca
Rancho S.P.

S1

49

50 Tierra Blanca Mtns.

Desert State

Canebrake

Park

El
Capitan
Lake

43
79

46-48

Laguna

Lakeside

8

56

Pine
Valley

57

Mountains

58

51

54-55

Alpine

Descanso

52

Ocotillo

53

El Cajon

Loveland
Reservoir

Cleveland
National
Forest

67

59

Spring
Valley

Jamul

Jacumba Mountains

60
Upper
Otay Lake

94

Barrett
Lake

65-66

64 Morena
Reservoir

69

8

68

62-63

Lower Otay
Lake

Potrero 61

94

Jacumba

San Ysidro Mountains

2

Tecate

2

2

Valle de
las Palmas

3

M E X I C O

© AVALON TRAVEL PUBLISHING, INC.

z

1 DOHENY STATE BEACH

Rating: 8

On Dana Point Harbor.

Map 15.1, page 788

Some campsites are within steps from the beach. Yet this state beach is right in town, set at the entrance to Dana Point Harbor. It is a pretty spot with easy access off the highway. Reservations are needed to guarantee a site at this popular campground. A lifeguard service is available in the summer, and campfire and junior ranger programs are also available. A day-use area has a five-acre lawn with picnic area and volleyball courts. Surfing is popular, but note that it is permitted at the north end of the beach only. San Juan Capistrano provides a nearby side trip, just three miles away.

Campsites, facilities: There are 115 sites for tents or RVs up to 35 feet, and hike-in/bike-in sites. No hookups are provided. Picnic tables and fire grills are provided. Restrooms, drinking water, flush toilets, coin showers, RV dump station, exhibits, and food service (summer only) are available. Propane gas is nearby. Some facilities are wheelchair-accessible. Leashed pets are permitted in campground only, not on the beach.

Reservations, fees: Reserve at 800/444-PARK (800/444-7275) or website: www.Reserve America.com ($7.50 reservation fee); $12 per night, $1 per person for hike-in/bike-in site (photo ID required). Senior discount available. Open year-round.

Directions: Drive on I-5 to the exit for Pacific Coast Highway/Camino delas Ramblas (three miles south of San Juan Capistrano). Take that exit and drive to Del Obispo/Dana Point Drive (second light). Turn left and drive one block to Park Lantern/Doheny State Beach Road. Turn left and drive one block to the park entrance. Doheny State Beach is about one mile from I-5.

Contact: Doheny State Beach, 949/496-6172 or 949/492-0802.

2 SAN CLEMENTE STATE BEACH

Rating: 8

Near San Clemente.

Map 15.1, page 788

The campground at San Clemente State Beach is set on a bluff, not on a beach. A few campsites here have ocean views. Surfing is popular on the north end of a one-mile beach. The beach here is popular for swimming, body surfing, and skin diving. Of the three local state beaches that provide easy access and beachfront camping, this one offers full hookups. The others are Doheny State Beach to the north and San Onofre State Beach to the south. A feature at this park is a two-mile long interpretive trail, along with hike-in/bike-in campsites. Surfing camp is held here during the summer.

Campsites, facilities: There are 160 sites, 72 with full hookups, for tents or RVs up to 30 feet, one hike-in/bike-in site, and one group site with no hookups for up to 50 people and 20 vehicles— RVs or tents. Picnic tables and fire grills are provided. Flush toilets, coin showers, RV dump station, summer lifeguard service, and summer programs are available. A store, coin laundry, and propane gas are nearby. Some facilities are wheelchair-accessible. Leashed pets are permitted.

Reservations, fees: Reserve at 800/444-PARK (800/444-7275) or website: www.Reserve America.com ($7.50 reservation fee); $12–18 per night, $1 per person for hike-in/bike-in sites. Open year-round.

Directions: From I-5 in San Clemente, take the Avenida Calafia exit. Drive west for a short distance to the park entrance on the left.

Contact: San Clemente State Beach, 949/492-3156 or 949/492-3281; Orange Coast District, San Clemente Sector, 949/492-0802.

3 SAN ONOFRE STATE BEACH: BLUFF AREA

Rating: 7

Near San Clemente.

Map 15.1, page 788

This camp may appear perfect at first glance, but nope, it is very noisy. Both the highway and train tracks are within very close range; you can practically feel the ground rumble, and that's not all. With Camp Pendleton just on the other side of the freeway, there is considerable noise from helicopters and other operations. Too bad. This is one of three parks set along the beach near San Clemente, just off the busy Coast Highway. The campground is set on top of a 90-foot bluff. This state beach covers more than 3,000 acres, featuring 3.5 miles of sandy beaches and access trails on the neighboring bluffs. This area is one of the most popular in California for surfing, with this state beach also good for swimming. The shadow of the San Onofre Nuclear Power Plant is nearby. Other state beaches in the area are San Clemente State Beach and Doheny State Beach, both situated to the north.

Campsites, facilities: There are 176 sites for tents or RVs up to 30 feet long, one group site for up to 50 people, and one hike-in/bike-in site. Picnic tables and fire rings are provided. Drinking water, flush toilets, and cold showers are available. A store, coin laundry, and propane gas are available within about five miles. Leashed pets are permitted.

Reservations, fees: Reserve at 800/444-PARK (800/444-7275) or website: www.Reserve America.com ($7.50 reservation fee); $12 per night, $50 for the group site, $1 per person per night for the hike-in/bike-in site. Open year-round.

Directions: From San Clemente, drive south on I-5 for three miles to the Basilone Road exit. Take that exit and drive south on Basilone Road for two miles to the park.

Contact: San Onofre State Beach, 949/492-4872; Orange Coast District Office, 949/492-0802 or 909/366-8500.

4 SAN ONOFRE STATE BEACH: SAN MATEO

Rating: 9

Near San Clemente.

Map 15.1, page 788

This state beach is considered one of the best surf breaks in the United States—it's well known as the outstanding Trestles Surfing Area. The camp is set inland and includes a nature trail, featuring a marshy area where San Mateo Creek meets the shoreline. Although this is a state beach, the camp is relatively far from the ocean; it is a 1.1-mile walk to the beach. But it sure is a lot quieter than the nearby option, Bluff Area Campground.

Campsites, facilities: There are 159 sites, 47 with partial hookups, for RVs or tents. Picnic tables and fire grills are provided. An RV dump station, showers, and flush toilets are available. A store, propane gas, and coin laundry are nearby. Leashed pets are permitted. Some facilities are wheelchair-accessible.

Reservations, fees: Reserve at 800/444-PARK (800/444-7275) or website: www.Reserve America.com ($7.50 reservation fee); $12–18 per night. Senior discount available. Open year-round.

Directions: Drive on I-5 to the southern end of San Clemente and the Cristianitos Road exit. Take that exit and drive east on Cristianitos Road for 1.5 miles to the park entrance on the right.

Contact: San Onofre State Beach, 949/492-4872; Orange Coast District Office, 949/492-0802 or 909/366-8500.

5 RANCHO CORRÌDO RV PARK

Rating: 7

Near the Pala Mission.

Map 15.1, page 788

This RV layover is 10 miles east of I-15, the main drag. A fishing pond is available for catch-

and-release fishing only. This park is very active on summer weekends, with music on Saturday night from May to September, arts and crafts on Saturday, and wagon rides. A full playground makes this a family-oriented camp. It is a short drive to the Pala Indian Reservation and the Pala Mission to the east. The Palomar Observatory is 20 miles to the east, another possible side trip.

Campsites, facilities: There are 210 sites, including 110 with partial hookups, for RVs or tents, and 100 sites for tents only. Picnic tables and fire pits are provided. Restrooms, drinking water, flush toilets, showers, RV dump station, modem access, cable TV hookups, clubhouses, gazebos, small store, fishing pond, and coin laundry are available. A playground with volleyball, horseshoes, tetherball, and basketball are on site. Leashed pets are permitted.

Reservations, fees: Reservations are accepted. The fee is $18–28 per night, $7 per person for more than two people, $3 per night. Weekly rates available. Open year-round. Major credit cards accepted.

Directions: Drive on I-15 to the Highway 76 exit (east of Oceanside). Take that exit east and drive on Highway 76 to the town of Pala. Continue east on Highway 76 for four miles to the camp on the right (14715 Hwy. 76).

Contact: Rancho Corrido, 760/742-3755, fax 760/742-3245; website: www.ranchocorrido.com.

⑥ PARADISE BY THE SEA RV RESORT

Rating: 7

In Oceanside.

Map 15.1, page 788

This is a classic oceanfront RV park, but no tenters need apply. It's an easy walk to the beach. For boaters, Oceanside Marina to the immediate north is the place to go. Oceanside is an excellent headquarters for deep-sea fishing, with charter trips available to Catalina Island, the kelp forests to the north off the shore of Camp Pendleton and San Onofre, as well as points south; contact Helgren's Sportfishing, 760/722-2133, to arrange charters. Camp Pendleton, a huge Marine Corps training complex, is to the north.

Campsites, facilities: There are 102 sites with full hookups, four drive-through, for RVs. Restrooms, flush toilets, showers, cable TV hookups, swimming pool, whirlpool, clubhouse, banquet room, coin laundry, RV supplies, telephone, and a small store are available. Boat rentals are nearby. Leashed pets are permitted with proof of vaccination.

Reservations, fees: Reservations are recommended. Fees are $35–45 per night, $2 per person for more than two people, $5 per night for each extra vehicle, $1 per night. Major credit cards accepted. Open year-round.

Directions: Drive on I-5 to Oceanside and the Oceanside Boulevard exit. Take that exit and drive west on Oceanside Boulevard for a half mile to South Coast Highway. Turn left on South Coast Highway and drive to the park on the right (1537 S. Coast Highway).

Contact: Paradise by the Sea RV Resort, 760/439-1376, fax 760/439-1919, website: www.paradise bythesearvresort.com.

⑦ OCEANSIDE RV PARK

Rating: 7

In Oceanside.

Map 15.1, page 788

There are three options for RV cruisers in the Oceanside area, and this is one of them. It's a short distance to the beach, about a 10-minute walk. It has a lifeguard and snack bar. A bowling alley is across the street. (For details on the area, see the entry for Paradise by the Sea RV Park.) Some may remember this park as "Casitas Poquitos." It has been renamed—same owners, nice folks.

Campsites, facilities: There are 140 sites with full hookups for RVs. Picnic tables and patios are provided. Flush toilets, showers, cable TV hookups, playground, coin laundry, recreation room, swimming pool, spa, billiard room, propane gas, and a general store are available. Leashed pets are permitted.

Reservations, fees: Reservations are recommended. The fee is $43 per night, $2 per person per night for more than two people, $1 pet fee. Winter discount available. Major credit cards accepted. Open year-round.

Directions: Drive on I-5 to Oceanside and the Oceanside Boulevard exit. Take that exit and drive west on Oceanside Boulevard for a half mile to South Coast Highway. Turn left on South Coast Highway and drive a half block to the park at 1510 S. Coast Highway.

Contact: Oceanside RV Park, 760/722-4404, fax 760/722-4080.

8 SOUTH CARLSBAD STATE BEACH

Rating: 9

Near Carlsbad.

Map 15.1, page 788

No reservation? Then likely you can forget about staying here. This is a beautiful state beach and, as big as it is, the sites go fast to the coastal cruisers who reserved a spot. The campground is set on a bluff, with half the sites overlooking the ocean. The nearby beach is accessible by a series of stairs. This is a phenomenal place for scuba diving and snorkeling, with a nearby reef available. This is also a popular spot for surfing and body surfing.

Campsites, facilities: There are 222 sites for tents or RVs up to 35 feet long, and one hike-in/bike-in site. Picnic tables and fire rings are provided. Restrooms, drinking water, flush toilets, coin showers, and RV dump station are available. A lifeguard service is provided in summer. Some facilities are wheelchair-accessible. Supplies and a coin laundry are available in Carlsbad. Leashed pets are permitted, but not on the beach.

Reservations, fees: Reserve at 800/444-PARK

(800/444-7275) or website: www.Reserve America.com ($7.50 reservation fee); $12 per night, $1 for hike-in/bike-in site. Senior discount available. Open year-round, with the possibility of closing November to January.

Directions: Drive on I-5 to Carlsbad and the exit for Palomar Airport Road. Take that exit and drive .3 mile to Carlsbad Boulevard. Turn south on Carlsbad Boulevard and drive two miles to Poinsettia Avenue. Turn right and drive a short distance to the park entrance.

Contact: South Carlsbad State Beach, 760/438-3143; San Diego Coast District office, 858/642-4200.

9 GUAJOME COUNTY PARK

Rating: 5

In Oceanside.

Map 15.1, page 788

Guajome means "home of the frog" and, yep, so it is with little Guajome Lake and the adjacent marsh, both of which can be explored with a delightful two-mile hike. The lake provides a bit of fishing for warm-water species, mainly sunfish and catfish. Because of the wetlands, a huge variety of birds will stop here on their migratory journeys, making this a favorite area for bird-watching. There are also trails available for horseback riding. A historic adobe house in the park is a must-see. The park covers 557 acres and features several miles of trails for hiking and horseback riding and a nearby museum with antique gas and steam engines.

Campsites, facilities: There are 35 sites, a few drive-through, with partial hookups for RVs. Picnic tables and fire grills are provided. Restrooms, drinking water, flush toilets, showers, RV dump station, and a playground are available. An enclosed pavilion and gazebo can be reserved for groups. A store and propane gas are nearby. Leashed pets are permitted.

Reservations, fees: Make reservations at 858/565-3600, fax 619/260-6492 ($3 reservation fee); $16 per night, eight-person maximum per site,

$1 per night. Major credit cards accepted. Open year-round.

Directions: From Oceanside, drive east on Highway 76/Mission Avenue for seven miles to Guajome Lakes Road. Turn right (south) on Guajome Lakes Road and drive to the entrance.

Contact: San Diego County Parks Department, 858/694-3049, fax 858/495-5841, website: www.sdparks.org.

10 DIXON LAKE RECREATION AREA

Rating: 7

Near Escondido.

Map 15.1, page 788

Little Dixon Lake is the centerpiece of a regional park in the Escondido foothills. The camp is set at an elevation of 1,405 feet, about 400 feet above the lake's shoreline. No private boats are permitted, and a 5-mph speed limit for rental boats keeps things quiet. The water is clear, with fair bass fishing in the spring and trout fishing in the winter and early spring. Catfish are stocked in the summer, trout in winter and spring. In the summer, the lake is open at night for fishing for catfish. A pretty and easy hike is the Jack Creek Nature Trail, a one-mile walk to a 20-foot waterfall. Note that no wood fires are permitted, but charcoal is allowed.

Campsites, facilities: There are 45 sites, 10 with full hookups, for tents or RVs. Picnic tables and fire grills are provided. Restrooms, drinking water, flush toilets, showers, boat rentals, bait, ice, snack bar, and a playground are available. No pets.

Reservations, fees: Reservations are accepted. The fee is $12–16 per night, maximum of eight people per site, $2 per night for each extra vehicle. Group sites available. Major credit cards accepted. Open year-round.

Directions: Drive on I-15 to the exit for El Norte Parkway (four miles north of Escondido). Take that exit northeast and drive four miles to La Honda Drive. Turn left and drive to Dixon Lake.

Contact: Dixon Lake Recreation Area, 760/741-3328 or 760/839-4345, website: www.ci.escondido.ca.us.

11 SAN ELIJO STATE BEACH

Rating: 9

In Cardiff by the Sea.

Map 15.1, page 788

As with South Carlsbad State Beach, about half the sites overlook the ocean, that is, these are bluff-top campgrounds. The swimming and surfing are good here. The narrow bluff-backed stretch of sandy beach has a nearby reef that is popular for snorkeling and diving. What more could you ask for? Well, for one thing, how about not so many trains? Yep, train tracks run nearby and the trains roll by several times a day. So much for a chance at tranquility. Regardless, it is a beautiful beach just north of the small town of Cardiff by the Sea. As at all state beaches, reservations are usually required to get a spot between Memorial Day weekend and Labor Day weekend. Nearby San Elijo Lagoon at Solana Beach is an ecological preserve. Though this is near a developed area, there are numerous white egrets, as well as occasional herons and other marine birds.

Campsites, facilities: There are 171 sites, four with full hookups, for tents or RVs up to 35 feet long (maximum of 24 feet at sites with hookups), and one hike-in/bike-in site. Picnic tables and fire rings are provided. Restrooms, drinking water, flush toilets, coin showers, coin laundry, RV dump station, and a small store are available. A lifeguard service is available in the summer. Some facilities are wheelchair-accessible. Leashed pets are permitted, but not on the beach.

Reservations, fees: Reserve at 800/444-PARK (800/444-7275) or website: www.ReserveAmerica.com ($7.50 reservation fee); $12–18 per night, $1 per person per night for hike-in/bike-in site. Senior discount available. Open year-round.

Directions: Drive on I-5 to Encinitas and the Encinitas Boulevard exit. Take that exit and drive west on Encinitas Boulevard for one mile to U.S. 101 (South Coast Highway). Turn south on U.S. 101 and drive two miles to the park on the right.

Contact: San Elijo State Beach, 760/753-5091; San Diego Coast District Office, 858/642-4200.

12 DRIPPING SPRINGS

Rating: 7

Near the Agua Tibia Wilderness in Cleveland National Forest.

Map 15.2, page 789

This is one of the premium Forest Service camps available, set just inside the national forest border near Vail Lake and adjacent to the Agua Tibia Wilderness. The Dripping Springs Trail is routed south out of camp, starting at 1,600 feet and climbing near the peak of Agua Tibia Mountain, 4,779 feet.

Campsites, facilities: There are 24 sites for tents or RVs up to 32 feet long. Picnic tables and fire rings are provided. Drinking water and vault toilets are available. Supplies are available nearby in Temecula. Leashed pets are permitted.

Reservations, fees: Reservations are not accepted. The fee is $12–20 per night, $2 per night for additional vehicle. Senior discount available. Open July through March. Closed April through June for protection of an endangered species, the arroyo southwestern toad.

Directions: From I-15 in Temecula, drive 11 miles east on Highway 79 to the campground.

Contact: Cleveland National Forest, Palomar Ranger District, 760/788-0250, fax 760/788-6130.

13 OAK GROVE

Rating: 4

Near Temecula Creek in Cleveland National Forest.

Map 15.2, page 789

Oak Grove camp is on the northeastern fringe of Cleveland National Forest at 2,800 feet. Easy access from Highway 79 makes this a popular camp. The Palomar Observatory is just five miles up the mountain to the west, but there is no direct way to reach it from the campground. Lake Henshaw is about a half-hour drive to the south. A boat ramp and boat rentals are available there.

Campsites, facilities: There are 81 sites for tents or RVs up to 32 feet long. Picnic tables and fire grills are provided. Drinking water and flush toilets are available. Propane gas and groceries are nearby. Leashed pets are permitted.

Reservations, fees: Reservations are not accepted. The fee is $15–20 per night. Senior discount available. Open year-round.

Directions: Drive on I-15 to the Highway 79 exit. Take that exit and drive east on Highway 79 to Aguanga. Continue southeast on Highway 79 for 6.5 miles to the camp entrance.

Contact: Cleveland National Forest, Palomar Ranger District, 760/788-0250, fax 760/788-6130.

14 PALOMAR MOUNTAIN STATE PARK

Rating: 8

Near the Palomar Observatory.

Map 15.2, page 789

This is one of the best state parks in Southern California for hiking. It features 14 miles of trails, including several loop trails, often featuring long-distance views. Yet forest covers much of this park, one of the few sites in this Southern California region with a Sierra Nevada-like feel to it This camp offers hiking trails and some fishing in Doane Pond (permit required—great for youngsters learning to fish). There are numerous excellent hikes, including the Boucher Trail (four miles) and Lower Doane Valley Trail (three miles). The view from Boucher Lookout is stunning, at 5,438 feet looking out over the valley below. This developed state park is a short drive from the Palomar Observatory. There are four other campgrounds in the immediate area that are a short distance from the observatory. At the Palomar Observatory (not part of the park) you'll find the 200-inch Hale telescope, America's largest telescope. This is a private, working telescope, run by the California Institute of Technology, so there are no tours or public stargazing through it. The elevation is 4,700 feet.

Campsites, facilities: There are 31 sites for tents or RVs up to 21 feet long, three group sites for 15–25 people, and one hike-in/bike-in site. Picnic tables, fire grills, and raccoon-resistant food lockers are provided. Drinking water, flush toilets, and coin showers are available. Some facilities are wheelchair-accessible. Leashed pets are permitted.

Reservations, fees: Reserve at 800/444-PARK (800/444-7275) or website: www.Reserve America.com ($7.50 reservation fee); $12 per night, $1 for hike-in/bike-in site, $20–32 for group sites. Permit required for fishing pond. Senior discount available. Open year-round.

Directions: Drive on I-15 to the Highway 76 exit (east of Oceanside). Take that exit and drive east on Highway 76 for 25 miles to County Road S6 (which brings you to the top of Palomar Mountain). At the top of the mountain, turn left, drive about 50 feet to State Park Road/County Road S7. Turn left on State Park Road/County Road S7 and drive about 3.5 miles to the park entrance.

Contact: Palomar Mountain State Park, 760/742-3462; Colorado Desert District, 760/767-5311.

15 FRY CREEK

Rating: 6

Near the Palomar Observatory in Cleveland National Forest.

Map 15.2, page 789

A small, seasonal stream, Fry Creek, runs near the camp. The elevation is 5,200 feet. On a clear night, you can see forever from Palomar Mountain. Literally. That's because the Palomar Observatory, just a short distance from this forested camp, houses America's largest telescope. With the 200-inch Hale telescope, it is possible for scientists to see 100 billion galaxies. It is not open to public touring.

Campsites, facilities: There are 12 tent sites and eight sites for tents or RVs up to 16 feet long. Picnic tables and fire rings are provided. Drinking water and vault toilets are available. A store is nearby. Leashed pets are permitted.

Reservations, fees: Reservations are not accepted. The fee is $12 per night. Senior discount available. Open May through November.

Directions: Drive on I-15 to the Highway 76 exit (east of Oceanside). Take that exit and drive east on Highway 76 for 25 miles to County Road S6 (which brings you to the top of Palomar Mountain). Turn left on County Road S6 and drive about nine miles to the campground entrance on the left. The road is not recommended for trailers.

Contact: Cleveland National Forest, Palomar Ranger District, 760/788-0250, fax 760/788-6130.

16 OBSERVATORY

Rating: 4

Near the Palomar Observatory in Cleveland National Forest.

Map 15.2, page 789

This popular Forest Service camp is used primarily as a layover spot for campers visiting the nearby Palomar Observatory, housing the largest telescope in America. There are four other camps in the immediate area. The elevation is 4,800 feet. The trailhead for the Observatory Trail starts at this camp. This two-hour hike from the campground to the observatory includes one short, steep climb through woodlands, highlighted by a vista deck with a beautiful view of Mendenhall Valley, and then onward to the top and to the telescope viewing area.

Campsites, facilities: There are 42 sites for tents or RVs up to 22 feet long (a few sites will accommodate RVs up to 28 feet long). Picnic tables and fire grills are provided. Drinking water and vault toilets are available. Leashed pets are permitted.

Reservations, fees: Reservations are not accepted. The fee is $12 per night, double sites $20 per night. Senior discount available. Open May through November.

Directions: Drive on I-15 to the Highway 76 exit (east of Oceanside). Take that exit and drive east on Highway 76 for 25 miles to County Road S6 (which brings you to the top of Palomar Mountain). Turn left on County Road S6 and drive about 8.5 miles to the campground entrance on the right. The road is not recommended for trailers.

Contact: Cleveland National Forest, Palomar Ranger District, 760/788-0250, fax 760/788-6130.

17 OAK KNOLL

Rating: 5

Near the Palomar Observatory.
Map 15.2, page 789
The camp is set at 3,000 feet in San Diego County foothill country among giant old California oaks. It is at the western base of Palomar Mountain, and to visit the Palomar Observatory and its awesome 200-inch telescope requires a remarkably twisty 10-mile drive up the mountain (the telescope is not open to the public). A good side trip is driving to the Boucher Lookout in Palomar Mountain State Park. Trailheads for excellent hikes on Palomar Mountain include the Observatory Trail (starting at Observatory) and the Doane Valley Loop (starting in Palomar Mountain State Park).

Campsites, facilities: There are 46 sites, many with full or partial hookups for tents or RVs up to 30 feet at all sites and of any size at four sites. Restrooms, drinking water, flush toilets, coin showers, playground, swimming pool, clubhouse, baseball diamond, coin laundry, propane gas, and groceries are available. Leashed pets are permitted, but some dogs are prohibited.

Reservations, fees: Call ahead for available space. Fees are $20–30 per night, $3 per person for more than two people, $1 per night for extra vehicle, $2 per night. Open year-round.

Directions: Drive on I-15 to the Highway 76 exit (east of Oceanside). Take that exit and drive east on Highway 76 for 25 miles to County Road S6 (which brings you to the top of Palomar Mountain). Turn left and drive a short distance to the campground on the left.

Contact: Oak Knoll, 760/742-3437, website: www.oakknoll.net.

18 CRESTLINE GROUP CAMP

Rating: 4

Near the Palomar Observatory in Cleveland National Forest.
Map 15.2, page 789
This Forest Service camp is designed expressly for large groups. (For adventure information, see the entry for Palomar Mountain State Park.) The elevation is 4,800 feet.

Campsites, facilities: There is one group campsite for tents only. Picnic tables and fire grills are provided. Drinking water and vault toilets are available. A store is nearby. Leashed pets are permitted.

Reservations, fees: Reservations are required. Reserve at 877/444-6777 ($9 reservation fee) or website: www.ReserveUsa.com; $75 group fee per night. Major credit cards accepted. Open May through November.

Directions: Drive on I-15 to the Highway 76 exit (east of Oceanside). Take that exit and drive east on Highway 76 for 25 miles to County Road S6 (which brings you to the top of Palomar Mountain). Turn left on County Road S6 and drive about 6.5 miles to the campground at the junction of County Roads S6 and S7. The road is not recommended for trailers.

Contact: Cleveland National Forest, Palomar Ranger District, 760/788-0250, fax 760/788-6130.

19 INDIAN FLATS

Rating: 6

Near the Pacific Crest Trail in Cleveland National Forest.

Map 15.2, page 789

Indian Flats is a remote campground, set at 3,600 feet just north of Pine Mountain. A highlight here is that the Pacific Crest Trail passes only two miles down the road to the south. A two-mile hike south on the PCT will take you down into a canyon and the home of Agua Caliente Creek.

Campsites, facilities: There are 17 sites for tents. Picnic tables and fire grills are provided. Drinking water and vault toilets are available. Leashed pets are permitted.

Reservations, fees: Reservations are not accepted. The fee is $10 per night. Senior discount available. Open May through March, closed April through June for protection of an endangered species, the arroyo southwestern toad.

Directions: From El Cajon, drive east on I-8 to Highway 79 (near Descanso Junction). Turn north on Highway 79 and drive to the town of Warner Springs. Continue two miles on Highway 79 to Forest Road 9S05. Turn right on Forest Road 9S05 and drive six miles to the campground.

Contact: Cleveland National Forest, Palomar Ranger District, 760/788-0250, fax 760/788-6130.

20 BORREGO PALM CANYON

Rating: 4

In Anza-Borrego Desert State Park.

Map 15.2, page 789

This is one of the best camps in Anza-Borrego Desert State Park with two excellent hikes available. The short hike into Borrego Palm Canyon is like being transported to another world, from the desert to the tropics, complete with a small waterfall, a rare sight in these parts. The Panorama Overlook Trail also starts here. An excellent visitor center is available, offering an array of exhibits and a slide show. The elevation is 760 feet. Anza-Borrego Desert State Park is the largest state park in the continental United States, covering more than 600,000 acres and with 500 miles of dirt roads. "Borrego" means bighorn sheep, appropriately named for the desert bighorn sheep that live in the mountains of this park.

Campsites, facilities: There are 65 sites for tents or self-contained RVs up to 31 feet, 52 sites with full hookups for RVs up to 35 feet, and five group sites for up to 24 people with tents. Picnic tables and fire grills are provided. Restrooms, drinking water, flush toilets, showers, and RV dump station are available. Some facilities are wheelchair-accessible. A store, coin laundry, and propane gas are nearby. Leashed pets are permitted.

Reservations, fees: Reserve at 800/444-PARK (800/444-7275) or website: www.Reserve America.com ($7.50 reservation fee); $10–16 per night, $18 group fee. Senior discount available. Open year-round.

Directions: From Julian, at the junction of Highway 78 and Highway 79, drive east on Highway 78 for 19.5 miles to Yaqui Pass Road/County Road S3. Turn left (north) and drive six miles to Borrego Springs Road. Turn left and drive five miles to Borrego Springs and Palm Canyon Drive. Turn west and drive 2.5 miles to the campground entrance on the right.

Contact: Anza-Borrego Desert State Park, 760/767-4205; Colorado Desert District, 760/767-5311, fax 760/767-3427.

21 ARROYO SALADO PRIMITIVE CAMP AREA

Rating: 5

In Anza-Borrego Desert State Park.

Map 15.2, page 789

This camp is a primitive spot set along (and named after) an ephemeral stream, the Arroyo Salado. A few miles to the west is the trailhead for the Thimble Trail, which is routed south into a wash in the Borrego Badlands. The elevation is 880 feet.

Campsites, facilities: This is an primitive, open camping area in Anza-Borrego Desert State Park for tents or small, self-contained RVs. Vault toilets are available. No drinking water is available. Garbage must be packed out. Open fires are not allowed. Leashed pets are permitted.

Reservations, fees: Reservations are not accepted. There is no fee for camping. Open year-round.

Directions: From Julian, at the junction of Highway 78 and Highway 79, drive east on Highway 78 for 19.5 miles to Yaqui Pass Road/County Road S3. Turn left (north) and drive six miles to Borrego Springs Road. Turn left and drive five miles to Borrego Springs and Palm Canyon Drive. Turn right on Palm Canyon Drive and drive 10 miles (past Fonts Pass) to the campground entrance on the right. The access road is very steep, curvy, and long.

Contact: Anza-Borrego Desert State Park, 760/767-4205; Colorado Desert District, 760/767-5311, fax 760/767-3427.

22 WOODS VALLEY KAMPGROUND

Rating: 5

Near Lake Wohlford.

Map 15.2, page 789

This privately operated park is set up primarily for RVs and is a short drive from Lake Wohlford to the south. Lake Wohlford has a 5-mph speed limit, which guarantees quiet water; canoes, inflatables, sailboats, and boats under 10 feet and over 18 feet are prohibited. It provides fair fishing for bass, bluegill, and catfish, best in late winter and spring.

Campsites, facilities: There are 59 sites, many with partial hookups, for RVs of any length, and 30 sites for tents. Picnic tables and fire barrels are provided. Restrooms, drinking water, flush toilets, showers, RV dump station, cable TV, coin laundry, swimming pool, catch-and-release fishing pond, small farm, playground, modem access, recreation room, and supplies are available. Group facilities are also available. Leashed pets are permitted, with some dogs prohibited.

Reservations, fees: Reservations are accepted. The fee is $27–39 per night, $3 per person for more than four people; $3 per night for each extra vehicle, $3 per night. Monthly rates available. Open year-round.

Directions: From Escondido, drive south on I-15 past Lake Hodges to the exit for Valley Parkway. Take that exit and drive east on Valley Parkway for about 15 miles to the town of Valley Center and Woods Valley Road. Turn right on Woods Valley Road and drive southeast for two miles the campground entrance on the left (15236 Woods Valley Road).

Contact: Woods Valley Kampground, 760/749-2905, website: www.woodsvalley.com.

23 LAKE HENSHAW RESORT RV

Rating: 7

Near Santa Ysabel.

Map 15.2, page 789

Lake Henshaw is the biggest lake in San Diego County, yet it has only one camp. It's a good one, with the cabin rentals a big plus. The camp is on the southern corner of the lake, at 2,727 feet near Cleveland National Forest. Swimming is not permitted and a 10-mph speed limit is in effect. The fishing is best for catfish, especially in the summer, and at times decent for bass, with the lake-record bass weighing 14 pounds, four ounces.

Campsites, facilities: There are 164 sites, many with full hookups, for tents or RVs, and 17 cabins. Flush toilets, showers, swimming pool, whirlpool, clubhouse, playground, RV dump station, coin laundry, propane gas, boat and motor rentals, boat launch, bait and tackle shop, restaurant, and store are available. Some facilities are wheelchair-accessible. A golf course is 10 miles away. Leashed pets are permitted.

Reservations, fees: Reservations are not accepted. The fee is $14–19 per night, $1 per night. Reservations accepted for cabins only. Major credit cards accepted. Open year-round.

Directions: From El Cajon, drive east on I-8 to Highway 79 (near Descanso Junction). Turn north on Highway 79 and drive to Santa Ysabel. Continue north on Highway 79 for seven miles to Highway 76. Turn left on Highway 76 and drive four miles to the campground on the left.

Contact: Lake Henshaw Resort RV, 760/782-3487 or 760/782-3501, fax 760/782-9224, website: www.lakehenshawca.com.

24 STAGECOACH TRAILS RV, EQUESTRIAN, AND WILDLIFE RESORT

Rating: 6

Near Julian.

Map 15.2, page 789

Mention this book and you get a 10 percent discount. You want space? You got space. That includes 600,000 acres of public lands bordering this RV campground, making Stagecoach Trails Resort ideal for those who love horseback riding and hiking. Seventy-five corrals at the campground let you know right away that this camp is very horse-friendly. In addition, Stagecoach Trails Resort provides the perfect jumping-off place for trips into neighboring Anza-Borrego Desert State Park. The resort's name comes from its proximity to the old Wells Fargo Butterfield Stage Route. While the scenic rating merits a 6, if the rating were based purely on cleanliness, professionalism, and friendliness, this resort would rate a 10.

Campsites, facilities: There are 286 sites, most drive-through, with full hookups for RVs, and a primitive camping area for tents with 75 horse corrals and five trailers. Picnic tables and fire rings are provided. Restrooms, drinking water, flush toilets, showers, a heated pool, recreation room, banquet room, store, modem access, coin laundry, two RV dump stations, and propane gas are available. The facilities are wheelchair-accessible. Pets are permitted.

Reservations, fees: Reservations are accepted. The fee is $22–50 per night, $5 for extra vehicle, $5 per night per horse. Major credit cards accepted. Open year-round.

Directions: From Escondido, drive east on Highway 78 to Ramona, and continue on Highway 78 for 15 miles to Santa Ysabel and Highway 79. Turn north (left) and drive 14 miles to County Road S2/San Felipe Road. Turn right and drive 17 miles to Highway 78. Turn right (west, toward Julian) and drive .4 mile to County Road S2 (Great Southern Overland Stage Route). Turn left and drive four miles to the resort on the right (at Mile Marker 21 on Road S2).

Contact: Stagecoach Trails Resort, 7878 Overland Stage Route, Julian, CA 92036, 760/765-2197, website: www.stagecoachtrails.com.

25 BUTTERFIELD RANCH

Rating: 3

Near Anza-Borrego Desert State Park.

Map 15.2, page 789

Butterfield Ranch is an ideal layover spot for RV cruisers visiting nearby Anza-Borrego Desert State Park who want a developed park in which to stay overnight. Note that there is no gas available in Julian after 6 P.M. and that the nearest gas station is 36 miles to the east. This camp was once pretty run-down and we almost removed it from the book, but new owners took over in 2002 and are promising major upgrades, so the future is bright. By early 2003, it was already looking a lot better.

Campsites, facilities: There are 300 sites, most drive-through, with full hookups for RVs, and 200 sites for tents. Restrooms, showers, playground, a swimming pool, recreation room, country store, and a fishing pond for children are available. Leashed pets are permitted.

Reservations, fees: Reservations are accepted. The fee is $16–26 per night, $2 per night. Open year-round.

Directions: From Escondido, drive east on Highway 78 to the town of Ramona and continue east on Highway 78 for 14 miles to County Road S2/San Felipe Road. Turn right (south) and drive 12 miles to the campground entrance on the right.

Contact: Butterfield Ranch, 760/765-1463.

26 CULP VALLEY PRIMITIVE CAMP AREA

Rating: 4

Near Peòa Springs in Anza-Borrego Desert State Park.

Map 15.2, page 789

Culp Valley is set near Peòa Springs and offers a trailhead for a hike routed to the northeast to the high desert. An enjoyable side trip is to the Panorama Outlook at Borrego Palm Canyon, about a 15-minute drive north on County Road S22. The elevation at this campground is 3,400 feet. The access road is steep, a 12 percent grade, with blind turns.

Campsites, facilities: This is a primitive, open camping area in Anza-Borrego Desert State Park for tents or small, self-contained RVs. Vault toilets are available. No drinking water is available. No open fires are permitted. Garbage must be packed out. Leashed pets are permitted.

Reservations, fees: Reservations are not accepted. There is no fee for camping. Open year-round.

Directions: From Julian, at the junction of Highway 78 and Highway 79, drive east on Highway 78 for 19.5 miles to Yaqui Pass Road/County Road S3. Turn left (north) and drive six miles to Borrego Springs Road. Turn left and drive five miles to Borrego Springs and Palm Canyon Drive. Turn west and drive 1.5 miles to Montezuma Valley Road/County Road S22. Turn left and drive eight miles to the camp entrance. The access road is very steep and curvy.

Contact: Anza-Borrego Desert State Park, 760/767-4205; Colorado Desert District, 760/767-5311, fax 760/767-3427.

27 TAMARISK GROVE

Rating: 5

In Anza-Borrego Desert State Park.

Map 15.2, page 789

This is the number one campground in Anza-Borrego Desert State Park, and it is easy to see why: big tamarisk trees provide shade, and the park provides drinking water. It is one of three camps in the immediate area, so if this camp is full, primitive Yaqui Well to the immediate west and Yaqui Pass to the north on Yaqui Pass Road provide alternatives. The Cactus Loop Trail, with the trailhead just north of camp, provides a hiking option. This is a 2.5-mile loop that passes seven varieties of cacti, some as tall as people. The elevation is 1,400 feet at this campground.

Campsites, facilities: There are 27 sites for tents or RVs up to 21 feet. Picnic tables and fire grills are provided. Restrooms, drinking water, flush toilets, and coin showers are available. Some facilities are wheelchair-accessible. Leashed pets are permitted.

Reservations, fees: Reserve at 800/444-PARK (800/444-7275) or website: www.Reserve America.com ($7.50 reservation fee); $10 per night. Open year-round.

Directions: From Julian, at the junction of Highway 78 and Highway 79, drive east on Highway

78 for 19.5 miles to Yaqui Pass Road/County Road S3. Turn left (north) and drive a quarter mile to the campground on the right.

Contact: Anza-Borrego Desert State Park, 760/767-4205; Colorado Desert District, 760/767-5311, fax 760/767-3427.

28 YAQUI PASS PRIMITIVE CAMP AREA

Rating: 1

In Anza-Borrego Desert State Park.

Map 15.2, page 789

This extremely primitive area is set beside rough Yaqui Pass Road at an elevation of 1,730 feet. The camping area is a large, open, sloping area of asphalt, where it is darn near impossible to get an RV level. The trailhead for the Kenyon Loop Trail is to the immediate south. This spot is often overlooked because the Tamarisk Grove Camp nearby provides shade, drinking water, and a feature trail.

Campsites, facilities: This is an primitive, open camping area in Anza-Borrego Desert State Park available for tents or small, self-contained RVs. No drinking water or toilets are available. Garbage must be packed out. Leashed pets are permitted.

Reservations, fees: No reservations are accepted and there are no fees. Open year-round.

Directions: From Julian, at the junction of Highway 78 and Highway 79, drive east on Highway 78 for 19.5 miles to Yaqui Pass Road/County Road S3. Turn left (north) and drive two miles to the campground on the right.

Contact: Anza-Borrego Desert State Park, 760/767-4205; Colorado Desert District, 760/767-5311, fax 760/767-3427.

29 YAQUI WELL PRIMITIVE CAMP AREA

Rating: 2

In Anza-Borrego Desert State Park.

Map 15.2, page 789

This camp is used primarily as an overflow area if the more developed Tamarisk Grove Camp is full. The Cactus Loop Trail, a 2.5-mile loop hike that passes seven varieties of cacti, starts at Tamarisk Grove. The elevation is 1,400 feet.

Campsites, facilities: This is an primitive, open camping area in Anza-Borrego Desert State Park for tents or small, self-contained RVs. Vault toilets are available. No drinking water is available. Garbage must be packed out. Open fires are not permitted. Leashed pets are permitted.

Reservations, fees: No reservations are accepted and there are no fees. Open year-round.

Directions: From Borrego Springs, drive south on Borrego Springs Road for five miles to Yaqui Pass Road/County Road S3. Turn right on Yaqui Pass Road and drive about six miles to the camping area on the right.

Contact: Anza-Borrego Desert State Park, 760/767-4205; Colorado Desert District, 760/767-5311, fax 760/767-3427.

30 OCOTILLO WELLS STATE VEHICLE RECREATION AREA

Rating: 4

In Ocotillo Wells.

Map 15.2, page 789

This can be a wild place, a giant OHV camp where the population of Ocotillo Wells can go from 100 to 5,000 overnight, no kidding. Yet if you arrive when there is no off-road event, it can also be a lonely, extremely remote destination. Some locals call the OHV crowd "escapees" and watch stunned as they arrive every February for two or three weeks. OHV events are held here occasionally as well.

Mountain bikers also use these trails. One great side note is that the first Saturday of November is "Desert Cleanup Day," when OHV users will clean up the place. The non-OHV crowd can still use this camp, but most come in the winter on weekdays, when activity is lower. The landscape is barren desert, dry as an iguana's back. A few shade ramadas are provided on-site. The area covers 72,000 acres, ranging from below sea level to an elevation of 400 feet. It is adjacent to Anza-Borrego Desert State Park, another 600,000 acres of wildlands. The wash-and-ridge terrain includes a butte with dunes, a sand bowl, a blow sand dune, and springs. After wet winters, the blooms of wildflowers can be excellent. While this area is well-known as a wild play area for the OHV crowd, it is also a place where on most days you can literally disappear and see no one. All drivers should watch for soft ground. Many vehicles get stuck here and have to be towed out.

Campsites, facilities: There are 60 dispersed primitive sites for RVs or tents. Picnic tables and fire rings are provided. Vault and chemical toilets and shade ramadas are available. No drinking water is available. A coin shower building is available near the ranger station, and another is 3.5 miles east at Holmes Camp. A store, restaurants, propane, and auto supplies are available four miles away in Ocotillo Wells. A gas station is seven miles from the ranger station. Leashed pets are permitted.

Reservations, fees: No reservations are accepted and there is no fee, with a 30-day maximum stay per year. Open year-round.

Directions: From Julian, at the junction of Highway 78 and Highway 79, drive east on Highway 78 for 31.5 miles to Ranger Station Road. Turn left and drive a quarter mile to the ranger station. (Note: for an alternative route, advisable for big rigs, that avoids curvy sections of Highway 78, see the detour route detailed in the listing for Stagecoach Trails RV.)

Contact: Ocotillo Wells SVRA, 760/767-5391, fax 760/767-4951.

31 PINEZANITA TRAILER RANCH

Rating: 6

Near Julian.
Map 15.2, page 789

Set at an elevation of 4,680 feet in dense pine and oak, this camp has had the same owners, the Stanley family, for more than 30 years. The fishing pond is a great attraction for kids (no license is required); no swimming allowed. The pond is stocked with bluegill and catfish, some of which are 12 inches or longer. Two possible side trips include Lake Cuyamaca, five miles to the south, and William Heise County Park, about 10 miles to the north as the crow flies.

Campsites, facilities: There are 160 sites with full hookups for RVs, 30 sites for self-contained RVs, 40 sites for tents, and a few furnished cottages. Picnic tables and fire rings are provided. Restrooms, drinking water, flush toilets, showers, a general store, ice, propane, fishing pond, and RV dump station are available. Leashed pets are permitted.

Reservations, fees: Reservations are accepted. Fees for campsites are $18 per night per vehicle (two people), cottages are $125 per night for two people (no children or pets in the cottages), $2 each additional camper, $2 per hookup and $2 pet fee. Major credit cards accepted. Open year-round.

Directions: From El Cajon, drive east on I-8 to Highway 79 (near Descanso Junction). Turn north on Highway 79 and drive 20 miles to Julian and the campground on the left.

Contact: Pinezanita Trailer Ranch, P.O. Box 2380, Julian, CA 92036-2380, 760/765-0429, website: www.pinezanita.com.

32 WILLIAM HEISE COUNTY PARK

Rating: 6

Near Julian.
Map 15.2, page 789

This is a beautiful county park, set at 4,200 feet,

that offers hiking trails and a playground, all amid pretty woodlands with a mix of oak and pine. A great hike starts right at camp (at the tent camping area), signed "Nature Trail." It joins with the Canyon Oak Trail and, after little more than a mile, links with the Desert View Trail. Here you will reach an overlook with a beautiful view of the Anza-Borrego Desert and the Salton Sea. The park features 900 acres of mountain forests of oak, pine, and cedar. A popular equestrian trail is the Kelly Ditch Trail, which is linked to Cuyamaca Rancho State Park and Lake Cuyamaca. The vast Anza-Borrego Desert State Park lies to the east, and the historic mining town of Julian is five miles away. Julian is known for its Apple Day Festival each fall.

Campsites, facilities: There are 40 sites, one drive-through, for tents or RVs, 43 sites for tents only, two group sites, and two cabins. Picnic tables and fire grills are provided. Restrooms, drinking water, flush toilets, showers, coin laundry, RV dump station, picnic areas, and a playground are available. Supplies are available five miles away in Julian. Leashed pets are permitted.

Reservations, fees: Reservations are accepted at 858/565-3600. The fee is $12 per night Monday through Thursday, $14 per night Friday through Sunday, $1 per night. Major credit cards accepted. Open year-round.

Directions: From El Cajon, drive east on I-8 to Highway 79 (near Descanso Junction). Turn north on Highway 79 and drive to Julian and Highway 78. Turn west (left) on Highway 78 and drive to Pine Hills Road. Turn south on Pine Hills Road and drive two miles to Frisius Drive. Turn left on Frisius Drive and drive two miles to the park.

Contact: San Diego County Parks Department, 858/694-3049.

33 FISH CREEK

Rating: 3

In Anza-Borrego Desert State Park.
Map 15.2, page 789
This primitive camp is set just inside the east-

ern border of Anza-Borrego Desert State Park at the foot of the Vallecito Mountains to the west. A few miles north of camp is the Elephant Tree Discovery Trail, a 1.5-mile hike highlighted by a weird tree about eight feet tall with crumpled, reddish bark. At one time there were several of these trees here, but they have been killed by the drought and now only one remains. This is the closest camp to the Ocotillo Wells State Vehicular Recreation Area, which is 12 miles to the north.

Campsites, facilities: There are eight sites for tents or small self-contained RVs. Vault toilets are available. No drinking water is available. Garbage must be packed out. Leashed pets are permitted.

Reservations, fees: Reservations are not accepted. There is no fee for camping. Open year-round.

Directions: From Ramona, drive east on Highway 78 to Julian. Continue east on Highway 78 for 34 miles to Ocotillo Wells and Split Mountain Road. Turn south and drive 12 miles to the campground entrance on the right.

Contact: Anza-Borrego Desert State Park, 760/767-4205; Colorado Desert District, 760/767-5311, fax 760/767-3427.

34 DE ANZA HARBOR RESORT

Rating: 5

On Mission Bay.
Map 15.3, page 790
Location means everything in real estate and campgrounds, and this private park passes the test. It is set on a small peninsula that is surrounded on three sides by Mission Bay, Sea World, and the San Diego Zoo. Premium sites overlook Mission Bay, but you pay the highest price for an RV site in California to get it. A beach and golf course are adjacent to the park. Mission Bay has 27 miles of shoreline, expansive beach frontage, great windsurfing, fantastic boating for water-skiing, and ocean access for deep-sea fishing. Note that a 5-mph speed limit is enforced on the northern bay and on the entire bay after sunset.

Campsites, facilities: There are 243 sites with full hookups and patios for RVs. Restrooms, drinking water, flush toilets, showers, playground, RV dump station, coin laundry, modem access, recreation room, pool tables, bike rentals, boat ramp, propane gas, and a store are available. Some facilities are wheelchair-accessible. Leashed pets are permitted.

Reservations, fees: Make reservations at 800/924-7529. Fees are $30–50 per night for sites with no hookups, $50–80 per night with full hookups. $3 per person per night for more than four people, $3 boat fee, $3 pet fee. Major credit cards accepted. Open year-round.

Directions: Drive on I-5 south to San Diego and the Clairemont Drive/Mission Bay exit. Take that exit (stay to your left) to a stop sign at Clairemont Drive. Turn left and drive west to East Mission Bay Drive. Turn right and drive north (the road becomes De Anza Road) .7 mile to the park at the end of the road (2727 De Anza Road).

Contact: De Anza Harbor Resort, 858/273-3211, fax 858/581-5748.

35 CAMPLAND ON THE BAY

Rating: 5

On Mission Bay.

Map 15.3, page 790

No kidding, this is one of the biggest campgrounds on this side of the galaxy. It has space for both tenters and RVers, and you can usually find a spot to shoehorn your way into. The park overlooks Kendall Frost Wildlife Preserve and is set on Mission Bay, a beautiful spot and a boater's paradise; it includes a private beach. Water-skiing, windsurfing, and ocean access for deep-sea fishing are preeminent. Note that a 5-mph speed limit is enforced on the northern bay and on the entire bay after sunset. Sea World, just north of San Diego, offers a premium side trip.

Campsites, facilities: There are 750 sites, most with full or partial hookups and 25 drive-

through, for RVs or tents. Picnic tables and fire grills are provided. Restrooms, drinking water, flush toilets, showers, cable TV, phone, and modem access, swimming pools, hot tub, recreation hall, arcade, playground, RV dump station, coin laundry, store, RV supplies, propane gas, boat ramp, boat docks, water toy rentals, boat and bike rentals, and groceries are available. Leashed pets are permitted.

Reservations, fees: Reservations accepted up to two years in advance at 800/422-9386 ($25 site guarantee fee); tent sites are $30–40 per night, RV sites $53–160 per night; eight people per site maximum, $5 for boats and trailers, $30 for boat slip up to 20 feet, $3 per night pet fee. Senior discount available. Major credit cards accepted. Open year-round.

Directions: Drive on I-5 south to San Diego and the Balboa-Garnet exit. Take that exit to Mission Bay Drive and drive to Grand Avenue. Turn right and drive one mile to Olney Street. Turn left on Olney Street and drive to Pacific Beach Drive. Turn left and drive a short distance to the campground entrance.

From northbound I-5 in San Diego, take the Grand-Garnet exit. Stay in the left lane to Grand Avenue. Turn left on Grand Avenue and drive to Olney Street. Turn left on Olney Street and continue as above.

Contact: Campland on the Bay, 800/422-9386, administration office, 858/581-4200, fax 858/581-4206; 20-minute waits can occur when making reservations.

36 SANTA FE TRAVEL TRAILER PARK

Rating: 3

In San Diego.

Map 15.3, page 790

This camp is a short drive from a variety of side trips, including the San Diego Zoo, Sea World, golf courses, beaches, sportfishing, and Tijuana. The owners here are smart and pleasant.

Campsites, facilities: There are 129 RV sites

with full hookups. No tent camping is allowed. Restrooms, drinking water, flush toilets, showers, playground, swimming pool, hot tub, RV dump station, cable TV, weight room, and coin laundry are available. Some facilities are wheelchair-accessible. Leashed pets are permitted.

Reservations, fees: Make reservations at 800/959-3787. Fees are $41–50 per night, $2 person for more than four people, $2 per pet per night. Weekly rates available. Major credit cards accepted. Open year-round.

Directions: Drive on I-5 south to San Diego and the Balboa-Garnet exit. Take that exit a short distance to Damon Street (the first left). Turn left and drive a quarter mile to Santa Fe Street. Turn left and drive one mile to the camp on the right (5707 Santa Fe Street).

On northbound I-5, drive to the exit for Grand-Garnet. Take that exit and continue as it feeds to East Mission Bay Drive. Continue six blocks to Damon Street. Turn right and drive a quarter mile to Santa Fe Street. Turn left and drive one mile to the camp on the right (5707 Santa Fe Street).

Contact: Santa Fe Travel Trailer Park, 858/272-4051, fax 858/272-2845.

᥇᥉ SANTEE LAKES REGIONAL PARK

Rating: 6

Near Santee.

Map 15.3, page 790

This is a 190-acre park built around a complex of seven lakes. Most campsites are lakefront and the park is best known for its fishing. The lakes are stocked with 44,000 pounds of fish, with fantastic lake records including a 39-pound catfish, 16-pound rainbow trout, 12-pound largemouth bass, and 2.5-pound bluegill. Quiet, low-key boating is the name of the game here. Rowboats, pedal boats, and canoes are available for rent. This small regional park is 20 miles east of San Diego. It receives more than 100,000 visitors per year. The camp is set at 400 feet.

Campsites, facilities: There are 172 sites, 23 drive-through, with full hookups for RVs and 61 sites for tents. Some sites have barbecue grills and picnic tables. Restrooms, drinking water, flush toilets, showers, RV dump station, boat rentals, playground, swimming pool, store, snack bar, recreation center, modem access, pay phone, propane, and coin laundry are available. Some facilities are wheelchair-accessible. Leashed pets are permitted at campsites only.

Reservations, fees: Make reservations at 619/596-3141. Fees are $20–35 per night with a six-person maximum, $2 per night for each extra vehicle, $1 per night. Monthly rates available. Major credit cards accepted. Open year-round.

Directions: Drive on I-8 to El Cajon and Highway 67. Turn north on Highway 67 and drive two miles to Santee and the Prospect Avenue exit. Take that exit and turn left and drive to Magnolia. Turn right on Magnolia and drive to Mission Gorge Road. Turn left on Mission Gorge Road and drive 2.5 miles to Carlton Hills Drive. Turn right and drive to Carlton Oaks Drive. Turn left and drive a mile to the park on the right.

Contact: Santee Lakes Regional Park, 619/596-3141.

᥈᥉ SAN DIEGO METROPOLITAN KOA

Rating: 2

In Chula Vista.

Map 15.3, page 790

This is one in a series of parks set up primarily for RVs cruising I-5. Chula Vista is between Mexico and San Diego, allowing visitors to make side trips east to Lower Otay Lake, north to the San Diego attractions, south to Tijuana, or "around the corner" on Highway 75 to Silver Strand State Beach. Nearby San Diego Bay is beautiful with excellent water-skiing (in designated areas), windsurfing, and a great swimming beach.

Campsites, facilities: There are 206 sites, 100

drive-through, with full hookups for RVs, 64 sites for tents, and a few cabins. Picnic tables and barbecue grills are provided. Restrooms, drinking water, flush toilets, showers, modem access, playground, RV dump station, coin laundry, swimming pool, whirlpool, bike rentals, propane gas, and groceries are available. Some facilities are wheelchair-accessible. Leashed pets are permitted.

Reservations, fees: Make reservations at 800/762-KAMP (800/762-5267); $31–35 for tent sites, $39–43 per night for RV sites, $5 for extra vehicle, $4 per person per night for more than two people. Major credit cards accepted. Open year-round.

Directions: Drive on I-5 to Chula Vista and the exit for E Street. Take that exit and drive east on E Street for three miles to 2nd Street. Turn north on 2nd Street and drive to the park on the right (111 N. 2nd Street).

Contact: San Diego Metropolitan KOA, 619/427-3601, fax 619/427-3622, website: www.koa.com.

39 CHULA VISTA MARINA AND RV PARK

Rating: 6

In Chula Vista.

Map 15.3, page 790

This RV park is close to San Diego Bay, a beautiful, calm piece of water where water-skiing is permitted in designated areas. An excellent swimming beach is available, and conditions in the afternoon for windsurfing are also excellent.

Campsites, facilities: There are 237 sites, a few drive-through, with full hookups for RVs. Restrooms, drinking water, flush toilets, showers, modem access, TV hookups, playground, heated swimming pool and spa, game room, marina, fishing pier, free boat launch, coin laundry, propane gas, and groceries are available. Some facilities are wheelchair-accessible. Leashed pets are permitted.

Reservations, fees: Make reservations at 800/770-

2878. Fees are $43–57 per night, $3 for each extra vehicle, $1 per night. Senior discount available. Major credit cards accepted. Open year-round.

Directions: Drive on I-5 to Chula Vista and the exit for J Street/Marina Parkway. Take that exit and drive west a short distance to Sandpiper Way. Turn left and drive a short distance to the park on the left (460 Sandpiper Way).

Contact: Chula Vista Marina and RV Park, 619/422-0111, fax 619/422-8872, website: www.chulavistarv.com.

40 INTERNATIONAL MOTOR INN RV PARK

Rating: 3

Near Imperial Beach.

Map 15.3, page 790

Easy access from I-5 is a big plus here, but call ahead for available space. For nearby side trips, head west to Imperial Beach, south to Tijuana, or east to Otay Lake with its megasized bass and catfish.

Campsites, facilities: There are 42 sites, a few drive-through, with full hookups for RVs. Picnic tables and patios are provided. Restrooms, drinking water, flush toilets, showers, swimming pool, whirlpool, and coin laundry are available. Leashed pets are permitted.

Reservations, fees: Reservations are accepted. The fee is $27 per night, $2 per person per night for more than two people. Senior discount available. Major credit cards accepted. Open year-round.

Directions: Drive on I-5 south of the San Diego area to San Ysidro and the Via de San Ysidro exit. Take that exit to Calle Primera. Drive south on Calle Primera to the park (190 E. Calle Primera, next to Motel 6).

Contact: International Motor Inn RV Park, 619/428-4486.

41 LA PACIFICA RV PARK

🏊 🐕 ♿ 🚐

Rating: 1

In San Ysidro.

Map 15.3, page 790

This RV park is less than two miles from the Mexican border, with regular Mexicoach bus service from the park to downtown Tijuana and back. Do this trip just once and you will find out how two miles can be the equivalent of a million miles.

Campsites, facilities: There are 177 sites, many drive-through, with full hookups, individual lawns, and patios for RVs. Flush toilets, showers, heated swimming pool, whirlpool, recreation room, RV dump station, coin laundry, and propane gas are available. All facilities are wheelchair-accessible. Leashed pets under 20 pounds are permitted.

Reservations, fees: Reservations are accepted at 888/786-6997. The fee is $28 per night. Major credit cards accepted. Open year-round.

Directions: From the San Diego area, drive south on I-5 to San Ysidro and the exit for Dairymart Road. Take that exit east to Dairymart Road and drive to San Ysidro Boulevard. Turn left and drive to the park on the left (1010 San Ysidro Boulevard).

Contact: La Pacifica RV Park, 619/428-4411, fax 619/428-4413.

42 DOS PICOS COUNTY PARK

🚶 🛶 🏕 🐎 ♿ 🚐 ⛰

Rating: 6

Near Ramona.

Map 15.4, page 791

Dos Picos means "two peaks" and is the highlight of a landscape featuring old groves of oaks and steep, boulder-strewn mountain slopes. Some of the oaks are 300 years old. The park covers 78 acres. As a county park, this camp is often missed by folks relying on less complete guides. The park is quite picturesque, with plenty of shade trees and a small pond.

Several nearby recreation options are in the area, including Lake Poway and Lake Sutherland. The elevation is 1,500 feet.

Campsites, facilities: There are 50 sites with electrical hookups for RVs and 14 tent sites. Picnic tables and fire grills are provided. Restrooms, drinking water, flush toilets, showers, RV dump station, and a playground, horseshoes, and soccer field are available. Supplies and a coin laundry are one mile away in Ramona. Leashed pets are permitted.

Reservations, fees: Make reservations at 858/565-3600. Fees are $12–16 per night, maximum of eight people per site, $1 per night. Senior discount available. Major credit cards accepted. Open year-round.

Directions: Drive on I-8 to El Cajon and the exit for Highway 67. Take that exit and drive north on Highway 67 for 22 miles to Mussey Grade Road. Turn right (a sharp turn) on Mussey Grade Road and drive two miles to the park.

Contact: San Diego County Parks Department, 858/694-3049, fax 858/495-5841, website: www.sd parks.org.

43 GREEN VALLEY-CUYAMACA RANCHO STATE PARK

🚶 🚴 🛶 🏕 ♿ 🚐 ⛰

Rating: 8

In Cuyamaca Rancho State Park.

Map 15.4, page 791

Green Valley is the southernmost camp in Cuyamaca Rancho State Park. It is set at 3,900 feet, with Cuyamaca Mountain (6,512 feet) looming overhead to the northwest. A trailhead is available (look for the picnic area) at the camp for an easy five-minute walk to Green Valley Falls, and it can be continued out to the Sweetwater River in a 1.5-mile round-trip. Newcomers should visit the park headquarters, where exhibits detail the natural history of the area. The park covers 25,000 acres with more than 100 miles of trails for hiking, mountain biking, and horseback riding.

Campsites, facilities: There are 81 sites for tents or RVs up to 27 feet, and one hike-in/bike-in site. Picnic tables and fire grills are provided. Restrooms, drinking water, flush toilets, coin-operated showers, and RV dump station are available. Some facilities are wheelchair-accessible. A store and propane gas are nearby. Leashed pets are permitted.

Reservations, fees: Reserve at 800/444-PARK (800/444-7275) or website: www.Reserve America.com ($7.50 reservation fee); $12 per night, $1 per person per night for hike-in/bike-in site. Senior discount available. Open year-round.

Directions: From El Cajon, drive east on I-8 to Highway 79 (near Descanso Junction). Turn north (left) on Highway 79 and drive seven miles to the campground entrance on the left (near Mile Marker 4).

Contact: Cuyamaca Rancho State Park, 760/765-0755, fax 760/765-3021.

44 PASO PICACHO

Rating: 8

In Cuyamaca Rancho State Park.
Map 15.4, page 791

This camp is set at 4,900 feet in Cuyamaca Rancho State Park, best known for Cuyamaca Peak, 6,512 feet. The Stonewall Peak Trail is accessible from across the street. This is a five-mile round-trip, featuring the climb to the summit at 5,730 feet. There are long-distance views from here highlighted by the Salton Sea and the Anza-Borrego State Desert. It's the most popular hike in the park, an easy to moderate grade, and completed by a lot of families. Another, more ambitious hike is the trail up to Cuyamaca Peak, starting at the southern end of the campground, a 6.5-mile round-trip tromp (alas, on a paved road; at least it's closed to traffic) with a climb of 1,600 feet in the process. The view from the top is breathtaking, with the Pacific Ocean and Mexico visible to the west and south, respectively. Park headquarters features exhibits about the area's Native

Americans, gold mining, and natural history. The Stonewall Mine was once the greatest of gold mines in Southern California. You can also learn here that Cuyamaca means "The Rain Beyond."

Campsites, facilities: There are 85 sites for tents or RVs up to 27 feet, two group camps for up to 60 people each, five cabins, a nature den cabin, and one hike-in/bike-in site. Fire grills and picnic tables are provided. Restrooms, drinking water, flush toilets, coin-operated showers, and RV dump station are available. Supplies are available nearby in Cuyamaca. Leashed pets are permitted.

Reservations, fees: Reserve at 800/444-PARK (800/444-7275) or website: www.Reserve America.com ($7.50 reservation fee); $12 per night, $75 for group sites, $15 for nature den cabin. Senior discount available. Open year-round.

Directions: From El Cajon, drive east on I-8 to Highway 79 (near Descanso Junction). Turn north (left) and drive nine miles to the park entrance on the left.

Contact: Cuyamaca Rancho State Park, 760/765-0755, fax 760/765-3021.

45 LOS CABALLOS EQUESTRIAN AND LOS VAQUEROS GROUP EQUESTRIAN

Rating: 8

In Cuyamaca Rancho State Park.
Map 15.4, page 791

These equestrian camps are among the most popular in Southern California, so reservations must be secured far in advance of a trip. There are 110 miles of trails accessible out of the camp, amid a landscape of pine and oaks, at the edge of forest, meadows, and small streams. Equestrians share the trails with hikers, and the fire roads are shared with mountain bikers as well.

Campsites, facilities: There are 16 equestrian sites for tents or RVs up to 27 feet, one group camp that accommodates up to 80 people and

45 horses, and one cabin. Fire rings and picnic tables are provided. Restrooms, drinking water, flush toilets, and coin-operated showers are available. Two corrals are available at each site, one horse per corral, and manure must be removed, with shovels and trailers provided. Supplies are available nearby in Julian. Leashed pets are permitted at campsites and on paved roads only.

Reservations, fees: Reserve at 800/444-PARK (800/444-7275) or website: www.Reserve America.com ($7.50 reservation fee); $12 per night, $150 for group site. Open April through November, weather permitting.

Directions: From El Cajon, drive east on I-8 to Highway 79 (near Descanso Junction). Turn north (left) on Highway 79 and drive 11 miles to Stonewall Road. Turn left and drive one-quarter mile to Los Caballos Camp on the right, or continue one-half mile to Los Vaqueros Group Camp on the right.

Contact: Cuyamaca Rancho State Park, 760/765-0755, fax 760/765-3021.

46 LAGUNA

Rating: 4

Near Little Laguna Lake in Cleveland National Forest.

Map 15.4, page 791

Laguna is set on Little Laguna Lake, one of the few lakes in America where "Little" is part of its official name. That's because for years everybody always referred to it as "Little Laguna Lake," and it became official. Yep, it's a "little" lake all right, a relative speck, with the camp on its eastern side at an elevation of 5,550 feet. A trailhead for the Pacific Crest Trail is a mile north on the Sunrise Highway/Laguna Mountain Road. Big Laguna Lake, which is actually a pretty small lake, is one mile to the west.

Campsites, facilities: There are 30 sites for tents only, and 73 sites for tents or RVs up to 50 feet. Picnic tables and fire grills are provided.

Restrooms, drinking water, flush toilets, and coin-operated showers are available. A store and propane gas are available nearby. Some facilities are wheelchair-accessible. Leashed pets are permitted.

Reservations, fees: Some sites are available by reservation only; reserve at 877/444-6777 ($9 reservation fee) or website: www.ReserveUsa.com; $14 per night. Open year-round.

Directions: From San Diego, drive east on I-8 about 50 miles to the Laguna Junction exit for the Sunrise Highway. Turn north on the Sunrise Highway and drive 11 miles to the town of Mount Laguna. Continue north on Sunrise Highway/Laguna Mountain Road for 2.5 miles to the campground entrance road on the left.

Contact: Cleveland National Forest, Descanso Ranger District, 619/445-6235, fax 619/445-1753.

47 EL PRADO GROUP CAMP

Rating: 3

In Cleveland National Forest.

Map 15.4, page 791

El Prado Group Camp is directly adjacent to Laguna and is a group camp option to Horse Heaven Group Camp. The elevation is 5,500 feet.

Campsites, facilities: There are five group sites for tents or RVs. Picnic tables and fire grills are provided. Drinking water and vault toilets are available. You can buy supplies in Mount Laguna. Leashed pets are permitted.

Reservations, fees: Reserve at 877/444-6777 ($9 reservation fee) or website: www.Reserve Usa.com; $45–150 per group per night. Open Memorial Day weekend through Labor Day weekend.

Directions: From San Diego, drive east on I-8 about 50 miles to the Laguna Junction exit for the Sunrise Highway. Turn north on the Sunrise Highway and drive 11 miles to the town of Mount Laguna. Continue north on Sunrise Highway/Laguna Mountain Road for 2.5 miles to the campground entrance road on the left.

Contact: Cleveland National Forest, Descanso Ranger District, 619/445-6235, fax 619/445-1753.

48 HORSE HEAVEN GROUP CAMP

Rating: 3

Near the Pacific Crest Trail in Cleveland National Forest.

Map 15.4, page 791

Horse Heaven is set on the northeastern border of Cleveland National Forest at 5,500 feet, near Mount Laguna in the Laguna Recreation Area. The Pacific Crest Trail passes near the camp. Laguna and El Prado Group Camp provide nearby options. Side-trip possibilities include visiting Little Laguna Lake to the immediate west and Desert View Picnic Area to the south at Mount Laguna.

Campsites, facilities: There are three group sites for tents or RVs. Picnic tables and fire grills are provided. Drinking water and vault toilets are available. You can buy supplies in Mount Laguna. Leashed pets are permitted.

Reservations, fees: Reserve at 877/444-6777 ($9 reservation fee) or website: www.Reserve Usa.com; $60–150 per group per night. Senior discount available. Open Memorial Day weekend through Labor Day weekend.

Directions: From San Diego, drive east on I-8 about 50 miles to the Laguna Junction exit for the Sunrise Highway. Turn north on the Sunrise Highway and drive 11 miles to the town of Mt. Laguna. Continue north on Sunrise Highway/Laguna Mountain Road for two miles to the campground entrance road on the left.

Contact: Cleveland National Forest, Descanso Ranger District, 619/445-6235, fax 619/445-1753.

49 VALLECITO COUNTY PARK

Rating: 3

Near Anza-Borrego Desert State Park.

Map 15.4, page 791

This county park in the desert gets little at-tention in the face of the other nearby attractions. This is a 71-acre park built around a sod reconstruction of the historic Vallecito Stage Station. It was part of the Butterfield Overland Stage from 1858 to 1861. The route carried mail and passengers from Missouri to San Francisco in 25 days, covering 2,800 miles. Vallecito means "little valley." It provides a quiet alternative to some of the busier campgrounds in the desert. One bonus is that it is usually 10∞ cooler here than at Agua Caliente. A covered picnic area is a big plus. Other nearby destinations include Agua Caliente Hot Springs, Anza-Borrego Desert State Park to the east, and Lake Cuyamaca and Cuyamaca Rancho State Park about 35 miles away. The elevation is 1,500 feet.

Campsites, facilities: There are 44 sites for tents or RVs. Picnic tables, fire rings, and barbecues are provided. Drinking water, flush toilets, and a playground are available. Leashed pets are permitted.

Reservations, fees: Make reservations at 858/565-3600, fax 619/260-6492; $14–18 per night, maximum of eight people per site, $1 per night. Major credit cards accepted. Open Labor Day weekend through Memorial Day weekend; closed June, July, and August.

Directions: From Julian, at the intersection of Highway 78 and Highway 79, take Highway 78 east and drive 12 miles to San Felipe Road (County Road S2). Turn right and drive 18 miles to the park entrance on the right.

Contact: San Diego County Parks Department, 858/694-3049, fax 858/495-5841, website: www.sd parks.org.

50 AGUA CALIENTE COUNTY PARK

Rating: 3

Near Anza-Borrego Desert State Park.

Map 15.4, page 791

This is a popular park in winter. It has two naturally fed pools: a large outdoor pool is kept at its natural 96°F, and an indoor pool is heated and outfitted with jets. Everything is hot here. The weather is hot, the coffee is hot, and the water is hot. And hey, that's what "Agua Caliente" means—hot water, named after the nearby hot springs. Anza-Borrego Desert State Park is also nearby. If you would like to see some cold water, Lake Cuyamaca and Cuyamaca Rancho State Park are about 35 miles away. The elevation is 1,350 feet. The park covers 910 acres with several miles of hiking trails.

Campsites, facilities: There are 104 sites, many with full or partial hookups for RVs, 36 sites for tents or self-contained RVs, and a caravan area for groups. Picnic tables and fire grills are provided. Restrooms, drinking water, flush toilets, showers, outdoor and indoor pools, and a playground with horseshoes and shuffleboard are available. Groceries and propane gas are nearby. Some facilities are wheelchair-accessible. No pets are allowed.

Reservations, fees: Make reservations at 858/565-3600. Fees are $10–14 per night, with a maximum of eight people per site. Major credit cards accepted. Open Labor Day weekend through Memorial Day weekend; closed June, July, and August.

Directions: From El Cajon, drive east on I-8 about 75 miles to the town of Ocotillo (the first town after crossing from San Diego County to Imperial County) and County Road S2/Imperial Highway. Turn north on County Road S2/Imperial Highway and drive 25 miles to the park entrance.

From Julian, take Highway 78 east and drive 12 miles to County Road S2/San Felipe Road. Turn right on County Road S2/San Felipe Road and drive 21 miles south to the park entrance.

Contact: San Diego County Parks Department, 858/694-3049, fax 858/495-5841, website: www.sdparks.org.

51 MOUNTAIN PALM SPRINGS PRIMITIVE CAMP AREA

Rating: 4

In Anza-Borrego Desert State Park.
Map 15.4, page 791

A plus for this camping area is easy access from County Road S2, but no water is a giant minus. Regardless of pros and cons, only hikers will get the full benefit of the area. A trail leads south to Bow Willow Creek (and Bow Willow) and onward into Bow Willow Canyon. The Carrizo Badlands Overlook is on the southeast side of Sweeney Pass, about a 10-minute drive south on County Road S2. The elevation is 760 feet.

Campsites, facilities: This is an primitive, open camping area for tents or self-contained RVs of any length. Chemical toilets are available. No drinking water is available. Open fires are not permitted. Garbage must be packed out. Leashed pets are permitted.

Reservations, fees: Reservations are not accepted. There is no fee for camping. Open year-round.

Directions: From El Cajon, drive east on I-8 about 75 miles to the town of Ocotillo (the first town after crossing from San Diego County to Imperial County) and County Road S2/Imperial Highway. Turn north on County Road S2/Imperial Highway and drive 15 miles to the camp entrance road on the left.

Contact: Anza-Borrego Desert State Park, 760/767-4205; Colorado Desert District, 760/767-5311, fax 760/767-3427.

52 BOW WILLOW

Rating: 4

Near Bow Willow Canyon in Anza-Borrego Desert State Park.
Map 15.4, page 791

Bow Willow Canyon is a rugged setting that can be explored by hiking the trail that starts at this camp. A short distance east of the camp, the trail forks to the south to Rockhouse Canyon. For a good side trip, drive back to County Road S2 and head south over Sweeney Pass for the view at the Carrizo Badlands Overlook.

Campsites, facilities: There are 16 sites for tents or small self-contained RVs. Picnic tables, fire rings, and shade ramadas are provided. Drinking water and vault toilets are available. Leashed pets are permitted.

Reservations, fees: Reservations are not accepted. The fee is $7 per night. Open year-round.

Directions: From El Cajon, drive east on I-8 about 75 miles to the town of Ocotillo (the first town after crossing from San Diego County to Imperial County) and County Road S2/Imperial Highway. Turn north on County Road S2/Imperial Highway and drive 14 miles to the gravel campground entrance road on the left.

Contact: Anza-Borrego Desert State Park, 760/767-4205; Colorado Desert District, 760/767-5311, fax 760/767-3427.

53 VACATIONER RV PARK

Rating: 1

Near El Cajon.

Map 15.4, page 791

This camp is 25 minutes from San Diego, 40 minutes from Mexico. Discount tickets to area attractions such as the San Diego Zoo, Sea World, and the Wild Animal Park are available. It's not a real pretty place, and that is compounded with the very real chance of getting highway noise if you have a site at the back of the park. The RV sites are on asphalt and gravel. The elevation is 260 feet.

Campsites, facilities: There are 158 sites with full hookups for RVs up to 40 feet long, including 20 pull-through sites. No tent camping is allowed. Restrooms, drinking water, flush toilets, showers, laundry, recreation room, volleyball court, horseshoe pits, modem access, swimming pool, hot tub, RV dump station, satellite TV, free video library, and a picnic

area with barbecues are available. A store is nearby. Some facilities are wheelchair-accessible. Leashed pets are permitted.

Reservations, fees: Reservations are accepted. The fee is $29–36 per night, $2 per person for more than two people. Major credit cards accepted. Open year-round.

Directions: From El Cajon, drive east on I-8 for three miles to the Greenfield Road exit. Take that exit, turn north and drive 100 feet to East Main Street. Turn left (west) and drive one-half mile to the park on the left.

Contact: Vacationer RV Park, 619/442-0904, fax 619/442-4378.

54 RANCHO LOS COCHES RV PARK

Rating: 2

Near Lake Jennings.

Map 15.4, page 791

Nearby Lake Jennings provides an option for boaters and anglers and also has a less developed camp on its northeast shore. Vista Point on the southeastern side of the lake provides a side trip. (For more information, see Lake Jennings County Park.)

Campsites, facilities: There are 137 sites with full hookups for RVs and four areas for tents. Restrooms, drinking water, flush toilets, showers, RV dump station, modem access, and coin laundry are available. A store is one mile away. Leashed pets are permitted.

Reservations, fees: Reservations are accepted at 800/630-0448. The fee is $37 per night, $3 per person for more than two people. Open year-round.

Directions: From El Cajon, drive east on I-8 to the Los Coches Road exit. Take that exit, and drive under the freeway to Highway 8 Business Route. Turn right on Highway 8 Business Route and drive to the park entrance on the left (13468 Hwy. 8 Business).

Contact: Rancho Los Coches RV Park, 619/443-2025, fax 619/443-8440, website: www.rancho loscochesrv.com.

55 LAKE JENNINGS COUNTY PARK

🦢 🛶 🏕 🚶 🚐 ⛰

Rating: 6

On Lake Jennings.

Map 15.4, page 791

Lake Jennings is a nice little backyard fishing hole and recreation area set at 850 feet, with easy access from I-8. Most people come here for the fishing. It has quality prospects for giant catfish, as well as largemouth bass, bluegill, and in cool months, rainbow trout. Note that while shorefishing is available on a daily basis, boats are permitted on the lake only on Saturday, Sunday, and Monday. A fishing permit is required. The highlights here are evening picnics, summer catfishing, and a boat ramp and rentals. Only one camp is available right at the lake, and this is it. This lake wasn't named after my late pal, Waylon Jennings, the legendary country singer (he's got a campground named after him in Littlefield, Texas), but he would have approved of it even if it were.

Campsites, facilities: There are 34 RV sites with full hookups, 34 RV sites with partial hookups, and 26 tent sites. Picnic tables and fire grills are provided. Restrooms, drinking water, flush toilets, showers, playground, and RV dump station are available. A store is nearby. Leashed pets are permitted.

Reservations, fees: Make reservations at 858/565-3600, fax 619/260-6492); $14–18 per night, maximum of eight people per site, $1 per night. Open year-round.

Directions: From El Cajon, drive east on I-8 for 16 miles to Lake Jennings Park Road. Turn north on Lake Jennings Park Road and drive to the park entrance.

Contact: San Diego County Parks Department, 858/694-3049, fax 858/495-5841.

56 ALPINE SPRINGS RV RESORT

🦢 🏕 🚐 ⛰

Rating: 3

Near Lake Jennings.

Map 15.4, page 791

This is one of the few RV parks in the area that welcomes tent campers. It is set in the foothill country in Alpine, eight miles from Lake Jennings to the west. (See the entry for Lake Jennings County Park, about 10 minutes away, for more information.) Other nearby lakes include larger El Capitan to the north and Loveland Reservoir to the south. The Viejas Casino and an outlet shopping center are also nearby.

Campsites, facilities: There are 250 sites, some with full or partial hookups, for RVs or tents. Picnic tables are provided. Restrooms, drinking water, flush toilets, showers, RV dump station, coin laundry, and a swimming pool are available. No pets over 15 pounds are permitted.

Reservations, fees: Reservations are accepted. Fees for tent sites are $18 per night, RV sites $25–30 per night, $3 per person for more than two people. Monthly rates available. Open year-round.

Directions: From San Diego, drive east on I-8 about 30 miles to Alpine, then continue just east of Alpine to the East Willows exit. Take that exit, cross over the freeway, and drive .3 mile to the park on the left (5635 Willows Drive).

Contact: Alpine Springs RV Resort, 619/445-3162.

57 WOODED HILL GROUP

🚶 🏕 🚐 ⛰

Rating: 4

Near the Pacific Crest Trail in Cleveland National Forest.

Map 15.4, page 791

This camp is set on the southern flank of Mt. Laguna. The Pacific Crest Trail passes right by Burnt Rancheria Campground, a mile up the road to the northwest. The elevation is 6,000 feet.

Campsites, facilities: There are 22 sites for tents or RVs for groups only. Picnic tables and fire grills are provided. Drinking water and vault toilets are available. A store is nearby. Leashed pets are permitted.

Reservations, fees: Reserve at 877/444-6777 ($18 reservation fee) or website: www.ReserveUsa.com; $165 group fee per night. Open Memorial Day weekend to Labor Day weekend.

Directions: From San Diego, drive east on I-8 about 50 miles to the Laguna Junction exit for the Sunrise Highway. Turn north on the Sunrise Highway/Laguna Mountain Road and drive about eight miles to the campground entrance road on the left.

Contact: Cleveland National Forest, Descanso Ranger District, 619/445-6235, fax 619/445-1753.

58 BURNT RANCHERIA

Rating: 6

Near the Pacific Crest Trail in Cleveland National Forest.

Map 15.4, page 791

Burnt Rancheria is set high on the slopes of Mt. Laguna in Cleveland National Forest, at an elevation of 6,000 feet. The Pacific Crest Trail runs right alongside this camp. It is quiet and private with large, roomy sites. Desert View Picnic Area, a mile to the north, provides a good side trip. Wooded Hill Group Campground is less than two miles away.

Campsites, facilities: There are 58 sites for tents or RVs up to 50 feet, and 51 sites for tents only. Picnic tables and fire grills are provided. Drinking water and vault toilets are available. Supplies are nearby in Mount Laguna. Leashed pets are permitted.

Reservations, fees: Some sites are available by reservation only; reserve at 877/444-6777 ($9 reservation fee) or website: www.ReserveUsa.com; $14 per night (two-vehicle maximum). Senior discount available. Open May through October.

Directions: From San Diego, drive east on I-8 about 50 miles to the Laguna Junction exit

for the Sunrise Highway. Turn north on the Sunrise Highway/Laguna Mountain Road and drive about nine miles north to the campground entrance road on the right.

Contact: Cleveland National Forest, Descanso Ranger District, 619/445-6235, fax 619/445-1753.

59 COTTONWOOD

Rating: 4

In the McCain Valley Recreation Area.

Map 15.4, page 791

This camp is set on the western edge of the McCain Valley Recreation Area. Like most Bureau of Land Management camps, it is little known and little used. It is occasionally frequented by backcountry horsemen. The elevation is 4,000 feet.

Campsites, facilities: There are 29 sites for tents or RVs. Picnic tables and fire grills are provided. Drinking water and vault toilets are available. Two group horse corrals are also available. Leashed pets are permitted.

Reservations, fees: Reservations are not accepted. The fee is $6 per night. Senior discount available. Open year-round.

Directions: From El Cajon, drive east on I-8 for 70 miles to the Boulevard/Campo exit. Take that exit right, then at the frontage road, turn left immediately and drive east (just south of the interstate) for two miles to McCain Valley Road. Turn left on McCain Valley Road and drive about 13 miles to the campground.

Contact: Bureau of Land Management, El Centro Field Office, 760/337-4400, fax 760/337-4490.

60 SWEETWATER SUMMIT REGIONAL PARK

Rating: 7

Near Sweetwater Reservoir in Bonita.

Map 15.4, page 791

This regional park overlooks the Sweetwater Reservoir in Bonita. The campground is set right on the summit, overlooking the Sweet-water Valley. This camp has equestrian sites with corrals for the horses, and only a $1 fee per horse. There are 15 miles of trails for horseback riding in the park. There are several golf courses nearby and it is 15 minutes from Tijuana. The Chula Vista Nature Center is nearby on the shore of South San Diego Bay.

Campsites, facilities: There are 60 sites with partial hookups for RVs or tents, including 22 with horse corrals. Picnic tables and fire grills are provided. Restrooms, drinking water, flush toilets, showers, and RV dump station are available. Leashed pets are permitted.

Reservations, fees: Make reservations at 858/565-3600, fax 619/260-6492; $16 per night, maximum of eight people per site, $1 per pet per night. Open year-round.

Directions: From San Diego, drive south on I-805 for 10 miles to Bonita Road. Turn east on Bonita Road and drive to San Miguel Road. Continue on San Miguel Road another two miles to the park entrance on the left.

Contact: San Diego County Parks Department, 858/694-3049, fax 858/495-5841, website: www.sdparks.org.

61 POTRERO COUNTY PARK

Rating: 3

Near the Mexican border.

Map 15.4, page 791

If you are looking for a spot to hole up for the night before getting through customs, this is the place. This park covers 115 acres, set at an elevation of 2,300 feet. It is a broad valley peppered with coastal live oaks amid grassy meadows and rocky foothills. The average summer high temperature is in the 90-degree range. Potrero means "pasturing place." Some of the summer grazers are rattlesnakes, occasionally spotted here. Side trips include the railroad museum and century-old historic stone store in Campo and the Mexican community of Tecate. In fact, it is just a heartbeat away from the cus-

toms inspection station in Tecate. A good side trip is to the nearby Tecate Mission Chapel, where you can pray that the guards do not rip your car up in the search for contraband.

Campsites, facilities: There are 32 sites with partial hookups for RVs or tents. Picnic tables and fire grills are provided. Restrooms, drinking water, flush toilets, showers, playground, and RV dump station are available. Picnic areas, ball fields, and a dance pavilion are available. You can buy supplies in Potrero. Leashed pets are permitted.

Reservations, fees: Make reservations at 858/565-3600. Fees are $10–12 per night, maximum of eight people per site, $1 pet fee. Open year-round.

Directions: From El Cajon, drive east on Highway 94 for 42 miles (near the junction of Highway 188) to Potrero Valley Road. Turn north on Potrero Valley Road and drive one mile to Potrero Park Road. Turn east on Potrero Park Road and drive one mile to the park entrance.

Contact: San Diego County Parks Department, 858/694-3049, fax 858/495-5841, website: www.sdparks.org.

62 LAKE MORENA COUNTY PARK

Rating: 7

Near Campo.

Map 15.4, page 791

Lake Morena is like a silver dollar in a field of pennies. It's a great lake for fishing and the campground was remodeled in 2002. Yes, Lake Morena is out in the boondocks, but it's well worth the trip. If you like to fish for bass, don't miss it. The county park camp is set on the southern shore at an elevation of 3,200 feet. The landscape is chaparral, oak woodlands, and grasslands, and the campsites are set in a grove of oaks. When full, the lake covers 1,500 acres, but water levels can fluctuate a great deal here. Catch rates for bass can be excellent, and some bass are big; the lake record for largemouth bass weighed 19 pounds, two ounces, and the lake record for trout weighed nine pounds, six ounces. Boat rentals are available nearby. The lake is just south of Cleveland National Forest and only seven or eight miles from the California/Mexico border.

Campsites, facilities: There are 90 sites, some with partial hookups, for RVs and tents, and two cabins. Picnic tables and fire grills are provided. Restrooms, drinking water, flush toilets, and showers are available. A store, boat ramp, and rowboat rentals are nearby. Leashed pets are permitted.

Reservations, fees: Make reservations at 858/565-3600, fax 619/260-6492; $12–16 per night, maximum of eight people per site, $1 per night. Senior discount available. Open year-round.

Directions: From El Cajon, drive east on I-8 to Pine Valley, then continue east for four miles to Buckman Springs Road/County Road S1. Take the exit, turn south, and drive 5.5 miles to Oak Drive. Turn right on Oak Drive and drive (well signed) to Lake Morena Drive. Turn left on Lake Morena Drive and drive to the park entrance.

Contact: San Diego County Parks Department, 858/694-3049, fax 858/495-5841, website: www.sdparks.org.

63 LAKE MORENA RV PARK

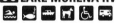

Rating: 6

Near Campo.

Map 15.4, page 791

This camp is near the southern side of Lake Morena, a great lake for fishing and off-season vacations. It is one of three camps near the lake and the best for RVs. Lake Morena, at 3,200 feet, is a large reservoir in the San Diego County foothills and is known for big bass. The lake record weighed 19 pounds, two ounces. The lake has a paved ramp and rowboat rentals.

Campsites, facilities: There are 27 sites with full hookups and 17 with partial hookups for RVs. Picnic tables are provided. Flush toilets, showers, propane gas, and coin laundry are

available. Leashed pets are permitted. Some facilities are wheelchair-accessible.

Reservations, fees: Reservations are recommended. The fee is $22 per night, $2 per person per night for more than four people. A deposit is required on three-day weekends. Open year-round.

Directions: From El Cajon, drive east on I-8 to Pine Valley, then continue east for four miles to Buckman Springs Road/County Road S1. Take the Buckman Springs off-ramp, turn right (south) on Buckman Springs Road, and drive 5.5 miles to Oak Drive. Turn right on Oak Drive and drive 1.5 miles to Lake Morena Drive. Turn left on Lake Morena Drive and drive to the park on the right (2330 Lake Morena Drive).

Contact: Lake Morena RV Park, 619/478-5677, fax 619/478-5031.

64 BOULDER OAKS

Rating: 4

Near Lake Morena in Cleveland National Forest.

Map 15.4, page 791

Boulder Oaks is easy to reach, just off I-8, yet it is a very small camp with an important trailhead for the Pacific Crest Trail running right by it. This camp also is designed as a trailhead camp for equestrians. The elevation is 3,500 feet, set in the southern end of Cleveland National Forest and the Laguna Mountains. This campground is closed March 1 to approximately May 31 to protect the breeding activity of the arroyo southwestern toad, an endangered species.

Campsites, facilities: There are 14 equestrian sites, 12 sites for tents or RVs, and six sites for tents only. Picnic tables and fire grills are provided. Drinking water and vault toilets are available. A store is nearby. Leashed pets are permitted.

Reservations, fees: Make equestrian site reservations at 877/444-6777 ($9 reservation fee) or website: www.ReserveUsa.com; $12 per night for equestrian sites, $10 per night for individual sites. Senior discount available. Open June through February.

Directions: From El Cajon, drive east on I-8 to Pine Valley, then continue east for four miles to Buckman Springs Road. Take the Buckman Springs off-ramp, turn right on Buckman Springs Road, and drive a short distance to a four-way stop sign at Old Highway 80. Turn left and drive 2.5 miles to the campground.

Contact: Cleveland National Forest, Descanso Ranger District, 619/445-6235, fax 619/445-1753.

65 BOBCAT MEADOWS

Rating: 6

In Cleveland National Forest.

Map 15.4, page 791

This camp, along with nearby Corral Canyon, caters primarily to OHV users. The camp is shaded with live oaks and is a 10-minute drive from Corral Canyon camp. This camp is similar, but it has no water. The more spacious sites and privacy can make up for that. The elevation is 3,800 feet.

Campsites, facilities: There are 16 sites for tents and pickup-truck campers. Picnic tables and fire pits are provided. Vault toilets are available. No drinking water is available. Garbage must be packed out. Leashed pets are permitted.

Reservations, fees: No reservations are accepted and there is no camping fee. Adventure Pass ($30 annual fee or $5 daily fee) is required. Senior discount available.Open year-round.

Directions: From El Cajon, drive east on I-8 to Pine Valley, then continue east for four miles to Buckman Springs Road. Take the Buckman Springs off-ramp, turn right (south) on Buckman Springs Road, and drive 3.6 miles to Corral Canyon Road, marked by a sign "Camp Morena." Turn right and drive 6.2 miles (the road becomes Forest Service Road 17S04) to the Four Corners Trailhead. Bear left (Forest Service Road 17S04) and drive a mile to the campground on the left.

Contact: Cleveland National Forest, Descanso Ranger District, 619/445-6235, fax 619/445-1753.

66 CORRAL CANYON

Rating: 6

In Cleveland National Forest.

Map 15.4, page 791

This camp is a primitive campsite set adjacent to a network of OHV trails leading 24 miles into the Corral Canyon area, hence the name. Most of the routes lead into a chaparral landscape. The camp is set at 3,500 feet and is primarily used by the OHV crowd. Drinking water available at this campground is a big plus.

Campsites, facilities: There are 20 sites for tents and pickup-truck campers. Picnic tables and fire rings are provided. Drinking water and vault toilets are available. Garbage must be packed out. Leashed pets are permitted.

Reservations, fees: No reservations are accepted and there is no camping fee. Adventure Pass ($30 annual fee or $5 daily fee) is required. Open year-round.

Directions: From El Cajon, drive east on I-8 to Pine Valley, then continue east for four miles to Buckman Springs Road. Take the Buckman Springs off-ramp, turn right (south) on Buckman Springs Road, and drive 3.6 miles to Corral Canyon Road, marked by a sign "Camp Morena." Turn right and drive 6.2 miles (the road becomes Forest Service Road 17S04) to the Four Corners Trailhead. Continue straight on Corral Canyon Road for one mile to the campground on the right.

Contact: Cleveland National Forest, Descanso Ranger District, 619/445-6235, fax 619/445-1753.

🐶 CIBBETS FLAT

Rating: 4

On Troy Canyon Creek in Cleveland National Forest.

Map 15.4, page 791

Cibbets Flat is at the southern flank of the Laguna Mountains near Troy Canyon Creek. It is an obscure, fairly remote camp and staging area for the Pacific Crest Trail. A trailhead for the PCT is a mile southeast of camp, mostly used by hikers heading north across the Laguna Mountains. The elevation is 4,000 feet.

Campsites, facilities: There are 23 sites for tents or small RVs. Picnic tables and fire grills are provided. Drinking water and vault toilets are available. Leashed pets are permitted.

Reservations, fees: Reservations are not accepted. The fee is $10 per night (two-vehicle maximum). Senior discount available. Open year-round.

Directions: From El Cajon, drive east on I-8 for about 50 miles to Boulder Oaks, then continue a short distance to the exit for Kitchen Creek/Cameron Station. Turn north on Kitchen Creek Road and drive 4.5 miles to the campground entrance on the right.

Contact: Cleveland National Forest, Descanso Ranger District, 619/445-6235, fax 619/445-1753.

🐶 OUTDOOR WORLD RV PARK AND CAMPGROUND

Rating: 4

In Boulevard.

Map 15.4, page 791

The town of Boulevard is centrally located for a wide variety of recreation possibilities. About 10 miles to the north is Mt. Laguna, with hiking trails available. About 30 minutes to the south is the nearest point of entry to Mexico at Tecate. Fishing at Lake Morena or Lake Cuyamaca is also a possibility, as is soaking in nearby hot springs.

Campsites, facilities: There are 138 sites, 122 with full hookups and 16 with partial hookups, for RVs or tents, and a primitive tent camping area. A clubhouse, pool table, restrooms, showers, horseshoes, fire rings, and a group camping area are available. Some facilities are wheelchair-accessible. Leashed pets are permitted, with some dogs prohibited.

Reservations, fees: Reservations are recommended. The fee is $15 per night for tent sites, $20 per night for RV sites, $2 per person for more than two people. Weekly and monthly rates available. Open year-round.

Directions: From El Cajon, drive east on I-8 for 65 miles (past Alpine) to the Live Oak Springs exit. Take that exit and turn south and drive three miles to Tierra del Sol Road. Turn right and drive one-quarter mile to Highway 94. Turn right and drive three miles to Shasta Lane. Turn left and drive three-quarters of a mile to the campground on the left.

Contact: Outdoor World RV Park and Campground, 37133 Hwy. 94, Boulevard, CA 91905, 619/766-4480, fax 619/766-4480.

🐶 LARK CANYON OHV

Rating: 5

In the McCain Valley Recreation Area.

Map 15.4, page 791

This is a small camp that few know of, set at 4,000 feet in the McCain Valley National Cooperative and Recreation Area. It is near a popular off-highway-vehicle area. Many dirt bikers use it as their base camp.

Campsites, facilities: There are 15 sites for tents or RVs. Picnic tables and fire grills are provided. Drinking water and vault toilets are available. Leashed pets are permitted.

Reservations, fees: Reservations are not accepted. The fee is $6 per night. Senior discount available. Open year-round.

Directions: From El Cajon, drive east on I-8 for 70 miles to the Boulevard/Campo exit. Take that exit right, then at the frontage road, turn left immediately and drive east (just south of the interstate) for two miles to McCain Valley Road. Turn left at McCain Valley Road and drive three miles to the campground.

Contact: Bureau of Land Management, El Centro Field Office, 760/337-4400, fax 760/337-4490.

© ROBERT HOLMES/CALTOUR

Chapter 16
The Southern Deserts

Chapter 16—The Southern Deserts

There is no region so vast in California—yet with fewer people—than the broad expanse of Anza-Borrego State Desert, Joshua Tree National Park, Mojave National Preserve, Salton Sea, and endless BLM land. And yet the area is best-loved not for the desert, but for the boating, water sports, and recreation of the Colorado River. Each of these respective areas has distinct qualities, separate and special, yet they are also joined at the edges.

What often attracts people to this region for the first time is a party at the Colorado River. On big weekends, it can even seem as if there is a party within close vicinity of every boat ramp on the river. The weather is hot, the boats are fast, and the body oil can flow as fast as the liquid refreshments. Campgrounds are available throughout this region for the best access to the water.

The rest of the area is far different.

Anza-Borrego (covered in the San Diego and Vicinity chapter) is so big that it seems to stretch to forever. That is because it does. The park covers 600,000 acres, the largest state park in California. The landscape features virtually every type of desert terrain, but most obvious are canyons, badlands, and barren ridges. In spring, the blooming cholla can be impressive. This is habitat for the endangered desert bighorn, and seeing one can be the highlight of a lifetime of wildlife viewing.

Joshua Tree National Park, on the other hand, features a sweeping desert landscape edged by mountains, peppered with the peculiar Joshua tree. It is best known by most as the place where the high desert (Mojave Desert, 4,000 feet elevation) meets the low desert (Colorado Desert). This transition and diversity create the setting for a similar diversity in vegetation and habitat. The strange piles of rocks often appear to have been left there by an ancient prehistoric giant, as if chipped, chiseled, and then left in rows and piles.

The national park is far different than Mojave National Preserve. The highlights here are the Kelso Dunes, a series of volcanic cliffs and a forest of Joshua trees. It is remote and explored by relatively few visitors. The Mojave is a point of national significance because it is where three major landscapes join; the Sonoran Desert, the Colorado Desert, and the Mojave Desert.

The Salton Sea and the endless BLM desert land provide one of the most distinct (and strange) lakes and terrain on earth. The Salton Sea, created in an accident from a broken dike, is one of the largest inland seas in the world. The desert land of the BLM, which stands for Bureau of Land Management, of course, is under BLM control only because no other agency wanted it.

Throughout this country, campgrounds are sprinkled in most of the best spots. In all, we found 66 camps. Some are extremely remote. Some consist of nothing but flat parking areas. Some are simple staging areas for OHV riders, and some serve as a base camp for a weekend party. Somewhere amid all this, a place like no other, you will likely be able to find a match for your desires.

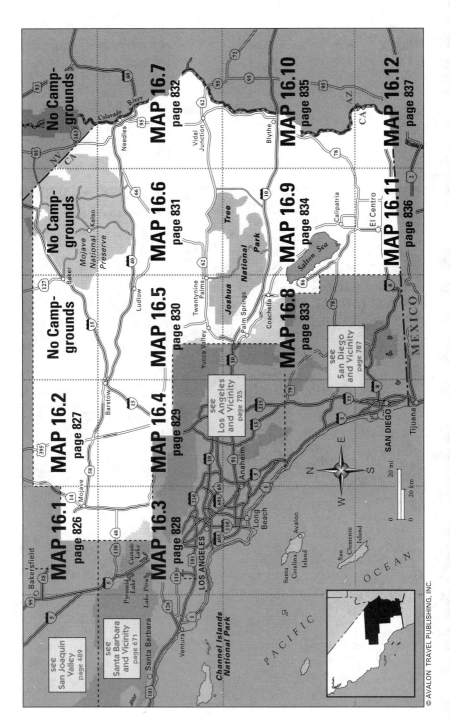

© AVALON TRAVEL PUBLISHING, INC.

Map 16.1

Campgrounds 1–3
Page 838

16.2

16.3

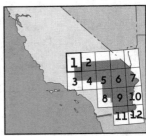

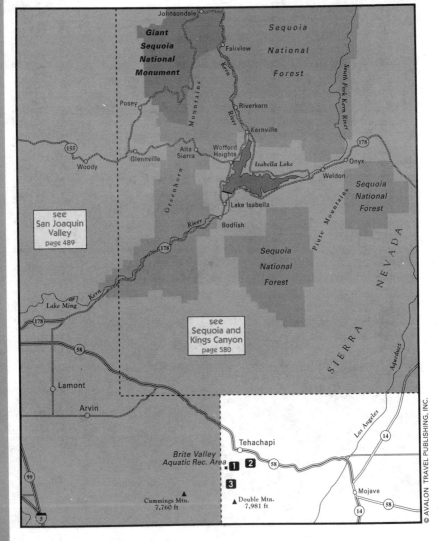

Map 16.2

**Campground 4
Page 839**

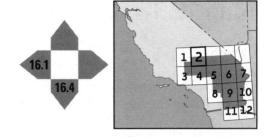

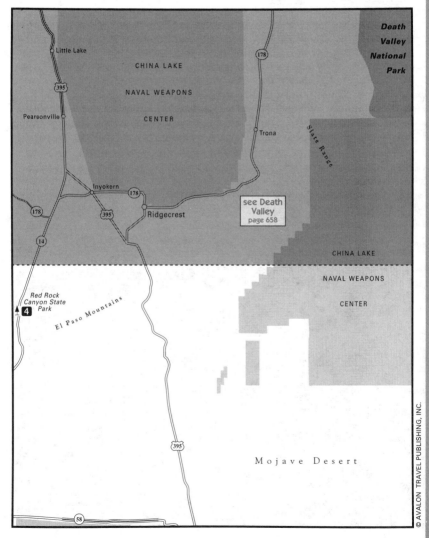

Death
Valley
National
Park

Little Lake

CHINA LAKE

395

NAVAL WEAPONS

CENTER

178

Pearsonville

Trona

Slate Range

Inyokern

178

178

395

Ridgecrest

see Death
Valley
page 658

14

CHINA LAKE

NAVAL WEAPONS

CENTER

Red Rock
Canyon State
Park

4

El Paso Mountains

395

Mojave Desert

© AVALON TRAVEL PUBLISHING, INC.

58

Map 16.3

Campgrounds 5–6
Pages 839–840

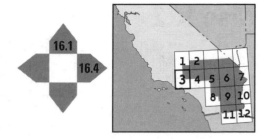

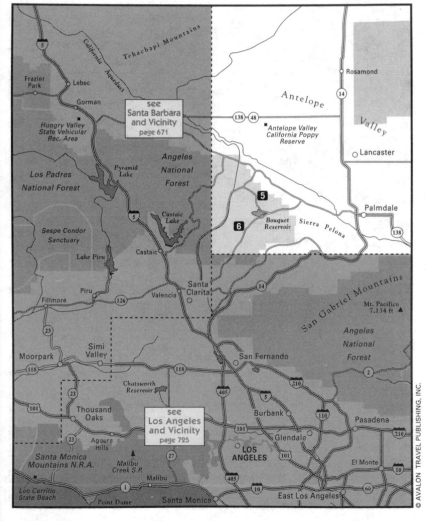

© AVALON TRAVEL PUBLISHING, INC.

Map 16.4

Campgrounds 7–12
Pages 840–842

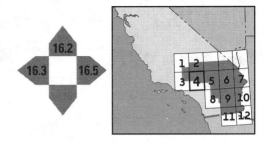

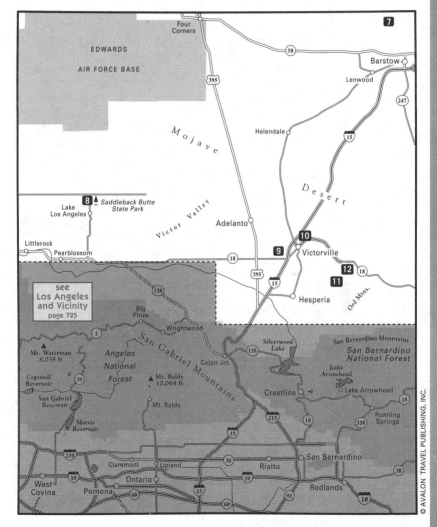

© AVALON TRAVEL PUBLISHING, INC.

Map 16.5

Campgrounds 13–17
Pages 843–845

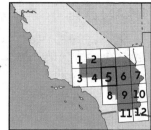

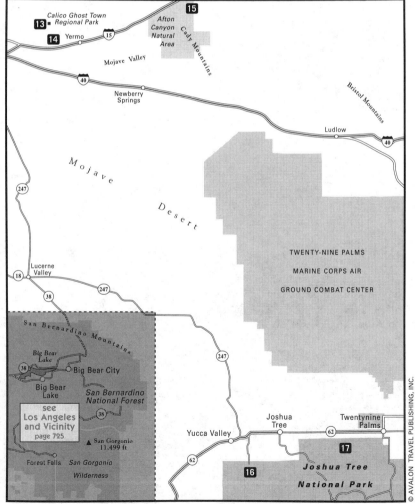

Map 16.6

Campgrounds 18–20
Pages 845–846

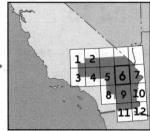

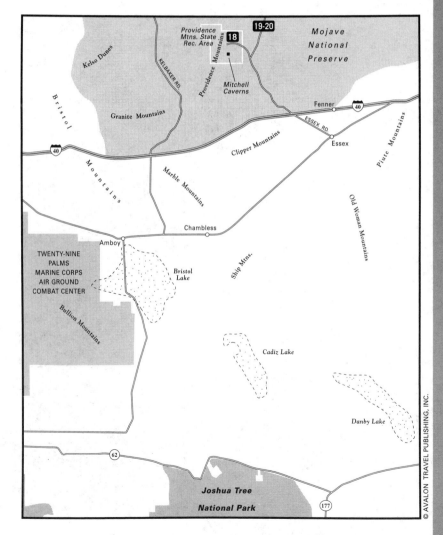

Map 16.7

Campgrounds 21–24
Pages 846–847

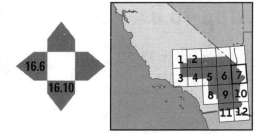

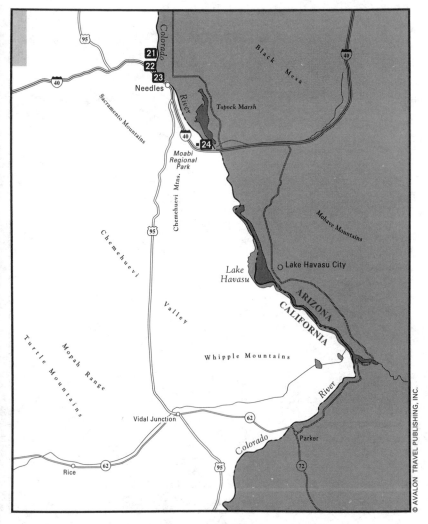

Map 16.8

**Campgrounds 25–38
Pages 848–853**

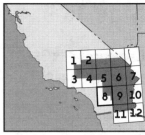

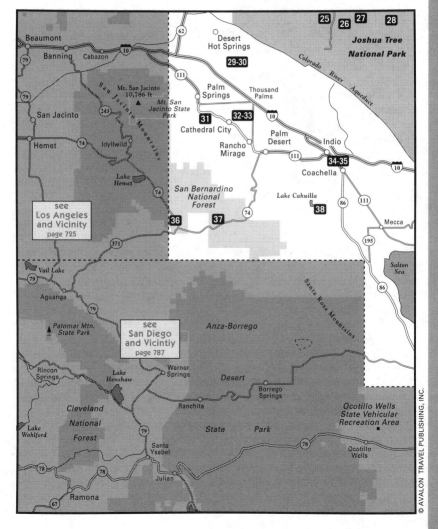

Map 16.9

Campgrounds 39–50
Pages 853–858

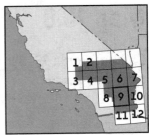

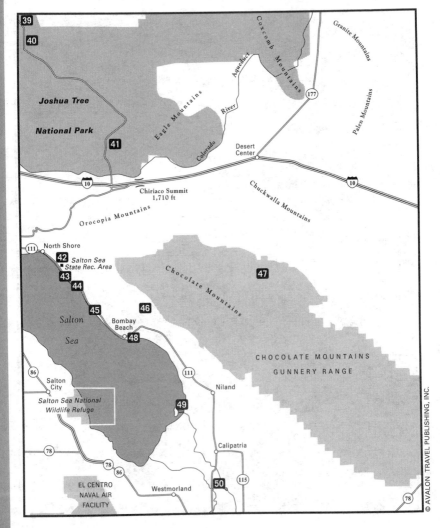

© AVALON TRAVEL PUBLISHING, INC.

Map 16.10

Campgrounds 51–57
Pages 858–861

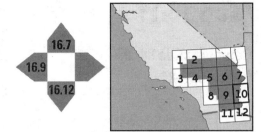

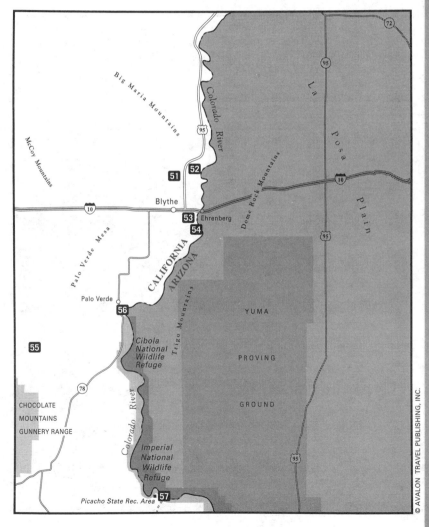

Map 16.11

Campgrounds 58–59
Pages 861–862

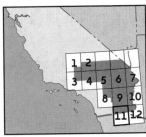

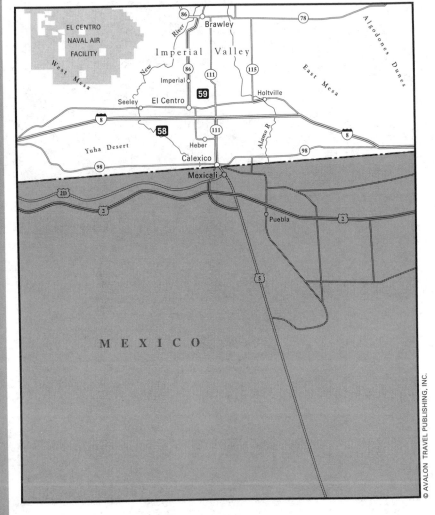

© AVALON TRAVEL PUBLISHING, INC.

Map 16.12

Campgrounds 60–64
Pages 862–864

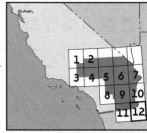

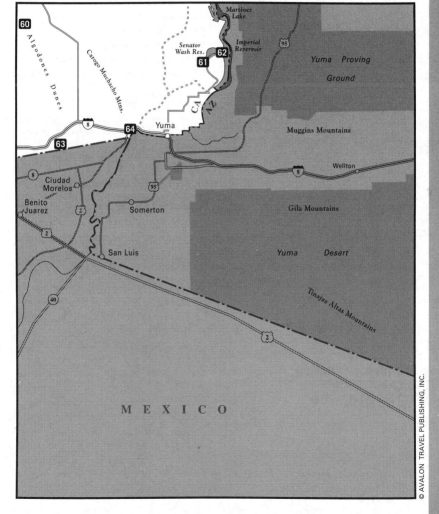

1 BRITE VALLEY AQUATIC RECREATION AREA

Rating: 7

At Brite Lake.

Map 16.1, page 826

Brite Valley Lake is a speck of a water hole (90 acres) on the northern flanks of the Tehachapi Mountains in Kern County, at an elevation of 4,000 feet. No gas motors are permitted on the lake, so it's perfect for canoes, kayaks, or inflatables. That makes the campground and lake ideal for a family camping experience. No swimming is permitted. Fishing is fair for trout in the spring, catfish in the summer.

Campsites, facilities: There are 12 sites with partial hookups for RVs and a tent camping area. Picnic tables and fire grills are provided. Restrooms, drinking water, flush toilets, showers, RV dump station, playground, three pavilions with electricity and tables, and a fish-cleaning station are available. Supplies are available about eight miles away in Tehachapi. Leashed pets are permitted.

Reservations, fees: Reservations are not accepted. The fee is $10–15 per night for each vehicle. Open late April to late October.

Directions: Drive on Highway 58 to Tehachapi and the exit for Tucker Road/Highway 202. Take that exit and drive a short distance to Highway 202. Turn west on Highway 202 and drive 3.5 miles to Banducci Road. Turn left on Banducci Road and follow the signs for about a mile to the park on the right.

Contact: Brite Valley Aquatic Recreation Area, 661/822-3228, fax 661/823-8529.

2 INDIAN HILL RANCH CAMPGROUND

Rating: 7

Near Tehachapi.

Map 16.1, page 826

This is a unique park with five ponds, all stocked with trout and catfish. The campground is open year-round and offers spacious, private sites with oak trees and a view of Brite Valley. The elevation is 5,000 feet.

Campsites, facilities: There are 46 sites, 21 drive-through and 37 with full hookups for RVs. Picnic tables and fire pits are provided. Flush toilets, showers, RV dump station, modem access, and five stocked fishing ponds are available. Leashed pets are permitted.

Reservations, fees: Reservations are accepted. The fee is $25–35, $6 per person for more than four people. Major credit cards accepted. Open year-round, with some sites closed from November to mid-May.

Directions: Drive on Highway 58 to Tehachapi and the exit for Tucker Road/Highway 202. Take that exit and drive a short distance to Highway 202. Turn west on Highway 202 and drive 3.5 miles to Banducci Road. Turn left and drive a mile to Indian Hill/Arosa Road. Turn left and drive 1.5 miles to the campground.

Contact: Indian Hill Ranch Campground, 661/822-6613, website: www.IndianHillRanch.com.

3 TEHACHAPI MOUNTAIN PARK

Rating: 5

Southwest of Tehachapi.

Map 16.1, page 826

This county park is overlooked by most out-of-towners. It is a pretty spot covering 570 acres, set on the slopes of the Tehachapi Mountains, with elevations in the park ranging from 5,500 to 7,000 feet. The roads to the campgrounds are steep, the sites are flat, and each site has its own toilet, a rarity (yes, it's really true—61 toilets). Trails for equestrians are available. This park is popular not only in spring, but also in winter, with the elevations sometimes high enough to get snow, offering a chance at winter sports (chains often required for access). The park lies eight miles southwest of the town of Tehachapi (pop. 6,550) on the southern side of Highway 58 between Mojave and Bakersfield. Woody's Peak (7,986 feet) overlooks the park from its dominion in the Tehachapi Mountains, the dividing line between the San Joaquin Valley and the Los Angeles Basin.

Campsites, facilities: There are 61 sites for tents or RVs, a group campsite, and 10 cabins with 10 beds each. Picnic tables and fire grills are provided. Restrooms, drinking water (natural spring), and pit and vault toilets are available. Some facilities are wheelchair-accessible. Leashed pets are permitted.

Reservations, fees: Reservations are not accepted. The fee is $10 per night, $2 per pet per night. Reserve group site and cabins at 661/868-7002. Senior discount available. Open year-round.

Directions: In Tehachapi, take Tehachapi Boulevard to the Cury Street exit. Take that exit south and drive about three miles to Highline Road. Turn right on Highline Road and drive two miles to Water Canyon Road. Turn left on Water Canyon Road and drive three miles to the park.

Contact: Kern County Parks Department, info line, 661/822-4632, website: www.co.kern.ca.us/parks/index.htm.

◪ RED ROCK CANYON STATE PARK

Rating: 8

Near Mojave.

Map 16.2, page 827

This unique state park is one of the prettiest spots in the region year-round. What makes it worthwhile in any season is the chance to see wondrous geologic formations, most of them tinted red. The park has paleontology sites and the remains of 1890s-era mining operations. A great, easy hike is the two-mile walk to Red Cliffs Natural Preserve, where there are awesome 300-foot cliffs and columns, painted red by the iron in the soil. Part of this area is closed from February through June to protect nesting raptors. For those who don't hike, a must

is driving up Jawbone Canyon Road to see Jawbone and Last Chance Canyons. Hikers have it better. The park also has excellent wildflower blooms from March through May. The elevation is 2,600 feet.

Campsites, facilities: There are 50 sites for tents or RVs up to 30 feet long. Picnic tables and fire grills are provided. Drinking water, pit toilets, RV dump station, picnic area, exhibits, and a nature trail are available. In spring and fall, nature walks led by rangers are available. Some facilities are wheelchair-accessible. Leashed pets are permitted.

Reservations, fees: Reservations are not accepted. The fee is $8 per night. Senior discount available. Open year-round.

Directions: Drive on Highway 14 to the town of Mojave (50 miles east of the Los Angeles Basin area). Continue northeast on Highway 14 for 25 miles to the park entrance on the left.

Contact: Red Rock Canyon State Park, Mojave Desert Sector, 661/942-0662, fax 661/940-7327.

◱ SPUNKY

Rating: 7

In Angeles National Forest.

Map 16.3, page 828

Spunky Camp is set at 3,000 feet elevation amid good tree cover, much of it large oaks. The campsites are open in a peaceful setting. The highlight is hiking, with the Pacific Crest Trail passing just 1.5 miles east of the camp. In addition, many campers will hike up the canyon behind the campground. The creek runs during the winter. Nearby Elizabeth Lake, 10 miles to the west, provides swimming, fishing, sailing, and low-speed power boating, with a 10-horsepower maximum on motors.

Campsites, facilities: There are eight tent sites. Picnic tables and fire pits are provided. Pit toilets are available. A camp host is often on-site. No drinking water is available. A restaurant, gas station, and minimart are available one mile away in Green Valley. Leashed pets are permitted.

Reservations, fees: No reservations and there is no camping fee. An Adventure Pass ($30 annual fee or $5 daily pass per parked vehicle) is required. Open year-round.

Directions: From the junction of I-5 and Highway 14, take Highway 14 to Santa Clarita and the exit for Valencia Boulevard. Take that exit east and drive five miles to Bouquet Canyon Road. Turn left on Bouquet Canyon Road and drive 19 miles to Spunky Canyon Road. Turn left and drive four miles to the campground on the right.

Contact: Angeles National Forest, Santa Clara/Mojave Rivers Ranger District, 661/296-9710, fax 661/296-5847.

6 STREAMSIDE

Rating: 7

On Bouquet Canyon Creek in Angeles National Forest.
Map 16.3, page 828

Streamside Camp is located along pretty Bouquet Canyon Creek at an elevation of 2,300 feet. This stream is typically stocked with trout twice a month in late spring and early summer. The creek and campgrounds are just downstream of Bouquet Reservoir, which provides stream flows in warm weather. Rangers advise not to drink the water from Bouquet Canyon Creek under any circumstances. Some may remember that this camp received damage in 2000 from mudslides. That damage has been repaired.

Campsites, facilities: There are nine tent sites. Picnic tables and fire pits are provided. Vault toilets are available. No drinking water is available. Leashed pets are permitted.

Reservations, fees: No reservations and there is no camping fee. An Adventure Pass ($30 annual fee or $5 daily pass per parked vehicle) is required. Open April through September.

Directions: From the junction of I-5 and High-

way 14, take Highway 14 to Santa Clarita and the exit for Valencia Boulevard. Take that exit east and drive five miles to Bouquet Canyon Road. Turn left on Bouquet Canyon Road and drive about 14 miles to the campground on the left.

Contact: Angeles National Forest, Santa Clara/Mojave Rivers Ranger District, 661/296-9710, fax 661/296-5847.

7 OWL CANYON

Rating: 3

Near Barstow.
Map 16.4, page 829

The primary attraction of Owl Canyon camp is that the surrounding desert is sprinkled with exposed fossils of ancient animals. Guess they couldn't find any water, heh, heh. Well, if people try hiking here without a full canteen, there may soon be some human skeletons out here, too. The sparse BLM land out here is kind of like an ugly dog you learn to love: after a while, when you look closely, you learn it has a heart of gold. This region is best visited in the spring and fall, of course, when hiking allows a fresh, new look at what may appear to some as a wasteland. The beauty is in the detail of it—tiny critters and tiny flowers seen against the unfenced vastness, with occasional fossils yet to be discovered. The elevation is 2,600 feet.

Campsites, facilities: There are 31 sites for tents or RVs. Picnic tables and fire grills are provided. Drinking water (limited) and vault toilets are available. Leashed pets are permitted.

Reservations, fees: Reservations are not accepted. The fee is $6 per night. Open year-round.

Directions: Drive on I-15 to Barstow to the exit for 1st Street. Take that exit and drive north on 1st Street (crossing the Mojave River Bridge) for three-quarters of a mile to Fort Irwin Road. Turn left and drive to Old Highway 58. Turn north and drive eight miles to Fossil Bed Road. Turn left and drive two miles to the campground on the right.

Contact: Bureau of Land Management, Barstow Field Office, 760/252-6000, fax 760/252-6099.

8 SADDLEBACK BUTTE STATE PARK

👣 🐕 ♿ 🚐 ⛰️

Rating: 8

Near Lancaster.
Map 16.4, page 829

This 3,000-acre park was originally established to preserve ancient Joshua trees. In fact, it used to be called Joshua Tree State Park, but folks kept getting it confused with Joshua Tree National Park, so it was renamed. The terrain is sparsely vegetated and desertlike, with excellent hiking trails up the nearby buttes. The best hike is the Saddleback Loop, a five-mile trip that features a 1,000-foot climb to Saddleback Summit at 3,651 feet. On rare clear days, there are fantastic views in all directions, including the Antelope Valley California Poppy Preserve, the surrounding mountains, and the Mojave Desert. On the typical hazy day, the poppy reserve might as well be on the moon; you can't even come close to seeing it. The elevation is 2,700 feet.

Campsites, facilities: There are 50 sites for tents, trailers, or self-contained RVs up to 30 feet long. A group camp is available for up to 30 people. Picnic tables and fire grills are provided. Drinking water, flush toilets, and RV dump station are available. A visitor center is nearby. Some facilities are wheelchair-accessible. Leashed pets are permitted.

Reservations, fees: No reservations accepted for single sites, but the group camp may be reserved at 800/444-PARK (800/444-7275) or website: www.ReserveAmerica.com ($7.50 reservation fee); $10 per night for individual sites, $22.50 per night for the group site. Senior discount available. Open year-round.

Directions: Drive east on Highway 14 to Lancaster and the exit for Avenue J. Take that exit and drive east on Avenue J for 17 miles to the park entrance on the right.

Or drive west on Highway 14 to Lancaster to the exit for 20th Street. Take that exit and drive to Avenue J. Turn east on Avenue J and drive 17 miles to the park entrance on the right.
Contact: Saddleback Butte State Park, Mojave Desert Information Center, 661/942-0662, fax 661/940-7327.

9 DESERT WILLOW RV PARK

🏊 🐕 ♿ 🚐

Rating: 2

In Hesperia.
Map 16.4, page 829

This is an RV park for I-15 cruisers looking to make a stop. Silverwood Lake, a 1,000-acre recreation lake with fishing, boating, and water sports, is 16 miles to the south. The elevation is 3,200 feet.

Campsites, facilities: There are 176 sites, 24 drive-through, with full hookups for RVs. Restrooms, hot showers, cable TV hookups, convenience store, groceries, ice, coin laundry, propane gas, swimming pool, indoor spa, recreation room, library, and cable TV are on the premises. Some facilities are wheelchair-accessible. Leashed pets are permitted.

Reservations, fees: Make reservations at 800/900-8114. Fees are $23–26 per night, $2 per person for more than two people, $2 per night. Major credit cards are accepted. Open year-round, with limited winter facilities.

Directions: Drive on I-15 to Hesperia and the exit for Main Street. Take that exit and drive west to the park on the right (12624 Main St. West).
Contact: Desert Willow RV Park, 760/949-0377, fax 760/949-4334.

10 SHADY OASIS VICTORVILLE KOA

🏊 🐕 👨‍👩‍👧 ♿ 🚐 ⛰️

Rating: 3

Near Victorville.
Map 16.4, page 829

Most long-distance trips on I-15 are grueling

endurance tests with drivers making the mistake of trying to get a decent night's sleep at a roadside rest stop. Why endure the torture, especially with a KOA way out here, in Victorville of all places? Where the heck is Victorville? If you are exhausted and lucky enough to find the place, you won't be making any jokes about it. By the way, if you visit, keep your eyes open for the ghost of Roy Rogers, the legendary cowboy singer. He lived just minutes away from this park, where he sat happily in his living room with his horse, Trigger, which he had stuffed. Happy trails to you, until we meet again.

Campsites, facilities: There are 136 sites, many with full or partial hookups, some drive-through, for RVs or tents, and cabins. Picnic tables and fire grills are provided. Restrooms, drinking water, flush toilets, showers, recreation room, swimming pool, playground, modem access, store, propane gas, and a laundry room are available. Some facilities are wheelchair-accessible. Leashed pets are permitted.

Reservations, fees: Make reservations at 800/KOA-3319 (800/562-3319); $22–24 per night, $2 per person for more than two people, $1 per night for extra vehicle. Major credit cards accepted. Open year-round.

Directions: Drive on I-15 to Victorville and Stoddard Wells Road (north of Victorville). Turn south on Stoddard Wells Road and drive a short distance to the campground (16530 Stoddard Wells Road).

Contact: Shady Oasis Victorville KOA, 760/245-6867, fax 760/243-2108, website: www.koa.com.

11 HESPERIA LAKE CAMPGROUND

Rating: 5

In Hesperia.
Map 16.4, page 829

This is a slightly more rustic alternative to Desert Willow RV Park in Hesperia. There is a small lake/pond for recreational fishing and there is a small fishing fee, but no fish-

ing license is required. No boating or swimming are allowed, but youngsters usually get a kick out of feeding the ducks and geese that live at the pond.

Campsites, facilities: There are 53 sites, 30 with electrical hookups, for RVs or tents, and two group areas for tents. Picnic tables and fire pits are provided. Restrooms, drinking water, flush toilets, showers, a playground, horseshoe pits, and a fishing pond are available. Some facilities are wheelchair-accessible. Leashed pets are permitted in the camp, but not around the lake.

Reservations, fees: Reservations are not accepted. The fee is $12–15 per night, $1 per person for more than six people, $2 pet fee. Senior discount available for fishing on Monday. Major credit cards accepted. Open year-round.

Directions: Drive on I-15 to Hesperia and the exit for Main Street. Take that exit and drive east on Main Street for 9.5 miles (the road curves and changes names) to the park on the left.

Contact: Hesperia Lake Campground, 800/521-6332 or 760/244-5951.

12 MOJAVE NARROWS REGIONAL PARK

Rating: 7

On the Mojave River.
Map 16.4, page 829

Almost no one except the locals knows about this little county park. It is like an oasis in the Mojave Desert. It is set at 2,000 feet and provides a few recreation options, including a pond stocked in season with trout and catfish, horseback riding facilities, and equestrian trails. Hiking includes a wheelchair-accessible trail. The Mojave River level fluctuates here, almost disappearing in some years in summer and early fall. One of the big events of the year here is on Fathers' Day in June, the Huck Finn Jubilee. Note: the gate closes each evening.

Campsites, facilities: There are 110 sites, seven

drive-through, 38 with full hookups, for tents or RVs. Picnic tables and barbecue grills are provided. Restrooms, drinking water, flush toilets, showers, RV dump station, snack bar, pay phone, playground, archery range, bait, boat rentals, horse rentals, and horseback riding facilities are available. A store, propane gas, and coin laundry are available three miles from the campground. Leashed pets are permitted.

Reservations, fees: Reservations accepted for RVs with full hookups; $10–17 per night, $2 per person for more than six people, $1 pet fee, $3 fishing fee. Weekly rates available. Major credit cards accepted. Open year-round.

Directions: Drive on I-15 to Victorville and the exit for Bear Valley Road. Take that exit and drive east on Bear Valley Road for six miles to Ridgecrest. Turn left on Ridgecrest, drive three miles, and make a left into the park.

Contact: Mojave Narrows Regional Park, 760/245-2226, website: www.co.san-bernardino.ca.us/parks/mojave.htm.

13 CALICO GHOST TOWN REGIONAL PARK

Rating: 4

Near Barstow.

Map 16.5, page 830

Let me tell you about this ghost town: there are probably more people here now than there have ever been. In the 1880s and 1890s it was a booming silver mine town, and there are still remnants of that. Alas, it now has lots of restaurants and shops. Recreation options include riding on a narrow-gauge railroad, touring what was once the largest silver mine in California, and watching an old-style play with villains and heroes. Whatever you do, don't take any artifacts you may come across, such as an old nail, a jar, or anything; you will be doomed with years of bad luck. No foolin'. This is a 480-acre park with self-guided tours, hiking trails, gold panning, summer entertainment, and museum, with festivals held through the year.

Campsites, facilities: There are 252 sites, 23 drive-through, 46 with full hookups, 58 with partial hookups, for RVs and tents, three group camping areas, cabins, and a bunkhouse. Fire grills are provided. Restrooms, drinking water, flush toilets, showers, and three RV dump stations are available. Pay phone, restaurants, and shops are on-site. Groceries, propane gas, and laundry facilities are available 10 miles away. Leashed pets are permitted.

Reservations, fees: Make reservations at 800/TO-CALICO (800/862-2542); $18–22 per night. Major credit cards accepted. Open year-round.

Directions: From Barstow, drive northeast on I-15 for seven miles to the exit for Ghost Town Road. Take that exit and drive north on Ghost Town Road for three miles to the park on the left.

Contact: Calico Ghost Town Regional Park, San Bernardino County, 760/254-2122, fax 760/254-2047, website: www.calicotown.com.

14 BARSTOW CALICO KOA

Rating: 3

Near Barstow.

Map 16.5, page 830

Don't blame us if you end up way out here. Actually, for vacationers making the long-distance grind of a drive on I-15, this KOA can seem like the promised land. It's clean, and a nightly quiet time ensures that you have a chance to get rested. It made a Gold Rating in 2002. But hey, as long as you're here, you might as well take a side trip to the Calico Ghost Town, about 10 miles to the northeast at the foot of the Calico Mountains. Rock-hounding and hiking are other nearby options. The elevation is 1,900 feet.

Campsites, facilities: There are 78 sites, many drive-through with full or partial hookups, for RVs or tents. Picnic tables and fire grills are provided. Restrooms, drinking water, flush toilets, showers, RV dump station, modem access, playground, swimming pool, recreation room, store, propane gas, ice, and laundry room facilities are available. Some facilities are wheelchair-accessible. Leashed pets are permitted.

Reservations, fees: Make reservations at 800/KOA-0059 (800/562-0059); $19–27 per night, $2.50 per person for more than two people, $1 per night for additional vehicle for more than two vehicles. Major credit cards accepted. Open year-round.

Directions: From Barstow, drive northeast on I-15 for seven miles to the exit for Ghost Town Road. Take that exit and drive left under the freeway to a frontage road. Turn left at the frontage road and drive a quarter mile to the campground on the right.

Contact: Barstow Calico KOA, 760/254-2311, fax 760/254-2247; website: www.koa.com.

15 AFTON CANYON

Rating: 6

Near Barstow in the East Mojave National Scenic Area.
Map 16.5, page 830

This camp is set at 1,400 feet elevation in a desert riparian habitat along the Mojave River. This is one of several Bureau of Land Management tracts in the East Mojave National Scenic Area. Side-trip options include the Rainbow Basin Natural Area, Soda Springs, and the Calico Early Man Site. Remember, rivers in the desert are not like rivers in cooler climates. There are no fish worth eating.

Campsites, facilities: There are 22 sites for tents or RVs. Picnic tables and fire rings are provided. Drinking water (limited) and vault toilets are available. Leashed pets are permitted.

Reservations, fees: Reservations are not accepted. The fee is $6 per night. Senior discount available. Open year-round.

Directions: From Barstow, drive east on I-15 for 40 miles to Afton Road. Turn right (south) and drive three miles to the campground on the left.

Contact: Bureau of Land Management, Barstow Field Office, 760/252-6000, fax 760/252-6099.

16 BLACK ROCK CANYON AND HORSE CAMP

Rating: 4

In Joshua Tree National Park.
Map 16.5, page 830

This is the fanciest darn campground this side of the desert. Why, it actually has drinking water. The camp is set at the mouth of Black Rock Canyon, 4,000 feet elevation, which provides good winter hiking possibilities amid unique (in other words, weird) rock formations. Show up in summer and you'll trade your gold for a sip of water. The camp is set near the excellent Black Rock Canyon Visitor Center and a trailhead for a four-mile round-trip hike to a rock wash. If you scramble onward, the route continues all the way to the top of Eureka Peak, 5,518 feet, an 11-mile round-trip. But hey, why not just drive there?

Campsites, facilities: There are 100 sites for tents or RVs up to 40 feet long, and 15 equestrian sites for up to six people and four horses per site. Picnic tables and fire grills are provided. Drinking water, flush toilets, and RV dump station are available. Some facilities are wheelchair-accessible. The horse camp has hitching posts and a water faucet and no tents are allowed. Leashed pets are permitted, but not on backcountry trails.

Reservations, fees: Reserve at 800/365-CAMP (800/365-2267) or website: reservations.nps.gov; $10 per night, plus $10 park entrance fee per vehicle. Senior discount available. Open year-round, weather permitting.

Directions: From the junction of I-10 and Highway 62 near Palm Springs, drive northeast on Highway 62 for 22.5 miles to Yucca Valley and Joshua Lane. Turn right (south) on Joshua Lane and drive about five miles to the campground.

Contact: Joshua Tree National Park, 760/367-5500, fax 760/367-6392; Black Rock Nature Center, 760/365-9585.

17 INDIAN COVE CAMPGROUND

Rating: 4

In Joshua Tree National Park.

Map 16.5, page 830

This is one of the campgrounds near the northern border of Joshua Tree National Park. The vast desert park, covering 1,238 square miles, is best known for its unique granite formations and scraggly looking trees. If you had to withstand the summer heat here, you'd look scraggly too. Drinking water is available at the Indian Cove Ranger Station.

Campsites, facilities: There are 101 sites for tents or RVs up to 40 feet long, and a group camp with 13 sites for tents only for up to 60 people. Drinking water is available at the Indian Cove Ranger Station. Pit toilets, picnic tables, and fire grills are provided. Gas, groceries, and laundry services are available in Joshua Tree, which is about 10 miles from camp. Leashed pets are permitted, but not on trails.

Reservations, fees: Reserve at 800/365-CAMP (800/365-2267) or website: reservations.nps.gov; $10 per night; $20–35 for group sites, plus $10 per vehicle park entrance fee. Senior discount available. Open year-round.

Directions: From the junction of I-10 and Highway 62 near Palm Springs, drive northeast on Highway 62 for 22 miles to Yucca Valley, continue to the small town of Joshua Tree, then continue nine miles to Indian Cove Road. Turn right and drive three miles to the campground.

Contact: Joshua Tree National Park, 760/367-5500, fax 760/367-6392.

18 PROVIDENCE MOUNTAINS STATE RECREATION AREA

Rating: 8

Near Mitchell Caverns.

Map 16.6, page 831

This remote desert park, set at 4,300 feet, offers guided tours of Mitchell Caverns ($1–3 tour fee, discounts available). These tours are available daily from early September through Memorial Day weekend, and on weekends from Memorial Day to early September. It's a good idea to make a reservation for the tour; phone 760/928-2586. The cavern tours are the reason most people visit and camp at this park. The caverns are classic limestone formations. There are additional recreational opportunities. From the campground the Nina Mora Overlook Trail is a short (quarter-mile) walk to a lookout of the Marble Mountains and the valley below. Another short hike with a great view is the steep, one-mile hike (one-way) on the Crystal Springs Trail, the best of the bunch. Another hike is the Mary Beale, an interpretive trail accessible from the visitor center, a one-mile loop.

Campsites, facilities: There are six sites for tents and self-contained RVs up to 32 feet long. Picnic tables and fire grills are provided. Drinking water and flush toilets are available. A pay phone is available nearby. Leashed pets are permitted.

Reservations, fees: Reservations are not accepted. The fee is $10 per night. Senior discount available. Open year-round.

Directions: Drive on I-40 to Essex Road (near Essex, 116 miles east of Barstow). Take that road and drive north on Essex Road for 16 miles to the park at road's end.

Contact: Providence Mountains State Recreation Area, 760/928-2586; Mojave Desert Information Center, 661/942-0662, fax 661/940-7327.

19 MID HILLS

Rating: 5

In the Mojave National Preserve.

Map 16.6, page 831

This is a primitive campground set among the junipers and piñon trees in a mountainous area at 5,600 feet. It is one of two little-known camps in the vast desert that is now managed by the

National Park Service. An attraction here is the privacy afforded by the vegetation in the sites. There is a eight-mile one-way trail that starts across from the entrance to Mid Hills and is routed down to the Hole-in-the-Wall Campground. It a pleasant walk in spring and fall.

Campsites, facilities: There are 35 sites for tents or RVs up to 22 feet long. Picnic tables and fire grills are provided. Drinking water and vault toilets are available. Leashed pets are permitted.

Reservations, fees: Reservations are not accepted. The fee is $12 per night. Senior discount available. Open year-round.

Directions: Drive on I-40 to Essex Road (near Essex, 116 miles east of Barstow). Take that exit and drive north on Essex Road for 10 miles to Black Canyon Road. Turn north and drive nine miles (at Hole-in-the-Wall Campground, the road becomes dirt) and continue seven miles to Wild Horse Canyon Road. Turn right and drive two miles (rough, dirt road) to the campground on the right.

Contact: Mojave National Preserve, 760/928-2572, fax 760/928-2072.

20 HOLE-IN-THE-WALL (AND BLACK CANYON GROUP AND HORSE CAMP)

Rating: 6

In the Mojave National Preserve.

Map 16.6, page 831

This is the largest and best-known of the camps in the vast Mojave National Preserve; the campgrounds are set at 4,400 feet in elevation, with a family camp, group camp, and equestrian camp situated across the road from each other. An interesting side trip is to the Mitchell Caverns in the nearby Providence Mountains State Recreation Area.

Campsites, facilities: There are 35 sites for tents or RVs, one group site for up to 50 people, and an equestrian camp. Picnic tables and fire grills are provided. Drinking water, vault toi-

lets, and RV dump station are available. Leashed pets are permitted.

Reservations, fees: Reservations are not accepted. The fee is $12 per night. Make reservations for group camp and horse camp at 760/326-6322; $25 per night, including horse corral if needed. Open year-round.

Directions: Drive on I-40 to Essex Road (near Essex, 116 miles east of Barstow). Take that exit and drive north on Essex Road for 10 miles to Black Canyon Road. Turn north and drive nine miles to the campgrounds.

Contact: Mojave National Preserve, 760/733-4040, fax 760/733-4027.

21 RAINBO BEACH RESORT AND MARINA

Rating: 6

On the Colorado River.

Map 16.7, page 832

The big bonus here is the full marina, making this resort on the Colorado River the headquarters for boaters and water-skiers. And headquarters it is, with tons of happy folks who are extremely well lubed, both inside and out. (For boating details, see the entry for Needles Marina Park.)

Campsites, facilities: There are 55 sites, 10 drive-through, with full hookups for RVs. Picnic tables are provided. Restrooms with showers, coin laundry, swimming pool, hot tub, recreation room, and a beer bar are available. A boat dock with gas is available nearby. Leashed pets are permitted.

Reservations, fees: Reservations are accepted. The fee is $26–31 per night. Senior discount available. Major credit cards accepted. Open year-round.

Directions: Drive on I-40 to Needles and River Road. Turn north on River Road and drive 1.5 miles to the resort on the right.

Contact: Rainbo Beach Resort and Marina, 760/326-3101, fax 760/326-5085, website: www.riverinfo.com.

22 NEEDLES MARINA PARK

Rating: 6

On the Colorado River.

Map 16.7, page 832

Bring your suntan lotion and a beach towel. This section of the Colorado River is a big tourist spot where the body oil and beer can flow faster than the river. Wakeboarding and water-skiing dominate the adjacent calm-water section of the Colorado River. Upstream is the prime area for canoeing or kayaking. Meanwhile, there's also an 18-hole golf course adjacent to the camp, but most folks head for the river. Compared to the surrounding desert, this park is almost a golden paradise.

Campsites, facilities: There are 158 sites, some drive-through, with full hookups for RVs, and six cabins. Picnic tables are provided. Restrooms, drinking water, flush toilets, showers, heated pool, whirlpool, recreation room, modem access, playground, boat ramp, boat slips, store, gas, and laundry facilities are available. Leashed pets are permitted.

Reservations, fees: Reservations are accepted. The fee is $28–30 per night, $7 per person for more than four people. Major credit cards accepted. Open year-round.

Directions: Drive on I-40 to Needles and the exit for J Street. Take that exit and drive to Broadway. Turn left on Broadway and drive three-quarters of a mile to Needles Highway. Turn right on Needles Highway and drive a half mile to the park on the left.

Contact: Needles Marina Park, 760/326-2197, fax 760/326-4125; website: www.needlesmarina.com.

23 NEEDLES KOA

Rating: 2

Near the Colorado River.

Map 16.7, page 832

At least you've got the Needles KOA out here, complete with swimming pool, where you can get a new start. Side trips include venturing to the nearby Colorado River or heading north to Lake Mead. Of course, you could always go to Las Vegas. Nah.

Campsites, facilities: There are 63 sites with full hookups, 30 sites with partial hookups and eight sites with no hookups for RVs or tents. Restrooms, drinking water, flush toilets, showers, recreation room, swimming pool, playground, store, snack bar, propane gas, and laundry facilities are available. Some facilities are wheelchair-accessible. Leashed pets are permitted.

Reservations, fees: Make reservations at 800/562-3407. Fees are $17.95–23.95 per night, $2 for more than two people. Major credit cards accepted. Open year-round.

Directions: Drive on I-40 to Needles and the exit for West Broadway. Take that exit and drive to Needles Highway. Turn left on Needles Highway and drive a short distance to National Old Trails Highway. Turn left and drive to the park on the right (5400 National Old Trails Highway).

Contact: Needles KOA, 760/326-4207, fax 760/326-6329; website: www.koa.com.

24 MOABI REGIONAL PARK

Rating: 7

On the Colorado River.

Map 16.7, page 832

Campsites are situated in the main area of the park along 2.5 miles of shoreline peninsula. One of the features here is 24 group areas. The adjacent Colorado River provides the main attraction, the only thing liquid around these parts that isn't contained in a can or bottle. The natural response when you see it is to jump in the water and everybody does so, with or without a boat. You'll see lots of wild and crazy types having the times of their lives on the water. The boating season is a long one here, courtesy of that desert climate. Fishing is available for trout, catfish, bass, striped bass, and crappie.

Campsites, facilities: There are more than 600 sites, many with full or partial hookups, 10 drive-through for RVs or tents, and 24 group camping areas. Picnic tables and fire grills are provided at most sites. Restrooms, flush toilets, showers, laundry facilities, store, ice, playground, two RV dump stations, and boat rentals (limited), bait, and a boat ramp are available. A softball field, volleyball, basketball, horseshoes, and putting green are also available. An 18-hole golf course is nearby. Some facilities are wheelchair-accessible. Leashed pets are permitted.

Reservations, fees: Reservations are accepted Monday through Friday, 8 A.M. to 4 P.M.; $12–35 per night per vehicle, $2 per person per night for more than six people, $1 pet fee. Long-term rates available, with limit of five months. Major credit cards accepted. Open year-round.

Directions: From Needles, drive east on I-40 for 11 miles to Park Moabi Road. Turn left on Park Moabi Road and continue a half mile to the park entrance at the end of the road

Contact: Moabi Regional Park, 760/326-3831, fax 760/326-3272; website: www.co.san-bernardino.ca.us/parks/moabi.

25 HIDDEN VALLEY

Rating: 7

In Joshua Tree National Park.
Map 16.8, page 833

This is one of California's top campgrounds for rock-climbers. Set at 4,200 feet in the high desert country, this is one of several camping options in the area. A trailhead is available two miles from camp at Barker Dam, an easy one-mile loop that features the Wonderland of Rocks. The hike takes you next to a small lake with magical reflections of rock formations off its surface. The RV sites here are snatched up quickly and this campground fills almost daily with rock-climbers.

Campsites, facilities: There are 39 sites for tents or RVs up to 40 feet long. Picnic tables and fire grills are provided. Pit toilets are available. No drinking water is available. Leashed pets are permitted.

Reservations, fees: No reservations are accepted and there is no camp fee, $10 park entrance fee per vehicle. Senior discount available. Open year-round.

Directions: From the junction of I-10 and Highway 62 near Palm Springs, drive northeast on Highway 62 for 22 miles to Yucca Valley, then continue to the small town of Joshua Tree and Park Boulevard. Turn south on Park Boulevard and drive 14 miles to the campground on the left.

Contact: Joshua Tree National Park, 760/367-5500, fax 760/367-6392.

26 RYAN

Rating: 4

In Joshua Tree National Park.
Map 16.8, page 833

This is one of the high desert camps in the immediate area (see also Jumbo Rocks). Joshua Tree National Park is a forbidding paradise: huge, hot, and waterless (most of the time). The unique rock formations look as if some great artist made them with a chisel. The elevation is 4,300 feet. The best hike in the park starts here—a three-mile round-trip to Ryan Mountain is a 1,000-foot climb to the top at 5,470 feet. The view is simply drop-dead gorgeous, not only of San Jacinto, Tahquitz, and San Gorgonio peaks, but of several beautiful rock-studded valleys as well as the Wonderland of Rocks.

Campsites, facilities: There are 31 sites for tents or RVs up to 40 feet long. Picnic tables and fire grills are provided. Pit toilets are available. No drinking water is available. Hitching posts are available (bring water for the horses). Leashed pets are permitted.

Reservations, fees: No reservations and there is no camp fee, but there is a $10 park entrance fee per vehicle. Senior discount available. Open year-round.

Directions: From the junction of I-10 and Highway 62 near Palm Springs, drive northeast on Highway 62 to Twentynine Palms and Utah Trail. Turn right (south) on Utah Trail and drive about 20 miles to the campground entrance on the left.

Contact: Joshua Tree National Park, 760/367-5500, fax 760/367-6392.

27 SHEEP PASS GROUP CAMP

Rating: 4

In Joshua Tree National Park.

Map 16.8, page 833

Several campgrounds are in this stretch of high desert. Ryan campground is just a couple of miles down the road from this one with an excellent trailhead for a trek to Ryan Mountain, the best hike in the park (see the entry for Ryan). Temperatures are routinely over 100°F here in the summer. (For details on this area, see the entry for White Tank.)

Campsites, facilities: There are two group camps for up to 20 people and up to 50 people. Picnic tables and fire grills are provided. Pit toilets are available. No drinking water is available. Leashed pets are permitted.

Reservations, fees: Reserve at 800/365-CAMP (800-365/2267) or website: reservations.nps.gov; $20–35 per night, plus $10 park entrance fee per vehicle. Open year-round.

Directions: From the junction of I-10 and Highway 62 near Palm Springs, drive northeast on Highway 62 to Twentynine Palms and Utah Trail. Turn right (south) on Utah Trail and

drive about 16 miles to the campground on the left.

Contact: Joshua Tree National Park, 760/367-5500, fax 760/367-6392.

28 JUMBO ROCKS

Rating: 4

In Joshua Tree National Park.

Map 16.8, page 833

Joshua Tree National Park covers more than 1,238 square miles. It is striking high-desert country with unique granite formations that seem to change color at different times of the day. This camp is one of the higher ones in the park at 4,400 feet, with adjacent boulders and rock formations that look as if they have been strewn about by an angry giant. It is a popular site for rock-climbing.

Campsites, facilities: There are 125 sites for tents or RVs up to 40 feet long. Picnic tables and fire grills are provided. Pit toilets are available. No drinking water is available. Leashed pets are permitted.

Reservations, fees: No reservations accepted and there is no camp fee, but there is $10 park entrance fee per vehicle. Senior discount available. Open year-round.

Directions: From the junction of I-10 and Highway 62 near Palm Springs, drive northeast on Highway 62 to Twentynine Palms and Utah Trail. Turn right (south) on Utah Trail and drive about nine miles to the campground on the left side of the road.

Contact: Joshua Tree National Park, 760/367-5500, fax 760/367-6392.

29 SAM'S FAMILY SPA

Rating: 3

Near Palm Springs.

Map 16.8, page 833

Hot mineral pools attract swarms of winter vacationers to the Palm Springs area. This park, set 10 miles outside of Palm Springs, provides an alternative to the more crowded spots. But note that half of the 170 sites are permanent rentals, and because of this, this park barely slipped into the book. The elevation of Sam's Family Spa is 1,000 feet. (For information on the tramway ride to Desert View west of Palm Springs, or the hike to Mt. San Jacinto, see the entry for Sky Valley Parks.)

Campsites, facilities: There are 170 sites, half available for overnighters, with full hookups for RVs. Picnic tables are provided. There is a separate area with fire grills. Restrooms, showers, playground, swimming pool, wading pool, four hot mineral pools, sauna, coin laundry, and a store are available. Some facilities are wheelchair-accessible. Leashed pets are permitted.

Reservations, fees: Reservations are not accepted. The fee is $38 per night, $6 per person for more than four people. Major credit cards accepted. Open year-round.

Directions: Drive on I-10 to the Palm Springs Area and the Palm Drive exit (to Desert Hot Springs). Take that exit and drive north on Palm Drive to Dillon Road. Turn right (east) on Dillon Road and drive 4.5 miles to the park on the right (70-875 Dillon Road).

Contact: Sam's Family Spa, 760/329-6457, fax 760/329-8267; website: samsfamilyspa.com.

30 SKY VALLEY PARKS

Rating: 2

Near Palm Springs.
Map 16.8, page 833

This park is a wonderful spot for family fun and relaxation. One of the best adventures in California is just west of Palm Springs, taking the tramway up from Chino Canyon to Desert View, a ride/climb of 2,600 feet for remarkable views to the east across the desert below. An option from there is hiking the flank of Mt. San Jacinto, including making the ascent to the summit (10,804 feet), a round-trip butt-kicker of nearly 12 miles.

Campsites, facilities: There are 614 sites with full hookups for RVs. Restrooms, showers, four swimming pools, nine natural hot mineral whirlpools, two laundry rooms, two large recreation rooms, modem access, social director, shuffleboard, tennis, horseshoes, crafts room, and walking paths are available. A store and propane gas are nearby. Some facilities are wheelchair-accessible. Leashed pets are permitted.

Reservations, fees: Make reservations at 888/893-7727. Fees are $33–35 per night, $4 per person for more than two people. Open year-round.

Directions: Drive on I-10 to the Palm Springs area and the Palm Drive exit (to Desert Hot Springs). Take that exit and drive north on Palm Drive to Dillon Road. Turn right on Dillon Road and drive 8.5 miles to the park on the right (74-711 Dillon Road).

Contact: Sky Valley Parks, 760/329-2909, fax 760/329-9473; website: www.skyvalleyresort.com.

31 HAPPY TRAVELER RV PARK

Rating: 1

In Palm Springs.
Map 16.8, page 833

Are we having fun yet? They are at Happy Traveler, which is within walking distance of Palm Springs shopping areas.

Campsites, facilities: There are 139 sites with full hookups for RVs. Picnic tables are provided. Restrooms, showers, recreation room, swimming pool, hot tub, and coin laundry are available. Leashed pets are permitted.

Reservations, fees: Reservations are accepted. The fee is $35 per night. Major credit cards accepted. Open year-round.

Directions: Drive on I-10 to Palm Springs and Highway 111/Palm Canyon Drive. Take Palm Canyon Drive and go one mile south (one block after Ramon) to Mesquite Avenue. Turn right on Mesquite Avenue and drive to the park on the left (211 W. Mesquite).

Contact: Happy Traveler RV Park, 760/325-8518, fax 760/778-6708.

32 OUTDOOR RESORT OF PALM SPRINGS

Rating: 6

Near Palm Springs.

Map 16.8, page 833

This is where "every day is considered a holiday." It's considered a Five-Star Resort, beautifully landscaped, huge, and offering many activities: swimming pools galore, three nine-hole golf courses, tons of tennis courts, spas, and on and on. The park is four miles from Palm Springs. One of the best adventures in California is just west of Palm Springs, taking the tramway up from Chino Canyon to Desert View, a ride/climb of 2,600 feet for remarkable views to the east across the desert below. An option from there is hiking the flank of Mt. San Jacinto, including making the ascent to the summit (10,804 feet), a round-trip butt-kicker of nearly 12 miles. If you still can't think of anything to do, you can always compare tires. This is the RV park that was voted the "Most Likely to Succeed as a City."

Campsites, facilities: There are 1,213 sites with full hookups for RVs. Restrooms, showers, eight swimming pools, 14 tennis courts, 10 spas, three nine-hole golf courses, two clubhouses, a health club with three saunas, a snack bar, a beauty salon, coin laundry, modem access, store, shuffleboard, and planned activities are available. Some facilities are wheelchair-accessible. Leashed pets are permitted.

Reservations, fees: Make reservations at 800/843-3131 (California only); winter rates $50–60 per night; summer rates $35–45 per night, $1 per night with a two-pet maximum. Major credit cards accepted. Open year-round.

Directions: Drive on I-10 to the Palm Springs area and continue to Cathedral City and the exit for Date Palm Drive. Take that exit and drive south on Date Palm Drive for two miles to Ramon Road. Turn left and drive to the resort on the right (69-411) Ramon Road.

Contact: Outdoor Resorts, 800/843-3131, 760/324-4005; website: www.outdoorresort.com.

33 PALM SPRINGS OASIS RV RESORT

Rating: 2

In Cathedral City.

Map 16.8, page 833

This popular wintering spot is for RV cruisers looking to hole up in the Palm Springs area for awhile. Palm Springs is only six miles away.

Campsites, facilities: There are 140 RV sites with full hookups. Restrooms, showers, cable TV and modem access, two swimming pools, whirlpool, 18-hole golf course, tennis courts, coin laundry, and propane gas are available. Some facilities are wheelchair-accessible. Leashed pets are permitted.

Reservations, fees: Reservations are accepted. The fee is $30–35 per night, $2 per person for more than two people. Weekly and monthly rates available. Major credit cards accepted. Open year-round.

Directions: Drive on I-10 to the Palm Springs area and continue to Cathedral City and the exit for Date Palm Drive. Take that exit and drive south on Date Palm Drive for four miles to Gerald Ford Drive and the park on the corner (36-100 Date Palm Drive).

Contact: Palm Springs Oasis RV Resort, 760/328-4813 or 800/680-0144, fax 760/328-8455, website: www.mhchomes.com.

34 INDIAN WELLS RV PARK

Rating: 1

In Indio.

Map 16.8, page 833

Indio is a good-sized town midway between the Salton Sea to the south and Palm Springs to the north. In the summer, it is one of the hottest places in America. In the winter, it is a favorite for "snowbirds," that is, RV and trailer owners from the snow country who migrate south to the desert for the winter. The park provides tons of drive-through sites.

Campsites, facilities: There are 381 sites, many drive-through and most with full hookups for RVs. Picnic tables and fire grills are provided. Restrooms, showers, cable TV hookups, three swimming pools, two therapy pools, fitness room, horseshoes, shuffleboard courts, putting green, planned activities, ice, dog run, barbecue, and coin laundry are available. Some facilities are wheelchair-accessible. Leashed pets are permitted.

Reservations, fees: Reservations are accepted. Feesa are $25–35.50 per night. Major credit cards are accepted. Open year-round.

Directions: Drive on I-10 to Indio and the exit for Jefferson Street. Take that exit, stay in the right lane, and drive to the light at Jefferson. Turn right at Jefferson and drive south for three miles to the park on the left (47-340 Jefferson Street).

Contact: Indian Wells RV Park, 760/347-0895 or 800/789-0895, fax 760/775-1147.

35 OUTDOOR RESORTS MOTORCOACH RESORT AND SPA

Rating: 7

In Indio.

Map 16.8, page 833

For owners of tour buses, motor coaches, and lavish RVs, it doesn't get any better than this in Southern California. This is the sole motorhome-only park in California and it is set close to golf, shopping, and restaurants. Jeep tours of the surrounding desert canyons and organized recreation events are available.

Campsites, facilities: There are 419 sites with full hookups including modem access for RVs only with a minimum length of 25 feet. No trailers or pickup-truck campers. Restrooms, showers, swimming pool, tennis court, sauna, whirlpool, coin laundry, and an 18-hole golf course are available. Some facilities are wheelchair-accessible. Leashed pets are permitted.

Reservations, fees: Reservations are accepted. The winter rates are $55–65 per night, summer rates are $40 per night. Major credit cards accepted. Open year-round.

Directions: Drive on I-10 to Indio and the exit for Jefferson Street. Take that exit, stay in the right lane, and drive to the light at Jefferson. Turn right at Jefferson and drive south to Highway 111. Continue on Jefferson for one block to 48th Avenue. Turn left and drive a quarter mile to the park on the left side of the road (80-394 48th Avenue).

Contact: Outdoor Resorts Motorcoach, 760/775-7255 or 800/892-2992 (outside California), fax 760/347-0875, website: www.outdoor-resorts.com.

36 TOOL BOX SPRING

Rating: 5

In San Bernardino National Forest.

Map 16.8, page 833

This is a lightly used campground well off the beaten track. More like off the beaten universe. That makes it perfect for people who want to be by themselves when they go camping. The Ramona trail begins at the campground, heads out to the north, and provides an easy hike-in backpack option, 3.5 miles one way. In the winter, call for road conditions to determine accessibility. The elevation is 6,500 feet.

Campsites, facilities: There are six tent sites. Picnic tables and fire grills are provided. Vault toilets are available. No drinking water is available. Garbage must be packed out. Leashed pets are permitted.

Reservations, fees: No reservations accepted and there is no camping fee. An Adventure Pass ($30 annual fee or $5 daily pass per parked vehicle) is required. Open year-round.

Directions: From Hemet, drive east on Highway 74 into San Bernardino National Forest and continue just past Lake Hemet to Forest Road 6S13. Turn right on Forest Road 6S13 (paved, then dirt) and drive four miles to Forest Road 5S13. Turn left on Forest Road 5S13 and drive 4.5 miles to the camp on the left.

Contact: San Bernardino National Forest, San

Jacinto Ranger District, 909/659-2117, fax 909/659-2107.

37 PINYON FLAT

Rating: 6

Near Cahuilla Tewanet Vista Point in San Bernardino National Forest.

Map 16.8, page 833

The Cahuilla Tewanet Vista Point is just two miles east of the camp and provides a good, easy side trip, along with a sweeping view to the east of the desert. A primitive trail is available two miles away to the southeast via Forest Road 7S01 off a short spur road (look for it on the left side of the road). This hike crosses a mix of sparse forest and high-desert terrain for 10 miles, passing Cactus Spring five miles in. Desert bighorn sheep are sometimes spotted in this area. The elevation is 4,000 feet.

Campsites, facilities: There are 18 sites for tents or RVs up to 22 feet long. Picnic tables and fire rings are provided. Drinking water and vault toilets are available. Some facilities are wheelchair-accessible. Leashed pets are permitted.

Reservations, fees: Reservations are not accepted. The fee is $8 per night. Senior discount available. Open year-round.

Directions: Drive on I-10 to Palm Springs and Highway 111. Turn south on Highway 111 and drive to Rancho Mirage and Highway 74. Turn right (south) on Highway 74 and drive 14 miles (a slow, twisty road) to the campground on the right.

Contact: San Bernardino National Forest, San Jacinto Ranger District, 909/659-2117, fax 909/659-2107.

38 LAKE CAHUILLA COUNTY PARK

Rating: 7

Near Indio.

Map 16.8, page 833

Lake Cahuilla covers just 135 acres, but those

are the most loved 135 acres for miles in all directions. After all, water out here is as scarce as polar bears. This Riverside County park provides large palm trees and a 10-acre beach and waterplay area. In the winter it is stocked with trout, and in the summer, with catfish. No swimming is allowed. Only car-top boats are permitted, and a speed limit of 10 mph is enforced. An equestrian camp is also available, complete with corrals. A warning: the wind can really howl through here, and temperatures well over 100ºF are typical in the summer. If it weren't for this lake, they might as well post a sign on I-10 that says, "You are now entering Hell." Actually, there really is a town on I-10 that is named "Hell."

Campsites, facilities: There are 60 sites with partial hookups and 10 sites with no hookups for RVs, a primitive camping area for tents and self-contained RVs, and a group area with horse corrals and equestrian trails. Fire grills and picnic tables are provided. Restrooms, showers, RV dump station, playground, swimming pool, and an unpaved beach boat launch are available. No gas motors are allowed. Leashed pets are permitted.

Reservations, fees: Make reservations at 800/234-PARK (800/234-7275; $6.50 reservation fee); $12–16 per night, $2 per pet per night. Weekly rates are available. Major credit cards accepted. Open year-round, closed Tuesday, Wednesday, and Thursday in summer.

Directions: Drive on I-10 to Indio and the exit for Monroe Street. Take that exit and drive south on Monroe Street to Avenue 58. Turn right and drive three miles to the park at the end of the road.

Contact: Lake Cahuilla County Park, 760/564-4712, fax 760/564-2506, website: www.riverside countyparks.org.

39 BELLE

Rating: 4

In Joshua Tree National Park.

Map 16.9, page 834

This camp is at 3,800 feet in rocky high

country. It is one of six camps in the immediate area. (For more details, see the entry for White Tank.)

Campsites, facilities: There are 18 sites for tents or RVs up to 40 feet long. Picnic tables and fire grills are provided. Pit toilets are available. No drinking water is available. Leashed pets are permitted.

Reservations, fees: No reservations are accepted and there is no camp fee, but there is a $10 park entrance fee per vehicle. Senior discount available. Open year-round.

Directions: From the junction of I-10 and Highway 62 near Palm Springs, drive northeast on Highway 62 to Twentynine Palms and Utah Trail. Turn right (south) on Utah Trail and drive eight miles to Cottonwood Springs Road. Turn left on Cottonwood Springs Road (heading toward I-10) and drive about 1.5 miles to the campground on the left.

Contact: Joshua Tree National Park, 760/367-5500, fax 760/367-6392.

40 WHITE TANK

Rating: 4

In Joshua Tree National Park.
Map 16.9, page 834

Joshua Tree National Park is a unique area where the high and low desert meet. Winter is a good time to explore the beautiful boulder piles and rock formations amid scraggly Joshua trees. There are several trails in the area, with the best near Black Rock Campground, Hidden Valley, and Cottonwood. The elevation is 3,800 feet.

Campsites, facilities: There are 15 sites for tents or RVs up to 25 feet long. Picnic tables and fire grills are provided. Pit toilets are available. No drinking water is available. Leashed pets are permitted.

Reservations, fees: No reservations are accepted and there is no camp fee, but there is $10 park entrance fee per vehicle. Senior discount available. Open year-round.

Directions: From the junction of I-10 and Highway 62 near Palm Springs, drive northeast on Highway 62 to Twentynine Palms and Utah Trail. Turn right (south) on Utah Trail and drive eight miles to Cottonwood Springs Road. Turn left on Cottonwood Springs Road (heading toward I-10) and drive three miles to the campground on the left.

Contact: Joshua Tree National Park, 760/367-5500, fax 760/367-6392.

41 COTTONWOOD

Rating: 4

In Joshua Tree National Park.
Map 16.9, page 834

If you enter Joshua Tree National Park at its southern access point, this is the first camp you will reach. The park visitor center, where maps are available, is a mandatory stop. This park is vast, high desert country, highlighted by unique rock formations, occasional scraggly trees, and vegetation that manages to survive the bleak, roasting summers. This camp is set at 3,000 feet. A trailhead is available here for an easy one-mile nature trail, where small signs have been posted to identify different types of vegetation. You'll notice, however, that they all look like cacti (the plants, not the signs, heh, heh).

Campsites, facilities: There are 62 sites for tents or RVs up to 40 feet long, and a group campground with three sites for up to 25 people each. Picnic tables and fire grills are provided. Drinking water and flush toilets are available. Some facilities are wheelchair-accessible. Leashed pets are permitted.

Reservations, fees: No reservations accepted for individual sites. Fees are $10 per night, plus $10 park entrance fee per vehicle. Reserve group sites at 800/365-CAMP (800/365-2267); $25 group fee per night, plus $10 park entrance fee per vehicle. Open year-round.

Directions: From Indio, drive east on I-10 for 35 miles to the exit for El Dorado Mine

Road/Twentynine Palms (near Chiriaco Summit). Take that exit and drive north for seven miles (entering the park) to the campground on the right.

Contact: Joshua Tree National Park, 760/367-5500, fax 760/367-6392.

42 HEADQUARTERS

Rating: 5

In the Salton Sea State Recreation Area.

Map 16.9, page 834

This is the northernmost camp on the shore of the giant Salton Sea, one of the campgrounds at the Salton Sea State Recreation Area. Salton Sea is a vast, shallow, and unique lake, the center of a 360-square mile basin and one of the world's inland seas. Salton Sea was created in 1905 when a dike broke, and in turn, the basin was flooded with saltwater. It is set at the recreation area headquarters, just south of the town of Desert Beach at an elevation of 227 feet below sea level. Fishing for corvina, tilapia, sargo, and croaker is popular, and it is also one of Southern California's most popular boating areas. Because of the low altitude, atmospheric pressure allows high performance for many ski boats. If winds are hazardous, a red beacon on the northeast shore of the lake will flash. If you see it, get to the nearest shore. The Salton Sea is about a three-hour drive from Los Angeles.

Campsites, facilities: There are 25 sites for tents, 15 with full hookups for RVs up to 40 feet, and several hike-in/bike-in sites. Picnic tables and fire grills are provided. Restrooms, drinking water, flush toilets, coin showers, RV dump station, and visitor center are available. A store is within two miles. Some facilities are wheelchair-accessible. Senior discount available. Leashed pets are permitted.

Reservations, fees: Reserve at 800/444-PARK (800/444-7275) or website: www.Reserve America.com ($7.50 reservation fee); $10–14 per night, and $1 per person per night for hike-

in/bike-in sites. Senior discount available. Open year-round.

Directions: From Indio, drive south on Highway 111 to Mecca. Continue southeast on Highway 111 for 11 miles to the entrance on the right.

Contact: Salton Sea State Recreation Area, 760/393-3052 or 760/393-3059.

43 MECCA BEACH

Rating: 4

In the Salton Sea State Recreation Area.

Map 16.9, page 834

This is one of the camps set in the Salton Sea State Recreation Area on the northeastern shore of the lake. (For details, see the entry for Headquarters.)

Campsites, facilities: There are 110 sites, 10 with full hookups, for RVs of any length and tents, and several hike-in/bike-in sites. Picnic tables and fire grills are provided. Restrooms, drinking water, flush toilets, and showers are available. An RV dump station is 1.5 miles north of Headquarters campground and a store is within 3.5 miles. Leashed pets are permitted.

Reservations, fees: Reservations are not accepted. The fee is $10 per night, $1 per night for hike-in/bike-in sites. Senior discount available. Open year-round.

Directions: From Indio, drive south on Highway 111 to Mecca. Continue southeast on Highway 111 for 12.5 miles to the entrance on the right.

Contact: Salton Sea State Recreation Area, 760/393-3052 or 760/393-3059.

44 CORVINA BEACH

Rating: 5

In the Salton Sea State Recreation Area.

Map 16.9, page 834

This is by far the biggest of the campgrounds on the Salton Sea. The campground is actually more of an open area on hard-packed dirt, best for parking an RV. (For details about the Salton Sea, see the entry for Headquarters.)

Campsites, facilities: There are 500 primitive sites in an open area for RVs of any length or tents and some hike-in/bike-in sites. Drinking water and chemical toilets are available. A store and gas station are available within five miles. Leashed pets are permitted.

Reservations, fees: Reservations are not accepted. The fee is $7 per night, $1 for hike-in/bike-in sites. Senior discount available. Open year-round.

Directions: From Indio, drive south on Highway 111 to Mecca. Continue southeast on Highway 111 for 14 miles to the entrance on the right.

Contact: Salton Sea State Recreation Area, 760/393-3052 or 760/393-3059.

45 SALT CREEK PRIMITIVE AREA

Rating: 4

In the Salton Sea State Recreation Area.
Map 16.9, page 834
The addition of water at this campground is a big plus, even though the campground consists of just an open area on hard-packed dirt. (For details on the Salton Sea State Recreation Area, see the entry for Headquarters.)

Campsites, facilities: There are 150 primitive sites for for RVs of any length or tents and several hike-in/bike-in sites. Drinking water and chemical toilets are available. Leashed pets are permitted.

Reservations, fees: Reservations are not accepted. The fee is $7 per night, $1 for hike-in/bike-in sites. Senior discount available. Open year-round.

Directions: From Indio, drive south on Highway 111 to Mecca. Continue southeast on Highway 111 for 17.5 miles to the entrance on the right.

Contact: Salton Sea State Recreation Area, 760/393-3052 or 760/393-3059.

46 FOUNTAIN OF YOUTH SPA

Rating: 4

Near the Salton Sea.
Map 16.9, page 834
Natural artesian steam rooms are the highlight here, but close inspection reveals that nobody seems to be getting any younger. This is a vast private park set near the Salton Sea. While this park has 1,000 sites for RVs, note than 400 of the sites have permanent rentals. (See the entry for nearby Red Hill Marina County Park for side-trip options.)

Campsites, facilities: There are 800 sites with full hookups and 200 sites with no hookups for RVs. Restrooms, flush toilets, showers, natural artesian steam rooms, hydrojet pools, swimming pools, recreation center, RV dump stations, modem access, coin laundry, barber shop, beauty parlor, masseur, church services, propane gas, and groceries are available. Some facilities are wheelchair-accessible. Leashed pets are permitted.

Reservations, fees: No reservations accepted. Winter rates are $16–25 per night, summer rates are $14–21 per night, $1 per person per night for more than two people. Major credit cards are accepted. Open year-round.

Directions: From Indio, drive south on Highway 111 for 44 miles to Hot Mineral Spa Road. Turn left (north) on Hot Mineral Spa Road and drive about four miles to the park on the left.

From Calipatria, drive north on Highway 111 to Niland, then continue north for 15 miles to Hot Mineral Spa Road. Turn right (north) on Hot Mineral Spa Road and drive about four miles to the park on the left.

Contact: Fountain of Youth Spa, 888/8000-SPA (888/800-0772) or 760/354-1340, fax 760/354-1558, website: www.foyspa.com.

47 CORN SPRINGS

Rating: 4

In BLM desert.

Map 16.9, page 834

Just think: if you spend a night here, you can say to darn near anybody, "I've camped someplace you haven't." I don't know whether to offer my condolences or congratulations, but Corn Springs offers a primitive spot in the middle of nowhere in desert country. A half-mile interpretive trail here can easily be walked in tennis shoes. It is divided into 11 stops with different vegetation, wildlife habitat, and cultural notes at each stop. The side trip to Joshua Tree National Park to the north is also well worth the adventure, as is the tramway ride available west of Palm Springs for an incredible view of the desert. On the other hand, if it's a summer afternoon, tell me, just how do you spend the day here when it's 115°F?

Campsites, facilities: There are nine sites for tents or RVs and one group site. Picnic tables and fire grills are provided. Drinking water, shade ramadas, and vault toilets are available. Leashed pets are permitted.

Reservations, fees: Reservations are not accepted. The fee is $6 per night. Open year-round.

Directions: From Indio, drive east on I-10 for 60 miles to Corn Springs Road. Exit right on Corn Springs Road and drive eight miles to the campground at the end of the road.

Contact: Bureau of Land Management, Palm Springs Field Office, 760/251-4800, fax 760/251-4899.

48 BOMBAY BEACH

Rating: 5

In the Salton Sea State Recreation Area.

Map 16.9, page 834

All in all, this is a strange-looking place, with the Salton Sea, a vast body of water, surrounded by stark, barren countryside. This camp is set in a bay along the northeastern shoreline, where a beach and nature trails are available. The campground is a flat, open area. Nearby to the south is the Wister Waterfowl Management Area. The Salton Sea is California's unique saltwater lake set below sea level, where corvina can provide lively sportfishing.

Campsites, facilities: There are 200 sites for tents or RVs of any length and several hike-in/bike-in sites. Drinking water and chemical toilets are available. A store, restaurant, marina, and boat launch are available nearby in Bombay Beach. Leashed pets are permitted.

Reservations, fees: Reservations are not accepted. The fee is $7 per night, $1 per night for hike-in/bike-in sites. Senior discount available. Open year-round.

Directions: From Indio, drive south on Highway 111 for 19 miles to Mecca. Continue southeast on Highway 11 for 25 miles to the campground entrance on the right.

From Calipatria, drive north on Highway 111 to Niland, then continue north 18 miles to the entrance on the left.

Contact: Salton Sea State Recreation Area, 760/393-3052 or 760/393-3059.

49 RED HILL MARINA COUNTY PARK

Rating: 3

Near the Salton Sea.

Map 16.9, page 834

This county park is near the south end of the Salton Sea, one of the weirdest places on earth. Set 228 feet below sea level, it's a vast body of water covering 360 square miles, 35 miles long, but with an average depth of just 10 feet. It's an extremely odd place to swim, where you bob around effortlessly in the highly saline water. Fishing is often good for corvina in spring and early summer. Several wildlife refuges are in the immediate area, including two separate chunks of the Imperial Wildfowl Management Area, to the west and south, and the huge Wister Waterfowl Management Area, northwest of Niland. (For side-trip options, see the entry for Bombay Beach.)

Campsites, facilities: There are 40 sites, 12 with electrical hookups, for RVs or tents. Picnic tables, cabanas, and barbecue pits are provided. Flush toilets, showers, and a boat launch are available. The water at this site is not certified for drinking. Leashed pets are permitted.

Reservations, fees: Reservations are not accepted. The fee is $7–12 per night, $2 per night for each extra vehicle, with a 14-day limit. Open year-round.

Directions: From El Centro, drive north on Highway 111 to Brawley and Highway 78/Main Street. Turn west (left) on Highway 78/Main Street and drive a short distance to Highway 111. Turn right (north) and drive to Calipatria. Continue north on Highway 111 just outside of Calipatria to Sinclair Road. Turn left on Sinclair Road and drive to Garst Road. Turn right and drive 1.5 miles to where it ends at Red Hill Road. Turn left at Red Hill Road and drive to the end of the road and the marina and the campground.

Contact: Red Hill Marina County Park, tel./fax 760/348-2310; Imperial County, 760/482-4384.

50 WIEST LAKE COUNTY PARK

Rating: 4

On Wiest Lake.

Map 16.9, page 834

This is a developed county park along the southern shore of Wiest Lake, which adjoins the Imperial Wildfowl Management Area to the north. Wiest Lake is just 50 acres, set 110 feet below sea level, and a prized area with such desolate country in the surrounding region. Water-skiing and windsurfing can be excellent, although few take advantage of the latter. The Salton Sea, about a 20-minute drive to the northwest, is a worthy side trip.

Campsites, facilities: There are 20 tent sites and 24 RV sites with full hookups. Picnic tables

and fire grills are provided. Restrooms, flush toilets, showers, and RV dump station are available. A store, coin laundry, and propane gas are nearby. Leashed pets are permitted.

Reservations, fees: Reservations are not accepted. The fee is $7–12 per night, $2 per night for each extra vehicle. Open year-round.

Directions: From El Centro, drive north on Highway 111 to Brawley and Highway 78/Main Street. Turn west (left) on Highway 78/Main Street and drive a short distance to Highway 111. Turn right (north) on Highway 111 and drive four miles to Rutherford Road (well signed). Turn right (east) and drive two miles to the park entrance on the right.

Contact: Wiest Lake County Park, 760/344-3712 or 760/339-4384, fax 760/339-4372; Imperial County, 760/482-4384.

51 MIDLAND LONG TERM VISITOR AREA

Rating: 4

West of Blythe.

Map 16.10, page 835

Like its neighbor to the south (Mule Mountain), this camp is attractive to snowbirds, rockhounds, and stargazers. Geodes and agates can be collected. The desert landscape is extremely stark. It is on the northern edge of the Palo Verda Mesa, with the campsites situated on flattened desert pavements consisting of alluvium derived from the Big Maria Mountains. Site elevations range from 600 feet on the northern boundary to 490 feet on the southern boundary.

Campsites, facilities: There are 13 sites for tents or RVs. No hookups. Picnic tables and fire grills are provided. Vault toilets are available. No drinking water is available. An RV dump station is nearby. Leashed pets are permitted.

Reservations, fees: Reservations are not accepted. The fee is $20 per week, $100 per season. Fees charged only during winter. Summer is free. Open year-round.

Directions: From Blythe, drive east on I-10 a

short distance to Lovekin Boulevard. Turn left and drive about three miles to the campground on the right.

Contact: Bureau of Land Management, Palm Springs Field Office, 760/251-4800.

52 MAYFLOWER COUNTY PARK

Rating: 6

On the Colorado River.

Map 16.10, page 835

The Colorado River is the fountain of life around these parts and, for campers, the main attraction of this county park. It is a popular spot for water-skiing. There is river access here in the Blythe area. This span of water is flanked by agricultural lands, although there are several developed recreation areas on the California side of the river south of Blythe near Palo Verde.

Campsites, facilities: There are 28 tent sites and 152 RV sites with piped water and electrical hookups provided. Picnic tables and fire grills are provided. Restrooms, drinking water, flush toilets, showers, RV dump station, and a boat ramp and docks are available. Leashed pets are permitted.

Reservations, fees: Reservations are accepted. The fee is $15–16 per night, $2 boat launch fee, $2 pet fee. Major credit cards accepted. Open year-round.

Directions: Drive on I-10 to Blythe and Highway 95. Take Highway 95 north (it becomes Intake Boulevard) and drive 3.5 miles to 6th Avenue. Turn right at 6th Avenue and drive three miles to the park entrance directly ahead.

Contact: Mayflower County Park, 760/922-4665; Riverside County, 760/922-9177.

53 DESTINY RIVIERA RESORT

Rating: 6

Near the Colorado River.

Map 16.10, page 835

This RV park is set up for camper-boaters who want to hunker down for awhile along the Colorado River and cool off. Access to the park is easy off I-10, and a marina is available, both big pluses for those showing up with trailered boats. A swimming lagoon is another bonus.

Campsites, facilities: There are 285 sites, some drive-through and many with full or partial hookups for RVs. Picnic tables are provided. Restrooms, showers, swimming pool, spa, cable TV, modem access, coin laundry, telephone room, store, card room, boat ramp, boat fuel, and propane gas are available. A golf course is within five miles. Leashed pets are permitted, with some restrictions.

Reservations, fees: Reservations are accepted at 800/RV-DESTINY (800/783-3784); $35–39 per night on weekends, three-day minimum; $18–25 per night weekdays, $4 per person for more than two people, $10 per night for each extra vehicle. Senior discount available. Major credit cards accepted. Open year-round.

Directions: Drive on I-10 to Blythe and continue east for two miles to the exit for Riviera Drive. Take that exit east and drive two miles to the park on the right (14100 Riviera Drive).

Contact: Riviera Blythe Marina, 760/922-5350, fax 760/922-6540, website: www.destinyrv.com.

54 DESTINY McINTYRE PARK

Rating: 3

On the Colorado River.

Map 16.10, page 835

This RV park sits on the outskirts of Blythe on the Colorado River, with this stretch of river providing good conditions for boating, water-skiing, and other water sports. A swimming lagoon is a big plus. Fishing is an option, with a variety of fish providing fair results, including striped bass, largemouth bass, and catfish roaming the area.

Campsites, facilities: There are 140 tent sites and 160 RV sites, including 11 pull-through sites, with full hookups. Picnic tables and fire rings are provided. Restrooms, drinking water, flush toilets, showers, RV dump station, propane gas, snack bar, store, bait, ice, and a boat ramp and boat fuel are available. Some facilities are wheelchair-accessible. Leashed pets are permitted from November 1 to March 31.

Reservations, fees: Make reservations at 800/RV-DESTINY (800/783-3784); $35–39 per night on weekends with a three-day minimum, $25 per night on weekdays, $4 per person for more than two people, $10 for extra vehicle. Senior discount available. Major credit cards accepted. Open year-round.

Directions: Drive on I-10 to Blythe to the exit for Intake Boulevard south. Take that exit and drive south on Intake Boulevard to the junction with 26th Avenue (it takes off to the right) and the park entrance on the left. Turn left and enter the park.

Contact: Destiny McIntyre Resort, 760/922-8205, fax 760/922-5695, website: www.destiny rv.com.

55 MULE MOUNTAIN LONG TERM VISITOR AREA

🚶 🐕 🚐 ⛺

Rating: 4

West of Blythe.

Map 16.10, page 835

Mule Mountain is out in the middle of nowhere, but rockhounds and stargazers have found it anyway; it's ideal for both sports. Rock-hounding, in particular, can be outstanding with several geode and agate beds nearby. Hobby rock collecting is permitted. Commercial rock poaching is not. The site, ideal for winter camping, attracts snowbirds and is set in a desert landscape at an elevation of 800 feet. The Bradshaw Trail runs east to west through the campground.

Campsites, facilities: There are 27 sites for tents or RVs. No hookups. Picnic tables and fire grills are provided. Vault toilets are available. No drinking water is available. An RV dump station is nearby. Leashed pets are permitted.

Reservations, fees: Reservations are not ac-

cepted. The fee is $20 per week, $100 per season. Fees charged only during winter. Summer is free. Open year-round.

Directions: From Blythe, drive west on I-10 about 15 miles to Wiley's Well Road. Turn left (south) and drive about six miles to the campground on the right.

Contact: Bureau of Land Management, Blythe Field Office, 760/337-4400, fax 760/337-4490.

56 PALO VERDE COUNTY PARK

🚐 🐕 🚐 ⛺

Rating: 5

Near the Colorado River.

Map 16.10, page 835

This is the only game in town, with no other camp around for many miles. It is set near a bend in the Colorado River, not far from the Cibola National Wildlife Refuge. A boat ramp is available at the park, making it a launch point for adventure. This stretch of river is a good one for powerboating and water-skiing. The best facilities for visitors are available here and on the west side of the river between Palo Verde and Blythe, with nothing available on the east side of the river.

Campsites, facilities: There are an undesignated number of sites for tents or RVs. Picnic tables, fire rings, and shade ramadas are available. Restrooms and flush toilets are available. No drinking water. A boat ramp is available. A store, coin laundry, and propane gas are available in Palo Verde. Leashed pets are permitted.

Reservations, fees: Reservations are not accepted. There is no fee for camping. Open year-round.

Directions: Drive on I-10 to Highway 78 (two miles west of Blythe). Take Highway 78 south and drive about 20 miles (past Palo Verde) to the park entrance road.

Contact: Palo Verde County Park, Imperial County, 760/482-4384.

57 PICACHO STATE RECREATION AREA

🧍 🛶 ⛴ 🐕 ♿ 🚐 ⛺

Rating: 6

Near Taylor Lake on the Colorado River.

Map 16.10, page 835

To get here, you really have to want it. Picacho State Recreation Area is way out there, requiring a long drive north out of Winterhaven on a spindly little road. The camp is on the southern side of Taylor Lake on the Colorado River. The park is the best deal around for many miles, though, with a boat ramp, water-skiing, good bass fishing, and occasionally, crazy folks having the time of their lives. The sun and water make a good combination. This recreation area includes eight miles of the lower Colorado River. Park wildlife includes wild burros and bighorn sheep, with thousands of migratory waterfowl on the Pacific Flyway occasionally taking up residence. More than 100 years ago, Picacho was a gold-mining town with a population of 100 people. Visitors should always carry extra water and essential supplies.

Campsites, facilities: There are 58 sites for tents or RVs up to 40 feet long, three group sites for 25–100 people, and three boat-in campsites. Picnic tables and fire grills are provided. Drinking water, pit toilets, RV dump station, solar showers, camp store, and two boat launches are available. Some facilities are wheelchair-accessible. Leashed pets are permitted.

Reservations, fees: No reservations are accepted except for groups. The fee is $7 per night. Group pricing based on group size with a $26 minimum. Senior discount available. Open year-round.

Directions: From El Centro, drive east on I-8 to Winterhaven and the exit for Winterhaven/4th Avenue. Take that exit to 4th Avenue. Turn left and drive a half mile to County Road S24/Picacho Road. Turn right and drive 18 miles (crossing rail tracks, a railroad bridge, and the American Canal, the road becoming

dirt) to the campground. The road is not suitable for large RVs. The drive takes one hour from Winterhaven. In summer, thunderstorms can cause flash flooding, making short sections of the road impassable.

Contact: Picacho State Recreation Area, c/o Salton Sea State Recreation Area, 760/393-3059 or 760/996-2963 (reservations); Colorado Desert District, 760/767-5311.

58 RIO BEND RV GOLF RESORT

🏊 🛶 🐕 ♿ 🚐 📼

Rating: 5

Near El Centro.

Map 16.11, page 836

This RV park is set at 50 feet below sea level near Mt. Signal, about a 20-minute drive south of the Salton Sea. For some, this region is a godforsaken wasteland, but hey, that makes arriving at this park all the more like coming to a mirage in the desert. The park is usually well maintained, and management does what it can to offer visitors recreational options. It's hot out here, sizzling most of the year, but dry and cool in the winter, the best time to visit. New owners took over in 2002, and their first mission was adding 200 sites with full hookups to this large park.

Campsites, facilities: There are 458 sites, 23 drive-through, with full hookups, 42 sites with partial hookups, and a group area with 42 sites with partial hookups for RVs. Picnic tables are provided. A heated pool, spa, shuffleboard, volleyball, two small stocked lakes, golf course, coin laundry, and telephone, cable, and modem access are available. Some facilities are wheelchair-accessible. A small store is nearby. Leashed pets are permitted.

Reservations, fees: Reservations are accepted. The fee is $32 per night, $3 per person for more than two people. Major credit cards accepted. Open year-round.

Directions: From El Centro, drive west on I-8 for seven miles to the Drew Road exit. Take that exit and drive south on Drew Road for one-quarter mile to the park on the right (1589 Drew Road).

Contact: Rio Bend RV Park, 760/352-7061, fax 760/352-0055; website: www.riobendrvgolf resort.com.

59 COUNTRY LIFE RV
🏊 🏕 ♿ 🚐 ⛺

Rating: 2

Near El Centro.
Map 16.11, page 836

You'd better have air conditioning. This is an RV parking lot on the desert flats about a 10-minute drive north of the Mexican border. Nearby side trips include the Salton Sea to the north, little Sunbeam Lake County Park to the west and, if you need to sober up, the Mexican border customs to the south.

Campsites, facilities: There are 150 sites with full hookups for RVs and six tent sites. Restrooms, drinking water, flush toilets, showers, limited modem access, swimming pool, clubhouse, coin laundry, propane gas, and groceries are available. Some facilities are wheelchair-accessible. Leashed pets are permitted.

Reservations, fees: Reservations are recommended. Fees are $15–18.50 per night, $1 per person per night for more than two people. Open year-round. Major credit cards accepted.

Directions: Drive on I-8 to El Centro and the Highway 111 exit. Take that exit north and drive a quarter mile to Ross road. Turn left on Ross Road and drive a short distance to the campground entrance on the left.

Contact: Country Life RV, 760/353-1040, fax 760/353-1948.

60 IMPERIAL SAND DUNES REC AREA
🥾 🏕 🚐 ⛺

Rating: 1

East of Brawley.
Map 16.12, page 837

Gecko, Roadrunner, and Midway camp-grounds are three of the many camping options at Imperial Sand Dunes Recreation Area. There isn't a tree within a million miles of this camp. People who wind up here all have the same thing in common: they're ready to ride across the dunes in their dune buggies or off-highway vehicles. The dune season is on a weather-permitting basis. There are opportunities for hiking on this incredible moonscape. Other recreation options include watching the sky and waiting for a cloud to show up. A gecko, by the way, is a harmless little lizard. I've had them crawl on the sides of my tent. Nice little fellows.

Campsites, facilities: There are numerous dispersed sites for tents or RVs. Vault toilets and a trash bin are available. No drinking water is available. Leashed pets are permitted.

Reservations, fees: Reservations are not accepted. The fee is $10 per week, $30 per season. Open year-round.

Directions: From Brawley, drive east on Highway 78 for 27 miles to Gecko Road. Turn south on Gecko Road and drive three miles to the campground entrance on the left. To reach Roadrunner Camp, continue for two miles to the campground at the end of the road.

Contact: Bureau of Land Management, El Centro Field Office, 1661 S. 4th St., El Centro, CA 92243, 760/337-4400, fax 760/337-4490.

61 SENATOR WASH RECREATION AREA
🏊 🚤 🏕 ♿ 🚐 ⛺

Rating: 6

Near Senator Wash Reservoir.
Map 16.12, page 837

Senator Wash Reservoir recreation area features two campgrounds, named (surprise) Senator Wash South Shore and Senator Wash North Shore. This recreation area is approximately 50 acres, with many trees of various types and several secluded camping areas. At Senator Wash North Shore (where there are fewer facilities than South Shore), these campsites are both on the water as well as further inland. Gravel beaches provide access to the reservoir. Boat ramps are nearby. This spot provides boating, fishing, OHV riding, wildlife viewing, and opportunities for solitude and sightseeing.

Campsites, facilities: There are an undesignated number of sites for tents or self-contained RVs. No drinking water is available. At South Shore, there are two restrooms with flush toilets, outdoor showers, and drinking water available. At North Shore, there are two vault toilets. A boat ramp is a quarter mile from South Shore. Some facilities are wheelchair-accessible. No camping at the boat ramp. Leashed pets are permitted.

Reservations, fees: Reservations are not accepted. The fee is $5 per night, $1 per person for more than four people. There is a maximum 14-day limit. Senior discount available. Open year-round.

Directions: Drive on I-8 to Yuma, Arizona, and the exit for 4th Avenue. Take that exit and drive to Imperial Highway/County Road S24. Turn north and drive 22 miles to Senator Wash Road. Turn left and drive about three miles to Mesa Campground. Turn left and drive 200 yards to the South Shore Campground access road on the right. Turn right and drive to the reservoir and campground.

Contact: Bureau of Land Management, Yuma Field Office, 520/317-3200, fax 520/317-3250.

62 SQUAW LAKE

Rating: 6

Near the Colorado River.
Map 16.12, page 837

Take your pick. There are two camps near the Colorado River in this area (the other is Senator Wash). This one is near Squaw Lake, created by the nearby Imperial Dam on the Colorado River. This sites provides opportunities for swimming, fishing, boating, and hiking, featuring direct boat access to the Colorado

River. Wildlife includes numerous waterfowl, as well as quail, coyotes, and reptiles. A speed limit of 5 mph enforced on the lake; no wakes permitted. The no-wake zone ends at the Colorado River.

Campsites, facilities: There are 125 sites for RVs and dispersed sites for tents. Picnic tables and barbecue grills are provided. Four restrooms with flush toilets and outdoor showers are available. Drinking water is available at a central location. Two boat ramps are nearby. Some facilities are wheelchair-accessible. Leashed pets are permitted.

Reservations, fees: Reservations are not accepted. The fee is $5 per night, $1 per person for more than four people. There is a maximum 14-day limit. Senior discount available. Open year-round.

Directions: Drive on I-8 to Yuma, Arizona, and the exit for 4th Avenue. Take that exit and drive to Imperial Highway/County Road S24. Turn north and drive 22 miles to Senator Wash Road. Turn left and drive about four miles (well signed) to the lake and campground on the right.

Contact: Bureau of Land Management, Yuma Field Office, 520/317-3200, fax 520/317-3250.

63 MIDWAY

Rating: 6

In the Imperial Sand Dunes Recreation Area.
Map 16.12, page 837

This is off-highway-vehicle headquarters, a place where people bring their three-wheelers, four-wheelers, and motorcycles and act like lunatics without anybody even raising an eyebrow. That's because a large area has been set aside just for this type of recreation. As you drive in you will enter the Buttercup Recreation Area, which is part of the Imperial Sand Dunes Recreation Area. You do what you please, camp wherever you like, and nobody beefs. (See listing for Imperial San Dunes for more options.)

Campsites, facilities: There are several primitive sites for tents or RVs. Pit toilets are available. No drinking water is available.

Reservations, fees: Reservations are not accepted. The fee is $10 per week, $30 per season. Open year-round, weather permitting.

Directions: From El Centro, drive east on I-8 for about 40 miles to Gray's Wells Road (signed Sand Dunes). Take that exit and drive (it bears to the right) to a stop sign. Continue straight on Gray's Wells Road and drive three miles (the road turns from pavement to dirt) and then dead-ends; camping is permitted anywhere in this region.

Contact: Bureau of Land Management, El Centro Field Office, 1661 S. 4th St., El Centro, CA 92243, 760/337-4400, fax 760/337-4490.

64 SANS END RV PARK

Rating: 5

In Winterhaven.

Map 16.12, page 837

Sans End is only seven miles from Mexico, and lots of people who stay here like to cross the border for shopping and fun. The high season at this RV park is January to March, and no wonder, because it is blazing hot here in the summer. The Colorado River provides recreational opportunities near Imperial Dam. Boat ramps are available in Yuma and Winterhaven. Some areas of this stretch of water are marshy wetlands that provide an opportunity for duck hunting in the fall and early winter. For anglers, there are some big catfish roaming these waters. The park is surrounded by palm trees, shielding your view of the junkyard across the road.

Campsites, facilities: There are 167 sites for RVs and a few sites for tents. Restrooms, showers, recreation hall with pool table, coin laundry, and shuffleboard are available. Leashed pets are permitted.

Reservations, fees: Reservations are not accepted. The fee is $21 per night. Open year-round.

Directions: Drive on I-8 to the exit for Winterhaven Drive (just west of Yuma, Arizona). Turn left (if arriving from the west) and drive a short distance to the park on the right.

Contact: Sans End RV Park, 2209 W. Winterhaven Dr., Winterhaven, CA 92283, 760/572-0797.

© TOM STIENSTRA

Resource Guide

Resource Guide

NATIONAL FORESTS

The Forest Service provides many secluded camps and allows camping anywhere except where it is specifically prohibited. If you ever want to clear the cobwebs from your head and get away from it all, this is the way to go.

Many Forest Service campgrounds are quite remote and have no drinking water. You usually don't need to check in or make reservations, and sometimes, there is no fee. At many Forest Service campgrounds that provide drinking water, the camping fee is often only a few dollars, with payment made on the honor system. Because most of these camps are in mountain areas, they are subject to winter closure because of snow or mud.

Dogs are permitted in national forests with no extra charge and no hassle. Leashes are required for all dogs in some places. Always carry documentation of current vaccinations.

National Forest Adventure Pass

Angeles, Cleveland, Los Padres, and San Bernardino National Forests require an Adventure Pass for each parked vehicle. Daily passes cost $5; annual passes are available for $30. You can buy Adventure Passes at national forest offices in Southern California and dozens of retail outlets and online vendors. The new charges are use fees, not entrance fees. Holders of Golden Age and Golden Access (not Golden Eagle) cards can buy the Adventure Pass at a 50 percent discount at national forest offices only, or at retail outlets for the retail price. A free annual Adventure Pass can be obtained when buying a Golden Eagle passport at participating forest service offices.

When you buy an annual Adventure Pass, you can also buy up to three additional annual Adventure Passes for $5 per family vehicle. Major credit cards are accepted at most retail and online outlets, but not at forest service offices. Adventure Passes can be purchased by telephone at 909/884-6634, ext. 3127, or by mail at San Bernardino National Forest, Fee Project Headquarters, 1824 S. Commercenter Circle, San Bernardino, CA 92408-3430. Checks should be made payable to USDA Forest Service.

You will not need an Adventure Pass while traveling through these forests, nor when you've paid other types of fees such as camping or ski pass fees. However, if you are camping in these forests and you leave the campground in your vehicle and park outside the campground for recreation purposes, such as at a trailhead, day use area, near a fishing stream, etc., you will need an Adventure Pass for your vehicle. You also need an Adventure Pass if camping at a no-fee campground. More information about the Adventure Pass program, including a listing of retail and online vendors, can be obtained by website: www.fsadventurepass.org.

National Forest Reservations

Some of the more popular camps, and most of the group camps, are on a reservation system. Reservations can be made up to 240 days in advance, and up to 360 days in advance for groups. To reserve a site call 877/444-6777 or visit the website: www.ReserveUsa.com. The reservation fee is usually $9 for a campsite in a national forest, and major credit cards are accepted. Holders of Golden Age or Golden Access passports receive a 50 percent discount for campground fees, except for group sites.

National Forest Maps

National Forest maps are among the best you can get for the price. They detail all backcountry streams, lakes, hiking trails, and logging roads for access. They cost $6 or more, and they can be obtained in person at forest service offices or by contacting U.S. Forest Service, Attn: Map Sales, P.O. Box 9035, Prescott, AZ 86313, 928/443-8285 with credit card, website: www.fs.fed.us/maps/.

Forest Service Information

Forest Service personnel are most helpful for obtaining camping or hiking trail information. Unless you are buying a map or Adventure Pass, it is advisable to phone to get the best service. For specific information on a national forest, contact the following offices:

USDA Forest Service
Pacific Southwest Region
1323 Club Dr.
Vallejo, CA 94592
707/562-USFS (707/562-8737)
website: www.r5.fs.fed.us

Angeles National Forest
701 N. Santa Anita Ave.
Arcadia, CA 91006
626/574-1613
fax 626/574-5233
website: www.r5 fs.fed.us/angeles

Cleveland National Forest
10845 Rancho Bernardo Rd., #200
San Diego, CA 92127-2107
858/673-6180
fax 858/673-6192
website: www.r5.fs.fed.us/cleveland

Eldorado National Forest
100 Forni Rd.
Placerville, CA 95667
530/622-5061
fax 530/621-5297
website: www.r5.fs.fed.us/eldorado
    or
Information Center
3070 Camino Heights Dr.
Camino, CA 95709
530/644-6048
fax 530/295-5624

Humboldt-Toiyabe National Forest
1200 Franklin Way
Sparks, NV 89431
775/331-6444
fax 775/355-5399
website: www.fs.fed.us/htnf

Inyo National Forest
873 N. Main St.
Bishop, CA 93514
760/873-2400
fax 760/873-2458
website: www.r5.fs.fed.us/inyo

Klamath National Forest
1312 Fairlane Rd.
Yreka, CA 96097-9549
530/842-6131
fax 530/841-4571
website: www.r5.fs.fed.us/klamath

Lake Tahoe Basin Management Unit
870 Emerald Bay Rd., Ste. 1
South Lake Tahoe, CA 96150
530/573-2600
fax 530/573-2693
website: www.r5.fs.fed.us/ltbmu

Lassen National Forest
2550 Riverside Drive
Susanville, CA 96130
530/257-2151
fax 530/252-6428
website: www.r5.fs.fed.us/lassen

Los Padres National Forest
6755 Hollister Ave., Ste. 150
Goleta, CA 93117
805/968-6640
fax 805/961-5729
website: www.r5.fs.fed.us/lospadres

Mendocino National Forest
825 N. Humboldt Ave.
Willows, CA 95988
530/934-3316
fax 530/934-7384
website: www.r5.fs.fed.us/mendocino

Modoc National Forest
800 W. 12th St.
Alturas, CA 96101
530/233-5811
fax 530/233-8709
website: www.r5.fs.fed.us/modoc

Plumas National Forest
P.O. Box 11500
159 Lawrence St.
Quincy, CA 95971
530/283-2050
fax 530/283-7746
website: www.r5.fs.fed.us/plumas

San Bernardino National Forest
1824 South Commercenter Circle
San Bernardino, CA 92408-3430
909/383-5588
fax 909/383-5770
website: www.r5.fs.fed.us/sanbernardino

Sequoia National Forest
Giant Sequoia National Monument
900 W. Grand Ave.

Porterville, CA 93257
559/784-1500
fax 559/781-4744
website: www.r5.fs.fed.us/sequoia

Shasta-Trinity National Forest
2400 Washington Ave.
Redding, CA 96001
530/244-2978
fax 530/242-2233
website: www.r5.fs.fed.us/shastatrinity

Sierra National Forest
1600 Tollhouse Rd.
Clovis, CA 93611
559/297-0706
fax 559/294-4809
website: www.r5.fs.fed.us/sierra

Six Rivers National Forest
1330 Bayshore Way
Eureka, CA 95501
707/442-1721
fax 707/442-9242
website: www.r5.fs.fed.us/sixrivers

Stanislaus National Forest
19777 Greenley Rd.
Sonora, CA 95370
209/532-3671
fax 209/533-1890
website: www.r5.fs.fed.us/stanislaus

Tahoe National Forest
631 Coyote St.
Nevada City, CA 95959
530/265-4531
fax 530/478-6109
website: www.r5.fs.fed.us/tahoe

STATE PARKS

The California State Parks system provides many popular camping spots in spectacular settings. These campgrounds include drive-in numbered sites, tent spaces, and picnic tables, with showers and bathrooms provided nearby. Reservations are often necessary during the summer. Although many parks are well known, there are still some little-known gems in the state parks system where campers can enjoy seclusion, even in the summer.

Because of fee reductions for camping, day use, tours, and boating, the state parks now provide about the best deal in camping in the country. Add-on fees for premium sites, peak season visitation, reservations, pets, extra vehicles, and boat launching have been eliminated at state parks. In addition, fees have been reduced for day use, museum and other tours, parking, boat mooring, swimming pool use, and cabin rentals. You can now camp at a state park for as little as $1 per person per night at many walk-in or bike-in sites.

State Park Reservations

Most of the state park campgrounds are on a reservation system, and campsites can be booked up to seven months in advance at these parks. There are also hike-in/bike-in sites at many of the parks, and they are available on a first-come, first-served basis. Reservations can be made by telephone or online by phoning 800/444-PARK (800/444-7275) or visiting the website: www.ReserveAmerica.com. The reservation fee is usually $7.50 for a campsite. Major credit cards are accepted for reservations but are generally not accepted in person at the parks.

Discounts are available for people age 62 and older. A reduced camping fee is also available to holders of the Disabled Discount Pass or the Disabled Veteran/Prisoner of War Pass.

For general information about California State Parks, contact:

California Department of Parks and Recreation
Communications Office
P.O. Box 942896
Sacramento, CA 94296
916/653-6995
fax 916/657-3903
website: www.parks.ca.gov

NATIONAL PARKS

California's national parks are natural wonders, varying from the spectacular yet crowded Yosemite Valley to the remote and rugged Lava Beds National Monument. Reservations for campsites are available five months in advance for many of the national parks in California. In addition to campground fees, expect to pay a park entrance fee ranging $5–20 per vehicle (you can buy a Golden Eagle annual pass that waives entrance fees). This entrance fee is valid for seven days. Various discounts are available for holders of Golden Age and Golden Access passports, including a 50 percent reduction of camping fees (group camps not included) and a waiver of park entrance fees.

For Yosemite National Park reservations, call 800/436-PARK (800/436-7275) or visit the website: http://reservations.nps.gov. Major credit cards accepted.

For all other national parks, call 800/365-CAMP (800/365-2267) or visit the website: reservations.nps.gov. Major credit cards are accepted.

National Park Service
Pacific West Region
One Jackson Center
1111 Jackson St., Ste. 700
Oakland, CA 94607
510/817-1300
website: www.nps.gov

Cabrillo National Monument
1800 Cabrillo Memorial Dr.
San Diego, CA 92106-3601
619/557-5450
fax 619/557-5469
website: www.nps.gov/cabr

Channel Islands National Park
1901 Spinnaker Dr.
Ventura, CA 93001
805/658-5730
fax 805/658-5799
website: www.nps.gov/chis

Death Valley National Park
P.O. Box 579
Death Valley, CA 92328-0579
760/786-3200
fax 760/786-3283
website: www.nps.gov/deva

Devils Postpile National Monument
c/o Sequoia and Kings Canyon National Parks
47050 Generals Hwy.
Three Rivers, CA 93271
760/934-2289 in summer only
559/565-3341 year-round
website: www.nps.gov/depo

Golden Gate National Recreation Area
Fort Mason, Bldg. 201
San Francisco, CA 94123-0022
415/556-4700
fax 415/561-4750
website: www.nps.gov/goga

Joshua Tree National Park
74485 National Park Dr.

Twentynine Palms, CA 92277-3597
760/367-5500
fax 760/367-6392
website: www.nps.gov/jotr

Lassen Volcanic National Park
P.O. Box 100
Mineral, CA 96063-0100
530/595-4444
fax 530/595-3262
website: www.nps.gov/lavo

Lava Beds National Monument
Indian Wells Headquarters
P.O. Box 867
Tulelake, CA 96134
530/667-2282
fax 530/667-2737
website: www.nps.gov/labe

Mojave National Preserve
P.O. Box 241
Baker, CA 92309
760/733-4040
fax 760/255-8809
website: www.nps.gov/moja

Pinnacles National Monument
5000 Hwy. 146
Paicines, CA 95043
831/389-4485
fax 831/389-4489
website: www.nps.gov/pinn

Point Reyes National Seashore
Point Reyes Station, CA 94956-9799
415/464-5100
fax 415/663-8132
website: www.nps.gov/pore

Redwood National and State Parks
1111 2nd St.
Crescent City, CA 95531
707/464-6101
fax 707/464-1812
website: www.nps.gov/redw

Santa Monica Mountains National
Recreation Area
401 W. Hillcrest Dr.
Thousand Oaks, CA 91360
805/370-2301
fax 805/370-1850
website: www.nps.gov/samo

Sequoia and Kings Canyon National Parks
47050 Generals Hwy.
Three Rivers, CA 93271-9651
559/565-3341 or 559/335-2856
website: www.nps.gov/seki

Smith River National Recreation Area
P.O. Box 228
Gasquet, CA 95543

707/457-3131
fax 707/457-3794

Whiskeytown National Recreation Area
P.O. Box 188
Whiskeytown, CA 96095
530/246-1225 or 530/242-3400
fax 530/246-5154
website: www.nps.gov/whis

Yosemite National Park
P.O. Box 577
Yosemite National Park, CA 95389
209/372-0200 for 24-hour recorded message or
209/372-0265
website: www.nps.gov/yose

U.S. ARMY CORPS OF ENGINEERS & RESERVATIONS

Some of the family camps and most of the group camps operated by the U.S. Army Corps of Engineers are on a reservation system. Reservations can be made up to 240 days in advance, and up to 360 days in advance for groups. To reserve a site, call 877/444-6777 or visit the website: www.ReserveUsa.com. The reservation fee is usually $9, and major credit cards are accepted. Holders of Golden Age or Golden Access passports receive a 50 percent discount for campground fees, except for group sites.

U.S. Army Corps of Engineers
South Pacific Division/San Francisco District
333 Market St.
San Francisco, CA 94105
415/977-8272
website: www.spn.usace.army.mil

U.S. Army Corps of Engineers
Sacramento District
1325 "J" St.
Sacramento, CA 95814
916/557-5100
website: www.spk.usace.army.mil

U.S. Army Corps of Engineers
Los Angeles District
911 Wilshire Blvd.
Los Angeles, CA 90017-3401
213/452-3908
fax 213/452-4191
website: www.spl.usace.army.mil

BUREAU OF LAND MANAGEMENT

Most of the BLM campgrounds are primitive and in remote areas. Often, there is no fee charged for camping. Holders of Golden Age or Golden Access passports receive a 50 percent discount, except for group camps, at BLM fee campgrounds.

Bureau of Land Management
California State Office
2800 Cottage Way, Room W-1834
Sacramento, CA 95825-1886
916/978-4400
website: www.ca.blm.gov

California Desert District Office
6221 Box Springs Blvd.
Riverside, CA 92507
909/697-5200
fax 909/697-5299
website: www.ca.blm.gov/cdd

Alturas Field Office
708 W. 12th St.
Alturas, CA 96101
530/233-4666
fax 530/233-5696
website: www.ca.blm.gov/alturas

Arcata Field Office
1695 Heindon Rd.
Arcata, CA 95521-4573
707/825-2300
fax 707/825-2301
website: www.ca.blm.gov/arcata

Bakersfield Field Office
3801 Pegasus Dr.
Bakersfield, CA 93308
661/391-6000
fax 661/391-6040
website: www.ca.blm.gov/bakersfield

Barstow Field Office
2601 Barstow Rd.
Barstow, CA 92311
760/252-6000
fax 760/252-6099
website: www.ca.blm.gov/barstow

Bishop Field Office
785 N. Main St., Ste. E
Bishop, CA 93514-2471
760/872-4881
fax 760/872-5050
website: www.ca.blm.gov/bishop

Eagle Lake Field Office
2950 Riverside Dr.
Susanville, CA 96130
530/257-0456
fax 530/257-4831
website: www.ca.blm.gov/eaglelake

El Centro Field Office
1661 S. 4th St.
El Centro, CA 92243
760/337-4400
fax 760/337-4490
website: www.ca.blm.gov/elcentro

Folsom Field Office
63 Natoma St.
Folsom, CA 95630
916/985-4474
fax 916/985-3259
website: www.ca.blm.gov/folsom

Hollister Field Office
20 Hamilton Ct.
Hollister, CA 95023
831/630-5000
fax 831/630-5055
website: www.ca.blm.gov/hollister

Palm Springs/South Coast Field Office
690 W. Garnet Ave.
North Palm Springs, CA 92258-1260
760/251-4800
fax 760/251-4899
website: www.ca.blm.gov/palmsprings

Redding Field Office
355 Hemsted Dr.
Redding, CA 96002
530/224-2100
fax 530/224-2172
website: www.ca.blm.gov/redding

Ridgecrest Field Office
300 S. Richmond Rd.
Ridgecrest, CA 93555

760/384-5400
fax 760/384-5499
website: www.ca.blm.gov/ridgecrest

Ukiah Field Office
2550 N. State St.
Ukiah, CA 95482
707/468-4000
fax 707/468-4027
website: www.ca.blm.gov/ukiah

OTHER VALUABLE RESOURCES
State Forests
Jackson Demonstration State Forest
802 N. Main St.
Fort Bragg, CA 95437
707/964-5674
fax 707/964-0941

Mountain Home Demonstration State Forest
P.O. Box 517
Springville, CA 93265
559/539-2321 (summer) or 559/539-2855
(winter)

County/Regional Park Departments
Del Norte County Parks
840 9th Street, Ste. 11
Crescent City, CA 95531
707/464-7230
fax 707/464-5824

East Bay Regional Park District
2950 Peralta Oaks Ct.
P.O. Box 5381
Oakland, CA 94605-0381
510/562-PARK/7275 or 510/544-2200
fax 510/635-3478
website: www.ebparks.org

Humboldt County Parks
1106 2nd St.
Eureka, CA 95501

707/445-7651
fax 707/445-7409

Marin Municipal Water District
220 Nellen Ave.
Corte Madera, CA 94925
415/945-1455
website: www.marinwater.org

Midpeninsula Regional Open Space District
330 Distel Circle
Los Altos, CA 94022-1404
650/691-1200
fax 650/691-0485
website: www.openspace.org

Pacific Gas and Electric Company
FERC/Land Projects
2730 Gateway Oaks, Ste. 220
Sacramento, CA 95833
916/386-5164
fax 916/923-7044
website: www.pge.com/recreation

Sacramento County Parks and Recreation Division
4040 Bradshaw Rd.
Sacramento, CA 95827
916/875-6961
website: www.sacparks.net

San Diego County Parks and Recreation Department
2454 Heritage Park Row
San Diego, CA 92110
858/694-3049
fax 619/) 260-6492
website: www.co.san_diego.ca.us/parks

San Luis Obispo County Parks Department
1087 Santa Rosa St.
San Luis Obispo, CA 93408
805/781-5930
fax 805/781-1102
website: www.slocountyparks.com

San Mateo County Parks and Recreation Department
455 County Center, 4th floor
Redwood City, CA 94063-1646
650/363-4020
fax 650/599-1721
website: www.eparks.net

Santa Barbara County Parks and Recreation Department
610 Mission Canyon Rd.
Santa Barbara, CA 93105
805/568-2461
fax 805/568-2459
website: www.sbparks.com

Santa Clara County Parks and Recreation
298 Garden Hill Dr.
Los Gatos, CA 95032-7669
408/355-2200
fax 408/355-2290
website: www.parkhere.org

Sonoma County Regional Parks
2300 County Center Dr., Ste. 120A
Santa Rosa, CA 95403
707/565-2041
fax 707/579-8247
website: www.sonoma-county.org/parks

State and Federal Offices
U.S. Fish and Wildlife Service
1849 "C" St. NW
Washington, DC 20240
website: www.fws.gov

U.S. Geological Survey
Branch of Information Services
P.O. Box 25286, Federal Center
Denver, CO 80225
888/ASK-USGS (888/275-8747) or
303/202-4700
website: www.usgs.gov

California Department of Fish and Game
1416 9th St., 12th floor
Sacramento, CA 95814
916/445-0411
fax 916/653-1856
website: www.dfg.ca.gov

Information Services
Lake County Visitor Information Center
875 Lakeport Blvd.
Lakeport, CA 95453
800/525-3743 or 707/263-9544
fax 707/263-9564
website: www.lakecounty.com

Mammoth Lakes Visitors Bureau
P.O. Box 48
437 Old Mammoth Rd., Ste. Y
Mammoth Lakes, CA 93546
888/GO-MAMMOTH or 888/466-2666
fax 760/934-7066
website: www.visitmammoth.com

Mt. Shasta Visitors Bureau
300 Pine St.
Mt. Shasta, CA 96067
800/397-1519 or 530/926-4865
website: www.mtshasta.com/chamber

The Nature Conservancy of California
201 Mission St., 4th floor
San Francisco, CA 94105-1832
415/777-0487
fax 415/777-0244
website: www.tnccalifornia.org

Plumas County Visitors Bureau
550 Crescent St.
P.O. Box 4120
Quincy, CA 95971
800/326-2247 or 530/283-6345
website: www.plumascounty.org

Shasta-Cascade Wonderland Association
1699 Hwy. 273
Anderson, CA 96007
800/474-2782 or 530/365-7500
fax 530/365-1258
website: www.shastacascade.org

Map Companies

Earthwalk Press
5432 La Jolla Hermosa Ave.
La Jolla, CA 92037
800/828-MAPS (800/828-6277)

Map Center
2440 Bancroft Way
Berkeley, CA 94704
510/841-6277
fax 510/841-0858

Map Link
30 S. La Patera Lane, Unit 5
Santa Barbara, CA 93117
805/692-6777
fax 800/627-7768
website: www.maplink.com

Olmstead Maps
P.O. Box 5351
Berkeley, CA 94705
tel./fax 510/658-6534

Tom Harrison Maps
2 Falmouth Cove
San Rafael, CA 94901-4465
tel./fax 800/265-9090 or 415/456-7940
website: www.tomharrisonmaps.com

U.S. Forest Service
Attn: Map Sales
P.O. Box 9035
Prescott, AZ 86313
928/443-8285
website: www.fs.fed.us/maps/

U.S. Geological Survey
Branch of Information Services
P.O. Box 25286, Federal Center
Denver, CO 80225
888/ASK-USGS (888/275-8747) or
303/202-4700
fax 303/202-4693
website: www.usgs.gov

Acknowledgments

For the willingness to create this new guidebook system, I am deeply appreciative to Bill Newlin, publisher of Avalon Travel Publishing, Marisa Solís, series manager of the Foghorn Outdoors books, and Krista Lyons-Gould, editorial director for Avalon. Bill Newlin is one of the finest editors and publishers in America, bar none, and I am thankful to work with him.

I am extremely grateful to Glenn Schwarz, executive sports editor of the *San Francisco Chronicle*, Larry Yant, assistant sports editor, and Phil Bronstein, executive editor, for allowing me to roam the state full-time, and in turn, best capture the outdoor experience. They have given me the opportunity that many might dream about, and I do my best to affirm they have made the right decision by turning me loose. They are lifetime friends and mentors I trust with my life.

I am also appreciative to Mike Morgenfeld, Kat Kalamaras, and Olivia Solís, who created the maps for this book and worked with me through the tedious yet exacting job of locating and sequencing the map numbers, a mind-bending job. It's also well known that I'm an outdoors guy who writes, but a pedestrian-level photographer, so I want to recognize the patience of Melissa Sherowski, the graphics cooridinator who helped work over the photography. My thanks also goes to Darren Alessi, the production coordinator who helped design the book and give it a new, updated look.

You know, people tell me I've always had too much juice for anything I care about—and thus can be a real load to work with (maybe that's why the *Chronicle* wants me out of the office, eh?). Yet working with Rebecca Browning, my editor for the book, has been seamless and nonpressured, except for the inevitable, "So, Tom, when did you say you're going to turn it in?"

The quality of detail in the listings is largely the result of the work by Senior Research Editor Stephani Cruickshank and Fact Checker Pam Padula. Stephani, in particular, has the best eye for detail I've ever seen, a fantastic curiosity for the natural world, and the ability to sustain excellence for remarkable duration. Pam and Stephani faxed every page of the 1,004-page manuscript to rangers, recreation specialists, and park owners to create a method of independent verification for everything in the book. Those who took part are noted in the acknowledgments that follow.

U.S. Forest Service

Matt Mathes, Pacific Region Headquarters
Cathie Andrews and Karen Finlaysen, Pacific Southwest Region
Kathy Peterson and Gail Wright, Angeles National Forest
Terrie Trippel, Angeles National Forest, Los Angeles River Ranger District
Patrick Hersey, Angeles National Forest, San Gabriel Ranger District
John Keeler, Angeles National Forest, Santa Clara/Mojave Ranger District
Virginia Krause, Pauline Bauer, and Susan Roder, Cleveland National Forest, Descanso
    Ranger District
Trish Huston, Cleveland National National Forest, Palomar Ranger District
Sandra Snorek and James Snow, Cleveland National Forest, Trabuco Ranger District
Joyce Pratt and Jean Clark, Eldorado National Forest, Eldorado Information Center
Dustin Swan and Lindsey Pulliam, Humboldt-Toiyabe National Forest, Bridgeport Ranger District
Ceva Andersen, Humboldt-Toiyabe National Forest, Carson Ranger District
Leslie Willoughby, Inyo National Forest, Inyo Information Center
Pennie Custer, Inyo National Forest, Mammoth Ranger District

Tim Bue, Inyo National Forest, Mono Lake Ranger District
K. C. Wylie, Inyo National Forest, Mt. Whitney Ranger District
Mary Loan and John Louth, White Mountain Ranger District
Karen Day and Jim Stout, Klamath National Forest, Goosenest Ranger District
Pat Garrahan, Klamath National Forest, Happy Camp Ranger District
Jim Lipke, Klamath National Forest, Salmon-Scott Rivers Ranger District
Dave Williams, Klamath National Forest, Ukonom Ranger District
Robert Becker and Robin Renteria, Lake Tahoe Basin Management Unit
Janie Ackley and Barbara Jackson, Lassen National Forest, Almanor Ranger District
Lenni Edgerton, Lassen National Forest, Big Valley Ranger District
Mike Zunio, Lassen National Forest, Eagle Lake Ranger District
Iris McCormick, Lassen National Forest, Hat Creek Ranger District
Loris Smith and Tim Oofterhous, Los Padres National Forest, Monterey Ranger District
Cheryl Dorsey and Ian Lauchlan, Los Padres National Forest, Mt. Piños Ranger District
Cindy Burkhart, Los Padres National Forest, Ojai Ranger District
Jim Lopez and Larry Griffith, Los Padres National Forest, Santa Barbara Ranger District
Jill Evans, Los Padres National Forest, Santa Lucia Ranger District
Kathi Schuster, Mendocino National Forest, Covelo Ranger District
Anna Fiorella, Jeff Applegate, Roxanne McGlothin, and Doris Blackmer, Mendocino
    National Forest, Grindstone Ranger District
Annie Downhour and Debbie McIntosh, Mendocino National Forest, Upper Lake
    Ranger District
Stephen Riley, Modoc National Forest, Devil's Garden Ranger District
Lorraine Worley, Modoc National Forest, Doublehead Ranger District
Jamie Neld, Modoc National Forest, Warner Mountain Ranger District
Trisha Humphreys and Linda Braxton, Plumas National Forest, Feather River Ranger District
Judy Abrams, Plumas National Forest, Mt. Hough Ranger District
Pandora Valle, Plumas National Forest, Beckwourth Ranger District
R. Dean Townsend, San Bernardino National Forest, Big Bear Discovery Center
Tahirih Vig and Bob Wood, San Bernardino National Forest, Front Country Ranger District
Gina Thompson and Norma Bailey, San Bernardino National Forest, Mountaintop
    Ranger District
Laura Verdugo, San Bernardino National Forest, San Jacinto Ranger District
Geri Adams and Dave Baskin, Sequoia National Forest, Greenhorn Ranger District
Carol Hallacy, Sequoia National Forest, Hume Lake Ranger District
Sandra York, Giant Sequoia National Monument, Tule River/Hot Springs Ranger District
Jean Cooke, Tim Clark, and Cindy Beckstead, Shasta-Trinity National Forest, Big Bar
    Ranger District
Jerry Kuczmanski, Shasta-Trinity National Forest, Hayfork Ranger District
Barbara Paolinetti and Lester Lloyd, Shasta-Trinity National Forest, McCloud Ranger District
Manny Navarro and Don Lee, Shasta-Trinity National Forest, Mt. Shasta Ranger District
Cathy Southwick and Ramona Brown, Shasta-Trinity National Forest, Shasta Lake Ranger
    District
Bev Heflin, Shasta-Trinity National Forest, Weaverville Ranger District
Judy Hanevold, Shasta-Trinity National Forest, Yolla Bolly Ranger District
Debe Arndt, Sierra National Forest, Bass Lake Ranger District

Leslie VanMeter and Mike Levre, Sierra National Forest, Kings River Ranger District
Mike Mitchell and Mark Burrows, Six Rivers National Forest, Lower Trinity Ranger District
Steve Pollard, Six Rivers National Forest, Mad River Ranger District
Bob Hemus, Six Rivers National Forest, Orleans Ranger District
Jim Fedderly, Stanislaus National Forest, Calaveras Ranger District
Linda Beck, Stanislaus National Forest, Groveland Ranger District
Bill Seib, Stanislaus National Forest, Mi-Wok Ranger District
Brenda J. Gorski and Dave Montoya, Stanislaus National Forest, Summit Ranger District
Ed Moore, Tahoe National Forest, Foresthill Ranger District
Patti Mahaffey, Tahoe National Forest, Nevada City Ranger District
Betty Leffew, Tahoe National Forest, North Yuba/Downieville Ranger District
Geneva May and Ricardo Buitron, Tahoe National Forest, Sierraville Ranger District
Molly Murphy and Diane Minutilli, Tahoe National Forest, Truckee Ranger District
Duane Sidebottom, Scott and Salmon River District, Klamath National Forest
Chele Morgan Sidebottom, Scott and Salmon River District, Klamath National Forest

U.S. Army Corps of Engineers
Mary Ann Deeming, Black Butte Lake
Greg Volkman, Eastman Lake
Carrie Richardson, Hensley Lake
Suzie Nichols, Lake Kaweah
Danielle Garrison and Greg Cox, Lake Mendocino
Tom Veader, Lake Sonoma
Ed Cole, Pine Flat Field Office
William "Skip" Sivertsen, Sacramento District
Nicole Adney and Lupe Moreno, Success Lake

Bureau of Land Management
Dolly Enderlein and Claude Singleton, Alturas Field Office
Jenny Weiss, Arcata Field Office
Ken Hock, Bakersfield Field Office
Bob Raver, Barstow Field Office
Jeff Yenez, Bishop Field Office
Stan Bales, Eagle Lake Field Office
Nicole Riven, El Centro Field Office
Jeff Horn and Lou Cutajar, Folsom Field Office
Ann Jacobson, Palm Springs Field Office
Tracy Hallstrom, Redding Field Office
Larry Ames, Jeff Wilbanks, and Deborah McAfee, Ukiah Field Office
Cori Bailey, Mirabella Lopez, and Denise Dorsey, Yuma Field Office

National Parks
Denise Badder and Carrie Coughlin, Death Valley National Park
Cindy Von Halle, Joshua Tree National Park
Nancy Bailey and Shandra Ochs, Lassen Volcanic National Park
George Freeland, Lava Beds National Monument

Andrea Morgan and Ruby Newton, Mojave National Preserve
Julie Burrill, Marin Headlands
Loretta Yarly, Point Reyes National Seashore
Steve Overman, San Francisco Presidio
Kris Fister, Sequoia and Kings Canyon National Parks
Phil Bono, Six Rivers National Recreation Area
Trisha Ford, Whiskeytown National Recreation Area
Raye Santos, Yosemite National Park

State Parks

John Ruddley, Ocotillo Wells State Vehicular Recreation Area
Liz Roth, Donner Memorial State Park
Tom Vinson, Sugar Pine Point State Park
Erin Hrimnak, Emerald Bay State Park
Mark Pupich, Grover Hot Springs State Park
Steve Johnson, Tahoe State Recreation Area
Rebecca Siller, D. L. Bliss State Park
Lynda Burman, Indian Grinding Rock State Historic Park
Sylvia Ramos, MacKerricher State Park
Anwar Verdun, Hendy Woods State Park
Kristina Moran and Adam Wolter, Sugarloaf Ridge State Park
Dena Morris, Bothe-Napa Valley State Park
Deborah Saylor, Lake Oroville State Recreation Area
Bob Silva, Colusa-Sacramento River State Recreation Area
Paul Anderson, Russian Gulch State Park
Debbie Joulian, Woodson Bridge State Recreation Area
Todd Kellogg, Fort Ross State Historic Park
Sandahl Nelson, Sonoma Coast State Beach
Kelly Setters, Auburn State Recreation Area
LeAnne Schaerer, Samuel P. Taylor State Park
Carlos Porrata, Marin District
John Kolsrud, Austin Creek State Recreation Area
Carl Nielson, Mt. Diablo State Park
Jorge Bayley, Butano State Park
Audrey Mitrevics, Plumas-Eureka State Park
Holly Huenemann, Portola Redwoods State Park
Bill Mentzer, Mt. Tamalpais State Park
Damien Jones, Carnegie State Vehicular Recreation Area
Ken Huie, Angel Island State Park
Jere Oliveira, Millerton Lake State Recreation Area
Jan Jeffers, Henry W. Coe State Park
Amber Bigler, Henry Cowell Redwoods State Park
Tess Cappieters, New Brighton State Beach
Bobbie Tate, Seacliff State Beach
Danielle Poret, Sunset State Beach
Robbie Wong, Manresa Beach State Park

Bob Stuart, Pfeiffer Big Sur State Park
Jared Ashton and Mateo Rebecchi, Hollister Hills State Vehicular Recreation Area
Meg Stoebner, Mojave Desert Sector
Margaret Beekman, Limekiln State Park
Sarah Bull, Morro Bay State Park
Kristyn Cornejo, Oceano Dunes State Vehicular Recreation Area
Wes Chapin, Channel Coast District
Irene Hamm and Bob Hamm, Pismo State Beach
Cindy Gustafson, San Simeon State Park
Lauren Goschke, Morro Strand State Beach
Curtis Price, Gavilan Sector
Sharon Nakayama, Brannan Island State Recreation Area
Nadine Vasquez, Caswell Memorial State Park
Danielle Davis, Turlock Lake State Recreation Area
Mike Martino, San Luis Reservoir State Recreation Area
Greg Kauffman, Four Rivers District, North Sector Office
Mary Pike, Colonel Allensworth State Historic Park
Randy Burt, Mojave Desert Information Center
Lauren Belch, Huntington State Beach
Erin Davis, Doheny State Beach
Rachel Hatcher, San Clemente State Beach
Robin Harding, Crystal Cove State Park
Jeff Lee, Palomar Mountain State Park
Maggie Aguilar, Cuyamaca State Park
Paul Pettit, South Carlsbad State Beach
Jane Singleton, Lake Perris State Recreation Area
Guillermo Suarez, Mt. San Jacinto State Park
Derek Jones, Orange Coast District
Casey Wear, San Diego Coast District
Joanie Cahill, Anza-Borrego Desert State Park
Rose Lambert, Salton Sea State Recreation Area
Yvette Lee, Silverwood Lake State Recreation Area
Bill Cardinal, Picacho State Recreation Area

State Forests
Norm Benson, Boggs Mountain Demonstration State Forest
Kelly Dressman and Shannon Everet, Latour Demonstration State Forest
Jose Medina and Rick Mejia, Mountain Home State Forest

Other
Christina Phillips, Hoopa Valley Tribal Council
Chuck Hamilton, Inyo County Parks
John Burns, Riverside County
Ivor Evans, Mono County
Paula Forgey, Mark Sanford, and Ross Jackson, Pacific Gas and Electric
Jeanette Buckley, U.S. Department of Reclamation

Pam Gallo, Ventura County
Roger Cummins, Siskiyou County
Marian Vigil, Yolo County
Duane Davis, Lake Solano County Park
Joe Anderson, Napa Valley Exposition
Diane Hawkeswood, Nevada County
Rick Madden, Livermore Area Recreation and Park District
Tim Stofleth, Placer County
Laurie Swason, Tahoe City Public Utility District
Judy Nagel, Alpine County
T. J. Lacoste, El Dorado Irrigation District
Nicole Welch, Sonoma County
Cheryl Bynum, Imperial County
Allyson Crawford, San Bernardino County

Index

Notes

Notes

Notes

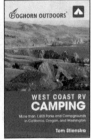
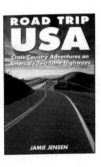